MANAGERIAL ECONOMICS

Analysis of Managerial Decision Making

ABOUT THE AUTHOR

Dr H L Ahuja, a distinguished academician, is a distinction holder in MA Economics. He was the recipient of McConnel Levin prize from Punjab University for his paper '*Investment Criteria in Development Planning*'. He continued his academic pursuit and received his doctorate from Delhi University in 1982 for his thesis '*Development Strategy for a Labour Surplus Economy with special reference to India*'.

An eminent professor, Dr Ahuja has taught Advanced Economic Theory (Micro and Macro), Development Economics and Problems of Indian Economy to postgraduate students at the Kurukshetra University. He subsequently taught at Zakir Husain Delhi College, Delhi University, where he taught Micro and Macro Economic Theories, Development Policy and Indian Economy. He was a member of the Academic Council of Delhi University for a period of five years (1987-92). A prolific writer, Dr Ahuja has more than a dozen books to his credit.

MANAGERIAL ECONOMICS

Analysis of Managerial Decision Making

Based on
UGC's Model Curriculum for MBA and IIMs Courses of Managerial Economics

For MBA, PGDM, MCom, MBE, MFC and Other Equivalent Courses

H L AHUJA
MA, PhD (DSE)
Former Associate Professor of Economics
Zakir Husain Delhi College
University of Delhi, Delhi
and
Former Visiting Professor of Managerial Economics
Maharishi Institute of Management, Noida

AMIT AHUJA

S. Chand And Company Limited
(ISO 9001 Certified Company)

S. Chand And Company Limited

(ISO 9001 Certified Company)

Head Office: D-92, Sector–2, Noida – 201301, U.P. (India), Ph. 91-120-4682700

Registered Office: A-27, 2nd Floor, Mohan Co-operative Industrial Estate, New Delhi – 110 044, Phone: 011-49731800

www.**schandpublishing.com;** e-mail: **info@schandpublishing.com**

Marketing Offices:

Chennai : Ph: 23632120; chennai@schandpublishing.com

Guwahati : Ph: 2738811, 2735640; guwahati@schandpublishing.com

Hyderabad : Ph: 40186018; hyderabad@schandpublishing.com

Jalandhar : Ph: 4645630; jalandhar@schandpublishing.com

Kolkata : Ph: 23357458, 23353914; kolkata@schandpublishing.com

Lucknow : Ph: 4003633; lucknow@schandpublishing.com

Mumbai : Ph: 25000297; mumbai@schandpublishing.com

Patna : Ph: 2260011; patna@schandpublishing.com

First Edition 2007
Subsequent Editions and Reprints 2008, 2009, 2010, 2011 (Twice), 2012
Eighth Edition 2014, Reprint 2015, 2016
Ninth Edition 2017, Reprints 2017, 2018, 2019, 2020 (Twice), 2021

Low Priced Students' Paperback Edition (LPSPE), 2022, 2023

Reprint 2024

ISBN: 978-93-550-1067-4 **Product Code:** H8MAE60ECON10ENAA21L

PRINTED IN INDIA

By Vikas Publishing House Private Limited, Plot 20/4, Site-IV, Industrial Area Sahibabad, Ghaziabad – 201 010 and Published by S. Chand And Company Limited, A-27, 2nd Floor, Mohan Co-operative Industrial Estate, New Delhi – 110 044.

To

Prem and Amit

With Love and Affection

PREFACE TO THE NINTH EDITION

It gives us great pleasure to bring out the **Ninth Edition** of the book after a short tenure of its eighth edition. This shows the growing popularity of the book, both among the students and teachers teaching the subject. As mentioned in the first edition, the book is based on the UGC model curriculum for MBA, MFC, M.Com and MBE. In writing the book, we have also kept in view the syllabi of managerial economics followed by IIM Ahmedabad, Bengaluru, Mumbai, Kolkata, Indore and Lucknow and prominent private institutions imparting education to students of postgraduation and business management.

In this ninth edition, important changes have been made with respect to micro and macro-economics. With respect to Microeconomics, in chapter 35, the explanation of decision making by risk averter and risk seeker under conditions of uncertainty has been revised. It also discusses why a risk averter buys insurance and risk seeker indulges in speculation and gambling.

Among the changes made in the Macroeconomics part, mention may be made of the following:

- **Chapter 37:** The recent data of balance of payments have been provided and the extent of *capital-inflows as percentage of GDP* in case of India has been specially explained.
- **Chapter 38:** Changes in *Gross Domestic Saving* (*GDS*) and *Gross Domestic Capital Formation* (*GDCF*) in case of India have been explained, and the chapter also examines how they explain the changes in GDP growth rate of India.
  - ➢ GDP growth rate of India and its sources have been discussed. The periods in which it has been *investment-led* and in which periods it has been *consumption-driven* have been explained.
  - ➢ In the section on Role of Capital Formation, we have explained its relation with tecnological change drawing distinction between *disembodied* and *embodied technological change*.
- **Chapter 38A:** The recent changes in valued added method to measure national income in India by CSO have been explained.
- **Appendix to Chapter 38A:** We have evaluated India's growth performance since 2001 and how it has overtaken China and has emerged as the fastest growing economy of the world.
- **Chapter 49:** The explanation of the role of monetary policy in economic development has been substantially revised especially how it can help achieve growth with price stability.
- **Chapter 50:** This has been divided into two chapters. We have discussed the objectives and role of fiscal policy in developing countries and how the resources can be mobilised for economic growth through taxes, both direct and indirect.
- **Chapter 51:** We have discussed the role of government borrowing for financing economic development and in this connection, we have explained the concept of fiscal deficit and to what extent it can be financed through government borrowing.

With the above significant changes in the book, we think the book will meet the requirements of MBA, M.Com., MFC, MBE and other equivalent courses of Indian universities and management institutes. Suggestions for further improvement of the book from fellow teachers are heartily welcomed. The authors can be contacted at drhlahuja@gmail.com.

H L AHUJA
AMIT AHUJA

PREFACE

In this revised edition in Chapter 35 of Microeconomics part we have revised the explanation of decision making by risk averter and risk-seeker under conditions of risk and uncertainty and have also discussed why a risk-averter buys insurance and risk-seeker indulges in speculation and gambling.

In recent years, there has been a revolution in management education in India. This is largely a result of liberalisation, privatisation and globalisation of the Indian economy. It has been felt that both private and public enterprises require management by professionally trained personnel. In last some years, an increasing number of students passing out from management institutes have got managerial jobs in MNCs and prominent Indian Corporate Companies with fabulous pay packages for working in both India and abroad. Consequently, there has been a craze among Indian students to get admission in various management institutes (especially IIMs) and university faculties. This is revealed by the fact that 1.77 lakh students appeared for CAT in December 2006 to get eligibility for admission in some prominent management institutes.

Managerial economics which is an application of economic theory and methods to managerial decision-making problems of business firms is a highly useful subject of the course of management science. Managerial economics is concerned with decisions regarding price and output of a commodity, its demand forecasting and sales, long-term investment and capital budgeting, use and allocation of resources within firm, multiple product pricing and transfer pricing. We feel that there is a dearth of good textbooks of managerial economics which approach the subject from the viewpoint of Indian students getting management education. The present work is an humble attempt to cater to their needs. The important feature of this book is that it makes exhaustive study of *managerial and behavioural (satisficing) models of the firm and managerial decision making under risk and uncertainty (including decision-tree approach)*.

The book is based on UGC Model Curriculum, FMS of Delhi University for MBA and courses of PGDBM of IIMs and other prominent management institutes and faculties of various Indian universities imparting postgraduate level management education. Traditionally, managerial economics course has been concerned with applied microeconomics for the decision making by the business firms. However, for making optimal business decisions, one requires the knowledge of how the economy as a whole functions, what determines the level of economic activity (*i.e.*, aggregate output and employment), price level and rate of inflation and what causes economic fluctuations or business cycles. Besides, in these days of globalisation a management student needs to understand the international economic linkages in terms of international flows of trade and capital. Therefore, UGC Model Curriculum contains the study of both micro and macro aspects of managerial economics. Some IIMs prescribe a separate course of macroeconomics which is essential for management students. Accordingly, *to make the book quite comprehensive and to fulfill the requirements of all universities and management institutes we have incorporated in the present work both the micro and macro-economic aspects of managerial economics.*

It may be noted that that some highly useful subjects such as demand estimation, multiple product pricing, transfer pricing, capital budgeting (*i.e.*, long–term investment analysis), cost of capital, the application of the theory of games and strategic behaviour and linear programming, the study of inflation and business cycles do not find mention in UGC Model Curriculum, though they form a part of the course of managerial economics prescribed by prominent management institutes (including IIMs) and other university faculties. Accordingly, we have made an in-depth analysis of these topics as well in the present book.

We hope both fellow teachers and the students will find the book useful for them. Suggestions from them for further improvement of the book are most welcome.

H L AHUJA
AMIT AHUJA

January 26, 2007
69, Vaishali
Pitampura
Delhi—110 034

UGC MODEL CURRICULUM FOR MBA

Managerial Economics

Objective:

The objective of the paper is to acquaint the participants with concepts and techniques used in economics and to enable them to apply the knowledge in business decision making. Emphasis is given to changes in the nature of business firms in the context of management of services and globalization.

Contents:

Concepts and Techniques – Nature of Business Decision Making, Marginal Analysis, Optimisation, Theory of Demand – Demand Functions, Income and Substitution Effects. Revealed Preference Approach and Demand Forecasts; Production and Cost – Returns to Scale. Cost Curves, Break-Even Analysis. Theory of Firm – The Profit-Maximizing Firm, Sales-Maximizing Firm. The Satisficing Theory of The Firm; Organisation Slack, Ownership and Control; Market Structure: Competition, Monopoly, Oligopoly, Non-price Competition; Pricing of Services; Decision-Making under Risk and Uncertainty.

Macroeconomic Aggregates and Concepts; GNP and GDP, Aggregate Consumption. Gross Domestic Savings, Gross Domestic Capital formation, WPI, CPI, and Inflation, Employment, Balance of Payments, Money Supply and Monetary Policy, Fiscal Policy; Concept and Measurement of National Income; Determination of National Income, Consumption Function. Fiscal Impact and Investment, Synthesis of Monetary and Real Factors, International Economic Linkages.

CONTENTS

PART–I

MANAGERIAL ECONOMICS: NATURE, SCOPE AND OPTIMISATION TECHNIQUES

PART–II

DEMAND ANALYSIS AND THEORY OF CONSUMER'S CHOICE

PART–III

THEORY OF PRODUCTION AND COST ANALYSIS

PART–IV

PRICING AND OUTPUT DECISIONS IN VARIOUS MARKET STRUCTURES

PART–V

PRICING PRACTICES AND STRATEGIES, MANAGERIAL AND BEHAVIOURAL MODELS OF THE FIRM

PART–VI

CAPITAL BUDGETING AND DECISION MAKING UNDER RISK AND UNCERTAINTY

PART–VII

MACROECONOMICS FOR MANAGEMENT

PART – I

MANAGERIAL ECONOMICS : NATURE, SCOPE AND OPTIMISATION TECHNIQUES

- The Nature and Scope of Managerial Economics
- The Basic Model of the Firm and Role of Profits
- Optimisation : Concepts and Techniques
- Marginal and Incremental Analysis

The Nature and Scope of Managerial Economics

What Managerial Economics is about

To begin with, it is important to understand what managerial economics is about? Managerial economics is concerned with the application of economic theory and methods of decision sciences to analyse decision-making problems faced by business firms. The first and most important problem faced by a business firm is the choice of a product to be produced or service to be provided. The second important problem dealt with in managerial economics is to decide by a firm about price and output of the product so as to maximise profits or to attain some other desired goal. The decisions regarding these require careful analysis of the demand for its product and costs of its production. The other important decision-making problems facing business firms relate to what methods or techniques of production are to be used in the production of commodities, and how much advertisement expenditure is to be incurred for promoting the sales of their products. A detailed study of the various types of business decisions will be made later in this chapter. In deciding about all these problems, a firm has to decide how it can use its limited resources to achieve its objective most efficiently.

The science of economics is concerned with the allocation of *scarce resources* to alternative uses so as to achieve maximum possible satisfaction of the people. Thus, Lord Robins defines economics as a "*Science which studies human behaviour as a relationship between ends and scarce means which have alternative uses*".[1] The type of decision-making by managers of business firms also usually involves question of resource allocation within a firm or organisation. The resources at the disposal of a firm are scarce or limited. What product to be produced, what price should be fixed, how much quantity of it should be produced, and what factor combination or production technique be used for the production of goods involve resource allocation by a firm. It is the task of a manager of a firm that it should take decisions regarding these resource allocation problems in a way that ensure most efficient use of resources. Only this will enable the firm to achieve the goal of maximisation of profits.

Thus, management science is concerned with the allocation of scarce resources at the

1. L. Robbins, *The Nature and Significance of Economic Science*, p.14.

disposable of the firm. While economics is primarily concerned with the allocation of scarce resources so as to achieve maximum social welfare management science deals particularly with organising and allocating a firm's scarce resources so as to achieve the objective of the individual *firm* which *generally* happens to be maximisation of its profits. Therefore, management science's is intimately related to economics.

Besides economic theory, managerial economics draws heavily on the **decisions sciences** for the techniques used for decision making. The techniques of decision sciences used especially for business decision making are **optimisation techniques**, particularly differential calculus and mathematical programming. These optimisation techniques are used in the analysis of alternative courses of action and the evaluation of results obtained so that best alternative which helps in attaining the objective efficiently is chosen. In addition to the optimisation techniques, methods of statistical estimation, game theory of decision sciences are extensively used in managerial economics for developing decision rules that can help managers in achieving firm's objectives. It may however be noted that these techniques of decision sciences have now become a part of modern economic theory. Thus, the role of economics and decision sciences in managerial decision-making is illustrated in Figure 1.1. *To conclude, managerial economics refers to the application of economic theory and methods of decision sciences to arrive at the optimal solution to the various decision-making problems faced by managers of business firms.*

It is important to note that managerial economics has both descriptive and prescriptive roles. Managerial economics not only *explains* how various economic forces affect the working of a firm but also *predicts* the consequences of the decisions made by it. This is its *positive* or *descriptive* role. In addition to this, managerial economics *prescribes* the rules for the improvement of decision making by firms or their managers so that they can achieve their objectives efficiently. This is its *prescriptive* role.

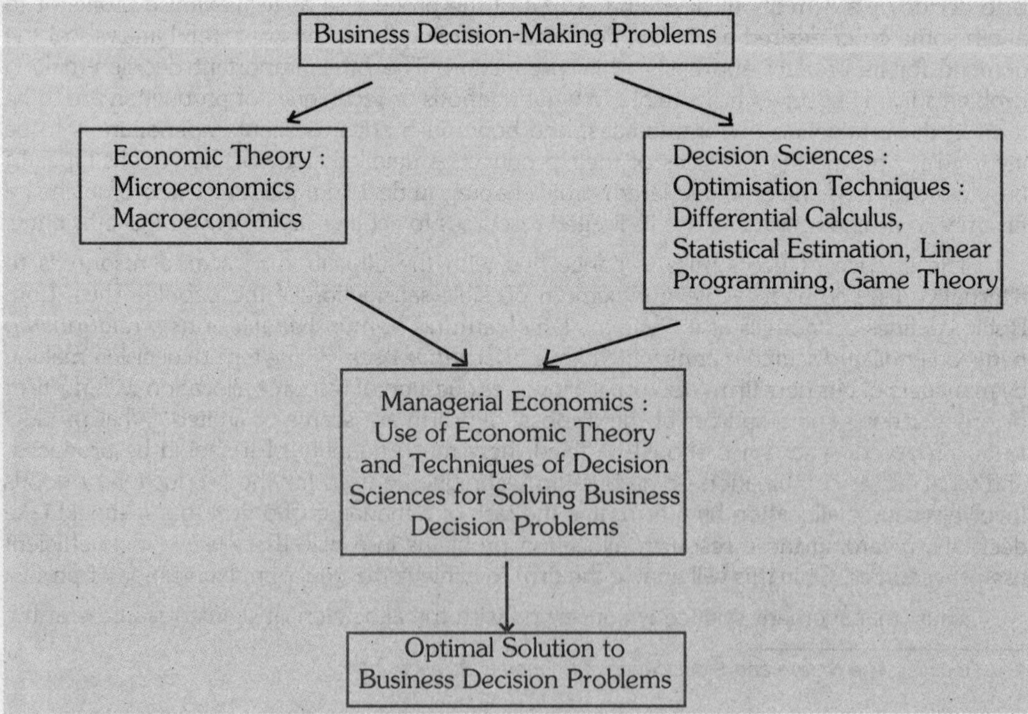

Fig. 1.1. *The Nature of Managerial Economics*

It may be noted that managerial economics deals with not only *private firms* but also *public enterprises*. Further, the technique, approach or way of thinking of managerial economics can also be profitably used in *non-profit making organisations* such as colleges, universities. This is because managers of all types of organisations face similar problems. In the last about three decades managerial economics has grown rapidly because it has been increasingly realised that economic theory and its methods and concepts can be used by managers to efficiently achieve the desired objectives of the firm.

Managerial Economics and Economic Theory

As has been stated above, managerial economics uses economic theory to solve business decision-making problems. Economic theory has been broadly divided into *microeconomics* and *macroeconomics*. Briefly, microeconomics deals with the theory of decision-making by individual consumers, resource owners and business firms in a free market economy. Macroeconomics, on the other hand, focuses on the study of economy as whole and its various aggregates such as national income, aggregate level of employment, general price level. It is important to note that though managerial economics draws on both microeconomics and macroeconomics. Managerial economics is however essentially a course in applied *microeconomics*, macroeconomic conditions of the economy such as level of aggrigate demand (which determines whether recessionary or boom conditions prevail in the economy), rate of inflation, rate of economic growth, that make up macroeconomic environment within which firms work are also very important for decision making by business firms.

Microeconomics has built models which explain how an individual consumer chooses among goods so as to maximise his satisfaction and individual business firm decides to fix price and output of its products to maximise profits and what factor combination it uses for producing them so as to minimise cost for a given level of output. The parts of microeconmomics which deal with demand theory, analysis of cost and production, theory of determination of price and output under different market structures are particularly useful in making business decisions about such matters.

The study of macroeconomics which focuses on the economy as a whole is also highly useful for management economist who is faced with various decision-making problems. This is because firms do not work in a vacuum. The level of overall economic activity, national income and employment, aggregate demand conditions, government policies (both fiscal and monetary), interest rate, the changes in price level greatly affect business firms.These aggregates of the economy make up the *macroeconomic environment* which affects business decisions of managers. Therefore, in recent years *macroeconomics for management* which is particularly relevant for business decision making has been developed. Forecasts of future demand, investment decisions by business firms are especially based on the overall situation of the economy and its growth prospects. Macro-theories of consumption, investment demand, the general price level and business cycles are particularly relevant for making capital investment expenditure which yields returns in future years.

Managerial Economics and Decision Sciences

Managerial economics depends on economic theory for theoretical framework for analysing the problems of business decision-making. On the other hand, *decision sciences* provide tools and techniques for constructing decision models and for evaluating the effect and results of alternative courses of action (i.e., alternative business strategies). Business economics uses *optimisation techniques* including differential calculus, linear and other types of mathematical programming for deriving decision rules which assist managers for achieving the objectives of business firms. Further *statistical tools* of the decision sciences are used to estimate the relationship between important variables which help in decision making. Besides, *forecasting techniques* of decision sciences are also widely used in business economics. Since most of business decisions require forecasting of future demand, and yield from capital investment, forecasting techniques play an important role in managerial decision-making. Thus, business economics draws heavily on decision sciences. As stated above, optimisation techniques, statistical estimation, and forecasting methods have now become an integral part of *modern* economic theory.

THE NATURE OF MANAGERIAL DECISION-MAKING

To solve the business decisions problems is the task of a managerial economist. Resources at the disposal of an organisation are scarce. Therefore optimum solution to the business decision-making problem requires that resources should be so used as to achieve the objective efficiently. The limited amount of resources is one type of constraint faced by the manager of a firm. The other type of constraint faced by the manager of a firm is imposed by the economic environment which includes the state of the economy, the phase of business cycles, the competition from the rival firms, government's fiscal and monetary policies, export and import policies etc. Given these constraints the manager has to make business decisions. Therefore, the decision-making problem faced by a manager is one of *constrained decision-making*.

Decision-making problem requires a choice among alternative courses of action so as to achieve the objective. These alternative courses of action among which choice has to made are often called *business strategies*. The nature of decision-making problem faced by business firms is therefore of the following type.

'To identify the alternative courses of action of achieving given objective(s), and then to select the course of action that achieves the objective in the economically most efficient way'.

An example will make clear the nature of decision-making problem requiring solution by the managers of business firms. Consider Maruti Udyog Limited which manufactures cars. Suppose it has identified two possible courses of action (generally called *strategies*) to meet the growing market demand for its products. First course of action or strategy is to plan for its internal expansion of productive capacity. The second course of action is to take over the premier Auto Limited and use its capacity to increase output to meet growing demand of its product.

The objective of Maruti Udyog Limited is to maximise profits (that is, the present value of expected returns) to be earned from expansion of output. Let S_1 stand for strategy 1 or the first course of action (that is, expanding its internal capacity), S_2 for strategy 2 or the second course of action, that is, to take over the other firm.

The objective function for the above decision-making problem can be stated as

Maximise profits (S_1, S_2)

To choose from the two alternative strategies, the following *decision rule* can be made :

Choose strategy S_1 *if profits from* S_1 > *profits from* S_2.

Choose strategy S_2 *if profits from* S_2 > *profits from* S_1.

The above simple example only brings out the essential feature of the decision-making problem faced by the managers of business firms and the rule for their rational solution. It is important to note that the knowledge of economic theory for decision-making by managers is important to formulate the objective function and to arrive at the decision rule for choosing a strategy or a course of action.

Modern economics is divided into two broad branches : microeconomics and macroeconomics. Microeconomics is concerned with theory of individual choice : Choice by a consumer and choice by a business firm. On the other hand, macroeconomics focuses on analysing the economy as a whole and its aggregates such as GNP, the general price level, the level of employment, etc. Managers or rational businessmen get assistance from both the microeconomics and macroeconomics while making business decisions, but concepts and techniques of microeconomic theory is of greater help for them. This is because microeconomics tells us how to make a rational choice in allocating scarce resources of the firm while making decisions regarding price, output, technology, advertising expenditure, and capital investment expenditure which are the direct concern of business management. Through their individual actions and choice managers can do little to affect the aggregate economy, with which macroeconomics is concerned. But macroeconomics tells him how his business environment will change as a result of movements in the aggregate economy such as situations of recession or inflation, changes in economy's balance of payments and the Government policy adopted to tackle them. All these factors which affect the outcome of business decisions. Thus, the managers during their decision-making process must take into the account the current macroeconomic outlook and likely changes in it in the future.

THE TYPES OF BUSINESS DECISIONS

Let us now explain at same length the various types of business decisions which managers of a firm are to make in the short run and long run. In the short run, the following decisions are to be made :

Price and Output Decision. Pricing of a product by a business firm is an important decision that has to be made by a manager. Price of a product will determine to a good extent how much quantity of its product it will be able to sell. Price along with cost per unit and output sold will determine its profits. In deciding about price of its products, a firm has to estimate demand for its product and also to estimate cost-output relationship. Its estimate of demand and production cost will determine how much quantity of output it should produce to maximise its profits. Profits is the difference between revenue and cost. Demand for a product tells the firms the quantities of a product that can be sold at various prices, and cost-output relationship (*i.e.*, cost function) determines the cost per unit that has to be incurred by producing different levels of output. Thus, demand together with cost determines the profit possibilities of producing a product.

It is important to note that price and output decisions made by a firm depends on the type of market structure, that is, the degree of competition prevailing in the market. As we will see later, a firm working in perfectly competitive market structure exercises no control over the price of the homogeneous product and is merely a price taker. Firms working in monopoly and monopolistic competition can take to a greater or lesser extent independent price-output decisions keeping in view the degree of competition they are facing in the market. The areas of microeconomics which deals with demand theory, cost theory, and product pricing are particularly useful for making decisions about what price to be charged and what quantity of output to be produced.

Demand Estimation. Making estimates about demand for a product is crucial for achieving the objective of profit maximisation. To arrive at correct estimates of demand, the firm has not only to study consumer's behaviour and their preferences but also the trends in macroeconomy regarding growth of GNP, price situation, changes in the level of employment and balance of payments which determine the demand for a product. Managers of business firms have not only to estimate *current* demand for their products but also the growth of demand for their products in future. Besides, firms have to estimate their own demand for the resources they need for manufacturing their products. And for this also they require to estimate the demand for their products. Theories of demand and forecasting are of great significance for estimating demand for the products.

Choice of a Technique of Production. The other important decision to be taken by business firms relates to the choice of a technique of production. A technique of production involves the use of particular combination of factors, especially labour and capital to produce a commodity. Usually various alternative techniques of producing a commodity are available among which a firm has to choose. Some production techniques involve the use of relatively more labour as compared to capital and are therefore called *labour-intensive techniques.* Some others use more capital relative to labour and are therefore called *capital-intensive techniques.* The choice between different techniques would depend on the available supplies of different factors of production and their relative prices.

Scarcity of resources demands that goods should be produced with the most efficient method. If the economy uses its resources inefficiently, the output would be smaller and there would be unnecessarily sacrifice of goods that otherwise would have been available. Therefore, it is in firm's interest that the technique of production which is used minimises the cost of production for producing a given lavel of output.

Advertising Decision. Advertising expenditure plays an important role in the market structure of monopolistic competition and differentiated oligopoly where firms have to compete to sell their products. Advertisement is required to promote sales of a product, and to create wants for the new product which is planned to be introduced in the market. Through advertisement management of a firm tries to influence the consumers about good quality of its product. Thus, how much expenditure has to be incurred on advertisement and through what madia (Newspapers, Television, Radio, Cable TV Network etc.) is an important decision to be made by a business firm. Theory of monopolistic competition and oligopoly is of great help in deciding about optimal advertisement expenditure to be made by business firms.

Long-run Production Decisions. Not only the decision regarding how much quantity of output is to be produced in the short run, but long-run decisions pertaining to production have also to be taken by firm's management. For example, where to locate the plant for manufacturing, what size of plant, that is, magnitude of productive capacity to be built up and which technology or production technique involving a particular factor-combination or factor proportion is to be used for producing a product. Besides, what product-mix should be produced to maximize profits. Developing and introducing a new product also falls in this category of long-run production decisions.

The choice among alternative courses in these matters obviously depends on the costs. The firms will aim at economising the use of scarce resources so as to achieve efficiency in production. They will decide to use technology or production technique that will minimise cost for producing a given level of output.

Cost depends on prices of resources or inputs such as capital, labour, raw materials on the one hand and productivity of these inputs on the other. Theory of production which analyses the relationship between output and inputs and theory of product pricing which are important branches of microeconomic theory are of great help in making decisions on these matters.

Investment Decision. The related type of long-run decision relates to investment or capital expenditure. Investment expenditure is required to expand the productive capacity, developing and introducing new products. Since they are of long-run nature, investment decision precedes other decisions. Investment decisions relate to how much investment or capital expenditure is to be undertaken in a period, what should be the rate of investment over the years, and on what projects capital expenditure is to be made. It is important to note that investment or capital expenditure on establishing or expanding production capacity yields returns in future periods. The theory of capital budgeting which has been developed in recent years is useful for deciding whether or not to undertake any specific investment or capital expenditure, or whether it is desirable to take over other firms to expand capacity.

Theory of capital budgeting essentially involves evaluating costs of an investment project and returns or profits flowing from it in future years. If the present discounted value (PDV) of expected returns from an investment project exceeds the cost, it is worthwhile to incur the particular capital expenditure.

MANAGERIAL DECISION MAKING PROCESS

Decision making is crucial for running a business enterprise which faces a large number of problems requiring decisions. Which product to be produced, what price to be charged, what quantity of the product to be produced, what and how much advertisement expenditure to be made to promote the sales, how much investment expenditure to be incurred are some of the problems which require decisions to be made by managers. Decision making process in each of these problems contains several phases or steps which are explained below:

1. Establishing the Objective. The first step in the decision making process is to establish the objective of the business enterprise. The important objective of a private business enterprise is to maximise profits. However, a business firm may have some other objectives such as maximisation of sales or growth of the firm.

But the objective of a *public enterprise* is normally not of maximisation of profits but to follow *benefit-cost criterion*. According to this criterion, a public enterprise should evaluate all *social costs and benefits* when making a decision whether to build an airport, a power plant, a steel plant, etc.

2. Defining the Problem. The second step in decision making process is one of defining or identifying the problem. Defining the nature of the problem is important because decision making is after all meant for solution of the problem. For instance, a cotton textile firm may find that its profits are declining. It needs to be investigated what are the causes of the problem of decreasing profits. Whether it is the wrong pricing policy, bad labour-management relations or the use of outdated technology which is causing the problem of declining profits. Once the source or reason for falling profits has been found, the problem has been identified and defined.

3. Identifying Possible Alternative Solutions (i.e. Alternative Courses of Action). Once the problem has been identified, the next step is to find out alternative solutions to the problem. This will require considering the variables that have an impact on the problem. In this way, relationship among the variables and with the problems has to be established. In regard to this, various hypotheses can be developed which will become alternative courses for the solution of the problem. For example, in case of the problem mentioned above, if it is identified that the problem of declining profits is due to be use of technologically inefficient and outdated machinery in production, the two possible solutions of the problem are : (1) Updating and replacing only the old machinery. (2) Building entirely a new plant equipped with latest machinery. The choice between these alternative courses of action depends on which will bring about larger increase in profits.

4. Evaluating Alternative Courses of Action. The next step in business decision making is to evaluate the alternative courses of action. This requires, the collection and analysis of the relevant data. Some data will be available within the various departments of the firm itself, the other may be obtained from the industry and government. The data and information so obtained can be used to evaluate the outcome or results expected from each possible course of action. Methods such as regression analysis, differential calculus, linear programming, cost-benefit analysis are used to arrive at the optimal course. The optimum solution will be one that helps to achieve the established objective of the firm. The course of action which is optimum will be actually chosen. It may be further noted that for the choice of an optimal solution to the problem, *a manager works under certain consraints*. The constraints may be legal such as laws regarding pollution and disposal of harmful wastes; they way be financial (i.e. limited financial resources); they may relate to the availability of physical infrastructure and raw materials, and they may be technological in nature which set limits to the possible output to be produced per unit of time. The crucial role of a business manager is to determine optimal course of action and he has to make a decision under these constraints.

5. Implementing the Decision. After the alternative courses of action have been evaluated and optimal course of action selected, the final step is to implement the decision. The implementation of the decision requires constant monitoring so that expected results from the optimal course of action are obtained. Thus, if it is found that expected results are not forthcoming due to the wrong implementation of the decision, then corrective measures should be taken.

However, it should be noted that once a course of action is implemented to achieve the established objective, changes in it may become necessary from time to time in response in changes in conditions or firm's operating environment on the basis of which decisions were taken.

The five steps in the decision making process are shown in Fig. 1.2

MANAGERIAL DECISION MAKING PROCESS

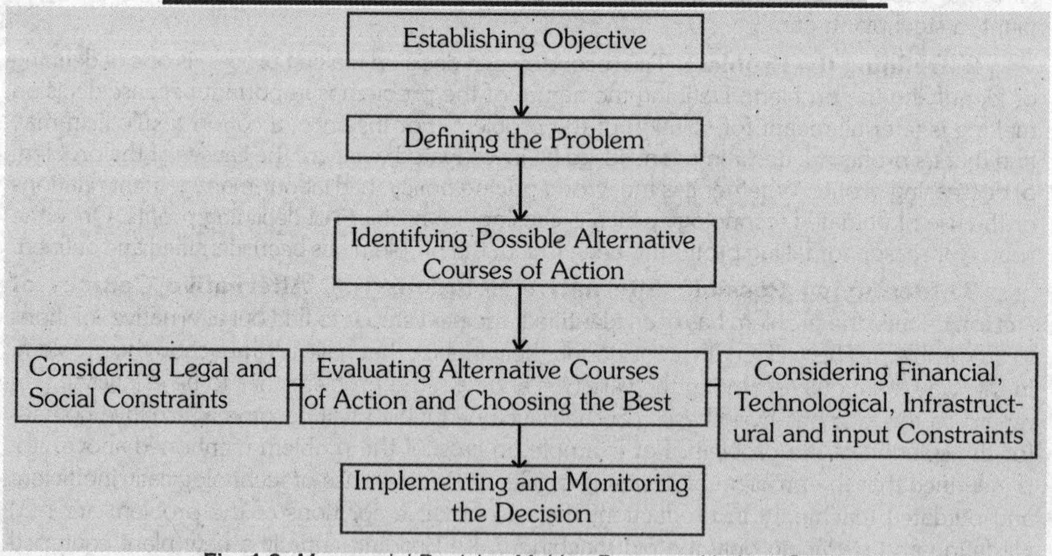

Establishing Objective

↓

Defining the Problem

↓

Identifying Possible Alternative Courses of Action

↓

Considering Legal and Social Constraints — Evaluating Alternative Courses of Action and Choosing the Best — Considering Financial, Technological, Infrastructural and input Constraints

↓

Implementing and Monitoring the Decision

Fig. 1.2. *Managerial Decision Making Process : Various Steps*

NATURE OF FIRM : THE FIRM AS AN AGENT OF PRODUCTION

The firm is an agent in the economy that produces goods and services to satisfy wants of the people. In its productive activity, it transforms inputs such as labour, raw materials, capital, natural resources into useful products which are demanded by consumers. Firms exist to use scarce resources of the society efficiently and thus help the economy to cope with the basic problem of scarcity. Business firms exist for three main reasons. (1) They exploit the economies of mass production, (2) They raise funds to finance its productive activities and (3) They organise the production process. The most important reason for organisation of production in firms is that *it enables us to take advantage of the economies of mass production.* Efficient production of goods requires the use of specialised machines and factories, assembly lines and division of labour into small operations which are performed by special groups of labour adequately trained for the operations done by them. Firms coordinate the process of production. They hire labour, get land of building and capital on rent, purchase raw materials, arrange for electric power to undertake the process of production. Emphasising the need for organising production in firms Prof. Samuelson writes *"If there were no need for specialisation and division of labour, we could each produce our own electricity, digital watch and fine-spun shirt in our backyard. We obviously cannot perform such feats, so efficiency generally requires large-scale production in business firms."*[2]

The second important function of firm is *raising of resources* for large-scale production of goods and services. A modern steel plant requires more than 200 crores of rupees to be set up, the expenditure on research and development to devise and develop a new type of aircraft might require even more funds. The supply of such a huge amount of funds cannot possibly come from wealthy individuals who in the past used to provide resources for production. Today, in a private-enterprise economy, the business firms are able to raise a large amount of funds through selling shares or bonds to the millions of people, borrowing funds from financial institutions and ploughing back their own profits for financing production.

The third important reason for the existence of firms is *management by someone* who organises production, arrange the required financial resources, introduce new products and processes, makes other business decisions and is responsible for the success or failure of the business venture. If a business venture fails and there are losses, it is the owners of firms which have to bear risk. To quote Prof. Samuelson again, *"Production is organised in firms because efficiency generally requires large-scale production, the raising of significant financial resources and careful management and monitoring of ongoing activities."*[3]

Why does a Firm Exist ? Coase's View

In a famous article in 1937, Ronald Coase[4], a Nobel Prize winner in economics in 1991 explained why a firm exists. In theory, the existence of a firm is not really necessary. One can think of separate contracts made by various individuals between them to produce without the existence of any institution of the firm, For example, consider production of a car. One individual can make a part of the car and sell it to another individual who could produce another part and add another part to the part bought from the first individual. Then, the second individual can sell these two parts of the car together to a third individual who in turn can add another part of car and then sell the three parts of the car together to a fourth individual and so on the chain of individuals adding their parts continue until the complete car is manufactured and sold to the ultimate buyer. In this way assembly line of manufacturing car will be replaced by a series of individual contracts made between various individuals selling and buying different parts of the car. This entire process of producing and selling different parts by individuals of the car is coordinated by prices at which different parts are bought and sold. In this way the firm is eliminated from the process.

Coase explained the existence of a firm producing the complete car in a single organisation rather than a series of contracts between individuals working independently to produce different parts and selling them to each other. Coase gives two reasons for the existence of

2. Paul, A. Samuelsun & William D. Nordhaus, *Economics,* Fourteenth Edition, 1992 McGraw Hill, P. 104.
3. Samuelson & Nordhaus, *op. cit,* p105.
4. Nature of the Firm, *Economica,* New Series, 4 (Now. 1937) 386-405.

firms. These are : (1) *lower transaction costs,* (2) *higher productivity under team work with division of labour.*

Transaction costs are costs of obtaining information about prices of components and inputs and also include the costs of negotiating contracts with the suppliers of inputs and purchasers of goods, writing bills and records and expenses made on getting contracts, if necessary, settled through courts and tribunals. The firm's transaction costs are reduced through bilateral contracts made by the firm. Each individual deals with the firm on bilateral basis rather than with other several individuals on a multilateral basis from whom the firm buys inputs and sells the products.

The second reason for the existence of a firm is that *production in it is done on a mass scale by a group or team of workers* among whom work is divided on the basis of their specialisation which greatly enhances productivity. Of course, there are some disadvantage of production by a group or team but its benefits outweigh its cost or disadvantages. Therefore, in modern times, it is team or group production with proper division of labour and specialisation in a firm that has made it possible to enjoy economies of scale and consequently lower cost per unit.

Decisions by Firms

To maximise profits and to use its resources for production of goods and services to satisfy wants of the buyers, the firm must make the following decisions :

1. Which goods and services to produce and in what quantities
2. Which production technique to use for production of a product
3. Which production resources or inputs to use and in what quantities
4. How to organise its management structure so as to coordinate the various activities of the process of production.
5. How to finance its productive activity, that is, how to raise resources or money capital to finance its investment in machines and factory building and pay wages to the workers and prices to the suppliers of other inputs.

ORGANISING PRODUCTIVE ACTIVITY BY A FIRM

Market Coordination Vs. Managerial Coordination

The primary objective of firms is to make maximum possible profits. Therefore, a firm makes the above decisions in a way that minimises its cost to produce a given level of output. The basic problem facing a firm is to organise the production of goods and services by combining and coordinating the productive resources it employs. Production in a modern economy is based on vast division of labour and specialisation among individuals. For efficient production of goods a firm must coordinate the activities of the individuals employed by it. Firms organise or coordinates its activities in the following two ways.

1. Market Coordination
2. Managerial Coordination or Command System.

We explain below these two ways of coordinating economic activity of a firm.

Market Coordination. Which goods and services a firm should produce is a significant decision a firm has to make and this decision relies on the market prices system that serves as a source of incentives and information network. As relative market prices of goods or services change due to the changes in their demand and supply, the buyers or users will substitute the relatively cheaper goods or services for the expensive ones. In response to the changes in demand for goods and guided by price signals, a firm will adjust the production of various goods produced by it. Besides, changes in relative prices of goods create new profit opportunities for firms who can plan expanding production of goods which are in greater demand and have higher prices. All these adjustments in productive activity of the firms is accomplished through changes in market demand, supply and prices of goods without any central coordinating authority issuing commands to the firms to change their production structure.

Managerial Coordination or Command System. There are many areas of firm's activity which do not rely on market system and instead are coordinated by management hierarchy. That is, these activities are coordinated within a firm by various layers of management. A senior manager issues commands or directions to their subordinates to do things in a way desired by him. Therefore, coordination by management within a firm is also called *command system*. At the top of managerial hierarchy within a firm is the Chief Executive Officer (CEO) who issues directions to the senior managers. The senior managers in turn give instructions to the middle-level managers and then middle level managers directs the operation managers. The operation managers represent the lowest level of management that controls the workers who produce goods and services as directed by the managers. While commands or directions pass downward through top management to the lowest level of workers, information passes upward. Managers at different levels of management hierarchy not only directs their subordinates but also collect and process information about the performance of the individuals under their control and supervision. They also ensure that the commands issued to their subordinates must be implemented properly and effectively. In the modern corporate form of business organisation, there are many layers of management and coordination of activities and collecting information and monitoring the activities of workers by them have become quite complex. However, since the 1980s, with the invention of micro computers and information revolution that has accompanied it has made the task of collecting information and coordinating efforts within a firm relatively much easier than before.

It is important to note that despite the enormous efforts made by owners and top level management and the recent information revolution, top managers lack the necessary and complete information about what is happening at the lowest level of actual implementation of commands issued. This affects the efficient working of the firm. Therefore, *large firms use incentive systems at various levels along with the command system to operate efficiently.* There is a need for the use of incentives for efficient operation because firm's owners and managers cannot have full information for efficient working of the firms. The use of incentives is necessary because contribution made by managers at various levels and workers at the floor level is very difficult to measure directly. At the floor level, some workers are more efficient and hard-working but for owners and managers it is often difficult to know who is efficiently working and who is shirking work. It is due to the lack of adequate information on the part of owners and CEO that it is difficult to fix responsibility on the sales-force when sales of the firm decline.

The above factors induce the firms to devise incentive systems within the organisation so as to ensure that all including managers, workers and sales-force work efficiently for better performance of the firm. It is due to the lack of complete information that firms do not simply employ productive resources and pay for them certain prices as if they were buying tangible goods with well known qualities. Instead they enter into contracts with managers of various levels, technical staff such as engineers, skilled labour and ordinary workers and pay them suitable compensation packages that give them adequate incentives so as to raise productivity. These contracts and incentive packages are known as **agency relationship.** These steps are adopted to solve what is called **principal-agent problem.** The principal agent problem arises because managers and workers do not always work in the best interests of the owners of shareholders in case of corporate form of business organisation. Instead, managers and workers often attempt to pursue their own goals which may conflict with the efficient and profitable working of the firm. To solve this principal-agent problem, suitable compensation packages that provide adequate incentives to the agents (*i.e.* managers and workers) to work in the interests of the principal (*i.e.* owners of the firm) are needed. In a later chapter we will discuss *agency theory of the firm* which is concerned with this principal-agent problem.

Boundaries of the Firm

Coase whose views about the nature of the firm has been explained above mentioned the two coordinating principles that determine the boundaries of the firm : (1) *market coordination principle,* (2) *managerial principle of coordination* internally which is also called the *command principle.* What limits the boundaries of a firm can be explained with these two *coordination principles. By boundaries of a firm we mean what parts of a product or what services a firm itself will produce and what parts or services it will get from outside using the market mechanism from other firms.* For example, if a firm requires some specific input such as a special component or a special service such as clearing the shop floor, it has two options; either it should do these itself inside the firm using command principle (that is, through managerial coordination and issuing commands to that effect) or it should buy them from other firms using market mechanism for that purpose. However, the boundaries between what components or services the firm should produce or do internally and what it should buy from the market differs in case of different firms. Each firm tends to grow until the cost of organising one extra task within the firm becomes equal to the cost of organising the same task outside the firm through the market. It may be further noted that boundaries of a firm go on changing over time with technological changes.

Coase's analysis of the boundaries of a firm is based on the concept of *transaction costs.* Transaction costs are those costs which are incurred by a firm when it buys a product or service from the market. For example, when a car manufacturing firm has to buy a component from outside the firm, it has to find the market in which that component is available and then to know the different quantities and qualities of the component are available in the market and at what prices. To collect all such information requires a lot of money expenditure which represents transaction costs.

On the other hand, when the firm decides to produce a component or provide any service within the firm itself, it opts for managerial coordination system. In this case using the command principle it can get produced a part or component of a product or provide any service internally of its desired specification and quality through issuing proper directions or commands to the managers at different levels of managerial hierarchy. It will also incur some extra costs of producing a component or service inside a firm. However, in deciding to produce a component or service internally, the firm is able to avoid some transaction costs but it no longer takes advantage of buying the component or service in a competitive market. As a firm expands its size and scale of production, it will face the inefficiencies of command system (that is, diseconomies of managing a large-sized firm) relative to the efficiencies involved in buying parts from the competitive markets.

It follows from above that the firms have to decide what components of a product it has to produce within the firm using managerial coordination system (that is, command principle) or get it from others through market mechanism. Most firms use both the systems; they buy some components from other firms through market mechanism and produce some other components themselves within the firm. Coase's view of the firm is that *it is the institution that economises on transaction costs.* The use of market mechanism to get parts or components is efficient or economical when its transactions costs are relatively small. When transaction costs of getting components or services through market are relatively high, it produces them within the firm using internal managerial command system. Thus, Lipsey and Chrystal write, "*Firms exist as an alternative to a pure market structure of transactions. Inside a firm there is a command economy. Managers of firms have always to be asking what activities should be done inside the firm and what should be obtained in the market from other suppliers.*"[5]

It is important to note that changes in technologies often change the relative costs of some components and services through market mechanism or producing them inside the firm. For example, the recent revolution in information technology that involves the use of computers and internet has reduced the transaction costs of getting some services or components through the market as compared to producing them 'in-house'. As a result, many firms which used to provide certain services or produce some components internally now get them from others through market. Small firms that supply certain specific services or produce components often do these things more efficiently as they acquire specialisation in them.

As is now well-known many American firms are getting several services done through *Call Centres* located in India, China and other developing countries. They are getting some services done through what is called BPO (Business Processing Outsourcing) while earlier they provided for these services internally. In this way the large firms are able to concentrate on what are called '*Core Competencies*' and contract out to get several other components produced and services done from other specialised firms. By doing so they are able to economise on transaction costs and increase their efficiency.

ROLE AND SOCIAL RESPONSIBILITY OF BUSINESS

An important issue which concerns business economics is to show the relationship between business firms and society. What role does business firms play in a society ? Do they behave in a socially responsible manner, that is, do they serve social interest or meely maximise their private profits at the expense of social welfare. These are the issues of business economics which we now analyse. Business economics clarifies the role business firms play in a society and also suggests ways of improving the benefits which firms provide to the society.

The vital role which business firms play in increasing social welfare is quite clear. It is due to the working of busines firms that a high rate of economic growth has been achieved in the United States and other western countries. Benefits of this economic growth have been widely shared. The high rate of economic growth has resulted in improving social well-being and removing poverty. To put in the words of Adam Smith, the father of economics, business firms have greatly increased the '*wealth of nations*' (that is, the volume of output of goods and services) in the capitalist world. The social benefits conferred by business firms on the communities is despite the fact that businesses work to maximise their profits or maximise the value of their firms. In their bid to maximise profits, business firms organise the work of production by engaging and combining the various productive resources and bringing about coordination between them. The suppliers of capital, labour, raw materials and other resources receive rewards from the firms for their contribution to the production of goods and services. These business firms generate income and employment for labour, the owners of capital, land and other resources. This has greatly benefited them and contributed to their well-being. Besides, consumers too have gained from increasing quantity of goods and services produced by business firms for their consumption.

Apart from the gain to the resource owners and consumers, business firms contribute a good deal of revenue to the government. Taxes on profits (*i.e.* income of business firms), excise duties on their production, sales tax on the goods produced by them and other such taxes yield a lot of public revenue which are used by the Government to expand the services provided by it and to increase public investment for economic growth.

---

5. Lipsey and Chrystal, *Economics*, 10th Edition, Oxford University Press, 2004.

All the above mentioned contributions of business firms to economic growth and social well-being depend on the efficiency with which they use national resources and allocate them among products and services, A fundamental question that has been often raised is how business firms, which in their productive activities are guided by maximisation of private profits, work to increase social welfare. The answer to this question was provided by Adam Smith, the author of now well-known classic '*Wealth of Nations*'. Advocating for a free market system he clarifies the role of business in promoting social well-being despite the fact that it pursues the goal of profit maximisation. Adam Smith argues that it is the profit-driven market system (also called price mechanism) that drives business firms to promise welfare though they work for privates gain. It is worth quoting him. "*Every individual endeveavours to employ his capital so that its produce may be of greatest value. He generally neither intends to promote the public interest, nor knows how much he is promoting it. He intends only his own security, only his own gain. And he is in this led by an invisible hand to promote an end which was no part of his intention. By pursuing his own interest, he frequently promotes that of society more effectively than when he realty intends to promote it.*[6]

Social Responsibility of Business

Now, an important questions is whether successful business-firms *always* behave in a socially responsible way, that is, promote social well-being without harming it in any way, the answer is 'no'. Some argues that businesses exist by public consent to serve the needs of society. Therefore, they survive only because they promote social welfare. However, this is not correct. Various problems are faced by society because of socially undesirable ways business firms perform their activities. Further, they impose certain social costs on the society for which they do not pay. However, society has taken steps to regularate and control them so as to induce or force them to serve social interest and minimise the harms done by them. We mention below the socially undersirable problems which the working of profit-driven business firms have created and how society has tried to regulate their activites to ensure that they work in public interest.

First problem that has been often faced is the emergence of monopolies in free market economies for the production of some important products or services. For example, economies of large-scale production and distribution are such that only one electricity producing and distributing company, only one company providing telephone service can efficiently serve a city. Such monopolistic firms are likely to exploit the consumers by charging higher prices and making excessive profits. It is in such cases that government on behalf of the society has intervened to directly regulate them. The Government has fixed fair prices for such commodities or services which are based on cost plus fair return on investment made by business firms.

The second problem posed by free private business is the emergence of olligopoly (that is, a few producers of a product competing with each other). In certain industries economies of scale are so large or barriers to entry into the industry are so strong that only a few firms serve a given market. If there exists competition among these few firms, no problem arises. But they formally or tacitly collude with each other and form a cartel, they pose a threat to social interest. Such collusion among the few firms eliminates or substantially reduces competition. Such collusion among the firms or formation of a cartel leads to higher monopoly price being charged and restriction of output. Such collusion or formation of a cartel has been sought to be controlled by the society through enacting laws such as antitrust law in the US and Monopolistic and Restrictive Trade Practices Act in India. These acts are designed to prevent collusion among firms and creation of monopolies through mergers. By promoting competition

6. Adam Smith, *An Equiry into the Nature and Causes of Wealth of Nations*, Random House/Modern Liabrary 1985.

these laws work for social betterment of the people and ensure social responsibility of business.

A further socially undersirable activity of free private business has been the exploitation of workers due to unequal bargaining power of the employers and workers. In India in private business enterprises, especially owned and managed by small-scale business firms, workers are paid very low wages because they are not well-organised and also because huge unemployment prevails in the Indian economy. Employers even do not make arrangements for their housing which have resulted in slums in the cities. Further, child labour and women are employed in private enterprises at very low wages while a lot of work is obtained from them. This has necessitated the regulation of business by the Government which have fixed minimum wages that must be paid to workers. The employment of child labour has been banned. Law regarding '*equal pay for equal work*' are being enforced under which women are to be paid equal wages as men.

But a very serious problem that arises in a business activity is that it imposes a heavy *social costs* on the economy. It is now common knowledge that productive activities of business firms have created an acute problem of **environment pollution**. They dump their toxic wastes into the air and water. The pollution creates lung ailments, asthma and other health hazards for the people. These are called social costs by the economists because while the firms impose these costs on the society, they do not pay for them. Often they do not provide safeguards so that undue smoke and other poisonous gases are not emitted by them. Bhopal gas tragedy is a shining example of how private business firms neglect their social responsibility by not providing adequate safeguards for leakage and emission of poisonous gases.

Now, a considerable attention is being paid by the society to internalise these social costs, that is, private business firms are forced to pay for these social costs. Safety standards are being laid down for emission limits on manufacturing processes and products that pollute the environment. Provision for heavy fines have been made who do not provide adequate safeguards. Firms that do not meet these safety standards are even closed down.

It may be noted that all the above measures, namely regulation of monopolies, antitrust laws, labour laws and anti-pollution policies are examples of actions that society has taken to modify the profit-maximising behaviour of business firms so that they perform their task of producing and distributing goods and service in a socially responsible way. These social constraints have an important bearing on the business activities of firms and hence on managerial decision making.

Social Responsibility and Value Maximisation Model of the Firm

With the above constraints imposed by the society on the working of business enterprises, does the value or profit maximisation model of the firm remain adequate when issues of social responsibility are included in it. Answer to this question is in affirmative. These are two ways in which the economic model of the firm retains its utility, validity and importance despite the social efforts to modify behaviour of business firms. One way is in so far as the social efforts are confined to inducements in the form of suitable fiscal and monetary measures such as taxes, subsidies, concessional rates of interest, these measures can be easily incorporated in the value-maximisation model of the firm. The second type of social measures such as licensing laws, anti-pollution measures, labour laws etc. can be considered as *constraints* of the model of the firms and managers have to take into account these constraints in decision making. Thus, with the constraints imposed on the business firms so that they should operate in socially responsible manner makes the decision-making model as one of '**constrained maximization**' of the value of the firm. This makes the process of decision making as "**constrained decision making**" by managers. Thus, in this sense the economic model of the firm still retains its usefulness despite measures adopted to ensure social responsibility of business firms.

QUESTIONS FOR REVIEW

1. What managerial economics is about ? Managerial economics has both descriptive and prescriptive roles. Explain.
2. What is the role of decision sciences in managerial decision making ?
3. What is the relationship between managerial economics and (*a*) microeconomics (*b*) macro-economics ?
4. Why are economic theory and its methods used by managers of business firms in their decision making ?
5. Explain the nature of business decision making problem. Explain the meaning of business strategy in this context. What criterion does manager of a business firm often follow in choosing a strategy ?
6. The decision-making problem faced by business firms process is one of constrained optimisation. Discuss.
7. Explain the various types of business decisions that mangers have to make.
8. Explain the various steps in managerial decision making prcoess. At what step does knowledge of economic theory and method help a manager to arrive at an optimum strategy ?
9. Explain the role of business in promoting social well-being. Does profit maximisation by businesses always promote social welfare ?
10. What is meant by social responsibility of business ? How do private business firms neglect social responsibility ? What measures can be adopted to force private firms to behave in a socially responsible way ?

Basic Model of the Firm and Role of Profits

THE FIRM'S OBJECTIVE : PROFIT MAXIMISATION

The efficient management of a business firm requires an optimal or best solution out of the available courses of action for a firm. This efficient or optimal decision making requires establishing the goal or objective to be achieved. Whether a management decision is optimal or not can be evaluated against the goal or objective that the firm seeks to achieve. In traditional economic model of the firm it is assumed that a firm's objective is to *maximise short-run profits,* that is, profits in the current period which is generally taken to be a year. In various forms of market structure such as perfect competition, monopoly, monopolistic competition the traditional microeconomic theory explains the determination of price and output by assuming that firm's aim is to maximise current or short-run profits. This current short-run profit maximisation model of the firm has provided decision makers with useful framework with regard to efficient management and allocation of resources.

Profit is a difference between total revenue and total cost. It may be noted that the concept of cost used in economic theory and managerial economics is different from the concept of accounting cost used by accountants. This difference in the concepts of costs makes the concept of profits used in economic theory different from that used in its calculation by the accountant. We will explain the concept of economic cost and concept of economic profits based on it in detail later in this chapter. It will suffice to state here that economic profits is the difference between total revenue and *economic* costs. Thus

$$\pi = TR - TC$$

Where π stands for total economic profits, *TR* for total revenue and *TC* for total economic costs. It is economic profits which firms try to maximise in their decision making about level of output to be produced and price to be charged for its product. This is illustrated in Fig.2.1. where *TR* curve[1] represents total revenue earned from selling varying amounts of output of a

1. It may be noted that the shape of the total revenue curve *TR* drawn in Fig. 2.1 is convex outward which indicates that price of the product falls as the firm produces and sells more of its product, that is, demand curve facing the firm is downward-shoping. Further, the shape of total cost curve is such that cost per unit of output falls in the beginning and then beyond a point it rises.

product. *TC* curve depicts total economic costs at different levels of output. It will be seen from the upper part of Fig.2.1 at *OM* level of output, total revenue equals total economic costs and therefore at this level of output the firm is just breaking even. Therefore, point *B* at which *TR* curve cuts *TC* curve is called *break-even point.* Beyond this break-even level of output positive profits start accruing to the firm as it expands its level of output. Profits go on increasing till output level *OQ* is reached. It will be seen from the upper part of Figure 2.1 that at output *OQ*, the difference between total revenue and total cost is maximum, that is, *JH* is the largest distance between the *TR* and *TC* curves. Therefore, *JH* is the maximum profits that can be earned by the firm, given the total revenue and total cost conditions.

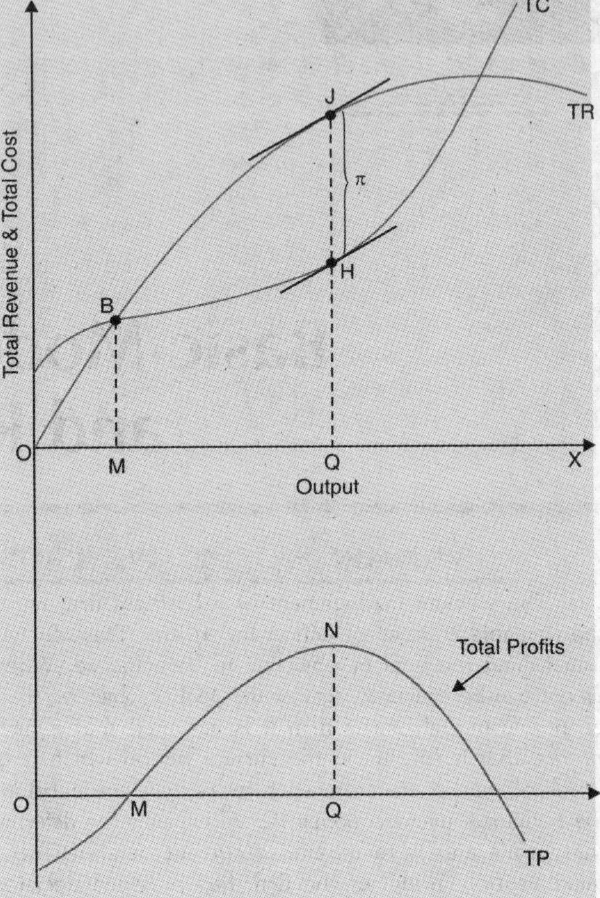

Fig. 2.1. *Profit-Maximising Model of the Firm*

That the profits are maximum at output level *OQ* can be shown mathematically as under :

$$\pi = TR - TC \quad ....(1)$$

For the total profits to be maximum, the first derivative of the total profit function should be zero. Thus, taking the first derivative of (1) above we have

$$\frac{d\pi}{dQ} = \frac{d(TR)}{dQ} - \frac{d(TC)}{dQ} = 0$$

or, $$\frac{d(TR)}{dQ} = \frac{d(TC)}{dQ}$$

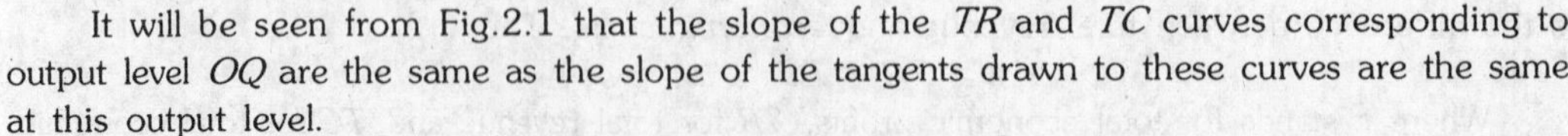

$\frac{d(TR)}{dQ}$ and $\frac{d(TC)}{dQ}$ are the slopes of *TR* and *TC* curves respectively.

It will be seen from Fig.2.1 that the slope of the *TR* and *TC* curves corresponding to output level *OQ* are the same as the slope of the tangents drawn to these curves are the same at this output level.

In the lower part of Figure 2.1 we have drawn a total profit curve *TP* which first rises and then beyond point *N* (corresponding to output level *OQ*) it starts falling indicating that profits are maximum at output level *OQ*.

It can be seen from the upper part of Figure 2.1 that profits start declining as output is expanded beyond *OQ*. Therefore, a firm which aims to maximise profits will produce output level of *OQ*, and will charge a price of its product which buyers are prepared to pay depending on the demand conditions. Since price or average revenue equals total revenue divided by a level of output, price charged by the firm at output level OQ is given by $\frac{TR}{OQ}$ or $\frac{QJ}{OQ}$.

The simple profit-maximising model of the firm provides very useful guidelines for the decision making by the firm with regard to efficient resource management. Thus, any business decision by a firm will increase its profits if the following conditions prevail :

1. It brings about increase in total revenue more than increase in costs.
2. It causes increase in revenue, costs remaining unchanged.
3. It reduces cost more than it reduces revenue.
4. It reduces costs, revenue remaining the same.

Limitations.Despite the merits of the profit maximising model of the firm, it has two important limitations. First, it does not incorporate time demension in the decision-making process by the firm. Secondly, *it does not analyse the firm's behaviour under conditions* of *risk and uncertainty.* The modern model of the firm known as *'Firm's value Maximization Model 'or Shareholder's wealth Maximising Model'* overcomes these limitations by incorporating time dimension into the managerial decision-making process. This model also considers risk involved in business decision-making. We explain this model below.

VALUE MAXIMIZATION MODEL OF THE FIRM

In modern managerial economics business decision making by managers are guided by the objective of maximising value of the firm. Since in a corporate form of business it is the shareholders who are the owners of the firm, value of a firm represents shareholders wealth. Thus, value maximisation of a firm implies maximisation of shareholder's wealth. Therefore, this model is also known as "*shareholders wealth maximisation model*".

Thus modern managerial economics departs from the traditional economic theory in which it is assumed that managers of corporate firms or owner-managers of self-owned business enterprises seek to maximise short-run profits. It has often been observed that firms sacrifice some short-run profits for the sake of higher profits in the future years. That is, they aim at maximising long-run profits. It is because of this objective that business enterprises incur huge expenditure on research and development, new capital equipment and expensive promotional schemes for their products. Therefore, incorporation of time in the analysis of decision making by managers of business enterprises is essential. Modern theory of the firm assumes that primary objective of the firm or their managers is to maximise value of wealth or shareholder's wealth.

Value of the firm is measured by calculating present value of cost flows of profits of the firm over a number of years in the future. To do so profits of future years must be discounted because money value a rupee of profit in a future year is worth less than a rupee of profit in the present. Therefore, the value of the firm or shareholder's wealth is given by the present value of all expected future profits of the firm. Thus, the value of a firm may be expressed as follows :

Value of the firm = Present value of expected future profits

$$PV = \frac{\pi_1}{(1+i)^1} + \frac{\pi_2}{(1+i)^2} \text{ .... } \frac{\pi_n}{(1+i)^n}$$

$$= \sum_{t=1}^{n} \frac{\pi_t}{(1+i)^t} \quad \text{...... (1)}$$

Since profits are the difference between revenue (R) and cost (C), the above equation (1) may be written as

$$\text{Value of the firm or } PV = \sum_{t=1}^{n} = \frac{(R-C)_t}{(1+i)^t} \quad ..... (2)$$

Where PV is the present value of the future expected profits and therefore represents the value of the firm. π_1, π_2 etc. are the expected profits in each of the future years t_1 t_2, t_3 and so forth upto any future year n which are considered by the firm for maximisation of expected future profits, i is the appropriate interest rate at which expected future profits are discounted to obtain the present value of the firm. Σ denotes the sum of the present values of expected future profits.

It may be noted that in the above equations (1) and (2) time dimension has been included in the maximisation model by considering the *expected future profits* rather than only the profits of the current year. Secondly, this model also allows for the consideration of risk and uncertainity. For intance, if a series of future profits is highly uncertain (that is, it is likely to differ, substantially from the expected values of future profits) it will involve a great deal of risk. To compensate the shareholders for bearing this risk, the discount rate of interest can be raised. Thus, the greater the risk involved in obtaining a future amount of profit, the lower will be the value placed by shareholders on future profits. We thus see that value maximisation model of the firm enables us to overcome the two major shortcomings of the static short run profit maximisation model.

Further insights regarding maximisation of value of the firm can be gained by decomposing *TR* and *TC* which determine profits made by the firm. *TR* is obtained from multiplying price with the quantity of output sold. Thus

$$TR = P_t \cdot Q_t$$

Where P_t stands for the price of the product of the firm in a period t and Q_t is the quantity sold in that period.

Cost can be obtained by taking a sum of variable cost and fixed costs. Thus

$$TC = V_t \cdot Q_t + F$$

Where V_t is the average variable cost and $V_t \cdot Q_t$ measures the total variable cost in a period. F_t represents the total fixed cost.

The present value of the firm measured in equation (2) can be written as :

$$PV = \sum_{t=1}^{n} = \frac{P_t Q_t - (V_t . Q_t + F)}{(1+i)^t} \quad ..... (3)$$

The term $P_t \cdot Q_t$ measures the total revenue generated by the sale of the product, while $(V_t \cdot Q_t + F)$ represents the total cost of the firm in period.

It is evident firm equation (3) that the value of the firm depends on the sales of the product (Q_t) and pricing decision (P_t) by managers on the one hand and firm's cost, both variable and fixed, on the other. Sales and pricing decision of a firm depends on demand function for the firm and its marketing strategy. These issues regarding demand function facing firms, demand estimation and forecasting will be explained in later chapters.

The choice of capital investment made by a firm or, in other words, capital budgeting decision determines the proportions of fixed and variable costs in the total cost function of the firm. The division of total cost into fixed cost and variable cost is determined by the choice of a production method to be used for the production of a commodity. Thus, choice of a capital-intensive method by the firm will mean a greater proportion of fixed cost and vice versa.

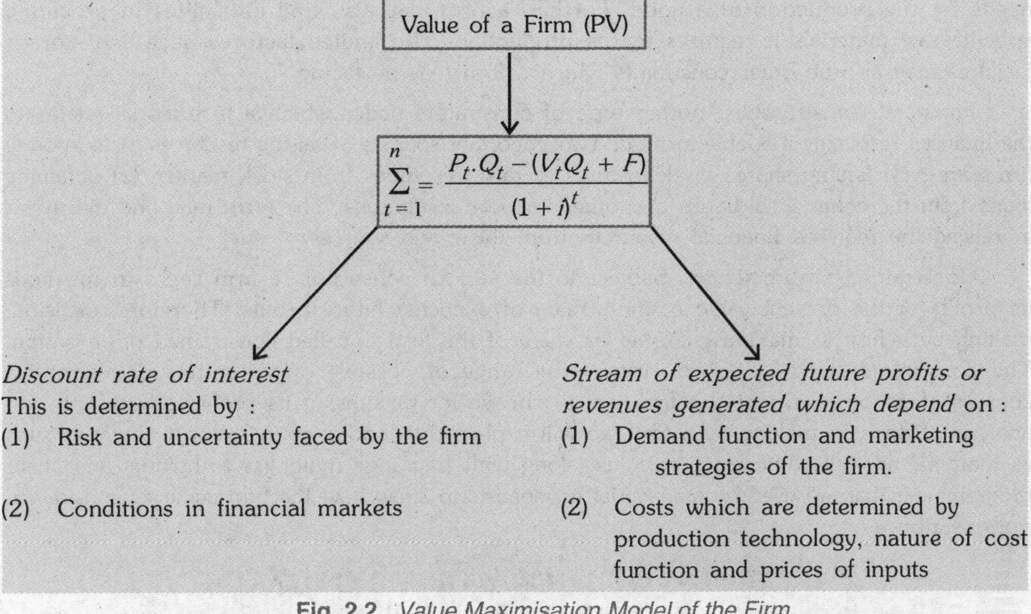

Fig. 2.2. *Value Maximisation Model of the Firm*

Cost of production also depends on physical production conditions including the technology used and prices of inputs. The determination of choice of a production method and costs of production will be discussed in later chapters.

The discount rate of interest that is used to find out the present value of the present value of the stream of expected future profits depends on the perceived risk of the firm, rate of expected inflation and conditions in the financial markets. Conditions in the financial markets determine interest rate and, therefore, the borrowing costs of the firm. It is thus clear that equation (3) provides us a unifying theme for the analysis of business decision by a firm. In various chapters of this book we will discuss several issues concerning the various terms of this equation.

Constrained Optimisation

We have explained above that primary goal or objective of the firm is to maximise value of the firm, that is, shareholders wealth. But to achieve its objective it faces many constraints. Thus, in making efficient or optimum decisions regarding pricing level of output, production method, costs, managers of the firms work under several constraints. These constraints are of the following types :

Legal Constraints. The legal constraints relate to such laws as minimum wage acts, company act to regulate corporate governance, Anti-Trust Act or Competition Promotion Act to prevent the emergence of monopolies and unfair trade practices, rules fixed by SEBI (Security and Exchange Board of India) regarding issue of shares and transactions in stock markets. Besides, There are laws which require the business firms to ensure pollution emission standard for protection of environment, required health and safety standards of the employees.

A society imposes these constraints on the firms in order to modify behaviour so as to make them consistent with the overall social objectives.

Input Constraints. Another important type of constraints relates to the limited availability of essential physical inputs. A firm may not be able to obtain as many skilled workers as it needs for the production of a good. Further, a firm may also find difficulties in procuring specific raw materials it requires for its production. The limited factory space and storage facilities may also be other constraints which a firm may be facing

Financial Constraints. Another type of constraints under which a firm works relates to the financial resources it is able to raise. Two important sources of raising resources for corporate firms are : (1) Issuing shares or debentures to raise resources from stock market, (2) obtaining loans from the commercial banks and other financial institutions. The firms may find difficulties in raising the required financial resources from these two sources.

Constrained Optimisation. Subject to the various constraints a firm seeks to maximes its profits or the present value of the stream of expected future profits. Therefore, decision-making by a firm to maximise profits or value of the firm is called constrained optimisation. The constraints faced by a firm restrict the range of possible opportunities or alternative courses of action from which a firm has to choose for maximsing its profits or value. In our analysis of decision making by a firm we will explain the various optimisation techniques such as marginal analysis, differential calculus (along with Lagrange multiplier technique) and linear programming that are used by managerial economists to show how the firm achieves constrained optimisation.

LIMITATIONS OF THE VALUE-MAXIMIZATION MODEL OF THE FIRM

The basic model of the firm outlined above which considers that the primary objective of the manager is to maximise value of the firm or shareholders wealth has been critieised on the ground that it is quite unrealistic. More specifically it has been alleged that maximising short-run profits or present value of the firm considers higher profits alone as the sale objective of the firm or the basis of firm's behaviour. It is pointed out that in the present-day corporate form of business firms, in their decision making managers strive to promote their own interest by enhancing their power, prestige, leisure. In fact, managers may maximise their utility rather than profits or value of the firm. Thus, William Baumol[2] has argued that managers seek to maximise sales rather than profits or value of the firm. He has put forward a *sales maximisation model* as an alternative *to profit or value maximisation model.*

Olivar Williamson[3] has argued that managers of modern corporate firms *seek to maximise their utility* rather than maximising short-run profits or value of the firm. According to him, utility of a manager depends on their salaries, fringe benefits, stock options, the number of subordinate staff under him, and the extent of his control on the company.

Finally, following the work of Herbert Simon[4], a Nobel prize winner in economics, Richard Cyert and James March[5] have suggested that in view of great uncertainty and a lot of constraints faced by a firm, the management of a modern corporation is a very difficult and complex task. According to them, managers are not able to maximise profits even if they so desire. Therefore, in their opinion, managers only *satisfice,* that is, they attempt to have a *satisfactory* performance in terms of profits, sales, market share or growth of the firm. Thus, according to Simon, Cyert and March, managers of business corporations try to *satisfice* rather than to *maximise.*

2. W.S. Baumol, *Economic Theory and Operations Analysis* .
3. O. Williamson, The Economics of Discretionery Behaviour : *Managerial Objectives in a Theory of the Firm,* Chicago, 1967.
4. Herbert A. Simon, Theories of Decision Making in Economic and Behavioural Sciences, *American Economic Review,* June 1959.
5. Richard Cyert and James March. *A Behavioural Theory of the Firm,* Prentice Hall, 1963.

Comments

While the alternative theories of firms lay stress on some relevant aspects of managerial behaviour, none of them provide a satisfactory substitute for the profit or value maximisation model of the firm. Managers who strive for maximisation of their own interests or utility rather than the firm's profits or value are likely to be replaced by the shareholders of the firm. Alternatively, if managers do not fully exploit profit opportunities, they will be taken over by other firm which sees its profit potential. Research has shown that in free market economies intense competition that prevails in the product and capital markets forces the managers to strive for maximising firm's profits or its value (*i.e.* shareholder's wealth) rather than promoting their own interest or maximising their utility. If they do not do so, they will be either replaced by the shareholders or the firms being managed by them will be taken over by others. Recent studies also show that there is a high correlation between profits and managerial compensation (i.e. their salaries and perks). Thus, in the free market economies today managers have strong incentives to pursue profit motive or value maximisation of the firm. Recent studies also show that there is a high correlation between profits and managerial compensation (*i.e.* their salaries and perks). Stock holders are interested in profit maximisation or value maximisation of the firm because it affects rate of return on capital investment. Therefore, in managerial economics, the theory of the firm based on profit maximisation or value maximisation is generally used in explaining managerial decision making. However, discussion of alternative theories of sales maximisation, managerial utility maximisation and satisficing behaviour provide us further significant insights into working of modern business corporations.

NATURE OF PROFITS

To understand the theory of the firm, it is necessary to know the nature of profits. How do profits arise, what determines the volume of profits or stream of expected future profits are important issues that require explanation in this regard. Profits or expected profit stream from a productive activity or an investment play a crucial role in decision making by managers. But, as mentioned earlier, the term profits, as used in economics, differs from that generally used by business community. Therefore, it is necessary to first explain the difference between business profits and economic profits. Business profits is an accounting concept and represents the residual sales revenue to the owners of the firm after making payments to all other factors or resources the firm uses. These payments to hired factors include the wages to hired labour, interest on borrowed capital, rent on land and factory buildings and expenditure on raw materials used by the firm. The expenditures on these factors or resources hired or purchased by the firms are call *explicit costs.* Business profit refers to the sales revenue of the firm minus its explicit costs. Thus

Business profits = Total sales revenue - Explicit costs

It is the concept of business profits that is generally used by the business community and accountants.

In their calculation of economic profit, the economists deduct not only explicit costs but also implicit costs from the sales revenue of the firm. The implicit costs refer to the *opportunity costs of the resources provided by the firm's owners* themselves including capital and entrepreneurial ability. These self-owned factors must be paid if they are to employed by the firm in its own production process otherwise they will be employed elsewhere on hired basis. Thus, economists take into account the *normal rate of return* on capital used by the owner of the firm in its own business and the *transfer earnings* of the owner-entrepreneur as costs of doing business.

The risk adjusted rate of return on capital is the minimum return that is necessary to attract or retain it in business and is equal to what the owner could earn from investing in other firms. Similarly, the opportunity cost of the entrepreneurial effort made by the owner entrepreneur is the salary that he could earn in his next best activity (say, as the manager of another firm). Likewise, the opportunity costs of other self-owned factors or inputs such as land, buildings used by the owner-entrepreneur in his own business will be counted as implicit costs.

The economic profit represents the sales revenue of the firm in exess of both explicit and implicit costs.

Economic profits = Sales revenue – Explicit costs – implicit costs.

While explaining maximisation of short-run profits or present value of the stream of expected profits in the future, economists assume that it is economic profits that owner-entrepreneur or managers of corporations seek to maximise. The concept of economic profits brings into sharp focus the question why such profits which is over and above the normal rate of return on equity capital and reward for entrepreneurial ability in case of owner-entrepreneur, exists and what is its role in a free enterprise system. In long-run equilibruim economic profits will be zero if all firms work in perfectly competitive market. Then, how does economic profits, positive or negative, come into existence. The various theories of profit provide explanation for the existence of economic profits. We briefly discuss them below.

Frictional Theory of Profits

According to this theory there exists a normal rate of profit which is a return on capital that must be paid to the owners of capital as a reward for saving and investment of their funds rather than to consume all their income or hoard them. In a static economy where no unanticipated changes in demand or cost conditions occur, in long-run equilibrium the firms would be earning only normal rate of profit on their capital and entrepreneurial talent. Under these conditions economic profits would not accrue to the firms. Frictional theory of profit explains that shocks or disturbances occasionally occur in an economy as a result of unanticepated changes in product demand or cost conditions which cause disequilibruim conditions. It is these disequilibrium conditions that brings into existence positive or negative economic profits for some firms.

Thus, according to frictional theory, economic profits exist for some time because of frictional factors which prevent an instanteous adjustment of the system to the new conditions. For example, at the time of sharp size in petroleum prices in the 1990 as a result of US-Iraq war many petroleum-refining firms enjoyed handsome economic profits. Similarly, as a result of slowdown in world trade in the years 1999-2001 many Indian firms doing export business suffered loses due to the decrease in the demand for their products, in the USA and other countries.

When economic profits are made in the short run, more firms will enter the industry in the long run until all economic profits are driven down to zero (that is, firms will be making only normal return or profits on their capital investment). On the other hand, when firms are making losses (*i.e.* negative profits), some firms will leave the industry. This will cause price of the product to rise so that losses are eliminated and the remaining firms make only normal profits.

Prof. G.J. Stigler, a winner of Nobel Prize in economics sums up the frictional theory of profits in the following words : "Firms in a competitive industry may receive profits..... because of a state of disequilibrium.... these profits can arise even if all entrepreneurs are identical for disequilibrium can characterise a whole industry. If prices are higher, or costs lower than were anticipated, entrepreneurs will receive a return in excess of the alternative product of their resources. If prices were lower or costs higher than were anticipated, entrepreneurs will receive less than the alternative product of their resources *i.e.*, negative profits. Positive profits may persist for a long time if firms outside the industry are show to enter the industry and negative profits can persist as long as specialised equipment yields more when used in the industry than used elsewhere, say as scrap."[6]

Monopoly Theory of Profits

Another explanation of above-normal profits attributes them to the monopoly power enjoyed by firms. Firms with monopoly power restrict output and charge higher prices than under perfect competition. This causes above-normal profits to be earned by the monopolistic firms. Joan Robinson, E.H. Chamberlin, M. Kalecki[7] associated super-normal profits with monopoly power enjoyed by some firms. Because of strong barriers to the entry of new firms, monopoly firms can continue to earn economic profits even in the long run. Monopoly power may arise due to sole control over some essential raw material required for the production of a commodity, from economies of scale, from legal sanction or from ownership patents, from Government restrictions on the import of a commodity. Various sources of monopoly power will be discussed in detail in a later chapter.

Innovations Theory of Profits

This theory of profits explains that economic profits arise because of successful innovations introduced by the entrepreneurs. It has been held by Joseph Schumpeter that the main function of the entrepreneur is to introduce innovations in the economy and profits are reward for his performing this function. Now, what is innovation ? Innovation, as used by Schumpeter, has a very wide connotation. Any *new* measure or policy adopted by an entrepreneur to reduce his cost of production or to increase the demand for his product is an innovation. Thus innovations can be divided into two categories.*First type of innovations are those which reduce cost of production.* In this first type of innovations are included the introduction of a new machinery, new and cheaper technique or process of production, exploitation of a new source of raw materials, a new and better method of orgainising the firm, etc.

Second type of innovations are those which increase the demand for the product. In this category are included the introduction of a new product, a new variety or design of the product, a new and superior method of advertisement, discovery of new markets etc. If an innovation proves successful, that is, if it achieves its aim of either reducing the cost of production or increasing the demand for a product, it will give rise to profits. *Profits emerge because due to successful innovations either cost falls below the prevailing price of the product or the entrepreneur is able to sell more and at a better price than before.*

It is here worth mentioning that *profits caused by a particular innovation* tend to be competed away as others imitate and also adopt it. An innovation ceases to be new or novel, when others also come to know of it and adopt it. When an entrepreneur introduces a new innovation, he is first in a monopoly position because the new innovation is confined to him only, He therefore makes large profits. When after some time others also adopt it in order to get a share, profits will disappear. If the law allows and the entrepreneur is able to get his new innovation e.g., new product patented, then he will continue to earn profits for a longer period. For example, Xerox corporation made a large economic profits because it successfully developed and marketed a superior copying technology. Xerox continued to make large profits until other firms entered the field to compete away these super-normal profits earned by it. Likewise, Bill Gates introduced Windows operating system and MS-office types of computure software and has become billionaire by making huge profit on his innovations.

6. G.J. Stigper, The *Theory of Price* (1952) In. 181.
7. M. Kalecki, The *Distribution of National Income in the Theory of the Firm.*

Risk and Uncertainty Bearing Theory of Profit

This theory explains that profits are a necessary reward of the entrepreneur for bearing risk and uncertainty in a changing economy. So this is functional theory of profits. Profits arise as a result of uncertainty of future. Entrepreneurs have to undertake the work of production under conditions of uncertainty. In advance they have to make estimates of the future conditions regarding demand for the product and other factors which affect price and costs. In view of their estimates and anticipations, they make contract with the suppliers of factors of production in advance at fixed rates of remuneration. They realise the value of output produced by the hired factors after it has been produced and sold in the market. But a good deal of time is spent in the process of producing and selling the product. But between the times of contracts and sale of output many changes may take place which may upset anticipations for good or for worse and thereby give rise to profits, positive and negitive.

Now if the conditions prevailing at the time of the sale of output could be known or predicted when the entrepreneurs enter into contractual relationships with the factors of production about their rates of remuneration, there would have been no uncertainty and, therefore, no profits. Thus *uncertainty, that is, ignorance about the future conditions of demand and supply, is the cause of profits.* It should be noted that positive profits accrue to those entrepreneurs who make correct estimate of the future or whose anticipations prove to be correct. Those whose anticipations prove to be incorrect will have to suffer losses.

Causes of Uncertainty. Now the questions is what types of changes cause uncertainty. Apart from the innovations which are introduced by the entrepreneurs themselves, changes which cause uncertainty are:

(1) changes in tastes and fashions of the people, (2) changes in Government policies and laws especially taxation, wage and labour policies and laws, liberalisation of imports, etc. (3) movements of prices as a result of inflation and depression, (4) changes in income of the people, (5) changes in production technology, (6) competition from the new firms that might enter the industry. All these changes cause uncertainty and bring profits, positive or negative, into existence.

F.H. Knight who propounded the uncertainty theory of profits draws distinction between *insurable* and *non-insurable risk.* Risks of factory catching fire, occurrence of any theft or accident which may cause huge losses to the entrepreneur are the kinds of risk which can be ensured against on payment of an insurance premium which forms a part of the cost of production. But there are risks that cannot be insured. These non-insurable risks relate to the outcome of price-output decisions made by the entrepreneur. Due to uncertainty his decisions may prove to be right or wrong. What output he should produce, what price, higher or lower, he should fix for his output. In view of uncertainty about future conditions he cannot be sure whether, given his price and output decisions, he will make profits or losses. Similarly, he has to bear risk as a result of his decision regarding mode of advertisement and expenditure made on it, regarding variation in product design. For taking all these decisions he has to guess about demand and cost conditions and there is always a risk of incurring losses as a result of his business decisions. No insurance company can insure the entrepreneur against business losses which result from his particular price, output, product design, and advertisement expenditure which fall upon him due to adverse changes that may take place in the economy. Thus, it is non-insurable risks that involves uncertainty and gives rise to economic profits, positive or negative.

Risk and uncertainty theory explains why super-normal profits (that is economic profits) are required by the firms who operate in such fields as petroleum exploration which involves relatively higher risks. Likewise, expected return on stocks has to be higher than the interest on bonds because of greater uncertainty and riskiness of investment in stocks of the companies .

Managerial Efficiency Theory of Profits

Lastly, this theory recognises that some firms are more efficient than others in terms of management of productive operations and successfully meeting the needs of consumers. Firms with average level of efficiency earns average rate of return. Firms with higher managerial skills and production efficiency are required to be compensated by above-normal profits (*i.e.* economic profits). Therefore, this theory is also called *compensatory theory of profits.*

Conclusion. All the theories of profits explained above have some element of truth. No single theory can adequately explain the existence of profits in all cases. Thus, economic profits can arise as a result of disequilibrium caused by dynamic changes in the economy and frictions in the instantaneous adjustment to the new conditions. They can arise due to the existence of monopoly in the product and factor markets, due to the introduction of innovations by the entrepreneurs, due to higher risk and correctly estimating the uncertain future and due to higher managerial efficiency and skills. B.S. Keirstead rightly writes, "Profits may come to exist as a result of monopoly or monopsony as a reward for innovation, as a reward for the correct estimate of uncertain factors either particular to the industry or general to the whole economy"[8].

Role and Functions of Profits

Profits play an important role in a free market economy. Profits perform two important primary roles in such an economy. First, profits serve as a signal to change the rate of output or for the firms to enter or leave the industry. Second, profits play a critical role in providing incentive to introduce innovations and increase productive efficiency and take risks.

Thus, high economic profits being earned in an industry serve as a *signal* that consumers want more of the commodity being produced by that industry. These profits indicate to the firm to expened output of the commodity and for the new firms to enter the industry to gain a share of economic profits that exist in the industry. As a result, more resources will be allocated to the output of that industry. On the other hand, below normal profits in an industry serve as a signal that either less output of the industry is demanded by the consumers or inefficient production methods are being used by the firms. In response to the lower demand for the product the firms will reduce their output and also some firms will leave the industry. As a result, some productive resources will be released from that industry and made available for the production of other goods. If the lower profits are due to the inefficient production and organisation, this will induce firm to improve efficiency by changing the production methods or make organisational changes to reduce costs.

As explained above, profit motive drives a free-market economy. Although it has been observed that sometimes managers and entrepreneurs in a free market system are swayed by greed and avarice, and break laws to make money or profits by exploiting the consumers or workers but in general profits perform useful function of sending signals for changing levels of output of various products and for reallocation of resources among them.

Secondly, above normal rate of profits in a free enterprise system is an essential reward for introducing innovations and taking risks. No entrepreneur will introduce new products or more efficient of production methods or undertake investment in risky projects unless there is

8. B.S. Keirstead, *Capital,, Interest and Profits* (1959), p.6.

prospect of making profits. Some firms continue to earn above-normal rate of profit year after year as they are continually introducing new products, new production methods and providing good customer services.

In the economy changes in demand for the product often occur due to cyclical and structural changes. Besides, new strategies of rival firms also affect the demand for the product of a firm. All these uncertain and unanticipated changes involve a good deal of risk. An important function of economic profits is to reward entrepreneurs for taking these risks involved in making investment and organising factors for the production of products.

However, in some cases firms are also able to make supernormal profits by virtue of their having monopoly power. Their monopoly power may be due to some legal patent and license obtained from the government, the economies of large scale production, exclusive control over essential raw materials which prevent the other firms from producing the same product or service. These enable the monopoly firms to charges higher prices and thereby make large economic profits. Therefore, even in free-market economies steps are taken to prevent the emergence of monopolies through anti-trust laws or Competition Acts as recently enacted in India. Of course, monopolies are legally permitted if they are needed in public interest. For example, in several cities Government grants license to some firms to provide public utility services such electricity, gas, telephone etc. In these cases of legal monopolies government regulates them and fix reasonable prices to be charged by them from the public but at the same time ensures fair return or normal profits to them on their investment.

Social Responsibility of Business and Profit Motive

It has been argued by some that business firms should be socailly responsible and works in a way that provides maximum benefits to the society. This implies that in their efforts to maximise private profits business firms should not harm social welfare. This implies that they should take steps to reduce pollution of environment caused by their activities and adopt measures for the safety and health of the workers and fulfill other social obligations. The experience of free market economices of the USA, Great Britain, Japan, Canada over the past several decades reveals that contribution of profit-driven business firms to their economic growth and increase in social welfare has been quite significant.

Despite this it is difficult to agree with the viewpoint of a noted American economist, Milton Friedman who states, "Business has only one social responsibility to make profits (so long as it stays within the legal and moral rules of the game established by the society). Few trends could so thoroughly undermine the very foundations of our society as the acceptance by corporate officials of a social responsibility other than to make as much money for their shareholders as possible".

This is an extreme view. Friedman has been an advocate of unregulated and unfettered capitalist system. Though, as stated above, profits in general play a useful role for allocating resources efficiently and promoting rapid economic growth, but it is difficult for us to agree with Freedman's view that business firms should not be guided by social responsibility. It has been seen that some business firms in their single-minded pursuit of maximising their private profits regardless of their harmful effect on social well-being behave in a socially irresponsible way. Thus, to make money at the expense of consumers, workers and society at large is not a socially responsible behaviour. That is why at present in all free-market economies some activities of business firms are regulated by government so that their decision making is consistent with the overall social goals.

QUESTIONS FOR REVIEW

1. How is the concept of economic profits different from the concept of business profits that is generally used by the accountants ? What role does the notion of normal profits play in this difference ?
2. Explain briefly profit-maximising model of the firm ? What are its limitations ?
3. Should profit motive be the main driving force of the economic system. Can you suggest an alternative to profit as an effective motivation for achieving economic efficiency ?
4. Explain briefy value maximisation theory of the firm. How does it differ from the short-run profit maximisation model ? Why is the former superior to the latter ?
5. How would each of the following affect the value of the firm.
   (a) The firm is required by the government to install new equipment to reduce air pollution
   (b) A successful advertising campaign by a firm leads to the increase in the sales of the firm substantially
   (c) The production department introduces new technology which significantly lowers production cost per unit of output.
   (d) Reserve Bank of India takes steps which leads to the lower lending rates of interest.
   (e) A new rival firm enters the industry.
   (f) Rate of inflation increases substantially
   (g) An economy is opened up with the result that foreign competitors enter market.
   (h) Workers organise themselves into a trade union when labour union did not exist before.
6. Profit or value maximisation model of the firm predicts the behaviour of the firm more accurately than does any of its alternative. Discuss.
7. What is meant by *social reponsibility of business* ? Do you feel it is reasonable to expect the private business firms to behave in a socially responsible manner ?
8. Some believe that managers of a big corporate firms make decisions so as to maximise their own utility or welfare as opposed to that of shareholders. Does such a behaviour create problem is using profit maximisation or value maximisation model as a basis for explaining managerial decision making.
9. What is meant by constrained optimisation ? Decision making by managers of firms is one of constrained optimisation ? Discuss.
10. Explain the role of profits in achieving efficiency in resource allocation and high economic growth. It is argued that former. Soviet economic system collapsed because profit motive and competition were absent in it. Do you agree ? Discuss.
11. Are profits a functional reward for entrepreneur ? What functions does an entrepreneur perform in a free market economy ?

Optimisation : Concepts and Techniques

Introduction

As explained in the previous chapter, managerial economics is concerned with decision making by managers of a firm. Managers of a firm have to take decisions regarding the level of output of a product to be produced, the price for a product to be charged, the size of the sales force to be engaged, the technique to be used for the production, the level of advertising expenditure to be incurred and many other such things. In business decision making a large number of options are open to a manager from which he has to make a choice. Obviously, a manager will try to make a best choice from among different options available to him. A best or optimum choice is one that best achieves the desired goal or objective of the firm. For example, a manager might consider what level of output of a product he should produce. Manager will produce the level of output which maximises firm's profit if he has set before himself the objective of profit-maximisation. This is a maximisation problem which he has to solve. Similarly, he may be considering to choose among the various combinations of factors or inputs that can be used for producing a level of output. To maximise profits he will choose the combination of inputs that minimises cost for producing a given level of output. Evidently, this is a minimisation problem which he has to solve.

Decision making that involves solving of maximisation and minimisation problems is called optimisation. Therefore, for making efficient decision it is neccessary for a successful manager to learn the techniques of optimisation. It may however he noted that popular techniques of optimisation are mathematical in nature. In recent year the use of analytical models of business decision making has increased the importance of the knowledge of techniques of optimisation for the students of business management. Mathematical formulations of these analytical models of managerial decision-making are expressed in terms of functions which describe economic relationship between various variables. Therefore, to begin with we will explain the concept of a function and its various important types. Besides, optimisation techniques involve the use of differential calculus and its concepts of deserivatives. Therefore, after studying the concept of function and its various types we will proceed to explain the concept of a derivative and rules of differentiation. At the end of this chapter we will give some examples of how differential calculus is used for optimisation problems in managerial economics.

FUNCTIONS

A function describes the relation between two or more than two variables. That is, a function expresses dependence of one variable on one or more other variables. Thus, if the value of a variable Y depends on another variable X, we may write

$$Y = f(X) \quad \text{.....(1)}$$

Where f stands for function.

This expression (1) is read as 'Y is function of X'. This implies that every value of the variable Y is determined by a unique value of the variable X. In the function (1), Y is known as the dependent variable and X is the independent variable. Thus in function (1) Y is called the dependent variable and its value depends on the value of X. Further, the independent variable is interpreted as the cause and the dependent variable as the effect. An important function which is extensively used in economics is a demand function which expresses quantity demanded of a commodity is a function of its price, other factors being held constant. Thus, demand for a commodity X is described as under

$$D_x = f(P_x)$$

Where D_x is the quantity demanded of commodity X and P_x is its price.

Similarly, supply function of a commodity X is expressed as

$$S_x = f(P_x)$$

When the value of the variable Y depends on more than two variables $X_1, X_2 \ldots\ldots\ldots X_n$ this function is written in general form as :

$$Y = f(X_1, X_2, X_3, X_4 \ldots\ldots\ldots\ldots\ldots\ldots X_n)$$

This shows the variable Y depends on several independent variables $X_1, X_2 \ldots\ldots\ldots\ldots X_n$ where n is the number of independent variables. Again note that in economics we write '*causes*' as the independent variables and '*effect*' as the dependent variable.

For example, demand for a product is generally considered to be a function of its own price, prices of other commodities (which may be substitutes or complements), income of the consumers, tastes and preferences of the consumers and advertising expenditure made by a firm to promote its product. Thus,

$$D_x = f(P_x, P_y, M, T, A)$$

Where

D_x = demand for the commodity X
P_x = price of the commodity X.
P_y = price of a substitute product Y.
M = income of the consumers
T = tastes and preferences of the consumer for the product.
A = advertising expenditure incurred by the firm.

The exact nature of relation of dependent variable with the independent variables can be known from the *specific form* of the function. The specific form of a function can take a variety of mathematical forms. We explain below some specific types of functions.

Linear and Power Functions

A widely used mathematical form of a function is a *linear function.* A linear function can be stated in the following general form :

$$Y = a + bX$$

Where a and b are positive constants and are called *parameters* of the function. Note that parameters of a function are variables that are fixed and given in a specific function. The values of constants a and b determine the specific nature of a linear function. The linear demand function with price as the only independent variable is written as

$$Q_d = a - bP$$

The minus sign before coefficient b indicates that quantity demanded of a commodity is negatively related with price of the commodity. That is, if price of a commodity falls, its quantity demand increases and vice versa. If a equals 7 and b equals 0.5, the linear demand function can be expressed in the following specific form :

$$Q_d = 7 - 0.5\,P$$

The above specific demand function shows that a unit fall in price of the commodity will cause 0.5 units increase in the quantity demanded of the commodity. If price (P) is zero, the second term ($0.5P$) in the demand function drops out and the quantity demanded is equal to 7.

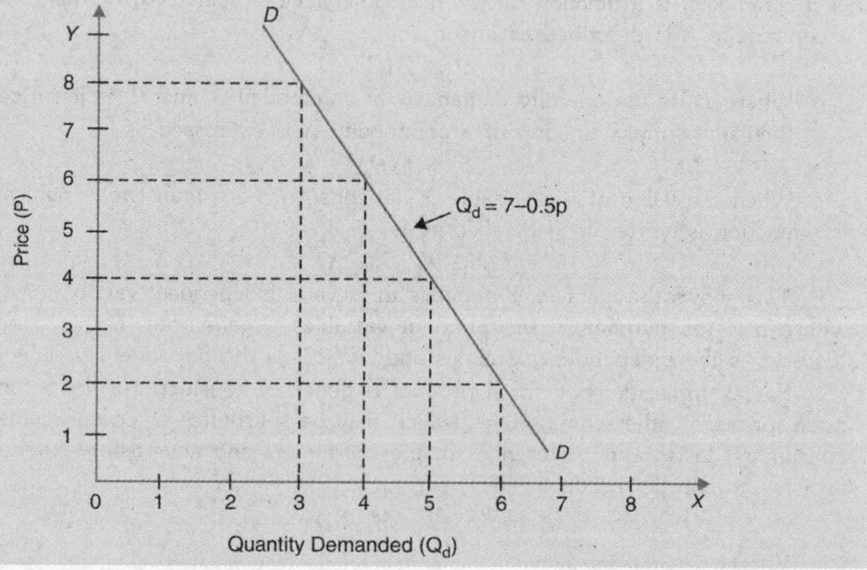

Fig. 3.1. *Graph of a Linear Demand Function ($Q_d = 7 - 0.5P$)*

We can take various values of P and find out different quantities (Q_d) of a commodity demanded at them. In Figure 3.1 we have noted these price-quantity combinations on a graph and have obtained demand curve *DD* of the commodity representing the given demand function ($Qd = 7 - 0.5P$).

It should be noted that, contrary to mathematical practice, by *convention* in economics to represent demand function we show the independent variable (price in the above case of demand function) on the y-axis and the dependent variable (the quantity demanded in the present case) on the x-axis. Graph of linear demand function is shown in Figure 3.1. It is worth noting that slope of the demand function curve in Figure 3.1 will represent $\frac{\Delta P}{\Delta Q}$. However, if we represent quantity demanded (Q_d) on the y-axis, and price (P_x) on the x-axis; the slope of the demand curve so drawn would be equal to $\frac{\Delta Q}{\Delta P}$.

Multivariate Linear Demand Function

Linear demand function with more than one independent variables, can be written in the following way

$$Q_x = a + b_1 Px + b_2 P_y + b_3 M + b_4 T + b_5 A$$

Where b_1, b_2, b_3, b_4 are the coeffieients of the respective variables. In economics the effect of variables other than the own price of a commodity in the demand function are depicted by *shifts in the demand curve.* For instance when income (M) of the consumers increases consumers will demand more of the product X at a given price. This implies shifting of the demand curve to the right.

The linear multivariate function is written in the following form

$$Y = 4 - 0.4X_1 + 0.2X_2 + 0.3X_3 + 0.5 X_4$$

In this function the coefficients 0.4, 0.2, 0.3 and 0.5 show the precise impact of the independent variables X_1, X_2, X_3, X_4 on the dependent variable Y.

Power Functions

The linear functions stated above are known as first degree functions where the independent variables X_1, X_2, X_3, etc are raised to the first power only. We now turn to explain power functions. In economics power functions of the quadratic and cubic forms are extensively used.

Quadratic Functions : In quadratic function one or more of the independent variables are squared, that is, raised to the second power. Note that power is also referred to as *exponent.* A quadratic function may be written as

$$Y = a + b X + c X^2$$

This implies that value of the dependent variable Y depends on the constant a plus the coefficient b times the value of the independent variable X plus the coefficient c times the square of the variable X. Suppose $a = 4$, $b = 3$ and $c = 2$ then quadratic function takes the following specific form.

$$Y = 4 + 3X + 2 X^2$$

We can obtain the different values of Y for taking different values of the independent variable X. Quadratic functions are of two types : convex quadratic functions and concave

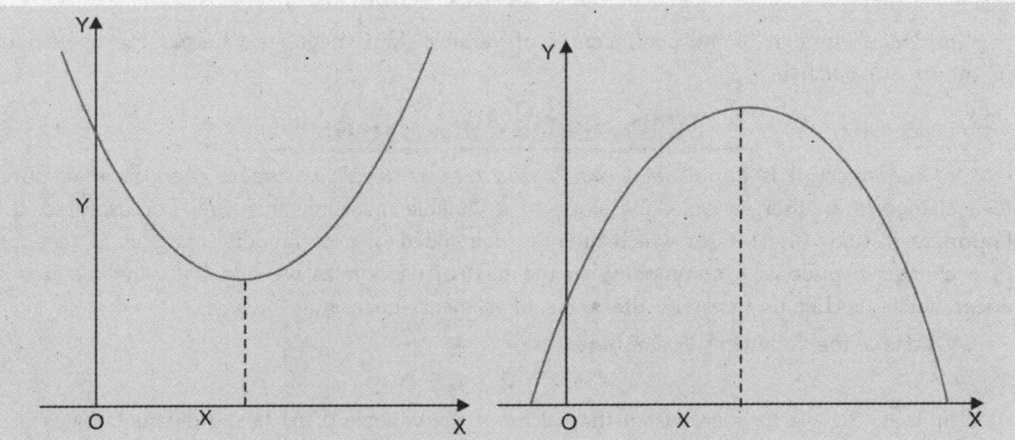

Fig.3.2. *Convex Quadratic function* **Fig.3.3.** *Concave Quadratic Function*

quadratic functions. The form of quadratic function depends on the sign of the coefficient c of X^2. The quadratic function, $Y = a + bX + cX^2$, where the coefficient c of X^2 is positive (i.e. $c > 0$) is called *convex* quadratic function, because its graph is U-shaped as shown in Figure 3.2. On the other hand, if coefficient of X^2 is negative ($c < 0$), that is, when $Y = a + bX - cX^2$, then we have *concave* quadratic function because its graphs is of inverted U- shape (*i.e.* ∩-shaped) as shown in Figure 3.3.

It is worth noting that slope of the curve of convex quadratic functions as is evident from U-shaped graph in this case where coefficient of X^2 is positive, slope is increasing every where. On the other hand, in case of concave quadratic function where coefficient of X^2 is negative ($c < 0$), slope of its graph is decreasing every where. It should be further noted that in analytical geometry it is proved that graph of any quadratic function is a *parabola* which may be be either convex or concave. A parabola is a curve which has a turning point and unlike the curve of a linear function, its slope is changing at different values of X.

Multivariable Quadratic Function. When there are more than one independent variable such as X_1, X_2, and they have a quadratic relationship with the dependent variable Y, such a function, is called multivariable quadratic function. In case of two independent variables X_1 and X_2 such a function may be expressed as under:

$$Y = a + bX_1 - cX_1^2 + dX_2 - eX_2^2$$

If such a function is graphically shown, it will be represented by a three - dimensional surface and not a two dimensional curve.

Cubic Function. A cubic function is the power function in which there is a *third degree term* relating to an independent variable. Thus, a cubic functions may have first degree, second degree and third degree terms. A cubic function may have the following form

$$Y = a + bX + cX^2 + dX^3$$

a is the intercept term, the dependent variable X has the first degree, second degree and third degree terms. When the signs of all the coefficients a, b, c and d are positive, then the values of Y will increase by progressively larger increments as the value of X increases. However, when the *signs* of various coefficients differ in the cubic function, that is, some have positive signs and some have negative signs, then the graph of the function may have both convex and concave segments depending on the values of the coefficients. Such a cubic function where signs of the coefficients of variables differ may be expressed as follows :

$$Y = a + bX - cX^2 + dX^3$$

in which the sign of the coefficient c of variable X^2 is negative whereas the coefficients of others are positive.

SLOPES OF FUNCTIONS

In economics it is important to know *the rate at which a variable changes* in response to a change in another variable, the slope of a variable measures this rate. For example, it is important to know the rate at which quantity demanded of a commodity changes in response to a change in price of a commodity. In the field of economics we find both linear and non-linear functions. Let us first take the slope of a linear function.

Consider the following linear function.

$$Y = f(X) = 2 + 0.5\ X$$

In Table 3.1 we have calculated the values of the variable Y *by* taking different values of X such as 1, 2, 3, 4 etc. Further, we have plotted the different values of Table 3.1 on a graph shown in Fig. 3.4. The slope of the function. ($Y = 2 + 0.5X$) between two points, say, A and B

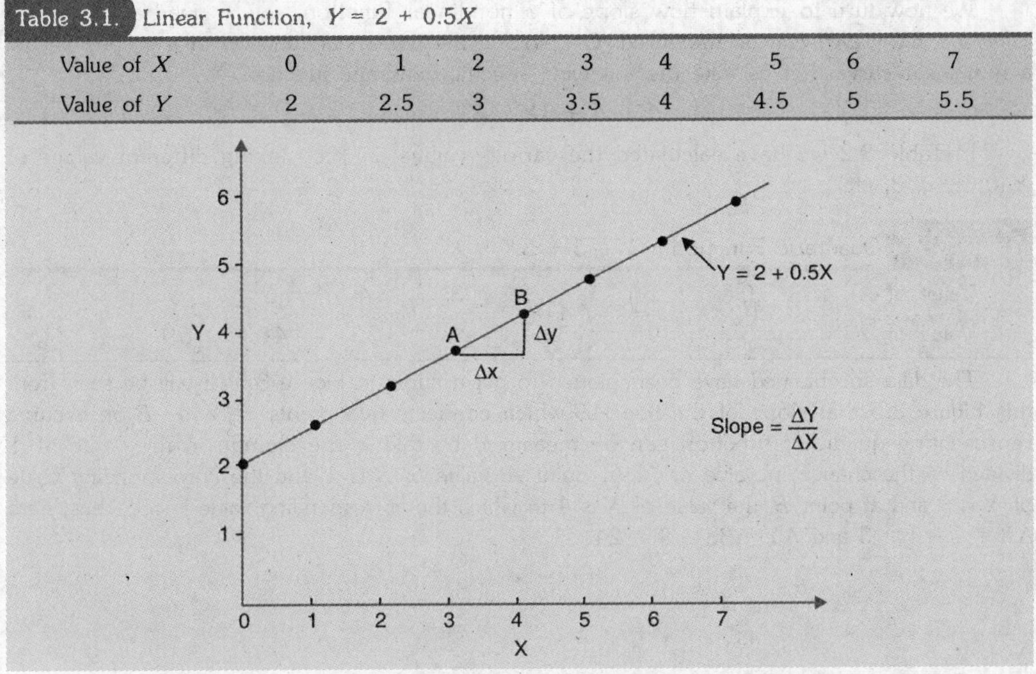

Table 3.1. Linear Function, $Y = 2 + 0.5X$

Value of X	0	1	2	3	4	5	6	7
Value of Y	2	2.5	3	3.5	4	4.5	5	5.5

Fig. 3.4. *Graph of $Y = 2 + 0.5X$*

in Figure 3.4 is given by the ratio of change in Y to the change in X. That is, slope $= \dfrac{\Delta Y}{\Delta X}$.

For example, at point A of the given function value of variable X is 3 and corresponding to it the value of variable Y is 3.5. When value of X rises from 3 to 4, value of Y increases from 3.5 to 4. Thus, the slope of the function ($Y = 2 + 0.5Y$) is :

$$\frac{\Delta Y}{\Delta X} = \frac{4-3.5}{4-3} = \frac{0.5}{1} = 0.5$$

This implies that value of Y increases by 0.5 when value of X increases by 1. It should be noted that slope of a linear function is constant throughout.

However, the slope of a linear function can be directly known from the linear function itself and for that purpose there is no need to plot the data. Consider the following linear function

$$Y = a + bX$$

It will be seen from this linear function that when the value of X is zero, the value of Y will be equal to a. Thus a is Y intercept. Further, in this function b is the coefficient of X and measures change in Y due to change in X, that is, $\dfrac{\Delta Y}{\Delta X}$. Thus, b represents the slope of the linear function. In linear function $Y = 2 + 0.5X$, 2 is the Y-intercept, that is, value of Y when X is zero, 0.5 is the b coefficient which measures the slope $\dfrac{\Delta Y}{\Delta X}$ of the linear function.

Slope of a Non-linear Function

We now turn to explain how slope of a non-linear function, say, a quadratic function ($Y = a + bX + cX^2$) can be measured. On plotting the non-linear function in a graph, we get a non-linear curve. Let us take the following specific quadratic function :

$$Y = 5 + 3X + X^2$$

In Table 3.2 we have calculated the various values of Y by taking different values of X (0, 1, 2, 3, etc)

Table 3.2. Quadratic Function : $Y = 5 + 3X + X^2$

Value of X	0	1	2	3	4	5	6
Value of Y	5	9	15	23	33	45	59

The data so obtained have been plotted to get a curve in Figure 3.5. It will be seen from this Figure 3.5 that slope of the line AB which connects two points A and B on a curve representing quadratic function can be measured by taking the change in the value of Y divided by the change in value of X. At point A, value of X is 1 and the corresponding value of Y is 9 and at point B, the value of X is 4 to which the corresponding value is 33. Thus, here $\Delta X = 4 - 1 = 3$ and $\Delta Y = 33 - 9 = 24$.

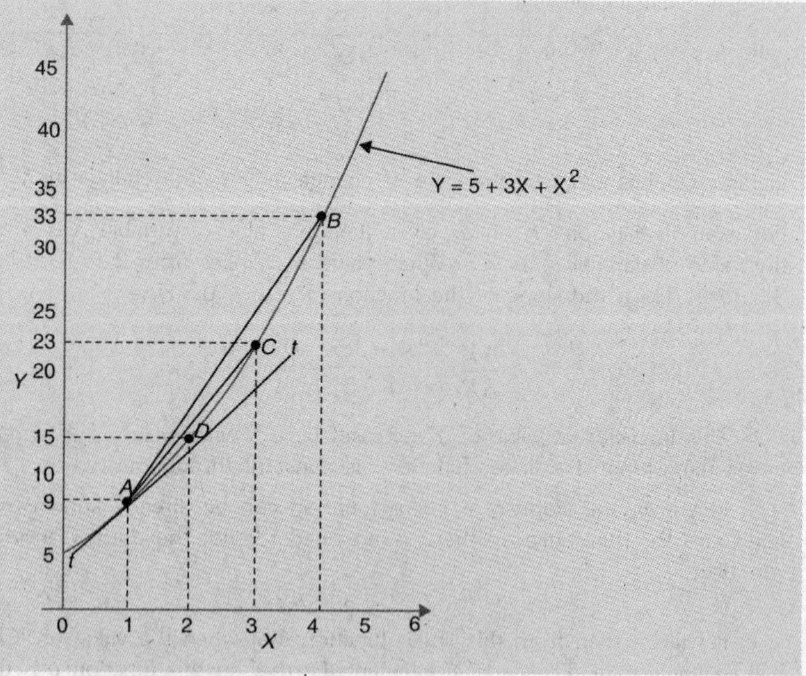

Fig. 3.5. *Slope of a Quadratic Function*

Thus, the slope of the line AB is

$$\frac{\Delta Y}{\Delta X} = \frac{24}{3} = 8$$

Similarly, slope of straight line AC in Fig.3.5. can be measured. Between two points A and C, $\Delta X = 3 - 1 = 2$ and $\Delta Y = 23 - 9 = 14$, Thus, the slope of straight line AC is

$$\frac{\Delta Y}{\Delta X} = \frac{14}{2} = 7$$

In a similar fashion, the slope of the straight line AD connecting points A and D on the non-linear quadratic function curve in Figure 3.5 is given by

$$\frac{\Delta Y}{\Delta X} = \frac{15-9}{2-1} = \frac{6}{1} = 6$$

It will thus be seen that as ΔX decreases; it was 3 between A and B, 2 between A and C and 1 between A and D, slope of the non-linear curve goes on declining. It was 8 of the line AB, 7 of the line AC and 6 of the line AD. As ΔX further decreases, slope of the line connecting two points of the non-linear curve will further decline,. It should also be noticed that the slope of the straight line AD connecting points A and D is very close to the slope of the tangent drawn to the curve at point A. As ΔX becomes smaller and smaller slope of the line connecting the two points on a curve will be come extremely close to the slope of the tangent tt drawn to the curve at point A. Therefore, *the slope at a point on the non-linear function curve can be measured by the slope of a tangent drawn to the curve at that point.*

OPTIMISATION TECHNIQUES : DIFFERENTIAL CALCULUS

Optimisation techniques are an important set of tools required for efficiently managing firm's resources. In what follows we will focus on the use of differential calculus to solve certain types of optimisation problems. In a later chapter we will explain linear programming technique used for solving constrained optimisation problem.

Diffential Calculus : The Concept of a Derivative

In explaining the slope of a continuous and smooth non-linear curve we explained above that when a change in the independent variable, that is, ΔX gets smaller and approaches zero, $\frac{\Delta Y}{\Delta X}$ becomes better approximation of the slope the function, $Y = f(X)$, at a particular point. Thus, if ΔX is infinitesimally small, $\frac{\Delta Y}{\Delta X}$ measures the slope of the function at a particular point and is called the derivative $\frac{dY}{dX}$ of the function with respect to X. *The derivative* $\frac{dY}{dX}$ *or more precisely the first derivative of a function is defined as limit of the ratio* $\frac{\Delta Y}{\Delta X}$ *as* ΔX *approaches zero.* Thus

$$\frac{dY}{dX} = \lim_{\Delta X \to 0} \frac{\Delta Y}{\Delta X}$$

It is thus evident that derivative of a function shows the change in value of the dependent variable when change in the independent variable (ΔX) becomes infinitesimally small. Note that derivative of a function [$Y = f(X)$] is also written as $\frac{d(fX)}{dX}$ or $f'(X)$.

As explained above, the derivative of a function at a point measures the slope of the tangent at that point. Consider Figure 3.6 when $\Delta X = X_3 - X_1$, the slope of the corresponding straight line AB is equal to $\frac{Y_3 - Y_1}{X_3 - X_1}$. When ΔX becomes smaller and is equal to $X_2 - X_1$, slope of the corresponding line AC is equal $\frac{Y_2 - Y_1}{X_2 - X_1}$. It will be seen from Figure 3.6 that slope of line AC is more near to the slope of the tangent *tt* drawn at point A to the function curve. Similarly, if ΔX is reduced further, slope of the straight line between the two corresponding points will go on becoming closer and closer to the slope of the tangent *tt* drawn at point A to the curve. At the limit of $\frac{\Delta Y}{\Delta X}$ *when ΔX approaches zero, slope of the tangent such as tt at a point on a function becomes the derivative* $\frac{dY}{dX}$ *of the function with respect to X.*

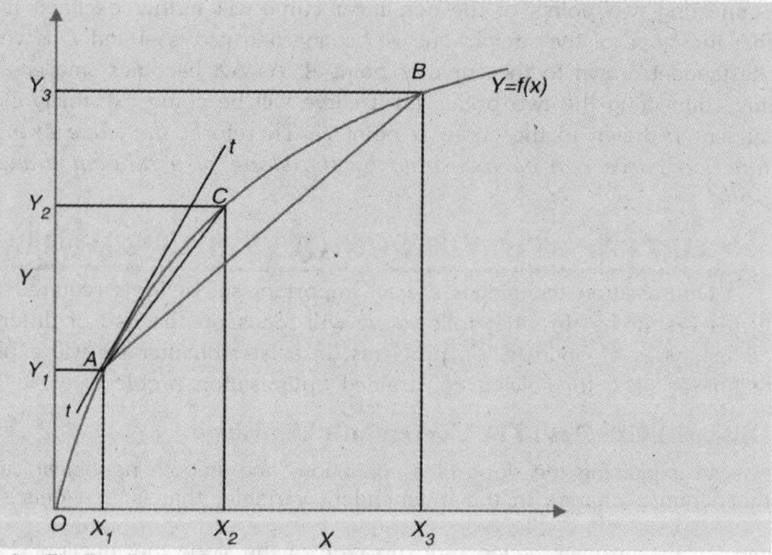

Fig 3.6. *Finding Derivative of a Function (Y = f(X) at a point*

Thus, derivative $\frac{dY}{dX}$ is slope of a function whether it is linear or non-linear and represents a change in the dependent variable due to a small change in the independent variable. The concept of a derivative is extensively used in economics and managerial decision making, especially in solving the problems of optimisation such as those of profit maximisation, cost minimisation, output and revenue maximisation.

There are various types of functions and for them there are different rules for finding the derivatives. We will explain below the basic rules of finding derivatives of the various types of functions.

RULES OF DIFFERENTIATION

Process of finding the derivative of a function is called differentiation. As stated above, derivative of a function represents the change in the dependent variable due to a infinitesimally small change in the independent variable and is written as $\frac{dY}{dX}$ for a function $Y = f(X)$. A series of rules have been derived for differentiating various types of functions. We describe below these rules of differentiation.

Derivative of a Constant Function. A constant function is expressed as

$$Y = f(X) = a$$

Where 'a' is constant. The constant 'a' implies that Y does not vary as X varies, that is, Y is independent of X. Therefore, the derivative of a constant function is equal to zero. Thus, in this constant function

$$\frac{dY}{dX} = 0$$

For example, let the constant function be

$$Y = 2.5$$

This is graphed in Figure 3.7(a). It will be seen that a constant function is a horizontal straight line (having a zero slope) which shows that irrespective of the value of the variable X, the value of Y does not change at all. Therefore, derivative $\frac{dY}{dX} = 0$.

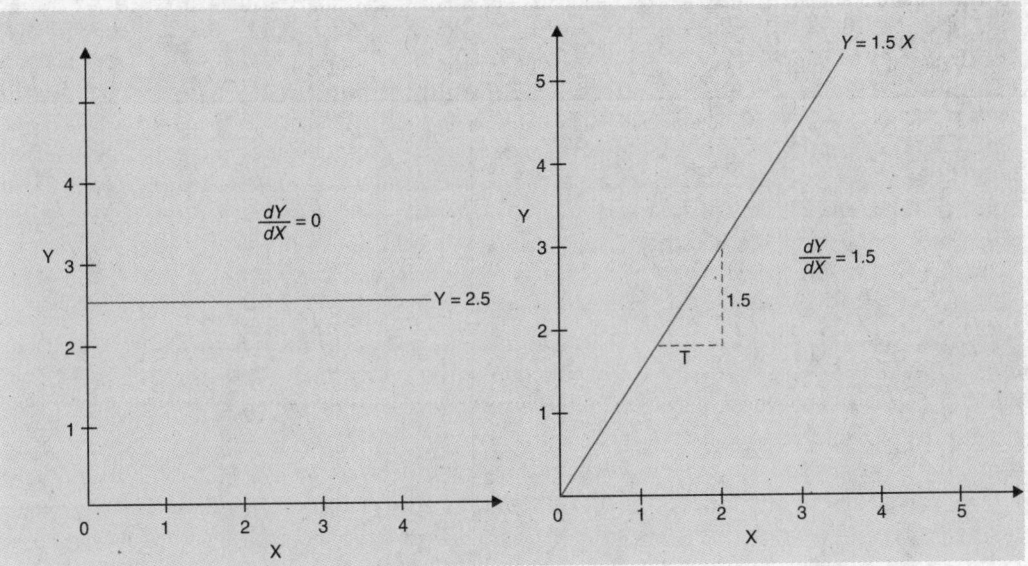

Fig. 3.7. (*a*) *Graph of a Constant Function* **Fig. 3.7.** (*b*) *Graph of a Linear Function*

Derivative of a Power Function

A power function takes the following form :

$$Y = aX^b$$

Where a and b are constants. Here a is the coefficient of the X term and the variable X is raised to the power b. The derivative of this power function is equal to the power b multiplied by the coefficient a times the variable X raised to the power $b - 1$. Thus rule for the derivative of power function ($Y = a\,X^b$) is

$$\frac{dY}{dX} = b.a.X^{b-1}$$

Let us take some examples of determining the derivative of a power function.

First, take the following power function :

$$Y = 1.5\,X$$

In this function 1.5 is the coefficient of variable X, that is, a and the power b of X is 1 (implicit). Using the above rule for the derivative of a power function we have

$$\frac{dY}{dX} = 1 \times 1.5\,X^{1-1} = 1 \times 1.5\,X^0 = 1.5$$

This is graphically shown in Figure 3.7(*b*). It will be seen from this figure that slope of the linear function ($Y = 1.5\ X$) is constant and is equal to 1.5 over any range of the values of the variables X.

Quadratic Power Function. Let us take the following example of a power function which is of quadratic type.

$$Y = X^2$$

$$\text{Its derivative,} \quad \frac{dy}{dx} = 2X^{2-1} = 2X^1 = 2X$$

To illustrate it we have calculated the values of Y, associated with different values of X such as 1, 2, 2.5 and –1, –2, –2.5 and have been shown in Table 3.3.

Table 3.3. Quardratic Power Function $Y = X^2$

Value of X	–2.5	–2	–1	+1	+2	+2.5
Value of Y	–6.25	–4	–1	+1	+4	+6.25

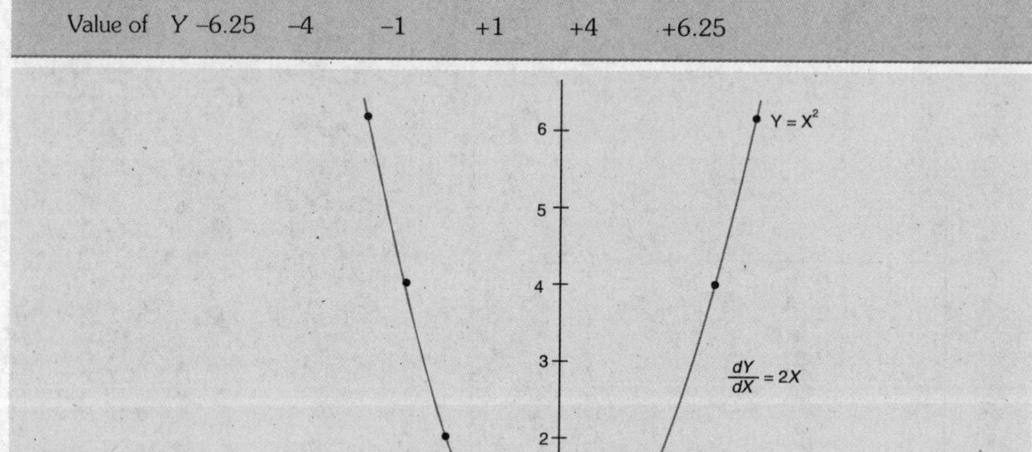

Fig. 3.8. *Graph of a Quadratic function*

We have plotted the values of X and corresponding values of Y to get a U-shaped parabolic curve in Figure 3.8. It will be seen that derivative $\frac{dY}{dX}$ or, in other words, slope of this quadratic function is changing at different values of X. *Some* other examples of power function and their derivatives are :

For power function,

$$Y = 3X^2$$

$$\frac{dy}{dx} = 2 \times 3.X^{2-1} = 6X$$

For power function; $\quad Y = X^5$

$$\frac{dY}{dX} = 5 \times 1.X^{5-1} = 5X^4$$

For power function; $Y = X$

$$\frac{dY}{dX} = 1 \times 1\,X^{1-1} = 1 \times 1.X^0 = 1$$

It should be noted that any variable raised to the zero power (as in our example X^0) is equal to 1

For power function, $Y = 3X^{-2}$

$$\frac{dY}{dX} = -2 \times 3.X^{-2-1} = -6X^{-3}$$

Derivative of a Sum or Difference of Two Functions

The derivative of a sum of the two functions is equal to the *sum* of the derivatives obtained separately of the two functions.

Suppose, $Y = f(X) + g(X)$

Where f(X) and g(X) are the two unspecified functions and Y is the sum of the two functions. Then the derivative of their sum is

$$\frac{dY}{dX} = \frac{df(X)}{dX} + \frac{dg(X)}{dX}$$

Likewise, the derivative of the difference of the two or more different functions is the difference of their separate derivatives. Thus, if

$$Y = f(X) - g(X)$$

then $$\frac{dY}{dX} = \frac{df(X)}{dX} - \frac{dg(X)}{dX}$$

To illustrate, we take some examples.

If, $Y = 4X^2 + 5X$

then $$\frac{dY}{dX} = 2 \times 4X^{2-1} + 1 \times 5X^{1-1} = 8X + 5$$

If $Y = 5X^2 - 2X^5$

$$\frac{dY}{dX} = 10X - 10X^4$$

Now, consider the following profit function where each of the three terms represents a function

$$\pi = -40 + 140Q - 10Q^2$$

Where π stands for profit and Q for level of output. Then, derivative of profit (π) with respect to output (Q) is

$$\frac{d\pi}{dQ} = 0 + 140 - 20\,Q$$

$$= 140 - 20\,Q$$

Note that derivative of a constant (–40) is zero, derivative of 140 Q is 140 and derivative 10 Q^2 = 20 Q.

Derivative of a Product of the Two Functions

Suppose Y is the product of the two separate functions $f(X)$ and $g(X)$.

$$Y = f(X) . g(X)$$

The derivative of the product of these two functions is equal to the first function multiplied by the derivative of the second function plus the second function multiplied by the derivative of the first function. Thus,

$$\frac{dY}{dX} = f(X).\frac{dg(X)}{dX} + g(X).\frac{df(X)}{dX}$$

For example, take the following function

$$Y = 5X^2 (2X + 3)$$

$f(X) = 5X^2$ and $g(X) = (2X + 3)$ are the two functions. Then, derivative of the product of these two functions,

$$\frac{dY}{dX} = 5X^2.\frac{d(2X+3)}{dX} + (2X+3).\frac{d(5X^2)}{dX}$$

$$\frac{dY}{dX} = 5X^2.2 + (2X + 3).10X$$

$$= 10X^2 + 20X^2 + 30X$$

$$= 30X^2 + 30X$$

$$= 30 (X^2 + X)$$

Take another example of the product rule. Let

$$Y = (X^3 + X^2 + 5) (2X^2 + 3)$$

then, $$\frac{dY}{dX} = (X^3 + X^2 + 5) . \frac{d(2X^2+3)}{dX} + (2X^2 + 3) . \frac{d(X^3+X^2+5)}{dX}$$

$$= (X^3 + X^2 + 5) . 4X + (2X^2 + 3) . (3X^2 + 2X)$$

$$= (4X^4 + 4X^3 + 20X) + 6X^4 + 9X^2 + 4X^3 + 6X$$

$$= 10X^4 + 8X^3 + 9X^2 + 26X$$

Derivative of the Quotient of the Two Functions

Suppose the variable Y is equal to the quotient of the two functions $f(X)$ and $g(X)$. That is,

$$Y = \frac{f(X)}{g(X)}$$

The derivative of the quotient of the two functions is equal to the denominator times the derivative of the numerator minus the numerator times the derivative of the denominator and the whole divided by the denominator squared. Thus,

$$\frac{dY}{dX} = \frac{g(X).\frac{df(X)}{d(X)} - f(X).\frac{dg(X)}{dX}}{[g(X)]^2}$$

To illustrate, consider the following example

$$Y = \frac{5X+2}{X-1}$$

Here Y is a quotient of two functions

$$f(X) = 5X + 2 \text{ and } g(X) = X - 1$$

$$\frac{dY}{dX} = \frac{(X-1)\,.\,\frac{d(5X+2)}{dX} - (5X+2)\,.\,\frac{d(X-1)}{dX}}{(X-1)^2}$$

$$= \frac{(X-1).5 - (5X+2).1}{(X-1)^2}$$

$$\frac{dY}{dX} = \frac{(5X-5)-(5X+2)}{(X-1)^2}$$

$$= \frac{dY}{dX} = \frac{5X-5-5X-2}{(X-1)^2}$$

$$= \frac{dY}{dX} = \frac{-7}{(X-1)^2}$$

Take another example. Let

$$Y = \frac{5-2X}{2X^2}$$

then,

$$\frac{dy}{dx} = \frac{2x^2 . \frac{d(5-2X)}{dX} - (5-2X).\frac{d(2X^2)}{dX}}{(2X^2)^2}$$

$$= \frac{2X^2.(-2) - (5-2X).4X}{4X^4}$$

$$= \frac{-4X^2 - 20X + 8X^2}{4X^4}$$

$$= \frac{4X^2 - 20X}{4X^4} = \frac{4X(X-5)}{4X(X^3)}$$

$$= \frac{X-5}{X^3}$$

Derivative of Function of a Function (Chain Rule)

When a variable Y is function of a variable U which in turn is related to another variable X, and if we wish to obtain a derivative of Y with respect to X, then we use chain rule for this purpose. Suppose variable Y is a function of the variable U, that is, $Y = f(U)$ and variable U is a function of variable X, that is, $U = g(X)$. Then, to obtain the derivative of Y with respect to X, that is $\frac{dY}{dX}$, we first find the derivative of the two functions, $Y = f(U)$ and $U = g(X)$ separately and then multiply them together. Thus,

For function, $$Y = f(U)$$

$$\frac{dY}{dU} = \frac{df(U)}{dU}$$

For function, $$U = g(X)$$

$$\frac{dU}{dX} = \frac{dg(X)}{dX}$$

Then $$\frac{dY}{dX} = \frac{dY}{dU} \cdot \frac{dU}{dX}$$

$$= \frac{df(U)}{dU} \cdot \frac{dg(X)}{dX}$$

Thus, *according to the chain rule if Y = f(U) and U = g(X), then derivative of Y with respect X, can be obtained by multiplying together the derivative of Ywith respect to U and the derivative of U with respect to X.*

Let us take some examples to illustrate this chain rule

Suppose $Y = U^3 + 15$ and $U = 3X^2$

$$\frac{dY}{dX} = \frac{dY}{dU} \cdot \frac{dU}{dX}$$

then $$\frac{dY}{dX} = \frac{d(U^3+15)}{dU} \cdot \frac{d(3X^2)}{dX} = 3U^2 \, . \, 6X$$

Substituting $U = 3X^2$ in the above we have

$$\frac{dY}{dX} = 3.(3X^2)^2 \, . \, 6X$$

$$= 3 \, . \, 9X^4 \, . \, 6X$$

$$= 27X^4 \, .6X$$

$$= 162X^5$$

SUMMARY OF RULES OF DIFFERENTIATION

Function	Derivative
1. Constant Function : $y = f(x) = a$	$\frac{dy}{dx} = 0$
2. Power Function : $y = ax^b$	$\frac{dy}{dx} = b.a. \, x^{b-1}$
3. Sum of functions : $y = f(x) + g(x)$	$\frac{dy}{dx} = \frac{df(x)}{dx} + \frac{dg(x)}{dx}$
4. Product of two Function : $y = f(x). \, g(x)$	$\frac{dy}{dx} = f(x) \, . \, \frac{dg(x)}{dx} + g(x) \, . \, \frac{df(x)}{dx}$
5. Quotient of two Finctions $y = \frac{f(x)}{g(x)}$	$\frac{dy}{dx} = \frac{g(x) \, . \, \frac{df(x)}{dx} - f(x) \, . \, \frac{dg(x)}{dx}}{[g(x)]^2}$
6. Function of a Function $y = f(u)$, and $u = g(x)$	$\frac{dy}{dx} = \frac{dy}{du} \cdot \frac{du}{dx}$

DIFFERENTIATION OF FUNCTIONS WITH TWO OR MORE THAN TWO INDEPENDENT VARIABLES

Partial Derivatives

So far we have been concerned with the differentiation of functions with one independent variable. However, both in economics and business economics, relations contain two or more than two independent variables about whose use economists and managers of business firms have to take decisions. For example, demands for the product of a firm depends on its price, income of the consumers, price of its substitute, advertising outlay made by the firm to promote the sales of its product and some others. Further, output of a product depends on the amounts of labour, capital, raw materials etc used for the production of a commodity. Other examples of functions from economics and business with two or more independent variables can be given.

When a function has two or more independent variables and each of them has an effect on the value of the dependent variable, we use the concept of a partial derivative. It is called partial derivative because in this the effect of only a part of influences on the dependent variable is examined. *A partial derivative of a function measures the marginal effect of a change in one variable on the value of the dependent variable, holding constant all other variables.*Thus,in a function, $y = f(x_1, x_2, x_3)$, partial derivative of y with respect to x_1, will show the marginal effect of a very small change in x_1, keeping constant x_2, x_3. By convention and to distinguish it from derivative of a function with one independent variable, for partial derivative we use lower case delta (∂) instead of lower case *d*. However, rules of differentiation in finding partial derivatives are the same as explained above in case of derivative of a function with a single independent variable.

It is worth nothing that in multivariable function, the partial derivative of one independent variable depends on the values at which other independent variables are held constant. That is why the expression for partial derivative of profit function of a firm with two independent variables products x and y, indicates that $\frac{\partial \pi}{\partial x}$ depends on the level at which the variable y is held constant. Similarly, the partial derivative of profit function with respect to y, indicates that it depends on the value of the variable x which is held constant. The economic reasoning for this will become clear if we take a two factor production function $q = f(L, K)$. In this partial derivative of production function with respect to labour (L), that is, $\frac{\partial q}{\partial L}$ implies marginal product of labour. Now, as is well known, marginal product of labour depends not only on its own skill and efficiency, but also on with how much capital (K) he has to work with. Generally, the greater the amount of capital, the higher will be marginal productivity of labour, the other things remaining the same.

To illustrate the concept of partial derivative we take the example of profit function with sales of two products as independent variables

$$\pi = f(x, y) = 50x - 3x^2 - xy - 4y^2 + 60y$$

where π represents profits, x and y are the sales of the two products being produced by a firm. The function represents that profits of a firm depend on the sales of two products produced by it.

Determining the partial derivative of profit (π) function with respect to sales of the product x treating sales of y as constant from the above profit function we obtain

$$\frac{\partial \pi}{\partial x} = 50 - 6x - y$$

Thus, with partial derivative we are able to isolate the marginal effect on profit (π) of the change in the sales of the product x, keeping the sales of products y as constant.

Note that in finding partial derivative of the profit function with respect to x, fourth and fifth terms in the profit function are not considered because they do not contain the variable x.

Likewise through partial derivative we can separate the marginal effect of the variation in sales of the product y on profit (π) while holding x constant.

Thus, partial derivative of profit (π) function with respect to y is

$$\frac{\partial \pi}{\partial y} = -x - 8y + 60.$$

APPLICATIONS OF DIFFERENTIAL CALCULUS (DERIVATIVES) TO OPTIMISATION PROBLEMS

We have explained above the concept of a derivative and rules for its differentiation in different types of functions because they are widely used in solving the problems of optimisation in economics and business management. *The process of optimisation often requires us to determine the maximum or minimum value of a function.* For a function to be a maximum (or minimum) its first derivative is zero. As explained above, derivative of a function measures its slope. Therefore, maximization of a function occurs where its derivative is equal to zero, Thus, an important optimisation problem facing a business manager is to produce a level of output which maximises firm's profits. Similarly, optimum use of resources requires that cost be minimised for producing a given level of output. These problems of maximisation and minimisation can be solved with the use of the concept of derivative.

Use in Profit Maximisation

For example, consider the following profit function :

$$\pi = -100 + 160Q - 10Q^2$$

where π = profits and Q is units of output

For the profit (π) function to be maximum, its first derivative must be equal to zero.

Therefore, to find the profit-maximising level of output we find the derivative of the given profit function and set it equal to zero. Thus

$$\frac{d\pi}{dQ} = 160 - 20Q.$$

Setting it equal to zero.

$$\frac{d\pi}{dQ} = 160 - 20\,Q = 0$$

$$20Q = 160$$

$$Q = \frac{160}{20} = 8$$

At 8 units of output profits will be maximum. Maximisation of profits through the use of derivative is graphically shown in Figure 3.9. It will be seen that profit maximisation curve reaches its maximum point at point *H*. Therefore, at point *H*, the slope of the tangent (which measures the value of derivative $\frac{d\pi}{dQ}$) drawn to the profit curve at this point is equal to zero. It will be seen that corresponding to maximum profit point *H* on the profit function level of output is 8 units.

Total profits made at 8 units of output can be obtained by substituting 8 for *Q* in the given profit function. Thus

$$\pi = -100 + 160 \times 8 - 10\,(8)^2$$
$$= 1280 - 740 = 540$$

Thus at output level of 8 units profits are equal to 540.

Graphical analysis *cannot tell us easily* exactly at what level of output, profits will be maximum, for it takes time to draw a graph and conclude from it. However, it is easier to use differential calculus to find the profit-maximising output. For this we simply find the first derivative of the profit function and set it equal to zero.

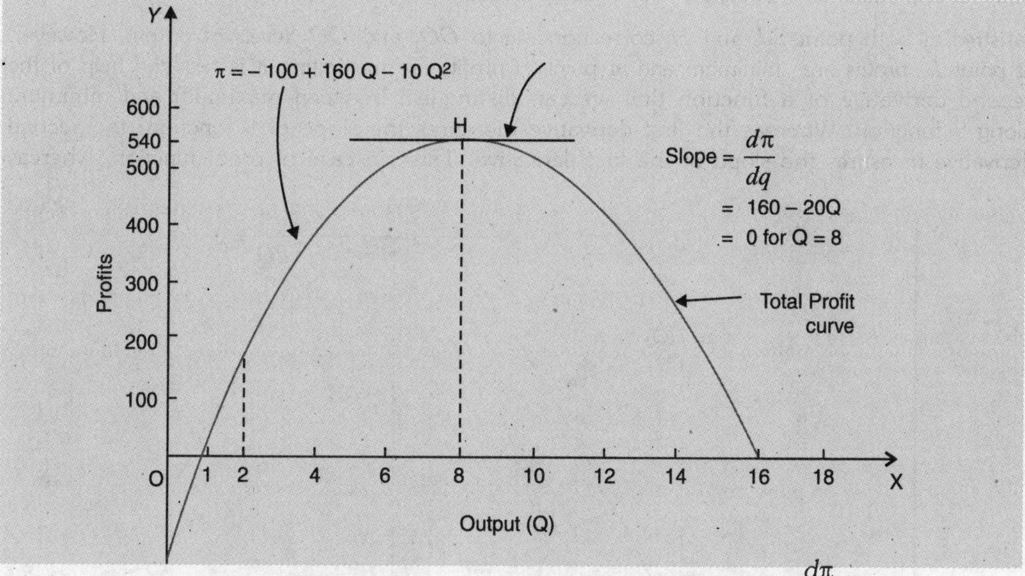

Fig. 3.9. *Profit Maximisastion is reached at output level where* $\frac{d\pi}{dQ} = 0$

Second Derivative and Second Order Condition for Optimisation

A problem arises when we use the first derivative of a function to determine its maximum or minimum value. For setting the first derivative of a function equal to zero and solving the resulting equation for the optimum value of the independent variable does not guarantee that optimum value (maximum or minimum as the case may be) will in fact he obtained. For the optimum value, the first derivative being equal to zero is a necessary condition for maximum or minimum, but it is not a sufficient condition : For example, in a profit function, first derivative is equal to zero, both at maximum and minimum profit levels. To ensure that the derivative is zero at the profit maximising level of the decision variable (*i.e.* output in the present case), we require to apply the second order condition. According to the second order condition, for profit *maximisation*, the second derivative of the profit function must be negative, that is, $\frac{d^2\pi}{dQ^2} < 0$. Thus, if optimisation requires maximisation of function say, $y = f(x)$, then the second derivative, which is written as $\frac{d^2y}{dx^2}$, must be negative.

It should be noted that the second derivative of a function is obtained by differenting the first derivative with respect to the independent variable. In case optimisation requires minimisation of a function as in case of minimisation of cost for producing a given level of output, the second derivative must be positive, that is, $\frac{d^2y}{dx^2} > 0$.

Consider again the case of profit maximisation explained above. A profit function curve such as the one drawn in Figure 3.10 may have both minimum point and maximum points. It will be seen from Figure 3.10 that point L represents the minimum point and H represents the maximum point of the profit curve. Important thing to note is that at both minimum point L and maximum point H, first order condition, that is, first derivative $\frac{d\pi}{dQ}$ be zero is satisfied at both points, L and H, corresponding to OQ_1 and OQ_2 levels of output. However, at point L profits are minimum and at point H profits are maximum. It is with the help of the second derivative of a function that we can distinguish between maximum and minimum along a function. Whereas the first derivative measures the slope of a function, the second derivative measures the slope of the first derivative. Thus, in case of profit function, whereas

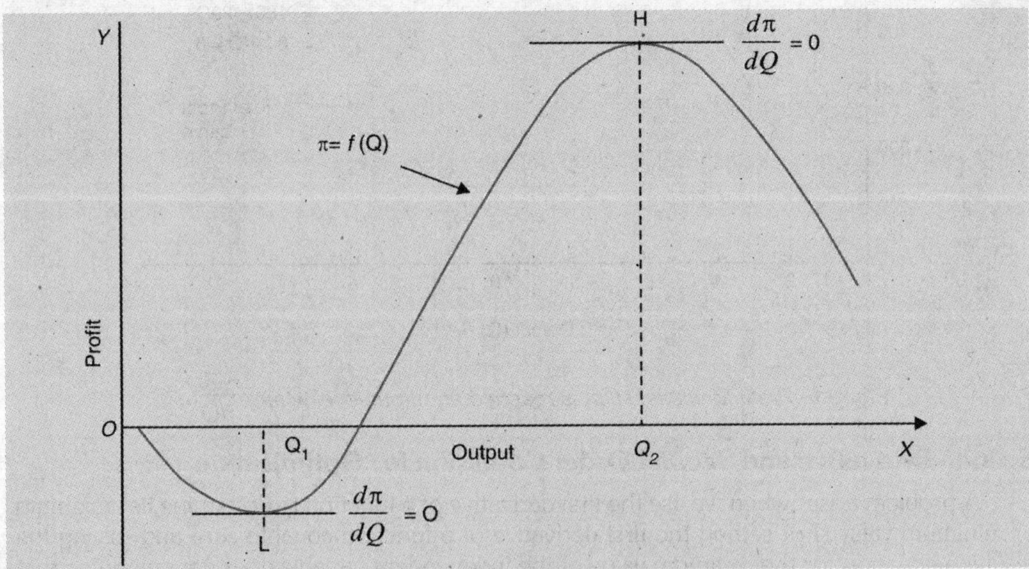

Fig. 3.10. *Second Order Condition for Optimisation*

first derivative, $\frac{d\pi}{dQ}$, measures the slope of the profit function curve, That is, marginal profit, its second derivative, $\frac{d^2\pi}{dQ^2}$, measures slope of the marginal profit function curve.

Since the second derivative of a function when measured at the maximisation level is always negative and when measured at the minimisation level is always positive, it can be used to distinguish between points of maximum and minimum. For example, if the second derivative in our profit function curve is negative, it implies that profits are maximum at the level where first derivative is equal to zero. On the other hand, if the second derivative at a point on a profit function where first derivative is zero is positive, it shows profits are in fact minimum rather than maximum. It can be easily known from having a look at Figure 3.10. It will be seen from this figure that up to point L, marginal profit $\left(\frac{d\pi}{dQ}\right)$, that is, slope of the total profit curve, is negative and has been causing the total profits to fall (in fact, up to L, due to negative marginal profits loses have been increasing. At point L, marginal profit $\left(\frac{d\pi}{dQ}\right)$ becomes zero and thereafter it becomes positive and therefore it will causes the total profit to increase. Hence, point L beyond which the second derivative (*i.e.* the slope of the first derivative) is positive, and therefore profits will be increasing cannot be point of maximum profits.

Now consider point H on the total profit corresponding to output level OQ_2. At point H, first derivative $\left(\frac{d\pi}{dQ}\right)$ is again equal to zero but after that marginal profit $\frac{d\pi}{dQ}$ becomes negative as the slope of total profit curve is negative as output is expanded beyond Q_2. This causes the total profits to fall. This shows that point H at which first derivative, $\frac{d\pi}{dQ}$ is zero and also beyond which second derivative $\left(\frac{d^2\pi}{dQ^2}\right)$, that is, slope of the first derivative becomes negative is indeed the point of maximum profit.

To conclude, we get a following general test for maximum and minimum.

(1) If the second derivative $\frac{d^2y}{dx^2}$ of a function is negative (< 0) at the point where first derivative $\left(\frac{dy}{dx}\right)$ is zero, it will represent a point of maximum.

(2) If the second derivative $\left(\frac{d^2y}{dx^2}\right)$ of a function is positive (> 0) at the point where first derivative is zero, it will represent a point of minimum.

Coming back to our profit function ($\pi = -100 + 160\ Q - 10\ Q^2$) in which case the first derivative is zero at 8 units of output, we test for the sign of second derivative. Thus,

$$\frac{d\pi}{dQ} = 160 - 20Q$$

$$\frac{d^2\pi}{dQ^2} = -20.$$

Thus, we find that at 8 units of output profits will in fact be maximum.

Minimisation Problem

In some decision making problems the objective of a manager is to minimise the objective function. For example, efficiency in the use of resources requires that a firm should produce at the minimum possible cost per unit of output. For example, the following average cost function of a firm is given :

$$AC = 25{,}000 - 180Q + 0.50Q^2$$

A manager is interested to find what level of output the firm will minimise its average cost. This can be obtained by differentiating the AC function with respect to output (Q) and setting it equal to zero, Thus

$$\frac{d(AC)}{dQ} = -180 + 1.0Q$$

Setting it equal to zero and solving for Q we have

$$-180 + 1.0\,Q = 0$$

$$Q = 180$$

Applying the second order condition to ensure whether it is really minimum we take the second derivative of AC function

$$\frac{d^2AC}{dQ^2} = +1.0$$

Since second derivative of AC function is positive, $\frac{d^2AC}{dQ^2} > 0$, output of 180 units of output is one that minimises average cost of production.

Multivariate Optimisation

As has been explained earlier, when a dependent variable is a function of many independent variables we use the concept of a partial derivative. Partial derivatives are therefore used to find optimal solution to maximisation or minimisation problem in case of two or more independent variables. Rules for finding maximisation and minimisation problems are the same as described above in case of one independent variable. To maximise or minimise a multivariate function we set partial derivative with respect to each independent variable equal to zero and solve the resulting set of simultaneous equations.

Consider that a firm is producing two products X and Y. Its profit function may be written as

$$\pi = f(X, Y).$$

Consider a firm producing the two products whose function is given below

$$\pi = 50X - 2X^2 - XY - 4Y^2 + 75Y$$

Where X and Y are two independent variables representing levels of outputs of two products. It is to decide what levels of output of the two products will maximise profits.

Differentiating the profit function with respect to X, while holding Y constant we have

$$\frac{d\pi}{dX} = 50 - 4X - Y$$

Differentiating the profit function with respect to y while holding x constant we have

$$\frac{d\pi}{dy} = -X - 8Y + 75$$

For maximisation of profits *we must set each partial derivative equal to zero* and then solve the resulting set of simultaneous equations for optimal values of independent variables *x* and *y*. Thus,

$$\frac{\partial \pi}{\partial X} = 50 - 4X - Y = 0 \quad \text{.... } (i)$$

$$\frac{\partial \pi}{\partial Y} = 75 - X - 8Y = 0 \quad \text{.... } (ii)$$

To solve the above two equations simultaneously we multiply equation (*i*) by – 8 and adding (*i*) and (*ii*) we have

$$-400 + 32X + 8Y = 0$$
$$75 - X - 8Y$$
$$-325 + 31X = 0$$
$$31X = 325$$
$$X = \frac{325}{31} = 10.45$$

Substituting $X = 10.45$ in equation (i) we have

$$50 - 4X\ 10.45 - Y = 0$$
$$50 - 41.80 - Y = 0$$

or $$Y = 50 - 41.80 = 8.20$$

Thus the firm will maximise profits of it produces and sells 10.45 units of product *x* and 8.2 units of product *y*.[1]

CONSTRAINED OPTIMISATION

So far we have been concerned with explaining unconstrained optimisation, that is, maximisation or minimisation of an objective function when there are *no constraints.* However, consumers and managers of business firms quite often face decision problems when there are constraints which limit the choice available to them for optimisation. For example, a business firm may face a constraint with regard to the limited availability of some crucial raw material, skilled manpower. Constraint may be of the limited productive capacity as determined by the size of the plant and capital equipment installed. Besides quite often marketing managers are required to maximise sales subject to the constraint of a given advertising expenditure at their disposal. Further, financial managers also work under the constraint of a given *investment requirements* of a firm and they are required to minimise the cost of raising capital for that purpose. Managers of business firms also face legal and environmental constraints.

In all these cases when managers face constraints in their decision making to maximise or minimise their objective functions we have a problem of *constrained optimisation.* It is worth nothing that the existence of constraints prevents the achievement of the unconstrained

1. It should be noted that the second order condition for maximisation is also satisfied. Recall that the second order condition which is based on the value of the second order derivative is used to distinguish between a maximum and minimum. However, the second-order condition in case of maximisation or minimisation of a multivariable function is very complex and therefore we do not attempt to explain that in this text in all maximisation and minimisation problems involving multivariable functions explained in this chapter. We therefore assume that the point at which all partial derivatives are zero, the second order condition for maximisation or minimisation is satisfied. Those readers who are interested in knowing the second order condition in case of multivariable functions may consult a textbook on differential calculus.

optimal. There are two techniques of solving the constrained optimisation problem[2]. They are : (1) substitution method, (2) Lagrangian multiplier technique. We explain them below.

1. Constrained Optimasation : Substitution Method. Substitution method to solve constrained optimisation problem is used when constraint equation is simple and not too complex. For example substitution method to maximise or minimise the objective function when it is subject to only one constraint equation of a very simple nature. In this method, we solve the constraint equation for one of the decision variables and substitute that variable in the objective function that is to be maximised or minimised. In this way this method converts the constrained optimisation problem into one of unconstrained optimisation problems of maximisation or minimisation. Then, the same procedure of optimisation is applied as the explained earlier in this chapter.

An example will clarify the use of substitution method to solve constrained optimisation problem. Suppose a manager of a firm which is producing two products x and y, seeks to maximise total profits function which is given by the following equation

$$\pi = 50x - 2x^2 - xy - 3y^2 + 95y$$

where x and y represent the quantities of the two products. The manager of the firm faces the constraints that the total output of the two products must be equal to 25. That is, according to the constraint,

$$x + y = 25$$

To solve this constrained optimisation problem through substitution we first solve the constraint equation for x. Thus

$$x = 25 - y$$

The next step in the substitution method is to substitute this value of $x = 25 - y$ in the objective function (*i.e.* the given profit function) which has to be maximised. Thus, substituting the constrained value of x in the profit function we have

$$\pi = 50\,(25 - y) - 2\,(25 - y)^2 - (25 - y)\,y - 3y^2 + 95y$$
$$= 1250 - 50y - 2\,(625 - 50y + y^2) - 25y + y^2 - 3y^2 + 95y$$
$$= 1250 - 50y - 1250 + 100y - 2y^2 - 25y + y^2 - 3y^2 + 95y$$
$$= 120y - 4y^2$$

To maximise the above profit function converted into the above unconstrained form we differentiate it with respect to y and set it equal to zero and solve for y. Thus,

$$\frac{d\pi}{dy} = 120 - 8y = 0$$

or, $8y = 120$

$$y = 15$$

Substituting $y = 15$ in the given constraint equation $(x + y = 25)$ we have

$$X + 15 = 25$$
$$X = 25 - 15 = 10$$

Thus, given the constraint, profit will be maximised if the manager of the firm decides to produce 10 units of the product x and 15 units of the product y. We can find the total profits

2. In this chapter we explain the techniques of solving the problems of constrained optimisation in those cases when constraints are expressed in the form of equations. Quite often constraints faced refer only to the upper or lower limits on the decision makers. These constraints are expressed as *inequalities.* A technique of linear programming has been development to deal with the problems of constrained optimisation in case constraints of inequality type are present. We will explain linear programming technique in a separate chapter of this book.

in this constrained optimum situation by substituting the values of x and y obtained in the given profit function. Thus,

$$\pi = 50x - 2x^2 - xy - 3y^2 + 95y$$
$$\pi = 50 \times 10 - 2(10)^2 - 10\times 15 - 3(15)^2 + 95 \times 15$$
$$= 500 - 200 - 150 - 675 + 1425$$
$$= 1925 - 1025$$
$$= 900$$

Lagrange Multiplier Technique

The substitution method for solving constrained optimisation problem cannot be used easily when the constraint equation is very complex and therefore cannot be solved for one of the decision variable. In such cases of constrained optimisation we employ the Lagrangian Multiplier technique. In this Lagrangian technique of solving constrained optimisation problem, a combined equation called Lagrangian function is formed which incorporates both the original objective function and constraint equation. This Lagrangian function is formed in a way which ensures that when it is maximised or minimised, the original given objective function is also maximised or minimised and at the same time it fulfils all the constraint requirements. In creating this Lagrangian function, an artificial variable λ (Greek letter Lamda) is used and it is multiplied by the given constraint function having been set equal to zero. λ is known as *Lagrangian multiplier.*

Lagrangian Multiplier

Since Lagrangian function incorporates the constraint equation into the objective function, it can be considered as unconstrained optimisation problem and solved accordingly. Let us illustrate Lagrangian multiplier technique by taking the constrained optimisation problem solved above by substitution method. In that problem manager of a firm was to maximise the following profit function :

$$\pi = 50x - 2x^2 - xy - 3y^2 + 95y$$

subject to the constraint,

$$x + y = 25$$

where x and y are the outputs of two products produced by the firm.

In order to constitute Lagrangian function we first set the constraint function equal to zero by bringing all the terms to the left side of the equation. In doing so we have

$$x + y - 25 = 0$$

The next step in creating the Lagrangian function is to multiply this form of the constraint function by the unknown artificial factor λ and then adding the result to the given original objective function. Thus combining the constraint and the objective function through Lagrangian multplier (λ) we have

$$L_\pi = 50x - 2x^2 - xy - 3y^2 + 95y + \lambda\,(x + y - 25)$$

where L_π stands for the expression of Lagrangian function.

As stated above, the Lagrangaion function can considered as unconstrained optimisation function. It will be seen that in this function there are three unknowns x, y and λ. Note that the solution that maximises Lagrangian function (L_π) will also maximise profit (π) function :

For maximising L_π, we first find partial derivatives of L_π with respect to three unknown x, y and λ and then set them equal to zero. Thus

$$\frac{\partial L_\pi}{\delta x} = 50 - 4x - y + \lambda = 0 \qquad ..... (i)$$

$$\frac{\partial L_\pi}{\delta y} = -x - 6y + 95 + \lambda = 0 \qquad \text{..... } (ii)$$

$$\frac{\partial L_\pi}{\delta \lambda} = x + y - 25 = 0 \qquad \text{..... } (iii)$$

Note that the last equation (iii) is the constraint subject to which the original profit function has to be maximised. In fact, Lagrangian function is so constructed that the partial derivative of L_π with respect to λ (Lagrangian multiplier) always yields the original constraint function. Further, since the portial derivative of L_π with respect to λ is set equal to zero, it not only ensures that the constraint of the optimisation problem is fulfilled but also converts the Lagrangian function into original constrained profit maximisation problem so that the solution to both of them will yield the same result.

Let us now solve the above system of three equations with three unknowns to find the optimal values of x and y. To do so we first substract the equation (ii) from equation (i) and get

$$-45 - 3x + 5y = 0 \qquad \text{..... (iv)}$$

Now, multiplying equation (iii) by 3 and adding it to equation (iv) we have

$$\begin{aligned} -45 - 3x + 5y &= 0 \\ -75 + 3x + 3y &= 0 \\ \hline -120 + 8y \quad - &= 0 \end{aligned}$$

Thus, $8y = 120$

$y = 15$

Substituting the value of $y = 15$ in the constraint function $x + y = 25$ we get x equal to 10. Thus, we find the same optimal values of x and y as we obtained in the substitution method.

Lagrange technique of solving constrained optimisation is highly significant for two reasons. First, as noted above, when constraint conditions are too many or too complex, it is not feasible to use substitution method and therefore in such cases it is easy to use Lagrange technique for solution of constrained optimisation problems. Second, the use of Lagrangian multiplier technique also provides the decision maker as additional important information. This information is the value of λ that is, Lagrangian multiplier itself. The value of λ has a significant economic interpretation. The value of λ shows the marginal effect on the solution of the objective function when there is a unit change in the constraint. Thus, in our example of profit maximization, value of λ indicates the *marginal profit* caused by a 1-unit change in the output of products, that is, change in the total profit when output constraint either increases from 25 to 26 or decreases from 25 to 24.

The value of λ can be obtained by substituting the solved values of x and y in a partial derivative equation containing λ in the Lagrangian function. Thus, in our above example, the value of λ can be obtained by substituting $x = 10$ and $y = 15$ in equation (ii) above

Thus, in the above equation (*ii*)

$$-x - 6y + 95 + \lambda = 0$$

$$\lambda = x + 6y - 95$$

$$\lambda = 10 + 90 - 95$$

$$\lambda = +5$$

Here λ can be interpreted as marginal profit at the production level of 25 units. It shows if the firm is required to produce 24 units instead of 25 units, its profits will fall by 5. On the other hand, if firm were to produce 26 instead of 25 units, its profits will increase by about 5.

Note that Lagrange technique maximises profits under a constraint. It does not solve unconstrained profit maximization.

QUESTIONS FOR REVIEW

1. What is meant by optimisation ? Explain its significance in managerial decision making.
2. Define the following terms
   (*i*) Function
   (*ii*) Dependent Variable
   (*iii*) Independent Variable
   (*iv*) Constant
   (*v*) Intercept
3. (*a*) What is a linear function ? What factors determine a specific form of a linear function ? How does its graph look like ?
   (2) (a) Write a linear demand function with a single independent variable.
   (*b*) Give an example of a specific linear demand function with a single independent variable.
   (*c*) How will you interpret the coefficient of the independent variable in a linear demand function ?
4. (*a*) Write a multivariable linear demand function ? How will you interpret the coefficients of various independent variables ?
   (*b*) How is the effect of non-price variables on demand for a commodity depicted in economics?
5. What is a quadratic function ? Distinguish between a convex and concave quadratic functions. How will their graphs look like ? Show them with diagrams.
6. Write a quadratic function with two independent variables. How will its graph look like ?
7. What is a cubic function ? Write a general form of a cubic function. Can a cubic function contain first degree, second degree and third degree terms in it ?
8. What does slope of a function indicate ? Plot the following linear function and measure its slope.

$$y = 5 + 0.8x$$

9. Draw a curve representing a quadratic function : How will you measure slope at a point on it? Does slope of a quadratic function remain constant along it ?

OPTIMISATION TECHNIQUES

10. (a) Explain the concept of a derivative of a function. Explain the logic of using the derivative of a function to find the maximum or minimum of that function.
    (b) What is the significance of the concept of derivative in business applications ?
11. Why is derivative of a constant function equal to zero? Draw a graph of a constant function.
12. You are given the following linear supply function :

$$Q = 2 + 1.5P$$

Draw its graph and show the value of its derivative.

13. Describe the following rules of differentiation

(1) Power rule of differentiation
(2) Function of a function rule of differentiation
(3) Chain rule of differentiation
(4) Product rule of differentiation

14. What is a partial derivative of a function ? In which type of function the concept of a partial derivative is applied ? What is the assumption that underlies the interpretation of any one variable?

15. What is a second derivative ? How is the second derivative used in distinguishing between a maximium and minimum point ?

16. Find the first and second derivative of the following total revenue (*TR*) and total cost (*TC*) functions. Find the values of these derivatives at the level of output of 10 units. Also interpret the values of the first and second derivatives so obtained

1. $TR = 40\,Q - 2Q^2$
2. $TR = 150 + 25Q + 10Q^2$
3. $TC = 300 + 15Q$
4. $TC = 150 + 7Q - 3Q^2 + Q^3$

17. You are given the following production functions where Q stands for output, L and K for units of labour and capital respectively used in the production process. Find the first and second derivatives of these functions with respect to labour and explain what these derivatives imply :

1. $Q = 3L^2 + 2\,LK - 5K^2$
2. $Q = 5L^2 + 10\,LK + 2K$
3. $Q = 100L^{0.5}\,K^{0.5}$

18. Consider the following demand function of a product facing a firm

$$P = 25 - Q$$

Where P = price and Q = quantity demand of the product measured in units

(*a*) Express the total revenue function
(*b*) Express the marginal revenue function
(*c*) At what quantity demanded total. revenue will be maximised.

19. How does the manager of a business firm determine the profit maximising level of output ? Use concept of derivatives.

20. Suppose objective function of a firm is to maximise its sales. How will it determine sales-maximisation level of output ?

(Hints. Sales is considered in value terms. Thus sales mean total revenue received from the output produced and sold) Take inverse demand function (that is, price expressed as a function of quantity demanded (Q) and multiply it with Q to get total revenue. Then use the concept of derivatives to determine sales maximisation level of output).

21. What is meant *by* partial derivative ? How is it obtained ? Can the partial derivative of a function with respect to one independent variable depend also on the value of the other independent variable ? If so, why ?

PROBLEMS ON CONSTRAINED OPTIMISATION

22. (a) What is meant *by* 'constrained optimisation'? What is its significance in managerial decision making ?
(b) How can a constrained optimisation problem be solved through Lagrangian multiplier technique?

23. Explain Lagrangian mutiplier method of solving constrained optimisation problem. How is Lagrangian function formed ? What is the economic significance of Lagrangian multiplier λ ?

24. Suppose that a firm is producing two models of a car, model *J* and model *T*. The total revenue function from the sales of two cars is

$TR = J.T$

where both J and T are measured in thousands of units Due to limited productive capacity the maximum number of cars (J models + T models) that can be produced is 10 thousands (that is $J + T = 10$)

Using lagrangion multiplier method determine the quantities of the two models is J and T that should be produced to maximise revenue. Also interpret the value of Lagrangian multiplier (λ) in this case.

25. Suppose Pepsi Cola estimates that sales of its drink is a function of the amounts of advertisement expenditure (measured in lakhs of rupees) in two different media, television and newspapers. If x stands for advertisement expenditure in lakhs on advertisement on television and y stands for expenditure in lakhs on advertisement in newspapers, sales of Pepsi Cola is given by

$$S = 200x + 100y - 10x^2 - 20y^2 + 20xy$$

Assume that advertising budget is restricted to Rs. 20 lakhs so that $x + y = 20$

(*i*) Using Lagrangian multplier technique find the amount of expenditure incurred on television and newspaper advertising separately to maximise sales subject to the bndgit constraint.

(*ii*) Calculate the sales of the firm at this constrained optimum level.

(*iii*) What economic interpretation will you give for the value of the Lagrangian multiplier obtained.

Marginal and Incremental Analysis

Role of Marginal Analysis in Managerial Decision Making

As stated earlier, managerial economics is the application of economic theory and method to examine how a business firm achieves its objective most efficiently. The objective of the firm generally is considered to be maximisation of profits or value of the firm. To achieve these objectives, firms have to minimise cost to produce a given level of output and, in the long run, to maximise yields from various investment projects undertaken by it. The methods of maximising or minimising the objective function are generally called *optimisation techniques.* Marginal analysis is one of the useful optimisation technique of managerial decision making. Managerial economics is chiefly concerned with resource allocation decisions by business firms: The resource-allocation decisions are frequently expressed in terms of the marginal conditions that must be met if optimal solution is to be obtained. The common element in all managerial decision making problem is: '*Is it worthwhile*' to take any action or decision in the performance of managerial functions. Whether a manager of firm is considering to produce more units of output, or it is considering to allocate more resources to advertising for the product, or it is planning to improve the quality of its product or to undertake any long-term investment project, he must ask the question: whether the action being considered will yield sufficient *additional* benefit to the firm to make it worthwhile to take it keeping in view the cost incurred on it. This is the essence of the managerial decision making for it shows that it is worthwhile to take an action if and only if it yields *net marginal benefits* to the firms and *net* marginal benefits means marginal benefits *net* of additional or marginal cost incurred to undertake that action.

It may be noted that marginal analysis is intimately related to mathematical tool of differential calculus which is also an important optimisation technique. A marginal number of units may be interpreted as the previous derivative of a function. We have studied differential calculus as an optimisation technique in the previous chapter. However, since marginal analysis can be conducted with the help of arithmetical examples and graphs or curves, it has a distinct pedagogical advantage over differential calculus. However, complex decision making problems involving several decision variables can be solved through differential calculus.

It should be noted that for finding an optimal solution to a problem through marginal analysis the decision-maker must be able not only to identify alternative courses of action in a given situation but also appropriate decision variables which have to be manipulated to achieve the goal. In addition, relevant benefits and costs of various alternatives must be capable of being estimated so that optimal solution to the problem be obtained. Many alternative techniques such as the use of total benefit and total cost, differential calculus, linear programming and others are available but in modern economic problems marginal analysis is the most widely used technique for finding optimal solution to a problem.

Fundamental Theorems of Resource Allocation

Before explaining the concept and technique of marginal analysis for finding optimum solution to managerial decision-making problems, it is desirable to state two fundamental theorems of resource allocation which make use of marginal analysis. These two theorems relate to the following two issues:

1. What is the *level or magnitude of an activity* which is optimal, that is, which best achieves the objective. The theorem is often referred to as theorem of *optimal activity level.* How much level of output a firm should produce which maximizes its profits, how many units of a factor or input a producer employs that minimizes cost for a given level of output or maximizes output for a given cost outlay ; how much quantity of a commodity a consumer should consume so as to maximize his satisfaction relate to optimal activity level.
2. *To what extent various activities involving allocation of given resources should be carried* to achieve the optimal results. This problem is therefore referred to as relative activity levels. We explain below two theorems concerning the above two problems, namely, (1) optimal activity level and (2) relative activity levels.

Optimal Activity Level

According to the first theorem of resource allocation, the level of output of a product, the amount of an input used or any other activity should be expanded so long as *marginal net yield* from it is *positive.* By marginal net yield of any activity we mean the addition to the total return or benefit made by one-unit increase in the activity level minus the additional cost incurred on it. *To achieve maximum total net yield or benefit, that is, to attain optimal level an activity should be expanded, if possible, to the point where marginal net yield is zero.* For example, the output of a product produced by a firm should be expanded to the level at which *marginal net profit is zero.* Marginal net profit is equal to the difference between marginal revenue and marginal cost of a unit of output. In other words, for optimal or profit-maximizing level of output marginal revenue must equal marginal cost of production. This is an important rule of managerial analysis which is extensively used in managerial economics for determining level of output of a product to be produced and price to be charged. We shall explain in more detail later in this chapter as to how a firm maximizes its profits by producing a level of output where marginal revenue (MR) equals marginal cost (*MC*) of production.

Similarly, to what extent a firm should use an input, say labour, is determined by the level at which marginal net yield from an extra unit of that input is zero. A firm pays price for an input (*e.g.*, wages to workers), a profit-cost maximizing level of employment of the labour is determined where wages (which constitute cost to the firm) equals marginal revenue product (MRP) of labour and therefore marginal net yield is zero. Another important application of this theorem of optimal level of activity lies in the field of long-term investment decisions which are also made using marginal analysis. According to this, an investment project should be undertaken if expected marginal return from it exceeds the marginal cost of capital funds. Further, to attain an optimal level investment in any particular field should be carried to the point where marginal net yield from it is zero.

We have given above only few examples from managerial economics where the theorem of optimal activity level based on marginal analysis is applied. This theorem of optimal activity level is, in fact, used in all fields of economics, namely, consumption, production, exchange, public finance, international economics.

Theorem on Relative Activity Levels

This is another significant theorem of marginal analysis. According to this, to achieve maximum gain or benefits from various activities, whenever possible *they should be carried to the levels where they provide equal marginal yield per unit of cost.* If this condition does not hold a decision maker will be missing the opportunity to obtain extra gain by reallocating his resources among them. For example, if a manager is considering use of various factors for production, *he will be maximising output from a given cost outlay if marginal product of a rupee spent on each factor* is the same (that is, $\frac{MP_L}{w} = \frac{MP_K}{r}$ where MP_L and MP_K are marginal products of labour and capital respectively, and w and r are the prices of labour and capital respectively). If it is not so (e.g., if $\frac{MP_L}{w} > \frac{MP_K}{r}$), then he can increase output for reallocating resources between them (*i.e.*, using resources to buy more labour and less capital until $\frac{MP_L}{w} = \frac{MP_K}{r}$). Similarly, to achieve maximum utility a consumer will be spending his money income on goods in such a manner that the marginal utility of a rupee spent on each good is the same

$$\left(\frac{MU_x}{P_x} = \frac{MU_x}{P_y} = \ldots\ldots\ldots \frac{MU_z}{P_z} = MU_m\right).$$

Take another example from managerial economics. Suppose a manager of a firm has to decide how much to spend his resources on (1) quality control, and (2) advertising for promoting sales of its product. The maximum benefits will be obtained if he allocates resources in a way that marginal yield of the resources from these two activities is the same.

TOTAL, AVERAGE AND MARGINAL RELATIONSHIP

Relationship between total, average and marginal concepts is highly useful in marginal analysis of optimum decision making. This relationship between total, average and marginal numbers holds in case of all concepts such as revenue, cost of production, profit, utility. We explain the relationship by taking total, average and marginal revenue concepts. Total revenue from a product of a firm is the total quantity of the product produced and sold multiplied by price of the product. Thus

$$TR = P.Q \qquad \ldots\ldots (1)$$

where TR stands for total revenue, P for price and Q for quantity of the product produced and sold.

Average revenue is the revenue earned per unit of output produced and sold. Thus

$$AR = \frac{TR}{Q} \qquad \ldots\ldots (2)$$

Average revenue (*AR*) is equal to price when a firm sells all units of output produced at the same price (that is, when it is not price discriminating).

However, it is marginal revenue concept that is of crucial importance in marginal analysis. Marginal revenue is defined as the extra revenue earned by producing and selling an extra unit of output. Stating algebraically, marginal revenue is the difference between total revenue earned by producing and selling '*n*' units of a product instead of '*n*-1' units. Thus

$$MR = TR_n - TR_{n-1} \qquad \text{......(3)}$$

Marginal revenue can also be defined in terms of differential calculus as

$$MR = \frac{\Delta TR}{\Delta Q}$$

Or $MR = \frac{dTR}{dQ}$, that is, limit of $\frac{\Delta TR}{\Delta Q}$ when $\Delta Q \Rightarrow O$,

$\frac{\Delta TR}{\Delta Q}$ or $\frac{dTR}{dQ}$ indicates that marginal revenue is given by the slope of the marginal revenue curve. The relationship between total, average and marginal revenue can be illustrated through equations, tables or graphs. We have explained the relation between these three concepts in Table 4.1 where we have given the data representing the following specific total revenue equation:

$$TR = 50Q - 5Q^2$$

By substituting the value of *Q* (0 to 7), we have obtained the total revenue, marginal revenue, average revenue figures at various levels of output or salses. It will be seen from the

Table 4.1. Relation between Total Revenue, Marginal Revenue and Average Revenue

Output (Q)	Equation $50Q - 5Q^2$		Total Revenue TR	Marginal Revenue (MR) $TR_n - TR_{n-1}$	Average Revenue (AR) TR/Q
0	$50(0) - 5(0)^2$	=	0	0	0
1	$50(1) - 5(1)^2$	=	45	45	45
2	$50(2) - 5(2)^2$	=	80	35	40
3	$50(3) - 5(3)^3$	=	105	25	35
4	$50(4) - 5(4)^2$	=	120	15	30
5	$50(5) - 5(5)^2$	=	125	5	25
6	$50(6) - 5(6)^2$	=	120	-5	20
7	$50(7) - 5(7)^2$	=	125	-15	15

table that when output is zero and nothing is sold, total revenue is zero and therefore marginal and average revenue (*AR*) are zero. As output is expanded and we substitute higher values of output (*Q*) are the total revenue equation, total revenue goes on increasing as will be seen from Col. III of Table 4.1. An important facts to be noted is that *when one unit of output is produced and sold, total revenue, marginal revenue and average revenue are equal.* All these are equal to Rs.45. This is quite obvious from the definition of total revenue, marginal revenue and average revenue and needs no explanation. It will be seen from Table 4.1 that if output is increased beyond five units of output, total revenue (*TR*) starts declining and marginal revenue (*MR*) becomes negative.

Relation between Total Revenue and Marginal Revenue

As stated above, marginal revenue is the addition to total revenue associated with a unit increase in output or sales. Therefore, total revenue (*TR*) increases when marginal revenue (*MR*) is positive and total revenue (*TR*) decreases when marginal revenue (*MR*) is negative. It will be seen from Table-I that up to 5 units of output and sales, marginal revenue is positive and as a result total revenue increases with output over this range. Marginal revenue of the 6th and 7th units of output are negative, it therefore causes total revenues (*TR*) to decrease. From this it follows that total revenue function will be maximized (or any function for that matter) at the point where marginal revenue (*MR*) changes from being positive to be negative. That is, total *revenue is maximised when marginal revenue (MR) is zero.* This is an important rule of marginal analysis.

Another important rule of marginal analysis can be derived from the relation between total revenue (*TR*) and marginal revenue (*MR*). Since marginal revenue is addition to total revenue by each successive units of output, *total revenue (TR) can be obtained by summering up marginal revenues of all the preceding units of output (including the last one).* Thus $TR = \Sigma MR$ of all the units of output produced and sold.

Thus with regard to relation between total revenue and marginal revenue we arrive at the following important rules:

1. Total revenue increases when marginal revenue is positive.
2. Total revenue is maximized at the output level where marginal revenue (MR) is equal to zero.
3. Total revenue at a certain level of output (or sales) is equal to the sum of all the preceding marginal revenues (including the last one) of the total units of output produced and sold.

The above relationships between total and marginal number apply equally to all the total and marginal concepts whether they relate to revenue, cost, profit or utility.

Relationship between Average and Marginal Revenue

There is an important arithmetical relationship between average and marginal revenue which is extensively used in optimization analysis. Since a marginal revenue represents the change in total revenue as a result of a unit change in output, it follows that when marginal revenue is greater than average revenue, average revenue increases (that is, higher *MR* pulls up *AR*). When marginal revenue is less than average revenue, average revenue declines. And when marginal revenue is equal to average revenue, average revenue remains unchanged.

It will be seen from Table 4.1 that when output increases from 2 units to 7 units, average revenue (*AR*) decreases from Rs. 40 to Rs. 15. This is because marginal revenue is less than average revenue over this range and therefore pulls down the average revenue. This relation between average and marginal numbers is more clearly evident is case of average and marginal costs. In the beginning when output increases, average cost of production falls because marginal cost remains less than average cost. Beyond a point average cost rises because marginal cost exceeds average cost of production. Marginal cost is equal to average cost when it stops falling and has not yet started rising. That is, marginal cost is equal to average cost at the latter's minimum point.

However, this relationship between average and marginal numbers is often misunderstood. It is often stated that when an average quantity *falls,* marginal quantity must also be *falling* and when average quantity *rises,* marginal quantity *must also be rising.* This is quite false. In fact what the relation between the two states is that *when average quantity falls* marginal quantity must be *less* than the average quantity; marginal quantity though remaining less than the average quantity may itself may be falling, rising on remain constant. If an average quantity is rising, marginal quantity need not be rising. What is true in this case is that when average is rising marginal *must be greater than average,* marginal number itself may be rising, falling or remaining constant. The relation between an average quantity (A) and marginal quantity (M) is illustrated in Figure 4.1.

It is worth noting that above relationship between average and marginal quantities is a purely arithmetical relation and does not represent any proposition or law of economics.

DERIVING AVERAGE AND MARGINAL REVENUE CURVES FROM TOTAL REVENUE CURVE

The relationship between total, average and marginal quantities can be illustrated geometrically. We explain this relationship by taking total revenue curve and deriving average and marginal revenue curves from it. Total revenue curve TR has been drawn in the upper panel of Fig. 4.1. This total revenue curve TR shows that total revenue ($P.Q$) earned increases with the increase in output up to output level OQ_3 and decreases beyond it. Average revenue is the total revenue (TR) divided by the corresponding level of output (that is, $AR = \frac{TR}{Q}$). Therefore, geometrically average revenue at a given level of output is given by the slope of a line from the origin to the corresponding point on the total revenue curve. For example, in Figure 4.1 at output level OQ_1, the corresponding point on the total revenue curve TR is R. Thus, average revenue at this point is given by the slope of the line OR, which is $\frac{RQ_1}{OQ_1}$, in the bottom panel of Figure 4.1, taken to be equal to Q_1r, (that is, $\frac{RQ_1}{OQ_1} = Q_1r$). Now, at output level OQ_2 corresponding to point S on the total revenue curve TR, average revenue is given by the slope of line OS, that is, $\frac{SQ_2}{OQ_2}$ which in the bottom panel is taken to be equal to Q_2S. Similarly, at point T on the total revenue curve TR or output level OQ_3 in the top panel of Figure 4.1, average revenue is given by the *slope of the line OT*, that is, $\frac{TQ_3}{OQ_3}$ which in the bottom panel has been taken to be equal to Q_3t. Thus, *at any point on the total revenue curve, the corresponding average revenue is given by the slope of a straight live from the origin to that point.*

Now, in the bottom panel of Figure 4.1 by joining points r, s and t we get average revenue curve AR which we have extended to the Y-axis.

Deriving Marginal Revenue Curve from the Total Revenue Curve

As stated above, marginal revenue is the addition to total revenue associated with a unit increase in output or sales by a firm. Therefore, marginal revenue (MR) at a point on the total revenue curve is given by the slope of the total revenue curve at a that point. The slope of the total revenue curve at a point is measured by the slope of the tangent drawn at that point to the total revenue curve. For example, at point R corresponding to output level OQ_1 in the top panel of Figure 4.1, marginal revenue at output level OQ_1 or point R on the TR curve can be obtained by measuring the slope of the tangent tt' drawn at point R which in the bottom panel of Figure 4.1 is taken to be equal to Q_1m_1. Similarly, at point S on the total revenue curve corresponding to output level OQ_2, marginal revenue can be measured by the slope the tangent JJ' drawn to the total revenue curve at point S, which is taken to be equal to Q_2m_2 in the bottom panel of Figure 4.1.

Further, at the highest point H on the total revenue curve TR corresponding to output level OQ_3, the slope of the tangent kk' drawn at point H is a horizontal straight line which implies that slope of the total revenue curve TR at this point is zero. Therefore, marginal revenue at OQ_3 in bottom panel is taken to be equal to zero. Now, joining points m_1, m_2, and Q_3 in the bottom panel gives us marginal revenue curve MR which we extend to the Y-axes. Thus, *at the point at which total revenue (TR) is maximum, marginal revenue (MR) is zero.*

It is important to note from the Figure 4.1 that beyond output level OQ_3, total revenue curve is sloping downward. This implies that beyond output level OQ_3, marginal revenue will be negative. Therefore, it *will* be seen from the bottom panel of Figure 4.1 that beyond output OQ_3 marginal revenue curve goes below the X-axes.

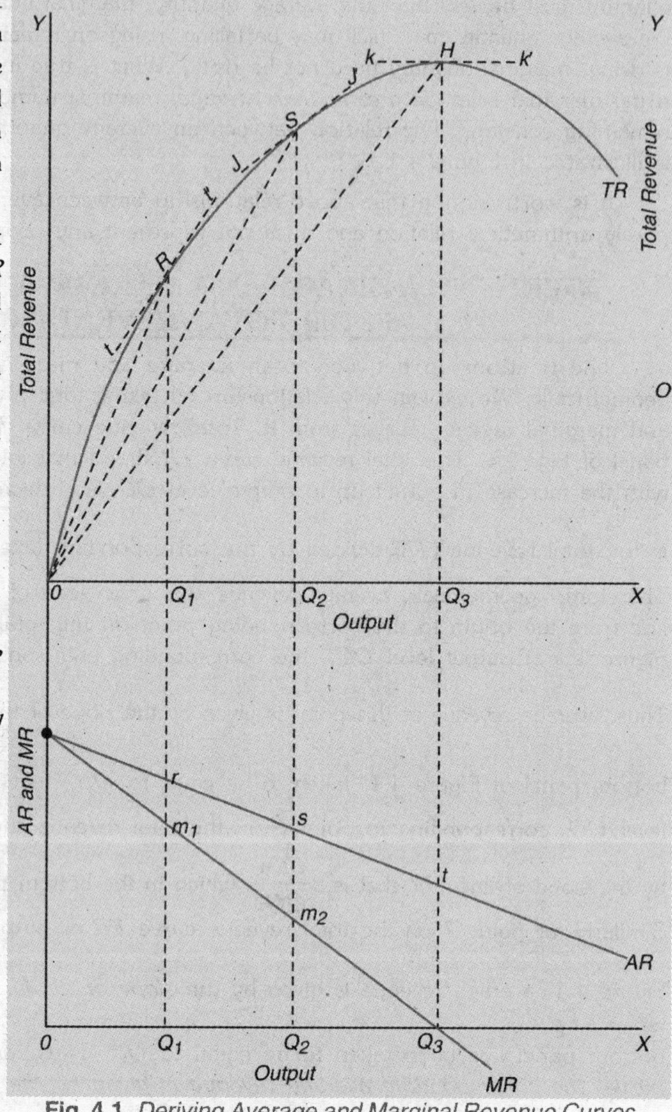

Fig. 4.1. *Deriving Average and Marginal Revenue Curves form Total Revenue Curve*

Average Revenue and Marginal Revenue Under Perfect Competition

We have explained above the concepts of total revenue, average revenue and marginal revenue when with the increase in output or sales by a firm, price of its product falls. However, when there prevails a perfect competition in the market for a product, price of the product is beyond the control of the firm, and it takes price as given and constant. As a result, demand curve facing a firm working in a perfectly competitive market is a horizontal straight line at the given level of price of the product. Thus, a perfectly competitive firm can sell as much as it likes at the prevailing price in the market. If the price or average revenue remains the same when more units of the good are sold, the marginal revenue will be equal to average revenue. This is so because if one more unit is sold and the price does not fall, the addition made to the total revenue by that unit will be equal to the price at which it is sold, since no loss in revenue is incurred on the previous units in this case.

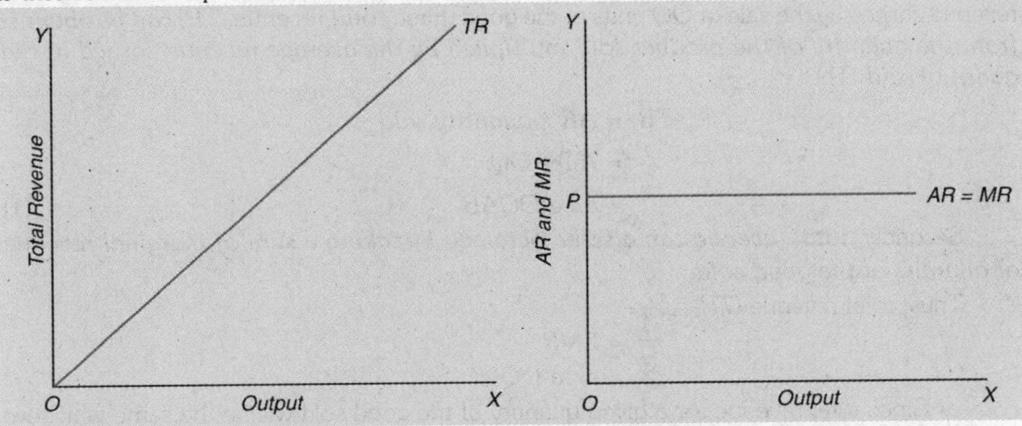

Fig 4.2. *Linear Total Revenue Curve of a Firm working Perfect Competition*

Fig. 4.3. *Average and Marginal Revenue Curves of a Firm working Under Perfect Competition*

The case of perfect competition when for an individual firm average revenue (or price) remains constant and marginal revenue is equal to average revenue is graphically shown in Fig. 4.2 and 4.3. Since marginal revenue under perfect competition remains constant and is equal to average revenue, total revenue curve under perfect competition will be a straight line from the origin as shown in Figure 4.2. Average revenue curve in this case is a horizontal straight line (*i.e.*, parallel to the *X*-axis) as shown in Fig.4.3. Horizontal-straight-line average revenue curve (*AR*) indicates that price or average revenue remains the same at *OP* level when more quantity of the product is sold. Marginal revenue (*MR*) curve coincides with average revenue (*AR*) curve since marginal revenue is equal to average revenue.

RELATIONSHIP BETWEEN AR AND MR CURVES

There is an important relationship between the average and marginal revenue curves *along a perpendicular to the Y-axis.* Given that the both average revenue (*AR*) and marginal revenue (*MR*) curves are of straight-line shape, it can be shown that (*MR*) curve will cut the distance between *AR* curve and *Y*-axis in the middle. In other words, when both *AR* and *MR* curves are linear, then if a perpendicular is drawn from a point on the *AR* curve to the *Y*-axis, *MR* curve will cut this perpendicular at its middle point. Consider Fig.4.4, where linear *AR* and *MR* curves are shown. Point *A* is taken on the average revenue curve and a perpendicular *AB* is drawn to the *Y*-axis. *MR* curve cuts perpendicular *AB* at point *C*. Now, if *MR* curve cuts halfway the distance between *AR* curve and *Y*-axis, then *AC* must be equal to *BC*. So in order to show that *MR* cuts halfway the distance between *AR* and *Y*-axis, we have to prove in Fig.4.4 that *AC* = *BC*.

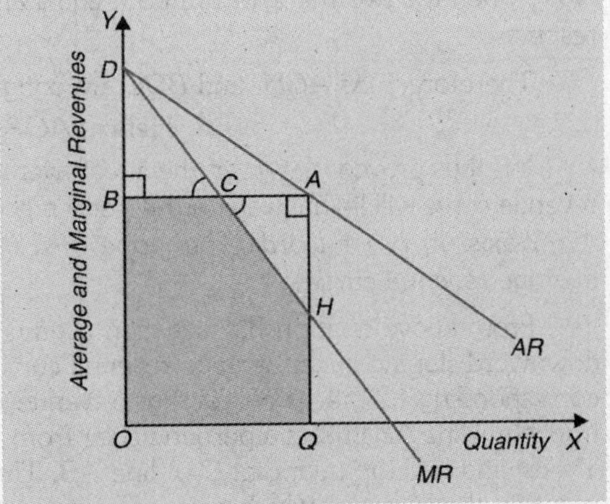

Fig.4.4. *MR curve cuts half-way the distance between AR curve and the Y-axis*

Draw a vertical straight line from *A* so as to meet the *X*-axis at *Q*. It means that when *OQ* quantity of the good is sold, average revenue is equal to AQ. Now, there are two ways in which we can find out the total revenue earned by the sale of OQ units of the good. First, *total revenue (TR) can be obtained from the quantity of the product sold multiplied by the average revenue earned at that quantity sold.* Thus

$$TR = AR \times quantity\ sold$$
$$= AQ \times OQ$$
$$= area\ OQAB \quad ..... (1)$$

Secondly, *total revenue can also be obtained by taking a sum of marginal revenues of all units of the good sold.*

Thus, total revenue (TR)

$$= \Sigma MR$$
$$= area\ OQHD$$

Since total revenue for a given quantity of the good sold will be the same whichever way it may be found, it follows that

$$OQAB = OQHD$$

But it will be noticed from the Figure 4.4 that

$$OQAB = OQHCB + ACH$$

And also $\quad OQHD = OQHCB + BDC$

From above it follows that

$$OQHCB + ACH = OQHCB + BDC$$

Or $\quad ACH = BDC$

Thus triangles ACH and BDC are equal in area

Now, in Δs ACH and BDC

$\angle HAC = \angle DBC$ (right angles)

$\angle ACH = \angle BCD$ (vertically opposite angles)

$\angle BDC = \angle AHC$ (alternate angles)

Therefore, ΔACH and ΔBDC are similar.

We have proved above that triangles ACH and BDC are equal in area as well as similar. Now, when the two triangles are both equal and similar, they are congruent (i.e. equal in all respects)

Therefore, Δs ACH and BDC are congruent

Hence, $AC = BC$

It is thus proved that given the linear average and marginal revenue curves, the marginal revenue curve will lie halfway on the perpendicular drawn from the average revenue curve to the Y-axis. *In other words, the slope of a marginal revenue curve is twice that of the average revenue curve.*

From above relationship between average revenue and marginal revenue in case of a downword-sloping linear average revenue curve, we can construct a marginal revenue curve corresponding to the given average revenue curve. For this purpose we draw any curve horizontal line AB (that is a perpendicular from any point on the average revenue curve to the Y-axis) and find the midpoint C of line AB. Then drawing a line DH starting from the same point on the Y-axis at which average revenue curve meets it.

Slope of liner *MR* Curve is Twice that of *AR* Curve: Mathematical Proof

That the linear marginal revenue curve has the same intercept on the *Y*-axis as the average revenue curve and its slope is twice that of average revenue curve of the firm can be mathematically proved.

Let the demand (or average revenue) curve be

$$P = a - bQ \qquad \text{.....}(i)$$

where P is price and Q is quantity demanded, 'a' is a constant term representing the intercept on the *Y*-axis and b is the slope of the demand or average revenue curve.

The total revenue curve (function) is

$$TR = P \,.\, Q = aQ - bQ^2$$

Differentiating the above total revenue function with respect to Q, we have

$$\frac{d(TR)}{dQ} = \frac{d(PQ)}{dQ} = a - 2bQ$$

Since $$\frac{d(TR)}{dQ} = MR$$

Therefore, $$MR = a - 2bQ \qquad \text{.....}(ii)$$

Comparing equations (*i*) and (*ii*), we see that intercept of the marginal revenue function (curve) on *Y*-axis is the same as of average revenue curve and the slope coefficient of the marginal revenue function is two times the slope coefficient b of the average revenue function. This implies that marginal revenue curve will cut half way the distance between the *Y*-axis and the average revenue curve.

Non-Liner *AR* and *MR* Curves

Marginal revenue curve corresponding to a *convex or concave* average revenue curve is not of straight-line shape but is either convex or concave to the origin. What relationship *MR* curve will bear to *AR* curve when average and marginal revenue curves are either convex or concave ? In either of these cases the marginal revenue curve will not lie halfway on the perpendicular from the average revenue curve to the *Y*-axis. If the average revenue curve is convex to the origin as in Fig.4.5 the marginal revenue curve *MR* will also be convex to the origin and will cut any perpendicular drawn from *AR* curve to the *Y*-axis *more than halfway* as measured from the average revenue curve. On the other hand, if the average revenue curve is *concave* to the origin as in Fig.4.6 the marginal revenue curve will also be concave and will cut any perpendicular line from the average revenue curve to the *Y*-axis *less than halfway* as measured from the average revenue curve. In Fig. 4.5 and 4.6, *C* is the middle point on the perpendicular line *AB* drawn to the *Y*-axis.

OPTIMISATION BY MARGINAL ANALYSIS

The most important use of marginal analysis in microeconomics is to determine optimum level of output by a firm, that is, to determine optimum activity level . The important objective of a firm is assumed to be maximisation of profits. In an earlier chapter we explained maximisation of profits by total revenue and total cost approach. In this section, we explain how a firm maximizes profits by equating marginal revenue with marginal cost. Marginal revenue (*MR*) is defined as the change in total revenue (*TR*) resulting from a unit change in output or sales and is measured by the slope of the total revenue curve at a level of

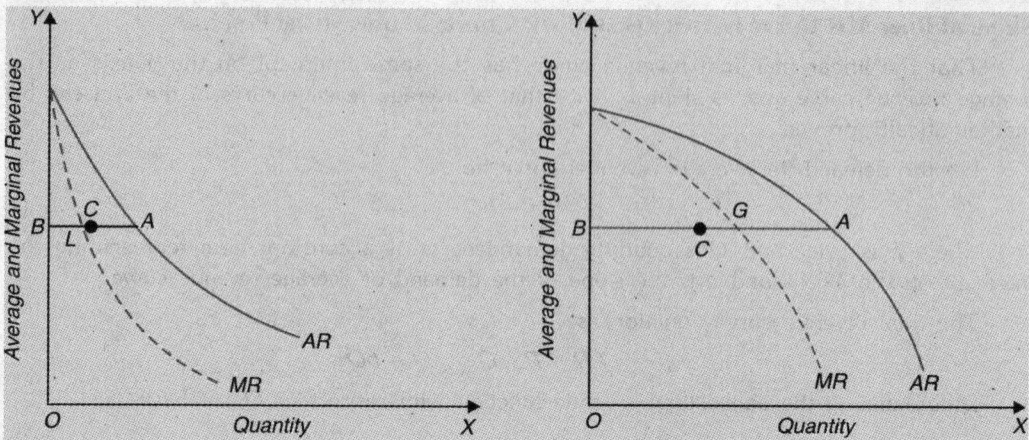

Fig. 4.5. *MR curve cuts the perpendicular from the AR curve to the Y-axis more than half way from AR curve when AR curve is convex*

Fig. 4.6. *Marginal Revenue curve cuts the perpendicular drawn from AR curve to the Y-axis less than half way from the AR curve when AR curve is concave*

output $\left(MR = \frac{\Delta TR}{\Delta Q}\right)$. Marginal cost is the addition to total cost caused by a unit change in output or sales and is measured by the slope of total cost curve corresponding to a level of output. Now, so long as marginal revenue exceeds marginal cost of production, it will profitable for the firm to expand output. This is because in this case the firm will be adding more to total revenue than to total cost and so its total profits will be increasing. It will be seen from the bottom panel of Figure 4.8 that up to output level *OQ*, marginal revenue (*MR*) is greater than marginal cost (*MC*) and at point *E* corresponding to output level *OQ* marginal revenue equals marginal cost of production. If output is expanded beyond output level *OQ*, marginal revenue is smaller than marginal cost, that is, in doing so the firm will be adding less to its total revenue than to its total cost. This means that expansion of output beyond *OQ* will not be profitable and will cause total profits to fall. It follows therefore that total profits will be maximized at point *E* or output level *OQ* at which marginal revenue equals marginal cost of

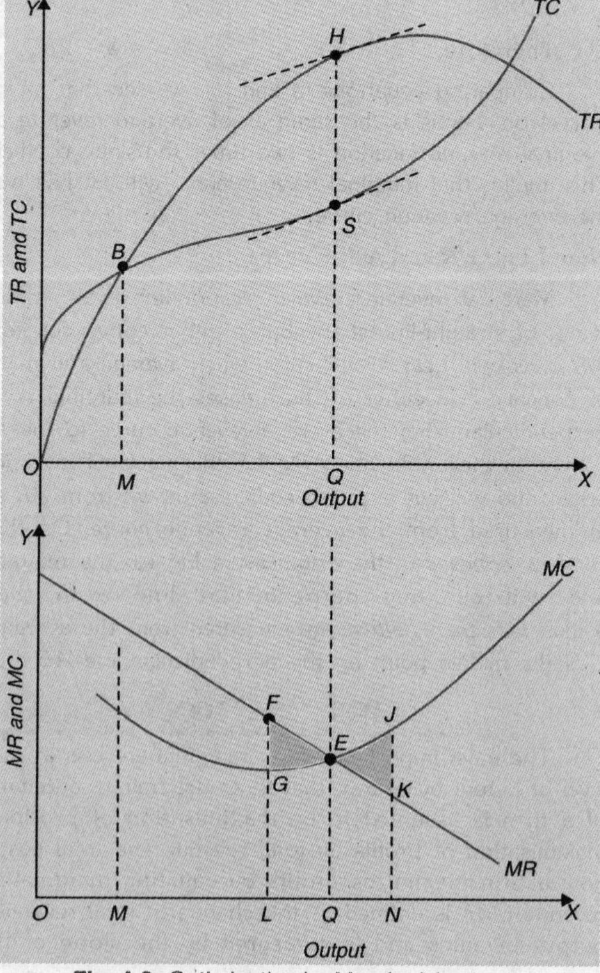

Fig. 4.8. *Optimisation by Marginal Analyses*

production. $MR = MC$ is the important rule for optimal activity level, that is, in the present case for profit-maximising level of output.

Now, it is important to note here that if a firm produces less than OQ level of output, say OL, it will not be earning maximum possible profits. This is because it will not availing of all the opportunities of earning profits. With OL level of output, it will be missing the opportunity of making additional profits equal to the shaded area FGE shown in the bottom panel of Figure 4.8.which it can earn by expanding output to OQ. On the other hand, if the firm produces output greater than OQ, say ON, in that case also its profits will not be maximum. This is because on the QN units of output produced more than OQ, marginal cost (MC) exceeds marginal revenue (MR) and is therefore incurring losses equal to EJK on these extra units of output. As a result, with ON output, firm's profits will be reduced by the shaded area EJK. It follows therefore, that firm's profits are maximum at the output level OQ at which marginal revenue equals marginal cost.

Now, consider the top panel of Fig. 4.8 where total revenue (TR) and total cost (TC) curves have been drawn. When the firm expands output to OM level, total revenue (TR) equals total cost (TC). Thus point B (or corresponding output level OM) is a *break-even point* which means at the output level OM neither profits nor losses are made. When the firm expands output beyond OM, the difference between TR and TC goes on increasing upto OQ level of output. At output level OQ, the vertical distance between total revenue and total cost curves is the maximum. Since profits are the difference between total revenue and total cost, profits are maximised at output level OQ. Geometrically, the vertical distance between the two curves are maximum at the points where the slopes of these two curves is the same. In the upper panel of Figure 4.8 we have drawn tangents to the total revenue and total cost curves at points H and S respectively corresponding to output level OQ. It will be seen from Figure 4.8, that tangents drawn to these curves at output OQ are parallel to each other which indicate that maximum possible profits are earned by producing output OQ.

A glance at the upper panel of Figure 4.8 will reveal that profit maximisation output OQ obtained through the maximum difference between TR and TC is the same as obtained through marginal revenue and marginal cost. This follows from the mathematical relationships between these curves. Marginal revenue is defined as the change in total revenue for a unit change in output *and is measured by the slope of the total revenue curve at a given output level* $\left(MR = \dfrac{\Delta TR}{\Delta Q}\right)$. Likewise, marginal cost is defined as a change in total cost for a unit change in output and *is measured by the slope of the total cost* curve *at a point corresponding to a level of output* $\left(MC = \dfrac{\Delta TC}{\Delta Q}\right)$. Thus, when at a certain level of output, slopes of the total revenue and total cost curves at the corresponding points are the same, and consequently the vertical distance between the two curves is the largest, marginal revenue and marginal cost at that level of output are the same. This also shows profits are maximum at the level of output at which marginal revenue equals marginal cost. A numerical example will help to clarify the use of marginal revenue and marginal cost for determining optimum or profit-maximising level of output.

Numerical Example : *Assume a firm has the following total revenue and total cost functions:*

$$TR = 320Q - 2Q^2$$

$$TC = 1800 + 50Q + 3Q^2$$

It is required to determine.

1. *The level of output at which the firm will be maximising profits.*
2. *The level of output at which total revenue will be maximum.*

The profit-maximising output can be found by obtaining *MR* and *MC* from the given total revenue and total cost function respectively. As has been noted above, marginal revenue (*MR*) and marginal cost (*MC*) are measured by the slopes at a point on these curves. Further, as has been explained in the previous chapter, slope at a point of a function is measured by the first derivative of the function. Taking the first derivative of total revenue function :

$$MR = \frac{\Delta TR}{\Delta Q} = 320 - 4Q$$

Taking the first derivative of the total cost function,

$$MC = \frac{\Delta TC}{\Delta Q} = 50 + 6Q$$

Setting MR = MC we have

$$320 - 4Q = 50 + 6Q$$

$$10Q = 320 - 50 = 270$$

$$Q = 27$$

Thus, profit-maximising level output of is 27.

It should be noted that if we use total revenue total cost approach to obtain optimum level of output, we will get the same results. Thus

$$\text{Profits } (\pi) = TR - TC$$

$$\pi = (320Q - 2Q^2) - (1800 + 50Q + 3Q^2)$$

$$= 320Q - 2Q^2 - 1800 - 50Q - 3Q^2$$

$$= 270Q - 5Q^2 - 1800$$

$$\frac{d\pi}{dQ} = 270 - 10Q$$

Now, profits will be maximized when the first derivative of total profit function is zero.

Thus, setting $\frac{d\pi}{dQ} = 0$, we have

$$270 - 10Q = 0$$

$$10Q = 270$$

$$Q = 27$$

We have explained above how we determine optimum activity level taking output of a product to be produced by a firm as an activity. Similarly, determination of optimal advertising expenditure to be incurred by a firm can be determined. The fundamental rule explained above will also hold in this case. Optimal advertising expenditure is obtained when marginal revenue obtained from increase in advertising expenditure is equal to marginal advertising expenditure, that is, when net marginal yield from advertising expenditure is zero.

The Second Order Condition

The marginal rule for optimal decision making explained above suffers from a serious limitation. The marginal rule for optimal activity level is that an activity should be carried if possible to the point where *net marginal yield* from it is zero. In the context of level of output to be produced, this means that the level of output at which marginal revenue from the sale of output is equal to marginal cost of production, that is, at output at which net marginal profit is zero. However, this marginal rule is *necessary but not a sufficient condition for an optimum.* This is because this marginal condition can be satisfied even in a *non-optional* situation. To ensure that a situation where marginal net yield is zero represents optimum a second order condition must also be fulfilled. This second order condition requires that whether a point determined from the first order condition is either a maximum point or a minimum point of a function. If a function is to be maximized to find optimal activity level, then slope of marginal value must be negative in the vicinity of the situation where marginal net yield is zero. On the other hand, if a function is to be minimised, for an optimum the slope of marginal net yield must be positive in the neighbourhood of the minimum value.

Marginal value of a function, that is, slope of a function is the first derivative $\left(\frac{dy}{dx}\right)$ of the function whereas slope of the marginal value is the derivative of the marginal value function, that is, the second derivative of the function $\left(\frac{d^2y}{dx^2}\right)$. The second order condition is therefore better explained in terms of differential calculas. As has been explained in the previous chapter, for a maximum point of a function to be attained, the second derivative of the function must be negative $\left(\frac{d^2y}{dx^2} < 0\right)$. And a minimum point of function is obtained if the second derivative of a function is positive $\left(\frac{d^2y}{dx^2} > 0\right)$.

Second Order Condition for Profit-Maximising Output in Terms of Marginal Revenue and Marginal Cost.

To further clarify the second order condition we explain it with reference to condition for profit-maximizing level of output. As explained above, for profit-maximizing level of output, marginal revenue must be equal to marginal cost. But equality of marginal revenue with marginal cost can be obtained both at the maximum profit and minimum profit points. This is illustrated in Fig.4.9 where we have drawn a U-shaped marginal cost curve *MC* and a linear marginal revenue curve *MR*. This is the situation that prevails when a firm is working under condition of perfect competition in the market. It will be seen from Figure 4.9 that marginal cost and marginal revenue are equal at two levels of output, *ON* and

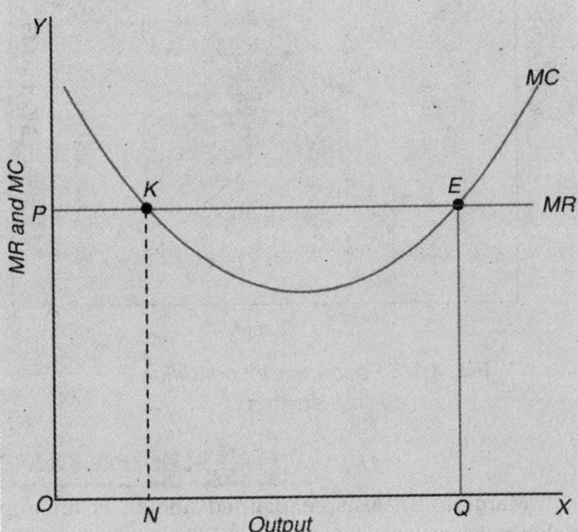

Fig. 4.9. *For optimal output MC curve must cut MR curve from below.*

OQ (that is, marginal net profit is equal to zero at both these output levels). However, output level *ON* or point *K* is not profit-maximising because beyond *point K marginal cost is lower than marginal revenue* and, therefore, it will be profitable for the firm to expand output beyond *ON*. Indeed, at output level *ON* firm's losses are maximum as upto point *K* marginal cost exceeds marginal revenue. Thus, point *K* or output level *ON* does not represent profit-maximizing or optimal activity level though marginal revenue is equal to marginal cost. It is worth nothing that at point *K marginal* cost curve is cutting *MR* curve *from above* so that beyond it marginal cost becomes lower than marginal revenue and as a result it pays the firm to expand output further.

Now, in Fig. 4.9 consider output *OQ* or point *E* where marginal revenue and marginal cost are again equal. However, at point *E* marginal cost curve is cutting marginal revenue curve from below so that beyond point *E* marginal cost is greater than marginal revenue. This shows that it will not be profitable for the firm to expand output beyond *OQ* output (or point *E*). We conclude that for profit maximizing output (i.e., optimal output level), the following two marginal conditions must be satisfied.

1. *First Order Condition.* Marginal revenue is equal to marginal cost of product (that is, marginal net profit is zero).

2. *The Second Order Condition.* The marginal cost curve should cut marginal revenue curve *from below.*

The above two conditions should be fulfilled even if both *MC* and *MR* curves are sloping downward. Thus consider Figure 4.10 and 4.11. In Figure 4.10 *MC* curve is cutting *MR* Curve *from above* so that beyond equality point *K* of *MR* and *MC*, *MR* exceeds *MC* and it pays the firm to expand output. Therefore, output *ON* or point *K* in Fig. 4.10 is not profit-maximizing output. On the other hand, in Figure 4.11 *MC* curve is cutting *MR* curve from below and after the equality point of *MR* and *MC*, *MR* is lower than *MC* and therefore it is not profitable to expand output beyond *OQ* level.

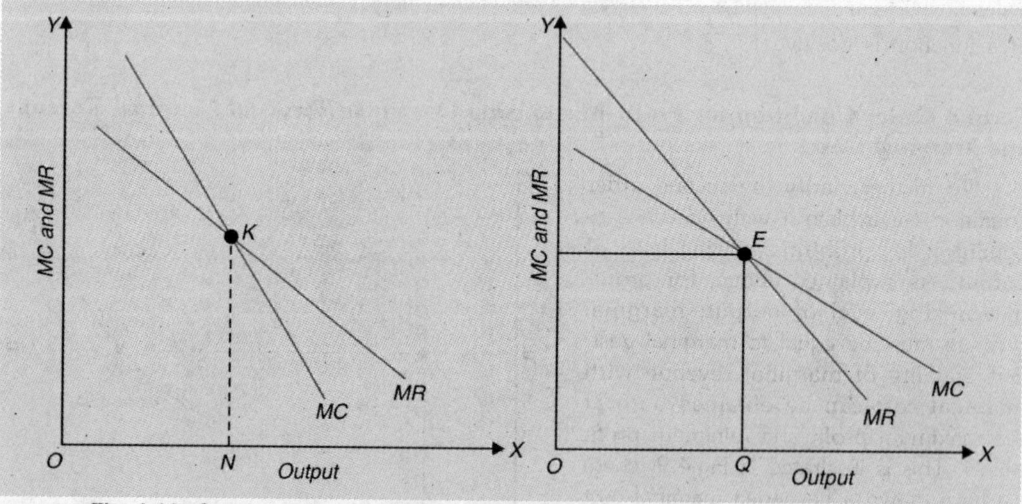

Fig. 4.10. *Second order condition is not staified*

Fig. 4.11. *Second order condition is satisfied*

INCREMENTAL ANALYSIS

Marginal analysis, explained above, is an important instrument of economic decision making. However, marginal analysis has some limitations for managerial decision making because it measures the effect (for example, on revenue, cost or profit) of only *one unit change* in output or some other independent variable. Most of the managerial decisions involve considerations of *changes that are broader in scope.* For example, a manager may be considering whether or not to expand output by 25 percent. Other examples of managerial decision making having a wider scope relate to the consideration of introducing a new product line, a new model of its product, a new technology in the production process, launching a new advertising campaigns, accepting or rejecting a new contract order. It is for evaluating such decisions which has wider and significant implications that the use of incremental analysis is made to select an optimal course of action.

Marginal analysis, though useful and vailid for evaluating the *effect of one unit change* in output or some other independent variable on revenue, cost or profit is too narrow and restricted to provide an optimal technique for making a business decision having a broader scope. On the other hand, incremental analysis is concerned with evaluating the *aggregate change* in revenue, cost and profit *resulting from a particular decision or a course of action* rather than from *one unit change* in output or some other independent variable. For example, *incremental profit* is not a marginal profit resulting from a one unit change in output but is the *change in total profit* that will accrue to the firm *when a new decision regarding introduction of a new product, new technology, making a significant cut in price, launching a new advertising campaign etc., is made. Similarly, incremental revenue of introduing a new product line is the change in total revenue* as estimated by the difference between total revenue with the new product and without it.

In order to evaluate the profitability of a new decision, the total *change in both total revenue and total cost* has to be evaluated. In other words, for making an optimal decision the *incremental revenue and incremental* cost of the new decision have to be measured. If a new decision adds more to total revenue than to total cost it will be profitable or optimal, that is, if incremental revenue exceeds incremental cost, the decision will result in positive profit. On the other hand, if incremental revenue is less than incremental cost that results from implementing a decision, incremental profits will be negative and it will not pay the firm to take that decision.

It is worth noting that for taking an optimal decision or choosing a course of action, one must take into consideration *all* increments in relevant revenues and relevant costs resulting from a particular decision. Therefore, caution must be exercised while measuring incremental revenue and incremental cost resulting from a decision. Therefore, it is worthwhile to explain the concepts of incremental cost and incremental revenue in some detail.

Incremental Cost

As stated above, incremental costs are defined as the *total change in cost that result from a particular decision.* Incremental cost may be either variable cost or fixed cost. This is because a business decision may require purchase of extra labour and raw materials to be used for implementing the decision. Besides, a business decision may need additional capital equipment on which extra cost have to be incurred. It should however be carefully noted that incremental cost differs from marginal cost. As mentioned above, marginal cost is the *change in total cost resulting* from a one-unit change in output or some other independent variable such as advertising outlay. On the other hand, incremental cost is the total change in costs that occurs as a result of a particular decision.

In fact, a managerial decision may not result in change in output at all though it will result in incremental cost. For example, if a manager takes a decision to *introduce a new technology* to produce a given level of output. The use of new technology will however involve change in both fixed and variable costs. It should however be noted that incremental costs must be correctly measured since in the real world managers quite often commit mistakes in the calculation of incremental costs which actually occur as a result of a particular business decision. Thus, for an optimal business decision, *all costs* that change as a result of a particular decision must be included while measuring incremental costs.

Let us further clarify the concept of incremental costs. If *some factors in a firm are lying idle and have no alternative use,* and if a particular decision involves the use of these idle factors, then for calculation of incremental cost, the costs incurred on these factors in the past (that is, *historical costs) must not be included* for a particular decision being presently considered. Since opportunity cost of these idle resources at present is zero, they are not relevant from the economic point of view to be included in the incremental cost. For example, if idle plant and machines purchased in the past and if costs incurred on them cannot be recovered by selling them at present, they are *sunk costs* and are therefore irrelevant to be considered for inclusion in incremental costs resulting from a decision. Thus, unless there is competing and profitable use for a firm's *own resources,* expenses made on them cannot be recovered, incremental cost of using them following a particular decision will be zero.

There are three type of incremental costs: (a) current period explict costs, (b) opportunity costs of self-owned factors, and (c) future costs. We explain them below briefly.

(*a*) Current Period Explicit Costs

Current period explicit costs include costs incurred on direct labour engaged, on purchase of new materials, certain types of variable overhead costs such as an electricity consumption required to implement the decision can be easily calculated. If the implementation of decision also requires the purchase of new additional capital equipment, cost on this should also be counted. However, those current period costs that have to be incurred regardless of the present decision should be excluded.

(*b*) Opportunity Costs : Suppose a firm is considering to launch a new project. The opportunity cost of undertaking and implementing a new project is *value of the resource* employees *in the best alternative* (that is, the current contribution made by these resources in their best alternative use) Therefore, if plant and machinery is currently lying idle with a firm, its opportunity cost for use in the new project will be zero. However, if the present plant and machinery is presently employed in a project, for its use in the new project, the current project would have to be cancelled, then its contribution to the revenue which that plant and machinery is currently making will constitute its opportunity cost which will be new project.

(c) Furtre Costs : Not only the current costs associated with a given decision be considered but also the likely future costs of any kind resulting from a given decision. It may however be noted that to the extent these costs can be foreknown their expected present value is estimated and included in the incremental cost of the decision.

Incremental Revenue

The incremental revenue is the total change in revenue resulting from the implementation of a decision. Increase in total revenue caused by deciding about a relatively large change in output, say by 25 per cent, introduction of a new product line or a new technology or launching an advertisement campaign expenditure is called incremental revenue. Since the revenue resulting from a decision may accrue over future years, their *expected present value* be estimated by discounting it at an appropriate rate. However, if the decision is implemented in a current year and all revenues resulting from a decision are received in the current period, it should be counted as incremental revenue without discounting.

Incremental analysis is widely used for pricing of new products, for deciding about use of new technology, undertaking of new investment projects and making a bid for a contract.

However, mistakes are generally committed by ill informed managers about all incremental costs and incremental revenues. As explained above, for optimal decision making only all relevant costs and revenues must be taken into consideration while evaluating the results of different decisions.

QUESTION FOR REVIEW

1. Explain the role of marginal analysis in managerial decision making for optimal resource allocation. Give some examples.
2. What is *optimal activity level?* Explain marginal conditions to find it.
3. Explain the theorem on *relative activity levels* regarding resource allocation by a firm. Give some examples.
4. Define total revenue, average revenue and marginal revenue. Explain the relationship between (*a*) total revenue and marginal revenue, (*b*) average revenue and marginal revenue.
5. (*a*) Draw total revenue (*TR*) curve representing the following total revenue function.

   $TR = 100 - 10Q^2$, where Q stands for output

   (*b*) Derive average and marginal revenue curves from the total revenue curve obtained in (*a*) above.
6. Show that marginal revenue curve cuts half-way the distance between the *Y*-axis and the linear downward-sloping average revenue curve.
7. Given the average revenue and marginal revenue curves. Explain the two ways of finding total revenue at a given level of output.
8. (*a*) Long-run average cost curve first falls as output increases due to economices of scale and then after a point rises due to diseconomies. Draw such an average cost curve and corresponding marginal cost curve. At what point the two curves will intersect and why ?

   (*b*) When average cost curve is falling, marginal cost curve must also be rising. True or false. Give reasons.
9. What is the value of marginal revenue (*a*) when total revenue increases, (*b*) when total revenue is maximum, and (*c*) when total revenue decreases.
10. Draw a graph showing total revenue curve (which is convex outward). Derive average and marginal revenue curves from it.
11. When for a firm price is given and constant, how will its total revenue, average revenue and marginal revenue curves look like ?
12. Show that total revenue is maximum at the level of output at which marginal revenue is zero.
13. Explain that a firm maximizes its profits at the level of output where marginal cost equals marginal revenue. Show graphically. Is equality of marginal cost with marginal revenue a sufficient condition for optimal output level?
14. Equality of marginal revenue with marginal cost of production is a necessary but not a sufficient condition for profit-maximizing output.
15. How as a manager of a firm would you determine optimal level of (*a*) advertising expenditure (*b*) size of investment, and (*c*) use of an input.
16. Assume that a firm's cost function is given by the following relationship:

    $TC = 20 + 5Q + Q^2$

    where Q represents the level of output produced and sold.

    Demand for the product of the firm is given by

$$Q = 25 - P$$

(*i*) Determine the output level where total profits are maximized

(*ii*) Calculate the total profits and selling price of the product at profit-maximizing output level.

(*iii*) If the fixed costs increase from Rs.20 to Rs.25, what would be its effect on profit-maximizing output level and total profits earned by the firm. (Hint: As regards part (*iii*) of the question, it may be noted that a change in fixed costs will not affect the profit-maximizing output level because marginal cost is independent of the fixed cost. However, as a result of increase in fixed cost, total profit will be reduced.

PART – II

DEMAND ANALYSIS AND THEORY OF CONSUMER'S CHOICE

- Demand and Demand Function
- Elasticity of Demand
- Consumer's Behaviour : Cardinal Utility Analysis
- Indifference Curve Analysis of Demand
- Revealed Preference Theory of Demand
- Demand Estimation
- Demand Forecasting

CHAPTER

Demand and Demand Function

Significance of Demand Function for a Business Manager

This chapter provides an introduction to the theory of demand and explains the various factors that determine demand for a product of a firm and an industry. In this context we will explain demand function and law of demand and the factors that account for it. We will also explain the effects of changes in factors that influence demand for products. In managerial economics we are primarily concerned with the demand for a product facing a firm. Demand for products plays crucial role in the determination of a firm's profitability. Therefore, estimates of future demand for a product are important for planning production activity and its expansion and also of marketing the product. For example, if demand for a firm's product is stable, then the same production schedule per period may be planned. On the other hand, if demand fluctuates very much, then flexible production processes must be used or arrangements for carrying large inventories of the product and raw materials must be made.

Demand conditions for a firm's product have also profound influence on its financial decisions. If product demand is strong and growing, the firm's financial manager must plan to arrange for sufficient funds to meet the growing capital requirements of the firm. The expansion of a firm needs not only increased finance but also increased human resources, especially skilled manpower. Therefore, human resource (HR) manager must plan not only to make arrangements for the recruitment of the new personnel but also for training programmes to ensure the availability of trained work force required for production and marketing the product. Further, demand conditions for a product together with the production technologies allow efficient production by a small-sized firm. If demand for a product is quite large, then it may cause a large number of firms producing a product which ensures a high level of competition in the industry. And if demand and production technology are such that lead to the existence of monopoly or oligopoly, then degree of competition will be low and firms will exercise large control over the price of the product. We will discuss in later chapters of this book the various forms of market structure and pricing and output decisions of the firms working in them.

INDIVIDUAL DEMAND

It is useful to know what economists mean by the demand for the goods by consumers. The demand for a commodity is consumer's desire to have it for which he is willing and able to pay. Demand for a good is in fact a photographic picture of consumers' attitude towards a commodity. This consumers' attitude gives rise to his actions in purchasing a certain number of units of a commodity at various given prices. *Precisely stated, the demand for a commodity is the amount of it that a consumer will purchase it at various given prices during a period of time.* This time period may be a week, a month, a year or any other given time period. The demand in economics implies both the desire to purchase and the ability to pay for a good. It is noteworthy that mere desire for a commodity does not constitute demand for it, if it is not backed by the ability to pay. For example, if a poor man who hardly makes both ends meet, wishes to have a car, his wish or desire for a car will not constitute the demand for the car because he cannot afford to pay for it, that is, he has no purchasing power to make his wish or desire effective in the market.

Thus, in economics unless demand is backed by purchasing power or ability to pay it does not constitute demand. Demand for a good is determined by several factors such as price of a commodity, the tastes and desires of the consumer for a commodity, income of the consumer, the prices of related goods, substitutes or complements. When there is a change in any of these factors, demand of the consumer for a good changes. Individual consumer's demand and market demand for a good may be distinguished. Market demand for a good is the total sum of the demands of individual consumers, who purchase the commodity in the market. We shall discuss in detail later in this chapter the various factors which determine the demand for a commodity and also how a market demand curve for a commodity is obtained.

Demand and Utility. People demand goods because they satisfy the wants of the people. *The utility means the amount of satisfaction which an individual derives from consuming a commodity.* It is also defined as want-satisfying power of a commodity. Utility of a good is the important determinant of demand of a consumer for the good. It is assumed that Individuals will try to maximise their utility or satisfaction from the goods they buy for consumption. Consumers' demand for consumer goods for their own satisfaction is called *direct demand.* Utility is a subjective entity and resides in the minds of men. Being subjective, it varies with different persons, that is, different persons derive different amounts of utility from a given good. People know utility of goods by means of introspection.

The desire for a commodity by a person depends upon the utility he expects to obtain from it. The greater the utility he expects from a commodity, the greater his desire for that commodity. It should be noted that no question of ethics or morality is involved in the use of the word, 'utility' in economics. *Thus desire to consume alcohol may be considered immoral by some relegious prople but no such meaning is attached to it in economics. Thus, in economics the concept of utility* is ethically neutral. Further a commodity may not be useful in the ordinary sense of the term, even then it may provide utility to some people. For instance, alcohol and cigarettes may actually harm persons but it possesses utility for those whose want they satisfy.

Consumer's choice of goods he buys is a difficult task in the modern economic system as thousands of goods and services are available in the market. But the quantities of goods consumers buy are constrained by their income or budget. Who would not like to 'buy City Honda Car, dine at Taj Hotel and live in a good bungalow in South Delhi. It is income which constrains consumers to buy goods they might want. Thus consumers face *constrained optimisation problem.*

Demand and Quantity Demanded. Demand for a good is determined by several factors such as tastes and desires of the consumer for a commodity, income of the consumer, the prices of related goods, substitutes or complements. When there is a change in any of these factors, demand of the consumer for a good changes. Individual consumer's demand

and market demand for a good may be distinguished. *Market demand for a good is the total sum of the demands of all individual consumers who purchase the commodity at various prices in the market in a period.* We shall discuss in detail later in this chapter the various factors which determine demand for a commodity.

It is worth noting that the demand for a commodity and quantity demanded are two different concepts. Whereas, demand refers to the quantities of a commodity which consumers plan to buy at *various prices of a good* during a period of time, the quantity demanded is the amount of a good or service which consumers plan to buy at a *particular price.* It is worth mentioning that quantity demanded is not necessary the amount *actually bought by* the consumers. Sometimes, the quantity demanded is greater than the quantity of the good available so that quantity of the good actually bought is less than the quantity demanded of it. The second thing worth mentioning about quantity demanded is that it is a *flow concept.* This means that quantity demanded is measured as an amount that consumers wish to buy per unit of time, which may be a day, a week a month or a year. Thus if you consume 5 cups of tea in a day, then your quantity demanded of tea is expressed as 5 cups per day or 35 cups per week or 150 cups per month and so on. Without specifying the time period, it is not possible to say whether the quantity demanded is large or small.

Demand Function

The demand function for a commodity describes the relationship between the quantity demanded of it and the factors that influence it. Individual's demand for a commodity depends on its own price, his income, prices of related commodities (which may be either substitutes or complements), his tastes and preferences, and advertising expenditure made by the producers for the commodity in question. Individual demand function for a commodity can be expressed in the folllowing *gereral form :*

$$Q_d = f(P_x, I, P_r, T, A) \qquad ...(1)$$

where P_x = Own price of the commodity X

I = Income of the individual

P_r = Prices of related commodities

T = Tastes and preferences of the individual consumer

A = Advertising expenditure made by the producers of the commodity.

We will explain in detail the above factors that determine demand later in this chapter.

For many purposes in economics, it is useful to focus on the relationship between quantity demanded of a good and its own price while *keeping other determining factors such as consumer's income, prices of other goods, his tastes and preferences constant.* With this we write the demand function of an individual in the following way.

$$Q_d = f(P_x) \qquad ...(2)$$

This implies that quantity demanded of a good X is function of its own price, other determinants remaining constant. As has been explained above, there is inverse relationship between price of a commodity and its quantity demanded. Thus, when price of a commodity falls, its quantity demanded will increase and when its price rises, its quantity demanded will decrease. Therefore, when we express this relationship through a curve we get a downard-sloping demand curve of a commodity as shown in Figure 5.1.

The individual's demand functon in (2) above is in *general* functional form and does not show how much quantity demanded of a consumer will change following a unit change in price (P_x). For the purpose of actually estimating demand for a commodity we need a specific form of the demand function. Generally, demand function is considered to be of a *linear* form. The specific demand function of a linear form is written as

$$Q_d = a - bP_x \quad \text{... (3)}$$

where a is a constant intercept term on the X- axis and b is the coefficient showing the slope of the demand curve. The coefficient of price (P_x), that is, b being negative implies that there is a negative relationship between price and quantity demanded of a commodity. If on estimating the demand functon (3) from the information about yearly quanties demanded of sugar at its various prices by an individual consumer, we find the constant a to be equal to 70 and the constant b to be equal to 2 we can write individual's demand function as

$$Q_d = 70 - 5P \quad \text{... (4)}$$

The above demand equation (4) is interpreted as one rupee fall in price of sugar will cause its quantity demanded to increase by 5 units of sugar and vice versa. It is this demand function that we have plotted on a graph and shown in Figure 5.1.

It should be noted that when there is a change in the other determining factors which are held constant such as income, tastes, prices of related commodities, the whole demand curve will shift. For example, if income increases, the whole demand curve will shift to the right and, on the contrary, if income decreases, then the whole demand curve will shift to the left. Similarly, changes in other determining factors such as tastes, prices of related commodities, advertising expenditure cause shift in the demand curve and are therefore called *shift factors.*

The demand function expressed in equation (1) above is of a general form and merely states the factors or variables that affect dmenad for a commodity. But to be useful for a manager in his decision making a demand function must be stated in explicit form which should show the precise effect on demand of changes in various individual variables. To illustrate an important form of a demand function that is generally used is the following linear form.

$$Q_d = a + b_1 P_x + b_2 P_1 + b_3 P_2 + b_4 I + b_5 I + b_6 A \quad \text{...(5)}$$

In the demand function (5), coefficient b_1, b_2, b_3, b_4 etc. shows the changes in quantity demanded of the commodity caused by one-unit change in the associated variables such as P, I T, price P_1 of a substitute, price P_2 of a complement and so on. Thus, if price of a product X is measured in rupees, the value of b will indicate the amount or quantity demanded of the commodity X resulting from a unit change in its price (P_x). For example, if $b_1 = -5$, then a fall in price of the commodity by one rupee will cause 5 units increase in the quantity demanded of the commodity. In a later chapter. we will examine various methods of estimating the values of the coefficients such as b_1, b_2, b_3 etc of various variables. If we know the values of coefficients of various variables of the demand function for a commodity we can accurately predict the demand for that commodity in the next year or in some other future years.

THE LAW OF DEMAND

An important information about demand is described by the law of demand. This law of demand expresses the functional relationhship between price and quantity demanded. The law of demand or functional relationship between price and quantity demanded of a commodity is one of the best known and most important laws of economic theory. *According to the law of demand, other things being equal, if the price of a commodity falls, the quantity demanded of it will rise, and if the price of the commodity rises, its quantity demanded will decline.* Thus, according to the law of demand, there is inverse relationship between price and quantity demanded, other things remaining the same. These other things which are assumed to be constant are the tastes and preferences of the consumer, the income of the consumer, and the prices of related goods. If these other factors which determine demand also undergo a change at the same time, then the inverse price-demand relationship may not hold good. Thus, the constancy of these other things which is generally stated as ceteris paribus is an important qualification of the law of demand.

Demand Curve and the Law of Demand. The law of demand can be illustrated through a demand schedule and a demand curve. A demand schedule of an individual consumer is presented in Table 5.1. It will be seen from this demand schedule that when the price of a commodity is Rs. 12 per unit, the consumer purchases 10 units of the commodity. When the price of the commodity falls to Rs. 10, he purchases 20 units of the commodity. Similarly, when the price further falls, quantity demanded by him goes on rising until at price Rs. 2, the quantity demanded by him rises to 60 units. We can convert this demand schedule into a demand curve by graphically plotting the various price-quantity combinatons, and this has been done in Fig. 5.1 where along the X-axis, quantity demanded is measured and along the Y-axis price of the commodity is measured.

Table 5.1. Demand Schedule of an Individual Consumer

Price (Rs.)	*Quantity Demanded*
12	10
10	20
8	30
6	40
4	50
2	60

By plotting 10 units of the commodity against price 12, we get a point in Fig. 5.1. Likewise, by plotting 20 units of the commodity demanded against price 10, we get another point in Fig. 5.1. Similarly, other points are plotted representing other combinations of price and quantity demanded of the commodity and are shown in Fig. 5.1. By joining these various points, we get a curve *DD*, which is known as the demand curve. Thus, this demand curve is a graphic representation of quantities of a good which will be demanded by the consumer at various possible prices in a given period of time.

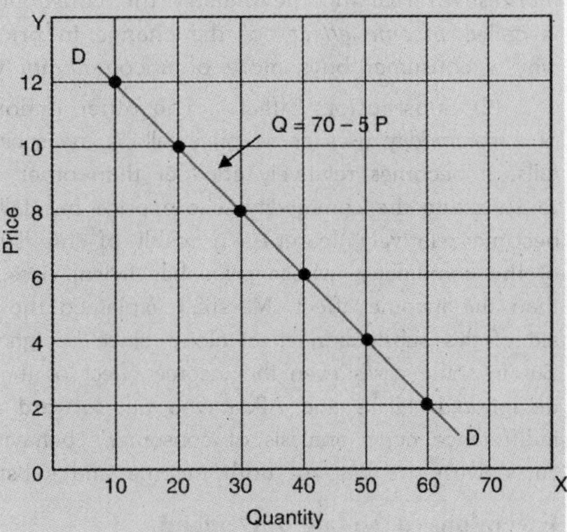

Fig. 5.1. *The Demand Curve of an Individual* $(Q^d = 70 - 5P)$

It should be noted that a demand schedule or a demand curve does not tell us what the price is; it only tells us how much quantity of the good would be purchased by the consumer at a various possible prices. Further, it will be seen from both the demand schedule and the demand curve that as the price of a commodity falls, more quantity of it is purchased or demanded. Since more is demanded at a lower price and less is demanded at a higher price, the demand curve slopes downward to the right. Thus, *the downward-sloping demand curve is in accordance with the law of demand which, as stated above, describes inverse price-demand relationship.*

It is important to note here that behind this demand curve or price-demand relationship always lie the tastes and preferences of the consumer, his income, the prices of substitutes and complementary goods, all of which are assumed to be constant in drawing a demand curve. If any change occurs in any of these other factors, the whole demand schedule or demand curve will change and new demand schedule or a demand curve will have to be drawn. Further, in drawing a demand curve, we assume that the buyer or consumer does not exercise any influence over the price of a commodity, that is, he takes the price of the commodity as given and constant for him.

Reasons for the Law of Demand : Why does Demand Curve Slope Downward?

We have explained above that when price falls the quantity demanded of a commodity rises and *vice versa,* other things remaining the same. It is due to this law of demand that demand curve slopes downward to the right. Now, the important question is why the demand curve slopes downward, or in other words, why the law of demand which describes inverse price-demand relationship is valid. We can prove this with marginal utility analysis which we shall explain in the next chapter. It may however be mentioned here that there are two factors due to which quantity demanded increases when price falls: (1) Income effect, (2) Substitution effect.

(1) Income Effect. When the price of a commodity falls the consumer can buy more quantity of the commodity with his *given income.* Or, if he chooses to buy the same amount of quantity as before, some money will be left with him because he has to spend less on the commodity due to its lower price. In other words, as a result of the fall in the price of a commodity, consumer's real income or purchasing power increases. This increase in real income induces the consumer to buy more of that commodity. This is called *income effect* of the change in price of the commodity. This is one reason why a consumer buys more of a commodity whose price falls.

(2) Substitution Effect. The other important reason why the quantity demanded of a commodity rises as its price falls is the substitution effect. When price of a conmmodity falls, it becomes relatively cheaper than other commodities . This induces the consumer to substitute the commodity whose price has fallen for other commodities which have now become relatively dearer.As a result of this *substitution effect,* the quantity demanded of the commodity, whose price has fallen, rises. This substitution effect is more important than the income effect. Marshall explained the downward-sloping demand curve with the aid of this substitution effect alone, since he ignored the income effect of the price change. But in some cases even the income effect of the price change is very signficant and cannot be ignored. Hicks and Allen who put forward an alternative theory of demand called as indifference curve analysis of consumer's behaviour explain this downward-sloping demand curve with the help of both income and substitution effects.

Exceptions to the Law of Demand

Law of demand is generally believed to be valid in most of the situations. However, some exceptions to the law of demand have been pointed out.

Goods having Prestige Value : Veblen Effect. One exception to the law of demand is associated with the name of the economist, Thorstein Veblen who propounded the doctrine *of conspicuous consumption.* According to Veblen, some consumers measure the utility of a commodity entirely by its price *i.e.,* for them, the greater the price of a commodity, the greater its utility. For example, diamonds are considered as prestige good in the society and for the upper strata of the society the higher the price of diamonds, the higher the prestige value of them and therefore the greater utility or desirability of them. In this case, some consumers will buy less of the diamonds at a lower price because with the fall in price its prestige value goes down. On the other hand, when price of diamonds goes up, their prestige value goes up and therefore their utility or desirability increases. As a result, at a higher price the quantity demanded of diamonds by a consumer will rise. This is called *Veblen effect.* Besides diamonds, other goods such as mink coats, luxury cars have prestige value and Veblen effect works in their case too.

Giffen Goods. Another exception to the law of demand was pointed out by Sir Robert Giffen who observed that when price of bread increased, the low-piad British workers in the early 19th century purchased more bread and not less of it and this is contrary to the law of demand described above. The reason given for this is that these British workers consumed a diet of mainly bread and when the price of bread went up they were compelled to spend more on given quantity of bread. Therefore, they could not afford to purchase as much meat as before. Thus, they substituted even bread for meat in order to maintain their intake of food. After the name of Robert Giffen, such goods in whose case there is a direct price-demand relationship are called *Giffen goods.* It is *important to note that with the rise in the price of a Giffen good, its quantity demand increases and with the fall in its price its quantity demanded decreases, the demand curve will slope upward to the right and not downward.*

MARKET DEMAND FUNCTION

So far we have been primarily concerned with an individual's demand for a commodity. However, manager of a business firm is more interested in the size of total market demand for the commodity and firm's share of it. This is because, for a manager of a firm market demand for a commodity and his firm's share in it forms the basis of his pricing and output decisions. Apart from the factors affecting individual's demand such as price of a product, his income, prices of related commodities individual's preferences, market demand for a product depends on an additional factor, namely the *number of consumers* which in turn depends on the population of a region or city or country (for which demand is being considered) who consume the product. Mathematically, market demand function of a product can be expressed in the general functional form as under.

$$Q_D = f(P_x, I, P_r, T, A, N)$$

where the additional factor is N which stands for the number of consumers or population.

As explained above, for the purpose of estimation of demand for a product we need a specific form of the above market demand function. Generally, it is the linear form which is chosen for estimating market demand function. So in the linear form, the market demand function is given below :

$$Q_D = C + b_1 P_x + b_2 I + b_3 P_y + b_4 T + b_5 A + b_6 N$$

C is a constant term which shows the intercept of the market demand curve on the

1. Veblen, ***The Economics of Leisure Class.***

X-axis. b_1, b_2, b_3 etc. are coefficients (these are generally called parameters) which show the quantitative relationship of various independent variables with the market demand. In other words, these coefficients, b_1, b_2, b_3 show how much market demand changes as a result of a unit change in various variables such as price, income, advertising expenditure, population (*i.e.*, the number of consumers).

Suppose we are interested in market demand for a specific brand of tea, say Brooke Bond tea. We assume that tastes (T) and the number of consumers for tea (N) remain the same and further if we have estimated the coefficients of other variables determining the market demand for Brooke Bond tea we can write market demand function for Brooke Bond tea as follows

$$Q_D = 2.0 - 1.5\ P_x + 0.6\ I + 0.8\ P_y - 0.7\ P_s + 1.5\ \text{A}$$

where Q_D represents market demand for Brooke Bond tea, P_x is the price of brooke bond tea per kilogram, I is disposable per capta income of the country, P_y is the price of Tata tea which is the competitor of Brooke Bond Tea, P_s is the price of sugar which is complementary with tea. A is advertisement expenditure made by manufacturers of Brooke Bond tea.

From the above market demand function, it follows that change of Re. 1 of Brooke Bond tea will cause 1.5 unit change in quantity demanded of Brooke Bond tea. Similarly, a fall in price by one rupee of Tata tea, a competing product, will cause 0.8 unit reduction in quantity demanded of Brooke Bond tea. On the other hand, one rupee fall in price of sugur will cause 0.7 change in the quantity demanded of Brooke Bond tea and similarly for other variables. Given these values of the coefficients, if we write the values of defferent determining variables such as price of Brooke Bond tea, per capita personal disposable income, price of sugur (P_s) we can calculate the change in market demand for Brooke Bond tea.

As pointed out in case of individual demand, in economics it is considered important and useful to focus on the relationship between quantity demanded of a product and its price, holding other factors constant. Therefore, if income (I), prices of other related commodities (P_r), tastes or preferences of the people (T), advertising expenditure are held constant, the market demand function can be written as

$$Q_D = a - b_1 P_x$$

where a is the constant term in the function or intercept of the market demand curve on the X-axis, b_1 is the coefficient which indicates how much quantity demanded of product X in the market will change as a result of a unit change in its own price, other factors held constant.

Market Demand Curve

We have drawn above an individual's demand curve of a commodity. We can graphically obtain the market demand curve by making horizontal addition of the demand curves of all individuals buying the commodity. In order to do so we add the various quantities demanded by the number of consumers in the market. In this way we can obtain the *market demand curve* for a commodity which like the individual consumer's demand curve will slope downward to the right. How this summation is done is illustrated in Fig. 5.2. Suppose there are two individual buyers of a good in the market. Fig. 5.2 (*a*) and (*b*) show the demand curves of the two independent individual buyers. Now, the market demand curve can be obtained by adding together the amounts of the good which individuals wish to buy at each price. Thus, at price P_1, the individual A wishes to buy 2 units of the good; individual B wishes to buy 3 units of the good. The total quantity of the good that the two individuals plan to buy at price P_1 is therefore 2 + 3 = 5, which is equal to OQ_1 in Fig. 5.2(*c*).

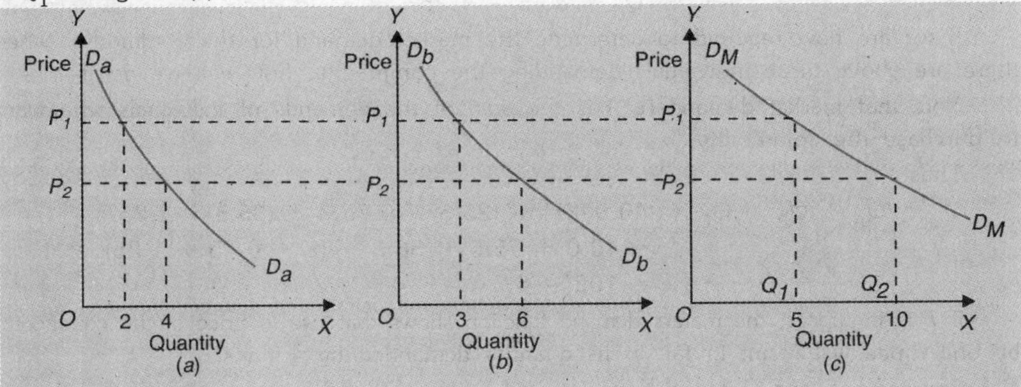

Fig. 5.2. *Horizontal Addition of Individual Demand Curves to get Market Demand Curve*

Now, as shall be seen from the figure, at price OP_2, individual A demands 4 units and individual B demands 6 units of the commodity. so the market demand at price OP_2 of the commodity is 4 + 6 = 10 units or OQ_2. Similarly, we can plot the quantity of the good that will be demanded by the two individuals at every other price of the good. When all the points showing the amounts demanded of the good by the two individuals at various prices are joined we get a market demand curve for the good. For the sake of convenience we have supposed that there are two individuals or buyers in the market for a good. Whatever be the number of individuals in the market, their demand curves can be added together, as illustrated above, to get a market demand curve for the good.

The market demand curve slopes downward to the right since the individual demand curves whose lateral summation gives us the market demand curve, normally slope downward to the right. Besides, as the price of the good falls, it is very likely that the new buyers will enter the market and will further raise the quantity demanded of the good. This is another reason why the market demand curve slopes downward to the right.

As in case of individuals' demand curves, factors other than price which affect market demand such as prices of related goods, per capital income of the individuals, their preferences for goods, number of consumers, etc are held constant while drawing the demand curve.

INDIVIDUAL DEMAND FUNCTIONS AND MARKET DEMAND FUNCTION

Market Demand Function

Adding up Individual Demand Functions. Demand for commodity by an individual depends on price of the commodity, his income, prices of related commodities. A simple demand function is expressed in terms of own price of the commodity, keeping other factors constant. Thus, such a linear demand function is

$$Q_A = 40 - 2P \qquad ...(i)$$

where Q_A is the quantity demanded of the commodity by individual A and P is the price of the commodity in rupees and 40 is constant (the intercept term). The above demand function shows that a rise in price of the commodity by one rupee causes 2 units decrease in quantity demanded by the individual A and vice-versa.

Likewise, demand functions of individuals B and C are as under :

$$Q_B = 25.5 - 0.75P \qquad ...(ii)$$

$$Q_C = 36.5 - 1.25P \qquad ...(iii)$$

If we are now required to determine the market demand for the commodity when there are above three individuals demanding the commodity, how will we do it ?

Note that market demand (Q_m) is the *sum* of the demands of indviduals who want to purchase the commodity.

Thus,

$$Q_m = Q_A + Q_B = Q_C = (40.0 - 2P) + (25.5 - 0.75P) + (36.5 - 1.25P)$$

$$= 40.0 + 25.5 + 36.5 - (2 + 0.75 + 1.25)\ P$$

$$= 102 - 4P$$

If P is in rupees, the market demand function shows that rise in price of the commodity by one rupee will result in fall in its quantity demanded by 4 units.

Relationship between Demand Function and Demand Curve

It is important to know the relationship between demand function and demand curve. While a complete demand function specifies the relationship between quantity demanded of a product and many variables such as the own price of the product, income of consumers, prices of related commodities, tastes and preferences, expected future prices etc. ($Q_x^d = f(P_x, I, P_y, T, A, N)$, the demand curve is a graphic represation of only a part of this demand function, namely, $Q_x^d = f(P)$, holding other independent variables in the demand function as constant. That is, while drawing a demand curve values of other variables in the demand function are kept constant at *particular levels*. The complete demand function with many variables cannot be shown by the two dimensional curve, the effect of changes in other variables or factors on the quantity demanded of a product is shown by shifts

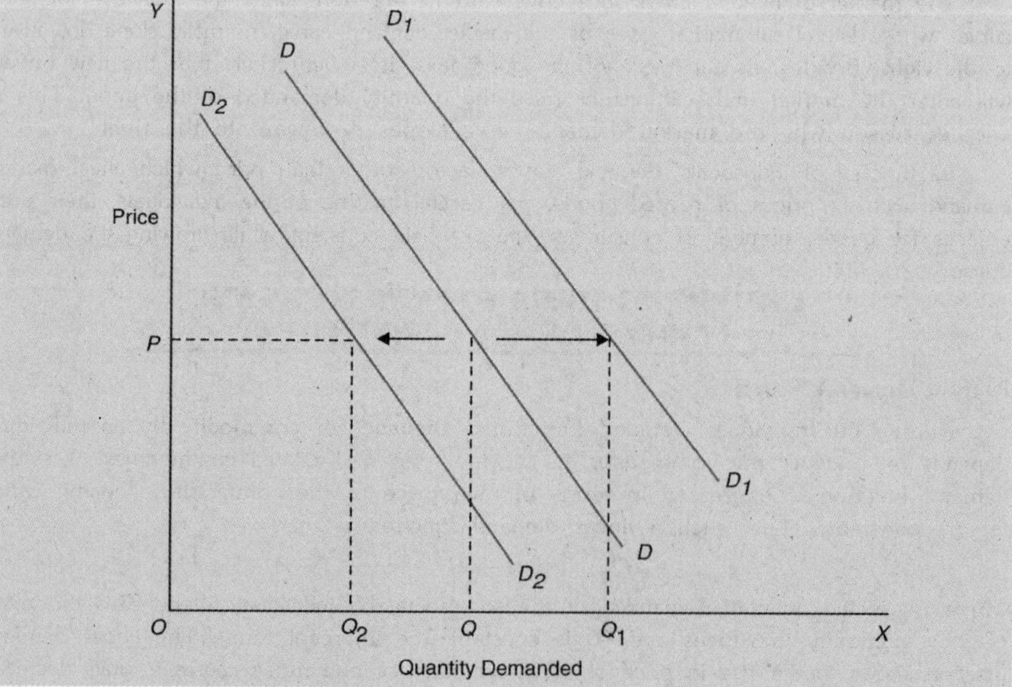

Fig. 5.3. *Shifts in Demand curve due to Changes in Variables other than Price*

in the whole demand curve. This is illustrated in Figure 5.3. To begin with *DD* is the market demand curve. Now, suppose income of consumers increases, say due to the hike in their wages and salaries. As a result, they will demand more of a product at each price causing a shift in the demand curve to the right as from *DD* to D_1D_1 in Figure 5.3. It will be seen that at a given price *OP*, with demand curve *DD* the consumers were buying *OQ* quantity of the product and with rightward shift in the demand curve to D_1D_1 they demand greater quantity OQ_1 of the product. Similarly, at other prices more is demanded at D_1D_1 as compared to the demand curve *DD*.

Similarly, increase in price of a substitute of a product, favourable change in preferences of consumers for a product, expectations of rise in price of a product in future will cause increase in the quantity demanded of a product and will therefore lead to the shift in demand curve for the product to the right.

On the other hand, decrease in consumers' income, fall in price of a substitute product, unfavourable change in consumers' preference for the product, aggressive advertisement expenditure by competitive firms will cause a decrease in demand for the product resulting in leftward shift in the demand curve from *DD* to D_2D_2. With lower demand curve D_2D_2 at each price consumers will demand less quantity of the product than before. Thus at price *OP* on demand curve D_2D_2 the consumers would now demand OQ_2 quantity of the product which is smaller than OQ.

To conclude, whereas demand function specifies relationship between quantity demanded of a product with many independent variables, demand curve of a product is a graphic representation of only a part of the demand function with price of the product as the only independent variable. The effects of change in variables other than price, as explained above, are shown through a shift in the demand curve.

Bandwagon Effect and Snob Effect

It is worth noting that making horizontal summation of individual demand curves to obtain market demand curve we have made an important assumption *that demand functions of individual consumers are independent.* This is however not always the case. Most important factor causing interdependence of demands of individual consumers is the bandwagon effect. Bandwagon effect arises because individuals demand some commodeties because others are doing so, that is, those commodities happen to be in fashion. The desire to look fashionable and to keep up with Joneses makes demands of individuals interdependent. For example, desire or demand for wearing jeans by girls has been influenced by the number of other girls purchasing and demanding jeans. The bandwagon effect tends to make the market demand curve flatter or more elastic than given by the simple horizontal summation of the individual demand comes.

The second factor which makes the demands of different individuals interdependent is snob effect. The *snob effect,* which is opposite of bandwagon effect, refers to the desire to purchase a commodity having prestige value so as to look different or exclusive than others. Therefore, individuals demand less of a commodity having a prestige value as more individuals buy it. This is because when more people have a commodity, it loses its prestige value. The existence of snob effect tends to make the demand steeper or less elastic than indicated by the horizontal summation of individual demand curves.

Industry (Market) Demand Versus Firm's Demand

Thus far we have discussed consumers' demand for a product of an industry. But from the viewpoint of a manager, it is the demand curve facing a firm is more relevant for making price-output decisions. The most important difference between the two is that in case of a demand curve facing a firm some different types of veriables have to be included in the demand function for a firm. The two important such variables which must be included in the demand function for a firm are : (1) prices charged by rival firms in the industry which significantly affects demand for individual firms whose products are similar and close substitutes of each other. (2) Advertising expenditure by rival firms. However in the extreme case when firm is the sole seller or producer a product, that is, if it has monopoly over its product, then demand function for it would not contain prices charged and advertising expenditure made by other firms. Therefore, in case of monopoly in the product market, a single firm faces the entire market demand for the product and will bear the full effect of changes in consumers' income, their tastes and preferences.

But in the real world monopolies are rare, what we actually find is market structure of monopolistic competition and oligopolies with product differentiation. In such cases prices charged and advertising expenditure by rival firms must be incorporated as independent variables in a demand function for a firm. Therefore, in such cases demand curve facing an individual firm is drawn keeping prices and advertising by rival firms as constant. Since in case of market structures of the form of monopolistic competition and oligopoly with product differentiation close substitutes of a firm's product are available, demand curve facing individual firms working in these market conditions will be relatively more elastic than the demand curve for the entire industry. It is worth noting that demand for a firm's product is negatively related to its own price but positively related to prices charged by rival firms.

However, in case of monopolistic competition where a large number of firms work and produce differentiated products which are close substitutes of each other, the quantitative impact on the demand for product of a firm of changes in prices of other products, income and tastes and preferences of the consumers will be much less as a firm's share is only small fraction of the total market for the product of the industry. For example, the effect of rise in price due to a hike in excise duty on the quantity demanded of an indvidual cotton textile firm as measured by the value of coefficient b of its price variable. It will be found much less as compared to the value of coefficient obtained in case of entire industry or market. Similarly, change in population will affect the demand for cotton textiles. But its coefficient will be much higher if estimated for the entire cotton textile industry than found in case of an individual firm producing cotton textiles.

In the extreme case when perfect competition prevails in the product market, whereas demand curve for the entire industry is downward-sloping, demand curve facing an individual firm is perfectly elastic (*i.e.* a horizontal straight) at the prevailing price. Since an individual firm working in perfectly competitive market produces only a small fraction of the total output of the industry, it has no influence over the price of the product. Whatever price is determind by demand for and supply of a product of the industry, a perfectly competitive individual firm takes it as given and constant for it. Hence, its demand curve is perfectly elastic at the prevailing price as shown in panel (*b*) of Figure 5.4 where *OP* is market price determined by the intersection of demand curve *DD* and supply curve *SS* a of a product of a perfectly competitive industry. An individual firm will take the price *OP* as given and constant for it. Since a firm can sell as much as it likes at this price, demand curve $D_F D_F$ facing it is perfectly elastic at this price (see panel (b) of Fig. 5.4).

It must however be emphasised that like a pure monopoly, perfect competition also rarely prevails in the real world.

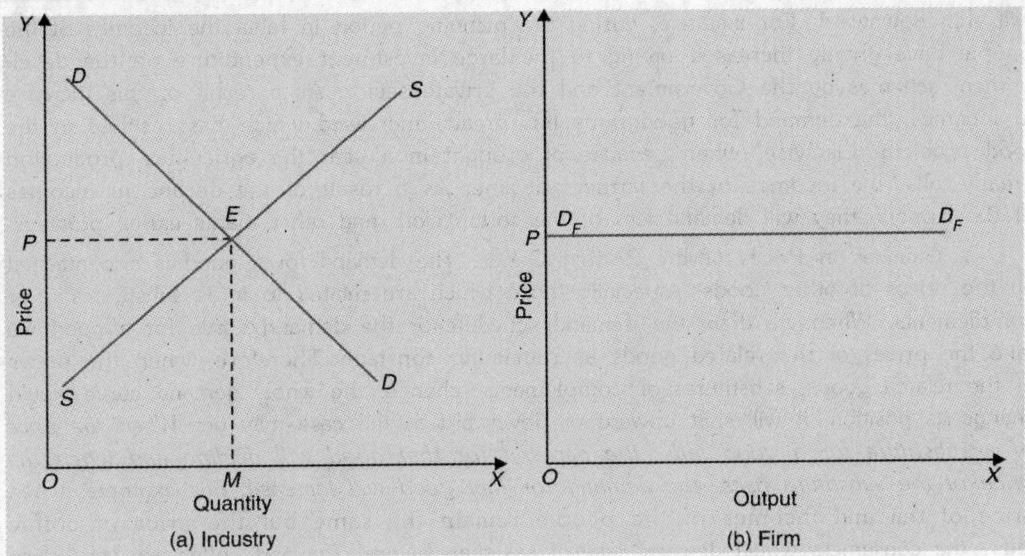

Fig. 5.4. *Demand Curve for Entire Industry and for an Individual Firm*

It is evident from above that since demand functions for industry and individual firms differ. Therefore, different demand equations must be specified for estimating demand for them.

FACTORS DETERMINING DEMAND

We have explained above how the demand changes as a result of changes in price, other factors determining it being held constant. We shall explain below in detail how these other factors determine market demand for a commodity. These other factors determine the position or level of demand curve of a commodity. It may be noted that when there is a change in these non-price factors, the whole curve shifts rightward or leftward as the case may be. The following factors determine market demand for a commmodity.

1. **Tastes and Preferences of the Consumers.** An important factor which determines the demand for a good is the tastes and preferences of the consumers for it. A good for which consumers' tastes and preferences are greater, its demand would be large and its demand curve will therefore lie at a higher level. People's tastes and preferences for various goods often change and as a result there is change in demand for them. The changes in demand for various goods occur due to the changes in fashion and also due to the *pressure of advertisements by the manufacturers and sellers* of different products. On the contrary, when certain goods go out of fashion or people's tastes and preferences no longer remain favourable to them, the demand for them decreases.

2. **Income of the People.** The demand for goods also depends upon the incomes of the people. The greater the incomes of the people, the greater will be their demand for goods. In drawing the demand schedule or the demand curve for a good we take income of the people as given and constant. When as a result of the rise in the income of the people, the demand increases, the whole of the demand curve shifts upward and *vice versa.* The greater income means the greater purchasing power. Therefore, when the incomes of the people increase, they can afford to buy more. It is because of this reason that increase in income has a positive effect on the demand for a good. When incomes of the people fall, they would demand less of a good and as a result the demand curve

will shift downward. For instance, during the planning period in India the incomes of the people have greatly increased owing to the large investment expenditure on the development schemes by the Government and the private sector. As a result of this increase in incomes, the demand for goodgrains has greatly increased which has resulted in the food problem. Likewise, when because of drought in a year the agriculture production greatly falls, the incomes of the farmers decline. As a result of the decline in incomes of the farmers, they will demand less of the cotton cloth and other manufactured products.

3. Changes in Prices of the Related Goods. The demand for a good is also affected by the prices of other goods, especially those which are related to it as substitutes or complements. When we draw the demand schedule or the demand curve for a good we take the prices of the related goods as remaining constant. Therefore, when the prices of the related goods, substitutes or complements, change, the whole demand curve would change its position; it will shift upward or downward as the case may be. *When the price of a substitute for a good falls, the demand for that good will decline and when the price of the substitute rises, the demand for that good will increase.* For example, when price of tea and incomes of the people remain the same but the price of coffee falls, the consumers would demand less of tea than before. Tea and coffee are very close substitutes. Therefore, when coffee becomes cheaper, the consumers substitute coffee for tea and as a result the demand for tea declines. The goods which are complementary with each other, the fall in the price of any of them would favourably affect the demand for the other. For instance, if price of milk falls, the demand for sugar would also be favourably affected. When people would take more milk, the demand for sugar will also increase. Likewise, when the price of cars falls, the quantity demanded of them would increase which in turn wil increase the demand for petrol.

4. Advertisement Expenditure. Advertisement expenditure made by a firm to promote the sales of its product is an important factor determining demand for a product, especially of the product of the firm which gives advertisements. The purpose of advertisement is to influence the consumers in favour of a product. Advertisements are given in various media such as newspapers, radio, television. Advertisements for goods are repeated several times so that consumers are convinced about their superior quality. When advertisements prove successful they cause an increase in the demand for the product.

5. The Number of Consumers in the Market. We have already explained that the market demand for a good is obtained by adding up the individual demands of the present as well as prospective consumers of a good at various possible prices. The greater the number of consumers of a good, the greater the market demand for it. Now, the question arises on what factors the number of consumers for a good depends. If the consumers substitute one good for another, then the number of consumers for the good which has been substituted by the other will decline and for the good which has been used in place of the others, the number of consumers will increase. Besides, when the seller of a good succeeds in finding out new markets for his good and as a result the market for his good expands, the number of consumers for that good will increase. Another important cause for the increase in the number of consumers is the growth in population. For instance, in India the demand for many essential goods, especially foodgrains, has increased because of the increase in the population of the country and the resultant increase in the number of consumers for them.

6. Consumers' Expectations with regard to Future Prices. Another factor which influences the demand for goods is consumers' expectations with regard to future prices

of the goods. If due to some reason, consumers expect that in the near future prices of the goods would rise, then in the present they would demand greater quantities of the goods so that in the future they should not have to pay higher prices. Similarly, when the consumers expect that in the future the prices of goods will fall, then in the present they will postpone a part of the consumption of goods with the result that their present demand for goods will decrease.

Increase in Demand and Shifts in Demand Curve

When demand changes due to the factors other than price, there is a shift in the whole demand curve. As mentioned above, apart from price, demand for a commodity is determined by incomes of the consumers, his tastes and preferences, prices of related goods. Thus, when there is any change in these factors, it will cause a shift in demand curve. For example, if incomes of the consumers increase, say due to the hike in their wages and salaries or due to the grant of dearness allowance, they will demand more of a good, say cloth, at each price. This will cause a shift in the demand curve to the right. Similarly, if preferences of the people for a commodity, say colour TV, become greater, their demand for colour TV will increase, that is, the demand curve will shift to the right and, therefore, at each price they will demand more colour TV.

The other important factor which can cause an increase in demand for a commodity is the *expectations about future prices.* If people expect that price of a commodity is likely to go up in future, they will try to purchase the commodity, especially a durable one, in the current period which will boost the current demand for the good and cause a shift in the demand curve to the right. As seen above, the prices of related commodities such as substitutes and complements can also change the demand for a commodity. For example, if the price of coffee rises, other factors remaining the constant, this will cause the demand for tea, a substitute for coffee, to increase and its demand curve to shift to the right.

Decrease in demand and Shift in the Demand Curve. If there are adverse changes in the factors influencing demand, it will lead to the decrease in demand causing a shift in the demand curve to the left as shown in Fig. 5.3. For eample, if due to inadequate rainfall agricultural production in a year declines, this will cause a fall in the incomes of the farmers. This fall incomes of the farmers will cause a decrease in the demand for industrial products, say cloth, and will result in a shift in the demand curve to the left. Similarly, change in preferences for commodities can also affect the demand. For example, when colour TVs came to India people's greater preference for them led to the increase in their demand. But this brought about decrease in demand for black and white TVs causing leftward shift in demand curve for these black and white TVs. The decrease in demand does not occur due to the rise in price but due to the changes in other determinants of demand. Decrease in demand for a commodity may occur due to the fall in the prices of its substitutes, rise in the prices of complements of that commodity and if the people expect that price of a good will fall in future.

DEMAND FOR DURABLE GOODS

Nature of demand for durable goods is of special interest in demand theory. Demand for durable goods is more volatile than the demand for non-durable goods. *In economics durable goods are defined as those goods that go on yielding services to the consumers over a number of periods in future.* Further, because of their durability they can be stored for longer periods of time. It is due to the use of services of durable goods for a relatively long term that consumer's' demand for them is more volatile, that is, fluctuates very much.

Now what accounts for the large volatility in demand for durable goods. First, since durable goods can be stored, producers, distributors and consumers usually keep a large inventories of such goods. Therefore, increase in demand for them may not show up in more production of such goods for quite some time because the greater demand for them can be met by drawing upon their inventories. On the other hand, when inventories of durable goods are low even a small increase in demand for them by their consumers may actually lead to greater market demand because producers and distributors would also tend to increase their demand for holding more inventories to accommodate their large demand in future.

The other factor responsible for volatility in demand for durable goods is that *replacement of these durable goods can be deferred* by undertaking additional maintenance expenditure on existing durable goods possessed by them. For example, an old car may be got replaced or its old model may be used for a longer period. Similarly, the purchase of new furniture may be postponed by tolerating the use of old furniture for one more year. Thus, analysis of demand for durable goods must consider not only new consumer's demand for them but also consider the need for building up their inventories by distributors and producers and replacement demand for them which may be deferred. It is not mere physical deterioration which calls for replacement of durable goods but more important is the fact that models of the durable goods being currently used may go out of fashion and therefore lose their prestige value.

However, the important difference between non-durable and durable goods is that non-durables are purchased for current consumption only, whereas durables are demanded for getting their services in future periods. Consequently, their demand for them crucially depends on consumers' expectations regarding their future incomes, especially when they buy them on credit, availability of these durables in future, expectations regarding future prices, rate of change in technology that make them obsolete. Thus, fluctuations in demand for durables is relatively greater as it depends on expectations of consumers about future developments. If the expectations of consumers are such that prices of durables will rise in future due to their short supply, their demand for them will increase not only to meet their current consumption needs but also for storing them for future use. Similarly, if consumers expect their prices will fall in future, they will postpone their purchases resulting in large decline in their demand.

Derived Demand

There are some goods which are not demanded by individuals to satisfy their wants directly but for using them to produce other consumer goods which directly satisfy their wants. Demand for them is called derived demand as its is derived from the demand for other goods. Thus, demand for car and housing loans is not determined directly but is derived from the demand for cars or houses which are purchased with the loan money. However, the important case of derived demand is demand for producers' goods such as raw materials, machines and other types of capital equipment, spare parts etc. These producers goods are not consumed directly by individuals to satisfy their wants. For example, demand for copper does not solely depend on individuals' desire for copper itself but rather for using it to produce products which are wholly or partly made of copper. In fact individuals, wants for them may be quite independent of the fact that copper is used in their production. Therefore, for the analysis of demand for the products for which there is derived demand we must consider the factors that affect demand for altimate goods in the production of which producer goods are used.

QUESTIONS AND PROBLEMS FOR REVIEW

1. Distinguish between a demand function and demand curve. What are the factors that cause a shift in the demand curve?
2. Distinguish between the movement along a demand curve and shift in the demand curve.
3. State the law of demand. How would you explain it with substitution effect and income effect? Are there any exceptions to this law?
4. Given the following market demand function for the commodity X

   $$Q_x = f(P_x, P_y, P_z, I, T, A)$$

   where

   P_x = Price of the commodity X

   P_y = Price of a substitute commodity Y

   P_z = Price of commodity Z which is complement of X

   I = Level of per capita income of consumers

   T = Tastes and preferences of consumers

   A = Advertising expenditure by a firm producing X

   How will the consumer demand for a commodity X change ?

   (*i*) if price of the commodity X rises,

   (*ii*) if price of the substitute good Y rises,

   (*iii*) if price of complementary commodity Z falls,

   (*iv*) per capita income (I) of the consumers rises, and

   (*v*) the firm producing X increases its advertisement expenditure.
5. Distinguish between industry demand curve and demand curve for the product of a single firm. Do you think demand curve for the product of a firm is more elastic than the demand curve for the commodity facing the industry? Give reasons.
6. How is the firm's demand curve affected by the degree of competition existing in its industry?

   (Hint : The degree of competition depends on the availability of substitutes and number of rival firms. When close substitutes of a product are available and the number of firms producing the commodity is very large, degree of competition is very high and consequently the demand curve for a firm's product is very elastic. When perfect competition prevails and different firms produce homogeneous product which are perfect substitutes of each other, though the demand curve for the industry as a whole slopes downward, demand curve for a firm is perfectly elastic at the price determined by the intersection of demand curve for industry and supply curve of the industry.)
7. What are the factors which determine market demand for a commodity? Explain what additional factors affect demand for individual firm's product.
8. Exaplain the nature of demand for durable goods. What factors are responsible for greater volatility in demand for them?
9. What is meant by derived demand? How is demand for producer goods a derived demand?
10. What is bandwagon effect and snob effect? How do they affect the demand for goods?
11. Explain 'Giffen Paradox' and Veblen Effect. Does usual law of demand apply in their case?

Elasticity of Demand

Various Concepts of Demand Elasticity

We have discussed in the preceding chapter that when price of a good falls, its quantity demanded rises and when price of it rises, its quantity demanded falls. This is generally known as *law of demand.* This law of demand indicates only the *direction of change in quantity demanded* of a commodity in response to a change in its price. This does not tell us by *how much* or *to what extent* the quantity demanded of a good will change in response to a change in its price. This information as to how much or to what extent the quantity demanded of a good will change as a result of a change in its price is provided by the concept of price elasticity of demand.

But, besides price elasticity of demand, there are various other concepts of demand elasticity. As we have seen in the previous chapter, demand for a good is determined by its price, incomes of the people, prices of related goods, etc. Quantity demanded of a good will change as a result of change in any of these determinants of demand. The concept of elasticity of demand therefore refers to the degree of responsiveness of quantity demanded of a good to a change in its price, consumers' income and prices of related goods. Accordingly, there are three concepts of demand elasticity : price elasticity, income elasticity, and cross elasticity. Price elasticity of demand relates to the degree of responsiveness of quantity demanded of a good to the change in its price. Income elasticity of demand refers to the sensitivenes of quantity demanded to a change in consumers' income. Cross elasticity of demand means the degree of responsiveness of demand of a good to a change in the price of a related good, which may be either a substitute for it or a complementary with it.

The concept of elasticity of demand has a very great importance in economic theory as well as formulation of suitable economic policies.

PRICE ELASTICITY OF DEMAND

As mentioned above, price elasticity of demand indicates the degree of responsiveness of quantity demanded of a good to the change in its price, other factors such as consumers' income, prices of related commodities that determine demand are held constant. Precisely, *price elasticity of demand is defined as the ratio of the percentage change in quantity demanded of a commodity to a given percentage change in price. Thus*

$$e_p = \frac{\text{Percentage change in quantity demanded}}{\text{Percentage change in price}}$$

For example, suppose 5 per cent rise in price of eggs causes its quantity demanded to fall by 10 per cent, we calculate price elasticity of demand for eggs as

$$\text{Price elasticity of demand} = \frac{10}{5} = 2$$

Strictly speaking, since as price of a commodity rises, its quantity demanded falls we should put negative sign before 10 and since price rises, we should put positive sign before 5., then we obtain the value of price elasticity as

$$\text{Price elasticity of demand} = \frac{-10}{+5} = -2$$

Thus, we get –2 as the price elasticity of demand. For the same changes in price and quantity demanded, we will get the same value of price elasticity of demand if price *falls* by 5 percent and quantity demanded rises by 10 percent. In this case we have

$$e_p = \frac{+10}{-5} = -2$$

However, it may be noted that a convention has been adopted in economics that price elasticity be expressed with a positive sign despite the fact that change in price and change in quantity demanded are inversely related to each other. This is because we are interested in measuring the *magnitude of responsiveness* of quantity demanded of a good to changes in its price.

It follows from the above definition of price elasticity of demand that when the percentage change in quantity demanded a commodity is greater than the percentage change in price that brought it about, price elasticity of demand (e_p) will be greater than one and in this case demand is said to be *elastic.* On the other hand, when a given prercentage change in price of a commodity leads to a smaller percentage change in quantity demanded, elasticity will be less than one and demand in this case is said to be *inelastic.* Further, when the percentage change in quantity demanded of a commodity is equal to the percentage change in price that caused it, price elasticity is equal to one. Thus. in case of elastic demand, a given percentage

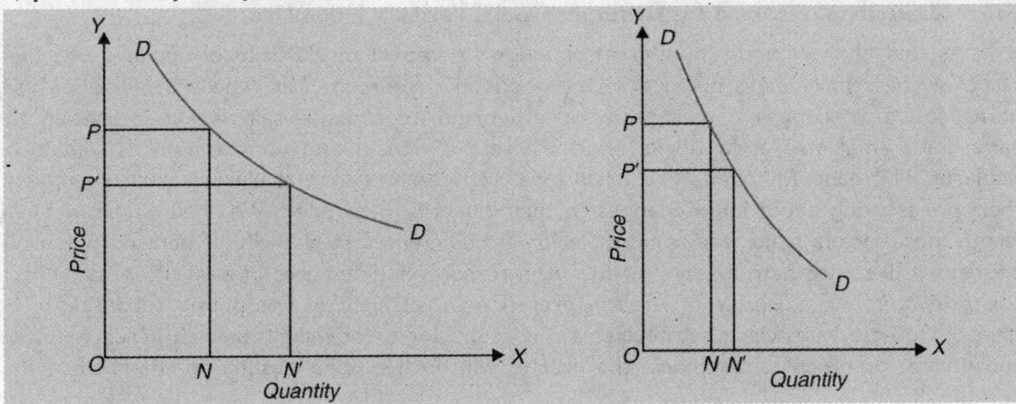

Fig. 6.1. *Elastic Demand* **Fig. 6.2.** *Inelastic Demand*

change in price causes quite a large change in quantity demanded. And in case of inelastic demand, a given percentage change in price brings about a very small change in quantity demanded of a commodity.

It is a matter of common knowledge and observation that there is a considerable difference between different goods in regard to the magnitude of response of demand to the changes in price. The demand for some goods is more responsive to the changes in price than those for others. In terminology of economics, we would say that demand for some goods is *more elastic* than those for the others or *the price elasticity of demand of some* goods is greater than those of the others. Marshall[1] who introduced the concept of elasticity into economic theory remarks that the elasticity or responsiveness *of demand in a market is great or small according as the amount demanded increases much or little for a given fall in price, and diminishes much or little for a given rise in price.* This will be clear from Figures 6.1 and 6.2 which respresent two demand curves. For a *given fall* in price, from *OP* to *OP′*, increase in quantity demanded is much greater in Figure 6.1 than in Figure 6.2. Therefore, demand in Figure 6.1 is more elastic than the demand in Figure in 6.2 for a given fall in price for the portion of demand curves considered. Demand for the good represented in Fig. 6.1 is generally said to be elastic and the demand for the goods in Fig. 6.2 to be inelastic.

It should, however, be noted that *terms elastic and inelastic demand are used in the relative sense.* In other words, elasticity is a matter of degree only. Demand for some goods is only more or less elastic than others. Thus, when we say that demand for a good is elastic, we mean only that the demand for it is relatively more elastic. Likewise, when we say that demand for a goods is inelastic, we do not mean that its demand is absolutely inelastic but only that it is relatively less elastic. In economic theory elastic and inelastic demands have come to acquire precise meanings. Demand for a goods is said to be *elastic* if price elasticity of demand for it is *greater than one.* Similarly, the demand for a goods is called *inelastic* if price elasticity of demand for it is *less than one.* Price elasticity of demand equal to one, or in other words, *unit elasticity* of demand therefore represents the dividing line between elastic and inelastic demands. It will now be clear that by inelastic demand we do not mean perfectly inelastic but only that price elasticity of demand is less than unity, and by elastic demand we do not mean absolutely elastic but that price elasticity of demand is greater than one.

Thus,

Elastic demand : $e_p > 1$

Inelastic demand : $e_p < 1$

Unitary elastic demand : $e_p = 1$

Price Elasticity of Demand for Different Goods Varies a Good Deal

As said above, goods show great variation in respect of elasticity of demand *i.e.,* their responsiveness to changes in price. Some goods like common salt, wheat and rice are very unresponsive to changes in their prices. The demand for common salt remains practically the same for a small rise or fall in its price. Therefore, demand for common salt is said to be 'inelastic'. Demand for goods like televisions, refrigerators etc., is elastic, since changes in their prices bring about large changes in their quantity demanded. We shall explain later at length those factors which are responsible for the differences in elasticity of demand of various goods. It will suffice here to say that the main reason for differences in elasticity of demand is the *possibility of substitution i.e.,* the presence or absence of competing substitues. The greater the ease with which substitutes can be found for a commodity or with which it can be substituted for other commodities, the greater will be the price elasticity of demand of that commodity.

1. Alfred Marshall, *Principles of Economics*, 8th Edition, Vol. 2.

Goods are demanded because they satisfy some particular wants and in general wants can be satisfied in a variety of alternative ways. For instance, the want for entertainment can be gratified by having television set, or by possessing a gramophone, or by going to cinemas or by visiting theatres. If the price of a television set falls, the quantity demanded of television sets will rise greatly since fall in the price of television will induce some people to buy television in place of having gramophones or visiting cinemas and theatres. Thus the demand for televisions is elastic. Likewise, if price of 'Lux' falls, its demand will greatly rise because it will be substituted for other varieties of soap such as Jai, Hamam, Godrej, Pears etc. On the contary, the demand for a necessary goods like common salt is inelastic. The demand for common salt is inelastic since it satisfies a basic human want and no substitutes for it are available. People would consume almost the same quantity of salt whether it becomes slightly cheaper or dearer than before.

Perfectly Inelastic and Perfectly Elastic Demand

We will now explain the two extreme cases of price elasticity of demand. First extreme situation is of perfectly inelastic demand which is depicted in Fig. 6.3. In this case changes in price of a commodity does not affect the quantity demand of the commodity at all. In this perfectly inelastic demand, demand curve is a vertical straight line as shown in Fig. 6.3. As will be seen from this figure, whatever the price the quantity demanded of the commodity remains unchanged at *OQ*. An approximate example of perfectly inelastic demand is the demand of acute diabetic patient for insulin. He has to get the prescribed doze of insulin per week whatever its price.

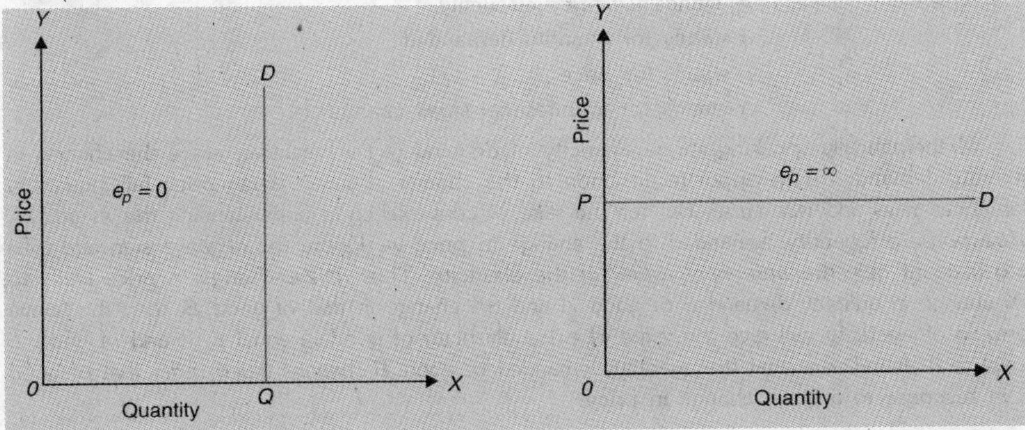

Fig. 6.3. *Perfectly Inelastic Demand ($e_p = 0$)* **Fig. 6.4.** *Perfectly Elastic Demand, $e_p = \infty$*

The second extreme situaiton is of perfectly elastic demand in which case demand curve is a horizontal straight line as shown in Fig. 6.4. This horizontal demand curve for a product implies that a small reduction in price would cause the buyers to increase the quantity demanded from zero to all they wanted. On the other hand, a small rise in price of the product will cause the buyers to switch completely away from the product so that its quantity demanded falls to zero. We will see in later chapters that perfectly elastic demand curve is found for the product of an individual firm working under perfect competition. Products of different firms working under perfect competition are completely identical. If any perfectly competitive firm raises the price of its product, it would lose all its customers who would switch over to other firms, and if it reduces its price somewhat it would get all the customers to buy the product from it.

MEASUREMENT OF PRICE ELASTICITY

As said above, price elasticity of demand expresses the response of relative change in quantity demanded of a good to relative changes in its price, given the consumer's income, his tastes and prices of all other goods. Thus price elasticity means the degree of responsiveness or sensitiveness of quantity demanded of a good to a change in its price. An important method to measure price elasticity of demand is the percentage method which we explain below.

Price elasticity can be precisely measured by dividing the percentage change in quantity demanded by the given percentage change in price that caused it. Thus we can measure price elasticity by using the following formula:

$$\text{Price Elaticity} = \frac{\text{Percentage change in quantity demanded}}{\text{Percentage change in price}}$$

$$= \frac{\text{Change in quantity demanded / Quantity demanded}}{\text{Chqnge in price /Price}}$$

or, in symbolic terms

$$e_p = \frac{\Delta q / q}{\Delta p / p} = \frac{\Delta q}{q} \div \frac{\Delta p}{p}$$

$$= \frac{\Delta q}{q} \times \frac{p}{\Delta p}$$

$$= \frac{\Delta q}{\Delta p} \times \frac{p}{q}$$

where e_p stands for price elastictity

q stands for quantity demanded

p stands for price

Δ stands for infinitesimal small change

Mathematically speaking, price elasticity of demand (e_p) is negative, since the change in quantity demanded is in opposite direction to the change in price; when price falls, quantity demanded rises and *vice versa.* But for the sake of convenience in understanding the *magnitude of response* of quantity demanded to the change in price we ignore the negative sign and take into account only the *numerical value* of the elasticity. Thus, if 2% change in price leads to 4% change in quantity demanded of good *A* and 8% change in that of good *B*, then the above formula of elasticity will give the value of price elasticity of good *A* equal to 2 and of good *B* equal to 4. It indicates that the quantity demanded of good *B* changes much more that of good A in response to a given change in price.

Midpoint Method of Calculating Percentage Changes

When we calculate the price elasticity of demand through percentage or proportionate method we face a problem whether to use the *initial price* as the base for calculating percent change in price and *initial quantity* as the base for calculating the percent change in quantity demanded in response to a given percent change in price. For example, suppose price of a commodity rises from Rs. 4 to Rs. 6 per unit and as a result, the quantity demanded falls from 120 units to 80 units. If we take initial price Rs. 4 as the base for change in price, then change in price by Rs. 2 amounts to 50 percent change in price $\left(\frac{6-4}{4} \times 100 = \frac{1}{2} \times 100 = 50\right)$ And taking intial quantity 120 units as the base for calculating percent change in quantity demanded, then there is 33.3 percent change in quantity demanded $\left(\frac{120-80}{120} \times 100 = \frac{1}{3} \times 100 = 33.3\right)$.

Thus we get price elasticity of demand as

$$e_p = \frac{33}{50} = 0.66$$

Let us now reverse the direciton. Suppose the price of the commodity falls from ₹ 6 to 4 per unit, and as a result quantity demanded increases from 80 units 120 units, then now taking initial ₹ 6 as the base for calculating percentage change in price, then there is 33 per cent change in price $\left(\frac{6-4}{6} \times 100 = \frac{2}{6} \times 100 = 33.\right)$ and taking 80 units as the base for calculating percentage change in quantity, then the quantity demanded rises by 50 percent $\left(\frac{120-80}{80} \times 100 = \frac{40}{80} \times 100 = 50\right)$. Thus, we will now get $\frac{50}{33.3}$ =1.5 as the price elasticity of demand. It therefore follows that for the same absolute change in price and absolute change in quantity demanded we get different values of price elasticity of demand if we use ₹ 4 or ₹ 6 as the base for calculating percentage change in price and 120 units or 80 units as the base for calculating percentage change in quantity demanded. To avoid this problem we use *midpoint method* for calculating the percentage changes in price and quantity demanded. In midpoint method we calculate the percentage change in price or quantity demanded by *taking midpoint of the initial and final values of price and quantity demanded* respectively as the base. Thus, in our above example, midpoint (or, in other words, average) of prices of ₹ 4 and ₹ 6 is $\frac{4+6}{2} = 5$ and midpoint (or average) of quantities demanded is $\frac{80+120}{2} = 100$.

Using this midpoint method the percentage change in price is $\frac{6-4}{5} \times 100 = 40$ and percentage change in quantity demanded is $\frac{120-80}{100} \times 100 = 40$. With these percentage changes in price and quantity demanded price of elasticity of demand will be

$$e_p = \frac{40}{40} = 1$$

It should be carefully noted that for *large changes in price, we must use midpoint method of calculating price elaticity of demand.* If change in price is *very small,* then we can use initial price and initial quantity demanded.

It p_1 stands for initial price and p_2 for the new price and q_1 for the initial quantity and q_2 for the new quantity, then midpoint formula for calculating price elasticity of demand (e_p) can be written as

$$e_p = \frac{(q_2 - q_1)}{\frac{q_1 + q_2}{2}} \div \frac{p_2 - p_1}{\frac{p_1 + p_2}{2}}$$

$$= \frac{\Delta q}{\frac{q_1 + q_2}{2}} \times \frac{\frac{p_1 + p_2}{2}}{\Delta p}$$

$$= \frac{\Delta q}{\Delta p} \times \frac{p_1 + p_2}{q_1 + q_2}$$

In a later section we will explain the concept of *arc elasticity of demand* which should be distinguished from the *point elasticity of demand.* Point elasticity of demand refers to the price elasticity at a point on a demand curve or, in other words, it refers to the price elasticity when the changes in the price and the resultant changes in quantity demanded are infinitestimally small. In this case if we take the initial or the original price and original quantity or the subsequent price and quantity after the change in price as the basis of measurement, there will not be any significant difference in the coefficient of elasticity.

Some Numerical Problems of Price Elasticity of Demand

Let us solve some numerical problems of price elasticity of demand (both point and arc) by percentage method.

Problem 1. *Suppose the price of a commodity falls from Rs. 6 to Rs. 4 per unit and due to this quantity demanded of the commodity increases from 80 units to 120 units. Find out the price elasticity of demand.*

Solution : Change in quantity demand $(Q_2 - Q_1) = 120 - 80$

$$\text{Percentage change in quantity demanded} = \frac{Q_2 - Q_1}{\frac{Q_2 + Q_1}{2}} \times 100$$

$$= \frac{40}{\frac{200}{2}} \times 100$$

$$= 40$$

$$\text{Change in price} = P_2 - P_1 = 4 - 6 = -2$$

$$\text{\% Change in price} = \frac{P_2 - P_1}{\frac{P_2 + P_1}{2}} \times 100 = \frac{-2}{\frac{10}{2}} \times 100$$

$$= -40$$

$$\text{Price elasticity of demand} = \frac{\text{\% change in quantity demanded}}{\text{\% Change in price}}$$

$$= \frac{40}{-40} = -1$$

We ignore the minus sign. Therefore, price elasticity of demand is equal to one.

Problem 2. *A consumer purchases 80 units of a commodity when its price is Re. 1 per unit and purchases 48 units when its price rises to Rs. 2 per unit. What is the price elasticity of demand for the commodity?*

Solution : It should be noted that the change in price from Re. 1 to Rs. 2 in this case is very large (*i.e.,* 100%). Therefore, to calculate the elasticity coefficient in this case midpoint elasticity formula should be used.

Change is price (Δp) = Rs. 2 – 1 = 1

$$\text{Average of the original and subsequent prices} = \frac{p_1 + p_2}{2}$$

$$= \frac{1+2}{2} = \frac{3}{2} = 1.5$$

Change in quantity demanded (Δq) = 80 − 48 = 32

Average of the original and subsequent quantities $= \frac{q_1 + q_2}{2} = \frac{80 + 48}{2} = \frac{128}{2} = 64$

$$e_p = \frac{\Delta q}{\frac{q_1 + q_2}{2}} \div \frac{\Delta p}{\frac{p_1 + p_2}{2}}$$

$$= \frac{32}{64} \div \frac{1}{1.5}$$

$$= \frac{32}{64} \times \frac{1.5}{1} = \frac{1}{2} \times \frac{15}{10} = \frac{3}{4} = 0.75$$

Thus, the price elasticity of demand obtained is equal to 0.75.

Problem 3. *Suppose a seller of a textile cloth wants to lower the price of its cloth form Rs. 150 per metre to Rs. 142.5 per metre. If its present sales are 2000 metres per month and further it is estimated that its price elasticity of demand for the product is equal to 0.7. Show*

(a) Whether or not his total revenue will increase as a result of his decision to lower the price; and

(b) Calculate the exact magnitude of its new total revenue.

Solution (*a*) Price elasticity $= \frac{\Delta q}{\Delta p} \cdot \frac{p}{q}$

$$p = \text{Rs. } 150$$

$$q = 2000 \text{ metres}$$

$$\Delta p = 150 - 142.5 = 7.5$$

$$e_p = 0.7$$

$$\Delta q = ?$$

Substituting the values of p, q., Δp and e_p in the price elasticity formula we have

$$0.7 = \frac{\Delta q}{7.5} \cdot \frac{150}{2000}$$

$$\Delta q = \frac{0.7 \times 7.5 \times 2000}{150} = 70$$

Since the price has fallen the quantity demanded will increase by 70 metres. So the new quantity demanded will be 2000 + 70 = 2070.

(*b*) Total Revenue before reduction in price = 2000 × 150 = Rs. 3,00,000

Total revenue after price reduction = 2070 × 142.5 = 2,94,975

Thus with reduction in price his total revenue has decreased.

Finding Price Elasticity from a Demand Function

Linear demand function for a commodity is of the following from

$$Q = a - bP \qquad \text{... (i)}$$

where Q stands for the quantity demanded and P for price of the commodity, a and b are constants.

Note that b represents the slope of the demand function which is negative and shows the ratio of change in quantity to a change in price, that is, $\frac{\Delta Q}{\Delta P}$.

Now, $$e_p = \frac{\Delta Q}{\Delta P} \cdot \frac{P}{Q}$$

Writing b for $\frac{\Delta Q}{\Delta P}$ we have

$$e_p = b\frac{P}{Q} \qquad \text{...... } (ii)$$

With the expression of above equation (*ii*) we can measure price elasticity from a given demand function. Let us take a numerical example.

Suppose we are given the following demand function for milk in the city of Delhi.

$$Q = 720 - 25\,P$$

Q is in thousands of litres. It is required to find out the price elasticity at price of Rs. 15 per litre.

b or $\frac{\Delta Q}{\Delta P}$ in the given demand function is 25. To obtain price elasticity we have first to calculate the quantity demanded at the given price of Rs. 15 per litre. Substituting 15 for P in the given demand function we have

$$Q = 720 - 25 \times 15$$

$$Q = 720 - 375 = 345$$

Now, substituting $P = 15$, $Q = 345$ and $b = 25$ in the elasticity expression of equation (*ii*) along we have

$$e_p = b.\frac{P}{Q} = 25 \times \frac{15}{345} = 1.08$$

Thus price elasticity at price Rs. 15 per litre is 1.08 and quantity demanded of milk is equal to 345 thousand litres

Price Elasticity of Demand and Changes in Total Expenditure

It is often useful to know what happens to total expenditure made by the consumers on a good when its price changes. In Figure 6.5, a demand curve *DD* of a good is shown. When the price of good is *OP*, its quantity demanded is *OQ*. Since the total expenditure is price multiplied by the quantity of the good purchased, therefore

Consumer's total expenditure

$$= OP \times OQ = \text{area } OQRP$$

Now, whether the total expenditure rises or falls or remains the same with the change in the price of the good depends upon the price elasticity of demand. The total expenditure bears an important relationship with the price elasticity of demand and this relationship is of great significance in the theory of price. The following is the relationship between changes in total expenditure and price elasticity of demand.

The relationship between price elasticity of demand for a goods and total expenditure or outlay made on it is of great significance because with this knowledge of relationship a producer or seller of the goods can estimate how his total revenue will change with the fall or rise in the price of the goods. As seen above, the price elasticity of demand measures the ratio of proportionate change in quantity demanded to the proportionate change in price. That is, ignoring signs, $e_p = \Delta Q/Q/\Delta/P/P$ or% ΔQ/% ΔP. If price elasticity of demand is greater than one, then ignoring the signs, %ΔQ > % ΔP. On the other hand, if price elasticity of demand is less than one, % ΔQ < % ΔP. And if price elasticity equals one or, in other words, demand is unitary elastic, %ΔQ = %ΔP. For the sake of convenience, we write the results of this relationship in Table 6.1.

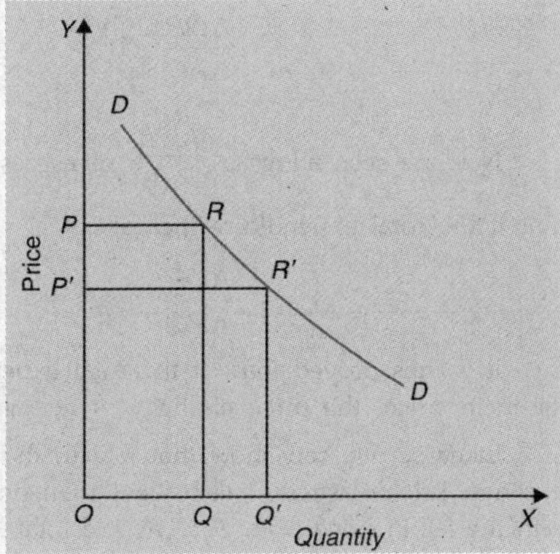

Fig. 6.5. *Changes in Price and Total Expenditure*

Table 6.1. Relationship Between Price Elasticity (e_p) and Total Expenditure (*TE*)

Price change	Elasticity greater than one (e_p > 1)	elasticity less than one (e_p < 1)	Elasticity equal to one (e_p = 1)
Price falls	*TE* increases	*TE* decreases	No change in *TE*
Price rises	*TE* decreases	*TE* increases	No change in *TE*

Proof of the Relation Between Price Elasticity and Total Expenditure

We can graphically prove the above-mentioned relationship between price elasticity of demand and the total expenditure. Consider Figure. 6.6 Suppose the price of a commodity falls from P to P_1 and in the response to it the quantity demanded increases from Q to Q_1. Since the total expenditure on a good equals the quantity demanded (Q) multiplied by the price of the good (P), that is, $TE = P.Q$, it will be seen from the diagram that at price OP the total expenditure equals the area of the rectangle $OPRQ$ and with the fall in price of the good the total expenditure equals OP_1TQ_1. Whereas the fall in price ($-\Delta P$) exerts a downward pressure on the total expenditure causing a decline in expenditure equal to $\Delta P.Q$. The increase in the quantity demanded caused by it ($+\Delta Q$) exerts an upward pressure on the total expenditure causing a gain in expenditure equal to ΔQP. If net total expenditure *increases* as price falls, then, as seen from Figure 6.6, the gain in expenditure ($+\Delta QP$) measured by the area of the rectangel $QLTQ_1$ must be greater than the decline in expenditure ($-\Delta P.Q$) as measured by the area of the rectangle $PRLP_1$. Thus, if with the fall in price from P to P_1, the total expenditure increases, we have

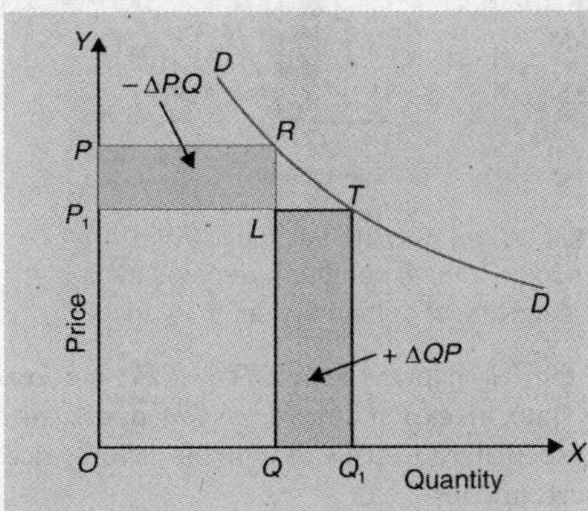

Fig. 6.6. *When Total expenditure increases with the fall in price, e_p is greater than one.*

$$\Delta QP > \Delta PQ.$$

Rearranging we have

$$\frac{\Delta QP}{\Delta PQ} > 1$$

Now, as seen above, $\frac{\Delta Q \cdot P}{\Delta P \cdot Q}$ measures the price elasticity of demand. It follows therefore that if the total expenditure increases

$$\frac{\Delta QP}{\Delta PQ} = e_p > 1$$

It is thus proved that if the total expenditure on a commodity increases resulting from a fall in its price, the price elasticity of demand is greater than one.

Likewise, we can show that if with the fall in price of a good the total expenditure on it declines, price elasticity will be less than one. Consider Figure 6.7 where it will be seen that with the fall in price from P to P_1 the total *net* expenditure decreases because as the decline in expenditure ($-\Delta PQ$) due to fall in price ($-\Delta P$) exceeds the gain in expenditure ($+\Delta QP$) due to the increase in quantity demanded ($+\Delta Q$) caused by it.

Thus, when total expenditure (*TE*) decreases with the fall in price we have

$$\Delta QP < \Delta PQ$$

Rearranging we have

$$\frac{\Delta QP}{\Delta PQ} < 1$$

$$\frac{\Delta QP}{\Delta PQ} = e_p < 1$$

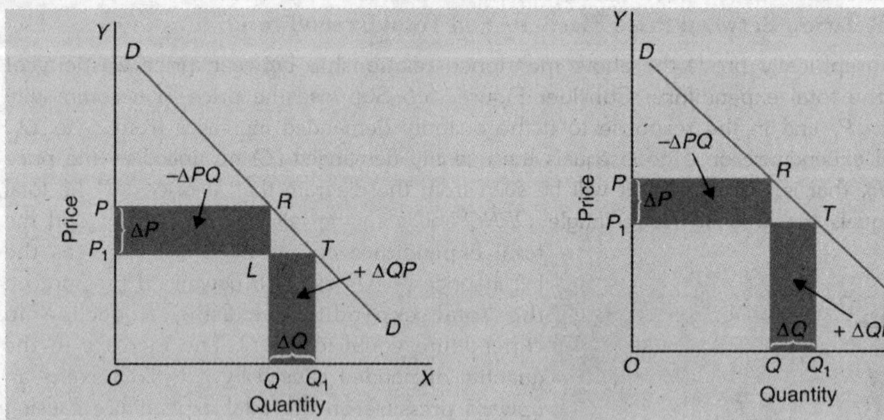

Fig.6.7. When with the fall in price of a commodity total expenditure decreases, price elasticity of demand is less than one.

Fig. 6.8. When with the fall in price of a commodity, total expenditure remains the same, price elasticity of demand is equal to unity.

Similarly, as will be seen from Figure 6.8, with the fall in price from OP to OP_1, the total expenditure on the good remains constant as the gain in expenditure ($+\Delta QP$) due to the increase in quantity demanded equals the decline in expenditure ($-\Delta PQ$) due to the fall in price. Thus, with the fall in price, constant total expenditure implies

$$\Delta QP = \Delta PQ$$

$$\frac{\Delta QP}{\Delta PQ} = 1$$

$$e_p = 1$$

As mentioned above, from the point of view of sellers and producers of goods the relation between price elasticity and total expenditure is of great importance. This relationship determines whether or not the seller's revenue or earnings would increase with the rise and fall in price. Total expenditure on a goods made by the consumers is revenue for the sellers. It is evident from the above relationship, that if a seller of a product *plans to cut the price* of his product, the total expenditure on it and therefore the total revenue of the seller will increase only if the demand for its product is elastic ($e_p > 1$) and his total revenue would decrease if the demand for its product is inelastic ($e_p < 1$). On the other hand, if the firm plans to raise the price of its product in a bid to increase its total revenue with the increase in its price, his total revenue will increase if the demand for its product is inelastic ($e_p < 1$).

MEASUREMENT OF PRICE ELASTICITY OF DEMAND AT A POINT ON A DEMAND CURVE

Let a straight line demand curve *DD'* is given and it is required to measure price elasticity at a point *R* on this demand curve. It will be seen from Fig. 6.10 that corresponding to point *R* on the demand curve *DD'*, price is *OP* and quantity demanded at it is *OQ*.

The measure of price elasticity of demand is given by :

$$e_p = \frac{\Delta Q}{\Delta P} \cdot \frac{P}{Q}$$

The first term in this formula, namely, $\frac{\Delta Q}{\Delta P}$ is the reciprocal of the slope of the demand curve *DD'* (Note that the slope of the demand curve *DD'* is equal to $\frac{\Delta P}{\Delta Q}$ which remains constant all along the straight-line demand curve). The second term in the above point elasticity formula is the original price (*p*) divided by the original quantity (*q*). Thus, at point *R*, on the demand curve *DD'*

$$e_p = \frac{1}{slope} \cdot \frac{P}{Q}$$

It will be seen from Fig. 6.9 that at point *R*, original price *P* = *OP* and original quantity *q* = *OQ*. Further, slope of the demand curve *DD*, is $\frac{\Delta P}{\Delta Q} = \frac{PD}{PR}$

Substituting these values in the above formula we have

$$e_p = \frac{1}{\frac{PD}{PR}} \times \frac{OP}{OQ}$$

$$= \frac{PR}{PD} \times \frac{OP}{OQ}$$

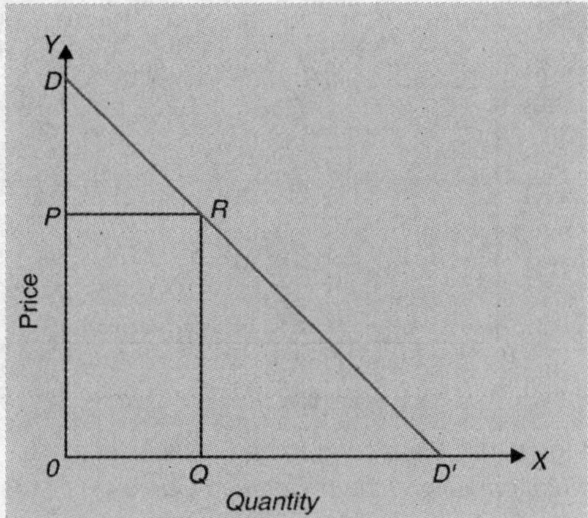

Fig. 6.9. *Measuring Price Elasticity at a point on a Straight-Line Demand Curve*

A glance at Figure 6.9 reveals that $PR = OQ$ and they will therefore cancel out in the above expression.

Therefore, $$e_p = \frac{OP}{PD} \quad \text{...(1)}$$

Measuring price elasticity by taking the *ratio of these distances on the vertical axis,* that is, $\frac{OP}{PD}$ is called *vertical axis formula.*

In a right-angled triangle ODD', PR is parallel to OD'. Therefore,

$$e_p = \frac{OP}{PD} = \frac{RD'}{RD}$$

RD' is the lower segment of the demand curve DD' at point R and RD is its upper segment. Therefore,

$$e_p = \frac{RD'}{RD} = \frac{\text{lower segment}}{\text{upper segment}}$$

Measuring price elasticity at a point on the demand curve by measuring the ratio of the distances of lower segment and upper segment is a popular method of measuring point price elasticity on a demand curve.

Measuring price elasticy on a non-linear demand curve. If the demand curve is not a straight line like DD' in Fig. 6.9 but is, as usual, a non-linear curve, then how to measure price elasticity at a given point on it? For instance, how price elasticity at point R on the demand curve DD in Fig. 6.10 is to be found. In order to measure price elasticity in this case, we have to draw a tangent TT' at the given point R on the demand curve DD' and then measure price elasticity by finding out the value of $\frac{RT'}{RT}$.

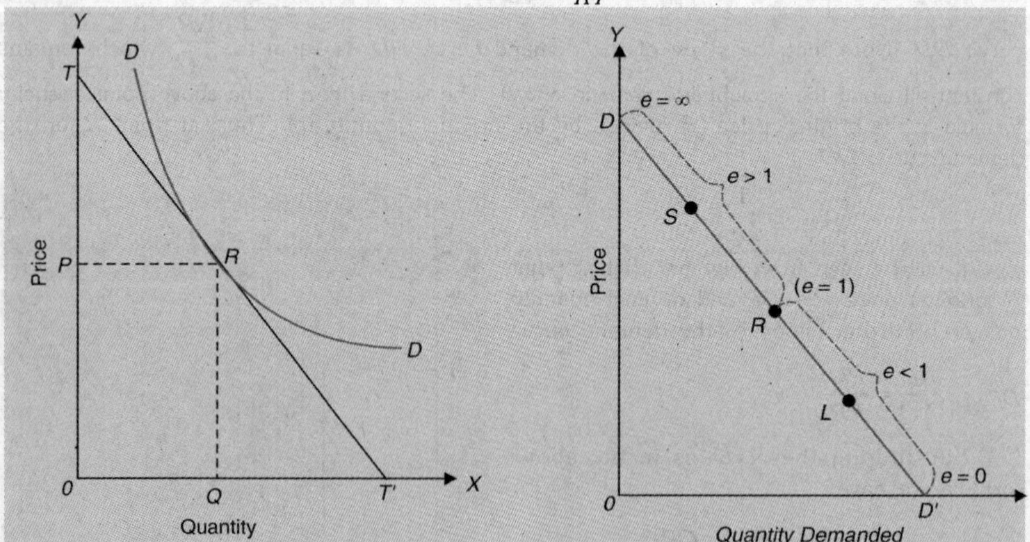

Fig. 6.10. *Measuring Price Elasticity at a Point on a Non-Linear Demand Curve*

Fig.6.11. *On a linear demand curve price elasticity varies from infinity to zero.*

On a linear demand curve price elasticity varies from zero to infinity. Now again, take the straight-line demand curve DD' (Fig. 6.11). If point R lies exactly at the middle of this straight-line demand curve DD', then the distance RD will be equal to the distance RD'.

Therefore, elasticity which is equal to $\frac{RD'}{RD}$ will be equal to one at the middle point of the straight-line demand curve. Suppose a point S lies above the middle point on the straight-line demand curve DD'. It is obvious that the distance SD' is greater than the distance SD and price elasticity, which is equal to $\frac{SD'}{SD}$ at point S, will be more than one. Similarly, at any other point which lies above the middle point on the straight-line demand curve, price elasticity will be greater than unity. Moreover, price elasticity will go on increasing as we move further towards point D and at point D price elasticity will be equal infinity. This is because price elasticity is equal to $\frac{\text{lower segment}}{\text{upper segment}}$ and as we move towards D the lower segment will go on increasing while the upper segment will become smaller and smaller. Therefore, as we move towards D on the demand curve, the price elasticity will be increasing. At point D, the lower segment will be equal to the whole DD', and the upper segment will be zero. Therefore,

$$\text{Price elasticity at point } D \text{ on the demand curve } DD' = \frac{DD'}{0} = \text{infinity.}$$

Now, suppose a point L lies below the middle point on the linear demand curve DD' in Fig. 6.11. In this case, the lower segment LD' will be smaller than the upper segment LD and therefore price elasticity at point L which is equal to $\frac{LD'}{LD}$ will be less than one.

Moreover, price elasticity will go on decreasing as we move towards point D'. This is because whereas lower segment will become smaller and smaller, the upper one will be increasing as we move towards point D'. At point D' the price elasticity will be zero, since at D' the lower segment will be equal to zero and the upper one equal to the whole DD'. At point D',

$$e_p = \frac{0}{DD'} = 0$$

Price Elasticity Varies at Different Points on a Non-linear Demand Curve

From above it is clear that price elasticity at different points on a given demand curve (or, in other words, price elasticity at different prices) is different. This is not only true for a straight-line demand curve but also for a non-linear demand curve. Take, for instance, demand curve DD in Fig. 6.12. As explained above, price elasticity at point R on the demand curve DD will be found out by drawing a tangent to this point. Thus elasticity at R will be $\frac{RT'}{RT}$.

Since distance RT' is greater than RT, price elasticity at point R will be more than one. How exactly it is equal to will be given by actual value

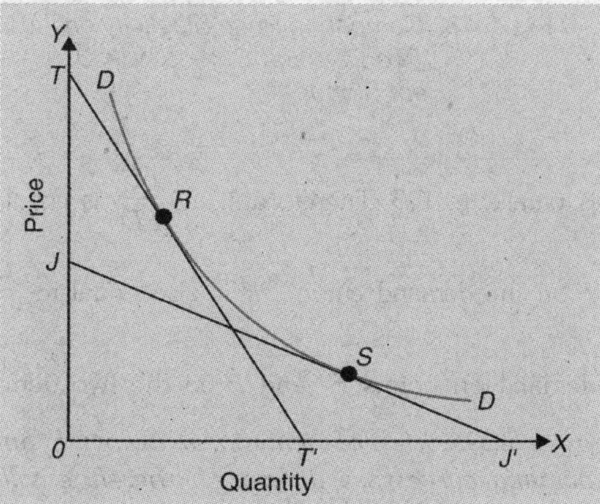

Fig. 6.12. *Price elasticity declines as we move down on a demaned curve.*

which is obtained from dividing RT' by RT. Likewise, price elasticity at point S will be given by $\frac{SJ'}{SJ}$. Because SJ' is smaller than SJ, elasticity point at S will be less than one. Again,how exactly it is, equal to will be found from actually dividing SJ' by SJ. It is thus evident that elasticity at point S is less than that at point R on the demand curve DD. Similarly, price elasticity at other points of the demand curves DD will be found to be different.

Comparing Price Elasticity at a Given Price on the Two Demand Curves with Different Slopes.

Having explained the measurement of price elasticity on a demand curve we will now explain how to compare price elasticity on two demand curves.

Let us take the case of two *demand curves with different slopes* starting from a given point on the Y-axis. This case is illustrated in Fig. 6.13 where two demand curves DA and DB which have different slopes but are starting from the same point D on the Y-axis. Slope of demand curve DB is less than that of DA. Now, it can be proved that at any given price the price elasticity on these two demand curves would be the same. If price is OP, then according to demand curve DA, quantity OL of the good is demanded and according to demand curve DB, quantity OH of the good is demanded . Thus, at price OP the corresponding points on the two demand curves are E and F respectively. We know that price elasticity at a point on the demand curve is equal to $\frac{\text{lower segment}}{\text{upper segment}}$.

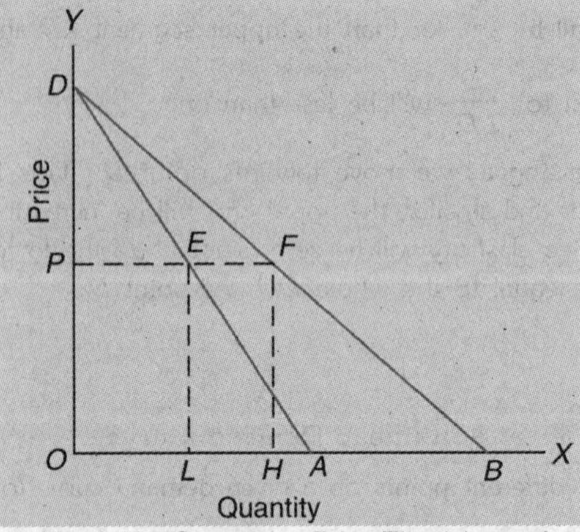

Fig. 6.13. *Comparing Price Elasticity on the Two Demand Curves with Different Slopes*

Therefore, the price elasticity of demand at point E on the demand curve DA is equal to $\frac{EA}{ED}$ and the price elasticity of demand at point F on the demand curve DB is equal to $\frac{FB}{FD}$.

Now, take triangle ODA which is a right-angled triangle in which PE is parallel ot OA. It follows that in it, $\frac{EA}{ED}$ is equal to $\frac{OP}{PD}$. Thus, the price elasticity at point E on the demand curve DA is equal to $\frac{OP}{PD}$.

Now, in the right-angled triangle ODB, PF is parallel to OB. Therefore, in it $\frac{FB}{FD}$ is equal to $\frac{OP}{PD}$. Thus, price elasticity of demand at point F on the demand curve DB is also equal to $\frac{OP}{PD}$. From above it is clear that price elasticity of demand on points E and F on the two demand curves respectively is equal to $\frac{OP}{PD}$, that is, *price elasticities of demand at points E and F are equal though the slopes of these two demand curves are differnt. It therefore follows that price elasticity is not the same thing as slope.* Therefore, price elasticity on two demand curves should not be compared by considering their slopes alone.

DETERMINANTS OF PRICE ELASTICITY OF DEMAND

We have explined above the concept of price elasticity of demand and also how it is measured. Now an important question is what are the factors which determine whether the demand for a goods is elastic or inelastic. The following are the main factors which determine price elasticity of demand for a commodity.

The Availabilty of Substitutes. Of all the factors determining price elasticity of demand the availability of the number and kinds of substiutes for a commodity is the most important factor. If for a commodity close substitutes are available, its demand tends to be elastic. If price of such a commodity goes up, the people will shift to its close substitutes and as a result the demand for that commodity will greatly decline. The greater the possibility of substitution, the greater the price elasticity of demand for it. If for a commodity goods substitutes are not available, people will have to buy it even when its price rises, and therefore its demand would tend to be inelastic.

For instance, if price of Coca Cola were to increase sharply, many consumers would turn to other kind of cold drinks, and as a result, the quantity demanded of Coca Cola will decline very much. On the other hand, if price of Coca Cola falls, many consumers will change from other cold drinks to Coca Cola. Thus, the demand for Coca Cola is elastic. It is the availability of close substitutes that makes the consumers senstive to the changes in price of Coca Cola and this makes the demand for Coca Cola elastic. Likewise, demand for common salt is inelastic because good substitutes for common salt are not available. If the price of common salt rises slightly, the people would consume almost the same quantity of common salt as before since good substitutes are not available. The demand for common salt is inelastic also because people spend a very little part of their income on it and even if its price rises, it makes only negligible difference in their budget allocation for common salt.

The Proportion of Consumer's Income Spent. Another important determinant of the elasticity of demand is how much it accounts for in cnsumer's budget. In other words, the proportion of consumer's income spent on a particular commodity also influences price elasticity of demand for it. The greater the proportion of income spent on a commodity, the greater will generally be its price elasticity of demand, and vice versa. The demand for common salt, soap, matches and such other goods tends to be highly inelastic because the households spend only a fraction of their income on each of them. When price of such a commodity rises, it will not make much difference in consumers' budget and therefore they will continue to buy almost the same quantity of that commodity and, therefore, demand for them will be inelastic. On the other hand, demand for cloth in a country like India tends to be elastic since households spends a good part of their income on clothing. If price of cloth falls, it will mean great saving in the budget of many households and therefore they will tend to increase the quantity demanded of the cloth. On the other hand, if price of cloth rises, many households will not afford to buy as much quantity of cloth as before, and therefore, the quantity demanded of cloth will fall.

The Number of Uses of a Commodity. The greater the number of uses to which a commodity can be put, the greater will be its price elasticity of demand. If price of a commodity having several uses is very high, its demand will be small and it will be put to the most important uses and if price of such a commodity falls it wil be put to less important uses also and consequently its quantity demanded will rise significantly. To illustrate, milk has several uses. If its price rises to a very high level, it will be used only for essential purposes such as feeding the children and sick persons. If price of milk falls, it would be devoted to other uses such as preparation of curd, cream, ghee and sweets. Therefore, the demand for milk tends to be elastic.

Complementarity Between Goods. Complementarity between goods or joint demand for goods also affects the price elaticity of demand. Households are generally less sensitive to the changes in prices of goods that are complementary with each other or which are jointly used as compared to those goods which have independent demand or used alone. For example, for the running of automobiles, besides petrol, lubricating oil is also used. Now, if price of lubricating oil goes up, it will mean a very small increase in the total cost of running the automobile, since the use of oil is much less as compared to other things such as petrol. Thus, the demand for lubricating oil tends to be inelastic. Similarly, the demand for common salt is inelastic, partly because consumers do not use it alone but along with other things.

It is worth mentioning here that for assessing elasticty of demand for a commodity all the above three factors must be taken into account. The three factors mentioned above may reinforce each other in determining the elasticity of demand for a commodity or they may operate against each other. The elasticity of demand for a commodity will be the net result of all the forces working on it.

Time and Elasticity. The element of time also influences the elasticity of demand for a commodity. Demand tends to be more elastic if the time involved is long. This is because consumers can substitute goods in the long run. In the short run, substitution of one commodity by another is not so easy. The longer the period of time, the greater is the ease with which both consumers and businessmen can substitue one commodity for another. For instance, if price of fuel oil rises, it may be difficult to substitute fuel oil by other types of fuels such as coal or cooking gas. But, given sufficient time, people will make adjustments and use coal or cooking gas instead of the fuel oil whose price has risen. Likewise, when the business firms find that the price of a certain material has risen, then it may not be possible for them to substitute that material by some other relatively cheaper one. But with the passage of time they can undertake research to find substitute material and can redesign the product or modify the machinery employed in the production of a commodity so as to economise in the use of the dearer material. Therefore, given the time, they can substitute the material whose price has risen. We thus see that demand is generally more elastic in he long run than in the short run.

CROSS ELASTICITY OF DEMAND

Very often demands for two goods are so related to each other that when price of any of them changes, the demand for the other goods also changes, when its own price remains the same. Therefore, the degree of responsiveness of change in the demand for one good in response to change in price of another good represents the corss elasticity of demand of one goods for the other.

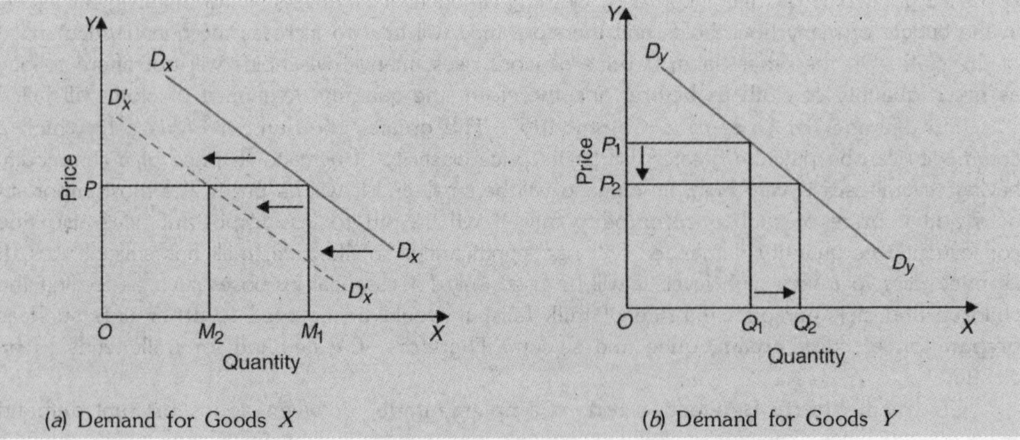

Fig. 6.14. *Demand Relations Between Two Substitutes Goods.*

The concept of cross elasticity of demand is illustrated by Figure 6.14 where demand curves of two goods *X* and Y are given. Initially, the price of goods *Y* is OP_1 at which OM_1 quantity of it is demanded.

Now suppose that the price of goods *Y* falls from OP_1 to OP_2, while price of goods *X* remains constant at *OP*. As a consequence of falls in price of good *Y* from OP_1 to OP_2, its quantity demanded rises from OQ_1 to OQ_2. In drawing the demand curve D_x D_x for good *X*, it is assumed that the prices of other goods (including good *Y*) remains the same. Now that the price of good *Y* has fallen and as *Y* is a substitute for good *X*, then as a result of the fall in price of good *Y* from OP_1 to OP_2, demand curve of good *X* will shift to the left, that is, demand for good *X* will decrease. This is because, as we shall see in the chapter on cardinal utility analysis, as the quantity of a good increases, the marginal utility of its substitute good declines and therefore the entire marginal utility curve of the substitute good shifts to the left. As shall be seen from the Figure 6.14 that as a result of the fall in price of good *Y*, the demand curve of goods *X* shifts from D_xD_x to the dotted position $D_x'D_x'$ so that now at price *OP* less quantity OM_2 of good *X* is demanded; M_1M_2 of good *X* has been substituted by Q_1Q_2, quantity good *Y*.

It should be noted that if good *X* instead of being substitue is *complement* of good Y, then the fall in price of good *Y* and resultant increase in its quanitity demanded would have caused the increase in the demand for good *X* and as a result the entire demand curve of good *X*, instead of shifting to the left, would have shifted to the right. This is because, as will be explained in the chapter on cardinal utility analysis, when the price of a good falls and consequently its quantity demanded increases, the marginal utility of its complements increases and therefore its entire demand curve of the good *X* would shift to the right. With the rightward shift of the demand curve of goods *X*, greater quantity of it would be demanded at price *OP*. It should be noted again that in the concept of cross elasticity of demand, in response to the change in price of *one*, the quantity demanded of *another good* changes.

When the quantity demanded of good *X* rises as a result of the fall in the price of good *Y*, the coefficient of cross elasticity of demand of *X* for *Y* will be equal to the relative change in the quantity demanded of goods *X* in response to a given relative change in the price of good *Y*. Therefore,

$$\text{Coefficient of corss elasticity of demand of } X \text{ for } Y = \frac{\text{Proportionate change in the quantity demanded of } X}{\text{Proportionate change in the price of good } Y}$$

$$or,\ e_c = \frac{\frac{\Delta q_x}{q_x}}{\frac{\Delta p_y}{P_y}} = \frac{\Delta q_x}{q_x} \div \frac{\Delta\, p_y}{p_y}$$

$$= \frac{\Delta q_x}{q_x} \times \frac{p_y}{\Delta p_y}$$

$$= \frac{\Delta\, q_x}{\Delta\, p_y} \times \frac{p_y}{q_x}$$

where e_c stands for cross elasticity of demand of *X* for *Y*.

q_x stands for the original quantity demanded of good *X*

Δq_x stands for change in quantity demanded of good X

p_y stands for the original price of good Y

Δp_y stands for a small change in the price of good Y

When change in price is large, we should use midpoint method for estimating cross elasticity of demand. We can write midpoint formula for measuring cross elasticity of demand as

$$e_c = \frac{q_{x2} - q_{x1}}{\frac{q_{x2} + q_{x1}}{2}} \div \frac{p_{y2} - p_{y1}}{\frac{p_{y2} + p_{y1}}{2}}$$

Numerical Problems

Problem 1. If *price of coffee rises from Rs. 45 per 250 grams pack to Rs. 55 per 250 grams pack and as a result the consumers demand for tea increases from 600 packs to 800 packs of 250 grams, then find the cross elasticty of demand of tea for coffee.*

Solution:

We use midpoint method to estimate cross elasticity of demand.

Change in quantity demanded of tea = $q_{t2} - q_{t1}$ = 800 – 600

Change in price of Coffee = $P_{C2} - P_{C1}$ = 55 – 45

Substituting the values of the various variables in the cross eleasticity formula we have

$$\text{Gross elasticity of demand} = \frac{800-600}{\frac{800+600}{2}} \div \frac{55-45}{\frac{55+45}{2}} = \frac{200}{700} \times \frac{50}{10} = \frac{10}{7} = 1.43$$

Problem 2. *Suppose the following demand function for coffee in terms of price of tea is given. Find out the cross elasticity of demand when price of tea rises from Rs 50 per 250 grams pack to Rs 55 per 250 grams pack.*

$$Q_c = 100 + 2.5P_t$$

where Q_c is the quantity demand of coffee in terms of packs of 250 grams and P_t is the price of tea per 250 grams pack.

Solution. The positive sign of the coefficient of P_t shows that rise in price of tea will cause an increase in quantity demanded of coffee. This implies that tea and coffee are substitutes.

The demand function equation implies that coefficient $\frac{dQ_c}{dP_t} = 2.5$.

In order to determine cross elasticity of demand between tea and coffee, we first find out quantity demanded of coffee when price of tea is Rs 50 per 250 grams pack. Thus,

$$Q_c = 100 + 2.5 \quad 50 = 225$$

$$\text{Cross elasticity,} \quad e_c = \frac{dQ_c}{dP_t} \times \frac{P_t}{Q_c}$$

$$= 2.5 \quad \frac{50}{225} = \frac{125}{225} = 0.51.$$

Cross Elasticity of Demand : Substitutes and Complements

As we have seen in the example of tea and coffee above, when two goods are substitutes of each other, then as a result of the rise in price of one good, the quantity demanded of the other good increases. Therefore, the cross elasticity of demand between the two substitute goods is *positive,* that is, in response to the *rise in price* of one good, the *demand for the other good rises.* Substitute goods are also known as *competing goods.* On the other hand, when the two goods are complementary with teath other such as bread and butter, tea and milk, etc., the *rise in price* of one good brings about the *decrease* in demand for the other. Therefore, the cross elasticity of demand between the two complementary goods is *negative.* Thus, *according to the classification based on the concept of cross elasticity of demand, goods X and Y are substitutes or complements according as the cross* elasticity of demand is *positive or negative.* However, these definitions of substitute and complementary goods in terms of cross elasticity of demand are not very satisfactory. While goods between which cross elasticity of demand is positive can be called substitutes, but the goods between which cross elasticity is negative are not always complements. This is because positive cross elasticity is also found when income effect of the price change is very strong.

Take two goods *X* and Y where the demand for good *X* is inelastic. Suppose the price of good *X* falls and as a result real income of the consumer increases. Since the demand for goods *X* is inelastic, the less moeny would now be spent on good *X* when its price has fallen. In this way a good amount of money income would now be released from good *X* which will be spent on good *Y*. Thus, the income effect of the fall in price of *X* on the demand for good *Y* will be very large and, as a result, the quantity demanded of good *Y* will increase (the demand curve for good Y will shift to the right). We thus see that the *fall in price of good X* has resulted in the *increase in demand for good Y* and therefore the cross elasticity and demand of *good Y* for good *X* is negative. But this negative cross elasticity of demand of *Y* for *X* is not due to the complementary relationship between the two but due to the strong income effect as compared to the substitution effect on the demand for good *Y* produced by the fall in price[2] of good *X*.

This can be easily understood from the aid of indifference curve diagram (Figure 6.15) With given prices of goods *X* and *Y* and a given money income as represented by the budget line *PL*, the consumer is in equilibrium at point *Q* on indifference curve IC_1, where he is purchasing OM_1 of good *X* and ON_1 of good *Y*. Now, suppose that the price of good *X* falls so that the budget line switches to the right to the position *PL'*. With *PL'* as the budget line, the consumer is in equilibrium at point *R* at which he is buying more of good *X* as well as more of good *Y*. This increase in the demand for good *Y* has come about as a result of stronger income effect on *Y* as compared to substitution effect on *Y*. Thus, in this case of strong income effect for good *Y*, the *quantity demanded of good Y increases* as a result of the fall *in price of good X,* and therefore the cross elasticity between the two is negative even though they are not complements.[3]

We have explained above important case where the cross elasticity between the two goods is negative even when they are not complements of each other. Thus, though the cross elasticity between the complements is negative, *but negative cross eleasticity, as we have seen above, cannot always be associated* with complements, since negative cross elasticity is also associated with relatively powerful income effect. Thus, Professor Ryan writes, "While we

---

2. It should be noted that the income effect and substitution effect on good Y produced by the fall in price of good X, work in the opposite direction. While the income effect on Y of the fall in price of X tends to increase the quantity demanded of Y, the substitution effect tends to reduce the quantity demanded of Y. This is because consumers would tend to substitue relatively cheapter good X for good Y. But if the income effect on Y is stronger, it would outweight the substituion effect.

3. That the two goods X and Y are not complements is evident from the shape of their indifference curves in Figure 6.15 As has been explained in the chapters on Indifference Curve Analysis of Demand, the shape of the indifiference curves of two complements is angular.

shall generally find that where the cross elasticity is negative, the goods would be regarded as complemntary in everyday usage.... We may associate negative cross elasticities of demand not only with complementarity but also with relatively strong income effect.[4]

It would be clear from the above analysis that cross elasticity approach to classify the goods as substitutes and complements is based upon the *total price effect on the quantity* demanded of a good resulting from a change in another good's price *without compensating for the change in the level of real* income, that is, without eliminating income effect. Thus, to quote professor Ferguson, "the cross elasticity approach to commodity classi-fication, directs attention to the change in quantity demanded resulting from a change in price without compensating for the change in the level of real income. The *total effect* of a price change is thus the criterion used in this classification scheme".[5]

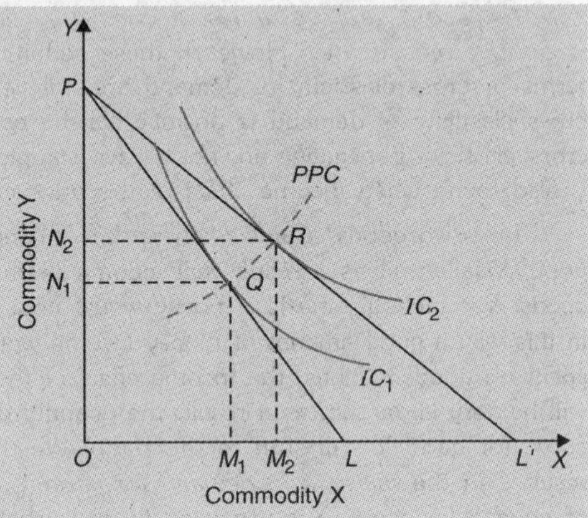

Fig. 6.15. *Demand for goods of goods Y increases due to stronger income effect of change in Price.*

it is because of this inherent shortcoming that cross elasticity approach to classify goods as substitutes and complements leads to misleading conclusions regarding complementary goods. Therefore, in his important work '*Value and Capital*', Professor Hicks pointed out that more accurate classification of substitutes and complements can be obtained on the basis of *substitution effect alone* of the price change, after the income effect has been eliminated. However, on an empirical level, it is very difficult to employ substiution effect alone, since it is based on individual's preference function about which data are not readily available. Thus, according to Professor Ferguson, a more accurate classification can be obtained by analysing the *substituion effect* alone. But while the latter method is more accurate, it is also more difficult to utilize on an empirical level. Thus in actual problems the older and less precise method must usualy be used.[6] He further says, "On an empirical level the cross elasticity approach is the only feasible method of commodity classification because market demand function can be computed while individual preference function cannot from readily available data."

Moreover, cross elasticity approach to commodity classification is very useful in applied economic problems because in such problems we are generally interested in knowing the *market relations* among various commodities rather than the relation among commodities as considered from the viewpoint of consumer preference functions. "Thus the cross-elasticity classification of commodity relations is *the one* most frequently encountered in applied studies."[7]

Importance of Cross Elasticity of Demand for Business Decision Making

The concept of cross elasticity of demand is of great importance in managerial decision making for formulating proper price strategy. Multiproduct firms often use this concept to measure the effect of change in price of one product on the demand for other products. For

4. W.J.L. Ryan *Price Theory,* Macmillan and Co. Ltd, London, 1959, p. 41.
5. C.F. Ferguson, *Microeconmic Theory.* Richard D. Irwin Inc., Illinois, 1967.
6. *Ibid,* p. 60.
7. *Ibid,* p. 63

example, Maruti Udyog Ltd. produces Maruti Zen, Maruti Swift and Maruti Esteem. These products are good substitutes of each other and therefore cross elasticity of demand between them is very high. If Maruti Udyog decides to lower the price of Maruti 800, it will significanty affect the demand for Maruti Vans and Maruti Esteem. So it will formulate a proper price strategy fixing appropriate price for its various products. Further, Gillete Company produces both razors and razors blades which are complements with high corss elasticity of demand. If it decides to lower the price of razors, it will greatly increase the demand for razor bladdes. Thus there is need for adopting a proper price stragegy when it produces products with high positive or negative cross price-easticity of demand.

Second, the concept of cross elasticity of demand is frequently used in defining the boundaries of an industry and in measuring interrelationship between industries. An industry is defined as a group of firms producing similar products (that is, products with a high positive cross elasticity of demand. For example, cross elasticity of demand between Maruti Esteem, Hydundai Assent, Opel Astra is postiive and quite high. They therefore belong to the same industry (*i.e.,* automobiles). It shuld be noted that because of interrelationship of firms and industries between which cross price-elasticity of demand is positive and high, any one cannot raise price of its product without losing sales to other firms in the related industries.

Further, the concept of cross elasticity of demand is extremly used in the United States in deciding cases relating to Anti-trust laws and monopolistic practices used by firms. It so happens that in order to reduce competition that one dominant firm producing a product with a high cross elasticity of demand with the products of other firms tries to take over them and thereby establish a monopoly or different firms try to merge with each other to form a cartel to enjoy monopolistic profits. These actions are held illegal by Anti-trust or anti-monopoly laws. An interesting attempt was made in India by Coca-Cola in 1995 when it returned to India following the adoption of policy of liberalisation. In order to reduce competition, Coca-Cola company purchased the firm producing Thums Up, Gold Spot, Limca which have high positive cross elasticity of demand with Coca-Cola. It further made efforts to take over 'Pure Drinks', the producer of Campa-Cola, another close substitutes but failed. If it had succeeded in its venture it could have significantly reduced competition. With this its competition would have been only with other multinational rival firm *Pepsi-Cola.*

INCOME ELASTICITY OF DEMAND

Another important concept of elasticity of demand is income elasticity of demand. Income elasticity of demand shows the degree of responsiveness of quantity demanded of a good to a small change in income of consumers. The degree of responsiveness of quantity demanded to a change in income is measured by dividing the proportionate change in quantity demanded by the proportionate change in income. Thus, more precisely, the income elasticity of demand may be defined as the ratio of the proportionate change in the quantity purchased of a good to the proportionate change in income which induces the former.

$$\text{Income Elasticity} = \frac{\text{Proportionate change in purchases of a good}}{\text{Proportionate change in income}}$$

Thus, if the proportionate change in purchases or quantity demanded of a good exceeds that of proportionate change in income, income elasticity will be greater than one. For example, if a 2 per cent change in income leads to 5 per cent change in quantity demanded of a good, income elasticity of the demand for the good will be 5%/2%=2.5.

Let M stand for an initial income, ΔM for a small change in income, Q for the initial quantity purchased demand, ΔQ for a change in quantity purchased as a result of a change in income and e_i for income elasticity of demand. Then

$$e_i = \frac{\frac{\Delta Q}{Q}}{\frac{\Delta M}{M}} = \frac{\Delta Q}{Q} \times \frac{M}{\Delta M}$$

$$= \frac{\Delta Q}{\Delta M} \cdot \frac{M}{Q}$$

Midpoint formula for measuring income elasticity of demand when changes in income are quite large can be written as

$$e_i = \frac{Q_2 - Q_1}{\frac{Q_2 + Q_1}{2}} \div \frac{M_2 - M_1}{\frac{M_2 + M_1}{2}}$$

$$= \frac{\Delta Q}{Q_2 + Q_1} \times \frac{M_2 + M_1}{\Delta M}$$

$$= \frac{\Delta Q}{\Delta M} \times \frac{M_2 + M_1}{Q_2 + Q_1}$$

Income Elasticity, Normal Goods and Inferior Goods

It is important to note that the value of *zero income elasticity of demand is of great singnificance.* Zero income elasticity of demand for a good implies that a given increase in income does not at all lead to any increase in quantity demanded of the good or increase in expenditure on it. In other words, zero income elasticity signifies that quantity demanded of the good is quite unresponsive to changes in income. Besides, zero income elasticity is significant because it represents a dividing line between positive income elasticity on the one side and negative income elasticity on the other. When income elasticity is more than zero (*that is, positive*), then an increase in income leads to the increase in quantity demanded of the goods. This happens in case of normal goods. On the other side there are all those goods which have income elasticity less than zero (that is, negative) and in such cases increase in income leads to the fall in quantity demanded of the goods. *Goods having negative income elasticity are known as inferior goods.* We thus see that zero income elasticity is a significant value, for it represents a dividing line between positive income elasticity and negative income elasticity and therefore helps us in distinguishing normal goods from inferior goods.

Income Elasticity, Luxuries and Necessities

Another significant value of income elasticity is unity. This is because when income elasticity of demand for a good is equal to one, then proportion of income spent on the good remains the same as consumer's income increases. Income elasticity of unity also represents a useful dividing line. If the income elasticity for a good is greater than one, the proportion of consumer's income spent on the good rises as consumer's income increases, that is, that good bulks larger in consumer's expenditure as he becomes richer. On the other hand, If income elasticity for a good is less than one, the proportion of consumer's income spent on it falls as his income rises, that is, the good becomes relatively less important in consumer's expenditure as his income rises. *A good having income elasticity more than one and which therefore bulks larger in consumer's budget as he becomes richer is called a luxury. A good with an income elasticity less than one and which claims declining proportion of consumer's income as he becomes richer is called a necessity.* It should, however, be noted that the definitions of luxuries and necessities on the basis of income elasticity may not conform to their definitions in English dictionary because the dictionary's luxuries may be necessities and its necessities may be luxuries according to the above definition. But in economic theory it is useful to call the goods with income elasticity greater than one as luxuries and goods with income elasticity less than one as necessities.

Income Elasticity and Proportion of Income Spent on a Good

Another important value of income elasticity is *the reciprocal of proportion of consumer's income spent on a good,* that is $1/K_x$ where K_x stands for the proportion of consumer's income spent on a good X. The value of $1/K_x$ for the income elasticity of demand is significant because when income elasticity for a good X equals $1/K_x$, then whole of the increase in consumer's income will be spent on the increase in quantity purchased of the good X.

Sum of income Elasticities, Budget Constraint and Expenditure

Increase in income can be spent on a number of goods and services demanded by a consumer. Given the budget constraint, when some part of an increase in income is not spent on a good, it must be spent on other goods and services, assuming that there is no saving and borrowing by the consumer. From this, a relationship can be derived which shows that *the sum of income elasticities for all good and services must be unity and further that income elasticity of demand for a good depends on income elasticity of other goods and services.*

Suppose that consumer has an income equal to M and further that all his income is spent on two goods X and Y. Let P_x and P_y represent the prices of two goods X and Y respectively. Let income increases by ΔM prices of the two goods semaining the same and as a result quantities purchased of two goods increase by ΔQ_x and ΔQ_y. Then, budget constraint can be written as

$$\Delta M = P_x \Delta\ Q_x + P_y . \Delta Q_y$$

Dividing both sides of the budget equation by ΔM we have

$$\frac{\Delta\ M}{\Delta\ M} = \frac{P_x . \Delta Q_x}{\Delta\ M} + \frac{P_y . \Delta Q_y}{\Delta\ M}$$

or, $$\frac{P_x . \Delta Q_x}{\Delta\ M} + \frac{P_y . \Delta Q_y}{\Delta\ M} = 1 \qquad \ldots (i)$$

The above equation implies that the sum of the proportion of increase in income spent on good X (*i.e.* $P_x \Delta Q_x / \Delta M$) and the proportion of increase in income spent on good Y (i.e. $P_y \Delta Q_y / \Delta M$) must be equal to one. Multiplying the first term on the left side of equation (i) by Q_x / Q_x and M/M and multiplying the second term by Q_y / Q_y and M/M, we have

$$\frac{P_x . Q_x}{M} . \frac{\Delta Q_x}{\Delta\ M} . \frac{M}{Q_x} + \frac{P_y . Q_y}{M} . \frac{\Delta Q_y}{\Delta\ M} . \frac{M}{Q_y} \qquad \ldots (ii)$$

It will be seen that the term $P_x Q_x / M$ represents the proportion of income spent on good X and $\frac{\Delta Q_X}{\Delta M} . \frac{M}{Q_X}$ is the income elasticity of demand for goods X. Similarly, term $P_y\ Q_y / M$ is the proportion of income spent on goods Y, and the term $\frac{\Delta P_Y}{\Delta M} . \frac{M}{Q_Y}$ is the income elasticity of demand for good Y. Using K_x to denote proportion of income spent on good X, K_y for the proportion of income spent on good Y, e_{xi} for income elasticity of demand for good X, and e_{yi} for income elasticity of demand for good Y, then from equations (*i*) and (*ii*) we have :

$$K_x e_{xi} + K_y\ e_{yi} = 1$$

The above equation reveals that the weighted sum of the income elasticities of demand for all goods (weights being the proportion of income spent on goods) must equal unity. This for example, means that when income increases by 10 per cent, the budget constraint requires that purchases or consumption of goods as a whole must also increase by 10 per cent. If there is a 10 per cent increase in income, if the consumption of some goods increases by less than 10 per cent, the consumption of others must increase by more than 10 per cent so that the increase in income must somehow be spent on the goods. That is, the increase in consumption of goods whose income elasticity of demand is less than one must be offset by increase in consumption of others for which income elasticity of demand is greater than one. Thus, on the average, consumption of goods must increase by the same proportion as income. If there are two goods X and Y, then the above equation $K_x\ e_{xi} + K_y e_{yi} = 1$ must hold. This equation implies that given the two goods on which a consumer spends his income, if we know the proportion of income spent of one good and the income elasticity for that good, we can calculate the income elasticity of demand for the other good.

Numerical Example

Assume that there are two commodities, rice and milk. If rice accounts for 75% of the budget and has income elasticity equal to 0.8, what would be the income elasticity of milk ?

Let us call rice as commodity X and milk as commodity y

$$K_x . e_{xi} + k_y . e_{yi} = 1$$

$$0.75\ (0.8) + o.25\ (e_{yi}) = 1$$

$$.600 + 0.25\ (e_{yi}) = 1$$

$$0.25(e_{yi}) = 1 - 0.6 = 0.4$$

$$e_{yi} = 0.4/0.25 = 1.6$$

Thus, income elasticity of demand for milk equals 1.6.

Importance of Income Elasticity for Business Firms

The concept of income elasticity is important for decision making both by business firms and industries. First, the firms producing products which have a high income elasticity have great potential for growth in an expending economy. For example, if for a firm's product income elasticity of demand is greater than one, it means that it will gain more than proportionately to the increase in national income. Thus firms which are producing products having high income elasticity are more interested in forecasting the level of aggregate economic activity (*i.e.*, level of national income) because the demand for their products greatly depends on the level of overall economic activity. Further, as seen above, the demand for luxuries is highly income elastic. Therefore, the demand for luxuries fluctuates very much during different phases of business cycles. During boom periods, demand for luxuries increases very much and declines sharply during recessionary periods.

On the other hand, the demand for products with low income elasticity will not be greatly affected by the fluctuations in aggregate economic activity. During booms the demand for these products will not increase much and during recessions it will not decrease sharply. Therefore, the firms with low income elasticity for their products would not be much interested in forecasting future business activity. Remember it is generally necessities for which demand is not much income elastic. However, there is one good thing for the firms which produce goods having low income elasticity. They are to a good extent recession-proof. In the periods of recession, their incomes do not fall to the extent of decline in aggregate income. Of course, to share the benefits of increasing national income firms currently producing products with low income elasticity would try to enter the industries demand for whose products is highly income elastic as this would ensure better growth opportunities.

The knowledge of income elasticity of demand also plays a significant role in designing marketing strategies of the firms. If income of people is an important determineant of demand for a product, the firms producing products with high income elasticity of demand will be located in those areas or set up their sales outlets in those cities or regions where incomes are increasing rapidly. Besides, the firms will direct their advertising campaigns and other sales promotion activities to those segments of people whose income is high and also increasing rapidly. This is to ensure higher growth of sales of their products.

The concept of income elasticity of demand shows clearly why farmers' income do not rise equal to that of urban people engaged in manufacturing industries. Income elasticity of demand for agricultural products such as foodgrains is less than one. This implies that it is difficult for the farmers' income from agriculture to increase in proportion to the expanding national income. Thus farmers' income cannot keep face with the urban people who derive their income from industries producing goods with high income elasticity of demand.

Some Numerical Problems on Income Elasticity

Problem 1. If a consumer's daily income rises from Rs. 300 to Rs. 350, his purchase of a good X increases from 25 units per day to 35 units, find income elasticity of demand for X.

Solution. Change in quantity demand (ΔQ) = ($Q_2 - Q_1$) = 35 – 25 = 10

Change in income (ΔM) = $M_2 - M_1$ = 350 – 300 = 50

$$e_i = \frac{\%\text{ Change in quantity demanded}}{\%\text{ Change in price}}$$

$$e_i = \frac{\Delta Q}{\Delta M} \times \frac{M_2 + M_1}{Q_2 + Q_1}$$

$$= \frac{10}{50} \times \frac{350 + 300}{25 + 35}$$

$$= \frac{10}{50} \times \frac{650}{60} = 2.17$$

Income elasticity of demand in this case is 2.17.

Problem 2. *Suppose demand for cars in Bombay as a function of income is given by the following equation :*

$$Q = 20{,}000 + 5M$$

where Q is quantity demanded, M is per capita level of income in rupees.

Find out income elasticity of demand when per capita annual income in Bombay is Rs 15,000.

Solution.

$$\text{Income elasticity } (e_i) = \frac{\Delta Q}{\Delta M} \cdot \frac{M}{Q}$$

In order to obtain income elasticity, we have to first find out quantity demanded (Q) at income level of Rs 15,000. Thus.

$$Q = 20{,}000 + 5 \times 15{,}000 = 95{,}000$$

It will be seen from the given income demand function that coefficient of income (M) is equal to 5. This implies that $\frac{\Delta Q}{\Delta M} = 5$. With this information we can calculate income elasticity.

$$e_i = \frac{\Delta Q}{\Delta M} \times \frac{M}{Q} = 5 \times \frac{15,000}{95,000} = 0.8$$

Problem 3. *The following demand function for readymade trousers has been estimated*

$$Q = 2,000 + 15Y - 5.5P$$

where Y is income in thousands of rupees, Q is the quantity demanded in units and P is the price per unit.

(a) *When P = Rs 150 and Y = 15 thousand rupees, determine the following :*

1. *Price elasticity of demand*
2. *Income elasticity of demand*

(b) *Determine what effect a rise in price would have on total revenue.*

(c) *Asses how sale of trousers would change during a period of rising incomes.*

Solution

(a) Coefficient of *P*, *i.e.*, $\frac{\Delta Q}{\Delta P} = 5.5$

Price elasticity of demand $\frac{\Delta Q}{\Delta P} \cdot \frac{P}{Q} = 5.5 \times \frac{150}{Q}$

Let us first find out the quantity demanded (*i.e.*, *Q*) at the given income (*Y* = 15 thousands) and given price (*P* = Rs 150 per unit). Substituting the values of income and price in the given demand function, we have :

$$\begin{aligned} Q &= 2,000 + 15 \times 15 - 5.5 \times 150 \\ &= 2,000 + 225 - 825 = 1,400 \end{aligned}$$

Thus, $e_p = \frac{\Delta Q}{\Delta P} \times \frac{P}{Q} = 5.5 \times \frac{150}{1400} = \frac{82.5}{140} = 0.59$

Income elasticity $= \frac{\Delta Q}{\Delta Y} \times \frac{Y}{Q}$

$\frac{\Delta Q}{\Delta Y} = 15$, $Q = 1400$, $Y = 15$ thousand rupees

$$e_i = 15 \times \frac{15}{1400} = \frac{9}{56} = 0.16$$

(b) Since price elasticity of demand for trousers is less than one, rise in price would cause increase in total revenue.

(c) Since income elasticity of demand for trousers is less than one, trousers are a necessity and therefore the increase in income of the people will lead to less than a proportionate increase in their sales.

SOME FURTHER EXERCISES ON ELASTICITY OF DEMAND

1. *Two goods have a cross price elasticity of demand of + 1.2. (a) Would you describe the goods as substitutes or complements? (b) If price of one of the goods rises by 5 percent, what will happen to the demand for the other good, holding other factors constant?*

Ans. (a) The goods with positive cross-price elasticity of demand are substitute goods. Therefore, the above two goods with cross-price elasticity of demand equal to + 1.2 will be substitute goods. (b) If price of one of the two goods increases by 5 per cent, it will be substituted by the other good so that the quantity demanded of it will rise. With positive cross-price elasticity being equal to 1.2, the quantity demanded of the good will increase by $1.2 \times 5 = 6$ per cent.

2. *In an attempt to increase revenues and profits, a firm is considering 5 per cent increase in price of its good and 15 per cent increase in advertising expenditure. If the price elasticity of demand is –1.5 and advertising elasticity of demand is + 0.6, would you predict an increase or decrease in total revenue? Explain.*

Ans. To answer this question, students should know the interpretation of the concept of elasticity. The price elasticity of demand equal to –1.5 means that 5 percent *increase* in price will result in $5 \times 1.5 = 7.5$ per cent *decrease* in quantity demanded of the good. On the other hand, advertising elasticity of demand being equal to + 0.6 means that 15 per cent increase in advertising expenditure will cause $1.5 \times 0.6 = 9$ per cent increase in quantity demanded. Therefore, there will be net 1.5 percent increase in quantity demanded of the good. Besides, there is 5 per cent rise in price. We therefore predict increase in revenue.

3. *For the following demand functions, determine whether demand is elastic, inelastic or unitary elastic at the given price:*

(i) $Q = 100 - 4P$ *and the given* $P =$ *Rs 20*

(ii) $Q = 1500 - 20P$ *and the given* $P =$ *Rs 5*

(iii) $P = 50 - 0.1Q$ *and the given* $P =$ *Rs 20*

Solution. (i) $Q = 100 - 4P$ where $P =$ Rs 20

In this demand function the derivative $\frac{dQ}{dP} = 4$.

Substituting the value of P in this demand function (i)

$$Q = 100 - (4 \times 20) = 20$$

$$e_p = \frac{dQ}{dP} \times \frac{P}{Q} = 4 \times \frac{20}{20} = 4.$$

Since $e_p > 1$, demand is elastic.

(ii) $Q = 1500 - 20P$ where $P =$ Rs 5

In this demand function equation, the derivative $\frac{dQ}{dP} = 20$

Substituting the value of P in this demand function

$$Q = 1500 - (20 \times 5) = 1400$$

$$e_p = \frac{dQ}{dP} \times \frac{P}{Q} = 20 \times \frac{5}{1400} = \frac{5}{70} = 0.07$$

Since $e_p < 1$, demand is inelastic.

(iii) $P = 50 - 0.1Q$ where $P =$ Rs 20

Let us first express this demand function in terms of quantity demanded as a function of price.

$$P = 50 - 0.1Q$$

$$0.1Q = 50 - P$$
$$Q = 50 \times 10 - 10P$$
$$Q = 500 - 10P$$

With given price equal to Rs 20,

$$Q = 500 - (10 \times 20) = 300$$

The derivative $\frac{dQ}{dP} = 10$

$$e_p = \frac{dQ}{dP} \times \frac{P}{Q} = 10 \times \frac{20}{300} = \frac{2}{3} = 0.66$$

Since $e_p < 1$, demand is inelastic.

Exercise 4. *Demand for "Advanced Economic Theory" by Dr H.L. Ahuja is given by $Q = 20,000 - 60P$.*

(a) Compute the point price elasticity of demand at price = Rs. 200.

(b) If the objective is to increase total revenue from the sales of the book, should the price be increased or reduced?

Solution. The given demand function is

$$Q = 20,000 - 60P$$

Substituting the value of $P = 200$ in the demand function equation

$$Q = 20,000 - (60 \times 200) = 8,000$$

The derivative $\frac{dQ}{dP} = 60$

$$e_p \text{ at Rs } 200 = \frac{dQ}{dP} \times \frac{P}{Q} = 60 \times \frac{200}{8,000} = \frac{3}{2} = 1.5$$

Since price elasticity of demand is greater than one, reduction in price will increase revenue. Therefore, price of the book should be reduced to increase revenue from the sales of the book.

PRICE ELASTICITY, TOTAL REVENUE AND MARGINAL REVENUE

The importance of price elasticity of demand for a business firm lies in the fact that it provides a useful measure of the effect of a change in price of its product by a firm on the total revenue obtained from it. Note that the total revenue (*TR*) is equal to the price (*P*) multiplied by the quantity sold ($TR = P.Q$). Further, since the quantity demanded and sold (*Q*) is inversely related to price, that is, when price falls, the quantity demanded sold increases and vice versa, the change in total revenue (*PQ*) depends on the price elasticity of demand, This is because $e_p = \frac{\%\Delta Q}{\%\Delta P}$. When demand is unitary elastic ($e_p = 1$), a given percentage fall in price (*P*) is offset by an equal percentage increase in the quantity demanded, therefore the total revenue remains unchanged.

When demand is elastic (*i.e.* $e_p > 1$), a given percentage in price leads to a larger percentage increase in the quantity demanded (*Q*) and as a result total revenue (*TR*) increases.

On the other hand, when demand is inelastic (*i,e.*$e_p < 1$), a given percentage fall in price causes a smaller percentage change in quantity demanded, the total revenue decreases. The effect of price elasticity of demand on changes in total revenue is illustrated in Table 6.2 where in the third column we have calculated price elasticity of demand corresponding to various quantities demanded in response to change in price of the commodity. It should be further noted that we use the formula, namely, $e_p = \dfrac{Q_2 - Q_1}{P_2 - P_1} \times \dfrac{P_2 + P_1}{Q_2 + Q_1}$ for measuring price elasticity.

It will be seen from the table 6, 2 that in the range of the demand function where price of the commodity falls from Rs. 50 to Rs. 30 per unit, price elasticity of demand exceeds unity ($e_p > 1$), total revenue (*TR*) increases over the range. When price falls from Rs. 30 to Rs 25, price elasticity is equal to unity ($e_p = 1$) total revenue remains constant. When price falls from Rs. 25 per unit downwards price elasticity is less than one ($e_p < 1$), and total revenue decreases.

In the last column of table 6.2 we give marginal revenue earned from sale of additional units of output at different prices. It will be seen from table 6.2 that over the range where $e_p > 1$ and total revenue (*TR*) is increasing, marginal revenue is positive and over the range of the demand function where price elasticity is less than one ($e_p < 1$) and total revenue deceases,

Table 6.2. Relationship between Price Elasticity of demand, Total Revenue and Marginal Revenue

Price (P)	Quantity Demanded (Q)	Price Elasticity (e_p) $\frac{\Delta Q}{\Delta P} \cdot \frac{P_1 + P_2}{Q_1 + Q_2}$	Total Revenue (TR)	Marginal Revenue (MR)
50	1	–	50	50
45	2	$\frac{1}{5} \times \frac{95}{3} = 16.33$	90	40
40	3	$\frac{1}{5} \times \frac{85}{5} = 3.40$	120	30
35	4	$\frac{1}{5} \times \frac{75}{7} = 2.14$	140	20
30	5	$\frac{1}{5} \times \frac{65}{9} = 1.44$	150	10
25	6	$\frac{1}{5} \times \frac{55}{11} = 1.00$	150	0
20	7	$\frac{1}{5} \times \frac{45}{13} = 0.69$	140	– 10
15	8	$\frac{1}{5} \times \frac{35}{15} = 0.47$	120	– 20
10	9	$\frac{1}{5} \times \frac{25}{17} = 0.29$	90	– 30

revenue (*MR*) is negative. When in the middle marginal of this demand function price falls from Rs. 30 to Rs. 25 per unit, price elasticity is equal to one, total revenue remains unchanged and therefore marginal revenue is zero.

Graphic Illustration. The relationship between price elasticity, total revenue and marginal revenue is further clarified through Figure 6.16 where in the upper panel a linear demand curve *DD'* has been drawn along with the marginal revenue (*MR*) curve lying below it. In the bottom panel of this figure total revenue curve has been drawn which first rises, reaches at the maximum point *H* at output level *OQ* and then falls downward. As we have been seen above) point price elasticity at the mid-point of the linear demand curve is equal to one and at points above it is greater than one and goes on increasing to the point at which the demand curve intercepts the vertical axis where it is equal to infinity.

On the other hand, below the *midpoint* of a demand curve price elasticity is less than one and goes on decreasing as we *move* downwards on *the demand curve DD′* in Figure 6.6 till it reaches zero at the point at which demand curve intercepts the *X*-axis.

Now, starting from point *D* as we move *downwards* to the midpoint *C*, absolute value of the elasticity of demand, though declining *remains* greater than one which causes total revenue (*P.Q*) to increase with the fall in price of the product. While reduction in price per unit (*P*) of the commodity *tends* to reduce revenue, increase in quantity sold caused by it tends to increase the revenue. Price elasticity *remaining* greater than one above the mid-point *C* implies that the percentage increase in quantity demanded exceeds the percentage fall in price which causes the total revenue (*PQ*) *to increase. Therefore, upto the level of output Q which corresponds to the mid-point C* of the demand curve, total revenue (*TR*) curve goes on increasing (see the bottom panel of Figure 6.16).

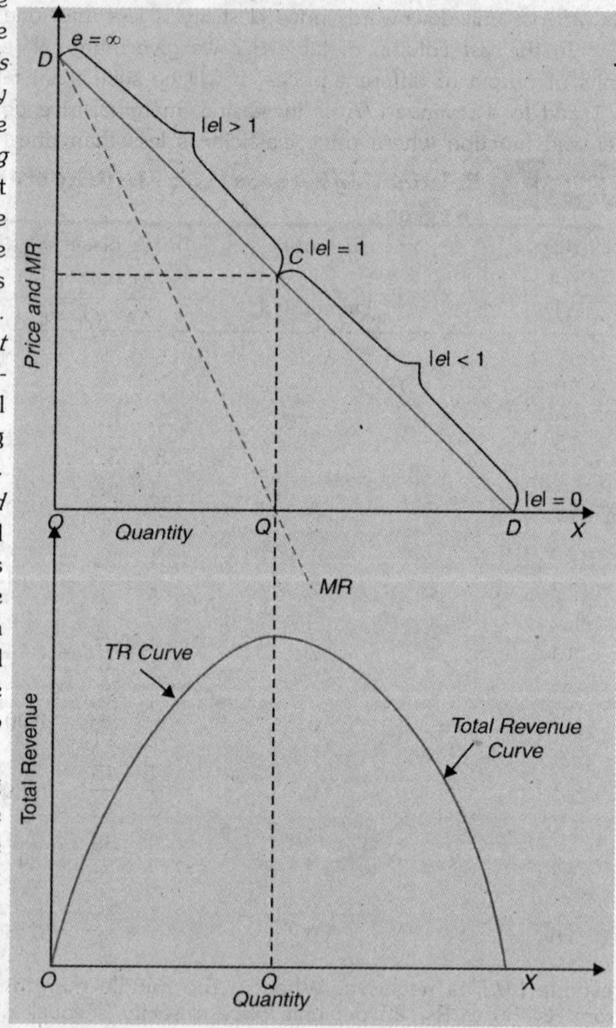

Figure 6.16. *Relationship between Price Elasticity of Demand, Total Revenue and Marginal Revenue*

Now, as we move *downword* from the mid-point *C* of the demand curve *DD′*, price elasticity being less than one implies that relative increase in the quantity demanded is less than relative fall in price which causes total revenue curve to decline. Therefore beyond output *OQ* corresponding to the mid-point *C* of the demand curve, total revenue (*TR*) curve is sloping downward as can be seen from the bottom panel of Figure 6.16. Since on a demand curve up to the mid-point *C* at which price elasticity is equal to one, total revenue goes on increasing as price elasticity is greater than one and below the mid-point *C*, total revenue decreases as price elasticity of demand is less than one, it follows therefore that the total revenue will be maximum at output *OQ* corresponding to the mid-point *C* of the demand curve at which price elasticity is equal to one.

Marginal Revenue and Total Revenue

Marginal revenue (*MR*) has an important relationship with total revenue (*TR*) as both depend on price elasticity of demand. Marginal revenue is defined as the additional revenue obtained when one more unit of output is sold. It will be seen from *MR* curve in 6.16 that marginal revenue is positive in the range of the demand curve above the mid-point *C* where price elasticity is greater than one and marginal revenue is negative below the mid-point *C* of the demand curve where price elasticity is less than one, and marginal revenue is zero corresponding to the mid-point *C* where price elasticity (e_p) is equal to one. How can we explain this?

Since imaginal revenue is the extra revenue earned from the sale of an additional unit of output where total revenue from the sale increases over the elastic *range* of a demand curve, it implies that marginal revenue (*MR*) is positive, An when *total revenue declines* over the inelastic raange that is, below the mid-point of the demand curve, it means marginal revenue is negative. When at the unitary elastic mid-point of the demand curve total revenue remains the same for a small change in price, it impiles that marginal revenue (*MR*) is zero. That is, at a unitary elastic mid-point of the linear demand curve, where total revenue is maximum, marginal revenue is zero.

The relationship between marginal revenue and price elasticity can be expressed algebraically as under.

$$MR = P\left(1 + \frac{1}{e_p}\right)$$

We can use this relationship to show that when demand is price elastic ($e_p > 1$), *MR* is positive and when demand is unitary elastic ($e_p < 1$), *MR* is equal to zero and when demand is price-inelastic ($e_p < 1$), *MR* is negative. We first derive below the above relationship between price elasticity and marginal revenue algebraically.

Derivation of Relationship between Marginal Revenue and Price Elasticity of Demand

There exists an important relationship between marginal revenue, Price (*i.e.*, *AR*) and price elasticity of demand which is extensively used in making price decisions by the firms. This relationship can be written algebraically as

$$MR = P\left(1 + \frac{1}{e}\right)$$

where P = price and e = point price elasticity of demand.

This relationship is mathematically derived as follows :

Marginal revenue (*MR*) is defined as the first derivative of total revenue (*TR*). Thus,

$$MR = \frac{d(TR)}{dQ} \qquad \text{....(1)}$$

Now, *TR* is the product of price and the quantity of the product sold ($TR = P.Q$). Thus,

$$MR = \frac{d(P.Q)}{dQ}$$

Using the rule of differentiation of a product, we have

$$MR = P\frac{dQ}{dQ} + Q\frac{dP}{dQ}$$

$$MR = P + Q\frac{dP}{dQ} \qquad \text{...... (2)}$$

This equation (2) can be rewritten as

$$MR = P\left(1 + \frac{Q}{P}\cdot\frac{dP}{dQ}\right) \qquad \text{...... (3)}$$

Now, recall that point price elasticity of demand $= \frac{P}{Q} \cdot \frac{dQ}{dP}$.

It will thus be noticed that the expression $\frac{Q}{P} \cdot \frac{dP}{dQ}$ in the equation (3) above is the reciprocal of point price elasticity of demand $\frac{P}{Q} \cdot \frac{dQ}{dP}$ · Thus,

$$\frac{Q}{P} \cdot \frac{dP}{dQ} = \frac{1}{e} \qquad \text{...... (4)}$$

Substituting equation (4) into equation (3), we obtain

$$MR = P\left(1 + \frac{1}{e}\right)$$

Remember that price elasticity of demand has a negative sign which is generally ignored. However, recognizing it, we have

$$MR = P\left(1 + \frac{1}{-e}\right)$$

or

$$MR = P\left(1 - \frac{1}{e}\right)$$

Let us use the above relationship between marginal revenue and price elastiaty of demand to show that when price elasticity of demand is greater than one, marginal revenue will be positive and when it is less then one, *MR* is negative and when price elasticity equals one, *MR* is zero To prove these relationships – we take the following demand function

$Q_d = 1000 - 200\ P$

At price Rs. 3 per unit,

$Q_d = 1000 - 200 \times 3 = 400$

Place elasticity (e_p) at price Rs. 3 and associated quantity of Rs 400 $= \frac{\Delta Q}{\Delta P} \cdot \frac{P}{Q}$

$$= 200 \times \frac{3}{400} = 1.5$$

MR at price (Rs.3) and quantity (400) $= P\left(1 + \frac{1}{e}\right) = 3\left(1 + \frac{1}{-1.5}\right)$

$$= 3\left(1 - \frac{1}{1.5}\right) = 1$$

Thus when price elasticity exceeds one, *MR* is positive

In the same demand function ($Q = 1000 - 200\ P$) at price Rs. 2.50, suppose price elasticity is equal to one. *MR* at this price is

$$= P\left(1 + \frac{1}{-1}\right) = P\left(1 - \frac{1}{1}\right) = 0$$

Again at price Rs. 2, quantity demanded is 600 units and price elasticity is equal to 2/3, then *MR* at price Rs. 2 is

$$= P\left(1+\frac{1}{-\frac{2}{3}}\right) = 2\left(1-\frac{3}{2}\right) = -1$$

Thus at price elasticity of less than one marginal revenue is found to be negative.

Having clarified the relationship between marginal revenue and price elasticity of demand we solve some important problems concerning this relationship.

SOME NUMERICAL PROBLEMS ON MR, TR AND PRICE ELASTICITY OF DEMAND

Problem 1. *The demand function equation faced by HCL for its personal computers is given by*

$$P = 50{,}000 - 4Q$$

1. *Write the marginal revenue equation.*
2. *At what price and quantity marginal revenue will be zero?*
3. *At what price and quantity will total revenue be maximized?*

Solution. To obtain total revenue function, we multiply the given demand equation by Q.

$$TR = PQ = 50{,}000Q - 4Q^2 \qquad \text{..... (1)}$$

Taking the first derivative of the total revenue function would give us marginal revenue equation. Thus,

$$MR = \frac{d(TR)}{dQ} = \frac{d(PQ)}{dQ} = 50{,}000 - 8Q \qquad \text{..... (2)}$$

(2) Setting MR equation equal to zero would give us the quantity at which MR is zero. Thus,

$$50{,}000 - 8Q = 0$$
$$8Q = 50{,}000$$
$$Q = 6250$$

Now, to obtain price associated with the quantity (6250), we substitute the value of Q into the demand equation ($P = 10{,}000 - 4Q$). Thus.

$$P = 50{,}000 - (4 \times 6250)$$
$$= 50{,}000 - 25{,}000 = 25{,}000$$

(3) To obtain quantity at which TR is maximum, we set the first derivative of TR function (*i*) equal to zero.

$$TR = 50.000Q - 4Q^2$$

---

1. Students should note that in each case given a price, we have found the quantity demanded (Q) by substituting the value of the given price in the demand function. Then with price and quantity demanded (Q) we have calculated e_p by using elasticity formula $\frac{dQ}{dP}\cdot\frac{P}{Q}$. The value of $\frac{dQ}{dP}$ is the same (*i.e* 200) in all cases as the given demand function is linear.

$$\frac{d(TR)}{dQ} = 50{,}000 - 8Q = 0$$

$$8Q = 50{,}000$$

$$Q = 6250$$

Thus, at the quantity of 6250 units the total revenue is maximum.

It follows from above that at the quantity of 6250 units and price of Rs. 25,000 per computer, marginal revenue is zero.

Important Conclusion. It is clear from the answers to the questions (2) and (3) of this problem that the *quantity at which MR is equal to zero, total revenue is maximum.* This is because, as stated above, it follows from the very definition of marginal revenue. Marginal revenue is the increase in total revenue resulting from the sale of an additional unit of output. As long as marginal revenue is positive, total revenue is increasing and beyond the output level where total revenue is maximum, marginal revenue becomes negative and, therefore, total revenue declines. Thus, at the output level where marginal revenue is zero, total revenue is maximum.

Problem 2. *From the demand function equation given in problem 1 show that price elasticity of demand is equal to one when total revenue is maximum.*

Solution. Total revenue is maximum at quantity 6250 units of computers and price Rs 25,000 per computer.

$$e_p = \frac{dQ}{dP} \cdot \frac{P}{Q} \qquad \text{..... } (i)$$

The given demand function is

$$P = 50{,}000 - 4Q \qquad \text{..... } (ii)$$

In order to obtain $\frac{dQ}{dP}$, we express demand function expressed in terms of quantity demanded as a function of price. Thus, rearranging the given demand function

$$4Q = 50{,}000 - P$$

$$Q = 12{,}500 - \frac{1}{4}P \qquad \text{..... } (iii)$$

From the demand function equation (iii), we find that the coefficient of P is $-\frac{1}{4}$ which means that $\frac{dQ}{dP} = -\frac{1}{4}$.

Further we found in problem I above that at the quantity (Q) equal to 6250 and price equal to 25,000, total revenue is maximum.

$$e_p = \frac{dQ}{dP} \times \frac{P}{Q}$$

$$= -\frac{1}{4} \times \frac{25{,}000}{6250} = -1$$

Thus, we find that output and price level at which TR is maximum, Price elasticity of demand is equal to one (e_p. = 1)

Problem 3. *Outside an airport, a shopkeeper is running a coffee shop. The demand function for coffee cups is*

$$Q = 150 - 10P$$

where Q is the quantity demanded of coffee cups and P is price per coffee cup.

1. Write total revenue function and determine at what quantity of coffee cups sold and price fixed, total revenue is maximised.

2. Find out value of marginal revenue at the quantity at which total revenue is maximised.

3. *Show that at the quantity sold where total revenue is maximised, price elasticity of demand is equal to unity.*

Solution. The given demand function is

$$Q = 150 - 10P \qquad \text{...... } (i)$$

In order to determine the total revenue, demand function can be rewritten in terms of price as a function of quantity demanded.

$$10P = 150 - Q$$

$$P = 15 - \frac{Q}{10} \qquad \text{...... } (ii)$$

Now,
$$TR = PQ$$

$$= Q\left(15 - \frac{Q}{10}\right)$$

$$TR = 15Q - \frac{Q^2}{10} \qquad \text{..... } (iii)$$

Taking the first derivative of the *TR* function

$$\frac{d(TR)}{dQ} = 15 - \frac{2}{10}Q = 15 - \frac{1}{5}Q$$

In order to find out quantity sold at which *TR* is maximised, we set first derivative of *TR* equal to zero.

$$15 - \frac{1}{5}Q = 0$$

$$\frac{1}{5}Q = 15$$

$$Q = 75$$

Substituting the value of *Q* into the demand equation (ii)

$$P = 15 - \frac{1}{10}.75 = 15 - 7.5$$

$$= \text{Rs. } 7.5$$

Thus, the quantity at which total revenue is maximized is 75 and associated price is Rs 7.5 per coffee cup.

2. *MR* Function

MR is obtained by taking the first derivative of *TR* function Thus,

$$TR = 15Q - \frac{Q^2}{10}$$

$$MR = \frac{d(TR)}{dQ} = 15 - \frac{1}{5}Q$$

Substituting the revenue-maximising quantity (= 75) into marginal revenue function

$$MR = 15 - \frac{1}{5}Q = 15 - \frac{1}{5} \times 75 = 0$$

Thus at the quantity sold at which *TR* is maximum, marginal revenue is zero.

3. Price elasticity of demand (e_p) = $\frac{dQ}{dP} \cdot \frac{P}{Q}$

From the demand function equation (i), we find that $\frac{dQ}{dP} = 10$.

We have found above that *TR*–maximizing quantity is 75 and associated price is 7.5, Substituting these values into the price elasticity formula

$$e_p = \frac{dQ}{dP} \cdot \frac{P}{Q} = 10 \times \frac{7.5}{75} = 1$$

Thus, price elasticity of demand at the *TR*–maximising quantity is equal to one.

QUESTIONS FOR REVIEW

1. Define price elasticity of demand. What are the factors that determine it? Explain
2. Distinguish between point price elasticity and arc price elasticity of demand. How will you measure them ?
3. (*a*) What is meant by (*i*) elastic demand, (*ii*) inelastic demand, and (*iii*) unitary elastic demand.

   (*b*) If price elasticity of demand for a commodity is – 2, how will you interpret it ?
4. Define perfectly elastic demand and perfectly inelastic demand. Why is demand curve facing a firm operating in a perfectly competitive market a perfectly elastic demand ? Explain
5. How is price elasticity of demand at a point on a demand carve measured? Show that on a linear demand curve price elasticity varies from infinity at the price axis to zero at the quantity axis.
6. Do you think that price elasticity of demand would be greater for car industry as a whole or for maruti 800 of Maruti firm.
7. Demand for a firm's product has been estimated to be

   $$Q_d = 1000 - 200P$$

   If the price of the product is Rs 3 per unit, find out the price elasticity of demand at this price.
8. *Given : P .Q = 500,* What happens to price elasticity of demand as price falls (*P* = price, and *Q* = quantity purchased) ?

   [Hints: *P. Q* represents expenditure on a commodity which remains constant at 500 even when price changes. When expenditure on a commodity remains constant as price changes, its price elasticity of demand is equal to one.]
9. An individual spends all his income on two goods, *X* and *Y*. If with the rise in price of good *X*, the quantity purchased of good *Y* remains unchanged, what is the price elasticity of demand for *X* ?

   [Hints: Quantity purchased of good *Y* remaining the same even when price of good *X* rises, means that expenditure on good *Y* i.e (*Py . Qy*) remains constant with a given income to spend on the two goods. This also means expenditure on good *X* remains constant when its price rises. This implies that price elasticity of demand for good *X* equals one.]
10. The price elasticity of demand of colour TVs is estimated to be – 2.5 If the price of colour TVs is reduced by 20 per cent, how much percentage increase in the quantity of colour TVs sold do you expect ?

[Hints : Price elasticity of demand being equal to – 2.5 means that one per cent change in price causes 2.5 per cent change in quantity demanded or sold. Besides, minus sign only indicates there is *inverse* relationship between price and quantity sold. Thus, 20 percent *reduction in price* of colour TVs will cause *increase in quantity* sold by 2.5 20 = 50 percent.]

12. Explain the relationship between the total revenue of a firm and the price elasticity of demand for price reduction .

13. (*a*) Explain why a firm facing a downward-sloping demand curve would never produce in the inelastice (e_p < 1) portion of the demand curve.

(*b*) When would the firm operate at the point where demand curve is unitary elastic?

[Hint : (*a*) In the inelastic portion of the demand curve, marginal revenue is negative. It is therefore not profitable to produce and sell the additional units of output which reduce total revenue.]

(*b*) [Hint : At the point where demand curve is unitary elastic, marginal revenue is zero It is profitable to produce a level of output at which *MR* is zero only when marginal court (*MC*) is zero]

14. Explain the concept of cross elasticity of demand. Using concept of cross elasticity of demand, define substitutes and complements.

15. Colgate sells its standard size toothpaste for Rs. 25. Its sales have been on an average 8000 units per month over the last year. Recently, its close competitor Binaca reduced the price of its same standard size toothpaste prom Rs 35 to Rs. 30. As a result, Colgate sales declined by 1500 units per month.

(*i*) Calculate the cross elasticity between the two products.

(*ii*) What does your estimate indicate about the relationship between the two ?

16. Explain the importance of the concept of cross elasticity in (a) formulating proper price strategy (b) analyzing the degree of competition prevailing in an industry.

17. Suppose the following demand function for Coffee in terms of price of tea is given. Found out the cross elasticity of demand when price of tea rises from Rs. 50 per 250 grams pack to Rs 55 per pack.

$$Q = 100 + 2.5\ P_t$$

where Q is the quantity demanded of coffee in terms of 250 grams and P_t is the price of tea per 250 grams pack.

18. Two goods have cross elasticity of demand equal to 1.2 (a) would you describe the two goods as substitutes or complements? It price of one of the goods rises by 5 per cent, What will happen to the demand for the other good, holding other factors constant?

19. Explain the concept of income elasticity of demand. How would you define necessities and luxuries on the basis of income elasticity of demand ?

20. Explain the importance of income elasticity of demand for a business firm, especially in designing marketing strategies ?

Consumer's Behaviour : Cardinal Utility Analysis

Introduction

The price of a product depends upon the demand for and the supply of it. In this part of the book we are concerned with the theory of consumer's behaviour, which explains his demand for a good and the factors determining it. Individual's demand for a product depends upon price of the product, income of the individual, the prices of related goods. It can be put in the following functional form:

$$D_x = f(P_x, I, P_y, P_z, T \text{ etc.})$$

where D_x stands for the demand of good X, P_x for price of good X, I for individual's income, P_y, P_z, for the prices of related goods and T for tastes and preferences of the individual. But among these determinants of demand, economists single out price of the good in question as the most important factor governing the demand for it. Indeed, the function of a theory of consumer's behaviour is to establish a relationship between quantity demanded of a good and its own price and to provide an explanation for it. From time to time, different theories have been advanced to explain consumer's demand for a good and to derive a valid demand theorem. Cardinal utility analysis is the oldest theory of demand which provides an explanation of consumer's demand for a product and derives the law of demand which establishes an inverse relationship between price and quantity demanded of a product. Recently, cardinal utility approach to the theory of demand has been subjected to severe criticisms and as a result some alternative theories, namely, *Indifference Curve Analysis, Samuelson's Revealed Preference Theory, Hicks' Logical Weak Ordering Theory* have been propounded. We shall discuss indifference curve analysis of demand and revealed preference approach in the next two chapters, while in the present chapter we shall be concerned with the cardinal utility analysis of consumer's demand. Though cardinal utility approach to the theory of demand is very old, its final shape emerged at the hands of Alfred Marshall. Therefore, it is Marshallian cardinal utility analysis of demand which has been discussed in this chapter.

Assumptions of Cardinal Utility Analysis

Cardinal utility analysis of demand is based upon certain important assumptions. Before explaining how cardinal utility analysis explains consumer's equilibrium in regard to the demand for a good, it is essential to describe the basic assumptions on which the whole utility analysis rests. As we shall see later, cardinal utility analysis has been criticised because of its unrealistic assumptions. The basic assumptions or premises of cardinal utility analysis are as follows:

The Cardinal Measurability of Utility. The exponents of cardinal utility analysis regard utility to be a cardinal concept. In other words, they hold that utility is a measurable and quantifiable entity. According to them, a person can express utility or satisfaction he derives from the goods in the quantitative cardinal terms. Thus, a person can say that he derives utility equal to 10 units from the consumption of a unit of good *A*, and 20 units from the consumption of a unit of good *B*. Moreover, the cardinal measurement of utility implies that a person can compare utilities derived from goods in respect of size, that is, how much one level of utility is greater than another. A person can say that the utility he gets from the consumption of one unit of good *B* is double the utility he obtains from the consumption of one unit of good *A*.

According to Marshall, marginal utility *is actually measurable in terms of money.*[1] Money represents the general purchasing power and it can therefore be regarded as a command over alternative utility-yielding goods. Marshall argues that the amount of money which a person is prepared to pay for a unit of a good rather than go without it is a measure of the utility he derives from that good. Thus, according to him, money is the measuring rod of utility. Some economists belonging to the cardinalist school measure utility in imaginary units called "utils". They assume that a consumer is capable of saying that one apple provides him utility equal to 4 utils. Further, on this ground, he can say that he gets twice as much utility from an apple as compared to an orange.

The Hypothesis of Independent Utilities. The second important tenet of the cardinal utility analysis is the hypothesis of *independent utilities*. On this hypothesis, the utility which a consumer derives from a good is the function of the quantity of that good and of that good only. In other words, the utility which a consumer obtains from a good does not depend upon the quantity consumed of other goods; it depends upon the quantity purchased of that good alone. On this assumption, then the total utility which a person gets from the whole collection of goods purchased by him is simply the total sum of the separate utilities of the goods. Thus, the cardinalist school regards utility as '*additive*', that is, separate utilities of different goods can be added to obtain the total sum of the utilities of all goods purchased.

Constancy of the Marginal Utility of Money. Another important assumption of the cardinal utility analysis is the constancy of the marginal utility of money. Thus, while the cardinal utility analysis assumes that marginal utilities of commodities diminish as more of them are purchased or consumed, but the marginal utility of money remains constant throughout when the individual is spending money on a good and due to which the amount of money with him varies. Daniel Bernoulli first of all introduced this assumption but later Marshall adopted this in his famous book "*Principles of Economics*'. As stated above, Marshall measured marginal utilities in terms of money. But measurement of marginal utility of goods in terms of money is only possible if the marginal utility of money itself remains constant. It should be noted that the assumption of constant marginal utility of money is very crucial to the Marshallian analysis, because otherwise Marshall could not measure the marginal utilities of goods in

1. Emil Kauder, *A History of Marginal Utility Theory*, (Princeton, New Jersy, 1965). p. 120.

terms of money. If money which is the unit of measurement itself varies as one is measuring with it, it cannot then yield correct measurement of the marginal utility of goods.

When price of a good falls and as a result the real income of the consumer rises, marginal utility of money to him will fall but Marshall ignored this and assumed that marginal utility of money did not change as a result of the change in price. Likewise, when price of a good rises, the real income of the consumer will fall and his marginal utility of money will rise. But Marshall ignored this and assumed that marginal utility of money remains the same. Marshall defended this assumption on the ground that "his (the individual consumer's) expenditure on any one thing.....is only a small part of his whole expenditure."

Introspective Method. Another important assumption of the cardinal utility analysis is the use of introspective method in judging the behaviour of marginal utility. "Introspection is the ability of the observer to reconstruct events which go on in the mind of another person with the help of self-observation. This form of comprehension may be just guesswork or intution or the result of long lasting experience."[1] Thus, the economists construct with the help of their own experience the trend of feeling which goes on in other men's mind. From his own response to certain forces and by experience and observation one gains understanding of the way other people's minds would work in similar situations. To sum up, in introspective method we attribute to another person what we know of our own mind. That is, by looking into ourselves we see inside the heads of other individuals. So the law of diminishing marginal utility is based upon introspection. We know from our own mind that as we have more of a thing, the less utility we derive from an additional unit of it. We conclude from it that other individuals' mind will work in a similar fashion, that is, marginal utility to them of a good will diminish as they have more units of it.

With the above basic premises, the founders of cardinal utility analysis have developed two laws which occupy an important place in economic theory and have several applications and uses. These two laws are : (1) Law of Diminishing Marginal Utility and (2) Law of Equi-Marginal Utility. It is with the help of these two laws about consumer's behaviour that the exponents of cardinal utility analysis have derived the law of demand. We explain below these two laws in detail and how law of demand is derived from them.

LAW OF DIMINISHING MARGINAL UTILITY

An important tenet of cardinal utility analysis relates to the behaviour of marginal utility. This familiar behaviour of marginal utility has been stated in the Law of Diminishing Marginal Utility according to which marginal utility of a good diminishes as an individual consumes more units of a good. In other words, as a consumer takes more units of a good, the extra utility or satisfaction that he derives from an extra unit of the good goes on falling. It should be carefully noted that it is the marginal utility and not the total utility that declines with the increase in the consumption of a good. The law of diminishing marginal utility means that the total utility increases at a decreasing rate.

Marshall who has been a famous exponent of the cardinal utility analysis has stated the law of diminishing marginal utility as follows:

"*The additional benefit which a person derives from a given increase of his stock of a thing diminishes with every increase in the stock that he already has.*"

This law is based upon two important facts. First, while the total wants of a man are virtually unlimited, *each single want is satiable*. Therefore, as an individual consumes more and more units of a good, intensity of his want for the good goes on falling and a point is reached where the individual no longer wants any more units of the good. That is, when saturation point is reached, marginal utility of a good becomes zero. Zero marginal utility of a good implies that the individual has all that he wants of the good in question. The second fact on which the law of diminishing marginal utility is based is that the different goods are not perfect substitutes for each other in the satisfaction of various wants. When an individual consumes more and more units of a good, the intensity of his particular want for the good diminishes but if the units of that good could be devoted to the satisfaction of other wants and yielded as much satisfaction as they did initially in the satisfaction of the first want, marginal utility of the good would not have diminished.

It is obvious from above that the law of diminishing marginal utility describes a familiar and fundamental tendency of human nature. This law has been arrived at by introspection and by observing how consumers behave.

Illustration of the Law of Diminishing Marginal Utility

Consider Table 7.1. where we have presented the total and marginal utilities derived by a person from cups of tea consumed per day. When one cup of tea is taken per day, the total utility derived by the person is 12 utils. And because this is the first cup its marginal utility is also 12 utils. With the consumption of 2nd cup per day, the total utility rises to 22 utils but marginal utility falls to 10. It will be seen from the table that as the consumption of tea increases to six cups per day, marginal utility from the additional cup goes on diminishing (*i.e.* the total utility goes on increasing at a diminishing rate). However, when the cups of tea consumed per day increases to seven, then instead of giving *positive* marginal utility, the seventh cup gives *negative* marginal utility equal to - 2 utils. This is because too many cups of tea consumed per day (say more that six for a particular individual) may cause acidity and gas trouble. Thus, the extra cups of tea beyond six to the individual in question gives him disutility rather than positive satisfaction.

Table 7.1 Diminishing Marginal Utility

Cups of tea consumerd per day (Q)	*Total Utility (utils)* TU	*Marginals Utility (utils)* $\frac{\Delta TU}{\Delta Q}$
1	12	12
2	22	10
3	30	8
4	36	6
5	40	4
6	41	1
7	39	-2
8	34	-5

Figure 7.1 illustrates the total utility and the marginal utility curves. The total utility curve drawn in Figure 7.1 is based upon three assumptions. First, as the quantity consumed per period by a consumer increases *his total utility increases* but *at a decreasing rate.* This implies that as the consumption per period of a commodity by the consumer *increases, marginal utility diminishes* as shown in the lower panel of Figure 7.1. Secondly, as will be observed from the figure, when the rate of consumption of a commodity per period increases to Q_4, the total utility of the consumer reaches its maximum level. Therefore, the quantity Q_4, of the commodity is called *satiation quantity or satiety point.* Thirdly, the increase in the

quantity consumed of the good per period by the consumer beyond the satiation point has an adverse effect on his total utility, that is, his total utility declines if more than Q_4 quantity of the good is consumed. This means beyond Q_4 marginal utility of the commodity for the consumer becomes negative as will be seen from the lower panel of Figure 7.1 beyond the satiation point Q_4 marginal utility curve *MU* goes below the *X*-axis indicating it becomes negative beyond quantity Q_4 per period of the commodity consumed.

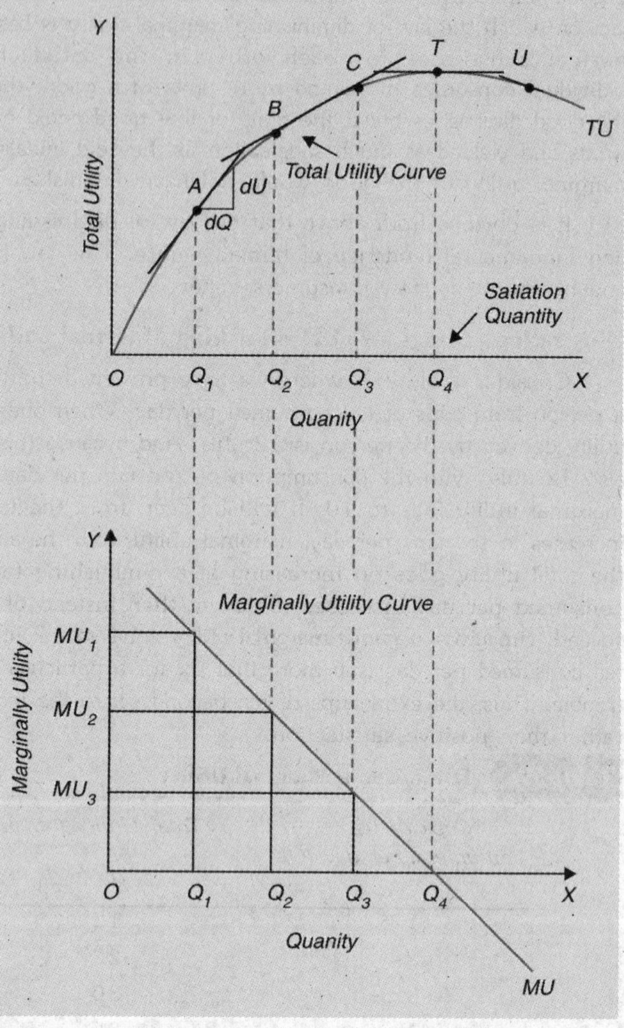

Fig. 7.1. Total Utility and Marginal Utility

It is important to understand how we have drawn the marginal utility curve. As stated above, marginal utility is the increase in total utility of the consumer caused by the consumption of an additional unit of the commodity per period. We can directly find out the marginal utility of the successive units of the commodity consumed by measuring the additional utility which a consumer obtains from successive units of the commodity and plotting them against their respective quantities. However, in terms of calculus, marginal utility of a commodity *X* is the slope of the total utility function $U = f(Q_x)$. Thus, we can derive the marginal utility curve by measuring the slope at various points of the total utility curve *TU* in the upper panel of Figure7.1 by drawing tangents at them. For instance, at the quantity Q_1 marginal utility (*i.e.* $\frac{dU}{dQ} = MU_1$) is found out by drawing tangent at point *A* and measuring its slope which is then plotted against quantity Q_1 in the lower panel of Figure 7.1. In the lower panel we measure marginal utility of the commodity on the *Y*-axis. Likewise, at quantity Q_2 marginal utility of the commodity has been obtained by measuring slope of the total utility curve *TU* at point *B* and plotting it in the lower panel against the quantity Q_2. It will be seen from the figure that at Q_4 of the commodity consumed, the total utility reaches at the maximum level *T*. Therefore, at quantity Q_4 the slope of the total utility curve is zero at this point. Beyond the quantity Q_4 the total utility declines and marginal utility becomes negative. Thus, quantity Q_4 of the commodity represents the satiation quantity.

Another important relationship between total utility and marginal utility is worth noting. At any quantity of a commodity consumed the *total utility is the sum of the marginal utilities.* For example, if marginal utility of the first, second, and third units of the commodity consumed are 15, 12, and 8 units, the total utility obtained from these three units of consumption of the commodity must equals 35 units (15 + 12 + 8 = 35). Similarly, in terms of graphs of total utility and marginal utility depicted in Figure 7.1 the total utility of the quantity Q_4 of the comomodity consumed is the *sum of the marginal utilities* of the units of commodity up to point Q_4. That is, the entire area under the marginal utility curve *MU* in lower panel up to the point Q_4 is the sum of marginal utilities which must be equal to the total utility Q_4T in the upper panel.

Marginal Utility and Consumer's Tastes and Preferences

The utility people derive from consuming a particular commodity depends on their tastes and preferences. Some consumers like oranges, others prefer apples and still others prefer bananas for consumption. Therefore, the utility which different individuals get from these various fruits depends on their tastes and preferences. An individual would have *different marginal utility curves* for different commodities depending on his tastes and preferences. Thus, *utility which people derive from various goods reflect their tastes and preferences for them.* However, it is worth noting that we cannot compare utility across consumers. Each consumer has a unique subjective utility scale. In the context of cardinal utility analysis, *a change in consumer's tastes and preferences means* a shift in his one or more marginal utility curves. However, it may be noted that a consumer's tastes and preferences do not frequently change, as these are determined by his habits. Of course, tastes and preferences can change occasionally. Therefore, in economic theory we generally assume that tastes or preferences are given and relatively stable.

Significance of Dimishing Marginal Utility

The significance of the diminishing marginal utility of a good for the theory of demand is that it helps us to show that the quantity demanded of a good increases as its price falls and *vice versa.* Thus, it is because of the diminishing marginal utility that the demand curve slopes downward. This will be explained in detail later in this chapter. If properly understood the law of diminishing marginal utility applies to all objects of desire including money. But it is worth mentioning that *marginal utility of money* is generally never zero or negative. Money represents purchasing power over all other goods, that is, a man can satisfy all his material wants if he possesses enough money. Since man's total wants are practically unlimited, therefore, the marginal utility of money to him never falls to zero.

The marginal utility analysis has a good number of uses and applications in both economic theory and policy. The concept of marginal utility is of crucial significance in explaining determination of the prices of commodities. The discovery of the concept of marginal utility has helped us to explain the *paradox of value* which troubled Adam Smith in *"The Wealth of Nations."* Adam Smith was greatly surprised to know why water which is so very essential and useful to life has such a low price (indeed no price), while diamonds which are quite unnecessary, have such a high price. He could not resolve this water-diamond paradox. But modern economists can solve it with the aid of the concept of marginal utility. According to the modern economists, the total utility of a commodity does not determine the price of a commodity and it is the marginal utility which is crucially important determinant of price. Now, the water is available in abundant quantities so that its relative marginal utility is very low or even zero. Therefore, its price is low or zero. On the other hand, the diamonds are scarce and therefore their relative marginal utility is quite high and this is the reason why their prices are high. Prof. Samuelson explains this paradox of value in the following words:— *"The more there is of a commodity, the less the relative desirability of its last little unit becomes, even though its total usefulness grows as we get more of the commodity. So, it is obvious why a large amount of water has a low price Or why air is actually a free good despite its vast usefulness. The many later units pull down the market value of all units."*[2]

Besides, the Marshallian concept of consumer's surplus is based on the principle of diminishing marginal utility.

CONSUMER'S EQUILIBRIUM : PRINCIPLE OF EQUI-MARGINAL UTILITY

Principle of equi-marginal utility occupies an important place in cardinal utility analysis. It is through this principle that consumer's equilibrium is explained. A consumer has a given income which he has to spend on various goods he wants. Now, the question is how he would allocate his given money income among various goods, that is to say, what would be his equilibrium position in respect of the purchases of the various goods. It may be mentioned here that consumer is assumed to be 'rational', that is, he carefully calculates utilities and substitutes one good for another so as to maximise his utility or satisfaction.

Suppose there are only two goods X and Y on which a consumer has to spend a given income. The consumer's behaviour will be governed by two factors: first, the marginal utilities of the goods and secondly, the prices of two goods. Suppose the prices of the goods are given for the consumer. *The law of equi-marginal utility states that the consumer will distribute his money income between the goods in such a way that the utility derived from the last rupee spent on each good is equal.* In other words, consumer is in equilibrium position when marginal utility of money expenditure on each good is the same. Now, the marginal utility of money expenditure on a good is equal to the marginal utility of a good divided by the price of the good. In symbols,

$$MU_m = \frac{MU_x}{P_x}$$

where MU_m is marginal utility of money expenditure and MU_x is the marginal utility of X and P_x is the price of X. The law of equi-marginal utility can therefore be stated thus: the consumer will spend his money income on different goods in such a way that marginal utility of money expenditure on each good is equal. That is, consumer is in equilibrium in respect of the purchases of two goods X and Y when

$$\frac{MU_x}{P_x} = \frac{MU_y}{P_y}$$

Now, if $\frac{MU_x}{P_x}$ and $\frac{MU_y}{P_y}$ are not equal and $\frac{MU_x}{P_x}$ is greater than $\frac{MU_y}{P_y}$, then the consumer will substitute good X for good Y. As a result of this substitution, the marginal utility of good X will fall and marginal utility of good Y will rise. The consumer will continue substituting good X for good Y until $\frac{MU_x}{P_x}$ becomes equal to $\frac{MU_y}{P_y}$. When $\frac{MU_x}{P_x}$ becomes equal to $\frac{MU_y}{P_y}$ the consumer will be in equilibrium.

2. Paul Samuelson, *Economics*, McGraw Hill, 8th edition, p. 417.

But the equality of $\frac{MU_x}{P_x}$ with $\frac{MU_y}{P_y}$ can be achieved not only at one level but at different levels of expenditure. The question is how far does a consumer go in purchasing the goods he wants. This is determined by the size of his money income. With a given income and money expenditure a rupee has a certain utility for him: this utility is the marginal utility of money to him. Since the law of diminishing marginal utility applies to money income also, the greater the size of his money income the smaller the marginal utility of money to him. Now, the consumer will go on purchasing goods until the marginal utility of money expenditure on each good becomes equal to the marginal utility of money to him. Thus, the consumer will be in equilibrium when the following equation holds good:

$$\frac{MU_x}{P_x} = \frac{MU_y}{P_y} = MU_m$$

where MU_m is marginal utility of money expenditure (that is, the utility of the last rupee spent on each good).

If there are more than two goods on which the consumer is spending his income, the above equation must hold good for all of them. Thus

$$\frac{MU_x}{P_x} = \frac{MU_y}{P_y} = \ldots\ldots\ldots\ldots = \frac{MU_n}{P_n} = MU_m$$

Let us illustrate the law of equi-marginal utility with the aid of an arithmetical table given below:

Table 7.2 **Marginal Utility of Goods X and Y**

Units	*MU_x (Utils)*	*MU_y (Utils)*
1	20	24
2	18	21
3	16	18
4	14	15
5	12	9
6	10	3

Let the prices of goods *X* and *Y* be Rs. 2 and Rs. 3 respectively. Reconstructing the above table by dividing marginal utilities (MU_x) of *X* by Rs. 2 and marginal utilities (MU_y) of *Y* by Rs. 3 we get the Table 7.3.

Table 7.3. **Marginal Utility of Money Expenditure**

Units	$\frac{MU_x}{P_x}$	$\frac{MU_y}{P_y}$
1	10	8
2	9	7
3	8	6
4	7	5
5	6	3
6	5	1

Suppose a consumer has money income of Rs. 24 to spend on the two goods. It is worth noting that in order to maximise his utility the consumer will not equate *marginal utilities of the goods* because prices of the two goods are different. He will equate the marginal utility of the last rupee (*i.e.* marginal utility of money expenditure) spent on these two goods. In other words, he will equate $\frac{MU_x}{P_x}$ with $\frac{MU_y}{P_y}$ while spending his give money income on the two goods. By looking at the Table 7.3 it will become clear that $\frac{MU_x}{P_x}$ is equal to 5 utils when the consumer purchases 6 units of good *X* and $\frac{MU_y}{P_y}$ is equal to 5 utils when he buys 4 units of good Y. Therefore, consumer will be in equilibrium when he is buying 6 units of good *X* and 4 units of good *Y* and will be spending (Rs. 2 6 + Rs. 3 4) = Rs. 24 on them that are equal to consumer's given income. Thus, in the equilibrium position where the consumer maximises his utility,

$$\frac{MU_x}{P_x} = \frac{MU_y}{P_y} = MU_m$$

$$\frac{10}{2} = \frac{15}{3} = 5$$

Thus, marginal utility of the last rupee spent on each of the two goods he purchases is the same, that is, 5 utils.

Consumers' equilibrium is graphically protrayed in Fig. 7.2. Since marginal utility curves of goods slope downward, curves depicting $\frac{MU_x}{P_x}$ and $\frac{MU_y}{P_y}$ also slope downward. Thus, when the consumer is buying *OH* of *X* and *OK* of *Y*, then

$$\frac{MU_x}{P_x} = \frac{MU_y}{P_y} = MU_m$$

Therefore, the consumer is in equilibrium when he is buying 6 units of *X* and 4 units of *Y*. No other allocation of money expenditure will yield him greater utility than when he is buying 6 units of commodity *X* and 4 units of commodity *Y*. Suppose the consumer buys one unit less of good *X* and one unit more of good *Y*. This will lead to the decrease in his total utility. It will be observed from Figure 7.2 (a) that the consumption of 5 units instead of 6 units of commodity *X* means a loss in satisfaction equal to the shaded area *ABCH* and from Fig. 7.2(b) it will be seen that consumption of 5 units of commodity *Y* instead of 4 units will mean gain in utility equal to the shaded area *KEFL*. It will be noticed that with this rearrangement of purchases of the two goods, the loss in utility *ABCH* exceeds gain in utility *KEFL*. Thus, his total satisfaction will fall as a result of this rearrangement of purchases. Thus when the consumer is making purchases by spending his given income in such a way that $\frac{MU_x}{P_x} = \frac{MU_y}{P_y}$, he will not like to make any further changes in the basket of goods and will therefore be in equilibrium situation by maximizing his utility.

Limitations of the Law of Equi-Marginal Utility

Like other laws of economics, law of equimarginal utility is also subject to various limitations. This law, like other laws of economics, brings out an important tendency among

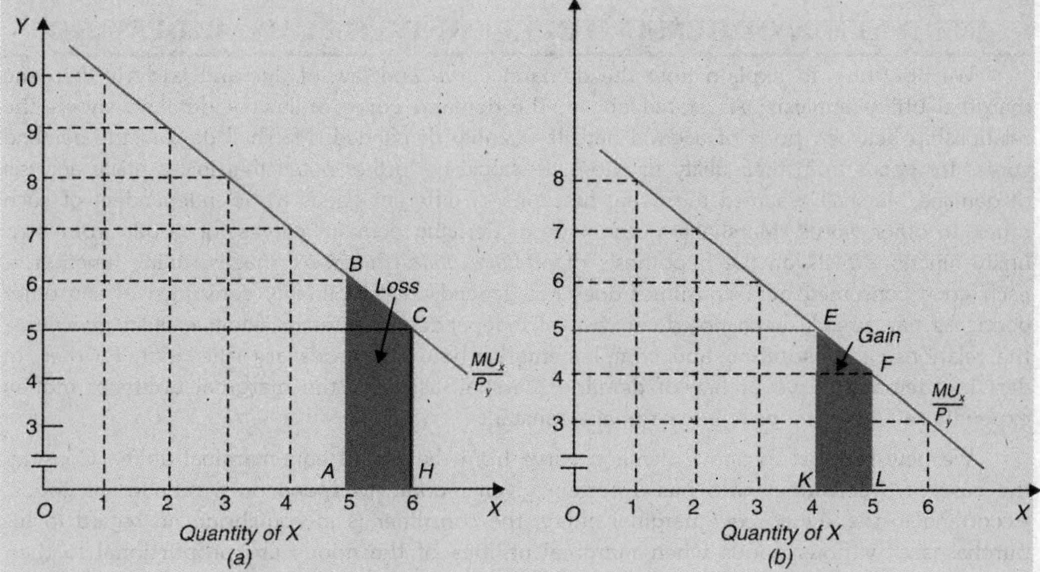

Fig. 7.2. *Equi-Marginal Utility Principle and Consumer's Equilibrium*

the people. This is not necessary that all people exactly follow this law in the allocation of their money income and therefore all may not obtain maximum satisfaction. This is due to the following reasons:-

(1) For applying this law of equi-marginal utility in the real life, consumer must weigh in his mind the marginal utilities of different commodities. For this he has to calculate and compare the marginal utilities obtained from different commodities. But it has been pointed out that the ordinary consumers are not so rational and calculating. Consumers are generally governed by habits and customs. Because of their habits and customs they spend particular amounts of money on different commodities, regardless of whether the particular allocation maximises their satisfaction or not.

(2) For applying this law in actual life and equate the marginal utility of the last rupee spent on different commodities, the consumers must be able to measure the marginal utilities of different commodities in cardinal terms. However, this is easier said than done. It has been said that it is not possible for the consumer to measure utility cardinally. Being a state of psychological feeling and also there being no objective units with which to measure utility, it is cardinally immeasurable. It is because of the immeasurability of utility in cardinal terms that the consumer's behaviour has been explained with the help of ordinal utility by J.R. Hicks and R.G.D. Allen. Ordinal utility analysis involves the use of indifference curves which we shall explain in the next chapter.

(3) Another limitation of the law of equi-marginal utility is found in case of *indivisibility* of certain goods. Goods are often available in large indivisible units. Because the goods are indivisible, it is not possible to equate the marginal utility of money spent on them. For instance, in allocating money between the purchase of car and foodgrains, marginal utilities of the last rupee spent on them cannot be equated. An ordinary car costs about Rs. 300,000 and is indivisible, whereas foodgrains are divisible and money spent on them can be easily varied. Therefore, the marginal utility of rupee obtained from cars cannot be equalised with that obtained from foodgrains. Thus, indivisibility of certain goods is a great obstacle in the way of equalisation of marginal utility of a rupee from different commodities.

DERIVATION OF DEMAND CURVE AND THE LAW OF DEMAND

We now turn to explain how the demand curve and law of demand is derived in the marginal utility analysis. As stated above, the demand curve or law of demand shows the relationship between price of a good and its quantity demanded. Marshall derived the demand curves for goods from their utility functions. It should be further noted that in his utility analysis of demand Marshall assumed the utility functions of different goods to be independent of each other. In other words, Marshallian technique of deriving demand curves for goods from their utility functions rests on the hypothesis of *additive utility functions*, that is, utility function of each good consumed by a consumer does not depend on the quantity consumed of any other good. As has already been noted, in case of independent utilities or additive utility functions, the relations of substitution and complementarity between goods are ruled out. Further, in deriving demand curve or law of demand Marshall assumes the marginal utility of money expenditure (MU_m) *in general* to remain constant.

We now proceed to derive demand curve from the law of equi-marginal utility. Consider the case of a consumer who has a certain given income to spend on a number of goods. According to the law of equi-marginal utility, the consumer is in equilibrium in regard to his purchases of various goods when marginal utilities of the goods are proportional to their prices. Thus, the consumer is in equilibrium when he is buying the quantities of the two goods in such a way that satisfies the following proportionality rule:

$$\frac{MU_x}{P_x} = \frac{MU_y}{P_y} = \text{MU}_m$$

where MU_m stands for marginal utility of money income in general.

With a certain given income for money expenditure the consumer would have a certain *marginal utility of money* (MU_m) *in general.* In order to attain the equilibrium position, according to the above proportionality rule, the consumer will equalise his marginal utility of money (expenditure) with the ratio of the marginal utility and the price of each commodity he buys. It follows therefore that a rational consumer will equalise the marginal utility of money (MU_m) with $\frac{MU_x}{P_x}$ of good x, with $\frac{MU_y}{P_y}$ of good Y and so on. Given *Ceteris Paribus* assumption, suppose price of good X falls. With the fall in the price of good X, the price of good Y, consumer's income and tastes remaining unchanged, the equality of the $\frac{MU_x}{P_x}$ with $\frac{MU_y}{P_y}$ and MU_m in general would be disturbed. With the lower price than before $\frac{MU_x}{P_x}$ will be *greater than* $\frac{MU_y}{P_y}$ or MU_m (It is assumed of course that the marginal utility of money does not change as a result of the change in the price of one good). Then, in order to restore the equality, marginal utility of X or MU_x must be reduced. And the marginal utility of X or MU_x can be reduced only by the consumer buying more of the good X. It is thus clear from the proportionality rule that as the price of a good falls, its quantity demanded will rise, other things remaining the same. This will make the demand curve for a good downward sloping. How the quantity purchased of a good increases with the fall in its price and also how the demand curve is derived in the cardinal utility analysis is illustrated in Fig. 7.3.

In the upper portion of Fig. 7.3, on the Y-axis $\frac{MU_x}{P_x}$ is shown and on the X-axis the quantity demanded of good X is shown. Given a certain income of the consumer, marginal utility of money in general for him is equal to OH. The consumer is buying Oq_1 of good X when price is P_{x1}, since at the quantity Oq_1 of X, marginal utility of money OH is equal to $\frac{MU_x}{P_{x_1}}$. Now, when price of good X falls to P_{x2}, the curve will shift upward to the new position $\frac{MU_x}{P_{x_2}}$. In order to equate marginal utility of money (OH) with the new $\frac{MU_x}{P_{x2}}$ the consumer increases the quantity demanded to Oq_2. Thus, with the fall in price of good X to P_{x2}, the consumer buys more of it.

It should be noted that no account is taken of the increase in real income of the consumer as a result of fall in price of good X. This is because if change in real income is taken into account, then marginal utility of money will also change and this would have an effect on the purchases of goods. Marginal utility of money can remain constant in two cases. First, when the elasticity of marginal utility curve (price elasticity of demand) is unity so that even with increase in the purchase of a commodity following the fall in price, the money expenditure made on it remains the same. Second, marginal utility of money will remain approximately constant for small changes in price of unimportant goods, that is, goods which account for negligible part of consumer's budget. In case of these unimportant goods increase in real income following the fall in price is negligible and therefore can be ignored.

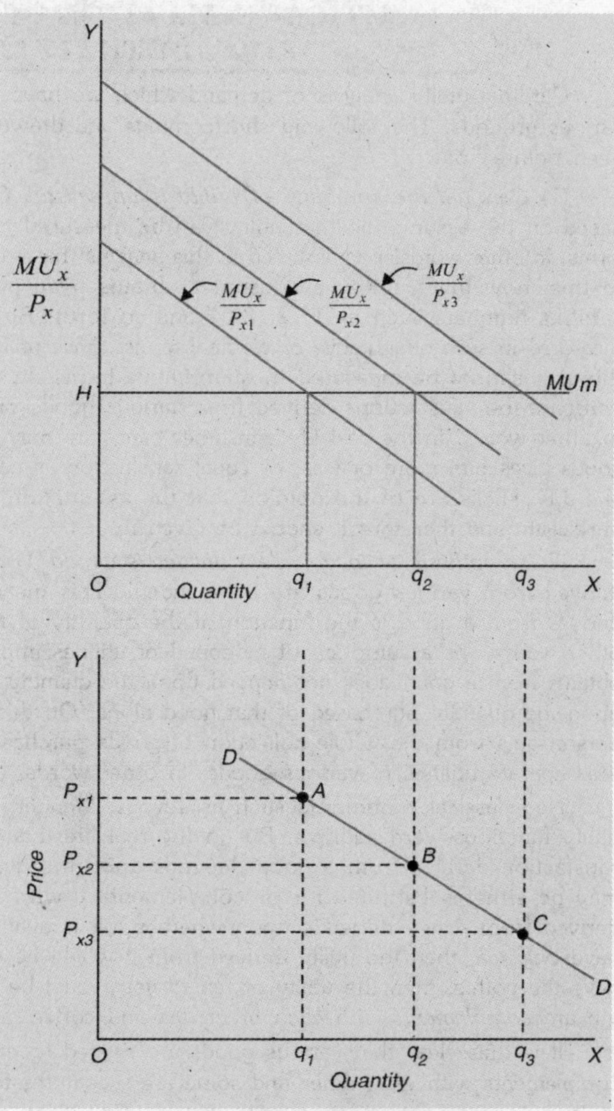

Fig. 7.3. *Derivation of Demand Curve*

At the bottom of Figure 7.4 the demand curve for X is derived. In this lower panel, price is measured the on the Y-axis. As in the upper panel the X-axis represents quantity. When the price of good X is Px_1, the relevant curve of $\frac{MU}{P}$ is $\frac{MU_x}{P_{x1}}$ which is shown in the upper portion. With $\frac{MU_x}{P_{x1}}$, as explained earlier, he buys Oq_1 of good X. Now, in the lower pannel this quantity Oq_1 is directly shown to be demanded at the price P_{x1}. When price of X falls to Px_2, the curve of $\frac{MU}{P}$ shifts upward to the new position $\frac{MU_x}{P_{x2}}$. With $\frac{MU_x}{P_{x2}}$ the consumer buys Oq_2 of X. This quantity Oq_2 is directly shown to be demanded at price Px_2 in the lower panel. Similarly, by varying price further we can know the quantity demanded at other prices. Thus, by joining points A, B and C we obtain the demand curve DD. The demand curve DD slopes downward which shows that as price of a good falls, its quantity purchased rises.

CRITICAL EVALUATION OF MARSHALL'S CARDINAL UTILITY ANALYSIS

Cardinal utility analysis of demand which we have studied above has been criticised on various grounds. The following shortcomings and drawbacks of cardinal utility analysis have been pointed out:

(1) *Cardinal measurability of utility is unrealistic.* Cardinal utility analysis of demand is based on the assumption that utility can be measured in absolute, objective and quantitative terms. In other words, it is assumed in this analysis that utility is cardinally measurable. According to this, how much utility a consumer obtains from goods can be expressed or stated in cardinal numbers such as 1, 2, 3, 4 and so forth. But in actual practice utility cannot be measured in such quantitative or cardinal terms. Since utility is a psychic feeling and a subjective thing, it cannot be measured in quantitative terms. In real life, consumers are only able to *compare* the satisfactions derived from various goods or various combinations of the goods. In other words, in the real life consumer can state only whether a good or a combination of goods gives him more or less, or equal satisfaction as compared to another. Thus, economists like J.R. Hicks are of the opinion that the assumption of cardinal measurability of utility is unrealistic and therefore it should be given up.

(2) *Hypothesis of independent utilities is wrong.* Utility analysis also assumes that utilities derived from various goods are independent. This means that the utility which a consumer derives from a good is the function of the quantity of that good and of that good alone. In other words, the assumption of independent utilities implies that the utility which a consumer obtains from a good does not depend upon the quantity consumed of other goods; it depends upon the quantity purchased of that good alone. On this assumption, the total utility which a person gets from the whole collection of goods purchased by him is simply the total sum of the separate utilities of various goods. In other words, utility functions are *additive.*

Neo-classical economists such as Jevons, Menger, Walras and Marshall considered that utility functions were additive. But in the real life this is not so. In actual life the utility or satisfaction derived from a good depends upon the availability of some other goods which may be either substitutes for or complementary with each other. For example, the utility derived from a pen depends upon whether ink is available or not. On the contrary, if you have *only* tea, then the utility derived from it would be greater but if along with tea you also have the coffee, then the utility of tea to you would be comparatively less. Whereas pen and ink are *complements* with each other, tea and coffee, are *substitutes for each other.*

It is thus clear that various goods are related to each other in the sense that some are complements with each other and some are substitutes for each other. As a result of this, the utilities derived from various goods are interdependent, that is, they depend upon each other. Therefore, the utility obtained from a good is not the function of its quantity alone but also depends upon the existence or consumption of other related goods (complements or substitutes).

It is thus evident that the assumption of the independence of utilities by Marshall and other supporters of marginal utility analysis is a great defect and shortcoming of their analysis. As we shall see below, the hypothesis of independent utilities along with the assumption of constant marginal utility of money reduces the validity of Marshallian demand theorem to the one-commodity model only.

(3) *Assumption of constant marginal utility of money is not valid:* An important assumption of cardinal utility analysis is that when a consumer spends varying amount on a good or various goods or when the price of a good changes, marginal utility of money remains unchanged. But in acutal practice this is not correct. As a consumer spends his money income on the goods, money income left with him declines. With the decline in money income of the consumer as a result of increase in his expenditure on goods, the marginal utility of money to him rises. Further, when price of a commodity changes, the real income of the consumer also changes. With this change in real income, marginal utility of money will change and this would have an effect on the demand for the good in question, even though the total money income available with the consumer remains the same. But utility analysis ignores all this and does not take cognizance of the changes in real income and its effect on demand for goods following the change in price of a good.

As has been explained earlier, according to Marshall, utility from a good can be measured in terms of money (that is, how much money a consumer is prepared to sacrifice for a good). But, to be able to measure utility in terms of money marginal utility of money itself should remain constant. Therefore, assumption of constant marginal utility of money is very crucial to Marshallian demand analysis. But in case the consumer has to spread his money income on a number of goods, there is a necessity for revision of marginal utility of money with every change in price of a good. In other words, in a multi-commodity model marginal utility of money does not remain invariant or constant.

J.R. Hicks and Tapas Majumdar have criticised Marshallian utility analysis on the ground that "Marshallian demand theorem cannot genuinely be derived from the marginal utility hypothesis except in a one-commodity model without contradicting the assumption of constant marginal utility of money".[3] In other words, Marshall's demand theorem and constant marginal utility of money are incompatible except in a one commodity case. As a result, Marshall's demand theorem cannot be validily derived in the case when a consumer spends his money on more than one good.

Now, whether following a fall in price of a good X, the new expenditure on it is equal to, smaller or greater than the initial expenditure depends upon the elasticity of marginal utility curve (i.e. price elasticity of demand). If elasticity of marginal utility curve of good X is unity, then the new expenditure on X after the fall in price of X will be equal to the initial expenditure. When the monetary expenditure made on the good remains constant as a result of change in price, then the Marshallian demand theory is valid. But the unitary elastic demand and therefore constant monetary expenditure on a commodity following a price change is only a rare phenomenon. Thus, in case of more than one good, Marshallian demand theorem cannot be genuinely derived while keeping the marginal utility of money constant.

(4) *Cardinal utility analysis does not split up the price effect into substitution and income effects:* The third shortcoming of the cardinal utility analysis is that *it does not distinguish between the income effect and the substitution effect of the price change.* We know that when price of a good falls, the consumer becomes better off than before, that is, a fall in price of a good brings about an increase in real income of the consumer. In other

3. Tapas Majumdar, *Measurement of Utility*, p. 55.

words, if with the fall in price the consumer purchases the same quantity of the good as before, then he would be left with some income. With this extra income he would be in a position to purchase more of this good as well as other goods. This is the income effect of the fall in price on the quantity demanded of the good. Besides, when price of a good falls, it becomes relatively cheaper than other goods and as a result the consumer is induced to substitute that good for others. This results in the increase in the quantity demanded of that good. This is the substitution effect of the price change on the quantity demanded of the good.

Thus, with the fall in price of a normal good, the quantity demanded of it rises because of income effect and substitution effect. But cardinal utility analysis does not make clear the distinction between the income and the substitution effects of the price change by assuming the constancy of marginal utility of money. Thus, according to Tapas Majumdar, "the assumption of constant marginal utility of money obscured Marshall's insight into the truly *composite character* of the price-demand relationship."[4] Marshall explained the changes in demand as a result of change in price of a good on the basis of substitution effect alone. Thus, J.R. Hicks rightly remarks, "*the distinction between income effect and substitution effect of a price change is accordingly left by the cardinal theory as an empty box which is crying out ot be filled*".[5] It is due to the failure to distinguish between income effect and substitution effect that Marshall could not explain a Giffen good in whose case price and quantity demanded are directly related.

Because of the above drawbacks, in modem economic theory demand is analysed with indifference curves which we shall explain in the next chapter.

QUESTIONS AND PROBLEMS FOR REVIEW

1. State and explain the law of diminishing marginal utility? How is law of demand derived from it ?
2. What is meant by consumer equilibrium ? How does a consumer maximise his satisfaction in cardinal utility analysis ?
3. Explain the Law of Equi-marginal utility ? How does it explain consumer equilibrium ?
4. You are given the following marginal utilities of goods *X* and *Y* obtained by a consumer. Given that price of *X* = Rs. 5, price of *Y* = Rs. 2 and income = Rs. 22, find out the optimal combination of goods.

Number of units consumed of a commodity	*MUx (utils)*	*MUy (utils)*
1	30	20
2	25	18
3	20	16
4	15	14
5	10	12
6	5	10
7	1	8

(Hint: Divide marginal utilities of goods *X* and *Y* by their prices and then compare.)

5. On what grounds Marshall's cardinal utility analysis has been criticised ?
6. Distinguish between cardinal utility and ordinal utility. Which is more realistic ?
7. What is Giffen Paradox ? Why Marshall could not explain it ?
8. Derive the demand curve for a commodity from Marshall's cardinal utility analysis. Explain in terms of cardinal utility theory why demand curve for a commodity slopes downward.
9. Deduce the inverse relationship between the quantity demanded of a commodity and its price in terms of Marshallian marginal utility analysis, indicating the underlying assumptions.
10. Suppose the *MU* of good *X* is 20, its price is Rs. 4, and the *MU* of good *Y* is 50 and its price is Rs. 5. The individual to whom this information applies is spending Rs. 20 on each good. Is he or she maximising satisfaction ? Why or why not ?

---

4. Tapas Majumdar, *ot.cit. p.*57.
5. J.R. Hicks, *A Revision of Demand Theory*, Oxford University Press, 1956.

Indifference Curve Analysis of Demand

Introduction

In the earlier two chapters we explained the demand for products and the factors that determine it. We also explained the elasticity or sensitivity of demand to changes in prices, income and prices of related goods. In the last chapter we explained and critically examined cardinal utility approach to consumer's demand. In the present chapter we shall explain the indifference theory of *consumer choice* underlying consumer's demand for products. Theory of *consumer choice* helps us to predict consumer's responses to changes in prices, income, tastes and preferences, prices of related goods, and advertising expenditure. With this understanding manager of a firm is better able to know the changes in firm's revenue consequent to the change in variables that the firm can control such as price of its product, advertising expenditure to promote its sales as well as consumer's responses to changes in variables such as consumer's income, prices of products of other rival firms and their promotional strategies. The indifference curve analysis is a popular theory of consumer's demand which forms the subject-matter of the present chapter. The technique of indifference curves was first of all invented by a classical economist Edgeworth but he used it only to show the possibilities of exchange between two persons and not to explain consumer's demand. Two English economists, J.R. Hicks and R.G.D. Allen in their now well-known paper '*A Reconsideration of the Theory of Value*' severely criticized Marshall's cardinal utility analysis based upon cardinal measurement of utility and put forward the indifference curve approach based on the notion of ordinal utility to explain consumer's behaviour. In 1939 Hicks reproduced the indifference curve theory of consumer's demand in his book '*Value and Capital*' modifying somewhat the version of the original paper.

INDIFFERENCE CURVE APPROACH

Indifference curve method has been evolved to supersede the cardinal utility analysis of demand which was discussed in the last chapter. The indifference curve method seeks to derive all rules and laws about consumer's demand that are derivable from the cardinal utility analysis. At the same time the inventors and supporters of new method contend that their analysis is based on fewer and more reasonable assumptions. The indifference curve analysis has, however, retained some of the assumptions of Marshall's cardinal utility analysis. Thus, the indifference curve approach, like the old cardinal utility approach, assumes that the *consumer possesses 'complete information'* about all the relevant aspects of economic environment in which he finds himself. For example, the prices of goods, the markets in which they are available, the satisfaction to be obtained from them etc. are all known to the consumer. Further, it is assumed that the *consumer acts rationally* in the sense that, given the prices of goods and the money income, he will choose the combination from among the various possible combinations that gives him maximum satisfaction. Moreover, the *assumption* of *'continuity'* has also been retained by Hicks-Allen indifference curve method. Continuity assumption means that the consumers are capable of ordering or ranking all *conceivable combinations of goods* according to the satisfaction they yield.

Ordinaal Utility

The fundamental approach of indifference curve analysis is that it has abandoned the concept of cardinal utility and instead has *adopted the concept of ordinal utility.* According to the supporters of the indifference curves theory, utility is a psychic entity and it cannot therefore be measured in quantitative cardinal terms. In other words, utility being a psychological feeling is not quantifiable. The concept of cardinal utility, according to the exponents of the indifference curve theory, is therefore untenable. On the other hand, the assumption of ordinal utility, according to them, is quite reasonable and realistic. *The ordinal utility implies that the consumer is capable of simply 'comparing the different levels of satisfaction'*. In other words, according to the ordinal utility hypothesis, while the consumer may not be able to indicate the exact amounts of utilities that he derives from commodities or any combination of them, but he is capable of judging whether the satisfaction obtained from a good or a combination of goods is equal to, lower than, or higher than another.

Notions of Preference and Indifference

For deriving the theory of consumer's behaviour, it is sufficient to assume that the consumer is able to rank his preferences consistently. Thus, the basis of indifference curve analysis of demand is the *preference-indifference hypothesis.* This means that if the consumer is presented with a number of various combinations of goods, he can order or rank them according to his '*scale of preferences*'. If the various combinations are marked *A, B, C, D, E,* etc. the consumer can tell whether he prefers *A* to *B*, or *B* to *A*, or is indifferent between them. Similarly, he can indicate his preference or indifference between any other pair of combinations. *The concept of ordinal utility implies that the consumer cannot go beyond stating his preference or indifference.* In other words, if a consumer happens to prefer A to B, he cannot tell by how much he prefers A to B. Thus, under ordinal utility hypothesis, the consumer cannot tell the '*quantitative differences*' between various levels of satisfaction; he can simply compare them 'qualitatively', that is, he can merely judge whether one level of satisfaction is higher than, lower than or equal to another. Further, according to the supporters of indifference-curve method, by 'how much' one combination of goods is preferred to another is not even needed for deriving laws concerning consumer's behaviour. It is sufficient to assume that the consumer is able to tell whether one combination of goods gives him greater, equal, or less satisfaction than another.

It may be noted that the *consumer formulates his scale of preferences independently of the market prices of goods keeping in view only the satisfaction which he hopes to get from various combinations of goods.* In consumer's scale of preferences some combinations will occupy the *same place, i.e.*, the consumer will be indifferent among them. Combinations occupying a higher place in his scale will be preferred to the combinations occupying lower places in the scale. Moreover, the indifference curve analysis assumes that the preference and indifference relations are '*transitive*'. The transitivity of preferences or indifference relations means that if a consumer prefers *A* to *B*, and *B* to *C*, then he will also prefer *A* to *C* and, likewise, if he is indifferent between *A* and *B*, and between *B* and *C*, then he will also be indifferent between *A* and *C*.

Assumptions of Indifferent Curves Analysis

Before explaining the properties or attributes which the indifference curves normally possess. It will be userful if we first mention the assumptions about the behaviour of the consumer which are generally made in indifference curve analysis.

1. More of a commodity is better than less. It is assumed that the consumer will always prefer a larger amount of a good to a smaller amount of that good, provided that the other goods at his disposal remains unchanged. This is a very reasonable and realistic assumption. This assumption implies that the consumer is not over-supplied with any good. When a consumer is over-supplied or over-satiated with one good, he will prefer a smaller quantity of that good to its larger quantity. It is thus assumed that the consumer has not yet reached the point of satiety in the consumption of any good. This assumption is therefore known as *non-satiety assumption*.

2. Preferences or indifferences of a consumer are transitive. Suppose there are three combinations of two goods, *A*, *B* and *C*. If the consumer is indifferent between *A* and *B* and also between *B* and *C*, it is then assumed that he will be indifferent between *A* and *C* too. This condition implies that consumer's tastes are quite consistent. This assumption is known as *assumption of transitivity*.

3. Diminishing marginal rate of substitution. In indifference curve analysis the principle of diminishing marginal rate of substitution is assumed. In other words, it is assumed that as more and more units of *X* are substituted for *Y*, the consumer will be willing to give up fewer and fewer units of *Y* for each additional unit of *X*, or when more and more of *Y* is substituted for *X*, he will be willing to give up successively fewer and fewer units of *X* for each additional unti of *Y*. This rule about consumer's behaviour is described as the principle of diminishing, marginal rate of substitution. This principle follows as a matter of logical necessity from the assumption that particular wants are satiable and that various goods are not perfect substitutes for one another.

WHAT ARE INDIFFERENCE CURVES ?

The basic tool of Hicks-Allen ordinal utility analysis of demand is the indifference curve which represents all those combinations of goods which give same satisfaction to the consumer. Since all the combinations on an indifference curve give equal satisfaction to the consumer, he will be indifferent between them, that is, it will not matter to him which one he gets. In other words, all combinations of two goods lying on a consumer's indifference curve are equally desirable to or equally preferred by him. To understand indifference curves, it is better to start with indifference schedules. In Table 8.1, two indifference schedules are given. In each schedule the amounts of goods *X* and *Y* in each combination are so much that the consumer is indifferent among the combinations in each schedule. In schedule 1, the consumer has to start with 1 unit of *X* and 12 units of *Y*. Now, the consumer is asked to tell how much of good *Y* he will be willing to give up for the gain of an additional unit of *X* so that his level of satisfaction remains the same. If the gain of one unit of *X* compensates him fully for the loss of 4 units of *Y*, then the next combination of 2 units of *X* and 8 units of *Y* ($2X + 8Y$) will give him as much satisfaction as the initial combination ($1X + 12Y$). Similarly, by asking the consumer further how much of Y he will be prepared to forgo for successive increments in his stock of X so that his level of satisfaction remains unaltered, we get combinations $3X + 5Y$, $4X + 3Y$, and $5X + 2Y$, each of which provides him same satisfaction as combination $1X + 12Y$ or $2X + 8Y$. Since his satisfaction is the same whichever combination of goods in the schedule is offered to him, he will be indifferent among the combinations of two goods included in the schedule.

Table 8.1 Two Indifference Schedules

I		II	
Good X	*Good Y*	*Good X*	*Good Y*
1	12	2	14
2	8	3	10
3	5	4	7
4	3	5	5
5	2	6	4

In schedule II, the consumer has initially 2 units of X and 14 units of Y. By asking the consumer how much of Y he will be prepared to abandon for the successive additions of X in his stock so that his satisfaction remains equal to what he derives from the initial combination $(2X + 14Y)$, we get combinations $3X + 10Y$, $4X + 7Y$, $5X + 5Y$ and $6X + 4Y$. Thus, each of the combinations in schedule II will be equally desirable to the consumer and he will be indifferent among them. But it should be borne in mind that the consumer will prefer any combination in schedule II to any combination in schedule I. That is, any combination in schedule II will give him more satisfaction than any combination in shcedule I. This is because it is assumed that more of a commodity is preferable to less of it (in other words, the greater quantity of a good

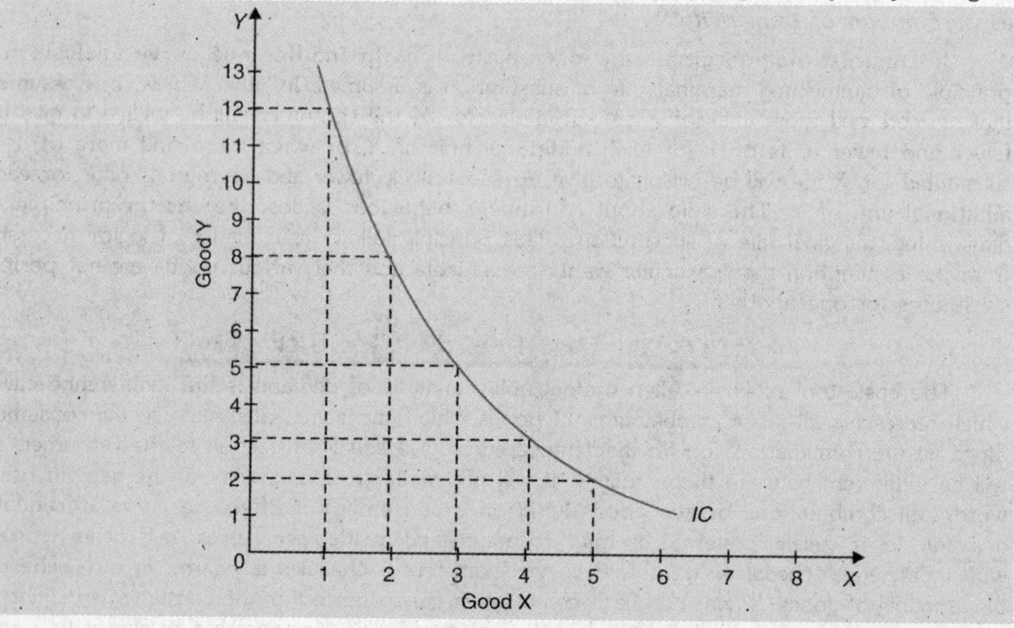

Fig. 8.1. *An Indifference Curve*

gives an individual more satisfaction than the smaller quantity of it), the quantities of other goods with him remaining the same. Initial combination in schedule II contains more of both the goods than the initial combination in schedule I, therefore the former will give greater satisfaction to the consumer than the latter. Now, since each of the other combinations in indifference schedule II provides the consumer same satisfaction as the initial combination ($2X + 14Y$) of the schedule and also each of other combinations in indifference schedule I gives the same satisfaction as the initial combination ($1X + 12Y$), any combination of the schedule II will be preferred to (will yield greater satisfaction) than any combination of schedule I.

Now, we can convert the indifference schedules into indifference curves by plotting the various combinations on a graph paper. In Fig. 8.1 an indifference curve *IC* is drawn by plotting the various combinations of the indifference schedule I. The quantity of good *X* is measured on the horizontal axis, and the quantity of the good *Y* is measured on the vertical axis. As in an indifference schedule, combinations lying on an indifference curve will also be equally desirable to the consumer, that is, will give him the same satisfaction. The smoothness and continuity of an indifference curve mean that goods in question are assumed to be perfectly divisible. If the indifference schedule *II* is also converted into indifference curve, this will lie above the indifference curve *IC*.

Any combination on a higher indifference curve will be preferred to any combination on a lower indifference curve. It is thus clear that the indifference curve lying above and to the right of an indifference curve will indicate a higher level of satisfaction. It may be noted that while an indifference curve shows all those combinations of two goods which provide equal satisfaction to the consumer, it does not indicate *exactly how much* satisfaction is derived by the consumer from those combinations. This is because the concept of ordinal utility does not involve the quantitative measurability of utility. Therefore, no attempt is made to label an indifference curve by the amount of satisfaction it represents.

Indifference Map

A complete description of consumer's tastes and preferences can be represented by an *indifference map* which consists of a set of indifference curves. Because the field in a two-dimensional diagram contains an infinite number of points, each representing a combination of goods X and Y, there will be an infinite number of the indifference curves each passing through combinations of goods that are equally desirable to the consumer. In Fig.8. 2 an indifference map of a consumer is shown which consists of five indifference curves. The consumer regards all combinations on the indifference curve *I* as giving him equal satisfactions. Similarly, all the combinations lying on indifference curve *II* provide the same satisfaction but the level of satisfaction on indifference curve *II*, for the reason already explained, will be greater than the level of satisfaction on indifference curve *I*. Likewise, all higher indifference curves, *III*, *IV* and *V* represent progressively higher and higher levels of satisfaction. It is importnat to remember that while the consumer will prefer any combination on a higher indifference curve to any combination on a lower indifference curve, but by *how much he prefers* one combination to another cannot be said. In other words, a higher indifference curve represents a higher level of satisfaction than a lower indifference curve but by "*how much higher*" cannot be indicated. This is because

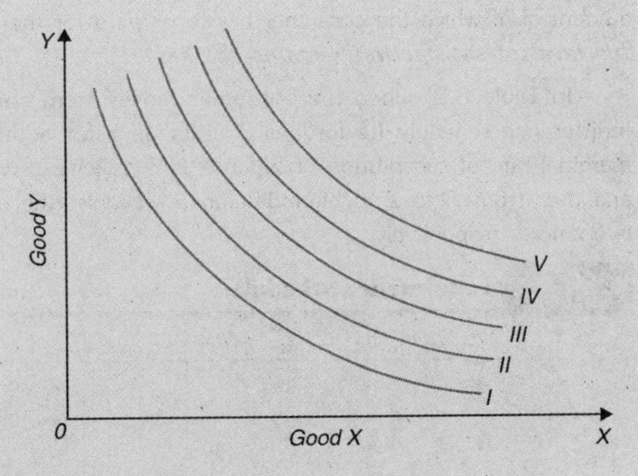

Fig. 8. 2. *Indifference Map*

the indifference curve system is based upon the concept of ordinal utility according to which the consumer is able to state only the '*qualitative*' differences in his various levels of satisfaction. It is not possible for the consumer to specify '*quantitative*' differences in his various levels of satisfaction (*i.e.*, by how much more or by how much less cannot be stated by him). Therefore, in an indifference map successively higher indifference curves can be denoted by any ascending series, 1,3,7, 9...; or 1, 4, 6, 8, 13...; or 1, 2, 5, 8, 10...; etc., the magnitude of these various numbers and the quantitative differences among them having no relevance. It is more usual to label the indifference curves by ordinal numbers as *I*, *II*, *III*, *IV*, *V* as is done in Fig. 8.2.

An indifference map of a consumer represents, as said earlier, his tastes and preferences for the two goods and his preferences between different combinations of them. In other words, *an indifference map portrays consumer's scale of preferences.* Scale of preferences of indifference curve analysis replaces Marshall's utility schedule. So long as consumer's tastes and preferences remain unchanged, the whole indifference map will remain the same. If the consumer's tastes and preferences undergo a change, then a new indifference map corresponding to new tastes and preferences will have to be drawn. If, for instance, good Y is eggs and good *X* is bread, and if the doctor advises our consumer to take more of eggs to overcome some diseases, the shapes of all his indifference curves will change and his indifference map will have to be redrawn. Since the doctor's advice will intensify our consumer's desire for eggs, now a smaller quantity of eggs than before will be given up by him for a given increment in bread.

MARGINAL RATE OF SUBSTITUTION

The concept of marginal rate of substitution is an important tool of indifference curve analysis of demand. The rate at which the consumer is prepared to exchange goods *X* and *Y* is known as marginal rate of substitution. In our indifference schedule I above, which is reproduced in Table 8.2, in the beginning the consumer gives up 4 units of *Y* for the gain of one additional unit of *X* and in this process his level of satisfaction remains the same. It follows that one unit gain in *X* fully compensates him for the loss of 4 units of *Y*. It means that at this stage he is prepared to exchange 4 units of *Y* for one unit of *X*. Therefore, at this stage consumer's marginal rate of substitution of *X* for Y is 4. Thus, *we may define the marginal rate of substitution of X for Y as the amount of Y whose loss can just be compensated by one unit gain in X.* In other words, marginal rate of substitution of X for Y represents the amount of Y which the consumer has to give up for the gain of one additional unit of *X so that his level of satisfaction remains the same.*

In Table 8.2, when the consumer moves from combination *B* to combination *C* on his indifference schedule he forgoes 3 units of *Y* for additional one unit gain in *X*. Hence, the marginal rate of substitution of *X* for *Y* is 3. Likewise, when the consumer moves from *C* to *D*, and then from *D* to *E* in his indifference schedule, the marginal rate of substitution of *X* for *Y* is 2 and 1 respectively.

Table 8.2. Indifference Schedule

Combination	*Good X*	*Good Y*	MRS_{xy}
A	1	12	
B	2	8	4
C	3	5	3
D	4	3	2
E	5	2	1

How to measure marginal rate of substitution on an indifference curve ? Consider Fig. 8.3 where an indifference curve is shown. When the consumer moves from point A to B on this indifference curve he gives up AS of Y and takes up SB of X and remains on the same indifference curve (or, in other words, at the same level of satisfaction). It means that the loss of satisfaction caused by giving up AS of Y equals the gain in satisfaction due to the increase in good X by SB. It follows that the consumer is prepared to exchange AS of Y for SB increase in X. In other words, marginal rate of substitution of X for Y (MRS_{xy}) is equal to $\frac{AS}{SB}$. Now, a small change in the amount of Y such as AS, along an indifference curve can be written as ΔY and the change in the amount of X as ΔX. Thus, ΔY shows the amount of Y which the consumer has to give up for the ΔX increase in X if he is to remain on the same indifference curve. Therefore, it follows that :

$$\text{Marginal rate of substitution of } X \text{ for } Y\,(MRS_{xy}) = \frac{AS}{SB} = \frac{\Delta Y}{\Delta X}$$

Now, suppose that points A and B are very close to each other so that it can be assumed that both of them lie on the same tangent tT (Fig. 8.3). Now, in a right-angled traingle ASB, $\frac{AS}{SB}$ is equal to the tangent of the angle ABS. It therefore follows that :

$$MRS_{xy} = \frac{AS}{SB} = \frac{\Delta Y}{\Delta X} = \text{tangent of } \angle ABS$$

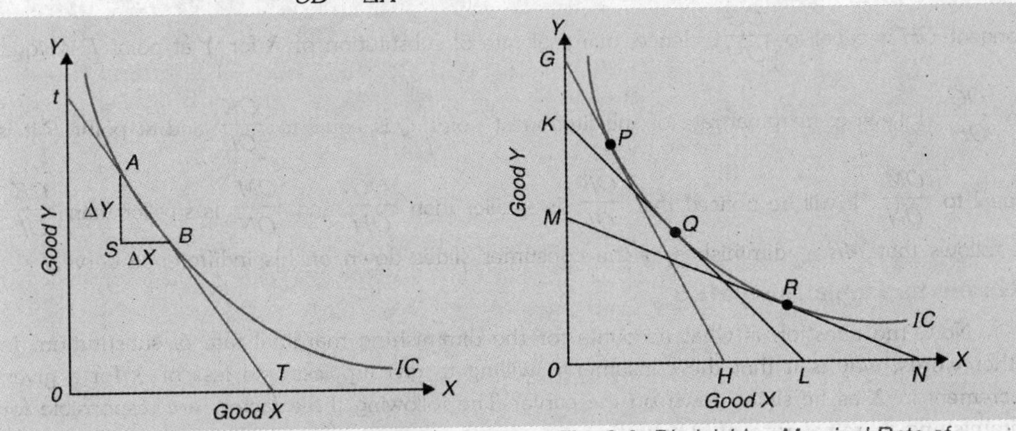

Fig. 8.3. *Graphic Illustration of the Concept of Marginal Rate of Substitution*

Fig. 8.4. *Diminishing Marginal Rate of Substitution*

But in Fig. 8.3 $\angle ABS = \angle tTO$

Hence MRS_{xy} = tangent of $\angle tTO$

But the tangent of $\angle tTO$ is equal to $\frac{Ot}{OT}$

Thus tangent of $\angle tTO$ indicates the slope of the tangent line tT drawn at point A or B on the indifference curve. In other words, the slope of the indifference curve at point of A or B is equal to the tangent of $\angle tTO$. It therefore follows:

$$MRS_{xy} = \text{tangent of } \angle tTO = \text{slope of the indifference curve on } A \text{ or } B = \frac{Ot}{OT}$$

It is thus clear from above that if we have to find out the MRS_{xy} at a point on the indifference curve we can do so by drawing a tangent at the point to the indifference curve and then measuring the slope by estimating the value of the tangent of the angle which the tangent line makes with the *X*-axis.

Principle of Diminishing Marginal Rate of Substitution

An important principle of economic theory is that marginal rate of substitution of *X* for *Y* diminishes as more and more of good *X* is substituted for good *Y*. In other words, as the consumer has more and more of good *X*, he is prepared to forego less and less of good Y. The principle of diminishing marginal rate of substitution is illustrated in Fig. 8.4.

That marginal rate of substitution falls is also evident from the Table 8.2. In the beginning the marginal rate of substitution of *X* for *Y* is 4 and as more and more of *X* is obtained and less and less of *Y* is left, the MRS_{xy} keeps on falling. Between *B* and *C* it is 3; between *C* and *D*, it is 2; any finally between *D* and *E*, it is 1. It means from Table 8.2 that as the consumer's stock of *X* increases and his stock of *Y* decreases, he is willing to forego less and less of *Y* for a given increment in *X*. In other words, marginal rate of substitution of *X* for *Y* falls as the consumer has more of *X* and less of Y. That the marginal rate of substitution of *X* for *Y* diminishes can also be known from drawing tangents at different points on an indifference curve. As explained above, marginal rate of substitution at a point on the indifference curve is equal to the slope of the indifference curve at that point and can therefore be found out by measuring the slope of tangent drawn at a point. In Fig. 8.4 three tangents *GH*, *KL* and *MN* are drawn at the points *P*, *Q* and *R* respectively to the given indifference curve. Slope of the tangent *GH* is equal to $\frac{OG}{OH}$. Hence, marginal rate of substitution of *X* for *Y* at point *P* is equal to $\frac{OG}{OH}$. Likewise, marginal rate of substitution at point *Q* is equal to $\frac{OK}{OL}$ and at point *R* it is equal to $\frac{OM}{ON}$. It will be noticed that $\frac{OK}{OL}$ is smaller than $\frac{OG}{OH}$ and $\frac{OM}{ON}$ is smaller than $\frac{OK}{OL}$. It follows that MRS_{xy} diminishes as the consumer slides down on his indifference curve.

Reasons for Diminishing MRS_{xy}

Now, the question is what accounts for the diminishing marginal rate of substitution. In other words, why is it that the consumer is willing to give up less and less of *Y* for a given increment in *X* as he slides down on the curve? The following three factors are responsible for diminishing marginal rate of substitution.

First, *the want for a particular good is satiable* so that as the consumer has more and more of a good the intensity of his want for that good goes on declining. It is because of this fall in the intensity of want for a good, say *X*, that when its stock increases with the consumer, he is prepared to forego less and less of good *Y* for every increment in *X*. In the beginning, when the consumer's stock of good *Y* is relatively large and his stock of good *X* is relatively small, consumer's marginal significance for good *Y* is low, while his marginal significance for good *X* is high. Owing to higher marginal significance of good *X* and lower marginal significance of good *Y* in the beginning the consumer will be willing to give up a larger amount of *Y* for one unit increase in good *X*. But as the stock of good X increases and intensity of desire for it falls, his marginal significance of good *X* will diminish and, on the other hand, as the stock of good *Y* decreases and the intensity of his desire for it increases, his marginal significance for good *Y* will go up. As a result, therefore, as the individual substitutes more and more of *X* for *Y*, he is prepared to give up less and less of *Y* for one unit increase in *X*.

The second reason for the decline in marginal rate of substitution is that the *goods are imperfect substitutes of each other.* If two goods are perfect substitutes of each other, then they are to be regarded as one and the same good, and therefore increase in the quantity of one and decrease in the quantity of the other would not make any difference in the marginal significance of the goods. Thus, in case of perfect substitutability of goods, the increase and decrease will be virtually in the same good which cancel out each other and therefore the marginal rate of substitution remains the same and does not decline.

Relationship Between MRS and Marginal Utilities

It can be shown mathematically that MRS_{xy} between goods is equal to the ratio of marginal utilities of goods X and Y.

An indifference curve can be represented by

$$U(x, y) = a \qquad \text{.......}(i)$$

where a represents a constant utility along an indifference curve. Taking total differential of (i) above, we have :

$$\frac{\partial U}{\partial X}dX + \frac{\partial U}{\partial Y}dY = 0$$

$$\frac{dY}{dX} = \frac{\frac{\partial U}{\partial X}}{\frac{\partial U}{\partial Y}}$$

$\frac{\partial U}{\partial X}$ and $\frac{\partial U}{\partial Y}$ are marginal utilities of goods X and Y respectively. Thus,

$$\frac{dY}{dX} = \frac{MU_x}{MU_y}$$

$\frac{dY}{dX}$ is the slope of indifference curve and represents MRS_{xy}. Thus,

$$MRS_{xy} = \frac{MU_x}{MU_y}$$

PROPERTIES OF INDIFFERENCE CURVES

We now proceed to deduce from the above-mentioned assumptions the important properties of typical indifference curves.

Property I : Indifference curves slope downward to the right.

This property implies that an indifference curve has a negative slope. This property follows from assumption I. Indifference curve being downward sloping means that when the amount of one good in the combination is increased, the amount of the other good is reduced. This must be so if the level of satisfaction is to remain the same on an indifference curve. If, for instance, the amount of good X is increased in the combination, while the amount of good Y remains unchanged, the new combination will be preferable to the original one and the two combinations will not therefore lie on the same indifference curve provided more of a commodity gives more satisfaction.

Property II : Indifference curves are convex to the origin.

Another important property of indifference curves is that they are usually convex to the origin. In other words, the indifference curve is relatively flatter in its right-hand portion and relatively steeper in its left-hand portion. This property of indifference curves follows from assumption 3, which is that the marginal rate of substitution of X for Y (MRS_{xy}) diminishes as more and more of *X* is substituted for Y. Only a convex indifference curve can mean a diminishing marginal rate of substitution of *X* for *Y*. If indifference curve was concave to the origin it would imply that the marginal rate of substitution of *X* for *Y* increased as more and more of *X* was substituted. for *Y*.

As shown in Fig. 8.4, when the indifference curve is convex to the origin, MRS_{xy} diminishes as more of *X* is substituted for *Y*. We therefore conclude that indifference curves are generally convex to the origin.

Our assumption regarding diminishing MRS_{xy} and the convexity of indifference curves is based upon the observation of actual behaviour of the normal consumer. *If indifference curves were concave or straight lines, the consumer would succumb to monomania, that is, he would buy and consume only* one good. We know that consumers in actual world do not generally buy and consume *one good.* It is for this reason that we reject indifference curves of concave or straight-line shapes and assume that indifference curves are normally convex to the origin. The degree of convexity of an indifference curve depends on the rate of fall in the marginal rate of substitution of *X* for Y. As stated above, when two goods are perfect substitutes of each other, the indifference curve is a straight line on which marginal rate of substitution remains constant. The better substitutes the two goods are for each other, the closer the indifference curve approaches to the straight line so that when the two goods are perfect substitutes, the indifference curve is a straight line.

Property III: Indifference curves cannot intersect each other.

Third important property of indifference curves is that they cannot intersect each other. In other words, only one indifference curve will pass through a point in the indifference map. This property can be easily proved by first making the two indifference curves cut each other and then showing the absurdity or self-contradictory result it leads to. In Fig. 8.5 two indifference curves are shown cutting each other at point *C*. Now take point *A* on indifference curve IC_2 and point *B* on indifference curve IC_1 vertically below *A*. Since an indifference curve represents those combinations of two commodities which give equal satisfaction to the consumer, the combinations represented by points *A* and *C* will give equal satisfaction to the consumer because both lie on the same indifference curve IC_2.

Likewise, the combinations B and C will give equal satisfaction to the consumer; both being on the same indifference curve IC_1. If combination *A* is equal to combination *C* in terms of satisfaction, and combination *B* is equal to combination *C*, it follows that the combination *A* will be equivalent to *B* in terms of satisfaction. But a glance at Fig.8.5 will show that this is absurd conclusion since combination *A* contains more of good *Y* than combination *B*, while the amount of good *X* is the same in both the combinations. Thus, the consumer will definitely prefer *A* to *B*, that is, *A* will give more satisfaction to the consumer than *B*. But the two indiffference curves cutting each other lead us to an absurd conclusion of *A* being equal to *B* in terms of satisfaction. We therefore conclude that indifference curves cannot cut each other.

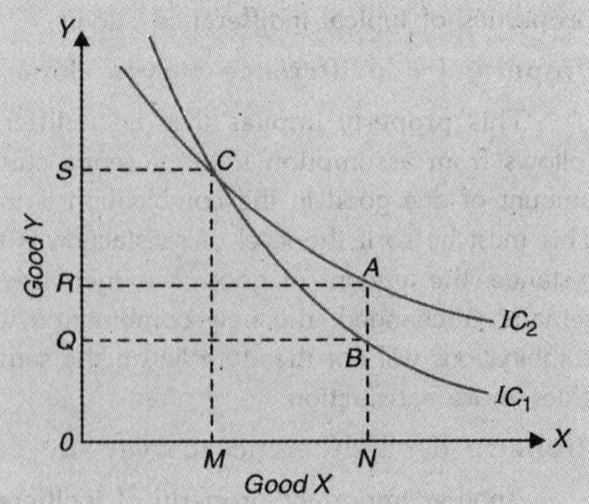

Fig. 8.5. *Indifference curves cannot cut each other.*

Another point which is worth mentioning in this regard is that indifference curves cannot even meet or touch each other or be tangent to each other at a point.The meeting of two indifference curves at a point will also lead us to an absurd conclusion. The same argument holds good in this case as developed above in the case of intersection of indifference curves.

Property IV: A higher indifference curve represents a higher level of satisfaction than a lower indifference curve.

The last property of indifference curve is that a higher indifference curve will represent a higher level of satisfaction than a lower indifference curve. In other words, the combinations which lie on a higher indifference curve will be preferred to the combinations which lie on a lower indifference curve. Consider indifference curves IC_1, and IC_2 in Fig. 8.6. IC_2 is a higher indifference curve than IC_1. Combination Q has been taken on a higher indifference curve IC_2 and combination S on a lower indifference curve IC_1. Combination Q on the higher indifference curve IC_2 will give a consumer more satisfaction than combination S on the lower indifference curve IC_1 because the combination Q contains more of both goods X and Y than the combination S. Hence the consumer must prefer Q to S. And by transitivity assumption, he will prefer any other combination such as combination R on IC_2 (all of which are indifferent with Q) to any combination on IC_1 (all of which are indifferent with S). We, therefore, conclude that a higher indifference curve represents a higher level of satisfaction and combinations on it will be preferred to the combinations on a lower indifference curve.

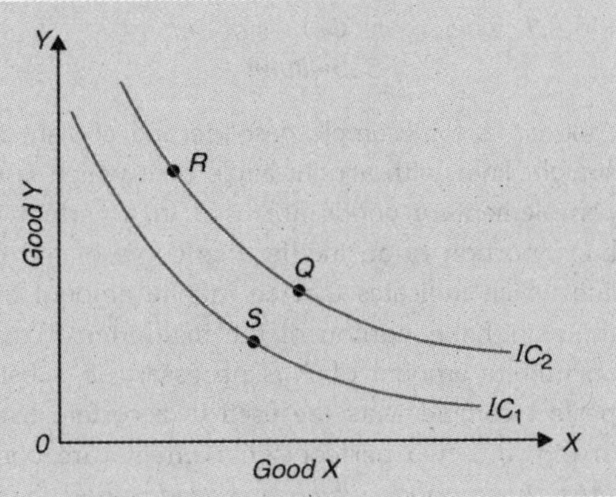

Fig. 8.6. *A higher indifference curve shows a higher level of satisfaction.*

Indifference Curves of Perfect Substitutes and Perfect Complements

The degree of convexity of an indifference curve depends upon the rate of fall in the marginal rate of substitution of X for Y. As stated above, when two goods are perfect substitutes of each other, the indifference curve is a straight line on which marginal rate of substitution remains constant. Straight-line indifference curves of perfect substitutes are shown in Fig. 8.7. The better substitutes the two goods are for each other, the closer the indifference curve approaches to the straight-line so that when the two goods are perfect substitutes, the indifference curve is a straight line. In case of perfect substitutes, the indifference curves are parallel straight lines because the consumer equally prefers the two goods and is willing to exchange one good for the other at a constant rate. As one moves along a straight-line indifference curve of perfect substitutes, marginal rate of substitution of one good for amother remains constant. Examples of goods that are perfect substitutes are not difficult to find in the real world. For example, Dalda and Rath Vanaspati, two different brands of cold drink such as Pepsi Cola and Coca Cola are generally considered to be perfect substitutes of each other.

The greater the fall in marginal rate of substitution, the greater the convexity of the indifference curve. The less the ease with which two goods can be substituted for each other, the greater will be the fall in the marginal rate of substitution. At the extreme, when two goods cannot at all be substituted for each other, that is, when the two goods are perfect complementary

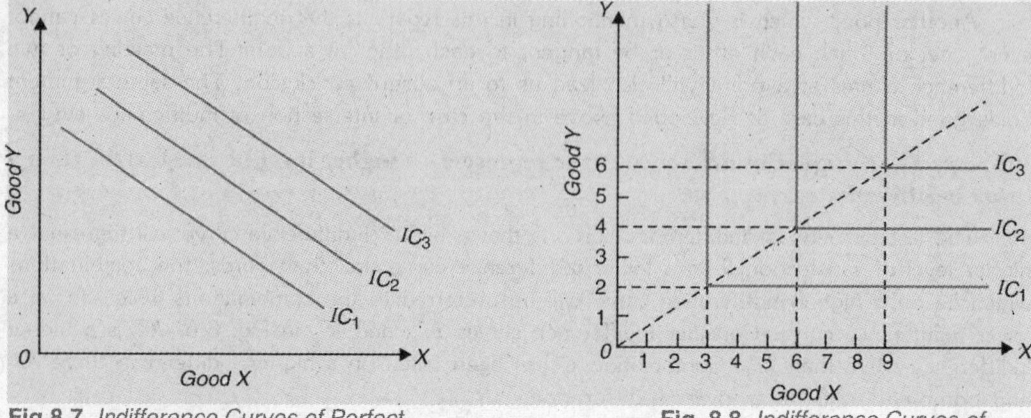

Fig.8.7. *Indifference Curves of Perfect Substitutes*

Fig. 8.8. *Indifference Curves of Perfect Complements*

goods, as for example gasoline and coolant in a car, the indifference curve will consist of two straight lines with a right angle bent which is convex to the origin as shown in Fig. 8.8. Perfect complementary goods are used in a certain fixed ratio. As will be seen in Fig. 8.8, the left-hand portion of an indifference curve of the perfect complementary goods is a vertical straight line which indicates that an infinite amount of *Y* is necessary to substitute one unit of *X*, and the right-hand portion of the indifference curve is a horizontal straight line which means that an infinite amount of *X* is necessary to substitute one unit of *Y*. All this means that the two perfect complements are used in a certain fixed ratio and cannot be substituted for each other. In Fig. 8.8 two perfect complements are consumed in the ratio, 3*X* : 2*Y*. *Complements are thus those goods which are used jointly in consumption so that their consumption increases or decreases simultaneously.* Pen and ink, right shoe and left shoe, automobile and petrol, sauce and hamburger, type writer and typists are some examples of perfect complements.

BUDGET LINE OR BUDGET CONSTRAINT

The knowledge of the concept of *budget line*[1] or what is also called *budget constraint* is essential for understanding the theory of consumer's equilibrium. As explained above, a higher indifference curve shows a higher level of satisfaction than a lower one. Therefore, a consumer in his attempt to maximise his satisfaction will try to reach the highest possible indifference curve. But in his pursuit of buying more and more goods and thus obtaining more and more satisfaction he has to work under two constraints: first, he has to pay the prices for the goods and, secondly, he has a limited money income with which to purchase the goods. Thus, how far he would go in for his purchases depends upon the prices of the goods and the money income which he has to spend on the goods. As explained above, indifference map represents consumer's scale of preferences between two goods. Now, in order to explain consumer's equilibrium there is also the need for introducing into the indifference curve analysis the budget line which represents the prices of the goods and consumer's money income.

Suppose our consumer has got income of Rs. 50 to spend on two goods *X* and *Y*. Let price of good *X* in the market be Rs. 10 per unit and that of *Y* Rs. 5 per unit. If the consumer spends his whole income of Rs. 50 on good *X*, he would buy 5 units of *X*; if he spends his whole income of Rs. 50 on good *Y* he would buy 10 units of *Y*. If a straight line joining 5*X* and 10*Y* is drawn, we will get what is called the price line or the budget line. *Thus budget line shows all those combinations of two goods which the consumer can buy by spending* *his given money income on the two goods at their given prices.* A look at Fig. 8.9 shows that with Rs. 50 and the prices of X and Y being Rs 10 and Rs. 5 respectively the consumer can buy $10Y$ and $0X$, or $8Y$ and 1X; or $6Y$ and $2X$, or $4Y$ and $3X$ etc. In other words, he can buy any combination that lies on the budget line with his given money income and given prices of the goods. It should be carefully noted that any combination of the two goods such such as H ($5Y$ and $4X$) which lies above and outside the given budget line will be beyond the reach of the consumer. But any combination lying within the budget line such as K ($2X$ and $2Y$) will be well within the reach of the consumer, but if he buys any such combination he will not be spending all his income of Rs. 50. Thus, with the assumption that whole of the given income is spent on the given goods and at given prices of them, the consumer has to choose from all those combinations which lie on the budget line.

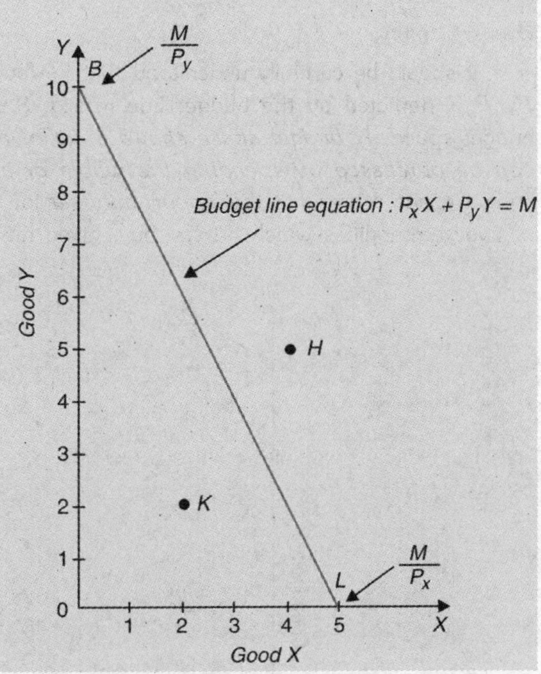

Fig. 8.9. *Budget Line or Budget Constraint*

It is clear from above that budget line graphically shows the *budget constraint.* The combinations of commodities lying to the right of the budget line are *unattainable* because income of the consumer is not sufficient to buy those combinations. Given consumer's income and prices of the two goods, the combinations of goods lying to the left of the budget line are *attainable*, that is, the consumer can buy any one of them. It is also important to remember that the intercept OB on the Y-axis in Fig. 8.9 equals the amount of his entire income (M) divided by the price (P_Y) of commodity Y. That is, $OB = M/Py$. Likewise, the intercept OL on the X-axis measures the total income divided by the price of commodity X. Thus $OL = M/P_x$.

The budget line can be written algebraically as follows :

$$P_x X + P_y Y = M \qquad \text{... (1)}$$

or

$$Y = \frac{M}{P_Y} - \frac{P_x}{P_Y} . X$$

where P_x and P_y denote prices of goods X and Y respectively and M stands for money income:

The above budget-line equation (1) implies that, given the money income of the consumer and prices of the two goods, every combination lying on the budget line will cost the same

1. The budget line has been variously named by different authors. Other names in the literature for the budget line are price line, price opportunity line, price-income line, outlay line, budget constraint, expenditure line and consumption possibility line.

amount of money and can therefore be purchased with the given income. The budget line can be defined as *a set of combinations of two commodities that can be purchased if whole of the given income is spent on them* and its slope is equal to the negative of the price ratio.

Budget Space

It should be carefully understood that the budget equation $P_xX + P_yY = M$ or $Y = M/P_y - Px/P_y.X$ depicted by the budget line in Fig. 8.9 only describes the budget line and not the budget space. A *budget space shows a set of all combinations of the two commodities that can be purchased by spending the whole or a part of the given income*. In other words, budget space represents the *opportunity set* for the consumer, that is, all those combinations of two commodities which he can buy, given his budget constraint. Thus, the budget space

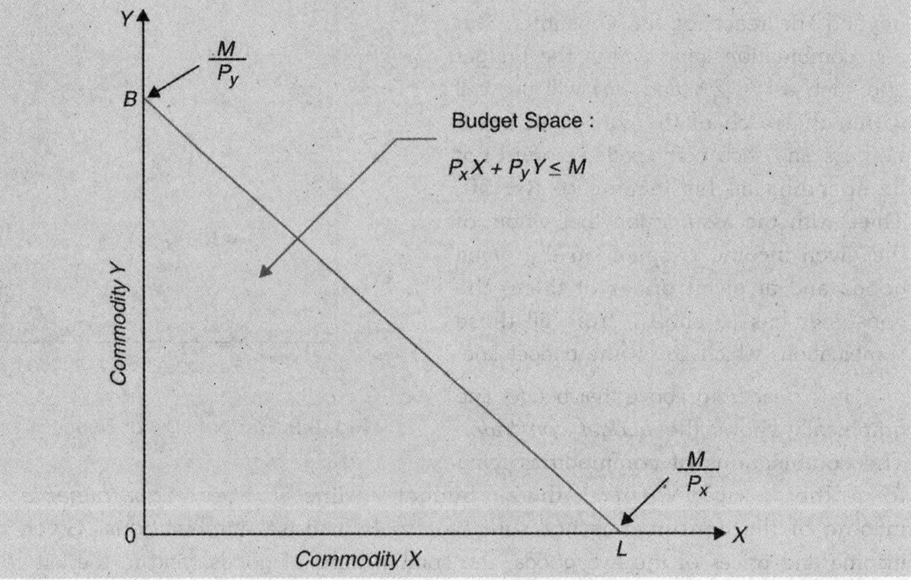

Fig. 8.10. *Budget Space or Opportunity Set*

implies the set of all combinations of two goods for which income spent on good X (*i.e.*, P_xX) and income spent on good Y (*i.e.* P_yY) *must not exceed* the given money income. Therefore, we can algebraically express the budget space in the following form of inequality :

$$P_xX + PyY \leq M, \text{ or } M \geq P_xX + P_yY$$

The budget space has been graphically shown in Fig. 8.10 as the shaded area. The budget space is the entire area enclosed by the budget line BL and the two axes.

Changes in Price and Shift in Budget Line

Now, what happens to the budget line if either the prices of goods change or the income changes. Let us first take the case of the changes in prices of the goods. This is illustrated in Fig. 8.11. Suppose the budget line in the beginning is BL, given certain prices of goods X and Y and a certain income. Suppose price of X falls, the price of Y and income remaining unchanged. Now, with a lower price of X the consumer will be able to purchase more quantity of X than before with his given income. Let at the lower price of X, the given income purchases OL' of X which is greater than OL. Since price of Y remains the same, there can be no change in the quantity purchased of good Y with the same given income and as a result there will be no shift in the point B. Thus, with the fall in price of good X, the consumer's money income and the price of Y remaining constant, the budget line will shift to the right to the new position *BL'*.

Now, what will happen to the budget line (initial budget line *BL*) if price of good *X* rises, the price of good *Y* and income remaining unaltered. With higher price of good *X*, the consumer can purchase smaller quantity of *X*, say *OL''* than before. Thus, with the rise in price of *X* the budget line will shift to the left to the new position *BL''*.

Figure 8.12 shows the changes in the budget line when price of good *Y* falls or rises, with the price of *X* and income remaining the same. In this the initial budget line is *BL*. With fall in price of good *Y*, other things remaining unchanged, the consumer could buy more of *Y* with the given money income and therefore budget line will shift above to *LB'*. Similarly, with the rise in price of *Y*, other things being constant, the budget line will shift below to *LB''*.

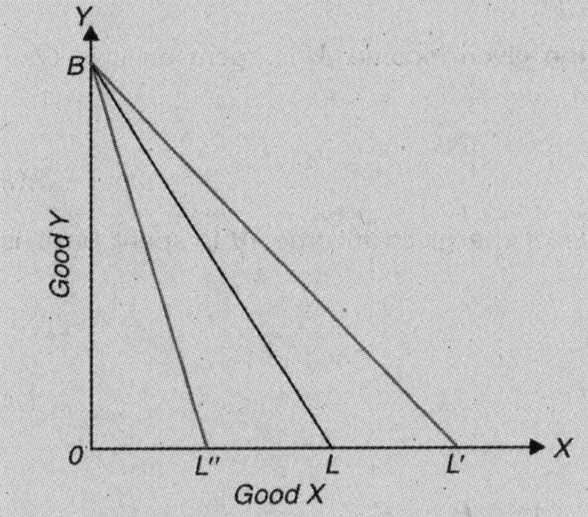

Fig. 8.11. *Changes in Budget Line as a Result of Changes of in Price of Good X*

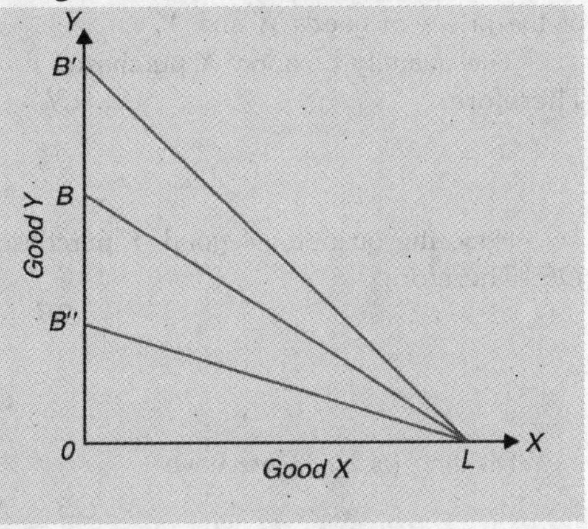

Fig. 8.12. *Changes in Budget Line as a Result Changes in Price of Good Y*

Changes in Income and Shifts in Budget line

Now, the question is what happens to the budget line if income changes, while the prices of goods remain the same. The effect of changes in income on the budget line is shown in Fig. 8.13. Let *BL* be the initial budget line, given certain prices of goods and income. If consumer's income increases while prices of both goods *X* and *Y* remain unaltered, the price line shifts upward (say, to *B'L'*) and is parallel to the original budget line *BL*. This is because with the increased income the consumer is able to purchase proportionately larger quantity of good *X* than before if whole of the income is spent on *X*, and proportionately greater quantity of good Y than before if whole of the income is spent on *Y*. On the other hand, if income of the consumer decreases, prices of both goods *X* and *Y* remaining unchanged, the budget line shifts downward (say, to B''L'') but remains parallel to the original price line *BL*. This is because a lower income will purchase a proportionately smaller quantity of good *X* if the whole of the income is spent on *X* and proportionately smaller quantity of good *Y* if the whole of the income is spent on *Y*.

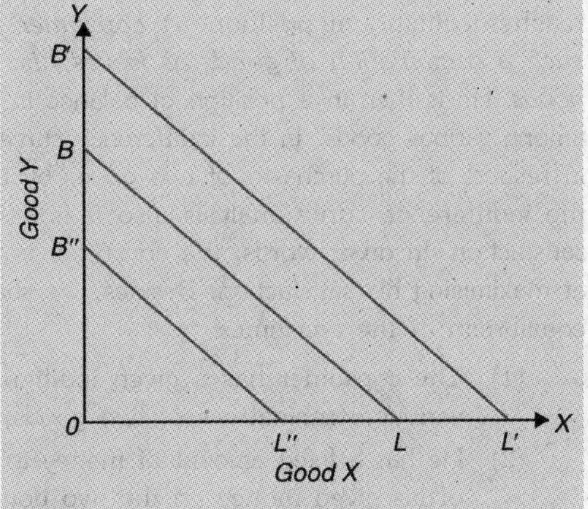

Fig. 8.13. *Shifts in Budget Line as a Result of Changes in Income*

It is clear from above that the budget line

will change if either the prices of goods change or the income of the consumer changes. Thus, the two determinants of the budget line are : *(a) the prices of goods, and (b) the consumer 's income to be spent on the goods.*

Slope of the Budget Line and Prices of Two Goods

It is also important to remember that the *slope* of the budget line is equal to the ratio of the prices of two goods. This can be proved with the aid of Fig. 8.9. Suppose the given income of the consumer is M and the given prices of goods X and Y are P_x and P_y respectively. The slope of the budget line BL is $\frac{OB}{OL}$. We intend to prove that this slope is equal to the ratio of the prices of goods X and Y.

The quantity of good X purchased if whole of the given income M is spent on it is OL. Therefore,

$$OL \quad P_x = M$$

$$OL = \frac{M}{P_x} \qquad \ldots(i)$$

Now, the quantity of good Y purchased if whole of the given income M is spent on it is OB. Therefore,

$$OB \quad P_y = M$$

$$OB = \frac{M}{P_y} \qquad \ldots(ii)$$

Dividing (*ii*) by (*i*) we have

$$\frac{OB}{OL} = \frac{M}{P_y} \qquad \frac{M}{P_x} = \frac{M}{P_y} \times \frac{P_x}{M} = \frac{P_x}{P_y}$$

$$\text{Thus, slope of budget line } = \frac{OB}{OL} = \frac{P_x}{P_y}$$

It is thus proved that *the slope of the budget line BL is equal to the ratio of prices of two goods.*

CONSUMER'S EQUILIBRIUM : MAXIMISING SATISFACTION

We are now in a position to explain with the help of indifference curves how a consumer reaches equilibrium position. *A consumer is said to be in equilibrium when he is buying such a combination of goods as leaves him with no tendency to rearrange his purchases of goods.* He is then in a position of balance in regard to the allocation of his money expenditure among various goods. In the indifference curve technique the consumer's equilibrium is discussed in respect of the purchases of two goods by the consumer. As in the cardinal utility analysis, in the indifference curve analysis also it is assumed that the consumer tries to maximise his satisfaction. In other words, the consumer is assumed to be rational in the sense that he aims at maximising his satisfaction. Besides, we shall make the following assumptions to explain the equilibrium of the consumer:

(1) The consumer has a given indifference map exhibiting his scale of preferences for various combinations of two goods, X and Y.

(2) He has a fixed amount of money to spend on the two goods. He has to spend whole of his given money on the two goods.

(3) Prices of the goods are given and constant for him. He cannot influence the prices of the goods by buying more or less of them.

(4) Goods are homogeneous and divisible.

To show which combination of two goods, X and Y, the consumer will decide to buy and will be in equilibrium position, his indifference map and budget line are brought together. As seen above, while indifference map portrays consumer's scale of preferences between various possible combinations of two goods, the budget line shows the various combinations which he can afford to buy with his given money income and given prices of the two goods. Consider Fig. 8.14 in which we depict consumer's indifference map together with the budget line *BL*. Good X is measured on the X-axis and good Y is measured on the X-axis. With a given money to be spent and given prices of the two goods, the consumer can buy any combination of the goods which lies on the budget line *BL*. Every combination on the budget line *BL* costs him the same amount of money. In order to maximise his satisfaction the consumer will try to reach the highest possible indifference curve which he could with a given expenditure of money and given prices of the two goods. Budget constraint forces the consumer to remain on the given budget line, that is, to choose a combination from among only those which lie on the given budget line.

It will be seen from Fig. 8.14 that the various combinations of the two goods lying on the budget line *BL* and which therefore the consumer can afford to buy do not lie on the same indifference curve; they lie on different indifference curves. The consumer will choose that combination on the budget line *BL* which lies on the highest possible indifference curve. The highest indifference curve to which the consumer can reach is the indifference curve to which the budget line *BL* is tangent. Any other possible combination of the two goods either would lie on a lower indifference curve and thus yield less satisfaction or would be unattainable.

In Fig. 8.14 budget line *BL* is tangent to indifference curve IC_3 at point *Q*. Since indifference curves are convex to the origin, all other points on the budget line *BL*, above or below the point *Q*, would lie on lower indifference curves. Take point *R* which also lies on the budget line *BL* and which the consumer can afford to buy. Combination of goods represented by *R* costs him the same as the combination *Q*. But, as is evident, *R* lies on the lower indifference curve IC_1 and will therefore yield less satisfaction than *Q*. Likewise, point *S* also lies on the budget line *BL* but will be rejected in favour of *Q* since *S* lies on the indifference curve IC_2 which is also lower than IC_3 on which *Q* lies. Similarly, *Q* will be preferred to all other points on the budget line *BL* which lies to the right of *Q* on the budget line, such as *T* and *H*. It is thus clear that of all possible combinations lying on budget line *BL*, combination *Q* lies on the highest possible indifference curve IC_3 which yields the consumer maximum possible satisfaction. Of course, combinations lying on indifference curves IC_4 and IC_5 will give greater satisfaction to the consumer than *Q*, but they are unattainable with the given money income and the given prices of the goods as represented by the budget line *BL*. It is therefore concluded that with the given money expenditure and the given prices of the goods as shown by *BL* the consumer will obtain maximum possible satisfaction

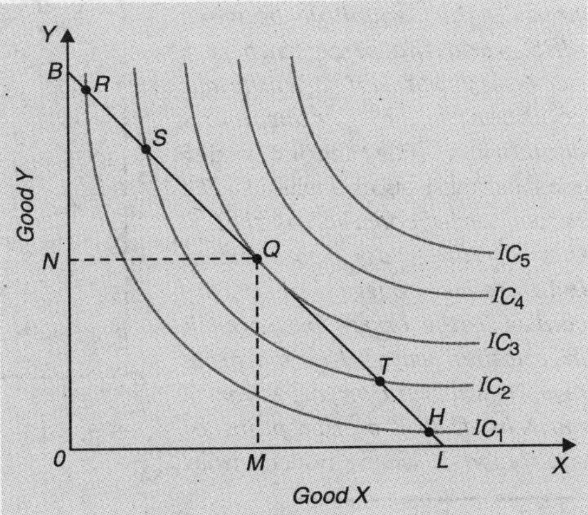

Fig. 8.14. *Consumer's Equilibrium*

and will therefore be in equilibrium position at point *Q* at which the budget line *BL* is tangent to the indifference curve IC_3. In this equilibrium position at *Q* the consumer will buy *OM* amount of good *X* and *ON* amount of good *Y*.

At the tangency point *Q*, the slopes of the budget line *BL* and indifference curve IC_3 are equal. Slope of the indifference curve shows the marginal rate of substitution of *X* for *Y* (MRS_{xy}), while the slope of the budget line indicates the ratio between the prices of two goods P_x/P_y. Thus, at the equilibrium point *Q*.

$$MRS_{xy} = \frac{\text{Price of good } X}{\text{Price of good } Y} = \frac{P_x}{P_y}$$

When the marginal rate of substitution of *X* for *Y* (MRS_{xy}) is greater or less than the price ratio between the two goods, it is advantageous for the consumer to substitute one good for the other. Thus, at points *R* and *S* in Fig. 8.14, marginal rates of substitution (MRS_{xy}) are greater than the given price ratio[2], the consumer will substitute good *X* for good *Y* and will come down along the budget line *BL*. He will continue to do so until the marginal rate of substitution becomes equal to the price ratio, that is, the given budget line *BL* becomes tangent to an indifference curve.

On the contrary, marginal rates of substitution at points *H* and *T* in Fig. 8.14 are less than the given price ratio. Therefore, it will be to the advantage of the consumer to substitute good *Y* for good *X* and accordingly move up the budget line *BL* until the MRS_{xy} rises so as to become equal to the given price ratio.

We can therefore express the condition for the equilibrium of the consumer by either saying that the given budget line must be tangent to the indifference curve, or the marginal rate of substitution of good X for good Y must be equal to the ratio between the prices of the two goods.

Second Order Condition for Consumer Equilibrium

The tangency between the given budget line and an indifference curve or, in other words, *the equality between MRS_{xy} and the price ratio is a necessary but not a sufficient condition of consumer's equilibrium*. The second order condition must also be fulfilled. *The second order condition is that at the point of equilibrium indifference curve must be convex to the origin, or to put it in another way, the marginal rate of substitution of X for Y must be falling at the point of equilibrium.* It will be noticed from

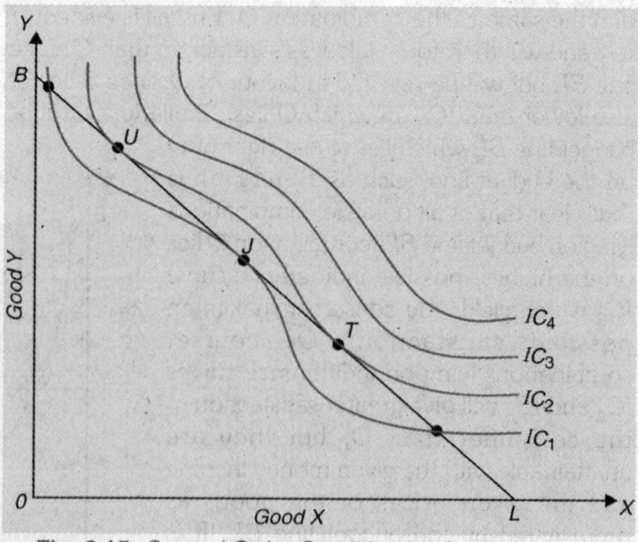

Fig. 8.15. *Second Order Condition for Consumer's Equilibrium*

2. Tangents drawn at point R and S on indifference curves IC_1 and IC_2 respectively in Fig. 8.14 have greater slopes than the given slope of the budget line *BL*.

Fig. 8.14 above that the indifference curve IC_3 is convex to the origin at Q, Thus at point Q both conditions of equilibrium are satisfied. Point Q in Fig. 8.14 is the optimum or best choice for the consumer and he will therefore be in stable equilibrium at Q.

But it may happen that while budget line is tangent to an indifference curve at a point but the indifference curve may be concave at that point. Take for instance, Fig. 8.15 where indifference curve IC_1 is concave to the origin around the point J. Budget line BL is tangent to the indifference curve IC_1 at point J and MRS_{xy} is equal to the price ratio, P_x/P_y. But J cannot be a position of equilibrium because consumer's satisfaction would not be maximum there. Indifference curve IC_1 being concave at the tangency point J, there may be some points on the given budget line BL such as U and T, which will lie on an indifference curve higher than IC_1. Thus the consumer by moving along the given budget line BL can go to points such as U and T and obtain greater satisfaction than at J. We therefore conclude that for the consumer to be in equilibrium, the following two conditions are required:

1. *A given budget line must be tangent to an indifference curve, or marginal rate of substitution of X for Y (MRS_{xy}) must be equal to the price ratio of the two goods* $\frac{P_x}{P_y}$.

2. *Indifference curve must be convex to the origin at the point of tangency.*

The above explanation of consumer's equilibrium in regard to the allocation of his money expenditure on the purchases of two goods has been made *entirely in terms of the consumer's relative preferences of the various combinations of two goods.* In this indifference curve analysis of consumer's equilibrium no use of cardinal utility concept has been made which implies that satisfaction or utility obtained from the goods is measurable in the quantitative sense.

INCOME EFFECT : INCOME CONSUMPTION CURVE

With a given money income to spend on goods, given prices of the two goods and given an indifference map (which portrays given tastes and preferences of the consumers), the consumer will be in equilibrium at a point in an indifference map. We are now interested in knowing how the consumer will react in regard to his purchases of the goods when his money income changes, prices of the goods and his tastes and preferences remaining unchanged. Income effect shows this reaction of the consumer. Thus, *the income effect means the change in consumer's purchases of the goods as a result of a change in his money income.* Income effect is illustrated in Fig. 8.16

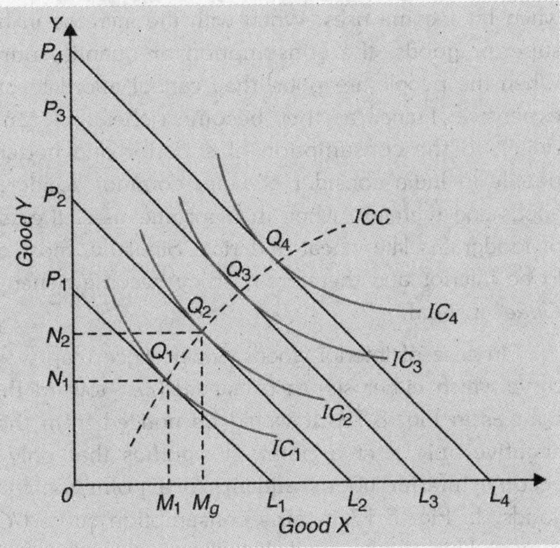

Fig. 8.16. *Income Consumption Curve: Income Effect*

With given prices and a given money income as indicated by the budget line P_1L_1, the consumer is initially in equilibrium at point Q_1 on the indifference curve IC_1 and is having OM_1 of X and ON_1 of Y. Now suppose that income of the consumer increases. With his increased income, he would be able to purchase larger quantities of both the goods. As a result, budget line will shift upward and will be parallel to the original budget line P_1L_1. Let us assume that the consumer's money income increases by such an amount that the new budget line is P_2L_2 (consumer's income has increased by L_1L_2 in terms of X or P_1P_2 in terms of Y). With budget line P_2L_2, the consumer is in equilibrium at point Q_2 on indifference curves IC_2 and is buying OM_2 of X and ON_2 of Y. Thus, as a result of the increase in his income the consumer buys more quantity of both the goods. Since he is on the higher indifference curve IC_2 he will be better off than before *i.e.*, his satisfaction will increase. If his income increases further so that the budget line shifts to P_3L_3, the consumer is in equilibrium at point Q_3 on indifference curve IC_3 and is having greater quantity of both the goods than at Q_2. Consequently, his satisfaction further increases. In Fig. 8.16 the consumer's equilibrium is shown at a still further higher level of income and it will be seen that the consumer is in equilibrium at Q_4 on indifference curves IC_4 when the budget line shifts to P_4L_4. As the consumer's income increases, he switches to higher indifference curves and as a consequence enjoys higher levels of satisfaction.

If now various points Q_1, Q_2, Q_3 and Q_4 showing consumer's equilibrium at various levels of income are joined together, we will get what is called *Income Consumption Curve* (*ICC*). Income consumption curve is thus the locus of equilibrium points at various levels of consumer's income. *Income consumption curve traces out the income effect on the quantity consumed of the goods.* Income effect can either be *positive or negative. Income effect for a good is said to be positive when with the increase in income of the consumer, his consumption of the good also increases.* This is the normal good case. When the income effect of both the goods represented on the two axes of the figure is positive, the income consumption curve (*ICC*) will slope upward to the right as in Fig. 8.16. Only the upward-sloping income consumption curve can show rising consumption of the two goods as income increases.

However, for some goods, income effect is negative. *Income effect for a good is said to be negative when with the increases in his income, the consumer reduces his consumption of the good.* Such goods for which income effect is negative are called *Inferior Goods.* This is because the goods whose consumption falls as income of the consumer rises are considered to be some way 'inferior' by the consumer and therefore he substitutes superior goods for them when his income rises. When with the increase in his income, the consumer begins to consume superior goods, the consumption or quantity purchased by him of the inferior goods falls. When the people are poor, they cannot afford to buy the superior goods which are often more expensive. Hence as they become richer and can afford to buy more expensive goods they switch to the consumption of superior and better quality goods. For instance, most of the people in India consider cheaper common foodgrains such as maize, jawar, bajra as inferior goods and therefore when their income rises, they shift to the consumption of superior varieties of foodgrains like wheat and rice. Similarly, most of the Indian people regard Vanaspati Ghee to be inferior and therefore as they become richer, they reduce its consumption and use '*Desi Ghee*' instead.

In case of inferior goods, indifference map would be such as to yield income consumption curve which either slopes backward (*i.e.*, toward the left) as in Fig. 8.17, or downward to the right as in Fig. 8.18. It would be noticed from these two figures that income effect becomes negative only after a point. It signifies that only at higher ranges of income, some goods become inferior goods and up to a point their consumption behaves like those of normal goods. In Fig. 8.17 income consumption curve (*ICC*) slopes backward *i.e.*, bends toward the Y-axis. This shows good X to be an inferior good, since beyond point Q_2, income effect is negative for good X and as a result its quantity demanded falls as income increases. In Fig.8.18

income consumption curve (*ICC*) slopes downward to the right beyond point Q_2 *i.e.*, bends towards the *X*-axis. This signifies that good *Y* is an inferior good because beyond point Q_2, income effect is negative for good *Y* and as a result its quantity demanded falls as income increases. It follows from above that the income consumption curve can have various possible shapes.

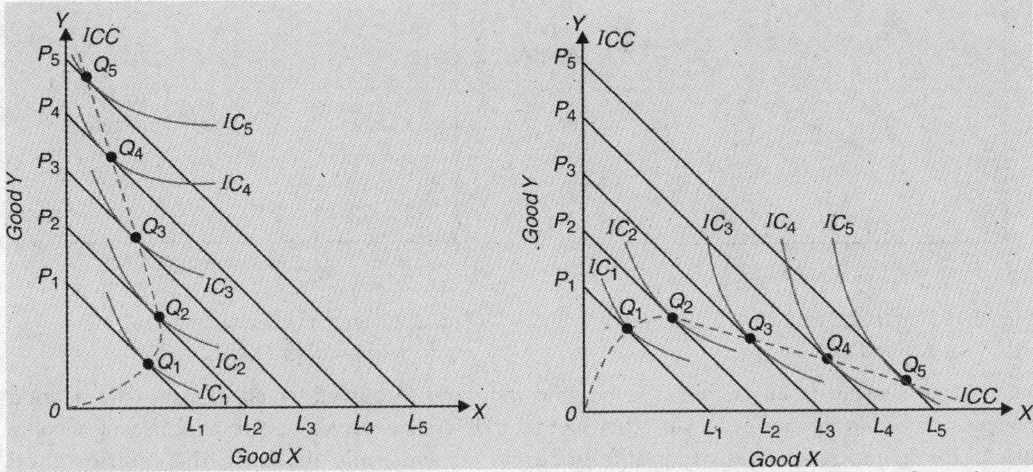

Fig. 8.17. *Income Consumption Curve in Case of Good X being Inferior Good*

Fig. 8.18. *Income Consumption Curve in Case of Good Y being Inferior Good*

But normal goods can be either necessities or luxuries depending upon whether the quantities purchased of the goods by the consumers increase less than or more than proportionately to the increases in income. If the quantity purchased of a commodity rises less than proportionately to the increases in consumer's income, the commodity is known as a *necessity*. On the other hand, if the quantity purchased of a commodity increases more than proportionately to the increases in income, it is called a *luxury*. In Fig. 8.19, the slope of income consumption curve ICC_1 is increasing which implies that the quantity purchased of the commodity *X* increases less than proportionately to the increases in consumer's income. Therefore, in this case of ICC_1, good *X* is a necessity and good *Y* is luxury. On the other hand, the slope of income consumption curve ICC_3 is decreasing which implies that the quantity purchased of good *X* increases more than proportionately to increases in income and therefore in this case good *X* is luxury and good *Y* is necessity. It will be seen from Fig. 8.19 that the income consumption curve ICC_2 is a *linear* curve passing through the origin which implies that the increases in the quantities purchased of both the goods are rising in proportion to the increase in income and therefore neither good is a luxury or a necessity.

If income effect is positive for both the goods *X* and *Y*, the income consumption curve will slope upward to the right as in Fig. 8.16. But upward-sloping income consumption curves to the right for various goods may be of different slopes as shown in Fig. 8.19 in which income consumption curves, with varying slopes, are all sloping upward and therefore indicate both goods to be normal goods having positive income effect. *If income effect for good X is negative, income consumption curve will slope backward to the left as ICC' in Fig. 8.20. If good Y happens to be an inferior good and income consumption curve will bend towards X-axis as shown by ICC' in Fig. 8.20. In Figs.* 8.19 and 8.20, various possible shapes which income consumption curve can take are shown *bereft of indifference curves and budget lines* which yield them. It may however be pointed out that given an indifference map and a set of budget lines there will be one income consumption curve.

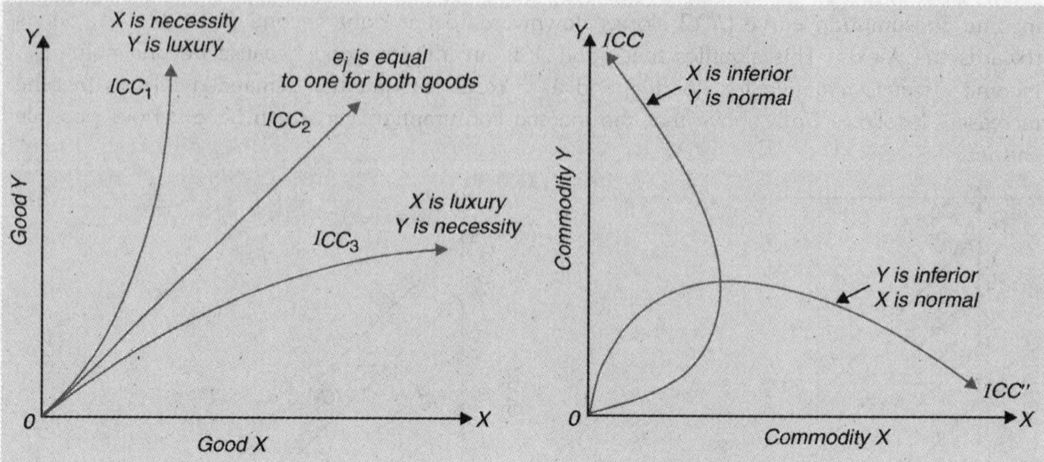

Fig. 8.19. *Income Consumption Curves of Normal Goods.*

Fig. 8.20. *Income Consumption Curves of Inferior Goods.*

A noteworthy point is that it is not the indifference curves which explain why a good happens to be an inferior good. In other words, indifference curves do not explain why income effect for a good is negative. Indifference curves can only illustrate the inferior-good phenomenon.

INCOME CONSUMPTION CURVE AND ENGEL CURVE

As seen above in indifference curve map, income consumption curve is the locus, of the equilibrium quantities consumed by an individual at different levels of his income. Thus, the income consumption curve (*ICC*) can be used to derive the relationship between the level of consumer's income and the quantity purchased of a commodity by him. A nineteenth century German statistician Ernet Engel (1821-1896) made an empirical study of family budgets to draw conclusions about the pattern of consumption expenditure, that is, expenditure on different goods and services by the households at different levels of income. The conslusions he arrived at are still believed to be generally valid. According to Engel's studies, as the income of a family increases, the proportion of its income spent on necessities such as food falls and that spent on luxuries (consisting of industrial goods and services) increases. In other words, the poor families spend relatively large proportion of their income on necessities, whereas rich families spend a relatively a large part of their income on luxuries. *This change in the pattern of consumption expenditure (that is, decline in the proportion of income spent on food and other necessities and increase in the proportion of income spent on luxuries) with the rise in income of the families has been called Engel's law.*

Though Engel dealt with the relationship between *income and expenditure* on different goods, in order to keep our analysis simple we will describe and explain the *relationship between income and quantities purchased of goods.* However, both types of relations will convey the same information about individual's consumption behaviour as in our analysis of Engel's curve, the prices of goods are held constant. *The curve showing the relationship between the levels of income and quantity purchased of particular commodities has therefore been called Engel curve.* In what follows we explain how an Engel curve is derived from income consumption curve. In our analysis of Engel curve we relate *quantity purchased* of a commodity, rather than *expenditure* on it, to the level of consumer's income.[3]

It is worth noting that like the demand curve depicting relationship between price and quantity purchased, other factors remaining the same, Engel curve shows relationship between income and quantity demanded, other influences on quantity purchased such as prices of goods, consumer preferences are assumed to be held constant.

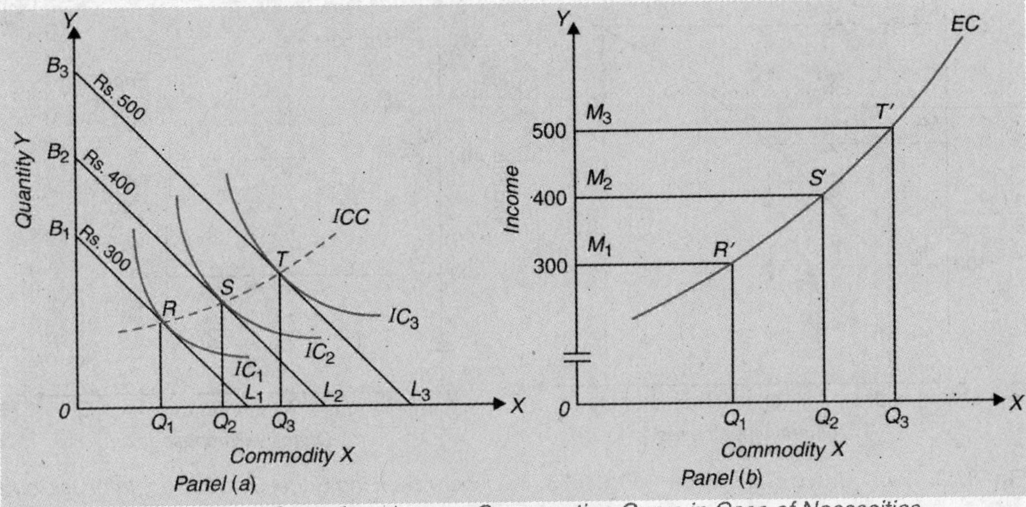

Fig. 8.21. *Deriving Engel Curve from Income Consumption Curve in Case of Necessities*

For deriving Engel curve from income consumption curve we plot level of income on the Y-axis and quantity purchased of a commodity on the *X*-axis. Consider panel (*a*) in Fig. 8.21. Given the indifference map representing the preferences of a consumer and the prices of two goods *X* and *Y*, *ICC* is the income consumption curve showing the equilibrium quantities purchased of commodities by the consumer as his income increases from Rs. 300 to Rs. 400 and to Rs. 500 per day. It will be seen from panel (*a*) of Fig. 8.21 that when income is Rs. 300, given prices of goods *X* and *Y*, the consumer is buying OQ_1 quantity of the commodity X.

In panel (*b*) of Fig. 8.21 in which level of income is represented on the vertical axis and quantity purchased of commodity *X* on the horizontal axis we directly plot quantity OQ_1 against income level of Rs. 300. As income increases to Rs. 400, prices of goods remaining constant, the budget line in panel (*a*) shifts outward to the left to the new position B_2L_2 with which consumer is in equilibrium at point *S* and the consumer buys OQ_2 quantity of good *X*. Thus, in panel (*b*) of Fig. 8.21 we plot quantity purchased OQ_2 of commodity *X* against income level of Rs. 400. Likewise, as income further rises to Rs. 500, budget line in panel (*a*) shifts to B_3L_3 and the consumer buys OQ_3 quantity of *X* in his new equilibrium position at *T*. Therefore, in panel (*b*) of Fig. 8.21. OQ_3 we plot OQ_3 against income of Rs. 500. Thus equilibrium points constituting the income consumption curve in consumer's indifference map have been transformed into Engel curve depicting quantity-income relationship. Each point of an Engel curve corresponds to a relevant point of income consumption curve. Thus *R*′ of the Engel curve *EC* corresponds to point *R* on the *ICC* curve. As seen from panel (*b*), *Engel curve for*

3. It may be noted that modern economists also study the relationship between expenditure and level of income and represent this by a curve which they call Engel Expenditure Curve. When they study the relationship between income and quantity purchased and derive a curve of this relationship, they call it simply Engel Curve as we are doing in the present chapter.

normal goods is upward-sloping which shows that as income increases, consumer buys more of a commodity.

The slope of Engel curve *EC* drawn in panel (*b*) of Figure 8.21 equals $\Delta M/\Delta Q$ where ΔM stands for chnage in income and ΔQ for change in quantity demanded of good *X* and has a positive sign. It is important to note that *the slope of the Engel curve in Fig.* 8.21 (*panel* (*b*)) *increases as income increases.* This indicates that with every equal increase in income, expansion in quantity purchased of the good successively declines. This upward-sloping Engel curve with increasing slope as income rises depicts the case of necessities, consumption of which increases relatively less as income rises. For instance, in Fig. 8.21 when income is initially Rs. 300 (= M_1) per week, the quantity purchased of the good *X* equals OQ_1 and when income rises by Rs. 100 to Rs. 400 (= M_2) per week he increases his consumption to OQ_2, that is, by quantity $Q_1 Q_2$. Now, when his income per week further increases by Rs. 100 to Rs. 500 per week, the quantity consumed increases to OQ_3, that is, by $Q_2 Q_3$ which is less than $Q_1 Q_2$. Thus, in Engel curve drawn in panel (*b*) of Fig. 8.21 quantity purchased of the commodity increases with the increase in income but at a *decreasing rate.* This shape of the Engel curve is obtained for *necessities.*

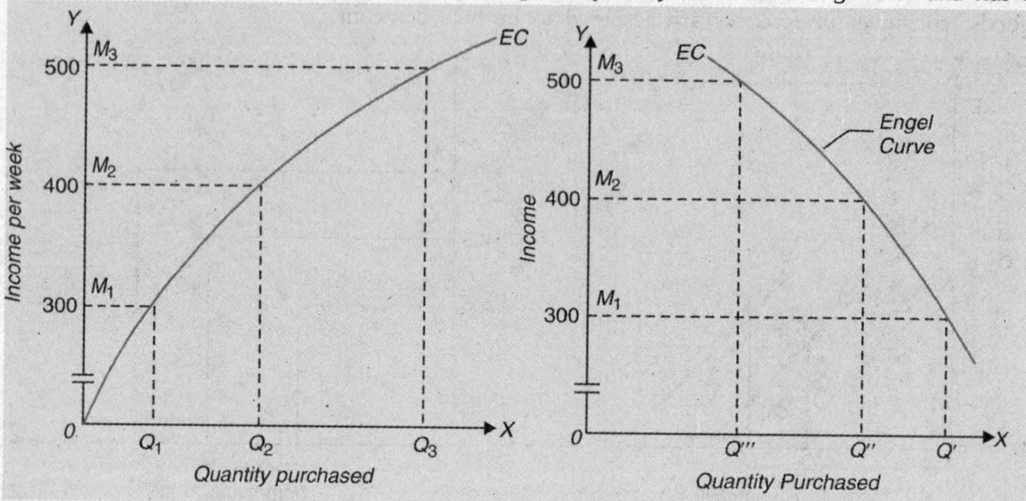

Fig. 8.22. *Engel Curve of a Luxury* **Fig. 8.23.** *Backward Bending Engel Curve of an Inferior Good*

The Engel curve drawn in Fig.8.22 is upward-sloping but is concave. This implies that slope of the Engel curve ($\Delta M/\Delta Q$) is declining with the increase in income. That is, in the Engel curve of a commodity depicted in Fig. 8.22 the equal increments in income result in successively larger increases in the quantity purchased of the commodity. Thus, in Fig. 8.22 at income of Rs. 300 the consumer purchases OQ_1 quantity of a commodity. The increase in income by Rs. 100 to Rs. 400 results in

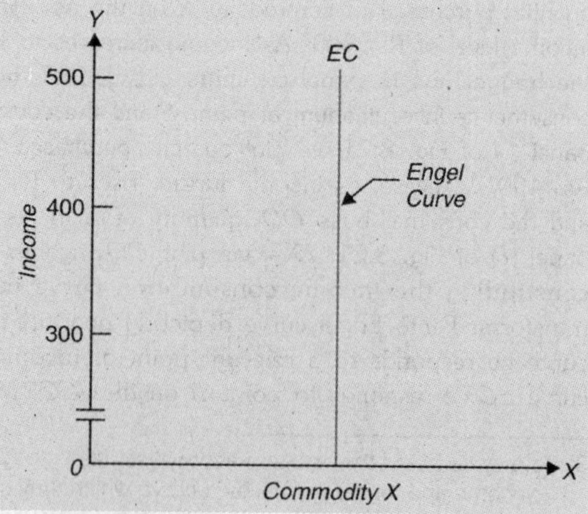

Fig. 8.24. *Engel Curve of a Neutral Good*

increase in quantity purchased of the commodity equal to Q_1Q_2. With the further increase in income by the same amount of Rs. 100 to Rs. 500, the quantity purchased increases by Q_2Q_3 which is much larger than Q_1Q_2. This implies that *as a consumer becomes richer he purchases relatively more of the commodity. Such commodities are called luxuries.* Example of luxuries are air travel, luxury cars, costly woollen suits, air conditioners, costly fruits, etc.

In case of *inferior goods*, consumption of the commodity declines as income creases. Engel curve of an inferior good is drawn in Figure 8.23 which is backward bending indicating a fall in the quantity purchased of the good as income increases.

An extreme case of Engel curve is *a vertical straight* line as drawn in Fig. 8.24. This represents the case of a *neutral* commodity which is quite unresponsive to the increase in income. The Engel curve of the shape of a vertical straight line shows that a person goes on consuming the same amount of a commodity whatever the level of his income. For example, the quantity of common salt purchased by a family remains the same, determined as it is by food habits, with the increase in their income.

SUBSTITUTION EFFECT

We have explained above the effect of changes in income on purchases or consumption of a good. Another important factor responsible for the changes in consumption of a good is the substitution effect. Whereas the income effect shows the change in the quantity purchased of a good by a consumer as a result of change in his income, prices of goods remaining constant, *substitution effect means the change in the quantity purchased of a good as a consequence of a change in its relative price alone, real income or level of satisfaction remaining constant.* When the price of a good changes, the real income or purchasing power of a consumer also changes. To keep the real income of the consumer constant so that the effect due to a change in the relative price alone may be known, price change is compensated by a simultaneous change in income. For example, when price of a good, say *X*, falls, real income of the consumer would increase. In order to find out the substitution effect *i.e.*, change in the quantity of *X* purchased which has come about due to the change only in its relative price, the consumer's money income must be reduced by an amount that cancels out the gain in real income that results from the decrease in price. Now, two slightly different concepts of substitution effect have been developed; one by J.R. Hicks and the other by E. Slutsky. These two concepts of substitution effect have been named after their authors. Thus, the substitution effect which is propounded by Hicks and Allen is called the *Hicksian Substitution Effect* and that developed by E. Slutsky is known as *Slutsky Substitution Effect*. The two concepts differ in regard to the magnitude of the change in money income which should be effected so as to neutralise the change in real income of the consumer which results from a change in the price. We shall explain here the Hicksian substitution effect.

In the Hicksian substitution effect price change is accompained by a so much change in money income that the consumer is neither better off nor worse off than before. In other words, money income of the consumer is changed by an amount which keeps the consumer on the same indifference curve on which he was before the change in the price. Thus the Hicksian substitution effect takes place on the same indifference curve. *The amount by which the money income of the consumer is changed so that the consumer is neither better off nor worse off than before is called compensating variation in income.* In other words, compensating variation in income *is a change in the income of the consumer which is just sufficient to compensate the consumer for a change in the price of a good.*

Thus, in the Hicksian type of substitution effect, income is changed by the magnitude of the *compensating variation in income.* Hicksian substitution effect is illustrated in Fig. 8.25. With a given money income and given prices of the two goods as represented by the budget line *PL*, the consumer is in equilibrium at point *Q* on the indifference curve *IC* and is pruchasing *OM* of good *X* and *ON* of good *Y*. Suppose that the price of good *X* falls (price of *Y* remaining unchanged) so that the budget line now shifts to *PL′*. With the fall in price of *X* the consumer's real income or purchasing power would increase. In order to find out the substitution effect, this gain in real income should be wiped out by reducing the money income of the consumer by such an amount that forces him to remain on the same indifference curve *IC* on which he was before the change in price of the good *X*. When some money is taken away from the consumer to cancel out the gain in real income, then the budget line which shifted to position *PL′* will now shift downward but will be parallel to *PL′*. In Fig.8.25 a budget line *AB* parallel to *PL′* has been drawn at such a distance from *PL′* that it touches the indifference curve *IC*. It means that reduction of consumer's income by the amount *PA* (in terms of *Y*) or *L′B* (in terms of *X*) has been made so as to keep him on the same indifference curve. *PA* or *L′B* is thus just sufficient to cancel out the gain in the real income which occurred due to the fall in the price of *X*. *PA* or *L′B* is therefore compensating variation in income.

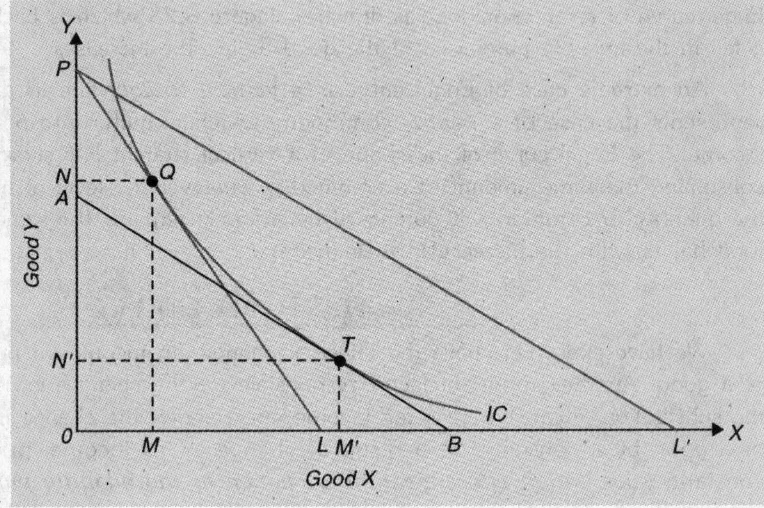

Fig. 8.25. *Hicksian Substitution Effect*

Now, budget line *AB* represents the new relative prices of goods *X* and *Y* since it is parallel to the budget line *PL′* which was obtained when price of good *X* had fallen. In comparison to the budget line *PL*, *X* is now relatively cheaper. The consumer would therefore rearrange his purchases of *X* and *Y* and will substitute *X* for *Y*. That is, since *X* is now relatively cheaper and *Y* is now relatively dearer than before, he will buy more of *X* and less of *Y*. It will be seen form Fig. 8.25 that budget line *AB* represents the changed relative prices but a lower money income than that of *PL*, since consumer's income has been reduced by compen-sating variation in income.

It will seen from Fig. 8.25 that with budget line *AB* the consumer is in equilibrium at point *T* and is now buying *OM* of *X* and *ON* of *Y*. Thus in order to buy *X* more he moves on the same indifference curve *IC* from point *Q* to point *T*. This increase in the quantity purchased of good *X* by *MM′* and the decrease in the quantity purchased of good *Y* by *NN′* is due to the change only in the relative prices of goods *X* and *Y*, since effect due to the gain in real income has been wiped out by making a simultaneous reduction in consumer's income. Therefore, movement from *Q* to *T* represents the substitution effect. Substitution effect on good *X* is the increase in its quantity purchased by *MM′* and substitution effect on *Y* is the fall in its quantity purchased by *NN′*. It is thus clear that as a result of the Hicksian substitution effect the consumer remains on the same indifference curve; he is however in equilibrium at a different point from that at which he was before the change in price of good X. *The less the convexity of the indifference curve, the greater will be the substitution effect.* As is known, the convexity of indifference curve is less in the case of those goods which are good substitutes. It is thus clear that the substitution effect in case of good substitutes will be large.

It is thus clear that a *fall* in relative price of a commodity always leads to the *increase* in its quantity demanded due to the substitution effect, the consumer's satisfaction or indifference curve remaining the same. Thus the *substitution effect is always negative*. The negative substitution effect implies that the relative price of a commodity and its quantity demanded change in opposite direction, that is, the *decline* in relative price of a commodity always causes *increase* in its quantity demanded. It is this negative substitution effect which lies at the root of the famous law of demand stating inverse relationship between price and quantity demanded.

PRICE EFFECT: PRICE CONSUMPTION CURVE

We will now explain how the consumer reacts to charges in the price of a good, his money income, tastes and prices of other goods remaining the same. Price effect shows this reaction of the consumer and measures the full effect of the change in the price of a good on the quantity purchased since no compensating variation in income is made in this case. When the price of a good charges, the consumer would be either better off or worse off than before,

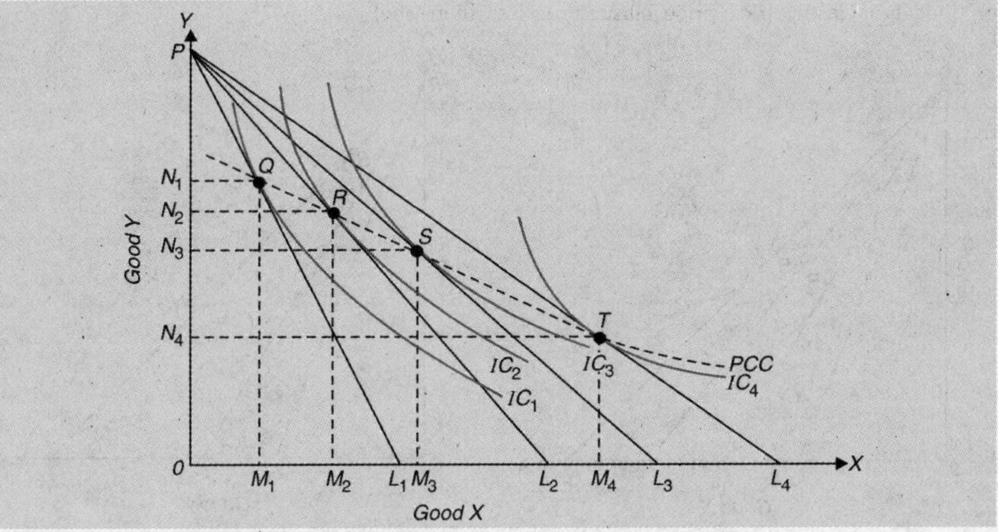

Fig. 8.26. *Downward-Sloping Price Consumption Curve*

depending upon whether the price falls or rises. In other words, as a result of change in price of a good, his equilibrium position would lie at a higher indifference curve in case of the fall in price and at a lower indifference curve in case of the rise in price.

Price effect is shown in Fig. 8.26. With given prices of goods X and Y, and a given money income as represented by the budget line PL_1, the consumer is in equilibrium at Q on indifference curve IC_1. In this equilibrium position at Q, he is buying OM_1 of X and ON_1 of Y. Let price of good X fall, price of Y and his money income remaining unchanged. As a result of this price change, budget line shifts to the position PL_2. The consumer is now in equilibrium at R on a higher indifference curve IC_2 and is buying OM_2 of X and ON_2 of Y. He has thus become better off, that is, his level of satisfaction has increased as a consequence of the fall in the price of good X. Suppose that price of X further falls so that PL_3 is now the relevant budget line. With budget line PL_3 the consumer is in equilibrium at S on indifference curve IC_3 where he has OM_3 of X and ON_3 of Y. If price of good X falls still further so that budget line now takes the position of PL_4, the consumer now attains equilibrium at T on indifference curve IC_4 and has OM_4 of X and ON_4 of Y. When all the equilibrium points such as Q, R, S, and T are joined together, we get what is called *Price Consumption Curve (PCC). Price consumption curve traces out the price effect. It shows how the changes in price of good X will affect the consumer's purchases of X, price of Y, his tastes and money income remaining unaltered,*

In Fig. 8.26 price consumption curve (*PCC*) is sloping downward. Downward-sloping price consumption curve for good X means that as price of good X falls, the consumer purchases a larger quantity of good X and a smaller quantity of good Y. This is quite evident from Fig. 8.26. As we shall discuss in detail in the chapter concerning elasticity of demand, we obtain downward-sloping price consumption curve for good X when demand for it is elastic (*i.e.*, price elasticity is greater than one). But downward sloping is one possible shape of price consumption curve. Price consumption curve can have other shapes also. In Fig. 8.27 upward-sloping price consumption curve is shown. *Upward-sloping price consumption curve for X means that when the price of good X falls, the quantity demanded of both goods X and Y rises.* We obtain the upward-sloping price consumption curve for good X when the demand for good is inelastic, (*i.e.*, price elasticity is less than one).

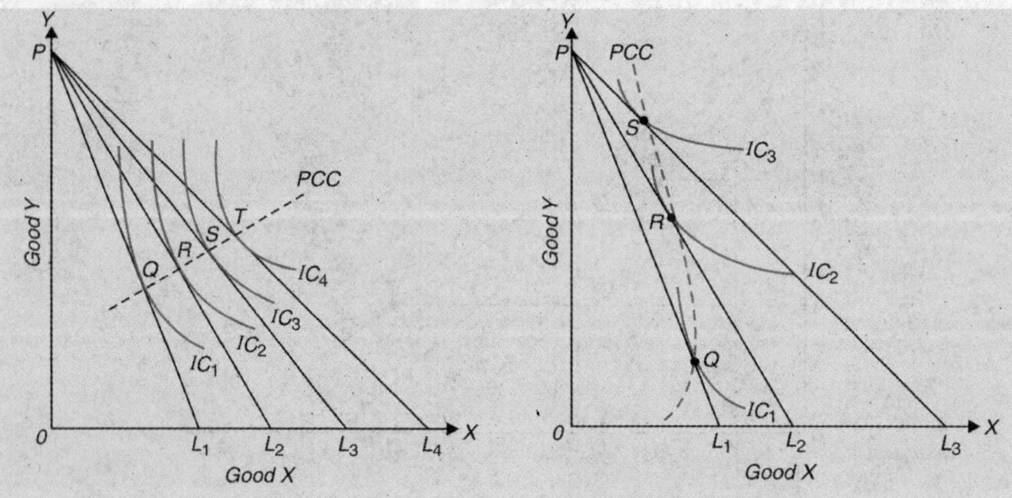

Fig. 8.27. *Upward-Sloping Price Consumption Curve*

Fig. 8.28. *Backward-Sloping Price Consumption Curve in Case of Giffen Goods*

Price consumption curve can also have a backward-sloping shape, which is depicted in Fig. 8.28. *Backward-sloping price consumption curve for good X indicates that when price of X falls, after a point smaller quantity of it is demanded or purchased.* We shall see later in this chapter that this is true in case of exceptional type of goods called Giffen Goods.

Price consumption curve for a good can take horizontal shape too. It means that when the price of the good X declines, its quantity purchased rises propor-tionately but quantity purchased of good Y remains the same. Horizontal price consumption curve is shown in Fig. 8.29. We obtain horizontal price consumption curve of good X when the price elasticity of demand for good X is equal to unity.

But it is rarely found that price consumption curve slopes downward throughout or slopes upward throughout or slopes backward throughout. More generally, price consumption curve has different slopes at different price ranges. At higher price levels it generally slopes downward, and it may then have a horizontal shape for some price ranges but ultimately it will be sloping upward. For some price ranges it can be backward sloping as in case of Giffen goods. A price consumption curve which has different shapes or slopes at different price ranges is drawn in Fig. 8.30. Such a type of price consumption curve means that price elasticity of demand varies at different price ranges.

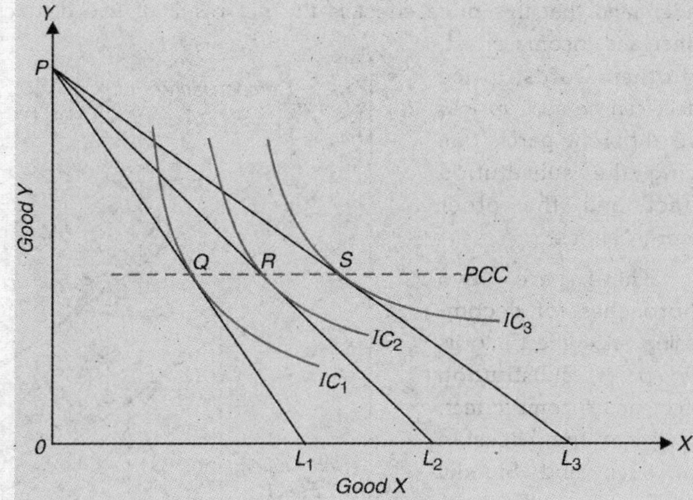

Fig.8.29. *Horizontal Price Consumption Curve.*

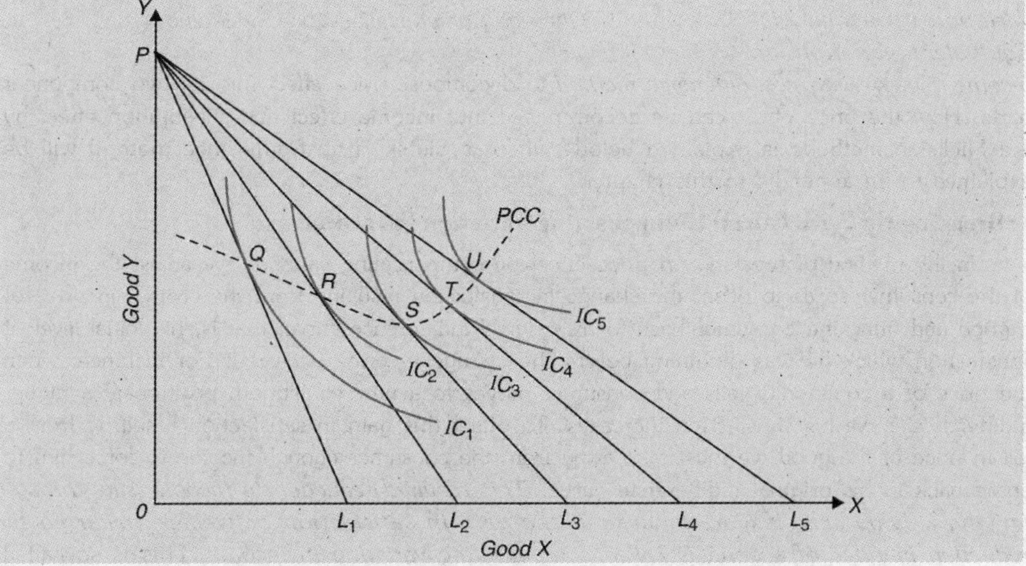

Fig. 8.30. *Price Consumption Curve with Varying Slopes*

BREAKING UP PRICE EFFECT INTO INCOME AND SUBSTITUTION EFFECTS

It has been explained above that as price of a good X falls, other things remaining the same, consumer would move to a new equilibrium position at a higher indifference curve and would buy more of good X at the lower price unless it is a Giffen good. Thus, in the Fig. 8.31 the consumer who is initially in equilibrium at Q on indifference curve IC_1 moves to the point R on indifference curve IC_2 when the price of good X falls and the budget line twists from PL_1 to PL_2. The movement from Q to R represents the price effect. It is now highly important to understand that this price effect is the net result of two distinct forces, namely, substitution effect and income effect. In other words, price effect can be split up into two different parts, one being the substitution effect and the other income effect.

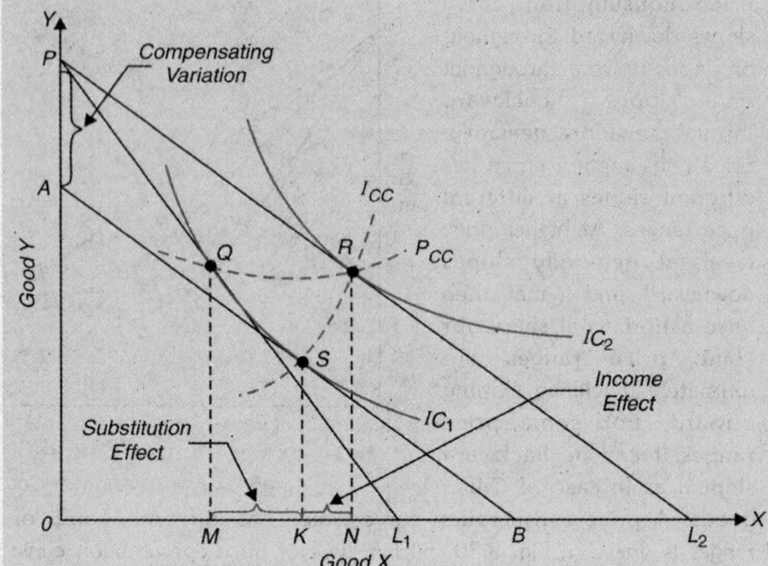

Fig. 8.31. *Price Effect Split up into Substitution and Income Effects through Compensating Variation Method*

There are two approaches for decomposing price effect into its two parts, substitution effect and income effect. They are the Hicksian approach and Slutsky approach. Further, Hicksian approach uses two methods of splitting the price effect, namely (*i*) *Compensating variation in income* (*ii*) *Equivalent variation in income.* Slutsky uses *cost-difference method* to decompose price effect into its two component parts. How the price effect can be decom-posed into income effect and substitution effect by the Hicksian methods is explained below, whereas Slutsky's cost-difference method will be explained in an appendix to this chapter.

1. Breaking Up Price Effect: Compensating Variation in Income

In the method of breaking up price effect by compensating variation we adjust the income of the consumer so as to offset the change in satisfaction resulting from the change in price of a good and bring the consumer back to his original indifference curve, that is, his initial level of satisfaction which he was obtaining before the change in price occurred. For instance, when the price of a commodity falls and consumer moves to a new equilibrium position at a higher indifference curve his satisfaction increases. To offset this gain in satisfaction resulting from a fall in price of the good we must take away from the consumer enough income to force him to come back to his original indifference curve. *This required reduction in income* (*say, through levying a lump sum tax*) *to cancel out the gain in satisfaction or welfare occurred by reduction in price of a good is called compensating variation in income.* This is so called because it compensates (in a negative way) for the gain in satisfaction resulting from a price reduction of the commodity. How the price effect is broken up into substitution effect and income effect through the method of compensating variation in income is illustrated in Fig 8.31.

When price of good X falls and as a result budget line shifts to PL_2, the real income of the consumer rises, *i.e.*, he can buy more of both the goods with his given money income. That is, price reduction enlarges consumer's opportunity set of the two goods. With the new budget line PL_2 he is in equilibrium at point R on a higher indifference curve IC_2 and thus gains in satisfaction as a result of fall in price of good X. Now, if his money income is reduced by the compensating variation in income so that he is forced to come back to the original indifference curve IC_1 he would buy more of X since X has now become relatively cheaper than before. In Fig. 8.31 as result of the fall in price of X, price line switches to PL_2. Now, with the reduction in income by compensating variation, budget line shifts to AB which has been drawn parallel to PL_2 so that it just touches the indifference curve IC_1 where he was before the fall in price of X. Since the price line AB has got the same slope as PL_2, it represents the changed relative prices with X being relatively cheaper than before. Now, X being relatively cheaper than before, the consumer in order to maximise his satisfaction in the new price-income situation substitutes X for Y. Thus, when the consumer's money income is reduced by the compensating variation in income (which is equal to PA in terms of Y or L_2B in terms of X), the consumer moves along the same indifference curve IC_1 and substitutes X for Y. With price line AB, he is in equilibrium at S on indifference curve IC_1 and is buying MK more of X in place of Y. This movement from Q to S on the same indifference curve IC_1 represents the substitution effect since it occurs due to the change in relative prices alone, real income remaining constant.

If the amount of money income which was taken away from him is now given back to him, he would move from S on indifference curve IC_1 to R on a higher indifference curve IC_2. The movement from S on a lower in difference curve to R on a higher in difference curve is the result of income effect. Thus the movement form Q to R due to price effect can be regarded as having been taken place into two steps : first from Q to S as a result of substitution effect and second from S to R as a result of income effect. In is thus mainfest that price effect is the combined result of a substitution effect and an income effect.

In Fig. 8.31 me various effects on the purchases of good X are:

$$\text{Price effect} = MN$$

$$\text{Substitution effect} = MK$$

$$\text{Income effect} = KN$$

$$MN = MK + KN$$

or

$$\text{Price effect} = \text{Substitution effect} + \text{Income effect}$$

From the above analysis, it is thus clear that price effect is the sum of income and substitution effects.

2. Breaking up Price Effect: Equivalent Variation in Income

As mentioned above, price effect can be split up into substitution and income effects through an alternative method of equivalent variation in income. The reduction in price of a commodity increases consumer's satisfaction as it enables him to reach a higher indifference curve. Now, the same increase in satisfaction can be achieved through bringing about an increase in his income, prices remaining constant. *The increase in income of the consumer, prices of goods remaining the same, so as to enable him to move to a higher subsequent indifference curve at which he in fact reaches with reduction in price of a good is called equivalent variation in income* because it represents the variation in income that is equivalent in terms of gain in satisfaction to a reduction in price of the good. Thus, in this equivalent income-variation method substitution effect is shown along the subsequent indifference curve rather than the original one. How this price effect is decomposed into income and substitution effects through equivalent variation in income is shown in Fig. 8.32.

When price of good X falls, the consumer can purchase more of both the goods, that is, the purchasing power of his given money income rises. It means that after the fall in price of X, if the consumer buys the same quantities of goods as before, then some amount of money will be left over. In other words, the fall in price of good X will release some amount of money. Money thus released can be spent on purchasing more of both the goods. It therefore follows that a change in price of the good produces an income effect. When the power to purchase goods rises due to the income effect of the price change, the consumer has to decide how this increase in his purchasing power is to be spread over the two goods he is buying. How he will spread the released purchasing power over the two goods depends upon the nature of his income consumption curve which in turn is determined by his preferences about the two goods.

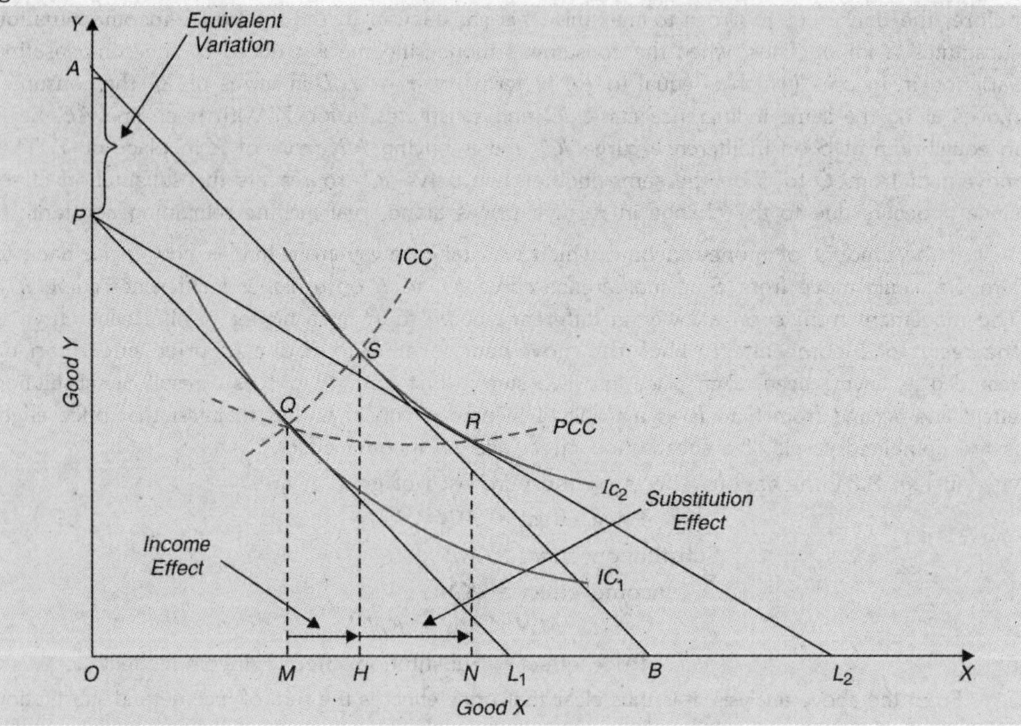

Fig. 8.32. *Price Effect Split Up into Income and Substitution Effects through Equivalent Variation Method*

From above it follows, that, as a result of the increase in his purchasing power (or real income) due to the fall in price, the consumer will move to a higher indifference curve and will become better off than before. It is as if price had remained the same but his money income was increased. In other words, a fall in price of good *X* does to the consumer what an equivalent rise in money income would have done to him. As a result of fall in price of *X*, the consumer can therefore be imagined as moving up to a higher indifference curve along the income consumption curve as if his money income had been increased, prices of *X* and *Y* remaining unchanged. Thus, a given change in price can be thought of as an equivalent to an appropriate change in income.

It will be seen from Fig. 8.32 that with price line PL_1, the consumer is in equilibrium at *Q* on indifference curve IC_1. Suppose price of good *X* falls, price of *Y* and his money income remaining unaltered, so that budget line is now PL_2. With budget line PL_2, he is in equilibrium at *R* on indifference curve IC_2. Now, a line *AB* is drawn parallel to PL_1 so that it touches the indifference curve IC_2 at *S*. It means that the increase in real income or purchasing power of the consumer as a result of the fall in price of *X* is equal to *PA* in terms of *Y* or L_1B in terms of *X*. Movement of the consumer from *Q* on indifference curve IC_1 to *S* on the higher indifference curve IC_2 along the income consumption curve is the result of income effect of the price change. But the consumer will not be finally in equilibrium at S. This is because now that X is relatively cheaper than Y, he will substitute X, which has become relatively cheaper, for good Y, which has become relatively dearer. It will be beneficial for the consumer to do so. Thus the consumer will move along the indifference curve IC_2 from S to R. This movement from S to R has taken place because of the change in relative prices alone and therefore represents substitution effect. Thus the price effect can be broken up into income and substitution effects, showing in this case substitution along the subsequent indifference curve. In Fig 8.32 the magnitudes of the various effects are :

Price effect = MN

Income effect = MH

Substitution effect = HN

In Fig. 8.32, $MN = MH + HN$

or Price effect = Income Effect + Substitution Effect

PRICE-DEMAND RELATIONSHIP: DERIVING LAW OF DEMAND

Indifference curve analysis with its technique of looking upon the price effect as a combination of income effect and substitution effect explains relationship between price and quantity demanded in a better and more analytical way. A distinct advantage of viewing the price effect as a sum of income effect and substitution effect is that through it the nature of response of quantity purchased to a change in the price of a good can be better and easily explained. In case of most of the goods, the income effect and substitution effect work in the same direction. But, in some cases, they may pull in different directions. The direction of substitution effect is quite certain. A *fall in the relative price* of a good always leads to the *increase in quantity demanded* of the good. In other words, substitution effect always induces the consumer to buy more of the cheaper good. But the direction of income effect is not so certain. With a rise in income, the individual will generally buy more of a good. But with the rise in income the individual will buy less of a good if it happens to be an inferior good for him since he will use better or superior substitutes in place of the inferior good when his income rises. Thus the income effect may be either positive or negative. For normal goods, the income effect is positive. Therefore, when price of a normal good falls and results in increase in the purchasing power, income effect will act in the same direction as the substitution effect, that is, both will work towards increasing the quantity demanded of the good whose price has fallen. For the inferior good in which case income effect is negative, income effect of the price change will work in opposite direction to the substitution effect. The net effect of the price change will then depend upon the relative strengths of the two effects. To sum up, price effect is composed of income effect and substitution effect and further that the direction in which quantity demanded will change as a result of the change in price will depend upon the direction and strength of the income effect on the one hand and strength of the substitution effect on the other.

Price Demand Relationship : Normal Goods

In order to understand the way in which price-demand relationship is established in indifference curve analysis, consider Fig 8.31. Given the price of two goods and his income represented by the budget line PL_1, the consumer will be in equilibrium at Q on indifference curve IC_1. Let us suppose that price of X falls, price of Y and his money income remaining unchanged so that budget line now shifts to PL_2. The consumer will now be in equilibrium at a point on the new budget line PL_2. If the equilibrium position on PL_2 lies to the right of Q

such as at *R* in Fig. 8.31, it will mean that the consumer buys more quantity of good *X* than at *Q*. Now, it can be proved that in case of normal goods the *new equilibrium point on budget line PL_2 will lie to the right of Q meaning thereby that the quantity demanded of the good X will increase as its price falls.*

As seen above, the direction and magnitude of the change in quantity demanded as a result of fall in price of a good depend upon the direction and strength of income effect on the one hand and substitution effect on the other. As for normal goods, the income effect is positive, it will work towards increasing the quantity demanded of good *X* when its price falls. The substitution effect which is always negative and operates so as to raise the quantity demanded of the good if its price falls and reduces the quantity demanded of the good if its price rises. Thus when both the income effect (when positive) and negative substitution effect work in the same direction, it will cause increase in the quantity purchased of good *X* whose price has fallen with the result that the new equilibrium point will lie to the right of the original equilibrium point *Q* such as point *R* in Fig. 8.31 above. Substitution effect causes *MK* increase in quantity demanded. Income effect which is positive here also leads to the increase in quantity demand by *KN*. Each effect therefore reinforces the other. As a result, the total effect of a fall in price of *X* from the level indicated by PL_1 to the level indicated by PL_2 is the rise in quantity demanded of good *X* from *OM* to *ON*, that is, quantity demanded increases by *MN* which is

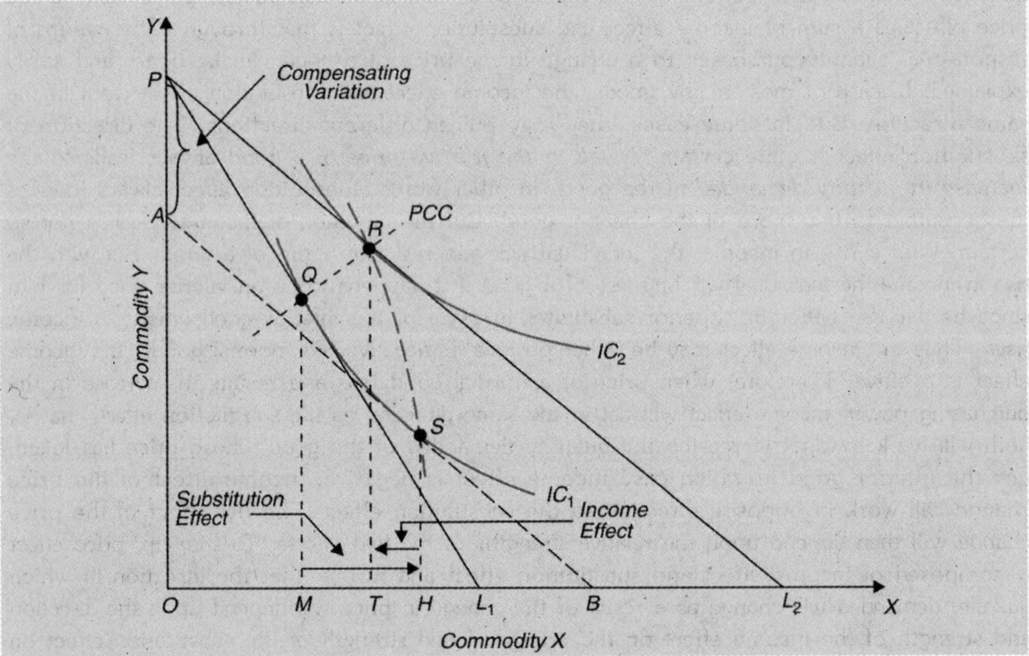

Fig. 8.33. *Price-Demand Relationship in case of an Inferior Good.*

equal to *MK* + *KN*. To sum up, *the income effect and substitution effect in case of normal goods work in the same direction and will lead to the increase in quantity demanded of the good whose price has fallen.* In other words, quantiy purchased of a normal good will vary inversely with its price as in its case income effect is positive.

Price-Demand Relationship : Inferior Goods. In case of inferior goods the income effect will work in opposite direction to the substitution effect. When price of an inferior good falls, its negative income effect will tend to reduce the quantity purchased, while the substitution effect will tend to increase the quantity purchased. But normally it happens that negative income effect of change in price is not large enough to outweigh the substitution effect. This is so because a consumer spends a very small proportion of his income on a single commodity and when price of a commodity falls, a very little income is released. In other words, income effect even when negative is generally too weak to outweigh the substitution effect. It follows therefore that as a result of fall in price of a good the substitution effect which always induces the consumer to buy more of the good whose price has fallen will usually outweigh the negative income effect. Thus even in most cases of inferior goods the net result of the fall in price will be increase in its quantity demanded. It is thus clear that in a majority of inferior goods quantity demanded of the good will vary inversely with price and the Marshallian law of demand will hold good.

The price-demand relationship in case of inferior goods having weaker income effect is illustrated in Figure 8.33. It will be seen from Fig. 8.33 that the fall in price of good *X* makes the consumer to shift from equilibrium at *Q* to a new equilibrium at *R*. As a result, quantity purchased of good *X* increases from *OM* to *OT*. But the income effect is negative and is equal to *HT*. If income effect alone was working, it would have caused the consumer to buy *HT* less of good *X*. But substituion effect is universally present and always induces the consumer to buy more of the relatively cheaper good. In Fig. 8.38 substitution effect is equal to *MH* and is greater than negative income effect *HT*. Therefore, the net effect of the fall in price of good X is the increase in quantity demanded by *MT*. Hence we conclude that *in case of inferior goods, quantity demanded varies inversely with price when negative income effect is weaker than the substitution effect.* In other words, even in case of inferior goods having weaker income effect, the demand curve will be downward sloping.

Price-Demand Relationship: Giffen Goods or Giffen Paradox. There is a third possibility. This is that there may be some inferior goods for which the negative income effect is strong or large enough to outweigh the substitution effect. In this case, quantity purchased of the good will fall as its price falls and quantity purchased of the good will rise as its price rises. In other words, in this case quantity purchased or demanded will vary directly with price. Now, the income effect can be substantial only when the consumer is spending a very large proportion of his income on the good in question so that when price of the good falls, a good amount of income is released. If that good happens to be inferior good, the income effect will be negative as well as strong and may outweigh

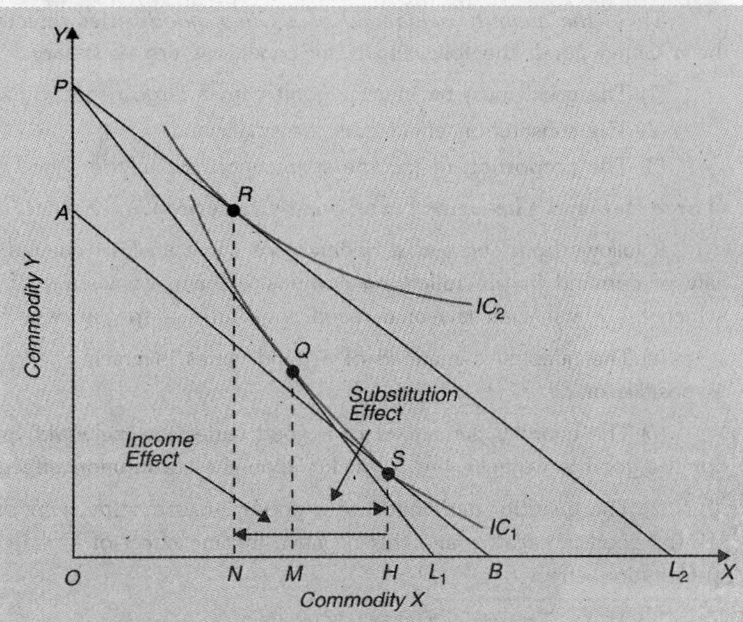

Fig. 8.34. *Price-Demand Relationship in Case of a Giffen Good*

the substitution effect so that with the fall in price, the consumer will buy less of the good. *Such an inferior good in which case the consumer reduces its consumption when its price falls and increases its consum-ption when its price rises is called a Giffen good* named after the British statistician, Sir Robert Giffen, who in the mid-nineteenth century is said to have claimed that when price of cheap common foodstuff like bread went up the people bought and consumed more bread. A rise in the price of bread caused such a large decline in the purchasing power of the poor people that they were forced to cut down the consumption of meat and other more expensive food. Since bread even when its price was higher than before was still the cheapest food article, people consumed more of it and not less when its price went up. Similarly, when price of an inferior good on which people spend a large proportion of their income falls, people will purchase less than before. This is because the fall in price of an inferior good on which they spend a very large portion of their income causes such a large increase in their purchasing power that creates a large negative income effect. They will therefore reduce the consumption of that good when its price falls since large negative income effect outweighs the substitution effect.

The price-demand relationship in case of a Giffen good is illustrated in Fig. 8.34. With a certain given price-income situation depicted by the budget line P_{L1}, the consumer is initially in equilibrium at Q on indifference curve IC_1. With a fall in price of the good, the consumer shifts to point R on indifference curve IC_2. It will be seen From Fig. 8.34 that with the fall in price and, as a result, the shift of the price line from PL_1 to PL_2 the consumer reduces his consumption of the good X from OM to ON. This is the net effect of the negative income effect which is here equal to HN which induces the consumer to buy less of good X and the substitution effect which is equal MH which induces the consumer to buy more of the good. Since the negative income effect HN is greater than the substitution effect MH, the net effect is the fall in quantity purchased of good X by MN with the fall in its price. Thus, *the quantity demanded of a Giffen good varies directly with price.* Therefore, if a demand curve showing price-demand relationship of a Giffen good is drawn, it will slope upward.

Thus, *the quantity demanded of a Giffen good* varies directly with price. For a good to be a Giffen good, the following three conditions are necessary:[4]

(1) The good must be inferior good with a large negative income effect;

(2) The substitution effect must be small; and

(3) The proportion of income spent upon the inferior good must be very large.

Three Demand Theorems Based on Indifference Curve Analysis

It follows from above that, indifference curve analysis enables us to derive a more general law of demand in the following composite form, consisting of three demand theorems to which the Marshallian law of demand constitutes a special case.[5]

(*a*) The quantity demanded of a good varies inversely with price when the income effect is positive or nil.

(*b*) The quantity demanded of a good varies inversely with price when the income effect for the good is negative but is weaker than the substitution effect.

(*c*) The quantity demanded of a good *varies directly with price when the income effect for* the good is negative and this negative income effect of a change in price is larger than the substitution effect.

4. J.R. Hicks, *A Revision of Demand Theory*, p. 66.
5. Tapas Majumdar, *Measurement of Utility*, pp. 74-75.

In the case, (*a*) and (*b*) the Marshallian law of demand holds good and we get a downward sloping demand curve. The case (*a*) applies to normal goods in which income effect and substitution effect work *in the same direction.* The case (*b*) applies to inferior goods which are not Giffen goods. When the third case occurs, we get a Giffen good of positively sloping demand curve. Marshallian law of demand does not hold true in the third case. Marshall mentioned a Giffen good case as an exception to his law of demand. Thus the indifference curve analysis is superior to Marshallian analysis in that it yields a more general law of demand which covers the Giffen-good case. The explanation for the occurrence of a Giffen good is that in its case the negative income effect outweighs the substitution effect. Since Marshall ignored the income effect of the change in price, he could not provide a satisfactory explanation for the reaction of the consumer to a change in price of a Giffen good.

However, it may be pointed out that it is very hard to satisfy the above mentioned third conditions for the occurrence of the Giffen good, namely, the consumer must be spending a very large proportion of his income on an inferior good. Therefore, although Giffen good case is theoretically possible the chance of its occurrence in the actual world is almost negligible.[6] This is because consumption of the people is generally diversified so that people spend a small proportion of their income on a single commodity with the result that price-induced income effect even when negative is generally small and cannot therefore outweigh the substitution effect. As mentioned earlier, Marshall believed that quantity demanded could vary directly with price, and, as mentioned above, Sir Robert Giffen is said to have actually observed this phenomenon. But there is a controversy about the intrepretation of this so-called Giffen good. But from our analysis it is clear that Giffen good case can occur in theory. As explained above, when negative income effect of the fall in the price of an inferior good is larger than substitution effect we get a positively-sloping demand curve of Giffen good. Thus Giffen good is theoretically quite possible. But, since income effect of the change in price of a single commodity in the real world is small, the negative income effect of the change in price of an inferior good is too weak to outweigh the substitution effect and therefore a Giffen good, although theoretically conceivable, rarely occurs in practice.

DERIVATION OF INDIVIDUAL'S DEMAND CURVE FROM INDIFFERENCE CURVE ANALYSIS

Price consumption curve traces the effect of a change in price on the quantity demanded of a good. But price consumption curve does not directly relate price with quantity demanded. In indifference curve diagram price is not explicitly shown on the *Y*-axis. On the other hand, demand curve directly relates price with quantity demanded, price being shown on the *Y*-axis and quantity demanded on the *X*-axis. A demand curve shows how much quantity of a good will be purchased or demanded at various prices, assuming that tastes and preferences of a consumer, his income, prices of all related goods remain constant. This demand curve showing explicit relationship between price and quantity demanded can be derived from price consumption curve of indifference curve analysis.

In Marshallian utility analysis, demand curve was derived on the assumptions that utility was cardinally measurable and marginal utility of money remained constant with the change in price of the good. In the indifference curve analysis, demand curve is derived without making these dubious assumptions.

Let us suppose that a consumer has got income of Rs. 300 to spend on goods. In Fig.

6. J.R. Hicks, *op.cit*, p. 67.

8.35 money is measured on the Y-axis, while the quantity of the good X whose demand curve is to be derived is measured on the X-axis. An indifference map of a consumer is drawn along with the various budget lines showing different prices of the good X. Budget line PL_1 shows that price of the good X is Rs. 15 per unit. As price of good X falls from Rs. 15 to Rs. 10, the budget line shifts to PL_2. Budget line PL_2 shows that price of good X is Rs. 10. With a further fall in price to Rs. 7.5 the budget line takes the position PL_3. Thus PL_3 shows that price of good X is Rs. 7.5. When price of good X falls to Rs. 6, PL_4 is the relevant budget line. The various budget lines obtained are shown in the column 2 of the Table 8.3. Tangency points between the various budget lines and indifference curves, which when joined together by a line constitute the price consumption curve which shows the amounts of good X purchased or demanded at various prices.

With the budget line PL_1 the consumer is in equilibrium at point Q_1 on the price consumption curve *PCC* at which the budget line PL_1 is tangent to indifference curve IC_1. In his equilibrium position at Q_1 the consumer is buying *OA* units of the good X. In other words, it means that the consumer demands *OA* units of good X at price Rs. 15. When price falls to Rs. 10 and thereby the budget line shifts to PL_2, the consumer comes to be in equilibrium at point Q_2 of the price-consumption curve *PCC* where the budget line PL_2 is tangent to indifference curve IC_2. At Q_2, the consumer is buying *OB* units of good X. In other words, the consumer demands *OB* units of the good X at price Rs. 10. Likewise, with budget lines PL_3 and PL_4, the consumer is in equilibrium at points Q_3 and Q_4 of price consumption curve and is demanding *OC* units and *OD* units of good X at price Rs. 7.5 and Rs. 6 respectively. It is thus clear that from the price consumption curve we can get information which is required to

Table 8.3. Demand Schedule

Price of good X Rs.	*Budget Line*	*Quantity Demanded*
15	PL_1	*OA*
10	PL_2	*OB*
7.5	PL_3	*OC*
6	PL_4	*OD*

draw the demand curve showing directly the amounts demanded of the good X against various prices. With the above information we draw up the demand schedule in Table 8.3 given above.

The above demand schedule which has been derived from the indifference curve diagram can be easily converted into a demand curve with price shown on the Y-axis and quantity demanded on the X-axis. It is easier to understand the derivation of demand curve if it is drawn rightly below the indifference curve diagram. This has been done so in Fig 8.35. In the diagram at the bottom, where on the X-axis the quantity demanded is shown as in indifference curves diagram in top where panel, but on the Y-axis in the diagram in the bottom panel *price per unit* of the good X is shown instead of total money. In order to obtain the demand curve, various points K, L, S and T representing the demand schedule of the above table are plotted. By joining the points K, L, S and T we get the required demand curve *DD*. In most cases the demand curve of individuals will slope downward to the right, because as the price of a good falls both the substitution effect and income effect pull together in increasing the quantity demanded of the good. Even when the income effect is negative, the demand curve will slope downward to the right if the substitution effect is strong enough to overwhelm the negative income effect. Only when the negative income effect is powerful enough to outweigh the substitution effect can the demand curve slope upward to the right instead of sloping downward to the left.

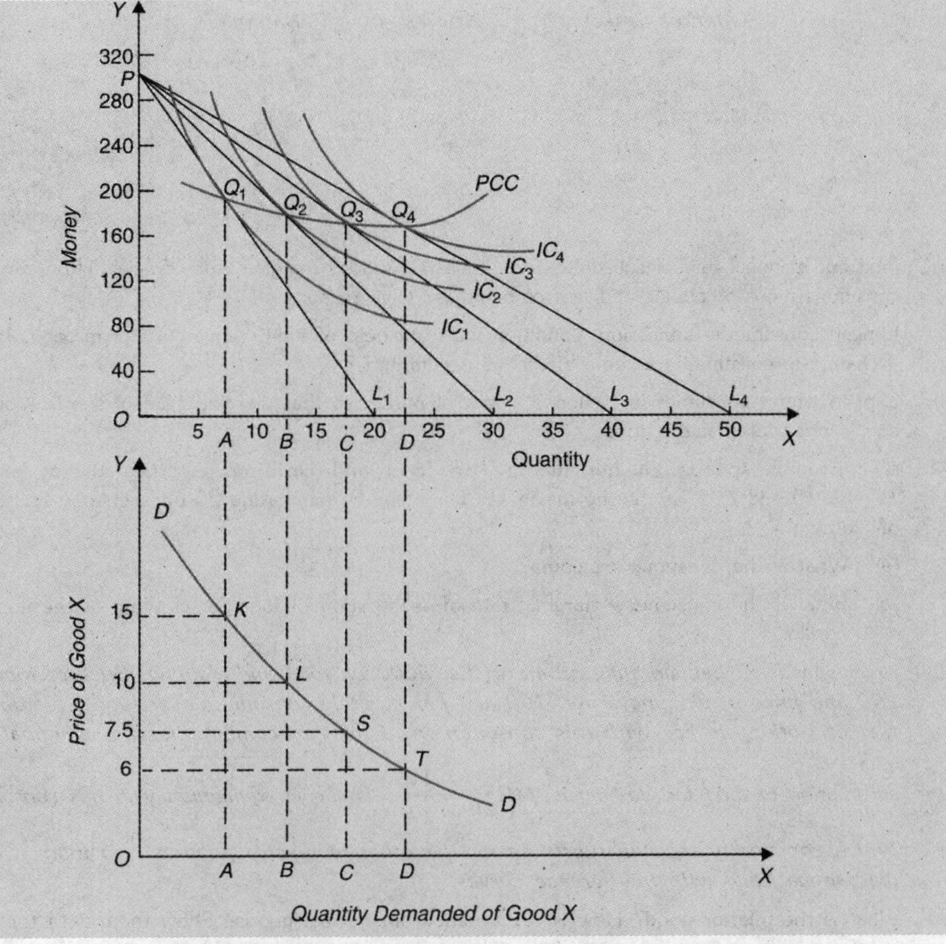

Fig. 8.35. *Derivation of Individual's Demand Curve*

QUESTIONS AND PROBLEMS FOR REVIEW

1. Distinguish between cardinal utility and ordinal utility? Which is more realistic?
2. What are indifference curves? What are the assumptions on which indifference curve analysis of demand is based?
3. (*a*) Explain why consumer's indifference curves (*i*) have negative slope, (*ii*) do not intersect and (*iii*) are convex to the origin.

   (*b*) Show that if indifference curves are concave, a consumer will consume only one of the two goods.
4. What is budget line? What does its intercept on *X*-axis show ? What does its intercept on Y-axis show? What does slope of the budget line measure ?
5. Amit's budget line relating good *X* and good Y has intercepts of 50 units of good *X* and 20 units of good *Y*. If the price of good *X* is 12, what is Amit's income? What is the price of good. *Y*? What is the slope of the budget line ?
6. What is marginal rate of substitution? An indifference curve of Sonia contains the following market baskets of apples and bananas. Each of these baskets gives her equal satisfaction.

Market basket	*Apples*	*Bananas*
1	2	16
2	3	11
3	4	7
4	5	4
5	6	2
6	7	1

Find out marginal rate of substitution of Sonia. How does marginal rate of substitution vary as she consumes more of apples and less of bananas? Give reasons.

7. Explain consumer's equilibrium condition with the help of indifference curve approach. How will a change in consumer's income affect his equilibrium ?

8. Explain why a consumer will choose a market basket so that marginal rate of substitution (*MRS*) equals price ratio of the goods.

9. A consumer spends all her income on food and clothing. At the current prices of P_f = Rs. 10 and P_c = Rs. 5, she maximises her utility by purchasing 20 units of food and 50 units of clothing.

   (*a*) What is the consumer's income?

   (*b*) What is the consumer's marginal rate of substitution of food for clothing at the equilibrium position ?

10. *Priya spends all her monthly income of Rs. 5000 on food and clothing. Price of food is Rs. 250 and price of clothing is Rs. 100 and her monthly consumption of food is 10 units and that of clothing is 25. With this consumption of the two commodities her marginal rate of substitution of food for clothing is* $MRS_{fc} = \frac{1C}{1F}$. *Is she in equilibrium with this consumption? Which commodity she will substitute for the other to reach equilibrium position ? Illustrate diagrammatically with indifference curves.*

11. What is the inferior good? How is it different from normal goods? Show them with the help of indifference curves.

12. Use indifference curves to explain what happens to the demand for an inferior good as consumers's real income increases at constant relative prices.

13. (a) What is price consumption curve? What is the relationship between price consumption curve and price elasticity of demand ?

    (*b*) Derive demand curve from Price Consumption Curve.

14. What is income consumption curve. Draw indifference curve diagrams showing the income consumption curve in case of (a) normal good, (b) inferior good.

15. (*a*) What is an Engel curve? How is Engel curve derived from income consumption curve ?

    (*b*) Draw an Engel curve for (*i*) a necessary good, (*ii*) luxury good (*iii*) neutral good.

16. Using indifference curve analysis, show how price effect of a commodity is decomposed into income effect and substitution effect.

17. With the help of indifference curve analysis, derive demand curve for a normal commodity? Explain why it slopes downward to the right.

18. What is Giffen good? How does indifference curve analysis explain Giffen Paradoix? What is the shape of price consumption curve for a Giffen good? Illustrate it with an indifference curve diagram.

19. Why demand curve for a Giffen good has a positive slope ?

20. What is an inferior good ? What is the shape of a demand curve for an inferior good which is not a Giffen good ?

21. What is compensating variation in income ? Using the concept of compensating variation in income distinguish between income and substitution effects of a fall in price of a commodity with the help of indifference curve technique in case of (*a*) normal good, and (*b*) an inferior good.

22. An individual's marginal utilities for commodities are given by the following relations :

$$MU_x = 40 - 5x \text{ and } MU_y = 20 - 3Y.$$

What is his marginal rate of substitution in consumption at the consumption basket $X = 3$, $Y = 5$? If P_x = Rs. 5 and P_y = Re. 1. Does the basket represent consumption equilibrium ?

APPENDIX A TO CHAPTER 8

MATHEMATICAL TREATMENT OF THE THEORY OF CONSUMER'S CHOICE

In this appendix we will study the mathematical derivation of consumer's equilibrium, the demand function and Slutsky equation which describes decomposition of price effect into substitution effect and income effect. We will also solve some numerical problems based on these concepts.

Mathematical Derivation of Conditions for Consumer's Equilibrium : Lagrangian Method

Those who know mathematics can understand the condition for consumer's equilibrium easily with the Lagrangian multiplier method which seeks to solve the maximisation and minimisation problems subject to some constraints.

Consider a consumer who intends to spends his entire given income (I) on the two goods, X and Y. P_x and P_y are the prices of two goods respectively which the consumer takes as given and constant for him. Consumer's budget constraint can be written by means of the following budget equation.

$$I = P_x \,.\, X + P_y \,.\, Y \qquad \text{...(1)}$$

where X and Y are the quantities of the two goods X and Y. The budget equation (1) describes that the expenditure on the two goods $P_x.X + P_y \,.\, Y$ equals (more generally speaking cannot exceed) his given income I.

The general ordinal utility function visualised by indifference curve analysis is given by

$$U = f(X, Y) \qquad \text{...(2)}$$

Equation (2) postulates that total utility (U) derived from consumption depends on the quantities X and Y of the two goods X and Y respectively. Note that in the indifference curve ordinal utility approach, total utility is not the *sum* of independent utilities derived separately from the two goods X and Y.

The aim of the consumer is to purchase such quantities of the two goods which maximise his total utility as given by the equation $U = f(x, y)$ subject to the budget constraint as given by equation (1). So this is a *constrained maximisation problem* which can be solved through a mathematical technique called Lagrangian method which is explained below.

First Step in this method is to form Lagrangian function from the above two equations which is as under :

$$L = f(X, Y) + \lambda(I - P_xX - P_yY) \qquad \text{...(3)}$$

where λ is Lagrangian multiplier. For maximisation of utility it is necessary that partial derivative of L with respect to x, y and λ of the above Lagraugian function be zero. Thus, for maximisation of utility.

$$\frac{\partial L}{\partial X} = \frac{\partial f}{\partial X} - \lambda P_x = 0 \quad \text{...(4)}$$

$$\frac{\partial L}{\partial Y} = \frac{\partial f}{\partial Y} - \lambda P_y = 0 \quad \text{...(5)}$$

$$\frac{\partial L}{\partial \lambda} = I - P_x X - P_y Y = 0 \quad \text{...(6)}$$

(Note that *'f'* in the above equation represents the utility function).

It will be noticed that equation (6) coincides with the budget equation (1). Knowing that $\frac{\partial f}{\partial x} = MU_x$ and $\frac{\partial f}{\partial y} = MU_y$ the above equations can be rewritten as

$$MU_x - \lambda P_x = 0 \quad \text{...(7)}$$

$$MU_y - \lambda P_y = 0 \quad \text{...(8)}$$

$$I - P_x X - P_x Y = 0 \quad \text{...(9)}$$

Rewritting the above equations we have

$$MU_x = \lambda P_x \quad \text{...(7)}$$

$$MU_y = \lambda P_y \quad \text{...(8)}$$

$$I = P_x \cdot X + P_y \cdot Y \quad \text{...(9)}$$

The above three equations can be solved simultaneously to obtain the values of X and Y. In order to do so we divide (7) by (8) we have

$$\frac{MU_x}{MU_y} = MRS_{xy} = \frac{\lambda P_x}{\lambda P_y}$$

or

$$MRS_{xy} = \frac{P_x}{P_y} \quad \text{....(10)}$$

In order to maximise satisfaction subject to the budget constraint, the equation (10) must be met along with the budget constraint equation (9).

It will be recalled that equality of MRS_{xy} with the price ratio is the necessary condition of consumer's equilibrium.

In order to obtain the values of X and Y we find out the value of X or Y from equation (10) and then substitute its value in the budget equation (9) to obtain the value of the other. This will become clear from the numerical problems solved below. Note that Lagrangean multiplier (λ) is equal to the marginal utility or satisfaction obtained from the last rupee spent on each commodity.

Numerical Problem 1

Utility function of an individual is given by $U = f(x, y) = x^{3/4} y^{1/4}$. Find out the optimal quantities of the two goods using Lagrangian method, if it is given that price of good x is Rs. 6 per unit, price of good y is Rs. 3 per unit and income of the individual (I) is equal to Rs. 120.

Solution:

Given : $U = x^{3/4}\ y^{1/4}$

$P_x = 6,\ P_y = 3$ and $I =$ Rs. 120

Lagrangian expression for the above problem is

$$L = x^{3/4}\ y^{1/4} + \lambda(120 - 6x - 3y)$$

Differentiating the Legrangian function (L) with respect to x, y, λ and setting them equal to zero we have

$$\frac{\partial L}{\partial x} = \frac{3}{4}x^{-1/4}y^{1/4} - 6\lambda = 0 \qquad \text{...(1)}$$

$$\frac{\partial L}{\partial y} = \frac{1}{4}x^{3/4}y^{-3/4} - 3\lambda = 0 \qquad \text{...(2)}$$

$$\frac{\partial L}{\partial \lambda} = 120 - 6x - 3y = 0 \qquad \text{...(3)}$$

Through rearrangement we have

$$\frac{3}{4}x^{-1/4}y^{1/4} = 6\lambda \qquad \text{...(4)}$$

$$\frac{1}{4}x^{3/4}y^{-3/4} = 3\lambda \qquad \text{...(5)}$$

$$6x + 3Y = 120 \qquad \text{...(6)}$$

To solve for x we divide the equation (4) by equation (5). Thus

$$\frac{\frac{3}{4}x^{-1/4}\ y^{1/4}}{\frac{1}{4}x^{3/4}y^{-\frac{3}{4}}} = \frac{6\lambda}{3\lambda}$$

$$3x^{-1}\cdot y = \frac{6}{3}$$

or

$$\frac{3y}{x} = 2 \text{ or } x = \frac{3y}{2}$$

Substituting the value of $x = \frac{3y}{2}$ in the budget equation (6) we have

$$6\frac{3y}{2} + 3y = 120$$

$$12y = 120$$

$$y = 10$$

Now, substituting the value of y = 10 in the budget equation (6) we have

$$6x + 30 = 120$$

$$x = 15$$

Thus the optimal quantities of x and y which maxise utility are $x = 15$ and $y = 10$.

Note. We can also find out the values of λ by substituting the values of x and y either in equation (4) or equation (5).

Numerical Problem 2

There are two commodities X_1 and X_2 on which a consumer spends his entire income in a day. He has utility function $U = \sqrt{X_1X_2}$. Find out the optimal quantities of X_1 and X_2 if prices of X_1 and X_2 are Rs. 5 and Rs. 2 respectively and his daily income equals Rs. 500.

Solution

Given utility function : $U = \sqrt{X_1X_2}$

or $U = X_1^{1/2}X_2^{1/2}$

and with $P_{x1} = 5$, $P_{x2} = 2$ and I = Rs 500, budget equation is

$$500 = 5X_1 + 2X_2$$

Defferentiating the given utility function with respect ot X_1 and X_2 we have

$$MU_{x1} = \frac{\partial U}{\partial X_1} = \frac{1}{2} X_1^{-1/2} X_2^{1/2} \quad ...(1)$$

$$MU_{x2} = \frac{\partial U}{\partial X_2} = \frac{1}{2} X_1^{1/2} X_2^{-1/2} \quad ....(2)$$

Dividing equations (1) by equation (2)

$$MRS_{xy} = \frac{MU_{x1}}{MU_{x2}} = \frac{\frac{1}{2}X_1^{-1/2} \cdot X_2^{1/2}}{\frac{1}{2}X_1^{1/2} \cdot X_2^{-1/2}} = X_1^{-1}X_2 = \frac{X_2}{X_1}$$

For maximisation of utility it is required that

$$MRS_{xy} = \frac{P_{x1}}{P_{x2}}$$

or

$$\frac{X_2}{X_1} = \frac{5}{2}$$

$$X_2 = \frac{5X_1}{2}$$

Substituting the value of X_2 in the budget equation, we have

$$I = X_1P_{x1} + X_2P_{x2} \text{ (Budget Equation)}$$

$$500 = X_1\, 5 + \frac{5X_1 .2}{2}$$

$$10\, X_1 = 500$$

$$X_1 = 50$$

Now substituting the value of X_1 in the budget equation

$$500 = 50 \times 5 + 2X_2$$

$$500 = 250 + 2X_2$$

$$2X_2 = 250$$

$$X_2 = 125$$

Thus the optimal quantities of X_1 and X_2 are 50 and 125 respectively.

DERIVATION OF DEMAND FUNCTION

In the above example we hav found the optimal values (i.e. utility-maximising values) of the goods for *specific* values of prices and income. A demand function represents how quantity demanded of a good changes when prices and income change. In other words, for deriving a demand function prices and income are treated as variables. This demand function can be derived with Lagrangian method.

To Illustrate the derivation of demand function, we take the utility function $U = f(x, y) = x^{3/4}\, y^{1/4}$ considered above. Thus, for derivation of demand function constrained maximisation problem is

Mamimise $U = x^{3/4}\, y^{1/4}$

Subject to $P_x.x + P_y.y = I$ (Budget equation)

Differentiating the utility function with respect to x and y we have

$$MU_x = \frac{\partial U}{\partial x} = \frac{3}{4} x^{-1/4} . y^{1/4}$$

$$MU_y = \frac{\partial U}{\partial y} = \frac{1}{4} x^{3/4} . y^{-3/4}$$

For maximisation of utility :

$$MRS_{xy} = \frac{MU_x}{MU_y} = \frac{P_x}{P_y} \quad \text{... (i)}$$

$$MRS_{xy} = \frac{MU_x}{MU_y} = \frac{\frac{3}{4} x^{-1/4} . Y^{1/4}}{\frac{1}{4} x^{\frac{3}{4}} . y^{-\frac{3}{4}}} = 3x^{-1} y = \frac{3y}{x}$$

Substituting the value of MRS_{xy} in equation (1) we have

$$\frac{3y}{x} = \frac{P_x}{P_y} \text{ or } y = \frac{x}{3} \frac{P_x}{P_y}$$

Substituting the value of $y = \frac{x}{3} \frac{P_x}{p_x}$ in the budget equation, we have

$$I = P_x \cdot x + P_y \cdot \frac{x}{3} \frac{P_x}{P_y}$$

or

$$I = P_x \left(x + \frac{1}{3} x \right) = P_x \left(\frac{4}{3} x \right)$$

$$x = \frac{3}{4} \frac{I}{P_x} \quad \text{...(2)}$$

x represents the quantity demanded of good x. The above equation (2) represents the demand function which states that quantity demanded of a good depends on its own price and income of the consumer, keeping the prices of other goods constant.

Likewise we can derive the demand function for y as

$$y = \frac{1}{4} \frac{I}{P_y} \quad \text{...(3)}$$

It is important to note that in the demand functions for goods X and Y, price of the good appear in the denominator which shows that the quantity demanded of the good is inversely related to the price of the good. That is demand curve of a good shopes downward to the right. Besides, I appear in the numerator of equations (2) and (3) which shows demand for a good varies directly with income.

Example 2. *Let us take another type of utility function and explain the mathematical derivation of demand function for a good following detailed procedure of Lagrangian method.*

Suppose the a general utility function $U = xy$ is given. I stands for income, and P_x and P_y denote prices of the two goods. Writing the constrained utility maximisation problem in this case we have

$$\text{Maximise } U = xy \qquad \text{...(1)}$$

$$\text{Subject to } P_x \cdot x + P_y y = I \qquad \text{...(2)}$$

Lagrangian expression for the above problem is

$$L = xy + \lambda(I - P_x x - P_y y)$$

For maximisation of utility it is required that

$$\frac{\partial L}{\partial x} = \frac{\partial U}{\partial x} - \lambda P_x = 0 \qquad \text{...(3)}$$

$$\frac{\partial L}{\partial y} = \frac{\partial U}{\partial y} - \lambda P_y = 0 \qquad \text{...(4)}$$

$$\frac{\partial L}{\partial \lambda} = I - P_x \cdot x + P_y y = 0 \qquad \text{...(5)}$$

Note that derivative $\frac{\partial U}{\partial x}$ of the utility function $U = xy$ is equal to y and derivative $\frac{\partial U}{\partial y}$ of the utility function $U = xy$ is equal to x. Further note that these derivatives represent marginal utilities of the goods. Rewriting the equation (3) and (4), we have

$$\frac{MU_x}{P_x} = \lambda$$

$$\frac{MU_y}{P_y} = \lambda$$

or

$$\frac{MU_x}{P_x} = \frac{MU_y}{P_y} \qquad \text{...(6)}$$

Since in the given utility function $MU_x = y$ and $MU_y = x$ we have

$$\frac{y}{P_x} = \frac{x}{P_y} \qquad \text{...(7)}$$

or

$$y = x\frac{P_x}{P_y} \qquad \text{...(8)}$$

Putting the value of y into the budget equation (2) we have

$$P_x \cdot x + P_y \cdot \frac{P_x}{P_y} \cdot x = I$$

$$P_x(x + x) = I$$

or $$P_x \,.\, 2x = I$$

$$x = \frac{I}{2P_x} \qquad \text{...(9)}$$

The equation (9) represents the demand function for good *X* with shows that quantity demanded (*x*) of good *X* is directly related to income (*I*) and inversely related to its own price (P_x), price of the other goods remaining constant.

Likewise, it can be shwn that demand function for *y* is given by :

$$y = \frac{I}{2P_y} \qquad \text{...(10)}$$

SLUTSKY EQUATION : DECOMPOSING PRICE EFFECT

In the chapter on indifference curve analysis we have graphically shown how the effect of change in price of a good can be broken up into its two component parts, namely, substitution effect and income effect. The decomposition of price effect into its two components can be derived and expressed mathematically. Suppose price of good *X* falls, its substitution effect on quantity demanded of the good arises due to substitution of the relatively cheaper good *X* for the now relatively dearer good *Y* so that his level of *real income* remains constant. The overall effect of change in its own price of a commodity on its quantity demanded can be expressed as $\frac{dq_x}{dp_x}$ and the substitution effect can be expressed as $\left.\frac{\partial q_x}{\partial p_x}\right|_{U=\bar{U}}$. The term $\left.\frac{\partial q_x}{\partial p_x}\right|_{U=\bar{U}}$ showschange in quantity demanded resulting from a relative change in price of X while real income of the consumer remains constant.

However, expressing income effect of the price change mathematically is rather a ticklish affair. Suppose a unit change in income (∂I) causes a ∂q_x change in quantity demanded of the good *X*. This can be written as $\frac{\partial q_x}{\partial I}$. But how much income changes due to a change in price of the good is determined by how much quantity of the good (q_x) the consumer was purchasing on the one hand and change in price of the good (∂p_x) that has taken place on the other. The change in income due to a change in price can be measured by $q_x . \partial p_x$. How much this change in income will affect the quantity demanded of the good *X* is determined by $\frac{\partial q_x}{\partial I}$ which shows the effect of a unit change in income on the quantity demanded of the good *X*. Thus the overall effect of change in price of the good *X* on its quantity demanded can be expressed by the following equation which is generally called *Slutsky equation* because it was Russian economist Slutsky who first of all divided the price effect into substitution and income effect.

$$-\frac{\partial q_x}{\partial p_x} = -\left.\frac{\partial q_x}{\partial p_x}\right|_{U=\bar{U}} - q_x \cdot \partial P_x \frac{\partial q_x}{\partial I} \qquad \text{.... } (i)$$

The first term on the right hand side of the equation represents the substitution affect obtained after income of the consumer has been adjusted to keep his level of real income or purchasing power constant. Since under the substitution effect, the *fall* in price of good leads to the *increase* in its quantity demanded, its sign is negative. The second term on the right hand side of the equation shows the income effect of the fall in price of the good X. The term $q_x.\partial p_x$ measures the increase in income or purchasing power caused by the fall in price of good X and $\frac{\partial q_x}{\partial I}$ measures the change in quantity demanded resulting from a unit increase in income (I). Therefore, income affect of the price change is given by $q_x.\partial p_x \frac{\partial q_x}{\partial I}$. Since the *fall* in price of a good *increases* real income or purchasing power of the consumer which in case of normal goods leads to the *increase in quantity demanded* of the good, sign of the income affect has been taken to be negative (–). Though income effect for a normal good as such is positive, but in the present case it is real income effect produced by *fall* in price that leads to *increase in quantity demanded* of good X which in mathematical terms is negative. Thus viewed from the viewpoint of *relationship between price and quantity* demanded both the effects are negative in mathematical terms and work in the *same direction* in case of normal goods. It should be noted that price effect *i.e.* $\frac{\Delta Q_x}{\Delta P_x}$ is itself negative showing the inverse relationship between price and quantity demanded. Remember that negative relationship in mathematics does not necessarily mean decrease in the variable, it means that the variables change in opposite directions.

Further, a point needs to be clarified. In the analysis of decomposing price effect into substitution and income effects Hicks considered substitution effect when with a change in price, consumer is so compensated as to keep his utility constant. However, in obtaining Slutsky substitution affect income of the consumer is adjusted to *keep his purchasing power constant* so that he could buy the original combination of goods if he so desires. This difference was later emphasied by J.R. Hicks Since it was Slutsky who first of all split up the price effect into substitution effect and income effect the above equation (*i*) is popularly known as Slutsky equation. It is proper to call it *Slutsky-Hicks equation.*

The second important conclusion which follows from Slutsky equation is that as the quantity of commodity (q_x) becomes smaller and smaller, the income effect of the price change will become smaller and smaller. Thus, if the quantity consumed of a commodity is very small, then the income effect is not very significant.

QUESTIONS FOR REVIEW

1. What is Slutsky Substitution effect ? Explain Slutsky substitution effect for a fall in price of good *X*.
2. Distingusih between Hicks and Slutsky approach to the measurements of income and substitution effects.
3. Show graphically the substitution and the real income effects by Hicks and Slutsky. What is the advantage of Slutsky measure ?
4. A consumer spends all his income on two goods *X* and *Y*. When the price of goods *X* is Rs. 2 he consumes 100 units of good *X*. If price of goods *X* increases to Rs. 3 and income is increased by Rs. 100 to enable him to purchase the original bundle, price of *Y* remaining constant, (*i*) would the level of satisfaction of the consumer change; and (*ii*) what would happen to the quantity consumed of *X* ?
5. State the Slutsky equation algebraically and explain each term in it. Using the equation explain (*i*) what must be the sign and magnitude of the income effect for a downward-sloping demand curve.

Revealed Preference Theory of Demand

BEHAVIOURISTIC APPROACH TO DEMAND ANALYSIS

In the previous two chapters the Marshallian utility theory and Hicks-Allen indifference curve theory of demand were discussed. In both these theories, introspective method has been applied to explain the consumer's behaviour. In other words, both these theories provide psychological explanation of consumer's demand; they derive laws about consumer's demand from how he would react psychologically to certain hypothetical changes in price and incomes. But the Revealed Preference Theory which has been put forward by Prof. Samuelson seeks to explain consumer's demand from his actual behavior in the market in various price-income situations. Thus, in sharp contrast to psychological or introspective explanation Prof. Samuelson's revealed preference theory is behaviouristic explanation of consumer's demand. Besides, revealed preference theory is based upon the concept of ordinal utility. In other words, revealed preference theory regards utilities to be merely comparable and not quantifiable. Prof. Tapas Majumdar has described Samuelson's revealed preference theory as "Behaviourist Ordinalist."[1] The description "Behaviourist Ordinalist" highlights the two basic features of the revealed preference theory : first, it applies behaviouristic method, and secondly it uses the concept of ordinal utility.

The revealed preference theory is regarded as "scientific" (meaning behaviouristic) explanation of consumer's behaviour as against the psychological explanation provided by Marshallian and Hicks-Allen theories of demand. This shift from psychological to behaviouristic explanation of consumer's behaviour is a landmark in the development of the theory of demand. The urge among economists to have scientific explanation led to the emergence of the behaviouristic method which seeks to derive the demand theorem from actually observed consumer's behaviour.

PREFERENCE HYPOTHESIS AND STRONG ORDERING

Prof. Samuelson's revealed preference theory has *preference hypothesis* as a basis of

1. Tapas Majumdar, *Measurement of Utility,* Chapter VII.

his theory of demand. According to this hypothesis when a consumer is observed to choose a combination *A* out of various alternative combinations open to him, then he 'reveals', his preference for *A* over all other alternative combinations which he could have purchased. In other words, when a consumer chooses a combination *A*, it means he considers all other alternative combinations which he could have purchased to be inferior to *A*. That is, he rejects all other alternative combinations open to him in favour of the chosen combination *A*. Thus, according to Prof. Samuelson, *choice reveals preference*. Choice of the combination A reveals his definite preference for A over all other rejected combinations. From the hypothesis of 'choice reveals preference' we can obtain definite information about the preferences of a consumer from the observations of his behaviour in the market. By comparing preferences of a consumer revealed in different price-income situations we can obtain certain information about his preference scale.

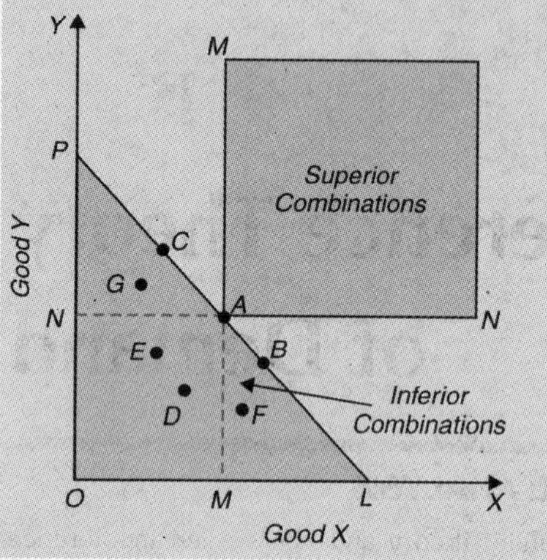

Fig. 9.1. *Choice reveals preference.*

Let us graphically explain the preference hypothesis. Given the prices of two commodities *X* and *Y* and the income of the consumer, price line *PL* is drawn in Fig. 9.1. The price line *PL* represents a given price-income situation. Given the price-income situation as represented by *PL*, the consumer can buy or choose any combination lying within or on the triangle *OPL*. In other words, all combinations lying on the line *PL* such as *A*, *B*, *C* and lying below the lime *PL* such as *D*, *E*, *F* and *G* are alternative combinations open to him, from among which he has to choose any combination. If our consumer chooses combination *A* out of all those open to him in the given price-income situation, it means he reveals his preference for *A* over all other combinations such as *B*, *C*, *D*, *E* and *F* which are rejected by him. As is evident from Fig. 9.1, in his observed chosen combination *A*, the consumer is buying *OM* quantity of commodity *X* and *ON* quantity of commodity *Y*.

It can be inferred from this choice of the consumer that he prefers *A* to other baskets of goods lying on the budget line *AB* or within the buget space. Thus, with the given *price-income situation PL*, when the consumer chooses *A* it is inferred that all other combitions of goods lying within the triangle *OPL* or on the line *PL* which he can afford to buy are revealed to be *inferior* to his chosen combination *A*. Besides , we can infer more from consumer's observed choice. As it is assumed that a rational consumer prefers more of both the goods to less of them or prefers more of at least one good, the amount of the other good remaining the same, we can infer that all combitions lying in the *rectangular shaded area* drawn above and to the right of chosen combition *A* are superior to *A* since in the rectangular shaded area there lie those combinations (baskets) of two goods which contain either more of both the goods or at least more of one good, the amount of the other remaining the same. This means that the consumer would prefer all combinations in the rectangular shaded area to the chosen combination *A*. In other words, all combinations in the shaded area *MAN* are superior to the chosen combination *A*.

As seen above, all other combinations lying in the budget-space *OPL* are attainable or affordable but are rejected in favour of *A* and are therefore revealed to be *inferior* to it. It should be carefully noted that Prof. Samuelson's revealed preference theory is based upon the strong form of preference hypothesis. In other words, in revealed preference theory, strong-ordering preference hypothesis has been applied. Strong ordering implies that there is *definite ordering* of various combinations in consumer's scale of preferences and therefore the choice of a combination by a consumer reveals his definite preference for that over all other alternatives open to him. *Thus, under strong ordering, relation of indifference between various alternative combinations is ruled out.* When in Fig. 9.1 a consumer chooses a combination *A* out of various alternative combinations open to him, it means he has a definite preference for *A* over all others; the possibility of the chosen combination *A* being indifferent to any other possible combination is ruled out by strong ordering hypothesis.

Prof. J. R. Hicks in his "*A Revision of Demand Theory*" does not consider the assumption of strong ordering as satisfactory and instead employs weak ordering hypothesis. Under weak ordering hypothesis (with an additional assumption that the consumer will always prefer a larger anount of a good to a smaller amount of it), the chosen combination A is preferred over all positions that lie within the triangle *OPL* and further that the chosen position *A* will be either preferred to or indfferent to the other positions on the price-income line *PL*. "The difference between the consequnces of strong and weak ordering, so interpreted amounts to no more than this that under strong ordeing the chosen position is shown to be preferred to all other positions *in* and *on* the triangle, while under weak ordering it is preferred to all positions *within* the triangle, but may be indifferent to other positions *on* the same boundary as itself."[1]

The revealed preference theory rests upon a basic assumption which has been called the '*consistency postulate*'. In fact, the consistency postulate is implied in the strong ordering hypothesis. The consistency postulate can be stated thus : '*no two observations of choice behaviour are made which provide conflicting evidence to the individual's preference.*" In other words, consistency postulate asserts that if an individual chooses *A* rather than *B* in one particular instance, then he cannot choose *B* rather than *A* in any other instance when both are available to the consumer. If he chooses *A* rather than *B* in one instance and chooses *B* rather than *A* in another when *A* and *B* are present in both the instances, then he is not behaving consistently. Thus, consistency postulate requires that if once *A* is revealed to be preferred to *B* by an individual, then *B* cannot be revealed to be preferred to *A* by him at any other time when *A* and *B* are present in both the cases. Since comparison here is between the two situations consistency involved in this has been called '*two term consistency*' by J.R. Hicks[1].

Weak Axiom of Revealed Preference (WARP)

If a person chooses combination *A* rather than combination *B* which he could purchase with the given budget constraint, then it cannot happen that he would choose (i.e. prefer) *B* over *A* in some other situation in which he could have bought A if he so wished. This means his choices or preferences must be consistent. This is called *revealed preference axiom.* We illustrate, revealed preference axiom in Figure 9.2. Suppose with the given prices of two goods *X* and *Y* and given his money income to spend on the two goods, *PL* is the budget line facing a consumer. In this budgetary situation *PL*, the consumer chooses *A* when he could have purchased *B* (note that combination *B* would have even cost him less than *A*). Thus, his choice of *A* over *B* means he prefers the combination *A* to the combination *B* of the two goods.

Now suppose that price of good *X* falls, and with some income and price adjustments, budget line changes to *PL'*. Budget line *PL'* is flatter than *PL* reflecting relatively lower price

1. J.R. Hicks, *A Revision of Demand Theory* (1956), p. 43.

of X as compared to the budget line PL. With this new budget line $P'L'$, if the consumer chooses combination B when he can purchase the combination A (as A lies below the budget line $P'L'$ in Fig. 9.2), then the consumer will be inconsistent in his preferences, that is, he will be violating the axiom of revealed preference. Such inconsistent consumer's behaviour is ruled out in revealed preference theory based on strong ordering. This axiom of revealed preference according to which consumer's choices are consistent is also called ' *Weak Axiom of Revealed Preference* or simply WARP. To sum up, according to the weak axiom of revealed preference, "*if combination A is directly revealed preferred to another combination B, then in any other situation, the combination B cannot be revealed preferred to combination A by the consumer when combination A is also affordable*". [2]

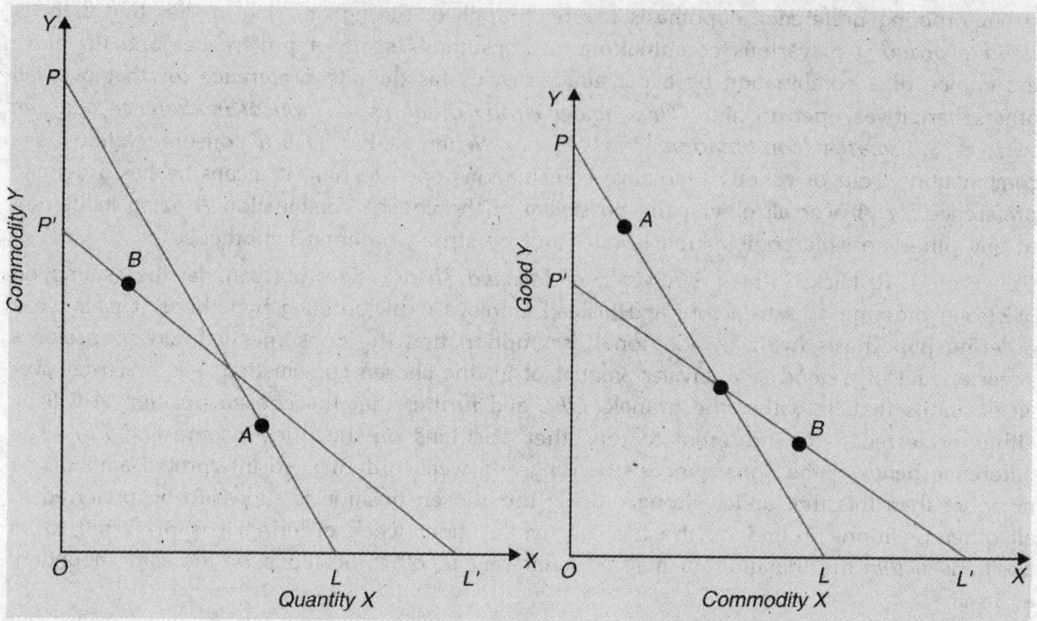

Fig.9.2. *Consumer's Preferences are Inconsistent*

Fig. 9.3. *Consumer's choices satisfy weak axiom of revealed preference.*

Now consider Figure 9.3 where to start with a consumer is facing budget line PL where he chooses combination A of two goods X and Y. Thus, consumer prefers combination A to all other combinations within and on the triangle OPL. Now suppose that budget constraint changes to $P'L'$ and consumer purchases combination B on it. As combination B lies outside the budget line PL it was not affordable when combination A was chosen. Therefore, choice of combination B with the budget line $P'L'$ is consistent with his earlier choice A with the budget constraint PL and is in accordance with the weak axiom of revealed preference.

Transitivity Assumption of Revealed Preference

The axiom of revealed preference described above provides us a consistency condition that must be satisfied by a rational consumer who makes an optimum choice. Apart from the axiom of revealed preference, revealed preference theory also assumes *that revealed preferences* are transitive. According to this, if an optimising consumer prefers combination

2. Hal Varian, *Intermediate Microeconomics*, 1963, p. 94.

A to combination B of the goods and combination B to combination C of the goods, then he will also prefer combination A to combination C of the goods. To put it briefly, assumption of transitivity of preferences requires that if $A > B$ and $B > C$, then $A > C$.

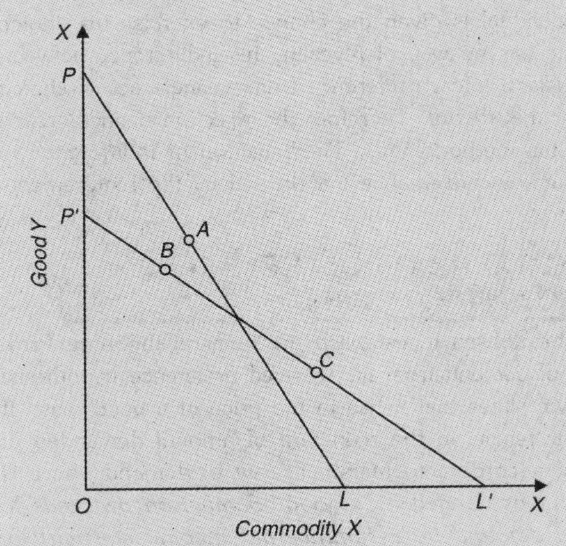

Fig. 9.4. *Revealed preferences are transitive.*

In this way we say that combination A is *indirectly* revealed to be preferred to combination C. Thus, if a combination A is either directly or indirectly revealed preferred to another combination we say that combination A is revealed to be preferred to the other combination. Consider Figure 9.4 where with budget constraint PL, the consumer chooses A and therefore reveals his preference for A over combination B which he could have purchased as combination B is affordable in budget constraint PL. Now suppose budget constraint facing the consumer changes to P'L', he chooses B when he could have purchased C. Thus, the consumer prefers B to C. From the transitivity assumption it follows that the consumer will prefer combination A to combination C. Thus, combination A is indirectly revealed to be preferred to combination C. We therefore conclude that the consumer prefers A either directly or indirectly to all those combination of the two goods lying in the shaded regions in Figure 9.4.

It is thus evident from above that concept of revealed preference is a very significant and powerful tool which provides a lot of information about consumer's preferences who behave in an optimising and consistent manner. By merely looking at the consumer's choices in different price-income situations we can get a lot of information about consumer's preferences.

It may be noted that the consistency postulate of revealed preference theory is the counterpart of the utility maximisation assumption in both Marshallian utility theory and Hicks-Allen indifference curve theory. The assumption that the consumer maximises utility or satisfaction is known as rationality assumption. It has been said that a rational consumer will try to maximise utility or satisfaction. Recently, some economists have challenged this assumption. They assert that consumers in actual practice do not maximise utility. The revealed theory has the advantage that its rationality assumption can be easily realised in actual practice. The rationality on the part of the consumer in revealed preference theory only requires that he should behave in a 'consistent' manner. Consistency of choice is a less restrictive assumption than the utility maximisation assumption. This is one of the improvements of Samuelson's theory over the Marshallian cardinal utility and Hicks-Allen indifference curve theories of demand.

It is important to note that Samuelson's revealed preference is not a statistical concept. If it were a statistical concept, then the preference of an individual for a combination A would have been inferred from giving him opportunity to exercise his choice several times in the same circumstances. If the individual from among the various alternative combinations open to him chooses a particular combination more frequently than any other, only then the individual's preference for A would have been statistically revealed. But in Prof. Samuelson's revealed preference theory preference is said to be revealed from a *single act of choice*. It is obvious that no single act of choice on the part of the consumer can prove his indifference between the two situations. Unless the individual is given the chance to exercise his choice several times in the given circumstances, he has no way of revealing his indifference between various combinations. Thus, because Samuelson infers preference from a single act of choice the relation of indifference is inadmissible to his theory. Therefore the rejection of indifference relation by Prof. Samuelson follows from his methodology. "The rejection of indifference in Samuelson theory is, therefore, not a matter of convenience but dicated by the requirements of his methodology."[3]

DERIVING DEMAND THEOREM FROM REVEALED PREFERENCE HYPOTHESIS

Revealed preference hypothesis can be utilised to establish the demand theorem. Prof. Samuelson has derived the Marshallian law of demand from his revealed preference hypothesis. Marshallian law of demand, as is well known, states that a rise in the price of a good must, if income and other prices are held constant, results in the reduction of amount demanded of the good, and *vice versa*. In other words, according to Marshall's law of demand, there is inverse relation between price and amount demanded of a good. *Samuelson proceeds to establish relationship between price and demand by assuming that income elasticity of demand is positive.* From positive income elasticity, he deduces the Marshallian inverse price-demand relationship. He states the demand theorem what he calls the *Fundamental Theorem of Consumption Theory as* under :

"Any good (simple or composite) that is known always to increase in demand when money income alone rises must definitely shrink in demand when its price alone rises".

Fundamental Consumption Theorem and Rise in Price

It is clear from the above statement of Fundamental Theorem that positive income elasticity of demand has been made a necessary qualification to the inverse price-demand principle. The geometrical proof of the Fundamental Theorem is illustrated in Fig. 9.5. Let us suppose that the consumer spends his entire income on the two goods *X* and *Y*. Further suppose that his income in terms of good *X* is *OB*, and in terms of good *Y* is *OA*. Now, the price line *AB* represents the price-income situation confronting the consumer. All the combinations of goods *X* and *Y* lying within or on the triangle *OAB* are available to the consumer, from which he can buy any combination. Suppose that the consumer is observed to choose the combination *Q*. This means that *Q* is revealed to be preferred to all other combinations that lie within or on the triangle *OAB*.

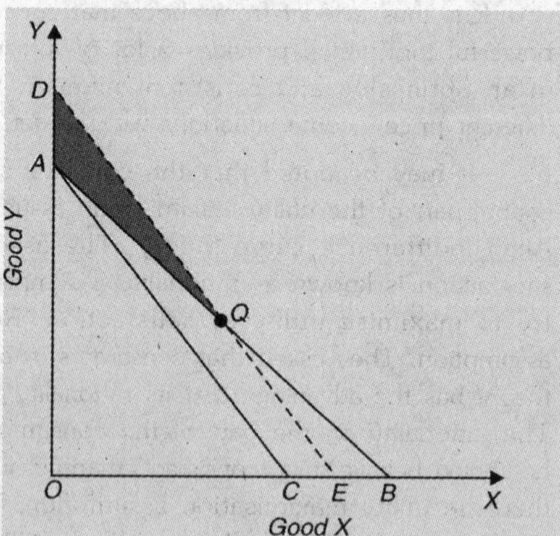

Fig. 9.5. Deriving Law of Demand through Revealed Preference Hypothesis

3. Tapas Majumbar, *Measurement of Utility*, p. 82

Now, suppose that the price of good *X* rises, his income and price of *Y* remaining unchanged. With the rise in price of *X* the price line shifts to the new position *AC*. The price line *AC* represents new price-income situation. We now want to know what is the effect of this rise in price of good *X* on its quantity demanded, assuming that demand varies directly with income (*i.e.*, income elasticity of demand is positive). It is evident from Fig. 9.5 that combination *Q* is not available to the consumer in price-income situation *AC*. Let us compensate the consumer for the higher price of *X* by granting him extra money so that he can buy the same combination *Q* even at the higher price of *X*. The amount of money which is required to be granted to the consumer so that he could buy the original combination *Q* at the higher price of *X* has been called *Cost-difference* by Prof. J. R. Hicks. In Fig.9.5. a line *DE* parallel to *AC* has been drawn so that it passes through *Q*. *DE* represents higher price of *X* and the money income after it has been increased by the cost difference.

Now, the question is which combination will be chosen by the consumer in price-income situation *DE*. The original combination *Q* is available in price-income situation *DE*. It is evident from Figure 9.5, that he will not choose any combination lying below *Q* on the line *DE*. This is because if he chooses any combination below *Q* on the line *DE*, his choice would be inconsistent. All combinations below *Q* on *DE*, that is, all combinations on *QE* could have been bought by the consumer but had been rejected by him in price-income situation *AB* in favour of *Q*. (All points on *QE* were contained in the original choice triangle *OAB*.). Since we are assuming consistency of choice behaviour on the part of the consumer he will not choose, in price-income situation *DE*, any combination below *Q* on *QE* in preference to *Q* when *Q* is available in the new situation. It follows, therefore, that in the price-income situation *DE* the consumer will either choose the original combination *Q* or any other combination on *QD* portion of *DE* or any combination within the shaded area *QDA*. (It should be noted that choice of any other combination on *QD* or within the shaded area *QDA* in preference to *Q* by the consumer will not be inconsistent since combinations lying above *Q* on *QD* or within the shaded region *QDA* were not available in price-income situation *AB*.)

In price-income situation *DE* if the consumer chooses the original combination *Q*, it means he will be buying the same amount of goods *X* and *Y* as before, and if he chooses any combination above *Q* on *QD* or within the shaded area *QDA*, it means that he will be buying less amount of commodity *X* and greater amount of *Y* than before. Thus, even after sufficient extra income has been granted to the consumer to compensate him for the rise in price of good *X*, he purchases either the *same* or the *smaller* quantity of *X* at the higher price. Now, if the extra money granted to him is *withdrawn*, he will definitely buy the smaller amount of *X* at the higher price, if the demand for good *X* is known always to fall with the decrease in income (that is, if income elasticity of demand fox *X* is positive). In other words, when the price of good *X* rises and no extra money is granted to the consumer so that he faces price-income situation *AC*, he will purchase less amount of good *X* than at *Q*. Thus assuming a positive income-elasticity of demand, the inverse price-demand relationship is established through revealed preference hypothesis so far as rise in price is concerned.

Proving Consumption Theorem in Case of Fall in Price

That the inverse price-demand relationship holds good in case of a fall in price also is demonstrated in Fig.9.6. Let us suppose that *AB* represents original price income situation and further that the consumer reveals his preference for *Q* over all other combinations within in or on the triangle *OAB*. Now, suppose that price of good *X* falls so that the price line shifts to the right to the position *AC'*. Let us take away some amount of money from the consumer so that he is left with just sufficient amount of money which enables him to purchase the original combination Q at the lower price of good X. Thus, in Figure.9.6, a line DE is drawn parallel to AC' so that it passes through Q. Price line DE represents lower price of X as given by AC and the money income after it has been reduced by the cost difference. It is obvious that in price-income situation DE, the consumer cannot choose any combination above Q on QD, since all such combinations were available to him in the original price-income situation AB and were rejected by him in favour of Q. The consumer will, therefore, choose either Q or any other combination on QE or from within the shaded region QEB. In price-income situation DE, his choice of Q means that he buys the same quantity of goods X and Y as in original price-income situation AB, and his choice of any other combination on QE or from *within the shaded region QEB* means that he buys larger amount of good X and smaller amount of good Y than in the original price-income situation AB. Thus, even after consumer's income has been reduced, he buys either the same quantity of X or more at the lower price. And if we give him back the amount of money taken away from him so that he confronts price-income situation AC he will definitely buy more of X at the lower price, provided that his demand for X rises with the rise in income (*i.e.* his income elasticity of demand for good X is positive).

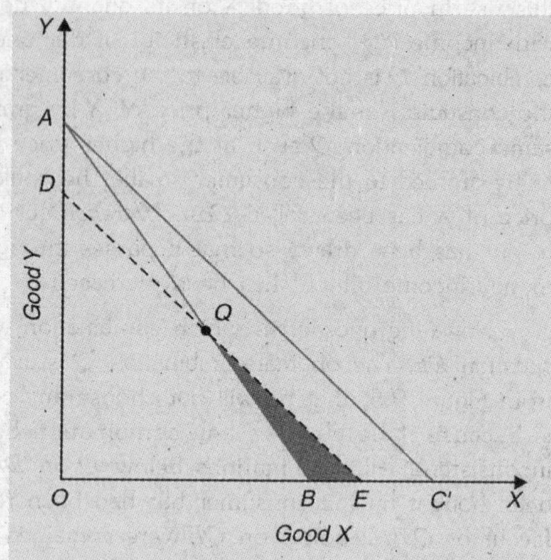

Fig. 9.6. *Proof of Consumption Theorem through Revealed Preference Approachs*

The two demonstrations given above together prove the fundamental theorem of consumption theory, according to which any good whose demand varies directly with income must definitely shrink in demand when its price rises and expands in demand when its price falls. It may be noted that Samuelson's theory involves two implicit assumptions which have not been explicitly stated. In the first place the consumer is always shown to choose a combination on the budget line. In other words, he is never shown to choose a combination from within the triangle. This is based upon the assumption that a *consumer always prefers a larger collection of goods to a smaller one.* Secondly, another implicit assumption involved in Samuelson's theory is that the consumer is shown to choose only one combination of goods in every price-income situation. With these two implicit assumptions the inverse price-demand relationship is deduced by Samuelson by making explicit assumptions of consistency of choice and a positive income- elasticity of demand.

Breaking up Price Effect into Substitution Effect and Income Effect

Having now explained the derivation of law of demand from revealed preference approach we are now in a position to show how in the revealed preference approach price effect can be broken up into substitution and income effects. We will explain this by considering the case of fall in price of a commodity. Now consider Figure 9.7 where, to begin with, price income situtation faced by a consumer is given by the budget line AB. With price income situation represented by the budget line AB, suppose the consumer chooses combination Q and buys OM qnatity of commodity X.

Now, suppose price of commodity *X* falls and as a result budget line shifts to the new position *AC*. Now, income of the consumer is reduced so much that the new budget line *DE* passes through the original chosen combination *Q*. That is, income is reduced equal to the cost difference so that gain in real income caused by the fall in price of commodity *X* is cancelled out. As seen above, with the new budget line *DE*, to be consistent in his behaviour the consumer can either choose the original combination *Q* or any combination lying on the segment *QE* of the budget line *DE* or from within the shaded area *QEB*. If he chooses again the original combination *Q*, the Slutsky substitution effect well be zero. However, suppose that the consumer actually chooses combination *S* on the segment *QE* of the new budget line *DE*.

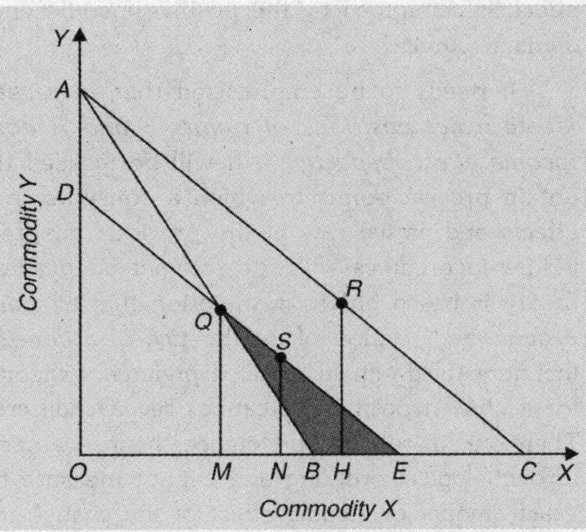

Fig. 9.7. *Breaking up Price Effect into Substitution and Income Effects.*

Now, choice of the combination *S* shows that there will be substitution effect due to which the consumer will buy *MN* more of good *X*. Note that subsitution effect is negative in the sense that the relative *fall* in price of good *X* has led to the *increase in quantity demanded* of *X*, that is, change in quantity demanded *is in opposite direction* to the change in price. It should be noted that choice of combination *S* on segment *QE* in preference to combination *Q* of the budget line *DE* is not inconsistent because combinations on *QE* segment and in the shaded area *QEB* were not available before when combination *Q* was earlier chosen in price-income situation *AB*. Thus, with the new budget line *DE* after consumer's income has been adjusted to cancel out the gain in real income resulting from a relative fall in price of *X*, the consumer chooses either *Q* (when substitution effect is zero or a combination such as *S* on segment *QE* when substitution effect leads to the increase in quantity demanded of good *X* by *MN*. This is generally known as Slutsky theorem *which states that if income effect is ignored substitution effect will lead to the increase in quantity demanded of the good whose price has fallen and therefore the Marshallian law of demand describing inverse relationship between quantity demanded and price of a good will hold good, that is, due to substitution effect alone demand curve slopes downward.*

Now, if the consumer chooses the combination *S* on the line segment *QE* of budget line *DE*, it means that he buys *MN* more due to the substitution effect. Thus he prefers combination *S* to combination *Q*. In other words, his choice of *S* instead of *Q* reveals that he will be *better off* at *S* as compared to *Q*. Now, if money income withdrawn from him is restored to him so that he is faced with the budget line *AC*. If income effect is positive, he will choose a combination, say *R*, on the budget line *AC* to the right of point *S* indicating that as a result of income effect he buys *NH* more of the commodity *X*. Thus quantity demanded of commodity *X* increases by *MN* as a result of substitution effect and by *NH* as a result of income effect. This proves the law of demand stating inverse relationship between price and quantity demanded.

On budget line *DE*, if the consumer chooses combination *Q* and consequently substitution effect is zero, the whole increase in quantity demanded *MH* as a result of decline in price of good *X* will be due to positive income effect. However, which is more likely the substitution effect will lead to the choice by a consumer a combination such as *S* that lies to the right of *Q* on the line segment *QE* and will therefore cause increase in quantity demanded. This substitution effect, is reinforced by the positive income effect and as result we get a downward-sloping demand curve.

It needs to be emphasised that *in revealed preference theory it is not possible to locate exact positions of points S and R obtained as a result of substitution effect and income effect respectively*. It will be recalled that with indifference curve analysis we could obtain precise points to which a consumer moves as a result of substitution and income effects and as we saw in the previous chapter that these were the points of tangency of indifference curves with the relevant budget lines. As explained above, revealed preference theory is based on the assumption that all points on or below the budget line are *strongly ordered* and relation of indifference of a consumer between some combinations of goods is therefore ruled out. In revealed preference theory, choice of a consumer reveals his preference for a chosen position; it cannot reveal indifference of the consumer between combinations. Therefore, in revealed preference theory we can say about the *direction* of substitution effect through logical ordering and cannot measure the exact size of it, nor we can measure the exact amount of income effect of the change in price.

Besides, the substitution effect obtained through variation in income through cost difference method, does not represent *pure* substitution effect in the Hicksian sense in which the consumer's satisfaction remains constant. In substitution effect obtained by the revealed preference theory through Slutskian method of cost difference, the consumer moves from point *Q* to point *S* on budget line *DE*. His choice of *S* on budget line *DE* instead of *Q* under the influence of substitution effect shows that he prefers *S* to *Q*. That is, he is *better off* in position *S* as compared to the position *Q*. Therefore, it is maintained by some economists that the substitution effect obtained in revealed preference theory is not a pure one and contains also some income effect.[4]

However, the present author is of the view that the two types of substitution effect (Hicksian and the one obtained in revealed preference theory) differ with regard to the *concept of real income* used by them. In indifference curve analysis the term real income is used in the sense of level of satisfaction obtained by the consumer, whereas in revealed preference theory real income is used in the sense of purchasing power. Thus, Hicksian substitution effect involves the change in the quantity demanded of a good when *its relative price alone changes, level of his satisfaction remaining the same.* On the other hand, *revealed preference theory* considers substitution effect as the result of change in relative price of a good on its quantity demanded, *consumer's purchasing power remaining the same.* In Fig.9.7. when we obtain budget line *DE* after reduction in income by the cost difference so that it passes through the original combination *Q* chosen by the consumer before the fall in price. This implies that with budget line *DE*, he can buy, if he so desires, the original combination *Q*, that is, the gain in purchasing power or real income caused by fall in price of *X* has been cancelled out by the reduction in his money income.

CRITICAL APPRAISAL OF REVEALED PREFERENCE THEORY

Samuelson's revealed preference theory has gained some advantages over the Marshallian cardinal utility theory and Hicks-Allen indifference curve theory of demand. It is the first to apply behaviouristic method to derive demand theorem from observed consumer's behaviour. In contrast, both the earlier theories, namely, Marshallian utility analysis and Hicks-Allen

4. See Stonier and Hague, *A Textbook of Economic Theory*, Orient Longman, 5th edition.

indifference curve theory were psychological and introspective explanations of consumer's behaviour. Both these earlier theories have been considered to be unsatisfactory by Samuelson who remarks, "For just as we do not claim to know by introspection the behaviour of utility, many will argue we cannot know the behaviour of ratio of marginal utilities or of indifference directions."[5] He further says, "The introduction and meaning of the marginal rate of substitution as an entity independent of any psychological, introspective implications would be, to say the least, ambiguous and would seem an artificial convention in the explanation of price behaviour."[6] Samuelson thinks that his revealed preference theory casts away the last vestiges of the psychological analysis in the explanation of consumer's behaviour.

It has been claimed that behaviouristic method is more scientific than the introspective method. In fact, the behaviouristic method has been called 'the scientific method'. Now, the question is whether it is the behaviouristic approach or the psychological approach which is more correct to explain consumer's demand. Two opinions are held in this regard. Prof. Samuelson and others of his way of thinking contend that the behaviouristic method is the only valid method of explaining consumer's demand. On other hand, Prof. Knight who belongs to the philosophical-psychological school of thought has called the scientific (behaviouristic) approach as the 'recourse' of those who worship the occam's razor.[7]

We are of the opinion that no prior grounds for choosing between behaviourist and introspective methods can be offered which would be acceptable irrespective of personal inclinations. Commenting on the behaviourist-ordinalist controversy, Professor Tapas Majumdar says, "*Behaviourism certainly has great advantages of treading only on observed ground; it cannot go wrong.*" But whether it goes far enough is the question. It may also be claimed for the method of introspection that operationally it can get all the results which are obtained by the alternative method, and it presumes to go further, *it not only states, but also explains its theorems.*"[8] We may conclude that which of the two methods is better and more staisfactory depends upon one's personal philosophical inclinations. However, behaviourist method has recently gained wide support from the economists and has become very popular.

Samuelson's revealed preference theory also marks an advance over the earlier theories of demand by giving up the dubious assumptions underlying them. Both the Marshallian utility analysis and Hicks-Allen indifference curve theory were based upon the utility-maximisation postulate. In these theories, rational behaviour on the part of consumer is interpreted as the attempt on his part to maximise utility or satisfaction. But this utility-maximising postulate has been objected to on the ground that it is very severe and is therefore difficult of realisation in actual practice. Prof. Samuelson has given up utility maxmisation assumption and has instead employed consistency postulate to derive the demand theorem,. Now, this assumption of consistency of choice in the consumer's behaviour is much less severe and conforms more to the real world behaviour of the consumers.

Professor Samuelson has likewise abandoned the assumption of continuity. The indifference curve theory involved the assumption of continuity. Indifference curves are continuous curves in which lie all conceivable combinations, whether they are actually available in the market or not. It may happen under indifference curve analysis that the budget line comes to be tangent to an indifference curve on the point which represents a combination which is not actually available. Thus, continuity assumption is quite unrealistic. The real

5. Samuelson. A Note on the Pure Theory of Consumer's Behaviour, *Economica*, Feb. 1938, p. 61.
6. *Ibid*, p. 62
7. *Introduction to Carl Menger's Principles of Economics*, p. 20.
8. Tapas Majumdar, *Measurement of Utility* (Italics Supplied).

economic world exhibits discontinuity. Now, the continuity assumption is not involved in the revealed preference theory. Of course, in the graphic explanation of the revealed preference theory a continuous price-income line, that is, a budget line is drawn within or on which the consumer has to choose any combination. But since the theory is based upon the actual observed choice of the consumer, and the consumer will choose a combination among all those actually available in the given price-income situation the continuity is not involved in the revealed preference theory.

The concept of reveal preference is a powerful tool which can provide a significant information about consumer's preferences from which we can derive law of demand or downward-sloping demand curve. Revealed preference theory does this without assuming that a consumer possesses complete information about his preferences and indifferences. In indifference curve analysis it is supposed that consumers have complete and consistent scale of preferences reflected in a set of indifference curves. His purchases of goods are in accordance with the scale of preferences. It is as if consumers were carrying complete indifference maps in their mind and purchasing goods accordingly. Therefore, it was considered better to derive demand theorem by observing consumer's behaviour in making actual choices. Most economists now-a-days believe that it is unrealistic to assume that a consumers have complete knowledge of their scale of preferences depicted in a set of indifference curves. The merit of revealed preference theory is that it has made possible to derive law of demand (i.e. downward-sloping demand curve) on the basis of revealed preference without using indifference curves and associated restrictive assumptions. Further, it has enabled us to divide the price effect into its two component parts, namely, substitution and income effects through cost difference method and axiom of revealed preference. Cost difference method requires only market data regarding increase of goods in different market situations. Cost difference (ΔC) can be simply measured by change in price (ΔP) multiplied by the quantity initially purchased by him. Thus,

$$\Delta C = \Delta P_x, Q_x$$

where ΔC stands for the cost difference, ΔP_x stands for the change in price of good X, Q_x is the quantity purchased by the consumer before the change in price of the good X.

Further, with revealed preference theory we can even establish the *existence* of indifference curves and their important property of *convexity*. However, it is notworthy that indifference curves are not required for deriving law of demand or downward sloping demand curve. Indifference curve analysis requires less information than Marshall's cardinal utility theory. But it still requires a lot of information on the part of a consumer since indifference curve analysis requires him to be able to rank consistently all possible combinations of goods. On the other hand, in Samuelson's revealed preference theory of demand the consumer does not require to rank his preferences on the basis of his introspection. It is based on the preferences revealed by his purchases or choices in the different market situations and on the axiom of revealed preference. If consumer's preferences and tastes do not change, revealed preference theory enables us to derive demand theorem just from observation of his market behaviour, that is, what purchases or choices he makes in different market situations. It is however assumed that his preference pattern or tastes do not change. As said above, we can even construct indifference curves from consumer's revealed preferences even though they are not required for establishing law of demand.

A Critique of Revealed Preference Theory

Although Samuelson's revealed preference approach has made some important improvements upon the earlier theories of demand but it is not free from all flaws. Various criticisms have been levelled against it.

First, Samuelson does not admit the possibility of indifference in consumer's behaviour. As has been explained above, the rejection of indifference by Samuelson follows from his strong ordering preference hypothesis. Prof. J.R. Hicks in his later work "*A Revision of Demand Theory*" does not consider the assumtion of strong ordering as satisfactory and instead employs weak ordering from of preference hypothesis. Whereas under strong ordering, the chosen combination is shown to be preferred to all other combinations *in* and *on* the triangle, under weak ordering the chosen combination is preferred to all positions *within* the triangle but *may be either preferred to or indifferent to other combinations on* the same triangle (*i.e.* on the budget line).

Further, in Samuelson's theory, preference is considered to be revealed from a single act of choice. It has been pointed out that if preference is to be judged from a large number of observations, then the possibility of indifference also emerges. Thus, an individual reveals preference for *A* over *B* if he chooses *A* rather than *B more frequently* than he chooses B rather than *A* over a given number of observations. Now, we can say that an individual is indifferent between the two situations *A* and *B* if a definite preference for either does not emerge from a sufficiently large number of observations. Thus only because Samuelson regards preference to be revealed from a single act of choice that indifference relation is methodologically inadmissible to his theory. The possibility of indifference relation clearly emerges if the existence of preference or otherwise is to be judged from a sufficiently large number of observations.

Furthermore, if we assume that an *individual is able to compare his ends,* which is a very valid assumption to be made about the individual's behaviour, then the possibility of indifference or in other words, remaining at the same level of satisfaction by sacrificing some amount of one good for a certain amount of another good will emerge clearly. Thus, commenting on the Samuelson's revealed preference theory from 'welfare' point of view Prof. Tapas Majumdar remarks : "It may be remembered that in all forms of welfare theory, indeed in any integral view of human activity, we have to assume that the individual can always compare his ends. If this axiom is not granted, the whole of welfare economics falls to the ground. And if this axiom is granted, then the idea of remaining on the same level of welfare while sacrificing something of one commodity for something else of another will emerge automatically."[9]

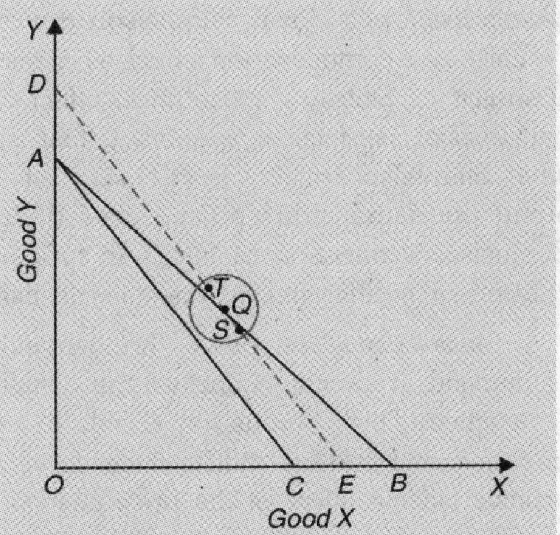

Fig. 9.8. *Armstrong's Notion of Indifference and Samuelson's Consumption* Theorem

Again, Mr. Armstrong has propounded the view that there are points of indifference on every side of a given chosen point. Thus, according to his view, the collection of goods actually selected by the consumer is one of the few between which the consumer is inidfferent. If this contention of armstrong is granted, then the proof which Samuelson's theory offers to establish the Fundamental Theorem of Consumption Theory breaks down. This is illustrated in Fig. 9.8. In price-income situation *AB*, the consumer chooses the combination *Q*. According

9. Tapas Majumdar, Measurement of Utility, p. 90

to Armstrong's notion, points around *Q* (within the circle) such as *S*, *T* etc. would be indifferent to *A*. Suppose that the price of good *X* rises so that the price-income situation is now *AC*. If an extra grantof money is given to the consumer so that he can buy the same combination *Q*, the price-income situation is *DE*. Now, in price-income situation *DE*, the consumer can pick up a point like *S* below *Q* on *QE*.

Thus, choice of *S* instead of *Q*, or *T* (or any other point in the circle) is not inconsistent to his previous choice because he was indifferent between points such as *Q*, *T*, *S* etc. But the choice of *S* in price income situation *DE* means that the consumer buys more of *X* now when its price is higher (since *DE* is parallel to *AC*, it represents the higher price of *X* as represented by *AC*). It follows, therefore, that if Armstrong's notion about points of indifference around the chosen point is granted, Samuelson's proof that the demand for a good shrinks when its price rises breaks down.

Further, it has been argued that Prof. Samuelson, because of his ruling out the relation of indifference, does not recognise or admit the substitution effect which is the operational consequence of the non-observable indifference hypothesis. It has been pointed out that Samuelson's revealed preference theory is based upon observed consumer's behaviour and on the plane of observation substitution effect cannot be distinguished from income effect. Since response of demand to a change in price is a composite of income and substitution effects, it is concluded, that Samuelson's theory offers a partial explanation of change in demand as a result of change in price. But to the present author, it seems that this criticism of Samuelson's theory is misplaced. In his article "*Consumption Theorems in Terms of Over Compensation*,'[10] Prof. Samuelson draws clear distinction between income effect and what he calls over-compensation effect as a result of change in price. His over-compensation effect is similar to Slutsky's substitution effect which involves the movement of the consumer from one level of satisfaction to another (that is, from one indifference curve to another). Therefore, what Samuelson rejects is Hicksian type substitution effect which permits only movement along the same indifference curve (that is, level of satisfaction remains the same). And Samuelson's rejection of Hicksian type substitution effect follows from his rejection of the relation of indifference in consumer's behaviour.

Since Samuelson proves his demand theorem on the basis of positive income elasticity of demand, it cannot enunciate the demand theorem when income effect or income elasticity is negative. Thus, Samuelson is able to enunciate the demand theorem in the case in which, in terms of Hicksain indifference curve theory, substitution effect has been reinforced by positive income effect of the price change. When the income elasticity is negative, Samuelson's revealed preference theory is unable to establish the demand theorem. In other words, given negative income elasticity of demand, we cannot know on the basis of revealed preference theory as to what will be the direction of change in demand as a result of change in price. Thus, Samuelson's revealed preference theory cannot enunciate the demand theorem when (*i*) the income elasticity is negative and the negative income effect is smaller than the substitution effect; and (*ii*) the income elasticity is negative and the negative income effect is greater than the substitution effect.

From above it follows that Samuelson's theory cannot account for Giffen's Paradox. The case of Giffen goods occurs when the income effect is negative and this negative income effect is so powerful that it outweighs the substitution effect. In case of Giffen goods, demand varies directly with price. Since he assumes income elasticity to be positive in his establishment of demand theorem, his theory cannot include the Giffen-good case. Prof. Samuelson denies

10. See *Economica*, February 1953, p. 2.

the validity of Giffen goods in which case demand seems to vary directly with price. He thus says, "but the phenomenon of Giffen's Paradox reminds us that the Marshallian proposition is not a true theorem and it is rather to a theory's credit than discredit if it refuses to enunciate a false theorem."[11] According to Samuelson, only valid theorem in demand theory is the one that establishes inverse relationship between price and demand. Against this we may, however, point out that Giffen good may not really exist in the world, but it is theoretically conceivable. Its theoretical possibility is clear when negative income effect of a change in price of an inferior good outweighs the substitution effect with the result that demand changes in the same direction as the price. Thus Hicks-Allen theorem of demand is more general than the Samuelson's Fundamental Theorem of Consumption theory since the former includes Giffen good case, while the latter does not. We thus conclude that though Samuelson makes improvement over the Hicks-Allen indifference curves theory of demand in respect of methodology adopted (that is, its behaviouristic method is superior to Hicks-Allen introspective method) but in respect of the content of the demand theorem enunciated by it, it is a few steps backward than the Hicks-Allen demand theorem.

In the end, we may emphasize the point that superiority of Samuelson's theory lies in his applying scientific or behaviouristic method to the consumer's demand and his enunciation of preference hypothesis.

QUESTIONS FOR REVIEW

1. What is meant by 'revealed preference hypothesis' ? Explain Samuelson revealed preference theory of demand based on it.
2. Carefully state the assumptions of the revealed preference theory of demand. Explain how law of demand is derived from these assumptions.
3. Define substitution effect. *Substitution effect is always negative.* How can you prove it with revealed preference approach to demand theory ?
4. Distinguish between strong-ordering and weak aordering forms of pregference hypothesis.
5. What is Slutsky theorem? How will you establish it with the help of revealed preference approach to demand analysis?
6. Explain how price effect is broken up into income effect and substitution effect with the aid of revealed preference theory of demand.
7. The price of a good increases. We know that the substitution effect is always negative. Does it follow that the income and substitution effects of the price rise always work in the same direction if the income elasticity of demand for the good is negative? Will the demand curve be downward sloping? Explain.
8. Show with the help of a diagram that the substitution effect of a fall in price of a commodity will make a consumer either consume the same quantity or more but not less of it.
9. (*a*) State Samuelson's "Weak Axiom of Recealed Preference" (WARP)

   (*b*) Consider two commodities, apples and oranges. Initially when both apples and oranges cost Re. 1 per unit each, a consumer buys 4 aspples and 6 oranges. When the price of apples rises to Rs. 2 per unit and that of oranges falls to Rs. 0.50 per unit, she buys 8 apples and 3 oranges. Does she violate WARP.
10. Revealed preference theory makes a major advancement in the study of consumer's behaviour. Discuss.

11. 'Consumption Theorems in Terms of Over-compensation', *Economica*, February 1953, p. 2.

Demand Estimation

Introduction

In some previous chapters we have explained the various theories of demand and have shown how demand for products plays a crucial role in business decision-making aimed at maximising profits or increasing the value of the firm. We have seen how the knowledge of price elasticity, income elasticity and cross elasticity of demand help the managers in making proper decisions regarding pricing of their products. A manager who is considering an increase in the price of a product of the firm should know the effect of this increase in the product-price on the quantity demanded, total revenue and profits of the firm. As we have seen, this effect depends on whether the demand for the product is elastic or inelastic. Similarly, the knowledge of income elasticity of demand of the products show what will happen if consumer's income increases or decreases as a result of expansion or recession in the economy. However, in our chapters on demand analysis we assumed that these elasticities were known to the managers of business firms. But this is not usually the case. Therefore, for proper decision-making regarding price and output of the product managers should collect adequate information and data from which *empirical relationship* between changes in factors affecting demand and the quantity demanded of a product can be established. Statistical methods can also be used to estimate a demand function from the relevant data from which elasticities or effects of changes in factors affecting demand can be calculated. From the estimated demand function the demand for the product can be predicted based on certain values of prices, income and other factors and their corresponding coefficients.

In this chapter, we explain the three important methods used to estimate the parameters (i.e., coefficients) of demand function. They are :

(1) Consumer Surveys
(2) Consumer Clinics
(3) Market Experiments
(4) Statistical Technique of Regression Analysis

Consumesr Surveys

The technique of consumer surveys involves questioning of a sample of consumers of a product about how they will respond to changes in prices of the product, changes in prices of related products (i.e., substitutes and complements), changes in advertising expenditure on a product, credit incentives etc. There are two ways of conducting such consumer surveys. First, they can be done by stopping and questioning consumers at shopping centres about their responses to the changes in prices of products, to the advertising campaigns launched by the producers etc. Secondly, consumer surveys can be made by preparing suitable questionnaires and providing or sending them to a *carefully chosen* representative sample of consumers. These consumers can then give their responses or reactions to the changes in factors affecting demand in writing or orally to the trained interviewers.

Merits and Shortcomings. Consumer surveys can provide useful information and data about demand relationships to the firms on the basis of which they can formulate their price, output and advertising strategies. On the basis of information and data collected through these surveys, a firm can predict the demand for its product and can at least roughly estimate some of the important parameters of the demand function.

However, despite its great usefulness this method has some shortcomings. Consumers are often unable and in some cases unwilling to provide correct answers to the hypothetical questions asked by the interviewers about how they would respond to the changes in the important variables in the demand function. Therefore, the quality or reliability of the information provided by such surveys is very poor and quite limited. For example, consider an example. If you are asked how you would react to 2 or 3 per cent reduction or increase in the price of Zen VX model of Maruti Car; would you be able to provide correct answer to this hypothetical question. Further, if the interviewers asks you about the effect on your demand for the car if Maruti Company increases its advertising expenditure on Zen VX or changes its advertising media from newspapers to television or improves its looks and comforts rather than fuel efficiency, it will indeed be very difficult for you to provide correct and reliable information. Thus, if people are unable to provide correct answer to the effects on demand of changes in price, advertising expenditure in case of major items such as cars, electrical appliances such as air conditioners, refrigerators, in case of most of ordinary consumer goods it will be very difficult to give correct response. For example, how would you react if price of Coca-Cola or Pepsi-Cola is raised by 5 per cent, would you be able to tell how much your monthly consumption of Coca-Cola/Pepsi-Cola will be affected. Thus, it is very difficult to correctly estimate the demand relationship for many consumer goods through survey method.

However, it should not be understood that consumer survey method does not at all provide any useful information about demand relationship. A trained interviewer can gather useful information about consumer behaviour by asking some probing questions. For example, by asking subtle questions about relative prices of competing goods might reveal that consumers are unaware of the price differences among competing goods. This is indicator that consumers are not much price conscious and their demand for goods is not highly responsive to price changes. With this information the firm will not reduce the price for the purpose of increasing the quantity demanded of its product. Similar probing questions can be asked by the interviewers to elicit useful information about the individuals' reaction to advertising campaigns of a firm as to what extent their demand is affected by certain advertising campaigns. Besides, interviews of consumers can provide information about consumers' expectations about future business and credit conditions and thus helps in predicting short-run demand or sales of the products, especially of durable goods. To conclude, though quite accurate estimate about demand cannot be made through survey technique, it may still provide useful information which is not much different from the correct estimate.

Consumer Clinics

Another important method of knowing about consumer response to the changes in the factors influencing demand is the use of consumer clinics. Consumer clinics are similar to laboratory experiments. In this method some selected individuals are given some amounts of money which they have to spend on certain goods kept in a particular store (termed as clinic). By making changes in prices of products, in prices of their competitive goods, and by making changes in product packages, displays and other factors affecting demand, the experimenter can assess their impact on the demand for the products. In order to provide incentives to the consumers to take interest in buying the goods they prefer most and to buy the quantities they desire most, in such experiments they are allowed to keep with themselves the goods they purchase in these experimental clinics. Better information can be obtained if participants in such experiments are so chosen as to form a true representative sample of socio-economic classes in the market of interest.

Besides being able to control the environment, information obtained from the consumer clinics is more realistic than that of consumer survey (that is, direct interview method) where the consumers are only faced with hypothetical situations. However, technique of estimating demand through consumer clinics suffers from certain shortcomings. First, the cost of setting up and running such clinics is very high and therefore the number of consumers who are chosen for such experiments to observe their purchasing behaviour and demand relationships is usually very small. As a result, reliable results from them cannot be obtained. Second, results of such experiments may not reveal their real purchasing behaviour of the consumers as they know that they are purchasing goods in an artificial market situation and that they are being observed in the experiment. As a result, they may attempt to act in a manner somewhat different from they *actually* or normally behave. Consumers participating in a consumer clinic suspect that the experimenter is interested in their revealing sensitivity to changes in prices, income, advertising expenditure etc. and as a result they become more conscious in their behaviour and show more sensitivity to these changes than they are actually so in a real market situation.

Despite the above shortcomings, consumer clinics provide some useful information which may be of great help in decision making, especially when they are supplemented by proper consumer surveys. Besides, as shall be known after the discussion of alternative methods of estimating demand, namely, direct market experiments, regression analysis that consumer surveys and clinics are the method of providing information about demand relationships only in certain cases.

Market Experiments

The demand for the products can be estimated through direct experiments in contrast to consumer clinics which are set up and run under strict laboratory environment. Market experiments examine consumer behaviour in actual market situation. One method of actual market experiments is that a firm may vary price or some other determinants of demand to estimate the effect on quantity demanded. For example, in India Hindustan Lever Company has offered two different types of bathing soaps, *Lux* and *Liril* with the same content but with a price differential and with different packagings. This has revealed that consumers' demand for Lux is more than that of Liril which is costlier. This shows sensitivity of consumers' demand to price changes. Similarly, several companies have conducted actual market experiments to examine sensitivity to changes in advertising expenditure and these experiments have shown that consumers' demand is quite responsive to changes in advertising expenditure.

Another method of conducting actual market experiments is to select various markets with similar socio-economic characteristics and to assess consumers' response by changing the price of the product in some markets, packaging in other markets, amount and type of advertising expenditure in some others. In this way different responses, that is, changes in purchases or sales of the product may be recorded. It may be noted that the firm should change one factor affecting demand at a time in different markets to correctly estimate consumers' response.

Actual market experiments has a merit in that they can be made on a scale large enough to ensure reliability of the result obtained and further that in this method consumers do not feel that they are the part of an experiment. However, this method has also some serious shortcomings. If such market experiments are conducted on a scale large enough to ensure reliability of results, it may be quite risky. For example, the firm may lose some customers permanently when it is making experiments with raising prices of the product to assess the price elasticity of demand. Second, if actual market experiments of examining the effects of changes in various factors affecting demand for the product are conducted on a large scale, they prove to be very costly. As a result, the cost of actual market experiments may be higher as compared to that of controlled experiments such as setting consumer clinics. Thirdly, the observed results of actual market experiments may get distorted due to all sorts of external disturbance factors. These factors such as bad weather conditions, adverse changes in market conditions or price reduction by rival firms when a firm is conducting its market experiments will provide unreliable results. Thus, due to high cost and large risk involved, the duration of market experiments of changing price, advertising expenditure etc. may be very short. Therefore, *long-term business decisions cannot be validly* made on the basis of such short-run experiments.

Despite the above drawbacks, market experiments may prove to be useful in a number of situations. First, for a firm market experiments happen to be useful means of arriving at a best pricing strategy after experimenting with prices of its product. Secondly, it is also useful in testing different packagings, different advertising media, and different product models to arrive at an optimal packaging, ideal model and most effective promotional activity. Thirdly, market experiments are of particular importance for launching a new product whose historical data do not exist and therefore statistical method of regression analysis cannot be used to estimate demand. Lastly, the market experiments can have an important role in verifying the results of statistical technique of regression analysis used for estimating demand. It can also provide data for use of statistical methods to estimate demand for product.

REGRESSION ANALYSIS

Regression analysis is a statistical technique to estimate demand for a product. With the help of regression analysis we can say precisely *to what extent* quantity demanded is responsive to changes in price of a product, prices of other goods, income of the people and promotional efforts such as advertising expenditure. For example, while law of demand says that quantity demanded is inversely related to the price of a product, it does not tell us to what extent quantity demanded changes in response to changes in these factors. With the help of regression analysis we can calculate demand coefficients and demand elasticities which measure quantitative relationship between demand and the factors that affect it. Thus, regression analysis is said to be superior to the methods of consumer survey, consumer clinics and market experiments. Regression analysis of demand estimation involve the following five steps :

1. Identifying the variables.
2. Collection of data.
3. Choice of a functional form of the demand equation that describes the relationship between the dependent and independent variables.
4. Estimating the parameters of the demand equation.
5. Interpretation of the results and making predictions based on the model used.

We explain below these steps of regression analysis for demand estimation in some detail.

Identifying Variables. In the analysis of demand function in a previous chapter, we have seen the quantity demanded is a function of price of the product, per capita income, prices of related goods, advertising expenditure, tastes and preferences of the consumers. It is important to note that the identification of independent variables that affect demand should be based on sound theoretical model describing economic relationship which tells us what independent variables should be included for estimating demand. The general demand function or model which is used to estimate demand is

$$Q_d = f(P_x, I, P_o, A, T)$$

where

Q_d = Quantity demand
P_x = Price of good X whose demand is to be estimated
I = Income of the consumers
P_o = Prices of other goods
A = Advertising expenditure by the firm to promote the sales of its product
T = Tastes and preferences of consumers.

The above demand function says that quantity demanded (which is dependent variable) of a product depends on its own price, per capita income of the consumers, prices of related goods, advertising expenditure, tastes and preferences which are independent variables. The one who conducts the regression analysis should seek to know as much as possible about factors that affect demand for the product before identifying the factors to be included in the demand equation as independent variables. If any important variable is omitted, the regression equation will be misspecied and therefore the estimates of parameters obtained may not be accurate. Thus, in the formulation of demand equation or model, all important variables should be included if we want accurate results.

However, the inclusion of more variables require more data to be collected which are not easily available or which are very costly to generate through consumer surveys or market experiments. Hence, researchers include important few variables, at the most upto six or seven variables.

It is important to note that economic theory can be used to examine the sign of the estimates of parameters obtained. If the sign of an estimated coefficient is contrary to the predictions of economic theory, the whole issue should be re-examined. For example, economic theory predicts that quantity demanded and price of a product are negatively related. But if regression analysis finds that the sign of the price coefficient is positive, it means that there is something wrong somewhere. Either the demand equation is not correctly specified or identified with some relevant variables being omitted or some error has been committed in the data collection or there is something special or unique about the product or service whose price demand relationship is being estimated.

Data Collection. Once the variables have been identified, the next step to estimate demand is the collection of relevant data. Required data can be obtained from a variety of sources. If demand for the product of a firm is being estimated, one important source of data is the past records of the firm. Secondly, data may be generated by conducting consumer surveys or market experiments. When demand for a product of the whole industry is being estimated, the relevant data may be obtained from the publications of the industry or of the State or of Central Government. Sometime the data is not available in the form required, researcher in that case has to make some transformation in the data to make it usable for regression analysis.

It is important to note that for estimating demand either *time-series or cross-section data* is used. Time-series data relate to period-wise (*i.e.*, monthly, quarterly or yearly) data of the market about the quantity demanded and the independent variables such as price, income, advertising expenditure that affect demand. For example, monthly data for 24 months about the sales, price advertising expenditure of '*Saffola*' edible oil in Delhi will be an example of time-series data that can be used for estimating demand for Saffola in Delhi.

On the other hand, *cross-section data* relate to the quantity demanded and the factors affecting it in a number of markets during a given time period. If the cross-section data show variation from market to market it can be used for estimating demand.

Choice of a Functional Form. The next step in the estimation of demand through regression analysis is to specify the form of the demand function that show the relationship between quantity demanded (*i.e.*, the dependent variable) and the independent variables such as price, income, advertising expenditure. The form of the demand function that should be chosen for estimation should show true or accurate relationship as closely as possible between the dependent and the independent variables. Various alternative forms should be tried for estimation and one which yields the best fit between the demand and independent variables affecting it should be used. The clue to which functional form should be initially used for estimation can be obtained by drawing a graph or scatter diagram between the dependent variable and the independent variable. The results of examining the scatter diagram will often show whether a linear equation model is the most appropriate or whether logarithmic, exponential or other functional forms is the proper one to estimate. Two important functional forms which are generally used to estimate demand are the linear demand model and multiplicative demand model.

Linear Demand Model. The linear demand equation is the simplest and most common form of the demand function used in the regression analysis. In the linear demand function the various factors affecting demand for a product of a firm are specified as follows :

$$Q_d = \alpha + \beta_1 P + \beta_2 I + \beta_3 P_o + \beta_4 A + e$$

where α, β_1, β_2, β_3 and β_4 are the parameters of the demand function and e is the error term. The values of these parameters are estimated using regression analysis which will be explained below later. The inclusion of error term in the demand equation implies that relationship between quantity demanded and the various independent variables is not an exact one. That is, estimated value of quantity demanded may not be equal to its real observed value. This divergence between the two is the indicator of error involved in estimating specified demand function. Ideally, the estimation technique should aim at minimising this divergence.

The linear form of demand function has several merits. First, it is easier to estimate it as it does not require the transformation of data to estimate it. Secondly, the coefficient of the independent variable is easily interpreted. A coefficient of an independent variable, say price of the product, means the change in quantity demanded of the product resulting from a unit change in the price. That is, it gives the value of the β-coefficient as partial derivative, $\frac{\partial Q_d}{\partial P}$. Thirdly, the estimates of β-coefficient are *constant* for each independent variable and are unaffected by the values of other variables in the demand function as the values of other variables are held constant. The constant term α has no special significance as it indicates what will be the value of the dependent variable (*i.e.*, demand) when the values of independent or explanatory variables are equal to zero. Therefore, caution must be exercised when on the basis of the estimated values of the parameters one predicts the demand or makes a forecast of demand that is very far off from the observed values used for estimating the demand function.

It is important to note that in this linear demand model each independent variable has a *constant impact* on a quantity demanded, that is, in linear demand model β-coefficient is constant throughout on every point on the linear demand curve regardless of the level of other independent variables. However, elasticity of demand with respect to each independent variable is not constant but in fact it depends on the point of the linear demand curve where it is measured. This is proved as under :

You may recall that price elasticity of demand in a previous chapter was defined as $\frac{\partial Q_d}{\partial P} \cdot \frac{P}{Q_d}$. Since $\frac{\partial Q}{\partial P}$ means the value of β-coefficient, which as mentioned above, remains constant on a linear demand curve. But since the term $\frac{P}{Q_d}$ in the elasticity formula varies at different points on the demand curve, the point price elasticity of demand varies at different points on the demand curve.

Because of merits and useful properties of the linear demand function it is widely used in empirical studies. Moreover, it is easier to make predictions on the basis of the values of parameters obtained from estimating linear demand function. For example, if the value of β-coefficient of price of a computer has been estimated to be 0.25, then reduction in price of computer of the company by Rs 5,000 per unit will lead to the increase in quantity demanded by 0.25 x 5,000 = 1,250 computers in a period. Likewise, if income coefficient for computer demand is 0.05 and if per capita income of the consumers increases by Rs 1,000, the quantity demanded will increase by 0.05 1,000 = 50 units per period.

With the help of β-coefficient obtained we can also calculate the elasticities of demand with respect to each independent variable. Thus, price elasticity of demand can be calculated from β-coefficient of price in the following manner :

$$e_p = \frac{\partial Q_d}{\partial P} \cdot \frac{P}{Q_d}$$

As explained above, $\frac{\partial Q_d}{\partial P} = \beta_1$

Substituting β_1 for $\frac{\partial Q_d}{\partial P}$ in the elasticity formula, we have

$$e_p = \beta_1 \times \frac{P}{Q_d}$$

Thus, by selecting the value of price (P) and using the estimated demand equation we can calculate quantity demanded (Q_d) at that price. Further, by multiplying the value of $\frac{P}{Q_d}$ so obtained with the value of β-coefficient (β_1), we can have the estimate of point price elasticity of demand.

Income and cross elasticity can also be determined in the same way as price elasticity of demand.

Multiplicative Demand Model: Another functional form of demand equation which is extensively used to estimate the demand is the multiplicative functional form. This multiplicative demand equation can be written as

$$Q_d = \alpha P^{\beta_1} \; I^{\beta_2} \; P_0^{\beta_3} \; A^{\beta_4}$$

In this form the demand equation cannot be estimated using ordinary least squares method because it is not linear. However, the use of this model is popular because there is a simple transformation of the multiplicative equation by converting all the data, both relating to the dependent and independent variables, into logarithmic values. In terms of logarithmic values, the above multiplicative demand equation becomes linear and can be written as

$$\log Q_d = \log \alpha + \beta^2{}_1 \log P + {}^2\beta_2 \log I + \beta^2{}_3 \log P_0 + \beta^2{}_4 \log A + e$$

---

* That the values of β-coefficients in this multiplicative form of demand function measures the elasticities can be proved as under :

Consider the price elasticity of demand taking the derivative of multiplicative equation ($Q_d = \alpha\ P^{\beta_1} I^{\beta_2} P_o^{\beta_3} A^{\beta_4}$) with respect to price, we have

$$\frac{\partial Q_d}{\partial P} = \beta_1 \alpha P^{\beta_1 ? 1} I^{\beta_2} P_o^{\beta_3} A^{\beta_4}$$

Multiplying both sides of the equation by $\frac{P}{Q_d}$, we have

$$\frac{\partial Q_d}{\partial P} \cdot \frac{P}{Q_d} = \frac{\beta_1 \alpha P^{\beta_1} I^{\beta_2} P_o^{\beta_3} A^{\beta_4}}{Q_d}$$

Since $\frac{\partial Q_d}{\partial P} \cdot \frac{P}{Q_d}$ represents price elasticity of demand and $\alpha\ P^{\beta_1}\ I^{\beta_2}\ P_o^{\beta_3}\ A^{\beta_4} = Q_d$, we have

$$e_p = \beta_1 \frac{Q_d}{Q_d}$$

or, $$e_p = \beta_1$$

Similarly, it can be shown that β_2 measures income elasticity of demand, β_3 represents cross elasticity of demand and β_4 measures elasticity with respect to advertising expenditure.

It is important to note that these days it is not necessary by researchers to calculate logarithmic values of the data by hand, since software packages are available with which a computer can accomplish this task in seconds.

The parameters α, β_1, β_2, β_3 and β_4 of the equation in logarithmic form can be estimated using ordinary least squares approach as with transformation into logarithmic form, the demand equation becomes linear. An important fact about this multiplicative demand model is that change in quantity demand associated with per unit change in an independent variable such as price $\left(\text{that is, } \frac{\partial Q_d}{\partial P}\right)$ is not constant but is dependent not only on the value of the concerned independent variable but also on the values of other independent variables. Further, estimation of demand function in this non-linear form, the *value of β–coefficient obtained directly yields elasticities of demand** and unlike the case of linear model *these elasticities are constant over* the range of data used for estimation of these parameters, that is, these elasticities are not dependent on the changes in the values of independent variables.

Estimating the Regression Coefficients

In order to explain the regression analysis to estimate the parameters of demand relationship let us assume that manager wants to know the relationship between the advertising expenditure for promotion of a product and demand for it, that is, sales revenue from it. Further, he wants to know the strength of this relationship, that is, how much sales revenue per period increases as a result of a unit increase in advertising expenditure. The following is the specification of the relationship between advertising expenditure and sales revenue (*i.e.*, demand) from the product :

$$Y = a + bX$$

where Y is the dependent variable and denotes sales revenue from a product, X is the amount of advertising expenditure which is the independent or explanatory variable, a is the intercept and b is the coefficient which shows the relationship between sales revenue and advertising expenditure. Note that b indicates the slope of the function and represents marginal sales revenue resulting from a unit increase in advertising expenditure.

We give in Table 10.1 below the data regarding advertising expenditure incurred by a firm to promote the sales of its product and sales revenue from it collected for the seven years, 1994-2000. Let Y stand for sales revenue, X for advertising expenditure. If the linear demand relationship between the two is hypothesised, then regression equation can be written as

$$Y = a + bX$$

The regression analysis is a statistical technique used for obtaining the line that best fits the data. For obtaining such a regression line ordinary least squares (*OLS*) method is used. According to the least squares method, regression line is the line that is obtained by *minimising the sum of squared vertical deviations of each observed or actual point from the regression line.*

The symbol e is used to denote the vertical deviation of the observed or actual of the dependent variable from its estimated value. (*i.e.*, the amount of sales revenue in our example and the corresponding estimated sales on the regression line). This vertical deviation of the estimated value of the dependent variable from the actual or observed value is also known as *error*. Thus, the vertical derivation or error is

$$e = Y_1 - \tilde{Y}_t$$

where Y_t is the actual or observed value of sales revenue in a year, $\hat{Y}_t$ is the estimated value for that year on the regression line. Note that this error or deviation arises because (1) some factors or independent variables that affect the dependent variable have been omitted in the regression equation, (2) possible mistakes in measurement of data, (3) errors of random human behaviour due to which we get different results (*i.e.*, different sales revenues from a product) under the same conditions.

Table 10.1

Year	1994	1995	1996	1997	1998	1999	2000
Advertising Expenditure (in thousands)	45	65	35	30	25	85	72
Sales Revenue (in thousand units)	370	480	450	360	250	550	620

Least Squares Method. Let us now analyse in some detail the regression method of least squares. To start with, we have plotted the data of sales revenue and corresponding advertising expenditure of various years in Fig. 10.1. A regression line that apparently fits the data best has been drawn. It will be noticed from this figure that a point on the regression line (that is, estimated value of the sales revenue) corresponding to the advertising expenditure of a year differs or deviates from the observed or actual values of sales revenue. It is this vertical deviation that represents the *error* in the estimated value of the sales revenue. It is the sum of the squares of these error terms that is minimised by the choice of parameters a and b in this regression technique of least squares. Thus, the regression equation representing the relationship between advertising expenditure and sales revenue can be written as

$$Y_t = \hat{a} + \hat{b} X_t + e_t \quad \text{... (1)}$$

where $\hat{a}$ is the estimated value of the intercept and $\hat{b}$ is the estimated value of β-coefficient showing the strength of relationship between advertising expenditure and sales revenue.

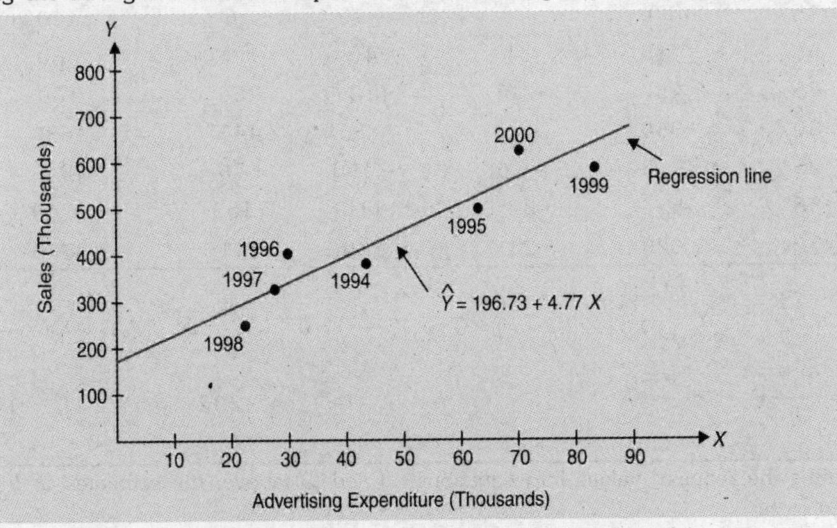

Fig. 10.1. *Advertising Expenditure (Thousands)*

From equation (1) it follows that

$$e_t = Y_t - \hat{a} - \hat{b} X_t \quad \text{...(2)}$$

Taking the sum of the squared error terms, we have

$$\sum_{t=1994}^{t=2000} e_t^2 = \sum_{t=1994}^{t=2000} (Y_t - \tilde{a} - \tilde{b}X_t)^2 \quad \ldots (3)$$

In the regression technique of least squares, it is the equation (3) above that is minimised by choice of the two parameters, *a* and *b*. Thus, in this method, the estimated values of *a* and *b* are :

$$\tilde{b} = \frac{\sum_{t=1994}^{t=2000} (X_t - \bar{X})(Y_t - \bar{Y})}{\sum_{t=1994}^{t=2000} (X_t - \bar{X})^2}$$

$$\tilde{a} = \bar{Y} - \tilde{b}\bar{X}$$

where $\bar{X}$ and $\bar{Y}$ are the mean *values* of actual or observed advertising expenditure and sales revenue respectively.

Now, given the observed data of advertising expenditure and sales revenue as given in Table 1 we can obtain estimated values of *a* and *b* as specified by the above formulations. Necessary calculations are shown in Table 10.2.

Table 10.2 Least Squares Method

Year	Advertising Expenditure X_t	Sales Revenue Y_t	$X_t - \bar{X}$	$Y_t - \bar{Y}$	$(X_t - \bar{X})^2$	$(X_t - \bar{X})(Y_t - \bar{Y})$
1994	45	370	- 6	- 70	36	420
1995	65	480	14	40	196	560
1996	35	450	- 16	10	256	160
1997	30	360	- 21	- 80	441	1680
1998	25	250	- 26	- 190	676	4940
1999	85	550	34	110	1156	3740
2000	72	620	21	180	441	3780
$n = 7$	$\bar{X} = \frac{\Sigma X_t}{7} = \frac{357}{7} = 51$	$\bar{Y} = \frac{\Sigma Y_t}{7} = \frac{3080}{7} = 440$	$\Sigma(X_t - \bar{X}) = 0$,	$\Sigma(Y_1 - \bar{Y}) = 0$	$\Sigma(X_t - \bar{X})^2 = 3202$	$\Sigma(X_t - \bar{X})(Y_t - \bar{Y}) = 15280$

Substituting the required values into equations (2) and (3) above, the estimates of *b* and *a* are calculated to be

$$\tilde{b} = \frac{\sum_{t=1994}^{t=2000} (X_t - \bar{X})(Y_t - \bar{Y})}{\sum_{t=1994}^{t=2000} (X_t - \bar{X})^2} = \frac{15280}{3202} = 4.77$$

$$\tilde{a} = \overline{Y} - b\overline{X} = 440 - 4.77 \times 51 = 196.73$$

Thus, the estimated equation for the demand function is

$$\tilde{Y} = 196.73 + 4.77\ X$$

196.73 is the vertical intercept of the regression line and indicates if there is no advertising expenditure to promote the sales of the product, total sales revenue from the product would be 196.73 thousand rupees. The coefficient b shows the eflect of change in advertising expenditure (X) on the change in the sales value (Y). As is expected on the basis of economic, theory that more advertising expenditure generally leads to the increase in demand for the product and therefore in sales revenue, the sign of the b-coefficient is positive and therefore correct. Further, estimated value of b being equal to 4.77 indicates that hike in advertising expenditure by one thousand rupees causes the sales revenue to increase by 4.77 thousand rupees.

It should be noted that we have omitted the error term at the last *stage because its expected* value is always zero. It should be further noted that actual calculation by hand or calculator is not difficult when there are a few observations. When the number of observations are very large, as is actually the case, software packages such as SPSS (Statistical Package for Social Sciences) are available which enable a researcher to make these difficult calculations with the aid of a computer in minutes by feeding the data indicating dependent and independent variables. Computer makes the necessary calculations as we have done in Table 2 above and gives us the estimates of the parameters a and b. Not only that, the computer very quickly calculates the value of R^2 and t-values and other necessary statistics which are needed to interpret the estimated values of the parameters.

Another Example : Estimating Demand-Price Relationship

In the above example we have explained the regression technique of relationship between demand and advertising expenditure using time-series data. Another important example of demand estimation refers to the demand-price relationship. We explain this with an example using cross-section data. In the Table 10.3, we have given the *number of meals* served per day (that is, demand for meals) and the price per meal in 8 ordinary hotels in North Delhi. Let Q_d stands for number of meals served per day by a hotel and P for the price per meal. The demand function which we seek to estimate is written as

$$Q_d = a + bP$$

Table 10.3

Hotel	1	2	3	4	5	6	7	8
Price per meal Rs.	30	36	38	281	26	38	32	28
Meals served per day	200	180	170	220	240	180	210	200

Since economic theory tells us that quantity demanded is inversely related to price of a product, demand equation can be written as

$$Q_i = a - bP_i$$

Necessary calculations to estimate the values of a and b of the above demand function are done in Table 10.4, Note that in this regression equation, price P_i is price per meal and Q_i is the number of meals served in a hotel per day, that is, Q_i is the quantity demanded of hotel meals and is dependent variable. It will be seen from Table 10.4 that mean value of price of per meal is Rs 32 and mean number of meals per day in a hotel has calculated to be equal to 200.

Table 10.4

Hotel	Price (P) (Rs)	Meals day (Q)	$(P_i - \bar{P})$	$(Q_i - \bar{Q})$	$(P_i - \bar{P})^2$	$(P_i - \bar{P})(Q_i - \bar{Q})$
1	30	200	– 2	0	4	0
2	36	180	4	–20	16	–80
3	38	170	6	–30	36	– 180
4	28	220	–4	20	16	–80
5	26	240	–6	40	36	–240
6	38	180	6	–20	36	–120
7	32	210	0	10	0	0
8	28	200	–4	0	16	0

$n = 8 \quad \bar{P} = \frac{256}{8} = 32 \quad \bar{Q} = \frac{1600}{8} = 200 \quad (P_i - \bar{P})^2 = 160 \quad \sum (P_i - \bar{P})(Q_i - \bar{Q}) = -700$

Now,
$$\hat{b} = \frac{\sum (P_i - \bar{P})(Q_i - \bar{Q})}{\sum (P_i - \bar{P})^2}$$

Substituting the calculated values, we have

$$\hat{b} = \frac{-700}{160} = -4.375$$

$$\hat{a} = \bar{Q} + b\bar{P}$$
$$= 200 - 4.375 \times 32$$
$$= 200 - 140 = 60$$

Thus, the estimated equation is

$$\hat{Q} = 60 - 4.375\,P$$

QUESTIONS FOR REVIEW

1. Explain the methods of (*a*) consumer survey, (*b*) consumer clinics for estimating demand for the product. What are their merits and shortcomings ?
2. How are actual market experiments conducted to estimate demand ? What are its main advantages and shortcomings ?
3. (*a*) What steps are usually involved in the estimation of demand equation by regression analysis ?

   (*b*) How does a researcher determine the demand model to estimate ?
4. What are the main advantages of regression analysis for estimating demand over the alternative methods of consumer surveys and market experiments ?
5. How does a researcher obtain the data to estimate demand equation by regression analysis ? What are some of the useful sources of data for Indian industries and trade ?
6. Why is the line connecting the *observed price-quantity data points* usually does not represent the demand curve for the commodity ? How is the demand curve for a commodity identified from these observed data points of price-quantity demanded ?

7. The following data of a manufacturing company is given. X is advertising expenditure in thousand rupees and Y is sales (in thousand units) at a product.

X	0	1	2	3	4
Y	1	2	4	5	6

Using least squares method of regression analysis, calculate the coefficients of this demand equation. Calculate standard error and t-statistics for b-coefficient of the regression equation ($Y = a + bX$).

7. Using a regression equation estimate the demand function for the new cotton shirt introduced by a garment company and sold in different cities in India. The data regarding price charged and quantity sold in different cities are as follows :

City	*Price charged (Rs)*	*Quantity sold (in thousand units)*
1	50	20.0
2	50	21.0
3	55	19.5
4	60	19.0
5	65	16.0
6	70	14.5
7	80	13.5
8	85	12.0
9	90	11.5
10	40	18.0

Interpret the value of intercept term a and b-coefficient of the estimated regression equation $Y = a + bX$. What is the price elasticity of demand at price Rs 60 per shirt ?

9. The following regression equation estimates are given for relationship between advertising expenditure (X) and sales of a product (Y). (The number of observed data points is 20).

$\tilde{Y} = 5.40 + 3.50\ X \qquad R^2 = 0.55$

(1.06) (3.05)

(Figures given in parameters are t-values)

Interpret the regression coefficient of X, the intercept term and coefficient of X estimated.

10. What is coefficient of determination (R^2) ? What does t-value of an estimate indicate ?

11. The General Manager of pen producing company has provided the following quarterly price-quantity data :

	QUARTERS									
	1	2	3	4	5	6	7	8	9	10
Price (Rs)	60	53	43	40	47	57	41	53	37	51
Quantity (in thousand)	83	93	100	108	97	80	105	86	110	90

Using ordinary least squares regression method, estimate the demand equation for the pens. The firm is considering an increase in price from Rs 60 to Rs 66. Would it be advisable for it to take this decision ?

Demand Forecasting

Demand Forecasting : Meaning, Need and Importance

Future is unknown and uncertain. However, managers have to make plans for future levels of production in the present. It always takes time for building up productive capacity to produce a product. Machines have to be ordered and installed, the required skilled labour has to be employed and trained, funds have to be arranged to fund production. If the future demand for the product is not known in advance proper planning for future production cannot be done. Thus, managers have to operate in uncertain environment. *To reduce this uncertainly in planning for future production levels, demand forecasting is essential. Forecasting demand means prediction of future demand.* Forecasting of future demand is one of the most important functions of managers of firms. Good forecasting of demand, reduces uncertainty of environment in which business decisions are made. If the future was known with certainty forecasting would not be required. If there is a certainty about future demand, decision about proper level of production could be taken on a once-for-all basis and no revision of it would be required. However, uncertainty is a fact of life and, therefore, a good forecast of future demand is necessary if proper planning for future level of production is to be made.

Good forecasting of future demand is also important for calculating rate of return on capital investment. Capital investment yields returns over a number of years in future, It is by comparing rate of return on capital investment with the current rate of interest that decision regarding investment is taken, Further, the demand for a firm's output depends on the price of its product, prices ol competing products, incomes of the people and advertisement expenditure by a firm to promote its sales. If the demand forecast of a firm reveals that the demand for its product is not enough it can think of stepping up expenditure on advertisement to increase the demand for its product. The firm can also increase its advertisement to raise its market-share (that is, share in the total market demand for the product). Further, to raise demand of its product or its market share, a firm can pursue other strategies such as properly adjusting its price policy or model of its product.

The demand forecast for a product may be in respect of (1) *aggregate demand*, that is, total demand for output in the economy at a future time. (2) Total demand for the product of an industry and (3) the demand for the product of an individual firm. As regards aggregate demand, it is usually measured by the level of gross national product (GNP). However, an individual firm is more interested in forecasting demand for its own product or its market share rather than gross nationat product. Demand forecast of an industry's product usually depends on the levels of overall economic activity or the performance of some major sectors of the economy. Demand forecasting by individual firms depend on an industry's demand forecast or its sales estimates. Generally, an individual firm estimates its future demand by considering industry's demand forecast (*i.e.* its sales forecast) and its expected market share.

Demand forecasts are needed not only by established firms but also by the new firms who are planning to enter an industry. If they think the demand for the product is large enough, it will decide to produce the product and thus enter the industry. Inadequate demand forecast for the product will prevent the entry of firms in the industry. Moreover, an established firm may be interested in predicting demand for a new product which it will be launching. It will forecast demand for the new product by taking into consideration its relative price, product design or model, and advertisement expenditure it wishes to make on it and overall future level of economic activity (*i.e.*, level of national income).

It is evident from above that *demand forecast plays an important role in planning for future level of production, for launching a new product, for expanding production capacity (i.e., making further capital investment) and for entering an industry.* This helps a manager to acquire the needed plant and capital equipment, the quantity of required raw materials, the necessary skilled labour and other type of human resources. There can hardly be any capital investment or planning for future production if uncertainty prevails about the likely demand for ihe product. Therefore, forecast of demand greatly helps in business decisions by reducing uncertainty under which firms operate.

There are two types of demand forecast : (1) *Short-term forecasts* are usually made for a period upto one year such as for a month, a quarter or a whole year. (2) *Long-term forecasts* which relates to the production for a year or more. Short-term demand forecasts are made in order to know the effect of present policies of the firm relating to relative price, advertising outlay, product model etc. on the demand for the product and also due to changes in government's fiscal and monestry policies. For the short-term demand forecast, it can be reasonably expected that the present demand will continue in the short run too or it will increase by a certain given proportion. For the short-term demand forecast, opinion of the experienced and well-informed managers can play an important role, Short-term forecasts of demand are made for the established products of the firms.

On the other hand, long-term demand forecasts relate to those forecasts which are made for a period of more than a year; it may even be five, ten or even twenty years. Long-term forecasts of demand are usually made when a *new product* has to be launched. More sophisticated techniques such as econometric or statistical methods are used to make long-term forecasts. The introduction of new products requires a large amount of capital investment in plant and equipment and therefore, in order to estimate returns from capital investment relatively more accurate demand forecasts are needed which should be made by using statistical methods.

METHODS OF DEMAND FORECASTING

There are several methods which can be used to forecast future demand for the products. The following are some of the important alternative techniques used for forecasting demand:

1. Consumer Survey Method
2. Expert Opinion
3. Market Experiments
4. Time Series Analysis
5. Econometric Method.

We shall explain below these alternative techniques of forecasting demand.

1. Consumer Survey Method

A direct method to obtain information about future demand for goods is to conduct a survey. Surveys are important technique for short-term forecasts. If data from existing sources do not meet their requirements or are not available, the firms conduct their own survey. This is especially the case when a firm is planning to introduce a new product or making substantial changes in the existing product. Surveys generally involve use of conducting consumer interviews or sending mailed questionnaire asking consumers about their *intentions* or *plans* about demand for goods. Consumers usually plan their spending on such goods as refrigerator, CTV, cars, housing well ahead of their future spending. Therefore, a survey indicates intentions of consumer about their future spending on consumer goods. Generally, individual firms make surveys when they are introducing a new product or making great changes in their existing product.

There are two types of surveys (1) Complete Enumeration and (2) Sample Survey.

Complete Enumeration. Just like population census in this all consumers of a product are asked questions about quantity of a product they plan to buy in future if the price of the good is increased, say by 10 per cent. With the information so gathered regarding intentions of all consumers to buy a commodity, total demand for the product and changes in it resulting from changes in price can be estimated. Thus, in a survey questions may be asked for consumer's reactions or response to proposed changes in price of a product, changes in their income, advertisement expenditure etc. The data and information gathered is classified and tabulated for analysing it. For example, if D stands for the quantity demanded of a product by each consumer, and N are the number of consumers then the total demand forecast for the product is given by

$$\sum_{i=1}^{N} D_i$$

The chief merit of this method of complete enumeration is that it is free from any bias or value judgement of the investigator. The investigator simply records the data or information. But it is very costly, tedious and cumbersome process. Therefore, it cannot be applied when a large number of consumers are involved.

Sample Survey Method. Though the technique of complete enumeration can provide useful data regarding demand of the consumers, it is *highly expensive, and time consuming.* Therefore, an alternative method of consumer survey, namely, sample survey is adopted. In this sample survey method, only a few consumers are selected at random or on a stratified basis. Through personal interviews or mailed questionnaire, questions are asked from them about their intended demand for a product and their response to changes in price of the product, their incomes, prices of competing products. The data so collected is classified and tabulated for analysis of consumers' demand. For example, if out of 2,500 consumers of a product in the survey a sample of 100 is selected for making a forecast, then the information collected through sample survey of 100 consumers would be deemed to apply to all the

2,500 consumers. Thus, in case of 100 selected consumers, the total demand is

$$\sum_{i=1}^{100} D_i = D_1 + D_2 + D_3 + ... + D_{100}$$

For all the consumers total demand forecast is given by the following ;

$$(D_1 + D_2 + D_3 + ... + D_{100}) \times \frac{2,500}{100}$$

Thus, the total demand of a sample of consumers is divided by the size of sample (i.e., 100) to arive at the average demand of a consumer in the sample and then this average is multiplied by the total number of consumers, *i.e.*, 2,500.

Compared to the complete enumeration method, sample survey techniques is *less costly* and less *cumbersome* method and involve *less data error.* But for getting accurate results from the sample survey method, choice of a sample is very critical. If a sample is small or it has a bias, it will not give correct results. If the sample is small, it will be subject to a large sampling error and if it has been selected with a bias, it will not provide reliable results. Therefore, for obtaining correct results, sample size should be sufficiently large to be a true representative of the population and further it should be selected at random so that it be free from bias.

Limitations of Survey Method

Apart from having a *sample bias*, survey method of forecasting demand has other draw-backs. First, it may also have a *response bias*, that is, the respondent may not give correct answers and simply report what the questioners would like to hear such as "your product is wonderful, I intend to buy it this year as soon as possible". Alternatively, some consumers may try to influence the decision-making and report that "if the price of the product is raised he will slop buying it". Neither of the two responses may reveal correct preferences of the consumers.

Secondly, in the survey method the consumers *may not be able to give accurate answer* to a given question with any degree of certainty. It is very difficult for a consumer to answer hypothetical questions such as "what would be his demand for the product, if price is raised, or if his income increases by 25% and so on". Potential consumers may not know how they will respond to a proposed rise in price of a product or his income or increase in advertisement expenditure by the firm.

Lastly, a chief drawback of the survey technique, both complete enumeration and sample survey method, is that it is *very costly.* In recent years, despite the fact that computer analysis of data have become possible and also firms specialising in conducting consumer surveys have come to exist, the fact remains that this is a very expensive method. Therefore, only a very big firms with huge resources can use consumer survey method. Consumer survey technique can provide useful and reliable data for the purpose of demand forecasting but much depends on the skills of the organisers conducting consumer surveys. For obtaining reliable information careful attention needs to be paid to each phase of the process of a survey. One important requirement is that questions should be properly worded to avoid ambiguity. Poorly worded questionnaires may yield data which are undependable and inaccurate. The investigator should avoid biasing or influencing the answers of the consumers surveyed.

2. Expert Opinion Method

An alternative method of demand forecasting is to *obtain views of specialists* who are well-informed about the market possibilities of a product. These specialists or experts may be of the organisation or firm itself. For example, the *executives* and *sales managers* of the firm may be asked to estimate future market possibilities of a product. There may be outside experts such as consultant firms, investment analysts, wbo are professionally trained for the purpose of forecasting demand. Although predictions of demand by experts are not always based on any hard data but they can provide useful information about demand for the product. There are various methods of confirming ihe opinion regarding future demand by experts. One such method is Delphi technique which we explain below:

Delphi Technique. In Delphi technique opinion of a number of experts about future demand is first obtained. Then, each expert is told about the prediction of the other experts and asked in the light of the other's views whether he would revise his prediction about future demand. The experts are again shown each other's revised forecasts and asked to reconsider their forecasts further till a consensus is reached or until referring the opinion of others again to the experts result in little or no change in demand forecasts.

Let us illustrate Delphi technique with an example. Suppose a business firm asks a panel of six experts to forecast a firm's sales for the next year (which indicates demand for its product). Suppose that, working independently, two experts predict that sales would increase by 10 per cent, two exerts predict 5 per cent increase and one predicts 3 per cent increase in sales while one forecasts no increase at all. All these responses will be shown to the experts to know from them whether in view of others' forecasts they would revise or adjust their earlier forecasts. This process of referring to them others' forecasts to each expert will continue until a final forecast is reached. It may happen that they revise the forecasts each time they are shown others' opinion and at the end of the process consensus emerges or the differences in their forecasts get substantially narrowed down.

Evidence from the USA shows that Delphi technique is widely used for demand forecasting as it is relatively less expensive. However, the usefulness of expert opinion depends on the skill and insight of the experts engaged for making forecasts. However, expert opinion method of forecasting is also not free from problems. Quite often the outside experts change huge fees for giving their opinion, Another problem faced in this method is that those who consider themselves experts may not like to be influenced by the predictions of others on a panel of experts. As a result, there may not be any revision in subsequent rounds of seeking their opinion about other's forecasts.

Survey of Sales Force

When it is very costly or otherwise not possible to conduct complete enumeration or a sample survey of consumer's intentions or seek expert opinion about future demand, a firm may enquire from its sales-representatives or salesmen about their estimates of sales of its product in future. Thus, in this method information regarding likely sales is obtained from those who are closest to the market and have a intimate insight of the market. The responses of the various salesmen or representatives are then aggregated to arrive at total demand forecast for the product.

This method has many advantages. It is cheap and easy to do. It has further advantage of increasing the motivation of salesmen to achieve the self-selected target for which they had made a forecast when they were asked to provide their prediction for future sales. However, method of sales force survey has also home disadvantages. First, sales representatives may not provide correct forecast. Some sales representative would like to impress the management for their being dynamic or efficient and as a result they are likely to make too optimistic sales forecast. On the other hand, some salesmen would make too pessimistic sales forecast so that they get higher payments for exceeding the targets based on their sales forecast.

Thus, sales forecasts provided by sales representatives are biased either upward or downward. However, as a result of experience some corrective factors are applied to sales estimates furnished by salesmen before aggregating them to arrive at a total demand forecast for the product.

3. Market Experiments

Business firms can also make market experiments to forecast demand for their products especially when they make changes in price, advertising expenditure, or want to introduce a new product in the market. A big problem with the survey technique of demand forecasting explained above is that consumer responses in the survey may not correspond to actual consumer behaviour. That is, consumers do not necessarily behave in the way they say when surveyed. This problem can be partly overcome by the use of market experiments. The two types of market experiments are generally used : (1) Test Marketing and (2) Controlled Experiments.

Test Marketing. In this technique the first step is to select a particular test area which accurately represents the whole market in which the new product is to be launched. Thus, market area for testing may consist of several cities and towns, or a particular representative region of the country or a sample of consumers taken from a mailing list. By introducing a new product in the test market consumers response about it can be judged. By choosing more than one test area, the firm can assess the effects on demand of the various alternative marketing strategies. For example, price, advertising, packaging, product model can be *different* in various market areas. Sales (*i.e.*, demand for the product) can he compared at different levels of price and advertising expenditure, and for different models of the product. In this way consumers' response to changes in price, advertising or product model can be known.

Market experiments have merits over consumer survey technique is that they are based on *actual consumer behaviour* and not on merely their *intentions* to buy the commodity. However, test experiments have some limitations. They are very costly and much *time consuming.* Another problem is risk involved in the test marketing. In test markets, where price is raised, the consumers may switch over to the products of the rival firms. Once the experiment is over and price is reduced to the original level it may be difficult to regain the lost customers. Thirdly, it is often difficult to select an area which accurately represents the potential market. For accurate forecast test area selected should be similar to the potential market with regard to socio-economic conditions, age pattern, occupational structure, advertising media available etc. The fourth limitation is that firm cannot control all the factors that influence demand for a product. The result of market experiments may get distorted by the counter moves of the competitors, changes in economic conditions, bad weather, etc. Lastly, because most test experiments last only for a short period, the changes in price or advertising to know consumer's response may go unnoticed by them in such a short period.

Controlled Experiments. An alternative type of market experiments is controlled experiments which are conducted to test the demand for a new product by a firm or to test the demands for various brands of a product. In a controlled experiment, a sample of some consumers of a product which are representative of the target market is selected. They are asked to visit a shopping store of a firm where various brands of a product are placed for sale.

These visiting consumers are asked which and how much of each brand they would buy at different prices. Their preferences are recorded. They are then provided advertising materials for various brands. Now, the selected sample of consumers are given a certain fixed money income and asked to make purchases of the products or various brands of a product. The quantity of the product or particular brands of a product purchased by them is recorded. A questionnaire may also be prepared to ask the reasons for the particular choice they have made. The price of the product or its model may be changed and the experiment is repeated.

The merit of controlled experiments is that they are likely to provide more accurate results than those of consumer surveys. This is because in controlled experiments consumers are asked to make *actual* decisions regarding their purchases, while consumer surveys show simply their *intentions to buy*. However, controlled experiments also suffer from similar limitations as consumer surveys.

First, the controlled experiments may be biased in the process of selection of a sample of consumers on which experiment is to be performed. Further, the selected consumers may not respond accurately when they know that they are a part of an experiment being conducted and their behaviour is being recorded. Therefore, the technique of controlled experiments is generally adopted as a supplement to statistical technique of forecasting demand.

4. Time Series Analysis

Time series analysis is an important technique of forecasting demand which is widely used by business world. As shall be explained below, time series analysis contains more than one technique of forecasting future value of a variable if it shows a *recognisable particular pattern over time*. Each technique of time series analysis uses *only past or historical values* of a variable to predict future values. It may be noted that the time-series analysis does not attempt to explain the causal *relationship* between variables that determine future value of a given variable. For example, if we are to predict future demand for a product, then the data of demand for past months, quarters or years are used. No attempt is made in the time-series analysis to establish causal relationship between future demand of a product on the one hand and the price of a product, advertising expenditure, prices of related products and income of consumers on the other. Instead, it is assumed that historic behaviour of a variable in the past will continue in the future also. The focus of time-series analysis is to identify and decompose the components of change in the data regarding past behaviour of a variable. These components of change in a variable over time are divided into the following four components:

1. Trends. These are *long-term increase* or *decrease* in time series of a variable (i.e., demand or sales of product in the present analysis of demand forecasting). For example, increasing population over time or changing consumer tastes may result in long-term increase or decrease of a demand for a product over time.

2. Seasonal variations. These are the changes in demand series over time due to changes in seasons during a year. Seasonal effects are generally *consistent* from year to year.

3. Cyclical variations. These are substantial expansion or contraction in an economic variable (demand or sales in the present analysis) that are *usually more than* a year's duration. In cyclical variations in an economic series sustained periods of high values of a variable are followed by its low values. In most industries cyclical changes in demand are not consistent or predictable over time. It may be noted that cyclical variations in a variable and secular trend in a variable are caused by different types of factors.

4. Random fluctuations. After accounting for trend, seasonal and cyclical variations in the time series of a variable the remaining changes in it which do not follow any regular

pattern are due to random factors. Caused as they are by random factors, random fluctuations are not predictable.

Various methods are used to isolate trend, seasonal fluctuations and cyclical changes in time series of a variable. We will explain below how to determine a trend in demand and thereby to forecast future demand for a product.

Forecasting Demand : Trend Projection

To forecast demand trend projection is a widely used technique. There are various models of trend projection.

Naive Models. These are simple test models which assume that future value of demand for a product is in some way a function of the present or recent value. One simplest naive model which is generally described as '*no change model*' states that the forecast value of demand for a product for the next period will be the same as the demand for the present period. Thus:

$$D_{t+1} = D_t$$

where D_t stands for demand or sale of a product in a quarter (say Quarter IV 2012), D_{t+1} for demand or sales in the next quarter (Quarter I, 2013). *The model simply states that demand for next quarter will be equal to its value in the present quarter.* In Table 11.1, we have given the data relating to demand (sales) of a two-wheeler firm. If it is required to forecast demand for the First Quarter of 2013. The above model will simply use the sales of Quarter IV of 2012 (₹ 550 lakhs) as the demand forecast for First Quarter of 2013. It is obvious that this technique of forecasting demand is very simple and cheapest. It is useful for forecasting demand over a very short period when historical evidence reveals no drastic short-term changes in demand for a product forecast for which is being made. Such a model is quite useful when demand for a product changes very slowly and forecast is being made for a very short period in future.

However, an important problem with this model is that data are not immediately available for the purpose of forecast for next month or even next quarter. Therefore, if this model is used, then to make forecast for the next period, the firm (or industry if it is forecast for an industry) must speed up the collection of data. Another problem with this model is that the effect of sales promotion efforts made by a firm in the present period or recent past are not incorporated in the demand forecast for the next or future periods. In case sales promotion efforts produce important affect on the demand for a product, then the recent or present data will be of little use in forecasting future demand.

Proportional Change Model. When the time series of demand or sales of a product show that there is a slight upward trend, as, for example, sales of a product in most months of a year are higher than in the same months of the previous year, then it is not appropriate to use 'no change model' for predicting future demand. Further, sales or demand of a product are somewhat seasonal, that is, they rise during some months in a year. Any demand forecast for future periods will be faulty if the above two types of effects, namely, (1) trend and (2) seasonal effects are not incorporated. Therefore, a better model than the above 'no change model' is the use of proportional change model. According to this, the forecast value of demand for a product for the next period D_{t+1} is obtained by adding the change in the current period over the previous period, (*i.e.*, $D_t - D_{t-1}$) to the current period demand (D_t). Thus

$$D_{t+1} = D_t + D_t - D_{t-1}$$

or

$$D_{t+1} = D_t + \Delta D_t$$

where

$$\Delta D_t = D_t - D_{t-1}$$

It may however be noted that even this 'proportional change model' does not fully capture the trend and seasonal variations for forecasting future demand.

Time Series Analysis : Trend Projection

One of the most widely used forecasting technique is trend projection. As mentioned above, a trend in time series of a variable is the *long-term change* (*increase or decrease*) in it. There can be a linear or non-linear trends in demand for a product. Mostly, *linear trend* and *constant rate* of growth trend are used to predict future demand. We explain below how future demand is forecasted on the basis of linear and constant rate of growth trends.

Trend Projection: Using Linear Trend Method. When data of a variable (demand or sales in the present case) show a generally increasing or decreasing trend over time we can forecast its future value by (1) *fitting a line to the data graphically* and (2) by *statistical curve fitting.*

Table 11.1 Sales Data of a Firm

Period No.	*Quarter*	*Sales Lakh (₹)*
1	2010 : I	300
2	2010 : II	335
3	2010 : III	375
4	2010 : IV	382
5	2011 : I	394
6	2011 : II	410
7	2011 : III	405
8	2011 : IV	460
9	2012 : I	475
10	2012 : II	505
11	2012 : III	480
12	2012 : IV	550

Graphic Curve Method. In Table 11.1 we have given the data regarding quarterly sales of a firm for the years, 2010, 2011 and 2012. Now, it is required to forecast the sales of the firm in the last quarter of 2013. The data shows that quarterly sales of the firm are generally increasing. However, for making forecast of future sales we have to know a more precise measure of the quarterly increase in sales. For this purpose *one method is to fit a line to the given data graphically so that it represents the trend in the data as correctly as possible.* For using this trend line for forecasting purpose we have to measure its slope which tells us the quarterly increase in the sales of the firm. Suppose the slope of the line so fitted is 18. Now, with sales of ₹ 550 lakhs in the last quarter of 2012, the sales in the first quarter of 2013 will be 550 + 18 = 568, in the second quarter, they will be 550 + 18 + 18 = 586, and in the last quarter of 2013 they will be 550 + 18 + 18 + 18 + 18 = ₹ 622 lakhs. Alternatively, the future sales at some future time can be predicted by extending the graphically drawn trend line to that point of time.

Statistical Curve Fitting. There is a limitation of the graphical curve fitting to predict future demand. The correctness of forecast depends on how much good fit curve is drawn by the analyst. A more accurate technique to draw a good fit curve to the sales (i.e., demand) data is the use of statistical method.

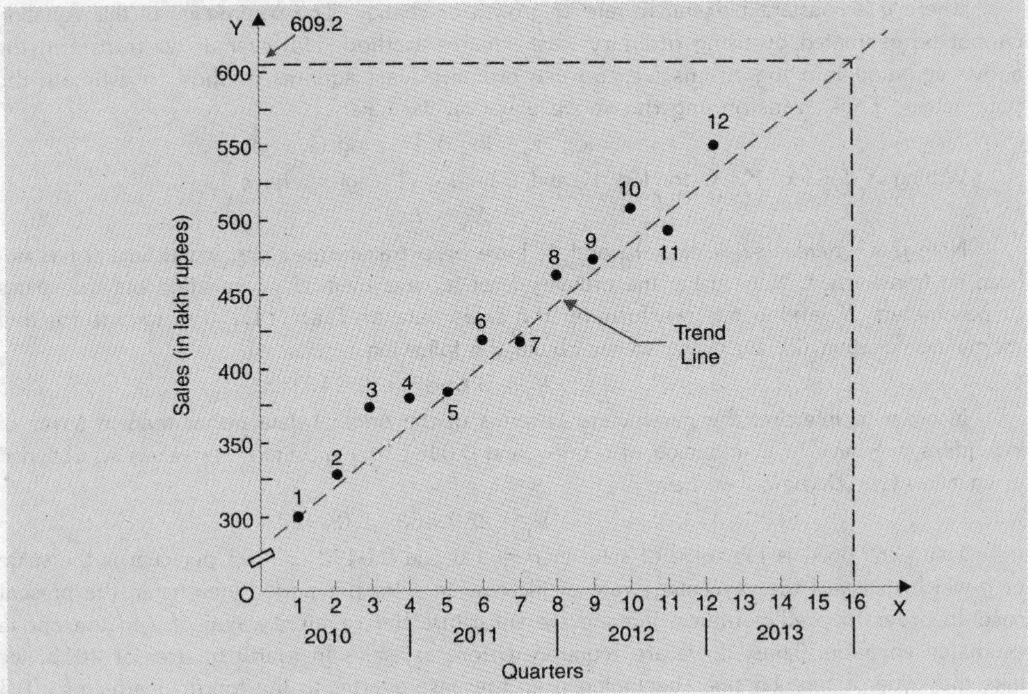

Fig. 11.1. *Predicting Future Demand or Sales through Statistical Curve Method*

Constant rate of change. Suppose it is assumed by an analyst that there is a constant rate of change in sales from one period (quarter) to another. This implies that demand or sales increase by the same amount every quarter. This increase in demand for a quarter can be obtained by estimating the parameters of the following regression equation:

$$Y_t = Y_0 + bt$$

Y_t denotes demand or sales in the period for which forecast is to be made, Y_0 is the parameter representing sales in the period 0, that is, it measures the intercept of the trend line on the *Y*-axis. The parameter *b* is constant rate of change and represents the slope of the trend line.

With the aid of calculators or computers, the regression equation can be estimated by using ordinary least squares method. On estimating the above equation through ordinary least squares method the following results are obtained:

$$Y_t = 290 + 19.95t$$

It will be noticed that the value of *b* is 19.95 which shows that in each quarter, sales increase by about 20 lakh rupees. A forecast of sales *for any future quarter* can be found out by substituting the value of *t*. Thus, with it we can obtain the forecast of the sales for the 4th quarter of 2013. Now, 4th quarter of 2013 will be 16th observation in the time series of quarters given in Table 11.1. Thus

$$Y_{16} = 290 + 19.95\ (16)$$
$$= 290 + 319.2 = 609.2$$

Constant percentage rate of change. Now suppose it is assumed by the analyst that sales increase by a constant percentage each period (*i.e.*, quarter). The equation expressing such a relation is as follows:

$$Y_t = Y_0\ (1 + g)^t \qquad \dots (i)$$

where g is constant percentage rate of growth or change. The parameters of this equation cannot be estimated by using ordinary least squares method. However, if we transform the above equation into logarithms we can use ordinary least squares method to estimate the parameters. Thus, transforming the above equation we have

$$\log Y_t = \log Y_0 + t \log (1 + g)$$

Writing X_t for $\log Y_t$, X_0 for $\log Y_0$ and b for $\log (1 + g)$ we have

$$X_t = X_0 + bt \qquad \text{... (2)}$$

Note that whereas sales data Y_0 and Y_t have been transformed into logarithms, t has not been so transformed. Now, using the ordinary least squares method we can find out the values of parameters X_0 and b on transforming the sales data of Table 11.1 into logarithms and estimating equation (2). By doing so we obtain the following results:

$$X_t = 5.6687 + 0.0481\ t$$

In order to interpret the parameters in terms of the original data rather than in terms of logarithms, we have to take antilog of 5.6687 and 0.0481 and substitute the values so obtained in equation (1) . Doing so we have

$$Y_t = 289.663\ (1.0492)^t$$

Thus, 289.663 is the value of sales in period 0 and 0.0492 or 4.92 per cent is the value of g which indicates the percentage rate of increase in sales per period (quarter in the present case).In order to predict future demand we substitute the required value of t in the above estimated equation. Thus, if we are required to forecast sales in fourth quarter of 2013, we take the value of t as 16 since beginning from the base quarter to the fourth quarter of 2013 in the time series is 16. Thus :

$$Y_{16} = 289.663(1.0492)^{16} = 624.63$$

5. Econometric Method

Another important forecasting technique used by the managerial economist is the econometric model. Econometrics is use of statistical methods and economic theory to estimate the causal relationship between economic variables. On the basis of economic theory a mathematical model describing relationship between economic variables is established. Then through the use of statistical methods estimates of parameters are made. With the help of these parameters forecasting of demand is made. Econometric technique has a number of important advantages over time-series analysis, survey technique, expert opinion or sales force polling and barometric methods. The most important advantage of econometric model is that it not only enables us to forecast an economic phenomenon but also *explains it.* That is, it establishes causal relationships between economic variables. Since management is able to manipulate some of the independent variables in a demand function such as price of product, advertising expenditure, variation in the product design, econometric method also helps the management to evaluate the impact of changes in its marketing strategies.

Another distinct merit of econometric technique is that it enables us not only to forecast the *direction of change* in an economic series but also the *magnitude of change.* Therefore, it helps to explain the *turning points* in economic series. Therefore, econometric method marks a great improvement over the trend projection technique which is unable to identify the turning points. It is also improvement over the barometric models which are incapable of predicting the *magnitudes of expected changes.* With regard to demand for the products econometric technique also helps to measure the elasticities of the various determinants of demand such as price elasticity, income elasticity, advertising elasticity and cross elasticity of demand. Having estimated these elasticities of demand we can know their relative importance.

Another advantage of econometric models is that they can be adjusted or adapted. On comparing the forecast values and actual values of a variable, if a large discrepancy between the two is found, then the model may be modified by including new variables on establishing new relationship between the variables.

Econometric model may be a *single equation model* or a *multiple equation model.* Single equation model is most widely used in empirical demand analysis. In this single equation model we estimate the parameters (i.e. coefficients) of demand equation and then use these parameters to forecast the future demand for a product.

Single equation demand model. Economic theory tells us the demand for a commodity is a function of its own price, disposable income of the people, prices of related commodities, advertising expenditure. We write below the demand model in an equation of linear form which is generally used to forecast future demand:

$$Q_d = a + b_1P_x + b_2Pc + b_3Y + b_4AD$$

where

P_x = own price of a good X

P_c = price of a competitive good

Y is disposable per capita income of the people

AD is advertising expenditure by the firm

a is a constant (intercept) term

b_1, b_2, b_3 and b_4 are the Coefficients of the various independent variables.

Through the regression technique of ordinary least squares method the above demand equation is estimated and the parameters of the equation such as a, b_1, b_2, b_3, b_4 etc. are obtained using the past data. Parameters of the equation which best represents the behaviour of the variables in the past are assumed to represent their behaviour in future also. The next step is to predict the values of the various variables such as price of goods (P), per Capita disposable income (Y), advertising expenditure (AD), etc. for the future period for which demand forecast is to be made. These future values may be predicted using time series analysis as explained earlier.

Now, in order to forecast demand for a given future period, the estimates of parameters such as a, b_1, b_2, b_3, b_4 etc. and the future values of P_x, P_c, Y, AD are substituted into the above demand equation. Then solving the demand equation will yield the forecast of the demand for the product (Q_d) which is the dependent variable.

QUESTIONS AND PROBLEMS FOR REVIEW

1. What is meant by demand forecasting ? Why is it so important for the management of business firms ?
2. Distinguish between short-term forecasts and long-term forecasts. For what purpose they are made ?
3. Explain consumer survey method. Discuss the merits and demerits of complete enumeration and sample survey methods of consumer survey.
4. Consumer survey method does not provide accurate results and it is also costly. Comment.
5. Critcially examine (a) Delphi technique and (b) Survey of Sales Force as methods of demand forecasting. What are their dadvantages and problems ?

6. Explain the role of market experiments by business firms of forecasting demand for their products. What types of market experiments are generally made ?
7. What is meant by time-series data ? What are the possible sources of variation in time-series data ? Why does time-series analysis deal primarily with trend and seasonal variations rather than with cyclical and irregular or random variations ? Why is time-series analysis often called "*naive forecasting*" ?
8. What is trend prediction ? Explain the method of predicting future demand through linear trend method. What is other most common trend forms used in time-series analysis ?
9. Explain the econometric method of forecasting demand. What are the advantages of econometric forecasting over the other forecasting techniques ?

PART – III

THEORY OF PRODUCTION AND COST ANALYSIS

- The Theory of Production : Returns to a Variable Factor
- Production Function with Two Variable Inputs
- Optimum Input Combination
- Cost Analysis
- Break-even Analysis
- Linear Programming

The Theory of Production: Returns to a Variable Factor

Introduction

So far we have been discussing the demand side of the pricing problems. In this chapter and the next few ones we shall be discussing the supply side of the pricing of products. The supply of a product, as we shall see in a later chapter, depends upon its cost of production, which in turn depends upon (a) the physical relationship between inputs[1] and output, and (b) the prices of inputs. The physical relationship between inputs and output plays an important part in determining the cost of production. It is the general description of this physical relation between inputs and output which forms the subject-matter of the theory of production. In other words, the theory of production relates to the physical laws governing production of goods.

The act of production involves the transformation of inputs into outputs. *The word production in economics is not merely confined to effecting physical transformation in the matter, it is creation or addition of value.* Therefore, production in economics also covers the rendering of services such as transporting, financing, marketing. Laws of production, or in other words, the generalisations regarding relations between inputs and outputs developed in this chapter will apply to all these types of production. *The theory of production provides a formal framework to help the managers of firms in deciding how to combine various factors or inputs most efficiently to produce the desired output of a product or service.*

The relation between inputs and output of a firm has been called the '*Production Function*'. Thus, the theory of production is the study of production functions. The production function of a firm can be studied by holding the quantities of some factors fixed, while varying the amount of other factors. This is called *short-run production function.* The time period in which at least one factor or input is fixed and production is increased by varying other factors is called the *short run.* The study of short-run production function when at least one factor is

1. The words "inputs" and "factors" of production are most often used interchangably. But, to some economists, meaning of inputs is broader. Inputs are all the things that firms buy, while the factors of production are taken to mean such things as labour, capital, land, entrepreneur.

kept fixed forms the subject of *law of diminishing returns* which is also known as *law of Variable Proportions.*On the other hand, the time period when *all factors* are variable is called the *long run.* The lenght of the long run, that is, the time period required for changes in all inputs depends on the industry. For some industries such as making of wooden chairs or tables the long run may be few weeks or months but for production of steel, it may be many years as it takes several yours to expend the capacity of steel production. The behaviour of production when all factors are varied proportionately is the subject-matter of *returns to scale.*Thus, in the theory of production, the study of (a) the returns to a variable factor and (b) the returns to scale is included. Besides this, the theory of production is also concerned with explaining *which combination of inputs (or factors of production) a firm will choose* so as to minimize its costs of production for producing a given level of output or to maximize output for a given level of cost.

PRODUCTION FUNCTION

Production, as said above, is transformation of physical inputs into physical outputs. The output is thus a function of inputs. The functional relationship between physical inputs and physical output of a firm is known as production function. Algebraically, production function can be written as :

$$q = f(a,\ b,\ c,\ d................) \qquad ...\ (i)$$

where q stands for the quantity of output, a, b, c, d etc., stand for the quantities of factors A, B, C, D respectively. This function shows that the quantity (q) of output produced depends upon the quantities, a, b, c, d of the factors A, B, C and D respectively. The above function shows that there exists *some relationship* between output q and the quantites of inputs a, b, c, d etc., but it does not tell us the specific form of this relationship. This unspecified relationship is denoted here by the letter f. If the form of the function f is given, that is, if right hand side of the equation (i) is given in a *specific* mathematical form[2], we can then fully find out we can then find out precisely the quantity of output that the firm would produce with each set of imputs such as labour and capital.

"*The production function is the name given to the relationship between the rates of input of productive services and the rate of output of product. It is the economist's summary of technological knowledge.*"[3] Thus, the production function expresses the relationship between the quantity of output and the quantity of various inputs used for the production. More precisely, the production function states the *maximium* quantity of output that can be produced from any given quantities of various inputs per period of time or, in other words, it states the *minimum* quantities of various inputs that are required to yield a given quantity of output per period of time, the technology being assumed to remain constant. It is important to note that when a change in technology occures, such as introduction of a new automated machine or the substitution of skilled labour for unskilled labour we will get a new production function. If a small firm produces wooden tables in a day, its production function will consist of the *maximum* number of tables that can be produced from given quantities of various inputs such as wood, varnish, labour time, machine time, floor space. Or, the production function of that firm may also be defined as the *minimum* quantites of wood, varnish, labour time, machine time, floor space, etc., that are required to produce a *given* number of tables per day.

---

2. A function is said to be in a specific form if we are able to find out the value of output q when the values of the independent variables (a, b, c, d etc.) are given.
3. G.J. Stigler, *The Theory of Price*, 1953, p.106.

Knowledge of the production function is a technological or engineeing knowledge and is provided to the firm by its engineers or production managers. Two things must be noted in respect of production function. First, production function, like the demand function, must be considered with reference to a *particular period of time, Production function expresses a flow of inputs resulting in a flow of output in a specific period of time.* Secondly, production function of a firm is determined by the state of technology. When there is advancement in technology, the production function changes with the result that the new production can yield greater flow of output from the given inputs, or smaller quantities of inputs can be used for producting a given quantity of output.

In economic theory we are intersted in two types of input-output relations or production functions. First , we study the production function when the quantities of some inputs are kept constant and the quantity of one input (or quantities of few inputs) are varied. This kind of input-output relation forms the subject-matter of the law of variable proportion. Since only in the short run, some factors are required to be held constant, the law of variable proportions relates to the short-run production function. Secondly, we study the input-output relation by varying all inputs proportionally. This forms the subject-matter of returns to scale. Since in the long-run all factors can be varied, the question of returns to scale relates to *long-run production function.*

Production function can be represented in verious forms; it can be represented by tables,graphs, mathematical equations, showing the maximum quantity of output that a firm can produce per period of time with various combinations of factors (*i.e.*, inputs). When two factors have to be explicity shown, production function can be represented by isoquants (*i.e.*, equal product curves). Production function can also be represented by *input-output tables.* However, it is worth mentaining that although production function provides quite a useful information about the production possibilities open to a firm, it does not given all the information required for efficient combination of inputs to produce a given level of output or to determine the profit maximising rate of output. As mentioned above, production function, while a fundamental part of managerial decision-making process, describes a physical relationship which must be combined with prices of inputs and output to determine the efficient resource combination of, producing a specific level of output and to find out the profit-maximising rate of output to produce.

PRODUCTION FUNCTION WITH ONE VARIABLE FACTOR

As mentioned above, in economic theory we are interested in two types of input-output relations or production functions. First, we study the production function when the quantities of some inputs are kept constant and the quantity of one input (or quantities of few inputs) are varied. This kind of input-output relations forms the subject-matter of the law of diminishing marginal returns which is also called *law of variable proportions* and describes *returns to a factor.* Secondly, we study the input-output relation by varying all inputs, that is, production function with two or more than two variable factors. The latter forms the subject-matter of the *returns to scale.* In the present chapter we shall explain the production function with one variable factor and in the next chapter we shall analysis returns to scale. It may be noted that concept of returns to a variable factor is relevent for the short run because in the short run some factors such as capital equipment, machines, land remain fixed and factors such as labour, raw materials are increased to expand output. Thus the short-run two factor prooduction function can be written as

$$Q = f(L, \overline{K})$$

where Q stands for output, L for labour and K for capital which is held constant in the short run. (Note that bar on K indicates that it is held constant). An important specific form of production function known as Cobb-Douglas production function which is most widely used in economics is written as

$$Q = A\, L^{\alpha} K^{\beta}$$

Where L is the amount of labour, K is the amount of capital used in the production process and A, α, β are constants. Either K or L can be held constant and the amount of the other factor can be a increased to study the returns to a factor. The concept of returns to a factor is concerned with the study of how output (Q) changes when the amount of a variable factor, such as labour, is increased. In what follows we will first explain some concepts of physical product that are generally used for the study of returns to a variable factor.

Total, Average and Marginal Physical Products

Regarding physical production of factors there are three concepts : (1) Total Product, (2) Average Product, and (3) Marginal Product. To study these concepts of a productivity relating to the use of a variable factor, say labour, we assume that a firm leases a machine with 1000 horse power and employs it in the production process as a fixed factor. Depending on the amount of a labour (*i.e.*, the number of workers) employed to operate the given machine, various quantities of output of the product will be produced. In Table 12.1 we give the quantities of output that is, produced by employing more workers with the given machine (*i.e.*, the fixed capital). Thus the data of Table 12.1 represents the production function with one variable input (labour), holding capital constant. We shall

Table 12.1 Total Product, Marginal Product, Average Product of Labour

Labour (i.e. No. of workers) L	Total Product (TP) Q	Marginal Product (MP) $\left(\frac{\Delta Q}{\Delta L}\right)$	Average Product (AP) $\left(\frac{Q}{L}\right)$	Output Elasticity of Labour (E_L)
1	80	80	80	1
2	170	90	85	1.06
3	270	100	90	1.11
4	368	98	92	1.06
5	430	62	86	0.72
6	480	50	80	0.62
7	504	24	72	0.33
8	504	0	63	0
9	495	-9	55	-0.16
10	480	-15	48	-0.31

now explain the concepts of total product, marginal product and average product of labour with the help of Table 12.1 and the curves.

Total Product (TP). The total product of a variable factor is the amount of total output produced by a given quantity of the variable factor, keeping the quantity of other factors such as capital, fixed. As the amount of the variable increases, the total output increases. But the rate of increase in total output varies at different levels of employment of the variable factor. It will be seen from Table 12.1 that as more workers are employed with a given quantity of capital (*i.e.*, the given machine), the total output of the product (TP) increases. When one worker is employed with a machine, total output is 80 units of output, with employment of 2 workers with the machine, the total output increase to 170 units, with employment of three workers, the total output incresases to 270. It will be seen from Table 12.1 that when more than 3 workers are employed, total output (*TP*) starts increasing at a diminishing rate and when more than 8 workers are employed, total output (*TP*) starts decreasing.

The behaviour of total product is graphically shown by the total product curve *TP* in Figure 12.1 where it will be seen that in the beginning total product curve rises at an increasring rate, that is, the slope of *TP* curve is rising in the beginning. After a point total product curve starts increasing at a diminishing rate as the employment of the variable factor labour is increased. The fact that ultimately total product increases at a diminishing rate has been proved to be valid on the basis of empirical evidence, as will be seen later in our discussion of the law of diminishing returns.

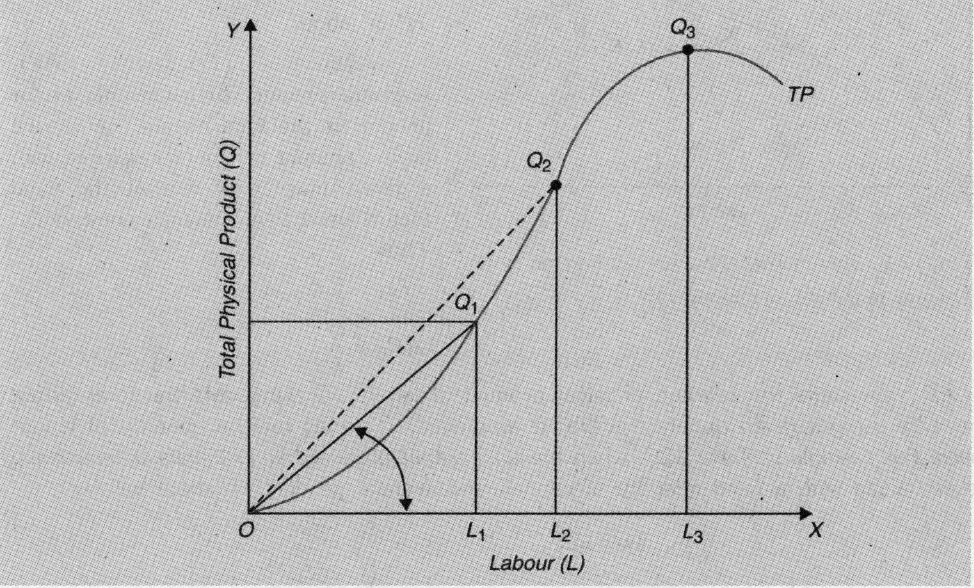

Fig. 12.1. *Total Product Curve of Labour.*

It may be emphasized again that the total product curve shows how the total output of the firm changes by increasing the quantities of a variable factor, say, labour assuming that the fixed factor (capital) is held constant. The total product curve of labour starts from the origin *O* because it is reasonable to assume that the fixed factor capital alone cannot produce any output. When the firm uses OL_1 amount of labour along with a fixed amount of capital, the total product equals $L_1\ Q_1$ units of total output. As employment of labour is increased to OL_2 the total product rises to $L_2\ Q_2$. Likewise, total product of the variable factor along with a fixed amount of capital continues to increase until OL_3 units of labour are employed at which the total production of labour with a given amount of capital reaches the maximum level $L_3 Q_3$. Further increases in employment of labour cause total product to decline. We shall discuss in detail later why total product of the variable labour decreases beyond a point.

Shift in the Total Product Curve. The total product curve of a variable factor (labour) is drawn on the assumption that the amount of a fixed factor capital is held constant. Now, any change in the magnitrude of the fixed factor capital will cause a shift in the total physical product curve of labour, the variable factor.

In Figure 12.2 the total product curve TP_1 of labour is drawn assuming that capital is held constant at a given amount K_1 of capital. (Note that for the sake of simplicity we have drawn in Fig. 12.2 the total product curves with decreasing slope only.) Now, if the amount of capital increases to K_2, the total product curve of the variable factor, labour, will shift upward as shown in Figure 12.2 by the curve TP_2, $(K = K_2)$. A further increase in capital to the amount K_3 will cause a further upward shift in the total product curve of labour to TP_3, $(K = K_3)$. It is thus evident that the total product curve of the variable factor, labour, depends upon how much quantity of the fixed factor capital it has to work with. The greater the available quantity of the capital, the higher will be the level of the total product curve *TP* of labour.

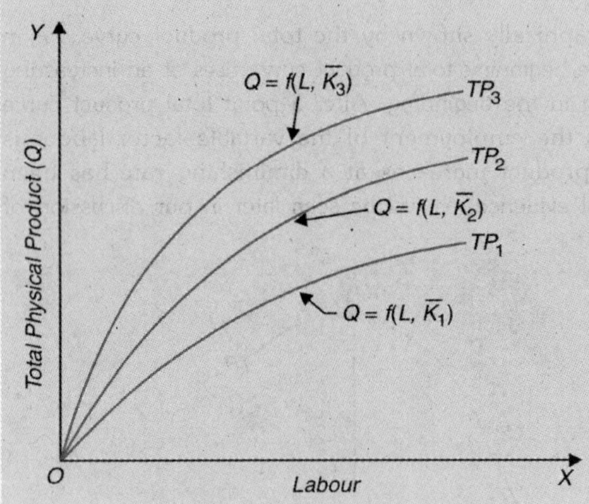

Fig. 12.2. *Shift in Total Product Curve Due to Increase in the Fixed Capital* $(\bar{K}_1 < \bar{K}_2 < \bar{K}_3)$.

Average Product (AP). Average product of a variable factor (labour) is the total output (*Q*) divided by the amount of labour employed with a given quantity of capital (the fixed factor) used to produce a commodity. Thus

$$AP_L = \frac{Q}{L}$$

where AP_L represents the average physical product of labour, *Q* represents the total output produced by using a given quantity of labour employed, *L* stands for the quantity of labour employed. For example in Table 12.1 when the total output produced is 170 units by employing 2 workers (along with a fixed quantity of capital), the average product of labour will be

$$AP_L = \frac{Q}{L} = \frac{170}{2} = 85$$

Similarly, in Table 12.1 when three workers are employed with the given capital, 270 units of output are produced, average product of labour,

$$AP_L = \frac{270}{3} = 90$$

It will be seen from Table 12.1 that average product of labour (*AP*) is increasing until 4 workers are employed and beyoud that average product (*AP*) of labour starts declining.

Derivation of Average Product Curve From the Total Product (TP) Curve. The average physical product curve can be easily derived from the total product curve of labour. This is illustrated in Fig. 12.3 where when OL_1 amount of labour is used, the total output is L_1Q_1. Thus, the average product of labour is equal to $\frac{L_1Q_1}{OL_1}$. But $\frac{L_1Q_1}{OL_1}$ is equal to the *slope of the line* connecting Q_1 with the point of origin (that is, tangent of angle $Q_1\ OL_1$). Similarly, average product of labour when OL_2 quantity of it used can be obtained by connecting the point Q_2 with a line to the origin and finding out its slope which will be equal to $\frac{L_2Q_2}{OL_2}$. In Fig. 12.3, it will be seen that the average product curve of labour, as derived from the total product curve *TP*, is changing with the increase in the variable factor, labour. As we increase

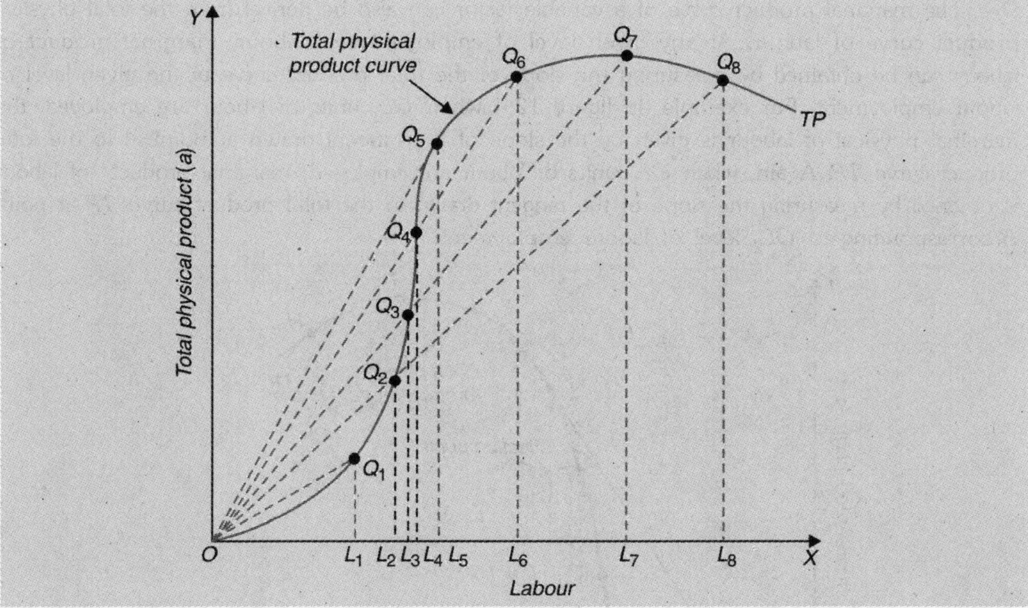

Fig. 12.3. *Changing Average Physical Product of Labour.*

the amount of labour from L_1 to L_5, we find that lines connecting points of total physical products, Q_1, Q_2, Q_3, Q_4 etc. on the total product curve with the origin have increasing slope up to Q_5 and then have a decreasing slope. Thus, average physical product of labour increases up to OL_5 quantity of labour used and thereafter it decreases.

It has been generally found that as more units of a factor are employed for producting a commodity with a fixed quantity of another, average product first rises and then it falls. As will be seen from Figure 12.3, the average product of labour first rises and then it diminishes That is, the average product curve of a factor would have an inverted U-shape.

Marginal Product (MP). Marginal product of a variable factor is the addition made to the total production by the employment of an extra unit of a factor. Suppose in Table 12.1 when two workers are employed to produce the product and they produce 170 units of output. Now, if instead of two workers, three workers are employed and as a result total product increases to 270 units metres of cloth, then the third worker has added 100 metres to the total production. Thus 100 metres is the marginal physical product of the thrid worker. Similarly, when four workers are employed with the given machine (capital), the total product increases to 368, that is, fourth factor has added 98 metres to total output. Thus, marginal product of workers has declined to 98. It will be seen from Table 12.1 that marginal product (*MP*) of labour rises initially but after 3 workers are employed marginal product of a worker diminishes and when 8 workers are employed, *MP* of labour has declimed to zero and on employing more than 8 workers *MP* of labour has become negative.

In general, if employment of labour increases by ΔL units yielding increases in total output by ΔQ units, the marginal product of labour* is given is by $\frac{\Delta Q}{\Delta L}$. That is,

$$MP_L = \frac{\Delta Q}{\Delta L}$$

* For *Infinitesimal changes* in labour, the marginal product of labour is the first desivative of the production function with respect to labour and is written as $\frac{dQ}{dL}$.

The marginal product curve of a variable factor can also be derivel from the total physical product curve of labour. At any given level of employment of labour, marginal product of labour can be obtained by measuring the slope of the total product curve at the given level of labour employment. For example, in figure 12.4 when OL_1 units of labour are employed, the marginal physical of labour is given by the slope of the tangent drawn at point *A* to the total product curve *TP*. Again, when OL_2 units of labour are employed, marginal product of labour is obtaned by measuring the slope of the tangent drawn to the total product curve *TP* at point *B* corresponding to OL_2 level of labour employment.

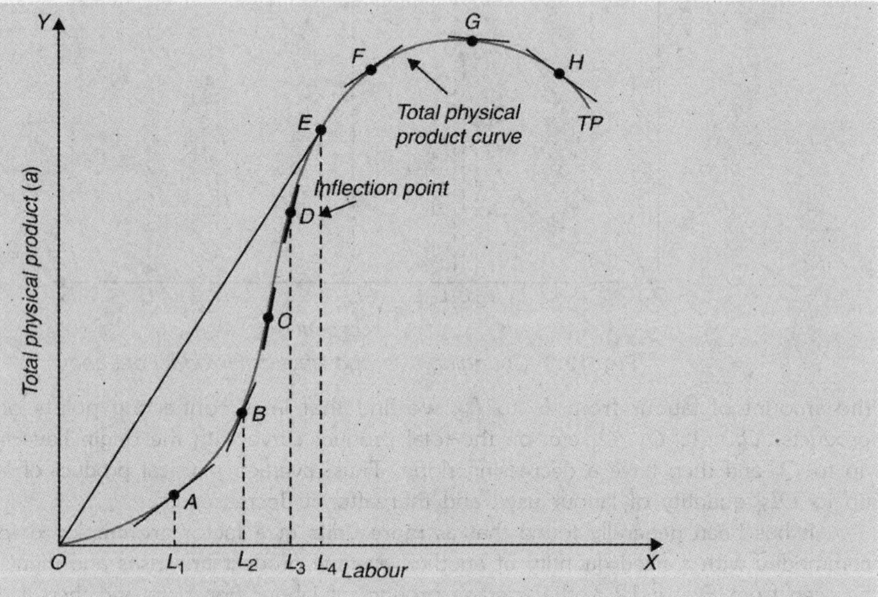

Fig. 12.4. *Deriving Mariginal Physical Product Curve*

The marginal product of a factor will change at different levels of employment of the factor. It has been found that marginal product of a factor rises in the beginning and then utimately falls as more of it is used for production, other things remaining the some. That is why in Fig. 12.4 marginal product (*MP*) has been shown to be rising in the beginning upto point *D,* that is, when OL_3 workers are employed and beyond that it starts diminishing. Point *D* is known as *point of inflection*. Marginal product of labour goes on diminishing beyond the inflection point *D* until it becomes negative beyond point G.

The relationship with average product and marginal product curves and how both of them are related to the total product curve has been graphically in Figure 12.5.

Output Elasticity of an Input

An important concept relating to production function with one variable input is output elasticity of an input. Just as price elasticity of demand for a good is defined as percentage change in quantity demanded of it that results from a given percentage change in price, the output elasticity of a variable input, say labour, is the percentage change in output that is brought about by a given percentage change in the quantity of variable input used, other factors such as capital remaining the same. That is,

$$E_L = \frac{\% \, \Delta \, Q}{\% \, \Delta \, L} \qquad \text{....(1)}$$

where E_L stands for output elasticity of labour

Rewriting equation (1) we have

$$E_L = \frac{\Delta Q}{Q} \div \frac{\Delta L}{L} = \frac{\Delta Q}{Q} \times \frac{L}{\Delta L}$$

$$E_L = \frac{\Delta Q}{\Delta L} \cdot \frac{L}{Q} \qquad \text{....(2)}$$

Since $\frac{\Delta Q}{\Delta L}$ represents marginal product of labour and $\frac{Q}{L}$ represents average product of labour, the equation (2) can be written as

$$E_L = \frac{MP_L}{AP_L}$$

Thus, output elasticity of labour is the ratio of marginal product of labour to its average product. In the last column of Table 12.1 we have calculated the output elasticity of labour from dividing MP_L by AP_L.

When use of labour, with a given quantity of capital is increased from one unit to 2 units of labour (that is, $\Delta L = 1$), output increses more that proportionately (i.e. by 1.06). The negative output elasticity of labour when more than 8 units of labour are employed means that output decreases with a given percentage increase in labour input.

Note that production elasticity greater that one means that one percentage change in input (labour) yields more than one percentage increase in output of the commodity. If elasticity of production of an input is less than one, it implies that one per cent increase in the variable input, keeping other factors constant, causes less than one per cent increase in output. Thus, the *elasticity of production of a variable input being less than one indicates diminishing returns to that factor.* Production elasticity of zero means that output does not change at all when a given percentage change in a variable input, keeping other factors constant, is used in the production process. If elasticity of production is less than zero (that is, it is negative), this implies that output of the commodity *decreases* as a result of a given percentage increase in the variable input.

Problem. *You are given the following production function*

$$Q = L^{0.75} K^{0.25}$$

(*i*) *Find the marginal product of labour*

(*ii*) *If the fixed quantity of capital in the short-run equals 10,000 units, what is the short-run production finction ?*

(*iii*) *Show that marginal product of labour (MP_L) is less than average product of labour (AP) in the short-run production function in (ii) above*

Solution. (*i*) To get marginal product of labour, we differentiate the given production fuction with respect to labour. Thus

$$MP_L = \frac{\partial Q}{\partial L} = 0.75 L^{-0.25} K^{0.25}$$

$$= 0.75 \left(\frac{K}{L}\right)^{0.25}$$

(*ii*) Note that in the short-run producton function, one factor is variable with the quantity of other fixed factor. Thus

$$Q = L^{0.75} K^{0.25}$$

$$Q = L^{0.75} (10{,}000)^{0.25}$$

Since the fourth root of 10,000 is 10

$$Q = L^{0.75} \,.\, 10 = 10L^{0.75}$$

Thus, short-run production function is $Q = 10\ L^{0.75}$.

(*iii*)

$$MP_L = \frac{\partial Q}{\partial L} = 10 \times 0.75 L^{-0.25}$$

$$= \frac{7.5}{L^{0.25}}$$

$$AP_L = \frac{Q}{L} = \frac{10L^{0.75}}{L} = 10L^{0.75-1}$$

$$= \frac{10}{L^{0.25}}$$

Comparing the values of MP_L and AP_L we find that $MP_L < AP_L$

Algebraic Determinination of Marginal Product and Average Product of a Factor from Short-run Production Function

It is useful to determine marginal and average products from the short-run production function. Let the following short-run algebraic production function of a business firm has been estimated. We have to determine the marginal and average products of labour

$$Q = 6L^2 - 0.4L^3$$

where Q is output and L is the quantity of labour used.

Note that the above function is short-run production functuion as there is no fixed term in it ; all terms in it contain the variable factor, labour (L).

To determine *marginal product of labour* (MP_L) we take the first derivative of output with respect to labour

$$MP_L = \frac{dQ}{dL} = 2 \times 6L - 3 \times 0.4L^2$$

$$= 12L - 1.2L^2$$

To determine *average product of labour*, we divide the total output by L. Thus,

$$AP_L = \frac{Q}{L} = \frac{6L^2 - 0.4L^3}{L} = 6L - 0.4L^2$$

We can find out the value of the variable factor L that maximises output (Q) and also the value of labour (L) at which its average product is maximum.

Value of L that maximises output (Q) : The value of variable input L that maximises output (Q) can be obtained by setting marginal product function of the variable input equal to zero. We have found above that . $MP_L = 12L - 1.2L^2$. Setting it equal, to zero we have

$$12L - 1.2L^2 = 0$$

$$1.2L^2 = 12L$$

$$\frac{1.2L^2}{L} = 12$$

$$1.2L = 12$$

$$L = 12 \times \frac{10}{12} = 10$$

At 10 units of labour, value of Q will be maximum.

Value of L at which its AP is maximum : Value of average product function will be maximised where its first derivative equals zero.

AP of labour obtained above $= 6L - 0.4L^2$

$$\frac{dAP}{dL} = 6 - 0.8L = 0$$

$$0.8L = 6$$

$$L = 6 \times \frac{10}{8} = \frac{60}{8} = 7.5$$

Thus, when 7.5 units of labour are used, its average product will be maximum.

Determination of Marginal and Average Products of a Variable Factor in Cobb-Douglas Production Function

An important production function called Cobb-Douglas production function widely used in empirical stitudies is of the following form

$$Q = AL^{\alpha} K^{\beta}$$

Let us first find out marginal products of labour, holding capital constant. This can be found by the first derivative of the function with respect to labour. Thus,

$$MP_L = \frac{\partial Q}{\partial L} = A\alpha\, L^{\alpha-1} K^{\beta}$$

$$= \alpha \frac{AL^{\alpha} K^{\beta}}{L} = \alpha \frac{Q}{L}$$

Marginal product of capital, holding labour constant, can be obtained by obtaining the first derivative of the function with respect to capital. Thus,

$$MP_k = \frac{\partial Q}{\partial K} = A\beta\, L^{\alpha} K^{\beta-1}$$

$$= B\frac{AL^{\alpha} K^{\beta}}{K} = \beta \frac{Q}{K}$$

Average product of labour, $\quad AP_L = \dfrac{Q}{L} = \dfrac{AL^{\alpha} K^{\beta}}{L}$

$$= AL^{\alpha-1} K^{\beta}$$

Average product of capital $\quad AP_L = \dfrac{Q}{L} = \dfrac{AL^{\alpha} K^{\beta}}{K}$

$$= AL^{\alpha} K^{\beta-1}$$

Exercise. *Suppose a firm producing cotton cloth has the following production function.*

$$Q = 2K^{1/2} L^{1/2}$$

Determine the marginal products of labour and capital.

Solution. This is Cobb-Douglas production function with the given specific values of exponents.

$$MP_L = \frac{\partial Q}{\partial L} = 2\left(\frac{1}{2}\right) K^{1/2}\, L^{1/2-1}$$

$$= K^{1/2} L^{-1/2}$$

$$= \left(\frac{K}{L}\right)^{1/2} = \sqrt{\frac{K}{L}}$$

$$MP_K = \frac{\partial Q}{\partial K} = 2\,.\left(\frac{1}{2}\right) K^{1/2-1}\, L^{1/2}$$

$$= K^{-1/2}\, L^{1/2} = \left(\frac{L}{K}\right)^{1/2}$$

$$= \sqrt{\frac{L}{K}}$$

NUMERICAL PROBLEM ON ELASTICITY OF OUTPUT

Given the following production function

$$Q = 1.50\, L^{0.75}\, K^{0.25}$$

Determine the elasticity of output with respect to (1) labour and (2) capital. Give an economic interpretation of these output elasticities.

Solution. Given production function is

$$Q = 1.50\, L^{0.75}\, K^{0.25}$$

output elasticity of labour (E_L) = $\dfrac{MP_L}{AP_L}$

$$MP_L = \frac{\partial Q}{\partial L} = 0.75 \times 1.50\, L^{-0.25}\, K^{0.25}$$

$$= 1.125\, L^{-0.25}\, K^{0.25}$$

$$AP_L = \frac{Q}{L} = \frac{1.50 L^{0.75} K^{0.25}}{L}$$

$$\frac{Q}{L} = 1.50\, L^{-0.25}\, K^{0.25}$$

$$E_L = \frac{MP_L}{AP_L} = \frac{1.125 L^{-0.25}\, K^{0.25}}{1.50\, L^{-0.25}\, K^{0.25}}$$

$$= 0.75$$

Output elasticity of capital (E_K) = $\dfrac{MP_K}{AP_K}$

$$MP_K = \frac{\partial Q}{\partial K} = 0.25 \times 1.50\ L^{0.75}\ K^{-0.75}$$

$$= 0.375\ L^{0.75}\ K^{-0.75}$$

$$AP_K = \frac{Q}{K} = \frac{1.50 L^{0.75}\ K^{0.25}}{K}$$

$$= 1.50\ L^{0.75}\ K^{-0.75}$$

$$E_K = \frac{MP_K}{AP_K} = \frac{0.375\ L^{0.75}\ K^{-0.75}}{1.50\ L^{0.75}\ K^{-0.75}}$$

$$= 0.25$$

From the value of output elasticity of labour equal to 0.75 it follows that 1 per cent increase in employment of labour causes 0.75 increase in output, that is, less than proportionately. Similarly, output elasticity of capital being equal to 0.25 implies that one per cent increase in capital causes 0.25 per cent increase in output of the commodity.

LAW OF DIMINISHING RETURNS

Law of diminishing returns occupies an important place in economic theory. This law examines the production function with one factor variable, keeping the quantites of other factors fixed. In other words, it refers to the input-output relation when output is increased by varying the quantity of one input. When the quantity of one factor is increased keeping the quantity of the other factors constant, the proportion between the variable factor and the fixed factor is altered ; the ratio of employment of the variable factor to that of the fixed goes on increaseing as the quantity of the variable factor is increased also. Since under this law we study the *effects on output of variations in factor proportions,* this is also known as the law of variable proportions. The law has played a vital role in the history of economic thought and occupies an equally important place in modern economic theory and has been supported by the empirical evidence about the real world. The law of diminishing returns has been stated by various economists in the following manner : G. J. Stigler, a Nobel prizer winner in economics writes, "*As equal increments of one input are added ; the inputs of other productive services being held constant, beyond a certain point the resulting increments of product will decrease, i.e., the marginal products will diminish.*[4]

Similarly, Samuelson, another Nobel Laureate, writes that when"An increase in some inputs relative to other fixed inputs will, in a given state of technology, causes output to increase; but after a point the extra output resulting from the same additions of extra inputs will become less and less.[5]

Assumptions of the Law of Diminishing Returns. The law of diminishing returns as stated above holds good under the following conditions:

1. First, the state of technology is assumed to be given and unchanged. If there is improvement in technology, then marginal and average product may rise instead of diminishing.

2. Secondly, there must be some other inputs such as capital must be kept fixed. It is only in this way then that we are able to measure the changes in output caused by increase in a

4. G.J. Stigler, *Theory of Price*, The Macmillan Co., 1953,p.111.
5. P.A . Samuelson, *Economics*, 8th edition, p.25.

variable factor that we can alter the factor proportions and know its effects on output. This law does not apply in case all factors are proportionately varied. Behaviour of output as a result of the variations in all inputs is discussed under "returns to scale".

3. Thirdly, the law is based upon the possibility of varying the proportions in which the various factors can be combined to produce a product. The law does not apply to those cases where the factors must be used in fixed proportions to yield a product. When the various factors are required to be used in rigidly fixed proportions, then the increase in one factor would not lead to any increase in output, that is, the marginal product of the factor will then be zero and not diminishing.' It may however be pointed out that products requiring fixed proportions of factors are quite uncommon. Thus the law of diminishing marginal returns also known as law of variable proportions applies to most of the cases of production.

Returns to a variable factor, say labour, keeping the quantity of a fixed factor land as constant is illustrated in Table 12.1 and Figure12.5. We shall first explain it by considering Table 12.1. Assume that there is a given fixed amount of land with which more variable factor, labour, is used to produce wheat. With a given fixed quantity of land, as a farmer raises employment of labour from one unit to 7 units, total product increases from 80 quintals to 504 quintals of wheat. Beyond the employment of 8 units of labour, total product diminishes. It is worth noting that up to the use of 3 units of labour, total product increases at an increasing rate and afterwards it increases at a diminishing rate. This fact is clearly revealed from column 3 which shows successive marginal products of labour as extra units of labour are used. Marginal product of labour, it may be recalled, is the increment in total output due to the use of an extra unit of labour.

It will be seen from col. 3 of Table 12.1 that the marginal product of labour initially rises and beyond the use of three units of labour, it starts diminishing. Thus when three units of labour are employed, marginal product of labour is 100 and with the use of 4th and 5th units of labour marginal product falls to 98 and 62 respectively. Beyond the use of eight units of labour, total product diminishes and therefore marginal product of labour becomes negative. As regards average product of labour, it rises up to the use of fourth unit of labour and beyond that it is falling throughout.

Three Stages of Production.

The behaviour of output when the varying quantity of one factor is combined with a fixed quantity of the other can be divided into three distinct stages. In order to understand these three stages it is better to graphically illustrate the production function with one factor variable. This is done in Fig. 12.5. In this figure, on the X-axis we measure the quantity of the variable factor and on the *Y*-axis we measure the total product, average product and the marginal product. How the total product, average product and marginal product of the variable factor change as a result of the increase in the quantity of one factor to a fixed quantity of the others will be seen from Fig. 12.5. The total product curve *TP* goes on increasing to a point and after that it starts declining. Average and marginal product curves also rise in the beginning and then decline; marginal product curve starts declining earlier than the average product curve. The behaviour of these total, average and marginal products of the variable factor consequent to the increase in its amount is generally divided into three stages which are explained below;

Stage 1: In this stage, total product increases at an increasing rate to a point. In Fig. 12.5 from the origin to the point *F*, slope of the total product curve *TP* is increasing, that is, up to the point *F*, *the total product increases at an increasing rate* (the total product curve *TP* is concave upwards to the point *F*), which means that the marginal product *MP* rises. From the point *F* onwards during the stage 1, the total product goes on rising but its slope is declining which means that *from point F to the point H the total product increases at a diminishing rate* (total product curve is concave downwards), i.e., marginal product falls but is positive. The point *F* where the total product stops increasing at an increasing rate and starts increasing at the diminishing rate is called the *point of inflecion*. Corresponding vertically to this point of inflecion marginal product is maximum, after which it starts diminishing.

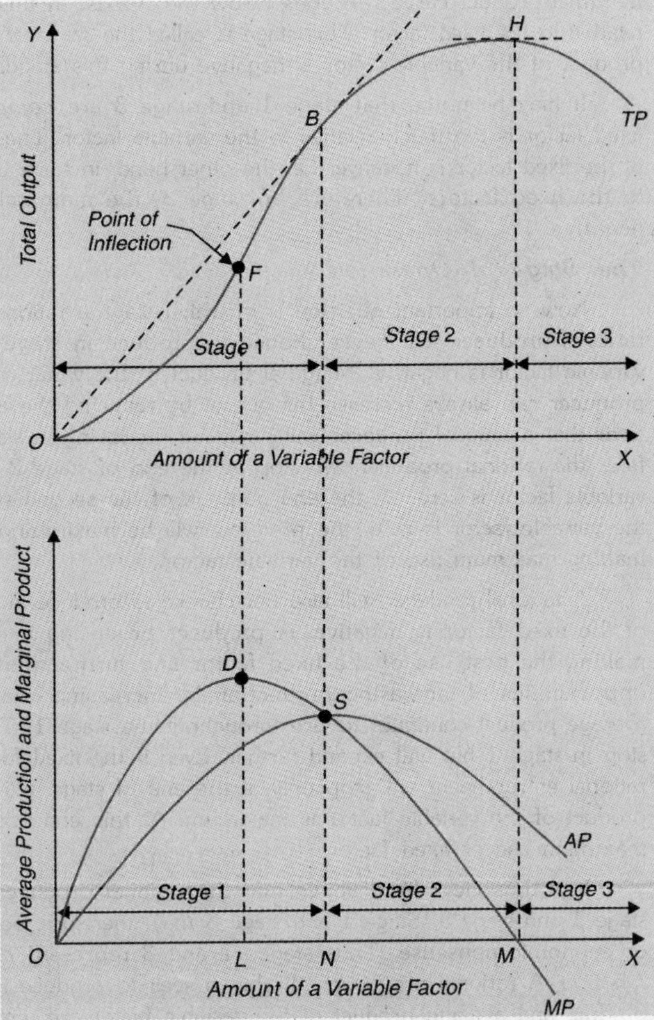

Fig. 12.5. *Three Stages of Production Function with one Variable Factor.*

The stage 1 ends where the average product curve reaches its highest point. During the stage 1, when marginal product of the variable factor is falling, it still exceeds its average product and so continues to cause the average product curve to rise. Thus, during the stage 1, whereas marginal product curve rises in a part and then falls, the average product curve rises throughout. In the first stage, the quantity of the fixed factor is are too much relative to the quantity of the variable factor so that if some quantity of the *fixed factor* is withdrawn, the total product would increase. Thus, in the first stage *marginal product of the fixed factor is negative.* Stage 1 is called by some economits as the *stage of increasing returns* because average product of the variable factor increases throughout this stage. It is notable that the marginal product in this stage initialy increases and in a later part it starts declining but remains greater than the average product throughout in stage 1 so that the average product continues to rise.

Stage 2: In stage 2, the total product continues to increase at a diminishing rate until it reaches its maximum point *H* where the second stage ends. In this stage both the marginal product and average product of the variable factor are diminishing but are positive. At the end of the second stage, that is, at point *M* marginal product of the variable factor is zero (corresponding to the highest point *H* of the total product curve *TP*). Stage 2 is very crucial and important because the firm will seek to produce in its range.

Stage 3: In stage 3 total product declines and therefore the total product curve *TP* slopes downward. As a result, marginal product of the variable factor is negative and the marginal product curve *MP* goes below the *X*-axis. In this stage, variable factor is too much relative to the fixed factor. This stage is called the *stage of negative returns,* since the marginal product of the variable factor is negative during this stage.

It may be noted that stage 1 and stage 3 are *completely symmetrical.* In stage 1 the fixed factor is too much relative to the variable factor. Therefore, in stage 1, marginal product of the fixed factor is negative. On the other hand, in stage 3 variable factor is too much relative to the fixed factors. Therefore, in stage 3, the marginal product of the variable factor is negative.

The Stage of Operation

Now an important question is in which stage a rational producer will seek to produce. A rational producer will never choose to produce in stage 3 where marginal product of the variable factor is negative. Marginal product of the variable factor being negative in stage 3, a producer can always increase his output by reducing the amount of variable factor. It is thus clear that a rational producer will never be producing in stage 3. Even if the variable factor is free, the rational producer will stop at the end of stage 2 where the marginal product of the variable factor is zero. At the end point *M* of the second stage where the marginal product of the variable factor is zero, the producer will be maximizing the total product and will thus be making maximum use of the variable factor.

A rational producer will also not choose to produce in stage 1 where the marginal product of the fixed factor is negative. A producer producing in stage 1 means that he will not be making the best use of the fixed factor and further that he will not be utilizing fully the opportunities of increasing production by increasing quantity of the variable factor whose average product continues to rise throughout the stage 1. Thus a rational entrepreneur will not stop in stage 1 but will expand further. Even if the fixed factor is free (i.e., costs nothing), the rational entrepreneur will stop only at the end of stage 1 (i.e., at point *N*) where the average product of the variable factor is maximum. At this end point *N* of stage 1 he will be making maximum use of fixed factor.[6]

It is thus clear from above that the rational producer will never be found producing in stage 1 and stage 3. Stage 1 and stage 3 may, therefore, be called stages of economic absurdity or economic nonsense. Thus stages 1 and 3 represent *non-economic region in production function.* A rational producer will always seek to produce in stage 2 where both the marginal product and average product of the variable factor are diminishing. At which particular point in this stage, the producer will decide to produce depends upon the price of the variable factor. The stage 2 represents the range of rational production decisions.

We have thus seen how the output varies as the factor proportions are altered at any given moment. We have also noticed that this input-output relation can be divided into three stages. Now the question arises as to what causes increasing marginal returns to a variable factor labour in the beginning in stage 1, diminishing marginal returns to the variable factor which start operating from point *D* in stage 1 and continues in stage 2 and ultimately we have negative marginal returns in stage 3. We explain below the factors which cause the increasing,

6. The statement in respect of the non-operation by a rational producer in stage 1 applies to the producer who is working under perfect competition in both the product and factor markets where the price of product sold by him and the prices of factors bought by him remain fixed. In monopoly and imperfect competition in product and factor markets where the prices of product and factors do not remain fixed with the changes in the level of output and employment, the producer might find his most profitable level of output in stage 1.

diminishing and genative marginal returns to the variable factor.

Causes of Initial Increasing Marginal Returns to a Variable Factor

In the beginning, the quantity of the fixed factor is abundant relative to the quantity of the variable factor. Therefore, when more and more units of the variable factor are added to the constant quantity of the fixed factor, then the fixed factor is more intensively and effectively utilized, that is, the efficiency of the fixed factor increases as additional units of the variable factors are added to it. This causes the production to increase at a rapid rate. When, in the beginning, the variable factor is relatively smaller in quantity, some amount of the fixed factor may remain unutilized and, therefore, when the variable factor is increased fuller utilisation of the fixed factor becomes possible with the result that increasing returns to a variable factor are obtained. The question arises as to why the fixed factor is not initially taken in a quantity which suits the available quantity of the variable factor. Answer to this question is provided by the fact that generally those factors are taken as fixed which are *indivisible*.[7]

Indivisibility of a factor means that due to technological requirements a minimum amount of it must be employed whatever the level of output. Thus, as more units of the variable factor are employed to work with an indivisible fixed factor, output greatly increases due to fuller and more effective utilization of the latter. Thus we see that it is the indivisibility of some factors which initially causes increasing returns to a variable factor.

The second reason why we get increasing returns at the initial stage is that as more units of the variable factor are employed the efficiency of the variable factor itself increases. This is because when there is a sufficient quantity of the variable factor, it becomes possible to introduce specialization or division of labour which results in higher productivity. The greater the quantity of the variable input, the greater the scope for specialization and hence greater will be the level of productivity and efficiency.

Causes of Diminishing Marginal Returns

The stage of diminishing returns in the production function with one factor variable is the most important. The question arises as to why we get diminishing marginal returns after a certain amount of the variable factor has been added to the fixed quantity of the other factor. It is important to note that the famous law of diminishing returns in fact concerned with *diminishing marginal returns* and not diminishing total returns i.e. total product of a factor.

Scarcity of the fixed factor. As explained above, increasing returns to a factor occur in the first stage primarily because of the more effective and efficient use of the fixed factor as more units of the variable factor are combined to work with it. Once the point is reached at which the amount of the variable factor is sufficient to ensure the efficient utilization of the fixed factor, further increases in the variable factor will cause *marginal and average products to decline because the fixed factor then becomes inadequate relative to the quantity of the variable factor.* In other words, the *contributions to the production made by the variable factor after a point becomes less and less because the additional units of the variable factor have less and less of the fixed factors to work with. The production is the result of the co-operation of various factors aiding each other.* In the beginning in stage 1, the fixed factor is abundant relative to the number of the variable factor and the former provides much aid to the latter. On the other hand, when with the increase in the variable factor the fixed factor becomes more and more scarce in relation to the variable factor so that as the units of the variable factor are increased they receive less and less aid from the fixed factor. As a result, the marginal and average products of the variable factor decline.

7. Moreover, a factor has to be taken in a fixed quantity because this is one way in which we can alter the factor proportion and judge its effect on output.

Indivisibility of the Fixed Factor. The phenomenon of diminishing marginal returns, like that of increasing marginal returns, rests upon the indivisibility of the fixed factor. As explained above, the important reason for increasing returns in stage 1 is the fact that the fixed factor is indivisible which has to be employed whether the output to be produced is small or large. In stage 1 when the indivisible fixed factor is not being fully used, successive increases in the variable factor add more and more to output since fuller and more efficient use is made of the indivisible fixed factor. But there is generally a limit to the range of the employment of the variable factor over which its average product will increase. There will usually be a level of employment of the variable factor at which indivisible fixed factor is being as fully and efficiently used as possible and therefore the marginal product is maximum. It will happen when the variable factor has increased to such an amount that the fixed indivisible factor is being used in the '*best or optimum proportion*' with the variable factor. Once the optimum proportion is disturbed by further increases in the variable factor, marginal returns to the variable factor (i.e., marginal product) will diminish primarily because the indivisible factor is being used in wrong proportion with the variable factor. Just as the marginal product of the variable factor increases in the beginning when better and fuller use of the fixed indivisible factor is being made, so the marginal product of the variable factor diminishes when the fixed indivisible factor is being worked too hard.

If the fixed factor was finely divisible, neither the increasing nor the diminishing marginal returns would have occurred. If the factors were perfectly divisible then there would not have been the necessity of taking a large quantity of the fixed factor in the beginning to combine with the varying quantities of the other factor. *In the presence of perfect divisibility of the factors, the optimum proportion between the factors could have been achieved in every case.* Perfect divisibility of the factors implies that a small farm with a miniature combine and one worker would be as efficient as a large farm with a large combine and many workers. The productivity would be the same in the two cases.

Thus we see that if the factors were perfectly divisible the question of varying factor proportions would not have arisen and hence the phenomena of increasing and diminishing marginal returns to a factor would not have occurred. It has been rightly said, "Let divisibility enter through the door, law of variable proportions rushes out through the window."

Imperfect Substitutability of the Factors. Joan Robinson goes deeper into the causes of diminishing returns. She holds that *the diminishing returns occur because the factors of production are imperfect substitutes for one another.* As seen above, diminishing marginal returns occur after a point since the fixed factor becomes inadequate relatively to the variable factor. Now, a factor which is scarce in supply is taken as fixed. When there is a scarce factor, quantity of that factor cannot be increased in accordance with the varying quantities of the other factors which beyond the optimum proportion of factors will result in diminishing marginal returns. If now some variable factor was perfect substitute of the scarce fixed factor, then the paucity of the scarce fixed factor after a stage would have been made up by increasing the supply of this perfect substitute with the result that output could be expanded without diminishing marginal returns. Thus, even if the variable factor which we add to the fixed factor were perfect substitute of the fixed factor, then when the fixed factor becomes relatively deficient, its deficiency would have been made up on account of the increase in the variable factor which is its perfect substitute.

Thus Joan Robinson says, "What the Law of Diminishing Returns really states is that there is limit to the extent to which one factor of production can be substituted for another, or, in other words, that the elasticity of substitution between factors is not infinite. If this were not true, it would be possible when one factor of production is fixed in amount and the rest are in perfectly elastic supply, to produce part of the output with the aid of the fixed factor, and then, when the optimum proportion between this and other factors was attained, to substitute some other factor for it and to increase output at constant cost."[8] We therefore see that *diminishing marginal returns operate because the elasticity of substitution between factors is not infinite.*

Causes of Negative Marginal Returns

As the amount of the variable factor continues to be increased to the constant quantity of the other, a stage is reached when the total product declines and the marginal product becomes negative. This phenomenon of negative marginal returns to the variable factor is due to the fact that the amount of the variable factor becomes too excessive relative to the fixed factor so that they get in each other's way with the result that the total output falls instead of rising. Besides, too large a number of the variable factor also impairs the efficiency of the fixed factor. The proverb "too many cooks spoil the broth" aptly applies to this situation. In such a situation, a reduction in the units of the variable factor will increase the total output. Just as in the first stage, marginal product of the fixed factor was negative due to its abundance, in the third stage the marginal product of the variable factor is negative due to its excessiveness.

GENERAL APPLICABILITY OF THE LAW OF DIMINISHING RETURNS

We have discussed above, the law of diminishing returns which states marginal physical product eventually diminishes, even if it is increasing in the beginning. Uptill Marshall, it was thought that three laws of production–diminishing, constant and increasing returns were quite distinct and separate. Now, modern economists have veered round to the view that diminishing, constant and increasing returns are not three separate laws but they are three phases of one general law of vâriable proportions. Moreover, uptill Marshall it was thought that law of diminishing returns applied to agriculture and the manufacturing industries were characterised by increasing or constant returns. But this is no longer believed; law of diminishing returns has vast general applicability. This law applies as much to industries as to agriculture. Whenever some factors are fixed and the amount of other increases, then the technology remaining the same, diminishing returns to a factor are bound to occur eventually both in agriculture and industries. We have given above the various definitions of law of diminishing returns which lay stress on its general applicability.

It is important to note that law of diminishing returns is *empirical generalisation* and not the law of economics derived through deductive logic. As for its validity is concerned, we have given the various reasons for the occurrence of diminishing returns. The occurrence of diminishing marginal physical returns to a factor after a point has been confirmed by the overwhelming empirical evidence. Indeed, if the diminishing returns did not occur we could grow sufficient amount of foodgrains even in a flower pot by using more dozens of labour and capital. If the constant returns could be obtained by applying more labour on a given piece of land, then as the population increased we could use more labour on that land to get proportionate increase in agricultural output. In that case world, especially developing countries like India, would not have to face problems of food shortage and overpopulation. Prof. R. G. Lipsey is right when he says, "Indeed, were the hypothesis of diminishing returns incorrect, there would need to be no fear that the present population explosion will bring with it a food crisis. If the marginal product of additional workers applied to a fixed quantity of land were constant, then

8. Joan Robinson, *The Economics of Imperfect Competition*, p. 330.

world food production could be expanded in proportion to the increase in population merely by keeping the same proportion of the population on farms. As it is, diminishing returns mean an inexorable decline in the marginal product of each additional labourer as an expanding population is applied, with static techniques, to a fixed world supply of agricultural land.[9]"

Thus, it should not be understood that because of diminishing returns there can be no hopes for raising the living standards of mankind, especially of the people in developing countries. Owing to the gloomy prognosis about the future of mankind made by the classical economists, especially Thomas Malthus, on the basis of diminishing returns, the subject of economics came to be called as a *dismal science.* However, to predict such a gloomy prospects for the future of mankind on the basis of law of diminishing returns is wholly unwarranted. Some people have misunderstood the law and have asserted that as the population will increase, the quantity of land remaining unchanged, the productivity per person will decline. But this is quite wrong. Law of diminishing returns, as stated above, has a great provision that technology, equipment, etc. remain the same. In the present-day developed countries, though population has increased, agricultural productivity has greatly gone up instead of diminishing. This is so because present-day developed countries have made an impressive progress in technical knowledge, resulting in new and superior machinery and other equipment, and the use of fertilizers. Capital equipment per worker engaged in agriculture has greatly increased. As a result, agricultural productivity has registered a phenomenal increase in the present-day advanced countries.

On the other hand, developing countries have not made much progress in technical knowledge and in capital accumulation and therefore do not use sufficient capital and equipment like machinery, tools, fertilizers, etc. It is no wonder, therefore, that agricultural productivity in them has not risen significantly. In fact, marginal productivity of labour has gone down. The phenomenon of disguised unemployment found in agriculture of developing countries reveals that marginal productivity of a worker is zero or nearly zero. It is thus clear that actual experience regarding the behaviour of agricultural productivity in both developed and developing countries is in no way a contradiction to the law of diminishing returns, the operation of which is subject to the condition that technical knowledge, capital equipment and other aids of production remain the same. Even in developing countries such as India where new agricultural technology represented by the use of HYV seeds, fertilizers, irrigation has been adopted, the productivety of labour and land has greatly increased which is described as green revolution. For India attaining food self-sufficiency, credit goes to the adoption of this new agricural technology.

Of course, if we fail to improve our technology sufficiently and to bring about rapid capital accumulation diminishing returns would assert themselves and create the problems of food crisis and starvation. We therefore conclude "*unless there is continual and rapidly accelerating improvement in the techniques of production, the population explosion must bring with it declining living standards over much of the world and the eventual widespread famine.*"[10]

OPTIMAL EMPLOYMENT OF THE VARIABLE FACTOR (INPUT)

How much variable input (labour in our analysis) will be used by a firm to maximise profits ? Ths guiding principle is the same that underlies marginal analysis. A firm that aims to maximise profits will use or employ the extra unit of a variable input such as labour as long as the additional revenue generated by it exceeds the marginal cost of hiring it. Suppose the marginal product of an extra unit of labour is 5 units of output and price of each unit of output

9. Richard, G. Lipsey, *Introduction to Positive Economics,* 3rd edition p. 216.
10. *Ibid.*

is Rs 10, then extra unit of input (labour) will generate additional revenue equal to 5 10 = Rs. 50. If the additional cost to the firm of hiring extra unit of labour is Rs. 30, then it will pay the firm to use and employ that unit for it adds to its revenue more than it adds to its cost and therefore hiring of it will increase its profits. The additional revenue generated by an extra unit of a variable input (*i.e.*, labour in our example) is called *marginal revenue product* (MRP_L) of it. This marginal revenue product (*MRP*) of variable input equals its marginal product (*MP*) times the marginal revenue*. Thus, if we take labour as a variable input, then

$$MRP_L = MP_L \,.\, MR$$

On the other hand, marginal cost of hiring labour which is generally denoted by *MFC* is addition to the total cost by hiring additional unit of labour. Thus,

$$MFC_L = \frac{\Delta TC}{\Delta L}$$

When a firm is facing perfectly competitive labour market, it has no influence over the price of labour, that is, wage rate (*W*) which, therefore, remains constant. Therefore, given the perfectly competitive labour market

$$MFC_L = W$$

In order to maximise profits a firm will go on using or employing more variable input labour until the marginal revenue product generated by the last unit of labour becomes equal to its marginal factor cost (*i.e.*, wage rate in case of perfectly competitive labour market). Thus, there will be optimum use or employment of labour when

$$MRP_L = MFC$$

or in case of perfect competition in the labour market

$$MRP_L = W$$

Likewise if the quantity of labour input was fixed, and capital is varied to increase output, the more capital will be used until marginal revenue product of capital becomes equal to its marginal factor cost or, under perfect competition in the capital market, the price of capital (*r*), that is,

$$MRP_K = MFC_K$$

In case of perfect competition in capital market, the condition for optimum use of capital is given by

$$MRP_K = r.$$

Table 12.2. Total and Marginal Products, MRP_L of Labour (Given $P_x = 2$ and $W = 100$)

Labour Input (*L*)	TP_L	MP_L	*TR* (TP_L P_x)	MRP_L (MP_L P_L)	*MFC* (= *W*)
1	80	80	160	160	100
2	170	90	340	180	100
3	270	100	540	200	100
4	368	98	736	196	100
5	430	62	860	124	100
6	480	50	960	100	100
7	504	24	1008	48	100
8	504	0	1008	0	100
9	495	–9	990	–18	100
10	480	–15	960	–30	100

*. Note that if perfect competition prevails in the market, marginal revenue equals the price of the product (*MR* = Price). Therefore, under conditions of perfect competition in the product market,

$$MRP_L = MP_L . P.$$

Let us illustrate the optimum employment of labour input by the firm given that perfect competition prevails in both product and labour market prevails so that both the price of the product and wage rate of labour are given and constant for the firm. Consider Table 12.2 where in the second and third columns we have given the data of total product and marginal product of labour respectively.

The total product of labour (TP_L) and marginal product of labour (MP_L) have been reproduced from Table 12.1. The total revenue (*TR*) generated by employment of more labour input has been obtained by multiplying total product of labour (TP_L) with the given price of product which is taken to be equal to Rs 2 per unit (P_x = Rs. 2). Marginal revenue product of labour can live found out in two alternative ways. First, marginal revenue product of labour (*MPL*) can be obtained directly by multiplying marginal product of labour (MP_L) with the given price of the product (*i.e.* Rs.2). Alternatively, marginal revenue product of labour (MRP_L) can be determined by finding the change in total revenue for each unit change in labour input. Both these methods will yield the same results. Thus,

$$MRP_L = MR \cdot MP_L$$

since $$MR = \frac{\Delta TR}{\Delta Q} \text{ and } MP_L = \frac{\Delta Q}{\Delta L}$$

We have $$MRP = \frac{\Delta TR}{\Delta Q} \cdot \frac{\Delta Q}{\Delta L} = \frac{\Delta TR}{\Delta L}$$

Thus marginal revenue product of labour (MRP_L) can also be obtained as change in total revenue resulting from one unit increase in labour input.

Optimal Employment of Labour

The number of optimal use or employment of labour depends the wage rate which measures marginal factor cost of labour (MFC_L). Suppose the given wage rate is equal to Rs.100 per worker. Now, the firm will hire or employ labour as long as marginal revenue product of labour (MRP_L) is greater than or equal to Rs.100. It will be seen from Table 12.2 that with 6 workers employed, marginal revenue product of labour (MRP_L) becomes equal to the given wage rate. With 7 workers employed, the firm will be maximising its profits. Given the wage rate equal to Rs 100, if the firm employs 7 workers, its profits will decrease became while seventh workers adds Rs 48 to total revenue, he will be paid wage equal to Rs 100. Thus, given the wage rate of workers equal to Rs 100, the optimum use or employment of labour will be 6 workers.

If the wage rate is raised to Rs. 124, then as will be seen from Table 12.2 workers will be employed. Thus, the rise in wage rate adversely affects employment of labour as it causes substitution of capital for labour.

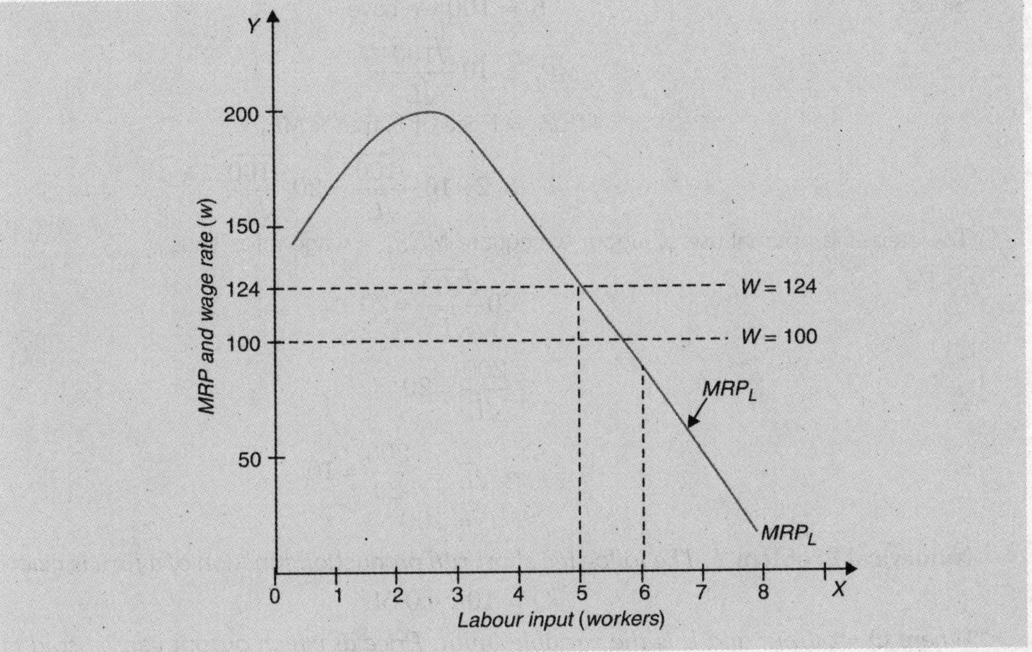

Fig. 12.6. *The Optimal Employment of variable Input (Labour).*

Marginal revenue product of labour (MRP_L) corresponding to Table 12.2 is graphically depicted in Figure 12.6. It will be seen from Figure 12.6 that at wage rate of labour equal to Rs 100, the firm employs 6 workers to equate marginal revenue product of labour with the given wage rate and thereby maximises its profits. If wage rate rises to Rs 124, it employs 5 workers to maximise its profits. Thus, labour demand curve for labour slopes downward. It should be remembered that downward-sloping labour demand curve is due to the operation of the law of diminishing marginal returns according to which marginal physical product of labour diminishes in the relevant stage of operation.

Numerical Problem 1 : The production function for the firm is $Q = 20\ K^{0.5}\ L^{0.5}$ *Suppose the quantity of capital is fixed at 100 . If the wage rate is Rs. 20 and price of output is Rs 2 per unit, determine the optimal use of labour input.*

Solution . In order to determine the optimal use of labour we first find out marginal product of labour from the given production function. Taking the first derivative of the given production function with respect to labour we have

The given production function is

$$Q = 20\ K^{0.5} L^{0.5}$$

$$MP_L = \frac{dQ}{dL} = 20 \times \frac{1}{2} K^{\frac{1}{2}} L^{-\frac{1}{2}}$$

$$MP_L = 10\ K^{\frac{1}{2}} L^{-\frac{1}{2}}$$

$$= 10\ \frac{\sqrt{K}}{\sqrt{L}}$$

Since $K = 100$ we have

$$MP_L = 10\frac{\sqrt{100}}{\sqrt{L}}$$

$$MRP_L = \text{Price of output} \times MP_L$$

$$= 2 \times 10\frac{\sqrt{100}}{\sqrt{L}} = 20\frac{\sqrt{100}}{\sqrt{L}}$$

To determine optimal use of labour we equate MRP_L = wage rate. Thus

$$20\frac{\sqrt{100}}{\sqrt{L}} = 20$$

$$\frac{200}{\sqrt{L}} = 20$$

$$= \sqrt{L} = \frac{200}{20} = 10$$

$$= L = 100$$

Numerical Problem 2. *The following short-run production function of a firm is given*

$$Q = 10L - 0.5L^2$$

Where Q = output and L is the variable input. Price at which output can be sold is Rs 10 per unit and given wage rate of labour for the firm is Rs 20 per labour unit.

(1) *find the marginal revenue product function of labour.*
(2) *What is marginal factor cost function of labour.*
(3) *Determine the optimum amount of labour used if the objective of the firm is to maximise profits.*

Solution :

The given short-run production function is

$$Q = 10\,L - 0.5L^2$$

(1) To find the marginal revenue product of labour (MRP_L) we have to first find out the total revenue generated by labour. Thus

$$TR = PQ = 10.P.\,L - 0.5P.\,L^2$$

The given price of output (P) = Rs 10. Therefore

$$TR = 10.10.L - 0.5.10\,L^2$$

$$= 100L - 5L^2$$

$$MRP_L = \frac{\Delta\,TR}{\Delta\,L} = 100 - 10L$$

(2) To obtain marginal factor cost function of labour we first find total factor cost function of labour. The given wage rate of labour is Rs 20 per unit of labour. Thus

$$\text{Total Factor cost } (TFC_L) = \text{Q.W.} = 10.W.L - 0.5\,WL^2$$

$$= 10 \times 20\,L - 0.5 \times 20L^2$$

$$= 200L - 10L^2$$

$$MFC_L = \frac{\Delta\,TFC}{\Delta\,L} = 200 - 20L$$

(3) In order to maximise profits, the firm will equate MRP_L with MFC_L. Thus,

$$MRP_L = MFC_L$$
$$100 - 10L = 200 - 20L$$
$$20L - 10L = 200 - 100 = 100$$
$$10L = 100$$
$$L = 10$$

Thus optimum use of labour is to employ 10 units of labour.

QUESTIONS FOR REVIEW

1. What is production function? Distinguish between fixed inputs and variable inputs. Is the distinction between the two relevant in the long run?
2. Explain the concept of production function? Why is it useful in the analysis of firm's behaviour?
3. What is the relationship between marginal product and average product of labour (or a variable input)?
4. State the law of diminishing returns. Why does diminishing marginal returns to a variable input occur eventually? Can they become negative? If so, why?
5. What are the three stages of short-run production function? Why does it not make any economic sense to produce in stage 1 or stage 3?
6. How is the law of diminishing returns reflected in the shape of the total product curve? If the total product increases at a decreasing rate from the very beginning what would be the shapes of corresponding marginal and average product curves?
7. Explain the law of diminishing returns. Mention on what assumptions it is based. How Malthus used the law to predict gloomy forecast for future mankind? What mistake did he commit in making this gloomy forecast?
8. If the law of diminishing marginal product did not hold, the world's food supply could be grown in a flower pot. Discuss.
9. The marginal revnue product function of factor is the demand curve for that factor. Explain
10. Fill in the blanks in the following table:

Number of variable input	*Total output (number of units)*	*Marginal product of the variable input*	*Average product of the variable input*
3	–	18	30
4	–	20	–
5	130	–	–
6	–	5	–
7	–	–	19½

Does the production function stated in the table given above exhibit diminishing returns? If so, at what number of units of the variable input do diminishing marginal returns begin to set in?

11. *As the quantity of a variable input increases, explain why the point where marginal product begins to decline is reached before the point where average product begins to decline. Also explain why the point where average product begins to decline is reached before the point where total output begins to decline.*

[Hints: This is due to the usual average-marginal relationship in the production process. Due to the operation of diminishing marginal returns, marginal returns begin to decline at some point but for some range though diminishing it remains greater than average product. Therefore, average product continues to increase. Only when in its diminishing phase marginal product becomes less than average product, average product starts declining. That is why marginal

product curve cuts the average product curve at the latter's highest point.
Marginal product continues diminishing after it is equal to the maximum average product but remains positive which causes the total output to continue increasing. Only when marginal product becomes zero, the total product reaches its maximum level. As a result, total output continues increasing after the maximum average product point and begins to decline only when marginal product becomes negative.]

12. Consider the following short-run production function (where X is the variable input and Q is the output).

$$Q = 6X^2 - 0.2X^3$$

(a) *Determine the marginal product function (MP_x).*
(b) *Determine the average product function (AP_x).*
(c) *Find the value of X that maximises Q.*
(d) *Find the value of X at which its average product takes on its maximum value.*

13. What is meant by output elasticity of an input ? Given the following production function, find the output elasticities of labour and capital.

$$Q = 50\ L^{0.70}\ K^{0.40}$$

where Q = output, L = labour and K = capital

14. Explain the condition for optimum use of a variable factor if the objective of the firm is to maximise profits.

15. Explain what considerations manager of a firm will keep in view white hiring labour. Explain and illustrate graphically how much labour a firm will employ to maximise profits ?

Production Function with Two Variable Inputs

In the last chapter we explained the production function with a single variable factor, holding other factors constant.In the present chapter we are concerned with the analysis of production function when two variable factors as used in the production process. For the analysis of a production function with two variable factors we make use of a concept called *isoquants* or *iso-product curves* which are similar to indifference curves of the theory of consumption.

ISOQUANTS

Isoquants, which are also called equal-product curves, are similar to the indifference curves of the theory of consumer's behaviour. An isoquant represents all those input combinations which are capable of producing the same level of output. The isoquants are thus contour lines which trace the loci of equal outputs. Since an isoquant represents those combinations of inputs which are capable of producing an equal quantity of output, the producer would be indifferent between them. Therefore, another name which is often given to the equal product curves is *production-indifference curves*.

The concept of isoquant can be easily understood from Table 13.1. It is presumed that two factors labour and capital are being employed to produce a product. Each of the factor combinations *A*, *B*, *C*, *D* and *E* produces the same level of output, say 100 units. To start with, factor combination *A* consisting of 1 unit of labour and 12 units of capital produces the given 100 units of output. Similarly, combination *B* consisting of 2 units of labour and 8 units of capital, combination *C* consisting of 3 units of labour and 5 units of capital, combination *D* consisting of 4 units of labour and 3 units of capital, combination *E* consisting of 5 units of labour and 2 units of capital are capable of producing the same amount of output, *i.e.,* 100 units. In Fig. Fig.13.1 we have plotted all these combinations and by joining them we obtain an isoquant showing that every combination represented on it can produce 100 units of output.

Table 13.1 Factor combinations to produce a given level of output

Factor Combinations	Labour	Capital
A	1	12
B	2	8
C	3	5
D	4	3
E	5	2

Though isoquants are similar to the indifference curves of the theory of consumer's behaviour, there is one important difference between the two. An indifference curve represents all those combinations of two goods which provide the same satisfaction or utility to a consumer but no attempt is made to specify the level of utility it stands for in exact quantitative terms. This is so because the cardinal measurement of satisfaction or utility in unambiguous terms is not possible. That is why we usually label indifference curves by ordinal numbers as I, II, III, etc. indicating that a higher indifference curve represents a higher level of satisfaction than a

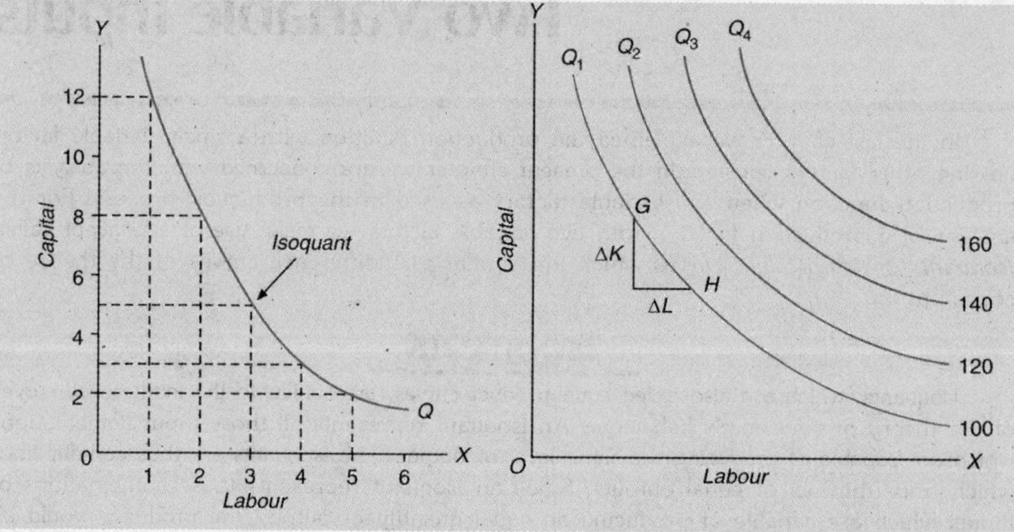

Fig. 13.1. *Isoquant* **Fig. 13.2.** *Isoquant Map*

a lower one, but the information as to by how much one level of satisfaction is greater than another is not provided. On the other hand, we can label isoquants in the physical units of output without any difficulty. Production of a good being a physical phenomenon lends itself easily to absolute measurement in physical units. Since each isoquant represents specified level of production, it is possible to say by how much one isoquant indicates greater or less production than another. In Fig. 13.2 we have drawn *an isoquant-map or equal-product map* with a set of four isoquants which represent 100 units, 120 units, 140 units and 160 units of output respectively. Then, from this set of isoquants it is very easy to judge by how much production level on one isoquant curve is greater or less than an another.

MARGINAL RATE OF TECHNICAL SUBSTITUTION

Marginal rate of technical substitution in the theory of production is similar to the concept of marginal rate of substitution in the indifference curve analysis of consumer's demand. Marginal rate of technical substitution indicates the rate at which factors can be substituted at the margin without altering the level of output. More precisely, *marginal rate of technical substitution of labour for capital may be defined as the number of units of capital which can be replaced by one unit of labour, the level of output remaining unchanged.* The concept of marginal rate of technical substitution can be easily understood from Table 13.2.

Each of the input combinations *A*, *B*, *C*, *D* and *E* yields the same level of output. Moving down the table from combination *A* to combination *B*, 4 units of capital are replaced by 1 unit of labour in the production process without any change in the level of output. Therefore, marginal rate of technical substitution of labour for capital is 4 at this stage. Switching from input combination *B* to input combination C involves the replacement of 3 units of capital by an additional unit of labour, output remaining the same. Thus, the marginal rate of technical substitution is now 3. Likewise, marginal rate of technical substitution of labour for capital between factor combinations *C* and *D* is 2, and between factor combinations *D* and *E* is 1.

Table 13.2. Marginal Rate of Technical Substitution

Factor Combinations	*Units of Labour (L)*	*Units of Capital (K)*	*MRTS of L for K*
A	1	12	
			4
B	2	8	
			3
C	3	5	
			2
D	4	3	
			1
E	5	2	

The marginal rate of technical substitution at a point on an isoquant (an equal product curve) can be known from the slope of the isoquant at that point. Consider a small movement down the equal product curve from *G* to *H* in Fig. 13.2 where a small amount of capital, say ΔK is replaced by an amount of labour say ΔL without any loss of output. The slope of the isoquant curve Q_1 at point *G* is therefore equal to $\frac{\Delta K}{\Delta L}$. Thus, marginal rate of technical substitution of labour for capital is equal to slope which is measured by $\frac{\Delta K}{\Delta L}$.

Slope of the isoquant at a point and hence the marginal rate of technical substitution (*MRTS*) between factors can also be known by the slope of the tangent drawn on the isoquant at that point. In Fig. 13.3 the tangent *TT'* is drawn at point *K* on the given equal product curve *Q*. The slope of the tangent *TT'* is equal to $\frac{OT}{OT'}$. Therefore, the marginal rate of substitution at point *K* on the equal product curve *Q* in Fig. 13.3 is equal to $\frac{OT}{OT'}$. *JJ'* is the

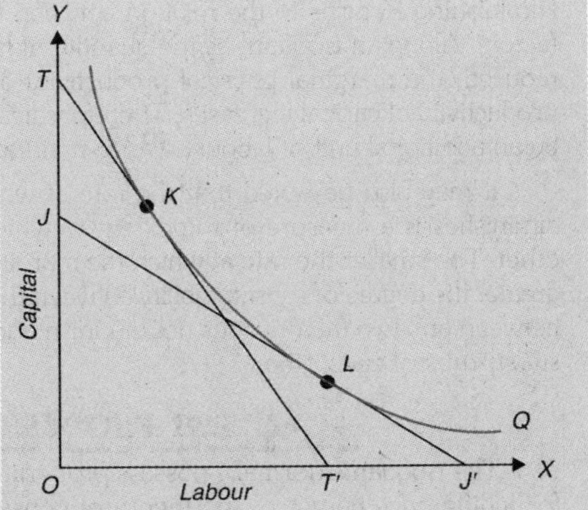

Fig. 13.3. *MRTS is given by the slope of the equal product curve.*

tangent at point L on the isoquant Q. Therefore, the marginal rate of technical substitution of labour for capital at point L is equal to OJ/OJ'.

An important point to be noted about the marginal rate of technical substitution is that it is equal to the ratio of the marginal physical products of the two factors. Since, by definition, output remains constant on as isoquant, the loss in physical output from a small reduction in capital will be equal to the gain in physical output from a small increment in labour. The loss in output is equal to the marginal physical product of capital (MP) multiplied by the amount of reduction in capital. The gain in output is equal to the marginal physical product of labour (MP) multiplied by the increment in labour.

Accordingly, along an isoquant

$$\Delta K . MP_k + \Delta L \,.\, MP_L = 0$$

$$\Delta K \times MP_k = \Delta L \times MP_L$$

$$\frac{\Delta K}{\Delta L} = \frac{MP_L}{MP_K}$$

But $\frac{\Delta K}{\Delta L}$, by definition, is the marginal rate of technical substitution of labour for capital

$$\therefore \qquad MRTS_{LK} = \frac{MP_L}{MP_K}$$

We thus see that marginal rate of technical substitution of labour for capital is the ratio of marginal physical products of the two factors.

Diminishing Marginal Rate of Technical Substitution. An important characteristic of marginal rate of technical substitution is that it diminishes as more and more of labour is substituted for capital. In other words, as the quantity of labour used is increased and the quantity of capital employed is reduced, the amount of capital that is required to be replaced by an additional unit of labour so as to keep the output constant will diminish. This is known as the *Principle of Diminishing Marginal Rate of Technical Substitution*. This principle of diminishing marginal rate of technical substitution is merely an extension of the Law of Diminishing Returns to the relation between the marginal physical productivities of the two factors. Along an isoquant as the quantity of labour is increased and the quantity of capital is reduced, the marginal physical productivity of labour diminishes and the marginal physical productivity of capital increases. Therefore, less and less of capital is required to be substituted by an additional unit of labour so as to maintain the same level of output.

It may also be noted that the rate at which the marginal rate of technical substitution diminishes is a measure of the extent to which the two factors can be substituted for each other. The smaller the rate at which the marginal rate of technical substitution diminishes, the greater the degree of substitutability between the two factors. If the marginal rate of substitution between any two factors does not diminish and remains constant, the two factors are *perfect substitutes* of each other.

GENERAL PROPERTIES OF ISOQUANTS

The isoquants normally possess properties which are similar to those generally assumed for indifference curves of the theory of consumer's behaviour. Moreover, the properties of isoquants can be proved in the same manner as in the case of indifference curves. The following are the important properties of isoquants.

1. Isoquants, like indifference curves, slope downward from left to right (*i.e.*, they have a negative slope.) This is so because when the quantity of factor, say labour, is increased, the quantity of other capital *i.e.*, capital must be reduced so as to keep output constant on a given isoquant. This downward-sloping property of isoquants follows from a valid assumption that the marginal physical products of factors are *positive*, that is, the use of additional units of factors yield *positive increments* in output. In view of this when one factor is increased yielding positive marginal products, the other factor must be *reduced* to hold the level of output constant; otherwise the output will increase and we will switch over to a higher isoquant.

The assumption that the marginal physical product of a foctor is positive is quite reasonable. In the discussion of the law of variable proportions we saw that in the stage III, when the units of the variable factor, say labour, become excessive, it causes such an overcrowding on a fixed capital equipment (or on a given piece of land if land is the fixed factor) that they obstruct each other resulting in negative marginal products of labour, that is, the use of additional units of labour reduces total output. This could happen but no rational producer who aims to minimize costs or maximize profits will employ units of a factor to the point where its marginal product has become negative because *positive prices* have to be paid for them. Thus, in view of the positive prices that have to be paid for the units of a factor, we rule out the use of the units of the factor that have negative or zero marginal products.

Thus, with labour measured on the *X*-axis and capital on the *Y*-axis, if the isoquant is a horizontal straight line, this would indicate that the marginal products of labour (MP_L) are zero. Likewise, vertical isoquant would indicate marginal products of capital (MP_K) are zero. Further, an upward-sloping isoquant implies that either the marginal products of the two factors are zero or one of the two factors has negative marginal products and the other has positive marginal products. It is also worth noting that the *upward-sloping isoquant implies that the same output can be produced with the use of less of both the factors,* that is, marginal products of at least one factor is negative. In this situation when every reduction in both the factors used does not affect output, the producer will not reach an equilibrium position. It follows from above that over the economically relevant stage of production when the marginal products of the factors are positive we have *downward-sloping isoquants.*

2. No two isoquants can intersect each other. If the two isoquants, one corresponding to 20 units of output and the other to 30 units of output intersect each other, there will then be a common factor-combination corresponding to the point of intersection. It means that the same factor combination which can produce 20 units of output according to one equal product curve can also produce 30 units of output according to the other equal product curve. But this is quite absurd. How can the same factor combination produces two different levels of output, techniques of production remaining unchanged.

3. Isoquants, like indifference curves, are convex to the origin. The convexity of isoquant curves means that as we move down the curve successively smaller units of capital are required to be substituted by a given increment of labour so as to keep the level of output unchanged. Thus, the convexity of equal product curves is due to the diminishing marginal rate of technical substitution of one factor for the other.

If the isoquants were concave to the origin, it would mean that the marginal rate of technical substitution increased as more and more units of labour substitute capital. This could be valid if the law of increasing returns applied. Since it is the law of diminishing returns which is more true of the real world, the principle of diminishing marginal rate of technical substitution generally holds good and it makes the isoquants convex to the origin. We have seen above that marginal rate of technical substitution diminishes because of diminishing marginal returns to a factor as we increase its quantity used. Therefore, *the convexity of iso-product curves implies the diminishing returns to a variable factor.* We have seen that there are diminishing returns to a factor because of the fact that different factors are *imperfect substitutes* of each other in the production of a good.

In general, convexity of isoquants implies that it *becomes progressively more difficult or harder to substitute one factor for another* as we move along an isoquant and increase the use of one factor substituting the other factor. Thus, when it is difficult to substitute a factor, say labour, for capital, it will then require a relatively larger amount of labour to replace a unit of capital, level of output being held constant.

The Rationale for Convexity of Isoquants

The main economic justification for the convexity of isoquants is that the producer's equilibrium in case of both concave isoquants or linear isoquants cannot occur with both factors used and instead it would occur when only one factor is being employed for production. Therefore, in case of concave or linear isoquants we would have *corner solution* where only one factor is being used for the production of a commodity. Since in practice more than one factor is used for production, both in the agricultural and industrial sectors, the isoquants are actually convex to the origin.

The convexity of isoquants follows from a valid assumption that marginal physical products of factors are positive, that is, the use of additional units of inputs (factors) yields positive increments in output. In view of this when only factor with positive marginal products is increased, the other factor in the production function must be reduced so as to keep the level of output constant, otherwise total output will increase and we will switch over to a higher isoquant. The assumption that marginal physical product of a factor is positive is quite reasonable. In the discussion of the law of variable proportions we saw that in stage III when the amount of a variable factor, labour, becomes excessive, it causes such an overcrowding in a given industrial plant or a given piece of agricultural land that workers obstruct each other in production resulting in negative marginal product. Of course, this could happen but no rational producer will employ a factor to the point where its marginal product has become negative (or even zero). This is because factors have to *be positive* prices and if they yield negative marginal returns, the producer will have to incur losses if he employs them. Thus, in view of the positive prices that have to be paid to the factors, we rule out the use of factors which have negative or zero marginal products.

Isoquants of Perfect Substitutes and Complements

There are two exceptions to this general property of the convexity of isoquants. One is the case of factors which are perfect substitutes of each other. When the two factors are perfect substitutes of each other, then each of them can be used equally well in place of the other. For all intents and purposes they can be regarded as the same factor. Therefore, the marginal rate of technical substitution between two perfect substitute factors remains constant. Since marginal rate of technical substitution remains the same throughout, the isoquants of perfect substitutes are straight lines, as shown in Fig. 13.4 instead of being convex to the origin.

Another exceptional case is of factors which are *perfect complements* and for which the isoquants are right-angled as shown in Fig. 13.5. The perfect complementary factors are those which are jointly used for production in a *fixed proportion.* Thus, in Fig. 13.5, *OA* of factor *X* and *OB* of factor *Y* are used to yield a level of output represented by isoquant Q_1. An increase in one factor without the required proportional increase in the other factor will yield no additional output whatsoever. That is why the isoquant is right-angled (with two arms, one is a vertical straight line and the other is a horizontal straight line) at the combination consisting of a given proportion of the two factors.

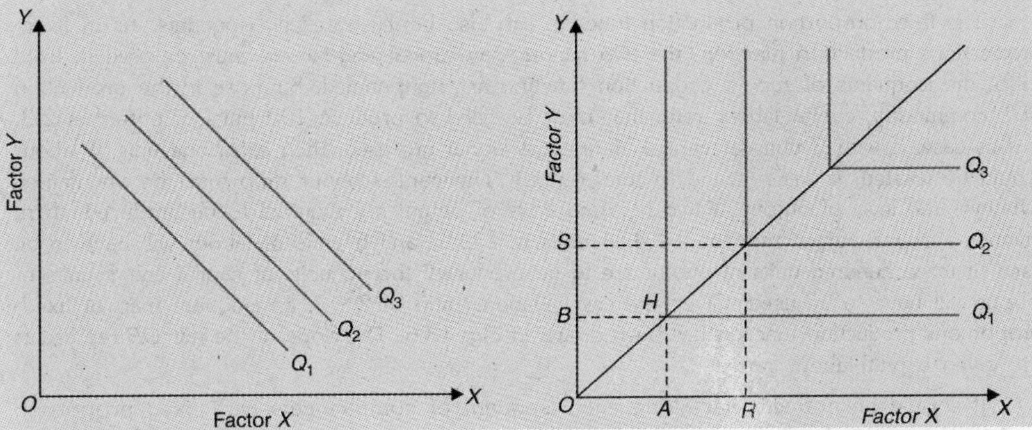

Fig. 13.4. *Perfect Substitutes* **Fig.13.5.** *Perfect Complementary Factors*

Consider isoquant or equal product curve Q_1 in Fig. 13.5 where output can be produced by the combination H consisting of OA of factor X and OB of factor Y. If now the amount of factor X is increased beyond OA without the increase in the factor Y, output will not rise and hence the lower portion of isoquant is a horizontal straight line. Likewise, if the amount of factor Y is increased beyond OB without the increase in factor X, the output will remain the same and hence the upper portion of the equal product curve is a vertical straight line. In case of perfect complementary factors, output can be increased only by increasing the amount of both the factors by the required given proportion. Thus in Fig. 13.5 if the amount of factor X is increased to OR (which is twice OA), then the amount of factor Y will have to increase by OS (which is twice OB) so that we have the same factor proportion, output increases by the same proportion as the increase in factors and we have a new isoquant Q_2 . It should be noted that no substitution is possible in case of perfect complements.

Fixed-Proportion and Variable-Proportion Production Functions

Production function is of two qualitatively different forms. It may be either *fixed-proportion production function or variable proportion production function.* Whether production function is of a fixed-proportion form or a variable-proportion form depends upon whether technical coefficients of production are fixed or variable. The amount of a productive factor that is essential to produce a unit of product is called the technical coefficient of production. For instance, if 25 workers are required to produce 100 units of a product, then 0.25 is the technical coefficient of labour for production. Now, if the technical coefficient of production of labour is fixed, then 0.25 of labour must be used for producing a unit of product and its amount cannot be reduced by using in its place some other factor. Therefore, in case of fixed-proportion production function, the factor or inputs, say labour and capital, must be used in a definite fixed proportion in order to produce a given level of output.

On the other hand, when technical coefficient of production is variable, that is, when the amount of a factor required to produce a unit of product can be varied by substituting in its place some other factor, the production function is of variable proportion form. Therefore, in case of variable-proportion production function, a given amount of a product can be produced by several alternative combinations of factors (inputs). The isoquant map shown in Fig. 13.2 represents variable proportion production function, since each isoquant drawn in it shows that various different combinations of factors, labour and capital, can be used to produce a given level of output. Several commodities in the real world are produced under conditions of variable proportion production function.

The fixed-proportion production function can also be illustrated by isoquants. As in fixed-proportions production function, the two factors, say capital and labour, must be used in fixed ratio, the isoquants of such a production function are right-angled. Suppose in the production of a commodity, capital-labour ratio that must be used to produce 100 units of output is 2:3. In this case, if with 2 units of capital, 4 units of labour are used, then extra one unit of labour would be wasted; it will not add to total output. The capital-labour ratio must be maintained whatever the level of output. If two hundred units of output are required to be produced, then, given the capital-output ratio of 2 : 3, 4 units of capital and 6 units of labour will have to be used, if three hundred units of output are to be produced, then 6 units of capital and 9 units of labour will have to be used. Given the capital-labour ratio of 2 : 3, an isoquant map of fixed-proportions production function has been drawn in Fig. 13.6. The slope of the ray *OR* represents the given capital-labour ratio.

It should be noticed that along each isoquant of complements with fixed proportion marginal product of a factor is zero. For instance, if we are at *B* on isoquant of 200, then capital being held constant at 4 units, use of more labour does not make any addition to total output, that is, marginal product of labour is zero. Likewise, if labour is held constant at 6 units, increase in the quantity of capital does not add to output. On the other hand, in a fixed-proportion production function, doubling the quantities of capital and labour at the required ratio doubles the output, trebling their quantities at the required ratio trebles the output.

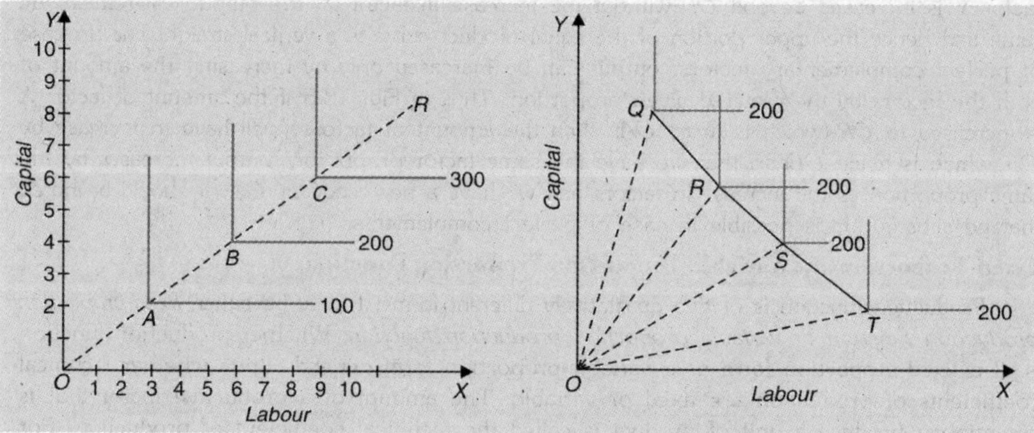

Fig. 13.6. *Isoquant Map of Fixed-Proportion Production Function*

Fig.13.7. *Four Fixed-Proportion production functions*

However, in the real world, instead of a single fixed-proportion production process, many (but not infinite) fixed-proportion production processes to produce a commodity are available, each process involves a given fixed factor ratio. Within one production process no factor substitution is possible. However, different processes use various factors in different proportions, since they involve different fixed-factor ratios. Such a production function of a commodity for which four fixed proportion processes are available is depicted in Fig. 13.7 where four isoquants representing four processes *i.e.*, four different capital-labour ratios have been drawn and all yield 200 units or output of the commodity. *OQ*, *OR*, *OS* and *OT* are the process-rays whose slopes represent different capital-labour ratios. By joining points *Q*, *R*, *S* and *T* by right-line segments we get a kinked (segmented) line *QRST*, each of the four points on which represents a factor-combination which can produce 200 units of the commodity. The kinked line *QRST* is similar to the ordinary isoquant, but there is an important difference between the two. Whereas every point on the ordinary isoquant is a feasible factor combination which itself is directly capable of producing a specified level of output, but every point on the kinked line *QRST* is not a feasible factor-combination capable of producing 200 units of output. Thus, factor combinations lying between *Q* and *R*, *R* and *S*, and *S* and *T* on the kinked line are not feasible factor combinations and cannot directly produce 200 units of output, for we have assumed that only four factor-combinations *Q*, *R*, *S* and *T* corresponding to four available processes are feasible factor-combinations capable of directly producing 200 units of output.

However, factor ratio corresponding to any point between *Q* and *R*, *R* and *S*, and *S* and *T* can be achieved by properly combining the two production processes. Thus, if factor ratio represented by a point between *R* and *S* is to be achieved, it can be done so by using a proper combination of two processes represented by *R* and *S*, that is, producing apart of the output with process *R* and a part with process *S*.

Linear Homogeneous Production Function

Production function can take several forms but a particular form of production function enjoys wide popularity among the economists. This is a linear homogeneous production function, that is, production function which is homogeneous of the first degree. Homogeneous production function of the first degree implies that if all factors of production are increased in a given proportion, output also increases in the same proportion. Hence linear homogeneous production function represents the case of constant returns to scale. If there are two factors *X* and *Y*, then homogeneous production function of the first degree can be mathematically expressed as :

$$mQ = f(mX,\ mY)$$

where *Q* stands for the total production and *m* is any real number.

The above function means that if factors *X* and Y are increased by *m*-times, total production *Q* also increases by m-times. It is because of this that homogeneous function of the first degree yields constant returns to scale.

More generally, a homogeneous production function can be expressed as

$$Qm^k = (mX,\ mY)$$

where *m* is any real number and *k* is constant. This function is homogeneous function of the *k*th degree. If *k* is equal to one, then the above homogeneous function becomes homogeneous of the first degree. If *k* is equal to two, the function becomes homogeneous of the 2nd degree. If *k* is greater, than one, the production function will yield increasing returns to scale. If on the other hand, *k* is less than 1, it will yield decreasing returns to scale.

Linear homogeneous production function is extensively used in empirical studies by economists. This is because in view of the limited analytical tools at the disposal of the economists, it can be easily handled and used in empirical studies. Further, because of its possessing highly useful economic features and properties, (for instance, constant returns to scale is a very important property of homogeneous production function of the first degree), it is easily used in calculations by computers and on account of this it is extensively employed in linear programming and input-output analysis, Moreover, because of its simplicity and close approximation to reality, it is widely used in model analysis regarding production, distribution and economic growth

As we shall prove in the next chapter, the expansion path of the homogeneous production function of the first degree is always a straight line through the origin. This implies that in case of homogeneous production function of the first degree, with constant relative factor prices, optimal proportions between the factors that will be used for production will always be the same whatever the amount of output to be produced. Because of the simple nature of the homogeneous production function of the first degree, the task of the entrepreneur is quite simple and convenient; he requires only to find out just one optimum factor proportions and so long as relative factor prices remain constant, he has not to make any fresh decision regarding factor proportions to be used as he expands his level of production. Moreover, the use of the same optimum factor proportions (with constant relative factor prices) at different levels of output in homogeneous production function of the first degree is also very useful in input-output analysis. Homogeneous production function of the first degree, which, as said above, implies constant returns to scale, has been actually found in agriculture as well as in many manufacturing industries. In India, farm management studies have been made for various States and data have been collected for agricultural inputs and outputs. Analysing the data collected in these farm management studies, Dr. A.M. Khusro reached the conclusion that constant returns to scale prevailed in Indian agriculture[1]. Likewise, empirical studies conducted in the United States and Britain have found that many manufacturing industries are characterised by a long phase of constant long-run average cost (*LAC*) curve which again implies constant returns to scale and homogeneous production function of the first degree.

COBB-DOUGLAS PRODUCTION FUNCTION

Many economists have studied actual production functions and have used statistical methods to find out relations between changes in physical inputs and physical outputs. A most familiar empirical production function found out by statistical methods is the *Cobb-Douglas production function.* Originally, Cobb-Douglas production function was applied not to the production process of an individual firm but to the whole of the manufacturing industry. Output in this function was thus originally whole manufacturing production. In Cobb-Douglas production function, there are two inputs, labour and capital, Cobb-Douglas production function takes the following mathematical form:

$$Q = AL^{\alpha}K^{\beta}$$

where Q is the manufacturing output, L is the quantity of labour employed, K is the quantity of capital employed, and A and a are positive constants. Roughly speaking, Cobb-Douglas production function found that about 75% of the increase in manufacturing production was due to the labour input and the remaining 25% was due to the capital input.

It is important to note that originally it was found that the sum of exponents of Cobb-Douglas production was equal to one, that is, $\alpha + \beta = 1$. However, from further research and analysis it was generalised and found that the sum of exponents ($\alpha + \beta$) could be equal to one, more than one and less than one. As we shall prove later when sum of exponents ($\alpha + \beta$) is equal to one, constant returns to scale (i.e., linear homogeneous production function) occur, when $\alpha + \beta > 1$, we get increasing returns to scale and when $\alpha + \beta < 1$, decreasing returns to scale occur.

Essential Features of Cobb-Douglas Production Function

Let us explain some of the essential features of linear homogeneous production function with special reference to Cobb-Douglas production, which is an important example of linear homogeneous production function.

---

1. See his article "Returns to Scale in Indian Agriculture", *The Indian Journal of Agricultural Economics*, Vol. XIX, July-Dec. 1964, reprinted in "*Readings in Agricultural Development*, edited by A.M. Khusro, Allied Publishers, 1968.

Average Product of Factors in Cobb-Douglas Production Function. The first important feature of Cobb-Douglas production function when the sum of its exponents is equal to one (*i.e.*, $\alpha + \beta = 1$) and therefore it is linearly homogeneous production function is that the *average and marginal products of factors depend upon the ratio in which factors are combined for the production of a commodity.*

Linear Cobb-Douglas function can be written as

$$Q = A\, L^{\alpha}\, K^{1-\alpha}, \qquad (\alpha + 1 - \alpha = 1)$$

Average product of labour can be obtained from dividing the production function by the amount of labour L. Thus,

$$\text{Average product of labour} = \frac{AL^{a}K^{1-\alpha}}{L} = \frac{AK^{1-\alpha}}{L^{1-a}}$$

$$= A\left(\frac{K}{L}\right)^{1-\alpha}$$

Since A and α are constants, average product of labour will depend on the *ratio of the factors* $\left(\frac{K}{L}\right)$ and will not depend upon the *absolute quantities* of the factors used. Let us take a numerical example: Suppose the constant term A in the Cobb-Douglas production is equal to 50 and constant exponent a is equal to $\frac{1}{2}$ and the quantity of capital used is 8 units and quantity of labour used is 2 so that, we get the capital-labour ratio equal to 4:1. The average product of labour will be equal to:

$$AP_L = A\left(\frac{K}{L}\right)^{1-\alpha}$$

$$= 50\left(\frac{8}{2}\right)^{1-\frac{1}{2}} = 50 \times (4)^{\frac{1}{2}} = 50.\sqrt{4} = 100$$

Now, if the quantities of factors used are increased to $K = 400$ and L 100, *keeping the factor-ratio constant* at 4:1, the average product of labour will still remain equal to 100.

$$AP_L = A\left(\frac{K}{L}\right)^{1-a} = 50\left(\frac{400}{100}\right)^{\frac{1}{2}} = 50.\sqrt{4} = 100$$

Marginal Product of Factors and Cobb-Douglas Production Function. Like the average product of a factor, the marginal product of a factor of *a linear* Cobb-Douglas production function also depends upon the *ratio* of the factors and is independent of the absolute quantities of the factors used. Note that marginal product of a factor, say labour, is the first derivative of the production function with respect to labour. The marginal product of labour from linear Cobb-Douglas production can be obtained as under:

$$Q = A L^{a} K^{1-a}$$

$$\text{Marginal Product of labour } \frac{dQ}{dL} = AaL^{a-1}K^{1-a}$$

$$= \frac{AaL^{a}k^{1-a}}{L}$$

$$= \frac{AaL^{a-a}K^{1-a}}{L^{1-a}} = \frac{AaK^{1-a}}{L^{1-a}}$$

$$= Aa\left(\frac{K}{L}\right)^{1-a}$$

Since A and α are constants, marginal product of labour will depend on captial-labour ratio, that is, capital per worker and is independent of the magnitudes of the factors employed.

Cobb-Douglas Production Function and Marginal Returns to a Variable Factor. In case of linear homogeneous Cobb-Douglas production function such as $Q = AL^{0.75} K^{0.25}$, marginal returns to a variable factor, say labour, diminishes as more labour is used. This will hold if the second derivative of the given Cobb-Douglas production function ($Q = AL^{0.75} K^{0.25}$ is be negative.

The first derivative $\frac{\partial Q}{\partial L}$ (i.e. MP_L) $= 0.75\ AL^{-0.25} K^{0.25}$

The second derivative, $\frac{\partial Q^2}{\partial^2 L} = -0.25 \times 0.75\ AL^{-1.25} K^{0.25}$

$$= -\ 1875\ AL^{-1.25}\ K^{0.25}$$

Since the second dervative is negative, MP_L will diminish with the increase in the amount of labour.

Cobb-Douglas Production Function and Marginal Rate of Substitution. Marginal rate of substitution is an important concept which is extensively used in the analysis of cost-minimizing choice of inputs for producing a given level of output of a commodity. As has been shown above, marginal rate of substitution between factors is equal to the ratio of the marginal physical products of the factors. Therefore, in order to derive marginal rate of substitution from Cobb-Douglas production function we need to obtain the marginal physical products of the two factors from the Cobb-Douglas production function. We now proceed to derive them below:

$$Q = AL^a K^\beta$$

Differentiating this with respect to L we have

$$\frac{dQ}{dL} = aAL^{a-1} K^\beta$$

$$= \frac{a\left(AL^a K^\beta\right)}{L}$$

Now, $AL^a K^\beta = Q$. Therefore,

$$\frac{dQ}{dL} = a\left(\frac{Q}{L}\right)$$

$\frac{dQ}{dL}$ represents marginal product of labour and $\frac{Q}{L}$ stands for the average product of labour.

Thus,

$$MP_L = a(AP_L) \qquad \text{... } (i)$$

Similarly, by differentiating Cobb-Douglas production function with respect to captial we can show that marginal product of captial,

$$\frac{dQ}{dK} = \beta\frac{Q}{K}$$

or,

$$MP_K = \beta(AP_K) \qquad \text{... } (ii)$$

It follows from (*i*) and (*ii*) above, that

$$MRS_{LK} = \frac{MP_L}{MP_K} = \frac{\alpha.Q/L}{\beta.Q/K} = \frac{\alpha}{\beta}.\frac{K}{L} \quad \text{... (iii)}$$

Cobb-Douglas Production Function and Elasticity of Substitution: Now, we can show that in *Cobb-Douglas production function elasticity of factor substitution* (e_s or σ) *is equal to unity.*

$$e_s \text{ or } \sigma = \frac{\text{Proportionate Change in Capital – Labour Ratio}\left(\frac{K}{L}\right)}{\text{Proportionate Change in } MRS_{LK}}$$

$$e_s \text{ or } \sigma = \frac{d\frac{K}{L}/\frac{K}{L}}{d(MRS_{LK})/MRS_{LK}}$$

Substituting the value of marginal rate of substitution obtained in (*iii*) above we have

$$e_s \text{ or } \sigma = \frac{d\left(\frac{K}{L}\right)/\left(\frac{K}{L}\right)}{d\left(\frac{\alpha}{\beta}.\frac{K}{L}\right)/\left(\frac{\alpha}{\beta}.\frac{K}{L}\right)}$$

Since $\frac{\alpha}{\beta}$ is constant and would not affect the derivative, it can therefore be factored out. Therefore,

$$\sigma = \frac{d\left(\frac{K}{L}\right).\frac{\alpha}{\beta}}{\frac{\alpha}{\beta}.d\left(\frac{K}{L}\right)} = 1$$

Cobb-Douglas Production Function and Returns to Scale

An important property of Cobb-Douglas production function is that the sum of its exponents measures returns to scale. Cobb-Douglas production function in general from, that is, when the sum of exponents is not necessarily equal to zero is given below:

$$Q = AL^{\alpha}K^{\beta}$$

In this production function the sum of exponents ($\alpha + \beta$) measures returns to scale. Multiplying each input, labour (*L*) and capital (*K*), by a constant factor *g*, we have

$$Q' = A(gL)^{\alpha}(gK)^{\beta}$$

$$= g^{\alpha}g^{\beta}\left(AL^{\alpha}K^{\beta}\right)$$

$$= g^{\alpha+\beta}\left(AL^{\alpha}K^{\beta}\right)$$

Expression in bracket $AL^{\alpha}K^{\beta} = Q$. Therefore

$$Q' = g^{\alpha+\beta}\,Q$$

This means that when each input is increased by a constant factor *g*, output *Q* increases by $g^{\alpha+\beta}$ Now, if $\alpha + \beta = 1$, then in this production function

$$Q' = g^1 Q$$

$$Q' = gQ$$

This is, when $\alpha + \beta = 1$, output (Q) also increases by the some factor g by which both inputs are increased. This implies that production function its *homogenous of first degree or,* in other words, returns to scale are constant.

When $\alpha + \beta > 1$, say it is equal to 2, then, in this production function new output

$$Q' = g^{\alpha+\beta} AL^{\alpha} K^{\beta} = g^2 Q$$

In this case multiplying each input by constant *g*, then output (Q) increases by g^2, that is by more than *g*. Therefore, when $\alpha + \beta > 1$. *Cobb-Douglas production function exhibits increasing returns to scale.*

When $\alpha + \beta < 1$, say it is equal to 0.8, then in this production function new output

$$Q' = g^{\alpha+\beta} AL^{\alpha} K^{\beta} = g^{0.8} Q$$

That is, increasing each input by constant factor *g* will cause output to increase by $g^{0.8}$, that is, less then g. Returns to scale in this case are decreasing.

It therefore follows from above that the sum of the exponents of Cobb-Douglas production function, that is, $\alpha + \beta$ measures returns to scale.

If $\alpha + \beta = 1$, returns to scale are constant.

If $\alpha + \beta > 1$, returns to scale are increasing.

If $\alpha + \beta < 1$, returns to scale are decreasing.

Cobb-Douglas Production Function and Output Elasticities of Factors

Thirdly, the exponents of labour and capital in Cobb-Douglas production function measure output elasticities of labour and capital. Output elasticity of a factor refers to a percentage change in output caused by a given percharge change in a variable factor, other factors and inputs remaining constant. Thus,

$$\text{Output elasticity of labour} = \frac{\partial Q}{Q} \div \frac{\partial L}{L} = \frac{\partial Q}{\partial L} \cdot \frac{L}{Q}$$

$\frac{\partial Q}{\partial L}$ = marginal product of labour and $\frac{Q}{L}$ = average product of labour

Thus, output elasticity of labour $= \frac{MP_L}{AP_L}$

We write Cobb-Douglas production function as under:

$$Q = AL^{\alpha} K^{\beta} \quad \text{......(1)}$$

Since output elasticity of labour is the ratio of its marginal product to the average product. Therefore, in order to find out the output elasticity of labour in Cobb-Douglas production function we have to first obtain marginal and average products of labour.

Taking the first derivative of the Cobb-Douglas production function with respect to labour:

$$MP_L = \frac{\partial Q}{\partial L} = A\alpha L^{\alpha-1} K^{\beta}$$

Average product of labour in the Cobb-Douglas production function:

$$AP_L = \frac{AL^{\alpha}K^{\beta}}{L}$$

$$= AL^{\alpha-1}K^{\beta}$$

Now, by taking the ratio of marginal and average products of labour we get elasticity of output of labour. Thus

$$E_L = \frac{MP_L}{AP_L} = \frac{A\alpha L^{\alpha-1}K^{\beta}}{AL^{\alpha-1}K^{\beta}}$$

$$= \alpha$$

Thus, output elasticity of labour in Cobb-Douglas production is *constant* and equal to its exponent α. This means that one percentage increase in labour input results in a increase in output.

Similarly, output elasticity of capital $= \frac{\partial Q}{\partial K} \cdot \frac{K}{Q} = \frac{MP_K}{AP_K}$

We take the first derivative of Cobb-Douglas production function ($Q = AL^{\alpha}K^{\beta}$) with respect to capital. Thus

$$MP_K = \beta AL^{\alpha}K^{\beta-1}$$

Average product of capital, $AP_K = \frac{AL^{\alpha}K^{\beta}}{K} = AL^{\alpha}K^{\beta-1}$

Output elasticity of capital, $E_K = \frac{\beta AL^{\alpha}K^{\beta-1}}{AL^{\alpha}K^{\beta-1}} = \beta$

Thus in Cobb-Douglas production function the exponents of inputs, labour and capital, measure their elasticities of output respectively.

Note that if output elasticity of a factor, that is, the value of α or β above is less than one, this will show diminishing marginal returns to a factor. Thus, if the value of α, that is, output elasticity of labour is less then one (say, it is equal to 0.7), this will mean, for example, one per cent increase in labour will cause 0.7 per cent increase in output. Therefore, when in Cobb-Douglas production function the sum of exponents ($a + b$) equals one, then the individual values of exponents α and β labour and capital respectively are less than one and Cobb-Douglas production function shows diminishing returns to a variable factor.

Cobb-Douglas Production Function and Euler Theorem

Cobb-Douglas production function, $Q=AL^aK^{\beta}$ where $a + b = 1$ helps to prove Euler theorem. According to Euler theorem, total output Q is exhausted by the distributive shares of all factors when each factor is paid equal to its marginal physical product. We give below a formal proof of it

As we saw above,

$$MP_L = Aa\left(\frac{K}{L}\right)^b \quad \text{... (1)}$$

fiberise,

$$MP_K = Ab\left(\frac{L}{K}\right)^a \quad \text{... (2)}$$

According to Euler theorem, if production function is homogeneous of first degree, then

Total output, $Q = L.MP_L + K.MP_K$.

Substituting the values of MP_L and MP_K we have

$$Q = L.Aa\left(\frac{K}{L}\right)^b + K.Ab\left(\frac{L}{K}\right)^a$$

$$Q = AaL^{1-b}K^b + AbL^aK^{1-a} \quad \ldots (3)$$

Now, in Cobb-Douglas production function with constant returns to scale, $a + b = 1$ and therefore $a = 1 - b$, and $b = 1 - a$. Substituting these in equation (3) we have

$$Q = AaL^aK^b + AbL^aK^b$$

$$= AL^aK^b(a+b)$$

Since $a + b = 1$, we have

$$Q = AL^aK^b$$

$$= Q.$$

Thus, in Cobb-Douglas production with $a + b = 1$ if wage rate $= MP_L$ and rate of return on capital (K) $= MP_K$, then total output will be exhausted.

Cobb-Douglas Production Function in the Extended Form

Cobb-Douglas production function can be extended to include more than two factors. For example, agricultural production depends not only on labour and capital used but also on the use of other inputs such as land, irrigation, fertilisers. Incorporating these inputs in the Cobb-Douglas production function we have:

$$Q = AL^aK^{b_1}D^{b_2}G^{b_3}F^{b_4}$$

where Q stands for output, L and K for labour and capital respectively, a and b are exponents of labour and capital respectively. D stands for land, G stands for irrigation, F for fertiliser and b_2, b_3, b_4 are exponents of land, irrigation and, fertilisers respectively.

The above Cobb-Douglas Production can be estimated by regression analysis by first converting it into the following log form.

$$\log Q = \log A + a\log L + b_1 \log K + b_2 \log D + b_3 \log G + b_4 \log F$$

Cobb-Douglas production function in log form is a linear function and therefore it can be estimated by least squares regression technique.

Cobb-Douglas production function is used in empirical production studies to estimate returns to scale in various industries as to whether they are increasing, constant or decreasing. Further, Cobb-Douglas production function is also frequently used to estimate output elasticities of labour and capital.

ELASTICITY OF TECHNICAL SUBSTITUTION (BETWEEN FACTORS)

In the theory of production we are concerned with the elasticity of substitution between factors (or inputs) in the production of goods. Thus, in the theory of production we are concerned with what may be called *elasticity of technical substitution.*

As seen above, marginal rate of technical substitution (*MRTS*) of factor X for factor Y declines as factor X is substituted for factor Y along an isoquant. In other words, marginal rate of technical substitution is different at different factor-proportions (*i.e.*, input ratios) used in the production of a good. This responsiveness of the proportions or ratios in which factors (or inputs) are used as there is a movement along an isoquant may be compared with the change in production possibilities as measured by the change in the marginal rate of technical substitution. *The relative change in the factor-proportions (or input ratios) as a consequence of the relative change in the marginal rate of technical substitution is known as elasticity of substitution between factors.*

The concept of elasticity of substitution has been widely discussed in economic literature in connection with the substitution between labour and capital. Therefore, we shall also explain the concept of elasticity of substitution with reference to capital and labour as factors of production. If K stands for the quantity of capital L for the quantity of labour and σ for the elasticity of substitution, then in accordance with the above definition, elasticity of substitution of capital for labour can be expressed as follows:

$$\sigma = \frac{\text{proportionate change in the ratio of inputs } (K \text{ and } L) \text{ used}}{\text{proportionate change in the marginal rate of technical substitution of } L \text{ for } K}$$

$$= \frac{\text{proportionate change in } K/L}{\text{proportionate change in } MRTS_{LK}}$$

$$= \frac{\frac{\Delta(K/L)}{K/L}}{\Delta(MRTS_{LK})/(MRTS_{LK})}$$

$$= \frac{\Delta(K/L)}{K/L} \cdot \frac{MRTS_{LK}}{\Delta(MRTS_{LK})}$$

$$= \frac{\Delta(K/L)}{\Delta(MRTS_{LK})} \cdot \frac{MRTS_{LK}}{K/L}$$

In order to understand the concept of elasticity of substitution, consider Fig. 13.8 where an isoquant or equal product curve q has been drawn. It will be seen that a point A on the given isoquant q, the capital-labour ratio used is K_1/L_1 which is equal to the slope of the ray OA. As labour is substituted for capital and therefore we move down along the isoquant q from point A to B, capital-labour ratio used is changed to K_2/L_2 which is equal to the slope of the ray OB. If further substitution of labour for capital takes place and welcome down to point C on the isoquant q, capital-labour ratio further falls to K_3/L_3 which is equal to the slope of the ray OC. It is therefore clear that as we substitute more labour for capital along the isoquant, capital-labour ratio is decreasing.

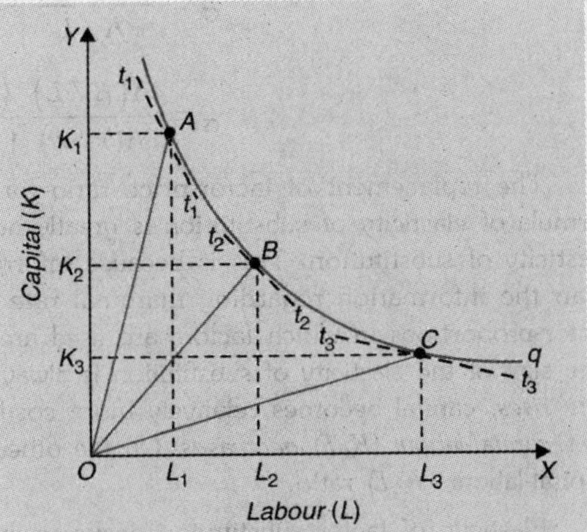

Fig. 13.8. *$MRTS_{LK}$ and Capital-Labour Ratios*

Now, as we have already seen, marginal rate of technical substitution at point A is given by the slope of the isoquant at that point (which is equal to the slope of the tangent t_1t_1 drawn at that point). At point *B*, the $MRTS_{LK}$ is equal to the slope of tangent t_2t_2 and at point *C*, the $MRTS_{LK}$ is equal to the slope of tangent t_3t_3. It will be seen that the slope of tangent t_2t_2 is less than that of t_1t_1; slope of t_3t_3 is less than that of t_2t_2.

It follows from above that geometrically the elasticity of substitution between factors is the ratio of proportionate change in the slopes of two rays from the origin to the two points on an isoquant to the proportionate change in the slopes of isoquants at those points. Thus

$$\sigma_{LK} = \frac{\text{proportionate change in the factor-proportions}}{\text{proportionate change in } MRTS_{LK}}$$

$$= \frac{\text{proportionate change in the slopes of two rays to two points}}{\text{porportionate change in the slopes of the tangents drawn to the isoquants at these points}}$$

Convexity of Isoquants and Elasticity of Substitution. The magnitude of the elasticity of substitution varies inversely with the curvature of the isoquants. The greater the convexity of isoquants, the less will be the substitution elasticity and *vice versa*. In the extreme case when the two factors are perfect complements and their isoquants are right-angled, the substitution elasticity between them is zero. On the other extreme, when the two factors are perfect substitutes and the isoquants between them are straight lines, substitution elasticity between them is equal to infinity. Moreover, since there is inverse relationship between marginal rate of technical substitutor and factor-ratio (as marginal rate of technical substitution of labour for capital *falls*, the labour-capital ratio *increases*), the elasticity of substitution is always negative.

Elasticity of Substitution and Factor-Price Ratio. Since, in equilibrium position the marginal rate of technical substitution is equal to the ratio of factor prices, the marginal rate of substitution in the formula for elasticity of substitution may therefore be replaced by the ratio of factor-prices.

Let *r* represent price of capital and *w* represent wage rate or price of labour. Thus,

$$\sigma_{LK} = \frac{\text{proportionate change in capital-labour ratio}}{\text{proportionate change in the ratio of } r/w}$$

$$\sigma = \frac{\Delta(K/L)}{K/L} \div \frac{\Delta(r/w)}{(r/w)} = \frac{\Delta(K/L)}{(K/L)} \cdot \frac{(r/w)}{\Delta(r/w)}$$

$$\sigma = \frac{\Delta(K/L)}{\Delta(r/w)} \cdot \frac{(r/w)}{(K/L)}$$

The replacement of factor-price ratio for marginal rate of technical substitution in the formula of elasticity of substitution is greatly helpful in practical application of the concept of elasticity of substitution. This is because information regarding prices is more easily available than the information regarding marginal rate of technical substitution. Further, changes in factor-proportions in which factors are used are generally induced by the relative factor prices. The sign of the elasticity of substitution is always negative (unless $\sigma = 0$). This is because *when r/w rises,* capital becomes relatively more costly and as a result it is substituted by labour so that *capital-labour (K/L) decreases.* On the other hand, a fall in *r/w* will lead to the increase in capital-labour (*K/L*) ratio.

Elasticity of factor substitution occupies an important place in the theory of distribution.

According to the neo-classical theory of distribution, distributive shares of labour and capital in national income depend on the elasticity of factor substitution.

THE ECONOMIC REGION OF PRODUCTION

Before explaining which factor combination a firm will use for production, it will be useful to demonstrate the region in which the optimal factor combination will lie. The economic theory focuses on only those combinations of factors which are technically efficient and the marginal products of factors are diminishing but positive. According to this, isoquants are slopping downward (*i.e.* their slope is negative) and convex to the origin. However, there are regions in a production function, where isoquants may have positively-sloping segments, that is, bend backwards. In Fig. 13.9 we represent a production function through isoquants and measure labour along the *X*-axis and capital along the *Y*-axis. It will be seen from this figure that above the line *OA* and below the line *OB* slope of the isoquants is *positive* which means that *increases in both capital and labour are required to produce a given fixed quantity of output.* Obviously the production techniques (that is, factor combinations) lying on these positively-sloping segments of the isoquants are technically inefficient. It may be recalled that a technique or factor combination is technically inefficient if it requires more quantity of both the factors for producing a given level of output. The positively-sloping segments of isoquants implies that marginal product of one of the factors has become negative. Thus, above the line *OA*, marginal product of capital has become negative, which means output decreases by using more capital, if the amount of labour is held constant. Therefore, to keep output constant along an isoquant when capital with negative marginal product increases, labour with positive marginal product has to be increased.

On the other hand, to the right of the line *OB*, marginal product of labour becomes negative, which means to keep output constant capital with positive marginal product has to be increased with the increase in labour input having negative marginal product. The lines *OA* and *OB* are called the *ridge lines* which bound a region in which marginal products of the two factors are positive. The ridge line *OA* connects those points of the isoquants where marginal product of capital is zero (MP_k = 0). On the other hand, the ridge line *OB* connects those points of the isoquants where marginal product of labour is zero (MP_L = 0). Thus, *the ridge lines are the locus of points of isoquants where marginal product of one of the factors is zero.*

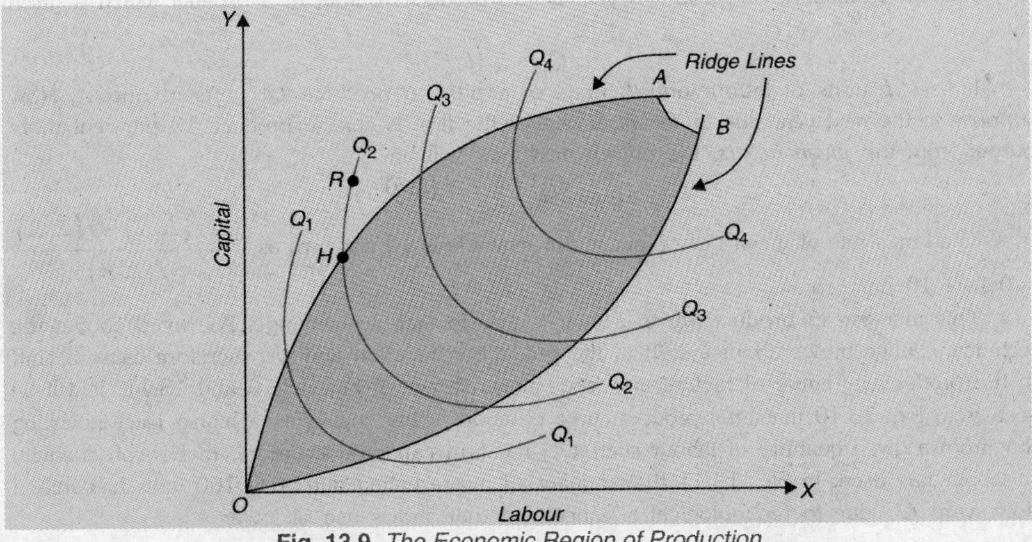

Fig. 13.9. *The Economic Region of Production*

The above analysis also shows that there is a limit to which one factor can be substituted for another. As the substitution of one factor for another is carried out more and more, it becomes progressively more difficult until a point is reached beyond which substitution between factors becomes impossible. As a result, the marginal product of the increasing factor first becomes zero and then it becomes negative so that isoquant becomes positively sloping.

No rational entrepreneur will operate at a point outside the ridge lines since marginal product of one of the factors is negative and production is technically inefficient. In other words, production outside the ridge lines is inefficient because *same output can be produced with less of the factors which therefore must be cheaper.* This can be better understood from Fig. 13.9. Consider point R on isoquant Q_2. It will be seen that R is the point where the isoquant is positively sloping and therefore lies outside the ridge line. It will be seen from Fig. 13.9 that at point R to produce output Q_2 requires more of both capital and labour than some other points, such as point H, on the same isoquant. Since, both capital and labour have to be paid positive prices, it will be cheaper to produce a given quantity of output at point H than at point R.

Thus, since production outside the ridge lines is technically inefficient and marginal product of one of the factors is negative, no rational entrepreneur will like to operate outside the ridge lines if he aims at minimising cost to produce a given output. Thus, *regions outside the ridge lines are called regions of economic nonsense.* A rational producer will produce in the region bounded by the two ridge lines OA and OB where the isoquants are negatively sloping and marginal products of factors are diminishing but positive. Therefore, the region bounded by the two ridge lines, OA and OB is called *economic region of production* which has been shaded by us. Exactly at what point in the economic region, a firm will operate depends on the outlay it has to make on purchasing the factors or the level of output it want to produce and also on prices of the factors.

PRODUCTION FUNCTION AND TECHNOLOGICAL CHANGE

For producing goods a firm tries to use the best available production process, given the state of technological knowledge. *Advance in technological knowledge that enables the firms to produce more output with the same quantities of inputs is called technical change or technological innovation.* It is important to note that technical progress changes or shifts the production function. Suppose this year a firm produces output of a product which is given by

$$Q_1 = f(L,K)$$

It uses L units of labour and K units of capital to produce Q_1 units of output. Now suppose in the next year due to *technical change* the firm is able to produce 10 per cent more output from the *given inputs,* the output next year will be

$$Q_2 = 1.1\ f(L,K)$$

The firm's rate of growth of output in our example is 10 per cent as $\dfrac{1.1f(L,K) - f(L,K)}{f(L,K)}$ = 0.1 or 10 per cent.

This increase in productivity in a year is due to technical change. As noted above, the technical change brings about a shift in the production function and will therefore cause a shift in the productivity curve of factors and isoquant as shown in Fig. 13.10 and 13.11. It will be seen from Fig. 13.10 that total product curve of labour shifts upward to a higher level indicating that from a given quantity of labour such OL, the firm can produce more, that is, productivity of labour has risen. In Fig. 13.11 the isoquant Q_1 representing output of 100 units has shifted downward Q'_1 due to technological advancement that shows use of lower

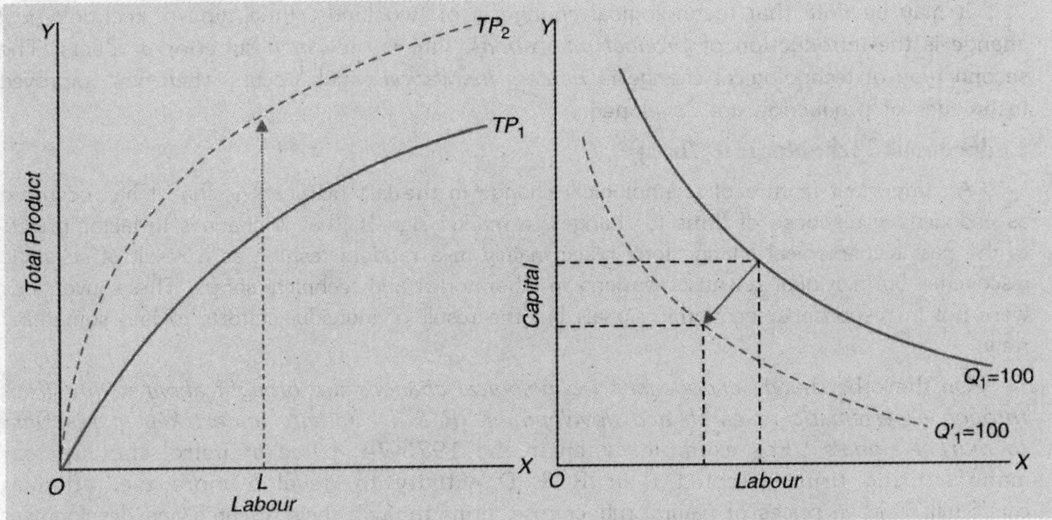

Fig. 13.10. *Upward Shift in the Total Product Curve of Labour due to Technological Change*

Fig. 13.11. *Downward Shift in the Isoquant due to Technological Change*

amounts of labour and capital can now yield 100 units of output. That is, productivity of both labour and capital or what is often called *total factor productivity* has gone up. In recent years various emprical studies have been made to measure technical change or growth in productivity. In Table 13.3 we have given the estimates of growth in productivity during 1 949-1983 in the USA. The growth in productivity varies in different industries.

It will be seen from Table 13.3 that in the manufacturing sector as a whole in the United States, productivity increased at the rate of 1.1 per cent annum during 1949-1983.

Table 13.3 Annual Rate of Productivity Growth in United States, 1949-83

Industry	*Growth rate (%)*
Food and Kindred products	0.7
Tobacco manufactures	0.2
Lumber and Wood Products	1.3
Paper and Allied Products	1.5
Total Manufacturing	1.1

Source: Gullickson and Harper, "*Multi-Factor Productivity in US Manufacturing,*1949-83"

Growth in productivity or technical change over years is an important factor in determining rate of economic growth of a country. The lower growth of productivity causes showdown in economic growth. If developing countries such as India is to catch up with the presently developed countries the key factor to achieve this is to bring about adequate technical change.

Since technological change raises productivity of inputs, it reduces average cost of producing output. Empirical evidence shows that possibilities of reducing cost of production through choice among available techniques of production are limited, while cost per unit can be reduced significantly through new inventions and innovations, that is, cost reduction through technological change is substantial. Lipsey and Chrystal rightly write, "*improvements by inventions and innovations are potentially limitless. Hence growth in living standards is critically linked to technological change.*[2]

2. Richard G. Lipsey, K. Alex Chrystal, *Economics*, 10th edition, 2004, p. 152.

It may be note that technological change is of two kinds. First type of technological change is the introduction of *product innovations,* that is, new and superior products. The second type of technological change is *process innovation* which occurs when new improved techniques of production are developed.

Endogenous Technological Change

An important feature of technological change in the last 50 years is that it has occurred as endogenous response of firms to changes in market signals, that is changes in factor prices. In the past technological change took place mainly in a random fashion as a result of scientific discoveries by individual scientists working in laboratories and technical shops. These inventions were not in response to economic signals but the result of individual efforts to find something new.

On the other hand, *endogenous technological changes are brought about within firms through a systematic research and development (R & D) activity undertaken in response to market signals.*[3] For example, when in the 1973-74, price of petrol shot up, car manufacturing firms directed their R & D activity to develop more fuel efficient cars.Similarly,when prices of natural rubber rose, firms through their research and development activity developed synthetic rubber and plastic to substitute natural rubber. Thus, Lipsey and Chrystal write, "Changes in technology are often *endogeneous responses to changing economic signals,* that is, they result from *responses by firms* to the same things that induce substitution of one input for another"[4] That is, as firms substitute one input for another within the confines of a given technology in response to change in relative prices of these inputs, similarly in the very long run firms develop new technologies in response to changes in market prices of inputs[5].

Regarding endogeneous technological change a significant example is furnished by Japanese experience. Japanese car manufacturing firms developed a new flexible manufacturing technology in response to scale disadvantage they suffered as compared to the car produces of the United States and Europe. Japanese firms could not attain the *minimum efficient scale* because they were then producing for home market with a small-size plants. But even *within the confines of small scale plants* they introduced new innovations which enabled them to produce superior cars at lower prices and almost drived out the American firms from competition within the United States. Production on a small scale but using a superior and efficient technology has been called '*Flexible Manufacturing*'. They repeated this same experience with regard to production of electronic products. This shows that for the introduction and use of new and improved technology, the production on a large scale is not necessary.

Conclusion. So far most of microeconomic theory explains the short-run and long-run responses of the firms to changes in prices of output and inputs within the confines of fixed plant and equipment. It has generally ignored the development of new technologies by the firms in response to economic signals. Thus, the response of firms to changes in prices of products and inputs should be analysed at three levels.

1. In the short run, the firms can change their output by changing the amounts of variable factors, fixed factors such as plant and equipment remaining the same.
2. In the long run, the firmss can change all inputs or factors, that is, both variable and fixed inputs but within the *confines of given* technology.
3. In the very long run firms respond to economic signals to introduce new inventions and

3. Lipsey and Chrystal, *op. cit.* p. 152.
4. *Ibid,* p. 153
5. In clarifying the concept of nature of technological change, N. Rosenberg has made an important contribution. See his work, *Inside the Black Box: Technology and Economics* (Cambridge University Press, 1982).

innovations (*i.e.*, new technologies) through their research and development activity

Types of Technical Change

Technical change has been classified into three categories: (1) Neutral technical change, (2) Labour-saving technical change and (3) Capital-saving technical change. *The technical change is neutral if more output can be produced by using the same ratio of inputs, say labour and capital.* This is depicted in Fig. 13.12 (a) where with the shift in production function, capital-labour ratio remains the same at a given MRS_{LK}.

On the other hand, if due to a technical change, the firm produces more output by using relatively less labour per unit of capital; the technological change will be labour-saving. For example, if a printing press that required two workers per machine is substituted by the production process that requires one worker per machine to produce the given quantity of printing material so that capital-labour ratio rises or labour-capital ratio falls, it will be labour saving. Thus, as a result of labour-saving technical change labour productivity increases with the increase in capital intensity. This is shown in Fig. 13.12 (b) where with the technological change, capital-labour ratio rises at a given MRS_{LK}.

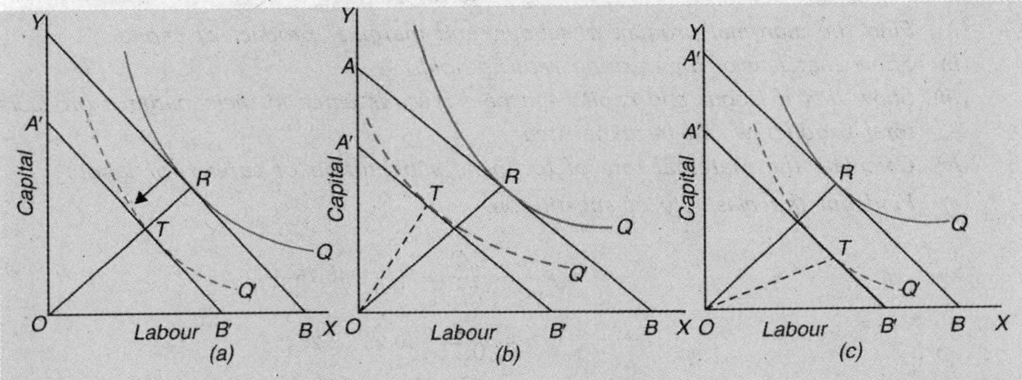

Fig. 13.12(a) *Neutral Technological Change*

Fig. 13.12(b) *Labour-Saving (or Capital-Bias) Technological Change*

Fig. 13.12(c) *Capital-Saving (or Labour-Bias) Technological Change*

On the other hand, *if as a result of technological change relatively less capital than labour is used to produce a given output so that capital-labour ratio falls, it will be capital-saving technological change.* As a result of capital-saving technical change, productivity of capital rises more than that of labour. This is depicted in Fig. 13.12 (c) where with the shift in production function capital-labour ratio falls at a given MRS_{LK}.

NUMERICAL PROBLEMS

Problem 1. *You are given the following production functions. What types of production function they are?*

(i) $Q = 2L + K$

(*ii*) $Q = Min\,(2L, K)$

Ans. (*i*) *Production function,* $Q = 2L + K$ is a *linear production* function. This is proved as under. Let L and K are increased by a given number λ

$$Q' = 2\lambda L + \lambda K$$

λ can be factored out. Thus,

$$Q' = \lambda(2L + K) = \lambda Q$$

Thus, increasing each inputs by λ, output also increases by λ. This shows this production function is linear homogeneous.

(ii) *Production function,* Q = Min $(2L, K)$ is a *Leontief production function.* This is so called because a noted American economist Wassily Leontief used this production function to describe the American economy. This a *fixed proportion production function* in which labour and capital are combined in the ratio of $2L$ and $1K$.

Problem 2. *The following production function is given:*

$$Q = L^{0.75} K^{0.25}$$

(*i*) *Find the marginal product of labour, and marginal product of capital*

(*ii*) *Show that law of diminishing returns holds*

(*iii*) *Show that if labour and capital are paid rewards equal to their marginal products, total product would be exhausted*

(*iv*) *Calculate the marginal rate of technical substitution of capital for labour*

(*v*) *Find out the elasticity of substituion.*

Ans. (*i*)

$$MP_L = \frac{\partial Q}{\partial L} = 0.75 L^{0.75-1} K^{0.25}$$

$$= 0.75 L^{-0.25} K^{0.25}$$

$$= 0.75 \left(\frac{K}{L}\right)^{0.25}$$

$$MP_K = \frac{\partial Q}{\partial K} = 0.25 . L^{0.75} K^{0.25-1}$$

$$= 0.25 . L^{0.75} K^{-0.75} = 0.25 \left(\frac{L}{K}\right)^{0.75}$$

(*ii*) *Law of diminishing returns holds, if marginal product of labour* $\left(MP_L = 0.75 \left(\frac{K}{L}\right)^{0.25}\right)$ *declinces with increases in the amount of labour.*

We have proved it earlier on page 280

(*iii*) For the total product to be exhausted if factors are paid rewards equal to their marginal products, the following equation which is called Euler's theorem must hold:

$$Q = MP_L . L + MP_K . K$$

Substituting the values of MP_L and MP_K obtained from the given production function in the above section (*i*) *in Euler's theorem* we have

$$Q = 0.75 \left(\frac{K}{L}\right)^{0.25} . L + 0.25 \left(\frac{L}{K}\right)^{0.75} . K$$

$$Q = 0.75 K^{0.25} L^{0.75} + 0.25 L^{0.75} K^{0.25}$$

$$Q = L^{0.75} K^{0.25} (0.75 + 0.25),$$

$$Q = L^{0.75} K^{0.25} \times 1 = L^{0.75} K^{0.25}$$

Since $L^{0.75} K^{0.25} = Q$ (given)

Therefore, $Q = Q$

Thus, product exhaustion of Euler's theorem applies to the given production function.

(*iv*) $MRTS_{LK}$ is equal to the ratio of marginal products of labour and capital. Using the marginal products of labour and capital we have

$$MRTS_{LK} = \frac{MP_L}{MP_K} = \frac{0.75\left(\frac{K}{L}\right)^{0.25}}{0.25\left(\frac{L}{K}\right)^{0.75}} = 3\left(\frac{K}{L}\right)$$

(*v*) Elasticity of substitution $= \dfrac{\Delta\left(\frac{K}{L}\right) / \frac{K}{L}}{\Delta MRS / MRS}$

Substituting the value of $MRS = 3\left(\frac{K}{L}\right)$ we have

$$\text{Elasticity of substitution} = \frac{\Delta\left(\frac{K}{L}\right) / \frac{K}{L}}{3\Delta\left(\frac{K}{L}\right) / 3\frac{K}{L}} = 1$$

RETURNS TO SCALE

Changes in Scale and Factor Proportions

In the previous chapter we explained the behaviour of output when alteration in factor proportions is made. Factor proportions are altered by keeping the quantity of one or some factors fixed and varying the quantity of the other. The changes in output as a result of the variation in factor proportions, as seen before, forms the subject-matter of the "law of variable proportions." We shall now undertake the study of changes in output when *all factors or inputs* in a particular production function are increased together *proportionately*. In other words, we shall now study the behaviour of output in response to the changes in the scale. The scale of production in the context of two factor production function means a *given amount of labour and capital* used in the production process. The proportionate changes in both the factors bring about a change in the scale. Thus *an increase in the scale means that all inputs or factors used in a production process are increased in the same proportion.* Increase in the scale thus occurs when all factors or inputs are increased keeping factor proportions unaltered. The term returns to scale refers to the degree by which output changes as a result of a given proportionate change in the amounts of all factors (inputs) used in production.

Before explaining returns to scale it will be instructive to make clear the distinction between changes in the scale and changes in factor proportions. The difference between the changes in scale and changes in factor proportions will become clear from the study of Fig. 13.13 where the two factors, labour and capital, have been measured on *X*-axis and *Y*-axis respectively. We suppose that only labour and capital are required to produce a particular product. An isoquant map has been drawn. *A* point *S* has been taken on the *Y*-axis and the horizontal line *ST* parallel to *X*-axis has been drawn. *OS* represents the amount of capital which remains fixed along the line *ST*. As we move towards right on the line *ST*, the amount of labour varies while the amount of capital remains fixed at *OS*. In other words, proportion between the two factors undergoes a change along the line *ST*; the ratio of the variable factor 'labour' to the fixed factor 'capital' rises as we move to the right on the line *ST*. Thus, the movement along the line *ST* represents variation in factor proportions. Likewise, a vertical line *GH* parallel to the *Y*-axis is drawn which will also indicate changes in factor proportions. But in this case the quantity of labour will remain fixed while the quantity of capital will vary.

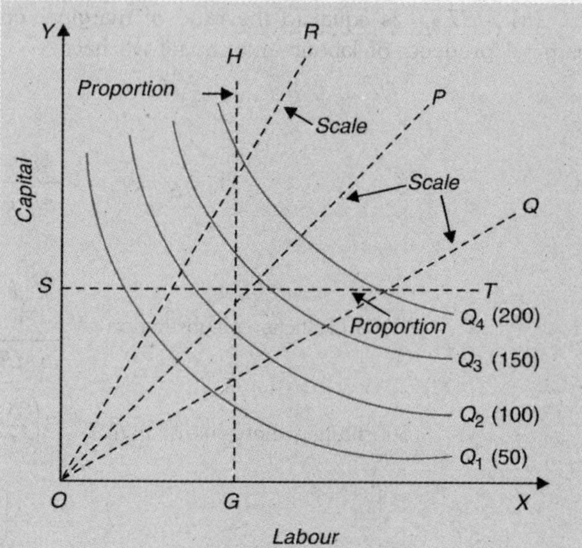

Fig. 13.13. *Changes in Scale and Factor Proportions*

Now, draw a straight line *OP* passing through the origin. It will be seen that along the line *OP* the inputs of both the factors, labour and capital, vary proportionately. Morover, because the line *OP* is a straight line through the origin, the ratio between the two factors along *OP* will remain the same throughout. Thus, the upward movement along the line *OP* indicates the increase in the absolute amounts of two factors employed with the proportion between two factors remaining unchanged. Assuming that only labour and capital are needed to produce a product, then the increase in the two factors along the line *OP* represents the *increase in the scale* since along the line *OP* both the factors increase in the same proportion and therefore proportion between the two factors remains unaltered. If any other straight line through the origin such as *OQ* or *OR* is drawn, it will show, like the line *OP*, the changes in the scale but it will represent a *different given proportion* of factors which remains the same along the line. That is, the various straight lines through the origin will indicate different proportions between the two factors but on each line the proportion between the two factors will remain the same throughout.

Returns to Scale. Let us explain further the meaning of returns to scale taking two factors (inputs) Cobb-Douglas production function, $Q = 100\ L^{0.5}\ K^{0.5}$. As explained above, returns to scale refer to the response of output to proportionate changes in all inputs used in production. For example, if the amounts of both labour and capital used in production are 10 in the above given production function we have

$$Q = 100(10)^{0.5}(10)^{0.5}$$

$$= 100\sqrt{100} = 1000$$

Now if we double the amounts of both factors (*i.e.*, if 20 units of labour and 20 units of capital) are used in production, then output will be

$$Q = 100(20)^{0.5}.(20)^{0.5}$$

$$= 100\sqrt{400} = 100 \times 20 = 2000$$

Thus in this case doubling of both inputs results in doubling of output. Thus this is a case of constant returns to scale. But we do not have always constant returns to scale. The output may increase more than in proportion to the increase in inputs when we will have *increasing returns to scale.* On the other hand, output may increase less than in proportion to the increase in inputs and this case we will have decreasing returns to scale.

Returns to scale are formally defined as follows. Let us take the general production function,

$$Q = f(L, K)$$

If both capital and labour are increased by some factor λ and output increases by factor h, we write it as follows :

$$hQ = f(\lambda L, \lambda K)$$

Now if $h = \lambda$, then it implies that output increases in the same proportion as inputs and therefore we have constant returns to scale. On the other hand, if $h > \lambda$, we will have *increasing returns* to scale. Further, if $h < \lambda$ we will have *decreasing returns* to scale.

In a previous section we have already shown that in Cobb-Douglas production of general form, that is when

$$Q = BAL^{\alpha}K^{\beta},$$

If the sum of exponents $a + \beta = 1$ we have constant returns to scale.

If the sum of exponents $a + \beta > 1$ we have increasing returns to scale

And if the sum of exponents $\alpha + \beta < 1$, we get decreasing returns to scale

We shall explain below the concept of returns to scale by assuming that only two factors, labour and capital, are needed for production. This makes our analysis simple and also enables us to make our analysis in terms of isoquants.

CONSTANT RETURNS TO SCALE

Returns to scale may be constant, increasing or decreasing. If we increase all factors (*i.e.,* scale) in a given proportion and the output increases in the same proportion, returns to scale are said to be constant. Thus, if a doubling or trebling of all factors causes a doubling or trebling of output respectively, returns to scale are constant. But, if the increase in all factors leads to a more than proportionate increase in output, returns to scale are said to be increasing. Thus, if all factors are doubled and output increases by more than a double, then the returns to scale are increasing. On the other hand, if the increase in all factors leads to a less than proportionate increase in output, returns to scale are decreasing. We shall explain below these various types of returns to scale.

As said above, the constant returns to scale mean that with the increase in the scale or the amounts of all factors leads to a proportionate increase in output, that is, doubling of all inputs doubles the output. In mathematics the case of constant returns to scale is called *linear homogeneous production function or homogeneous production function of the first degree.* Production function exhibiting constant returns to scale possesses very convenient mathematical properties which make it very useful for theoretical analysis. There are a number of special theorems which apply when production function exhibits constant returns to scale. Empirical evidence suggests that production function for the economy as a whole is not too far from being homogeneous of the first degree Empirical evidence also suggests that in the production function for an individual firm there is a long phase of constant returns to scale.

Let us illustrate diagrammatically the constant returns to scale with the help of equal product curves i.e. isoquants. Fig. 13.14 depicts an isoquant map. It is assumed that, in the production of a good, only two factors, labour and capital, are used. In order to judge whether or not returns to scale are constant, we draw some straight lines through the origin. As shown above, these straight lines passing through the origin indicate the increase in scale as we move upward. It will be seen from the figure that successive isoquants showing equal increments in output are equidistant from each other along each straight line drawn from the origin. Thus, along the line *OP*, *AB* = *BC* = *CD*, and along the line *OQ*, *A′ B′* = *B′ C′* = *C′ D′* and along the ray *OR*, *A′′ B′′* = *B′′ C′′* = *C′′ D′′*. The distance between the successive isoquants being the same along any straight line through the origin, means that if both labour and capital are increased in a given proportion, output expands by the same proportion. Therefore, Fig. 13.14 displays constant returns to scale.

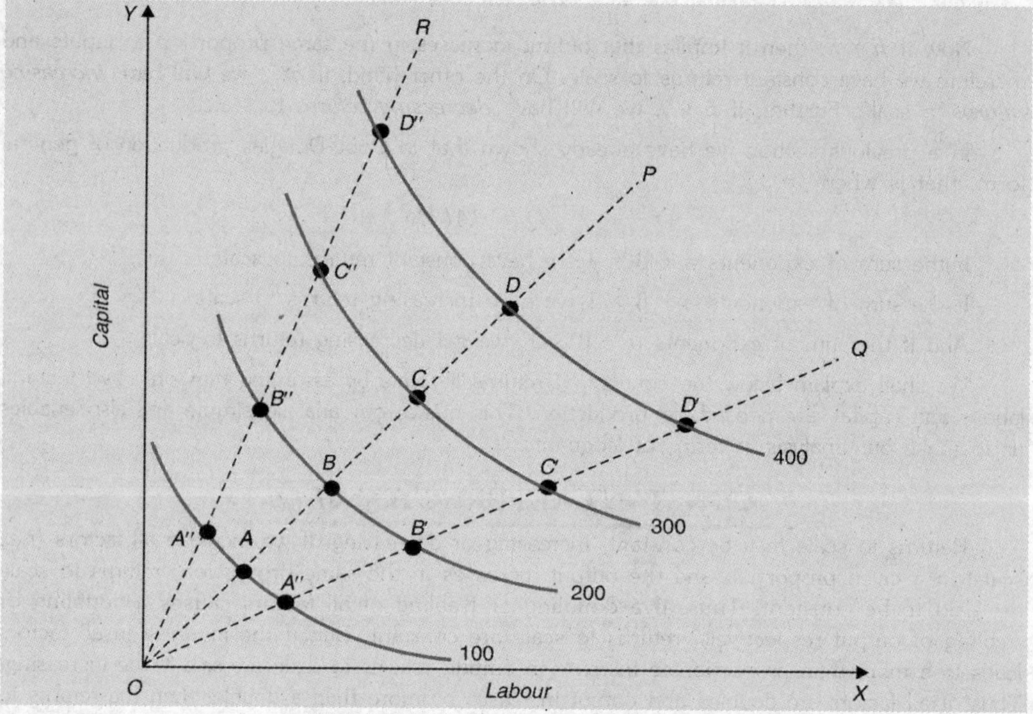

Fig. 13.14. *Constant Returns to Scale*

Divisibility of Factors, Proportionality and Constant Returns to Scale

Some economists are of the view that if the factors of production are perfectly divisible, production function must necessarily exhibit constant returns to scale. It is thus argued by them that if, for instance, all factors or inputs are doubled, then what is there to prevent the output from being doubled. Suppose we build three exactly same types of factories by using exactly same type of workers, capital equipment and raw materials, will we not produce three times the output of a single factory? Economists such as Joan Robinson, Nicholas Kaldor, A.P. Lerner, F.H. Knight who hold this view argue that if it is possible to increase or diminish all factor inputs in the same proportion, then the constant returns to scale must occur. They say that if constant returns to scale does not prevail in some industries it is because it is not possible to increase or diminish factors used in them in exactly the same proportion.

They advanced two reasons for our inability to vary the factors in the same proportion. First, there are some factors whose amount cannot be increased in a given proportion because their supplies are scarce and limited. The scarcities of these factors cause diminishing returns to scale. Secondly, it is pointed out that some factors are *indivisible* and full use of them can be made only when production is done on quite a large scale. Because of the indivisibility they have to be exployed even at a small level of output. Therefore, when output is sought is to be expanded, these indivisible factors will not be increased since they are already not being fully utilized. Thus, with the increase in output, cost per unit will fall because of the better utilization of indivisible factors. Indivisibilities are a source of a good many economies of large-scale production. It is thus clear that in the presence of indivisible factors their amount cannot be varied in the required proportion. According to this view, if the limited supply of some factors and the existence of indivisibilities would not have stood in the way of increasing the amounts of all factors in the same proportion, then there must have been constant returns to scale.

The above explanation of the absence of economies of scale when the factors of production are perfectly divisible, stresses the role of *factor proportionality* in production. According to this view, for achieving best results in production there is a certain *optimum proportion* of factors. When the factors of production are perfectly divisible, they can be increased or decreased by suitable amounts so as to achieve always the optimum proportion between the factors. When factors are indivisible, that is, available in discrete units, some of them quite large or lumpy, production on a small scale would mean the use of non-optimum factor proportions and therefore the inefficiency of small-scale production. Thus, in case of perfect divisibility, factors could be divided and subdivided by appropriate amounts and any amount of output, no matter how small or large, can be produced with optimum factor proportions and as a result economies and diseconomies of scale would be non-existent and we would get constant returns to scale.

The above view has been criticized by E.H. Chamberlin. Chamberlin and others of his view have argued that constant returns to scale cannot prevail. They say that even if all factors could be varied in required quantities and even if all factors were perfectly divisible, there could be increasing returns to scale. In their view even in case of perfect divisibility and variation of the factors, increasing returns to scale can occur with the increase in the scale or size (*i.e.*, increase in all factors or resources) because at a larger scale, (1) greater specilization of labour becomes possible and (2) introduction of specialized machinery or other inputs of a superior technology is made possible by a wise selection from among the greater range of technical possibilities opened up by greater resources. Thus, Chamberlin lays stress on *size* (or *scale*), in causing economies of scale. According to him, when the size or scale of operations, or in other words when the *absolute amounts* of all factors increase, the efficiency of the factors is increased by the use of greater specialisation of labour and by the introduction of specialised and superior machinery. Thus, according to Chamberlin, the above view which stresses divisibility and proportionality neglects the effect of *scale* on the efficiency of factors.[6]

It has been further pointed out that one cannot meaningfully speak of doubling all the factors in a given situation. For instance, two factories existing nearby is simply not the same thing as doubling of one factory in isolation. The existence of another factory in close distance affects labour discipline, air pollution, cost of labour training etc. It is thus argued that in practice it is not possible to vary all the factors in a given proportion and obtain increases in output in the same proportion.

More significantly, it is pointed out that if a large single factory is more efficient than two small factories (the two having total capacity equal to the large one), then there would be no incentive on the part of an entrepreneur to double or duplicate his factors in the sense of

6. For the views of Professor Chamberlin regarding the controversial question of divisibility, proportionality and economies of scale, see his article in *Quarterly Journal of Economics*. Vol. LXII, Feb. 1948.

setting up another small factory near to his previous one. In other words, when the entrepreneur sees the opportunity of getting increasing returns to scale by setting up a large factory, then he would not set up a duplicate factory of his previous size and obtain constant returns to scale. In this connection, it is pointed out that there are many types of economies of scale due to which there is a great possibility of getting, at least in the beginning, increasing returns to scale.

INCREASING RETURNS TO SCALE

As stated above, increasing returns to scale means that output increases in a greater proportion than the increase in inputs. If, for instance, all inputs are increased by 25%, and output increases by 40%, then the increasing returns to scale will be prevailing. When a firm expands, the increasing returns to scale occur at least in the initial stages.

Indivisibility of the Factors. Many economists, such as Joan Robinson, Kaldor, Lerner and Knight ascribe increasing returns to scale to the indivisibility of factors. Some factors are available in large and lumpy units and can therefore be utilised with utmost efficiency at a large level of output. Therefore, in the case of some indivisible and lumpy factors, when output is increased from a small level to a large one, indivisible factors are better utilized and therefore increasing returns are obtained. According to this view, as stated above, if all factors are perfectly divisible, increasing returns to scale would not occur.

Greater Possibilities of Specialisation of Labour and Machinery. As stated above, Chamberlin is of the view that returns to scale increase because of greater possibilities of specialization of labour and machinery. According to him, even if the factors were perfectly divisible, with the increase in the scale, returns to scale can increase because the firm can introduce greater degree of specialization of labour and mjachinery (because now greater resources or amounts of factors become available) and also because it can install technologically more efficient machinery.

At a larger scale of production, instead of being generalists workers can specialise in performing a particular task in the production process. Generally, a worker who does one task repeatedly will do it more efficiently and accurately than the one who has to perform various tasks in the production process. By concentrating on one task, the time of the worker is also saved as he does not have to move from one machine to another.

Similarly, the use of techologically superior machine and specialised equipment is cost effective at larger scale of production as at lower scale its capacity will not be fully utilised. For example, installing an expensive automated binding machine for books will make little sense for use by small book-binding firm as it will not be using its full capacity.

Dimensional Economies. Another important cause of increasing returns to scale lies in dimensional relations, which have been emphasized by Professor Baumol.[7] A wooden box of 3 foot-cube contains 9 times greater wood than the wooden box of 1 foot-cube, that is, 3 foot-cube wooden box contains 9 times greater input. But the capacity of the 3 foot-cube wooden box is 27 times greater than that of 1 foot-cube. Another example is the construction of warehouse. Suppose a rectangular whorehouse is proposed to be constructed. Most important input used in this construction work is the number of bricks and other inputs which almost vary in proportion to the number of bricks used. The number of bricks used depneds upon the wall area of the building. The elementary mathematics tells us that the wall area will increase equal to the square of the perimeter of the warehouse, while its volume, that is, its storage area will increase equal to the cube of the perimeter. In other words, double the number of bricks and other inputs that go with them, the storage capacity of the warehouse will be more than

7. W.J. Baumol, *Economic Theory and Operations Analysis*, 3rd edition, p. 382.

doubled. This is thus a case of increasing returns to scale. Similarly, if the diameter of a pipe is doubled, the flow through it is more than doubled.

Increasing returns to scale can be shown through isoquants. When increasing returns to scale occur, the successive isoquants representing equal increments in output will lie at successively smaller distances along a straight line ray *OR* through the origin. In Fig. 13.15 the various isoquants Q_1, Q_2, Q_3, are drawn which represent 100, 200 and 300 units of output respectively. It will be seen that distances between the successive isoquants decrease as we

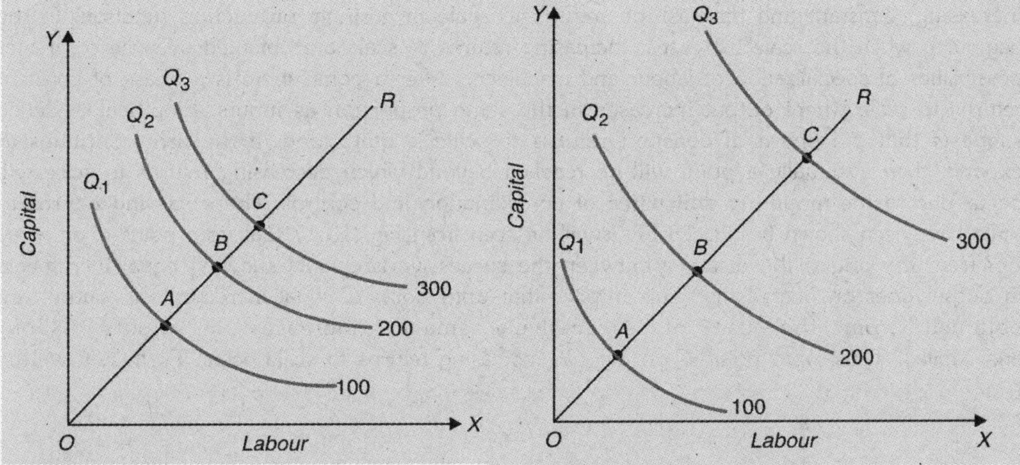

Fig. 13.15. *Increasing Returns to Scale*

Fig. 13.16. *Decreasing Returns to Scale*

expand output by increasing the scale. Thus, increasing returns to scale occur since AB < *OA* and *BC* < *AB* which means that equal increases in output are obtained by successively smaller and smaller increments in inputs.

DECREASING RETURNS TO SCALE

As stated above, when output increases in a smaller proportion than the increase in all inputs, decreasing returns to scale are said to prevail. When a firm goes on expanding by increasing all his inputs, *eventually* diminishing returns to scale will occur. But among economists there is no agreement on a cause or causes of diminishing returns to scale. Some economists are of the view that the entrepreneur is a fixed factor of production; while all other inputs may be increased, he cannot be. According to this view, decreasing returns to scale is therefore actually a special case of the law of variable proportions. Thus, they point out that we get diminishing returns to scale beyond a point because varying quantities of all other inputs are combined with a fixed entrepreneur. Thus, according to this view, decreasing returns to scale is a special case of the law of variable proportions with entrepreneur as the fixed factor. Other economists do not treat decreasing returns to scale as the special case of the law of variable proportions and argue that decreasing returns to scale eventually occur because of the *increasing difficulties of management, co-ordination and control.* When the firm has expanded to a too gigantic size, it is difficult to manage it with the same efficiency as previously. For example, managing a large number of workers and coordinating the activities of several divisions of the firm is quite difficult and results in decline in productivity of inputs used.

The case of decreasing returns to scale can be shown on an isoquant map. When successive isoquants representing increments in outputs lie at progressively larger and larger distance on a ray through the origin, returns to scale will be decreasing. In Fig. 13.16 successively decreasing returns to scale occur since *AB* > *OA*, and *BC* > *AB*. It means that *more and more of inputs (labour and capital) are required to obtain equal increments in output.*

Varying Returns to Scale in a Single Production Process

It should be noted that it is not always the case that different production functions should exhibit different types of returns to scale. It generally happens that there are three phases of increasing, constant and diminishing returns to scale in a single production function. In the beginning when the scale increases, increasing returns to scale are obtained because of greater possibilities of specialization of labour and machinery. After a point, there is a phase of constant returns to scale where output increases in the same proportion as inputs. Empirical evidence suggests that the phase of constant returns to scale is quite long. If the firm continues to expand, then eventually a point will be reached beyond which decreasing returns to scale will occur due to the mounting difficulties of co-ordination and control. These varying returns to scale have been shown in Fig. 13.17. It will be seen from Fig. 13.17 that upto point *C* on a ray *OR* from the origin, the distance between the successive isoquants showing equal increments in output goes on decreasing. This implies that upto point *C* equal increments in output are obtained from the use of successively smaller increases in inputs (labour and capital). Thus, upto point *C* on ray *OR* increasing returns to scale occur. Further, it will be

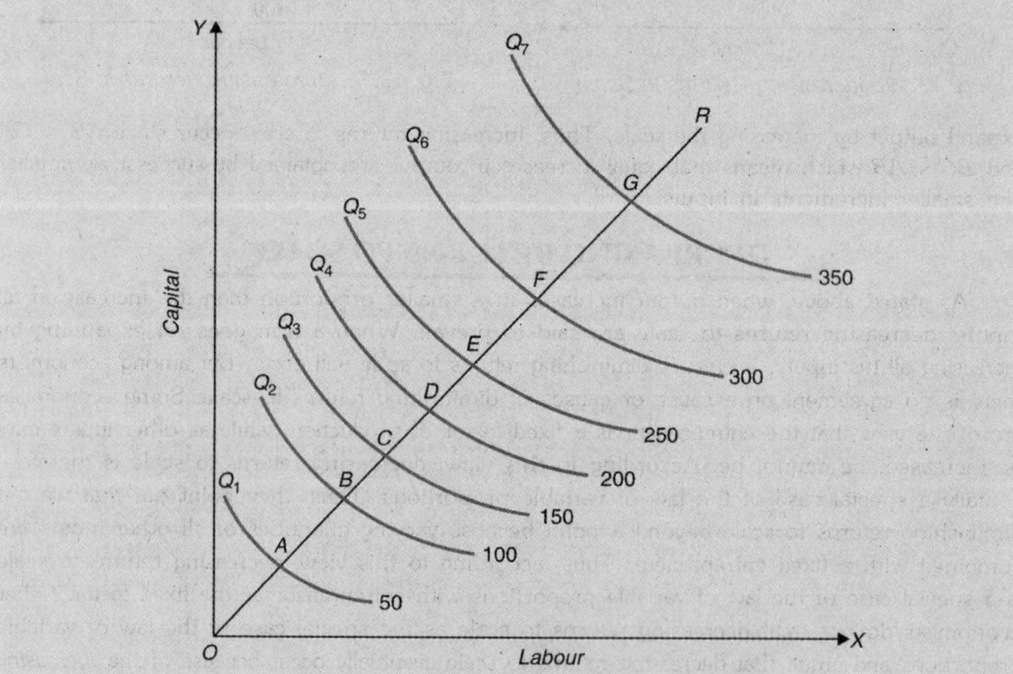

Fig.13.17. *Varying Returns to Scale in a Single Production Process*

seen form Fig.13.17 that from point *C* to point *E* constant returns to scale are obtained as the same proportionate increments in output are obtained from the proportional increase in inputs of labour and capital. Beyond point *E*, the distance between the successive isoquants representing equal increments in output is decreasing along the ray *OR* from the origin which implies that less than proportionate increase in output is obtained from the same proportionate increments in the use of the two factors, labour and capital on the ray *OR* from the origin; *EF* > *DE* and *FG* > *EF*. Thus decreasing returns to scale occur beyond point *E* on the process ray *OR*.

RETURNS TO SCALE AND MARGINAL RETURNS TO A VARIABLE FACTOR

Constant Returns to Scale and Returns to a Variable Factor

We now turn to study the relationship between returns to scale and marginal returns to a variable factor. In other words, we want to study whether marginal productivity of a factor diminishes or rises when the returns to scale are constant, diminishing and increasing. We first take the case of constant returns to scale. As seen above, in case of constant returns to scale, or what is called in mathematics, homogeneous production function of the first degree, the distance between the successive isoquants representing equal increments in output along a straight line through the origin is alqways the same. Consider Fig. 13.18 in which three equal product curves showing 100, 200 and 300 units of output respectively are drawn. A straight line *OL* through the origin and cutting the isoquants is drawn. Line *OL* displays returns to scale. Since returns to scale are constant, *PQ* is equal to *QR*. A horizontal line *ST* is also drawn, which shows the behaviour of output when the amount of the variable factor labour is increased to a fixed quantity *OS* of capital. Now, it is to be proved that when the returns to scale are constant, the marginal physical product of the variable factor diminishes. In terms of Fig. 13.18 where returns to scale are constant, for showing dimainishing marginal returns to the variable factor (labour) we have to prove that *more units of the variable factor labour will be required to be added to a fixed quantity of capital to obtain equal increments in output*, that is, *QN* is greater than *MQ*. Thus, given that *PQ* = *QR* (*i.e.*, returns to scale are constant), we have to prove that *QN* is greater than *MQ*. *QN* being greater than *MQ* means that marginal physical product of labour diminishes as varying amounts of it are added to the fixed quantity of capital. This can be proved in the following way :

In triangles *QRF* and *QPE* in Fig. 13.18

QR = *PQ* (given, because of constant returns to scale)

∠*QRF* = ∠*QPE*, (alternate angles)

∠*RQF* = ∠*PQE*, (vertically opposite angles)

Therefore, triangles *QRF* and *QPE* are congruent, *i.e.*, equal in every respect.

Hence, *QF* = *EQ*

It will be seen from Fig. 13.18 that *MQ* is less than *EQ* and *QN* is greater than *QF*.

Therefore, *QN* is greater than *MQ*.

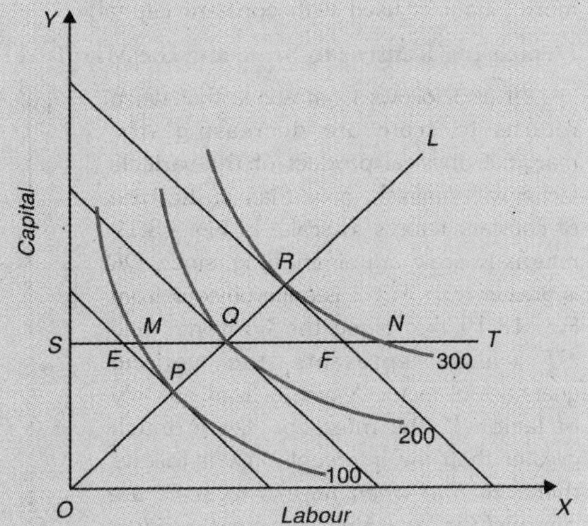

Fig. 13.18. *When Returns to Scale are Constant, Returns to a Variable Factor Diminish.*

It is thus proved that *when returns to scale are constant, (or when production function is homogenours of the first degree), marginal physical product (i.e., marginal returns) to a variable factor diminishes.* In other words, constant returns to scale implies diminishing returns to a variable factor.

Constant Returns to Scale and Marginal Product of a Variable Factor : Mathematical Proof

When returns to scale are constant, marginal product of a variable factor, say labour, diminishes. We can prove it mathematically. Let us take *Cobb-Douglas production function* with sum of exponents equal to 1 which implies constant returns to scale. Such a Cobb-Douglas production function can be written as

$$Q = AL^{a}K^{1-a}$$

Since their sum of $a + 1 - a$ equals 1, this represents constant returns to scale.

Now, suppose $\alpha = 0.75$ and then $1 - \alpha = 1 - 0.75 = 0.25$. With this Cobb-Douglas production function with constant returns to scale can be written as

$$Q = AL^{0.75}K^{0.25}$$

In order to obtain marginal product of labour, we differentiate the given production function with respect to labour. Thus,

$$MP_L = \frac{\partial Q}{\partial L} = 0.75\ AL^{0.75-1}K^{0.25}$$

$$= 0.75\ AL^{-0.25}K^{0.25}$$

For the marginal products of the variable factor labour to diminish the second derivative of the function $Q = AL^{0.75}K^{0.25}$ should be negative Taking its second derivative we have

$$\frac{\partial Q^2}{\partial^2 L} = -0.25 \times 0.75\ AL^{-1.25}\ K^{0.25}$$

$$= -\ 0.1875\ AL^{-1.25}\ K^{0.25}$$

Since the second derivative of the constant returns to scale of production function, $Q = AL^{0.75}\ K^{0.25}$ is negative marginal returns to the variable factor labour will diminish as more labour is used with constant capital.

Decreasing Returns to Scale and the Marginal Physical Product of the Variable Factor

It also follows from above that when returns to scale are decreasing, the marginal physical product of the variable factor will diminish more than in the case of constant returns to scale. In Fig. 13.19 returns to scale are diminishing, since *QR* is greater than *PQ*. It is quite obvious from Fig. 13.19 that along the horizontal line *ST* which represents the varying quantities of factor *X* with a fixed quantity of factor *Y*, the intercept *QN* is much greater than the intercept *MQ*. It follows therefore *that when returns to scale are diminishing, marginal physical product of the variable factor falls rapidly.*

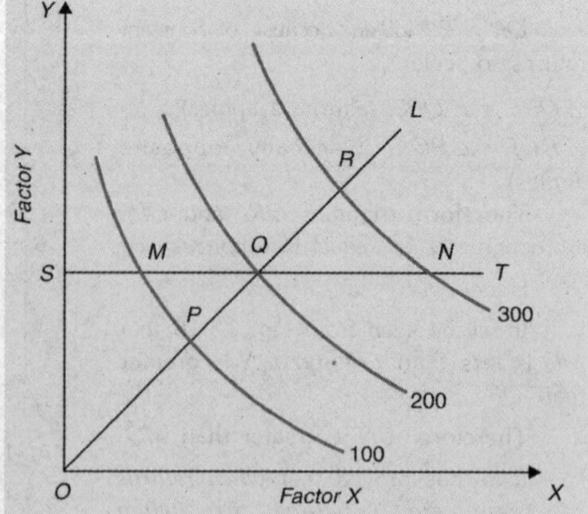

Fig. 13.19. *When Returns to Scale are Decreasing Returns to a Variable Factor Diminish*

Increasing Returns to Scale and Marginal Physical Product of the Variable Factor

Finally, how the marginal physical product of the variable factor behaves when returns to scale are increasing. This case is illustrated in Fig. 13.20 where returns to scale are increasing strongly. *QR* is much smaller than *PQ*. It will be seen from Fig. 13.20 that along the horizontal line *ST*, *QN* is less than *MQ*. It means that as the varying quantities of factor *X* are successively added to the given quantity of the fixed factor *Y*, smaller quantity of factor X than before is required to be increased to get an equal increment in output. Thus, *QN* being less than *MQ* means that marginal physical product of the variable factor *X* increases.

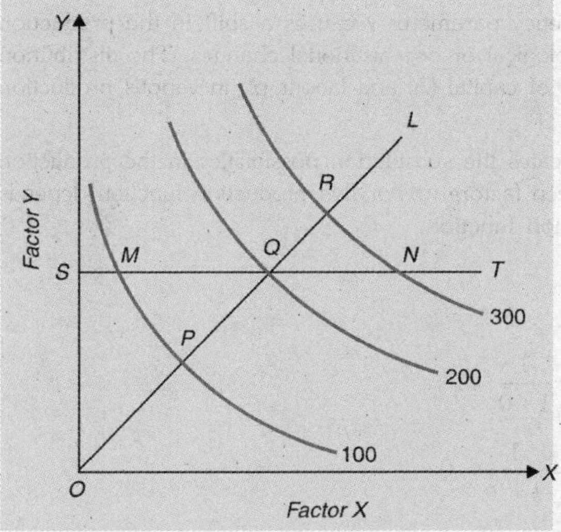

Fig. 13.20. *Marginal Physical Product of a factor increases when Returns to Scale are Increasing*

It is therefore concluded that when returns to scale are *strongly* increasing, the marginal returns to a variable factor (used with a fixed quantity of the other factor) increases. However, when the returns to scale are slightly increasing, then the marginal returns of the variable factor will be diminishing. *Thus, the law of diminishing marginal returns to a factor is even consistent with increasing returns to scale. As just seen above, increasing returns to scale can yield increasing marginal returns as well as diminishing marginal returns to a variable factor depending upon whether returns to scale are strongly increasing or slightly increasing.*

From the foregoing analysis we conclude that *if returns to scale are constant the marginal physical product of a variable factor used in combination with a fixed factor will always diminish as more of the variable factor is used. Similarly, when returns to scale are decreasing, marginal physical product of a variable factor will always diminish, and when returns to scale are increasing marginal physical product of a factor will still diminish unless the returns to scale are increasing sufficiently strongly.*

CONSTANT ELASTICITY OF SUBSTITUTION (CES) PRODUCTION FUNCTION

A general production function which can have any constant value of elasticity of factor substitution has been developed jointly by Arrow, Chenery, Minhas and Solow is the Constant Elasticity of Substitution (CES) Production Function.[8] The two types of production function with either elasticity of factor-substitution equal to zero, and infinity are rarely found in the production processes of the industrial world. Cobb-Douglas production function with elasticity of factor substitution being equal to one has been found to be approximately valid for several industries and agricultural crops. But it is still restrictive and is lacking in general application. CES production function is quite a general production function wherein elasticity of factor substitution can take any positive constant value. However, CES production function is of complex mathematical form given below :-

$$Q = \gamma\,[\delta K^{-p} + (1 - \delta)L^{-p}]^{-1/p}$$

where

γ is an efficiency parameter

8. A. J. Arrow, H. B Chenery, B. S. Minhas and R. M Solow, "Capital-Labour Substitution and Economic Efficiency". *The Review of Economics and Statistics.* August, 1961, pp. 225-250.

δ is a distribution parameter

p is a substitution parameter.

and where $\delta > 0$

$0 \leq \delta \leq 1$

$p \geq 1$

It may be noted that a change in efficiency parameter γ causes a shift in the production function that can occur as a result of technological or organisational changes. The distribution parameter δ indicates the relative importance of capital (K) and labour (L) in various production processes.

Lastly, the substitution parameter p indicates the substitution possibilities in the production processes. The elasticity of substitution between factors (σ) for this production function depends upon this parameter. Thus, for this production function.

$$\sigma = \frac{1}{1+p}$$

When $p = 0, \sigma = 1$, as $\sigma = \frac{1}{1+p} = \frac{1}{1+0} = 1$

When $p = \infty, \sigma = 0$, as $\sigma = \frac{1}{1+p} = \frac{1}{1+\infty} = 0$

When $p = -1, \sigma = \infty$, as $\sigma = \frac{1}{1+p} = \frac{1}{1+(-1)} = \frac{1}{0} = \infty$

It is evident from above that CES production is quite general and it includes $\sigma = 1$, $\sigma = 0$, and $\sigma = \infty$ as special cases.

Isoquants of CES production are also of normal convex shape. Further, CES production also exhibits constant returns to scale which can be proved as under

$$Q = \gamma\,[\delta K^{-p} + (1-\delta)L^{-p}]^{-\frac{1}{p}}$$

Let capital (K) and labour (L) inputs be increased by a positive number m. Thus

$$Q = f(mk,\ mL) = \gamma\,[\delta\ (mk)^{-p} + (1-\delta)\ (mL)^{-p}]^{-\frac{1}{p}}$$

In this $[m^{-p}]^{-\frac{1}{p}}$ can be factored out and we have

$$Q = f(mk,\ mL) = \gamma\ [m^{-p}]^{-\frac{1}{p}}\ [\delta K^{-p} + (1-\delta)L^{-p}]^{-\frac{1}{p}}$$

$$= mf(K,\ L)$$

In recent years, economists are making extensive use of CES production function in their empircal studies of production processes because this production function permits the determination of the value of elasticity of factor substitution from the data itself rather than prior fixing of the value of substitution elasticity (σ).

NUMERICAL PROBLEMS ON RETURNS TO SCALE

Problem 1. *Given the production function* $Q = f(x_1, x_2) = x_1^2\, x_2^3$ *where* x_1, x_2 *are two inputs and Q is production. Does this show constant, decreasing or increasing returns to scale ?*

Solution. $Q = x_1^2 \ x_2^3$

Increasing both inputs x_1 and x_2 by m, we get

$$Q' = (mx_1)^2 \,.\, (mx_2)^3 = m^2 m.^3 \ x_1^{\,2} x_2^{\,3}$$

$$Q' = m^5 \ x_1^2 \ x_2^3 = m^5 \ Q$$

Thus, increase in both inputs by m causes output to increase by m^5. Hence, increasing returns to scale prevail in this case. (Students should see that the sum of the exponents of two inputs x_1 and x_2 is 2 + 3 = 5. As explained above, in the case of Cobb-Douglas production function, if the sum of exponents is greater than one, increasing returns to scale occur. Note further that $Q = x_1^{\,2} x_2^{\,3}$ is a production function of Cobb-Douglas variety).

Problem 2. *Consider production function $Q = 5L^{0.5} \ K^{0.3}$. Does it represent increasing, decreasing or constant returns to scale ?*

Solution. Increasing both labour and capital inputs by m, we have :

$$Q' = 5 \ (mL)^{0.5}. \ (mK)^{0.3}$$

$$Q' = m^{0.5} m^{0.3} \ 5L^{0.5} K^{0.3}$$

$$Q' = m^{0.8} \ Q$$

That is, by increasing labour and capital by m, output increases by $m^{0.8}$, that is, less than m. Thus, in this case decreasing returns to scale occur.

Problem 3. *Do each of the following production functions exhibit decreasing, constant or increasing returns to scale ?*

(a) $Q = 0.5KL$ *(b) $Q = 2K + 3L$*

Solution. (*a*) $Q = Q.5KL$

Increasing K and L by m, we have :

$$Q' = 0.5mK \ . \ mL$$

$$Q' = m^1 m^1 \ 0.5KL$$

$$= m^2.0.5KL = m^2 Q$$

Increasing K and L by m, output increases by m^2, that is, increasing returns to scale operate in this case.

(*b*). $Q = 2K + 3L$

Increasing K and L by m, we have :

$$Q' = 2mK + 3mL$$

$$Q' = m(2K + 3L) = mQ$$

That is, increasing K and L by m in this production function results in increase in output also by m. That is, constant returns to scale occur in this case.

Problem 4. *Suppose a commodity is produced with two inputs, labour and capital, and the production function is given by*

$$Q = 10\sqrt{LK}$$

where Q is output and L and K are amounts of labour and capital. What type of returns to scale does it exhibit ?

Solution. The above production function can be rewritten as

$$Q = 10L^{1/2}K^{1/2}$$

Hence, this is a Cobb-Douglas production function. To show the nature of returns to scale, let us multiply L and K by λ

$$Q' = 10(\lambda L)^{1/2}(\lambda K)^{1/2}$$

$$= \lambda^{1/2}\lambda^{1/2}10L^{1/2}K^{1/2}$$

$$Q' = \lambda Q$$

Increasing L and K by λ results in increase in output (Q) by λ. Hence, this shows constant returns to scale.

Problem 5. *Econometric studies of jute industry in India show that Cobb-Douglas production function can be applied and the exponent of labour is 0.84 and exponent of capital is 0.14. If both labour and capital are increased by one per cent, by what amount output of jute will increase ?*

Solution. As shown above, an exponent of an input in Cobb-Douglas production function can be interpreted as the percentage increase in output resulting from one per cent in increase in input. Thus, the exponent of 0.84 of labour means that one per cent increase in labour leads to 0.84 per cent expansion in output of jute. Similarly, the exponent of 0.14 of capital means *one per cent increase in capital* leads to 0.14 per cent increase in output. Thus, one per cent increase in both labour and capital will result in 0.84 + 0.14 = 0.98 per cent expansion in output.

Problem 6. *Suppose you find that a paper mill which uses capital and labour is subject to the production function $Q = L^{0.75}K^{0.25}$. Will it be right to say that in the paper mill, output per worker will be a function of capital per worker ?*

Solution. Note that capital per worker means capital-labour ratio $\left(\frac{K}{L}\right)$. The given production function $Q = L^{0.75}K^{0.25}$ is a Cobb-Douglas production function where sum of exponents is equal to one (0.75 + 0.25 = 1). Let a represent 0.75, then 0.25 will be $1 - a$. Now, rewriting the production function

$$Q = L^a K^{1-a}$$

Now, Average Product of Labour $(AP) = \frac{Q}{L} = \frac{L^a\,K^{1-a}}{L}$

Now, dividing the term L in both numerator and denominator by a, we have:

$$AP_L\left(\text{or } \frac{Q}{L}\right) = \frac{L^{a-a}K^{1-a}}{L^{1-a}}$$

Since $L^{a-a} = L^0 = 1$, we have

$$AP_L = \frac{K^{1-a}}{L^{1-a}} = \left(\frac{K}{L}\right)^{1-a}$$

Since a is constant, it follows that average product of labour or output per worker depends on capital-labour ratio, that is, capital per worker.

Problem 7. *Suppose we are interested in determining the returns to scale of Britannia Company whose production function is as follows:*

$$Q = 10XY - 2X^2 - Y^2$$

where Q = output, X and Y are inputs.

Solution. Multiplying each input in the above production function by a constant g, we have

$$Q' = 10(gX)(gY) - 2(gX)^2 - (gY)^2$$
$$= 10g^2 XY - 2g^2X^2 - g^2y^2$$
$$= g^2 (10XY - 2X^2 - Y^2)$$

Note that expression in bracket = Q

Thus, $$Q' = g^2 Q$$

This means that output increases by a factor *more than g*, that is, by a factor g^2.

Thus production function of Britannia Company shows increasing returns to scale.

Problem 8. *The production function of a firm is given by:*

$$Q = 0.6X + 0.2Y$$

where Q = output, X and Y are inputs.

Determine returns to scale.

Solution. To determine returns to scale we multiply each input by a constant factor g. Thus,

$$Q' = 0.6gX + 0.2gY$$

g can be factored out

Therefore, $$Q' = g(0.6X + 0.2Y)$$

or $$Q' = gQ.$$

Thus, increasing each input by a constant g leads to increase in output by the same constant g. Thus, it shows that production function is *homogeneous of first degree* and returns to scale are constant.

Problem 9. *Determine returns to scale of the following production function*

$$Q = aL + bK.$$

Solution. To determine returns to scale we multiply each input by a constant factor g. Thus,

$$Q' = a \,.\, gL + b \,.\, gK$$
$$= g\,(aL + bK)$$
$$= gQ.$$

This shows returns to scale are constant..

THE ESTIMATION OF PRODUCT ION FUNCTION

Having explained the theory of production, we now turn to explain how the economists estimate production function. The estimation of production function which applies to the productive activity of the firm is one of the important tasks of its manager. In what follows we will discuss the possible forms of production function and its implications for the productive activity of a firm. Second, we shall explain the estimation of Cobb-Douglas production which is most commonly used by the economists. Third, we will examine the data required for estimation of production function. Finally, we will present the estimates of the production function studies made by some economists.

Various Forms of Production Functions

There are many forms of production functions and therefore the first task of a manager is to select *a form of production function* that applies well to the productive activity of the firm. It may be noted that a functional form of production describes the *specific relationship among the factors* used in the production process.

In our analysis of production theory the distinction has been drawn between the short-run production function and long-run production function. The short-run production function describes the existence of a fixed factor to which the different amounts of a variable factor are added to produce output. In the short-run production function of a manufacturing industry, the economists generally take capital as a fixed factor and labour as a variable factor. Thus, the form of this two factor production function can be written as

$$Q = f(L)_k \quad \text{....(1)}$$

According to this, output of a product in the short-run is determined by the amount of the variable factor labour (L), given the quantity of the fixed factor capital (k).

In the discussion of general production function with one factor variable we have seen that in the beginning we get increasing marginal returns and beyond a point we have diminishing marginal returns to a variable factor. This implies a cubic form of production function which can be written as

$$Q = a + bL + CL^2 - dL^3 \quad \text{....(2)}$$

Where a is constant (intercept term), b, c and d are the coefficients. This cubic production function with labour as the variable factor is shown in Fig. 13.21 where panel (a) depicts the total product curve of labour and panel (b) shows the average and marginal product curves.

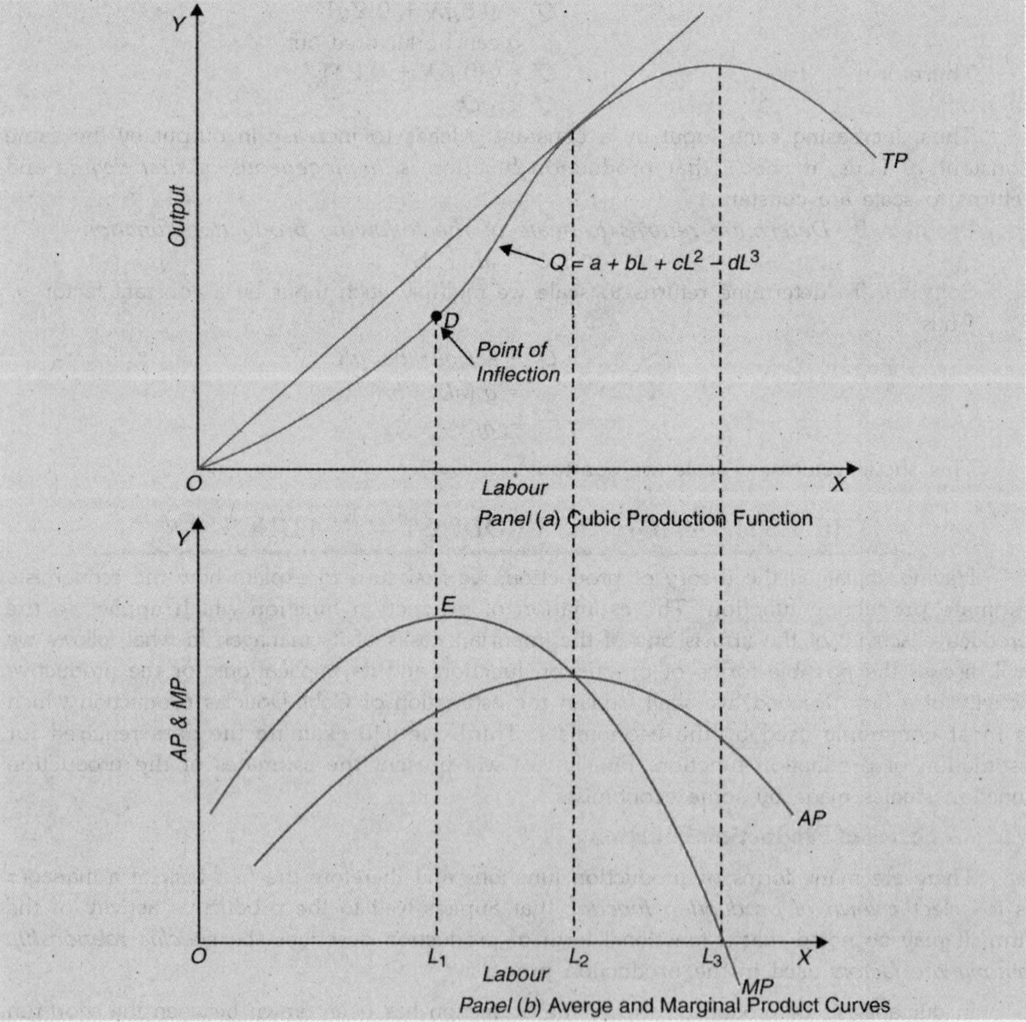

Fig. 13.21. *Cubic Production Function and its Associated Average and Marginal Product Curves*

It may be noted that total product curve (*TP*) of labour has been drawn beginning from the origin. This is because it is assumed that no production is possible without the use of a variable factor. However, in the cubic production function equation (2), an intercept term *a* appears. This is because when such a production function is estimated we are likely to get the fitted curve with a positive or negative constant term.

It is possible that production data used to estimate the production function may exhibit only diminishing marginal returns to a variable factor (*i.e.* the absence of stage 1.). In such a situation the short-run production function is represented by a quadratic production function as given below

$$Q = a + bL - CL^2 \qquad ....(3)$$

This quadratic production function is shown in Figure 13.22 where in panel (*a*) we have drawn the total product curve (*TP*) of labour which is concave inside indicating that both average and marginal product curves will be sloping downward as shown in panel (*b*) of Fig. 13.22. This shows that stage of increasing marginal returns to the variable factor is not present in the quadratic production function.

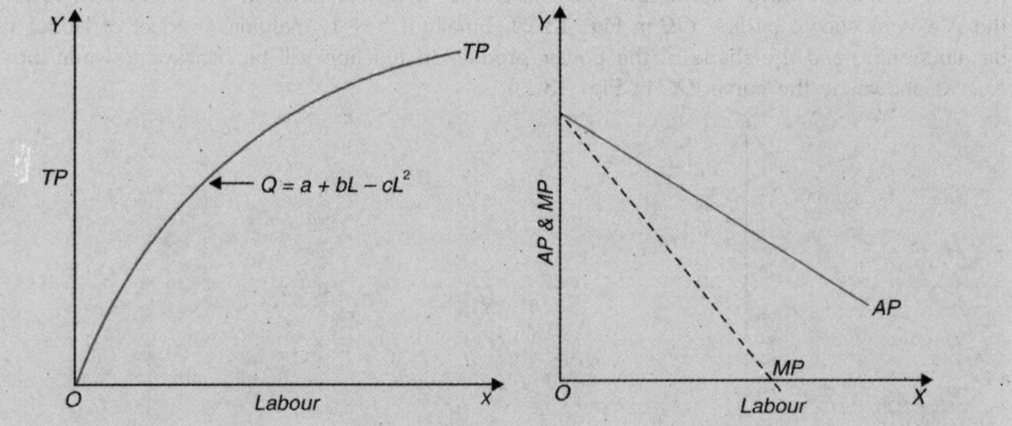

Fig. 13.22. *Quadratic Production Function and its Associated AP and MP Curves.*

Finally, in an empirical study it is likely that data used exhibits no increasing or diminishing marginal returns to a variable factor. Thus production function obtained by an emperical study may indicate linear production function of the following type :

$$Q = a + bL \qquad .....(3)$$

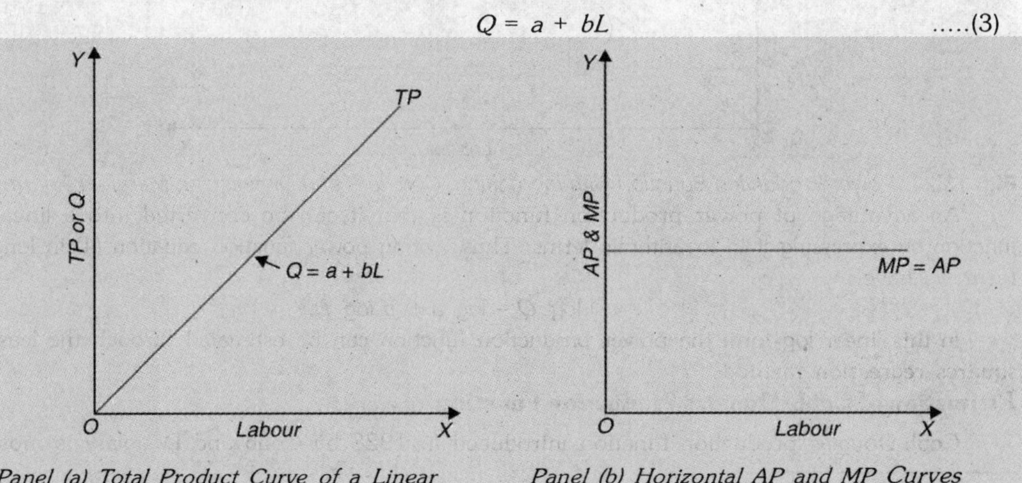

Panel (a) Total Product Curve of a Linear Production Function *Panel (b) Horizontal AP and MP Curves*

Fig. 13.23. *Linear Production Function and its Associated AP and MP Curves*

In this case of linear production function with one variable factor we get a straight-line total product curve with slope (*b*) equal to average product (*AP*) and marginal product as shown in Figure 13.23. Therefore, in this linear production function *AP* and *MP* curves will coincide and are horizontal straight line as shown in panel (*b*) of Fig. 13.23. A linear production function may be obtained in some real situations. However, given the fact that there is a fixed factor in the short-run production function, linear production function may not hold over a wide range of output.

Power Production Function

Another important form of production function usually obtained in emperical studies is power function which can be written as

$$Q = a\,L^{b} \qquad \text{..... (4)}$$

The shape of power production function depends on the value of exponent *b*. If $b = 1$ in the above power production function, the marginal product of the variable factor (*e.g.* labour) will be straight line from the origin as shown in Fig. 13.24. by line *OA* . If $b > 1$ the marginal product of labour will be increasing and the shape of power function will be convex towards the *X*-axis as shown by line *OB* in Fig. 13.24. Finally if $b < 1$, marginal product of labour will be diminishing and the shape of the power production function will be concave towards the *X*-axis as shown by the curve *OC* in Fig. 13.24.

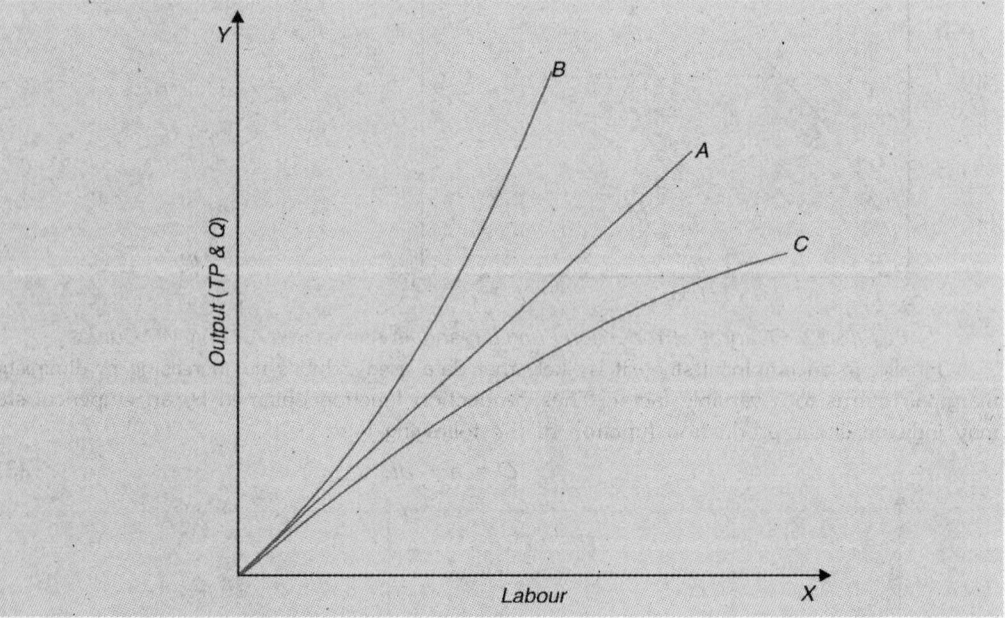

Fig. 13.24. *Power Production Function with Increasing, Constant and Diminishing Marginal Returns*

An advantage of power production function is that it can be converted into a linear function by expressing it in logarithmic terms. Thus writing power function equation (4) in long form we have

$$\log Q = \log a + b \log L$$

In this linear log form the power production function can be estimated through the least squares regression method.

Estimation of Cobb-Douglas Production Function

Cobb-Douglas production function introduced in 1928 by Cobb and Douglas[9] is most

9. See C.W. Cobb and P.H. Douglas, 'A Theory of Production, *American Economic Review* 8, (March 1928)

commonly used in empirical studies for the estimation of production function. It is of the following general form[10] :

$$Q = AL^a K^b \qquad \text{... } (i)$$

Note that estimation of production function requires to estimate the values of parameters, that is, constant A and coefficient a and b. To estimate these measures we use the time series data of inputs and output of a firm or industry or cross section analysis of firm in an industry. The time series data of inputs and output of the whole manufacturing can be used. The value of the parameters A, a and b will measure the production relationship between inputs (L and K) and output (Q). An important feature of Cobb-Douglas production is that it is of multiplicative form. This implies that both inputs must be used to get a positive output[11] (Q).

It is worth mentioning that as proved in the analysis of the theory of production function, the marginal products of labour and capital are functions of the parameters A, a, and b and the quantities of labour (L) and capital (K) inputs used for production. Thus

$$MP_L = \frac{\partial Q}{\partial L} = a\, AL^{a-1} K^b = \frac{a\, AL^a K^b}{L}$$

$$MP_K = \frac{\partial Q}{\partial K} = b\, AL^a K^{b-1} = \frac{b\, AL^a K^b}{K}$$

Further, as shown earlier, the sum of exponents of Cobb-Douglas ($a + b$) shows the returns to scale. Thus

If $a + b = 1$, returns to scale are constant. If $a + b > 1$, returns to scale are increasing.

If $a + b < 1$, returns to scale are decreasing.

Since Cobb-Douglas production function describes non-linear relationship between inputs and output, it cannot be directly estimated by the least squares regression technique. Therefore, for estimation of Cobb-Douglas production we have first to transform it in logarithmic form. That is,

$$\log Q = \log A + a \log L + b \log K \qquad \text{... } (ii)$$

In this logarithmic form Cobb-Douglas production is linear and therefore can be estimated through least squares method of regression analysis[12], as illustrated in estimation of demand in an earlier chapter.

A merit of Cobb-Douglas production function is that it can be used not only for just two variable inputs but for any number of independent input variables. Thus

$$Q = AX_1^{b_1}.X_2^{b_2}.X_3^{b_3}.X_4^{b_4} \ldots\ldots\ldots\ldots X_n^{b_n}$$

10. Originally Cobb-Douglas production used was of the form where the sum of exponents was equal to one, that is, it was of the form, $Q = AL^a K^{1-a}$ where (a + 1 − a = 1).Later on it was generalised so that the sum of exponents may be equal to one, greater than one or less than one.
11. On the other hand, if additive function such as $Q = a + bL + CK$ is used, output could be positive even if one of the two inputs is zero
12. There are many software packages such as Excel of Microsoft, SPSS which are available to estimate the values of parameters through least squares regression. The use of these software packages has made the calculation involved in estimating Cobb-Douglas production quite easier.

It may be noted that in theoretical discussion of Cobb-Douglas production function, it is assumed that technology remains constant. However, when using a time series data of a firm or industry, it may be found that technology has progressed over time. To capture the effect of technological change on output a trend variable can be included in the production function where $t = 1$, $t = 2$, $t = 3$, etc. over a time span can be taken.

On estimating Cobb-Douglas production function we can easily know the elasticities of output and marginal products. Note that the elasticity of output with respect to any input shows the percentage change in output in response to one per cent change in an input. As mentioned above, the exponents such as *a* and *b* of independent variables (*L* and *K*) measure the output elasticities of labour and capital.

Having estimated the parameters of functional equation (*ii*) we can obtain from these equations marginal products of labour and capital by using the specified values of inputs, labour and capital.

For example, using time series data in natural log form of the Indian jute manufacturing industry the following estimate of Cobb-Douglas production function in long form has been obtained

$$\log Q = 2.501 + 0.84 \log L + 0.14 \log K \qquad R^2 = 0.98$$

The estimated value of coefficient $a = 0.84$ and $b = 0.14$. To determine the value of A we take antilog of 2.501 (which is equal to 12.19). Thus estimated Cobb-Douglas production function can be written as

$$Q = 12.19\, L^{0.84}\, K^{0.14}$$

The returns to scale are $0.84 + 0.14 = 0.98$ which is very close to one. This means that the Indian jute industry exhibits constant returns to scale. Output elasticity of labour is 0.84 and output elasticity of capital 0.14. The marginal products of labour and capital are given by

$$MP_L = \frac{\partial Q}{\partial L} = 0.84\,(12.19).L^{-0.16} K^{0.14}$$

$$MP_K = \frac{\partial Q}{\partial L} = 0.14\,(12.19).L^{0.84} K^{-0.86}$$

Now MP_L and MP_K can be obtained by substituting the specified values of labour and capital (say 50 units of labour and 10 units of capital) in the above marginal product functions of labour and capital.

Estimates of production function made for some industries of India and the USA are given in the following table. It is useful to know the estimates of parameters especially β_1, β_2. For example, the estimate of β_1 shows elasticity of production with respect to labour, that is, it shows how much per cent output increases when there is one percentage increase in labour input. Likewise, estimate of β_2 shows the production elasticity with respect to capital input. Thus, the β_1 coefficient of labour equal to 0.59 obtained for sugar industry shows that one percentage increase in labour causes 0.59 per cent expansion in sugar output in India. Similarly, the value of β_2 coefficient of 0.33 of capital for Indian sugar Industry show that one percentage increase in capital input leads to 0.33 per cent increase in sugar output.

Table 13.4. Estimates β_1 and β_2 for Some Industries

Industry	*Country*	β_1	β_2	β_3	$\beta_1 + \beta_2$
Cotton	India	0.92	0.12		1.04
Jute	India	0.84	0.14		0.98
Sugar	India	0.59	0.33		0.92
Coal	India	0.71	0.44		1.15
Paper	India	0.64	0.45		1.09
Chemicals	India	0.80	0.37		1.17
Electricity	India	0.20	0.67		0.87
Food	United States	0.63	0.44		1.07
Paper	United States	0.62	0.37		0.99
Rail Roads	United States	0.70	0.41		1.11
Aircraft	United States	0.54	0.38	0.11	1.03
Gas	France	0.83	0.10		0.93
Coal	U.K.	0.79	0.29		1.08

Source. A.A. Walters, "Production and Cost Function", *Econometrica,* January 1963.

J. Moroney, "Cobb-Douglas Production Function and Returns to Scale in U.S. Manufacturing". *Western Economic Journal,* 1967.

In the last column of table 13.4, we have shown the sum of the exponents of labour and capital of the two-factor Cobb-Douglas production function. A look at this table will reveal that in 7 out of 13 cases, the sum of the parameters ($\beta_1 + \beta_2$) is greater than one and therefore increasing returns to scale occur in these cases. In the two cases (jute industry in case of India and paper industry in case of the USA), the sum of $\beta_1 + \beta_2$ is *near unity* (0.98 and 0.99 respectively) and hence constant returns to scale occur in these cases. In the remaining cases, decreasing returns to scale are obtained as the sum of $\beta_1 + \beta_2$ is less than one.

Problems in Estimation of Production Functions

Some important problems encountered in the production function studies are noteworthy. First, whereas production function theoretically includes only technically efficient combinations of inputs and output, the actual data used for measurement of production function may not actually represent the efficient input combinations. This may cause some error in the estimation of production function.

The second important problem in estimating production function relates to the measurement of capital input. The main difficulty in this regard is that stock of capital is heterogeneous, that is, it is composed of different types of machines, buildings and inventories. to obtain *a single measure* of the quantity of capital input used poses a very difficult problem.

A third problem which arises in case of time series and cross-section studies of production function is that errors can arise because the various data-points which are assumed to be on the same production function may belong in fact to different production functions.

Cobb-Douglas production function cannot show the changes in marginal product of a variable factor *over all the three stages of short-run production function in one specification.* As explained above, a cubic type of production function is needed to represent all the three stages of production function with one variable factor. Thus Cobb-Douglas production when estimated for a firm or an industry cannot represent changes in marginal returns over stages of increasing, constant and decreasing returns. As seen above, the estimation of Cobb-Douglas function can show either increasing or constant or decreasing returns to scale.

Ideally, inputs should be measured as *'flow'* rather than *'stock'* variables. However, this is not always possible, especially in case of measurement of capital used in production. This is because capital which is of heterogenous type is available in stock and it is difficult to measure *how much capital is actually* utilised during a period for producing a commodity. Thus, Like other production functions the estimation of Cobb-Douglas production is also not without problems.

QUESTIONS FOR REVIEW

1. Distinguish between returns to scale and returns to a variable factor with the help of isoquants.
2. What are isoquants ? Why does an isoquant slope downward? Why do they cannot cut each other ? Why are they convex to the origin ?
3. What is meant by marginal rate of technical substitution between factors ($MRTS_{LK}$). How is it related to marginal products of factors ? Why does marginal rate of technical substitution of labour for capital diminishes as more labour is used by substituting capital?
4. "*The slope of an isoquant is a measure of the relative marginal productivities of the factors.*" *Explain.*

   OR

   Show that marginal rate of technical substitution between two factors is the equal to the ratio of marginal products of the two factors.
5. Distinguish between fixed proportion and variable proportion production function. Draw the isoquants of fixed proportion production function.
6. Define substitute and complementary factors. Draw isoquants of perfect substitutes and perfect complements in production. Give examples.
7. What are increasing returns to scale? Show them on an isoquant map. Explain the causes of increasing returns to scale.
8. Show the increasing, constant and decreasing returns to scale through isoquents. What causes decreasing returns to scale beyond a certain point?
9. Is increasing marginal returns to a variable factor compatible with increasing returns to scale?
10. Show that when returns to scale are constant, marginal returns to a variable factor diminishes, (*a*) Prove geometrically, (*b*) Give an algebraic proof of it using a linear homogeneous production function.
11. What are ridge lines? Draw an isoquant map showing ridge lines. Why does a rational producer not operate outside the ridge lines? Indicate in the isoquant map the area where a rational producer will possible operate.
12. What is linear homogeneous production function? What are its properties ?

    [Hint: Cobb-Douglas production function is linear homogeneous when sum of its exponents, $a + b = 1$. Therefore, the properties of Cobb-Douglas production function explained in the chapter are the properties of linear homogeneous production function.]
13. What is Cobb-Douglas production function ? What are its useful properties ? Why is it extensively used in empirical studies for estimation of production ?
14. When the sum of exponents ($a + b$) of two factor Cobb-Douglas production function is equal to one, it shows constant returns to scale. Prove it ?
15. What is meant by constant returns to scale? Show them with an iso-product map. Is it correct to say that returns to scale would have been constant if the factors of production had been perfectly divisible?

16. You are given the following production functions. Which ones represent constant returns to scale, which ones increasing returns to scale and decreasing returns to scale and why?

(*a*) $Q = AK^{0.5} L^{0.7}$ (*b*) $Q = AK^{0.25} L^{0.75}$

(*c*) $Q = AK^{0.3} L^{0.6}$ (*d*) $Q = 10\sqrt{L}\sqrt{K}$

17. A firm has the following production function:

$$Q = 2L^{\frac{1}{2}} K^{\frac{1}{3}}$$

Calculate marginal product functions for labour and capital. Does this show increasing, decreasing or constant returns to scale ?

18. (*a*) What would the isoquants look like if both inputs are perfect substitutes in the production process? What if there was zero substitutability between inputs?

(*b*) What does the isoquants of perfect substitutes imply for the least-cost combination of inputs ?

19. Consider the production function represented by $Y = AL^{\alpha} K^{\beta}$ where Y is output and α. and β are positive constants.

(*a*) Show that this production function exhibits constant returns to scale when $\alpha + \beta = 1$.

(*b*) Show that marginal product of labour depends on the input ratio $\frac{K}{L}$ only.

(*c*) When is the expansion path linear ?

20. State the form of Cobb-Douglas production function which exhibits constant returns to scale. Prove that returns to a variable factor diminishes in this production function.

21. What is meant by marginal rate of technical substitution (MRTS) between the two factors? If $MRTS_{xy}$ is –3. If same output is to be produced, then with reduction in use of factor X by 3 units, how many units of factor Y will be required to be added ?

22. Show three kinds of returns to scale with help of isoquants. Why do we get initially increasing returns to scale and eventually decreasing returns to scale ?

Optimum Input Combination

Introduction

In the last three chapters we explained the law of variable proportions and returns to scale which underlil the process of production. An important problem facing an enterpreneur is to decide about the particular combination of factors which should be employed for producing a product. There are various technical possibilities open to a firm from which it has to choose, that is, there are various combinations of factors which can yield a given level of output and from among which producer has to select one for production. As explained in an earlier chapter, various combinations of factors which produce equal level of output are represented by an equal product cure or what is also called insoquant. An isoquant map or isoproduct map represents various technical possibilities of producing different levels of output.

It is assumed that the entrepreneur aims at maximizing his profits. A profit-maximizing entrepreneur will seek to minimise his cost for producing a given output, or to put it in another way, he will try to maximise his output for a given level of cost outlay. The choice of a particular combination of factors by an entrepreneur depends upon (*a*) technical possibilities of production, and (*b*) the prices of factors used for the production of a particular product. Technical possibilities of production are represented by the isoquant map. Before explaining how producer will arrive at the least-cost combination of factors, we shall first explain how the prices of factors can be introduced our analysis.

ISO-COST LINE

The prices of factors are represented by the iso-cost line. The iso-cost line plays an important role in determining what combination of factors the firm will choose for production. An iso-cost line shows various combinations of two factors that the firm can buy with a given outlay. How the iso-cost line is drawn is shown in Fig.14.1 where on the *X*-axis we measure units of labour and on the *Y*-axis we measure units of capital. We assume that prices of factors are given and constant for the firm. In other words, we are considering a firm which is working under perfect competition in the factor markets. Further suppose that the firm has Rs. 300 to spend on the factors, labour and capital and price of labour is Rs.4 per labour hour and the price of capital is Rs. 5 per machine hour. With outlay of Rs. 300 he can buy 75 units of labour or 60 units of machine hours (*i.e.*, capital). Let *OB* in Fig.14.1 represent 75 units of labour and *OA* represent 60 units of capital. In other words, if the firm spends its entire outlay of Rs. 300 on laour it buys 75 units or *OB* of labour hours and if it spends its entire outlay of Rs. 300 on capital it buys 60 units or *OA* of machine hours. The straight line *AB* which joins points *A* and *B* will pass through all combinations of labour and capital which the firm can buy with cost outlay of Rs. 300 , if it spends the entire sum on them at the given prices. This line *AB* is called *iso-cost* line, for whichever combination lying on it the firm buys it has to incur the same cost-outlay at the given prices. *An iso-cost line is defined as the locus of various combinations of factors which a firm can buy with a constant outlay. The iso-cost line is also called the price line or outlay line.*

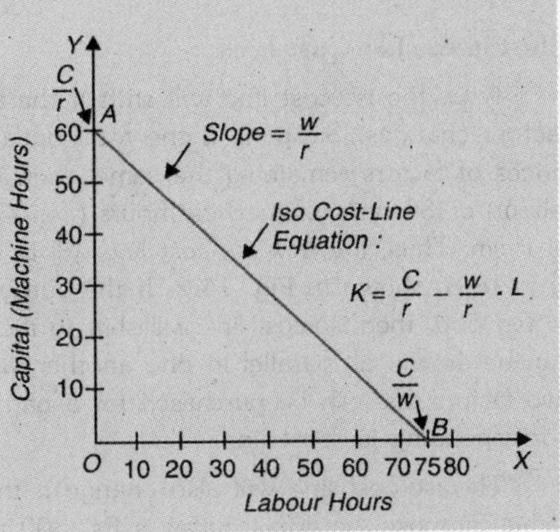

Fig. 14.1. *Iso-Cost Line*

The Equation of the Iso-Cost Line. The total cost incurred on the factors of production for production of a commodity is equal to the sum of the payments made for labour and capital. Now, payment for the labour used is equal to the wage rate (w) multiplied by the amount of labour used (L). Thus $W.L$ represents the total payment made for labour. Similarly, rK is the total payment made for capital where r is the price per unit of capital and K is the quantity of capital used. The total cost equation can therefore be described as follows.

$$C = w.L + rK$$

Where C is the total cost incurred by the firm on purchasing the quantities of factors used for production. Given the prices of factors, the iso-cost equation can be rearranged as under to express it in the intercept-slope form :

$$C = wL + rK$$

$$rK = C - w.L$$

$$K = \frac{C}{r} - \frac{w}{r}.L \qquad \ldots(ii)$$

Where $\frac{C}{r}$ represents the intercept of the iso-cost line on the Y-axis and $\frac{w}{r}$ represents the factor price ratio and is equal to the slope of the iso-cost line.

Slope of the Iso-Cost Line. The slope of the iso-cost line can be proved to be equal to the ratio of price of labour (w) and price of capital (r). Let, according to the iso-cost line *AB*, which, given the factor prices, represents the total cost outlay incurred on the two factors, labour and capital, the total cost equals C.

As explained above, the vertical intercept *OA* that represents the quantity of factor capital if entire cost-outlay is spent on it is equal to $\frac{C}{r}$. Similarly, the horizontal intercept *OB* representing the quantity of labour purchased if entire cost-outlay is incurred on purchasing it is equal to $\frac{C}{w}$.

Now, the slope of the iso-cost line is

$$\frac{OA}{OB} = \frac{C}{r} \div \frac{C}{w} = \frac{C}{r} \cdot \frac{w}{C} = \frac{w}{r}$$

Thus the slope of the iso-cost line $\frac{OA}{OB}$ is equal to the ratio of factor-prices $(\frac{w}{r})$

Shift in the Iso-Cost Line

Now, the iso-cost line will shift if the total outlay which the firm wants to spend on the factors changes. Suppose if the total outlay to be made by the firm increases to Rs. 400, prices of factors remaining the same, then it can buy 100 units of labour hours (*i.e., OB'* of labour) or 80 units of machine hours (*i.e., OA'* of capital) if it spends the entire sum on either of them. Thus, the new iso-cost line will be *A'B'* which will be parallel to the original iso-cost line *AB* as shown in Fig. 14.2. If the outlay which the firm intends to make further increases to Rs. 500, then iso-cost line will shift to the position *A''B''*. Thus any number of iso-cost lines can be drawn, all parallel to one another, and each representing the various combinations of two factors that can be purchased for a particular outlay. The higher the outlay, the higher the corresponding iso-cost line.

The iso-cost line will also change if the prices of factors change, outlay remaining the same. Suppose the firm's outlay is Rs. 300 and the prices of labour and capital are Rs. 4 and Rs. 5 respectively the iso-cost line will then be *AB* as shown in Fig. 14.3. If now the price of labour falls to Rs. 3, then with the outlay of Rs. 300 and Rs. 3 as the price of labour the firm

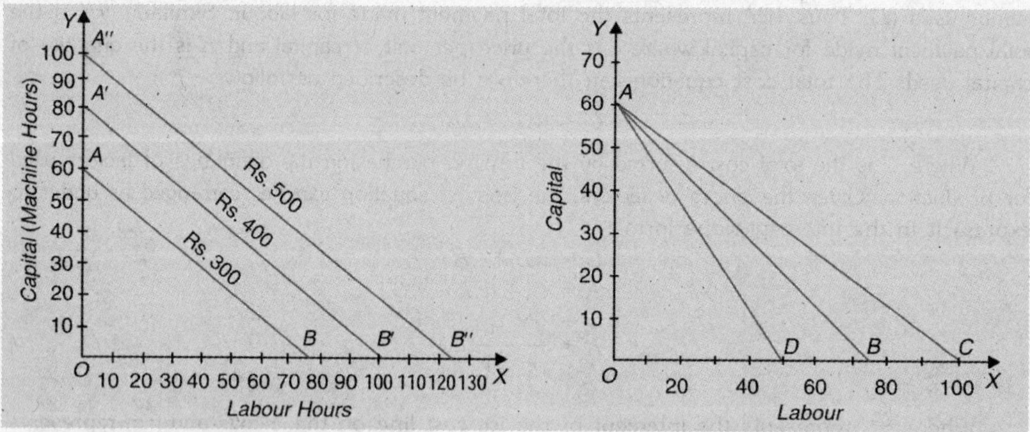

Fig. 14.2. *Shift in Iso-Cost line Resulting from Increase in Outlay or Total Cost*

Fig. 14.3. *Changes in Iso-cost line as a Result of Changes in the Price of Labour*

can buy 100 units of labour if it spends the entire outlay on it. *OC* represents 100 units of labour. Therefore, as a result of the fall in price of labour from Rs. 4 to 3, the price line changes from *AB* to *AC*. If price of labour rises from Rs. 4 to Rs. 6 per hour the iso-cost line will shift to *AD*. Likewise, if price of capital changes, the outlay and price of labour remaining the same, the iso-cost line will shift.

It is clear from above that the iso-cost line depends upon two things : (i) prices of the factors of production, and (ii) the total cost outlay which the firm has to make on the factors. Given these two things, an iso-cost line can be drawn. It should also be noted that the slope of the iso-cost line, like that of the price line in indifference curve analysis and demand, is equal to the ratio of prices of two factors. Thus, slope of the iso-cost line *AB*

$$= \frac{\text{Price of Labour}}{\text{Price of Capital}} = \frac{w}{r}$$

OPTIMUM INPUT COMBINATION

An equal product map of isoquant map represents the various factor combinations which can yield various levels of output, every isoquant showing those factor combinations each of which can produce a specified level of output. Thus, an isoquant map represents the production function of a product with two variable factors. Therefore, an isoquant map represents the technical conditions of production for a product. On the other hand, a family of iso-cost line represents the various levels of total cost outlay, given the prices of two factors. The entrepreneur may desire to minimize his cost for producing a given level of output, or he may desire to maximize his output level for a given cost outlay. Let us suppose that the entrepreneur has already decided about the level of output to be produced. Then the question is with which factor combination the entrepreneur will try to produce the given level of output. To produce a given level of output, the entrepreneur will choose the combination of factors which minimizes his cost of production, for only in this way he will be maximizing his profits. Thus a producer will try to produce a given level of output with *least-cost combination* of factors. This least-cost combination of factors will be optimum for him.

Which will be the least-cost combination of factors can be understood from considering Fig. 14.4. Suppose the entrepreneur has decided to produce 500 units of output which is represented by isoquant *Q*. The 500 units of output can be produced by any combination of labour and capital such as *R*., *S*., *E*., *T*. and *J* lying on the isoquant *Q*. Now, a glance at the figure will reveal that for producing the given level of output (500 units) the cost will be minimum at point *E* at which the iso-cost line *CD* is tangent to the given isoquant. At no other point such as *R*.*S*.*T*. and *J*, lying on the isoquant *Q* the cost is minimum. It will be seen from Fig.14.4 that all other points on isoquant *Q*, such as *R, S, T, J* lie on higher iso-cost lines than *CD* and which will therefore mean greater total cost-outlay for producing the given output. Therefore, the entrepreneur will not chose any of the combinations *R, S, T* and *J*.

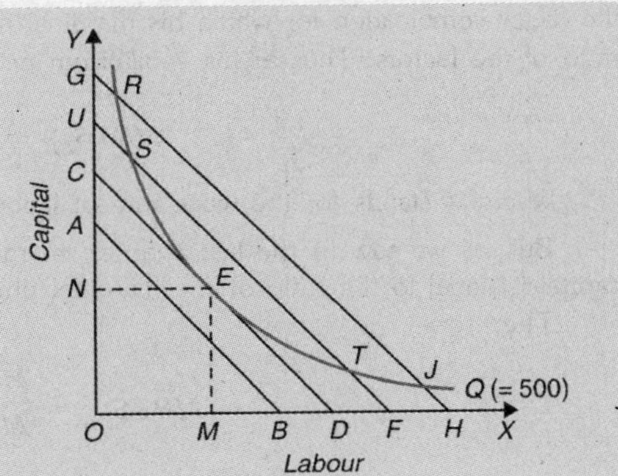

Fig. 14.4. *Minimising Cost for a Given Lavel of Output*

We thus see that factor combination *E* is the least-cost combination of labour and capital for producing a given output. Factor combination *E* is therefore an optimum combination for him under the given circumstances. Hence we conclude that the entrepreneur will choose factor combination *E* (that is, *OM* units of labour and *ON* units of capital) to produce 500 units of output. It is thus clear that the tangency point of the given isoquant with an iso-cost line represents the least-cost combination of factors for producing a given output.

How the entrepreneur will arrive at the least-cost factor combination can also be explained with the help of the concept of marginal rate of technical substitution (*MRTS*) and the price ratio of the two factors. As has been shown earlier, the marginal rate of technical substitution (*MRTS*) is given by the slope of the isoquant at its various points. On the other hand, the price ratio of the factors is given by the slope of the iso-cost line. The entrepreneur will not choose to produce the given output at point *R* because at point *R* marginal rate of technical substitution of labour for capital is greater than the price ratio of the factors (at point *R* the slope of the isoquant *Q* is greater than the slope of the iso-cost line *GH*). Therefore, if he is at point *R* he will be reducing his cost by using more of labour in place of capital and go down on the isoquant. Likewise, he will not stop at point *S*, since the marginal rate of technical substitution of labour for capital is still greater than the price ratio of the factors; slope of the isoquant at point *S* being greater than the slope of the iso-cost line *UF*. Therefore, the entrepreneur will further substitute labour for capital and will go down further on the isoquant *Q*.

When the entrepreneur reaches point *E*, the marginal rate of technical substitution of labour for capital is there equal to the price ratio of the factors, since the slopes of the isoquant and the iso-cost; line *CD* are equal to each other. The entrepreneur will have no incentive to go down further, for he will not be lowering his cost in this way, but in fact he will be reaching higher iso-cost lines. At points *J* and *T* on the isoquant *Q* the marginal rate of technical substitution of labour for capital is smaller than the price ratio of the factors and the entrepreneur will try to substitute capital for labour and move upward on the isoquant *Q* until he reaches the point of tangency *E*, where marginal rate of technical substitution is equal to the price ratio of the factors. It is thus clear that the entrepreneur will be minimizing his cost when he is using the factor combination for which his marginal rate of technical substitution is equal to the price ratio of the factors. Thus at his equilibrium point *E*.

$$MRTS_{LK} = \frac{w}{r}$$

where *w* stands for the wage rate of labour and *r* for the price of capital

But, as we saw in the last chapter, marginal rate of technical substitution of labour for capital is equal to the ratio of the marginal physical products of the two factors. Therefore

$$MRTS_{LK} = \frac{MP_L}{MP_k} = \frac{w}{r}$$

$$\frac{MP_L}{MP_k} = \frac{w}{r}$$

We can rearrange the above equation to have

$$\frac{MP_L}{w} = \frac{MP_K}{r}$$

We therefore reach an important conclusion about the entrepreneur's choice of the quantities of the two factors. The entrepreneur will be in equilibrium in regard to his use and purchases of the two factors when he is using such quantities of the two factors that the marginal physical products of the two factors are proportional to the factor prices. If, for instance, the price of factor *X* is twice as much as that of factor *Y*, then the entrepreneur will purchase and use such quantities of the two factors that the marginal physical product of factor *X* is twice the marginal physical product of factor *Y*.

We can extend the above condition for least-cost combination of factors when more than two factors are involved. Suppose there are three factors, labour, capital and land. From the above condition for least cost or optimal combination of factors to produce a given level of output, it follows that in case of these three factors also the ratio of marginal physical product of factor to its price will be the same in case of all the three factors. Thus, the equilibrium to produce a given level of output will be achieved when the following condition holds

$$\frac{MP_L}{w} = \frac{MP_K}{r} = \frac{MP_D}{t}$$

where

w = price of labour, *i.e.,* its wage rate

r = price of capital

t = price of the use of land, that is, rent of land

MP_D = the marginal physical product of land

It is quite clear from above that the entrepreneur's behaviour in choosing the quantities of factors is exactly symmetrical with the behaviour of the consumer. Both the entrepreneur and the consumer purchase things in such quantities as to equate marginal rate of substitution with the price ratio. The consumer, to be in equilibrium, equates his marginal rate of substitution (or the ratio of the marginal utilities of two goods) with the price ratio of the goods. The entrepreneur equates the marginal rate of technical substitution (or, the ratio of the marginal physical products of the two factors) with the price ratio of the factors.

Output Maximisation Subject to Cost Constraint

The dual of cost-minimisation problem for a given level of output is of output maximisation for a given level of cost or outlay. Suppose the firm has decided upon the cost-outlay which it has to incur for the production of a commodity. With a given level of cost outlay, there will be a single iso-cost line that represents the outlay that firm has decided to spend. The firm will have to choose a factor combination lying on the given iso-cost line. Obviously, with a given cost-outlay, a rational producer will be interested in maximising output of the commodity. Consider Fig. 14.5. Suppose the firm has decided to incur an outlay of Rs. 5000 on labour and capital which is represented by the iso-cost line *AB*. The firm has a choice to use any factor combination of labour and capital such as *R, S, E, T, J* etc. lying on the given iso-cost line *AB* to produce the product, An isoquant map showing a set of isoquants that represents various levels of output (200, 300, 400, 500 units) has been superimposed on the given iso-cost line *AB*. A glance at the Fig. 14.5 reveals that the firm will choose the factor combination *E* consisting of *ON* of labour and *OH* of capital. This is because of all the factor combinations that lie on the given iso-cost line *AB*, only the factor combination *E* enables the firm to reach the highest possible isoquant Q_3 and thus produce 400 units of output. All other combinations of labour and capital on the given iso-cost line *AB* such as *R, S, T, J* etc., lie on lower isoquants showing lower level of output than 400 units.

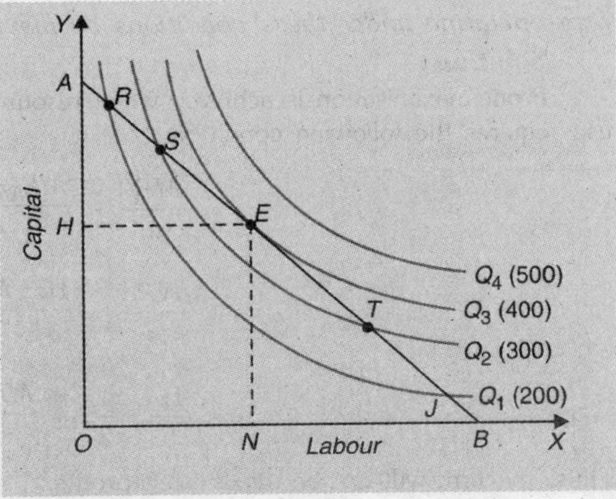

Fig. 14.5. *Maximization of Output for a Given Cost*

NUMERICAL PROBLEMS

Problem 1. *A firm is producing output using labour and capital in such quantities that marginal product of labour is 15, and marginal product of capital is 8. The wage rate of labour is Rs 3 and price of capital is Rs 2. Is the firm using efficient factor combination for production? If not, what it should do to achieve economic efficiency ?*

Solution :

Efficiency condition for factor use (that is, optimal factor combination) requires that the following condition should be fulfilled:

$$\frac{MP_L}{w} = \frac{MP_K}{r}$$

Now, $$\frac{MP_L}{w} = \frac{15}{3} \text{ and } \frac{MP_K}{r} = \frac{8}{2}$$

Now, $$\frac{15}{3} > \frac{8}{2}$$

The given factor combination cannot therefore be efficient or optimal factor combination because the firm is getting more output from a rupee spent on labour than on capital. To achieve economic efficiency in the use of resources and to maximise profits the firm should substitute labour for capital

so that $\frac{MP_L}{w}$ becomes equal to $\frac{MP_K}{r}$.

Problem 2. *The wage rate of labour is Rs 6 and price of raw materials is Rs 2. The marginal product of labour is 16 while the marginal product of raw materials is 4. Can a firm operating under these conditions be maximising profits ?*

Solution :

Profit maximisation is achieved when resources are efficiently used. Efficiency in resource use requires the following condition :

$$\frac{MP_L}{w} = \frac{MP_{RM}}{P_{RM}}$$

$$\frac{MP_L}{w} = \frac{16}{6}, \frac{MP_{RM}}{P_{RM}} = \frac{4}{2}$$

$$\frac{16}{6} > \frac{4}{2} \text{ or } \frac{MP_L}{w} > \frac{MP_{RM}}{P_{RM}}$$

Thus, the firm will not be maximising profits. To maximise profits, it should substitute labour for raw materials

Problem 3. *A firm reports that marginal product of labour is 5 and marginal rate of technical substitution of labour for capital is 2. What is the marginal product of capital?*

Solution : $$MRTS_{LK} = \frac{MP_L}{MP_K} \qquad 2 = \frac{5}{MP_K}$$

$$MP_K = \frac{5}{2} = 2.5$$

Problem 4. *A firm employs labour as the only variable factor along with a fixed quantity of capital. Wage rate of labour is Rs 100 per day and its marginal product is 20 units of output. What is marginal cost of the product?*

Solution.

Marginal cost is the additional cost incurred on producing an extra unit of output. Marginal cost can be obtained from dividing the wage that has to be paid to the additional unit of labour by the number of units of output produced by it (that is, marginal product). Thus,

$$MC = \frac{w}{MP_L}$$

$$= \frac{100}{20} = 5.$$

Problem 5. *A biscuit producing company reports the following data about its production and factors used:*

Q	*K*	*L*	*Q*	*K*	*L*
490	15	99	470	14	100
500	15	100	500	15	100

where Q = output, K = capital, L = labour.'

If wage rate of labour is Rs 5 and price of capital is Rs 10, does the input combination of 15K and 100L represents the least-cost factor combination? If not, should it use more labour and less capital or less labour and more capital?

Solution.

Least-cost factor combination requires that the following condition must be met

$$\frac{MP_L}{w} = \frac{MP_K}{r},$$

where w is wage rate and r is price of capital.

Now, in the problem when factor combination is changed from $15K + 100L$ to $15K + 99L$, the output declines by 10 units (500 – 490 = 10). Thus, $MP_L = 10$. Similarly, when factor combination is changed from $15K + 100L$, to $14K + 100L$, output declines by 30(500 – 470 = 30). Thus, $MP_k = 30$. Substituting these values of marginal products of labour and capital and the factor prices in the condition for least-cost factor combination, we have

$$\frac{MP_L}{w} = \frac{MP_K}{r}$$

$$\frac{10}{5} \neq \frac{30}{10} \text{ or } \frac{10}{5} < \frac{30}{10}$$

The company will use more capital and less labour as output per unit of a rupee (3) spent on it is greater than the output per unit of a rupee $\left(\frac{10}{5} \text{ or } 2\right)$ spent on labour.

EXPANSION PATH

We explained above which factor combination a firm will choose to produce a specified level of output, given the prices of the two factors. We are now interested in studying how the entrepreneur will change his factor combination as he expands his output, given the factor prices. To begin with, suppose the prices of the two factors labour and capital are such that are represented by the slope of the iso-cost line *AB*. In Fig. 14.6 four iso-cost lines, *AB*, *CD*, *UF* and GH are drawn which show different levels of total cost outlay. All iso-cost lines are parallel to one another indicating that prices of two factors remain the same. If the firm wants to produce the output level denoted by Q_1 (= 100 units of output), it will chose the factor combination E_1 which minimizes cost of production; E_1 being the point of tangency between the isoquant Q_1 and the iso-cost line AB. Now, if a firm wants to produce a higher level of output denoted by the isoquant Q_2 (=200), it will choose the factor combination E_2 which is the least-cost combination for new output. Likewise, for still higher output levels denoted by Q_3 and Q_4 , then firm will choose tangency combination E_3 and E_4 respectively which minimize cost for the given outputs.

The line joining the minimum cost combinations such as E_1, E_2, E_3, E_4 is called the *expansion path* because it shows how the factor combination with which the firm produces will alter as the firm expands its level of output. Thus *the expansion path may be defined as the locus of the points of tangency between the iso product curves (i.e., isoquants) and the iso-cost lines.* The expansion path is also known as *scale-line* because it shows how the entrepreneur will change the quantities of the two factors when it increases the level of output. The expansion path can have different shapes and slopes depending upon the relative prices of the productive factors used and the shape of the isoquants. As we shall prove below, when the production function exhibits constant returns to scale, the expansion path will be a straight line through the origin. Further, for a given isoquant map there will be a different expansion path for each different relative prices of the factors.

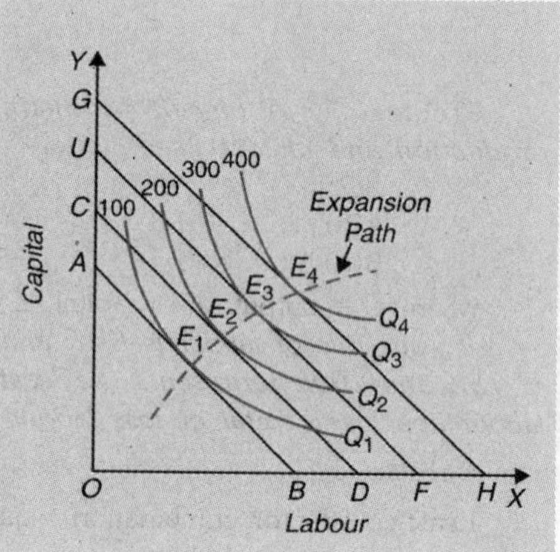

Fig. 14.6. *Expansion Path.*

Since expansion path represents minimum cost combinations for various levels of output, it shows the cheapest way of producing each output, given the relative prices of the factors. When two factors are variable, the entrepreneur will choose to produce at some point on the expansion path. One cannot say exactly at which particular point on the expansion path the entrepreneur will in fact be producing unless one knows either the output which he wants to produce or the size of the cost-outlay it wants to incur. But this is certain that when both factors are variable and the prices of factors are given, a rational entrepreneur will seek to produce at one point or the other on the expansion path.

Derivation of Equation for Expansion Path (in Cobb-Douglas Production Function)

As explained above, expansion path shows how *optimal factor combination changes* when a firm expands its level of output *at the given factor prices.* We can mathematically derive equation for expansion path which plays an important role in the production analysis. To derive the equation for expansion we take the following Cobb-Douglas production function.

$$Q = 100\ K^{0.5}\ L^{0.5}$$

We have seen above at optimal factor combinations the following condition holds :

$$MRTS_{LK} = \frac{w}{r} \qquad \text{......(1)}$$

and $$MRTS_{LK} = \frac{MP_L}{MP_K} \qquad \text{......(2)}$$

To obtain MP_L or $\frac{\partial Q}{\partial L}$ we differentiate the given production function ($Q = 100\ K^{0.5}\ L^{0.5}$) with respect to labour. Thus.

$$MP_L = 100 \times \frac{1}{2} K^{1/2} L^{-1/2} = 50 \frac{K^{1/2}}{L^{1/2}}$$

and $$MP_K \text{ or } \frac{\partial Q}{\partial K} = 100 \times \frac{1}{2} K^{-1/2} L^{1/2} = 50 \frac{L^{1/2}}{K^{1/2}}$$

Therefore, $$MRTS_{LK} = \frac{MP_L}{MP_K} = \frac{50 \frac{K^{1/2}}{L^{1/2}}}{50 \frac{L^{1/2}}{K^{1/2}}} = \frac{K}{L} \qquad \text{.....(3)}$$

Substituting $\frac{K}{L}$ for $MRTS_{LK}$ in equation (1), we have

$$\frac{K}{L} = \frac{w}{r}$$

or $$K = \frac{w}{r} . L \qquad \text{....(4)}$$

The expression in equation (4) is the equation for expansion path for the production function, $Q = 100K^{1/2}L^{1/2}$. If the prices of labour and capital, *i.e.*, w and r respectively are known, equation (4) defines the *optimal combinations of factors* (that is, least-cost combinations of factors for various levels of output or output-maximising factor combinations for various cost outlays)

The equation (4) for expansion path reveals that the quantities of labour and capital used to produce a level of output, given the production function, depends on prices of factors, w and r. For example, if prices of labour and capital are equal, say Rs. 50 per hour as wage rate (w) of labour and Rs. 50 per hour as rental (r) of machine (*i.e.*, capital) used, then from the expansion path equation (4) we obtain

$$K = \frac{w}{r} . L = \frac{50}{50} L$$

$$K = L$$

That is, when prices of two factors are the same, given the Cobb-Douglas production function, equal quantities of the two factos will be used.

Suppose the wage rate of labour rises to Rs. 100 per hour, while rental of the machine remains fixed at Rs. 50 per hour, we obtain the following equation for expansion path

$$K = \frac{w}{r} . L = \frac{100}{50} L$$

$$K = 2L$$

This means that with rise in wage rate of labour from Rs. 50 per hour to Rs. 100 per hour, the quantity of capital used will be two times labour input. That is, rise in wage rate has resulted in substitution of capital for labour in the production process.

Finding Output Level with given Factor Prices

It should be noted that expansion path $\left(K = \frac{w}{r} L\right)$ shows various optimal factor combinations for the given factor prices, *it does not indicate the specific level of output for a given optimal factor combination.* However, the level of output produced with an optimal factor combinations can be determined by substituting the equation for expansion path into the original production function. Thus, in our example, to determine the specific level or rate of output,. we substitute the equation for expansion path $\left(K = \frac{w}{r}. L\right)$ into the production function $Q = 100\ K^{1/2}.L^{1/2}$ we have

$$Q = 100\left(\frac{w}{r}. L\right)^{1/2} L^{1/2}$$

$$Q = 100\ L\left(\frac{w}{r}\right)^{1/2}$$

If the value of L and $\frac{w}{r}$ are known, we can find out the value of Q.

Numerical Problem : *Given the production function $Q = 100\ K^{0.5}\ L^{0.5}$. Determine the optimal input combination for producing 1444 units of output if wage rate of labour (w) is Rs. 30 and price per unit of capital (r) is Rs. 40. What is the minimum cost of production ?*

Solution :

The given production function is

$$Q = 100K^{0.5}.\ L^{0.5}$$

$$MP_L = \frac{\partial Q}{\partial L} = 100 \quad 0.5\ K^{0.5}\ L^{-0.5}$$

$$= 50K^{0.5}\ L^{-0.5}$$

$$MP_K = \frac{\partial Q}{\partial K} = 100 \times 0.5K^{-0.5}\ L^{0.5}$$

$$= 50\ K^{-0.5}\ L^{0.5}$$

$$\frac{MP_L}{MP_K} = \frac{50K^{0.5}\ L^{-0.5}}{50K^{-0.5}\ L^{0.5}} = \frac{K}{L}$$

In equilibrium $MRS_{LK} = \frac{MP_L}{MP_K} = \frac{w}{r}$ Thus, in optimal input combination, $\frac{K}{L} = \frac{w}{r}$

or
$$K = \frac{w}{r} L.$$

To obtain the value of L we substitue $K = \frac{w}{r} L.$ in the production function with $Q = 1444$ units. Thus

$$1444 = 100\, K^{0.5}\, L^{0.5}$$

$$= 100\left(\frac{w}{r}L\right)^{0.5} L^{0.5}$$

$$1444 = 100\, L\left(\frac{w}{r}\right)^{0.5}$$

Substituting $w = 30$ and $r = 40$

$$1444 = 100L \times \left(\frac{30}{40}\right)^{0.5}$$

$$1444 = 100\, L \times (0.75)^{0.5}$$

$$= 100\, L \times 0.866 = 86.6L$$

$$L = \frac{1444}{86.6} = 16.67$$

Now, using the equation for expansion path ($K = \frac{w}{r}$ L) we can obtain the value of K by substituting the values of L, w and r. Thus

$$K = \frac{30}{40} \times 16.67$$

$$= 0.75 \times 16.67$$

$$= 12.5$$

Thus optimum combination of inputs consists of 16.67 units of labour and 12.5 units of capital. This will ensure minimum possible cost for producing 1444 units of output.

In order to determine this minimum cost we substitute the optimum values of L and K obtained above and the given prices of labour and capital (*i.e.*, w and r) in the cost function. Thus

$$C = wL + rK$$

$$= 30 \times 16.67 + 40 \times 12.50$$

$$= 500 + 500$$

$$= \text{Rs. } 1000$$

Thus minimum cost of producing 1444 units of output is Rs. 1000.

Numerical Problem 2

Given : $Q = 100K^{0.5} L^{0.5}$, C = Rs. 1200, $w = 30$ and $r = 40$. Determine the quantity of labour and capital that the firm should use in order to maximise output. What is this level of output ?

Solution. The problem of constrained maximisation is :

$$\text{Maximise } Q = 100\, K^{\frac{1}{2}}\, L^{\frac{1}{2}}$$

Subject to cost constraint : $1200 = 30\, L + 40\, K$

$$MP_K = \frac{\partial Q}{\partial K} = \frac{1}{2}\, 100\, K^{-1/2}\, L^{1/2}$$

$$MP_L = \frac{\partial Q}{\partial L} = \frac{1}{2}\ 100\, K^{1/2}\, L^{-1/2}$$

$$\frac{MP_K}{MP_L} = \frac{50K^{-1/2}\, L^{1/2}}{50K^{1/2}\, L^{-1/2}} = \frac{L}{K} \qquad ...(1)$$

For output maximisation

$$\frac{MP_K}{MP_L} = \frac{r}{w} \qquad ...(2)$$

Substituting $\frac{MP_K}{MP_L} = \frac{L}{K}$ and $w = 30$ and $r = 40$ in equation (2) we have

$$\frac{L}{K} = \frac{4}{3} \text{ or } L = \frac{4K}{3} \qquad ...(3)$$

Putting the value of $L = \frac{4}{3}K$ in cost-constraint equation we get

$$1200 = wL + rK$$

$$= 30 \times \frac{4K}{3} + 40K = 80\,K$$

$$K = \frac{1200}{80} = 15$$

Substituting $K = 15$ in the cost-constraint equation we have

$$1200 = 30 \times L + 40 \times 15$$

$$30L + 600 = 1200$$

$$L = \frac{1200 - 600}{30} = 20$$

Thus output-maximising amounts of capital and labour are 15 and 20 respectively. To get the level of output produced we substitute these amounts of capital and labour in the given production function

$$Q = 100K^{1/2}\, L^{1/2}$$

$$Q = 100\sqrt{15}\,\sqrt{20}$$

$$= 100\sqrt{300}$$

$$= 100 \times 17.32$$

$$= 1732$$

PROFIT MAXIMISATION AND OPTIMUM INPUT COMBINATION

The optimum combination of factors (inputs) is a necessary but not sufficient for profit maximisation which is the objective of the firm. If a firm is not working with an optimum input combination it can substitute one for another to reduce cost for a given output and thereby to increase its profits. But there are several optimum input combinations depending on the level of output to be produced . For example, on expansion path in Figure 14.6 there are several points of tangency between isoquants and isocosts such as E_1, E_2 and E_3 which are all optimum or efficient input combinations. The problem is to determine which one of these optimum input combinations will ensure maximum profits for the firm. Thus, for determining profit maximisation only optimum combination lying on the expansion need to be considered.

To arrive at profit maximisation we should consider *the optimum use of each variable factor* explained earlier . As shown above, for optimum use of a variable factor it must be used until marginal revenue product (*MRP*) of the factor is equal to marginal factor cost (*MFC*) of the factor. When the price of an input such as wage rate of labour or rental cost (*r*) of capital is given and constant for the firm marginal factor cost for the firm equals the price of the factor or input (that is, wage rate of labour or rental cost of capital). Thus, for a perfectly competiive firm to achieve profit maximization labour and capital should be used in such amounts that marginal revenue product of each should be equal to wage rate and rental cost of capital respectively. Thus, the conditions for profit maximization with regard to the use of the factors when the factor prices for the firm are given and constant are :

$$MRP_L = w \quad \ldots(1)$$

and

$$MRP_K = r \quad \ldots(2)$$

As mentioned above, marginal revenue product of a factor is the additional revenue generated by using an extra unit of a factor (input). Thus, if the use of an additional unit of a factor generates more revenue than the price of the factor, the firm's profits will rise by hiring and using it . And the profits will increase until marginal revenue product of each variable factor equals the price of the factor. That is, for maximization of profits, in case of two factor production function the above condition (1) and (2) must be satisfied.

The above conditions for profit maximisation imply that the condition for optimum factor combination, namely, $MP_{Ls}/w = MP_k/r$ will also be fulfilled. This can be proved as follows.

As explained earlier marginal revenue product of a factor, given the price of output, is equal to the marginal physical product of the factor times the *price of output* in the market. Keeping this in view we rewrite the above conditions (1) and 2) for profit maximisation. Thus

$$MP_L.P = w \quad \ldots(3)$$

and

$$MP_K.P = r \quad \ldots(4)$$

when P is price of output,

Dividing equation (3) by (4) we get

$$\frac{MP_L}{MP_K} = \frac{w}{r} \quad \ldots(5)$$

The equation 5 is the condition for optimum factor combination which can also be written as

$$\frac{MP_L}{w} = \frac{MP_K}{r} \quad \ldots(6)$$

Thus, from equation (1) and (2) and (6) we conclude that *if a firm is maximising profits, it will also be working with optimum input combination and thus working efficiently.*

Numerical Problem. *The following production function of a firm is given*

$$100\ L^{0.5}K^{0.5}$$

It is also given that K = 100 and price (P) of output is Rs. 2 per unit, wage rate of labour is Rs. 50 and rental cost (r) of capital is Rs. 40 per machine hour. Determine the quantity of labour the firm should hire to maximise profits. Find the maximum profits of the firm.

Solution :

To maximise profits the firm will hire labour until MRP_L equals its wage rate. Thus

$$MRP_L = w$$

or $$P.MP_L = w \quad \text{...(1)}$$

Similarly, the firm will equate marginal revenue product of capital with rental cost of capital

$$MRP_K = r$$

or $$P.MP_K = r \quad \text{....(2)}$$

Dividing equation (1) by (2) we have

$$\frac{P.MP_L}{P.MP_K} = \frac{w}{r}$$

or $$\frac{MP_L}{MP_K} = \frac{w}{r} \quad \text{...(3)}$$

From the given production function $Q = 100\, L^{0.5}\, K^{0.5}$ we obtain marginal products of labour and capital by differentiating it with respect to labour and capital. Thus

$$MP_L = 50L^{-0.5}\, K^{0.5}$$

and $$MP_K = 50L^{0.5}\, K^{-0.5}$$

Dividing MP_L by MP_K we have

$$\frac{MP_L}{MP_K} = \frac{50L^{-0.5}K^{0.5}}{50\, L^{0.5}K^{-0.5}}$$

$$= \frac{K}{L}$$

Substituting $\frac{K}{L}$ for $\frac{MP_L}{MP_K}$ in equation (3)

$$\frac{K}{L} = \frac{w}{r}$$

$$L = K.\frac{r}{w} \quad \text{...(4)}$$

Substituting the given values of K and $\frac{r}{w}$ in expansion path equation (4) we have

$$L = 100\ \frac{40}{50}$$

$$= 80$$

Now, substituting values of L and K in the given production function we have

$$Q = 100\ (80)^{0.5}\ (100)^{0.5}$$

$$= 100 \times 8.944 \times 10$$

$$= 8944$$

The profit (π) function can be stated as under

$$\pi = TR - TC$$

$$TR = PQ \text{ and } TC = wL + rK$$

Therefore
$$\pi = P.Q. - wL - rK$$
$$= 2 \times 8944 - 50 \times 80 - 40 \times 100$$
$$= 17888 - 4000 - 4000$$
$$= 9888$$

Thus 80 units of labour will be employed and total profits made are Rs. 9888.

EFFECT OF CHANGES IN FACTOR PRICES : FACTOR SUBSTITUTION

We have seen above that the cost-minimising factor combination depends on the relative prices of factors used. As shown above, given the prices of factors, the cost of producing a level of output is minimised by using a factor combination at which

$$MRTS_{LK} = \frac{w_0}{r_0}$$

or, where
$$\frac{MP_L}{w_0} = \frac{MP_K}{r_0}$$

Now, if either the price of labour (w) or the price of capital (r) changes, the producer will respond to this change in factor prices as his cost-minimisation state will be disturbed. For example, if wage rate rises from w_0 to w_1, then at the initial equilibrium position,

$$\frac{MP_L}{w_1} < \frac{MP_K}{r_0} \quad \text{or,} \quad \frac{MP_K}{r_0} > \frac{MP_L}{w_1}$$

This will induce a rational producer to substitute capital for relatively more expensive labour. That is, he will try to use more capital and less labour and continue substituting capital for labour until $MRTS_{LK} = \frac{w_1}{r_0}$ or $\frac{MP_L}{w_1} = \frac{MP_k}{r_0}$. Substitution of one factor for another is graphically illustrated by using isoquants in Fig. 14.7 where with factor prices w_0 and r_0 respectively of labour and capital, AB, which is the iso-cost line for a given amount of outlay, is tangent to the isoquant Q_0 at point E. In this equilibrium situation, he is using OL_0 of labour and OK_0 of capital. Now, suppose price of labour (*i.e.*, wage rate) rises so that the iso-cost line, price of capital (r) and outlay remaining constant, rotates to the new position AC. It will be seen from Fig. 14.7 that none of the factor combinations lying on the iso-cost line AC will be sufficient to produce the level of output Q_0 as the iso-cost line AC lies at a lower level than the isoquant Q_0. In other words, with higher wage rate w_1, the given amount of outlay is not enough to buy the required amounts of the two factors to produce the level of output Q_0. Thus, if producer wants to produce the same level of output Q_0 it will have to increase its outlay,. The increase in outlay on factors implies moving to a higher iso-cost line that will be parallel to the new iso-cost line AC. Now, with the new relative prices of labour and capital, the iso-cost line GH is drawn parallel to AC so that it is tangent to the isoquant Q_0. It will be seen from the Fig. 14.7 that the iso-cost line GH will not be tangent at the initial equilibrium point E since its slope reflecting the new relative factor prices differs from the slope of the initial iso-cost line *AB*. Thus, *the initial point E no longer minimises cost in the context of new relative factor prices.* Now that the wage rate is higher, that is, the labour is relatively more expensive, to produce the initial level of output, the producer will substitute capital for labour by moving upward along the isoquant Q_0.

It will be observed from Fig.14.7 that the new iso-cost line *GH* which is parallel to *AC* and therefore reflects the relatively higher wage rate as compared to the iso-cost line *AB*, is tangent to the isoquant Q_0 at point *R* showing that in order to minimise cost with the new relative factor prices, the producer has substituted K_0 K_1 amount of capital for L_0 L_1 amount of labour to reach the new cost-minimizing factor combination *R* where he uses smaller amount OL_1 of labour and larger quantity OK_1 of capital. It may be noted again that substitution of capital for labour and thereby changing the factor-proportion used to reach the equilibrium point *R* for producing a given level of output Q_0 involves the increase in cost of production resulting from the rise in the price of labour (iso-cost line *GH* lies further away from the iso-cost line *AC* when viewed from the origin).

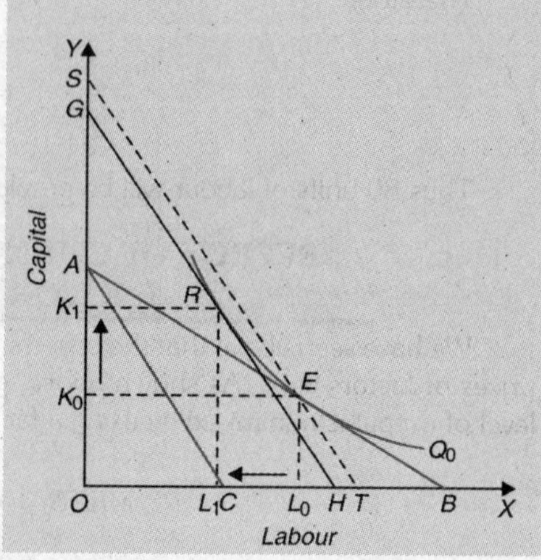

Fig. 14.7. *Rise in wage rate (price) of labour causes substitution of capital for labour.*

However, if with the new higher price of labour, the producer had used the original factor combination *E*, he would have incurred still higher cost or expenditure for producing the output level Q_0. An isocost line *ST* that is drawn parallel to *AC* reflecting new relative factor prices passes through the original factor combination point *E* but lies still further away from *GH* indicating that if with new relative prices of labour and capital the firm uses the same labour-capital combination *E* to produce the initial level of output Q_0, it will involve still higher cost. Thus, by changing the factor combination from *E* to *R*, following the rise in price of labour by substituting capital for now relatively more expensive labour, the firm has succeeded in lowering its cost than it would have incurred if it had continued to use the original factor combination *E* to produce output Q_0 even after the change in the factor price situation.

From the foregoing analysis we arrive at the conclusion that change in relative factor prices causes a substitution of a factor that has become relatively more expensive by a factor that has become relatively cheaper. In the real world there are several examples of factor substitution in response to changes in relative factor prices. When price of petroleum increased many countries tried to substitute other types of energy resources using inputs such as coal, electricity to reduce costs of production. Again, in the United States the firms use more machines (*i.e.*, capital) and relatively less labour as labour there is very costly than is the case in some developing countries where wages are comparatively low. Further, recently when prices of computers have fallen, there has been substitution of manual labour for doing such work as book-keeping, making architectural maps, composing books and journals by computers (*i.e.*, capital).

SUBSTITUTE AND COMPLEMENTARY FACTORS

When a fall in the price of one of the two variable factors leads to the decline in the quantity purchased of the other factor, the two factors are said to be substitutes of each other in production. The substitute factors are also called *rival factors.* It should be carefully understood why when the price of a factor falls and as a result its quantity used increases, the quantity employed of its substitute factor decreases. The answer is that *in case of substitute factors, the increase in the use of one factor actually reduces the marginal physical product of its substitute factor.* This reduction in marginal physical product of the factor, given its price, causes the decrease in its quantity used to attain cost-mimimising or optimal factor combination. The examples of substitute or rival factors are male and female labour, capital and labour in several production processes, jumbo jets and small jets, electronic typewriter and word processors etc.

The Fig. 14.8. illustrates the case of two factors which are substitute of each other. The effect of change in price of a factor on the use of the factors can be divided into two parts, namely, the substitution effect and output effect. The fall in price (wage rate) of labour, price of capital and cost outlay remaining the same, makes it relatively cheaper than capital. This causes substitution of relatively cheaper labour for capital which becomes relatively expensive. This is substitution effect. Besides, the fall in price of labour enables the producer to produce more output because with lower price of labour the producer can buy more quantities of both the factors with the same cost-outlay. This leads to the increase in use of both the factors resulting in more output. This is the output effect of the change in price of a factor.

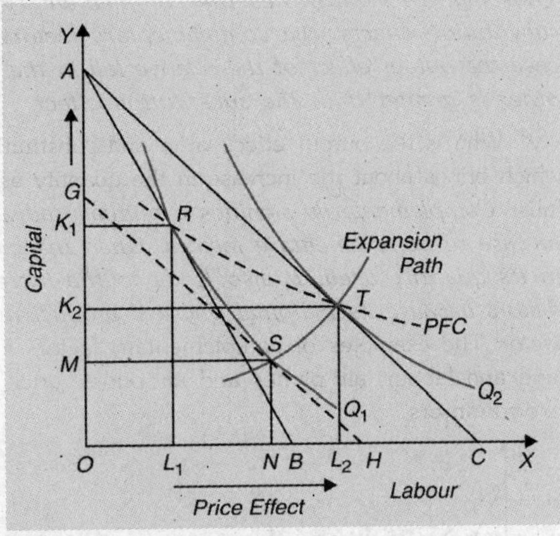

Fig. 14.8. *Substitution and Output Effects of the Change in Factor Price*

Now consider Figure 14.8. to begin with, given the factor prices and cost outlay, the iso-cost line is *AB* and the producer is in equilibrium at point *R* on isoquant Q_1. Now, with the fall in wage rate, price of capital and cost outlay remaining the same, iso-cost line shifts to *AC* and the producer's equilibrium is at point *T* on higher isoquant Q_2 and with this the producer uses L_1L_2 more labour and K_1K_2 less capital. This is the factor price effect of fall in wage rate of labour. To separate the two effects we reduce the cost-outlay of the producer so that iso-cost -line shifts to *GH* which is tangent to the original isoquaut Q_1 at new point *S*. It should be noted that the fall in the price of labour has led to the decline in quantity used of capital, because the substitution effect of the fall in wage rate which causes substitution of capital by labour is greater than its output, effect. We may therefore say *two factors X and Y are substitutes if the substitution effect on Y of the change in price of X is greater than the output effect on it.* Fig. 14.8 the substitution effect of the fall in the price of labour on the use of capital is K_1 *M* which is greater than the output effect MK_2 on it. The two effects work in opposite direction on the quantity used of capital; the substitution effect tends to reduce it and output effect tends to increase it. Since the substitution effect on capital is greater than the output effect, the net result is the fall in the quantity used of capital by K_1K_2. Thus Fig. 14.8 represents the case of the two factors which are substitutes of each other.

In Fig. 14.9 the marginal rate of technical substitution diminishes rapidly along the isoquants, that is, the isoquants are highly convex when looked form origin. In this case, therefore, the substitution effect will be very small. Thus, in Fig. 14.9 the output effect of the fall in price of factor X on the quantity used or purchased of factor Y is greater than the substitution effect and therefore the net effect of the fall in price of X on Y is the increase in the quantity purchased of Y. In Fig 14.9 the substitution effect on Y as a result of the fall in the price of factor X is (–) K_1M, whereas the output effect on Y is (+) MK_2 which is greater than K_1M. In this case, therefore, the fall in price of X leads to the increase in the quantity purchased and used of both the factors. *When a fall in the price of one of the two factors causes the increase in quantity purchased of both the factors, they are said to be complementary. Thus Fig. 14.9 illustrates the complementary factors. In terms of output and technical substitution effects, the complementary factors may be defined as those factors in which case the output effect of the relative fall in the price of one factor on the purchases of the other is greater than the substitution effect.*

Why is the output effect large and substitution effect very small in case of some factors which brings about the increase in the quantity used of both the factors when the price of one falls. *Complementarily signifies a mutually advantageous cooperation of factors. Therefore, in case of complementary factors, when the price of one factor falls resulting in increase in its quantity used, it also leads to the increase in the quantity of its complementary factors because its marginal physical productivity rises due to the greater use of the other factor.* The examples of complementary factors in the real world are irrigation and fertilizers, land and labour, air planes and air pilots, brick layers and bricks, computers and computer programmers.

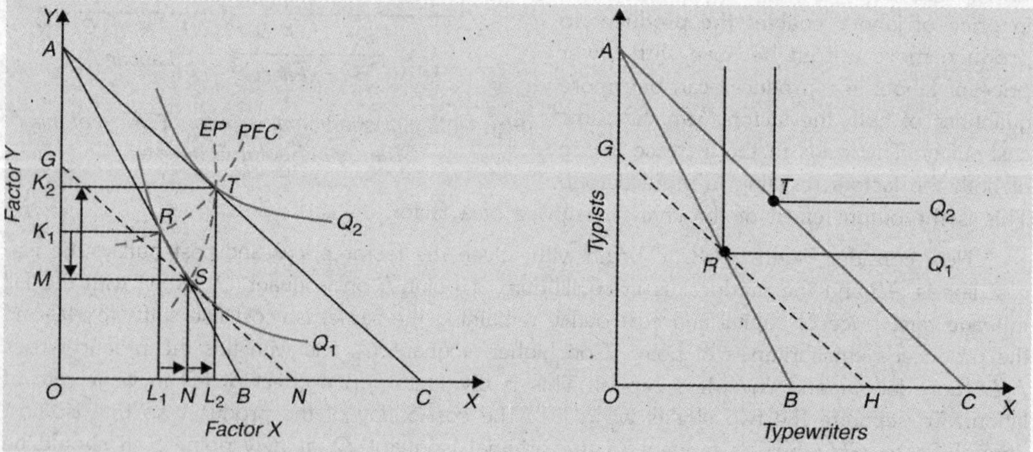

Fig. 14.9. Complementary Factors Fig. 14.10. Perfect Complimentsary Factors

It should be noted that the factors represented in Fig.14.9 are complements but not perfect complements. The two perfect complementary factors are used in a given fixed proportion and, as explained in the previous chapter, the isoquants of the two perfect complementary factors are right-angled and the *technical substitutions effect in case of the two perfect complements* is therefore zero. The case of perfect complements is illustrated in Fig. 14.10 where substitution effect being nil, price effect consists of only the output effect and the quantities of both factors change in a given proportion as a result of the fall in price of a factor and the resultant change in the iso-cost line from AB to AC. It will be seen from Fig. 14.10 that when iso-cost line GH is drawn parallel to AC so as to be tangent to the initial isoquant Q_1, it touches the same point R where the original iso-cost AB is tangent to the isoquant Q_1. This shows that substitution effect is zero and price effect contains only the output effect.

THE EXPANSION PATH OF THE LINEAR HOMOGENEOUS PRODUCTION FUNCTION

We shall now establish an important relationship between the linear production function exhibiting constant returns to scale and the nature of the expansion path. The following proposition holds good in this connection:

The expansion path in case of the linear homogeneous production function (i.e., production function with constant returns to scale) is always a straight line through the origin.

Whether expansion path is linear or non-linear, depends on the nature of technology involved in the production function. *Expansion path of a linear homogeneous production path is a straight line from the origin.* This is an important property of linear homogeneous production function. Recall that expansion path shows optimal factor combinations as firm expands its output, given the prices of factors. Since at optimal factor combination $MRS_{LK} = \frac{w}{r}$, given the constant factor prices along an expansion path, this implies that given the factor price ratio, *MRS* will remain the same. Expansion path being a straight line from the origin implies that $\frac{K}{L}$ ratio remains constant as we move from one optimal point to another on it. To prove that expansion path of a linear homogeneous production function is a straight line from the origin we take Cobb-Douglas production function ($Q = AK^{1/2} L^{1/2}$) which is linear homogeneous production function.

Differentiating the production function with respect to labour

$$\frac{\partial Q}{\partial L} = \frac{1}{2} AK^{1/2} L^{-1/2} \quad \text{...(1)}$$

Differentiating the production function with respect to capital

$$\frac{\partial Q}{\partial K} = \frac{1}{2} AK^{-1/2} L^{1/2} \quad \text{...(2)}$$

Dividing (1) by (2), we have

$$MRTS_{LK} = \frac{MP_L}{MP_K} = \frac{\frac{\partial Q}{\partial L}}{\frac{\partial Q}{\partial K}} = \frac{\frac{1}{2} AK^{1/2} L^{-1/2}}{\frac{1}{2} AK^{-1/2} L^{1/2}} = \frac{K}{L} \quad \text{...(3)}$$

Thus, $MRTS_{LK}$ in linear homogeneous Cobb-Douglas production is equal to $\frac{K}{L}$. Since, as explained above, at optimal factor combinations on the expansion path,

$$MRTS_{LK} = \frac{w}{r}$$

As $MRTS_{LM}$ in linear homogeneous Cobb-Douglas production is equal to $\frac{K}{L}$, it follows that on expansion path

$$\frac{K}{L} = \frac{w}{r}$$

With given prices of labour and capital, w and r, capital-labour $\left(\frac{K}{L}\right)$ ratio will remain constant. This means that expansion path of this production function is a straight line from the origin.

We therefore conclude that, in a linear homogeneous production function, $MRTS_{LK}$ *depends on the capital-labour ratio which remains constant.* This is graphically illustrated in Figure 14.11 where linear homogeneous production has been represented by isoquants Q_1 (=100), Q_2 (= 200) and Q_3 (=300) units of output. Two rays OR and OS from the origin have been drawn which represent two different capital-labour ratios but along each capital-labour ratio remains the same. Now, on the ray OR from the origin which passes though A, B and C on the isoquants Q_1, Q_2 and Q_3, tangents have been drawn at points A, B, and C. These tangents depicting the slopes of the isoquants representing $MRTS_{LK}$ at points A, B, and C on the isoquants Q_1, Q_2 and Q_3 respectively are parallel to each other. Thus the marginal rate of technical substitution ($MRTS_{LK}$) along the straight-line ray OR, which depicts a given and constant capital-labour ratio $\left(\frac{K}{L}\right)$ as we move along it, remains the same. Likewise, on a straight-line ray OS from the origin the tangents representing slope of the isoquants drawn at the points E, F and G on the successive isoquants Q_1, Q_2 and Q_3 are parallel which show that with a constant capital-labour ratio (K/L), the marginal rate of substitution remains the same.

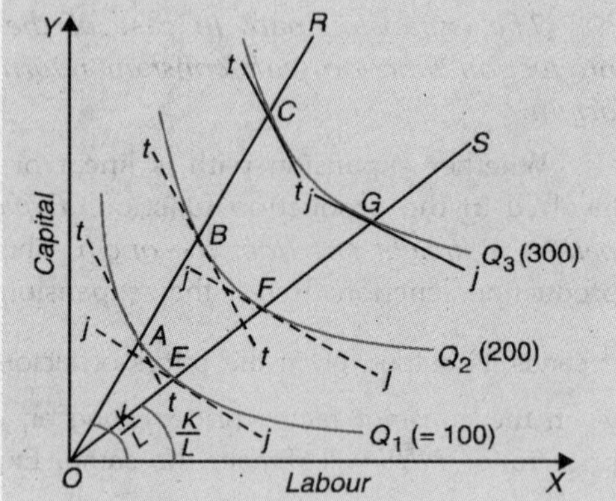

Fig. 14.11. Expansion path in case of a Linear Homogeneous Production Function is a straight line from the origin

Now, since the marginal rate of technical substitution on a straight-line ray from the origin in a linear homogeneous production function remains the same and, given the factor prices, the successive iso-cost lines have the same slope at the cost-minimisation points the expansion path of the firm will be located on the given straight line from the origin at which $MRTS_{LX}$ will be equal to the factor price ratio (w/r) at the tangency points of the successive isoquants and iso-cost lines. Thus, it is evident that expansion path of a linearly homogeneous production function is a straight line through the origin. However, it is important to notice that with a different factor price ratio, the expansion path of a linear homogeneous production function will be a different straight line from the origin. Thus in Fig. 14.11. If the factor-price ratio is given by the slope of the tangent tt, the expansion path will be the straight line OR from the origin and if the factor price ratio is given by the slope of the tangent jj, the expansion path will be the straight line OS from the origin.

It follows from above that the expansion path of a production function exhibiting constant returns to scale will always be a straight line through the origin. But, as is known, all points on a straight line through the origin involve the same proportion between the two factors. It follows therefore that with constant returns to scale and given factor prices there will be only one *optimum factor proportion (say, 5 units of a particular raw material per unit of labour which remains the same whatever the firm's level of output. Thus, in case of constant returns to scale, the task of an entrepreneurs is quite simple and convenient. He requires only to find out just one optimum factor proportion and so long as factor prices do not change he does not face any decision-making problem regarding factor proportions to be used for production.* Moreover, this result is also very useful for input-output analysis in economics.

QUESTIONS FOR REVIEW

1. Explain the concept of production function. The information about production function facing a firm is inadequate for making decision regarding economically efficient use of factors or resources. Explain

   [Hints : Production function describes the technological aspect of production, that is, maximum possible output that can be produced by various combination of factors. On the other hand, economic efficiency in resource use implies least-cost combination of factors to produce a given output or alternatively it implies maximisation of output for a given cost. Thus, for deciding about optimal or economically efficient resource use we require not only the data about the production function but also about prices of factors.]

2. What is meant by efficient or optimum factor combination in production? Explain with the help of isoquants and iso-cost lines how a producer achieves this combination of factors.
3. Show with the help of isoquants that a firm will be in equilibrium regarding use of a factor combination when marginal rate of technical subsititution (*MRTS*) between factors is equal to the ratio of factor prices.
4. Given the prices of the two factors for the individual firm, explain the conditions for producing a given output at the least cost.
5. Capital-labour ratio has been increasing in the Indian manufacturing industry over time. What possible explanations can be offered for this increase in capital intensity.

   [Hints: One possible reason is that the rise in wage rate of labour due to which factor price ratio $\frac{w}{r}$ has been increasing which has led the producers to substitute capital for labour. As a result, capital-labour ratio has risen. An alternative explanation can be the nature of technology used which determines the nature of production function which, with given factor prices, influences the shape of the expansion path. Besides, change in technology over time can be such that makes the production function capital-biased. In both these, the nature of production function and therefore the expansion path is such that, with given prices of labour and capital, capital-labour ratio will be increasing).

6. Show with the help of isoquant diagram how a rise in wage rate of labour, price of capital remaining the same, will affect the use of labour and capital.
7. Show with the isoquant-iso-cost apparatus, a firm is in equilibrium with regard to the use of factors when the ratios of marginal products of factors to their respective prices are equal.
8. Show that maximisation of output subject to a given cost constraint and minimisation of cost subject to a given output yield identical results.
9. What is an expansion path? Show that expansion path of a linear homogeneous production function is a straight line from the origin.
10. Explain using isoquants (*a*) the effect of rise in wage rate of labour, price of capital remaining constant, on the use of labour and capital, (*b*) the effect of fall in price of capital, wage rate of labour remaining the same.
11. Explain using isoquants-iso-cost apparatus how a change in price of a factor is split up into output effect and substitution effect.
12. What is meant by economic efficiency in the use of resources in production? In the diagram given below, *AB* is the given iso-cost line and Q_1 is the isoquant representing 100 units of output. Does the factor combination depicted by point *N* in the diagram represent economically efficient use of resources?

[**Hints:** Economic efficiency in the use of resources means either minimisation of cost for a given output or maximisation of output for a given cost-outlay. In the diagram point *N* does not represent economically efficient use of resource, because this does not ensure maximum output for a given iso-cost line. It will be rational behaviour on the part of the firm to move down along the given iso-cost line *AB* by substituting labour for capital as in doing so it will be reaching higher isoquants representing higher levels of output. As shown in Fig. 14.12, the firm will reach the efficient factor combination at point *E* at which the given iso-cost line is tangent to the isoquant Q_2 representing 150 units of output. Thus, at point *E* the firm uses L_2 amount of labour and K_2 amount of capital and maximises output with a given iso-cost line. Note that at point *E*, $MRTS_{LK} = \frac{w}{r}$.]

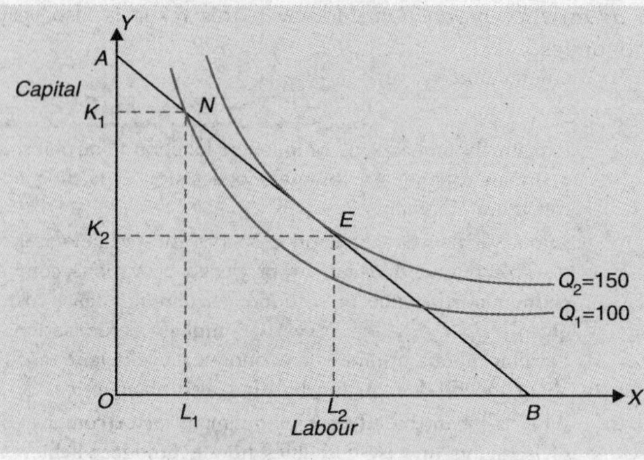

Fig. 14.12.

13. A firm is operating with a optimum factor combination of laour and capital. How will it be affected if wage rate of labour rises ?

14. Given the two factor product in, $Q = 150\ L^{0.5}\ K^{0.5}$, wage rate of labour equal to Rs 50 and rental cost of capital equal to Rs 40. Determine the amounts of labour and capital that will minimise the cost of producing 1118 units of output.

APPENDIX TO CHAPTER 14

MATHEMATICAL TREATMENT OF PRODUCTION THEORY

This appendix deals with the mathematical derivation of cost minimisation and its dual output maximisation problems of production theory.

Choice of Inputs : Cost Minimisation for a Given Output

Consider a firm that uses labour (*L*) and capital (*K*) to produce output (*Q*). Let *w* is the price of labour, that is, wage rate and *r* is the price of capital and *C* is the cost incurred to produce a level of output is given by

$$C = wL + rK \qquad \ldots(i)$$

The objective of the firm is to minimise cost for producing a given level of output. Let the production function is given by the following

$$Q = f(L,K)$$

In general there are several labour-capital combinations to produce a given level of output. Which combination of factors a firm should choose that will minimise its total cost of production to produce a given level of output. Thus, the problem of constrained minimisation is:

$$\text{minimise } C = wL + rK$$

subject to produce a given level of output, say Q_1, that satisfies the following production function

$$Q = f(L, K)$$

The choice of an optimal factor combination can be obtained through using Lagrangian method. Let us first form the Lagrangian function which is given below

$$Z = wL + rK + \lambda\,[Q_1 - f(L, K)] \qquad ...(ii)$$

where λ is Lagrangian multiplier

For minimisation of cost it is necessary that partial derivatives of Z with respect to L, K and λ be zero

$$\frac{\partial Z}{\partial L} = w - \frac{\lambda \partial f(L, K)}{\partial L} = 0 \qquad ...(iii)$$

$$\frac{\lambda \partial Z}{\partial K} = r - \frac{\lambda \partial f(L, K)}{\partial K} = 0 \qquad ...(iv)$$

$$\frac{\partial Z}{\partial \lambda} = Q_1 - f(L, K) = 0 \qquad ...(v)$$

Note that $\frac{\partial f(L, K)}{\partial L}$ and $\frac{\partial f(L, K)}{\partial K}$ are the marginal physical products of labour and capital respectively. It will also be noticed that the equation (v) is the given production function. Rewriting the above equations we have

$$w - \lambda\, MP_L = 0 \qquad ...(vi)$$

$$r - \lambda\, MP_K = 0 \qquad ...(vii)$$

$$Q_1 = f(L, K) \qquad ...(viii)$$

By combining the two equations (vi) and (vii) we have

$$\frac{w}{r} = \frac{MP_L}{MP_K} \qquad .....(ix)$$

Equation (ix) shows that total cost is minimised when the factor price ratio $\frac{w}{r}$ equals the ratio of marginal physical products of labour and capital. Since the ratio of marginal products of the two factors equals the marginal rate of technical substitution ($MRTSxy$), optimal or cost-minimising quantities of the two factors are obtained when we have

$$\frac{w}{r} = \frac{MP_L}{MP_K} = MRTS_{LK}$$

By rearranging the equation (ix) we get the following necessary condition for choice of optimal factor combination :

$$\frac{MR_L}{w} = \frac{MR_K}{r} \qquad ...(x)$$

From the above equation (x) it follows that when price of capital (r) falls, wage rate remaining constant, $\frac{MR_K}{r} > \frac{MR_L}{w}$. This will induce the firm to substitute capital for labour so that MP_K falls and in this way $\frac{MP_K}{r}$ becomes equal to $\frac{MP_K}{w}$ again to obtain a new cost-minimising factor combination.

Finally, we combine the two equations (vi) and (vii) in an alternative way to obtain the value of Lagrangian multiplier λ. Thus

$$\lambda = \frac{w}{MP_L} \text{ and } \lambda = \frac{r}{MP_K}$$

$$\lambda = \frac{w}{MP_L} = \frac{r}{MP_K}$$

Suppose output is increased by one unit. Since the marginal product of labour measures the extra output obtained by using an additional unit of labour, $\frac{1}{MP_L}$ represents the extra labour required to produce one unit of output, $\frac{w}{MP_L}$ measures the extra or marginal cost on labour of producing an additional unit of output. Similarly, $\frac{r}{MP_K}$ measures the marginal cost of producing an extra unit of output by using an additional unit of capital. It is thus clear that Lagrange multiplier (λ) equals marginal cost of output because it tells us how much addition to cost occurs when an extra unit of output is produced by using an additional unit of labour or capital.

Duality of Cost-Minimisation Problem : Output-Maximisation With a Given Cost

In the field of both consumer theory and production theory, for every minimisation problem there is corresponding maximisation problem and vice versa. In other words, for every minimisation problem there is corresponding dual problem of maximisation and vice versa. The solution of both the primal problem and its dual is the same. We explain below the dual nature of optimal choice of factor combination used for production of a commodity.

The dual of the primal problem of cost-minimisation for producing a given level of output is maximisation of output for a *given cost*. In other words, for a given iso-cost line the dual problem for a firm is to choose a factor combination that enables it to reach the highest production isoquant which is tangent to the given iso-cost line. Thus the dual problem of cost minimisation is of the following type

$$\text{Maximise } Q = f(L, K) \quad \ldots(i)$$

Subject to cost constant: $$C_0 = r.L + rK \quad \ldots(ii)$$

Lagrangian expression for the above constrained maximisation problem is

$$Z = f(L, K) + \lambda\,(C_0 - w.L - rK)$$

where C_0 is the given amount of cost, λ is the Lagrangian multiplier. For maximisation of output with a given cost, the necessary conditions are that partial derivatives of Lagrangeian function with respect to L, K and λ be zero, Thus

$$\frac{\partial Z}{\partial L} = \frac{\partial f(L,K)}{\partial L} - \lambda w = 0 \quad \ldots\text{(iii)}$$

$$\frac{\partial Z}{\partial K} = \frac{\partial f(L,K)}{\partial K} - \lambda r = 0 \quad \ldots\text{(iv)}$$

$$\frac{\partial Z}{\partial \lambda} = C_0 - w.L - rK = 0 \quad \ldots\text{(v)}$$

Note that $\frac{\partial f(L,K)}{\partial L} = MP_L$ and $\frac{\partial f(L,K)}{\partial K} = MP_K$. Further note that the equation (*v*) represents the budget constraint (that is, the equation of the iso-cost line). Therefore, rewriting the above equations we have

$$MP_L - \lambda w = 0 \quad \ldots(vi)$$

$$MP_K - \lambda r = 0 \quad \ldots(vii)$$

$$wL + rK = C_0 \quad \ldots(viii)$$

Combining the equations (*vi*) and (*vii*) we have

$$\frac{MP_L}{w} = \frac{MP_K}{r} \quad \ldots(ix)$$

It will be seen from equation (*ix*) that necessary condition for output maximisation with a given cost is the same for as the one we obtained for cost-minimisation problem for a given level of output.

Cost Analysis

Introduction

In the last two chapters we studied the nature of production function underlying the production process of goods. The production function, along with the prices of factors, and the state of technology determine to an appreciable degree the supply of goods. In this chapter we carry further the analysis of the forces determining supply of goods. We shall examine here how the costs of production of the firm depend on the nature of physical production function. We will be mainly concerned with how the cost of production varies with the increase in the level of output of the firm. In other words, we shall study how the cost and level of output are related to each other. The relation between cost and output is called "*cost function*". The cost function of the firm depends upon the physical production function, the prices of the factors used for production and the technology used for production. How much cost a firm will incur on production depend on the level of output, given the factor prices and the state of technology. The quantity of a product that will be offered by the firm for supply in the market will depend to a great degree upon the cost of production incurred on the various possible levels of output. Cost of production is the most important factor governing the supply of a product. It should be pointed out here that it is assumed that for each level of output, the firm chooses least-cost combination of factors. We shall explain below the various concepts of costs that are used in modern economic theory and then turn to study the derivation of the short-run and the long-run cost curves, However, to begin with, we shall draw distinction between technical efficiency and economic efficiency as they are intimately connected with the study of costs of production.

TECHNICAL EFFICIENCY VERSUS ECONOMIC EFFICIENCY

Before explaining the theory of cost, it is worthwhile to make clear the notion of economic efficiency in the use of resources as it is intimately related to the cost of production. In the last few chapters we have studied the concepts of physical production function and isoquants. In the study of both the production function and the isoquants representing it, economists take it granted that resources are used by the producers with technical efficiency. By *technical efficiency we mean that the maximum possible output is obtained from a given set of inputs*. It may be noted that in the description of production function and in drawing the isoquants it is assumed that producer has in fact attained the technical efficiency in the use of resources or factors. If the use of resources is not technically efficient, it will involve the *waste of resources*. However, it is primarily the concern of management and engineers to attain this technical efficiency in the use of resources so that scarce resources are not wasted.

Though this question of technical efficiency is highly important, economists are not generally concerned with it. Economists examine the question that with, the given prices of various resources or factors, which production process or factor combination, a producer will employ for producing a *given level of output* of a commodity which minimises the cost of production. *The economic efficiency therefore implies the use of production process or resource combination which ensures the minimisation of cost incurred on using resources to produce a given level of output.* Thus whereas engineers are primarily concerned with getting *maximum output* from a given amount of physical inputs, economists are essentially concerned with *maximising the output* from a given level of *cost* (i.e. value of inputs used) or minimising cost for a given level of output. Economic efficiency is achieved when a rupee's worth of inputs yields largest possible output. In the theory of production and cost, the prices of inputs and outputs are assumed to be given and constant for the producer. As explained in a previous chapter, for deciding which factor combination or production process a firm will choose to produce a level of output, given the prices of inputs, the problem which a firm faces is not of technical efficiency but of economic efficiency. Indeed, in that analysis, it was taken for granted that technical efficiency of resources had already been attained and the isoquants depicting the production function drawn represented only the technically efficient combinations of factors; each isoquant represents various technically efficient factor combinations to produce a given level of output. The achievement of economic efficiency requires that the firm should choose a factor combination that minimises cost of production for producing a given level of output or that maximises output for a given level of cost outlay. We saw in a previous chapter that the producer achieves economic efficiency in resource use when for the production of a commodity he chooses a factor combination at which marginal rate of substitution between two factors equals the ratio of factor prices $(MRS_{LK} = \frac{w}{r})$. It is thus clear that to make economically efficient use of resources, the producer has to take into account not only the physical productivity of factors (*i.e.* MRS_{LK} which is equal to the ratio of $\frac{MPP_L}{MPP_K}$) but also the prices of factors employed for production.

It is important to note that in the theory of cost we assume that for each level of output a producer uses economically efficeint production process or the least-cost factor combination. In other words, a producer chooses a factor combination which lies on the expansion path corresponding to a given level of output. In fact, as we will explain later, how the long-run total cost curve is derived from the firm's expansion path which represents economically efficient factor combinations for the production of different levels of output.

THE CONCEPTS OF COST

The term cost has different meaning. Accountants view of cost is different from that of economists. The accountants tend to focus on the explicit and historical costs. On the other hand, economists emphasise that for efficient decision making by the firm it is the *opportunity cost* rather than explicit and historical cost that must be considered. And, as will be explained below, the opportunity cost concept includes both the explicit and implicit costs. It is therefore necessary that we should explain the meaning of cost as used by economists and which is relevant for managerial decision making.

Opportunity Cost

The concept of opportunity cost is a basic concept of cost in economics. As the resources of the society are scarce, we cannot produce all goods that the people may desire. Therefore, when more resources are allocated to one product, some other product has to be foregone or sacrificed. The opportunity cost of a product is therefore the value of the next best alternative product that is forgone so as to release resources for greater production of the former.

The knowledge of opportunity cost is essential for managerial decision making as the manager is also faced with the problem of constrained optimisation. He works with a budget constraint. Whenever more resources are allocated by him to one division or department of the firm, they have to be withdrawn from another and therefore the opportunity cost is involved. For example, if some resources are allocated to Research and Development (R & D) Division, it may result in withdrawal of resources from Production Department which means reduction in the current output of the product, though allocation of more resources to R & D may result in more and better products in future yielding more profits to the firm in future. Of course, such a decision should be made if the management is quite sure that greater profits in future will outweigh the loss of output and profits in the current period.

However, in the theory of costs we are more concerned with opportunity cost of a factor of production used in the production of a commodity. In this sense the opportunity cost of an input or factor of production is *its value* (*i.e. earnings*) *in the next best alternative use or employment.* The firm must consider the opportunity cost of all inputs and factors of production. If a firm pays a factor lower price than it can get in any other firm or use, it will not be able to retain it. That is, actual payment to an input or a factor of production which is called explicit cost must not be less than its opportunity cost, otherwise it will not be able to retain it.

Similarly, it will not be worthwhile for the firm to use a self-owned factor in its business if it can get a higher price by *selling* it to others, or hiring it out to others. For example, if an entrepreneur has set up his firm and manages his own business, he foregoes the salary that he could have earned for working as a manager in another's firm. Similarly, if an entreprenur invests his own financial capital in his firm, he foregoes interest or return that he could earn by investing that in fixed deposits in banks or purchasing shares of companies. The interest which he could earn on fixed deposits or return which he could get by making investment of his financial capital in shares of other companies is the opportunity cost of financial capital which he invests in his own business. The salary which an entrepreneur gets elsewhere by working as a manager and return on his financial capital which he can get by investing elsewhere are the implicit costs which are not generally considered by accountants in their financial statement of the firm must be taken into account in rational decision making by management of the firm.

It follows from above that economic opportunity costs include both explicit and implicit costs and therefore both should be taken into account in rational decision making by management. Thus both the explicit and implicit costs are relevant and therefore must be considered while making decision regarding whether to produce a product or use inputs for its production. The failure to consider the opportunity cost and rely on historical cost will lead to inefficient decision. An example will bring out the importance of the opportunity cost in making optimal managerial decisions. Let us consider the problem of *inventory evaluation.* Suppose a firm purchased a raw material at price of Rs. 1000 per quintal. The accountant would continue to consider the value of the inventory of raw material at its historical cost, namely, Rs.1000 per quintal. However, the economists would consider the value of inventory of raw material at its current price at which it can be presently replaced . If a firm considers the historical cost of inventories of raw materials rather than their current replacement value, it may take a wrong decision. For example, on the basis of higher historical cost of the raw material it may decide not to produce the commodity in whose production it is used because it would involve losses. But if the raw material is valued at its current replacement price of Rs. 600 per quintal it may be profitable to produce the commodity.

The resources which are used for the manufacture of armaments may also be used for the production of cars or other automobiles. Therefore, the opportunity cost of production of an armament is the output of cars and other automobiles foregone or sacrificed, which could have been produced with the same amount of factors that have gone into the making of an armament. To lake another example, a farmer who is producing wheat, can also produce potatoes with the same factors. Therefore, the opportunity cost of a quintal of wheat is the amount of output of potatoes given up. Thus, the opportunity-cost of anything is the next best alternative that could be produced instead by the same resources having the same monetary value.

The alternative or opportunity cost of a good can be given a money value. In order to produce a good the producer has to employ various factors of production and has to pay them sufficient prices to get their services. These factors have alternative uses. The factors must be paid at least the price they are able to obtain in the alternative uses. The opportunity cost of a factor to a firm is its earnings in the next best alternative use. For instance, consider the case of a farmer who works on his own farm. While calculating cost he must take into account the wages of his own labour rendered on his farm. These wages must be equal to the maximum wages that he would earn if he worked as hired labour on other farms. The maximum wages earned elsewhere by a farmer is the opportunity cost of his labour rendered on his own farm. The total alternative earnings in the next best use of the various factors, both supplied by others to the entrepreneur and those supplied by the entrepreneur himself employed in the production of a good will constitute the opportunity cost of the good.

A significant fact worth mentioning is that *relative prices of goods tend to reflect their opportunity costs*. The resources will remain employed in the production of a particular good when they are being paid at least the money rewards that are sufficient to induce them to stay in the industry, *i.e.*, equal to the value they are able to obtain and create elsewhere. In other words, a collection of factors employed in the production of a good must be paid equal to their opportunity costs. The greater the opportunity cost of the collection of factors used in the production of a goods, the greater must be the price of the goods. Thus, if the same collection of factors can produce either one tractor or 2 scooters, then the price of one tractor will be twice that of one scooter.

However, it may be noted that *market prices of goods do not always reflect their true social opportunity costs*. This is because the market prices of factors or resources used for the production of commodities may fail to reflect their opportunity costs from the social point of view (*i.e.* their true scarcity value or the true cost of diverting resources from alternative uses in the economy as a whole). This may occur for a number of reasons such as government regulation and control of prices of some inputs and resources, imposition of indirect taxes on various inputs, presence of monopoly or imperfect competition in the production and supply of resources or inputs under which higher prices are charged than justified on the basis of their scarcity values. For example, labour in India is abundant and a large magnitude of unemployment of labour prevails in the Indian economy and therefore its scarcity value is zero, that is, from the social point of view, opportunity cost of labour is zero. But due to several social and institutional factors, labour commands a price in the market which the entrepreneurs will have to include in their private costs of production. Similarly, in India due to the cheap credit policy, liberal depreciation allowance on investment granted to the business entrepreneurs in the corporate taxation policy and until recently before the policy of liberalisation the higher exchange rate of rupee kept by the government had made the effective price of capital lower than warranted by its scarcity in the Indian economy. Thus, the higher market price of labour and the lower price of capital than their social opportunity costs or their scarcity values have encouraged the chioce of capital-intensive techniques and production processes in the Indian industries. This has stood in the way of minimizing social opportunity costs which is generaly assumed in the economic theory.

Historical Costs as Sunk Costs. There is an important difference between the approach of economists from accountants regarding the treatment of fixed costs incurred on durable capital goods such as machines, buildings. The accountants take *historical costs* of these capital goods, that is, the price at which they were originally purchsed and a given percentage of the original price is taken as *depreciation* which is charged to current costs of production per year. However, economists consider the historical costs as *sunk cost* which is irrelevant to the current costs of production and therefore cannot be the basis of decision-making with regard to production and pricing of commodities. Sunk costs are those expenditures that cannot be recovered. The economists adopt the principle that "bygones are bygones" and consider the current opportunity costs of these capital goods after they have been acquired that is relevant for decision making in the current period. If the capital goods can be put to an alternative use or can be let out to others, the earnings in the next best alternative or the rental value of the machines if they are hired by others would constitute the opportunity costs of these capital goods and could be counted by the economists as part of the current cost of production. However, if the durable capital goods, especially specialised equipment such as machines, have no alternative use, their opportunity cost will be zero and economists would not include them in current costs of production, despite their depreciation during a year. It may, however, be noted that conventional accounting method of including depreciation charge in current cost of production may be useful for other purposes, for instance, for determining income tax liability. But economists look at things from the point of view of opportunity costs which affect the decision-making process. Thus, when determining the rental value of specialised capital equipment, economists consider its opportunity cost and ignore its historical price.

Accounting Costs and Economic Costs

The difference between accounting costs and economic costs requires further consideration. This difference also makes clear the meaning of economic profits. The accounting costs are called *explicit costs* which include wages to hire labour, prices of raw materials fuel and semifinished products purchased for use in production and rental price of capital equipment and buildings. When an entrepreneur undertakes an act of production, he has to pay prices for the factors which he employs for production. He thus pays wages to the labourers employed, prices for the raw materials, fuel and power used, rent for the building he hires for the production work, and the rate of interest on the money borrowed for doing business. All these are included in his cost of production. *An accountant will take into account only the* expenditure incurred on buying or hiring various inputs or factors for use in production.

But an economist's view of cost is somewhat different from this. It generally happens that the entrepreneur invests a certain amount of his own money capital in his business. If the money capital invested by the entrepreneur in his own business had been invested elsewhere, it would have earned a certain amount of interest or dividends. Further, an entrepreneur devotes times to his own work of production and contributes his entrepreneurial and managerial ability to it. If the entrepreneur had not set up his own business, he would have worked as manager in some other's firm on salary basis. The economists, therefore, also include in his costs of production the opportunity costs of the self-owned factors. Thus, in calculation of costs the economists will include *(i) the normal return on money capital* invested by the enterpreneur himself in his own business, which he could have earned if invested elsewhere. Normal return on his own capital invested by the entrepreneur in his own business is in fact the opportunity cost of his money capital, and *(ii) the wages or salary* he could have earned if he sold his services to others as a manager or consultant. The accountants do not include these two items in cost of production but the economists consider them as bona fide costs and will accordingly include them. Likewise, the money rewards for other factors such as building owned by the entrepreneur himself and employed by him in his own business are also considered by the economists as costs of production.

Thus, the accountants consider those costs which involve actual *cash payments by the entrepreneur of the firm to others*, the economists take into account all of these *accounting costs*, but in addition, they also take into account the amount of money the entrepreneur could have earned if he had invested his money capital and sold his own services and other factors in the next best alternative uses. *The accounting costs or actual contractual cash payments which the firm makes to other factor owners for purchasing or hiring the various factors are also known as explicit costs.* The normal return on money capital invested by the entrepreneur and the wages or salary for his services and the opportunity costs of the other factors the entrepreneur himself owns and employs them in his firm are known as *implicit costs or imputed costs.* The economists take into consideration both the explicit and implicit costs. Therefore,

Economic Costs = Accounting costs (i.e. explicit costs) + Implicit costs

It is worthwhile to note that the concept of opportunity cost explained above is not confined to the firm's implicit cost alone. The concept of opportunity cost applies to the explicit costs also. For example, when a firm buys raw materials, it foregoes the opportunity of purchasing something else with the same amount of money that he has spent on the raw materials. Therefore, from the point of view of the firm money value of the raw materials paid by it reflects their opportunity cost. Thus the explicit costs are also the private opportunity costs.

It may be pointed out that the firm will earn *economic profits* only if it is making revenue *in excess of the total of explicit and implicit costs.* Thus, when the firm is in no profit and no loss position, it means that the firm is making revenue equal to the sum of explicit and implicit costs and no more. Therefore,

Economic Profits = Total Revenue – Economic Costs

Since the economic costs are sum of the explicit and implicit costs, economic profits can be defined and measured as under:

Economic Profits = Total Revenue – (Explicit costs + Implicit costs)

Among the implicit costs which economists take into account but accountants ignore them, mention may be made of *normal profits.* These normal profits are not the true profits as understood in economics. The normal profits are defined as the necessary payments that must be made to the entrepreneur in order to retain him in the present business or industry. Obviously, if the entrepreneur leaves his own business, he can be employed by another firm as a manager or executive which is generally taken to be his next best occupation or job. If the entrepreneur in his next best job of a manager earns Rs. 50,000 per month as salary or wages, he must earn this much amount in his own business and therefore this would constitute his normal profits. As a matter of fact, in his own business he does perform certain managerial functions such as bringing together various factors, bringing about coordination among them to do a particular work of production and supervising them. Thus normal profits are actually wages or salary for managerial services rendered by the entrepreneur in his own business which he must earn if he is to stay in his own business. If he is unable to get this normal reward for this managerial services performed, he will go to his next best alternative as a manager in another's firm. It is thus clear that normal profits are his opportunity costs or transfer earnings and like other opportunity costs of other productive services, they should also be included in the implicit costs of production.

THE THEORY OF COST

Cost Functions : Short Run and Long Run

From the view point of the changes in cost of production, the economists draw distinction between the short-run costs and long-run costs. The short-run costs are those costs which are incurred by the firm during a period in which some factors, especially, capital equipment, land and management are held constant. The short-run costs are incurred on the purchases of labour, raw materials, chemicals, fuel etc. which vary with the changes in the level of output. On the other hand, the long-run costs are the costs incurred during a period which is sufficiently long to allow the variation in all factors of production including capital equipment, land and managerial staff to produce output.

As explained earlier, the long-run cost function refers to the change in cost when output is varied by changing the quantities of all factors used for the production of a commodity. Besides, as emphasised earlier, the long-run cost function represents the minimum cost incurred on factors used for producing various levels of output, given the prices of factors or inputs. Further, the level of technology is also assumed to remain constant in deriving the long-run cost function. We shall explain later how a *long-run average cost curve representing the long-run cost function is derived from the expansion path* of the firm. Recall that expansion path is the locus of optimum or least-cost factor combinations used for producing various levels of output.

It is important to note that *effect of changes in technology and factor prices on cost of production are shown to cause a shift in the function,* either downward or upward as the case may be. For instance, the improvement in technology raises the productivity of factors and will therefore cause the long-run cost function to shift downward. On the other hand, increase in factor prices will raise the cost of production and shift the cost function upward. Therefore, the determinants of cost of production other than the level of output are called *shift factors.*

Short-Run Cost Function

The short-run is defined as a period of time in which output of a firm can be increased or decreased by changing the amounts of variable factors such as labour, raw materials, chemicals, fuel etc. while the quantity of such factors as capital equipment, building remaining fixed. Thus in the short run a firm's manager cannot decide to build a new plant or abondon an old one. If a firm wants to increase output in the short run, it can do so only by using more labour and raw materials. It cannot increase output in the short run by expanding the capacity of the existing plant or building a new plant with a larger capacity. Therefore, the short-run cost function relates the cost of production with level of output where capital (and other fixed factors) are held constant along with the given technology and given factor prices. The difference between the short-run and long-run cost function is that whereas in the former the cost-output relation is studied with a certain amount of capital or land fixed, the long-run cost function examines the relation between cost output when capital and land also vary along with the variable factors such as labour, raw materials. In both the short-run and long-run cost functions we study the relation between the cost and level of output *i.e.*, $C = f(Q)$, the difference lies in factors that are varied to expand or contract output . Whereas in the long run, the advancement in technology and changes in factor prices cause a shift in the long-run cost function, in the short-run, besides technology and factor prices some fixed factors such as capital or land also bring about a shift in the cost function.

As has been pointed out above, in deriving the cost function or cost curve, especially in the long run it is assumed that every level of output of a commodity is produced at the minimum possible cost. This implies that it is assumed that the firm employs optimum or economically efficient resource combinations. Thus every point on the long-run cost function or long-run cost curve represents the use of optimum resource combination so as to ensure minimum cost of production for each level of output. Even in the short run, it is assumed that given the size of the plant (*i.e.*, capital equipment), the firms operate to minimise cost for producing various levels of output.

Total Fixed and Variable Costs in the Short Run

There are some inputs or factors which can be readily adjusted with the changes in the output level. Thus, a firm can readily employ more workers, if it has to increase output. Likewise, it can secure and use more raw materials, more chemicals without much delay if it has to expand production. Thus, labour, raw materials, chemicals etc., are the factors which can be readily varied with the change in output. Such factors are called variable factors. On the other hand, there are factors such as capital equipment, factory building, top management personnel which cannot be so readily varied. It requires a comparatively long time to make variations in them. It takes time to expand a factory building or to build a new factory building with larger area or capacity. Similarly, it also takes time to order and install new machinery. The factors such as raw materials, labour, etc., which can be readily varied with the change in the output level are known as variable factors and the factors such as capital equipment, building which cannot be readily varied and require comparatively a long time to make adjustment in them are called fixed factors.

Corresponding to this distinction between variable factors and fixed factors, economists distinguish between the short run and the long run. *The short run is a period of time in which output can be increased or decreased by changing only the amount of variable factors such as labour, raw materials, chemicals,* etc,. In the short run, quantities of the fixed factors such as capital equipment, factory building etc., cannot be varied for making changes in output. Thus, in the short run, the firm cannot build a new plant or abandon an old one. If the firm wants to increase output in the short run, it can only do so by using more labour and more raw materials, it cannot increase output in the short run by expanding the capacity of its existing plant or building a new plant with a larger capacity. Thus, the short run is a period of time in which only the quantities of variable factors can be varied, while the quantities of the fixed factors remain unaltered.

On the other hand, *the long run is defined as the period of time in which the quantities of all factors may be varied.* All factors being variable in the long run, the fixed and variable factors dichotomy holds good only in the short run. In the long run, the output can be increased not only by using more quantities of labour and raw materials but also by expanding the size of the existing plant or by building a new plant with a larger productive capacity. It may be noted that the word 'plant' in economics stands for a collection of fixed factors, such as factory building, machinery installed, the organisation represented by the manager and other essential skilled personnel. As mentioned above, even in the long run, it is assumed that while calculating costs and drawing cost curves, *prices* of inputs, (*i.e.*, the prices of resources and factors) and the *technology* (*i.e.*, the state of arts) remain constant. Whenever there is change in prices of inputs or the progress in technology, even the long-run cost curves will shift.

Total Fixed Costs. Having explained the difference between the fixed factors and the variable factors and also between the short run and the long run, we are in a position to distinguish between the fixed costs and the variable costs which when added together make up total costs of a business. Fixed costs are those which are independent of output, that is, they do not change with changes in output. These costs are a 'fixed' amount which must be incurred by a firm in the short run, whether the output is small or large. Even if the firm closes down for some time in the short run but remains in business, these costs have to be borne by it. Fixed costs are also known as *overhead costs* and include charges such as contractual rent, insurance fee, maintenance costs, property taxes, interest on the borrowed funds, minimum administrative expenses such as manager's salary, watchman's wages etc. Thus fixed costs are those which are incurred in hiring the fixed factors of production whose amount cannot by altered in the short run.

Total Variable Cost. Variable costs, on the other hand, are those costs which are incurred on the employment of variable factors of production whose amount can be altered in the short run. Thus, the total variable costs change with changes in output in the short run, i.e., they increase or decrease when the output rises or falls. These costs include payments to labour employed, the prices of the raw material, fuel and power used, the expenses incurred on transportation and the like. If a firm shuts down for some time in the short run, it will not use the variable factors of production and will not therefore incur any variable costs. Variable costs are made only when some amount of output is produced and the total variable costs, increase with the increase in the level of production. Variable costs are also called *prime costs or direct costs*. Total costs of a business are the sum of its total variable costs and total fixed costs. Thus:

$$TC = TFC + TVC$$

Because one component, *i.e.*, the total variable cost (TVC) varies with the change in output, the total cost of production will also respond to changes in the level of output. The total cost increases as the level of output increases. The way in which fixed, variable and total costs are estimated are shown in Table 15.1 where for the sake of convenience it is assumed that labour is the only variable factor and daily wage per worker is Rs. 60. The second column gives how the output changes with the increase in the number of workers to produce cloth. It is further assumed that "fixed cost is Rs. 120 per day whether or not cloth is produced on any day. By multiplying the wage rate W (Rs. 60) with the number of workers (L) employed for the production of cloth we get the total variable costs ($W.L$) in the short run which is given in the column IV. By adding the fixed cost of Rs. 120 to the variable costs at different levels of labour employment we get the short-run total cost ($STC = TVC + TFC$) which is given in

Table 15.1. Fixed, Variable and Total Costs in the Short Run

Number of Workers (*L*)	Output (Metres of Cloth Produced Per Day) (*Q*)	Daily Wages per Worker (*W*)	Total Variable Costs (*W.L.*)	Total Fixed Costs (*TFC*)	Short-Run Total Cost (*TVC+TFC*)
I	II	III	IV	V	VI
0	0	Rs. 60	0	Rs. 120	Rs. 120
1	10	60	Rs. 60	120	180
2	22	60	120	120	240
3	36	60	180	120	300
4	52	60	240	120	360
5	70	60	300	120	420
6	86	60	360	120	480
7	100	60	420	120	540
8	112	60	480	120	600
9	122	60	540	120	660
10	130	60	600	120	720
11	137	60	660	120	780
12	143	60	720	120	840
13	148	60	780	120	900
14	152	60	840	120	960
15	155	60	900	120	1020

column VI. It will be seen from column V that total fixed costs remain fixed at Rs. 120 whatever the level of output. Column VI reveals that short-run total cost increases as output is expanded by increasing the employment of workers. The short-run total fixed and variable costs curves are portrayed in Fig. 15.1 where output is measured on the *X*-axis and cost on *Y*-axis. Since the total fixed cost remains constant whatever the level of output, the total fixed cost curve (*TFC*) is parallel to the *X*-axis. It will be seen from Fig. 15.1 that total fixed cost curve (*TFC*) starts from a point on the *Y*-axis meaning thereby that the total fixed cost will be incurred even if the output is zero. On the other hand, the total variable cost curve (*TVC*) rises upward showing thereby that as the output is increased, the total variable cost also increases. The total variable cost curve *TVC* starts from the origin which shows that when output is zero the variable costs are also nil.

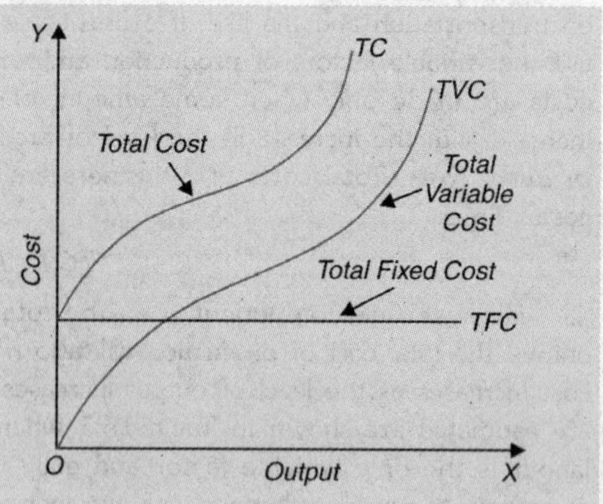

Fig. 15.1. *Short-Run Total Cost Curves*

It should be noted that total cost (*TC*) is function of the total output (*Q*); the greater the output, the greater will be the total cost. In symbols, we write:

$$TC = f(Q)$$

We can prove this as follows:

$$TC = TFC + TVC$$

Suppose *TFC* is equal to *K* which is a constant amount whatever the level of output. *TVC* is equal to the amount used of the variable factor say, labour, *L*, multiplied by the given price of the variable factor, say, *w*,

$$TVC = L.w$$

$$TC = \overline{K} + L.w. \qquad ...(i)$$

Now, *L.w.*, that is, *TVC* must rise with the increase in output in the short run because only by increase in the amount of variable factor, that is, by increase in *L*, that the output can be increased. From equation (*i*) it follows that with the increase in *L.w* as output rises, *TC* must also rise. In other words, total cost (*TC*) is a function of total output (*q*) and varies directly with it.

Total cost curve (*TC*) has been obtained by adding up vertically total fixed cost curve and total variable cost curve because the total cost is sum of total fixed cost and total variable cost at various levels of output. It will be seen that the vertical distance between the *TVC* and *TC* curves in Fig. 15.1 is constant throughout. This is because the vertical distance between the *TVC* and *TC* curve represents the amount of total fixed cost which remains unchanged as output is increased in the short run. It should also be noted that the vertical distance between the total cost curve (*TC*) and total fixed cost curve (*TFC*) represents the amount of total variable costs which increase with the increase in output. The shape of the total cost curve (*TC*) is exactly the same as that of total variable cost curve (*TVC*) because the same vertical distance always separates the two curves.

THE SHORT-RUN AVERAGE AND MARGINAL COST CURVES

We have explained above the short-run total cost curves. However, the cost concept is more frequently used both by businessmen and economists in the form of cost per unit, or average costs rather than total costs. We, therefore, pass on to the study of short-run *average cost curves.*

Average Fixed Cost (*AFC*)

Average fixed cost is the total fixed costs divided by the number of units of output produced. Therefore,

$$AFC = \frac{TFC}{Q}$$

where *Q* represents the number of units of output produced.

Thus, the average fixed cost can be obtained from dividing the total fixed cost by the level of output. In the Table 15.2 the column *VI* gives the average fixed cost as output increases. It will be seen from the table that average fixed cost is the fixed cost per unit of output. Since total fixed cost is a constant quantity (Rs. 120) average fixed cost steadily falls as output increases. Therefore, average fixed cost curve slopes downward throughout its length but it does

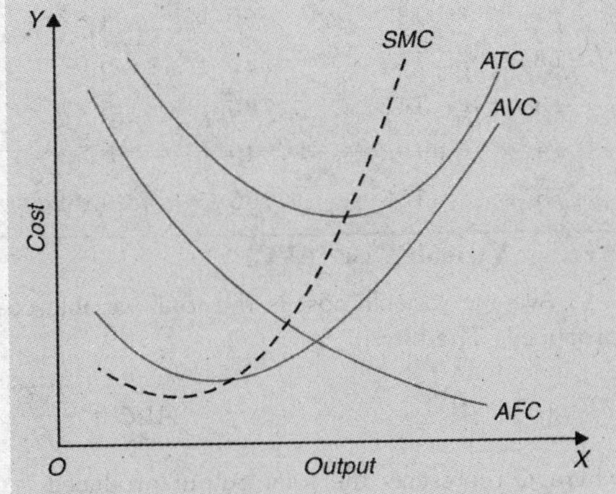

Fig. 15.2. *Short-run Average and Marginal Cost Curves*

not touch the X-axis. As output increases, the total fixed cost spreads over more and more units and therefore average fixed cost becomes less and less. When output becomes very large average fixed cost approaches zero. Average fixed cost curve (*AFC*) is shown in Fig. 15.2. It will be seen that average fixed cost curve continuously falls throughout. Mathematically speaking, average fixed cost curve approaches both axes asymptotically. In other words, the *AFC* curve gets very nearer to but never touches either axis.

The average fixed cost curve, *AFC*, possesses another important property. If we pick up any point on the average fixed cost curve and multiply the average fixed cost at that point with the corresponding quantity of output produced, then the product is always the same. This is because the product of the average fixed cost and the corresponding quantity of output will yield the total fixed cost which remains constant throughout. A curve with such a property is called *rectangular hyperbola*.

Table 15.2. Average Variable Cost, Average Fixed Cost, Average Total Cost and Marginal Cost

Number of Workers (L)	Output of Cloth (Q)	TVC (w=Rs. 60) w.L	AFC $\frac{TVC}{Q}$	TVC	AFC $\left(\frac{TFC}{Q}\right)$	ATC $\left(\frac{TVC+TFC}{Q}\right)$	MC $\left(\frac{\Delta TVC}{\Delta Q}\right)$
I	II	III	IV	V	VI	VII	VIII
0	0	0	0	Rs. 120	0	0	–
1	10	60	6	120	12	18	6.0
2	22	120	5.45	120	5.45	10.9	5
3	36	180	5.0	120	3.35	8.33	4.28
4	52	240	4.61	120	2.30	6.92	3.75
5	70	300	4.28	120	1.71	6.00	3.33
6	86	360	4.19	120	1.39	5.58	3.75
7	100	420	4.20	120	1.20	5.40	4.28
8	112	480	4.29	120	1.07	5.36	5.00
9	122	540	4.42	120	0.98	5.41	6.00
10	130	600	4.62	120	0.92	5.54	7.50
11	137	660	4.82	120	0.87	5.69	8.57
12	143	720	5.03	120	0.84	5.87	10.00
13	148	780	5.27	120	0.81	6.08	12.00
14	152	840	5.52	120	0.79	6.32	15.00
15	155	900	6.00	120	0.77	6.58	20.00

Average Variable Cost (AVC)

Average variable cost is the total variable cost divided by the number of units of output produced. Therefore,

$$AVC = \frac{TVC}{Q}$$

where Q represents the total output produced.

Thus average variable cost is variable cost per unit of output. In Table 15.2 we have obtained the average variable cost per unit of output from dividing column III which gives total variable cost (*TVC*) by column *II* which gives total output (*Q*). It will be seen that average variable cost falls until 86 units of output and thereafter it increases. The average variable cost will generally fall as output increases from zero to the normal capacity output due to the occurrence of increasing returns. But beyond the normal capacity output the average variable cost will rise steeply because of the operation of diminishing returns. The average variable cost curve is shown in Fig. 15.2 by the curve *AVC* which first falls, reaches a minimum and then rises.

Average total cost (*ATC*) is the sum of the average variable cost and average fixed cost. Therefore, as output increases and average fixed cost becomes smaller and smaller, the vertical distance, representing average fixed cost between the average total cost curve (*ATC*) and average variable cost curve (*AVC*) goes on diminishing and the average variable cost curve approaches the average total cost curve (*ATC*).

Average variable cost bears an important relationship with the average product per unit of the variable factor. Let Q stand for quantity of total product produced; L for the amount of the variable factor, say labour, used and w for the price per unit of the variable factor and AP for the average product of the variable factor. We assume that the price of the variable factor remains unaltered as more or fewer units of it are employed.

Total product (or output Q) $= AP.L$

Average variable cost, $AVC = \dfrac{TVC}{Q}$

Since the total variable cost (*TVC*) is equal to the amount of the variable factor (L) employed multiplied by the price per unit (w) of the variable factor, ($TVC = L.w$). Therefore,

$$AVC = \frac{L.w}{Q}$$

Since $$Q = AP.L,$$

$$\therefore \quad AVC = \frac{L.w}{AP.L} = \frac{w}{AP} = w\left(\frac{1}{AP}\right)$$

Thus, given the price of the variable factor w, the average variable cost is equal to the reciprocal of the average product ($\frac{1}{AP}$ is the reciprocal of AP) multiplied by the constant w. It follows that average variable cost and average product vary inversely with each other. Therefore, when average product rises in the beginning as more units of the variable factor are employed, the average variable cost must be falling. And when the average product of the variable factor falls, the average variable cost must be rising. At the level of output at which the average product is maximum the average variable cost is minimum. Thus, the average variable cost (*AVC*) curve looks like the average product (*AP*) curve turned upside down with minimum point of the *AVC* curve corresponding to the maximum point of the *AP* curve.

Average Total Cost (ATC)

The average total cost or what is called simply average cost is the total cost divided by the number of units of output produced. Thus

$$\text{Average total cost} = \frac{\text{total cost}}{\text{output}}$$

or $$ATC = \frac{TC}{Q}$$

Since the total cost is the sum of total variable cost and total fixed cost, the average total cost is also the sum of average variable cost and average fixed cost. This can be proved as follows :

$$ATC = \frac{TC}{Q}$$

Since $$TC = TVC + TFC$$

Therefore, $$ATC = \frac{TVC + TFC}{Q}$$

In Table 15.2 we have obtained the average total cost by first adding up the total variable cost and total fixed cost ($TVC + TFC$) and then dividing it by total output. Thus, in Table 15.2 we have calculated the average total cost by adding up column *III* and *V* and then dividing by output figures of column *II*. Since average total cost is sum of average variable cost and average fixed cost, we can also compute the average total cost by adding up the average variable cost, *AVC* (given in Column *IV*) and average fixed cost, *AFC* (given in Column VI). Thus :

$$ATC = \frac{STC}{Q}$$

$$= \frac{TVC + TFC}{Q} = AVC + AFC$$

It will be seen from Table 15.2 that as output increases, in the initial stages, that is, upto 112 meters of cloth production, average total cost falls and thereafter it is rising. This implies that short-run average total cost (*ATC*) curve will have a U-shape, which is shown in Figure 15.2.

ATC Curve. It needs to be emphasized that the behaviour of the average total cost curve will depend upon the behaviour of the average variable cost curve and average fixed cost curve. In the beginning, both *AVC* and *AFC* curves fall, the *ATC* curve therefore falls sharply in the beginning. When *AVC* curve begins rising, but *AFC* curve is falling steeply, the *ATC* curve continues to fall. This is because during this stage the fall in *AFC* curve weighs more than the rise in the *AVC* curve. But as output increases further, there is a sharp rise in *AVC* which more than offsets the fall in *AFC*. Therefore, the *ATC* curve rises after a point. Therefore, the average total cost curve (*ATC*) like the *AVC* curve first falls, reaches its minimum value and then rises. The average total cost curve (*ATC*) is therefore almost of a 'U'-shape.

Short-Run Marginal Cost (SMC)

The concept of marginal cost occupies an important place in economic theory. Marginal cost is *addition* to the total cost caused by producing one more unit of output. In other words, marginal cost is the addition to the total cost of producing n units instead of $n - 1$ units (*i.e.*, one less) where n is any given number. In symbols:

$$MC_n = TC_n - TC_{n-1}$$

Suppose the production of 5 units of a product involves the total cost of Rs. 206. If the increase in production to 6 units raises the total cost to Rs. 236, then marginal cost of the sixth unit of output is Rs. 30, (236 – 206 = 30). Let us illustrate the computation of marginal cost from a table of total cost and output.

Since marginal cost is a change in total cost as a result of a unit change in output, it can also be written as:

$$MC = \frac{\Delta TC}{\Delta Q}$$

where ΔTC represents a change in total cost and ΔQ represents a small change in output.

In the Table 15.3 we have explained the method of computing short-run marginal cost. When output is zero in the short run, the producer is incurring total cost of Rs. 120 which represents the total fixed cost of production. When 10 units of output are produced, the total cost rises to Rs. 180.

Table 15.3 Computation of Short-Run Marginal Cost

Output of Cloth in metres (Q)	Change in Output (ΔQ)	Total Cost (TC)	Change in Total Cost (ΔTC)	Marginal Cost (MC) $\left(\frac{\Delta TC}{\Delta Q}\right)$
0	—	Rs. 120	—	–
10	10	180	Rs. 60	Rs. 6
22	12	240	60	5
36	14	300	60	4.28
52	16	360	60	3.75
70	18	420	60	3.33
86	16	480	60	3.75
100	14	540	60	4.28
112	12	600	60	5.00
122	10	660	60	6.00
130	8	720	60	7.50
137	7	780	60	8.57
143	6	840	60	10.00
148	5	900	60	12.00
152	4	960	60	15.00
155	3	1020	60	20.00

The marginal cost of a unit of output is therefore Rs. 6 which has been obtained from dividing change in total cost (Rs. 180 - 120 = 60) by change in total output ΔQ *i.e.*, 10 – 0 = 10). Thus $MC = \frac{\Delta TC}{\Delta Q} = \frac{60}{10} = 6$. When output increases to 22 metres of cloth, the total cost increases to Rs. 240. This gives us short-run marginal cost to be equal to $\frac{240-180}{22-10} = \frac{60}{12} = 5$. Similarly, for further increases in output, the short-run marginal cost can be computed.

It will be seen from Table 15.3 that the short-run marginal cost declines until output of 70 metres of cloth is produced. With the further increases in output beyond 70 metres, short-run marginal cost rises. This means that short-run marginal cost will have a U-shape. This short-run marginal cost has been shown in Fig. 15.2 by the curve labelled as *SMC*.

If we consider the total cost curve, $\frac{\Delta TC}{\Delta Q}$ represents the slope of it. Therefore, if we want to measure the marginal cost at a certain output level, we can do so by measuring the slope of the total cost curve corresponding to that output by drawing tangent to it.

It is worth pointing out that *marginal cost is independent of the fixed costs.* Since fixed costs do not change with the change in output, there are no *marginal fixed costs* when output is increased in the short run. It is only the variable costs that vary with output in the short run. Therefore, the marginal costs are in fact due to the change in variable costs, and whatever the amount of fixed cost, the marginal cost is unaffected by it.

The independence of the marginal cost from the fixed cost can be proved algebraically as follows :

$$\begin{aligned} MC_n &= TC_n - TC_{n-1} \\ &= (TVC_n + TFC) - (TVC_{n-1} + TFC) \\ &= TCN_n + TFC - TVC_{n-1} - TFC \\ &= TVC_n - TVC_{n-1} \end{aligned}$$

Hence marginal cost is the *addition to the total variable costs* when output is increased from $n - 1$ units to n units of output. It follows, therefore, that the marginal cost is independent of the amount of the fixed costs.

Relationship Between Marginal Cost and Marginal Physical Product

It should be noted that marginal cost of production is intimately related to the marginal product of the variable factor. As explained above,

$$MC = \frac{\Delta TC}{\Delta Q}$$

Since MC is independent of fixed cost and is directly attributed to the change in total variable cost,

$$MC = \frac{\Delta TVC}{\Delta Q}$$

Since price of the variable factor *i.e.,* w is assumed to be constant, the change in total variable cost can occur due to the change in the amount of the variable factor. Threrfore,

$$MC = \frac{w \cdot \Delta L}{\Delta Q} = w \cdot \frac{\Delta L}{\Delta Q} \quad \ldots(i)$$

From our prior study of the theory of production we know that marginal product of the variable factor is the change in total product as a result of a unit change in the variable factor

$$MP = \frac{\Delta Q}{\Delta L},$$

where ΔQ stands for change in total product, ΔL stands for the change in the amount of the variable factor.

The reciprocal of the marginal product of the variable factor is

$$\frac{1}{MP} = \frac{\Delta L}{\Delta Q}$$

Substituting $\frac{1}{MP}$ for $\frac{\Delta L}{\Delta Q}$ in equation (*i*), we get

$$MC = w.\frac{1}{MP} = \frac{w}{MP} \quad ...(ii)$$

Thus, marginal cost of production is equal to the reciprocal of marginal product of the variable factor multiplied by the price of the variable factor. Therefore, marginal cost varies inversely with marginal product of the variable factor. Now, if price of the variable factor i.e. w is assumed constant, then from the relation between MC and MP represented in equation (ii), we can ascertain the shape of the marginal cost curve. We know from the study of the law of variable proportions that as output increases in the beginning, marginal product of the variable factor rises. This means that the constant w in equation (ii) is being divided by increasingly larger MP. This will cause the marginal cost (MC) to decline as output increases in the beginning. Further, according to the law of variable proportions, marginal product declines after a certain level of output, which means that now the constant w in equation (ii) is being divided by increasingly smaller MP. This causes the marginal cost (MC) to rise after a certain level of output. Thus, the fact that marginal product rises first, reaches a maximum and then declines, ensures that the marginal cost curve of a firm declines first, reaches a minimum level and then rises. In other words, marginal cost curve of a firm has a U shape.

It is clear from the above that the law of variable proportions, or in other words, the behaviour of marginal product (MP) curve determines the shape of marginal cost (MC) curve. Indeed, marginal cost (MC) curve is an inversion of the marginal product (MP) curve, with the maximum of marginal product corresponding to the minimum of marginal cost. Marginal cost is simply the transformation of marginal product from physical terms into money terms. The relation between marginal product and marginal cost is quite similar to the relationship between average product and average cost.

Three points are worth noting in regard to our above analysis of marginal cost. First, marginal cost is due to the changes in variable cost and is, therefore, independent of the fixed cost. Secondly, the shape of the marginal cost curve is determined by the law of variable proportions, that is, by the behaviour of the marginal product of the variable factor. Thirdly, the assumption that the price of variable factor remains constant as the firm expands its output is greatly significant, since a change in factor price may disturb our conclusion.

DERIVATION OF THE SHORT-RUN AVERAGE AND MARGINAL COST CURVES FROM THEIR TOTAL COST CURVES

In a previous chapter we explained how average and marginal physical product curves were derived from a total physical product curve. Likewise, average and marginal cost curves can be derived from the total cost curves. In the short run there are three types of total costs : (*i*) Total Fixed Cost (*TFC*), (ii) Total Variable Cost (*TVC*) and Short-Run Total Cost (*STC*) which is equal to the sum of total fixed cost and total variable cost ($STC = TFC + TVC$). Accordingly, there are three types of total cost curves in the short run, *TFC*, *TVC* and *STC* curves.

We will derive the average fixed curve, average variable cost and short-run average total cost curves from their respective total cost curves. This analysis of derivation of average and marginal cost curves from their total cost curves will reveal how the average and marginal cost curves are related to the total cost curves.

Derivation of Average Fixed Cost Curve from Total Fixed Cost Curve

We have seen above that the total fixed cost is a fixed amount of expenditure per time period incurred on some fixed factors such as managerial staff, capital and land. The total fixed cost curve is invariant to the changes in the level of output in the short run and is therefore a horizontal straight line. How the average fixed cost curve is derived from the *TFC* curve is illustrated in Figure 15.3. It will be seen from this figure that at all levels of output the total fixed cost remains constant at Rs. 100 per period. At the level of output OQ_1 (or 10

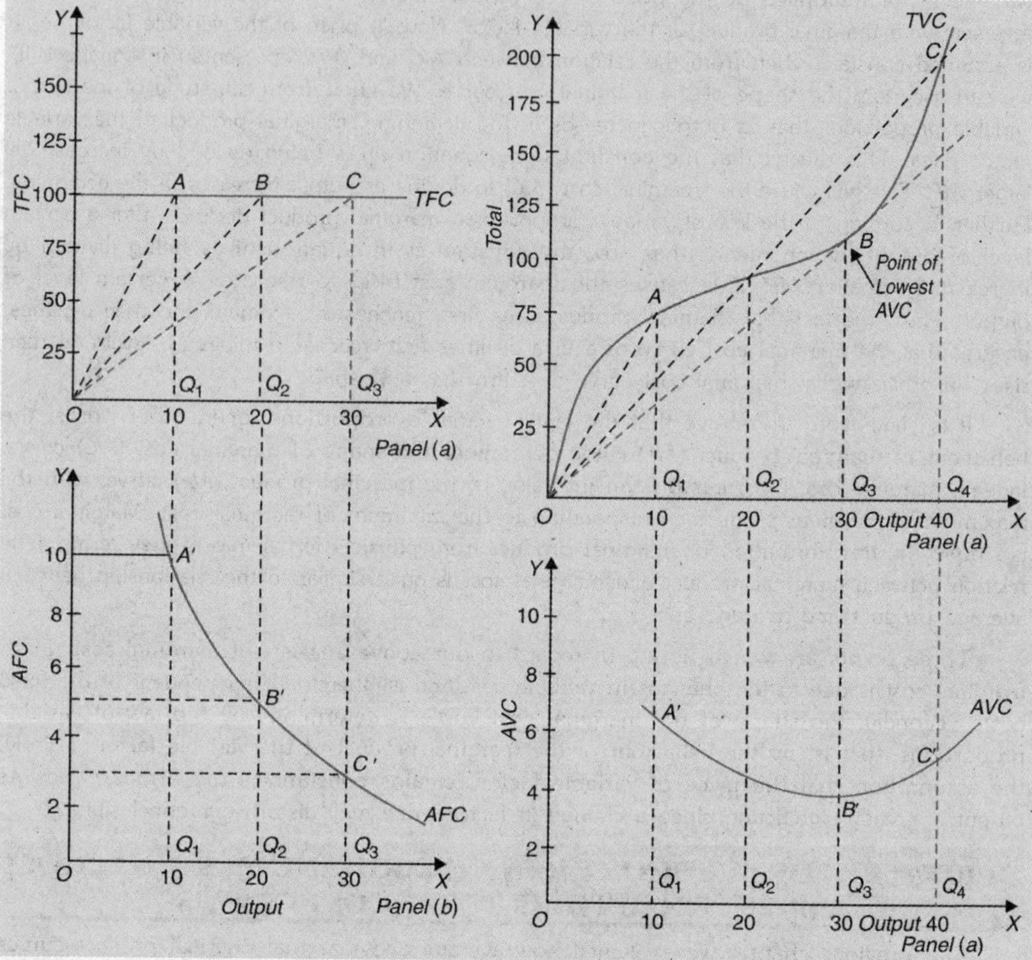

Fig.15.3. *Derivation of Average Fixed Cost Curve from Total Fixed Cost Curve*

Fig.15.4. *Derivation of Average Variable Cost Curve from Total Variable Cost Curve*

units), the average fixed cost is given by $\frac{AQ_1}{OQ_1}$ or $\frac{100}{10} = 10$. Geometrically, the average fixed cost at OQ_1 level of output is given by the *slope of the ray OA* drawn from the origin to the point *A* on the total fixed cost curve *TFC* which is equal to $\frac{AQ_1}{OQ_1}$ or 100/10 =10 in our Figure 15.3

In the lower panel (*b*) we have directly plotted this average fixed cost of Rs. 10 or AQ_1/OQ_1 as point *A*' against the output level of OQ_1 or 10 units. Note that in the lower panel (*b*) the scale on the vertical axis is different from that in the upper panel (*b*). Similarly, at output level of OQ_2 or 20 units, the average fixed cost is given by the slope of the ray *OB* which equals BQ_2/OQ_2 or 100/20 = Rs. 5. Again, this average fixed cost is plotted in the lower panel (*b*) as point B' against the output level OQ_2 or 20 units. Further, at output level OQ_3 or 30 units of output, the average fixed cost is given by slope of the ray OC which equals $\frac{CQ_3}{OQ_3} = \frac{100}{30}$ = Rs.3.33 which is plotted as point C' in the lower panels (*b*) against output level OQ_3 or 30 units. On joining points A', B' and C in the lower panel (*b*) of Figure 15.3 we get the average fixed cost curve *AFC* as derived from the total fixed cost curve *TFC*. Since total fixed cost equals *AFC* multiplied by output, the area at every point under the average fixed cost curve *AFC* will be equal to the total fixed cost. As the total fixed cost does not vary with the change in output in the short run, the area under every point of the average fixed cost curve will be equal to the constant total fixed cost. It follows therefore that the shape of the average fixed cost curve is of *rectangular hyperbola*.

Derivation of Average Variable Cost Curve

The average variable cost (*AVC*) curve can be derived from the total variable cost (*TVC*) curve. Unlike the total fixed cost curve, the total variable cost is function of output, that is, it varies with the changes in the level of output. The total variable cost curve is drawn as *TVC* curve in panel (*a*) of Figure 15.4. Since average variable cost at any given level of output is given by the total variable cost divided by the quantity of output produced, it can be measured by the slope of the ray (i.e., straight line) from the origin to a point on the *TVC* curve corresponding to a given level of output. Thus, in Figure 15.4 at output level OQ_1 the average variable cost curve is given by $\frac{AQ_1}{OQ_1} = \frac{75}{10} = 7.5$ which is equal to the slope of the ray *OA* drawn from the origin. The average variable cost so obtained is plotted in the panel (*b*) below as Q_1A' (= Rs. 7.5). Note that the scale on the vertical axis in panel (*b*) is not the same as in panel (a) above. Similarly, at a higher level of output OQ_3, the average variable cost is given by the slope of the ray *OB* drawn from the origin which equals BQ_3/OQ_3 or 110/30 = Rs. 3.7 which in panel (*b*) is plotted as Q_3B' (= Rs. 3.7). Again, at a still' higher level of output OQ_4, the average variable cost is measured by the slope of the ray *OC* drawn from the origin which is equal to CQ_4/OO_4 or $\frac{200}{40}$ = Rs. 5 and this is plotted in the lower panel (*b*) as Q_4C'.

It will be seen from panel (*a*) of Figure 15.4 that the slope of the ray drawn from the origin to a point on the *TVC* curve goes on declining until the output level OQ_3 is reached. It should be carefully noted that the slope of the ray *OB* from the origin at point *B* or output level OQ_3 is also the tangent to the *TVC* curve. This implies that beyond output level OQ_3, or point *B* on the *TVC* curve, the slope of the ray from the origin starts increasing. Thus, at point *C* on the *TVC* curve corresponding to the output level OQ_4, the slope of ray *OC* from the origin is greater than the slope of the ray *OB*. Thus, until output level OQ_3 the average variable cost curve, as will be seen from panel (*b*) below, is declining and beyond output level Q_3 it rises. This implies that the *AVC* curve is roughly of U-Shape.

Derivation of the Short-Run Average Total Cost (ATC) Curve

Derivation of the short-run average total cost curve from the short-run total cost curve (*STC*) is similar to the derivation of *AVC* curve from the *TVC* curve as explained above.It can be derived by drawing *rays from the origin to the points on total short-run cost curve (STC)* corresponding to various levels of output and then *measuring the slope* of these rays from the origin. Since the short-run total Cost (*STC*) curve is generally of *S* shape as the total variable cost curve *TVC* in Fig. 15.4, the average total cost curve (*ATC*) which we will get will also be of U shape, that is, first sloping downward and then rising. Besides, since average total cost is the sum of average fixed cost and average variable cost (*ATC* = *AFC* + *AVC*), average total cost (*ATC*) curve falls in the beginning because both *AFC* and *AVC* decline upto a point and then *ATC* rises beyond a point because due to diminishing returns to the variable factors, average variable cost (*AVC*) curve rises more rapidly than the fall in the average fixed cost (*AFC*) curve.

Derivation of Short-Run Marginal Cost Curve

Since marginal cost is defined as $\frac{\Delta TC}{\Delta Q}$, that is, addition made to the total cost resulting from a small change in output, it can be derived form the total cost curve. The derivation of the marginal cost curve from the total cost curve is illustrated in Figure 15.5 in which *STC* is the short-run total cost curve with its usual shape. As output increases from OQ_1, to OQ_2, the producer moves from point *A* to *B* on the total cost curve *STC* and his total cost increases from C_1 to C_2. From this, marginal cost is obtained as under :

$$MC = \frac{\Delta TC}{\Delta Q} = \frac{C_2 - C_1}{Q_2 - Q_1} = \frac{BH}{AH}$$

Now, if point *A* is brought closer to point *B* on the total cost curve, the distance between *A* and *B* becomes smaller so that the slope of the tangent drawn at point *B* becomes a better measure of the $\frac{BH}{AH}$, that is, marginal cost. Thus movement in the small neighbourhood around point *B*, the slope of the tangent geometrically measures the marginal cost of production at the output level Q_2.

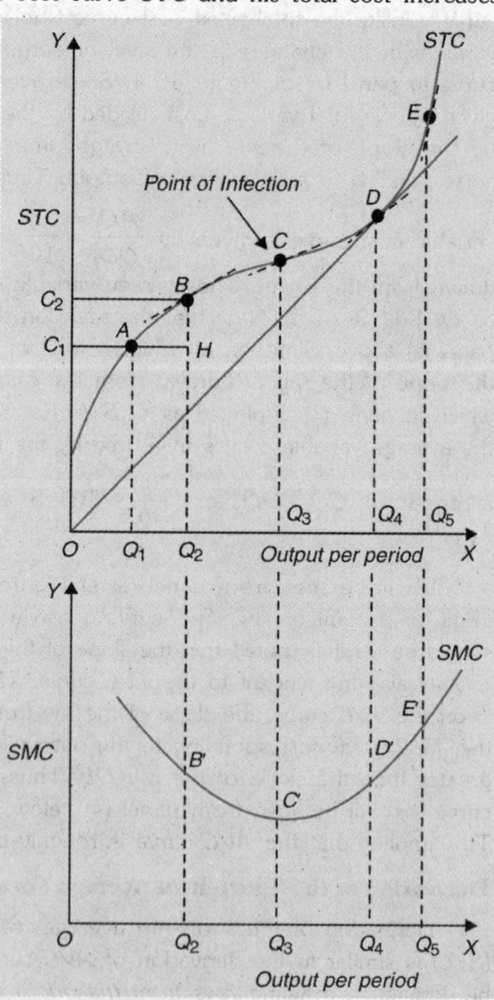

Fig. 15.5. *Derivation of Short-Run Marginal Cost Curve from Short-Run Total Cost Curve*

Now, consider the *STC* curve in Figure 15.5. It will be seen that the slope of the tangents drawn to the *STC* curve at various points corresponding to successively higher levels of output, diminishes until output Q_3 is reached. Thereafter, the slope of the tangent, that is, marginal cost increases. Thus, as the output increases upto Q_3, marginal cost decreases and beyond that it increases. This implies that the marginal cost is minimum at output level OQ_3. It should be further noted that at point *D* on the short-run total cost curve (*STC*) corresponding to output level Q_4, the ray from the origin is also the tangent at this point. This means that at output level Q_4, the marginal cost which is given by the slope of the tangent drawn to the *STC* curve becomes equal to the average cost which is given by the slope of the ray from the origin to a point on *STC*. Beyond point *D*, the slope of the tangent at a point on the total cost curve, for instance, at point *E* becomes greater than the slope of the ray from the origin drawn to that point. This implies that beyond point *D* on the short-run total cost curve, marginal cost curve would lie above the average cost curve, cutting the latter from its minimum point. Figure 15.5 therefore also brings out the relationship between the marginal cost and average cost curves. The slope of short-run total cost curve (*STC*) at any point to the left of point *D* is less than the slope of the ray from the origin which means that marginal cost curve (*SMC*) would lie below the average cost curve. In fact, it is the lower marginal cost than the average cost before point *D* that pushes down the average cost. On the other hand, to the right of point *D*, the slope of the total cost curve at any point is greater than the slope of the ray drawn from the origin, which means that the marginal cost is greater than the average cost to the right of point *D*. As a matter of fact, the higher marginal cost than average cost pushes up the latter.

The Relation Between the Average and Marginal Cost Curves

We have explained above the concepts of average and marginal cost curves. There is an important relation between the two which is explained below.

The relationship between the marginal cost and average cost is the same as that between any other marginal-average quantities. When marginal cost is less than average cost, average cost falls and when marginal cost is greater than average cost, average cost rises. This marginal-average relationship is a matter of mathematical truism and can be easily understood by a simple example. Suppose that a cricket player's batting average is 50. If in his next innings he scores less than 50, say 45, then his average score will fall because his marginal (additional) score is less than his average score. If instead of 45, he scores more than 50, say 55, in his next innings, then his average score will increase because now the marginal score is greater than his previous average score. Again, with , his present average runs as 50, if he scores 50 also in his next innings, then his average score will remain the same i.e. 50, since his marginal score is just equal to the average score. Likewise, a producer is producing a certain number of units of a product and his average cost is Rs. 20. Now, if he produces one unit more and his average cost falls, it means that the additional unit must have cost him less than Rs. 20. On the other hand, if the production of the additional unit raises his average cost, then the marginal unit must have cost him more than Rs. 20. And finally, if as a result of production of an additional unit, the average cost remains the same, then marginal unit must have cost him exactly Rs. 20, that is, marginal cost and average cost would be equal in this case.

The relationship between average and marginal cost can be easily remembered with the help of Fig. 15.6. It is illustrated in this figure that when marginal cost (*MC*) is above average cost (*AC*), the average cost rises, that is, the marginal cost (*MC*) pulls the average cost (*AC*) upward. On the other hand, if marginal cost (*MC*) is below the average cost (*AC*), average cost falls, that is, the marginal cost pulls the average cost downward. When marginal cost (*MC*) stands equal to the average cost (*AC*), the average cost remains the same, that is, the marginal cost pulls the average cost horizontally.

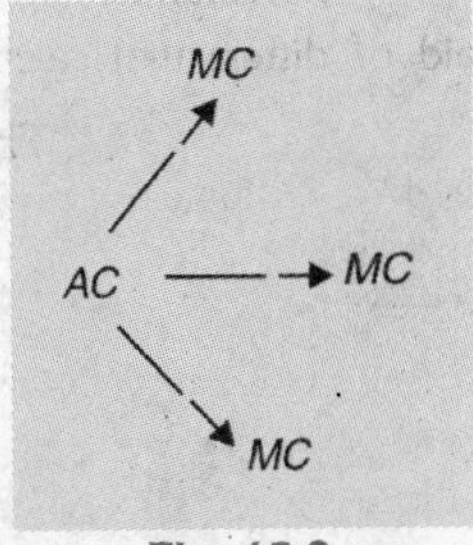

Fig. 15.6

Now, take Fig. 15.7 where short-run average cost curve *AC* is drawn. As long as short-run marginal cost curve *MC* lies *below* short-run average cost curve AC, the average cost curve *AC* is falling. When marginal cost curve *MC lies above* the average cost curve *AC*, the average cost curve *AC* is rising. At the point of intersection *L* where

MC is equal to *AC*, *AC* is neither falling nor rising, that is, at point *L*, *AC* has just ceased to fall but has not yet begun to rise. It follows that point *L*, where the *MC* curve crosses the *AC* curve to lie above the *AC* curve, is the minimum point of the *AC* curve. Thus marginal cost curve cuts the average cost curve at the latter's minimum point.

It is important to note that we cannot generalise about the *direction* in which marginal cost is moving from the way average cost is changing, that is, when average cost is falling we cannot say that marginal cost will be falling too. When average cost is falling, what we can say definitely is only that the marginal cost will be *below* it but marginal cost itself may be either rising or falling. Likewise, when average cost is rising, we cannot deduce that marginal cost will be rising too. When average cost is rising, the marginal cost must be *above* it but the marginal cost itself may be either rising or falling. Consider Fig. 15.7 where up to the point *K*, marginal cost is falling as well as below the average cost. As a result, the average cost is falling. But beyond point *K* and up to point *L*, marginal cost curve lies below the average cost curve with the result that the average cost curve is falling. But it will be seen that between *K* and *L* when the marginal cost is rising, the average cost is falling. This is because though *MC* is rising between *K* and *L*, it is below *AC*. It is therefore clear that when the average cost is falling, marginal cost may be either falling or rising. This can also be easily illustrated by the example of batting average. Suppose a cricket player's present batting average is 50. If in his next innings he scores less than 50, say, 45, his batting average will fall. But his marginal score of 45, though less than the average may have risen. For instance, he might have scored 25 in his previous innings so that his present marginal score of 45 is much greater than his previous marginal score. Thus one cannot deduce about the *direction* of marginal cost as to whether it will be falling or rising when the average cost is falling or rising.

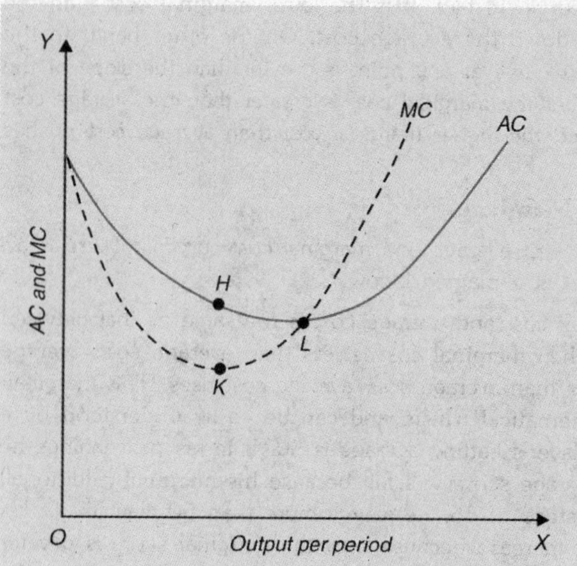

Fig. 15.7 The Relation between *AC* and *MC* curves

The relationship between average cost and marginal cost can be easily proved with the aid of differential calculus. Let *AC* stand for average cost per unit and *Q* for total output,

Then, total cost $(TC) = AC.Q$

$$MC = \frac{d(TC)}{dQ}$$

Since $TC =$ output x average cost

$= AC.Q$

$$MC = \frac{d(AC.Q)}{dQ}$$

$$MC = Q\frac{d(AC)}{dQ} + AC \qquad \ldots(i)$$

$\frac{d(AC)}{dQ}$ measures the slope of the average cost curve. Because total output Q is positive, from equation (*i*) above, it follows that when

$$\frac{d(AC)}{dQ} < 0,\ MC < AC \qquad \ldots(ii)$$

$$\frac{d(AC)}{dQ} > 0,\ MC > AC \qquad \ldots(iii)$$

$$\frac{d(AC)}{dQ} = 0,\ MC = AC \qquad \ldots(iv)$$

From the condition (iv), it follows that marginal cost is equal to average cost at its minimum. From condition (*ii*), it follows that when the slope of the average cost curve is negative, that is, when AC is falling marginal cost (MC) would be below it. From the above condition (*iii*) it follows that when the slope of the average cost curve is greater than zero (*i.e.*, positive) or, in other words when, the average cost curve is rising, marginal cost will be greater than it.

THEORY OF LONG-RUN COSTS

We now begin to explain the cost curves in the long run. It may be noted that the long run refers to a time period during which full adjustment to a change in environment can be made by the firm by varying all inputs, including capital equipment and factory building. An important aspect of the long run is that it represents a *planning horizon* because in it the firm plans its size of the plant which is appropriate to the specific level of output. However, all production is done in the short run during which the size of plant (*i.e.*, the capital equipment, factory building) is given. Thus, the long run consists of all possible short-run situations among which a firm has to choose to produce a target level of output. It needs to be carefully understood that *before* an investment is made, a firm is in a long-run situation; it can choose among a number of possible sizes of plant, in which to invest. But once investment is made in a particular capital equipment and plant has been set up, the firm operates in the short run.

In what follows we shall first explain how a long run average and marginal cost curves are derived from a number of short-run average cost and marginal cost curves. Having done so we shall explain why the long-run average cost curve is of approximately U-shape. Further we shall show how the long-run total cost curve is derived from the production function or the expansion path of the theory of production.

Long-Run Average Cost Curve

We now turn to explain the cost curves in the long run. The long run, as noted above, is a period of time during which the firm can vary all its inputs. In the short run, some inputs are fixed and others are varied to increase the level of output. In the long run, none of the factors is fixed and all can be varied to expand output. The long-run production function has therefore no fixed factors and the firm has no fixed costs in the long run. It is conventional to regard the size or scale of plant as a typical fixed input. The term 'plant' is here understood to be as consisting of capital equipment, machinery, land, etc. In the short run, the size of the plant is fixed and it cannot be increased or reduced. That is to say, one cannot change the amount of capital equipment in the short run, if one has to increase or decrease output. On the other hand, long run is a period of time sufficiently long to permit changes in plant, that is, in capital equipment, machinery, land, etc. in order to expand or contract output. Thus, whereas in the short run the firm is tied with a given plant, in the long run the firm moves from one plant to another; the firm can make a larger plant if it has to increase its output and a smaller plant if it has to reduce its output. The long-run cost of production is the least possible cost of producing any given level of output when all inputs are variable, including of course the size of the plant. A long-run cost curve depicts the functional relationship between output and the long-run cost of production, as just defined.

Long-run average cost is the long-run total cost divided by the level of output. Long-run average cost curve depicts the least possible average cost for producing various levels of output. In order to understand how the long-run average cost curve is derived, consider the three short-run average cost curves as shown in Fig. 15.8. These short-run average cost curves are also called *plant curves,* since in the short run plant is fixed and each of the short-run average cost curves corresponds to a particular plant. In the short run, the firm can be operating on any short-run average cost curve, given the size of the plant. Suppose that only these three are technically possible sizes of plant and that no other size of the plant can be built. Given the size of the plant or short-run average cost curve the firm will increase or decrease its output by varying the amount of the variable inputs. But, in the long run, the firm can choose among the three possible sizes of plant as depicted by short-run average cost curves SAC_1, SAC_2 and SAC_3. In the long run the firm will examine with which size of plant or on which short-run SAC_2 curve it should operate to produce a given level of output at the minimum possible cost.

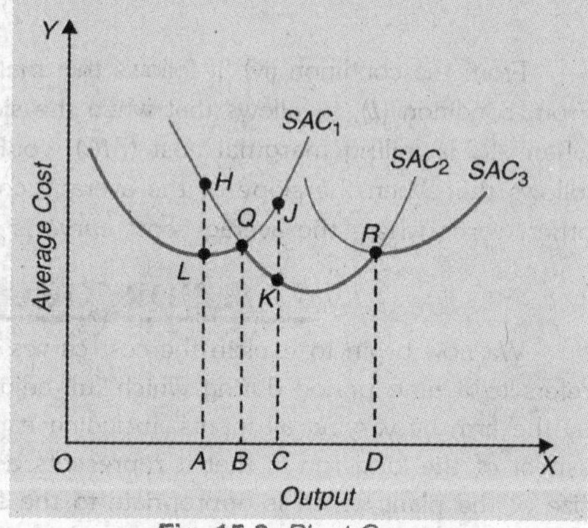

Fig. 15.8. *Plant Curves*

It will be seen from Fig. 15.8 that upto *OB* amount of output, the firm will operate on the short-run average cost curve SAC_1, though it could also produce with short-run average cost curve SAC_2, because upto *OB* amount of output, production on SAC_1 curve entails lower cost than on SAC_2. For instance, if the level of output *OA* is produced with SAC_1 it will cost *AL* per unit and if it is produced with SAC_2 it will cost *AH* per unit. It will be seen from the figure that *AL* is smaller than *AH.* Similarly, all other output levels up to *OB* can be produced more economically with the smaller plant SAC_1 than with the larger plant SAC_2. It is thus clear that in the long run the firm will produce any output upto *OB* on SAC_1. If the firm plans to produce an output which is larger than *OB* (but less than *OD*), then it will not be economical to produce on SAC_1. It will be seen from Fig. 15.8 that the outputs larger than *OB* but less than *OD,* can be produced at a lower cost per unit on SAC_2 than on SAC_1. Thus, the output *OC* if produced on SAC_2 costs *CK* per unit which is lower than *CJ* which is the cost incurred when produced on SAC_1. Therefore, if the firm plans to produce between outputs *OB* and *OD,* it will employ the plant corresponding to the short-run average cost curve SAC_2. If the firm has to produce an output which exceeds *OD,* then the cost per unit will be lower on SAC_3 than on SAC_2. Therefore, for outputs larger than *OD,* the firm will employ plant corresponding to the short-run average cost curve SAC_3.

It is thus clear that in the long run the firm has a choice in the employment of a plant, and it will employ that plant which yields minimum possible unit cost for producing a given output. The long-run average cost curve depicts the least possible average cost for producing various levels of output when all factors including the size of the plant have been adjusted. Given that only three sizes of plants as shown in Fig. 15.8 are technically possible, then the long-run average cost curve is the curve which has scallops in it. This heavily scalloped long-run average cost curve consists of some segments of all the short-run average cost curves as explained above.

Suppose now that the size of the plant can be varied by infinitely small gradations so that there are infinite number of plants corresponding to which there will be numerous short-run average cost curves. In that case, the long-run average cost curve will be a smooth and continuous curve without any scallops. Such a smooth long-run average cost curve has been shown in Fig. 15.9 and has been labelled as *LAC*. There will be infinite short-run average cost curves in such a case, though only seven have been shown in Fig. 15.9. This long-run average cost curve *LAC* is so drawn as to be tangent to each of the short-run average cost curves. Since an infinite number of short-run average cost curves is assumed, every point on the long-run average cost curve will be a tangency point with some short-run average cost curve. In fact, the long-run average cost curve is nothing else but the locus of all these tangency points. It is again worth noting that the long-run average cost curve shows the least possible average cost of producing any output, when all productive factors are variable. If a firm desires to produce a particular output in the long run, it will pick a point on the long-run average cost curve corresponding to that output and it will then build a relevant plant and operate on the corresponding short-run average cost curve.

In the situation as depicted in Fig. 15.9 for producing output *OM* the corresponding point on the long-run average cost curve *LAC* is *G* at which the short-run average cost curve SAC_2 is tangent to the long-run average cost curve *LAC*. Thus, if a firm desires to produce output *OM*, the firm will construct a plant corresponding to SAC_2 and will operate on this curve at point *G*. Similar would be the case for all other outputs in the long run. Further, consider that the firm plans to produce output *ON*, which corresponds to point *K* on the long-run average cost curve *LAC*. As already noted, every point on the long-run average cost curve is a tangency point with some short-run average cost curve and that there are infinite number of short-run average cost curves, so there will be some short-run average cost curve (not shown in Fig. 15.9) which will be tangent to the long-run average cost curve *LAC* at the point *K* corresponding to *ON* output. Thus, for producing output *ON*, the firm will build a plant which will correspond to that short-run average cost curve which is tangent to the long-run average cost curve *LAC* at point *K* corresponding to *ON* output. The long-run average cost curve *LAC* is also called '*envelope*' since it envelops or supports a family of short-run average cost curves from below.

It is evident from Fig. 15.9 that larger outputs can be produced at the lower cost with the larger plants, whereas smaller outputs can be produced at the lower cost with smaller plants. Thus, output *OM* can be produced with the lowest possible cost with the plant represented by SAC_2. To produce *OM* output with a larger plant corresponding to SAC_3 will entail higher unit cost than that of SAC_2. But a larger output *OV* can be produced most economically with a larger plant represented by SAC_3, while to produce *OV* with the smaller plant of SAC_2 will mean higher unit cost. This is, as it will be expected, a larger plant with a greater productive capacity is more expensive when employed to produce a small output will not be fully utilized and its under-utilization will cause higher unit cost. In other words, using a larger plant and to operate it much below its capacity in order to produce a small output will naturally mean higher average cost. On the other hand, a large output with a small-sized plant will also involve higher cost per unit because of its limited capacity.

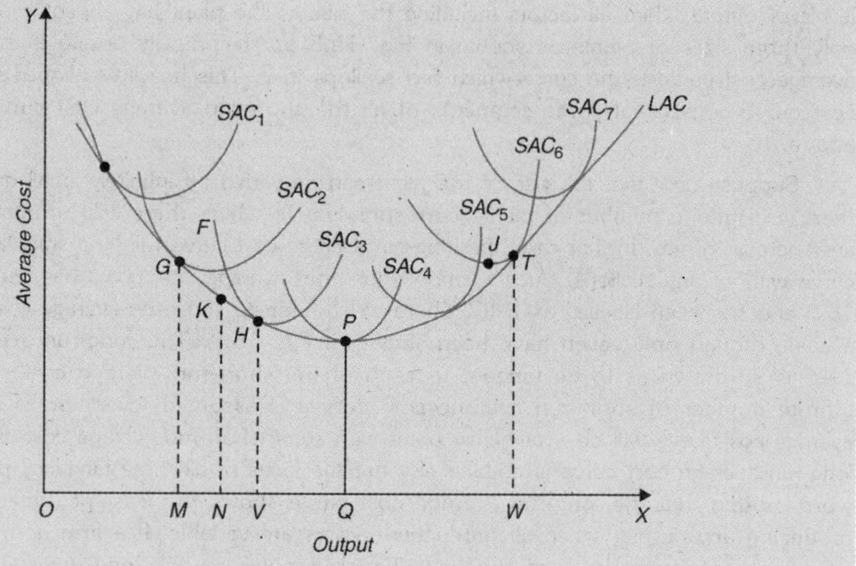

Fig. 15.9. *Deriving Long-Run Average Cost Curve from a Family of Short-Run Average Cost Curves*

It will be seen from Fig. 15.9 that the long-run average cost curve first falls and then beyond a certain point it rises, that is, the long-run average cost curve is U-shaped, though the U-shape of the long-run average cost curve is less pronounced than that of the short-run average cost curve. In Fig. 15.9 long-run average cost is minimum at output *OQ*. The long-run average cost falls upto the output *OQ* and it rises beyond it. Why does the long-run average cost first decline and then rise will be explained a little later.

An important fact about the long-run average cost curve is worth mentioning. It is that the *long-run average curve LAC is not tangent to the minimum points of the short-run average cost curves.* When the long-run average cost curve is declining, that is, for outputs less than *OQ*, it is tangent to the *falling portions* of the short-run average cost curves. This means that for any output smaller than *OQ*, it will not pay to operate a plant at its minimum unit cost. Consider, for instance, the plant corresponding to the short-run average cost curve SAC_2, which is operated at point *G* in the long run to produce output *OM*. The point *G* lies on the falling portion of the short-run average cost curve SAC_2 which has a minimum point *F*, By working on point *G* of SAC_2, the firm is using the given plant below its full capacity. The plant of SAC_2 will be utilized to its full capacity if it is operated at minimum unit cost point *F* to produce a larger output than *OM*. But, in the long run, it does not pay the firm to produce with the plant of SAC_2, an output larger than *OM*. This is because output larger than *OM* can be produced at a lower unit cost with a plant larger than the plant of SAC_2. It is thus clear that for producing an output less than *OQ* at the lowest possible unit cost the firm will construct an appropriate plant and will operate it at less than its capacity, that is, at less than its minimum average cost of production.

On the other hand, when the long-run average cost curve is rising, it will be tangent to the *rising portions* of the short-run average cost curves. This implies that outputs larger than *OQ* will be produced most cheaply by constructing a plant with a given optimal capacity and operating it to produce larger than its capacity, that is, using it to produce at more than its minimum unit cost of production. Consider, for instance, the short-run average cost curve SAC_6 which is tangent to the long-run average cost curve *LAC* at point *T*. Point *T* lies on the rising portion of SAC_6 which has a minimum unit cost point *J* to the left of the point *T*. This means that the firm is producing output *OW* by operating at point *T* on the plant of SAC_6 which has a optimum capacity less than *OW*. That is, for producing output *OW* at lowest possible cost the firm has built a plant corresponding to SAC_6 and works it at more than its capacity.

Long-run average cost curve is often called the *'planning curve'* of the firm by some economists because a firm plans to produce any output in the long run by choosing a plant on the long-run average cost curve corresponding to the given output. The long-run average cost curve reveals to the firm that how large should be the plant for producing a certain output at the least possible cost. Thus while making decisions regarding the choice of a plant, the firm has to look at its long-run average cost curve enveloping a family of plant curves. What different sizes of plants are available at a time and what short-run average cost curves they will have on being used for production are known to the firm either from experience or from engineering studies.

Long-Run Average Cost Curve in Case of Constant Returns to Scale

If the production function is linear and homogeneous (that is, homogeneous of the first degree) and also the prices of inputs remain constant, then the long-run average cost will remain constant at all levels of output. As explained in the previous chapter, linear homogeneous production function implies constant returns to scale which means that when all inputs are increased in a certain proportion, output increases in the same proportion. Therefore, with the given prices of inputs, when returns to scale are constant, cost per unit of output remains the same. In this case, the long-run average cost curve will be a horizontal straight line as depicted in Fig. 15.10. Though there will be infinite number of short-run average cost curves as we continue to assume that the size of the plant can be varied by infinitely small gradations, only the *SAC* curves of three plants have been shown in Fig. 15.10

It will be noticed from Fig. 15.10 that all short-run average cost curves such as SAC_1, SAC_2, SAC_3 have the same minimum average cost of production. This means whatever the size of the plant, the minimum average cost of production is the same. This implies that all factors can be adjusted in the long run in such a way that the proportions between them always remain optimum. In such a case, the optimum size of the firm is indeterminate, since all levels of output can be produced at the same long-run average cost which represents the same minimum short-run average cost throughout. It is useful to note that though all levels of output will be produced at the same minimum cost of production the different sizes of plants will be used for producing different levels of output. Thus, for producing output *OA*, the plant of SAC_1 will be employed; for output *OB*, the plant of SAC_2 will be employed; and for output *OC* the plant of SAC_3 will be employed. This is because the production at the lowest possible cost for output *OA* is possible with plant SAC_1, and for output *OB* with plant SAC_2 and for output *OC* with plant SAC_3.

Some economists like Kaldor, Joan Robinson, Stigler are of the view that when all factors of production are "*perfectly divisible*" then there would be no internal economies of scale (and no internal diseconomies). Therefore, according to them, in case of 'perfect divisibility' of all factors, the long-run average cost curve will be a horizontal straight line showing that the long-run average cost is constant whatever the level of output. In their view, all internal economies of scale are due to the indivisibility of some factors. Therefore, they argue that if perfect divisibility of factors is assumed, then it implies the absence of internal economies of scale and therefore in such a case the long-run average cost curve will be a horizontal straight line. But E.H. Chamberlin has challenged this viewpoint. According to him, perfect divisibility has nothing to do with efficiency, that is to say, perfect divisibility does not mean the absence of internal economies of scale. Thus, according to him, even if all factors were perfectly divisible, the economies of scale will be reaped due to the use of more specialized machinery and a greater degree of division of labour at higher levels of output. Therefore, according to Chamberlin, constant returns to scale cannot exist and long-run average cost cannot remain constant. even when factors are perfectly divisible.

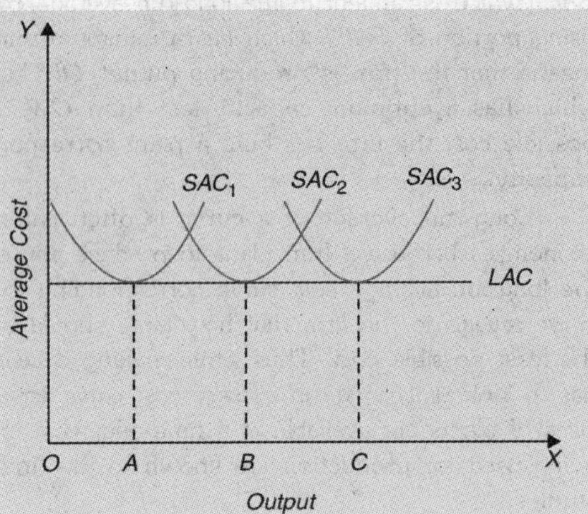

Fig. 15.10. *When Returns to Scale are Constant, Long-run Average Cost Curve is a Horizontal Straight Line.*

However, many empirical studies have shown that U-shape of the long-run average cost curve is not smooth and regular but a wavy and irregular one. Further, a very important feature of long-run average cost curve revealed by empirical studies is that there is a relatively very large flat portion or, in other words, a large horizontal region in the centre of long-run average cost curve, as is depicted in Figure 15.11. In such a real case, long-run average cost curve has a saucer-shaped appearance. Such a long-run cost curve with a very large flat portion in the centre can arise if the economies of scale are exhausted at a very modest scale of operation and then for a relatively large further expansion in output, diseconomies of scale do not occur. Only after a very large increase in output, diseconomies of scale exert themselves and bring about a rise in the long-run average cost. A long horizontal or flat section in the long-run average cost curve can also occur because economies of scale which are mostly of technological type may offset the diseconomies over a wide range of output.

Minimum Efficient Scale

It is clear from Fig. 15.9 that in the continuous long-run average cost curve both for outputs less than OQ and more than OQ no plant is used at its point of minimum cost. It is only the plant, the minimum point of whose short-run average cost curve coincides with the minimum point of the long-run average cost curve, which is operated at the point of its minimum average cost of production. In Fig. 15.9 for producing output OQ, the plant of SAC_4 is being efficiently utilized to produce output with minimum long-run average cost, that is, it is being used at its full capacity. The *minimum efficient scale* of plant is the level of output at which long-run average cost is minimum. This is also optimum size of the firm.

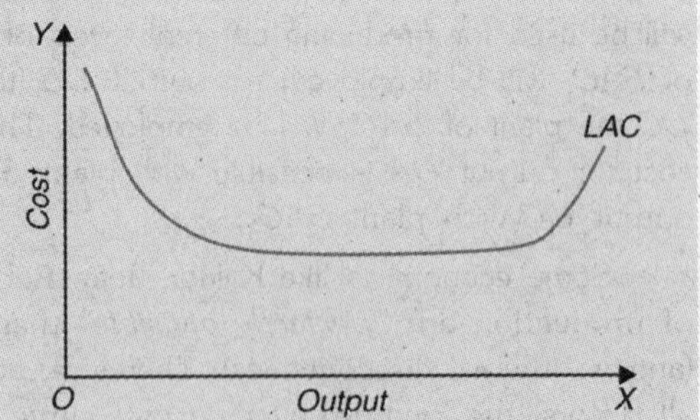

Fig . 15.11. *Saucer-Shaped Long-Run Average Cost Curve*

It should be noted that in Fig 15.9 the plant of SAC_4 is optimum plant, since its minimum cost of production is the lowest of the minimum costs of all other plants. If the size of the plant is increased beyond SAC_4, it results in higher average cost of production. Similarly, if the size of the plant is smaller than SAC_4, average cost of production is higher. Further, the least-cost output of plant SAC_4 is OQ. Now, if the firm produces output OQ with the optimum plant SAC_4, it is said to have achieved the *minimum efficient scale.* In our Fig 15.9 the firm will be working with efficient scale if it employs plant SAC_4 and uses it to produce OQ. Since the point of minimum cost of the optimum plant (SAC_4) coincides with the minimum point of the long-run average cost curve, the *minimum efficient scale can also be defined as the level of output when the firm operates at the minimum point of the long-run average cost curve (LAC).*

The minimum efficient scale of the firm varies a great deal in different industries. In agriculture, extractive industries, wholesale and retail trade, the minimum efficient scale is relatively small, that is, the minimum point of the long-run average cost curve is reached at a comparatively small output. Fig.15.12 shows a firm whose minimum efficient size is relatively small. On the other hand, the minimum efficient scale of the firm in steel industry, automobile industry, other heavy industries and public utilities is relatively very large, that is, the minimum point of their long-run average cost curve is reached at a relatively very large output. Fig.15.13 depicts a firm whose minimum efficient size is very large . Whether market for a good of a

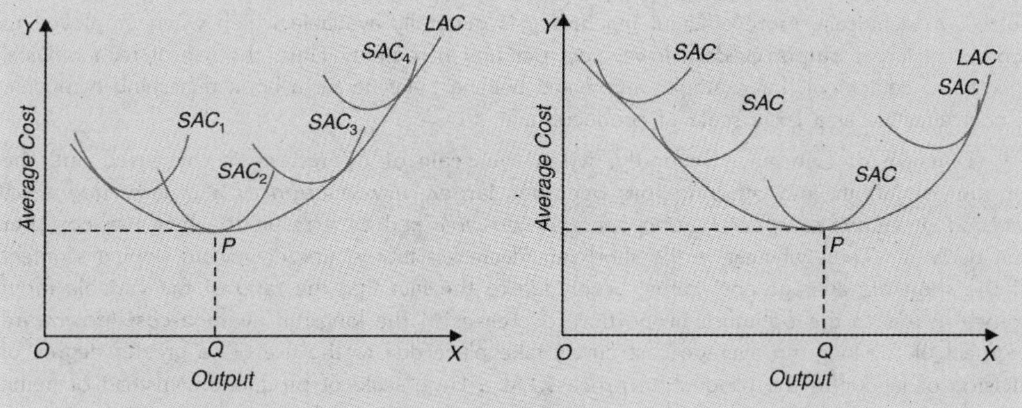

Fig.15.12. *Small Minimum Efficient Scale* **Fig. 15.13.** *Large Minimum Efficient Scale*

given size is supplied by a large number of relatively small-scale firms or by a small number of relatively large size firms depends on the minimum efficient scale of firms in the industry. And this minimum efficient scale is largly determined by the technology of production of an industry. In the industry in which the efficient size of the firm is very large, there are generally a few number of firms, each with a large size.

EXPLANATION OF THE U-SHAPE OF THE LONG-RUN AVERAGE COST CURVE

In Fig. 15.9 we have drawn the long-run average cost curve as having an approximately U-shape. It is generally believed by economists that the long-run average cost curve is normally U-shaped, that is, the long-run average cost first declines as output is increased and then beyond a certain point it rises. Now, what is the proper explanation for such a behaviour of the long-run average cost ?

We saw above that the U-shape of the short-run average cost curve is explained with the law of proportions. But *the long-run average cost curve depends upon the returns to scale.* In the long run all inputs including the capital equipment can be altered, therefore, the relevant principle governing the shape of the long-run average cost curve is that of returns to scale. In a previous chapter we explained that returns to scale increase at the initial increases in output and after remaining constant for a while, the returns to scale decrease. It is because of the increasing returns to scale in the beginning that the long-run average cost of production falls as output is increased and, likewise, it is because of the decreasing returns to scale that the long-run average cost of production rises beyond a certain level of output.

Economies of Scale

But the question is why we first get increasing returns to scale due to which cost falls and why after a certain point we get decreasing returns to scale that result in rise in cost per unit of output. In other words, what are the reasons for the firm to enjoy *economies of scale* up to a certain point and then beyond it why it encounters *diseconomies of scale.* The following factors are said to be responsible for the economies of scale which accrue to the firm and due to which cost per unit falls.

Use of Technically Efficient Machines : First, as the firm increases its scale of operations, it becomes possible to *use more specialized and technically more efficient form of all factors, especially capital equipment and machinery.* For producing higher levels of output, a technically more efficient machinery is generally available which when employed to produce a larger output yields a lower cost per unit of output. Thus, the use of technological specialised equipment, for example, automated buiding machine for a book publishing company, is cost effective at a large scale of production.

Division of Labour : Secondly, when the scale of operations is increased and the amount of labour and other factors becomes larger, *introduction of a greater degree of division of labour or specialisation becomes possible* and as a result the long-run cost per unit declines. Thus, whereas in the short run, decreases in cost (the downward sloping segment of the short-run average cost curve) occur due to the fact that the ratio of the variable input comes nearer to the optimum proportion, decreases in the long-run average cost (downward segment of the long-run average cost curve) take place due to the use of a greater degree of division of labour in the production process. At a large scale of production, instead of being generalists workers can specialise in performing a particular task in the production process. Generally, a worker who has to perform one task in the production process of a commodity can do it more efficiently than the one who has to perform several tasks in it. Besides, under division of labour time of the workers is also saved as they do not have to move from one machine to another.

Indivisibility and Economies of Scale. Some economists as Nicholas Kaldor and Joan Robinson explain economies of scale as arising from the *imperfect divisibility of factors.* In other words, they think that the economies of scale occur and therefore the long-run average cost falls because of the 'indivisibility' of factors. They argue that most of the factors are 'lumpy'. That is, they are available in *large indivisible units*, which can therefore yield lower cost of production when they are used to produce a large output. If a small output is produced with these costly indivisible units of the factors, the average cost of production will naturally be high. If the factors of production were perfectly divisible, they say, then suitable adjustment in the factors could be made so that the optimum proportions between the factors were maintained even for producing small outputs and hence the average cost of production would not have been higher. Thus, according to them, if the factors were perfectly divisible the small-scale production would be as good and efficient as the large-scale production and the economies of scale would be non-existent. Thus, Kaldor writes: "It appears methodologically convenient to treat all cases of large-scale economies under the heading 'indivisibility.'"[1] Likewise, Joan Robinson remarks,[2] "if all the factors were finely divisible, like sand, it would be possible to produce the smallest output of any commodity with all the advantages of large-scale industry."

We have outlined above the two different opinions regarding the emergence of economies of scale and hence the downward sloping segment of the long-run average cost curve. Both the above views are currently held by economists, some economists aligning themselves with the first line of reasoning which is associated with the name of Chamberlin and some other economists believe in the second view which is advanced by Joan Robinson, Nicholas Kaldor, J. Stigler and some others.

Financial Economies. Besides the above technological factors accounting for economies of scale there are financial reasons for reduction in unit cost of production as the size of the firm increases. Due to bulk purchases large firms generally get large quantity discounts in buying raw materials and intermediate products than the small-sized firms. Similarly, large firms can borrow funds from the commercial banks at relatively lower interest rate than smaller firms. Further, large firms can sell bonds and stocks in the capital market at more favourable terms. This reduces the cost of raising funds required for business purposes. Finally, large firms are able to take advantage of economies that result from spreading out of advertisiment and other promotional costs.

Economies of Scope. Economies of scope should be distingwished from economies of scale. Economies of scope refer to the reduction in costs that occur when a firm produces two or more commodities together rather than a single one. Many examples of economies of scope can be given. For example, a passanger air line can profitably extend its operations by using the same air plane for providing cargo services which lowers its cost of operation. In such an airoplane seats have to be removed and packets and bags containing goods can be placed to carry to their places of destination.

Another example of benefit from economies of scope which is often cited is when a firm extends its product line by utilising its waste product to produce a useful commodity for which there is demand in the market. Before this, the firm may be disposing of its waste product at a cost. Besides, a firm may have excess capacity that can be utilised to produce other products with little or no increase in capital cost. This results in lowering cost per unit of output of a firm.

In the real world the firms greatly benefit from their comparative advantage in the production of related products. For example, Hindustan Lever does not produce only bathing soap 'Lux' but a whole range of detergents and cleansing products. This is quite cost effective and lowers the overall unit cost of products.

Diseconomies of Scale

So much for the downward-sloping segment of the long-run average cost curve. As noted above, beyond a certain point the long-run average cost curve rises which means that the long-run average cost increases as output exceeds beyond a certain point. In other words, beyond a certain point a firm experiences *net diseconomies of scale.* There is also divergence of views about the proper explanation for this upward-sloping segment of the long-run average cost curve. The first view as held by Chamberlin and his followers is that when the firm has reached a size large enough to allow the utilization of almost all the possibilities of division of

1. Nicholas Kaldor, The Equilibrium of the Firm, *Economic Journal*, Vol. 44, reprinted in *Readings in Price Theory* (A.E.A.).
2. Joan Robinson, *The Economics of Imperfect Competition*, p.334.

labour and the employment of more efficient machinery, further increase in the size of the plant will entail higher long-run unit cost because of the difficulties of management. When the scale of operations exceeds a certain limit, the management may not be as efficient as when the scale of operations is relatively small.

With too large a scale of operations, it becomes difficult for the top management to exercise control and to bring about proper coordination. When the scale of operations is enlarged, it ordinarily becomes necessary to employ more assistants and supervisors and to effect more delegation of powers. Thus, increase in the firm's plant beyond a certain size involves more bureaucracy, more red tape, and lengthens the chain of communication and command between the top management and the men on the production line. Thus, increase in the plant beyond a certain sufficiently large size makes the managerial structure more cumbersome and reduces the overall efficiency of management. After a certain sufficiently large size these inefficiencies of management more than offset the economies of scale and thereby bring about the rise in long-run average cost and make the *LAC* curve upward-sloping. It should be noted that this view regards the entrepreneurial or managerial functions to be divisible and variable and explains the diseconomies of scale or the rising part of the long-run average cost curve as arising from the mounting difficulties of management (i.e., of supervision and coordination) beyond a certain sufficiently large scale of operations.

The Entrepreneur as a Fixed and Indivisible Factor. The second view regards the entrepreneur to be a fixed and indivisible factor. In this view, though all other factors can be increased, the entrepreneur cannot be. The entrepreneur and his functions of decision-making and ultimate control are indivisible and cannot be increased. Therefore, when a point is reached where the abilities of the fixed and indivisible entrepreneur are best utilized, further increases in the scale of operations *by increasing other inputs* cause increases in the cost per unit of output. In other words, there is a certain optimum proportion between an entrepreneur and other inputs and when that optimum proportion is reached, further increases in the other inputs to the fixed entrepreneur means the proportion between the inputs is moved away from the optimum and, therefore, results in the rise in the long-run average cost. Thus, in this view, increases in the long-run average cost is explained by the law of variable proportions. Economists who hold this view think that the decreasing returns to scale or rising long-run average cost is actually a special case of variable proportions, with entrepreneur as the fixed factor.

Long-Run Marginal Cost Curve

In a previous section we explained what is the marginal cost and how the short-run marginal cost curve is obtained and what relation it bears to the short-run average cost curve. Since marginal cost curve is important both from the viewpoint of the short run and the long run, it will be useful to know how the long-run marginal cost curve can be directly derived from the long-run total cost curve, since the long-run marginal cost at a level of output is given by the slope of the total cost curve at the point corresponding to that level of output. Besides, the long-run marginal cost curve can also be derived from the long-run average cost curve, because the long-run marginal cost curve is related to the long-run average cost curve in the same way as the short-run marginal cost curve is related to short run average cost curve. In Fig.15.14, it is depicted how the long-run marginal cost curve *LMC* is derived from a long-run average cost curve *LAC* enveloping a family of short-run average and marginal cost curves.

If the output *OA* is to be produced in the long run, then it must be produced on the long-run average cost curve *LAC* at point *H* which is a tangency point with the short-run average cost curve SAC_1. Thus, when output *OA* is to be produced in the long run, it will be produced with the plant corresponding to the short-run average cost curve SAC_1 and the short-run marginal cost curve SMC_1.

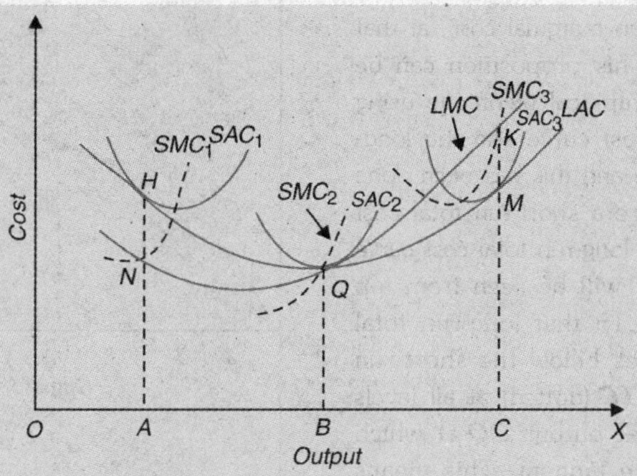

Fig.15.14. *Derivation of Long-Run Marginal Cost Curve*

Corresponding to the tangency point *H* between the short-run average cost curve SAC_1 and the long-run average cost curve *LAC*, there is point *N* on the short-run marginal cost curve SMC_1. This means that the production of output *OA* in the long run involves the marginal cost *AN*. Therefore, point *N* must lie on the long-run marginal cost curve corresponding to output *OA*. If output *OB* is to be produced in the long run, it will be produced at point *Q* which is the tangency point between *LAC* and SAC_2. *Q* is also the point on the short-run marginal cost curve SMC_2 corresponding to output *OB*. (*Q* is the common point between SAC_2 at which the SMC_2 cuts it from below). Thus *Q* must also lie on the long-run marginal cost curve corresponding to output *OB*. Similarly, if output *OC* is to be produced in the long run, it will be produced at point *M* which is the tangency point between *LAC* and SAC_3. Corresponding to point *M*, the relevant point on the SMC_3 is *K* which means that the long-run marginal cost of producing *OC* is *CK*. Thus point *K* must lie on the long-run marginal cost curve corresponding to output *OC*. By connecting points *N*, *Q* and *K* we obtain the long-run marginal cost curve *LMC*.

It will be seen from Fig. 15.14. that long-run marginal cost curve *LMC*, like the long-run average cost curve *LAC*, is U-shaped. It will be further seen that the long-run marginal cost curve *LMC* is flatter than the short-run marginal cost curves. This is what one would expect because the long-run average cost curve *LAC* is flatter than the short-run average cost curves. It should also be remembered that the relationship between the long-run marginal cost curve *LMC* and the long-run average cost curve *LAC* is the same as that between the short-run marginal cost curve and the short-run average cost curve (*SAC*). Thus, when the long-run marginal cost curve (*LMC*) lies above the long-run average cost curve, the latter will be rising. When the long-run marginal cost is equal to the long-run average cost, the latter will be neither rising nor falling. In other words, the long-run marginal cost curve will cut long-run average cost curve at the latter' s minimum point.

RELATIONSHIP BETWEEN STC AND LTC AND BETWEEN LAC AND SAC CURVES

It is useful to note that *LAC* and *SAC* curves are related in an important way with the *SMC* and *LMC* curves. This relationship shows, as will be seen from Fig. 15.14, that *at the level of output at which a particular SAC curve is tangent to the LAC curve, the corresponding SMC curve intersects the LMC curve.* In other words, the level of output where the short-run average cost is equal to the long-run average cost the corresponding short-run marginal cost is equal to the long-run marginal cost at that level of output. This proposition can be proved with the graphical technique using a short-run total cost curve and the long-run total cost curve and this has been done in Fig. 15.15 where a short-run total cost curve *STC* and the long-run total cost curve *LTC* are drawn. It will be seen from top panel of Fig.15.15 that long-run total cost curve *LTC* lies below the short-run total cost curve *STC* (dotted) at all levels of output except at output *OQ* at which the two curves are tangent. This means that at output level *OQ*, the slope of the ray *OP* measures both the short-run average cost (*SAC*) and long-run average cost, (*LAC*). Therefore, in the panel at the bottom of Fig. 15.15 at output *OQ* and corresponding to tangency point *P* in the top panel, *SAC* and *LAC* curves are tangent to each other at point *E* indicating that *SAC* equals *LAC* at the output level *OQ* at which *STC* is tangent to *LTC*.

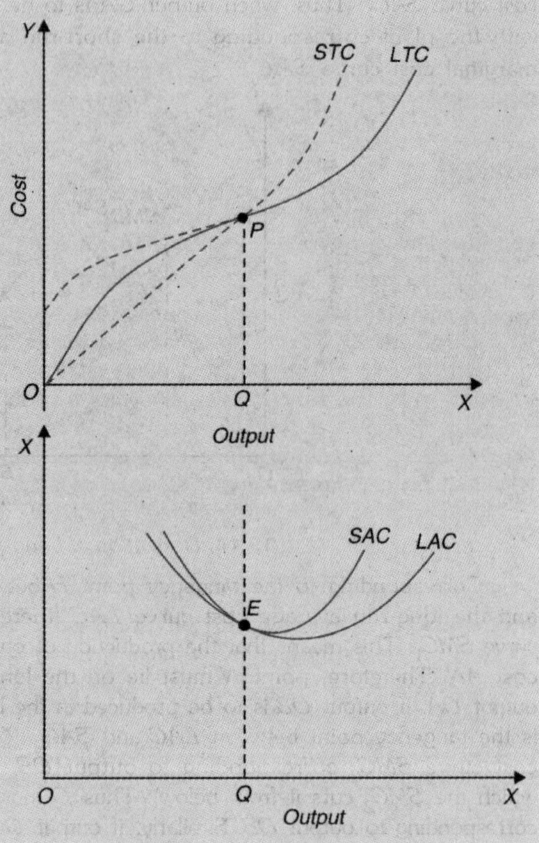

Fig.15.15. *Relationship between STC and LTC and between SAC and LAC.*

Further, the above relation implies that *LAC* is less than *SAC* at all levels of output until *OQ* is reached, as can be ascertained by drawing rays from the origin to *LTC* and *STC* at various levels of output before point *Q*. Beyond *OQ* output *SAC* becomes greater than *LAC* as will be known by drawing rays from the origin to the corresponding points on the *STC* and *LTC* curves at a given level of output beyond *OQ*. As will be seen from the panel at the bottom of the Fig. 15.15, the long-run average cost *LAC* is therefore equal to the short-run average cost *SAC* at output *OQ* at which *LTC* is tangent to the *STC*. How do we explain this relationship between short run and long run cost curves ? In the long-run adjustment is made in all factors including fixed factors such as capital equipment to minimise cost of production. In the short run some factors remain fixed and therefore cannot be suitably adjusted to minimise cost of production. As a result, short run cost, both total and average, exceed long-run cost except at one point where the given quantity of the fixed factor is in optimum proportion with the variable factor. A glance at the Figure 15.15 will make this point quite clear.

But the long-run marginal cost *LMC* must also be equal to short-run marginal cost *SMC* at output *OQ i.e.* the tangency point *P* of *STC* and *LTC* in Fig.15.15. This is because marginal cost is given by the slope of the total cost curve at any point, and the *LTC* curve and *STC* curve have the same slope at the tangency point *P*. It is thus clear that at output level *OQ*, where the *SAC* is equal to the *LAC*, *SMC* is also equal to the *LMC*. Though *SMC* and *LMC* will be equal to each other at output level *OQ*, they will be less than *SAC* and *LAC* because the slope of the tangent at point *P* is less than the slope of the ray *OP* from the origin. Thus the long-run marginal cost (*LMC*) curve will cut the short run marginal cost (*SMC*) at output level *OQ*, that is, exactly vertically below the point of equality of *SAC* and *LAC*.

LONG-RUN TOTAL COSTS AND EXPANSION PATH

Costs are related to the expansion path of the isoquant analysis of the production theory. We can derive the total cost curve from the expansion path. It may be recalled that given the nature of production function and factor prices, expansion path depicts the combinations of factors which an entrepreneur uses to produce various levels of output at the minimum possible cost. Once the long-run total cost curve is derived from the expansion path we can then derive the long-run average cost and marginal cost curve from the long-run total cost curve in a similar way that was adopted in case of derivation of short-run average and marginal cost curves. Let us take two factor production function which is assumed in the isoquant analysis. These two factors which we take are labour and capital. To minimize cost for a given level of output an entrepreneur will use such capital-labour ratio which equates marginal rate of technical substitution with factor price ratio. This is realised at the tangency point between an isoquant (representing a given level of output) with an iso-cost curve. Now, we are interested in knowing how the total cost changes when output is expanded by the entrepreneur along the expansion path as this would enable us to derive the long-run total cost curve. This is illustrated in Figure 15.16. We select three isoquants Q_1, Q_2, Q_3, representing three levels of output.

To find out the minimum-cost combination of capital and labour to produce a level of output Q_1, we draw an iso-cost line (which has a slope equal of price of labour and capital, $\frac{w}{r}$) which is tangent to the given isoquant Q_1. It will be seen from Figure 15.16 that resulting iso-cost line is C_1L_1. This will give us the total cost incurred on producing rate of output *Q*, equal to $\frac{OC_1}{r}$ or $\frac{OL_1}{w}$ which we call as TC_1. Now, we take the higher isoquant representing a higher rate of output Q_2. With factor prices remaining the same we draw an iso-cost line which is tangent to the isoquant Q_2. We find that the iso-cost line C_2L_2 giving us total cost equal to TC_2 is tangent to the isoquant Q_2. Next we draw an iso-cost line which is tangent to the isoquant representing higher level of output Q_3 and find that this iso-cost line C_3L_3 is tangent to it which gives us total cost equal to TC_3. Connecting the tangency points A, B, and C we get the expansion path.

It is thus evident from the expansion path that when output level is Q_1, the minimum total cost to produce it is TC_1. When rate of output is Q_2, the minimum total cost to produce it is TC_2 and when output expands to Q_3, the minimum total cost for its production rises to TC_3. Now, plotting TC_1, TC_2 and TC_3 against output levels Q_1 Q_2 and Q_3 respectively in panel (*b*) of Figure 15.16 we get the long-run total cost curve (*LTC*). Note that on an expansion path in the input space of panel (*a*) of Figure 15.16, there are numerous points of tangency of isoquants and iso-cost lines (only three are actually shown) which give us the combinations of long-run total cost and different rates of output. This gives us a smooth long-run total cost curve *LTC* in panel (*b*) of Figure 15.16

It is now easy to derive the long-run average cost curve and marginal cost curve from the total cost curve. The long-run average cost curve can be derived from the long-run total cost

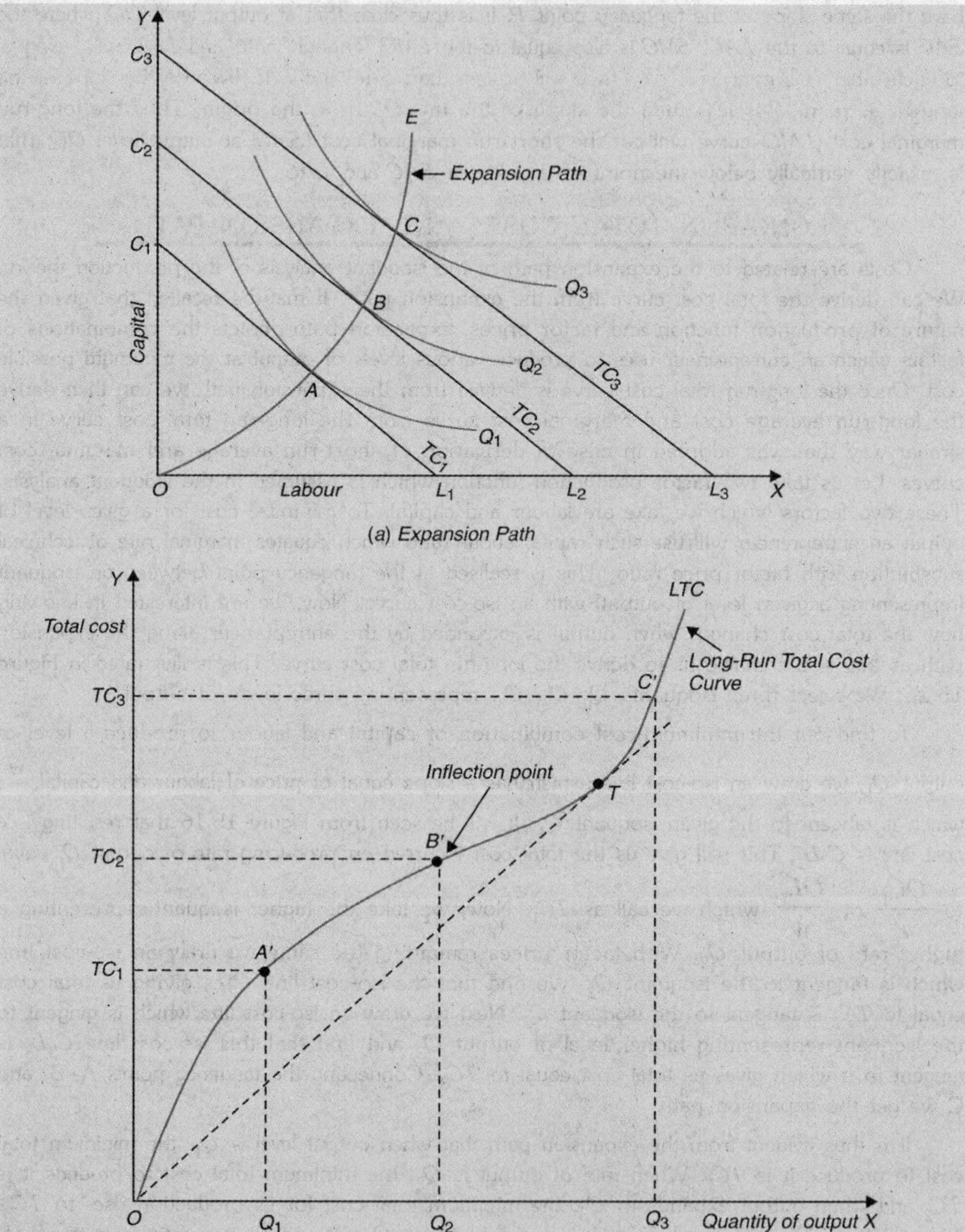

Fig. 15.16. *Derivation of Long Run Total Cost Curve from the Expansion Path*

curve by *measuring the slopes of the rays* drawn from the origins to various points on the *LTC* curves corresponding to different levels of output, as we have explained above in case of the derivation of short-ran average cost curve from the short-run total cost curve (*STC*). The long-run marginal cost curve is derived by *measuring slopes of LTC curve* by drawing tangents at various points corresponding to different levels of output. We have derived the *LAC* and *LMC* curves from the *LTC* in Figure 15.17. This also shows not only the relationship between the *LAC* and *LMC* curves with the *LTC* curve but also between the *LAC* and *LMC* curves. The relationship between *LAC* and *LMC* is the same as that between *SAC* and *SMC* curves explained above.

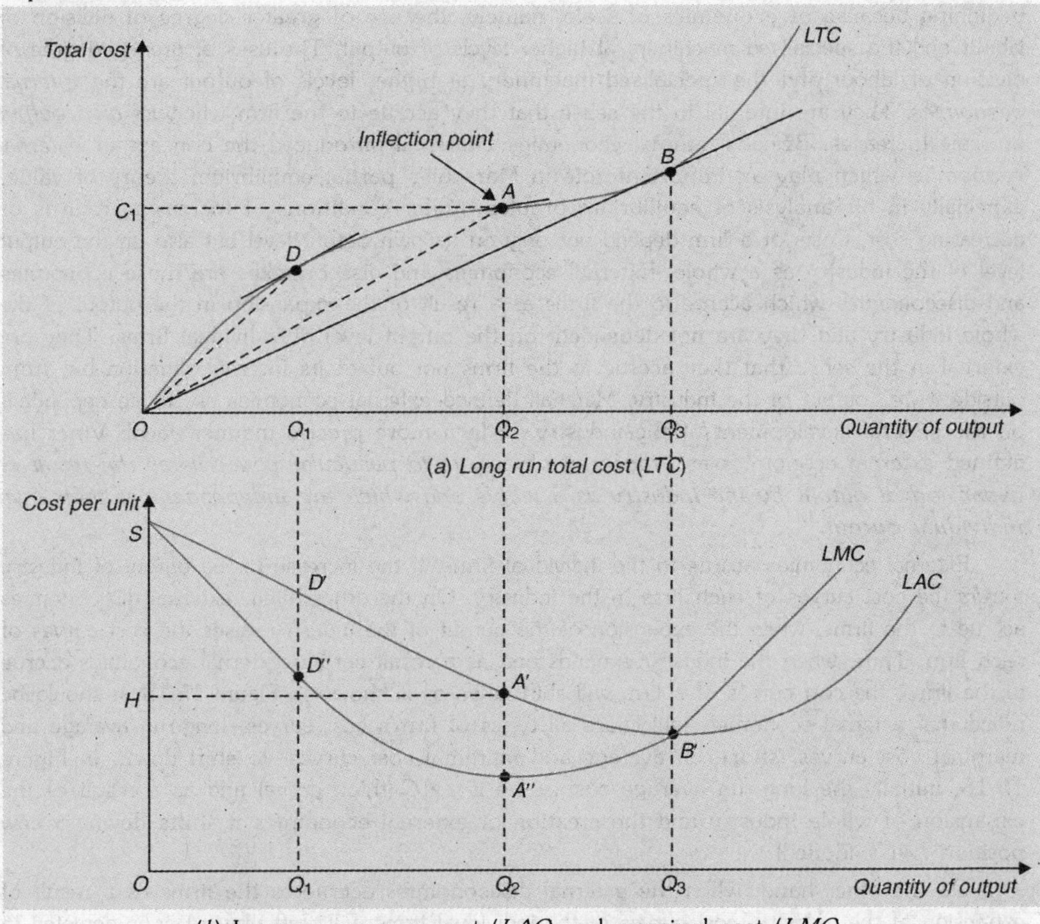

(*b*) Long-run average cost (*LAC*) and marginal cost (*LMC*)

Fig. 15.17. *Derivation of LAC and LMC from Long-Run Total Cost Curve (LTC).*

It is important to note that at different points of the expansion path, that is, at different levels of output, the firm may use a different capital-labour ratio as we are here concerned with the long run in which quantities of both capital and labour can be changed. The entirely different factor-ratio, that is, the production process may be used to minimize cost for producing output levels Q_1, Q_2, and Q_3 respectively. It is only when production function is linearly homogeneous and expansion path is a straight line from the origin, that the same factor ratio or the production process will be used to produce different levels of output. It needs to be emphasised that the long run represents a planning horizon where all productive factors (in our case both labour and capital) are variable, except factor prices and technology (i.e. the state of arts) and the firm has to decide which combination of factors (capital and labour) it has to choose. Whereas the change in factor prices will shift the iso-cost line, a change in technology will cause a change in the production function which will require a different isoquant map. This will change the expansion path and the long-run total cost curve derived from it.

EXTERNAL ECONOMIES AND DISECONOMIES AND COST CURVES

We have explained above that the long-run average cost curve falls downward in the beginning because of economies of scale, namely, the use of greater degree of division of labour and the specialised machinery at higher levels of output. The uses of greater degree of division of labour and the specialised machinery at higher levels of output are the *internal economies*. They are internal in the sense that they accrue to the firm when *its own output* or scale increases. Besides internal economies, Marshall introduced the concept of *external economies* which play an important role in Marshall's partial equilibrium theory of value, especially in his analysis of equilibrium problem under conditions of increasing returns or decreasing cost. Costs of a firm depend not only on its own output level but also on the output level of the industry as a whole. External economies and diseconomies are those economies and diseconomies which accrue to the firms as a result of the expansion in the output of the whole industry and they are not dependent on the output level of individual firms. They are external in the sense that they accrue to the firms not out of its internal situation but from outside it *i.e.,* output of the industry. Marshall defined external economies as "those dependent on the general development of the industry.[3]". In a more precise manner Jacob Viner has defined external economies as "*those which accrue to particular concerns as the result of expansion of output by the industry as a whole and which are independent of their own individual output.*"[4]

External economies accrue to the individual firms, if the increase in the output of industry *lowers* the cost curves of each firm in the industry. On the other hand, external diseconomies accrue to the firms, when the expansion of the output of the industry raises the cost curves of each firm. Thus, when the industry expands and as a result certain external economies accrue to the firms, the cost curves of a firm will shift down as is shown in Figure 15.18. It should be noted that external economies will cause all types of firm's cost curves—long-run average and marginal cost curves, short-run average and marginal cost curves—to shift down. In Figure 15.18, initially the long-run average cost curve is *LAC* (thick curve) and as a result of the expansion of whole industry and the creation of external economies it shifts down to new position *LAC′* (dotted).

On the other hand, when the external diseconomies accrue to the firms as a result of expansion of the industry, cost curves of the individual firms will shift upward as is depicted in the Fig.15.19. In the beginning, the long-run average cost curve is *LAC* and with the expansion of the industry output and consequent emergence of external diseconomies cause the long-run average cost curve (along with its short-run average and marginal cost curves) to shift upward to new position *LAC′* (dotted).

We noted above in a previous section that internal economies and diseconomies of scale affect the shape that the long-run average cost curve takes; internal economies of scale cause the long-run average cost to fall as output is increased in the initial stage and internal diseconomies of scale cause the long-run average cost curve to rise. On the other hand, external economies and external diseconomies cause the long-run average cost curve to shift down or up, as the case may be. Moreover, when we are considering the effect of external economies and external diseconomies on the cost curves, it is not only the long-run cost curves, but all short-run and long-run cost curves, whether total, average or marginal, shift together up or down as the case may be. In this connection, it is also worth noting that shifts in cost curves of a firm are not always, nor necessarily brought about by the expansion or

3. A Marshall, *Principles of Economics,* 8th ed., p. 266.
4. Jacob Viner, Cost Curves and Supply Curves, *Readings in Prices Theory,* AEA, p. 217.

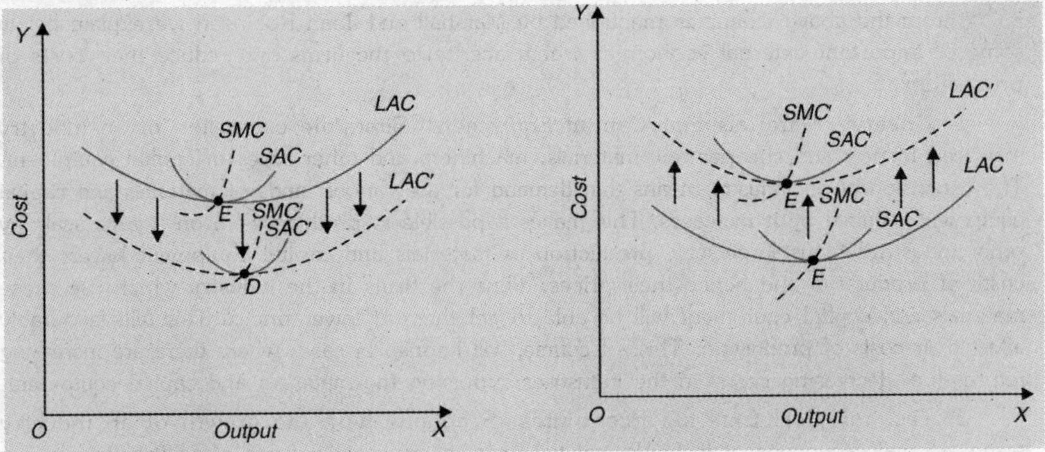

Fig. 15.18. *Downward Shift of the Cost Curves due to External Economies*

Fig. 15.19. *Upward Shift of the Cost Curves due to External Diseconomies*

contraction of an industry's output. For instance, a *general increase* in the prices of machinery and equipment, an all-round increase in wages and interest rates in the economy will also shift up the cost curves of a firm. Therefore, in microeconomics when we speak of increasing-cost industries, and decreasing-cost industries, we consider *only the effect of expansion of industry's own output* on costs of materials, labour, capital equipment etc. incurred by the firms in that industry and rule out any general increase in these costs in the whole economy.

Now, the question arises when an industry grows or expands its output, what types of external economies it generates which reduce the costs of all firms in it. The chief examples of external economies provided by Marshall are :

(*i*) "improved methods or machinery which are accessible to the whole industry"[5] when it expands;

(*ii*) economies which result from "development of mechanical appliances, of division of labour and of the means of transport and improved organisation of all kinds"[6] with the growth of an industry;

(*iii*) economies which result from the growth of correlated branches of industry which mutually assist one another and "being concentrated in the same localities"[7] encourage the development of 'hereditary skill"[8], 'the growth of subsidiary trades supplying it with implements and machinery and the "economic use of expensive machinery"[9]

(*iv*) economies which are "connected with the growth of knowledge and the progress of arts, especially in matters of trade knowledge: newspapers, trade and technical publications[10].

Like Marshall, Joan Robinson who analysed the *phenomenon of increasing returns* (i.e., decreasing costs) in the context of partial equilibrium analysis, provided the following main examples of external economies:

(*i*) the cases "where the machinery can be bought more cheaply when the industry presents a large market to the machine-making industry"[11] and

(*ii*) the cases "where a large labour force is accustomed to work at a certain trade" and develops "traditional skill"[12]

5. A Marshall, *Principles of Economics,* 8th edition, p.615.
6. *Ibid,* p. 808.
7. *Ibid,* p. 317.
8. *Ibid,* p. 217.
9. *Ibid,* p. 267.
10. *Ibid,* p. 284.
11. Joan Robinson, *The Economics of Imperfect Competition,* p.340.

From the above examples mentioned by Marshall and Joan Robinson we explain below some of important external economies which accrue to the firms and reduce their costs of production.

1. Cheaper Materials and Capital Equipment. First, the expansion of an industry may lead to new and cheaper raw materials, machinery and other types of capital equipment. The expansion of an industry means that demand for the various kinds of materials and capital equipment required by it increases. This makes it possible to produce them on a large scale by other industries. This large-scale production of materials and capital equipment lowers their costs of production and hence their prices. Thus the firms in the industry which use these materials and capital equipment will be able to get them at lower prices. This will favourably affect their costs of production. This, of course, will happen in cases where there are increasing returns (i.e. decreasing costs) in the industries supplying the materials and capital equipment.

2. Technological External Economies. Secondly, with the growth of an industry some external economies of technological type may accrue to the firms of an industry. In our discussion of returns to scale we mentioned that as an individual firm expands its scale, it may become possible for it to use more specialised and productive machinery and to introduce greater degree of division of labour. These are internal technological economies which change the technical coefficients of production and improve the firm's productivity. Similarly, when the whole industry in expands, it may lead to the discovery of new technical knowledge and in accordance with that the use of improved and better machinery than before becomes possible. This will also change the technical coefficients of production and will enhance the productivity of the firms in the industry and will reduce their costs of production.

3. Development of Skilled Labour. Another example of external economies that has been suggested is the development of hereditary or traditional skills among labour. When an industry expands in an area, the labour in that area is well accustomed to do the various productive processes and learns a good deal from the experience. As a result, with the growth of an industry a region a pool of trained labour equipped with the traditional skills is developed which has a favourable effect on the level of productivity and costs of the firms in the industry.

4. The Growth of Subsidiary and Correlated Industries. Another external economy accruing to the firms from the growth of an industry is the growth of subsidiary and correlated industries. These subsidiary and correlated industries may specialise in the production of raw materials, tools and machinery and therefore can provide them at lower prices to the main industry. Likewise, some specialised firms may come into existence, which process the 'waste product' of the industry into some useful product as a result of expansion of the industry when the waste product is large enough to make it worthwhile to set up separate plants for transforming the waste products into useful ones. When this happens, then the firms of the industry can sell their waste products at a good price. This will tend to reduce their cost of production.

5. Improved Transportation and Marketing Facilities. These external economies are greatly relevant when an infant industry grows up in a new territory. In the beginning, transportation and marketing facilities both for the purchase of materials and for the sale of its product may not be well-developed. However, the expansion of the industry by the entry of new firms in it may make possible the development of transportation and marketing facilities which will greatly reduce the costs of the firms.

---

12. *Ibid*, p. 341.

6. Development of Industry Information Services. As an industry expands, the firms may form a trade association that distributes information regarding technical knowledge and market possibilities about the industry through publication of trade and technical journals. With the expansion of the industry the firms may jointly set up a central research institute which will be engaged in discovering new improved techniques for the firms in the industry. Thus, besides providing market information, the growth of the industry may help in discovering and spreading improved technical knowledge.

External Diseconomies

We have explained above the external economies which accrue to the firms as a result of the growth of the industry. But, as said above, the expansion of an industry is also likely to generate external diseconomies which raise the cost curves of the firms. The main example of external diseconomies is the *rise in some factor prices* when the industry expands and its demand for various factors needed by it increases. The expansion of an industry will definitely raise the prices of those raw materials and capital goods which are in short supply. Likewise, the expansion of the industry is likely to raise the wages of skilled labour, at least in the short run, since it always takes time for the labour to get training and acquire specialised skills needed in a particular industry.

Since the productive factors such as various types of raw materials, cement, steel, various kinds of machinery and tools and skilled labour are scarce, the increase in demand for them resulting from the expansion in the industry is likely to push up their prices. In the context of scarcity of resources, an industry in an attempt to snatch away the resources from other industries, it will bid up their prices. Thus, in the real world of scarcity, an expanding industry will create more external diseconomies than external economies. Therefore, most industries in the real world encounter rising costs when they expand.

MODERN DEVELOPMENTS IN COST THEORY

Until recently it was widely believed that both the short-run and long-run average costs are of roughly U-shape. But in recent years, U-shape of the cost curve has been questioned by some economists, mainly on the empirical grounds. This challenge to U-shape average cost curve relates to both the short-run and long-run average cost curve. We first explain the shape of the short-run average variable cost according to the recent developments in economic theory.

Saucer-Shaped Short-Run Average Variable Cost Curve (SAVC)

The recent empirical studies have found that the short-run average variable cost curve has a saucer type shape rather than U-shape of the traditional economic theory. The saucer type shape of the average variable cost curve implies that there is a *flat stretch over a certain range of output* in it. It has been pointed out that this flat stretch in the short-run average cost curve is due to the reserve capacity that is consciously built in the plant size while designing it. This reserve capacity is built in the plant size with a view to impart flexibility in production so that the firm can expand output over a certain range without a rise in unit cost to meet any greater demand for its output in the future. On the contrary, the traditional theory assumes that there is single optimum level of output of a plant or firm after which unit cost starts rising. This short-run average variable cost curve with a saucer shape has been shown in Fig.15.20 where it will be seen that in the beginning the short-run average variable cost declines and the remains constant over the range of output $Q_1 Q_2$ and thereafter it rises. Corresponding to the output range $Q_1 Q_2$, the short-run average variable cost curve has a flat stretch.

The decline in average variable cost as output is expanded in the beginning has been explained to be the result of (1) better utilization of the fixed factor with increase in the variable factor, (2) the improvement in skills and productivity of labour, and (3) reduction in wastes of raw materials due to better skills and productivity of both management and labour ensuring better efficiency in the operation of the firm. On the other hand, the rising part of the *SAVC* curve after a flat stretch has been attributed to the fall in labour productivity as a result of long hours of work, overtime payment to labour, wastage in raw materials and more frequent breakdown of machinery as plant is operated for a longer time or with more shifts per day.

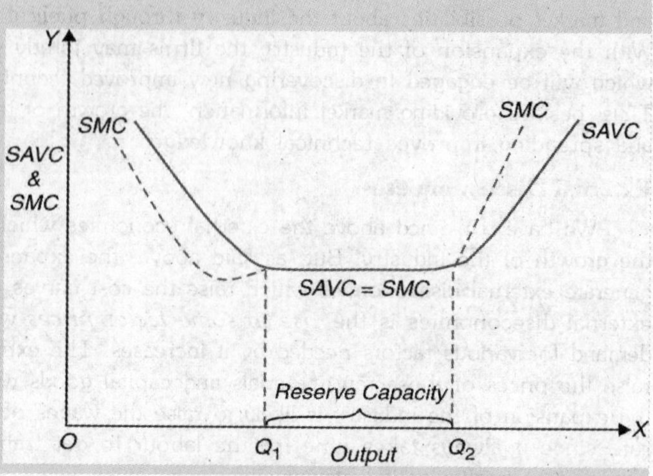

Fig.15.20. *Saucer-Shaped Average Variable Cost Curve*

In the initial stages when *SAVC* curve falls, marginal cost curve (*MC*) lies below it, in its flat stretch portion the marginal cost curve coincides with it and ultimately when *SAVC* curve rises after the full utilization of the reserve capacity of the plant, the marginal cost curve lies above it.

Average Total Cost Curve

Now, it is interesting to note that what will be the shape of the short-run average total cost curve when average variable cost curve has a saucer type shape. Average total cost is obtained by adding the average fixed cost to the average variable cost. Since average fixed cost falls continuously as output is expanded, the *SATC* curve declines up to the level of output at which reserve capacity is fully exhausted. Beyond that level of output, *SATC* will be rising with the further increases in output. This *SATC* curve when *SAVC* is of saucer shape is shown in Fig. 15.21 which illustrates how *SATC* is obtained by adding vertically *SAVC* and *AFC*.

L-Shaped Long Run Average Cost Curve

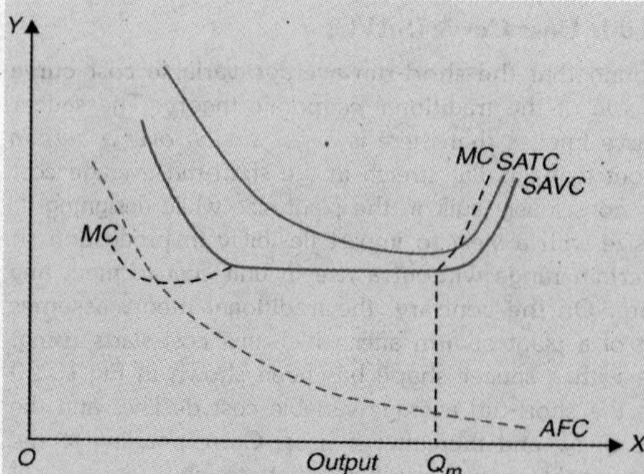

Fig. 15.21. *Short-Run Average Total Cost Curve when Average Variable Cost Curve has a Saucer-Shape*

A significant recent development in cost theory is that the long-run average cost theory is L-shaped rather than U-shaped. The L-shape of the long-run average cost curve implies that in the beginning when output is expanded through increase in plant size and associated variable factors, cost per unit falls rapidly due to economies of scale. Even after a sufficiently large scale of output, the long-run average cost curve does not rise; it may either remain constant or it may even go on falling slightly. At a very large scale of production, the managerial cost per unit of output may rise, but the technical or production economies more than offset the managerial diseconomies so that the total long-run average cost does not rise or even falls continuously though at a very small rate. Thus the empirical evidence gathered by economists in recent years does not indicate any U-shape in the long-run average cost curve. Empirical evidence indicates that the long-run average cost rapidly falls but after a point it remains flat throughout or at its right-hand end it may even slope gently downward.

L-shaped long-run average cost curve is illustrated in Fig.15.22. The difference between L-shaped *LAC* of Fig.15.22 and the U-shaped *LAC* is that there is no rising portion in the former. Indeed, as stated just above, the empirical evidence shows that *LAC* may even slope gently downward at its right-hand end. Thus, there is an apparent contradiction between traditional economic theory according to which *LAC* is U-shaped and the results of empirical investigations which find *LAC* to be L-shaped. However, there is controversy about whether the long-run average cost is really L-shaped when for deriving the long-run average cost curve usual assumptions made in traditional theory hold.

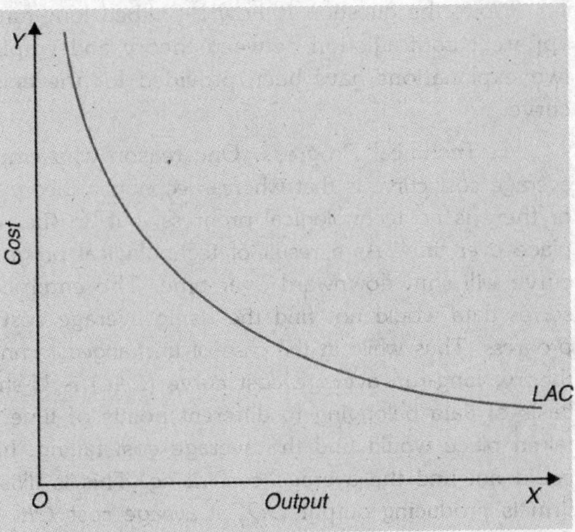

Fig. 15.22. *L-Shaped Long-Run Avarage Cost Curve*

Two explanations have been given for the explanation of L-Shape of *LAC*. First, it is pointed out that a firm continues to enjoy some technical or production'economies even after a *minimum optimal scale* is reached. Secondly, the modern developments in managerial science ensuring optimal managerial set-up for a larger scale of production prevents the long-run average cost to rise. We explain them below in some detail.

Production or Technical Economies. These are substantial economies of scale enjoyed by a firm when it expands its scale of output in the beginning. This causes the long-run average cost to fall steeply with the initial increases in scale of production. However, it has been asserted that even after most of the economies of scale have been achieved and the firm reaches a minimum optimal scale, given the technology of the industry, the unit cost of production may fall due to some technical eonomies which it can continue to enjoy even after the minimum optimal scale. First, the *new techniques* of production are adopted at a large scale of production due to which cost per unit falls. But even with the existing known techniques some economies can always be obtained due to (1) decentralisation and improved skills and productivity of labour, (2) lower repair costs after a certain scale is achieved, and (3) manufacturing by a firm itself some of the materials and equipment at lower cost which it needs for its production process instead of buying them from other firms.

Managerial Costs, In the traditional cost theory, the rising part of the *LAC* is explained by the difficulties in management, supervision, coordination and control which pushes up the unit cost of production after a certain scale of production is attained. In this regard, it has been pointed out that modern management science has developed for each plant size appropriate organizational and managerial, set-up for efficient working of the firm. For different scales of plant and sizes of firms different appropriate management techniques have been evolved and each management technique is applicable to a range of output. Only at a very large scale, managerial costs may rise. However, it has been claimed that any rise in managerial costs after a very large scale of output may be offset by production economies.

L-Shape Long-Run Cost Curve and Empirical Evidence : A Critical Evaluation

Now, the question is how L-Shaped long-run average cost curve can be explained and apparent contradiction between theory and empirical evidence be removed. The following two explanations have been provided for the existence of L-shaped long-run average cost curve.

1. Technical Progress. One reason why empirical studies don't find U-shape long-run average cost curve is that whereas economic theory assumes that technology remains unchanged or there is no technological progress, but, in the real world, technological progress does take place over time. As a result of technological progress in the real world, long-run average cost curve will shift downward over time. The empirical investigations which are based on time series data would not find the rising average cost in view of the existence of technological progress. Thus while in the case of unchanged technology, as is assumed in traditional economic theory, long-run average cost curve (*LAC*) is U-shaped, empirical studies conducted on the basis of data belonging to different points of time between which technological progress had taken place would find the average cost falling. In view of the technological progress, they could not find the average cost rising. This is illustrated in Fig. 15.23. Suppose initially the firm is producing output OQ_1 at aveage cost OK_1 by operating on LAC_1. If the demand for the firm's product increases to OQ_2, then in the context of unchanged technology the firm will expand production along LAC_1 and will produce OQ_2 output at average cost *OH*. Now, if the technological progress has taken place and in accordance with new technology the firm has a new plant whose long-run average cost is LAC_2, the firm will produce on the new curve LAC_2 output OQ_2 at OK_2 cost per unit which is less than both OK_1 and *OH*.

Likewise, when the firm at some later date has expanded output to OQ_2 in response to the increase in demand for its product, the technology might have advanced in the mean time so that the firm produces OQ_3 at OK_3, cost per unit which is less than OK_2. By joining the minimum points of long-run average cost curves we get a curve *LAC* which gently slopes downward due to technological progress that has taken place over time, whereas with unchanged technology long-run average cost curves LAC_1, LAC_2 and LAC_3 each with a different but unchanged technology is U-shaped.

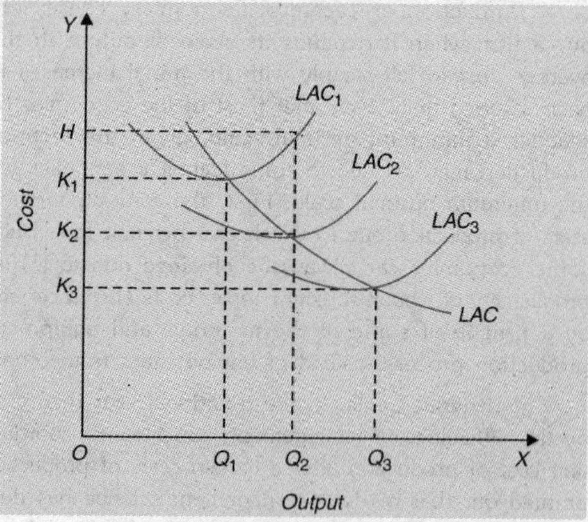

Fig. 15.23. *L-Shaped Long-Run Average Cost Curve*

Empirical studies made by economists at different points of time would estimate OK_1, OK_2 and OK_3 costs at output OQ_1, OQ_2 and OQ_3 respectively and would therefore suggest that long-run average cost curve was like the L-shaped curve *LAC*. We therefore conclude that while with a given and unchanged technology long-run average cost curves are U-shaped, empirical studies would find L-shaped long-run average cost curve due to technological progress that takes place over time. "The fact that technology changes does not in itself contradict our contention that, if only because it is harder to manage a larger firm than a smaller one, long-run average cost curves will be U-shaped in a given state of technology. What the empirical evidence does suggest is that technological progress may often be rapid enough to reduce unit costs even in a situation where, with given technology, the problem of managing a bigger firm would increase unit costs."[13]

Learning by Doing. Learning by doing is another factor which causes the long-run average cost to slope downward throughout. It is now common knowledge that a person learns while doing some productive work, the greater the amount of work he has done since the time he started doing a particular work, the greater the experience he attains and with the experience he learns to do things in a better way than before. This tends to reduce the cost per unit. A firm learns to produce a commodity more efficiently as the aggregate amount of output produced by it increases over time. A good deal of empirical evidence is available which goes to prove that firm's cost of production depends not only on the amount of output of a commodity it produces each month or year but also on the aggregate amount of that commodity produced since the time it started its production. This is because the aggregate output by a firm to date determines the degree of learning it has acquired and the efficiency gained by it.

Therefore, we can draw a learning curve which relates the average cost of production of a commodity to the *aggregate amount* of output produced over time by a firm of that commodity. This learning curve will be sloping downward indicating thereby that as the aggregate amount of output produced of a commodity by a firm increases over time, cost per unit goes on declining. This is because, as said above, with greater production, a firm learns to produce a commodity more efficiently and therefore cost per unit declines. It should be noted that with the increase in aggregate production of a commodity over time, learning gained by a firm is not only in respect of improving efficiency in physical operations in the production of a commodity but also in respect of improving the organisation of the plant. Thus, besides the factor of technological progress, learning provides us another reason why long-run average cost curve is L-shaped rather than U-shaped. To quote Stonier and Hague, "Even with a given technology, a firm can 'learn' to produce at a lower unit cost the longer the period of time that has elapsed since a previous observation and the greater the aggregate amount of that product that has consequently been made. It may be, therefore, that technological change is not the only reason why long-run average cost curves are L-shaped rather than U-shaped."[14]

Validity of Empirical Evidence Regarding the Behaviour of Long-Run Average Cost

We have stated above that according to empirical evidence gathered by economists long-run average cost is L-shaped rather than U-shaped. In other words, according to the empirical evidence, long-run average cost after the initial rapid fall, either remains constant or declines throughout; it does not rise. That is, long-run average cost does not turn up as is required if it is U-shaped. Professor C.A. Smith who has examined empirical evidence in this connection has concluded that with a very large size of firm, labour costs, assembly costs and distribution costs increase very much and therefore large-sized plants with *increasing average cost are not set up in actual practice* and therefore empirical evidence cannot assess the cost situation in them. Therefore, according to Professor Smith, empirical evidence does not refute the U-

13. Stonier and Hangue, *A Textbook of Economic Theory*, 4th edition, 1972, p.140.
14. Op. cit, p. 141.

shaped nature of long-run average cost curve. To quote him, "(1) With increasing size of plant, at least from small to medium size, average cost of production declines as size increases if factor costs are held constant. (2) There is no substantial evidence that the decline in unit costs stops before the maximum size of plant available for study if factor costs are held constant and the product is the same. On the other hand, the *little evidence available does not refute the idea that the long-run average cost curves even with factor prices constant turns up at some attainable size.* We can hardly hope to find an answer to this question as to whether there is in practice a plant so large that the cost of producing specific products does not increase even if factor prices are held constant because : (*a*) Factor costs, especially labour cost, seem to vary with size of plant : (*b*) Assembly costs and distribution costs per unit decline for a time with increasing size of plant but usually start to increase within the range of size of plant available for study"[15].

From his analysis of empirical evidence he concludes that "increases in factor prices and in assembly and distribution costs result in cost increases which make it impractical to build plants which might be large enough to have higher average cost. Therefore, *we have no opportunity to study the costs of such plants.* The hypothesis that the long-run cost function for the production of a product typically turns up at some very large size cannot be subjected to empirical verification."[16]

In view of the limited empirical evidence about the correct shape of the long-run average cost curve we shall continue to assume in our analysis throughout that the typical shape of the long-run average cost curve is U-shaped, though its U-shape is less pronounced than that of short-run average cost curve. However, there is in fact a long flat region *i.e.*, horizontal portion in this long-run average cost curve, which we shall not be showing in the diagrams.

THE LEARNING CURVE

The learning curve is an important modern concept according to which cumulative experience by a firm in the production of a product over time increases efficiency in the use of inputs such as labour and raw materials and thereby lowers cost per unit of output. Arrow, one of the pioneers in putting forward this concept calls it "*Learning by Doing*"[17]. According to Arrow, as a firm or its manager produces successive lots of output over various periods of time, it learns to produce 'more with a given quantity of resources or it is capable of producing a given output by using lesser quantities of inputs or resources than before. Thus, either with the increase in efficiency of resources or with saving in resources such as labour and raw materials, cost per unit of output declines. This learning curve effect mostly occurs in the reduction of labour requirements per unit of output.

A number of factors bring this learning curve effect. As cumulative volume of output over successive periods of time increases, labour and supervisors become more familiar with the work methods or the production process, which leads to the reduction in the amount of scrap and other types of wastes. Besides, raw materials cost per unit of output may also decline as cumulative volume of output in successive periods over time increases and as a result a firm gains more experience in doing a production process repeatedly over successive time periods.

15. C.A. Smith, *Empirical Evidence of Economies of Scale,* printed in Business Concentration and Price Policy, Universities National Bureau Committee for Economic Research, Princeton University press, 1955.
16. Op. cit, p. 42.
17. K.J. Arrow, "The Economic Implications of Learning by Doing", *Review of Economic Studies*, Vol. 29 (June 1962) pp. 154-179.

The learning curve is graphically shown in Fig, 15.24. where on the *X*-axis cumulative total output over successive periods of time and on the *Y*-axis cost per unit of output are measured. It will be seen from Fig. 15.24 that the learning curve slopes downward which shows declining cost per unit of output as cumulative output increases over time and the firm learns from its work experience.

The learning curve effect is usually expressed as a *constant percentage.* This percentage represents the proportion by which cost per unit of output declines with the increase in cumulative output in each successive time period. For example, if in a production process labour-input cost experiences 80 per cent learning-curve effect, this means that if in the first period production of a unit of output requires labour cost of Rs 1000, in the next period labour cost per unit will decline to Rs 800 and so forth. This learning curve relationship between cost and output is expressed algebraically as follows

$$C = aQ^b$$

where C is the input cost of Qth unit of output, Q is successive unit of output produced, a is the input cost per unit of output in the first period and b is the rate of decline in cost per unit of output in the successive periods. Since the learning curve is downward-sloping, the value of b is negative.

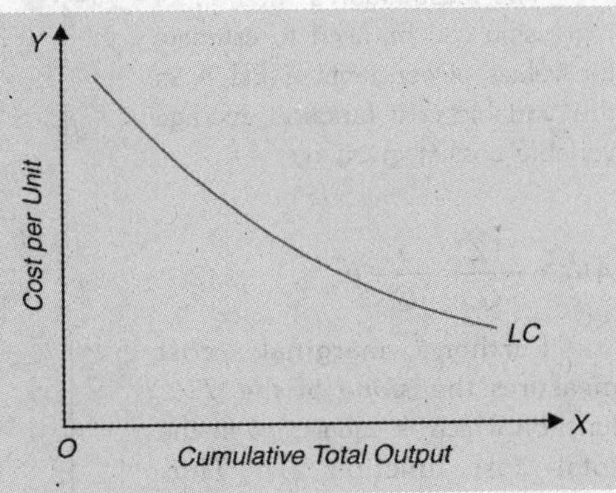

Fig. 15.24. *The Learning Curve*

It is important to note that reduction in cost per unit due to the learning-curve effect is different from economies of scale. Whereas economies of scale refer to decline in cost per unit of output as a *firm's output per time period* increases, the learning curve describes the reduction in cost per unit of output as a *firm's cumulative output over successive time periods increases, while output per period* may remain the same.

THE ESTIMATION OF COST FUNCTION

As in case of production function, managerial decisions require quantitative estimates of cost function. Management decision-making requires the estimates of both short-run and long-run cost functions. The estimation of short-run cost function helps the manager to know about the *quantitative estimates of marginal costs* which are required to determine profit-maximising output and price of products. In the long-run the manager requires to know which size of plant will be most efficient, that is, has a minimum long-run average cost. This most efficient size of plant depends on the economies and diseconomies of scale. We explain below the estimation of both shortrun and long-run cost functions.

The Estimation of Short-run Cost Function

The short-run costs consist of both fixed costs and variable costs. Though the fixed costs must be identified and measured, they are not estimated in cost-function studies because they do not very with changes in output. In the estimation of short-run cost function one requires data wherein changes in both output and cost occur as a result of changes in some factors, holding the quantities of other factors fixed. If estimate of total cost function is required, the fixed cost is added to the variable cost function.

Assume that the appropriate data on variable cost and output have been collected, then for estimation of parameters of the cost function one needs the suitable functional form which gives a best fit to the data collected over the observed range of output. If the relationship between the variable cost and output is approximately of linear form, then the following cost function should be used to estimate its parameters

$$TVC = a + b\,Q \quad .....(1)$$

The least-squares method of regression can be used to estimate the values of constants *a* and *b*. In this variable cost function average variable cost is given by

$$AVC = \frac{TVC}{Q} = \frac{a}{Q} + b \quad .....(2)$$

Further, marginal cost measures the *slope* of the *TVC* function which is equal to *b* in the total cost function (1). Thus marginal cost function is given by

$$MC = \frac{dTVC}{dQ} = b \quad .....(3)$$

TVC, *AVC* and *MC* functions of the linear variable cost are illustrated in Fig. 15.25. In panel (*a*) of Fig.15.25. linear total variable cost curve with an intercept is drawn and corresponding to this in panel (*b*) *AVC* curve has been drawn which is given by $AVC = \frac{a}{Q} + b$, is falling with increase in output. Since *TVC* is linear, marginal cost (*MC*) which is equal to its slope (*b*) remains constant and therefore *MC* curve is a horizontal straight line. It should be carefully noted that as output increases, $\frac{a}{Q}$ will become successively smaller and therefore *AVC* curve depicting $\frac{a}{Q} + b$ will tend to be closer to *b*, that is, marginal cost but will not touch it.

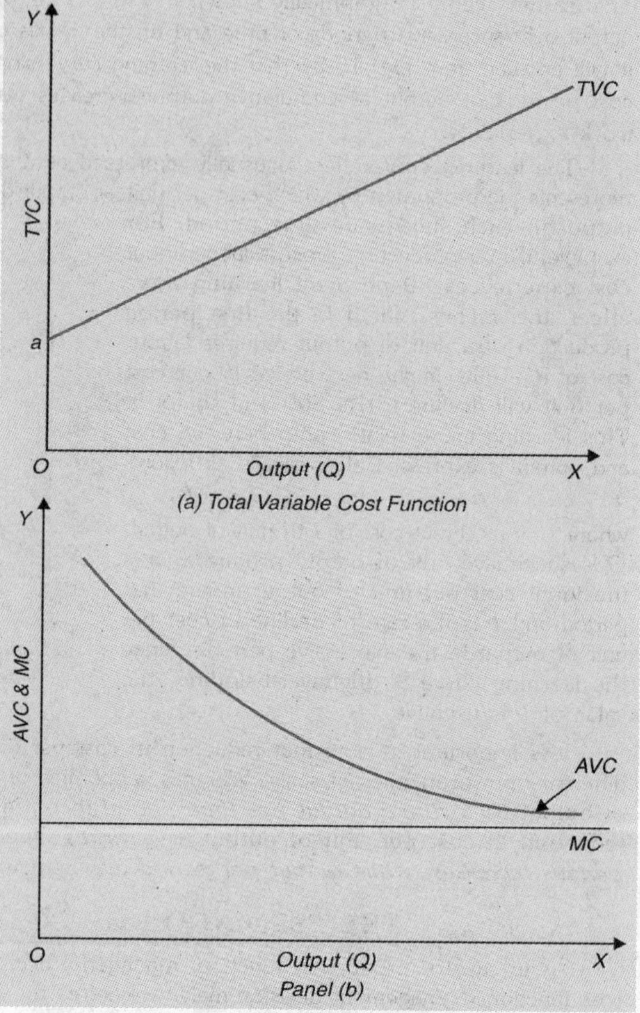

Fig. 15.25. *Total Variable, Cost, AVC and MC Functions*

The Cubic TVC Function

In economic theory it is hypothesized that *TVC* function is *S* shaped (*i.e.* cubic) which corresponds to U-shaped *AVC* and *MC* curves as indicated in Fig. 15.26. The empirical data about output and cost may also indicate cubic form of *TVC* function and hence U-shaped *AVC* and marginal cost functions are given by

$$TVC = aQ + bQ^2 + cQ^3$$

$$AVC = \frac{TVC}{Q} = a + bQ + cQ^2$$

$$MC = \frac{dTVC}{dQ} = a + 2bQ + 3cQ^2$$

Through the variable cost functions are non-linear in variables Q, Q^2 and Q^3 but are linear in parameters a, b and c. Therefore, these parameters can be estimated by least squares regression technique without transformation of the functional equations. The cubic total variable cost function and its associated *AVC* and *MC* functions are shown in Fig.15.26. In the upper panel of this figure *S*-shaped *TVC* curve has been drawn and in the lower panel corresponding to it, U-shaped *AVC* and *MC* curves have been shown. It should be noted that *AVC* and *MC* curves are equal at the level of output corresponding to which the tangent drawn to the *TVC* curve meets the point of origin. Further note that up to the inflection point of the *TVC* curve *MC* is falling and beyond that *MC* will be rising. It is worth noting that actual shapes of these cost functions depend on the values of estimated parameters (*i.e.* a, b and c)

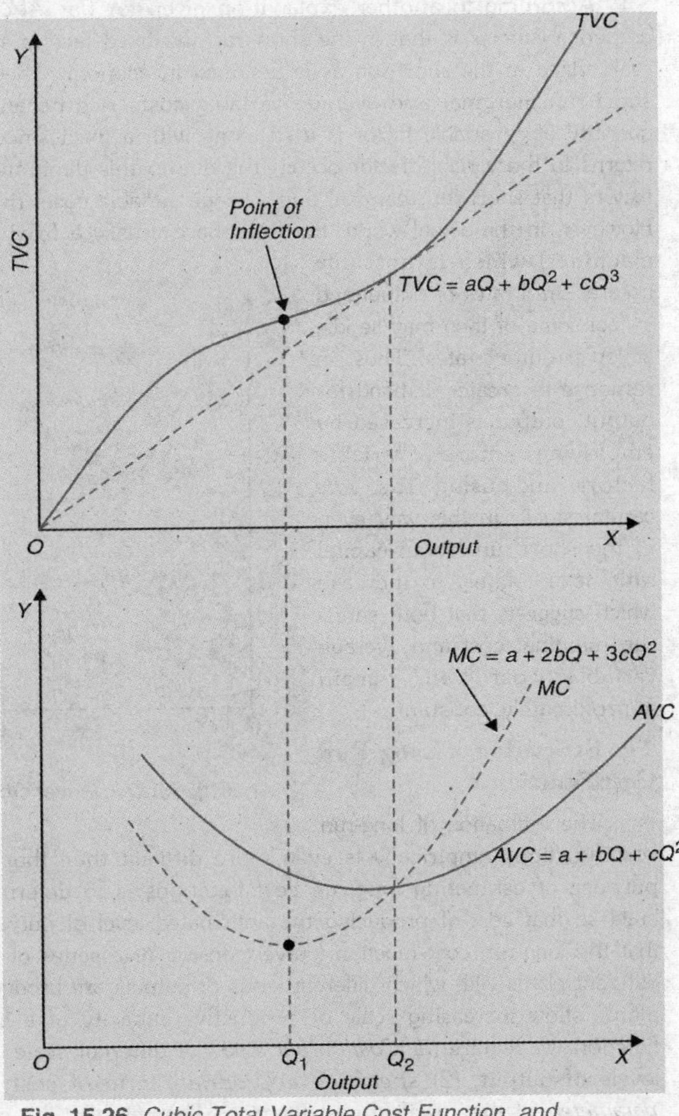

Fig. 15.26. *Cubic Total Variable Cost Function and Corresponding AVC and MC Function*

Explanation of Flat AVC and MC Curves

It will be noticed from Fig. 15.25 that *MC* curve is a horizontal straight line and *AVC* curve becomes flat and approaches the value of b (*i.e.* *MC*) towards its right end. Emfirical studies of short-run cost functions have found that marginal cost and average variable cost are constant over a wide range of output rates. Thus seems to be inconsistent to the convenional economic theory according to which average variable cost and marginal cost curves are U-shaped, that is, in the beginning they slope downward and beyond a certain level of output, they rise due to diminishing returns to the variable factors. How can we then explain this inconcistency between economic theory and empirical studies. One explanation that is offerred is that average variable cost and short-run marginal cost curves are saucer-shaped as shown in Fig.15.27. The saucer-shaped of these curves show that they have a negative slopes at low levels of output and positive slopes (rising) at high levels of output with a flat portion over a wide range of output in between. Since efficient working generally requires that firms in the real world should operate in the flat portion of these curves, most of the data regarding actual production rates and costs would reveal approximately constant costs .

According to another explanation given for flat *AVC* and *MC* cost functions found in emperical studies is that in the short run the fixed factors such as physical capital may not be really fixed in the short-run as is assumed in economic theory. Economic theory explains that short-run marginal and average variable costs rise because in the short run, as a greater quantity of a variable factor is used along with a fixed amount of capital, diminishing marginal returns to the variable factor occur. It is due to this diminishing marginal returns to the variable factors that short-run marginal and average variable costs rise beyond a certain level of output. However, in the actual world, the firms have usually a fixed stock of capital (*i.e.* the number of machines) which is not fully used at small rates of output and in fact some of then may lie idle at lower output rates. Thus, in response to greater demand for output, output is increased by employing more variable factors and using the *idle* capital stock. In this way even in the short-run labour-capital ratio is not likely to increase which suggests that both short-run marginal cost and average variable cost will remain approximately constant.

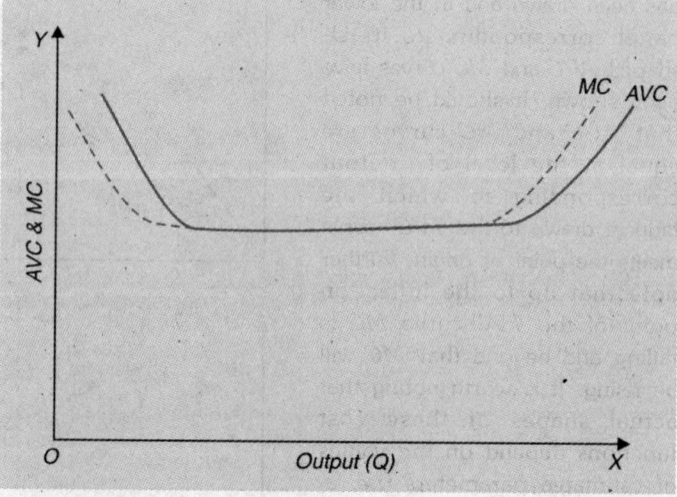

Fig. 15.27. *Sancer Shaped AVC and MC Curves*

The Estimation of Long-Run Cost Functions

The estimation of long-run cost functions empirically is even more difficult than that of short-run cost functions. The purpose of estimating long-run cost functions is to determine the *optimal scale of plant* to build so that cost of producing the anticipated level of output is minimised. It may be recalled that the long-run cost function (curve) consists of a series of short-run cost functions (curves) of different plants with which different levels of outputs are produced in the long run. The successive plants show increasing scale or productive capacity of a firm. For estimating long-run cost function we require (*a*) *Cost-output data* of different scales of plants appropriate to different levels of output, (2) *specfying appropriate* form of cost function, and (*c*) *estimating the parameters* of the specified cost function. Theoretically, the estimation of long-run cost function requires either time-series analysis of a firm or cross section analysis of firms. The main problem in using time-series data of a plant or firm for making regression analysis is that if period is long enough for the scale of plant to have changed, it *will also involve changes in production technology and input prices.* The changes in technology and input prices will distort the estimation of true long run cost function. It will be recalled that in deriving cost functions, both short-run and long run, the economists assume the production technology and input prices to remain constant.

In view of the above problems with time-series analysis of estimating long-run cost function, the cross-sectional approach is generally used to estimate the long-run cost function. For this purpose we require cost-output data of a number of firms at a given point in time.

However, in regression analysis of cross-sectional data to estimate the long-run cost function we also face difficult problems. First, the firms whose cost and output data are collected for estimation of long-run cost function may belong to different geographical regions and therefore they are likely to pay different input prices, for example different wage rates. To allow for such differences, wage rates of labour and prices of other inputs have to be included in the cost function as independent variables. Besides, the various firms are likely to use different depreciation rules that may distort the cost data of the firms and vitiate our estimates of long-run cost function.

However, the major problem faced in estimation of long-run cost function using cross-sectional cost-output data of a number of firms is that it is difficult to determine if each firm

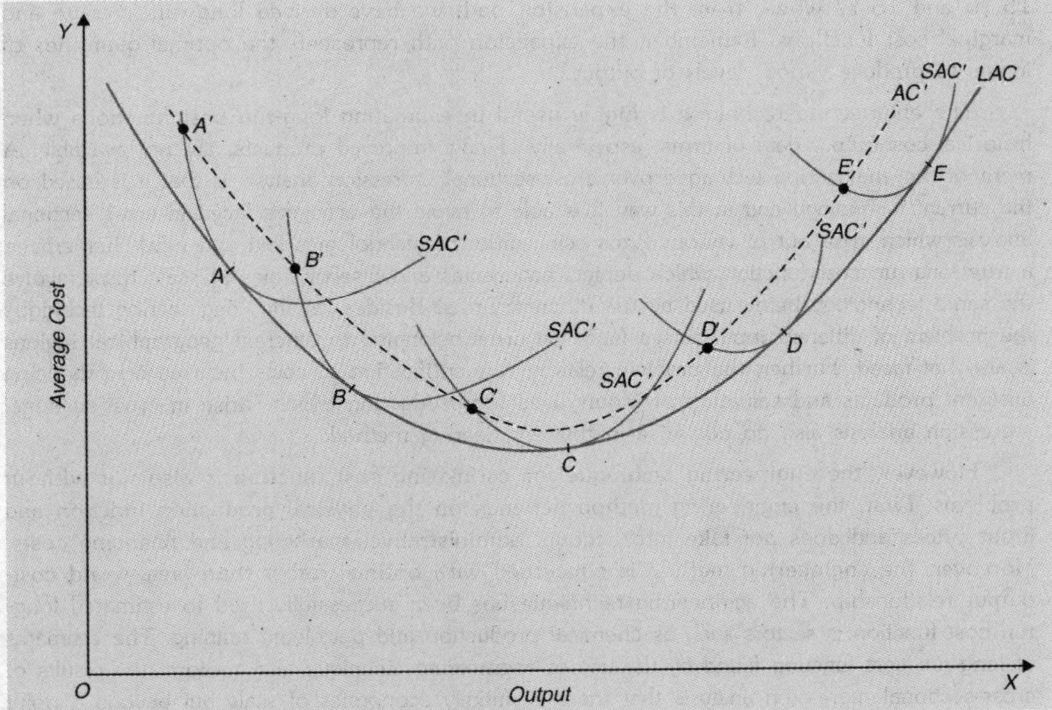

Fig. 15.28. *Estimation of Long-run Cost Function*

in the sample is producing with optimal plant and its optimal output (that is, at which its short-run average cost is tangent to the long-run cost function curve). For example, the correct estimate of the long-run cost function requires that the firms must operate at points *A*, *B*, *C*, *D* and *E* that are tangency points of various plant curves (*i.e.* short-run avarage cost curves) such as SAC_1, SAC_2, SAC_3, SAC_4, and SAC_5. These tangency points represent optimal cost-output data of the firms in the longrun.

However, the firms in the real world may be producing at A', B', C', D' and E' and therefore cost-output data collected may correspond to these points and on estimation we get the *dotted long-run average cost function (curve) LAC'* which will be biased in an upward direction and will overestimate the degree of economies and diseconomies of scale.

A large number of emperical studies of cost functions suggests that there are sharply increasing returns to scale in the beginning and near constant returns to scale at higher levels of output are obtained that is *LAC appears to be L-shaped.* However, some emperical studies do show the diseconomies of scale for large firms and plants.

Estimation of Long-run Cost Functions with Engineering and Survival Techniques

When adequate cross-sectional cost-output data of firms is not available, long-run cost function is estimated by either engineering technique or survivor technique. Engineering technique is based on the costs involving the physical relationship between inputs used and output produced. In other words, the engineering technique uses the knowledge of production function expressing physical relationship between inputs used and output produced and from it determine the optimal input combinations required to produce various levels of output. *The optimal quantities* of inputs to produce different levels of output so obtained are multiplied by the prices of inputs to obtain long-run costs of various output levels. This is illustrated in Fig. 15.16 and 15.17 where from the expansion path we have derived long-run average and marginal cost functions. Remember, the expansion path represents the optimal quantities of inputs to produce various levels of output.

The engineering technique is highly useful in estimating long-run cost functions when historical cost-output data of firms, especisally of new improved products, are not available. A merit of the engineering technique over cross-sectional regression analysis is that it is based on the current technology and in this way it is able to avoid the problems faced in cross sectional analysis which arise out of various firms using different technologies (old and new). Remember, a true long-run cost function which depicts economies and diseconomies of scale must involve the same technology being used by the different firms. Besides, in the engineering technique the problem of different input prices faced by firms belonging to different geographical regions is also not faced. Further, the problem relating to identification of costs incurred on producing different products and valuation of inputs used for production which arise in cross-sectional regression analysis also do not arise in this engineering method.

However, the engineering technique for estimating cost function is also not without problems. First, the engineering method depends on the physical production function and input prices and does not take into account administrative, marketing and financing costs. Moreover, the engineering method is concerned with optimal rather than real world cost-output relationship. The engineering technique has been successfully used to estimated long-run cost function is sectors such as chemical production and petroleum refining. The estimates of long-run cost function found by the use of engineering technique also conform the results of cross-sectional regression analysis that there is initially economies of scale but beyond a point constant returns to scale occur, that is, long-run cost curve is L-shaped.

The Survival Technique

An eminent American economist and a Nobel Laureate George J. Stigler has suggested a simple method of estimating long-run cost[2]. Stigler expressed the view that for estimating long-run cost function, the cross-sectional studies make use of accounting cost-output data that are full of distortions. We therefore require adjustments in the data before they are used in the regression analysis they are of doubtful validity. In his study he postulated if large-size firms coexist with small-size firms it means constant returns to scale prevail. This is because if there exist large economies of scale over an extensive range of output, then being cost-efficient the large firms will compete away the small firms from the industry. As a result, the share of large firms in the total capacity or output of the industry will increase while that of small firms will decline. In his formal empirical study of steel industry in the United States he *observed the industry over time.* He classified the firms in the steel industry into various categories according to their *size* which he measured by percentage share of the firm in total output or total capacity of the industry. Using data for 1930, 1938 and 1951 he arrived at the conclusion that while the share of medium-size firms (defined as between 2.5 per cent and 25 per cent of the industry capacity) increased over the 21 years period (1930-1951) from 35 per cent to 46 per cent of the total, whereas the share of small steel firms each with less than 2.5 per cent of the industry capacity and of large firms (actually there was one large firm accounting for over 25 per cent of industry capacity) declined over the time period. This Stigler's study suggested that *LAC* was U-shaped but had a flat bottoms shown in Fig. 15.29. This implies that in the beginning while there are economies of scale followed by constant returns to scale over a wide range of output and then beyond an output level, the firm experiences diseconomies of scale.

Stilger also used his survival technique to estimate long-run cost function in case of Automobile industry of the United States and found that there existed economies of scale at the intial increases in the outputs of firms and thereafter constant returns to scale prevailed. Thus Stilger's empirical study of the US automobile industry suggested L-shaped long-run average cost curve.

Stilger's survival technique is quite appealing due to its simplicity and avoidance of unreliable cost-output data furnished by the firms. However, Stilger's technique is also not without some serious problems. First, it does not help us in estimating long-run cost function for managerial decision making for the purpose of planning to set up a plant of an appropriate size for which such cost-estimation is needed. It says nothing directly about relative costs of various plant sizes, Second, Stigler implicitly assumes that the form of industry structure is highly competitive in which survival depends on the efficiency due to economies of scale. It does not consider that inefficient firms may survive if they are provided shelter by government regulation or if they enjoy market power due to strong barriers to the entry in the industry. In such cases Stigler's survival principle gets distorted or becomes inoperative. Changes in technology and inflation over a long period of time also cause distortions in Stigler's analysis of long-run cost estimation. Besides, the imperfections such as product differentiation by firms or local advantages enjoyed by them also permit inefficient firms to survive even

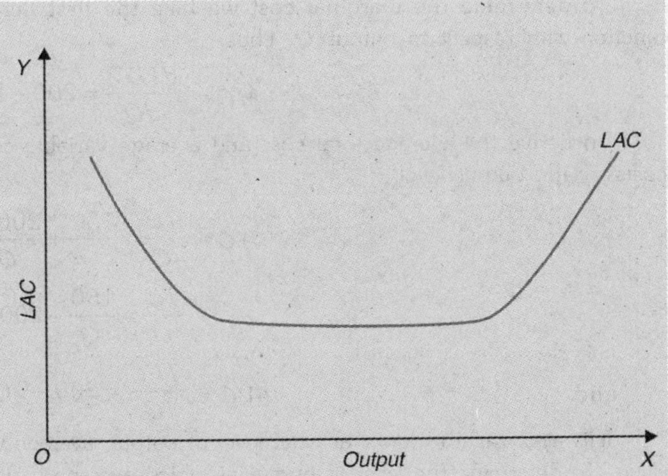

Fig. 15.29. *Long-run Average Cost Function as per Stilger's Study of the US Steel Industry.*

though they are inefficient in terms of cost of production. Finally, survival technique does not permit us to measure the degree of economies or diseconomies of scale.

NUMERICAL PROBLEMS ON COST FUNCTIONS

Problem 1. *Suppose a firm faces a cost function of* $C = 8 + 4q + q^2$

(*i*) *What is the firm's fixed cost ?*

(*ii*) *Derive an expression for the firm's average variable cost and marginal cost.*

Solution. (*i*) As fixed cost of the firm does not vary with output, the term in the given cost function which has no output (q) term will be the fixed cost. From the given cost function it is evident that fixed cost is 8.

(*ii*) Total variable cost $(TVC) = TC - TFC$

$$= (8 + 4q + q^2) - 8 = 4q + q^2$$

and
$$AVC = \frac{TVC}{q} = \frac{4q + q^2}{q} = 4 + q$$

Marginal cost is the first derivative of total cost function or total variable cost function.

Thus, $$MC = \frac{\Delta TVC}{\Delta q} = 4 + 2q$$

Problem 2. *A biscuit producing company has the following variable cost function :*

$$TVC = 200Q + 9Q^2 + 0.25Q^3$$

If the company's fixed costs are equal to Rs. 150 lakhs find out :

(*a*) *total cost function*

(*b*) *marginal cost function*

(*c*) *average variable cost function*

(*d*) *average total cost function*

(*e*) *at what output levels average variable cost and marginal cost will be minimum.*

Solution. Since total cost is the sum of total fixed cost and total variable cost ($TC = TFC + TVC$), we get the total cost function as under:

$$TC = 150 + 200Q - 9Q^2 + 0.25Q^3$$

To determine the marginal cost we take the first derivative of the total variable cost function with respect to output Q. Thus,

$$MC = \frac{d(TC)}{dQ} = 200 - 18Q + 0.75Q^2$$

To derive the average total cost and average variable cost we divide the respective total costs by the output level.

$$AC = \frac{TC}{Q} = \frac{150}{Q} + \frac{200Q}{Q} - \frac{9Q^2}{Q} + \frac{0.25Q^3}{Q}$$

$$= \frac{TC}{Q} = \frac{150}{Q} + 200 - 9Q + 0.25Q^2$$

and
$$AVC = \frac{TVC}{Q} = 200 - 9Q + 0.25Q^2$$

It is also useful to know at what level of output, average variable cost takes on its minimum value. To determine the level of output at which average variable cost is minimum, we have to take first derivative of the average variable cost (AVC) function and set this derivative equal to zero.

Thus, taking the first derivative of AVC function ($AVC = 200 - 9Q + 0.25Q^2$), we have :

$$\frac{d(AVC)}{dQ} = -9 + 0.50Q$$

Setting it equal to zero we have

$$-9 + 0.50Q = 0$$
$$0.50Q = 9$$
$$\frac{1}{2}Q = 9$$
$$Q = 18$$

Thus, at output level equal to 18, average variable cost will be minimum.

Output at which MC Function is Minimum

$$MC = 200 - 18Q + 0.75Q^2$$

To find the output level at which MC is minimum, we have to set the first derivative of MC function equal to zero. The first derivative of MC function is

$$\frac{d(MC)}{dQ} = -18 + 1.50\ Q$$

Setting $\frac{d(MC)}{dQ}$ equal to zero, we have :

$$-18 + 1.50\ Q = 0$$
$$1.50Q = 18$$
$$Q = -18 \times \frac{10}{15} = 12$$

Thus, at output level 12, MC is minimum.

It is thus clear from above that marginal cost takes on the minimum value at an output level smaller than that at which AVC is minimum.

Problem 3. *A firm producing hockey sticks has a production function given by $Q = 2\sqrt{KL}$. In the short run, the firm's amount of capital equipment is fixed at $K = 100$. The rental rate for K is Re. 1 and the wage rate is Rs. 4.*

(*i*) *Calculate the firm's short run total and average costs.*

(*ii*) *What are STC, SAC and SMC for producing 25 sticks.*

Solution. The given production function of the firm is

$$Q = 2\sqrt{KL}$$

With $K = 100$ in the short run, the short-run production function is

$$Q = 2\sqrt{100L} = 2 \times 10\sqrt{L} = 20\sqrt{L}$$

Cost, $C = \omega L + rK$

Given that $w = 4$ and $r = 1$

$$C = 4L + 1K$$

With the given $K = 100$

$$C = 4L + 100 \quad \ldots(1)$$

The short-run production function when $K = 100$ as obtained above is:

$$Q = 20\sqrt{L}$$

Taking square of both sides we have

$$Q^2 = 400\ L$$

or

$$\frac{Q^2}{400} = L. \quad \ldots(2)$$

Substituting (2) in (1) we have

$$C = 100 + 4.\frac{Q^2}{400}$$

$$C = 100 + \frac{Q^2}{100} \quad \ldots(3)$$

The above equation (3) represents the short-run total cost function.

To get the short-run average cost function we divide the short-run total cost function in (3) by output (Q). Thus,

$$SAC = \frac{100 + \frac{Q^2}{100}}{Q} = \frac{100}{Q} + \frac{Q}{100}$$

Short-run Marginal Cost Function :

Short-run marginal cost function can be obtained by taking the first derivative of the short-run total cost function.

Short-run total cost function as found above is

$$C = 100 + \frac{Q^2}{100}$$

$$SMC = \frac{dC}{dQ} = \frac{2Q}{100} = \frac{Q}{50}$$

(*ii*) If output of hockey sticks = 25, then

$$STC = 100 + \frac{(25)^2}{100} = 100 + \frac{625}{100}$$

$$STC = 106.25$$

$$SAC = \frac{STC}{Q} = \frac{106.25}{25} = 4.25$$

$$SMC = \frac{Q}{50} = \frac{25}{50} = 0.5$$

Problem 4. *If $Q = A(KL)^{0.5}$, what is short-run cost function when $K = 100$? What is MC function ?*

Solution. With $K = 100$, the short-run production function can be written as

$$Q = A\ (100\ L)^{0.5} = 10A\ (L)^{0.5}$$

Squaring both sides we have

$$Q^2 = 100A^2L \quad ...(i)$$

Now, the short-run cost function is

$$C = TFC + TVC$$

$$TFC = Kr = 100r \text{ and } TVC = wL$$

where r is the rental price of capital and w is wage rate of labour and given $K = 100$

Therefore $$C = 100r + wL \quad ...(ii)$$

From equation (*i*) we have

$$L = \frac{Q^2}{100A^2}$$

Substituting the value of L in (*ii*) we get the following short-run cost function :

$$C = 100r + w.\frac{Q^2}{100A^2} \quad ...(iii)$$

Note that total variable cost function is $w\frac{Q^2}{100A^2}$

Differentiating the total variable cost (TVC) function with respect to output (Q) we have the following marginal cost function :

$$MC = \frac{dTVC}{dQ} = \frac{2wQ}{100A^2}$$

QUESTIONS FOR REVIEW

1. Distinguish between economic costs and accounting costs. Which should be taken into account for calculating the economic profits of the firm?
2. What is the difference between explicit costs and implicit costs? Should both be considered for optimal business decision-making by the firm?
3. Explain the concepts of total fixed cost, total variable costs and total costs. How are they related to each other? Illustrate them through curves. Is the distinction between the fixed costs and variable costs relevant in the long run ?
4. Explain the following concepts of cost:

   (*a*) Average fixed cost (AFC)

   (*b*) Average variable cost (AVC)

   (*c*) Average total cost (ATC)

   (*d*) Marginal cost (MC)

   Why does ATC curve reach its lowest point after the AVC curve? Why does the MC curve intersect below the AVC and ATC curves at their minimum points ?
5. Derive long-run total cost curve from expansion path. How are average cost curve and marginal cost curve derived from total cost curve.
6. *Short-run* total and average cost will exceed *long-run* total and average cost respectively. Explain and illustrate graphically.

7. We give below short-run total cost function :

$$TC = 100 + 50Q - 12Q^2 + Q^3$$

where TC is total cost and Q is level of output.

(*i*) Determine : (*a*) total fixed cost function, (*b*) total variable cost function, (*c*) average variable cost function, (*d*) marginal cost function.

(*ii*) Calculate total cost, *ATC*, *AVC* and *MC* when the firm produces 10 units of output.

(*iii*) Calculate the level of output at which *AVC* is minimum.

8. What is the relationship between average cost and marginal cost? If the marginal cost is rising, does it mean that average cost must also be rising?

9. Derive long-run average cost curve from short-run average cost curves. How are they related to each other? Does the curve joining the minimum points of the short-run average cost curves constitutes long-run average cost curve? Give reasons.

10. Give reasons for the U-shape of long-run average cost curve. Why is long-run average cost curve usually called 'planning curve'?

11. Explain the various economies of scale and diseconomies of scale that accrue to the firm when it expands its scale of production.

12. Modern empirical studies have found that long-run average cost curve (*LAC*) is L-shaped. How would you explain it? Does it not contradict the U-shaped long-run average cost curve of the traditional cost theory?

13. What would be the shape of long-run average cost (*LAC*) curve when constant returns to scale occur? How would you explain the occurrence of constant returns to scale?

14. What is the Learning Curve? What are the factors that bring about learning curve effect? How does reduction in cost per unit due to the learning curve effect differ from economies of scale?

15. (a) Describe relationship between *AVC* and average product and between marginal cost and marginal product.

(b) How is U-shape of average variable cost curve explained by law of variable proportions?

16. Define marginal cost. How is it related to marginal product of a factor. As output is increased, marginal cost first falls and then beyond a certain point it rises. How would you explain it ?

Appendix To Chapter 15

Derivation Of Long-run Cost Function

Total cost incurred by a firm is the sum of costs of all the inputs or factors used. In symbolic terms for the two factor production function, total cost is given by

$$C = L \,.\, w + K \,.\, r$$

where L and K are the quantities of labour and capital employed and w and r are the prices of these factors respectively. As has been discussed in the chapters on production theory that a profit-maximising firm must seek to use the specific combination of factors (or inputs) that minimises its cost and to adjust its use of factors as it increases its level of output along a particular expansion path which is determined by the underlying production function and relative factor prices. Points along that expansion path then determine the specific relation between costs and output constituting the firm's cost function which can be expressed as

$$C = f(Q)$$

As the cost function is essentially the relationship between costs and outputs along an expansion path, it is strictly defined for the *given factor prices*. This means that any change in factor prices causes a change in the expansion path and, therefore, causes a shift in the associated cost function.

In the light of the above we proceed to derive the long-run cost function. We are given the following production function.

$$Q = L^{1/2}\ K^{1/2} \qquad \ldots(i)$$

and cost equation is given by

$$C = w \,.\, L + rK \qquad \ldots(ii)$$

It may be reiterated that long-run cost function depicts the expenditure incurred on cost-minimising combinations of factors (labour and capital in our example) to produce various levels of output. We explain below step-wise procedure of deriving long-run cost function.

First step in deriving the long-run cost function from a given production function and cost equation is to obtain the value of $MRTS_{LK}$ or ratio of marginal products of the factors. Thus, for the given production function,

$$MP_L = \frac{1}{2}\ L^{-1/2}\ K^{1/2}$$

$$MP_K = \frac{1}{2}\ L^{1/2}\ K^{-1/2}$$

$$MRTS_{LK} = \frac{MP_L}{MP_K} = \frac{\frac{1}{2}L^{-1/2}\ K^{1/2}}{\frac{1}{2}\ L^{1/2}\ K^{-1/2}} = \frac{K}{L} \qquad \ldots(iii)$$

The *second step* is to substitute the value of $MRTS_{LK}$ in the condition for minimising cost, namely, $MRTS_{LK} = \frac{w}{r}$ and to find out the equation for expansion path. Thus, in our example

$$\frac{K}{L} = \frac{w}{r}$$

$$K = \frac{w.L}{r} \qquad .....(iv)$$

The equation (*iv*) describes the expansion path of the firm

The *third step* is to substitute the equation for expansion path, $K = \frac{w.L}{r}$ in the given production function to obtain the cost-minimising quantity of labour to produce an output. In our example

$$Q = L^{1/2}\left(\frac{w.L}{r}\right)^{1/2}$$

or
$$L = w^{-1/2}.\ r^{1/2}\ .\ Q \qquad ...(v)$$

The *fourth step* is to estimate the cost-minimising quantity of capital to produce an output. The equation for expansion path derived above can be rewritten as $L = \frac{Kr}{w}$. In order to obtain the cost-minimising quantity of capital to produce an output substitute $L = \frac{Kr}{w}$ in the given production function. Thus, in our example

$$Q = \left(\frac{Kr}{w}\right)^{1/2} K^{1/2}$$

or
$$K = r^{-1/2}.\ w^{1/2}\ .\ Q \qquad ...(vi)$$

The final step in the derivation of cost function is to substitute the cost-minimising quantities of inputs (labour and capital) as given by equation (v) and (vi) in the iso-cost equation.

$$C = w.L + rK$$

$$C = w\ \ (w^{-1/2}\ .\ r^{1/2}\ Q) + r\,(r^{-1/2}\ .\ w^{1/2}\ Q)$$

$$= 2w^{1/2}\ r^{1/2}\ Q \qquad ...(vii)$$

The equation (*vii*) *represents the long-run cost function according to which long-run cost depends on factor prices and output.* It is evident from equation (*vii*) that, *given the factor prices*, we can find out the cost by taking different amounts of output (*i.e.*, *Q*). It will also be noticed from the cost function that rise in price of either factor will cause the total cost to increase This can be easily shown by differentiating the cost function ($C = 2w^{1/2}\ r^{1/2}\ Q$) with respective to wage, the price of labour. Thus

$$\frac{\partial C}{\partial w} = w^{-1/2}\ r^{1/2}\ Q$$

It will be seen that this partial derivative of cost function with respect to wage rate is positive ($w^{-1/2}\ r^{1/2}\ Q > 0$). The positive partial derivative with respect to wage rate shows that cost increases with the rise in wages. It will also be noticed this partial derivative of the cost function with respect to wage equals the cost-minimising quantity of labour (described by equation (*v*) above). This is an important finding. *In general, the derivative of cost function with respect to a factor price is the cost-minimising quantity of that factor.*

Break-Even Analysis (Cost-Volume Profit Analysis)

Introduction

Theory of costs has an important application in the decision making of a firm regarding the level of output at which it will break even, that is, *at which its total revenue will equal total cost and therefore it will attain no profit, no loss position. Break-even analysis is also called cost-volume profit analysis* since it is based on the relationship among total cost, total revenue and profits at various levels of output. The break-even analysis is also called *Contribution marginal analysis* because in it contribution margin, as will be seen below, is used to determine the break-even point.

Break-even analysis is also applied to determine the quantity of output sold at which the firm will realise its target level of profits. Break even analysis can be made by assuming firstly linear cost-output and revenue-output relationships and, secondly, by assuming non-linear cost and revenue functions. Besides, break-even analysis can be either made through graphical method or algebraic method. In our analysis below, we will explain break-even analysis through both these methods. The break-even analysis or cost-volume profit analysis is extensively used by businessmen and managers of corporate firms for making business decisions.

Linear Break-Even Analysis : Graphic Method

As mentioned above, break-even analyses is based on revenue-output functions and cost-output functions. Figure 16.l, graphically shows a typical linear break-even analysis chart. When price of the product remains constant as the firm expands its production and sales, the total revenue will be linearly related to output. Thus, the total revenue function *TR* in Fig. 16.1 represents the total revenue that the firm will earn at each level of output, *assuming that the price* (*P*) *of product for the firm remains constant.* Similarly, total cost function *TC* is a straight line starting from point *F* on the Y-axis and thus represents the linear relationship between total cost and output. It may be noted that in our analysis of cost function in the previous chapter we have explained that average variable cost falls over a range of output in the beginning and then begins to rise. However, the managers of business firms who use the break-even analysis are interested in a *relevant middle ranges of output* without considering

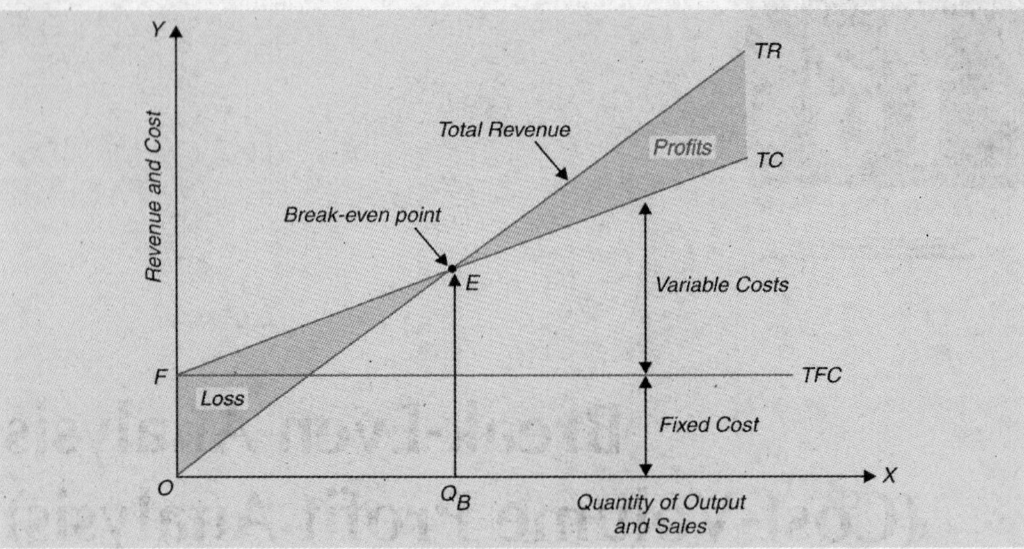

Fig. 16.1. *Break-Even Level of Output and Sales*

the extremes of low and very high ranges of output at which average variable cost falls or rises. Hence linear cost function represented by the straight-line curve is generally used in break-even analysis.

TFC is the total fixed cost line, with the given fixed cost equal to *OF*. The vertical distance between the total cost line *TC* and total fixed cost line *TFC* represents the total variable cost. As will be seen from Fig. 16.1, the vertical distance between the *TC* and *TFC* curves representing the total variable cost increases as quantity of output produced and sold increases. But, *TC* line is linear starting from point *F*, which shows that average variable cost is constant. It will be further seen that the slope of the total revenue curve (which indicates the price at which additional units of the good are sold) is greater than the slope of the total cost curve (which indicates the additional variable cost incurred per unit of output by the firm). This means the price which the firm receives for every unit of the good sold exceeds the additional cost incurred per unit of output on labour, raw materials and other variable factors.

The total profit-loss position depends on total revenue on the one hand and total cost (*i.e.* variable costs plus fixed cost) on the other. It will be seen from Fig. 16.1, that up to quantity Q_B of the commodity produced and sold total cost exceeds total revenue indicating that the firm will suffer losses if it produces and sells less than Q_B quantity of the commodity. At output Q_B produced and sold, the total revenue received equals the total cost ($TR = TC$) and therefore at this output level the firm neither makes profits, nor incurs losses. In other words, at Q_B quantity of output produced and sold, the firm just breaks even. Therefore, output level Q_B or intersection point *E* at which the firm neither make profits, nor suffers losses is called a break-even point. *Break-even level of output shows the minimum level of output required to be sold if the firm will just be in no profit, no loss position.* If the firm's estimate of demand for its product falls short of this break-even level, it would not produce the product. The firm will undertake the production of a commodity if it estimates that it will be able to sell the quantity of output equal to or greater than the break-even point.

Cost-Volume Profit Analysis for Achieving Target Profits

Further, the break-even analysis is also useful for determining the level of output *required to make a certain target amount of profits.* Suppose if the firm sets a target amount of profits for a period equal to 20 lakhs (which is supposed to be equal to *ET* in Fig. 16.2 then the level of output required to be produced and sold to obtain the given target amount of profit exceeds the break-even level. It will been seen from Fig. 16.2 that to realise target amount of profits π or *ET*, the level of output necessary to be produced and sold increases to Q_T

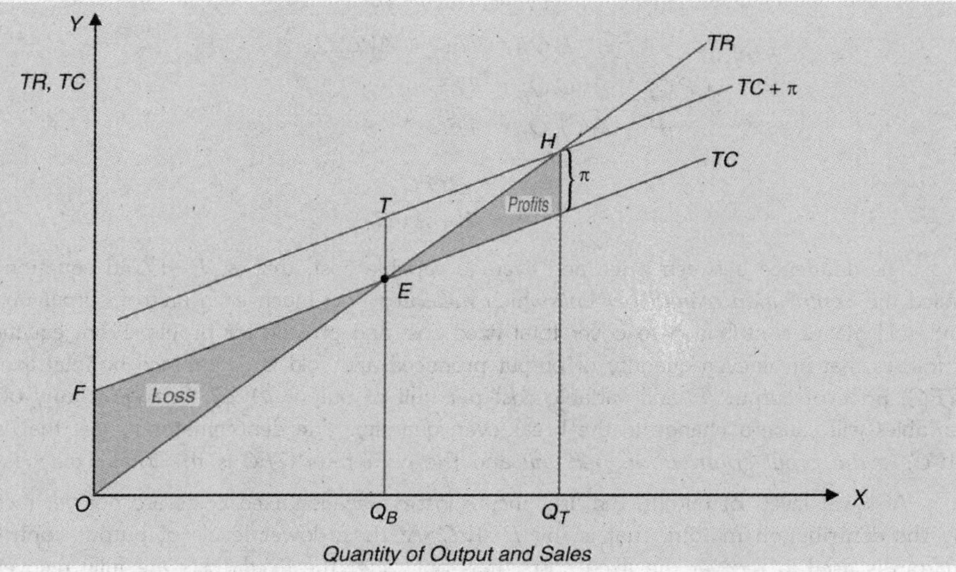

Fig. 16.2. *Level of Output and Sales to Achieve a Target Amount of Profits.*

Linear Break-Even Analysis (Cost-Volume Profit Analysis) : Algebraic Method

Although graphic method of break-even analysis is useful way of illustrating cost-output, revenue-output and profit-output relationships break-even analysis through algebraic model is of great help in decision-making problems by a firm.

Let P = Price per unit of commodity sold

Q = Quantity produced and sold

TFC = Total fixed cost

AVC = Average variable cost per unit of output.

π = Profits

Recall that profit π is the difference between total revenue (TR) and total cost (TC). To write in symbolic terms

$$\pi = TR - TC$$

Total revenue (TR) is equal to the price (P) per unit of the commodity times the quantity of output sold.

Therefore,

$$TR = P.Q \quad \ldots(i)$$

On the other hand, total cost is the sum of total variable cost (TVC) and total fixed cost (TFC). Total variable cost (TVC) is the variable cost per unit multiplied by the output produced and sold ($TVC = AVC.Q$). Therefore

$$TC = TVC + TFC$$

$$TC = AVC.Q + TFC \quad \ldots(ii)$$

As explained above, break-even quantity of output produced and sold occurs at the level at which total revenue (*TR*) equals total cost (*TC*).

Let Q_B indicates the break-even quantity. From (*i*) and (*ii*) above, at the break-even quantity (Q_B) we have

$$TR = TC$$

$$P.Q_B = TFC + AVC.Q_B$$

$$P.Q_B - AVC.Q_B = TFC$$

$$(P - AVC)\, Q_B = TFC$$

$$Q_B = \frac{TFC}{P - AVC} \qquad \text{...(iii)}$$

The difference between price and average variable cost, that is, *P-AVC* in equation (*iii*) is called the *contribution margin per unit* which measures how much each unit of output produced and sold makes contribution to cover total fixed cost and provide for profits. From equation (*iii*) it follows that break-even quantity of output produced and sold is determined by total fixed cost *(TFC)*, price of output *(P)* and variable cost per unit of output *(AVC)*. Change in any of these variables will cause a change in the break-even quantity. The denominator in (*iii*), that is, *P – AVC, is the profit contribution per unit* and the numerator *TFC* is the total fixed cost.

At lower levels of output, the firm incurs losses because fixed costs are not yet recovered by the contribution margin, that is, by *P–AVC*. At these lower levels of output contribution margin is used to recover the fixed costs. It is only after the fixed costs are fully recovered by the contribution per unit of output (*P–AVC*), then the firm starts making operating profits. The break–even level of output is thus given by the total fixed cost divided by the contribution margin per unit of output.

Linear Break-Even Analysis and Target Amount of Profits

Break-even analysis can be used to determine the quantity of output required to be produced and sold to achieve a target amount of profits. Let π stand for a profit target. Then this target profit π can be added to total fixed cost in the numerator in equation (iii) and dividing it by the contribution margin per unit (*i.e. P–AVC*). Thus

$$Q_T = \frac{TFC + \pi}{P - AVC} \qquad \text{...(iv)}$$

The expression *(iv)* shows that to achieve a profit objective, the contribution margin per unit, that is, difference between *P* and *AVC* must be large enough to recover the total fixed cost *(TFC)* and to achieve target amount of profits.

A Numerical Example of Break-Even Analysis

Break-even analysis can be easily understood from a numerical example. Let us take the case of a book-publishing company. The total fixed cost incurred on typesetting, providing illustrations, proof reading etc. incurred is Rs. 50,000. Variable cost incurred per copy on printing paper, binding, author's royalty per copy, book seller's commission is equal to Rs. 15 per copy. Suppose he fixes Rs. 40 as price per copy of the book. We have to find out the break-even number of copies of the book printed and sold.

Thus, in this example

$$TFC = \text{Rs. } 50{,}000$$

$$AVC = \text{Rs. } 15$$

$$P = \text{Rs. } 40$$

$$\text{Break-even quantity} = \frac{TFC}{P - AVC}$$

$$Q_B = \frac{50{,}000}{40 - 15}$$

$$= 2000 \text{ copies}$$

Thus, 2000 copies of the book represents the break-even output and sales of the book. That is, if the publisher produces and is able to sell 2000 copies, he will achieve no profits, no loss situation.

If the publishing company expects or estimates to sell less than 2000 copies (say 1800 copies) of the book, it will incur losses. As a result, the publisher may consider cutting production costs such as using lower grade paper, negotiating with the author to reduce the royalty rate, etc. so as to break-even or even achieve some profits. In the alternative, he can think of fixing a higher price. If he fixes price equal to Rs. 55 per copy, his costs and estimates of sales remaining the same, we can calculate the new break-even sales of the book.

$$Q_B = \frac{5{,}000}{55 - 15} = \frac{50{,}000}{40}$$

$$= 1250$$

Thus, the break-even quantity produced and sold of the book are 1250 copies. If he is able to sell 1800 copies at price Rs 55 per copy, his sales will exceed the break-even point and will therefore yield profits to him.

Now, suppose the publishing company has a profit objective of making Rs. 10,000 from the book, then the required quantity of sales can be calculated to realise the target amount of profits of Rs. 10,000 by using expression (iv) above. Thus,

$$= \frac{TFC + \pi}{P - AVC}$$

$$= \frac{50{,}000 + 10{,}000}{55 - 15}$$

$$= \frac{60{,}000}{40} = 1500$$

It follows from above, that if he is able to sell 1500 copies of the book he will recover the fixed and variable costs and also make profits of Rs. 10,000. His profits will be greater if his sales exceed 1500 copies.

LINEAR BREAK-EVEN ANALYSIS : CHANGES IN BREAK-EVEN OUTPUT

As seen above, break-even output depends on the following three factors :

(1) Price per unit of the product
(2) Variable cost per unit
(3) Fixed cost on capital and equipment incurred by a firm

Firms often analyse the effects of changes in any one or more of the above variables on the break-even output. The effect of the following two factors on the break-even output is often considered by the firms:

(1) Changing the selling price of the product; and

(2) Substituting fixed costs for variable costs.

1. Changing the Selling Price

We have seen in our numerical analysis of break-even output that if a firm raises the selling price of its product, the break-even output decreases. This can be graphically shown by a break-even chart which we have done in Fig. 16.3 It may be noted that hike in the selling price of the product would make the total revenue curve *TR* more steep. In Figure 16.3 *TC* curve portrays the change in total cost as firm expands its output. Note that it is only the total variable cost that changes, fixed cost remain constant at *OF.* *TR* is the total revenue curve whose stope measures the price of the product. With *TC* and *TR* as total cost and total revenue curves respectively, OQ_B is the break-even output. When the selling price of the product is raised, *TR* curve rotates to the new position *TR′*. It will be seen from Fig. 16.3 that this new total revenue curve *TR′* intersects the given *TC* curve at point *E′* and determines OQ'_B as break-even output which is less than the previous break-even output OQ_B obtained before the hike in price of the product. Thus, increase in selling price results in lowering of the break-even output.

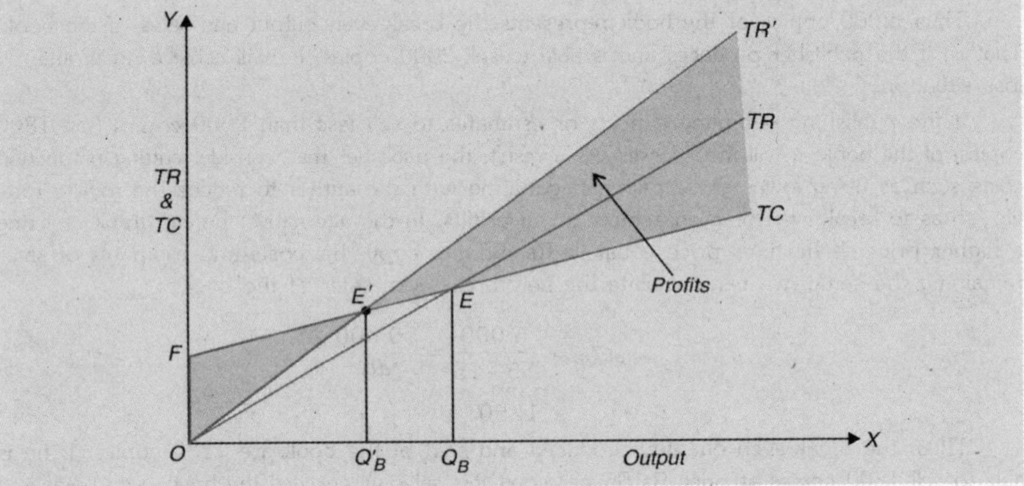

Fig.16.3. *Impact of Increase in Selling Price on Break-Even Output*

Substituting Fixed Costs for Variable Costs

Instead of raising the selling price per unit, the firm may consider to substitute fixed costs for variable costs in some of its operations. For example, when machines are substituted for labour, the firm's fixed cost rises and the variable costs decrease. Thus, when wage rates of labour rise, it has been found that many firms seek to reduce the variable labour costs through undertaking automation of some operations of its production process. Automation of some operations implies that the firm substitutes fixed capital equipment for labour. As shall be seen from Figure 16.4 (*a*) and (*b*) that when machines are substituted for labour, and consequently fixed cost rises and variable cost falls, the total cost curve *FTC* in Figure 16.4 (a) changes to *F TC′* in Figure 16.4 (*b*). The break–even level of output increases from OQ_B in Figure 16.4 (a) to OQ_B in Figure 16.4 (b). Substitution of fixed capital for variable cost generally raises the break-even point.

OPERATING LEVERAGE

Operating leverage refers to the ratio of a firm's total fixed costs to the total variable costs. The greater the ratio of fixed costs to the variable costs, the more highly leveraged the firm is. The degree of operating leverage increases as a firm substitutes fixed capital and equipment for variable factors such as labour when the firm introduces automation of some of its operations. Thus, with increase in operating leverage *whereas fixed or overhead costs increase, its average variable cost declines.* The degree of operating leverage

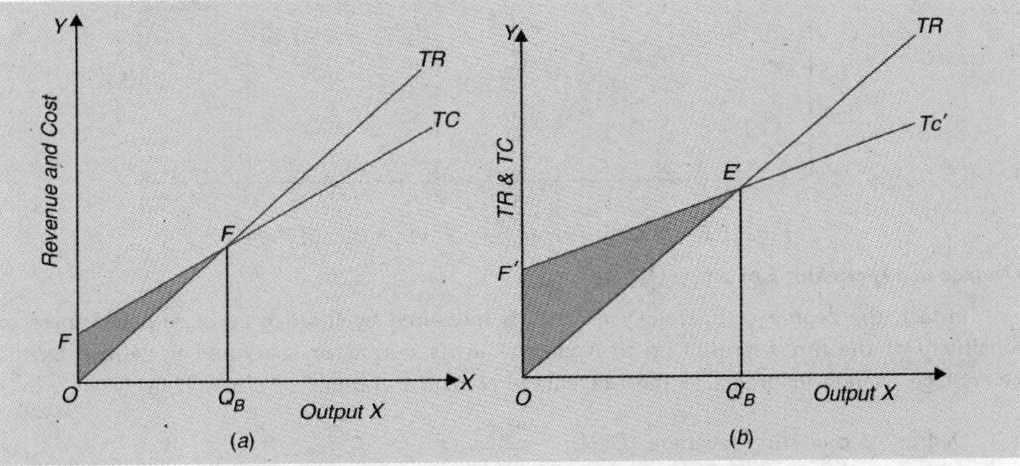

Fig. 16.4. *Operating Leverage and Break-Even Output.*

may also increase when a firm makes more borrowing causing increase in its interest costs which are of fixed nature and have to be incurred regardless of the level of output in a period.

Since with the increase in operating leverage, the firm's fixed costs rise, the break-even output generally increases. This is shown in Fig. 16.4 where in Panel (a) *TC* is the total fixed cost curve starting from point *F* on the vertical axis indicating that *OF* is the fixed cost of the firm. Now, when the firm substitutes fixed capital plant and equipment for variable labours costs and consequently the firm becomes more highly leveraged, fixed costs rise to *OF '* and total cost curve shifts to *TC '* in Panel (*b*) which has a less slope than the original total cost curve *TC* showing that now variable costs have fallen. It will be observed from Fig. 16.4 that with the increase in the degree of operating leverage, the break-even output has risen to Q'_B corresponding to which new total cost curve *TC'* intersects the given total revenue curve *TR*.

An important feature of a high-leveraged firm is that *it experiences a more variability in profits* for a given percentage change in output or sales as compared to the low-leveraged firm. This is due to the fact that for a high-leveraged firm the proportion of fixed cost is higher and therefore *total cost (TFC + TVC) will change less in proportion to the changes in level of output.* Therefore, as a result, in a high leveraged firm profits will vary more than in proportion to the changes in levels of output. Thus sensitivity (*i.e.* variability) of profits to output changes rises as a firm becomes more highly leveraged. This, is illustrated in Fig. 16.5 where at output level *OM*, profits of the firm with *TC* and *TC'* of less-leveraged firm and high leveraged firm respectively are equal to *KL*. However, when the firm's output and sales increase to *ON*, with lower degree of operating leverage represented by total cost curve *TC*, firm's profits go up to *DH* whereas in case of a firm with greater degree of operating leverage represented by total cost curve *F TC*, profits rise more to *UH* as will be seen from Fig. 16.5.

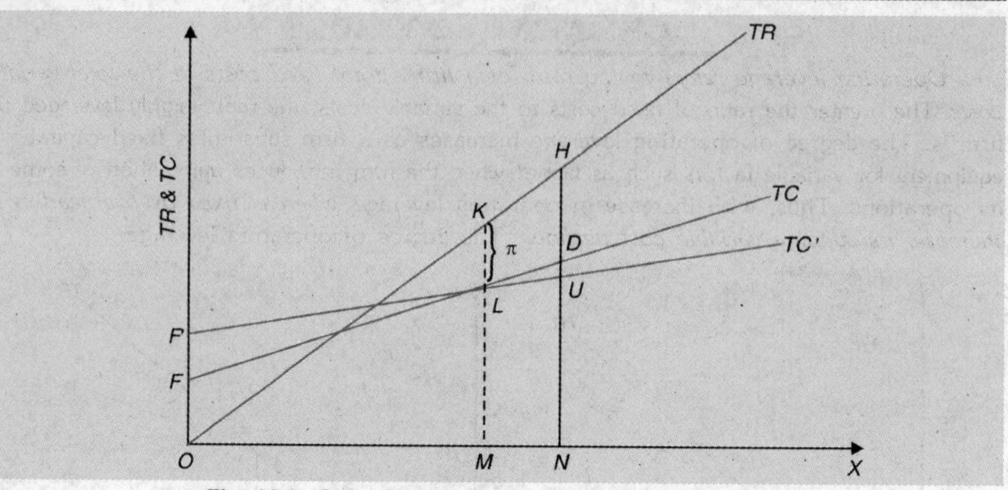

Fig. 16.5. *Operating leverage and Variability of Profits*

Degree of Operating Leverage (*DOL*).

In fact, the degree of operating leverage is measured by the degree of responsiveness or sensitivity of the firm's profits (π) to a change in its output or sales and is defined as the percentage change in profits to the percentage change in output or sales. Thus,

$$\text{Degree of operating leverage } (DOL) = \frac{\%\Delta\pi}{\%\Delta Q} \quad \text{... } (i)$$

$$= \frac{\Delta\pi/\pi}{\Delta Q/Q}$$

$$\text{DOL} = \frac{\Delta\pi}{\Delta Q}.\frac{Q}{\pi} \quad \text{...}(ii)$$

where
$\Delta\pi$ = Change in Profits.
ΔQ = Change in output or sales
Q = Original output or sales
π = Original profits

It will be observed from equation (*i*) and (*ii*) that degree of operating leverage conceived in terms of variability of firm's profits is the same things as the *output or sales elasticity of profits*.

The output elasticity of profits, given the constant price of output, depends on the level of output, the total fixed cost and average variable cost per unit of output. This can be proved as follows.

$$\text{The profits } (\pi) = TR - TVC - TFC$$
$$= PQ - (AVC)\, Q - TFC$$

and change in profits $\Delta\pi = \Delta Q.P - (AVC)\, \Delta Q$

Note that both price (*P*) and total fixed cost (*TFC*) remain constant. Now substituting the expressions for profit (π) and change in profit (Δ π) into equation (*ii*) we have

$$DOL = \frac{\Delta Q.P-(AVC).\Delta Q}{\Delta Q} \times \frac{Q}{PQ-AVC(Q)-TFC}$$

$$= \frac{\Delta Q(P-AVC)Q}{\Delta Q[(P-AVC)Q-TFC]}$$

$$= \frac{Q(P-AVC)}{Q(P-AVC)-TFC} \quad \ldots(iii)$$

The numerator in (*iii*), that is, $Q(P - AVC)$ measures the total contribution to the fixed cost and profits of the firm while the denominator $Q(P - AVC) - TFC = QP - Q.AVC - TFC$ measures profits made by the firm.

We can calculate the degree of operating leverage from our above numerical example of finding level of output required to yield a target amount of profits. In our case the fixed cost is Rs 50, 000, price is Rs. 55 and $AVC = 15$ and level of output required to recover fixed cost and provide for profits of Rs 10,000 was found to be equal to 1500 units. Substituting these into the operating leverage equation (*iii*) we get

$$DOL = \frac{Q(P-AVC)}{Q(P-AVC)-TFC} = \frac{1500\ (55-15)}{1500\ (55-15)-50{,}000}$$

$$= \frac{1500\ (40)}{1500\ (40)-50{,}000} = \frac{60{,}000}{60{,}000-50{,}000} = 6$$

Now if the firm becomes more highly leveraged, the total fixed cost will increase and average variable cost will decline resulting in larger output required to recover fixed cost and to yield targetted profits. This will lead to the greater degree of operating leverage (*DOL*).

Analysis of Break-Even Point In Case of Non-Linear Total Revenue and Cost Curves

In our above analysis of break-even point we have assumed that both cost-output and revenue-output relationships are linear. However, in the market forms of monopoly and imperfect competition such as monopolistic competition and oligopoly revenue-output relationship is non-linear. In these market forms, total revenue curve increases at a diminishing rate. On the other hand, short-run total cost curve generally first rise at a diminishing rate and then it starts rising at an increasing rate. We will now explain the break-even point of a firm with non-linear cost-output and revenue-output relationships. This is illustrated in Fig. 16.6, where *TR* represents total revenue curve. This total revenue curve is increasing at a diminishing rate. This is because for a firm working under monopoly or imperfect competition, price of its product falls as it sells more and marginal revenue is less than price. However, it will be seen that total cost curve *TC* starts from a point *F* which lies above the origin. It means that *OF* is the fixed cost which the firm has to incur even if it stops production in the short-run. It will be seen that total short-run cost curve *TC* initially increases at a decreasing rate and then after a point it increases at an increasing rate. This implies that average total cost curve is roughly of U-shape. Total profits can be measured as the vertical distance between *TR* and *TC* curves.

It will be observed from Fig. 16.6 that up to the level of output OQ_B, *TC* curve lies above *TR* curve showing that as the firm raises its output in the initial stages total cost is greater than total revenue and the firm is incurring losses. When it produces OQ_B level of output, total revenue just equals total cost and the firm is therefore neither making profits nor incurring losses. That is, the firm is only breaking even at output level OQ_B. Thus the point *B* or output level OQ_B is called *Break-Even Point.*

When the firm increases its output beyond OQ_B, total revenue becomes larger than total cost and profits begin to accrue to the firm. It will be noticed from the figure that profits are increasing as the firm increases production to output OQ_M, since the distance between the total revenue curve (*TR*) and total cost curve (*TC*) is widening. At OQ_M level of output, the distance between the *TR* curve and *TC* curve is the largest and therefore profits will be maximum. If the firm expands output beyond Q_M, the gap between *TR* and *TC* curves goes on narrowing down and therefore the total profits will be declining. It is therefore clear that at OQ_M level of output where total revenue exceeds total cost by the largest amount firm's profits are maximum.

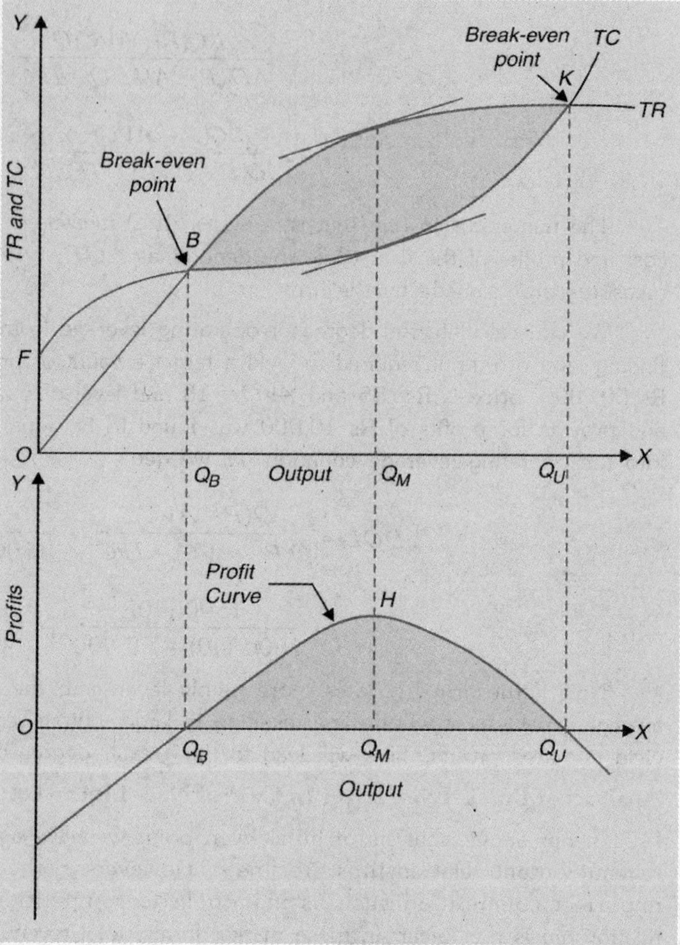

Fig. 16.6. *Break-Even Chart Showing Break-Even Point and Profit Maximising Output in Case of Non-linear Revenue and Cost Functions*

It will be observed from Fig. 16.6 that at output level Q_u, total revenue is again equal to total cost (*TR* curve cuts *TC* curve at point *K* corresponding to output Q_u). Thus, point *K* is again a break-even point, usually called *upper break-even point.* It may however be noted that this upper break-even point *K* or output level Q_u is not of much relevance as it lies beyond firm's profit-maximising level and may actually lie beyond firm's capacity to produce. It is the first break-even point *B* or output level OQ_B which is highly significant as a firm will not plan to produce if it cannot sell output equal to at least OQ_B at which total revenue just covers total cost of production so that its economic profits are zero.

For a more vivid representation of break-even point and its comparison with profit-maximising point in the lower panel of Fig. 16.6 we have drawn the profit curve which measures the distance between *TR* and *TC* curves. It will be seen from this panel that up to output level. OQ_B profit curve lies below the *X*-axis showing that the firm is making losses if it produces less than OQ_B. At output level Q_B, the firm's net profits are zero because at this output level total revenue just covers total cost of production. Therefore, OQ_B is break-even level of output. As the firm expands its level of output beyond OQ_B, profit curve is rising until it reaches at its maximum profit point *H* corresponding to the level of output OQ_M. Beyond level of output OQ_M, profit curve slopes downward indicating that total profits decline beyond output Q_M. Thus, at output level OQ_M, the firm maximises its profits. At a higher output level OQ_u, net profits are again zero indicating the upper break-even point which is not relevant.

Limitations of Linear Break-Even Analysis

Limitations of linear break-even analysis, or what is also called linear *Cost-Volume Profit Analysis* should be noted. While linear break-even analysis is very useful and is often used by business firms to know their no-profit, no-loss level of output and also to know the amount of losses or profits they would earn at different levels of output or sales. However, linear break-even analysis can be applied only in cases where the assumption of *constant* selling prices and *constant* average variable costs hold good. Further, break-even analysis also assumes that a firm produces a single product or a constant mix of products. This does not represent the real-world situation where the firms often produce multiple products. When this is the case or when over time the product mix changes, it may be difficult to opportion the fixed costs among various products. However, despite these limitations, when properly used break-even analysis can prove to be very useful in managerial decision making.

QUESTIONS AND PROBLEMS FOR REVIEW

1. What is a break-even point? Taking a linear revenue and cost functions, graphically show the level of output at which a firm breaks even.
2. Fixed costs of a firm are Rs. 10,000, average variable cost (*AVC*) per unit of output is Rs. 15 and the firm sells its product at Rs. 20 per unit. Determine break-even level of output.
3. *What is contribution margin ?* Show graphically through break-even diagram, the level of output or sales to achieve a target amount of profits. Use linear revenue and cost functions.
4. Suppose fixed costs of a firm are Rs. 10,000, price (*P*) at which the firm sells its product is Rs. 20 and AVC = Rs. 15. The firm has set a required profit target of Rs. 20,000, Find out the level of output to achieve the target level of profits.
5. Given the following total cost and revenue functions

   $TC = 15000 + 45Q$

   $TR = 75Q$

   (*a*) Find the break-even rate of output

   (*b*) Find the rate of output required to earn profits of Rs 35000
6. How is a break-even point different from profit maximisation point? Using non-linear cost and revenue functions curves illustrate break-even point and profit maximisation level of output.
7. What is break-even output? Using linear revenue and cost functions show how the level of break-even output would be affected by the following changes:

   (a) Increase in selling price of the product.

   (*b*) Increase in fixed cost.

   (*c*) Substitution of fixed cost for variable costs (*i.e.*, using more machines in place of labour)
8. Explain the concept of operating leverage. How does increase in operating leverage affect the break-even output ?
9. A firm has a fixed cost of Rs 2100 and sells output at Rs 120 per unit. Contribution margin is 25 per cent of price.

   (*a*) Determine the break even rate of output.

   (*b*) What is the profit elasticity at an output rate of 90 ?
10. How is break-even analysis useful and important for a firm for making business decisions? What are its limitations ?

Linear Programming

Introduction

The central problem of economics is how the maximum possible satisfaction of the people can be achieved through proper allocation of scarce or limited resources among different uses. Several economists attempted to analyse this central problem of economics with the use of marginal analysis. But the marginal analysis involves several practical difficulties due to which it has not succeeded in solving some practical economic problems. In order to solve the some practical problems, especially decision-making by the business firms, the technique of linear programming has been developed. First of all, an American mathematician, D.B. Dantzig developed the technique of linear programming after the Second World War in 1946. A Russian mathematician L.V. Kantorvich also had evolved independently the technique of linear programming. Linear Programming has also been called *mathematical programming and activity analysis.*

Linear programming technique is concerned with constrained optimization problem. In such problem, there is one objective function and one or more constraints. In the theory of production we dealt with such problem when we explained how to minimise cost subject to the production of *a given level of output.* Here minimisation of cost was the objective function and a given level of output was the constraint. Another common example of constrained optimisation problem is maximisation of profits subject to the constraints such as the capacity of machine used in production, availabilty of raw materials etc.

An important feature of linear programming technique is that in it both the objective function and constraints are linear, that is, they describe linear relationship between the variables. Hence the name of the technique as linear programming, Since all managers of business firms face constrainted optimization problems, linear programming technique is used in solving a number of business problems. Leanear programming problem is also widely used in agriculture, especially by agribusiness. Such problems as determination of least cost minimisation of feeds given to animals that meet their minimum nutritional requirements, the problem of allocation of land to different crops subject to constraints such as fixed land area, limited availability of irrigation facilities. We will explain the use of linear programming technique to some important problems of constrained optimisation facing managers of businesses. Both graphical and algebraic methods will be used to solve linear programming problems.

Meaning of Linear Programming

The term 'Linear Programming' consists of two words: (a) linear and (2) programming. The linear programming considers only *linear relationship* between two or more variables. By linear relationship we mean that relations between the variables can be represented by straight lines. Programming means planning or decision-making in a systematic way. "Linear programming refers to a technique for the formulation and solution of problems in which some linear function of two or more variables is to be optimized subject to a set of linear constraints, at least one of which must be expressed as inequality." The American mathematician George B. Dantzig who invented the linear programming technique used it for the purpose of scheduling the procurement activities of the United States Air Force. Since 1946 linear programming has been greatly developed both in theory and its application to several practical problems of the firm, industry and the economy. Since linear programming requires a lot of numerical calculations, the development of electronic computer after the Second World War has contributed to the development of this method and its application to practical problems.

Since leading concepts, principles and ideas of linear programming involve the use of advanced mathematics, a complete analysis of linear programming theory and its application cannot be given here. We shall confine ourselves to the explanation of linear programming technique with special reference to the theory of the firm and will briefly describe its applications to other fields at the end. Further, we shall only make graphical and simple mathematical analysis of linear programming and will avoid the use of higher mathematics as far as possible. A firm has to face two important production problems. In the first place, a firm has to decide about which particular production process from several alternative processes available it should choose for production of a commodity. This problem has been successfully analysed with linear programming technique. Second important production problem which a firm faces is what amounts of output of various products it should produce so as to maximise its profits. Linear programming technique also helps to solve this problem of the firm. But before explaining the applications of linear programming to these aspects of the theory of the firm, we shall explain the basic concepts and terms used in linear programming.

BASIC CONCEPTS AND TERMS OF LINEAR PROGRAMMING

The linear programming as applied to the theory of the firm explains decision-making by a firm about output and processes it will choose, given the prices of both inputs and products. Thus in the analysis of the firm conducted through the linear programming, it is assumed that prices for the products as well as the inputs used by them will remain constant. With the given constant prices of inputs and outputs, the linear programming provides numerical solution to the problem of making optimum choice by the firm when it has to work within certain given constraints. The optimization can refer to either maximization or minimization. For instance, objective may be maximization of profits for a given level of outlay or minimization of cost for a given level of output. Optimizaton and choice are thus central features of linear programming problem.

The Linearity Assumption. The principal characteristic of a problem that can be solved through linear programming technique is linearity. By linearity we mean that the problem which is to be analysed through linear programming must be formulated in terms of *linear functions* of two or more variables which are also subject to a set of *linear constraints*, at least one of which must be expressed as inequality. That is, the problem to be analysesd through linear programming is expressed entirely in terms of linear equations and inequalities.

It may be noted that the correctness of the solution reached through linear programming depends crucially upon the validity of this assumption of linearity. The assumption of linearity makes the complicated mathematical programming simpler than it otherwise would have been. Linearity is not only a merely simplifying assumption but also a realistic description of the real world situation.

The economic implications of linearity in the field of production are that constant returns to scale prevail and average cost is constant and consequently marginal products and average products are equal. Empirical evidence has revealed that over a wide range of output, constant returns to scale prevail and average cost curve is a horizontal over this range. Besides, the implications of linearity assumption are that prices of inputs and outputs are given for the firm. It is because of the constant prices of inputs and outputs that they can also be shown by straight lines on price-quantity diagrams. Even though returns and costs may not be exactly linear they may be so close to it that it may be justified to make the linearity assumption.

Objective Function. Objective function, also called criterion function, describes the "determinants of the quantity to be maximised or to be minimised."[1] If the objective of a firm is to maximise output or profits, then this is the objective function of the firm. If the linear programming requires the minimisation of cost, then this is the objective function of the firm. An objective function has two parts—*the primal and dual.* If the primal of the objective function is to maximise output subject a cost outlay, then its dual will be the minimisation of cost subject to a given output.

Constraints. The maximization of the objective function is subject to certain limitations which are called constraints. The budget or income of a consumer is constraint on him for maximizing his satisfaction. A firm which aims to maximize its output is constrained by the fact that it has, say, only 13 machines to work with and a certain limited floor space on which work has to be performed. Besides, constraints on a firm may be of the type that for a particular machine, say A, at least two labourers are needed to operate it, and for another machine B, at least 5 labourers are required to operate it. *Constraints are also called inequalities* because they are generally expressed in the form of inequalities. The constraint regarding the availability of 10 machines for production is generally expressed as 10 or fewer machines (that is, ≤ 10 machines hours) are available for production. If the constraint is that at least two workers are required to operate a machine, then it is written as ≤ 2 workers are needed to operate a machine.

Feasible Region. After knowing the constraints, feasible solutions of the problem for a consumer, a producer, a firm or an economy can be ascertained. Feasable region contains those solutions which *meet or satisfy the constraints of the problem* and therefore it is possible to attain them. For a consumer which aims to maximize his satisfaction from his purchases of goods, feasible solutions are those which lie at or to the left of the given budget line, which in turn is determined by the constraints of the

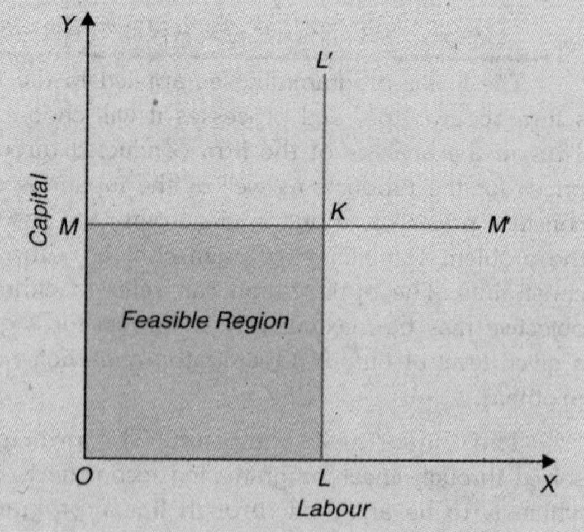

Fig. 17.1. *Region of Feasible Solutions.*

1. D. S. Watson, *Price Theory and Its Uses*, 4th edition, p. 206.

given income and the given prices of goods. Likewise, feasible solutions for a firm using two inputs, labour and capital, and seeking to maximize his output, are those possible combinations of inputs which lie on or to the left of the given iso-cost line which in turn is determined by the given total outlay and given prices of the two inputs. The shape of the area or region of feasible solutions depends upon the nature of constraints.

Some Illustrations. The constraints of a firm for the production of a commodity are given by a certain amount of physical capital, say, *OM* and a certain amount of labour, say, *OL*, then the region of feasible solutions is represented in Figure 17.1 by the area *OMKL*. Since no more than *OL* amount of labour and no more than *OM* amount of capital is available, in Figure 17.1 a vertical line *LL'* at *OL* amount of labour has been drawn to represent the constraint of labour and a horizontal straight line *MM'* at the amount of capital *OM* has been drawn to represent the constraint of capital. Any combination of factors which lies on or within the rectangle *OMKL* is feasible to be used for production. And any combination of inputs which is outside the region *OMKL* is not feasible to be used for production.

Another example of the region of feasible solutions is depicted in Figure 17.2. It has been assumed that two goods *X* and *Y* are to be produced. The machine *A* which is used for the production of a commodity has the capacity to work for 12 hours a day and the machine *B* has the capacity to work for eight hours a day. The production of a unit of commodity *X* requires 2 hours work each on machine *A* and *B*. To produce a unit of commodity *Y* requires three hours work on machine A and one hour work on machine *B*. These constraints can be expressed in the form of following inequalities :-

$$2X + 3Y \leq 12$$

$$2X + 1Y \leq 8$$

These constraints are represented in Figure 17.2. If the entire capacity of 12 machine hours of machine *A* is devoted to production of *X*, then 6 units of commodity *X* are produced. If entire capacity of 12 hours of machine *A* is used for the production of commodity *Y*, then 4 units of product *Y* are produced. Thus, the line *AB* in Figure 17.2 represents the constraint imposed by machine *A*, that is, it represents $2X + 3Y \leq 12$. The area to the left of the line *AB* represents the feasible region from the viewpoint of the given capacity of machine *A*.

In the same way, constraint $2X + 1Y \leq 8$ regarding the available capacity of machine *B* has been represented in Figure 17.2 by the line *CD*, the area to the left of which represents the area of feasible solutions from the viewpoint of the capacity of machine *B*. But from the viewpoint of the constraints imposed by the two machines together, the region of feasible solutions is given by the shaded area *OAKD*.

We have given above some examples of region of feasible solutions. The shape of the feasible region would differ as the number and nature of constraints vary.

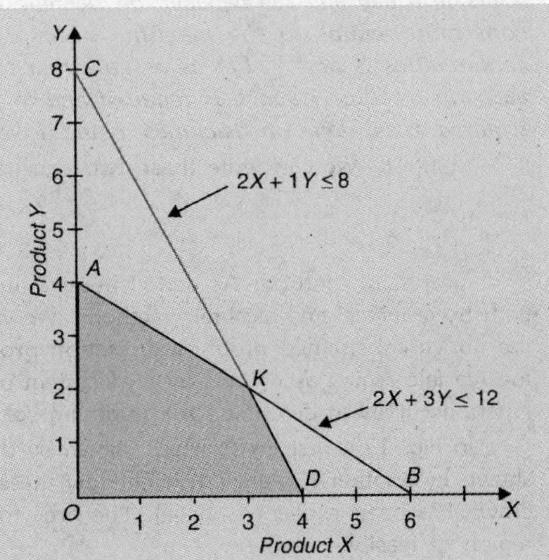

Fig. 17.2. *Feasible Region*

Optimum Solution

The best of all feasible solutions is the optimum solution. In other words, of all the feasible solutions, the solution which maximizes or minimizes the objective function is the optimum solution. For instance, if the objective function is to maximize profits from the production of two goods, then the optimum solution will be that combination of two products that will maximize the profits for the firm. Similarly, if the objective function is to minimize cost by the choice of a process or combination of processes, then the process or a combination of processes which actually minimizes the cost for a given level of output will represent the optimum solution. It is worthwhile to repeat that optimum solution must lie within the region of feasible solutions.

In linear programming there are two alternative methods of finding the optimum solution. One is the non-mathematical or graphical method of obtaining the optimal solution. This graphical method can handle only simple linear programming problems. The other method of finding the optimum solution of the linear programming problem is the *simplex method.* The simplex method involves a set of successive mathematical calculations with which feasible solutions are successively tested during which the poorer solutions (*i.e.* which are not optimal) are successively eliminated until ultimately the optimum solution is obtained. Thus, the simplex method uses a mathematical and computational procedure to find out the optimal solution for the problem in question. Though the graphical and simplex methods follow different procedures to obtain the optimal solution for the problem, they reach identical numerical results.

CHOICE OF PRODUCTS : CONSTRAINED PROFIT MAXIMIZATION

An important linear programming relates to the maximization of profits in the production of two products when it is subject to some contraints. That is, what quantities of the two products are produced so that the profits of the firm are maximized when their production is subject to some constraints. Such analysis is highly relevant for a multiple product firm *i.e.* for a firm which produces more than one product. In this regard it is worthwhile to know that production is subject to what constraints.

The Problem : *Let us suppose that the production of two products X and Y requires the use of two machines I and II. The available capacity of machine I is to work for 12 hours in a day and the capacity of machine II is to work for eight hours a day. The other constraint relates to the machine hours required for the production of each unit of commodities X and Y. Let us assume that to produce a unit of product X, 2 hours work each on machine I and II is required and to produce a unit of product Y, 3 hours work is required to be done on machines 1 and 1 hour work is needed to be done on machine II.*

Solution. We can write these two constraints in the following manner :

$$2X + 3Y \leq 12 \quad \ldots(i)$$

$$2X + 1Y \leq 8 \quad \ldots(ii)$$

Graphical Method. As stated above, the linear programming problem can be solved both by graphical and algebraic methods. We will first explain the graphical method of solving the above constrained profit-maximisation problem. In this graphical method we first graph the feasible region as defined by the system of linear constraints and then draw linear profit-function curves to determine the optimum solution.

In Fig. 17.4 first constraint is shown by the straight line *AB* and the second constraint is shown by another straight line *CD* (How these straight lines representing the constraints are drawn has been explained above). The area to the left of the thick line *AQD* represents the region of feasible solutions.

To show which combination of two products X and Y, the firm will produce so as to maximise its profits, it is necessary to explain first the concept of *iso-profit curves* which represent the given profit function. To draw iso-profit curves one needs to know the profit per unit produced of the two products. *The profits or net revenue earned per unit of a product can be obtained by deducting the average variable cost from the price pet unit of the product.* Let us assume that profits obtained in this way from product X are Rs. 10 and from product Y are Rs. 6 per unit of output. We can therefore write the objective function as follows:

$$\pi = 10X + 6Y$$

Where π (i.e. profits) are to be maximised subject to the constraints stated above in (i) and (*ii*), and X and Y represent the quantities of two products.

In order to represent the profits through iso-profit curves we shall have to fix the various amounts of profits. With different amounts of profits, the level of iso-profit curve will vary; the larger the amount of profits to be earned, the higher the level of iso-profit curve. If the amount of profits to be made is Rs. 30, then the equation of the objective function will be as follows :

$$30 = 10X + 6Y$$

If the product X is not to be produced at all and therefore its amount is zero, we will get the following equation of the objective function :

$$30 = 10(0) + 6Y$$

$$Y = 5$$

This means that with the production of 5 units of product Y and none of product X, amount of profits made will be Rs. 30. The point 5 is plotted on the Y-axis in Fig. 17.3 Likewise, if no amount of product Y is produced, then

$$30 = 10X + 6(0)$$

$$X = 3$$

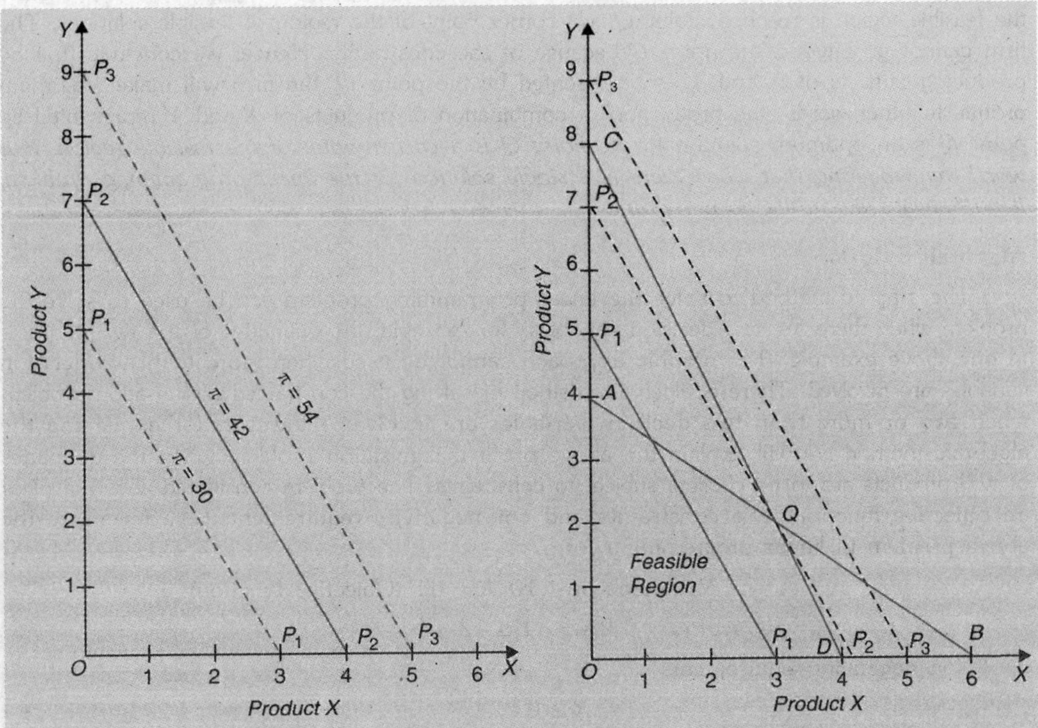

Fig. 17.3. *Iso-Profit Curves*

Fig. 17.4. *Optimal Solution : Constrained Profit Maximisation*

This means that the production of 3 units of X alone and none of Y will fetch the profit of Rs. 30. Therefore, point 3 is plotted of the X-axis. Thus, by joining the points 5 on the Y-axis and point 3 on the X-axis through a straight line, we get an iso-profit curve P_1P_1 representing the amount of profits equal to Rs. 30. All combinations of two products lying on the iso-profit curve P_1P_1 will yield profit equal to Rs. 30. Similarly, iso-profit curves P_2P_2, P_3P_3 showing successively higher levels of profits can be drawn. Given that profits per unit of products X and Y remain unchanged, various iso-profit curves will be parallel to each other.

Now, consider Figure 17.4 where iso-profit curves have been superimposed on the region of feasible solutions. As noted above, the higher the level of iso-profit curve, the greater the amount of profits. Therefore, a firm whose objective is to maximise profits, will seek to go to the highest possible iso-profit curve. However, it cannot go beyond the region of feasible solutions because constraints prevent it to do so. A glance at Figure 17.4 will reveal that the firm will make maximum possible profits by producing at point Q where an iso-profit curve P_2P_2 is touching the boundary of the region of feasible solutions. The firm will not produce at any other point since any point other than Q on or within the region of feasible solutions will lie at a lower iso-profit curve.

It is worthwhile to note that the optimum solution of the linear programming problem will always lie at the boundary of the region of feasible solutions. This follows from a simple logic even without reference to the iso-profit curves. It may be recalled that in linear programming constant returns to scale are assumed to be prevailing and also prices of products and inputs are assumed to remain constant. Therefore, if the production of a commodity is profitable, a firm will continue to expand output because neither diminishing returns to scale will occur nor there will be any adverse effects on the prices of output and inputs. Therefore, it will always be worthwhile to increase output until some capacity limit is reached, that is, until the boundary of the feasible region is reached. Point Q is a corner point of the region of feasible solutions. The firm cannot go beyond the point Q because of the constraints. Hence, we conclude that by producing outputs of X and Y as represented by the point Q, the firm will make maximum profits. In other words, the production of combination of products of X and Y represented by point Q is an optimum solution for it. *Point Q is a corner point of the feasible region. It is worth remembering that when there is a single solution for the linear programming problem, it will always lie at the corner point.*

Algebraic Solution

The graphic method to solve the linear programming problem can be used to solve the problem when there are two decision variables for example, the quantities of the two products in our above example. The graphic approach cannot be used when more than two decision variables are involved. There is algebraic method of solving the constrained optimisation problem when two or more than two decision variables are involved. However, for explaining the algebraic method we will explain the above profit maximisation problem when the quantities of two products are to be chosen, subject to constraints. The problem considered above involves an objective function, two constraints and non-negativity requirements. We formulate the above problem in linear programming form.

Maximise : $\pi = 10X + 6Y$ (Objective function)

Subject to : $2X + 3Y \leq 12$

Non negativity requirements

$$X \geq 0$$

$$Y \geq 0$$

The general algebraic approach to solve the problem is to *identify the corners* (*i.e.* extreme points including the zero value of each decision variable) of the feasible region by graphing the constraints. The corner points are either extreme points of zero value of the variables or the intersection points of the two constraints. We then solve the two constraint equations for the values of the decision variables (the quantities of the two products to be produced at the point of the intersection. With the values of the decision variables so obtained we solve the objective function. In our example we calcuate the profits for each set of the values of decision variables corresponding to different corner extreme points. This is explained below.

Consider Fig. 17.4 where the feasible region has been shown with corner points *A*, *Q* and *D*. Thus the present linear programming problem can be solved by calculating the profits for the quantities of the two products at these corner points,

(1) The given profit function is $\pi = 10X + 6Y$. At point *A* of the feasible region the quantity of *X* is zero and the quantity of *Y* is 4. Thus, at point *A*

$$\pi = 10(0) + 6\,(4)$$

$$= 24 \qquad \ldots(i)$$

(2) At corner point *D* of the feasible region, the quantity of product X is 4 and the quantity of product *Y* is zero. Thus at corner point *D*

$$\pi = 10\,(4) + 6\,(0)$$

$$= 40 \qquad \ldots(ii)$$

(3) Now at the corner point *Q*, the two constraint equation curves intersect. That is, point Q satisfies the two constraint equations. The values of variables (*i.e.* outputs of the two products corresponding to this can be obtained by solving them simultaneously. The two constraint equations are :

$$2X + 3Y = 12 \qquad \ldots(a)$$

$$2X + 1Y = 8 \qquad \ldots(b)$$

Substracting equation (*b*) from equation (*a*) we have

$$2Y = 4$$

$$Y = 2$$

Substituting the value of *Y* into equation (*a*) we have

$$2X + 3\,(2) = 12$$

$$2X = 12 - 6 = 6$$

$$X = 3$$

Thus at the corner point *Q*, the outputs of X and *Y* are 3 and 2 units respectively. Now substituting these values of X and *Y* in the profits-function equation we can find the profits at the corner points Q.

Thus

$$\pi = 10X + 6Y$$

with $X = 3$ and $Y = 2$ we have

$$\pi = 10 \times 3 + 6 \times 2 = \text{Rs. } 42 \qquad \ldots\ldots(iii)$$

Given the profit function, profits at the corner points *A*, *D* and *Q* are Rs. 24, 40 and 42 respectively. Thus, given the constraints, profits at corner point *Q* are the maximum and corresponding to this the firm produces 3 units of X and 2 units of *Y*. It is thus clear in linear programming solution optimal solution occurs at a corner of the feasible region. This is because both the objective function and constraints are linear.

Problem 2

Let us take another linear programming problem and solve it by algebraic method.

An important thing the students should understand is how to formulate the given problem as a linear programming problem, that is, to write the objective function and the constraints in the form of *equations or inequalities. Let us first state the problem.*

Suppose a firm produces two products X_1 and X_2. Each unit of product X_1 contributes Rs. 30 to profit and each unit of product X_2 contributes 40 to profits. The production of these products require inputs A, B and C and their available quantities are 14, 10 and 4 respectively. It is given that production of one unit of product X_1 requires 2 units of input A, 1 unit of input B and does not require input C. And the production of one unit of product X_2 requires 2 units of input A, 2 units of input B and 4 units of input C.

Formulate the above problem as a linear programming problem and solve it by algebraic method.

Solution:

We write below the above problem as a linear programming problem.

Maximise : $\pi = 30X_1, + 40X_2$ (objective function)

Subject to : $2X_1 + 2X_2 \leq 14$ (Input A constraint)

$1X_1 + 2X_2 \leq 10$ (Input B constraint)

$X_2 \leq 4$ (Input C constraint)

$X_1, X_2 \geq 0$ (non-negativity constraint)

In order to solve the above linear programming problem by algebraic method we first determine feasible region and its extreme or corner points. This has been done in Fig. 17.5 Three constraint lines *AB*, *CD* and *EG* representing input constraints have been drawn to get the area *EFKB* as the feasible region. There are three *E, F, K,* and *B* corner points of this feasible region.

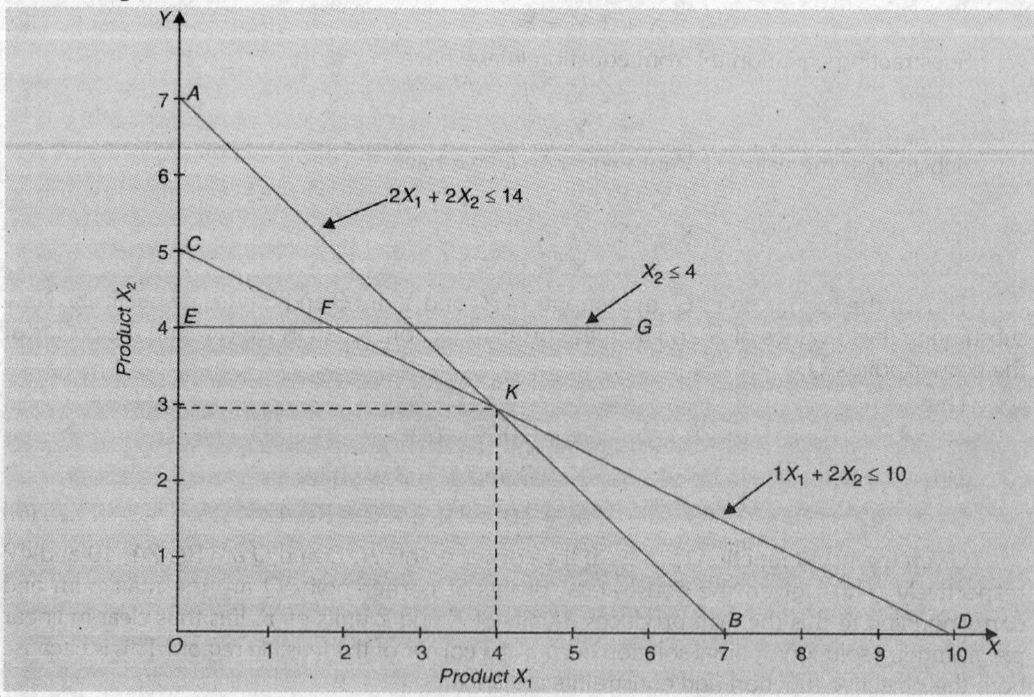

Fig.17.5. *Feasible Region and Corner Points*

The corner point E is determined by only one constraint of input C and according to it 4 units of product X_2 and 0 amount of X_1 are produced. Substituting this in profit function we get profits at corner point E.

Thus profits at corner point $E = 30 \times 0 + 40 \times 4 = 160$.

At corner point B, 7 units of product X_1 and zero output of product X_2 are produced. Thus

$$\pi \text{ at corner point } B = 30 \times 7 + 40 \times 0 = \text{Rs. } 210$$

The corner point F is determined by the intersection of constraints of inputs B and C. As will be seen from the feasible region, according to the corner point F, 4 units of product X_2 are produced. To get the quantity produced of product X_1 we substitute $X_2 = 4$ in the constraint equation of input B

Thus,

$$X_1 + 2 \times 4 = 10$$

$$X_1 = 10 - 8 = 2$$

Now with $X_1 = 2$ and $X_2 = 4$ at the corner point F, profits are

$$\pi = 30\,X_1 + 40\,X_2$$

$$= 30 \times 2 + 40 \times 4 = 60 + 160 = 220$$

Now, take corner point K which is determined by intersection of the constraints of inputs A and B. The output of two products at the corner point can therefore be obtained by solving the constraints equation of the input A and B. Thus

$$2\,X_1 + 2\,X_2 = 14 \quad \ldots(i)$$

$$1\,X_1 + 2\,X_2 = 10 \quad \ldots(ii)$$

Substracting equation (ii) from equation (i) we have

$$1\,X_1 = 4$$

Substituting the value of $X_1 = 4$ into equation (*ii*) we have

$$4 + 2\,X_2 = 10$$

$$2X_2 = 10 - 4 = 6$$

$$X_2 = 3$$

Thus at corner point K, 4 units of product X_1 and 3 units of product X_2 are produced. With these outputs of X_1 and X_2 profits are :

$$\pi = 30\,X_1 + 40\,X_2$$

$$= 30 \times 4 + 40 \times 3$$

$$= 120 + 120 = 240$$

It is evident from above that at corner points E, B, F and K the profits earned are Rs. 160, 210, 220 and 240 respectively.

Table 17.1 : ***Outputs and Profits at Different Corners of the Feasible Region***

Corner Point	Outputs of Two Products	Profits Rs.
E	$X_1 = 0;\ X_2 = 4$	160
F	$X_1 = 2;\ X_2 = 4$	220
K	$X_1 = 4;\ X_2 = 3$	240
B	$X_1 = 7;\ X_2 = 0$	210

K represents the optimum or profit-maximising outputs of two products, namely, 4 units of product X_1 and 3 units of product X_2. We summarise these results in the Table 17.1.

CHOICE OF A PROCESS : OUTPUT MAXIMIZATION SUBJECT TO SOME CONSTRAINTS

Another important problem of firm which can be solved through the method of linear programming is that of choosing a best process for production of a commodity. In this analysis of choice of a process it is generally assumed that a firm seeks to maximize its output subject to the constraint of (*i*) a given cost outlay or (*ii*) some available inputs. On the other hand, if the level of output is given, the choice of a process by a firm is analysed by assuming that a firm will aim to minimize cost for the given level of output. We shall discuss all these cases of choice of a best process. But before we explain the optimal solution in these cases we will explain the various concepts in this regard.

Processes and Process Rays. A process is another fundamental concept of linear programming as applied to the theory of production and firm. A process is a particular method of producing goods and requires various inputs (or factors) in fixed proportions. A process is also called *activity* or *complex*. The constant or fixed proportions between inputs to produce a particular product is an essential property of a production process. Thus, a process is a complex of workers and capital equipment. Since each process requires the use of fixed proportions between factors, say between capital and labour, no substitution within a process is possible. This is in sharp contrast to the neo-classical theory of production which assumes easy substitution among factors of production and accordingly a smooth isoquant is drawn. If a production process A involves 8 machine hours and one worker (that is, per unit of labour time) and another production method B involves 5 machine hours per unit of labour, they are by definition two different production processes. The level of a process means how many machine hours and units of labour within that process are used for production. The assumption of linearity implies that 16 machine hours and 2 workers will produce twice as much as 8 machine hours and 1 worker and so on in case of process A. Similarly, for process B. Some processes used for the production of a commodity are capital-intensive and some are labour-intensive.

The concept of a process is technological in nature. Depending upon available technologies, several processes are available to a firm for producing a particular product. Each production process can be used at several levels to produce a particular product. The higher the level at which the process is used, the greater the output produced. It is worth mentioning that one process can be substituted for another. Besides, when a commodity is produced with two or more processes at the same time in a community, it is generally assumed that the two processes do not interfere with each other or do not increase the productivity of one another. A typical linear programming is to choose a process or a combination of processes, given the constraints, that minimizes cost of production for producing a given level of output.

Representation of Process : Process Rays. Given the linearity assumption, in each production process proportion between factors remains fixed or constant. As a result, each production process can be expressed through a straight line passing through the origin. In a diagram whose two axes represent the two factors, say labour and capital, the straight line passing through the origin which is the locus of points involving fixed proportions between the two factors is called a process ray. In Figure 17.6 a process ray OA has been drawn which represents a fixed ratio between capital and labour which is given by the slope of the ray. It may be noted that on the process ray OA points Q_1, Q_2, Q_3 etc are the various levels at which the given process can be used. It will be further noticed that the process A is a relatively capital-intensive method of production. Similarly, in Fig.17.6 process rays *OB*, *OC* and *OD* representing different factor proportions and therefore representing different processes *B*, *C* and *D* have been drawn which are respectively less and less capital-intensive. R_1, R_2, R_3 etc are the different levels of the process *B*. S_1, S_2, S_3 etc are the different levels of process *C*, and T_1, T_2, T_3 etc are the different levels of process *D*. Because linear relationship between inputs and outputs has been assumed, as the amounts of inputs or factors are increased along a given process ray, output will increase in the same proportion as inputs, that is, constant returns to scale will occur. Since point Q_1, Q_2, Q_3 and Q_4 have been taken at the same distance from each other, the increment in output between them will also be the same.

On process ray *OB*, points R_1 R_2, R_3 and R_4 lying on it represent a different factor proportion (*i.e.* capital-labour ratio) from that on various points at process ray *OA*. It is worth mentioning that it is not necessary that to produce a given output along process ray *B*, one has to work at the same level of process *B* as of *A*, that is, distance OR_1 on *OB* may not be equal to the distance OQ_1 on *OA* ; both O_1, and R_1 yielding the same level of output. Likewise, factor combination R_2 and Q_2 which yield the same level of output may not be equidistant from the origin *O*. Similarly, points S_1, S_2, S_3 and S_4 have been taken on process ray *OC* and points T_1, T_2, T_3 and T_4 have been taken on process ray *OD*. With factor combination S_1 of process *C*, T_1 of process *D*, output equal to that of Q_1 or R_1 is obtained. With factor combination S_2 of process *C* and factor combination T_2 of process *D*, output equal to that of Q_2 or R_2 is obtained.

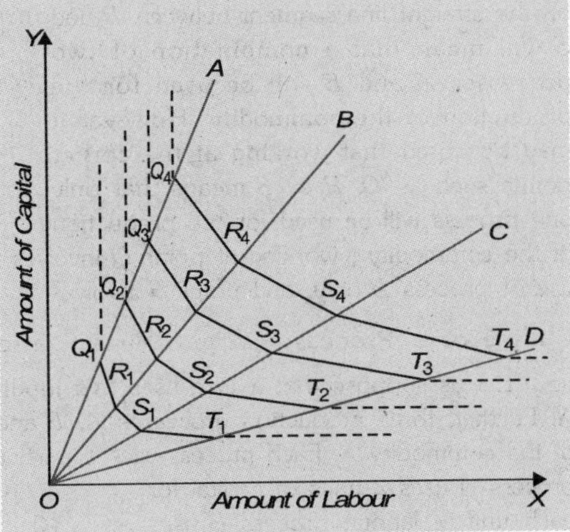

Fig. 17.6. *Process Rays*

Likewise, on process ray *OD*, points T_1, T_2, T_3, T_4 represent output equal to Q_1, Q_2, Q_3 and Q_4 respectively. On joining points Q_1, R_1, S_1 and T_1, we get a kinked curve (with right linear segments) $Q_1R_1S_1T_1$ which is called isoquant which is similar to equal product curves of the traditional production theory. Further, points Q_2, R_2, S_2 and T_2 are joined together to obtain another iso quant representing a higher level of output. Likewise, higher isoquants are obtained by joining points on different process rays. In order to make it more similar to the iso-product curves of traditional production theory, the extremes of isoquants of linear programming theory are usually extended by vertical and horizontal lines as shown in Figure 17.6 by the dotted lines. Another point worth mentioning is that iso-product curves or isoquants of traditional production theory are smooth or continuous, whereas isoquants in linear programming theory are kinked having right-line segments.

Combination of Processes. As mentioned above, more than one processes are generally available to produce a commodity and various levels of output of the commodity can be produced by working at different levels of the process. It is worthwhile to note that instead of producing a commodity with a single production process a combination of two processes can also be used to produce a commodity. A part of the output of a commodity can be produced with one process and a part with another process. This happens when a firm is working at a point like *K* on segment *QR* in Figure 17.7. In this figure three process rays, *OA, OB*, and *OC* have been depicted and an iso-quant *QRS* has been drawn. If a firm decides to work at point *K* to produce a given level of output represented by the isoquant *QRS*, it will employ two processes *A* and *B* to produce the commodity. Now, the question is at what levels of the processes *A* and

B the firm will work when it is producing at K. In order to know that a line from point K parallel to OB is drawn which meets OA at L and, similarly, a line from K parallel to OA is drawn which meets OB at T. Thus, to produce the output corresponding to point Q on isoquant QRS, the firm will work at the level of OL of process A and at OT of process B.

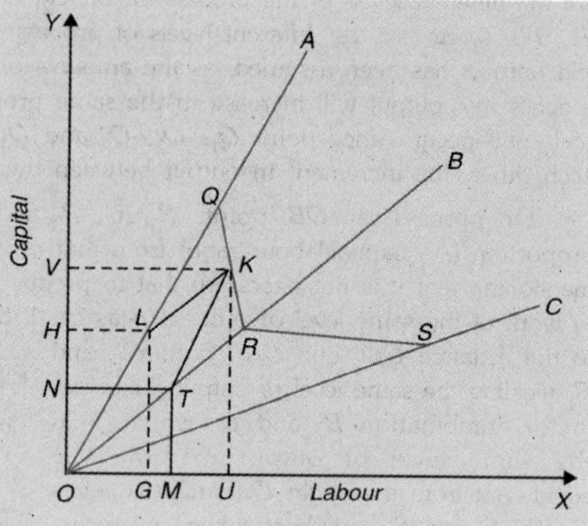

Fig. 17.7. *Combination of Processes*

It can be proved that the total amounts of factors, labour and capital, used at point L and T will be equal to the factor combination represented by K (*i.e.* OV of capital and OU of labour). That is, $OG + OM = OU$ of labour and $OH + ON = OV$ of capital.[2]

In the same way, working at any point on the straight line segment between R and S will mean that a combination of two processes A and B will be used for the production of the commodity. However it may be noted that working at the corner points such as Q, R or S means that only one process will be used for the production of the commodity ; working at point Q involves the use of process A only, point R involves the use of process B only, and point S involves the use of process C only.

Choice of a Process: Output Maximization with Cost-Outlay Constant

Let us suppose that a firm uses two inputs, labour and capital, to produce a commodity X. Further, three production processes A, B and C are available to the firm for the production of the commodity X. Each process uses a particular ratio of two inputs capital and labour. Thus process A uses 2 units of capital for each unit of labour, process B uses one unit of capital for each unit of labour and process C uses 0.5 units of capital for each unit of labour. The slope of the each process ray measures the ratio of the two inputs, capital and labour. These processes are represented by the process rays OA, OB, and OC in Figure 17.8 wherein along X-axis amount of labour is measured and along the Y-axis amount of capital is measured. The process rays, OA, OB and OC are successively more and more labour-intensive. Points L, M and N on the process rays OA, OB and OC represent the levels of these processes respectively, the working at which yields the same level of output, say 40. By joining these

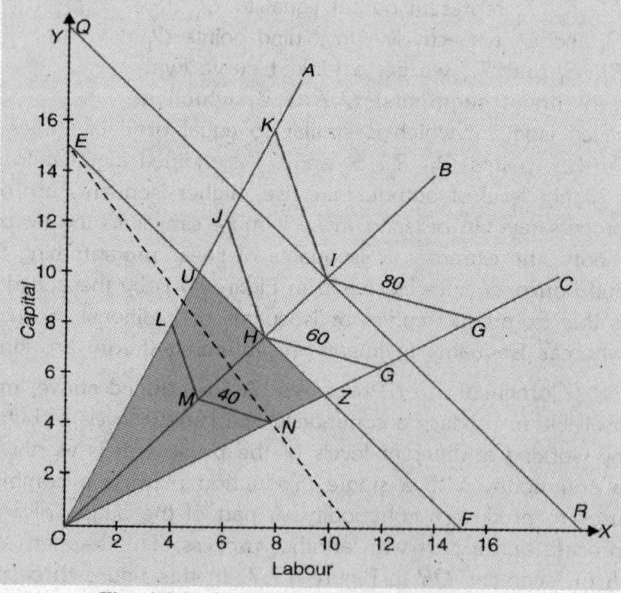

Fig. 17.8. *Optimum Choice of Processes*

2. For proof Sec J. Baumol, *Economic Theory and Operations Analysis*, 4th edition, p. 305.

points we get an isoquant *LMN* representing 40 units of commodity *X*. Likewise, we join points *J, H, G*, on various process rays to represent an isoquant representing output level of 60 units of commodity *X*.

Let us assume that with a given cost-outlay, say *T* (= Rs 300) the firm can buy *OF* amount of labour at its given price or wage rate *w* or *OE* amount of capital at its given price *r*. Then, in Fig. 17.8 on a straight line *EF*, called an iso-cost line, any combination of two factors can be purchased with the given cost-outlay (= Rs 300). Writing this in the from of equation :

$$T (= \text{Rs } 300) = L.w + Kr$$

$$\text{or } 300 = L.\ w + Kr$$

where *T* stands for the given cost outlay, *L* for the amount of labour, *w* for the given price of labour, *K* for the amount of capital and *r* for the given price of capital. With the constraint of given total cost-outlay, the area to the left or on the line *EF* represents the feasible region. But, as noted above, since only three processes of production represented by process rays *OA*, *OB* and *OC* are available, choice of process will be confined to the area within process rays *OA* and *OC*. With these constraints imposed by the availability of only 3 production processes, the feasible region is reduced to the shaded area *OUZ*. Since with a given cost-outlay, a firm will seek to maximize production the actual choice of process will be made from among the process lying on segment *UZ* of the iso-cost line *EF*.

It will be seen from the Figure 17.8 that the iso-cost line is touching the corner point *H* of isoquant *JHG* representing 60 units of output. No point other than *H* lying on the given isocost line *EF* will yield greater output. Thus, the factor combination *H* is the optimum solution of the problem, that is, output-maximizing combination for the given cost-outlay. It will be observed that point *H* lies on the process ray *OB*. It follows therefore that firm will employ process *B* for the production of the commodity.

Cost–Minimisation for a Given Output : It is worthwhile to mention here that if the problem is to choose a process subject to the given output of 60 units of product *X*, even then the firm will choose the point *H* on the process ray *OB*. In this case output of 60 units or isoquant *JHG* will be the constraint and the firm will aim at minimising cost for its production. It will be seen from Figure 17.8 that on the isoquant *JHG*, point *H* will lie on the lowest possible iso-cost line *EF*. It means cost-minimizing solution for the production of 60 units of output will also be *H* which, as seen above, is the output-maximising solution for the cost outlay represented by the iso-cost line *EF*. Since cost-minimization for producing a given output is the dual of the primal problem of output maximization with a given cost-oulay, it follows that the *optimum solution for the dual of the linear programming problem is the same as that of its primal problem.* It should be noted that choice of optimum process depends on the relative prices of inputs. If capital is relatively cheaper than labour, a capital intensive process will be chosen. On the other hand, if labour is relatively cheaper, more labour intensive process will be selected for production.

Another interesting question is how the change in the total cost-outlay, prices of both inputs, capital and labour, remaining the same, will affect the choice of process. Suppose in Figure 17.8, as a result of the increase in total cost outlay iso-cost line shifts to a higher position *QR* which is parallel to the initial iso-cost outlay *EF*. It will be seen from Figure 17.8 that the higher isocost line *QR* will touch the corner of the higher isoquant and but will lie on the same process line *OB* as point *H*. It means change in total-cost outlay, input prices remaining unchanged, will not affect the choice of the process ; only the firm will now be at different level of the same process.

It should be further noted that due to the linearity assumption in linear programming that the higher iso-quants are so drawn as to reflect the operation of constant returns to scale. For example in our Fig. 17.8 when we increase inputs by 50 percent (from $8K + 4L$ to $12K + 6L$) on process ray *OC* we obtain higher isoquant *JHG* of 60 units of output which is 50 per cent greater then 40 units of output at lower isoquant *LMN*.

It is also clear from the above analysis that when there exists only one constraint, namely, total cost-outlay in the above case, there will be only one process which will be optimal and will be used by the firm for the production of the goods.

Multiple Optimal Solutions

It may be noted that in a linear programming there is usually a *single* optimum solution for the choice of process. But there can be an unusual case where there are *multiple optimum* solutions of the problem. This can happen when the factor prices are such that the given isocost line coincides with a segment of an iso-cost line. This is depicted in Figure 17.9 where it is assumed that four processes *A, B, C* and *D*, represented by process rays *OA, OB, OC*, and *OD* respectively, are available for the production of a commodity. Factor prices are such that *EF* is the iso-cost line. It will be observed that the iso-cost line *EF* coincides with the segment *RS* of the isoquant *QRST*. It is thus obvious that either processes *B* or *C* or any other combination of these processes lying on segment *RS* are optimum solution for the firm; any of which can be used to maximise production. Thus, in this case, there are more than one optimum solution. However, normally there is one optimum solution which may be at the corner or an extreme point of the isoquant.

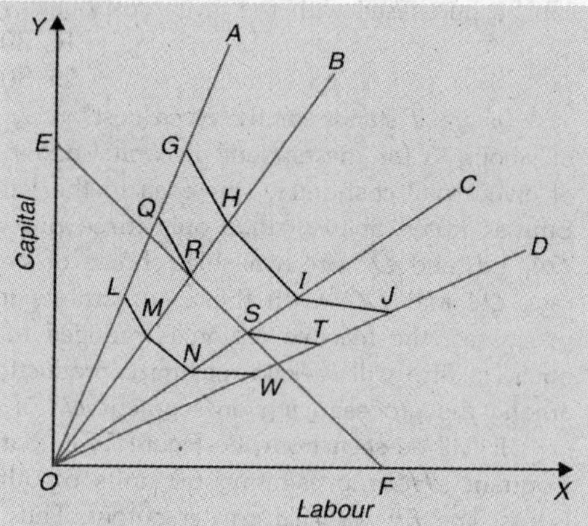

Fig. 17.9. *Choice of a Process : Mulitiple Optimum Solutions*

Choice of a Process: Output Maximization with Two Inputs as Constraints

Now, if instead of cost-outlay as constraint, the firm is faced with constraints of two inputs which are available to it in limited quantities. Evidently, with the given amounts of inputs, the firm will try to maximise output so as to maximise its profits. Let us assume that three processes *A, B* and *C* are available for the production of the commodity produced by the firm. In Figure 17.10 process rays *OA* , *OB* and *OC* represent the three processes *A* , *B* and *C*. *OL* and *OK* are the available quantities of labour and capital, Thus, the horizontal straight line *KT* represents the constraint of available capital and the vertical line *LG* represents the constraint of available labour. These two lines interact at point *S*. The area *OKSL* represents the region of feasible solutions.

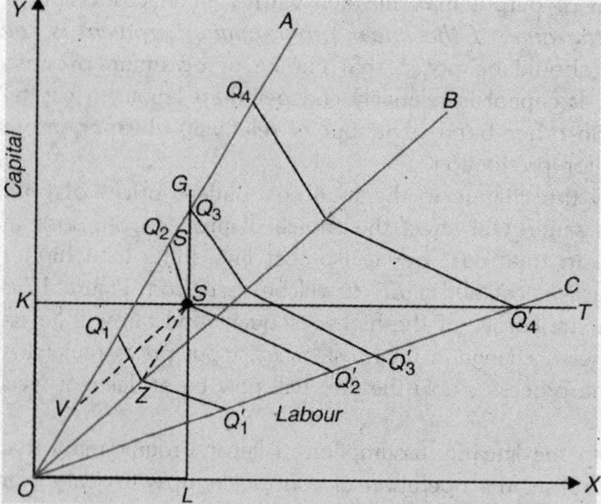

Fig. 17.10. *Output Maximisation with Two Inputs as Constraints*

As the firm will be interested in maximizing output; with the given constraints it will try to reach the highest attainable isoquant. So it will go to the boundary of the feasible region because production at this will ensure its maximum output which is possible within the constraints. It will be observed from the Figure 17.10 that the feasible region is touching the isoquant $Q_2Q'_2$ at the corner point S. So the firm will produce maximum possible output represented by isoquant $Q_2Q'_2$ by working at point S. The point S therefore is the optimum solution for the choice of the process. A glance at Figure 17.10 will reveal that the boundary or corner point S lies at the segment of the isoquant Q_2Q_2 in between the process rays OA and OB. It is thus clear that at the optimum solution point S, the firm will use a combination of two processes A and B. By drawing a line SV parallel to OB and line SZ parallel to OA we determine that the firm will work at the level OV of process A and at the level OZ of process B to reach the optimum input combination S.

Output-Maximisation with One Limited Input

Instead of two limited inputs, there may be one limited input which constitutes the constraint, while the other input is available in any desired amount. It may happen that in case of capital, capacity of a machine is limited or a ware house of a limited given capacity is available. Or, it may happen that a limited amount of capital is available while there does not exist any constraint regarding labour. Consider Figure 17.10 again. If labour is available in any amount desired by the firm but only OK amount of capital is available for production. In this case constraint line LG would not be there and only the horizontal line KT representing the constraint of limited capital will be there. A firm with its objective of maximization of output will move along the capital-constraint line KT so as to reach highest achievable isoquant. $Q_4Q'_4$. Since only three processes are available, the firm cannot go to the right of process ray OC. It will be observed that with OK as limited capital at the most the firm will go upto point Q'_4 on process C. Thus Q'_4 will be the optimum solution with only OK amount of capital as the constraint.

If there were no limitations in regard to the availability of capital, while labour was available only in limited quantity, such as the amount OL in Figure. 17.10 Now, the vertical line LG representing the given labour constraint meets the ray OA at point Q_3. Since only three process rays are available, the firm cannot go above (*i.e.* to the right) of process ray OA, Thus, with OL as the maximum amount of labour available, the firm will use the process A and work at its level OQ_3.

SOME ADDITIONAL PROBLEMS AND THEIR LINEAR PROGRAMMING SOLUTIONS

We shall now explain some additional problems which are generally encountered and their linear programrning solutions. First, take the case which is illustrated in Figure 17.11

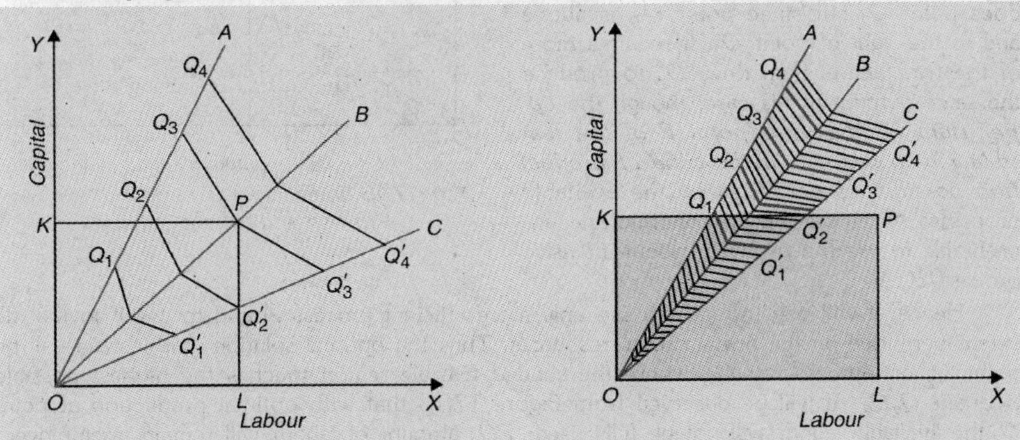

Fig. 17.11. *Full Utilisation of Given Input* **Fig. 17.12.** *Labour as Slack Variable*

where three processes *A, B* and *C* represented by process rays *OA, OB* and *OC* respectively are available. Furthermore, labour and capital are available in limited quantities, *OL* and *OK* respectively. *OKPL* is thus feasible region $Q_1Q'_1$, $Q_2Q'_2$, $Q_3Q'_3$, $Q_4Q'_4$, are the isoquants indicating various levels of output. It will be seen from Fig. 17.11 that in this case the upper right hand comer of the feasible region *OKPL* happens to touch the process ray *OB* at corner point *P*. This means that optimal linear programming solution will be to use only one production process *B*; *the other two processes, A and C will not be used at all.* In equilibrium, the firm will work with the process *B* at the level *OP* and produce the amount of the product indicated by the isoquant $Q_3Q'_3$. It will also be seen that with the corner point *P* as the production point, the available quantities of both the factors, labour and capital, are being fully used.

Now, consider the problem represented in Fig.17.12. In this there are two constraints regarding the availabilities of factors, labour and capital. *OL* is the amount of labour available and *OK* is the amount of capital available. Consequently, *OKPL* is the feasible region. It will be further seen that three processes, *A, B* and *C* are available and striped region *AOC* between them represents the cone of production possibilities as permitted by the availability of three production processes. In this case which represents a rather common situation in real economic life, the upper right hand corner (*i.e.* point *P*) of the feasible region lies outside the cone of production possibilities *AOC*. *In this case, the corner point P does not represent the optimal solution of the problem.* Instead, point Q'_2, from where the feasible region passes through provides the optimal solution. It will be noticed from Figure 17.12 that in this case with O'_2 as the optimal production point labour will not be fully used. The magnitude of labour unused is equal to PO'_2. Further, in this case also only one process *C* will be employed for production.

Another similar case which is commonly found is represented in Figure 17.13. Here there are two factors, labour and capital. Their available quantities yield *OKPL* as the feasible region. *A* and *B* are the two production processes represented by the process rays *OA* and *OB*. The process *A* is relatively capital-intensive and process *B* is relatively labour-intensive. The special thing about this case is that labour-intensive method is highly inefficient with the result that *isoquants* $Q_1Q'_1$, $Q_2Q'_2$ *etc, are positively sloping*. Because of this, for instance, on the same isoquant higher level point O_2 on the labour-intensive process ray *OB* yields the same output as the lower level point Q_2, on the relatively capital-intensive process ray *OA*. Point Q'_2 yields the same output as does point Q_2 but since point Q'_2 is above and to the right of point Q_2, it requires more of the two factors than does Q_2 to produce the same output. In this case, though the *upper right hand corner point P of the feasible region lies within the cone of production possibilities* permitted by the available processes, yet it will be uneconomic and unprofitable to use the relatively labour-intensive process *B*.

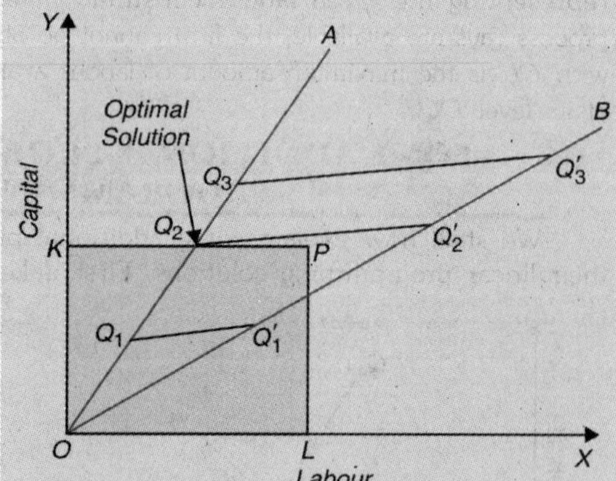

Fig. 17.13. *Inefficiency of Labour-intensive Process and Labour Surplus*

Hence, it will pay the firm to use only more efficient process *A* and to use it to the full extent permitted by the firm's capital resources. Thus the optimal solution in this case will be point Q_2 on process ray *OA* where the shaded feasible region touches the highest possible isoquant Q_2Q_2'. It will be observed from Figure 17.13 that with optimal production at point Q_2,the available labour will not be fully used; PQ_2 amount of labour will remain unemployed.

A SPECIAL PROBLEM OF COST-MINIMIZATION : DIET PROBLEM

In the modern days linear programming technique has been used to solve several types of business and social problems. A social problem in which linear programming has been used to find an optimum solution relates to the problem of feeding diet to the animals. The problem of feeding optimum diet is the problem in minimizing cost of feeding various grains so that the animals are provided with minimum nutritional requirements which constitute the constraints. Various grains or foodstuffs have different prices and a pound of each grain contains different amounts of various nutrients—vitamins, minerals, calories, proteins, etc. Thus the problem is to find a least-cost combination of various grains which meet the minimum nutritional requirements.

Suppose a farmer feeds two types of grains. *A* and *B* to the animals reared by him. Constraint facing him is that the animals must be fed with certain minimum amounts of three nutrients-proteins, carbohydrates and calcium. Thus in this simplified example there are two variables, each with a price, represented by grains, three constraints regarding the minimum quantities of three nutrients which must be provided. The objective function is minimization of cost of providing the required diet to the animals.

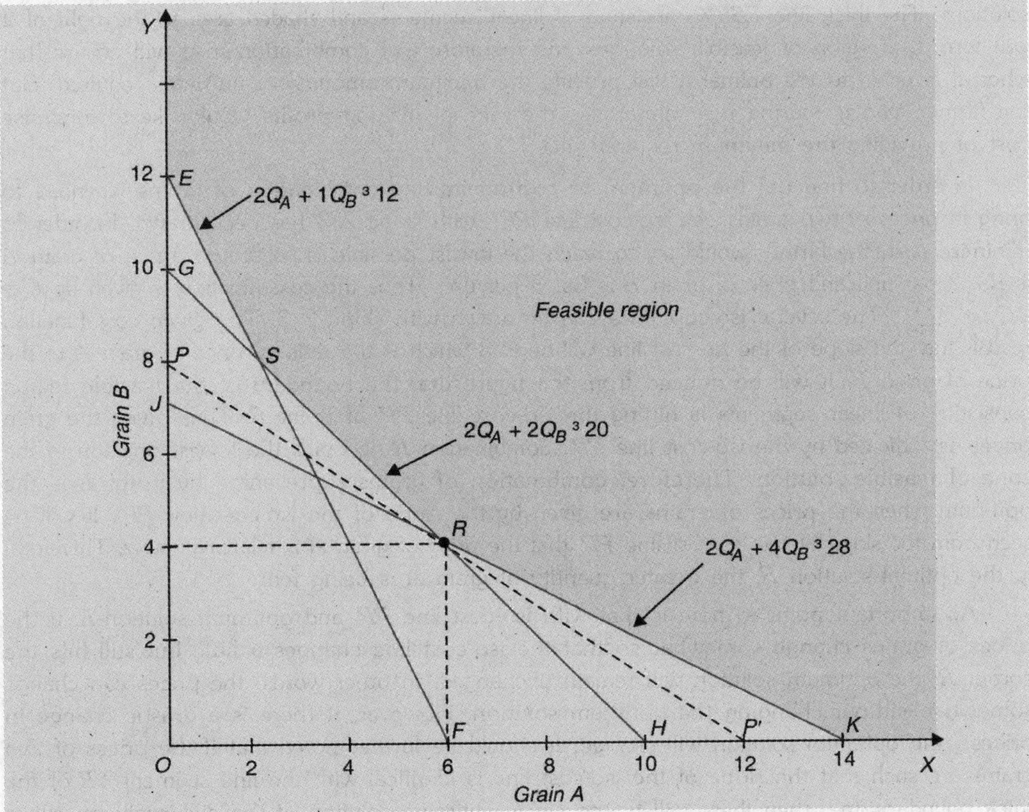

Fig. 17.14. *Solution of Diet Problem through Linear Programming*

What is the feasible region in this case and what will be the optimum solution is illustrated in Figure 17.14 where the *X*-axis measures the quantity of grain *A* and the *Y*-axis measures the quantity of grain *B*. The line *EF* represents the protein constraint ($2Q_A + 1Q_B \geq 12$) and shows the various combinations of quantities of grains *A* and *B* which meet the minimum requirements of protein Similarly, the line *GH* represents calcium constraint ($2Q_A + 2\ Q_B$

$\geq$20) and shows the combinations of two grains which provide the minimum requirements of calcium and the line *JK* represents the combinations which fulfil the minimum requirements of carbohydrates. It should be noted that the steeper slope of the line *EF* shows that one pound of grain *A* contains relatively more amount of proteins than grain *B*. We write below the cost-minimising problem of providing proper diet to the animals.

Minimise : $C = 2\,Q_A + 3Q_B$

Subject to :

$$2Q_A + 1Q_B \geq 12$$
$$2Q_A + 2Q_B \geq 20$$
$$2Q_A + 4Q_B \geq 28$$
$$Q_A, Q_B \geq 0$$

Now, we are interested in obtaining the region of feasible solutions. Since any combination of grains lying *below the lines* showing the three constraints will not meet the minimum nutritional requirement, the outer segments of the three lines which have been thickened constitute the boundary, the combinations lying on it and to the right of it will be feasible solutions. The thick line *ESRK* consisting of linear segments and shaded area to the right of it will form the region of feasible solutions and therefore any combination in it will ensure that when it is given to the animal it will provide the minimum amounts of nutrients required. But the farmer who is rearing the animals for the sake of making profits would like to minimise cost of providing the minimum required diet.

In order to find out the optimum or cost-minimizing combination of grains we need to bring in prices of two grains. An iso-cost line *PP′* with slope 2/3 has been drawn. In order to minimize cost, the farmer would try to reach the lowest possible iso-cost line. Price of grain *A* is Rs. 2 per unit and price of grain *B* is Rs. 3 per unit. Thus the cost function is given by $C = 2Q_A + 3Q_B$. The several iso-cost lines can be drawn with slope 2/3. The given cost function reveals that the slope of the iso-cost line will be 2/3 which is the ratio of price of grain *A* to the price of grain *B*. It will be noticed from the figure that the boundary of the feasible region consisting of linear segments is hitting the iso-cost line *PP′* at point *R*. Thus given the grain prices as indicated by the iso-cost line *PP′*, combination *R* occupies the lowest position in the zone of feasible solution. Therefore, combination of grains represented by point *R* is the optimum when the prices of grains are given by the slope of the iso-cost line *PP′*. It will be seen from the slope of the iso-cost line *PP′* that the price of grain *A* is relatively lower. Therefore, in the optimal solution *R*, the greater quantity of grain *A* is being fed.

An important point to note is that with iso-cost line *PP′* and optimum solution-*R*, if the prices of grains change somewhat so that the iso-cost line changes a little but still hits the corner *R*, the optimum solution will remain unchanged. In other words, the prices can change somewhat without changing the optimum solution. However, if there is a drastic change in prices , the optimum solution will change. It should be further noted that if the prices of two grains are such that the slope of the iso-cost line is identical with the line segment *SR* of the thick boundary line, then there will be *no single* optimum solution of the diet problem; either *R* or *S* or any other point between them on the line segment *SR* will be the optimum.

Algebraic Solution

The cost minimization problem to provide minimum required neutrients to the animals which we have graphically explained above can be solved by algebraic method. For doing so we do not have to draw iso-cost lines but consider only the corner points of the feasible region and then compare the costs at the corner points. The corner point at which the total cost will be minimum will give us the optimum solution.

It will be seen from the boundary of the feasible region that we have to compare the costs at corner points *E, S, R* and *K*. At corner point *E* only 12 units of grain *B* are fed to the animal ($Q_A = 0$; $Q_B = 12$) which will cost C = 3 × 12 = Rs. 36

Now consider the corner point *S* which is formed by the intersection of the constraints of protein and calcium. We solve the equations of these two nutrients simultaneously

Thus

$$2Q_A + 2Q_B = 20 \quad \text{...(i)}$$

$$2Q_A + 1Q_B = 12 \quad \text{...(ii)}$$

Substracting equation (*ii*) from equation (i) We have

$$1Q_B = 8$$

Now, substituting $Q_B = 8$ into equation (*ii*) we have

$$2Q_A + 8 = 12$$

$$Q_A = 2$$

Now we calculate the cost of combination *S* of two grains, $Q_A = 2$, $Q_B = 8$

Cost at corner point *S* = 2 × (2) + 3 (8) = 4 + 24 = 28

Now we consider corner point *R* which is formed by the intersection of constraints of calcium ($2Q_A + 2Q_B \geq 20$) and of carbohydrates ($2Q_A + 4Q_B \geq 28$). In order to find the quantities of two grains *A* and *B* at the corner point *R*, we solve these two constraint equations. Thus

$$2Q_A + 4Q_B = 28 \quad \text{...(a)}$$

$$2Q_A + 2Q_B = 20 \quad \text{...(b)}$$

Subtracting equation (*b*) from equation (*a*) we have

$$2Q_B = 8$$

$$Q_B = \frac{8}{2} = 4$$

Substituting the value $Q_B = 4$ into equation (*b*) above we have

$$2Q_A + 2 \times 4 = 20$$

$$2Q_A = 20 - 8 = 12$$

$$Q_A = 6$$

The cost of combination of two grains at corner point *R* is *C* = 2 × (6) + 3 (4) = **24**

Now consider corner point of the boundary. *K* containing only 14 units of grain *A* and zero grain *B*. Thus cost of grains at corner point *K* is *C* = 2 × 14 = **28**

It is evident from above that given the cost-function and the constraints, the corner point *R* where the quantity of grain A is 6 units and the quantity of grain *B* is 4 units which provides the optimal solution where the cost is minimum.

QUESTIONS FOR REVIEW

1. Explain the linear programming technique to solve the problems of constrained optimization. Why is the assumption of linearity important in linear programming?
2. Explain the following concepts as used in linear programming technique.

   1. Objective function
   2. Feasible region
   3. Constraints

   Write some objective functions and give some examples of different forms of feasible region
3. State the three broad types of problems for which linear programming is used and solve them. A firm is producing two products *A* and *B* and face constraints in the form of limited quantities of two inputs *X* and *Y* which are available for use in the production of two commodities. Explain the linear programming techniques in general to solve the profit maximization problem given the constraints in the form of limited availabilities of two inputs.
4. Explain the primal and dual problems in the theory of linear programming technique. Is optimum solution of the dual problem the same as of the primal problem? Explain.
5. Why does optimum solution in linear programming always lie at the corner of the feasible region? When do we get multiple optimal solutions in the linear programming. Show graphically
6. A firm uses two machines *A* and *B* to produce two products *X* and *Y*. Each unit of product *X* requires two hours of time on both machines. Each unit of product *Y* requires three hours of time on machine A and one hour on machine *B*. The profit contribution of product *X* is Rs. 6 per unit and of product *Y* is Rs 7 per unit.

   Assuming that the objective is to maximize profits, how many units of product *X* and *Y* should be produced. Formulate this problem as linear programming problem and solve graphically and by algebraic method.
7. You are given the following linear programming problem.

   Maximize : $\pi = 2Q_A + 5Q_B$

   Subject to

   $1Q_A + 3Q_B \leq 16$

   $4Q_A + 1Q_B \leq 20$

   $1Q_B \leq 4$

   $Q_A, Q_B \geq O$

   π stands for profits, Q_A and Q_B are the quantities of two products. 16, 20, 4 are the quantities of three inputs available for use in production.

   Solve the above problem graphically.
8. A manager of a milk producing firm has to decide how much of two feeds *A* and *B* be given to milch cattle to minimise cost. The minimum requirement of adequate feed intake of a milch cattle consists of 40 units of protein, 60 units of calcium and 60 units of carbohydrates. It is given that price of feed *A* is Rs 100 per ton and price of feed *B* is Rs. 200 per ton.

   Find the quantities of two feeds to be purchased for feeding milk cows that minimizes cost subject to the minimum nutritional requirements of feed intake. Formulate the above problem as linear programming problem and solve both by graphic and algebraic methods.

Supply and Its Elasticity

The Meaning of Supply

As demand is defined as a schedule of the quantities'of good that will be purchased at various prices, similarly the supply refers to the schedule of the quantities of a good that the firms are able and willing to offer for sale at various prices. How much of a commodity the firms are able to produce depends on the resources available to them and the technology they employ for producing a commodity. How much of a commodity the firms will be willing to offer for sale depends on the profits they expect to make on producing and selling the commodity. Profits in turn depends on the price of the commodity on the one hand and unit cost of production on the other.

Supply should be distinguished from the *quantity supplied*. Whereas supply of a commodity is the entire schedule of the quantities of a commodity that would be offered for sale at all possible prices during a period of time, for example, a day, a week, a month and so on, the quantity supplied refers to the quantity of a commodity which the firms are able and willing to sell at a *particular price* of the commodity. Thus the term supply refers to the entire relationship between the price of a commodity and the quantity supplied at various possible prices and is illustrated by the entire supply curve or supply schedule as given in Figure 17A.1 and Table 17A.1, where the term quantity supplied refers to a *point* on a given supply curve, that is, quantity supplied at a particular price.

Two things are worth mentioning about the concept of supply. First, supply is a *flow concept*, that is, it refers to the amount of a commodity that the firms produce and offer for sale in the market *per period of time*, say a week, a month or a year. Without specifying the time period, supply of a commodity has a little meaning. Second, the quantity supplied at a commodity which the producers plan to produce and sell at a price is not necessarily the same as the *quantity actually sold*. Sometimes the quantity which the firms are willing to produce and sell at a price is greater than the quantity demanded, so the quantity actually bought and sold is less than the quantity supplied.

Supply Function

The quantity of a commodity that firms will be able and willing to offer for sale in the market depends on several factors. The important factors determining supply of a commodity are :

1. The price of the commodity
2. The prices of inputs (*i.e.*, resources) used for the production of the commodity
3. The state of technology
4. The number of firms producing and selling the commodity
5. The prices of related goods produced
6. Future expectations regarding prices.

We will explain these factors determining supply of a commodity in detail in a later section. However, it may be noted that out of the above determinants of supply the own price of the commodity, the prices of inputs (*i.e.*, resources) used to produce the commodity, and the technology used in production are three important factors and therefore the supply function of a commodity is often written taking these factors as independent variables. *Thus, supply function of a commodity is written as*

$$Q_x^s = S(P_x, F_1, F_2 \text{ .... } F_m)$$

where Q^s_x is the quantity supplied of the commodity X, P_x is it own price, F_1, F_2,... F_m are the prices of inputs used to produce the commodity X. The state of technology determines the form of supply function S.

It must however be noted that the *form of the supply function* refers to the precise quantitative relation between the quantity supplied and the independent variables such as the own price of the commodity P_x and prices of factors such as, F_1, F_2 etc. and technology that determine it.

In economics when describing supply of a commodity prices of factors and technology that determine it are generally assumed to remain constant and supply is expressed as a function of price of the commodity alone. Thus, supply function is generally written as

$$Q_x^S = f(P_x)$$

That is, other factors such as factor prices and technolgoy remaining the same, the quantity supplied of a commodity X is a function of price of the commodity X. When these other factors change, the whole supply, function ($Q_x^s = f(Px)$) and the supply curve describing it will change. For example, if there is improvement in technology, the supply curve will shift to the right. On the other hand, if prices of factors rise (for example, if wages of labour increase or fuel prices rise), the whole supply curve will shift to the left.

The Relation between Price and Quantity Supplied : Law of Supply

Supply of a commodity is functionally related to its price. The law of supply relates to this functional relationship between price of a commodity and its quantity supplied. In contrast to the inverse relationship between the quantity demanded and the changes in price, *the quantity supplied of a commodity generally varies directly with price.* That is, the higher the price, the larger is the quantity supplied of a commodity.

The supply schedule and the upward-sloping supply cruve reflect the law of supply. According to the law of supply, *when the price of a commodity rises, the quantity supplied of it in the market increases, and when the price of the commodity falls, its quantity supplied decreases, other factors determining supply remaining the same.* Thus, according to the law of supply, the quantity supplied of a commodity is directly or positively related to price. It is due to this positive relationship between price of a commodity and its quantity supplied that the supply curve of a commodity slopes upward to right as seen from supply curve *SS* in Figure. 17A.1. When price of wheat rises from ₹ 520 to ₹ 530 per quintal, the qunatity supplied of wheat in the market increases from 200 quintals to 225 quintals per period.

Table 17A.1. Supply Schedule of Wheat

Price Per Quantity (₹)	*Quantity Supplied* (in quintals)
500	100
510	150
520	200
530	225
540	250
550	275

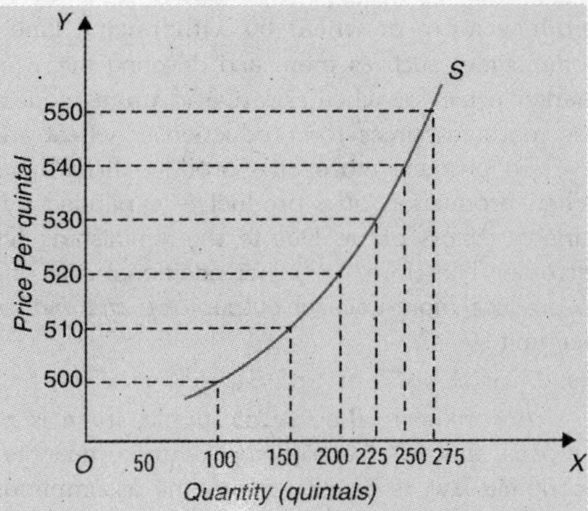

Fig. 17A.1. *Supply Curve Showing Direct Relationship Between Price and Quantity Supplied*

Similar to the demand schedule we can construct a commodity supply schedule. By totalling up the quantity supplied of a commodity at various prices by all the sellers in a market, we can obtain the market supply schedule of the commodity. Supply schedule represents the relation between prices and the quantities that the firms are able and willing to produce and sell at various prices. We have given in Table 17A.1 a supply schedule of wheat per day in a market.

It will be seen from the above table that when price of wheat is ₹ 500 per quintal, the 100 quintals of wheat are supplied in the market. When price of wheat rises to ₹ 510 per quintal, 150 quintals of wheat are supplied. When price of wheat goes up to ₹ 550 per quintal, its quantity supplied in the market rises to 275 quintal. By plotting the above supply schedule of wheat on a graph paper we have obtained supply curve *SS* in Fig. 17A.1. In Fig. 17A.1, the quantity supplied has been measured along the *X*-axis and price of wheat has been measured along the *Y*-axis. It will be seen from this figure that supply curve slopes upward from left to right, which indicates that as price of wheat rises, quantity supplied increases and vice versa. This is in a sharp contrast to the demand curve of a commodity which slopes downward from left to right.

Explanation of the Law of Supply: Why does Supply Curve Generally Slope Upward ?

It has been observed that price of a product and quantity supplied of it by firms producing it are positively related to each other, that is, at a higher price more is supplied and vice versa, other things remaining the same. In analysing the relation between price of a commodity and the quantity supplied, given *ceteris paribus* assumption we are in fact dealing with the supply function, $Q^S_x = f(P_x)$. This positive relationship between price and quantity supplied is an important law of economics. How do we explain it? It should be remembered that firms are driven by profit motive. The higher price of a product, given the cost per unit of output, makes it profitable to expand output and offer more quantity of the product for sale. Thus, higher price serves as an incentive for the producer to produce more of it. The higher the price, the greater the incentive for the firm to produce and supply more of a commodity in the market, other things remaining the same. The basic reason behind the law of supply (*i.e.,* positive relationship between price and quantity supplied) is the way cost changes as output is expanded to offer more for sale.

Further, the changes in quantity supplied of a product following the changes in its price also depends on the *possibilities of substitution of one product for an other.* For example, if price of wheat in the market rises, the farmers will alter the cropping pattern so as to produce more of wheat by withdrawing land and other resources from the cultivation of commodities such as gram and devoting them to the production of wheat. This is because high market price for wheat relative to gram induces farmers, who aim at maximising profits, to use more resources for production of wheat and fewer resources for the production of gram.

To produce more of a product, firms have to devote more resources to its production. When production of a product is expanded by using more resources, diminishing returns to variable factors occur. Due to the diminishing returns average and marginal costs of production increase. Therefore, at higher additional cost of producing more units of output; it is profitable to produce more units of output *only at a higher price* so as to cover the rise in additional cost per unit.

Assumption of Law of Supply

According to the law of supply, there is positive relationship between price and quantity supplied, that is, at a higher price more quantity of a good is supplied. This law, like any other economic law, is based upon some assumptions which are stated below.

First, for the law of supply to apply the producers or sellers should aim at maximing profits from production or sale of a commodity. The higher price, the cost per unit of the commodity remaining the same, means more profit in a competitive enviornment and therefore when price rises, the profit-maximising firms will expand output and supply more to avail of the profit opportunities.

Second, the law of supply is based on the assumption that short-run marginal cost curve *rises* above the minimum point of average variable cost curve due to diminishing marginal returns to variable factors on expansion of output. Therefore, higher price is needed to cover higher marginal costs as output or supply is expanded by the firm.

Thirdly, the law supply of assumes that firms operate in a competitive environment and no individual firm has a monopoly over the production of the commodity. The monoplist has a control over the supply of a commondity and therefore fixes price of the commodity to maximise profits. The monopolist is a price maker and not a price taker. What is true of monopoly also applies to the other cases of imperfect competition such as monopolistic competition and oligopoly where the undividual firms have some degree of control over the supply and price of a commodity. In fact, the firms in these imperfect markets face a downward sloping-demand curve and choose on it a price-quantity combination rather than reacting to a given price.

In our above analysis we have explained the assumptions of law of supply from the viewpoint of a short-run supply of a firm or industry. In case of long run, the law of supply applies in case of only the increasing-cost industry which on expansion expercences rising costs due to external diseconomies outweighing external economies. The rising costs of an industry in the long run implies that higher price is required to cover higher cost when more is produced and supplied.

In case of constant-cost and decreasing-cost industries, the law of supply will not apply. In case of constant-cost industry the equilibrium long-run average cost remains constant and therefore more quantity of the good is supplied at the same price by the industry in the long run. In case of *decreasing-cost industry*, equilibrium long-run average cost declines as industry expands because external economies outweigh external diseconomies and therefore more will be supplied at a lower price by the industry in the long run. This behaviour is quite opposite to the law of supply.

The Concept of Supply Curve is Relevant only in Case of Perfect Competition

It is worth nothing here that the concept of supply curve, as it is used in economic theory, is relevant only for the case of perfect or pure competition and it is quite inapplicable to the cases of imperfect competition—monopolistic competition, monopoly and oligopoly. This is because the *notion of supply curve refers to the question as to how much quantity of a commodity a firm will supply at various given prices.* In other words, notion of supply curve refers to the quantity reactions of a firm when the firm itself exercises no influence over the determination of price and takes price as given datum for it and adjusts its quantity produced or supplied. Since only in perfect or pure competition a firm exercises no influence over the price which is determined by impersonal market mechanism of demand and supply and is beyond the control of individual firms, the concept of supply curve is relevant only for perfect or pure competition. So far as short-run supply curve of the industry under perfect competition is concerned, it is a mere lateral summation of the short-run supply curves of the firms.

Under various forms of imperfect competition, an individual firm does not take the price as given and is not a mere quantity adjuster. In fact, under various forms of imperfect competition, a firm sets its own price. For a firm under imperfect competition it is not a question of adjusting output or supply at a given price but of choosing *price-output combination* which maximises its profits. Commenting on the relevance of supply curve, Prof. Baumol writes, "*The supply curve is, strictly speaking, a concept which is usually relevant only for the case of pure (or perfect) competition. The reason for this lies in its definition–the supply curve is designed to answer question of the form, 'How much will firm A supply if it encounters a price which is fixed at P dollars*[1]. But such a question is most relevant to the behaviour of firms that actually face prices over whose determination they exercise no influence. This is relevant only under conditions of perfect competition. Elaborating the point that supply curve concept does not apply to the market conditions of monopoly and other forms of imperfect competition where competition is restricted.

Profs. Nellis and Parker write, "*A monopoly firm is not at the mercy of the market like a competitive firm, it does not have to take the market price as given and react to it. On the countrary, the monopolist has the power to select the price-output combination on its demand curve that it prefers so as to maximise profits*"[2]. In fact a monopolist is a price maker and not a price taker. What is true of monopoly is also valid in case of less extreme forms of imperfect competition such as monopolistic competition and oligopoly in which also firms do not take price of their products as given.

It may however be noted that if in the long run marginal or avergae cost of the whole industry do not rise due to the easy availability of all factors such as labour, factory space and machinery (that is, the external diseconomies are absent and external economies do not accrue to the expanding industry) with the expansion of an industry the supply curve of output of the industry will be a horizontal straight line in the long run and the law of supply will not hold. Thus, it is the rising marginal cost of additional units of output coupled with the objective of maximising profits on the part of producers that explain the upward-sloping supply curve of output which reflects the law of supply.

It is important to note that each point on the supply curve indicates the price at which a given quantity of output the producers will be willing to supply, that is, make it available in the market. *The price at which a given quantity of the commodity is supplied by the sellers is called supply price.* As there is expansion in output of industry, it draws away more scarce resources from other industries and as a result opportunatly cost of output of an expanding industry rises and therefore it has to pay higher prices for the extra resources employed by it for its expansion of output. This raises the supply price of output of an expanding industry. The upward-sloping supply curve indicates that the supply price increases if more quantity of the good is to be supplied in the market. Thus, the greater the quantity which the consumers would like to buy, generally the higher the price necessary to induce the industry to produce a commodity and make it available in the market.

1. Baumol, *Economic Theory and Operations Analysis,* Prentice Hall,.
2. Joseph G. Nellis and David Parker, *The Essence of Business Economics,* Prentice Hall, p.65.

Shifts in Supply : Increase and Decrease in Supply

As stated above, the supply of a commodity in economics means the entire schedule or curve depicting the relationship between price and quantity supplied of the commodity, given the other factors influencing supply. These other factors are the state of technology, prices of inputs (resources), prices of other related commodities, etc., which are assumed constant when the relationship between price and quantity supplied of a commodity is examined. It is the change in these factors other than price that cause a shift in the supply curve. For example, when prices of inputs such as labour and raw materials used for the production of a commodity decline, this will result in lowering the cost of production which will induce the producers to produce and make available a greater quantity of the commodity in the market at each price. This increases in supply of a commodity due to the reduction in prices of inputs will cause the

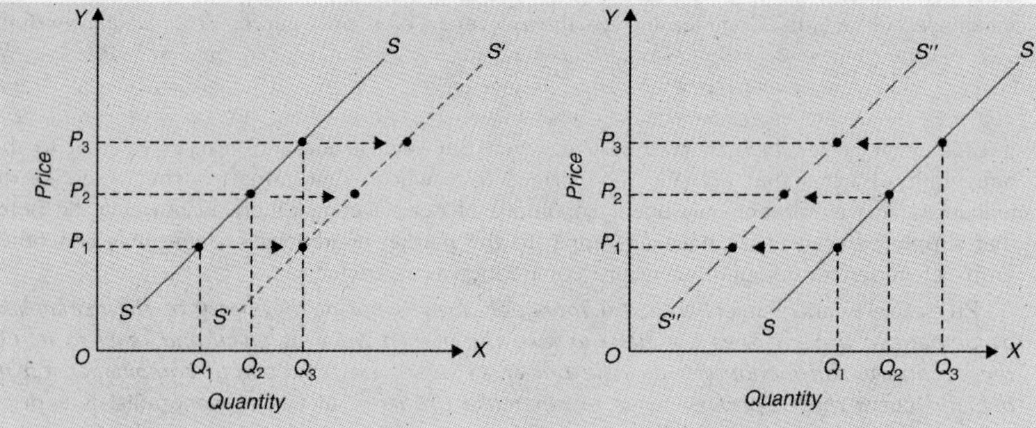

Fig. 17A.2. *Increase in Supply Causing a Rightward Shift in the Supply Curve*

Fig. 17A.3. *Decrease in Supply Causing a Leftward Shift in the Supply Curve*

entire supply curve to shift to the right as shown in Figure 17A.2 where the supply curve shifts from *SS* to *S′ S*. As shown by arrow marks, at price P_1, P_2 and P_3 quantity supplied increases when supply increases causing a rightward shift in the supply curve. Similarly, progress in technology used for production of a commodity which increases productivity and reduces cost per unit will also cause the supply curve to shift to the right.

On the other hand, *decrease in supply means the reduction in quantity supplied at each price of the commodity* as shown in Figure 17A.3 whereas a result of decrease in supply the supply curve shifts to the left from *SS* to *S′S′*. As shown by the arrow marks, at each price such as P_1, P_2, P_3, the quantity supplied on the supply curve *S′S′* has declined as compared to the supply curve *SS*. The decrease in supply occurs when the rise in prices of factors (inputs) used for the production of a commodity produced leads to higher cost per unit of output which causes a reduction in quantity supplied at each price. Similarly, the imposition of an excise duty or sales tax on a commodity means that each quantity will now be supplied at a higher price than before so as to cover the excise duty or sales tax per unit. This implies that quantity supplied of the commodity at each price will decrease as shown by the shift of the supply curve to the left.

Another important factor causing a decrease in supply of a commodity is the *rise in prices of other commodities* using the same factors. For example if the price of wheat rises sharply, it will become more profitable for the farmers to grow it. This will induce the farmers to reduce the cultivated area under other crops, say pulses, and devote it to the production of wheat. This will lead to the decrease in supply of pulses whose supply curve will shift to the left.

Further, agricultural production in India greatly depends on the rainfall due to monsoons. If monsoon come in time and rainfall is adequate, there are bumper crops, the supply of agricultural products increases. However, in a year when Monsoons are untimely or highly inadequate, there is a sharp drop in agricultural output which causes a shift in the supply curve of agricultural output to the left.

The supply of a commodity in the market at any time is also determined by *sellers' expectations of future prices.* If, as happens during inflationary periods, sellers expect the prices to rise in future, they would reduce current supply of a product in the market and would instead hoard the commodity. The hoarding of huge quantities of goods by traders is an important factor in reducing their supplies in the market and thus causing further rise in their prices.

Taxes and subsidies also influence the supply of a product. If an excise duty or sales tax is levied on a product, the firms will supply the same amount of it at a higher price or less quantity of it at the same price. This is because excise duty on a commodity is included in price by the sellers to pass it on to the buyers. This implies that imposition of a sales tax or excise duty will cause a leftward shift in the supply curve. On the other hand, when government provides subsidy on a commodity, it will reduce the supply price of a commodity. This implies that grant of subsidy on a commodity will cause the supply curve to shift to the right.

It follows from above that technology, prices of factors and products, expectations regarding future prices and taxes and subsidies are the important determinants of supply which cause rightward or leftward shift in the whole supply curve.

We thus see that *there are several factors other than price which determine the supply of a commodity and any change in these other factors will cause a shift in the entire supply curve.*

ELASTICITY OF SUPPLY

The concept of elasticity of supply, like the elasticity of demand, occupies an important place in price theory. The elasticity of supply is the degree of responsiveness of supply to changes in price of a good. More precisely, the elasticity of supply can be defined as a percentage change in quantity supplied of a good in response to a given percentage change in price of the good. Therefore :

In terms of symbols, we can wrie :

$$e_s = \frac{\Delta q}{q} \div \frac{\Delta p}{p} = \frac{\Delta q}{q} \times \frac{p}{\Delta p} = \frac{\Delta q}{\Delta p} \times \frac{p}{q}$$

For an accurate measure of elasticity of supply *midpoint method*, as explained in case of elasticity of demand, should be used. Using midpoint formula, elasticity of supply can be measured as

$$e_s = \frac{q_2 - q_1}{\frac{q_1 + q_2}{2}} \div \frac{p_2 - p_1}{\frac{p_1 + p_2}{2}},$$

where $q_2 - q_1 = \Delta q$ and $P_2 - P_1 = \Delta P$

Therefore, $$e_s = \frac{\Delta q}{q_1 + q_2} \times \frac{p_1 + p_2}{\Delta P} = \frac{\Delta q}{\Delta P} \times \frac{p_1 + p_2}{q_1 + q_2}$$

The elasticity of supply depends upon the ease with which the output of an industry can be expanded and the change in marginal cost of production. Since there is greater scope for increase in output in the long run than in the short run, the supply of a good is more elastic in the long run than in the short run.

Measurement of Elasticity of Supply at a Point on the Supply Curve

The elasticity of supply at a point on the supply curve can be easily measured by a formula. We shall derive this formula below.

In Fig. 17A.4 supply curve *SS* is given and elasticity of supply at point *A* is required to be measured. At price *OP* the quantity supplied is *OQ*. With the rise in price from *OP* to *OP*′, the quantity supplied increases from *OQ* to *OQ*′. Extend supply curve *SS* downward so that it meets *X*-axis at point *T*.

$$\text{Then, elasticity of supply at point } A = \frac{\Delta q}{q} \div \frac{\Delta p}{p} = \frac{\Delta q}{\Delta p} \times \frac{p}{q}$$

A glance at Figure 17A.4 reveals that $\Delta q = QQ'$, $\Delta p = PP'$. Therefore, writing *QQ*′ for Δq, *PP*′ for Δp, we have elasticity of supply equal to :–

$$e_s = \frac{\Delta q}{\Delta p} \cdot \frac{p}{q} = \frac{QQ'}{PP'} \times \frac{OP}{OQ}$$

It will be further seen from Figure 17A.4 that $QQ' = AC$, $PP' = BC$ and $OP = QA$. Therefore, substituting *AC* for *QQ*′, *BC* for *PP*′ and *QA* for *OP* we have

$$e_s \text{ at point } A = \frac{\Delta q}{\Delta p} \cdot \frac{p}{q} = \frac{QQ'}{PP'} \times \frac{OP}{OQ} = \frac{AC}{BC} \cdot \frac{QA}{OQ} \quad ...(i)$$

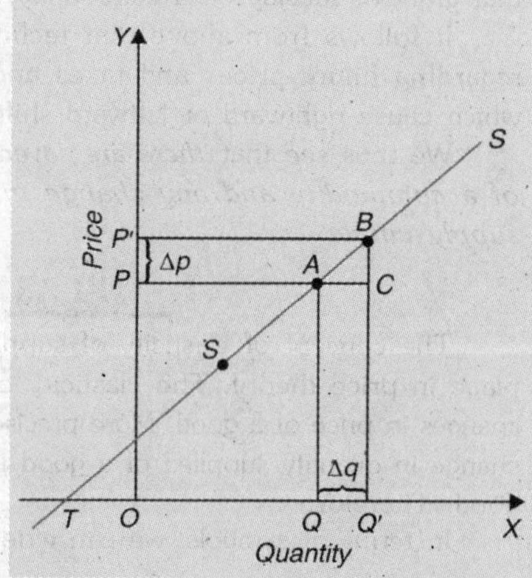

Fig. 17A.4. *Measurement of elasticity of supply at a point on a linear supply curve.*

Now, in triangles *ACB* and *TQA*

$\angle ACB = \angle TQA$ (rt. angles)

$\angle BAC = \angle ATQ$ (corresponding angles)

$\angle ABC = \angle TAQ$ (corresponding angles)

Therefore, triangles *ABC* and *TAQ* are similar.

$$\text{Hence, } \frac{AC}{BC} = \frac{TQ}{QA}$$

Substituting $\frac{TQ}{QA}$ for $\frac{AC}{BC}$ in (*i*) above, we have

$$e_s \text{ at } A = \frac{TQ}{QA} \cdot \frac{QA}{OQ} = \frac{TQ}{OQ}$$

Thus, we can measure the value of elasticity of supply from dividing *TQ* by *OQ*. Since in Fig. 17A.4, *TQ* is greater than *OQ*, supply elasticity $\frac{TQ}{OQ}$ will be greater than one.

In Fig. 17A.5 supply curve when extended meets the *X*-axis to the right of the point of origin so that *TQ* is smaller than *OQ*. Therefore, in Fig. 17A.5 the elasticity of supply at point A, which is equal to $\frac{TQ}{OQ}$ is less than unity. In Fig. 17A.6 supply curve *SS* when extended meets the *X*-axis exactly at the point of origin so that *TQ* is equal to *OQ*. Therefore, in Fig. 17A.6 elasticity of supply at point A will be equal to one.

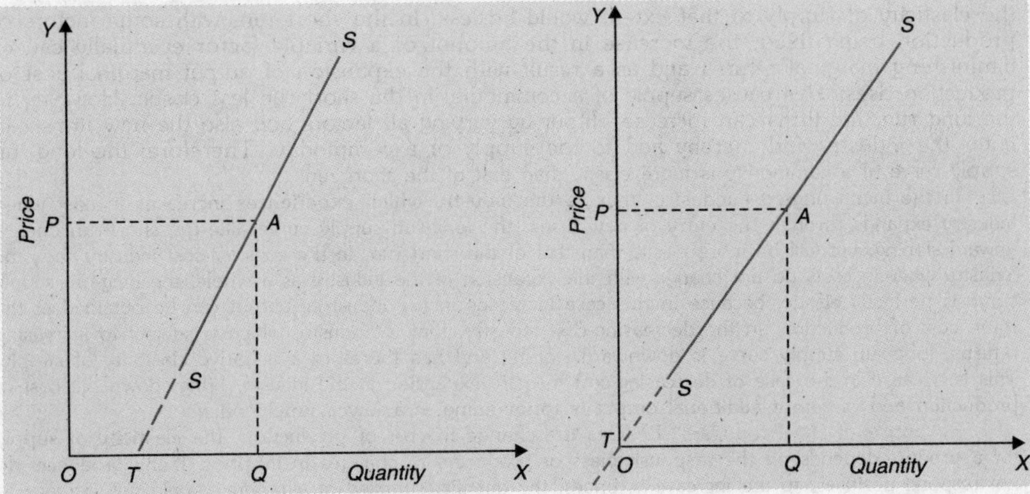

Supply Function and Elasticity of Supply

Let us explain price elasticity of supply using the supply function for a commodity. The linear supply function for a commodity is of the following form :

$$Q = c + dP$$

where Q is quantity supplied of a commodity, P is its price and c and d are constants. The constant coefficient d represents the slope of the supply function and indicates how much quantity supplied changes in response to a change in price. That is, $d = \frac{\Delta Q}{\Delta P}$. Since d is positive, it shows how much quantity supplied of a commodity increases as its price rises.

Now, elasticity of supply is

$$e_s = \frac{\Delta Q}{\Delta P} \cdot \frac{P}{Q}$$

Substituting d for $\frac{\Delta Q}{\Delta P}$ we have $e_s = d\frac{P}{Q}$

We take the following specific supply function to estimate elasticity of supply

$$Q = 90 + 15P$$

It is required to estimate elasticity of supply at price ₹ 20 per unit of the commodity from the above supply function. In the above supply function 90 is the constant intercept term c and 15 measures slope of the function (d) and is equal to $\frac{\Delta Q}{\Delta P}$.

In order to obtain elasticity of supply at price of ₹ 20, we first find out the quantity supplied at this price. Therefore, substituting 20 for P in the supply function we get

$$Q = 90 + 15 \times 20 = 390$$

Now, as shown above, elasticity of supply is

$$e_s = b\frac{P}{Q} = 15 \times \frac{20}{390} = \frac{20}{26} = 0.77$$

This means 1 per cent rise in price will lead to 0.77 per cent increase in quantity supplied.

FACTORS DETERMINING ELASTICITY OF SUPPLY

Elasticity of supply plays an important role in determining prices of products. To what extent price of a product will rise following the increase in demand for it depends on the elasticity of supply. The greater the elasticity of supply of a product, the less the rise in its price when demand for it increases. We explain below the factors which determine elasticity of supply of a product.

Changes in Marginal Cost of Production. Elasticity of supply of a commodity depends upon the ease with which increases in output can be obtained without bringing about rise in cost of production. If with the increase in production, the marginal cost of production goes up the elasticity of supply to that extent would be less. In the short run, with some factors of production being fixed, the increase in the amount of a variable factor eventually causes diminishing marginal returns and as a result with the expansion of output marginal cost of production rises. This causes supply of a commodity in the short run less elastic. However, in the long run, the firms can increase output by varying all factors and also the new firms can enter the industry and thereby add to the supply of a commodity. Therefore, the long-run supply curve of a commodity is more elastic than that of the short run.

In the increasing-cost industry, that is, the industry which experiences increases in cost when industry expands through the entry of new firms, the long-run supply curve, like the short-run one, is upward sloping, but will be more elastic than that of the short run. In the constant-cost industry, *i.e.*, the industry wherein costs do not change with the expansion of the industry as a whole, the long-run supply curve is perfectly elastic, because in this case increases in the industrial output can be obtained at the same cost of production. In the decreasing-cost industry, that is, industry which is subject to increasing returns, long-run supply curve is downward sloping and has therefore a negative elasticity of supply. This is because in the case of decreasing-cost industry expansion in the industry brings down the cost of production and therefore additional output is forthcoming at a lower supply price.

Response of the Producers. Besides the change in cost of production, the elasticity of supply for a product depends on the responsiveness of producers to changes in its price. If the producers do not respond positively to the increase in prices, the quantity supplied of a product would not increase as a result of rise in its price. A profit-maximising producer will increase the quantity supplied of a product following the rise in its price. However, producers who not always exhibit profit-maximising behaviour may not raise supply in response to the rise in price. For example, it has been argued by some with some empirical evidences that farmers in developing countries respond negatively to the rise in price of their agricultural products. They point out that with the higher agricultural prices, their need for fixed money income is met by selling smaller quantities of foodgrains and therefore at higher prices they may produce and sell smaller quantities rather than more. However, recent evidence does not indicare this negative response of farmers in the developing countries.

Availability of Inputs for Expanding Output. The extent to which the producers would raise supply of their products also depends on the availability of inputs required for the production of goods. If inputs used in the production of a commodity are easily available at going market prices, then output of the commodity can be easily expanded with little rise in price. This would show price elasticity of supply is relatively large. On the other hand, if production capacity for producing a product is limited or infrastructure facilities for expanding output of a commodity are not adequately available, then even sharp increase in price of the product will cause only a small expansion in output. This indicates relatively inelastic supply. For example, when there is lack of fertilisers and irrigation facilities, the farmers would not be able to raise the supplies of agricultural products in response to the rise in their prices even if they want to do so. Likewise, in the industrial field if there is shortage of power, fuel, essential raw materials, the expansion in supply would not be forthcoming in response to the rise in prices of industrial products.

Possibilities of Substitution of one Product for the Others. The change in quantity supplied of a product following the change in its price also depends on the possibilities of substitution of one product for others. For example, if market price of wheat rises, the farmers will try to shift resources such as land, labour, fertilisers away from other products such as pulses to devote them to the production of wheat. The greater the extent of possibilities of shifting of resources from the other products to the production of a given product, the greater the elasticity of supply of wheat.

The Length of Time. The elasticity of supply of a product also depends on the length of time during which producers have to respond to a given change in price of a product. Generally, the longer the time producers get to make adjustments for changing the level of output in response to the change in price, the greater the response of output, that is, the greater the elasticity of supply. In the immediate and short period following a rise in price of a commodity, it may not be possible for the firms to increase the inputs of labour (especially skilled labour), materials and capital and therefore the supply may be price inelastic. However, over a long period the firm can hire more labour, build new capacity to expand output. This means long-run supply is price elastic. From the viewpoint of the influence of the length of time on the elasticity of supply we distinguish between three time periods : (1) market period or very short run, (2) short run and (3) long run. The market period is a very short period and during this no more production is possible. Therefore, market-period supply curve is a vertical straight line (*i.e.*, perfectly inelastic). In the short run, firms can change output by changing the amounts of only variable factors, short-run supply curve is somewhat elastic. In the long run since firms can adjust all factors of production and also new firms can enter or leave the industry, long-run supply curve is more elastic.

PART – IV

PRICING AND OUTPUT DECISIONS IN VARIOUS MARKET STRUCTURES

- Market Structures and Price and Output Determination Under Perfect Competition
- Pricing and Output Decisions Under Monopoly
- Pricing and Output Decisions Under Monopolistic Competition
- Price and Output Determination Under Oligopoly
- Non-Price Competition : Advertising Expenditure
- Government Policies Towards Monopoly and Competetion

Market Structures and Price and Output Determination Under Perfect Competition

The determination of prices and outputs of various products depends upon the type of market structure in which they are produced, sold and purchased. In this connection economists have classified the various markets prevailing in a capitalist economy into (*a*) perfect competition or pure competition, (*b*) monopolistic competition, (*c*) oligopoly and (*d*) monopoly. Three market forms, monopolistic competition, oligopoly and monopoly, are generally grouped under the general heading of imperfect competition, since these three forms of market differ with respect to the degree of imperfection in the market. Monopolistic competition is slighly imperfect and monopoly is the most imperfect form of market structure.

But before explaining the salient features of various market forms, it will be useful to explain what is meant by market in economics.

Meaning of Market

Market is generally understood to mean a particular place or locality where goods are sold and purchased. However, in economics, by the term market we do not mean any particular place or locality in which goods are bought and sold. The idea of a particular locality or geographical place is not necessary to the concept of the market. What is required for the market to exist is the contact between the sellers and buyers so that transaction (*i.e.*, sale and purchase of a commodity) at an agreed price can take place between them. The buyers and sellers may be spread over a whole town, region or a country but if they are in close communication with each other either through personal contact, exchange of letters, telegrams, telephones, etc. so that they can sell and buy a good on agreed price, the market would be said to exist. Further, it is noteworthy that because in a market, there is close and free communication between various buyers and sellers price of a homogeneous commodity settled between different sellers and buyers tends to be the same. Thus, in the words of Cournot, a French economist, *"Economists understand by the term market not any particular market place in which things are bought and sold but the whole of any region in which buyers and sellers are in such free intercourse with one another that the price of the same good tends to equality easily and quickly".*

Thus, the essentials of a market are: (*a*) commodity which is dealt with, (*b*) the existence of buyers and sellers, (*c*) a place, be it a certain region, a country or the entire world, and (*d*) such communication between buyers and sellers that only one price should prevail for the same commodity at the same time.

CLASSIFICATION OF MARKET STRUCTURES

The popular basis of classifying market structures rests on three crucial elements, (1) the number of firms producing a product, (2) the nature of product produced by the firms, that is, whether it is homogeneous or differentiated, and (3) the ease with which new firms can enter the industry. The price elasticity of demand for a firm's product depends upon the number of competitive firms producing the same or similar product as well as on the degree of substitution which is possible between the product of a firm and other products produced by rival firms. Therefore, a distinguishing feature of different market categories is the degree of price elasticity of demand faced by an individual firm.

We present in the table given below the classification of market forms based on the number of firms, the nature of product produced by them and price elasticity of demand.

1. Perfect Competition. As is evident from Table 18.1 perfect competition is said to prevail where there is a large number of producers (firms) producing a homogeneous product. The maximum output which an individual firm can produce is very small relatively to the total demand of the industry product so that a firm cannot affect the price by varying its supply of output.

There are following four important features of perfect competition :

1. There is a large number of firms (producers and sellers) and buyers of a product,
2. Products of all firms are homogeneous,
3. There is freedom of new firms to enter the industry and old ones to leave it,
4. All firms and buyers have perfect information about the prevailing market price of the product.

With many firms and homogenous product under perfect competition, no individual firm in it is in a position to influence the price of the product and therefore the demand curve facing it will be a horizontal straight line at the level of prevailing price of the product in the market, that is, price elasticity of demand for a single firm will be infinite. Mrs, Joan Robinson writes: "Perfect competition prevails when the demand for the output of each producer is perfectly elastic. This entails, first, that the number of sellers is large, so that the output of any one seller is negligibly small proportion of the total output of the commodity, the second, that the products of various sellers are homogeneous from the viewpoint of consumer's[1].

2. Imperfect Competition. Imperfect competition is an important market category wherein individual firms exercise control over the price to a smaller or larger degree depending upon the degree of imperfection present in a case. Control over price of a product by a firm and therefore the existence of imperfect competition can be caused either by the 'fewness' of the firms or by the product differentiation. Therefore, imperfect competition has several sub-categories.

1. Joan Robinson, *The Economics of Imperfect Competition*. Macmillan and Co., London, 1954, p. 18.

Table 18.1. The Classification of Market Structures

Form of Market Structure	*Number of Firms*	*Nature of Product*	*Price Elasticity of Demand for an Individual Firm*	*Degree of Control over Price*	*Ease of Entry*
(*a*) Perfect Competition	A large number of firms	Homogeneous product	Infinite	None	Free Entry
(*b*) Imperfect Competition					
(*i*) Monopolistic Competition	A large number of firms	Differentiated Products (but they are close substitutes of each other)	Large	Some	Free entry but for producing close substitutes
(*ii*) Pure Oligopoly, (*i.e.*, Oligopoly without Product Differentiation)	Few firms	Homogeneous Product	Small	Some	Limited entry
(*iii*) Differentiated Oligopoly (*i.e.*, Oligopoly with Product Differentiation)	Few firms	Differentiated Products (which are close substitutes of each other)	Small	Large	Limited entry
(*c*) Monopoly	One	Unique Product without Close Substitutes	Very Small	Very Large	Strong Barriers to Entry

(*a*) Monopolistic Competition. The first important sub-category of imperfect competition is monopolistic competition on which Professor E.H. Chamberlin laid a great stress in his original thought-provoking work "*The Theory of Monopolistic Competition*". Monopolistic Competition, as is now understood, is characterised by a large number of firms and product differentiation.[2] That is, in *monopolistic competition* a large number of firms produce somewhat different products which are close substitutes of each other. As a result, demand curve facing a firm under monopolistic competition is highly elastic and this indicates that a firm working in it enjoys some control over the price. Besides, there is freedom of entry and exit under monopolistic competition.

(*b*) Pure Oligopoly. The second sub-category of imperfect competition is oligopoly without product differentiation which is also known as *pure oligopoly*. Under it there is competition among the few firms producing homogeneous or identical product. The fewness of the firms ensures that each of them will have some control over the price of the product and

2. It should be carefully noted that Prof. E.H. Chamberlin called any market structure, which was a blend of monopoly and competition as monopolistic competition. A blend of monopoly and competition could be there if there was either a few firms producing an identical or differentiated product or there was a large number of firms producing differentiated products. The former is the case of oligopoly with and without product differentiation and the latter is the monopolistic competition with many firms. Thus, in Chamberlin's terminology, the concept of monopolistic competition covers both oligopoly (with as well as without product differentiation) and monopolistic competition with a large number of firms producing differentiated products. However, in standard modern economic theory, the term monopolistic competition is used only for the latter.

the demand curve facing each firm will be downward sloping which indicates that the price elasticity of demand for each firm will not be infinite.

(c) Differentiated Oligopoly. The third sub-category of imperfect competition is oligopoly with product differentiation which is also called *differentiated oligopoly.* As its name shows, it is characterised by competition among the few firms producing differentiated products which are close substitutes of each other. The demand curve facing individual firms under oligopoly with product differentiation is downward stoping[3] and the firms have fairly large control over the price of their individual products.

Monopoly.[4] Monopoly, as is now generally understood, means the existence of a *single producer or seller which is producing or selling a product which has no close substitutes.* Since a monopoly firm has a sole control over the supply of a product, which can have only remote substitutes, it has a very large control over the price of its product. The expansion and contraction in output of the product by a monopolist will considerably affect the price of the product, contraction in output will raise its price and expansion in output will lower it. Therefore, the demand curve facing a monopolist is downward sloping and has a steep slope. Thus, according to Prof. F. Machlup, "Monopolistic competition would then comprise the cases of closer substitutes and more elastic demand curves, while monopoly would comprise those of remote substitutes and steeper demand curves."[5] Besides, in monopoly there are strong barriers to the entry of new firms in the industry.

The classification of market forms made on the basis of *(i) number af firms in the industry, (ii) the nature of product* (*i.e., the closeness or remoteness of substitution among products and (iii) the ease with which new firms can enter the industry or the old ones can leave it, which we have explained above, is quite adequate and satisfactory.*

PRICING AND OUTPUT UNDER PERFECT COMPETITION

Conditions of Perfect Competition

In an earlier chapter we made a general analysis of the equilibrium of the firm and its conditions. In this chapter we will study the equilibrium of the firm and industry under conditions of perfect competition and explain how price and output are determined under it. It would be in the fitness of things if we first describe what we mean by perfect competition. As mentioned above, perfect competition, as is generally understood, is said to prevail when the following conditions are found in the market:

1. There are a large number of firms producing and selling a product. .
2. The product of all firms is homogeneous.
3. Both the sellers and buyers have perfect information about the prevailing price in the market.

3. The nature of demand curve under oligopoly is, however, a controversial matter. In some models of oligopoly without product differentiation, it is assumed that the demand curve for an oligopolist is perfectly elastic (*i.e.*, horizontal straight line). Further, another important model of oligopoly assumes a kinked demand curve (with a kink at the prevailing price) for an oligopoly firm.
4. For monopoly, sometimes the terms *absolute* monopoly, *pure* monopoly, *complete* monopoly are used. All these terms have the same meaning since all visualise a single producer or seller producing a product which has no close substitutes. However, Sraffa used the term 'Pure Monopoly' in a different 'sense. *By pure monopoly Sraffa means that a single seller of a product is so powerful that he is in a position to take the whole income of all the consumers whatever the level of his output. Obviously, such a pure or absolute monopoly cannot exist in the real world.*
5. Fritz Machlup, Monopoly and Competition: A Classification of Market Positions, *American Economic Review*, September 1937, p.448.

4. Entry into and exit from the industry is free for the firms.

We shall discuss below in detail the above four conditions of perfect competition.

A Large Number of Firms. The first condition of perfect competition is that there are a large number of firms in the industry. The position of a single firm in the industry containing numerous firms is just like a drop in the ocean. The existence of a large number of firms producing and selling the product ensures that an individual firm exercises no influence over the price of the product. The output of an individual firm constitutes a very small fraction of the total output of the whole industry so that any increase or decrease in output by an individual firm has a negligible effect on the total supply of the product of industry. As a result, a single firm is not in a position to influence the price of the product by increasing or reducing its output. The individual firm under perfect competition therefore takes the price of the product as a given datum and adjusts its output to earn maximum profits. In other words, a firm under perfect competition is price-taker and output-adjuster.

Homogeneous Products. The second condition of perfect competition is that the products produced by all firms in the industry are fully homogeneous and identical. It means that the products of various firms are indistinguishable from each other; they are perfect substitutes for one another. In other words, cross elasticity between the products of the firms is infinite. In case of homogeneous products, trade marks, patents, special brand labels etc. do not exist since these things make the products differentiated. It should be noted that if there are many firms, but they are producing differentiated products, each one of them will have influence over the price of his own variety of the product. The control over price is completely eliminated only when all firms are producing homogeneous products.

But whether or not products are homogeneous should be judged from the viewpoint of the buyers. Products would be homogeneous only when the buyers consider them to be so. Even if the buyers find some imagined differences between the products, the products would not be homogeneous, howsoever physically alike they may be. Anything which makes buyers prefer one seller to another, be it personality, reputation, convenient location, or the tone of his shop, differentiates the product to that degree, since what is bought is really a bundle of utilities of which these things are a part. Therefore, for the products to be homogeneous utilities offered by all sellers to buyers must be identical. If the bundle of utilities offered by all sellers is not the same, then the buyers would have a preference for some sellers who will have a degree of control over their individual prices. Thus the existence of homogeneous products signifies that the products of all sellers are completely identical in the eyes of consumers who therefore do not have any preference for one seller over another. Under such conditions it is evident that "buyers and sellers will be paired in random fashion in a large number of transactions. It will be entirely a matter of chance from which seller a particular buyer makes his purchases, and purchases over a period of time will be distributed among all sellers according to the law of probability. After all this is only another way of saying that the product is homogeneous."[6]

Perfect Information about the Prevailing Price. Another condition for perfect competition to prevail is that both the buyers and sellers are fully aware of the ruling price in the market. Because only when all buyers know fully the current price of the product in the market, sellers cannot charge more than the prevailing price. If any seller tries to charge a higher price than that ruling in the market, the buyers will shift to some other sellers and buy the good at the ruling price since they know what the ruling price in the market is. Similarly, all sellers are also aware of the prevailing price in the market and no one will charge less price than this.

---

6. E.H. Chamberlin, *Theory of Monopolistic Competition*, 7th ed, p.8.

Free Entry and Exit. Lastly, perfect competition requires that there must be complete freedom for the entry of new firms or the exit of the existing firms from the industry in the long run. There must be no barriers to the entry of firms. Since, in the short run, firms can neither change the size of their plants, nor new firms can enter or old ones can leave the industry, the condition of free entry and free exit therefore applies only to the long-run equilibrium under perfect competition. If the existing firms are making super-normal profits in the short run, this condition requires that in the long run new firms will enter the industry to compete away the profits. If, on the other hand, firms are making losses in the short run, some of the existing firms will leave the industry in the long run with the result that the price of the product will go up and the firms left in the industry will be earning at least normal profits.

PRICE DETERMINATION UNDER PERFECT COMPETITION : EQUILIBRIUM BETWEEN DEMAND AND SUPPLY

Before Marshall there was a dispute among earlier economists as to whether it is supply of a good or the demand for it that determines its price. Broadly speaking, there were two schools of thought in this regard. One school of thought believed that it is cost of production, that is, the force that determines the supply, which determines the price of the product. The other school of thought held the view that it is the utility or more precisely the marginal utility that determines the demand and therefore the price of the product. But each school of thought took one-sided view of the pricing problem. The credit of finding the true answer to the pricing problem gees to Marshall who held that both demand and supply were equally important in determining the price of a good. In other words, Marshall said that both the marginal utility of a good and the cost of producing it took part in determining price. He compared the price determination to the cutting of a piece of a paper by a pair of scissors. This famous analogy is worth quoting here. "We might as reasonably dispute whether it is the upper or the under blade of a pair of scissors that cuts a piece of paper as to whether value is governed by utility or cost of production. It is true that when one blade is held still and the cutting is effected by moving the other, we may say with careless brevity that the cutting is done by the second, but the statement is not strictly accurate and is to be excused only so long as it claims to be merely a popular and not a strictly scientific account of what happens."[7]

Neither the upper blade nor the lower one taken individually can cut the paper; both are required to do the work of cutting. The lower blade may be held stationary and only the upper one may be moved, yet both are indispensable for cutting the paper. Similarly, both demand and supply are essential forces for determining price. The only right answer to the question whether it is supply or demand which determines price is that it is both. At sometimes it appears that one is more important than the other, because one is active and the other passive. Thus, if demand remains constant but supply conditions change, it is demand which is passive and supply active. But both are equally important in determining price.

In the chapters on theory of demand we have explained that the demand curve of a commodity normally slopes downward. In other words, with the fall in price, quantity-demanded rises and *vice versa*. In the theory of production and cost we have studied that the supply curve of a commodity usually slopes upward. In other words, an industry will offer to sell more quantity of a good at a higher price than at a lower one. The level of price at which demand and supply curve intersect each other will finally come to stay in the market. In other words, the price which will come to prevail in the market is one at which quantity demanded is equal to quantity supplied. *The price at which quantity demanded equals quantity supplied is*

7. **A. Marshall, *Principles of Economics*, 8th edition, p. 344.**

called equilibrium price, for at this price the two forces of demand and supply exactly balance each other. *The quantity of the good which is purchased and sold at this equilibrium price is called equilibrium amount.* Thus, the intersection of demand and supply curves determines price-quantity equilibrium. This price-quantity equilibrium is *static equilibrium* because, other factors influencing demand and supply have been held constant.

Only at the equilibrium price wishes of both the buyers and sellers are satisfied. If price was greater or less than the equilibrium price the buyers' and sellers' wishes would be inconsistent: either the buyers would demand more than the amount offered by sellers, or the sellers would be ready to supply more than the amount demanded by the buyers. If price was greater than the equilibrium price, quantity supplied would exceed quantity demanded and thus giving rise to *excess supply* of the good at the current price. It means some of the sellers will not be able to sell the amount of the good they wanted to supply. These unsatisfied sellers would try to dispose of the unsold goods by bidding price down. The price will go on declining until the quantity demanded equals quantity supplied.

On the other hand, if price were lower than the equilibrium price, the quantity demanded would exceed quantity supplied giving rise to *excess demand* for the commodity. Some buyers would not be able to obtain the amount of the good they wanted to purchase at the prevailing price. They will therefore bid price up in their effort to get all that they desired to buy. The price will go on rising until the quantity demanded and quantity supplied are again equal. We thus see that the price which will settle down can be neither greater nor less than the equilibrium price. It is the equilibrium price which will finally come to stay in the market.

Graphic Illustration

We illustrate below the process of price determination with the aid of demand and supply curves which will make the whole pricing process in perfectly competitive markets very clear. The equilibrium between demand and supply is depicted in Fig. 18.1 where demand curve *DD* is sloping downward and the supply curve *SS* is sloping upward. Demand and supply are in equilibrium at point *E* where two curves intersect each other. It means that only at price *OP* (corresponding to the intersection point), the quantity demanded is equal to quantity supplied. *OQ* is the equilibrium quantity which is exchanged at price *OP*. If price is greater than the equilibrium price, say *OP*, the quantity demanded by the buyers is *P′ L*, while the quantity offered to supply by the sellers is *P′ K*. Thus *LK* is the excess supply which the buyers will not take off the market at price *OP ′*. In order to dispose of this excess supply, the sellers will compete with each other and in doing so they will bring down the price. Thus there will be tendency for the price to fall to the level of equilibrium price *OP*.

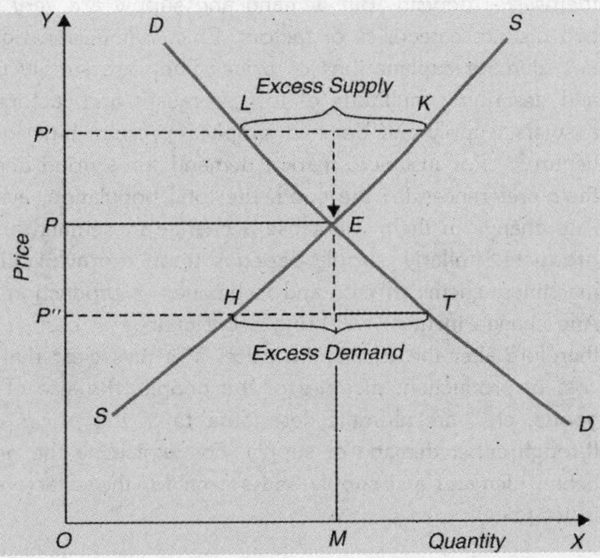

Fig. 18.1 *Determination of Price Through Intersection of Demand and Supply Curves*

At price OP', which is less than the equilibrium price, the buyers demand $P'T$, the sellers are prepared to supply only $P'H$. The quantity, HT represents excess demand. The unsatisfied buyers will compete with each other to obtain the limited supply of cloth and in this effort they will bid up the price. Thus there will be tendency for the price to rise to the level of equilibrium price OP where all wanting to buy and all wanting to sell will be satisfied.

From above it follows that if the price was above or below the equilibrium price, certain forces in the system would operate to bring the price to the level of the equilibrium price OP. We thus see that price is determined by the equilibrium between demand and supply. The price at which demand and supply curves intersect each other will eventually come to prevail in the market.

Method of adjustment of market to the equilibrium position explained above considers change in price as the driving force in the process. In this process of adjustment to equilibrium between demand and supply, when buyers and sellers (firms) find themselves in disequilibrium, they move along their respective demand and supply curves until the equilibrium price-quantity combination is reached. As seen above, when price is above equilibrium price, quantity demanded falls short of quantity supplied (that is, the excess demand is negative, $ED < 0$.) As a result of this excess supply, price falls. On the other hand, when price is below the equilibrium price, the quantity demanded exceeds the quantity supplied (that is, excess demand is positive, $ED > 0$). This pulls up the price of the product.

Are Demand and Supply Final Answers to the Pricing Problem ?

From above it follows that price is determined by equilibrium between demand and supply. But it is worth mentioning that demand and supply do not provide final answers to the pricing problem. Demand and supply which by their intersection determine price are themselves governed by several factors. There are many forces or factors which work behind demand and supply to determine price of a product. 'Demand and supply' is only a superficial formula. The ultimate factors that determine the prices of goods are those upon which demand and supply themselves depend. But demand and supply are very useful concepts serving outer cover for two distinct categories of factors. Prof. Samuelson rightly remarks: "Supply and demand are not ultimate explanations of price. They are simply useful catch-all categories for analyzing and describing multitude of forces, causes and factors impinging on price. Rather than final answers, supply and demand simply represent initial questions. Our work is not over but just begun."[8] For instance, market demand for a good depends upon the incomes of the people, their preferences for the good, the total population, availability and prices of substitute goods. Any change in them will cause a change in demand and hence in the equilibrium price of the product. Similarly, supply depends upon the availability and price of labour, raw materials, machines, chemicals etc., and techniques of production, all of which govern cost of production. Any change in them will bring about change in cost of production that governs supply and will therefore alter the equilibrium price. It is thus clear that factors like availability of raw materials, cost of production, incomes of the people, the size of population, consumers' preferences for goods, etc., are ultimate determinants of the prices of various goods but all of them work through either demand or supply. For explaining the price behaviour of a good we have to go behind demand and supply and search for those factors which are responsible for the changes in its price.

8. P. A. Samuelson, *Economics*, 8th edition, 1970, pp. 369-70.

Importance of Time Element in Price Determination

Marshall, who propounded the theory that price is determined by both demand and supply, also gave a great importance to the time element in the determination of price. Time element is of great relevance in the theory of value, since one of the two determinants of price, namely, supply depends on the time allowed for its adjustment. It is worth mentioning that Marshall divided time into different periods from the viewpoint of supply and not from the viewpoint of demand. Time is short or long according to the extent to which supply can adjust to the change in demand. Marshall felt it necessary to divide time into different periods on the *basis of response of supply* because it always takes time for the supply to adjust fully to the changed conditions of demand. The reason why supply takes time to adjust itself to a change in the demand condition is that the nature of technical conditions of production is such as to prohibit instantaneous adjustment of supply to changed demand conditions. A period of time is required for changes to be made in the size of plant, new machinery to be installed, and for the new firms to enter the industry or the old ones to leave the industry.

Another point is worth noting. When Marshall distinguished short and long periods he was not using clock or calendar time as his criterion, but *'operational'* time in terms of economic forces at work. In this regard, as said above, supply forces were given the major attention and a time was short or long according to the extent of adjustment in the forces of supply. The greater the adjustability of the supply forces the greater the length of the time, irrespective of the length in clock-time. Marshall divided time into three periods on the basis of response of supply to a given and permanent change in demand : (i) Market period, (2) short run, and (3) long run. The market period is very short period in which the supply is fixed, that is, no adjustment can take place in supply conditions. Short run is a period in which supply can be adjusted to a limited extent. During the short period the firms can expand output with given equipment by changing the amounts of variable factors employed. Short period is not long enough to allow the firm to change the plants or given capital equipment.

The long run is a period long enough to permit the firms to build new plants or abandon old ones. Further, in the long run, new firms can enter the industry and old ones can leave it. Since in the long run all factors are subject to variation, none is a fixed factor. During the long period forces of supply fully adjust themselves to a given change in demand; the size of individual firms as well as the size of the whole industry expands or contracts according to the requirements of demand.

From above, it is clear that because of the varying response of supply over a period of time to a sudden and once-for-all increase in demand that Marshall found it necessary and useful to study the pricing process in (*a*) the market period, (*b*) the short run, and (*c*) the long run depending respectively upon whether the supply conditions have time to make (*i*) *no adjustment,* (*ii*) *some adjustment of labour and other variable factors*, and (*iii*) *full adjustment of all factors and all costs*. Therefore, Marshall explained how the equilibrium between demand and supply was established in three time periods which consequently determine market price, short-run price and long-run price.

Demand-Supply Model of Price-Output Determination: Mathematical Analysis

As we have seen both demand for and supply of a commodity determine price and the quantity sold and purchased in a competitive market. In this model quantity demanded is inversely related to price, that is, demand curve for a commodity slopes downward to the right. On the other hand, quantity supplied of a commodity is directly related to price, that is, supply curve slopes upward to the right.

Thus, assuming that both demand and supply curves are linear, demand-supply model can be stated in the form of the following three equations:

$$q^d = a - bp \quad ...(1)$$

$$q^s = c + dp \quad ...(2)$$

$$q^d = q^s \quad ...(3)$$

where q^d and q^s are the quantities demanded and supplied respectively, a and c are intercept coefficients of demand and supply curves respectively, b and d are the coefficients that measure the slopes of these curves and (3) is the equilibrium condition. Thus, in equilibrium

$$a - bp = c + dp$$

$$a - c = dp + bp = p\,(d + b)$$

Dividing both sides by $d + b$ we have

$$\frac{a-c}{d+b} = \frac{p(d+b)}{d+b}$$

or equilibrium price $$p = \frac{a-c}{b+d} \quad ...(4)$$

Substituting (4) into (1) we have

equilibrium quantity $$q^d = a - b\,\frac{a-c}{b+d}$$

$$= \frac{ad + bc}{b+d} \quad ...(5)$$

Equations (4) and (5) describe the qualitative results of the model. If the values of parameters a, b, c and d are given we can obtain the equilibrium price and quantity by substituting the values of these parameters in the qualitative results of equation (4) and (5).

A Numerical Example

Suppose the following demand and supply functions of a commodity are given which is being produced under conditions of perfect competition. Find out the equilibrium price and quantity

$$q^d = 750 - 25p$$

$$q^s = 300 + 20p$$

Solution. There are two alternative ways of solving for equilibrium price and quantity. First, we can find out the equilibrium price and quantity by using the equilibrium condition, namely, $q^d = q^s$. Secondly, we can obtain equilibrium price and quantity by using the qualitative results of the demand-supply model, $p = \frac{a-c}{b+d}$ and $q = \frac{ad+bc}{b+d}$

1. Since in equilibrium, $q^d = q^s$

$$750 - 25p = 300 + 20p$$

$$45p = 750 - 300$$

$$p = \frac{450}{45} = 10$$

Now, substituting the value of p in the demand equation

$$q^d = 750 - 25 \times 10$$

$$= 500$$

Alternative Method

$$p = \frac{a-c}{b+d}$$

$$a = 750,\ b = 25,\ c = 300,\ d = 20$$

$$p = \frac{750 - 300}{25 + 20} = \frac{450}{45} = 10$$

$$q^d = \frac{ad + bc}{b + d}$$

$$= \frac{750 \times 20 + 25 \times 300}{25 + 20} = \frac{15000 + 7500}{45}$$

$$= \frac{22500}{45} = 500$$

Thus both methods yield the same results.

Demand Curve of a Product Facing a Perfectly Competitive Firm

The first three conditions ensure that a single price must prevail under perfect competition and demand curve or average revenue curve faced by an individual firm under perfect competition is perfectly elastic at the ruling price in the market. Perfectly elastic demand curve signifies that the firm does not exercise any control over the price of the product but can sell any amount of the product as it likes at the ruling price. If the firm raises its price slightly above the ruling price, it will lose all its customers to its rivals. Because it can sell as much as it likes at the prevailing price it has no incentive to lower it. Without being able to raise the price and having no incentive to lower it, the firm is content to accept the ruling price in the market.

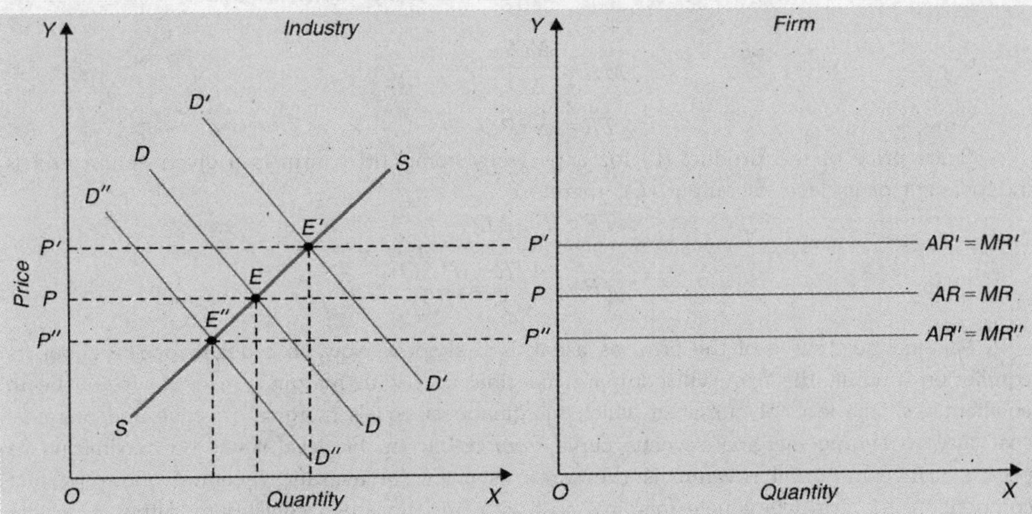

Fig.18.2. *Demand curve facing a perfectly competitive firm is perfectly elastic.*

Once the price in the market is established, a firm accepts the price as a given datum and adjusts its output at the level which gives it maximum profits. Consider Fig.18.2. To begin with, demand curve *DD* and supply curve *SS* intersect at point *E* and determine price *OP*. Now, the firm, having no influence over the price, will take the price *OP* as given and therefore average-marginal revenue curve facing it will be a horizontal straight line at the level of *OP*. When the demand increases and as a result price rises to *OP*′, the firm will now confront average-marginal revenue curve at the level of *OP*′. And if the demand decreases and price falls to *OP*′′, the firm's average-marginal revenue curve will shift below to the level of *OP*′′.

SHORT-RUN EQUILIBRIUM OF THE COMPETITIVE FIRM

As explained in a previous chapter, the short run means a period of time within which the firms can alter their level of output only by increasing or decreasing amounts of variable factors such as labour and raw materials, while fixed factors like capital equipment, machinery etc. remain unchanged. Moreover, in the short run, new firms can neither enter the industry, nor the existing firms can leave it. Before explaining competitive equilibrium we assume that a firm tries to maximize money profits. We shall explain the equilibrium of a perfectly competitive firm in two stages : first, by assuming that all firms are working under identical cost conditions and, secondly, by assuming that they are working under differential cost conditions.

The working of firms under identical cost conditions implies that all firms are facing same cost conditions, that is, their average and marginal cost curves are of the same level and shapes. This would be so if the entrepreneurs of all firms are of equal efficiency and also the other factors of production used by them are perfectly homogeneous and are available to all of them at the same prices.

As explained earlier, under perfect competition, an individual firm is a *price taker*, that is, it has to accept the prevailing price as a given datum. It cannot influence the price by its individual action. As a result, demand curve or average revenue curve of the firm is a horizontal straight line (*i.e.*, perfectly elastic) at the level of the prevailing price. Since, a perfectly competitive firm sells additional units of output at the same price, marginal revenue curve coincides with average revenue curve. That the marginal revenue of a perfectly competitive firm equals price or average revenue can be mathematically shown as under

$$MR = \frac{\Delta TR}{\Delta Q}$$

Now, $\Delta TR = \Delta\ (P.Q)$

Since price of the product (P) for a perfectly competitive firm is a given datum and is independent of its level of output (Q), therefore,

$$\Delta TR = P\ .\ \Delta Q$$

Thus, $$MR = \frac{\Delta TR}{\Delta Q} = \frac{P.\Delta Q}{\Delta Q} = P$$

Marginal cost curve of the firm, as usual, is U-shaped. Now, in order to decide about its equilibrium output, the firm will compare marginal cost with marginal revenue. It will be in equilibrium at the level of output at which marginal cost equals marginal revenue and marginal cost curve is cutting marginal revenue curve *from below.* At this level it will be maximizing its profits. Since marginal revenue is the same as price (or average revenue) under perfect competition, the firm will equate marginal cost with price to attain equilibrium output. Consider Fig. 18.3 in which price *OP* is prevailing in the market. *PL* would then be the demand curve or the average and marginal revenue curve of the firm. It will be seen from Fig. 18.3 that marginal cost curve cuts average and marginal revenue curve at two different points, *F* and *E*. *F* cannot be the position of equilibrium, since at *F* second order condition of firms equilibrium, namely, that the marginal cost curve must cut marginal revenue curve from below at the point of equilibrium is not satisfied. The firm will be increasing its profits by producing beyond *F* because marginal revenue is greater than marginal cost. The firm will be in equilibrium at point *E* or output *OM* since at *E* marginal cost equals marginal revenue (or price) as well as marginal cost curve is cutting marginal revenue curve from below. As under perfect competition marginal revenue curve is a horizontal straight line, the marginal cost curve must be rising so as to cut the marginal revenue curve from below. Therefore, in case of perfect competition the second order condition of firm's equilibrium requires that marginal cost curve must be rising at the point of equilibrium. Hence the twin conditions of firm's equilibrium under perfect competition are:

(1) $MC = MR = Price$

(2) MC curve must be rising at the point of equilibrium.

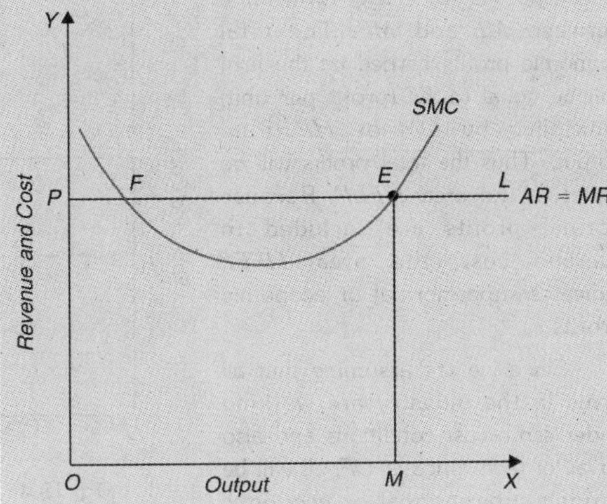

Fig. 18.3. *Firm's Equilibrium Under Perfect Competition.*

Conditions for Profit Maximization; Algebraic Analysis. That a competitive firm will maximise its total profits when marginal cost (MC) equals price (P) can be easily proved with differential calculus. Note that both the total cost (TC) and total revenue (TR) are functions of output (Q). This implies that total profits are also function of output (Q). Let π represent total profits. Thus

$$\pi = f(Q)$$

$$\pi = TR - TC = P.Q - TC \quad ...(i)$$

For maximisation of profits, the first derivative of the profit function has to be set equal to zero.

Thus, for maximum profits $\dfrac{d\pi}{dQ} = 0$

Since $d\pi = d(P.Q) - dTC$, for maximization of profits

$$\frac{d\pi}{dQ} = \frac{d(P.Q)}{dQ} - \frac{dTC}{dQ} = 0 \qquad ....(ii)$$

$\dfrac{d(P.Q)}{dQ}$ represents marginal revenue, and $\dfrac{d(TC)}{dQ}$ represents marginal cost.

Assuming that second order condition for profit maximization holds, it follows from (*ii*) above that for maximization of profits

$$\frac{d(P.Q)}{dQ} = \frac{dTC}{dQ} \text{ or } MR = MC$$

Now, because price of the product for a perfectly competitive firm is constant, marginal revenue, $\dfrac{d(P.Q)}{dQ}$ = Price. It follows therefore that for maximization of profits by a perfectly competitive firm,

$$\text{Price} = MC$$

But the fulfilment of the above two conditions does not guarantee that positive profits will be earned by the firm. In order to know whether the firm is making profits or losses and how much of them, average cost curve must be introduced in the figure. This has been done in Fig. 18.4, where SAC and SMC curves are short-run average cost and short-run marginal cost curves respectively. Profit per unit of output is the difference between average revenue (price) and average cost. In Fig. 18.4 at the equilibrium output *OM*, average revenue is equal to *ME*, and average cost is equal to *MF*.

Therefore, the profit per unit of output is *EF*, the difference between *ME* and *MF*. The total economic profits earned by the firm will be equal to *EF* (profit per unit) multiplied by *OM* or *HF* (total output). Thus the total profits will be equal to the area *HFEP*. Because normal profits are included in average cost, the area *HFEP* indicates super-normal or economic profits.

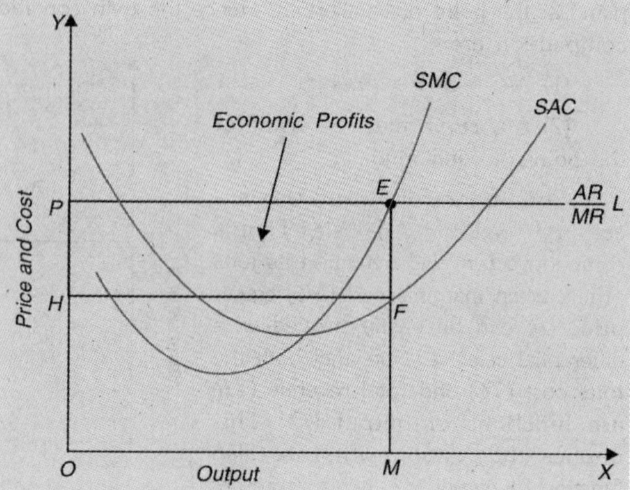

Fig. 18.4. *Short-Run Equilibrium with Profit.*

Since we are assuming that all firms in the industry are working under same cost conditions and also for all of them price is *OP*, all will be earning super-normal or economic profits equal to the area *HFEP*. Thus while all firms in the industry will be in short-run equilibrium, but the industry will not be in equilibrium since there will be a tendency for the new firms to enter the industry to compete away the super-normal profits. But the short run is not a period long enough for the new firms to enter the industry. The existing firms will therefore continue earning super-normal profits equal to *HFEP* in the short period. It is evident that in the situation depicted in Fig. 18.4 all firms will be in equilibrium at *E* and each will be producing *OM* output, but the industry will not be in equilibrium since the tendency for the new firms to enter the industry will be present, though they cannot enter during the short period.

Short-Run Equilibrium of a Firm in Case of Losses

Now suppose that the prevailing market price of the product is such that the price line or average and marginal revenue curve lies below average cost throughout. This case is illustrated

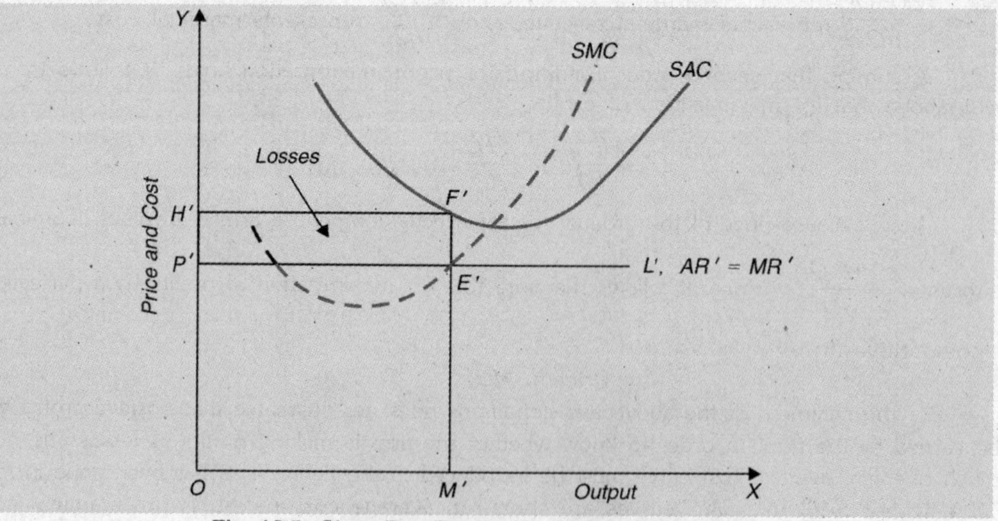

Fig. 18.5. *Short-Run Equilibrium: Minimizing Losses*

in Fig. 18.5 where the ruling price is *OP* which is taken as given by the firm. *PL'* is the price line which lies below *AC* curve at all levels of output. The firm will be in equilibrium at point *E* at which marginal cost is equal to price (or marginal revenue) and marginal cost curve is rising. Firm would be producing *OM* output but would be making losses, since average revenue, (or price) which is equal to *ME* is less than average cost which is equal to *MF*. The loss per unit of output is then equal to *EF* and total loss will be equal to *PEFH* which is the minimum loss that a firm can make under the given price-cost situation. Since all the firms are working under same cost conditions, all would be in equilibrium at point *E* or output *OM* and every one will be making losses equal to *PEFH*. As a result, the firms will have a tendency to quit the industry in order to make a search for earning at least normal profits elsewhere. We thus see that at price *OP* firms will be in equilibrium at *E*.

But the question arises as to why at all the firms should continue producing the product if they are to make losses. In the short run if they cannot go out of the industry by disposing of the plant, why do they not at least close down, that is, stop producing, when they are making losses. In other words, why do they not suspend production during the short period while remaining in the industry. This is because they cannot alter the fixed capital equipment in the short run and will therefore have to incur losses equal to the fixed costs even if they choose to shut down and stop producing the product. We thus see that if *the firm shuts down in the short run, it can avoid only variable costs, fixed costs have to be borne by it in the short run whether it is producing or not.* Therefore, if the firm can earn revenue which covers variable costs as well as a part of the fixed costs, it will be quite rational for it to keep operating and go on producing the product since stopping production under such circumstances will mean greater losses. *If the firm stops production in the short run, losses will be equal to the fixed cost.* Losses will be less than the fixed costs if a firm while operating earns revenue which covers variable costs fully as well as a part of the fixed costs.

It is thus quite rational for the firm to continue producing in the short run when it is earning more than variable costs even though it may be producing at a loss. For by doing so it will be *minimizing its losses in* the short run. It is prudent to continue working in the short run if the firm is covering variable costs and also making something to meet a part of the fixed costs. The saying 'half a loaf is better than none' is suggestive of rational action, for it is better to obtain some revenue to meet a part of the fixed costs than not to meet them at all. We conclude therefore that as long as price exceeds average variable cost, the firm should continue operating in the short run.

Shutting Down in the Short Run

But if the price falls below average variable cost, the firm will lose its fixed costs plus some of its variable costs, that is, it will make losses greater than the total fixed costs. Under such circumstances, it will be rational for the firm to close down, because by suspending production it can avoid losses incurred on variable costs. We conclude therefore that if the firm is not able to cover even its variable costs fully it will shut down even in the short run to avoid unnecessary losses.

The whole argument of the above two paragraphs can be easily grasped with the help of Fig.18.6 where along with short-run average cost and marginal cost curves, average variable cost curve is also drawn. When the price in the market is OP_1, the firm will be in equilibrium at point *R* and will therefore produce *OQ* output. Since average cost which is equal to *QS* is greater than the average revenue or price which is equal to *QR* or OP_1, the firm will be making losses equal to P_1RST. But it will be in the interest of the firm to continue producing at point *R* because the price OP_1 or *QR* is greater than the average variable cost which is here equal to QB. By operating at price OP_1, the firm is covering total variable costs (area $OQBA$) and a part of the fixed costs (area $ABRP_1$). The part of the fixed costs equal to area P_1RST is not being covered. The firm should operate and bear the losses equal to P_1RST because by closing down in the short run the firm will have to bear the losses equal to the whole fixed costs, the area $ABST$. Thus the losses will be smaller in case the firm is working than if it stops producing.

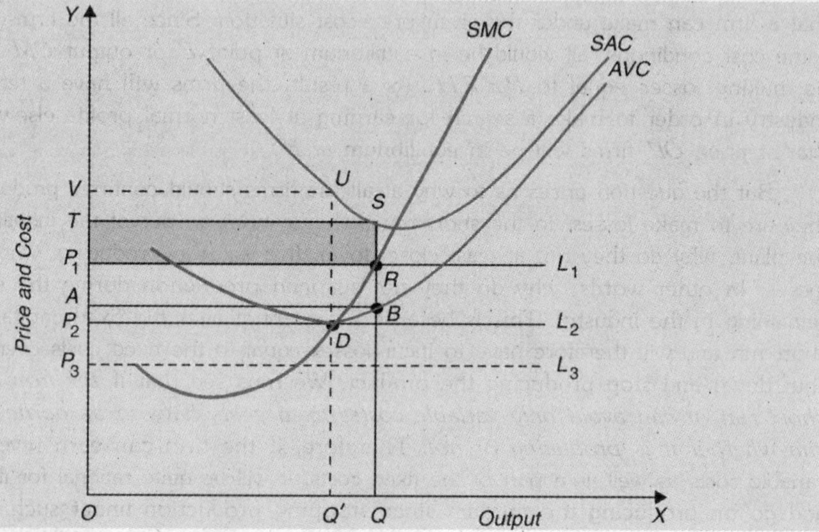

Fig.18.6. *Shut-Down Point for the Perfectly Competitive Firm.*

If the price in the market happens to be OP_2, the firm will be in equilibrium at point D. Price is here equal to average variable cost. At point D the firm is covering the variable costs fully, but it is not meeting any part of the fixed costs. Therefore, its losses are equal to the whole fixed costs equal to the area P_2DUV. Even if the firm stops operating, its losses will be equal to the whole fixed cost, therefore it will be a matter of indifference for the firm to operate at price OP_2 or not. But if the price falls below average variable cost or OP_2, for instance, if the price falls to OP_3, the firm will simply shut down since the firm will not cover even its variable costs fully. Therefore, the firm will suspend production at price OP_3 or any other price below OP_2 and will wait for some good time to come.

From the above analysis of equilibrium of the competitive firm in the short run, it follows that the firm in the short run may earn supernormal profits or losses or normal profits depending upon the price prevailing in the market. Firm's short-run equilibrium is possible in all these three situations. If the prevailing price is such that the price line is tangent to the minimum point of the average cost curve, then the firm would make only normal profits even in the short run.

LONG-RUN EQUILIBRIUM OF THE FIRM UNDER PERFECT COMPETITION

The long run is a period of time which is sufficiently long to allow the firms to make changes in all factors of production. In the long run, all factors are variable and none fixed. The firms, in the long run, can increase their output by changing their capital equipment; they may expand their old plants or replace the old lower-capacity plants by the new higher-capacity plants or add new plants. Besides, in the long run, new firms can enter the industry to compete the existing firms. On the other hand, in the long run, the firms can contract their output level by reducing their capital equipment; they may allow a part of the existing capital equipment to wear out without replacement or sell out a part of the capital equipment. Moreover, the firms can leave the industry in the long run. The long-run equilibrium then refers to the situation when free and full adjustment in the capital equipment as well as in the number of firms has been allowed to take place. It is therefore long-run average and marginal cost curve which are relevant for deciding about equilibrium output in the long run. Moreover, in the long ran, it is the average total cost which is of determining importance, since all costs are variable and none fixed.

As explained above, a firm is in equilibrium under perfect competition when marginal cost is equal to price. But for the firm to be in long-run equilibrium, besides marginal cost being equal to price, the price must also be equal to average cost. For, if the price is greater or less than the average cost, there will be tendency for the firms to enter or leave the industry. If the price is greater than the average cost, the firms will earn more than normal profits. These supernormal profits will attract other firms into the industry. With the entry of new firms in the industry, the price of the product will go down as a result of the increase in supply of output and also the cost will go up as a result of more intensive competition for factors of production. The firms will continue entering the industry until the price is equal to average cost so that all firms are earning only normal profits.

On the contrary, if the price is lower than the average cost, the firms would make losses. These losses will induce some of the firms to quit the industry. As a result, the output of the industry will fall which will raise the price. On the other hand, with some firms going out of the industry, cost may go down as a result of fall in the demand for certain specialised factors of production. The firms will continue leaving the industry until the price is equal to average cost so that the firms remaining in the field are making only normal profits. It, therefore, follows that for a perfectly competitive firm to be in long-run equilibrium, the following two conditions must be fulfilled.

1. *Price = Marginal Cost*
2. *Price = Average Cost*

If price is equal to both marginal cost and average cost, then we have a double condition of long-run perfectly competitive equilibrium :

Price = Marginal Cost = Average Cost

But from the relationship between marginal cost and average cost we know that marginal cost is equal to average cost only at the minimum point of the average cost curve. Therefore, the condition for long-run equilibrium of the firm can be written as :

Price = Marginal Cost = Minimum Average Cost

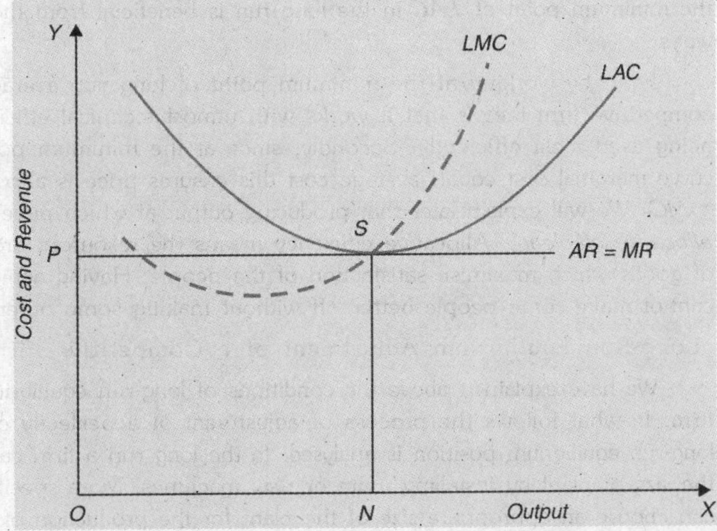

Fig. 18.7. *Long-run Equilibrium of the firm*

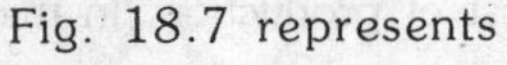
Fig. 18.7 represents

long-run equilibrium of firm under perfect competition. The firm cannot be in the long-run equilibrium at a price greater than *OP* in Fig.18.7. This is because if price is greater than *OP*, then the price line (demand curve) would lie somewhere above the minimum point of the average cost curve so that marginal cost and price will be equal where the firm is earning super-normal profits. Since there will be tendency for new firms to enter and compete away these super-normal profits, the firm cannot be in long-run equilibrium at any price higher than *OP*. Likewise, the firm cannot be in long-run equilibrium at a price lower than *OP* in Fig. 18.7 under perfect competition. If price is lower than *OP*, the average and marginal revenue curve will lie below the average cost curve so that the marginal cost and price will be equal at the point where the firm is making losses. Therefore, there will be tendency for some of the firms in the industry to go out with the result that price will rise and the firms left in the industry make normal profits. We therefore conclude that the firm can be in long-run equilibrium under perfect competition only when price is at such a level that the horizontal demand curve (that is, *AR* curve) is tangent to the average cost curve so that price equals average cost and firm makes only normal profits.

It should be noted that a horizontal demand curve can be tangent to a U-shaped average cost curve only at the latter's minimum point. Since at the minimum point of the average cost curve the marginal cost and average cost are equal, price in long-run equilibrium is equal to both marginal cost and average cost. In other words, double condition of long-run equilibrium is fulfilled at the minimum point of the average cost curve.

It is clear from above that *long-run equilibrium of the firm under perfect competition is established at the minimum point of the long-run average cost curve.* Working at the minimum point of the long-run average cost curve signifies that the firm is producing with the plant of optimum scale, that is, with lowest possible level of short-run average cost curve. Besides, the perfectly competitive firm by producing at the minimum point of the long-run average curve *LAC is enjoying all possible economies of scale*, or in other words, it has exhausted the economies of scale and has no incentive to move to any other point on the long-run average cost curve *LAC*. Working at the minimum point of long-run average cost curve implies that; it is working *at the optimum or efficient scale*. The fact that the firm working under conditions of perfect competition tends to be working with optimum scale plant and at the minimum point of *LAC* in the long run is beneficial from the social point of view in two ways.

First, by working at the minimum point of long run average cost curve by a perfectly competitive firm means that it works with utmost technical efficiency and thus resources are being used most efficiently. Secondly, since at the minimum point of long-run average cost curve marginal cost equals average cost this ensures price is also equal to marginal cost (Price = *MC*). We will explain later that producing output at which price equals marginal cost ensures *allocative efficiency*. Allocative efficiency means the resources are allocated to the production of goods which maximise satisfaction of the people. Having achieved allocative efficiency, we cannot make some people better off without making some others worse off.

Long-Run Equilibrium Adjustment of a Competitive Firm

We have explained above the conditions of long-run equilibrium of a perfectly competitive firm. In what follows the process of adjustment of a perfectly competitive firm to attain its long-run equilibrium position is analysed. In the long run a firm can change all factors including the size of plant by installing more or new machines. More specifically, in the long run a firm can choose an appropriate size of the plant for the production of the product depending upon the price of the product and the long-run average and marginal cost of production. In the long run, a firm can even decide to leave the industry to avoid losses or if it thinks it can earn more profits elsewhere. The long-run equilibrium adjustment of competitive firm is illustrated in Fig. 18.8.

As in the short run, in the long run also a competitive firm faces a perfectly elastic (horizontal) demand curve as being incapable of influencing the price, it takes the market price as given. In Fig.18.8, the price of the product in the market, to begin with, is equal to OP_1 and therefore the demand curve facing the firm is P_1L_1. Suppose the firm is working with a plant of the size having short-run average cost curve, SAC_1, with its short run marginal cost curve SMC_1. With P_1L as the demand curve, the firm will maximise its profits in the short run by producing level of output equal to OQ_1 where its SMC_1 = Price OP_1. With this short-run equilibrium output OQ_1, the firm is making positive economic profits equal to the area of the rectangle $ABEP_1$ (Note that EB is the difference between AR and AC and therefore represents profit per unit).

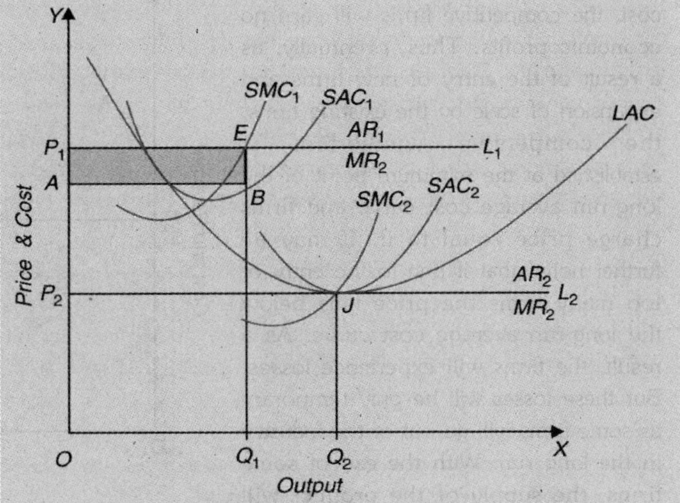

Fig. 18.8. *Long-run Adjustment of a Competitive Firm*

Though the firm is making positive economic profits in the short run by producing output OQ_1, this does not represent its long-run equilibrium position. This is because the firm can increase its profits by expanding the size of plant and other associated factors. The decision regarding which plant size to employ and what level of output to produce with it is governed by the long-run average and marginal cost curves. The long-run average cost curve is also U-shaped which shows that as the firm expands the size of its plant and output there are economies of scale up to an output level OQ_2 and beyond this the diseconomies of scale occur. As long as the firm is earning economic profits and economies of scale exist, the firm will expand its scale.

It will be seen from Figure 18.8 that if firm can reduce its average cost of production by expanding output to the level OQ_2 and installing a plant of scale whose short-run average cost curve is SAC_2. Thus, the firm will tend to shift to SAC_2 and produce output OQ_2. However, at the same time lured by the economic profits made by the existing firms, new firms having same costs as the existing firm will enter the industry which will cause the supply of output to increase. Thus supply of output of the product increases in two ways: First, the existing firms expand their size to take advantage of the economies of scale and secondly new firms enter the industry to take advantage of the profit opportunities in the industry.

As a consequence of the expansion of output by all the existing firms and the entry of new firms in the industry, the supply of the product of the industry will increase which will cause a reduction in its price. The entry of new firms will continue and price go on falling under the pressure of more supply until the price falls to OP_2 equal to the level of minimum long-run average cost curve. It will be seen from Fig.18.8 that with price OP_2, the competitive firm will be in equilibrium by producing output equal to OQ_2 where the following conditions hold good:

Price $(OP_2) = LMC = SMC =$ Minimum LAC

Since price is equal to average cost, the competitive firms will earn no economic profits. Thus, eventually, as a result of the entry of new firms and expansion of scale by the existing firms, the competitive equilibrium is established at the minimum point of the long-run average cost curve and firms charge price equal to it. It may be further noted that if due to the entry of too many firms the price falls below the long-run average cost curve. As a result, the firms will experience losses. But these losses will be only temporary as some firms will go out of the industry in the long run. With the exit of some firms, the supply of the product will decrease and consequently price will rise resulting in elimination of profits and with this the existing firms can hope to earn only normal profits. The eventual long-run equilibrium of the competitive firm when it makes zero economic profits or in other words, earns only normal profits has been shown in Fig. 18.9.

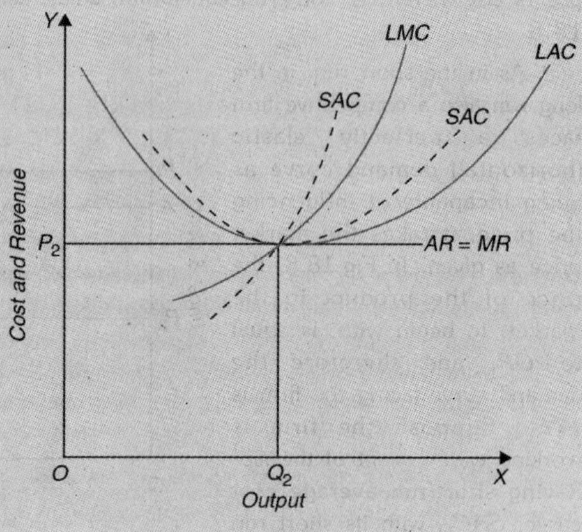

Fig.18.9. *Long-Run Equilibrium of the Competitive Firm with zero economic Profits*

Why do Competitive Firms Stay in Business if They Make Zero Economic Profits in the Long Run ?

The earning of zero economic profits by the competitive firms in the long run poses a great puzzle for the students of economics. The competitive firms which aim to maximize profits and adjust their plant size to increase profits in the long run finally end up in zero economic profits. As has been explained above, this is mainly due to the free entry and exit of the firms which is an important feature of perfect competition model. In the perfect competition model it is assumed that there are no legal restrictions on the entry of new firms and further that there are no entry costs apart from the direct cost of production and capital investment. Besides, the zero economic profit situation arises because we have assumed that all firms have the same cost functions which implies that not only all the factors used by the firms are homogeneous and equally productive but also the owner-entrepreneurs themselves are equally efficient.

But the most important issue raised by zero economic profits in the long-run competitive equilibrium is one of survival of the firms. In view of zero-economic profits, how do they survive ? Further, why don't these firms quit the industry to search for profits elsewhere ? To understand this issue one should remember the distinction between *economic profits* and *accounting profits.* As has been explained in the chapter on costs, the *accounting profits* are measured by the difference between the revenue and the explicit costs (*i.e.*, actual expenditure incurred by the firms for buying and hiring factors plus depreciation), whereas economic profits also take into account the *opportunity costs* of self-owned factors employed by the entrepreneur in the firm. The two important factors supplied by the owner-entrepreneurs to their firms are capital investment and the managerial services rendered by them. Economists include the opportunity costs of capital invested (*i.e.*, the reasonable rate of return on capital which can be earned elsewhere) and the opportunity costs of managerial services rendered by the owner-entrepreneurs (*i.e.*, wages of management), which are generally called normal profits, in the costs of production. Thus, when the competitive firms earn zero economic profits, it means that they are in fact earning a fair rate of return on capital invested and wages for the managerial services performed which are included in the average cost of production. Thus, in long-run competitive equilibrium, all factors including the capital investment and the managerial services by the entrepreneurs are rewarded equal to their opportunity costs. That is why the firms survive and also stay in the competitive industry.

Of course, the firms would like to earn positive economic profits. The goal of earning positive economic profits motivates the entrepreneurs to invovate and develop new ideas for commercial use so that they can either lower the cost of production or raise the demand for their product. But, as seen above, in competitive markets as a result of adjustment expansion of output by all firms and the entry of new firms, economic profits tend to be zero in the long run. But it takes time for the full adjustment to take place and economic profits to be reduced to zero. Therefore, by introducing innovations and also as a result of frequent changes in tastes, incomes and demand of the people entrepreneurs can earn positive economic profits in the short run as depicted in Figure18.4 by the area *PEFH*. Indeed, the long run, like tomorrow, never comes as the demand and supply conditions change frequently as a result of changes in both the external and the internal factors. For example, innovations introduced by the entrepreneurs themselves cause the emergence of economic profits in the short run.

SHORT-RUN SUPPLY CURVE OF THE PERFECTLY COMPETITIVE FIRM

As is known, the short run is a period in which more quantity of the good is produced by working the given capital equipment or plant more intensively by employing more amounts of the variable factors. We have seen above that the firm under perfect competition produces that amount of the good at which marginal cost equals price. Since the price for a perfectly competitive firm is given and constant for it, price line will be a horizontal straight line. The horizontal coordinate of a point on the rising marginal cost curve measures the quantity of the good that the firm will produce at that price. The short-run marginal cost curve of the firm therefore indicates the quantities which the firm will produce in the short run at different prices.

Consider Figure 18.10. At price OP_3 the firm will produce and offer for sale *OM* quantity of the good, because at *OM* quantity of the good, price OP_3 equals marginal cost. Similarly, at price OP_4 the quantity produced or supplied will be *ON*, since price OP_4 equals marginal cost at output *ON*. Likewise, at price OP_2 the firm will produce and supply *OL* quantity of the product. It is thus

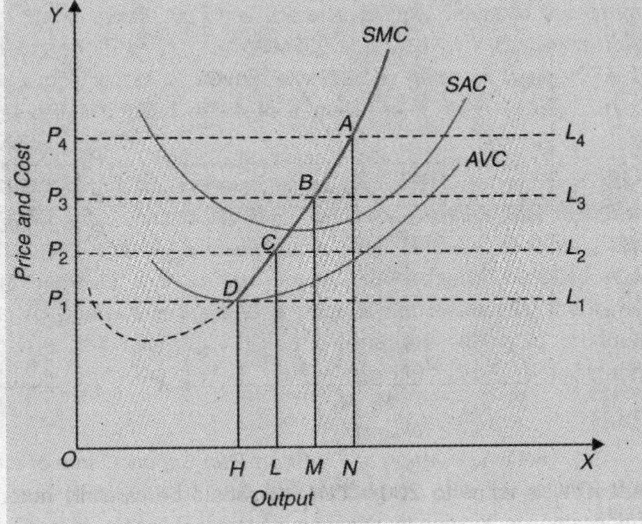

Fig. 18.10 *Short-Run Supply Curve of the Firm.*

clear that *short-run marginal cost curve of the firm is in fact the short-run supply curve of the firm*. The firm will not produce any output at a price below OP_1, since it will not be fully recovering its variable costs at a price below OP_1. Thus, *only the part of the short run marginal cost curve which lies above the average variable cost forms the short-run supply curve of the firm*. In the Fig. 18.10 thick portion of the short-run marginal cost curve *SMC* represents the short-run supply curve of the firm. Since under perfect competition marginal cost must be rising above the minimum point of the average variable cost curve, *the short-run supply curve of the firm must always slope upward to the right.*

It should be noted that in our analysis of deriving short-run supply curve of the firm, we have assumed that following the rise in price when the firm expands its output or supply, prices of resources or inputs it uses for production do not go up. It is a valid assumption because an individual firm under perfect competition is only one among many and its demand for inputs or resources is insignificant part of the total market demand for them and therefore the increase in demand for these resources by the firm as it expands will have no effect on their prices.

SHORT-RUN SUPPLY CURVE OF THE COMPETITIVE INDUSTRY

We now proceed to derive the short-run supply curve of the competitive industry. As the market demand curve is found by the horizontal summation of demand curves of all individual consumers of a product, similarly *the supply curve of the industry is obtained by lateral summation (horizontal addition) of short-run supply curves of all individual firms in the industry*. How the short-run supply curves (short-run marginal cost curves) of the firms are added to obtain the short-run supply curve of the competitive industry is illustrated in 18.11. Suppose there are 200 firms in the competitive-industry. We further assume that all firms are alike in respect of cost of production. In Fig. 18.11 (a), *SMC* represents short-run supply curve of an individual firm. At price OP_1 an individual firm will produce and supply OM_1 quantity of the product. Since there are 200 such firms in the industry, the whole industry will produce and supply 200 OM_1 quantity of the product. Therefore, in Fig. 18.11(*b*), 200 OM_1, quantity is plotted against the price OP_1.

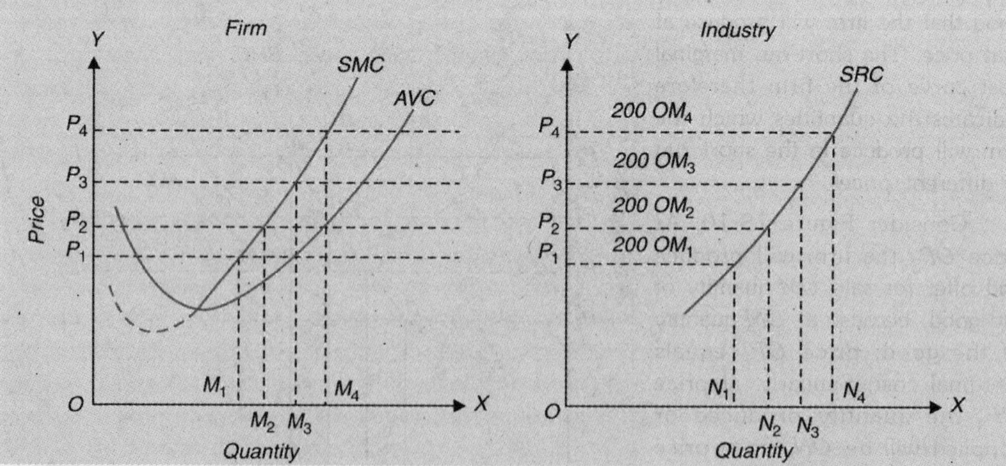

Fig. 18.11. *Derivation of the Short-Run Supply Curve of the Perfectly Competitive Industry*

ON_1 is equal to 200 OM_1. It should be carefully noted that in Fig.18.11 (*a*) and (*b*) while the scale on *X*-axis is the same, the scale on *Y*-axis differs very much. The scale on *X*-axis in Fig. 18.11, has been compressed very much to accommodate large quantities. At price OP_2 an individual firm will produce and supply OM_2 amount of the good, while the whole industry will supply ON_2 which is equal to 200 OM_2 amount of the product. In the same way, industry will produce and supply (200 OM_3) = ON_3 output at price OP_3 , and (200 OM_4) or ON_4 at price OP_4. Likewise, the industry's supply can be determined for all other prices. *The short-run supply curve of the industry will always slope upward.* This is because the short-run marginal cost curves of the firms (*i.e.*, their short-run supply curves) always slope upward above the minimum point of the averae variable cost curves. The slope and the elasticity of short-run supply curve of the industry will obviously depend upon the slope and elasticity of the marginal cost curves of individual firms in the industry.

That the short-run supply curve of the industry under perfect competition is a lateral or horizontal summation of the short-run curves (*i.e.*, *SMC*) of the firms in it is subject to an important qualification. This is that the simultaneous expansion of output by all the firms in it (*i.e.*, the expansion of output by the industry) and therefore the increase in demand for the resources or inputs to be used for production will have no effect on the prices of these resources, that is, for the whole industry these resources or inputs are perfectly elastic. But whereas the expansion or contraction of output of the individual firm and therefore the changes in its demand for resources is not likely to affect their prices, the simultaneous expansion or contraction of all firms in the industry may mean a significant change in the demand for these resources and will therefore affect their prices. If expansion of industry output and therefore the increase in demand for resources raises the prices of these resources, then the cost curves of the individual firms will shift upward. On the other hand, if the expansion of the industry brings about a fall in the prices of resources, the cost curves of individual firms will shift downward. It may be that prices of some resources may rise and some others may fall with the expansion of the industry. In that case, the shift in the cost curves of the firms will depend upon whether the increase or decrease in resource prices is predominant.

When the cost curves of individual firms shift due to the change in resource prices, then the supply curve of industry cannot be obtained by summing up laterally the short-run supply curves of the firms, because then with every increase in the industry output, cost curves of firms change. In this case, therefore, when external effects are present, that is, when resource prices change with the expansion of industry, the short-run supply curve of the industry can be obtained by summing up the *equilibrium outputs* with different cost curves of all firms at each possible market price of the product.

ECONOMIC EFFICIENCY OF PERFECTLY COMPETITIVE MARKET

We have explained above how in a perfectly competitive market price and output are determined through equilibrium between demand for and supply of goods. Now, an important question is how well do the competitive markets perform to allocate society's scarce resources? Do they use and allocate society's resources efficiently for satisfying the satisfaction of wants of the people ? To answer this question we must first explain what we mean by *economic efficiency or allocative efficiency. The resources of a society are efficiently used if they are so used and allocated that the consumers get the maximum possible satisfaction. When such an efficiency has been achieved, it is then not possible through any reorganisation of resources and production of goods and services to make anyone better off without making someone worse off.* Under such conditions of efficiency, the satisfaction of one individual can be increased only at the loss of utility by another. This concept of efficiency is generally referred to as *Pareto efficiency* as it was first developed by the Italian economists Vilfredo Pareto (1848-1923). We will use the concepts of consumer surplus and producer surplus to explain whether competitive markets achieve economic or allocative efficiency as defined above.

Consumer Surplus. Recall that consumer surplus obtained by the consumers from buying a product is the price that they are willing to pay over and above the market price which they actually pay for a commodity. It is important to note that *demand curve of a commodity reflects what price the consumers are willing to pay for various units of a goods.* This willingness to pay for a unit of a commodity by consumers measures the *utility or satisfaction* they hope to get from it. In economics the *well-being* of an individual is measured by the utility or satisfaction individuals obtain from the consumption of goods. The market demand curve of a commodity is obtained through the horizontal addition of the demand curves of individuals for the commodity. The consumer surplus obtained by all individuals is the gain in utility or well-being from consuming a good over and above the price they pay for it. Thus consumer surplus represents the *net gain* of utility or benefit or well-being the individuals get from consuming a commodity. It is measured by the area under the given demand curve as shown in Figure 18.12 where *DD′* is the demand curve of a commodity, *OP* is the market price as determined by demand for and supply of a commodity. The consumers will buy *OQ* quantity of the commodity and will pay total value equal to the *OPEQ* for the commodity while total value (equal to the money value of satisfaction they will get) which they are willing to pay for the commodity is equal to the total area under the demand curve upto the quantity *OQ* purchased, which is equal to the area *ODEQ*. Thus, total value they are willing to pay for *OQ* quantity of the commodity, that is, *ODEQ minus* the value *OPEQ* they actually pay for it gives us the amount of consumer surplus they obtain from buying the commodity. Remember consumer surplus measures the net gain or well-being by the consumer for buying the commodity from the market.

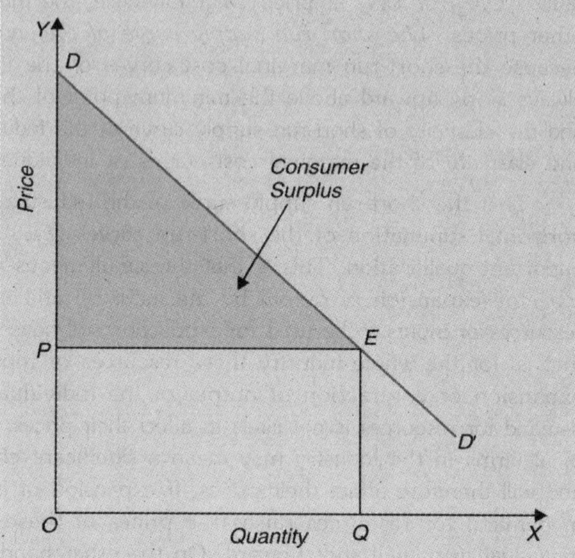

Fig. 18.12. *Measurement of Consumer Surplus*

Producer Surplus. *Similarly, producer surplus is the excess of market price at which producers sell the quantity of a commodity over and above the minimum price at which they would be willing to supply it.* The minimum price which the producers would accept to supply a unit of the commodity is its marginal cost which reflects the opportunity cost of resources used for its production. Consider Figure 18.13 where demand curve *DD* and supply curve *SS* of a commodity intersect at point *E* and determine *OP* as the market price and *OQ* as the quantity sold and bought. It will be seen from the supply curve *SS* of Figure 18.13 that producers produce the last *Q*th unit of the commodity at the marginal cost which is just equal to the market price *OP*. However, as is indicated by the supply curve *SS* the producers will be ready to supply the earlier successive units from zero to *Q*th unit at much less than the market price *OP*. Thus, from these earlier units the producers actually get more than their minimum acceptable supply price. The area *OSEQ* below the supply curve is indicator of the aggregate supply price of *OQ* units of the commodity produced and supplied by the producers. On the other hand, the total revenue earned by them is equal to the area *OPEQ* (market price *OP* x quantity *OQ* sold). Thus, the producers earn revenue equal to the shaded area *SEP* more than the aggregate supply price. This excess amount *SEP* over the aggregate supply price is the aggregate producer surplus earned by the producers. *The producer surplus earned by the producers is the measure of benefits obtained by them for producing and exchanging the commodity.*

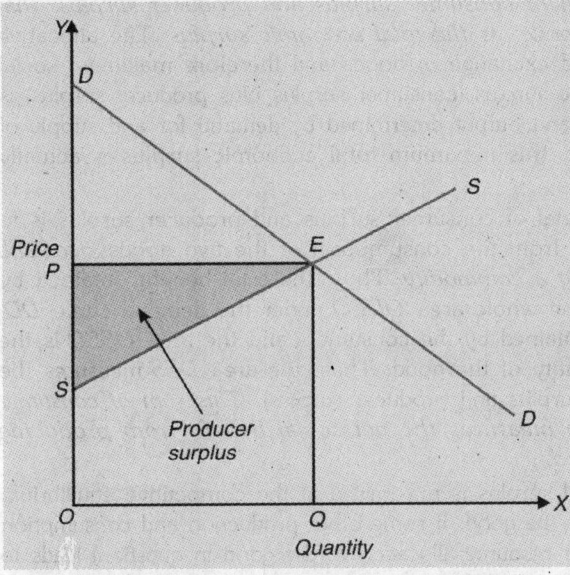

Fig. 18.13. *The Concept of Producer Surplus*

Allocative Efficiency of Perfectly Competitive Equilibrium

One of the most beneficial feature of perfectly competitive market is that it results in allocative efficiency which means that it enables the use of resources for production of goods that ensures maximum welfare benefits to the persons in a society. Allocative efficiency of perfectly competitive markets also implies the mutually beneficial exchange between consumers and producers of goods.That is, both are better off in participating in the exchange. Under conditions of perfectly competitive markets optimum production and exchange of goods takes place which ensures the achievement of maximum social welfare. This can be shown by the concept of producer surplus and consumer surplus.

Recall that consumer surplus measures the welfare gain to the consumers from buying a commodity equal to the amount which they are willing to pay (which reflects their utility derived from the commodity) over and above the market price they actually pay for the good which they buy from the producers. Consumer surpluse is measured by the area under the demand curve over the market price.

Thus, in Figure 18.14 where demand curve *DD* of consumers and supply curve *SS* of consumers through their intersection at point *E* determine market price *OP* and quantity *OQ* of the good produced and exchanged between them. Consumer surplus obtained by the consumers is equal to the area *DPE*. On the other hand, as explained above, *PES* is producer surplus obtained by the producers which measures the excess revenue obtained by them over and above the sum of marginal costs (*i.e.* supply price) incurred by them for producing *OQ* amount of the good.

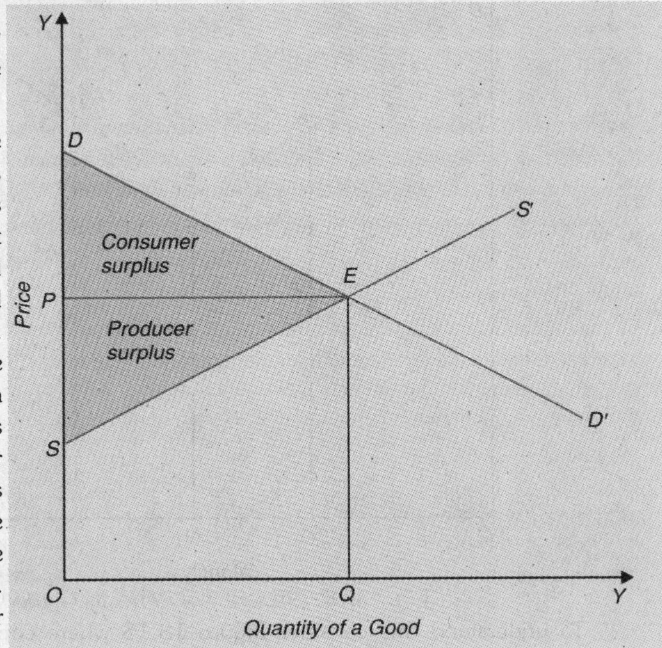

Fig. 18.14. *Maximisation of Total Economic Surplus*

It follows from above that both the consumers and producers gain from exchange and production of goods. *From the society's point of view, the total gain is the sum of consumer surplus and producer surplus. This sum of consumer surplus and producer surplus, that is, the sum of areas DPE and PES is known as the total economic surplus.* The allocative efficiency in consumption, production and exchange of goods and therefore maximum social benefit is attained when the total economic surplus (consumer surplus plus producer surplus) is maximised. And, as seen above, at price and output determined by demand for and supply of goods in a perfectly competitive market, this maximum total economic surplus is actually attained.

An alternative way of viewing the total of consumer surplus and producer surplus is to consider it as the *total benefits* obtained from the consumption of the two goods *over and above the total variable cost of producing a commodity.* Thus, the total benefit obtained by consuming *OQ* quantity of the good is the whole area *ODEQ* under the demand curve *DD'* which means the total utility or benefit obtained by the consumers and the area *OSEQ* is the sum of total costs of producing *OQ* quantity of the good. Thus, the area *DES* measures the total surplus (*i.e.*, the sum of consumer surplus and producer surplus). *This sum of consumer surplus and producer surplus therefore measures the net social benefit from producing and consuming OQ quantity of the good.*

The key question is whether the total surplus is maximised at the competitive equilibrium as determined by demand for and supply of the good. If some other production and consumption of the good (or in other words, some other resource allocation to the good in question) leads to a higher total surplus, the output *OQ* of the good determined by competitive equilibrium would not be efficient. This is because it would then be possible to make consumers and producers better off collectively. On the other hand, if there is no alternative resource allocation to the good in question which generates a higher level of total surplus, the competitive equilibrium is economically efficient.

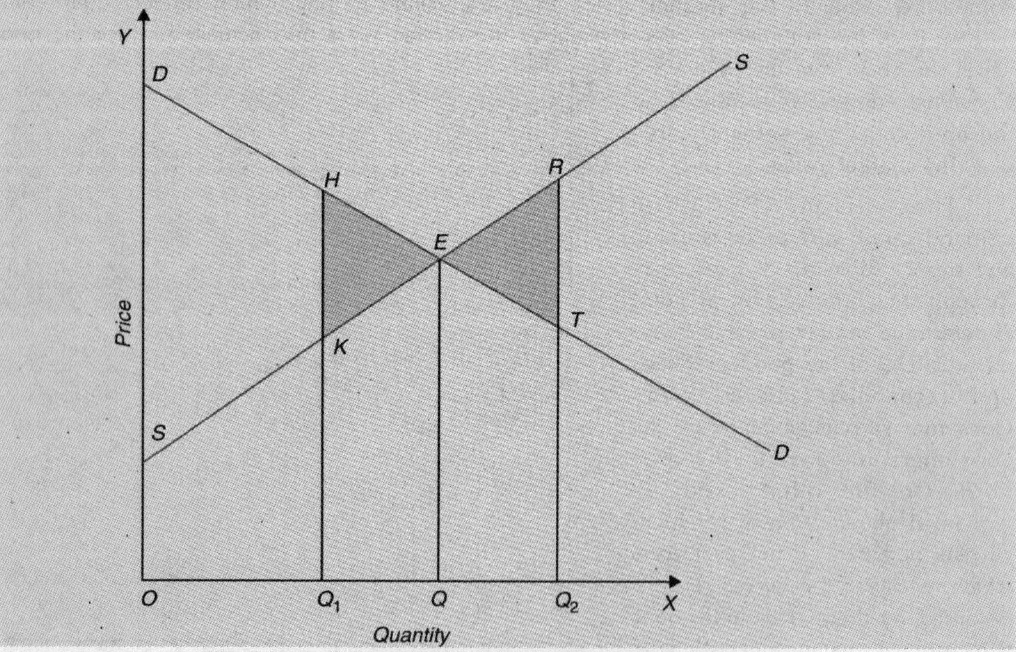

Fig. 18.15. *Efficiency of Perfectly Competitive Equilibrium*

To understand this consider Figure 18.15 where competitive equilibrium is attained by producing *OQ* quantity of the good. Now, suppose a smaller quantity OQ_1 of the good is produced, then as will be seen from Figure18.15 the consumers and producers will suffer a loss of total economic surplus equal to the area *HKE*. Likewise, any other quantity smaller than *OQ* would mean a lower total economic surplus than that obtained from producing and consuming *OQ* quantity of the good by allocating required resources to its production.

If a greater quantity than *OQ*, say OQ_2 *is produced and consumed, the consumers would get less* utility (or welfare benefit) as indicated by the demand curve in the *range of quantity* QQ_2 which is lower than the cost of producing the good as indicated by the higher level of the supply curve in this quantity range (*i.e.*, QQ_2). Thus, the production of greater quantity OQ_2 of the good than the competitive output *OQ* leads to the loss of total economic surplus equal to the area *ERT*.

From above it follows that production of *OQ* quantity of the good competitive equilibrium ensures maximum total economic surplus and therefore leads to maximum social benefit. This is an important conclusion which tells us that *competitive markets perform quite well in allocating scarce social resources.*

But perfect competition rarely exists in the real world. It is market forms of monopolies, oligopolies and monopolistic competition that exist in the real world and not perfect competition. We shall study in the next few chapters how market categories of monopolies, oligopolies and monopolistic competition create economic inefficiencies in resource allocation and hence loss of social welfare.

Further, the *economic efficiency is achieved under conditions of perfect competition only when there do not exist any externalities, negative or positive.* The existence of externalities causes divergence between private benefit and social benefit as well as between private cost and social cost. Thus, perfectly competitive equilibrium based on private cost and private benefit would not lead to the maximum social welfare when externalities are present.

Economic Efficiency and Equity

That under conditions of perfect competition the conclusion that welfare is maximum is based on the thinking that the total economic surplus is the true measure of social welfare. To consider so is to ignore the effect of distribution of output and income on social welfare. *The equity, that is, fairness in distribution is as important as maximisation of total economic surplus.* To consider the size of total economic surplus as the sole criterion of assessment of social welfare is to implicitly make the value judgement that a rupee gives each person the same satisfaction irrespective of whether the person is consumer or producer, rich or poor. To clarify this let us consider that price of a product is raised. As a result, the consumers would lose some consumer surplus and producers would gain some extra producer surplus. The criterion of total economic surplus is based on the net change in surplus in rupee terms. Suppose as a result of rise in price of a good consumers suffer a loss of consumer surplus of Rs. 1000 and producers gain extra producer surplus of Rs. 1000. Thus, the total economic surplus remains unchanged.

But, if consumers are poor households whereas producers are rich individuals, the redistribution of income from the poor consumers to the rich producers, the total economic surplus remaining the same, will lead to the *net* loss of social welfare. To conclude that in this case social welfare remains unchanged is based on the implicit assumption that the poor derive utility from Rs. 1000 equal to that of the rich. That is, marginal utility of one rupee is the same for the rich and the poor. This is a questionable assumption and involves value judgement which is not justified on any scientific grounds. In other words, *maximising total economic surplus leads to economic efficiency but it will not be necessarily 'fair' or 'equitable'.* The maximisation of total economic surplus does not capture the equity aspect of social welfare. In the light of this fact, the total economic surplus (*i.e.*, the sum of producer surplus and economic surplus) is not a very good measure of social well-being. Thus, maximisation of total surplus leads to the outcome which is economically efficient but it may not be necessarily fair or equitable.

It may be noted that some economists consider maximisation of total surplus as a valid criterion of social welfare as they think that once total surplus is maximised, it can be redistributed in accordance with society's notion of equity or fairness. It is argued that "*make the pie as big as possible and then distribute it according to society's notion of equity.*" However, in our view, it is difficult to redistribute output and income so as to ensure equity and thereby to increase social well-being. Besides, in the redistribution, demand and supply curves of a good which generated the maximum total surplus, are likely to change which may result in deviation of the outcome from the maximum total economic surplus (or economic efficiency).

NUMERICAL PROBLEMS ON PERFECT COMPETITION MODEL

Let us solve some numerical problems to make clear the conditions of profit maximisation under perfect competition.

Problem 1. *For a perfectly competitive firm, the following short-run function is given*

$$TC = 2 + 4Q + Q^2$$

If price of the product prevailing in the market is Rs. 8, at what level of output the firm will maximise profits ?

Solution. Since total revenue is price multiplied by quantity of output, total revenue function is

$$TR = P \,.\, Q = 8Q$$

$$TC = 2 + 4Q + Q^2$$

We explain below the profit maximisation with both the *TR* – *TC* approach and *MC* – *MR* approach,

TR–TC Approach

Profits

$$\pi = TR - TC$$

$$= 8Q - (2 + 4Q + Q^2)$$

$$= 8Q - 2 - 4Q - Q^2$$

$$= 4Q - 2 - Q^2 \quad \ldots(i)$$

Now, profits will be maximum at the output level at which first derivative of profit function with respect to the quantity of output equals 0. Thus, by taking the first derivative of profit function (*i*) and setting it equal to zero, we have :

$$\frac{d\pi}{dQ} = 4 - 2Q = 0$$

$$2Q = 4$$

$$Q^* = 2$$

MR–MC Approach

In this approach profits are maximum at the output level at which *MR* equals *MC*. We therefore first derive the marginal revenue and marginal cost from *TR* and *TC* functions.

$$TR = 8Q \quad \ldots(ii)$$

$$MR = \frac{d(TR)}{dQ} = 8$$

$$TC = 2 + 4Q + Q^2 \quad ...(iii)$$

$$MC = \frac{d\ (TR)}{dQ} = 4 + 2Q$$

In order to determine profit-maximising output we set MR equal to MC. Thus,

$$MR = MC$$
$$8 = 4 + 2Q$$
$$2Q = 8 - 4 = 4$$
$$Q^* = 2.$$

Problem 2. *In a city there are a large number of firms selling a product and no single firm has any control over the price of the product. The following total revenue and cost functions are given for a single seller*

$$TR = 10Q$$
$$TC = 1000 + 2Q + 0.01Q^2$$

Determine how many units of the product a firm will produce per annum if it aims at profit maximisation. Also find out the total profits made by it in the equilibrium situation.

Solution. We determine MR and MC form the given revenue and cost functions. Thus,

$$TR = 10Q$$

$$MR = \frac{d\ (TR)}{dQ} = 10$$

(Note that since MR is constant, price will be equal to it.)

$$TC = 1000 + 2Q + 0.01Q^2$$

$$MC = \frac{d\ (TC)}{dQ} = 2 + 0.02Q$$

For profit maximisation

$$MC = MR$$
$$2 + 0.02Q = 10$$
$$0.02Q = 8$$
$$Q = \frac{8 \times 100}{2} = 400.$$

Profits

$$\pi = TR - TC$$
$$TR = P.Q = 10 \times 400 = 4000$$
$$TC = 1000 + 2 \times 400 + 0.01\ (400)^2$$
$$= 1800 + 1600 = 3{,}400$$
$$\pi = 4000 - 3400 = \text{Rs } 600$$

Problem 3. *A firm producing bread is operating in a perfectly competitive market. The firm's variable cost function is given by*

$$TVC = 150Q - 20Q^2 + Q^3$$

where Q is level of output.

Determine below what price the firm should shut down production in the short run.

Solution. In the short run a firm will shut down operations if the price falls below the level of minimum average variable cost. So we first determine the minimum average variable cost.

$$AVC = \frac{TVC}{Q} = \frac{150Q}{Q} - \frac{20Q^2}{Q} + \frac{Q^3}{Q}$$

$$AVC = 150 - 20Q + Q^2$$

To determine the level of output at which average variable cost is minimum we take the first derivative of the *AVC* function and set it equal to zero.

$$\frac{d(AVC)}{dQ} = -20 + 2Q = 0$$

$$2Q = 20$$

$$Q = 10$$

Now, substituting the valve of *Q* in the *AVC* function we know the minimum average variable cost.

$$AVC = 150 - 20 \times 10 + (10)^2$$

$$= 150 - 200 + 100 = 50$$

Thus, if price falls below Rs. 50 per unit the firm will shut down.

Problem 4. *A firm's total variable cost is given by the following :*

$$TVC = 75Q - 10Q^2 + Q^3$$

Will the firm produce the product if price of the product is Rs. 40 ?

Solution. A firm produces a product if price of the product exceeds its minimum average variable cost

$$\text{AVC} = \frac{TVC}{Q} = \frac{75Q - 10Q^2 + Q^3}{Q}$$

$$= 75 - 10Q + Q^2 \qquad ...(i)$$

AVC is minimised at the output level at which

$$\frac{d\,(AVC)}{dQ} = 0$$

Taking the derivative of *AVC* we have :

$$\frac{d\,(AVC)}{dQ} = -10 + 2Q$$

Therefore, *AVC* will be minimum when

$$-10 + 2Q = 0$$

$$2Q = 10$$

$$Q = \frac{10}{2} = 5$$

Now substituting the value of *Q* in equation for *AVC* we have

$$\text{Minimum } AVC = 75 - 10 \times 5 + 25$$

$$= 100 - 50 = 50$$

Thus, price of Rs. 40 of the product is less than the minimum average variable cost, the firm will not produce the product.

Problem 5. *Given the following short-run cost function of a firm*

$$TC = 1000 + 10Q^2$$

Derive the expression for firm's short-run supply curve.

Solution: A firm's short-run supply curve is firm's short-run marginal cost curve. To obtain marginal cost function we have to obtain the first derivative of total cost function. Thus,

$$MC = \frac{dTC}{dQ} = 2 \times 10Q = 20Q.$$

To get the short-run supply curve of a firm we set price equal to marginal cost. Thus,

$$P = 20Q$$

or $$Q = \frac{P}{20} \quad \text{...(1)}$$

Since the supply curve of a firm is that portion of marginal cost curve that lies above the minimum point of the average variable cost (AVC) curve. AVC is minimised at the output level where its first derivative equals zero. From the given cost function we find that $TFC = 1000$ and TVC is $10Q^2$

$$AVC = \frac{TVC}{Q} = \frac{10Q^2}{Q} = 10Q$$

Setting its derivative equal to zero we have

$$\frac{d(10Q)}{dQ} = 0$$

or $$Q = 0$$

Thus, AVC is minimised when output (Q) is equal to zero. It therefore follows that the entire supply function found in (1) above, namely, $Q = P/20$ or $P = 20Q$ represents the short-run supply curve of the firm.

Problem 6. *A firm operating in a purely competitive environment is faced with a market price of Rs. 250 per unit of the product. The firm's total short-run cost function is*

$$TC = 6000 + 400Q - 20Q^2 + Q^3$$

(i) *Should the firm produce at this price in the short-run?*

(ii) *If the market price is Rs. 300 per unit, what will total profits (losses) be if the firm produces ten units of output? Should the firm produce at this price?*

(iii) *If the market price is greater than Rs. 300, should the firm produce at this price?*

Solution. (*i*) A firm will continue producing in the short run if price of the product of Rs. 250 exceeds the minimum average variable cost. So we have first to find out the minimum average variable cost.

Note that in the given cost function Rs. 6,000 is the total fixed cost because it does not contain any output element (Q). Thus,

$$TVC = 400Q - 20Q^2 + Q^3$$

$$AVC = \frac{TVC}{Q} = \frac{400Q - 20Q^2 + Q^3}{Q}$$

$$AVC = 400 - 20Q + Q^2$$

To determine the level of output at which average variable cost is minimum, we take the first derivative of *AVC* function and set it equal to zero.

$$\frac{d(AVC)}{dQ} = -20 + 2Q$$

$$\text{Setting } \frac{d(AVC)}{dQ} = 0 \text{ we have}$$

$$-20 + 2Q = 0$$

$$2Q = 20$$

$$Q = 10$$

Substituting the value of *Q* in the *AVC* function we have

$$\text{Minimum } AVC = 400 - 20 \times 10 + (10)^2 = 300$$

Since the price of Rs. 250 is less than the minimum average variable cost of Rs. 300, the firm will not produce in the short run because it will not even recover variable costs.

(*ii*) If the market price of the product is Rs. 300, it may continue producing in the short run because it will be covering the variable costs fully, though it will not be recovering any part of the fixed costs and therefore suffering losses.

It should be noted that at price Rs. 300, the firm shall produce 10 units. This can be known by equating this price with marginal cost which is the profit-maximising condition under perfect competition. Thus,

$$MC = \frac{d(TVC)}{dQ} = 400 - 40Q + 3Q^2$$

$$MC = \text{Price} = 300$$

$$400 - 40Q + 3Q^2 = 300$$

$$Q = 10$$

Now $$ATC = \frac{6000 + 400Q - 20Q^2 + Q^3}{Q}$$

$$= \frac{6000}{Q} + 400 - 20Q + Q^2$$

ATC at output 10= 600 + 400 – 200 + 100 = 900

Losses at Price Rs 300 :

$$\pi = TR - TC$$

$$TR = P \,.\, Q - ATC \times Q$$

$$= (300 \times 10) - (900 \times 10)$$

$$= 3000 - 9000 = -6000$$

Thus, the firm will be suffering losses equal to Rs 6,000 at price Rs 300 per unit (that is, losses are equal to the total fixed cost).

Problem 7: *Suppose a firm is operating under perfectly competitive conditions in the market. It faces the following revenue and cost conditions:*

$$TR = 12Q$$
$$TC = 2 + 4Q + Q^2$$

Determine the equilibrium level of output using both the first order and second order conditions of equilibrium. Calculate total profits made.

Solution. Profits are maximised when the firm equates marginal cost with MR and marginal cost is rising. Thus, in order to obtain the equilibrium output we equate $MC = MR$.

$$TR = 12Q$$

$$MR = \frac{dTR}{dQ} = 12$$

$$MC = \frac{dTC}{dQ} = 4 + 2Q$$

In equilibrium,

$$MC = MR$$
$$4 + 2Q = 12$$
$$Q = 4$$

Total profits (π)

$$= TR - TC$$
$$= 12Q - (2 + 4Q + Q^2)$$

Substituting $Q = 4$, we have

$$\pi = (12 \times 4) - 2 - (4 \times 4) - 16$$
$$= 48 - 34 = 14$$

Note that in order to ensure for the fulfillment of second order condition, we have to test whether MC is rising. For this, we take the derivative of MC *i.e.* second derivative of TC

Thus, $$MC = \frac{dTC}{dQ} = 4 + 2Q$$

$$\frac{d^2TC}{dQ^2} = +2$$

The positive sign of the second derivative of TC implies that MC is rising.

Problem 8. *Suppose that revenue and total cost of a firm are given by the equations:*

$$R = 60Q$$

and $C = 10 + 5Q^2$, *(Q = output).*

Using TR-TC approach find what will be the profit-maximising output and total profit of the firm?

Solution :

$$\pi = TR - TC$$
$$= 60Q - 10 - 5Q^2$$

Profits will be maximum at the level of output at which the first derivative of total profit function = 0. Thus,

$$\frac{d\pi}{dQ} = 60 - 10Q$$

Setting $\frac{d\pi}{dQ}$ equal to zero we have

$$60 - 10Q = 0$$
$$10Q = 60$$
$$Q = 6$$

For the second order condition to be fulfilled, the second order derivative of profit function should be negative. Taking the second derivative of the profit function, we have

$$\frac{d^2\pi}{dQ^2} = -10$$

Thus, the second order condition is satisfied.

Substituting $Q = 6$ in the profit function, we have

$$\pi = 60 \times 6 - 10 - 5(6)^2$$
$$= 360 - 10 - 5 \times 36$$
$$= 360 - 10 - 180 = \text{Rs } 170$$

Problem 9. *The following table shows the total cost schedule of a competitive firm. What is total fixed cost of the firm. Using marginal analysis find the profit-maximising level of output if price of the product for the firm is Rs. 8. Calculate the profits at this output level.*

Quantity sold (units)	*TC* (Rs.)
0	5
1	7
2	10
3	12
4	15
5	23
6	33
7	40

Solution. Since the firm incurs a cost of Rs. 5 even at zero level of output, the firm's total fixed cost is Rs. 5. In order to determine the profit-maximising level of output (i.e. equilibrium output) we have to first calculate marginal costs at different levels of output. We do so in the following table.

Quantity sold (units)	*TC* (Rs.)	*MC* (Rs.) ($TC_n - TC_{-1}$)
0	5	
1	7	2
2	10	3
3	12	2
4	15	3
5	23	8
6	33	10
7	45	12
8	58	13

To maximise profits the competitive firm will equate price with the marginal cost. It will be seen from the table that at output level of 5 units, the given price equals marginal cost (Rs. 8). Thus the firm's maximising-profit level of output is 5 units.

$$\text{Profits} = TR - TC = (P.Q) - TC$$
$$= 8 \times 5 - 23 = \text{Rs. } 17$$

Problem 10. *A competitive firm has the following data*

Output, (Q)	*TFC (Rs.)*	*TVC (Rs.)*
0	100	0
1	100	50
2	100	90

3	100	140
4	100	200
5	100	280
6	100	380

(*i*) *If price = Rs. 60, how many units will the firm produce ?*
(*ii*) *What will be level of profits/losses at this level of production ?*
(*iii*) *Will the firm operate in the short run ?* (*iv*) *What happens in the long run ?*

Solution. (*i*) In order to obtain how many units of output, the competitive firm will produce given the price, depends on the marginal cost of production. Note that $MC = \frac{\Delta TVC}{\Delta Q}$ where $\Delta Q = 1$ or, in other words, $MC = TVC_n - TVC_{n\text{-}1}$. We calculate below MC at different levels of output.

Output (Q)	*TVC (Rs.)*	*MC* $TVC_n - TVC_{n-1}$
0	0	–
1	50	50
2	90	40
3	140	50
4	200	60
5	280	80
6	380	100

In order to be in equilibrium a perfectly competitive firm will produce the number of units of output at which price = *MC*. It will be seen from the above table that price of Rs. 60 equals marginal cost when it is producing 4 units of output.

(*ii*) With 4 units of output total cost = *TVC* + *TFC* = 200 + 100 = 300. Total revenue (*TR*) earned by producing 4 units of output will be *P* *Q* = 60 4 = 240. Since total cost (Rs. 300) exceeds total revenue (Rs. 240), the firm will be incurring losses equal to 300 – 240 = 60 rupees through it will be minimising losses.

(*iii*) Since at 4 units of output total revenue of Rs. 240 exceeds the total variable cost (200), the firm will continue to operate in the short run.

(*iv*) In the long run, some firms will leave the industry causing price of the product to rise. The firms that remain in the industry must earn zero economic profits, that is, for them price must be equal to the long-run average cost.

QUESTIONS FOR REVIEW

1. Explain the various features of a perfectly competitive market. How is price of a commodity determined under it?
2. What is meant by firm's equilibrium? Explain the conditions of short-run equilibrium of a firm under perfect competition. Is equality of marginal revenue with marginal cost sufficient condition for equilibrium of the firm?
3. Can a firm under perfect competition operate in the short run when it is making losses? If so, under what conditions?
4. When does a firm working under perfect competition decide to (*a*) shut down in the short run, (*b*) leave the industry in the long run ?
5. Explain the conditions of long-run equilibrium of a firm operating under conditions of perfect competition. A firm operating under perfect competition tends to be of optimum size. Explain. What is the significance of this for the consumer and the community as a whole?
6. "If there is free entry of new firms in the competitive industry, price must fall to the level of minimum long-run average cost." Explain.

7. "In the long-run equilibrium, every firm in a competitive industry earns zero profits. Why do not these firms leave the industry and go elsewhere to make some positive economic profits.?" Examine this statement.
8. A perfectly competitive firm has the following total cost function:

Total output (Units)	*Total cost (Rs)*
0	20
1	30
2	42
3	55
4	69
5	84
6	100
7	117

How much will the firm produce if the price of the product in the market is Rs 14 per unit? How will it change its output if price rises to Rs 16 per unit?

[Hint. Under perfect competition *MR* = Price which is given to be equal to Rs 14 or Rs 16. For equating this *MR* or Price with *MC*, make the third column in the above table calculating *MC* at various levels of output and see at what output level *MC* = Price.]

9. (*a*) Explain the concept of supply curve. How is this relevant only under perfect competition?
   (*b*) Derive a short-run supply curve of the firm operating under perfect competition. Explain that short-run supply curve of a firm always slopes upward.
10. What is meant by economic efficiency? Explain how economic efficiency is achieved under perfect competition.
11. Distinguish between *productive efficiency in resource use and allocative efficiency*. Explain how both are achieved under perfect competition.
12. Explain the concept of economic efficiency using the concepts of consumer surplus and producer surplus. Show how does a perfectly competitive market achieve economic efficiency?

Pricing and Output Decisions Under Monopoly

In a few previous chapters we have discussed the equilibrium of the firm and industry under perfect competition and as a consequence the determination of price and output under it. Monopoly is another important market form which merits detailed study in respect of output equilibrium of the firm as well as how price is determined under it. About seventy years ago it was thought that the existence of monopoly was an exceptional case. But nowadays monopoly form of market structure extensively prevails in capitalist economies of the world, including that of India. Monopolistic market structure prevails in many large-scale manufacturing industries and public utility services. Therefore, the analysis of price and output determination under monopoly has assumed vital importance. Monopoly, as it is now generally understood, is an extreme form of imperfect competition. Perfect competition and pure or absolute monopoly are the two extreme opposite cases and between them the various intermediate market situations lie, which differ from each other in respect of the degree of monopoly. In this chapter we will explain the principles which underlie the price and output equilibrium under monopoly and will compare them with those of perfectly competitive equilibrium.

MONOPOLY: ITS MEANING AND CONDITIONS

What is monopoly ? *Monopoly is said to exist when one firm is the sole producer or seller of a product which has no close substitutes.* Three points are worth noting in this definition. First, there must be a *single producer or seller of a product* if there is to be monopoly. This single producer may be in the form of an individual owner or a single partnership or a joint stock company. If there are many producers producing a product, either perfect competition or monopolistic competition will prevail depending upon whether the product is homogeneous or differentiated. On the other hand, when there are few producers or sellers of a product, oligopoly is said to exist. If then there is to be monopoly, there must be one firm in the field. Even literally monopoly means one seller. 'Mono' means one and 'poly' means seller. Thus monopoly means one seller or one producer.

But to say that monopoly means one seller or producer is not enough. A second condition which is essential for a firm to be called monopolist is that *no close substitutes for the product of that firm should be available.* If there are some other firms which are producing close substitutes for the product in question there will be competition between them. In the presence of this competition a firm cannot be said to have monopoly. Monopoly implies absence of all competition. For instance, there is one firm in India which produces 'Colgate' toothpaste but this firm cannot be called monopolist since there are many other firms which produce close substitutes of Colgate toothpaste such as Binaca, Forhans, etc. These various brands of toothpaste compete with each other in the market and the producer of any one of them cannot be said to have a monopoly. Thus the privilege of being the single seller of a product does not by itself make one a monopolist in the sense of possessing the market power to set the price. As a single seller, he may be a king without a crown.

We can express the second condition of monopoly in terms of cross elasticity of demand also. Cross elasticity of demand shows the degree of change in the demand for a good as a result of a change in the price of another good. Therefore, if there is to be monopoly *the cross elasticity of demand between the product of the monopolist and the product of any other producer must be very small.*

The fact that there is one firm under monopoly means that other firms for one reason or another are prohibited to enter the monopolistic industry. In other words, *strong barriers to the entry of new firms exist* wherever there is one firm having a sole control over the production of a commodity. The barriers which prevent the firms to enter the industry may be economic in nature or else of institutional and artificial nature. In case of monopoly, barriers are so strong that they prevent entry of all firms except the one which is already in the field.

From above it follows that for the monopoly to exist, the following three conditions are necessary

1. There is a single producer or seller of a product.
2. There are no close substitutes for the product.
3. Strong barriers to the entry of new firms in the industry exist.

SOURCES OR CAUSES OF MONOPOLY

There are five major reasons or sources of monopoly. It is because of these reasons that monopolist enjoys a high degree of monopoly power. These sources relate to the factors which prevent the entry of new firms in an industry. Thus, these factors serve as barriers to the entry of new firms. We have explained earlier that strong barriers to the entry of new firms is an essential condition for the existence of monopoly. We explain below some of the important factors that serve as barriers to the entry of new firms and therefore constitute sources of monopoly.

1. Patents or Copyright. First important source of monopoly is that a firm may posses a patent or copyright which prevent others to produce the same product or use a particular production process. Generally, when the firms introduce *new products,* they get patent rights from the Government so that others cannot produce them. These patent rights are granted for a certain period of time. For example, when copying machine was invented, its inventor 'Xerox' company had monopoly in its production based on a patent granted to it by the Government. Likewise, when a new medicine is invented by a medical company, it gets, patent right from the Government so that it retains monopoly power over its production. Patents and copyrights constitute strong barrier to the entry of potential competitors.

2. Control over the Essential Raw Material. Another source of monopoly is a control by a particular firm over an essential raw material or input used in the production of a commodity. For example, before World War II, Aluminium Company of America exercised exclusive control over almost every source of bauxite, which is an essential input for the manufacture of aluminium, had the monopoly power over the production of aluminium in the USA. Likewise, OPEC (Organisation of Petroleum Exporting Countries) exercises monopoly power in the world over the supply of petroleum products from the Middle East countries as it has control over the supply of Crude Oil of these countries.

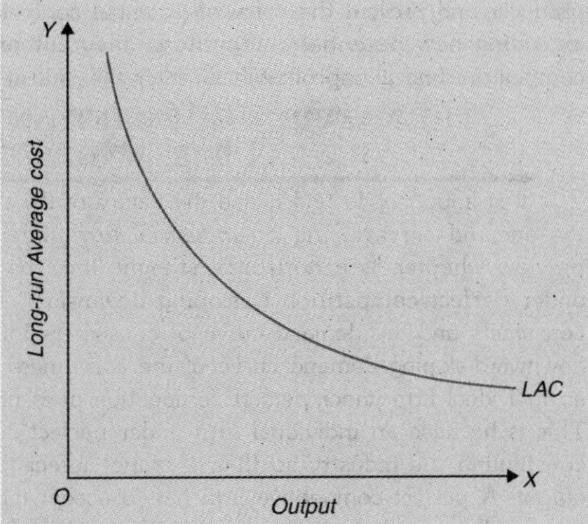

Fig.19.1. *Significant Economies of Scale of a Natural Monopoly*

3. **Grant of Franchise by the Government.** Another important reason for monopoly is the grant of franchise by the Government to a firm. A firm is granted the exclusive legal right to produce a given product or service in a particular area or region. For example in a large part of Delhi Government has granted the exclusive right to TATA-owned Company NDPL to provide or distribute electricity in Delhi. Likewise, Mahanagar Telephone Nigam Ltd. (MTNL) enjoys exclusive legal rights to provide land-line telephone service in Delhi. It may be noted that when a company is given a franchise to produce a particular product or provide a particular service by the Government, the Government keeps with itself the right to regulate its price and quality.

4. **Economies of Scale: Natural Monopoly.** Another important source of monopoly is significant economies of scale over a wide range of initial output. When significant economies of scale are present, *long-run average cost of production goes on falling over a wide range of output and reaches a minimum at an output rate that is large enough for a single firm to meet the entire market demand at a price that is profitable.* In such a situation if more than one firm operate to produce the product each firm must be producing the product at a higher than minimum level cost per unit. In such a situation each firm is inclined to cut price to increase its output and reduce average cost of the product. This leads to price warfare and one who survives in this economic warfare emerges as a monopolist.

When there are significant economies of scale and as a result average cost decreases over a wide range of output (as shown in Fig. 19.1), *natural monopoly is said to exist.* Natural monopolies are regulated by the Government so that they should not charge high prices and exploit the consumers.

5. **Advertising and Brand Loyalties of the Established Firms.** Another important reason that prevents the entry of new competitors in the industry is the strong loyalties to the brands of the established firms and their heavy advertising campaigns to promote their brand. For example, strong loyalty of the consumers for 'Britannia Bread' makes it difficult for the potential competitors to enter. Further, for a long time in the USA the firm producing Coca Cola was well-established firm to produce a famous cold drink and no one dared to enter this field till Pepsi Cola, another giant, came and broke its monopoly. Huge advertising campaigns and customer service programmes are often undertaken to enhance the market power of the

producer and prevent the entry of potential competitors. Besides, if well-established firms are expecting new potential competitors, they cut prices of their products so that potential competitors find it unprofitable to enter the industry.

THE NATURE OF DEMAND AND MARGINAL REVENUE CURVES UNDER MONOPOLY

It is important to understand the nature of the demand curve facing a monopolist. Whereas the demand curve facing *an industrial firm* under perfect competition, as explained in a previous chapter, is a horizontal straight line, the demand curve facing the *whole industry* under perfect competition is sloping downward. This is so because the demand is of the consumers and the demand curve of consumers for a product usually slopes downward. The downward-sloping demand curve of the consumers faces the whole competitive industry. But an individual firm under perfect competition does not face a downward-sloping demand curve. This is because an individual firm under perfect competition is one among numerous firms constituting the industry so that it cannot affect the price by varying its individual level of output. A perfect competitive firm has to accept the ruling price as given and constant for it. It can sell as much as it likes at the ruling price of the product. Therefore, the demand curve facing an individual firm under perfect competition is a horizontal straight line at the level of prevailing price of the product. A perfectly competitive firm is a mere quantity adjuster; it has no influence over price.

But in the case of monopoly one firm constitutes the whole industry. Therefore, the entire demand of the consumers for a product faces the monopolist. Since the demand curve of the consumers for a product slopes downward, the monopolist faces a downward-sloping demand curve. If he wants to increase the sales of his good, he must lower the price. He can raise the price if he is prepared to sacrifice some sales. To put it in another way, monopolist can lower the price by increasing his level of sales and output, and he can raise the price by reducing his level of sales or output. A perfectly competitive firm merely adjusts the quantity of output he has to produce, price being a given and constant datum for it. But the monopolist encounters a more complicated problem. He cannot merely adjust quantity for a given price because each quantity change by it will bring about a change in the price at which product can be sold. Consider Fig. 19.2. *DD* is the demand curve facing a monopolist. At price *OP* the quantity demanded is *OM*, therefore he would be able to sell *OM* quantity at price *OP*. If he wants to sell greater quantity *ON*, then the price would fall to *OL*. If he restricts his quantity to *OG*, the price will rise to *OH*. Thus, every quantity change by him entails a change in price at which the product can be sold. Thus the problem faced by a monopolist is to choose the price-quantity combination which is optimum for him, that is, which yields him maximum possible profits.

Relation between Marginal Revenue and Price

It is important to know the relationship between marginal revenue and price under monopoly which faces a downward-sloping demand curve (*i.e.* average revenue curve). To explain this relationship let us write the expression for marginal revenue :

$$MR = \frac{\Delta TR}{\Delta Q} = \frac{\Delta (PQ)}{\Delta Q}$$

where ΔTR stands for change in total revenue, P for price and Q for quantity of output sold. Now consider Figure 19.3 where *DD* is the demand curve and when price falls from *OP* to *OP′* the quantity demanded increases from *OQ* to *OQ′*. The change in total revenue [ΔTR or $\Delta(P.Q)$] is equal to the gain in revenue from extra unit sold (i.e. $P. \Delta Q$) following the decline in price and the loss in revenue incurred on all the previous intramarginal units due to the fall in price equals $Q.\ \Delta P$. Thus, for small values of ΔP and ΔQ, the change in total revenue can be obtained as under:

$$\Delta TR = P.\Delta Q + Q.\Delta P$$

Dividing both sides by ΔQ we have

$$\frac{\Delta TR}{\Delta Q} = P + Q\ .\ \frac{\Delta P}{\Delta Q}$$

or

$$MR = P + Q\ .\ \frac{\Delta P}{\Delta Q} \qquad \text{... } (i)$$

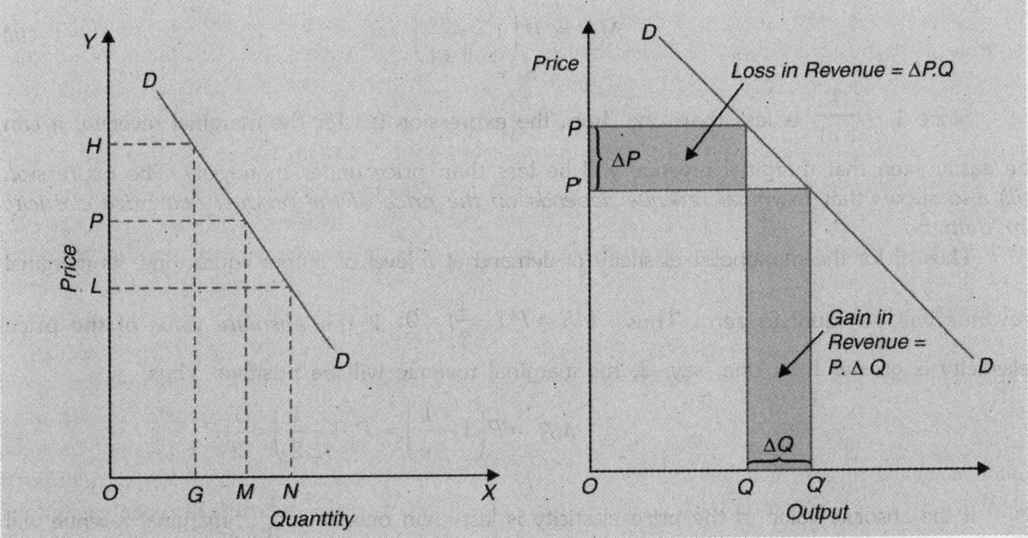

Fig. 19.2. *Demand curve of the monopolist slopes downward.*

Fig. 19.3. *MR is less than price when demand curve Is downward sloping.*

Since demand curve facing the monopolist is downward sloping, ΔP is *negative* whereas ΔQ is positive, the term $Q\frac{\Delta P}{\Delta Q}$ will be negative. It therefore follows from the above expression (*i*) that marginal revenue (*MR*) will be less than price (*P*)

MR, Price and Elasticity of Demand Under Monopoly

By further manipulation of the expression (*i*) for marginal revenue we can explain relationship between marginal revenue, price and elasticity of demand. Let us *multiply and divide* by *P* the *second term* of the right hand side of equation (*i*) above

$$MR = P + \frac{P}{P}\ Q.\ \frac{\Delta P}{\Delta Q}$$

$$= P + P.\frac{Q}{P}.\frac{\Delta P}{\Delta Q} \qquad \text{... } (ii)$$

Recall that price elasticity of demand, $e = \frac{\Delta Q}{\Delta P}.\frac{P}{Q}$

Therefore, $\frac{1}{e} = \frac{\Delta P}{\Delta Q}.\frac{Q}{P}$

Thus we see that the second term $\frac{\Delta P}{\Delta Q} \cdot \frac{Q}{P}$ in the expression (*ii*) for marginal revenue is the reciprocal of the price elasticity of demand. Therefore substituting $\frac{1}{e}$ for $\frac{\Delta P}{\Delta Q} \cdot \frac{Q}{P}$ in expression (*ii*) above we have

$$MR = P + P.\frac{1}{e} = P\left(1 + \frac{1}{e}\right)$$

Since demand curve facing the monopolist has a negative slope, elasticity *e* will be negative. Therefore,

$$MR = P\left(1 - \frac{1}{|e|}\right) \qquad ...(iii)$$

Since $1 - \frac{1}{|e|}$ is less than one, from the expression (*iii*) for the marginal revenue, it can be easily seen that marginal revenue will be less than price under monopoly. The expression (*iii*) also shows that *marginal revenue depends on the price of the product and price elasticity of demand.*

Thus, if for the monopolist elasticity of demand at a level of output equals one, its marginal revenue will be equal to zero. Thus, $MR = P(1 - \frac{1}{1}) = 0$. If the *absolute value* of the price elasticity is greater than one, say, 2, his marginal revenue will be positive. Thus,

$$MR = P\left(1 - \frac{1}{e}\right) = P\left(1 - \frac{1}{2}\right) = \frac{1}{2}P$$

If the absolute value of the price elasticity is less than one, say, $\frac{1}{3}$, marginal revenue will be negative. Thus,

$$MR = P\left(1 - \frac{1}{e}\right) = P\left(1 - \frac{1}{1/3}\right) =$$

$P(1-3) = -2P$

Demand curve facing the monopolist will be his average revenue curve. Thus the average revenue curve of the monopolist slopes downward throughout its length. We have seen above that marginal revenue is less than price when demand curve slopes downward. Therefore, marginal revenue curve will lie below the average revenue curve. When monopolist sells more, the price of his product falls, marginal revenue therefore must be less than price. In Fig. 19.4. *AR* is the average revenue curve of the monopolist and slopes

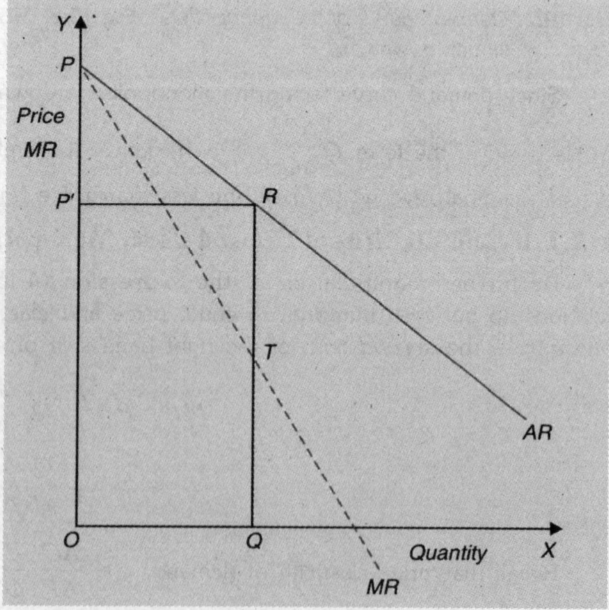

Fig.19.4. *Average and Marginal Revenue Curves of the Monopolist.*

downward, *MR* is the marginal revenue curve and lies below *AR* curve. At quantity *OQ* average revenue (or price) is *QR* or *OP* and marginal revenue is *QT* which is less than *QR*. We have explained that average and marginal revenue at a quantity are related to each other through elasticity of demand and in this connection we derived the following formula: *MR* = Price$\left(\frac{e-1}{e}\right) = P\left(1-\frac{1}{2}\right)$ where *e* stands for absolute value of elasticity.

Since *AR* is the same thing as price

Therefore, $MR = AR\left(1-\frac{1}{e}\right)$

Since the expression $1 - \frac{1}{e}$ will be less than unity, *MR* will be less than price, or price will be greater than *MR*. The extent to which *MR* curve lies below *AR* curve depends upon the value of the fraction $1 - \frac{1}{e}$.

The monopolist has a clearly distinguished demand curve for his product, which is identical with the consumers' demand curve for the product in question. It is also worth mentioning that, unlike oligopolist or a firm under monopolist competition, monopolist does not consider the repercussions of a price change by him upon those of other firms. Monopoly, as defined here, requires that the gap between the monopoly product and those of other firms is so large that changes in the price policies of the monopolist will not affect other firms and will therefore not evoke any readjustments of the price-output policies by these firms.

PRICE-OUTPUT EQUILIBRIUM UNDER MONOPOLY

Monopolist, like a perfectly competitive firm, tries to maximize his profits. Profit maximization assumption on which is based the equilibrium analysis of the perfectly competitive firm is also taken to be the most valid assumption about the behaviour of the monopolist too. The motive of monopolist is the same as the motive of the perfectly competitive firm, that is, both aim at maximizing money profits. We thus do not attribute any more sinister motive to the monopolist. If the results of monopolist's behaviour on the basis of profit maximization motive are different from those of the firm under perfect competition, it is not due to any more sinister motive of monopolist but due to the circumstances and situation in which he is placed. A firm under perfect competition faces a horizontal straight-line demand curve and marginal revenue is equal to average revenue (or price), but a monopolist faces a downward-sloping demand (or *AR*) curve and his marginal revenue curve lies below the average revenue curve. This difference in the demand conditions facing the monopolist and the perfectly competitive firm makes all the difference in the results of their equilibrium, even though both work on the basis of the same profit maximization motive.

Monopoly equilibrium is depicted in Fig. 19.5. The monopolist will go on producing additional units of output as long as marginal revenue exceeds marginal cost. This is because it is profitable to produce an additional unit if it adds more to revenue than to cost. His profits will be maximum and he will attain equilibrium at the level of output at which marginal revenue equals marginal cost. If he stops short of the level of output at which *MR* equals *MC*, he will be unnecessarily foregoing some profits which otherwise he could make. In Fig.19.5 marginal revenue is equal to marginal cost at *OM* level of output. The firm will be earning maximum profits and will therefore be in equilibrium when it is producing and selling *OM* quantity of the product. If he increases his output beyond *OM*, marginal revenue will be less than marginal cost, that is, additional units beyond *OM* will add more to cost than to revenue. Therefore, the monopolist will be incurring a loss on the additional units beyond *OM* and will thus be reducing his total profits by producing more than *OM*. He is therefore in equilibrium at *OM* level of output at which marginal cost equals marginal revenue.

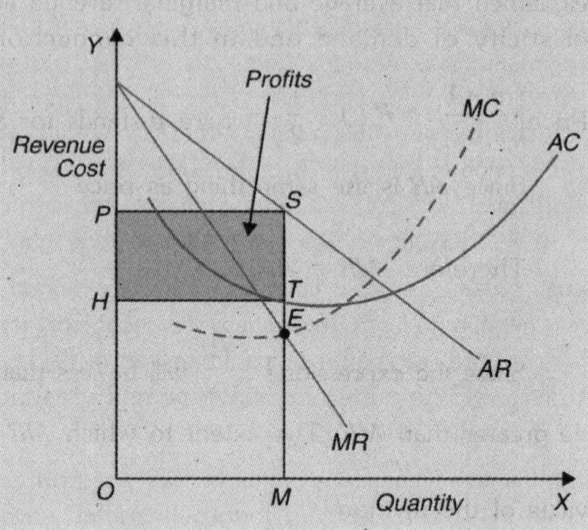

Fig. 19.5. *Firm's Equilibrium Under Monopoly : Mamimization of Profits.*

It will be seen from the *AR* curve in Figure 19.5 that equilibrium output *OM* can be sold at price *MS* or *OP*. It therefore follows that the monopolist will produce output equal to *OM* and fix price of its product equal to *OP*. It will be further observed from Figure 19.5 that at the level of equilibrium output, average cost of production is equal to *MT*. With equilibrium price equal to *OP* or *MS*, the profit per unit is equal to *TS*. Profit per unit *TS* multiplied with output *OM* gives us the total economic profits made by the monopolist being equal to the shaded area *HTSP*.

Price and Marginal Cost Under Monopoly

There is a significant difference between monopoly equilibrium and perfectly competitive equilibrium. The price under perfectly competitive equilibrium is equal to marginal cost, but price exceeds marginal cost under monopoly. This is so because the monopolist, unlike perfectly competitive firm, faces a downward-sloping average revenue curve and his marginal revenue curve lies below average revenue curve. Therefore, in monopoly equilibrium when marginal cost is equal to marginal revenue, it is less than price (or average revenue). From Fig. 19.5 it will be noticed that at equilibrium output *OM*, marginal cost and marginal revenue are equal and both are here equal to *ME*, and are less than price or average revenue which is equal to *MS* = *OP*. It thus follows that price under monopoly is greater than marginal cost. But it is worth pointing out that although price under monopoly will not be equal to marginal cost it will stand in a certain relation to the marginal cost. We know that:

$$\text{Price} = MR\,\frac{e}{e-1}$$

where *MR* stands for marginal revenue and *e* for price elasticity of demand.

But, in equilibrium, *MR* = *MC*

Therefore, $\text{Price} = MC\,\frac{e}{e-1}$.

Since $\frac{e}{e-1}$ will be more than unity for a given value of elasticity, it follows that under monopoly :

$$\text{Price} > MC$$

Furthermore, from the fact that price $= MC\frac{e}{e-1}$ under monopoly it follows that the extent to which price would differ from marginal cost (*MC*) depends upon the value of elasticity on the average revenue curve at the point corresponding to the equilibrium output. The precise extent to which price will be greater than marginal cost (*MC*) will be given by the value of expression $\frac{e}{e-1}$. The smaller the elasticity, the greater the value of $\frac{e}{e-1}$ expression and hence greater the extent to which price would diverge from marginal cost. *Monopoly price is thus the function of marginal cost of production and elasticity of demand.*

Monopoly Equilibrium and Price Elasticity of Demand

Another important feature of monopoly equilibrium is that the *monopolist will never be in equilibrium at a point on the demand curve or average revenue curve at which elasticity of demand is less than one.* In other words, the monopolist will never fix his level of output at which price elasticity of demand or average revenue curve is less than one, provided the marginal cost is positive which is most usually the case. Since marginal cost can never be negative, equality of marginal revenue and marginal cost cannot be achieved where price elasticity of demand is less than one and marginal revenue is therefore negative. We know from the relationship between price elasticity and marginal revenue that whenever elasticity is less than one, marginal revenue is negative. Therefore, no sensible monopolist will produce on that portion of the demand or average revenue curve which gives him negative marginal revenue, that is, which reduces his total revenue, while the production of additional marginal units adds to his total cost.

That the equilibrium of the monopolist will never be at the level of output at which price elasticity of demand on average revenue curve is less than one is illustrated in Figure 19.6. It will be seen from Figure 19.6 (upper panel) that up to *ON* level of output, *MR* is positive and total revenue is increasing as up to this output level, price elasticity of demand on the demand or average revenue curve is greater than one. Equilibrium will always lie where elasticity is greater than one. We know that at the middle point *R* of the straight-line demand or *AR* curve, elasticity is equal to one and corresponding to this unit elasticity point, marginal revenue is equal to zero. Below the middle point *R* on the average revenue curve, elasticity is less than one and marginal revenue is negative. The equilibrium of the monopolist will, therefore, never lie below the middle point of the average revenue curve *AR* as over this range, marginal revenue becomes negative and total revenue (*TR*) decreases as is evident from the falling *TR* curve beyond *ON* output. Thus, given that *MC* is positive, *TR* equilibrium cannot lie below the middle point of the average revenue curve where price elasticity is less than one. It will always lie above the middle point of the average revenue curve where elasticity is greater than one. The precise point on which equilibrium point lies depends, as already explained, upon the position of marginal cost curve and its intersection point with the marginal revenue curve.

Monopoly Equilibrium in Case of Zero Marginal Cost

There are however, some cases where marginal cost is zero, that is, it costs nothing to produce additional units of output. For instance, in case of mineral water spring, cost of production of mineral water is zero. Furthermore, in the very short period when a product is already on hand in excessive amount, it is not relevant to consider cost of production while determining the quantity of output to sell. In these cases where cost of production is either zero or is irrelevant to consider, the monopoly equilibrium will lie at a unit elasticity point on the demand curve. This is because in such cases monopolist has only to decide at which output the total revenue will be maximum. And total revenue is maximum at the output level at which marginal revenue is zero. When marginal cost is zero, the condition of profit maximization, that is, the equality between marginal cost and marginal revenue can be achieved only at the output where the latter is also zero. It will be seen from upper panel of Fig. 19.6 that when marginal cost is zero, monopoly equilibrium will be achieved at *ON* level of output at which *MR* is zero. The price set by him in this situation will be *NR* or *OP*. *ON* quantity of output will yield maximum total revenue since beyond this marginal revenue becomes negative and total revenue will therefore start declining. Since cost of production is zero, the whole revenue will represent profits and because total revenue is maximum at *ON* output, the total profits will be maximum at this output. As at *ON* level of output *MR* is zero and, as already seen, corresponding to zero marginal revenue, elasticity of the demand on the average revenue curve is equal to one. We therefore conclude that when cost of production is zero, monopoly equilibrium will be established at a level where price elasticity of demand is one. If the marginal cost is positive, then, as explained above, monopolist will be in equilibrium at a point where price elasticity on average revenue curve is greater than one.

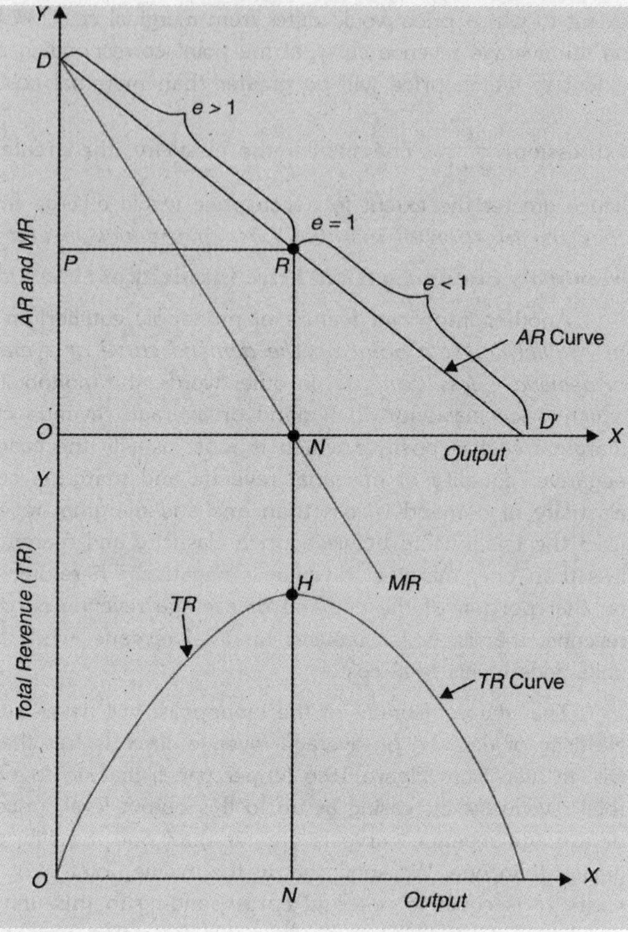

Fig. 19.6. *Monopolist cannot be in equilibrium at a level of output where elasticity of demand is less than one.*

Long-Run Equilibrium under Monopoly

In the long run monopolist would make adjustment in the size of his plant. The long-run average cost curve and its corresponding long-run marginal cost curve portray the alternative plants, *i.e.*, various plant sizes from which the firm has to choose for operation in the long run. The monopolist would choose that plant size which is most appropriate for a particular level of demand. In the short run the monopolist adjusts the level of output while working with a given existing plant. His profit-maximizing output in the short run will be where only the short-run marginal cost curve (*i.e.*, marginal cost curve with the existing plant) is equal marginal revenue. But in the long run he can further increase his profits by adjusting the size of the plant. So in the long run he will be in equilibrium at the level of output where given marginal revenue curve cuts the long-run marginal cost curve. Fixing output level at which marginal revenue is equal to long-run marginal cost shows that the size of the plant has also been adjusted. That plant size has been chosen which is most optimal for a given demand for the product. It should be carefully noted that, in the long run, marginal revenue is also equal to short-run marginal cost curve. But this short-run marginal cost curve is of the plant which has been selected in the long run keeping in view the given demand for the product. Thus while, in the short run, marginal revenue is equal only to the short-run marginal cost of a given existing plant, in the long run marginal revenue is equal to the long-run marginal cost as well as to the short-run marginal cost of that plant which is appropriate for a given demand for the product in the long run. In the long-run equilibrium, therefore, both the long-run marginal cost curve and the short-run marginal cost curve of the relevant plant intersect the marginal revenue curve at the same point.

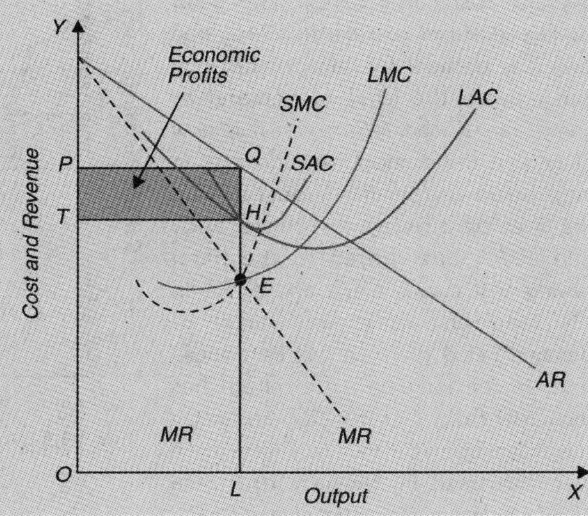

Fig. 19.7. *Long-run Equilibrium under Monopoly*

Further, it is important to note that, in the long run, the *firm will operate at a point on the long-run average cost curve* (*LAC*) at which the short-run average cost is tangent to it. This is because it is only at the tangency point that short-run marginal cost (*SMC*) of the optimal plant equals the long-run marginal cost (*LMC*). Figure 19.7 portrays the long-run equilibrium of the monopolist. He is in equilibrium at *OL* output at which long-run marginal cost curve *LMC* intersects marginal revenue curve *MR*. Given the level of demand as indicated by positions of *AR* and *MR* curves he would choose the plant size whose short-run average and marginal cost curves are *SAC* and *SMC*. He will be charging price equal to *LQ* or *OP* and will be making profits equal to the area of rectangle *THQP*.

It therefore follows that for the monopolist to maximize profits in the long run, the following conditions must be fulfilled

$$MR = LMC = SMC$$

$$SAC = LAC$$

$$P \geq LAC$$

The last condition implies in *long-run monopoly equilibrium* price of the product should be either greater than long-run average cost or at least equal to it. The price cannot fall below long-run average cost because in the long run the monopolist will quit the industry if it is not even able to make normal profits.

Long-Run Equilibrium Adjustment under Monopoly

In order to understand fully the difference between the short-run equilibrium and long-run adjustment under monopoly, it is necessary to show short-run equilibrium and long-run equilibrium in one figure. This is done in Fig. 19.8 which shows that for a given level of demand, the monopolist will be in short-run equilibrium at point *E* or at output OQ_1 if he has plant size SAC_1 at that time. But in the long run he would not be in equilibrium at *E* since in the long run he can also change the plant and will employ that plant which is most appropriate for a given level of demand. In the long run he will be in equilibrium at point *F* where marginal revenue curve cuts his long-run marginal cost curve. But every point of the long-run marginal cost curve corresponds to a point of some short-run marginal cost curve Long-run equilibrium point *F* at which marginal revenue curve cuts long-run marginal cost curve is also the point on short-run marginal cost curve SMC_2 which corresponds to the short-run average cost curve SAC_2. The plant having short-run cost curves SAC_2 and SMC_2 is optimal for him in the long run, given the level of demand as shown by *AR* and *MR* curves. It is now clear that the monopolist who was in equilibrium at *E* in the short run with the given plant having cost curves SAC_1 and SMC_1 has shifted to the plant having cost curves SAC_2 and SMC_2 in his long-run adjustment, level of demand being given. It will be noticed that, in the long run, the output has increased from OQ_1 to OQ_2 and price has fallen from *OP* to *OJ*. Profits have also increased in the long run; area *GHKJ* is larger than the area *TRSP*.

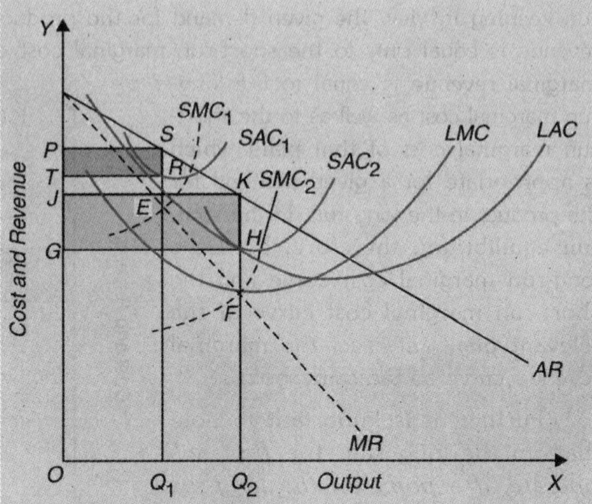

Fig. 19.8. *Shift from a Short-Run to Long-run Equilibrium Position under Monopoly*

In Monopoly Equilibrium Price is Higher and Output Lower than under Perfect Competition.

Another important difference between monopoly equilibrium and perfectly competitive equilibrium is that *under monopoly price is higher and output smaller than under perfect competition,* assuming demand and cost conditions in the two cases are the same. Suppose a number of firms are producing homogeneous products and pure or perfect competition in the sense that no one can individually affect the price exists among them. Price and output will be determined at the level where demand and supply curves intersect each other. Suppose that all the firms constituting the competitive industry combine together so as to form a monopoly. We assume that no economies, internal or external, accrue when the firms combine together so that the cost or supply conditions remain unchanged. Now, the price and output under monopoly are determined by the equality between marginal cost and marginal revenue.

Price-output equilibrium under perfect competition and monopoly are graphically shown in a single diagram (Fig.19.9). Curves *DD* and *SS* are respectively demand and supply curves of the perfectly competitive industry. It should be noted that the supply curve *SS* of a product under perfect competition is obtained by horizontal summation (ΣMC) of the marginal cost curves of all the firms in the competitive industry. The two curves intersect each other at point *E* and as a result price *QE* or OP_1 and output *OQ* are determined under perfect competition. The marginal revenue curve *MR* is drawn corresponding to the demand curve *DD*. The supply curve *SS* of the perfectly competitive industry which is obtained by summing up laterally the marginal cost curves of the firms in it will now constitute the marginal cost curve under monopoly. It will be seen from Fig. 19.9 that the marginal revenue curve *MR* cuts the marginal cost curve *SS* (*i.e.* ΣMC) of the monopolist at point *B* and as a consequence monopoly price OP_2 and monopoly output *OM* are determined. It is thus clear that if cost conditions remain unchanged, the merger of firms to form monopoly has resulted in a higher price and a lower output of the product. As a result of monopoly coming into existence price has risen from OP_1 to OP_2 and output has fallen from *OQ* to *OM*. Monopolist thus restricts output to raise price.

If the price elasticity of demand for his product changes to – 4, how will he change his price?

Solution :

)

$$TC = 10 + 5Q$$

$$MC = \frac{\Delta TC}{\Delta Q} = 5 \quad ...(1)$$

The relationship between MR, price and price elasticity of demand (e) is

$$MR = P\left(1+\frac{1}{e}\right)$$

Given that price elasticity of demand is – 2.

$$MR = P\left(1+\frac{1}{-2}\right) = P\left(1-\frac{1}{2}\right)$$

$$MR = \frac{1}{2}P \quad ...(2)$$

In equilibrium,

$$MR = MC$$

$$\frac{1}{2}P = 5$$

$$P = 5 \times 2 = \text{Rs } 10$$

Given that $e = -4$

$$MR = P\left(1+\frac{1}{-4}\right) = P\left(1-\frac{1}{4}\right) = \frac{3}{4}P$$

In equilibrium

$$MR = MC$$

$$\frac{3}{4}P = 5$$

$$P = 5 \times \frac{4}{3} = 6.67$$

Thus, with the increase in absolute value of price elasticity of demand, monopolist will reduce the price of his product.

Problem 4. *Suppose price elasticity of demand for the product of a monopolist is – 2.0. Show that price fixed by him will be twice the marginal cost of production.*

Solution. In price-output equilibrium of the monopolist

$$MR = MC$$

Since $MR = P\left(1-\frac{1}{|e|}\right)$

$$MC = P\left(1-\frac{1}{|e|}\right)$$

If $e = -2.0$

$$MC = P\left(1-\frac{1}{2}\right) = \frac{1}{2}P$$

Now, a pertinent question is whether cost conditions are likely to remain the same when a number of firms combine to become a monopoly ? In other words, whether some extra economies will not accrue when the monopoly comes into existence and works on a larger scale than that of a large number of separate firms under perfect competition. There are two opinions on this issue.

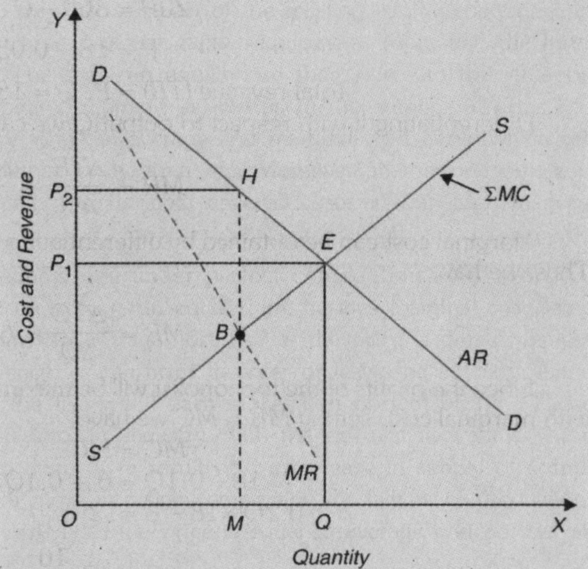

Fig. 19.9. *Under monopoly, price is higher and output smaller than under perfect competition.*

One view is that monopolist can introduce various economies such as greater specialization in the work by bringing about suitable lateral and vertical integration, organization of sales on a large scale, buying raw materials and machinery on a big order, getting cheap credit, discovering and introducing new methods of production, and undertaking various measures which are generally associated with rationalization. These economies, it is held, will lower the cost of production of the monopolist with the result that the marginal cost cure (SS) in Fig. 19.9 will shift to a downward position when monopoly comes into existence. If these economies are good enough so that there is substantial downward fall in the cost curve, the monopoly price will be lower than the competitive price OP_1 or QE and monopoly output will be larger than the competitive output.

But in view of Mrs. Joan Robinson, "perfect competition would bring about all the economies which monopoly could introduce".[1] She holds therefore that the cost curve will not shift downward as a result of the establishment of monopoly in place of the large number of firms working perfect competition. Thus, according to her, monopoly price is always higher and monopoly output always smaller than that under perfect competition.

NUMERICAL PROBLEMS ON MONOPOLY EQUILBRIUM

Problem 1. *Let us illustrate the monopoly equilibrium with a numerical example. Suppose for a monopolist the following demand and total cost function are given. Find out how much he will produce and what price he will charge*

$$Q = 360 - 20P \text{ (demand function)}$$

$$TC = 6Q + 0.05Q^2 \text{ (cost function)}$$

Solution : In order to find the profit-maximizing solution we have to derive the marginal revenue and marginal cost from the demand and cost equations given above. In order to find out the marginal revenue we have to first obtain the total revenue function.

Thus we first derive the inverse demand function as under:

$$Q = 360 - 20P$$

1. See her *Economics of Imperfect Competition*, p.168

$$20P = 360 - Q$$

$$P = 18 - 0.05\,Q \quad \text{......}(i)$$

$$\text{Total revenue } (TR) = P.\,Q = 18Q - 0.05Q^2$$

Differentiating it with respect to output Q we can get MR. Thus

$$MR = \frac{\Delta TR}{\Delta Q} = \frac{\Delta(P.Q)}{\Delta Q} = 18 - 0.1Q \quad \text{...}(ii)$$

Marginal cost can be obtained by differentiating the total function ($TC = 6Q + 0.05Q^2$). Thus, we have

$$MR = \frac{\Delta TC}{\Delta Q} = 6 + 0.1Q$$

Since the profits of the monopolist will be maximized when he equates marginal revenue with marginal cost, setting $MR = MC$ we have

$$MC = MC$$

$$18 - 0.1Q = 6 + 0.1Q$$

$$0.2Q = 18 - 6 = 12$$

$$Q = 12.\frac{10}{2} = 60$$

To find out price we substitute the value of output Q in the demand function (i) above we have

$$P = 18 - 0.05Q$$

$$= 18 - 0.05 \times 60 = 18 - 3 = 15$$

To obtain total profits we calculate total revenue and total cost

$$TR = P.Q = 15 \times 60 = 900$$

$$TC = 6Q + 0.05Q^2 = 6 \times 60 + 0.05\,(60)^2$$

$$= 360 + \frac{5}{100} \times 3600 = 540$$

$$\text{Profit} = TR - TC = 900 - 540 = 360$$

Thus, output (Q) = 60; price (P) = Rs. 15 and Profits = Rs. 360.

Problem 2. *A monopolist firm producing and supplying cooking gas to a city faces the following demand function*

$$Q = 400 - 20P$$

The firm has the following cost function

$$TC = 5Q + \frac{Q^2}{50}$$

Determine the quantity of the cooking gas he will produce and price he will charge to maximize profits. What will be amount of profits made by him ?

Solution.

[Note that the given cost function does not contain the fixed cost component as all terms in it contain the element of output (Q). Therefore, this represents the long-run cost function as in the long-run all factors are variable and there are no fixed costs.]

It should be carefully noted that for the problem of profit maximization we are required to obtain total revenue function, from which marginal revenue can be derived. In order to obtain *TR* and *MR inverse demand function* is required, that is, demand expressed in terms of "*Price as a function of quantity*". Thus,

$$Q = 400 - 20P$$

$$20P = 400 - Q$$

$$P = \frac{400}{20} - \frac{Q}{20}$$

Thus, inverse demand function is : $P = 20 - \frac{Q}{20}$

Multiplying both sides by Q

$$PQ = TR = 20Q - \frac{Q^2}{20}$$

$$MR = \frac{d(TR)}{dQ} = 20 - \frac{Q}{10}$$

The given cost function is

$$TC = 5Q + \frac{Q^2}{50}$$

$$MC = \frac{d(TC)}{dQ} = 5 + \frac{Q}{25}$$

For profit maximisation

$$MR = MC$$

$$20 - \frac{Q}{10} = 5 + \frac{Q}{25}$$

$$\frac{Q}{25} + \frac{Q}{10} = 20 - 5 = 15$$

$$\frac{7Q}{50} = 15$$

$$7Q = 50 \times 15 = 750$$

Profit maximising output $Q^* = \frac{750}{7} = 107$ (rounded off)

To solve for P we substitute the value of Q^* in the demand function equation (i) above.

$$P = 20 - \frac{Q}{20}$$

$$P = 20 - \frac{107}{20} = 20 - 5.35 = 14.65$$

Thus, profit maximising price is Rs 14.65.

Profits

$$\pi = TR - TC$$

$$TR = 14.65 \times 107 = 1568$$

$$TC = 5Q + \frac{Q^2}{50} = 5 \times 107 + \frac{(107)^2}{50} = 764$$

$$\pi = 1568 - 764 = 804.$$

Problem 3. *A monopolist has the following total cost function*

$$TC = 10 + 5Q$$

(1) *If the price elasticity of demand for his product is – 2, find out wh* *fix for his product.*

Now, a pertinent question is whether cost conditions are likely to remain the same when a number of firms combine to become a monopoly ? In other words, whether some extra economies will not accrue when the monopoly comes into existence and works on a larger scale than that of a large number of separate firms under perfect competition. There are two opinions on this issue.

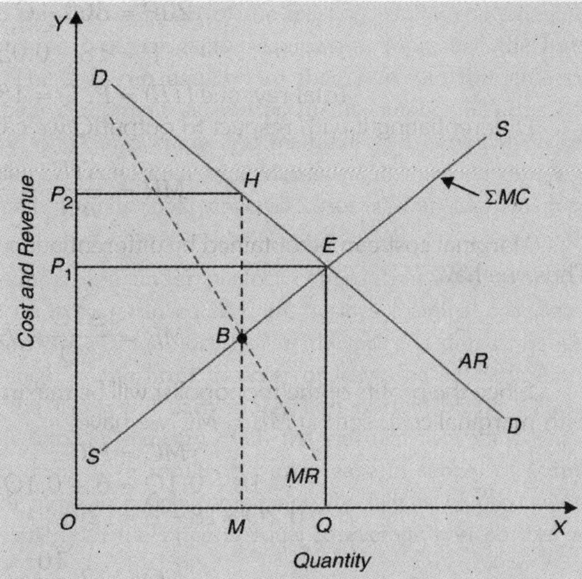

Fig. 19.9. *Under monopoly, price is higher and output smaller than under perfect competition.*

One view is that monopolist can introduce various economies such as greater specialization in the work by bringing about suitable lateral and vertical integration, organization of sales on a large scale, buying raw materials and machinery on a big order, getting cheap credit, discovering and introducing new methods of production, and undertaking various measures which are generally associated with rationalization. These economies, it is held, will lower the cost of production of the monopolist with the result that the marginal cost cure (*SS*) in Fig. 19.9 will shift to a downward position when monopoly comes into existence. If these economies are good enough so that there is substantial downward fall in the cost curve, the monopoly price will be lower than the competitive price OP_1 or *QE* and monopoly output will be larger than the competitive output.

But in view of Mrs. Joan Robinson, "perfect competition would bring about all the economies which monopoly could introduce".[1] She holds therefore that the cost curve will not shift downward as a result of the establishment of monopoly in place of the large number of firms working perfect competition. Thus, according to her, monopoly price is always higher and monopoly output always smaller than that under perfect competition.

NUMERICAL PROBLEMS ON MONOPOLY EQUILBRIUM

Problem 1. *Let us illustrate the monopoly equilibrium with a numerical example. Suppose for a monopolist the following demand and total cost function are given. Find out how much he will produce and what price he will charge*

$$Q = 360 - 20P \text{ (demand function)}$$

$$TC = 6Q + 0.05Q^2 \text{ (cost function)}$$

Solution : In order to find the profit-maximizing solution we have to derive the marginal revenue and marginal cost from the demand and cost equations given above. In order to find out the marginal revenue we have to first obtain the total revenue function.

Thus we first derive the inverse demand function as under:

$$Q = 360 - 20P$$

1. See her *Economics of Imperfect Competition*, p.168

$$20P = 360 - Q$$

$$P = 18 - 0.05\,Q \qquad \text{......}(i)$$

$$\text{Total revenue } (TR) = P.\,Q = 18Q - 0.05Q^2$$

Differentiating it with respect to output Q we can get MR. Thus

$$MR = \frac{\Delta TR}{\Delta Q} = \frac{\Delta(P.Q)}{\Delta Q} = 18 - 0.1Q \qquad \text{...}(ii)$$

Marginal cost can be obtained by differentiating the total function ($TC = 6Q + 0.05Q^2$). Thus, we have

$$MR = \frac{\Delta TC}{\Delta Q} = 6 + 0.1Q$$

Since the profits of the monopolist will be maximized when he equates marginal revenue with marginal cost, setting $MR = MC$ we have

$$MC = MC$$

$$18 - 0.1Q = 6 + 0.1Q$$

$$0.2Q = 18 - 6 = 12$$

$$Q = 12.\frac{10}{2} = 60$$

To find out price we substitute the value of output Q in the demand function (i) above we have

$$P = 18 - 0.05Q$$

$$= 18 - 0.05 \times 60 = 18 - 3 = 15$$

To obtain total profits we calculate total revenue and total cost

$$TR = P.Q = 15 \times 60 = 900$$

$$TC = 6Q + 0.05Q^2 = 6 \times 60 + 0.05\,(60)^2$$

$$= 360 + \frac{5}{100} \times 3600 = 540$$

$$\text{Profit} = TR - TC = 900 - 540 = 360$$

Thus, output (Q) = 60; price (P) = Rs. 15 and Profits = Rs. 360.

Problem 2. *A monopolist firm producing and supplying cooking gas to a city faces the following demand function*

$$Q = 400 - 20P$$

The firm has the following cost function

$$TC = 5Q + \frac{Q^2}{50}$$

Determine the quantity of the cooking gas he will produce and price he will charge to maximize profits. What will be amount of profits made by him ?

Solution.

[Note that the given cost function does not contain the fixed cost component as all terms in it contain the element of output (Q). Therefore, this represents the long-run cost function as in the long-run all factors are variable and there are no fixed costs.]

It should be carefully noted that for the problem of profit maximization we are required to obtain total revenue function, from which marginal revenue can be derived. In order to obtain TR and MR *inverse demand function* is required, that is, demand expressed in terms of "*Price as a function of quantity*". Thus,

$$Q = 400 - 20P$$

$$20P = 400 - Q$$

$$P = \frac{400}{20} - \frac{Q}{20}$$

Thus, inverse demand function is :$P = 20 - \frac{Q}{20}$ ...(*i*)

Multiplying both sides by Q

$$PQ = TR = 20Q - \frac{Q^2}{20}$$

$$MR = \frac{d(TR)}{dQ} = 20 - \frac{Q}{10} \quad \text{...(ii)}$$

The given cost function is

$$TC = 5Q + \frac{Q^2}{50}$$

$$MC = \frac{d(TC)}{dQ} = 5 + \frac{Q}{25} \quad \text{...(iii)}$$

For profit maximisation

$$MR = MC$$

$$20 - \frac{Q}{10} = 5 + \frac{Q}{25}$$

$$\frac{Q}{25} + \frac{Q}{10} = 20 - 5 = 15$$

$$\frac{7Q}{50} = 15$$

$$7Q = 50 \times 15 = 750$$

Profit maximising output $Q^* = \frac{750}{7} = 107$ (rounded off)

To solve for P we substitute the value of Q^* in the demand function equation (*i*) above.

$$P = 20 - \frac{Q}{20}$$

$$P = 20 - \frac{107}{20} = 20 - 5.35 = 14.65$$

Thus, profit maximising price is Rs 14.65.

Profits

$$\pi = TR - TC$$

$$TR = 14.65 \times 107 = 1568$$

$$TC = 5Q + \frac{Q^2}{50} = 5 \times 107 + \frac{(107)^2}{50} = 764$$

$$\pi = 1568 - 764 = 804.$$

Problem 3. *A monopolist has the following total cost function*

$$TC = 10 + 5Q$$

(1) If the price elasticity of demand for his product is – 2, find out what price he will fix for his product.

(2) *If the price elasticity of demand for his product changes to – 4, how will he change his price?*

Solution :

(1)
$$TC = 10 + 5Q$$
$$MC = \frac{\Delta TC}{\Delta Q} = 5 \qquad ...(1)$$

The relationship between MR, price and price elasticity of demand (e) is

$$MR = P\left(1+\frac{1}{e}\right)$$

Given that price elasticity of demand is – 2.

$$MR = P\left(1+\frac{1}{-2}\right) = P\left(1-\frac{1}{2}\right)$$
$$MR = \frac{1}{2}P \qquad ...(2)$$

In equilibrium,

$$MR = MC$$
$$\frac{1}{2}P = 5$$
$$P = 5 \times 2 = \text{Rs } 10$$

Given that $e = -4$

$$MR = P\left(1+\frac{1}{-4}\right) = P\left(1-\frac{1}{4}\right) = \frac{3}{4}P$$

In equilibrium

$$MR = MC$$
$$\frac{3}{4}P = 5$$
$$P = 5 \times \frac{4}{3} = 6.67$$

Thus, with the increase in absolute value of price elasticity of demand, monopolist will reduce the price of his product.

Problem 4. *Suppose price elasticity of demand for the product of a monopolist is – 2.0. Show that price fixed by him will be twice the marginal cost of production.*

Solution. In price-output equilibrium of the monopolist

$$MR = MC$$

Since
$$MR = P\left(1-\frac{1}{|e|}\right)$$
$$MC = P\left(1-\frac{1}{|e|}\right)$$

If $e = -2.0$

$$MC = P\left(1-\frac{1}{2}\right) = \frac{1}{2}P$$

or $$P = 2MC.$$

Problem 5. *Given the following linear demand and cost functions, show that monopolist will produce half the output under perfect competition*

$$Q = 300 - 2P \quad \text{(Linear demand function)}$$

$$TC = 150 + 10Q$$

Solution : $$TC = 150 + 10Q$$

$$MC = \frac{\Delta TC}{\Delta Q} = 10 \quad ...(i)$$

Now, the given linear demand function is

$$Q = 300 - 2P$$

$$2P = 300 - Q$$

$$P = 150 - 0.5Q \quad ...(ii)$$

$$TR = PQ = 150Q - 0.5Q^2$$

$$MR = \frac{\Delta(PQ)}{\Delta Q} = 150 - Q \quad ...(iii)$$

Output under perfect competition is determined where $MC = P$

Thus, under perfect competition

$$10 = 150 - 0.5Q$$

$$0.5Q = 150 - 10 = 140$$

Hence, $$Q_{pc} = 280 \quad ...(iv)$$

In equilibrium under monopoly,

$$MR = MC$$

From (*iii*) we know $MR = 150 - Q$ and from (*i*) we know that $MC = 10$

Thus, in equilibrium under monopoly

$$150 - Q = 10$$

$$Q = 150 - 10 = 140$$

Thus, $$Q_m = 140 \quad ...(v)$$

Comparing (*iv*) and (*v*) we find that output under monopoly is half of that produced under perfect competition.

ABSENCE OF SUPPLY CURVE UNDER MONOPOLY

An important feature of the monopoly equilibrium is that unlike a competitive firm, the *monopolist does not have the supply curve.* It is worthnoting that the supply curve shows how much output a firm will produce at various *given prices* of a product. The supply curve of a product by a firm traces out the *unique price-output relationship*, that is, against a given price there is a particular amount of output which the firm will produce and sell in the market. As explained in a previous chapter, the concept of supply curve is relevant only when the firm exercises no control over the price of the product and takes it given. Therefore, it is perfectly competitive firm which is a price taker and demand curve facing it is a horizontal straight line that unique price-output relationship is established. For a perfectly competitive firm, marginal revenue (*MR*) equals price and therefore to maximize profits, the firm equates the new higher price (*i.e.* new *MR*) with its marginal cost at higher level of output. In this way under perfect competition, marginal cost curve becomes the supply curve of the firm.

But for a monopoly firm demand curve slopes downward and marginal revenue (*MR*) curve lies below it. Therefore, a monopolist in order to maximize profits does not equate price with marginal cost; instead he equates marginal revenue with marginal cost. As a result, shifts in demand causing changes in price do not trace out a unique price-output series as happens in case of a perfectly competitive firm. In fact, under monopoly shifts in demand can lead to a change in price with no change in output or a change in output with no change in price or they can lead to changes in both price and output. This renders the concept of supply curve inapplicable and irrelevant under conditions of monopoly.

That, under monopoly, we do not get a series of unique price-output relationship or supply curve of a product is illustrated in Figure 19.10. Suppose the demand curve is initially D_1 corresponding to which MR_1 is the marginal revenue curve. Given the marginal cost curve *MC*, monopolist is in equilibrium at *OM* level of output and charging price OP_1. Now, suppose that demand curve shifts to the position D_2 corresponding to which MR_2 is the marginal revenue curve. It will be seen from Fig. 19.10 that the new marginal revenue curve MR_2 also intersects the given marginal cost curve *MC* at the same level of output *OM* as before the shift in the demand curve but the price has risen to OP_2. Thus we see that, under monopoly, a shift in demand leads to the production and *supply of the same output at two different prices.* This clearly shows that there is no unique price-output relationship which is essential for the concept of supply curve to be applicable.

Figure 19.11 illustrates another special case where shift in demand leads to the *different levels of output being supplied at the same price.* Initially, with D_1 and MR_1 as the demand

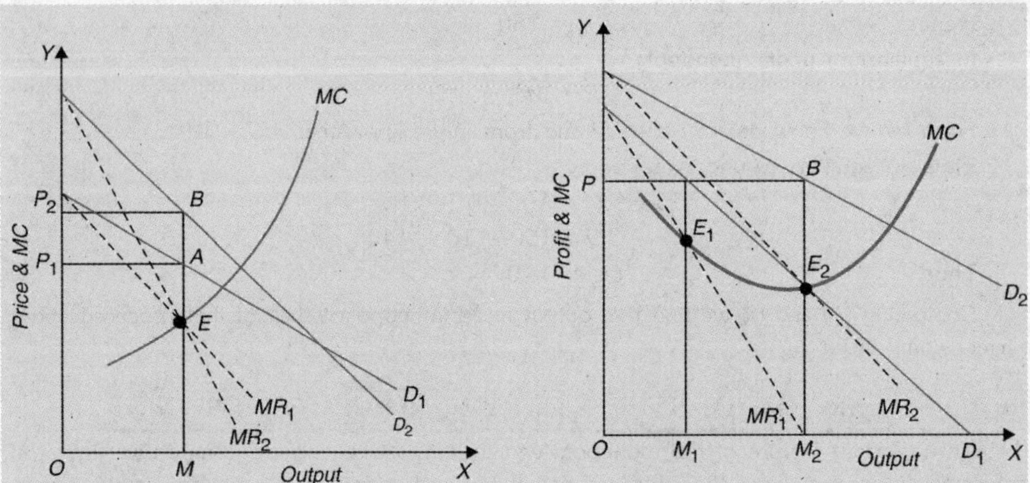

Fig. 19.10. *Under monopoly a shift in demand leading to the same output being supplied at two different prices.*

Fig. 19.11. *Under monopoly a shift in demand leading to a change in output supplied at the same price.*

and marginal revenue curves respectively, the monopolist maximizes his profits by producing OM_1 and charging price *OP*. The shift in demand curve to D_2 and the marginal revenue curve to MR_2, the marginal cost curve *MC* cuts the new MR_2 curve at E_2 and it will be observed from Figure 19.11 that in the new equilibrium, the monopolist produces higher quantity OM_2 at the same price *OP*. This again shows that under monopoly there is no any *specific* quantity of the product supplied at a price.

To sum up, under monopoly, there is no supply curve associating unique output with a price. Shift in demand may lead to either change in price with the same output being produced and supplied or it may lead to the change in output with same price. However, usually the shift in demand would lead to the changes in both output and price. *How price and output will change as a result of shift in demand depends not only on the marginal cost curve but also on the price elasticity of demand.* The important thing to remember is that in sharp contrast to the case of a perfectly competitive firm, under monopoly marginal cost curve does not serve as the supply curve of the firm and further that there is no supply curve under monopoly depicting unique price-output relationship.

MONOPOLY, RESOURCE ALLOCATION AND SOCIAL WELFARE

Monopoly is often criticized that it causes misallocation of resources or economic inefficiency in resource allocation. *By economic efficiency we mean that resource allocation to the production of a good is such that it maximizes social welfare, that is, the satisfaction of the consumers.* Thus, whereas under perfect competition allocation of resources is pareto optimum and therefore social welfare is maximum, under monopoly resources are misallocated causing loss of social welfare.

As seen above, when a product is produced and sold under conditions of monopoly, the monopolist gains at the expense of consumers, who have to pay a price higher than the marginal cost of production. This results in loss of consumers' welfare. Which is greater ? Monopolist's gain or consumers' loss and how total social welfare is affected by a monopoly. The two methods are used by economists to measure the loss of welfare or degree of economic inefficiency caused by monopoly. One method to evaluate the loss in welfare is the adoption of partial equilibrium approach by using the concepts of consumer surplus and producer surplus. The second method to evaluating the loss of welfare caused by monopoly is the use of general equilibrium approach and employing the technique of production possibility curve and social indifference curves. We explain here the first method.

1. Net Welfare Loss under Monopoly: Loss of Consumer Surplus and Dead-Weight Loss Approach

To measure welfare gain or loss economists often use the concept of consumer's surplus. Consumer's surplus, it will be recalled, is the surplus of price which consumers are prepared to pay for a commodity rather than go without it over and above what they actually pay for it. The net loss in consumer's welfare, also called *dead weight loss* of welfare, due to monopoly, can be shown through Figure 19.12 where *TD* is the demand curve for the monopolist's product, *MR* is the corresponding marginal revenue curve. It is assumed that the industry is a constant cost industry so that average cost (*AC*) remains the same as output is increased and marginal cost is equal to it.

Under perfect competition, industry will be in equilibrium with *ON* output being produced and price OP_c or *NA* of the product is determined by the forces of demand for and supply of the product and is equal to marginal cost of production. It will be seen from Figure 19.12 that under perfect competition, price will be *NA* (or OP_c) which is equal to marginal cost at *ON* level of output. It will be seen from Figure 19.12 with OP_c or *NA* as the market price, buyers obtain consumers' surplus equal to area ATP_c. This is because total utility which they get by consuming *ON* output will be equal to the area *OTAN* (*i.e.*, the area under the demand curve) and the total price they actually pay for it is measured by OP_cAN.

Now, the monopolist would produce output *OM* of the product as this will maximize his profits (It will be seen from Fig. 19.12, that marginal revenue (*MR*) and marginal cost of the monopolist are equal at output level *OM*). The monopolist will set price OP_m or *ML* of the product. With output equal to *OM* and price OP_m, the monopolist gain is P_mLEP_c. On the other hand, with the rise in price to OP_m and fall in output to *OM* under monopoly, the consumer surplus has been reduced to LTP_m. That is, under monopoly consumers have suffered a loss of consumer surplus equal to the area ALP_mP_c. Out of the total loss of consumer surplus monopoly has gained profits equal to the area P_mLEP_c. Thus whereas consumers lose, the producers gain due to monopoly. In this way, there has been redistribution of income in favour of the monopolist. But the consumers' loss of consumer surplus is more than the gain of profits by the monopolist. It will be seen there is net loss of consumer's welfare equal to the area of triangle *LEA*. Monopoly has caused this net welfare loss because it has reduced output from *ON* to *OM*. Between *OM* and *ON* outputs, consumers are prepared to pay higher price as indicated by portion of the demand or average curve in this region than the marginal cost which the society has to incur on producing units of output between *OM* and *ON*.

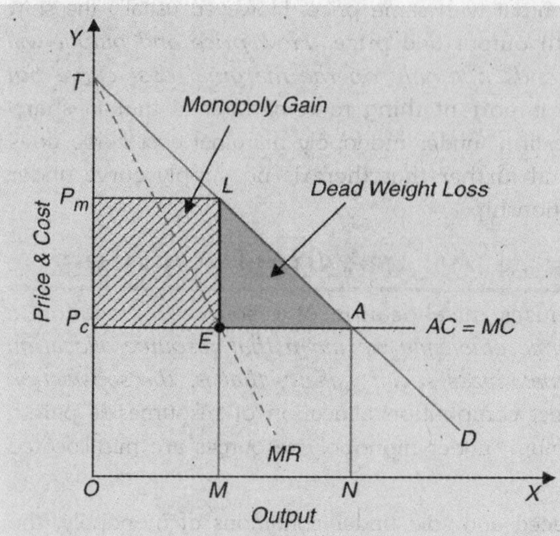

Fig. 19.12. *Welfare Loss due to Monopoly under Constant Cost Conditions.*

With lower production of the product by the monopolist, relatively less resources will be allocated to its production. For optimum allocation of resources or for being economically efficient (*i.e.* achieving pareto optimality) *ON* amount of the product, at which marginal cost equals price, should have been produced and resources allocated accordingly. To conclude, monopoly causes misallocation of resources and net loss of welfare (which is also known as *dead weight loss*) by not producing the level of output of the commodity at which price equals marginal cost of production. It should be noted that in addition to causing net welfare loss monopoly has also caused *transfer of income* away from the consumers. The monetary gain of the monopolist equal to the area P_mLEP_c represents this transfer of income to the monopolist producer; the monopolist has gained at the expense of consumers. Thus monopoly adversely affects income distribution in an economy. However, it is worth mentioning that in sharp contrast to this adverse distribution effect under which one's gain is other's loss, the net welfare loss measured by the area *AEL* represents a loss for which no one has gained. That is why it is often referred to as *dead-weight loss*. This is due to the economic inefficiency or misallocation of resources caused by monopoly.

Net Loss of Welfare under Monopoly in Case of Increasing Marginal Cost

In our above analysis of net welfare loss due to reduction in output and hike in the price by a monopolist as compared to the perfectly competitive equilibrium, it has been assumed that marginal cost curve is a horizontal straight line. When marginal cost curve is a horizontal straight line, the loss in welfare occurs only in consumer surplus. But when marginal cost curve is rising, the loss in welfare due to reduction in output by the monopolist will occur not only in reduction in consumer surplus but also in producer surplus. Producer surplus, it will be recalled, is the total revenue earned over and over all the opportunity costs (explicit and implicit) represented by the marginal cost curve. It may be noted that *maximum social welfare or economic efficiency is achieved when the sum of consumer surplus and producer surplus is the maximum.* In a perfectly competitive equilibrium where quantity demanded equals quantity supplied or price equals marginal cost, the sum of consumer surplus and producer surplus is maximum and therefore perfect competition ensures maxi-mum social welfare or economic efficiency. But to be in equilibrium and maximize profits monopolist does not equate price with marginal cost. Instead, he equates marginal revenue with marginal cost and therefore reduces output and raises price and thereby causes loss of welfare. Loss in welfare as measured by the reduction in the sum of consumer surplus and producer surplus is illustrated in Figure 19.13. It will be seen that, under perfect competition, equilibrium will be at point *D* where price is equal to marginal cost (*MC*) and *OQ* output is being produced and P_c price is being charged.

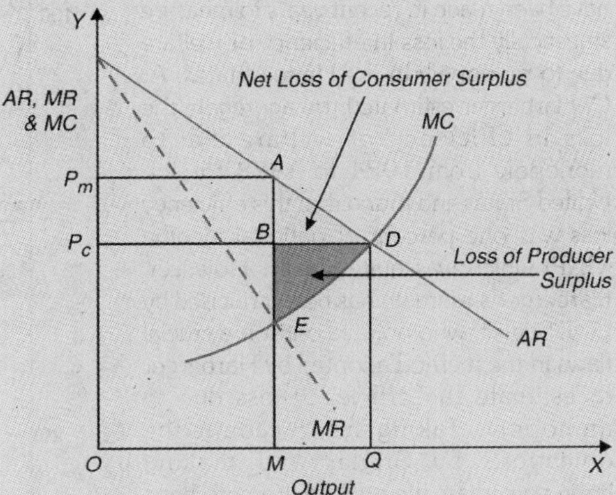

Fig. 19.13. *Dead-weight loss in welfare due to reduction in output and hike in price by the monopolist in case of increasing marginal cost*

Now, if monopoly comes into existence, the monopolist-producer will maximize profits by producing lower output *OM* and will charge higher price P_m. It will be observed that the loss in consumer surplus suffered by the buyers is equal to area P_cDAP_m. Due to the higher price charged by the monopolist, his gain in profits or producer surplus equals the rectangle P_cBAP_m. (It may be noted that this gain in producer surplus by the monopolist occurs at the expense of consumers who suffer a loss in consumer surplus and is equal to the price differential $P_m - P_c$ or *AB* times the monopoly output *OM*). Thus the gain in producer surplus represented by the area P_cBAP_m is just a transfer of income from the consumers to the monopolist. Net loss of consumer surplus or welfare is therefore the area of the triangle *ABD*.

However, in the situation depicted in Figure 19.13 where marginal cost is rising, apart from the net loss of consumer surplus, there is also a loss of producer surplus due to reduction in output by *QM* amount under monopoly. It will be seen from Figure 19.13 that under perfect competition with price equal to OP_c or *QD*, the extra revenue or producer surplus earned over and above the marginal costs in the region of *MQ* output equals the area *BDE* which is lost due to the reduction in output equal to *QM* by the monopolist. This loss in producer surplus *BDE* is also a *dead weight loss* caused by the inefficiency or lower production due to monopoly because this has not transferred to or benefited any other. Thus, the total dead weight loss of welfare caused by the monopoly is equal to the whole area *AED* which is the sum of net loss of consumer surplus (*ABD*) and the loss of producer surplus equal to *BDE* represents *social cost of monopoly.*

It follows from the partial equilibrium approach to the measurement of loss of welfare that monopoly is economically inefficient and causes misallocation of resources as it does not extend production of a product to the level desired by the consumers. Some attempts have been made in recent years to measure statistically the loss in efficiency or welfare due to monopoly in the United States. A. C. Harberger estimated the aggregate the loss in efficiency or welfare due to monopoly from 1924 to 1928 for the United States and found that this efficiency loss was one percent of national income (GNP) which was quite small[2]. However, Harberger's estimate has been criticised by G. J. Stigler[3] who pointed out some crucial flaws in the method adopted by Harberger to estimate the efficiency loss due to monopoly. Taking into account the objections by Stigler and making improvements in the method, Kamerschen[4] estimated that welfare loss due to monopoly for the period 1956-1961 in the United States was quite large, around 6 per cent of national income. However, the exact estimate of welfare or efficiency loss due to monopoly still remains a controversial issue.

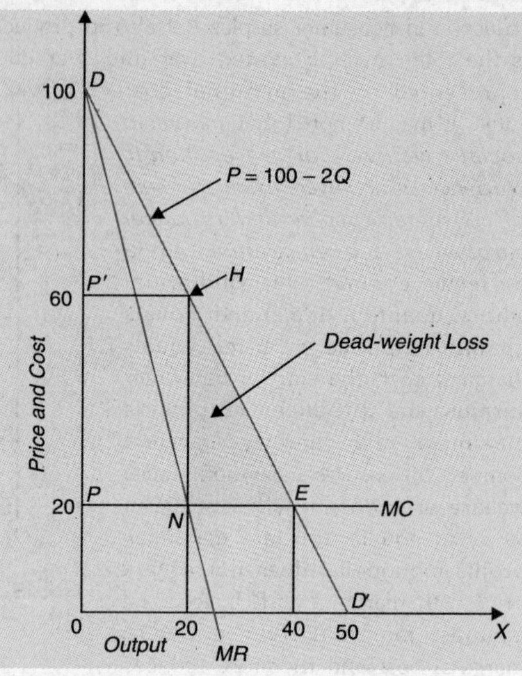

Fig. 19.14. *Dead-Weight Loss of Welfare.*

NUMERICAL PROBLEMS ON DEAD-WEIGHT LOSS

Problem 1. *A monopolist faces a demand curve, P = 700 — 2Q. If marginal cost is constant and is equal to 20. What is the amount of profits made by the monopolist? What is dead-weight welfare loss on account of monopoly ?*

Solution. For monopoly equilibrium, $MR = MC$.

The given demand curve is : $P = 100 - 2Q$

$$TR = P.Q = 100Q - 2Q^2$$

$$MR = \frac{d(TR)}{dQ} = \frac{d(PQ)}{dQ} = 100 - 4Q$$

Equating MR with MC (= 20) we have

$$100 - 4Q = 20$$

$$4Q = 100 - 20 = 80$$

$$Q = \frac{80}{4} = 20$$

To obtain equilibrium price we substitute $Q = 20$ in the given demand function. Thus,

$$P = 100 - 2 \times 20 = 100 - 40 = \text{Rs. } 60$$

2. A. C. Harberger, "Monopoly and Resource Allocation", *American Economic Review*, May, 1954.
3. G. J. Stigler, "The Statistics of Monopoly and Merger", *Journal of Political Economy*, February, 1956.
4. D. R Kamerschen, "An Estimation of the Welfare Losses from Monopoly in the American Economy", *Western Economic Journal*, Vol. 4,1966.

Welfare is maximised when at the output produced price equals marginal cost as under conditions of perfect competition. Thus, equating price with marginal cost we have

$$P = MC$$
$$100 - 2Q = 20$$
$$2Q = 100 - 20 = 80$$
$$Q = 40.$$

Dead-weight loss of welfare from monopoly is depicted in Figure 19.4. Consumer's surplus with output equal to 40 and price equal to 20 is equal to the area *DPE*. Monopoly restricts output to 20 and raises price to 60 or *OP′*. Therefore, under monopoly, consumer surplus is reduced to the area *DP′H*. Thus, consumers suffer a loss of welfare (*i.e.*, consumer's surplus) equal to the area *PP′HE*. The monopolist's profits as a result of restriction of output from 40 units to 20 units and raising of price of the product from 20 to Rs.60, is equal to the area *PNHP¢* (*i.e.*, 40 × 20 = Rs. 800). But consumers suffer a greater loss of consumer surplus equal to the area *PP HE*, that is, *NHE* more than the gain in profits of the monopolist. The welfare loss of consumers equal to the area *NHE* represents the *dead weight loss* of welfare and is

$$= \frac{1}{2}(40 \times 20) = \frac{1}{2}(800)$$
$$= 400$$

This dead-weight loss represents social cost of monopoly.

Problem 2. *The following demand function and total cost function of a monopolist are given. Calculate his marginal revenue and marginal cost. At what level of output, the monopolist will be in equilibrium. What price will be set at the equilibrium output and calculate total profits made by him.*

Price (Rs.)	Quantity sold	Total cost (Rs.)
15	1	12
14	2	22
13	3	31
12	4	39
11	5	46
10	6	54
9	7	64
8	8	75

Solution. In order to find marginal revenue (*MR*) we have first to calculate total revenue $MR = TR_n - TR_{n-1}$ and marginal cost which is $TC_n - TC_{n-1}$ The monopolist will be in equilibrium at the level of output at which *MR* = *MC*. Calculating *TR*, *MR* and *MC* we have the following table.

It will be seen from the table given below that *MC* = *MR* when 5 units of output are sold. Therefore, to be in equilibrium the monopolist will produce 5 units to maximise his profits.

Table : Finding Equilibrium Output

Price (P) Rs.	Quantity sold (Q)	*TR* (P × Q)	*MR* $TR_n - TR_{n-1}$	*TC* Rs.	*MC* $TC_n - TC_{n-1}$
15	1	15	15	12	12
14	2	28	13	22	10
13	3	39	11	31	9
12	4	48	9	39	8
11	5	55	7	46	7
10	6	60	5	54	8
9	7	63	3	64	10
8	8	64	1	75	11

$$\text{Price} = \text{AR} = \frac{TR}{Q} = \frac{55}{5} = 11$$

$$\text{Total profits} = TR - TC = 55 - 46 = 9$$

Problem 3. *Suppose a monopolist faces the following demand schedule*

(i) Calculate the marginal revenue. If marginal cost is Rs. 50, what is the profit-maximising level of output and price?

(ii) If price is set equal to marginal cost, what will be the output that the monopoly will produce ?

Demand	Schedule
Price, P	Quantity, Q
100	0
90	5
80	10
70	15
60	20
50	25
40	30
30	35

Solution. Note that in this problem quantity demanded (or sold) increases by blocks of 5 units and price changes by blocks of Rs. 10. This should be kept in mind while calculating marginal revenue.

To obtain marginal revenue we have first to calculate total revenue (*TR*) which is equal to $P \quad Q$. Then marginal revenue (MR) $= \frac{\Delta TR}{\Delta Q}$. We calculate MR below.

Price (P) Rs.	Quantity demanded or sold (Q)	Total Revenue (TR) ($P \quad Q$)	$MR\left(=\frac{\Delta TR}{\Delta Q}\right)$
100	0	0	0
90	5	450	$\frac{450}{5}=90$
80	10	800	$\frac{350}{5}=70$
70	15	1050	$\frac{250}{5}=50$
60	20	1200	$\frac{150}{5}=30$
50	25	1250	$\frac{50}{5}=10$
40	30	1200	$\frac{-50}{5}=-10$
30	35	1050	$\frac{-150}{5}=-30$

Given marginal cost equal to Rs.50, the profit-maximising condition of $MC = MR$ is satisfied when 15 units of the product are sold. It will be seen from the above table that with 15 units of output sale price of the product is Rs. 70 per unit.

(*ii*) If price is set equal to marginal cost, that is, at Rs. 50, then as will be seen from the above table, 25 units of output will be produced and sold by the monopolist.

QUESTIONS AND PROBLEMS FOR REVIEW

1. What is monopoly? Explain the three conditions necessary for the existence of monopoly.
2. Explain the relationship between average revenue, marginal revenue and price elasticity of demand under the conditions of monopoly.
3. Explain the equilibrium of a monopoly firm ? Show that price fixed by the monopolist is less than marginal cost of production.
4. How are price and output determined under monopoly ? Show that under monopoly price is higher and output smaller than under perfect competition.
5. Show that a monopolist will always operate on the elastic part of the demand curve.
6. A monopolist will never be in equilibrium on the *inelastic* ($e_p < 1$) portion of the demand curve. Explain.
7. A monopolistic firm has the following total cost function and demand function.

Price (Rupees)	*Quantity demanded (Units)*	*Total cost (Rs)*
8	5	20
7	6	21
6	7	22
5	8	23
4	9	24
3	10	25

Explain what price will be charged and what output will be produced.

[Hint: From the given data of price and quantity demanded, first find out total revenue ($TR = P.Q$). From TR, marginal revenue can be obtained at different levels of quantity demanded or sold. From total cost data, MC can be obtained. Then the output level at which $MC = MR$, will be the equilibrium output and price at that will be equilibrium price. In the above table, MC is constant at Rs. 1. When 6 units of sold, $MR = 2$ and when 7, units are sold, $MR = 0$, therefore the firm should produce 6 units of output to maximise profits.]

8. How is monopoly power measured ? State Lerner's measure of degree of monopoly power. Show that degree of monopoly power is inverse of the price elasticity of demand.
9. A simple monopolist is in equilibrium. At the point of equilibrium the coefficient of price elasticity is – 2.0 and the marginal cost is Rs. 4.0. Calculate his equilibrium price. How will this price be affected by an increase in the fixed cost of the monopolist ? **[Hints** : In equilibrium, $MC = MR$

Since $MR = P(1 - \frac{1}{|e|})$

Given $MC = 4$ and $e = -2$

i.e., $4 = P\left(1 - \frac{1}{2}\right)$

$P = 4 \times \frac{2}{1} = 8$]

10. When a monopolist is maximising profits, price is greater than marginal cost. Thus consumers will be paying more for additional units of output than it costs to produce. So why does not the monopolist produce more ?
11. A monopolist plans to produce 100 units of a commodity and observes that the price elasticity of demand at this output is 0.5. What advice would you give to the monopolist ?

[Hints. Since MR is negative at an output level where price elasticity is less than one, the monopolist will not be making maximum profits. In fact, he may be making losses if he pursues his plan. Therefore, the monopolist should restrict output of the commodity to the level where price elasticity of demand is greater than one and where his $MC = MR$]

12. A monopolist will never sell its product at a price less than its average total cost. Is it true or false? Give reasons.

13. Explain why marginal revenue of a monopolist is less than the price charged.

14. Explain why a perfectly competitive firm will never operate when marginal cost is declining but a monopoly firm can do so.

15. If a price making monopolistic firm wants to maximise its sales revenue, it should :

 (*a*) set the highest price it can get.

 (*b*) set the lowest price it can get.

 (*c*) choose a selling price at which the elasticity of demand for its product is unity.

 (*d*) choose a selling price where the extra revenue received from the last unit sold exceeds the extra cost of making that unit.

Tick the right answer

16. Suppose that at the profit maximising output, a monopolist price is twice as high as his marginal cost. What is the price elasticity of demand?

17. Does a monopolist always set his price above marginal cost ? Will he ever produce at the minimum point of long-run average curve.

 [Hints. As explained in the text a monopolist always sets his price above marginal cost of production. Further, in the long run he usually produces less than the minimum point of *LAC*, that is, he produces with excess capacity in the long run. *However, this is not necessary* as it depends on the demand conditions facing him. If demand for his product is sufficiently large he may produce at or near the minimum point of long-run average curve, that is, produces with a optimal scale of plant and uses it at its full capacity (see Fig. 19.15). However, there is no certainty that monopolist will produce at this optimal level, as is the case under perfect competition. This is because unlike in competitive market conditions, no market forces operate under monopoly that compel the monopolist to work with optimum plant size and uses it at its full capacity.

18. A monopolist has attained equilibrium on a point on the demand curve where the coefficient of price elasticity is – 2.5 and the equilibrium price is Rs. 20.00. Calculate his marginal revenue.

19. What do you understand by 'dead-weight loss' of monopoly ? If the gains to producers be redistributed to consumers, would the "dead-weight loss" be eliminated ?

20. What is a social cost of monopoly ? If the gains to the monopolist could be redistributed to consumers, would the social cost of monopoly be eliminated. Explain briefly.

21. Let the demand function for an industry's output be $Q = 50 - 5P$, where P is price and Q is the output. Assume constant costs at Rs. 6 per unit of output.

 (*i*) How much would a profit-maximising monopolist produce ? What would be the equilibrium price ?

 (*ii*) Now assume the commodity is produced by a public sector undertaking which follows the *marginal cost pricing principle*. What would be the optimal quantity produced ?

 [Hints. (*ii*) A public sector undertaking following marginal cost-pricing principle would set the price equal to marginal cost of production. Thus

 $Q = 50 - 5P$ ...(1)

 $5P = 50 - Q$

 $P = 10 - 1/5Q$ ...(2)

 Setting price (P) equal to marginal cost we have

 $6 = 10 - 1/5\ Q$

 $1/5Q = 10 - 6 = 4$, or $Q = 20$]

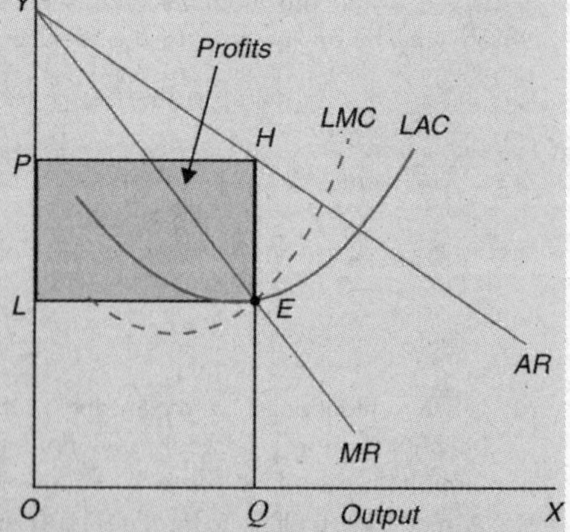

Fig. 19.15. *Monopolist working at the minimum point of LAC.*

22. Consider a shift in demand under monopoly. In two separate diagrams, show that this can result in:

 (*i*) Different quantities being supplied at the same price.

(*ii*) Different prices supporting the same quantity. Hence show that a monopolist does not have a unique supply curve.

23. We write the percentage make-up of price over marginal cost as $(P - MC)/P$. For a profit maximising monopolist, how does this mark-up depend on the elasticity of demand ? Why can this mark-up be viewd as a measure of monopoly power ?

24. Show why supply curve does not exist under monopoly.

25. Explain how average revenue curve, marginal revenue curve and elasticity of demand are related to one another. Why should a monopoly firm not sell below the price where elasticity of demand is less than one?

26. Explain the long-run equilibrium under monopoly. Explain the adjustment process. How a monopoly firm will shift from the short-run equilibrium to the long-run equilibrium position. Why is monopoly profits not likely to be eliminated ?

27. Show how monopoly causes misallocation of resources and thereby causes loss of social welfare.

OR

Monopoly is said to be economically inefficient. Explain and show how it causes dead weight loss.

20 CHAPTER

Pricing and Output Decisions Under Monopolistic Competition

Imperfect Competition : Monopolistic Competition and Oligopoly

Perfect competition and monopoly are rarely found in the real world and thus they do not represent, for the most part, the actual market situations. Therefore, the conclusions which follow from the theories of pure competition were found to be inapplicable to the behaviour of business firms in the actual world. For instance, in the real world, firms were found to be enjoying 'internal economies of scale' which were incompatible with the theory of perfect competition. The urgent need was therefore felt to reformulate the theory of price so as to bring it nearer to the actual world. This was accomplished by E.H. Chamberlin and Joan Robinson who worked quite independently and brought out simultaneously "*The Theory of Monopolistic Competition*" and "*The Economics of Imperfect Competition*" respectively. Joan Robinson got the clues for her theory of imperfect competition from Sraffa who in his article "The Laws of Returns under Competitive Conditions" in *Economic Journal* asserted, "*It is necessary, therefore, to abandon the path of free competition and turn in the opposite direction, namely, towards monopoly.*"

Monopolistic competition theory of Prof. Chamberlin and imperfect competition theory of Joan Robinson, though similar in various ways differ in some important respects. The nutshell of these theories, especially of the theory of monopolistic competition, is that the pure competition and pure monopoly are the two opposite limiting cases, lying between which is a series of intermediate cases, which differ from each other in relative strengths of monopoly and competitive elements, or in other words, in *degrees of imperfection*. It may be noted that the extreme limit of monopoly is reached when a seller does not face competition from any substitute product. Since every good has to compete with others for buyer's money income, every good is a substitute of others to some extent. It follows that the extreme limit of monopoly, which Sraffa denotes as *pure monopoly*, will be reached only when a single person or agency comes to have a "control over the supply of all economic goods." At the other extreme is pure or perfect competition in which case an individual seller has to compete with the products (of rival sellers) which are perfect substitutes of his own product, since products of all sellers are completely identical or homogeneous. Between these two extremes of pure monopoly and pure competition, there are all gradations in which both the monopolistic and competitive elements are present. In the terminology of Robinson and Chamberlin, pure monopoly in the sense of a single seller of a product which has got no close substitutes is an extreme form of imperfect competition. *The two important forms of imperfect competition are : (a) monopolistic competition, (b) oligopoly.*

The fundamental distinguishing feature of imperfect competition is that unlike that under perfect or pure competition, the demand curve confronting an individual firm under it slopes downward. As a result, the marginal revenue curve lies below it. Marginal revenue curve plays such a crucial role because of its definite relation with price and elasticity (MR = Price $\frac{e-1}{e}$). It is the nature of this relation which distinguishes a state of competition that is pure from one that is impure or imperfect. The difference between marginal revenue and price at an output level depends upon the size of price elasticity of demand at it. Under perfect competition, price is equal to marginal revenue since price elasticity of demand is infinite, while under imperfect competition, price is greater than marginal revenue since price elasticity of demand is less than infinite. Therefore, the difference between the price and marginal revenue (or marginal cost) at equilibrium output is regarded as the *degree of monopoly*. Thus, the relative magnitudes of price and marginal revenue at equilibrium output help us to distinguish between different degrees of monopoly power in various market structures. The greater the difference between the price and the marginal revenue, the greater the degree of monopoly element and *vice versa*.

PRODUCT DIFFERENTIATION AND MONOPOLISTIC COMPETITION

The concept of monopolistic competition put forth by Chamberlin is a true revolutionary as well as more realistic than either perfect competition or pure monopoly. Before Chamberlin, monopoly and competition were regarded as two mutually exclusive alternatives; one would be absent when the other exists. On the other hand, according to Chamberlin, in most of the real world economic situations, both monopoly and competitive elements are present. Chamberlin's concept of monopolistic competition is thus a blending of competition and monopoly.

The distinguishing feature of monopolistic competition which makes it as a blending of competition and monopoly is the *differentiation of the product*. This means that the products of various firms are not homogeneous but differentiated though they are closely related to each other. Product differentiation does not mean that the products of various firms are altogether different. They are only slightly different so that they are quite similar and serve as close substitutes of each other. When there is any degree of differentiation of products, monopoly element enters the situation. And, the greater the differentiation, the greater the element of monopoly involved in the market situation. When there is a large number of firms producing differentiated products, each one has a monopoly of its own product but is subject to the competition of close substitutes. Since each is a monopolist and yet has competitors, we have a market situation which can be aptly described as "monopolistic competition." It is thus clear that monopolistic competition involves both the monopoly and competitive elements. Here, it is worth quoting Chamberlin himself "With differentiation appears monopoly and as it proceeds further, the element of monopoly becomes greater. Where there is any degree of differentiation whatever, each seller has an absolute monopoly of his own product, but is subject to the competition of more or less imperfect substitutes. Since each is a monopolist and yet has competitors we may speak of them as 'competing monopolists' and with peculiar appropriateness, of the forces at work as those of monopolistic competition."[1]

It is thus clear from above that in monopolistic competition, products are not identical as in perfect competition, but neither are they remote substitutes as in monopoly. The products of various sellers are fairly similar (but not the same) and serve as close substitutes of each other. Every seller has a monopoly of his own differentiated product but he has to face a stiff competition from his rival sellers which are selling close substitutes of his product.

Many examples of product differentiation can be given from the Indian scene. For instance, in India there are various manufacturers of toothpaste which produce different brands such as Colgate, Binaca, Forhans , Pepsodent , Signals, Neem etc. Thus, the manufacturer of 'Colgate' has a monopoly of producing it (nobody else can produce and sell the toothpaste with the name 'Colgate') but he faces competition from the manufacturers of Forhans, Binaca, Pepsodent etc. which are close substitutes of Colgate. The manufacturer of Colgate cannot therefore decide about its price-output policies without considering the possible reactions of rival firms producing close substitutes. Other examples of monopolistic competition are the producers of bathing soaps (Lux, Godrej, Breeze, Hamam, Palmolive, Jai etc.); the manufacturers of tooth brushes (Colgate, Dr. West's, Wisdom, Binaca, etc.); retailers' shops in the towns; barbers' shops in the towns, etc. We thus see that monopolistic competition corresponds more to the real world economic situation than perfect competition or monopoly.

A general class of product is differentiated if a basis exists for preferring goods of one seller to those of others. Such a basis for preference may be real or fancied, it will cause differentiation of the product. When such differentiation of the product exists, even if it is slight, buyers will be paired with sellers not in a random fashion (as in perfect competition) but according to their preferences. There are, broadly speaking, two bases of product differentiation. Firstly, differentiation may be based upon certain *characteristic of the product itself* such as exclusive patented features, trade marks and trade names, peculiarities of packages or wrappers if any, or difference in quality, design, colour or style. Real qualitative differences like those of materials used, design and workmanship are no doubt important means of differentiating products. But imaginary differences created through advertising, the use of attractive packets, the use of trade marks and brand names are more usual methods by which products are differentiated, even if physically they are identical or almost so. Secondly, differentiation may be based upon the *conditions surrounding the sale of the product.* This means that product is differentiated if the services rendered in the process of selling the product by one seller or firm are not identical with those rendered by any other seller or firm. Thus, in retail trade to take only one instance, the conditions surrounding the sale of the product include "the convenience of the seller's location, the general tone or character of his establishment, his way of doing business, his reputation for fair dealing, courtesy, efficiency, and all others which attach his customers either to himself or to those employed by him".[2] If these and other intangible factors surrounding the sale of the product are different in case of different sellers, the product in each case will be different since the buyers take these intangible factors into consideration while making purchases. These factors like the patents, trade marks etc. serve as a basis for preference.

If the above two aspects of differentiation are borne in mind, then it will be quite manifest that virtually all products in the real world are more or less differentiated. It should be carefully noted that even when product differentiation is caused by the circumstances surrounding the sale of the products, both monopolistic and competitive elements are present. In retail trade, to take the above example, every product is rendered differentiated by the individuality of the

1. E.H. Chamberlin, *The Theory of Monopolistic Competition, 7th ed., 1956, p. 904.*
2. E.H. Chamberlin, *op. cit.*, p. 68

establishment in which it is sold including the location factor, the general tone, reputation, goodwill of the establishment, way of dealing with customers etc. Each retail trader has complete and absolute control over the supply of his 'product' when this is taken to include location factor, general tone and reputation, way of dealing with the customers etc; this is the monopolistic aspect. Again, every retail trade is subject to the competition of other 'products' sold under different conditions and at different locations; this is the competitive aspect. Thus, as in the case of patents and trade marks, both monopoly and competition are present in the case of 'products' differentiated by the conditions surrounding their sale.

Under monopoly, the demand curve for the product of the monopolist is given. But the demand curve for the product of an individual producer or seller under monopolistic competition cannot be taken as given since there exist, in monopolistic competition, close competitive interrelationships among various producers selling close substitutes. The demand curve for the product of an individual depends upon the nature and prices of its closely competing substitutes. Thus, according to Chamberlin, "Monopolistic competition concerns itself not only with the problem of an *individual equilibrium* (the ordinary theory of monopoly), but also with that of a *group equilibrium* (the adjustment of economic forces within a group of competing monopolists, ordinarily regarded as merely a group of competitors). In this, it differs both from the theory of competition and from the theory of monopoly".[3]

This leads us to Chamberlin's concepts of group and group equilibrium. Chamberlin has used the word group instead of industry in order to draw distinction between pure competition and monopolistic competition. The word industry is generally used in economics in the context of pure or perfect competition and *refers to a collection of firms that produce homogeneous products.* But, as explained above, under monopolistic competition we have product hetrogeneity. Therefore, the word 'industry' loses its significance under monopolistic competition. Therefore, Prof. Chamberlin has used the word 'group'. *By group he means "a number of producers whose goods are fairly close substitutes."* We thus see that the Chamberlin's 'group' refers to a collection of firms that produce closely related but not identical products. It became necessary for Prof. Chamberlin to evolve the concept of 'group' as distinct from industry because in the case of group where products are differentiated there are special problems which are absent in the case of industry where products are homogeneous. The various firms in a given group produce products which are close substitutes of each other and therefore compete with each other in the market. The demand for the product of one producer depends upon the price and the nature of the products of his close rivals. These competitive inter-relationships among firms are absent in the case of an industry under pure or perfect competition since all of them produce homogeneous products and each of them can sell his entire supply of the product at the going market price.

An individual producer in the 'group' under monopolistic competition cannot therefore be treated in complete isolation from his rivals producing close substitutes, since the demand for his product depends upon the nature and price of the close substitutes. To quote Prof. Chamberlin: "From our point of view, each producer within the group is a monopolist, yet his market is interwoven with those of his competitors, and he is no longer to be isolated from them."[4]

Lastly, it may be noted that the sense in which the word 'competition' is generally used in the business world is in conformity more with the monopolistic competition than with the

3. *Ibid.*, p. 69,
4. E.H. Chamberlin, *op. cit.* p.8.

perfect competition. The phrases such as price cutting, under-selling, unfair competition, meeting competition, cut-throat competition, securing market etc. often used in the business world are irrelevant in the context of perfect competition. This is because each seller under so-called 'perfect competition' accepts the going market price and can dispose of his entire supply of the product without affecting price. For a perfect competitor there is no problem of choosing a price policy, problem of advertising in order to attract customers. Thus, the competition in the ordinary sense of the competitive phrases, just noted above, has meaning only in the context of monopolistic competition (and also of oligopoly) where products of various sellers are differentiated but closely related. Sellers really compete in the ordinary sense of the word only under the monopolistic competition and oligopoly.

IMPORTANT FEATURES OF MONOPOLISTIC COMPETITION

It is important to understand the important characteristics of monopolistic competition. The knowledge of these features will enable the students to know how this form of market structure is different from perfect competition and oligopoly. We explain below its important features.

1. A large number of firms. The first important feature of monopolistic competition is that under it there are a relatively large number of firms each satisfying a small share of the market demand for the product. Because there is a large number of firms under monopolistic competition, there exists stiff competition between them. Unlike perfect competition these large number of firms do not produce identical products. Instead, they produce and sell differentiated products which are close substitutes of each other. This makes the competition among firms real and tough.

Further, the fact that there is a large number of firms under monopolistic competition, size of each firm will be relatively small. This is unlike oligopoly where there are a few firms of big size.

2. Product differentiation. The second important feature of monopolistic competition is that the products produced by various firms are not identical but are slightly different from each other. Though different firms make their products slightly different from others, they remain close substitutes of each other. In other words, the products of various firms working under monopolistic competition are not the same but are similar. Therefore, their prices cannot be very much different from each other. It is because of the fact that their products are similar and close substitutes of each other that the various firms under monopolistic competition compete with each other.

3. Some influence over the price. Each firm under monopolistic competition produces a product variety which is close substitute of others. Therefore, if a firm lowers the price of its product variety, some customers of other product varieties will switch over to it. This means as it lowers the price of its product variety, quantity demanded of it will increase. On the other hand, if it raises the price of its product, some of its customers will leave it and buy the similar products from its competing firms. This implies that demand curve facing a firm working under monopolistic competition slopes downward and marginal revenue curve lies below it. This means that under monopolistic competition an individual firm is not a price taker but will have some influence over the price of its product. If it fixes a higher price, it will be able to sell a relatively smaller quantity of output. And if it fixes a lower price, it will be able to sell more. *Thus under monopolistic competition, a firm has to choose a price-output combination which will maximise its profits.*

4. Non-price competition: Expenditure on advertisement and other selling costs. An important feature of monopolistic competition is that firms incur a considerable expenditure on advertisements and other selling costs to promote the sales of their products. Promoting sales of their products through advertisement is an important example of non-price competition. The expenditure incurred on advertisement is prominent among the various types of selling costs. The advertisement and other selling outlays by a firm change the demand for its product as well as its costs. Like the adjustments of price and product, a seller under monopolistic competition will also adjust the amount of his advertisement expenditure so as to maximise his profits. This problem of adjusting one's selling outlay is unique to monopolistic competition, because the firm under perfect competition has not to incur any expenditure on advertisement. The advertisement expenditure by a purely competitive firm will be without purpose since it can sell as much amount as it pleases at the going market price without any advertisement expenditure. The rival firms under monopolistic competition keenly compete with each other through advertisement by which they change the consumers' wants for their products and attract more customers. Thus, a full explanation of the equilibrium under monopolistic competition must also involve equilibrium in regard to the amount of expenditure on advertisement and other sales promotion activities.

5. Product variation. Another form of non-price competition which a firm under monopolistic competition has to face is the variation in products by various firms. A firm, under perfect competition, does not confront this problem, for the product is homogeneous under perfect competition. The problem of product variation under monopolistic competition exists because there is differentiation of products of various firms. The firm will try to adjust its product so as to conform more to the wishes of the buyers. The variation of the product may refer to a change in the quality of the product itself, technical changes, a new design, better materials, and it may mean only a new package or container. It may also mean more prompt or courteous service, and a different way of doing business. The amount of the product which a firm will be able to sell in the market depends in part upon the manner in which its product differs from others. Where the possibility of product differentiation exists, sales depend upon the skill with which a product is distinguished from others and made to appeal to a particular group of buyers. The profit maximisation principle applies to the choice of the nature of the product as to its price. In other words, a firm will choose that nature of the product, given its price, which gives it maximum profits. Therefore, in a full explanation of the firm's equilibrium under monopolistic competition we have also to explain product equilibrium in addition to price equilibrium and selling-costs equilibrium.

6. Freedom of entry and exit. This is another important feature of monopolistic competition. In a monopolistically competitive industry it is easy for the new firms to enter and the existing firms to leave it. Free entry means that when in the industry existing firms are making super-normal profits, the new firms enter the industry which leads to the expansion of output. As a result, price of product tends to fall in the long run. However, it may be noted that under monopolistic competition entry may not be as easy or free as under perfect competition. Whereas under perfect competition the new firms which enter the industry can produce identical products, but under monopolistic competition, the new firms can produce only new brands or product varieties which may initially find it difficult to compete with the already well-established brands and product varieties.

The Nature of Demand and Marginal Revenue Curves under Monopolistic Competition

It is important to understand the nature of the demand curve facing an individual firm under monopolistic competition. As has been explained in previous chapters, demand curve facing a firm working under perfect competition is perfectly elastic at the ruling market price since it has absolutely no control over the price of the product. On the contrary, a firm working under monopolistic competition enjoys some control over the price of its product since its product is somewhat differentiated from others. If a firm under monopolistic competition raises the price of its product, it will find some of its customers going away to buy other products. As a result, the quantity demanded of its product will fall. On the contrary, if it lowers the price, it will find that buyers of other varieties of the product will start purchasing its product and as a result the quantity demanded of its product will increase. It therefore follows that the demand curve facing an individual firm under monopolistic competition slopes downward.

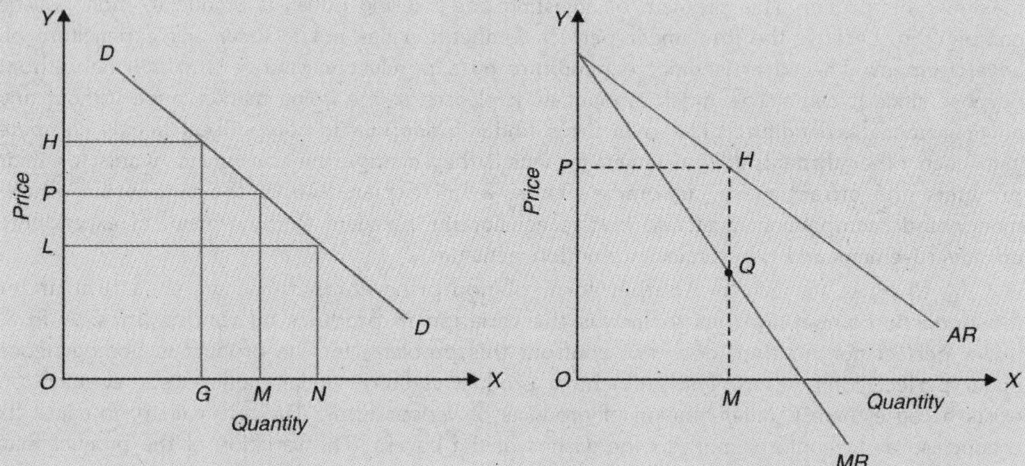

Fig. 20.1. *Demand Curve Facing a Monopolistically Competitive Firm*

Fig. 20.2. *Average and Marginal Revenue Curves under Monopolistic Competition*

If a firm working under monopolistic competition wants to increase the sales of its product, it must lower the price. It can raise the price if it is prepared to sacrifice some sales. To put it in another way, a firm working under monopolistic competition can lower the price by increasing its level of sales and output. A purely competitive firm merely adjusts the quantity of output it has to produce, price being a given and constant datum for it. But a firm working under monopolistic competition faces a more complicated problem. It cannot merely adjust quantity at a given price because each quantity change by it will bring about a change in the price at which the product can be sold. Consider Fig. 20.1. *DD* is the demand curve facing an individual firm under monopolistic competition. At price *OP* the quantity demanded is *OM*. Therefore, the firm would be able to sell *OM* quantity at price *OP*. If it wants to sell greater quantity *ON*, then it will have to reduce price to *OL*. If it restricts its quantity to *OG*, price will rise to *OH*. Thus, every quantity change by it entails a change in price at which the product can be sold. Thus *the problem faced by a firm working under monopolistic competition is to choose the price-quantity combination which is optimum for it, that is, which yields it maximum possible profits.*

Demand curve facing a firm will be his average revenue curve. Thus the average revenue curve of the monopolistically competitive firm slopes downward throughout its length. Since average revenue curve slopes downward, marginal revenue curve lies below it. This follows from usual average-marginal relationship. The implication of marginal revenue curve lying below average revenue curve is that the marginal revenue will be less than the price or average revenue. When a firm working under monopolistic competition sells more, the price of its product falls; marginal revenue therefore must be less than price. In Fig. 20.2 *AR* is the average revenue curve of the firm under monopolistic competition and slopes downward. *MR* is the marginal revenue curve and lies below *AR* curve. At quantity *OM*, average revenue (or price) is *OP* and marginal revenue is *MQ* which is less than *OP*. In an earlier chapter we have explained that average and marginal revenues at a level of output are related to each other through price elasticity of demand and in this connection we derived the following formula:

$$MR = AR\left(1 - \frac{1}{e}\right),$$ where *e* stands for *absolute value* of price elasticity of demand.

PRICE-OUTPUT EQUILIBRIUM UNDER MONOPOLISTIC COMPETITION

A firm under monopolistic competition has to face various problems which are absent under perfect competition. Since the market of an individual firm under perfect competition is completely merged with the general one, it can sell any amount of the good at the ruling market price. But, under monopolistic competition, individual firm's market is isolated to a certain degree from those of its rivals with the result that its sales are limited and depend upon (1) its price, (2) the nature of its product, and (3) the advertising outlay it makes. Thus, the firm under monopolistic competition has to confront a more complicated problem than the perfectly competitive firm. Equilibrium of an individual firm under monopolistic competition involves equilibrium in three respects, that is, in regard to the price, the nature of the product, and the amount of advertising outlay it should make.

Equilibrium of the firm in respect of three variables simultaneously—price, nature of product, selling outlay—is difficult to discuss. Therefore, the method of explaining equilibrium in respect of each of them separately is adopted, keeping the other two variables given and constant. Moreover, as noted above, the equilibrium under monopolistic competition involves "individual equilibrium" of the firms as well as "group equilibrium." We shall discuss these two types of equilibrium first in respect of price and output and then in respects of product and advertising expenditure adjustments.

Individual Firm's Equilibrium under Monopolistic Competition

The demand curve for the product of an individual firm, as noted above, is downward sloping. Since the various firms under monopolistic competition produce products which are close substitutes of each other, the position and elasticity of the demand curve for the product of any of them depend upon the availability of the competiting substitutes and their prices. Therefore, the equilibrium adjustment of an individual firm cannot be defined in isolation from the general field of which it is a part. However, for the sake of simplicity in analysis, conditions regarding the availability of substitute products produced by the rival firms and prices charged for them are held constant while the equilibrium adjustment of an individual firm is considered in isolation. Since close substitutes for its product are available in the market, the

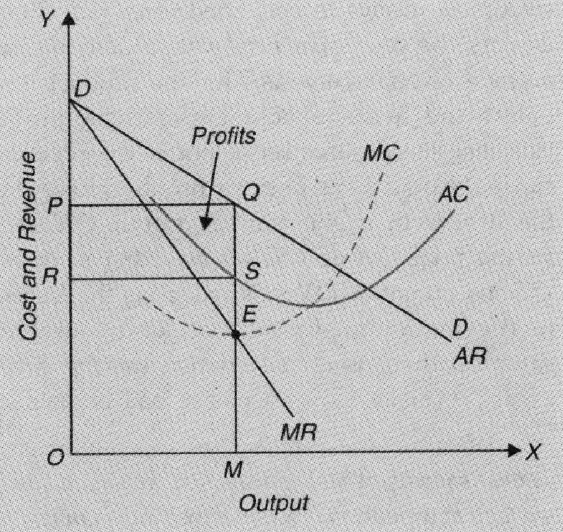

Fig. 20.3. *Individual Firm's Equilibrium under Monopolistic Competition (with Profits)*

demand curve for the product of an individual firm working under conditions of monopolistic competition is fairly elastic. Thus, although a firm under monopolistic competition has a monopolistic control over its variety of the product but its control is tempered by the fact that there are close substitutes available in the market and that if it sets too high a price for its product, many of its customers will shift to the rival products.

Assuming the conditions with respect to all substitutes such as their nature and prices being constant, the demand curve for the product of a firm will be given. We further suppose that the product of the firm is held constant, only variables are price and output in respect of which equilibrium adjustment is to be made. The individual equilibrium under monopolistic competition is graphically shown in Fig. 20.3. *DD* is the demand curve for the product of an individual firm, the nature and prices of all substitutes being given. This demand curve *DD* is also the average revenue (*AR*) curve of the firm. *AC* represents the average cost curve of the firm, while *MC* is the marginal cost curve corresponding to it. It may be recalled that average cost curve first falls due to internal economies and then rises due to internal diseconomies.

Given these demand and cost conditions a firm will adjust its price and output at the level which gives it maximum total profits. Theory of value under monopolistic compe-tition is also based upon the profit maximisation principle, as is the theory of value under perfect competition. Thus a firm in order to maximise profits will equate marginal cost with marginal revenue. In Fig. 20.3, the firm will fix its level of output at *OM*, for at *OM* output marginal cost is equal to marginal revenue. The demand curve *DD* facing the firm in question indicates that output *OM* can be sold at price *MQ* = *OP*. Therefore, the determined price will evidently be *MQ* or *OP*. In this equilibrium position, by fixing its price at *OP* and output at *OM*, the firm is making economic profits equal to the area *RSQP* which is maximum. It may be recalled that profits *RSQP* are in excess of normal profits because the normal profits which represent the minimum profits necessary to secure the entrepreneur's services are included in average cost curve *AC*. Thus, the area *RSQP* indicates the amount of supernormal or economic profits made by the firm.

In the short-run, the firm, in equilibrium, may make economic profits, as shown in Fig. 20.3 above, but it may make losses too if the demand conditions for its product are not so favourable relative to cost conditions. Fig. 20.4 depicts the case of a firm whose demand or average revenue curve *AR* for the product lies below the average cost curve throughout indicating thereby that no output of the product can be produced at positive profits. However, the firm is in equilibrium at output *ON* and setting price *NK* or *OT*, for by fixing price at *OT* and output at *ON*, it is rendering the losses to the minimum. In such an unfavourable situation there is no alternative for the firm except to make the best of the bad bargain.

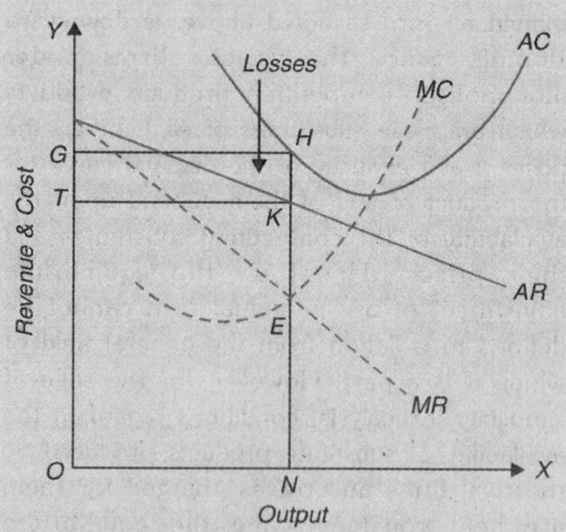

Fig. 20.4. *Individual Firm's Equilibrium under Monopolistic Competition (with Losses).*

We thus see that a firm in equilibrium under monopolistic competition, as under perfect competition, may be making economic profits or incurring losses depending upon the position of the demand curve relative to the position of the average cost curve. Further, a firm may be making only normal profits even in the short run if the demand curve happens to be tangent to the average cost curve.

It should be carefully noted that in individual equilibrium of the firm both in Fig. 20.3 and Fig. 20.4, the firm having once fixed adjusted price at *OP* and *OT* respectively will have no tendency to vary the price any more. If it varies its price upward, the loss due to fall in quantity demanded will be more than made up by the higher price. If it cuts down its price, the gain due to the increase in quantity demanded will be less than the loss due to the lower price. Hence, price will remain stable at *OP* and *OT* in the two cases respectively.

Long-Run Firm's Equilibrium and Group Equilibrium under Monopolistic Competition

We may now turn to see how the 'group' comes to be in equilibrium. In other words, we have now to explain how the equilibrium adjustment of prices and outputs of a number of firms whose products are close substitues comes about. As explained above, each firm within a group has monopoly of its own particular product, yet its market is interwoven with those of his competitors who produce closely related products. The price and output decisions of a firm will affect his rival firms who may in turn revise their price and output policies. This dependence of the various producers upon one another is a prominent feature of monopolistic competition. The question now is: what characterises the system of relationship into which the group tends to fall as a result of producers's influence on each other ?

A difficulty faced in describing the group equilibrium is the vast diversity of conditions which exist in respect of many matters between the various firms constituting the group. The product of each firm has special characteristics and adapted to the tastes and preferences of its customers. The qualitative differences among the products lead to the large variations in cost and demand curves of the various firms. The demand curves of the products of various firms differ in respect of elasticity as well as position. Similarly, cost curves of the various firms differ in respect of shape and position. As a result of these heterogeneous conditions surrounding each firm, there will be differences in prices, outputs (scales of production) and profits of the various firms in the group. Putting this matter in another way, E.H. Chamberlin says: "*The differentiation of the product is not, so to speak, 'uniformly spaced'; it is not distributed homogeneously among all the products which are grouped together. Each has its own individuality, and the size of its market depends on the strength of the preference for it over other varieties.*"[5]

In order to simplify the analysis of equilibrium, Chamberlin ignores these diverse conditions surrounding each firm and takes an assumption what has been called "*uniformity assumption*". Thus Chamberlin says: "*We, therefore, proceed under the heroic assumption that both demand and cost curves for all the 'products' are uniform throughout the group.*"[6] Chamberlin points out that by taking this assumption we do not reduce the differentiation of products. Under the uniformity assumption, "It is required only that *consumer's preferences be evenly distributed among the different varieties*, and that differences between them be not such as to give rise to differences in cost."[7]

Further, to facilitate exposition of his theory, Chamberlin introduces a further assumption which has been called '*symmetry assumption*' by Prof. Stigler. It is that the number of firms being large under monopolistic competition, an individual's actions regarding price and output adjustment will have a negligible effect upon its numerous competitors so that they will not

5. *Op. cit.* p.82
6. *Ibid.*, p. 82
7. *Ibid*, p. 83 (*italics added*)

think of retaliation for readjusting their prices and outputs. He thus says, specifically, we assume for the present that any adjustment of price of a "product" by a single producer spreads its influence over so many of his competitors that the impact felt by any one is negligible and does not lead him to any readjustment of his own situation. A price cut, for instance, which increases the sales of him who made it draws inappreciable amounts from the markets of each of his many competitors, achieving a considerable result for the one who cut, but without making incursions upon the market of any single competitor sufficient to cause him to do anything he would not have done any way."[8]

Given the above assumptions, we proceed to explain how under monopolistic competition an individual firm and a group of firms producing close substitutes come to be in equilibrium position. To begin with, suppose that the demand and cost curves of each of the firms in the group are *DD* and *AC* as depicted in Fig. 20.3. Each firm will set price *OP* at which marginal cost is equal to marginal revenue and hence profits are maximum. Although all firms are making economic profits, there is no reason for any one to cut down price below *OP* because the sales gained thereby will be insufficient to make up the loss due to the lower price. These economic profits will, however, attract new firms into the field in the long run.

Here it may be pointed out that full freedom of entry cannot prevail under monopolistic competition. Entry can be fully free only if the new firms who propose to enter the field can produce exactly identical products as those of the existing firms. But under monopolistic competition, this is not possible. Therefore, entry in the full and strict sense cannot exist under monopolistic competition. However new entrants are free to produce closely related products which are very similar to the products of the existing firms. Thus, *under monopolistic competition there can be freedom of entry only in the sense of a freedom to produce close substitutes.*

Turning to the above argument, when the new firms lured by the economic profits enjoyed by the existing firms enter the field, the market would be shared between more firms and as a result the demand curve (or average revenue curve) for the product of each firm will shift downward *i.e.*, to the left. This process of entry of new firms and the resultant shift in the demand (average revenue) curve to the left will continue until the average revenue curve becomes tangent to the average cost curve and the economic profits are completely wiped out. This is shown in Fig. 20.5 where average revenue curve is tangent to average cost curve at point *T*. Marginal cost and marginal revenue curves intersect each other at point *E* exactly vertically below *T*. Therefore, *the firm is in long-run equilibrium by setting price QT or OP and producing OQ quantity of its product.* Because average revenue is equal to average cost, the firm will be making only normal profits. Since all firms are alike in respect of demand and cost curves (by assumption), the average revenue of all will be tangent to their average cost curves and all firms will, therefore, be earning only normal profits. Because only normal profits are accruing to the firms there will be no more tendency for the new competitors to enter the field and the group as a whole will, therefore, be in equilibrium.

An important point is worth noting here. It is that a *firm in long-run equilibrium under monopolistic competition makes only normal profits, as in perfect competition, but its price is higher and output smaller than under perfect competition.* Under perfect competition, long-run equilibrium of the firm is established at the minimum point of the average cost curve. In other words, a firm under perfect competition tends to be of the optimum size. But a firm in the long run under monopolistic competition, as is evident from Fig. 20.5, stops short of the optimum point and operates at the point at which average cost is still falling. In Fig. 20.5 the firm produces output *OQ*, while a firm under perfect competition would have

8. *Ibid.*, p. 83

produced output *OR* at which average cost is minimum. The firm under monopolistic competition can reduce its cost of production by expanding output to the point *R* but it will not do so because by expanding output beyond *OQ* it will be reducing price more than the average cost. It is, therefore, clear that by producing *OQ* instead of *OR*, the firm under monopolistic competition does not use its capacity fully. (The firm would be using its capacity fully, if it produces optimum or full capacity output *OR*). Thus capacity equal to *QR* is lying unused in the firm's long-run equilibrium under monopolistic competition. This *unused capacity is called excess capacity which is a prominent feature of long-run equilibrium under monopolistic competition.*

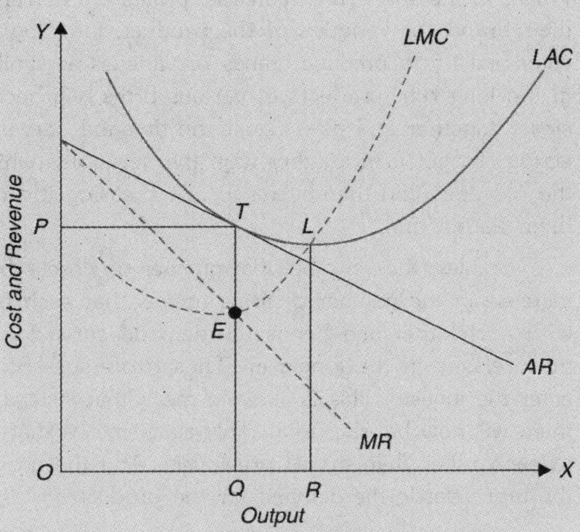

Fig. 20.5. *The Long-run Equilibrium : The group is in equilibrium when average revenue curves of the firms are tangent to their long-run average cost curves.*

Further, it may be noted that in the long-run equilibrium, firms under monopolistic competition make only normal profits as under perfect competition, but the price set under monopolistic competition is higher than competitive price. In Fig. 20.5, price set in long-run equilibrium under monopolistic competition is *QT* while competitive price would have been equal to *RL*. This higher price under monopolistic competition is due to monopoly element contained in it. The monopoly element involved in monopolistic competition makes the demand or average revenue curve facing an individual firm downward sloping and a downward-sloping average revenue curve can be tangent to the average cost curve only to the left of its minimum point.

Thus price under monopolistic competition will be higher than the competitive price due to the monopoly element in monopolistic competition. But, in spite of the higher price, a firm under monopolistic competition will not be making profits above normal in the long run. We may, therefore, say that a *firm under monopolistic competition, in the long-run equilibrium, charges higher price without enjoying monopoly profits.* A significant result follows from this. It is that the non-existence of economic profits is no indicator of the absence of monopoly element. In long-run equilibrium under monopolistic competition, as seen above, the firm has monopoly power (it has a sole control over its own differentiated product with the result that demand curve for it slopes downward) but does not make any economic or supernormal profits. Further, the existence of economic profits does not necessarily mean the presence of monopoly power. Under perfect competition, a firm in the short run may enjoy economic or supernormal profits due to the increase in demand for the product. Thus it has been rightly said that "*he skates on thin ice who identifies profits with monopoly and monopoly with profits.*"

Another noteworthy point about long-run equilibrium under monopolistic competition is that with the increase in the number of firms in the long run *demand curves facing individual firms will become more elastic in the sense that they will flatten out.* Although Chamberlin denies it, it is now commonly believed that as the number of firms gets larger in the long run, the cross elasticities of demand between the products of various firms will increase and as a result the demand curves of the firms will become more elastic (or graphically less steep). When, in the short run, economic profits are accruing to the firms due to the large demand for their brands or varieties of the product, lured by these economic profits the new firms will enter and try to produce brands or varieties as similar to the existing brands as possible. Thus, in the long run, products of various firms will become more similar or in other words, come closer together and as a result the demand curves facing individual firms will become more elastic. To put it in another way, the new firms which enter the group will come "in between" the old ones and thereby result in increasing the elasticities of demand curves (that is, make them flatten out).

Besides, the very fact that number of close substitutes in the long run increases due to the increase in the number of firms means that each brand will become more closely competitive with each other and hence the demand curve for the product of any one firm will become more elastic in the long run. Thus Professors Stonier and Hague write: "If new producers enter the industry, this is likely to mean that instead of, say, twenty similar cars being produced there will now be, say, forty. This again means that each of the cars is likely to be more similar to each other than it was previously. And the more closely competitive substitutes there are, the more elastic the demand for the product of any one firm in the group will be."[9]

EXCESS CAPACITY UNDER MONOPOLISTIC COMPETITION

Theories of Chamberlin's monopolistic competition and Joan Robinson's imperfect competition have revealed that a firm under monopolistic competition or imperfect competition in long-run equilibrium produces an output which is less than socially optimum or ideal output. This means that firms operate at the point on the falling portion of long-run average cost curve, that is, they do not produce the level of output at which long-run average cost is minimum. Long-run equilibrium of a firm under monopolistic competition is achieved when the demand curve (or average revenue curve) facing a firm becomes tangential to the long-run average cost curve so that it earns only normal profits. Under such circumstances a firm can reduce average cost (and hence price) by expanding output to the minimum level of long-run average cost, but it will not do so because its profits are maximised (equality of marginal revenue with marginal cost is attained) at the level of output smaller than that at which its long-run average cost is minimum.

Society's productive resources are fully utilised when they are used to produce the level of output which renders long-run average cost minimum. Thus a monopolistically competitive firm produces less than the socially optimum or ideal output, that is, the output corresponding to the lowest point of long-run average cost curve. This is in sharp contrast to the position of the firm in long-run equilibrium under perfect competition, which operates at the minimum point of the long-run average cost curve. The amount by which the actual long-run output of the firm under monopolistic competition falls short of the socially ideal output is a measure of *excess capacity* which means unutilised capacity.

The existence of excess capacity under monopolistic competition can be understood from Figures 20.6 and 20.7. Figure 20.7 depicts the long-run position of a perfectly competitive firm which is in long-run equilibrium at the level of output *ON* corresponding to which long-run average cost is minimum. It is at output *ON* that the double condition of long-run equilibrium, namely Price = *MC* = *AC* is fulfilled. It is thus clear that firms under perfect competition produce socially ideal output. On the other hand, a firm under monopolistic competition

9. Stonier and Hague, *A Textbook of Economic Theory*, 4th edition, 1972, p.209

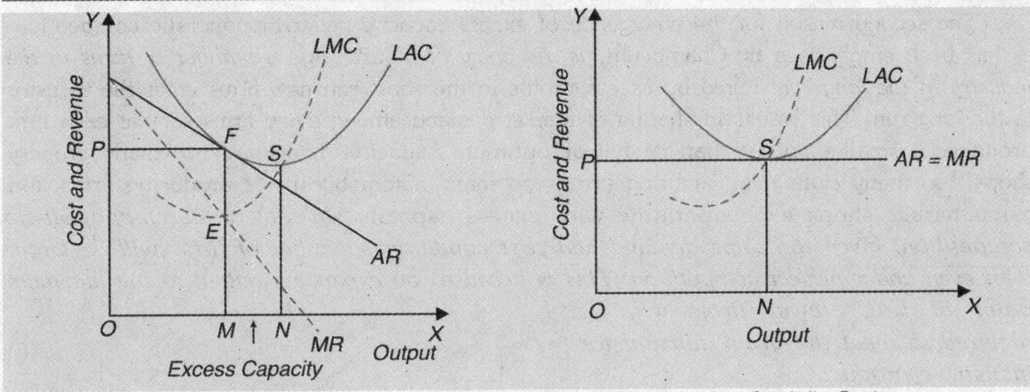

Fig. 20.6. *Excess Capacity under Monopolistic Competition*

Fig. 20.7. *Ideal or Socially Optimum Output under Perfect Competition*

depicted in Fig. 20.6 is in long-run equilibrium at output *OM* at which its marginal revenue is equal to marginal cost and price is equal to average cost (Average revenue curve *AR* is tangential to average cost curve *LAC* at point *F* corresponding to output *OM*). It will be noticed that at output *OM* long-run average cost (*LAC*) is still falling and goes on falling up to output *ON*. This means that the firm can expand its production up to *ON* and reduce his long-run average cost to the minimum. Ideal output is the output at which long-run average cost is minimum. Therefore, the firm is *producing MN less than the ideal output. Thus MN output represents the excess capacity which emerges under monopolistic competition.* It is worth noting that the concept of excess capacity refers only to the long run. This is because in the short run under any type of market structure (including perfect competition) there can be all sorts of departures from the ideal reflecting incomplete adjustment to the existing market conditions.

Causes of Excess Capacity

What factors are responsible for the existence of excess capacity under monopolistic competition? It is due to the existence of excess capacity that average cost of production and price of product are higher and output smaller monopolistic competition than under perfect competition. There are three main causes of the emergence of excess capacity under monopolistic competition. First, the most important cause of the existence of excess capacity under monopolistic competition is *downward-sloping demand curve* (*or average revenue curve*) *of the firm*. A downward-sloping average revenue curve can be tangent to a U-shaped average cost curve only at the latter's falling portion. It is only the horizontal demand curve or average revenue curve (as is actually found under perfect competition) which can be tangent to a U-shaped average cost curve at the latter's minimum point. From this, it also follows that the greater the elasticity of average revenue (or demand) curve confronting a monopolistically competitive firm, the less the excess capacity and *vice versa*. When the demand curve facing a firm is perfectly elastic, there is no excess capacity, as is the case under perfect competition.

Now, demand curve facing individual firms under monopolistic competition slopes downward due to *product differentiation* found in it. Various firms produce different varieties and brands of product and each has a certain degree of monopoly power over the variety or brand it produces for fixing price and output. If products were homogeneous, the demand curve would not have been downward sloping and long-run equilibrium would have been established at the minimum point of *LAC* without there being any excess capacity.

The second reason for the emergence of excess capacity under monopolistic competition, as has been emphasised by Chamberlin, *is the entry of a very large a number of firms in the industry in the long run.* Lured by excess profits in the short run new firms enter the industry in the long run. This results in sharing of market demand among many firms so that each firm produces a smaller output than its full or optimum capacity. There are too many grocery shops, too many cloth manufacturing firms, too many automobile parts producing firms, too many barber shops each operating with excess capacity. *In fact, under monopolistic competition, given the same demand and cost conditions, number of firms will be larger than even under perfect competition. This is because by expanding output to the minimum point of LAC, fewer firms will be required to meet the given demand for industry's product.*

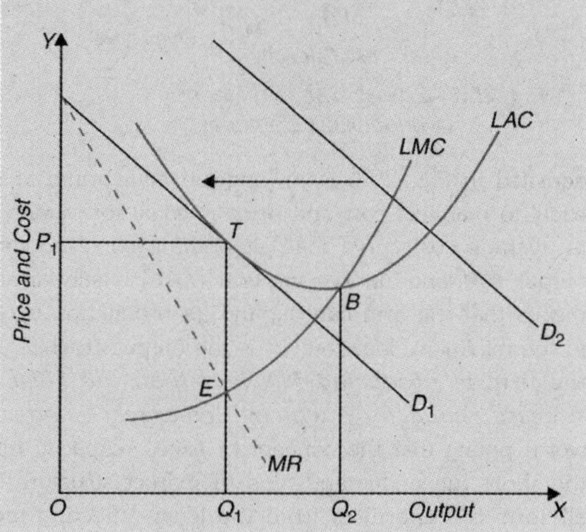

Fig. 20.8. *Emergence of Excess Capacity due to the Entry of Firms in the Long Run*

How entry of firms in the long run under monopolistic competition leads to the emergence of excess capacity is illustrated in Figure 20.8. Since there are no restrictions on the entry of new firms under monopolistic competition, lured by economic profits earned by the existing firms the new firms enter the industry in the long run. As a result, the number of firms in the industry increases so that market demand is shared among more firms resulting in the reduction in output of each firm. Consider Figure 20.8. Initially, the demand curve for firm's product is D_2 and the firm is in equilibrium at output level Q_2 by equating marginal revenue corresponding to the given demand curve D_2 with short-run marginal cost (To avoid confusion, marginal revenue curve and short-run marginal cost curve are not drawn). The firm will be making economic profits in the short run. Output Q_2 represents the ideal output as at it the long-run average cost (*LAC*) is minimum and society's resources are used efficiently. Lured by economic profits earned by the existing firms, new firms enter the industry and as a result the demand curve facing each firm shifts to the left. The demand curve will go on shifting to the left until it becomes tangent to the long-run average curve *LAC* at point *T*. But with the shift in the demand curve to D_1, the profit-maximising quantity has fallen to Q_1. Thus with the entry of new firms the excess capacity equal to Q_1Q_2 has emerged in the firm. Besides, as a consequence, *the consumer pays a price higher than the minimum long-run average cost* Q_2B.

The conception and the measure of excess capacity as enunciated above is based upon a particular notion of ideal output. Marshall, Kahn[10], Harrod[11], Cassels[12] and Joan Robinson have regarded *ideal output or optimum size of the firm as that output at which its long-run average cost is minimum.* To quote Joan Robinson, "In a perfectly competitive industry each

10. R.F. Kahn, "Some Notes on Ideal Output"', *Economic Journal*, XIV (1935), pp. 1-35.
11. R.F. Harrod, Doctrines of Imperfect Competition, *Quarterly Journal of Economics*, XLIX (1934-35), pp. 442-70.
12. J.M. Cassels, Excess Capacity and Monopolistic Competition, *Quartely Journal of Economics*, LI (1936-37), pp. 426-43.

firm in full equilibrium will produce that output at which its average costs are minimum. Each firm will then be of the optimum size. If competition is imperfect, the demand curve for the output of the individual firm will be falling and the double condition of equilibrium can only be fulfilled for some output at which average cost is falling. The firms will, therefore, be of less than optimum size when profits are normal... It is only if conditions of perfect competition prevail that firms will be of the optimum size and there is no reason to expect that they will be of optimum size in the real world since in the real world competition is not perfect."[13]

How Excess Capacity is Beneficial ? However, many modern economists are of the view that excess capacity under monopolistic competition is *desirable in some respects.* According to them, excess capacity under monopolistic competition provides some benefits which increase consumer welfare. As mentioned above, the excess capacity comes into existence mainly due to product differentiation under monopolistic competition. Now, this *product differentiation leads to product variety* which is highly beneficial to the consumers. The ability to choose among a wide variety of clothes, furniture, restaurant meals and various types of product designs add greatly to the satisfaction or welfare of the consumers. Therefore, according to this view, social benefits of excess capacity should be weighed against the cost to the society of excess capacity.

PRICE-OUTPUT EQUILIBRIUM UNDER MONOPOLISTIC COMPETITION COMPARED WITH THAT UNDER PERFECT COMPETITION

It is useful to explain how price-output equilibrium under monopolistic competition differs from that under perfect competition.

1. Price is greater than MC under monopolistic competition. A significant difference between the two relates to the relation between price and marginal cost. Whereas in equilibrium under perfect competition, price is equal to marginal cost, in equilibrium under monopolistic competition price is greater than marginal cost. Since under perfect competition, an individual firm cannot influence the price of its product and takes price as given and constant, the demand or average revenue curve facing it is a horizontal straight line and marginal revenue (*MR*) is equal to average revenue (*AR*) or price. Therefore, under perfect competition when a firm equates marginal cost with marginal revenue so as to maximise its profits, the former also becomes equal to price.

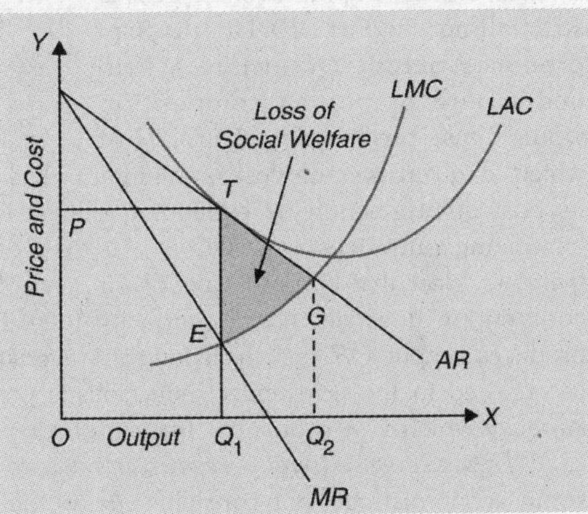

Fig. 20.9. *Inefficiency of Monopolistic Competition and Loss of Social Welfare.*

On the other hand, under monopolistic competition, a firm exercises some control over the price of its product and the demand curve for it, representing prices at various quantities, slopes downward. As a result, marginal revenue (*MR*) curve lies below average revenue (*AR*) curve. Therefore, in order to maximise profits when a firm under monopolistic competition equates marginal cost with marginal revenue, price stands at a higher level than marginal cost. This is clear from Fig.20.9 where, in equilibrium, price determined is equal to

13. Joan Robinson, *Economics of Imperfect Competition*, pp. 96-97.

OP or Q_1T, which is greater than marginal cost (Q_1E).

It should be noted that *producing level of output much less than at which marginal cost equals price implies a loss of social welfare.* It should be noted that social welfare is maximum when output is extended to the point where price is equal to long-run marginal cost. It will be seen from Fig. 20.9 that such point is G where price or $AR = LMC$. But as will be seen from Fig. 20.9 the firm working under conditions of monopolistic competition produces OQ_1 in the long-run equilibrium. Thus, the area *TEG represents loss of social* welfare which is also called *dead weight loss.* This indicates inefficiency of monopolistic competition.

2. Long-run equilibrium under monopolistic competition is established at less than the technically efficient scale size

Another important difference between the equilibrium under monopolistic competition and perfect competition is that whereas a firm in long-run equilibrium under monopolistic competition produces less than its technically efficient scale (that is, the level of output at which long-run average cost is minimum), as under perfect competition where long-run equilibrium of the firm is established at the minimum point of the long-run average cost curve. In other words, a firm under perfect competition tends to be of technically efficient scale. But a firm under monopolistic competition, as is evident from Fig. 20.10 stops short of the technically efficient scale and operates in the long run at the point at which long-run average cost is still falling. In Fig. 20.10 the firm produces output OQ, while a firm under pure or perfect competition would have produced output OR at which long-run average cost is minimum. The firm under monopolistic competition can reduce its cost of production by expanding output to the point R but it will not do so because by expanding output beyond OQ it will be reducing price more than the average cost. It is, therefore, clear that by producing OQ instead of OR in the long run, the firm under monopolistic competition does not use its capacity fully. (The firm would be using its capacity fully if it produces output OR at which long-run average cost is minimum). Thus, capacity equal to QR lies unused in the firm under monopolistic competition. This unused capacity is called *excess capacity* which is a prominent feature of long-run equilibrium under monopolistic competition.

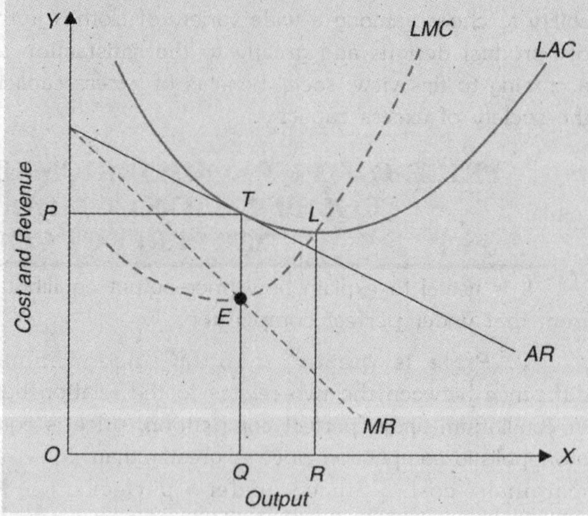

Fig. 20.10. *Production at less than Technically Efficient Scale*

This excess capacity represents waste of resources. However, as mentioned above, some economists do not consider QR as the excess capacity. According to them, this small loss of output and consequently higher average cost is price which people are paying for the product variety which they get under monopolistic competition due to product differentiation as compared to perfect competition. Further, *firms under monopolistic competition spend a lot of money on advertisement and other sales promotion activities which also represents* wastes of competition.

It needs to be emphasised that, according to Chamberlin, *a lot of excess capacity is created under monopolistic competition as a result of entry of a large number of firms only if price competition does not prevail.* If price competition prevails then there is not much excess capacity under monopolistic competition. However, in the long run many firms enter the industry so that market is shared among many and *in the absence of price competition* each produces much less than its full capacity.

3. Price under monopolistic competition is greater than competitive price.

Further, it may be noted that in the long-run equilibrium, firms under monopolistic competition make only normal profits as under perfect competition, but the price set under monopolistic competition is higher than competitive price, given the long average cost curve. In Fig. 20.10, price set in long-run equilibrium under monopolistic competition is *QT* while competitive price in the long run would have been equal to *RL*. This higher price under monopolistic competition is due to monopoly element contained in it. The monopoly element involved in monopolistic competition makes the demand or average revenue curve facing an individual firm downward sloping and a downward-sloping average revenue curve can be tangent to the long-run average cost curve only to the left of its minimum point.

Thus price under monopolistic competition will be higher than the perfectly competitive price due to the monopoly element in monopolistic competition. But, in spite of the higher price, a firm under monopolistic competition will not be making profits above normal in the long run. We may, therefore, say that a firm under monopolistic competition, in the long-run equilibrium, charges higher price without enjoying monopoly profits. A significant result follows from this. It is that the *non-existence of super-normal profits is no indicator of the absence of monopoly element.* In long-run equilibrium under monopolistic competition, as seen above, the firm has some monopoly power (it has a sole control over its own differentiated product) with the result that demand curve for it slopes downward) but it does not make any super-normal profits in the long run.

MONOPOLISTIC COMPETITION AND ECONOMIC EFFICIENCY

Perfect competition is said to be the ideal market form as it ensures maximum possible social welfare. In partial equilibrium analysis welfare is measuerd by the consumer surplus gained by the consumers and producer surplus earned by the producers. Under perfect competition, given the demand and cost conditions the maximum possible sum of consumer surplus and producer surplus is achieved so that social welfare is maximised. Besides, under perfect competition in the long run firms operate at the minimum point of the long-run average cost curve which ensures maximum efficiency in the use of resources. According to this, not only *optimum scale of plant* (*i.e*, plant with minimum *LAC*) is set up but also that plant is operated at its *optimum* or *full capacity*, that is, at the minimum point of short-run average cost curve of the plant.

On the other hand, firms operating in monopolistic competitive environment earn zero economic profits in their long-run equilibrium but they operate with *two types of inefficiencies.* First, as discussed above in detail, firms operate in the long run with *excess capacity* which implies inefficiency or waste in the use of resources and this impedes the achievement of maximum social welfare. In long-run equilibrium under monopolistic competition, firms operate at less than the scale of output at which long-run average cost is minimum. In this long-run equilibrium situation, neither the optimum scale of plant is set up, nor the plant actually set up is operated at its optimum capacity (*i.e.*, at minimum point of short-run average cost). This implies higher cost and price as well as lower output than if production had been done at minimum point of *LAC*. Thus, the existence of excess capacity under monopolistic competition causes inefficiency in the use of resources and loss of consumer welfare.

The second type of inefficiency that prevails under monopolistic competition is called *allocative inefficiency* which refers to the misallocation of resources among products which also causes loss of welfare. *Allocative efficiency is achieved if price of a product is fixed equal to the marginal cost of production*. However, under monopolistic competition firms are in long-run equilibrium at the level of output at which price exceeds marginal cost of production. Consider Fig. 20.9, the firm is in long-run equilibrium at output OQ_1 at which MR equals MC but price fixed is Q_1T or OP which exceeds marginal cost Q_1E at the equilibrium output. The ideal output from the viewpoint of allocative efficiency is OQ_2 at which price equals MC. It will be observed from the AR curve in the figure that the price which consumers are willing to pay for additional units from Q_1 to Q_2 exceeds the marginal cost of production to be incurred by the society. If output were extended to Q_2 at which demand (AR) curve cuts the long-run marginal cost curve LMC, the total surplus (sum of consumer surplus and producer surplus) could be increased by an amount equal to the shaded area ETG. This shaded area ETG represents *dead weight loss* of welfare. This dead-weight loss accrues due to the monopoly element involved in monopolistic competition. It may be recalled that monopoly element is present in monopolistic competition because products of different firms are differentiated and each of them has some control over the price of its product. Expansion of output to Q_2 requires allocation of more resources to the production of the product. By restricting output to Q_1 and thereby raising price of the product, firms operating under monopolistic competition do not allocate resources efficiently which cause dead-weight loss in social welfare. This is called dead-weight loss because there is no any compensating gain by any one else. Because of these inefficiences, monopolisitc competition was considered as socially undesirable form of market structure. However, many modern economists do not think so. This is for two reasons. First, the excess capacity that exists under monopolistic competition is very small because in the long run under monopolistic competition demand curve facing each firm becomes highly elastic as a result of the entry of new firms in the industry making available more close substitutes in the market.

Second, due to the demand (AR) curve becoming highly elastic in the long run monopolistic competition ensures that the difference between the price and marginal cost will also be very small which means whatever dead-weight loss in welfare occurs is not very significant. Above all there is gain or benefits to consumers because of *product variety* found in this market structure. Most consumers derive great satisfaction from the ability to choose among a wide variety of products and brands that exist under monopolistic competition. The gain in consumer welfare or benefits due to product diversity may be weighed against the cost of little inefficiency that prevails under monopolistic competition.

QUESTIONS AND PROBLEMS FOR REVIEW

1. What is monopolistic competition? Explain the important features of monopolistic competition.
2. What is product differentiation? What role does it play in the determination of price and output under monopolistic competition?
3. Analyse the short-run and long-run equilibrium of a firm working under monopolistic competition.
4. What is group equilibrium? Explain how group equilibrium is achieved under monopolistic competition.
5. (*a*) What is meant by excess capacity? Show that how a firm working under monopolistic competition works with excess capacity in the long run.
   (*b*) What causes excess capacity under monopolistic competition? Why is it undesirable?
6. *Are there any benefits of excess capacity associated with monopolistc competition?*
7. What are wastes of competition? How are they found under monopolistic competition?
8. Compare price-output equilibrium under monopolistic competition with that under (*a*) perfect competition, (*b*) monopoly.
9. Explain Chamberlin's concept of excess capacity. What, according to him, is responsible for the emergence of excess capacity under monopolistic competition?
10. Explain the concept of economic efficiency. Evaluate economic inefficiency of firms operating under monopolistic competition.
11. "Monopolistically competitive industries are characterised by too many firms each of which produces too little."

21

CHAPTER

Price and Output Determination Under Oligopoly

Introduction

We have studied price and output determination under three market forms, namely, perfect competition, monopoly, and monopolistic competition. However, in the real world economies we find that many of the markets or industries are oligopolistic. Oligopoly is an important form of imperfect competition. Oligopoly is said to prevail when there are few firms or sellers in the market producing or selling a product. In other words, when there are two or more than two, but not many, producers or sellers of a product, oligopoly is said to exist. Oligopoly is also often referred to as "*Competition among the Few*". *The simplest case of oligopoly is duopoly which prevails when there are only two producers or sellers of a product.* Analysis of duopoly raises all those basic problems which are confronted while explaining oligopoly with more than two firms.

Although there is no borderline between few and many but when the number of sellers of a product are two to ten, oligopoly situation is said to exist. When products of a few sellers are homogeneous, we talk of *Oligopoly without Product Differentiation or Pure Oligopoly.* On the other hand, when products of the few sellers or firms, instead of being homogeneous, are differentiated but close substitutes of each other, *Oligopoly with Product Differentiation or Differentiated Oligopoly* is said to prevail.

CHARACTERISTICS OF OLIGOPOLY

In oligopoly some special characteristics are found which are not present in other market structures. We discuss some of these characteristics below:

Interdependence. The most important feature of oligopoly is the interdependence in decision-making of the few firms which comprise the industry. This is because when the number of competitors is few, any change in price, output, product design etc. by a firm will have a direct effect on the fortune of its rivals, which will then retaliate in changing their own prices, output or products as the case may be. It is, therefore, clear that the oligopolistic firm must consider not only the market demand for the industry's product but also the reactions of the other firms in the industry to any action or decision it may take. Since more than one reaction-pattern is possible from the other firms, we have to make some assumptions about the reaction of the others before we can provide a definite and determinate solution of price-output fixation under oligopoly.

Importance of Advertising and Selling Costs. A direct effect of interdependence of oligopolists is that the various firms have to employ various aggressive and defensive marketing weapons to gain a greater share in the market or to prevent a fall in their market share. For this various firms have to incur a good deal of costs on advertising and on other measures of sales promotion. Therefore, there is a great importance of advertising and selling costs under conditions of market situation characterised by oligopoly. Prof. Baumol rightly says that "it is only under oligopoly that advertising comes fully into its own."[1] Under perfect competition, advertising by an individual firm is unnecessary in view of the fact that it can sell any amount of its product at the going price. A monopolist has also not to make any competitive advertisement since he is the only seller of a product. A monopolist may, perhaps, advertise when he has to inform the public about his introduction of a new model of his product or he may advertise in order to attract potential consumers who have not yet tried his product. Under monopolistic competition, advertising plays an important role because of the product differentiation that exists under it, but not as much important as under oligopoly. "Under oligopoly, advertising can become a life-and-death matter where a firm which fails to keep up with the advertising budget of its competitors may find its customers drifting off to rival products."[2]

In view of the fact that a firm in an oligopolistic industry competes by changing the advertisement costs, quality of the product, prices, output etc., *the presence of competitive conditions in it can hardly be denied.* To an oligopolist "Competition can consist not in the quiescent stalemate of perfect competition where there is no battle because there is never anyone strong enough to disturb the peace. Rather to him, true competition consists of the life of constant struggle, rival against rival, which one can only find under oligopoly (or, on a smaller scale, under conditions of monopolistic competition)."[3]

Group Behaviour. Further, another important feature of oligopoly is that for the proper solution to the problem of determination of price and output under it, analysis of group behaviour is important. Theories of perfect competition, monopoly and monopolistic competition present no difficult problem of making suitable assumption about human behaviour. In cases of perfect competition and monopolistic competition (with a large number of firms), the economists assume that the business firms behave in such a way as to maximise their profits. Assumption of profit maximisation gives overall good results in these situations where mass of people are involved and there is no interdependence of firms. On the other end, the theory of monopoly deals with a sole individual and it is also appropriate to assume profit maximising behaviour on his part.

But, the theory of oligopoly is a theory of *group behaviour* not of mass or individual behaviour, and to assume profit-maximising behaviour on the part of a producer of a group may not be very valid. In oligopoly, there are a few firms in a group which are very much interdependent. Given the present state of our economic and social science, there is no generally accepted theory of group behaviour. Do the members of a group will cooperate with each other in promotion of common interests or will they fight to promote their individual interests? Does the group possess any leader? If so, how does he get the others to follow him? These are some of the questions that need to be answered by the theory of group behaviour.

1. William J. Baumol, *Economic Theory and Operations Analysis,* 3rd ed., p. 352.
2. *Ibid*, p. 352.
3. *Ibid*, p. 352

Indeterminateness of Demand Curve Facing an Oligopolist. Another important feature is the indeterminateness of the demand curve facing an oligopolist. The demand curve shows what amounts of its product a firm will be able to sell at various prices. Now, under perfect competition, an individual firm's demand curve is given and definite. Since a perfectly competitive firm is one among a large number of firms producing an identical product, it is incapable of influencing the price of its product by its own individual action. Therefore, a firm under perfect competition faces a perfectly elastic demand curve at the level of the going price in the market. On the other hand, a monopolist produces a product which has only remote substitutes. Therefore, a monopolist can safely ignore the effects of its own price changes on his distant rivals and, therefore, the monopolist faces a given and definite demand curve depending upon the consumer's demand for his product. Under monopolistic competition, where there is a large number of firms producing products which are close substitutes of each other, changes in price by an individual firm will have a negligible effect on each of its many rivals. Therefore, a firm under monopolistic competition can validly assume the prices of its rivals to remain unchanged when it makes changes in the price of its product. Thus, the demand curve for a firm under monopolistic competition can be taken as definite and is given by the buyers' preferences for its product.

But the situation under oligopoly is quite different because of interdependence of the firms in it. Under oligopoly, a firm cannot assume that its rivals will keep their prices unchanged when it makes changes in its own price. As a result of this, the demand curve facing an oligopolistic firm loses its definiteness and determinateness because it goes on constantly shifting as the rivals change their prices in reaction to price changes by a firm.

CAUSES FOR THE EXISTENCE OF OLIGOPOLIES

Oligopolies dominate in many industries in the free market economies. Some of the factors responsible for the existence of oligopolies are natural in the sense that they are based on underlying production technologies and demand conditions for the products and some are created by the firms themselves. We explain below both these causes of the existence of oligopolies.

1. Economies of Scale. One important reason that a market may have few firms is the existence of economies of scale. When the economies of scale are quite strong, then the market for a product may be too small to support a large number of firms. When economies of scale exist, average cost falls rapidly over a large range of increase in the level of output. As a result of large economies of scale, a few firms can fulfil the demand for the product by producing on a large scale and thus lowering their average cost of production. These economies of scale may be based on division of labour when production of a complex product is split up into several simple tasks each of which is accomplished by the specialised workers using machines in an assembly-line production. The use of division of labour and large-scale production is limited by the size of market, as was pointed out by Adam Smith in his well-known book "*Wealth of Nations*'. Therefore, big firms have advantage over small firms on account of economies of scale based on division of labour. The larger the scale of production, the lower the average variable cost of production.

A Large Amount of Fixed Cost. Apart from the falling average variable cost due to the use of greater degree of division of labour, economies of scale also exist due to a large fixed cost incurred on developing and designing a new product. If the sales by a firm of a new product that has been developed after incurring a large fixed cost increase, its average fixed cost declines. This helps the firm to recover its fixed cost if it is produced on a large scale resulting in a lower average fixed cost. With a lower average fixed cost at a large scale of product, the firm will be able to sell it at a lower price and compete away its rival firms producing on a small scale. Thus, Lipsey and Chrystal write, "*With enormous development cost of some of today's high technology products, firms that can sell a large volume have a distinct pricing advantage over firms that sell a smaller volume. Firms with large product development costs face downward-sloping average total cost curve even if their average variable costs are constant.*"[4]

Economies of Scope. Similar to the economies of scale, there are economies of scope which arise in case of multiproduct firms when some of their resources can be used for the production of a number of products. *Economies of scope arise when production of different products within one firm leads to the lower average cost of production than if they were produced in independent firms.* Such economies of scope arise because some activities such as marketing and distribution can be shared by many products or there might be some skills available to the firm that can be used for the production of more than one product. The economies of scope also lower average cost of production and provide competitive advantage to large firms.

It follows from above that economies of scale arising out of division of labour and having a large fixed costs of product development and economies of scope enable a few large firms to lower unit cost of production. Market size of the product may be such that only a few large firms are able to exist and meet the demand for the product.

Barriers to Entry. A few firms in the industry may exist due to the barriers of entry. There are two types of barriers : technological and legal. A technological barrier to entry arises when the potential firms do not have the required knowledge or access to inputs as the existing firms. A legal barrier arises when government imposes restrictions on the entry of new firms to avoid harmful competition among the firms. For example, governments of many countries permit only a few firms to provide long-distance telephone calls or air-line services. Patents are another source of legal barriers to the entry of firms imposed by government as they provide incentives for future invention of new products.

Product-Differentiation. When products produced by various firms are differentiated, it provides some market power to the producers of different varieties of the product. It may be noted that the names such as Maruti, Indica, Santro are the brand names of cars manufactures in India. When the existing firms enjoy good reputation for their brands of the product, it is difficult for the new firms to enter the market with the new products to compete the existing ones. Besides, the existing firms even make strategic threats to potential entrants against entering the markets. Such threats may take the form of lowering the price of the product so as to make it unviable or unprofitable for the new entrants to operate in the industry. Product differentiation along with economies of scale are significant causes of the existence of oligopolies in the industry.

Firm-created Causes of Oligopolies. Product differentiation is not the only reason for the existence of a few big firms in the industries. Some existing firms may take strategic moves to take over other firms in the industry. Firms may grow and become big by *merging* with other firms. Firms may even drive out their rivals from the market by making them bankrupt through *predatory* practices. Thus, through takeovers, mergers and predatory practices, some firms in an industry become big and dominate it. By eliminating competitors, a few big firms are able to make large profits. However, the large profits made by the existing firms will attract the new firms in the industry. Therefore, unless the existing few firms can create and sustain strong barriers to the entry of new firms, oligopolies may not last long if they do not arise due to the technological factors such as economies of scale and scope.

4. Lipsey and Chrystal, *Economics*, 10th edition., p. 200.

Are Oligopolies due to Economies of Scale or Firms-Created Causes ?

As explained above, oligopolies exist both due to economies of scale and firms-created causes such as product-differentiation, moves to prevent entry of new firms, takeover of other firms or merging with them. In some industries, the few firms dominate because due to the economies of scale efficient size of the firm is large enough relative to the size of the market so that only a few firms can meet the demand for the products. Harward economist Alfred D. Chandler in an important work has given evidence that the *major reason for the existence of oligopolies in the United States, the United Kingdom and Germany is efficiency of the big firms gained through economies of scale and scope.*

ARE PRICE AND OUTPUT UNDER OLIGOPOLY INDETERMINATE ?

We have explained above the various characteristics and problems of oligopoly. The readers will now like to know how the economists analyse the determination of price and output under oligopoly. Because of the interdependence of firms in oligopoly and the uncertainty about the reaction patterns of the rivals, the easy and determinate solution to the oligopoly problem is not possible. In other words, interdependence of firms in an oligopoly and consequently firm's reactions to each other's behaviour poses serious difficulties in establishing the theory of the determination of price and output in an oligopolistic market.

Interdependence of Firms in Oligopoly

A significant consequence of interdependence of firms in an oligopolistic market situation is that under it a *wide variety of behaviour patterns becomes possible.* "Rivals may decide to get together and co-operate in the pursuit of their objectives, at least so far as the law allows or, at the other extreme, they may try to fight each other to the death. Even if they enter into an agreement it may last or it may break down. And the agreements may follow a wide variety of patterns."[5] Therefore, a large variety of models analysing price-output determination under oligopoly have been evolved by the economists depending upon the different assumptions about the behaviour of the oligopolistic group and the reaction patterns of rivals to a change in price or output by a firm.

Another difficulty that arises from interdependence of oligopolistic firms is the *indeterminateness of the demand curves facing individual firms.* As has been stated earlier, because of the interdependence an oligopolistic firm cannot assume that its rival firms will keep their prices and quantities constant when it makes changes in its price. When an oligopolistic firm changes its price, its rival firms will retaliate or react and change their prices which in turn would affect the demand for the product of the former firm. Therefore, an oligopolistic firm cannot have sure and definite demand curve, since it keeps shifting as the rivals change their prices in reaction to the price changes made by it. Moreover, there is quite an uncertainty about the rival's reactions to a price change by one firm. That is, when an oligopoly firm cuts its price, whether its rivals will also cut their prices similarly, or whether they will keep their prices unchanged. If they cut their prices, whether they will cut their prices by the same amount, or by a smaller or greater amount. A definite and determinate demand curve for a firm can be drawn if its rival's prices remain unchanged or if it is known before hand that they will change their prices in a *certain particular way* in response to price changes by one firm. But under oligopoly there is no certainty about the reactions of the rivals to the price changes made by a firm. Hence the demand curve of an oligopolistic firm cannot be easily determined.

Now, when an oligopolist does not know the demand curve confronting him, what price and output he will fix cannot be ascertained by economic analysis. In other words, in view of

5. William J Baumol, *op. cit*, pp. 223–24.

the indeterminateness of demand curve for a firm under oligopoly, the solution for the determination of price and output under oligopoly cannot be provided by the economic theory. Under conditions of perfect competition, monopoly and monopolistic competition, an individual firm faces a determinate demand curve which has a corresponding definite marginal revenue curve. Then, on the basis of profit maximisation principle, the determinate solution to the price and output fixation under perfect competition, monopoly and monopolistic competition is found by the equality of marginal revenue with marginal cost. This solution cannot be applied to price and output determination under oligopoly without qualification or making some additional assumptions because the individual firm's demand curve and, therefore, the marginal revenue curve is indeterminate or unknown. Thus even if profit maximisation assumption is considered as valid under conditions of oligopoly, no determinate solution for price-output fixation can be provided because of the indeterminateness of demand curve.

Even when the firms of an oligopoly do not enter into collusion, tacit or formal, or choose a leader from among themselves and instead try to compete with each other no single and simple solution is possible as to how a firm will fix its price and output. This is because of the uncertainty about the reaction patterns of the rivals to a move by one firm. This uncertainty about the reaction patterns of competitors poses a serious analytical difficulty in the way of providing a determinate solution for the oligopoly problem. Quoting Prof. Baumol again, "When a businessman wonders about his competitors' likely response to some move which he is considering, he must recognize that his competitors, too, are likely to take this interdependence phenomenon into account. The firms attempts to outguess one another are then likely to lead to an *interplay of anticipated strategies and counterstrategies which is tangled beyond hope of direct analysis*."[6] Thus under oligopoly a firm is likely to imagine an infinite sequence of compounded hypotheses such as "If I make move A, he may consider making countermove B, but he may realise that I might then respond by making move C, in which case..., and so an *ad infinitum*."

Profit-Maximising Assumption Challenged in Case of Oligopoly

Again, a determinate solution to the price-output problem in other market forms (perfect competition, monopoly and monopolistic competition) is arrived at by assuming profit-maximising motive on the part of the firms. But some economists have challenged the validity of the profit-maximising hypothesis in oligopolistic situations. According to Prof. Rothschild, *oligopolists aim at maximising their amount of stable profits over a long period of time rather than maximising profits at a time.*[7] On the other hand, Prof. Baumol thinks that in oligopolistic circumstances it is legitimate to assume *sales maximising objective* on the part of the firms.[8] Some other economists think that managers of oligopolistic firms maximise their own *utility function*. Still others like R.L. Morris think that firms try to maximise their *growth rate*. Finally, some economists assert that oligopolists do not maximise anything, they merely *satisfice*. In other words, they aim to achieve satisfactory performance in terms of profits, sales, market share rather than maximum profits. All this controversy about the real objective of the firms relates especially to the oligopolistic firms. This controversy about the most probable objective of the oligopolists further introduces indeterminacy in the analysis of price and output under oligopoly.

In view of above, there is no single determinate solution of the oligopoly problem but a wide variety of possible solutions, each depending upon different assumptions. It is worth

6. *Op. cit.*, p. 224 (italics added).
7. K.W. Rothschild, Price Theory and Oligopoly, *Economic Journal*, Vol. 57, 1947.
8. For Baumol's view about sales maximization objective, see chapter 29.

noting as to what exactly economists mean by *indeterminacy.* When no single solution of a problem is possible, economists generally say that the problem has no determinate solution. Thus economists usually speak of indeterminacy where mathematicians would speak of a multiplicity of solutions. Prof. Fritz Machlup explains the meaning of indeterminacy as follows:

"In a general way, economists speak of indeterminacy if not enough information is available to give a safe and unambiguous answer to a question before them. If they wish to solve a problem—for example, how the price of a certain commodity will change under certain conditions—but find that the data which are assumed to be "given" *would permit of two or more perhaps of an infinite number of* answers, they will say that the problem has no determinate solution."[9]

VARIOUS APPROACHES TO DETERMINATION OF PRICE AND OUTPUT UNDER OLIGOPOLY

It may, however, be pointed out that in spite of what has been said above, economists have tried to provide a determinate solution to the oligopoly problem. But there is no any *single determinate solution, but a number of determinate solutions* depending upon different assumptions. The determinate solution to the oligopoly problem has been provided in the following ways.

Ignoring Interdependence. First, for providing a determinate solution to the price-output determination, some economists have assumed that oligopolistic firms *ignore interdependence.* Now, when interdependence disappears from decision-making of the oligopolistic firms, the demand curve facing them becomes determinate and can be ascertained. With this, the standard analysis of the theory of the firm can be applied to provide a determinate solution for price and output problem of oligopoly. Classical models of duopoly put forward by Cournot and Bertrand fall in this category. In both those models, oligopolistic interdependence has been ignored. Cournot[10] in his famous model assumed that each oligopolistic firm would set its output in the belief that its rival firm's output would remain constant. On the other hand, Bertrand[11] assumed that an oligopolistic firm would set its price in the belief that its rival firm would keep its price unchanged. But for providing a solution for price and output determination under oligopoly by ignoring the interdependence is a fundamentally mistaken approach. Rothschild rightly writes, "The determinate solution can be reached.... if it is assumed that the oligopolists do not take into account the effect of their action on the policy of their rivals as in the famous Cournot and Bertrand's solutions; ...But this type of approach is absolutely valueless, because it only solves the oligopoly problem by removing from the analysis its most essential differentiating aspect: the oligopolists' consciousness of their interdependence."[12]

Predicting Reaction Pattern and Counter-moves of Rivals. The second approach to provide a determinate solution to the price and output problem of oligopoly is to assume that oligopolistic firm is able to *predict the reaction patterns and counter-moves of his rivals.* In this approach various oligopoly models based on different assumptions regarding the particular reaction patterns have been propounded. Chamberlin[13] while recognizing that

9. Fritz Machlup, The *Economics of Sellers' Competition,* p. 415 (italics added).
10. A. Cournot, "*Researches into the Mathematical Principles of the Theory of Wealth*", translated by Nathaniel T. Bacon, the Macmillan Co., New York, 1897.
11. J. Bertrand, "Theorie Mathematique de la Richesse Sociale", *Journal des Savants,* Paris, September 1893.
12. K.W. Rothschild, "Price Theory and Oligopoly", *'Economic Journal,'* Vol. 57, 1947, reprinted in *Reading in Price Theory* (AEA).
13. E.H. Chamberlin, *The Theory of Monopolistic Competition,* chapter 3 and Appendix A.

oligopolistic firms are conscious of their interdependence took some assumptions regarding the reaction pattern and provided a determinate solution according to which, under duopoly or oligopoly, monopoly output and price are determined so that *profits of duopolists (oligopolists) are jointly maximised.* P.M. Sweezy and Oxford economists, Hall and Hitch, assume that an oligopolist firm considers that while the price increase by it will not be followed by its rival firms, the price reduction will be matched by them. With such an assumption about the reaction pattern, demand curve facing an individual oligopolistic firm is of a kinked type with a kink at the current price. We shall discuss the kinked demand curve approach to oligopoly problem in detail later in this chapter. Many other economists assuming other reaction patterns have propounded various other oligopoly models.

Cooperative Behaviour :- Forming a Collusion to Maximise Joint Profits. The third approach to oligopoly problem assumes that oligopolistic firms, realising their interdependence, will pursue their common interests and will form a collusion, formal or tacit, that is, will enter into agreement and work in the pursuit of their common interests. They will maximise joint profits and share profits, market or output as agreed to between them. A variant of this approach is that firms in an oligopoly would accept one firm as a leader, which may be a dominant or low-cost firm, and they will follow their leader in the fixation of price of the product. Both the collusive and price leadership oligopoly models will be critically examined later in this chapter. In case of collusion and price leadership, the problem of indeterminateness of demand curve is not encountered.

Game Theory Approach to Oligopoly. Another significant approach to the oligopoly is that of the *theory of games*, put forward by Neumann and Morgenstern. In the theory of games, an oligopolistic firm does not guess at its rivals' reaction pattern, but *calculates the optimal moves by rival firms*, that is, their best possible strategies and in view of that adopts its own policies and counter-moves. The explanation of the application of the theory of games to the oligopoly problem will be discussed in a separate chapter in this book.

From our above analysis it follows that there is no single determinate solution to the price-output fixation under oligopoly. As said above, economists have developed a large number of models by taking different assumptions regarding the behaviour of the oligopolistic group (that is, whether they will cooperate together or fight with each other), regarding the objective they seek to achieve (that is, whether they are assumed to maximise individual or joint profits or they are assumed to maximise sales etc.), and regarding the *different reaction patterns* of rival firms to price and output changes by one firm.

COOPERATIVE VS. NON COOPERATIVE BEHAVIOUR : BASIC DILEMMA OF OLIGOPOLY

An important difference between oligopoly on the one hand and perfect competition and monopolistic competition on the other is that behaviour of oligopolistic firms can be strategic in deciding about their price and output policies. *The strategic behaviour means that the oligopolistic firms must take into account the effect of their price-output decisions on their rival firms and on the reactions they expect from them.* On the other hand, the firms working in perfect competition about their price and output and monopolistic competition while deciling about their price and output engage in non-strategic behaviour which means that while making decisions they do not take into account the likely reactions of their large number of competitors. Instead, in making decisions about their price and output, they are guided by their own demand and cost curves. The behaviour of monopolist is also non-strategic as he has no competitors with whom to compete and interact. A monopolist sets his price and output quite independently of others.

However, behaviour of an oligopolistic firm is a strategic one as it interacts with a few rivals who are affected by its decisions. There are mainly two types of strategies open to the oligopolists : *compete with their rivals to promote their individual interests or cooperate with them to promote their mutual interests, namely, to maximise joint profits*. This is the basic dilemma facing oligopolistic firms. The oligopolistic firms can make more profits as a group if they cooperate. However, any one oligopolistic firm can make more profits for itself by taking an appropriate price-output decision provided others continue to cooperate. In a perfectly competitive industry there are such a large number of firms that it is not possible to reach a cooperative solution unless some central authority enforce a cooperative decision on them. In contrast, in an oligopolistic industry the few firms can recognise their interdependence and realise the loss they may incur if they compete with each other instead of cooperating. Therefore, they can adopt cooperative behaviour to maximise their joint profits. In what follows we explain in brief the cooperative and non-cooperative behaviour in the context of oligopolistic market structure.

Cooperative Solution

If the few firms cooperate they can form a cartel *overtly* if permitted by law and *tacitly* if formal formation of cartel is prohibited by law. By deciding not to compete with each other they can decide to charge a monopoly price and reach an agreement on the outputs produced by each. In this way the cooperative behaviour results in maximisation of joint profits, that is, monopoly profits if they worked as one firm. We will explain later the *collusive oligopoly model which* provides an example of cooperative behaviour. However, we will see there how individual firms in a cartel has a tendency to cheat and try to undercut price to make more profits.

Another model of cooperative behaviour is *price-leadership model* where the few firms in an oligopolistic industry accept one firm as leader and accept the price set by it. Another cooperative model is put forward by Chamberlin who explains *how firms working independently* realise their interdependence and realise the prospects of making losses if they compete with each other. This leads them to charge a monopoly price which maximises their joint profits.

The Non-Cooperative Equilibrium : Nash Equilibrium

If few firms in the industry do not cooperate and compete with each other, even then they can reach an equilibrium, which is called *non-cooperative equilibrium*. This type of equilibrium is also called *Nash Equilibrium*, named after John Nash, the well-known US mathematician who was awarded the Nobel Prize in economics for his work in 1994[14], Nash equilibrium is reached when each firm thinks that *its present strategy is the optimum strategy given the present strategy of other firms*. That is, each firm in an oligopolistic industry has reached a strategy that it thinks is best under the circumstances provided others continue to follow their present strategies. The oldest model of duopoly was propounded by a French economist, A Cournot (1801-1876). In Cournot model the two firms do not cooperate but compete with each other. In Cournot's duopoly model each firm decides about the output it will produce, *assuming that its rival firm will keep its output constant at the present level.* Even competing through changes in output, the two duopolistic firms will reach the Nash equilibrium in which *each* thinks its present strategy is the best, given the output of the other firm. The other important model based on non-cooperative behaviour has been propounded

14. On the whole life of John Nash a motion picture *'A Beautiful Mind'* has been made by the Hollywood. It is quite interesting to see this picture (now available in a CD form) to know the working of the mind of this great thinker.

by the French Mathematician Bertrand (1822-1900). In Bertrand model it is assumed that in making price decision, *a firm assumes that the other firm will keep its price constant.* After engaging in price war, in Bertrand model the duopolists reach the equilibrium state in which each firm thinks it is setting the best or optimum price, given the present price of the other firm. From the foregoing analysis we see that economists have built models assuming both cooperative and non-cooperative behaviour of the firms.

COLLUSIVE OLIGOPOLY : CARTEL AS A COOPERATIVE MODEL

In order to avoid uncertainty arising out of interdependence and to avoid price wars and cut throat competition, firms working under oligopolistic conditions often enter into agreement regarding a uniform price-output policy to be pursued by them. The agreement may be either formal (open) or tacit (secret). But since formal or open agreements to form monopolies are illegal in most countries, agreements reached between oligopolists are generally tacit or secret. When the firms enter into such collusive agreements formally or secretly, collusive oligopoly prevails. But collusions are of two main types: (*a*) cartels and (*b*) price leadership. In a cartel type of collusive oligopoly, firms jointly fix a price and output policy through agreements. But under price leadership one firm sets the price and others follow it. The one which sets the price is a price leader and the others who follow it are its followers. The follower firms adopt the price of the leader even though they have to depart from their profit-maximising position, as they think that it is to their advantage not to compete with their leader and between themselves. In this present section we confine ourselves to explain the determination of price and output under the cartel type of collusive oligopoly and in the next section we will explain price and output determination under price-leadership form of collusive oligopoly.

Originally, the term 'cartel' was used for the agreement in which there existed a common sales agency which alone undertook the selling operations of all the firms that were party to the agreement. But now-a-days all types of formal or informal and tacit agreements reached among the oligopolistic firms of an industry are known as cartels. Since these cartels restrain competition among the member firms, their formations have been made illegal in some countries by the Governments passing laws against them. For instance, the formation of a cartel is illegal in U.S.A. under the Anti-Trust Laws passed there. However, in spite of the illegality of cartels they are still formed in U.S.A. through secret devices and by adopting some means or the other shrewd businessmen are able to evade the anti-monopoly laws.

Formal collusion or agreement among the oligopolists may itself take various forms. An extreme form of collusion is found when the member firms agree to surrender completely their rights of price and output determination to a 'Central Administrative Agency' so as to secure maximum joint profits for them. Formation of such a formal collusion is generally designated as *perfect cartel.* Thus under perfect cartel type of collusive oligopoly, the price and output determination of the whole industry as well as of each member firm is determined by the common administrative authority so as to *achieve maximum joint profits for the member firms.*

The total profits are distributed among the member firms in a way already agreed between them. The share from total profits of each member firm is not necessarily in proportion to the output quota it has to supply and the cost it incurs on it. The output quota to be produced by each firm is decided by the central administrative authority in such a way that the total costs of the total output produced is minimum. In fact, under perfect cartel, the central authority determines the separate outputs to be produced by the various members and the price they have to charge in the same way as a monopolist operating multiple plants would do. Now, the question arises as to what outputs different firms in a cartel will be asked to produce so that the total cost is made minimum. Total cost will be minimised when the various firms in the cartel produce such separate outputs so that their marginal costs are equal. This is because if the marginal costs of the member firms are not equal, then the marginal units of output could be produced at a smaller cost by the firms with a lower marginal cost than by those with a higher marginal cost.

Let us now see how the cartel works and determines its price and output. Let us assume that two firms have formed a cartel by entering into an agreement. We assume that the *cartel*

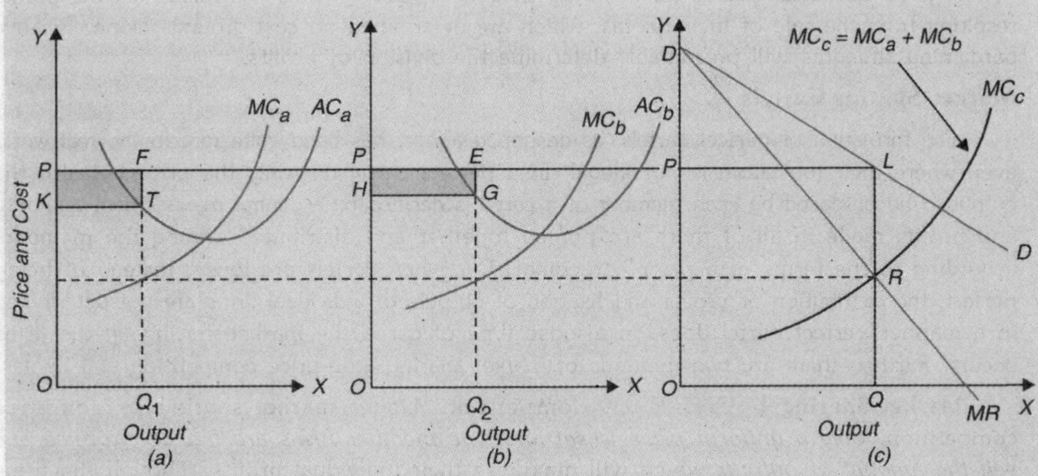

Fig. 21.1. *Price and Output Determination under Cartel: Joint Profit Maximisation*

will aim at maximising joint profits for the member firms. First of all, the cartel will estimate the demand curve of the industry's product. As the demand curve facing a cartel will be the aggregate demand curve of the consumers of the product, it will be sloping downward as is shown by the curve *DD* in Fig. 21.1(*c*). Marginal revenue curve *MR* showing the addition to cartel's revenue for successive additions to its output and sales will lie below the demand curve *DD*. Cartel's marginal cost curve (MC_c) will be given by the horizontal addition of the marginal cost curves of the two firms. This has been done in Fig. 21.1(*c*) where MC_c curve has been obtained by adding horizontally marginal cost curves MC_a and MC_b of firms *A* and *B* respectively. It should be noted that cartel's marginal cost curve MC_c, obtained as it is by horizontal addition of marginal cost curves of the two firms, will indicate the minimum possible total cost of producing each industry output on it; each industry's output being distributed among the two firms in such a way that their marginal costs are equal.

Now, the cartel will maximise its profits by fixing the industry's output at the level at which *MR* and *MC* curves of the cartel intersect each other. It will be seen in Fig. 21.1(*c*) that *MR* and *MC* curves cut each other at point *R* or output *OQ*. It will also be seen from the demand curve *DD* that the output *OQ* will determine price equal to *QL* or *OP*. Having decided the total output *OQ* to be produced, the cartel will allot output quota to be produced by each firm so that the marginal cost of each firm is the same. This can be known by drawing a horizontal straight line from point *R* towards the *Y*-axis. It will be seen from the figure that when firm *A* produces OQ_1 and firm *B* produces OQ_2, the marginal costs of the two firms are equal. The output quota of firm *A* will be OQ_1, and of firm *B* will be OQ_2. It is worth noting that the total output *OQ* will be equal to the sum of OQ_1 and OQ_2.

Thus, the determination of output *OQ* and price *OP* and the outputs OQ_1 and OQ_2 by the two firms *A* and *B* will ensure the maximum joint profits for the member firms constituting the cartel. It will be seen from Fig. 21.1(*a*) that with output OQ_1 and cartel price *OP*, the profits made in firm *A* are equal to *PFTK* and with output OQ_2 and cartel price *OP* the profits made in firm *B* are equal to *PEGH*. The sum of profits, that is, the joint profits made by the cartel will be maximum under the given demand and cost conditions as they have been arrived at as a result of equating combined marginal cost (MC_c) with the combined marginal revenue (*MR*). *The allocation of output quota to each of them is made on the grounds of minimising cost and not as a basis for determining profit distribution.* Prof. J.S. Bain rightly says, "There is no particular reason for believing that the operating firms will retain just the profits resulting from the sale of their quotas, which are determined on cost grounds alone. Relative bargaining strengths will presumably determine the division of profits."[15]

Market-Sharing Cartels

The formation of perfect cartels, as described above, has been quite rare in the real world even where their formation is not illegal. In a perfect cartel not only the price but also the output to be produced by each member of a cartel is decided by a central management authority and profits made in all of them are pooled together and distributed among the members according to the terms of a prior agreement. But when cartels are loose, instead of being perfect, the distribution of profits and fixation of outputs of individual firms are not determined in a manner perfect cartel does. In a loose type of cartel the market-sharing by the firms occurs. Further, there are two methods of market sharing: non-price competition and quotas.

Market-Sharing by Non-Price Competition. Under market sharing by non-price competition, *only a uniform price is set and, the member firms are free to produce and sell the amount of outputs* which will maximise their individual profits. Though the firms agree not to sell at a price below the fixed price they are free to vary the style of their product and the advertising expenditure and to promote sales in other ways. That is, the price being a fixed datum, the firms compete on non-price basis. If the different member firms have identical costs, then the agreed uniform price will be the monopoly price which will ensure maximisation of joint profits. But when there are cost differences between the firms as is generally the case, the cartel price will be fixed by bargaining between the firms. The level of this price will be such as will ensure some profits to high-cost firms.

But with cost differences such loose cartels are quite unstable. This is because the low cost firms will have an incentive to cut price to increase their profits and therefore they will tend to break away from the cartel. However, they may not openly charge lower price than the fixed one and instead cheat the other firms by giving secret price concessions to the buyers. However, as the rivals gradually lose their customers, the cheating by the low-cost firms will be ultimately discovered and consequently open price war may commence and cartel breaks down.

Market-Sharing by Output Quota. The second type of market-sharing cartel is the agreement reached between the oligopolistic firms regarding quota of output to be produced and sold by each of them at the agreed price. If all firms are producing homogeneous product and have same costs, the monopoly solution (that is, the maximisation of joint profits) will emerge with the market being equally shared by them. However, when costs of member-firms are different, the different quotas for various firms will be fixed and, therefore, their market shares will differ. The quotas and market shares in case of cost differences are decided through bargaining between the firms. During the bargaining process, two criteria are usually adopted to fix the quotas of the firms. One is the past level of sales of the various firms and the second is the productive capacity of the firms. However, the 'past-period sales' and 'productive capacity'

15. J.S. Bain, *Pricing, Distribution and Employment*, 1953, p. 286.

of various firms are not very firm criteria as they can be easily manipulated. Ultimately, the quotas fixed for various firms depend upon their bargaining power and skill.

The second common basis for the quota system and market sharing is the division of market regionwise, that is, the geographical division of the market between the cartel firms. In this arrangement, price and also style of the product of cartel firms may vary.

Instability of a Cartel

It is worth noting that all types of cartels are unstable when there exists cost differences between firms. The low-cost firms always have a tendency to reduce price of the product to maximise their profits which ultimately results in the collapse of the collusive agreement. Further, if the entry of firms in the oligopolistic industry is free, the instability of the cartel is intensified. The new entrants may not join the cartel and may fix a lower price of the product to sell a large quantity. This may start a price war between the cartel firms and the new entrants. We thus see that the stability of the cartel arrangement is always in danger.

Graphical illustration. The strong incentive to cheat on the part of cartel members and consequently causing a break-down of a cartel is graphically illustrated in Fig. 21.2, where *DD* is market demand curve facing the cartel consisting of two firms *A* and *B*. MC_a in panel (*i*) is the marginal cost curve of the firm *A*. Summing up horizontally marginal cost curves of the two firms forming a cartel we get the combined marginal cost curve MC_{a+b}. The cartel maximises its profits by equating *MR* with MC_{a+b} and accordingly output *OQ* and price *OP* are fixed. The output share of each firm will be fixed where marginal cost of each firm equals the combined marginal cost of the cartel members. Accordingly, the output share of firm *A* shown in panel (*i*) is Oq_a at which marginal cost of firm *A* equals the combined marginal cost *OT* or *QE* in the equilibrium situation. Oq_a will be the agreed share of output of firm *A*. To simplify our analysis we have not shown the cost situation of firm *B*, the other member of the cartel.

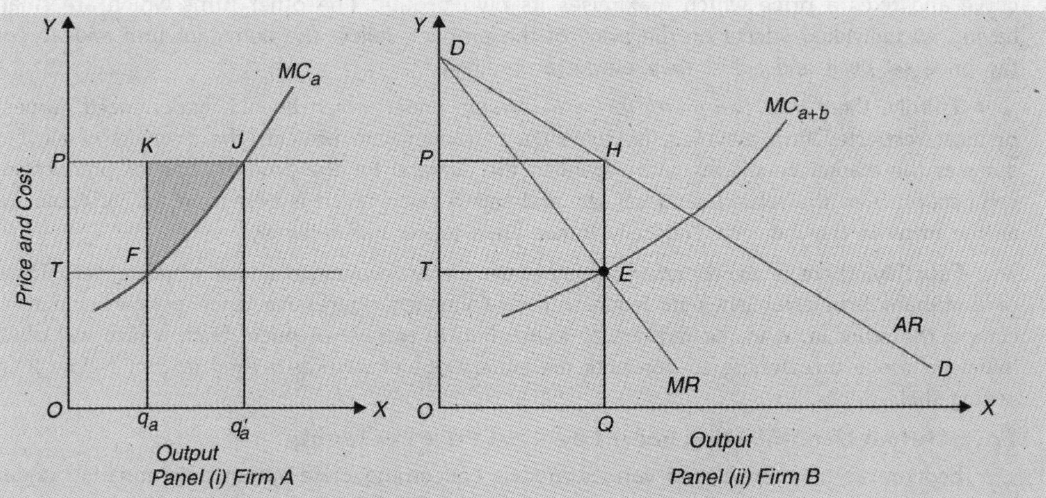

Fig. 21.2. *Instability of a Cartel Due to Cheating by a Member*

Thus, under the cartel agreement, firm *A* will be producing Oq_a, and charging price *OP*. Now, a glance at panel (*i*) in Fig. 21.2, reveals that given the price *OP*, fixed by the cartel, if the firm *A* increases its output from agreed share Oq_a to Oq'_a, it can increase its profits by the shaded area *FKJ*. This means that in order to increase its profits the firm *A* will have incentive to cheat by trying to produce and sell more at the agreed price *OP*. Similarly, the firm *B*, other member of the cartel (not shown in Fig. 21.2) will also find that it can increase its profits by violating the cartel agreement by producing and selling more than its agreed output share. To sum up, *it is due to the promotion of self-interest by cartel members that accounts for the instability of cartel arrangements and frequent price wars.*

PRICE LEADERSHIP

As mentioned above, price leadership is an important form of collusive oligopoly. Under it, one firm sets the price, others follow it. Price leadership also comes into existence either through tacit or formal agreement. But as the formal or open agreement to establish price leadership are generally illegal, price leadership is generally established as a result of *informal and tacit understanding* between the oligopolists. The competing oligopolists in an informal meeting choose a leader and agree to follow him in setting price.

Types of Price Leadership

Price leadership is of various types. Firstly, there is a *price leadership by a low-cost firm.* In order to maximise profits the low-cost firm sets a lower price than the profit-maximising price of the high-cost firms. Since the high-cost firms will not be able to sell their product at the higher price, they are forced to agree to the low price set by the low-cost firm. Of course, the low-cost price leader has to ensure that the price which he sets must yield some profits to the high-cost firms—their followers.

Secondly, there is a *price leadership of the dominant firm.* Under this one of the few firms in the industry may be producing a vary large proportion of the total production of the industry and may, therefore, dominate the market for the product. This dominant firm wields a great influence over the market for the product, while other firms are small and are incapable of making any impact on the market. As a result, the dominant firm estimates its own demand curve and fixes a price which maximises its own profits. The other firms which are small having no individual effects on the price of the product, follow the dominant firm and accept the price set by it and adjust their output accordingly.

Thirdly, there is a *barometric price leadership* under which an old, experienced, largest or most respected firm assumes the role of a custodian who protects the interests of all. He assesses the market conditions with regard to the demand for the product, cost of production, competition from the related products etc. and sets a price which is best from the viewpoint of all the firms in the industry. Naturally, other firms follow him willingly.

Fourthly, there is *exploitative or aggressive price leadership* under which a very large or dominant firm establishes its leadership by following aggressive price policies and thus compel the other firms in the industry to follow him in respect of price. Such a firm will often initiate a move threatening to compete the others out of market if they do not follow it in setting their prices.

Price-Output Determination under Low-Cost Price Leadership

Economists have developed various models concerning price-output determination under price leadership making different assumptions about the behaviour of price leader and his followers. We shall first explain price-output determination under price leadership by a low-cost firm. In order to simplify our analysis we make the following assumptions:

(1) There are two firms, *A* and *B*. The firm *A* has a lower cost of production than firm *B*.

(2) The product produced by the two firms is homogeneous so that the consumers have no preference between them.

(3) Each of the two firms has equal share in the market. In other words, demand curve facing each firm will be the same and will be half of the total market demand curve of product.

Given the above assumptions, price and output determination under price leadership is illustrated in Fig. 21.3. Each firm is facing demand curve *Dd* which is half of the total market demand curve *DD* for the product. *MR* is the marginal revenue curve of each firm. AC_a and MC_a are the average and marginal cost curves of firm *A* and AC_b and MC_b are the average and marginal cost curves of firm *B*. Cost curves of firm *A* lie below the cost curves of firm *B* because we are assuming that firm *A* has a lower cost of production than firm *B*.

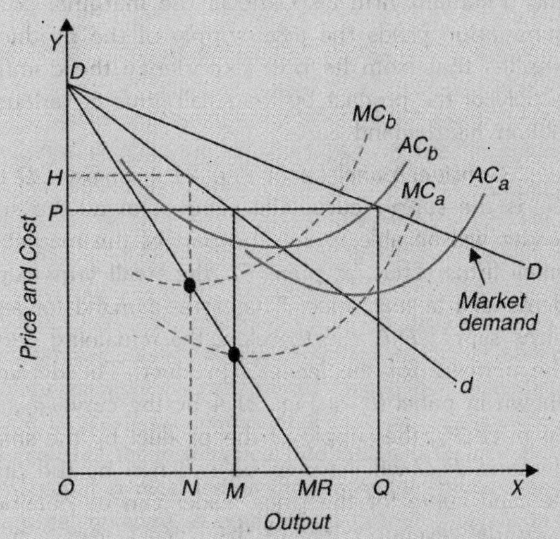

Fig. 21.3. *Price-Output Determination under Low-Cost Price Leadership*

The firm *A* will be maximising its profits by selling output *OM* and setting price *OP*, since at output *OM*, its marginal cost is equal to the marginal revenue. Firm *B*s profits will be maximum when it fixes price *OH* and sells output *ON*. It will be seen from the figure that profit-maximising price *OP* of firm *A* is lower than the profit-maximising price *OH* of firm *B*. Since the two firms are producing a homogeneous product, they cannot charge two different prices. Because the profit-maximising price *OP* of firm *A* is lower than the profit-maximising price *OH* of firm *B*, firm *A* will dictate price to the firm *B* or, in other words, firm *A* will win if there is price war between the two and will emerge as a price leader and firm *B* will be compelled to follow. Given these facts, the agreement reached between them, even though tacit it may be, will require that the firm *A* will act as the price leader and firm *B* as the price follower.

It should be noted that firm *B* after having accepted firm *A* as the price leader will actually charge price *OP* and produce and sell *OM*. This is because at price *OP*, it can sell *OM* output like firm *A* because the demand curve facing each firm is the same. Thus, both the firms will charge the same price *OP* and sell the same amount (*OM*). Note that the total output of the two firms will be *OM* + *OM* = *OQ* which will be equal to the market demand for the good at price *OP*. But there is an important difference between the two. While firm *A*, the price leader, will be maximising its profits by selling output *OM* and charging price *OP*, the firm *B* will not be making maximum profits with this price-output combination because its profits are maximum at output *ON* and price *OH*. Profits earned by firm *B* by producing and selling output *OM* and charging price *OP* will be smaller than those of firm *A* because its costs are greater.

When the products of the price leader and his price followers are differentiated, then the price charged by them will be different but the prices charged by the followers will be only slightly different either way from that of the price leader and they will conform to a definite pattern of differentials.

Price-Output Determination Under Price Leadership by the Dominant Firm

We now proceed to explain the determination of price and output when there exists price leadership by a dominant firm which is having a large share of the market with a number of small firms as followers each of which has a small share of the market. To explain this we assume that the dominant firm knows the total market demand curve for the product. Further, the dominant firm also knows the marginal cost curves of the smaller firms whose lateral summation yields the total supply of the product by the small firms at various prices. This implies that from its past experience the dominant firm can estimate fairly well the likely supply of the product by the small firms at various prices. With this information, the leader can obtain his demand curve.

Consider panel (*a*) of Fig. 21.4 where *DD* is the market demand curve for the product, S_m is the supply curve the product of all the small firms taken together. At each price the leader will be able to sell the part of the market demand not fulfilled by the supply from the small firms. Thus, at price P_1, the small firms supply the whole of the quantity of the product demanded at that price. Therefore, demand for leader's product is zero. At price P_2, the small firms supply P_2C and therefore the remaining part of *CT* of the market demand will constitute the demand for the leader's product. The demand for leader's product has been separately shown in panel (*b*) of Fig. 21.4 by the curve d_L. P_2Z in panel *(b)* is equal to *C T* in panel *(a)*. At price P_3, the supply of the product by the small firms is zero. Therefore, the whole market demand P_3U will have to be satisfied by the price leader. Likewise, the other point of the demand curve for the price leader can be obtained. In panel (*b*) of Fig. 21.4 the MR_L is the marginal revenue curve of the price leader corresponding to his demand curve d_L. *AC* and *MC* are his average and marginal cost curves. The dominant price leader will maximise his profits by producing output *OQ* (or *PH*) and setting price *OP*. The followers, that is, the small firms will charge the price *OP* and will together produce *PB*. [*PH* in panel (*b*) equals *BS* of panel (*a*) in Fig. 21.4].

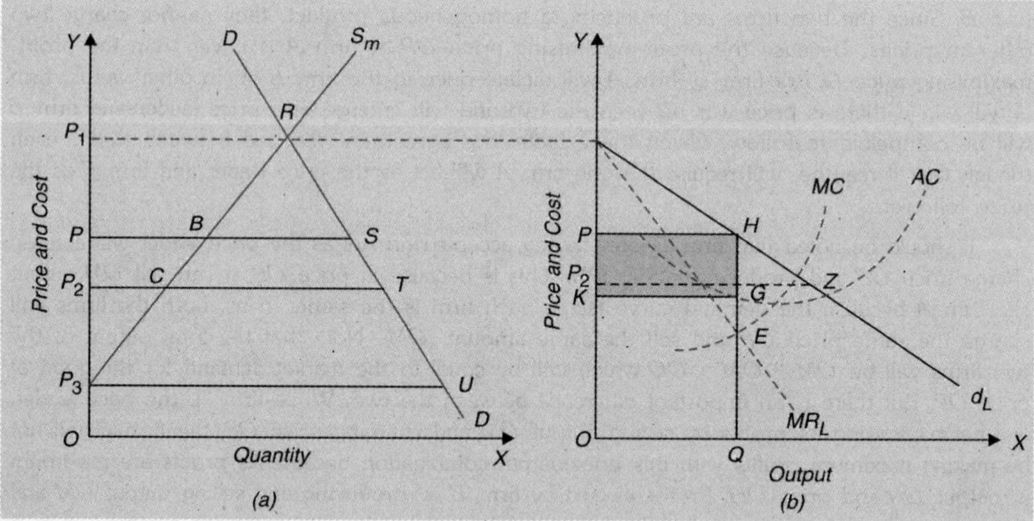

Fig. 21.4. *Price Leadership by the Dominant Firm*

It is worth noting that in order that profits of the leader are maximised it is not enough that followers should charge profit-maximising price *OP* set by him; he will also have to ensure that they produce output *PB*. If the followers produce more or less than this, given the market demand *DD*, the leader will be pushed to a non-profit maximising position. This implies that if price-leadership is to remain, there must be some definite market-sharing agreement, tacit though it may be.

Difficulties of Price Leadership

Price leadership involves many difficulties in the real world. First, the success of price leadership of a firm depends upon the correctness of his estimates about the reactions of his followers. If his estimates about the reactions of his rivals to price changes by it prove to be incorrect, then not only the success of his price policy but also his leadership in the market will be jeopardised. Secondly, when a price leader fixes a higher price than the followers would prefer, there is a strong tendency for the followers to make hidden price cuts in order to increase their shares of the market without openly challenging the price leader. A good number of devices which amount to secret price cutting are used by business firms. Some of these secret price-cutting devices are the offer of rebates, favourable credit terms, 'money back' guarantees, after-delivery free services, sale on the payment of price in easy installments with low rates of interest etc., and liberal entertainment of the buyers. Price leaders are generally fed up with the increasing number of concessions granted by their rivals and they make an open price cut to prevent further fall in their share of the market. In such circumstances price leadership becomes infructuous.

Another important difficulty of maintaining price leadership is the tendency on the part of the rivals to indulge in *non-price competition* to increase sales while charging the price set by the price leader. The devices used under 'non-price competition' include advertising and other methods of the sales promotion, like improvement of the quality of the product, in addition to the hidden price-product concessions mentioned above. While charging the same price, the rivals try to increase their share of the market by increasing the advertisement expenditure. As a result of this non-price competition, the price leader has also to adopt similar devices to prevent the fall in its sales or has to make outright cut in price in order to achieve his objective. In view of these facts, the price leader may not be able to maintain his leadership for a long time.

Further, there is a great limitation on the price leader to fix a high price of his product. This is because the high price will induce the rivals to make secret price cuts which will adversely affect the sales of the price leader. Moreover, a high price fixed by the price leader will attract new competitors into the industry which may not accept his leadership. Lastly, differences in costs also pose a problem. If the price leader has higher costs, then the high price fixed by him will, as mentioned above, induce the rivals to undercut price or will attract the entry of new firms into the industry. If the price leader has lower costs than his rivals, he will set a low price which will antagonise his rivals who will disturb him quite frequently.

THE KINKED DEMAND CURVE THEORY OF OLIGOPOLY

It has been observed that many oligopolistic industries exhibit an appreciable degree of price rigidity or stability. In other words, in many oligopolistic industries prices remain sticky or inflexible, that is, there is no tendency on the part of the oligopolists to change the price even if the economic conditions undergo a change. Many explanations have been given of this price rigidity under oligopoly and most popular explanation is the kinked demand curve hypothesis. The kinked demand curve hypothesis was put forward independently by Paul M. Sweezy[16], an American economist, and by Hall and Hitch[17], Oxford economists.

It is especially for explaining price and output *under oligopoly with product differentiation* that economists often use the kinked demand curve hypothesis. This is because when under

16. Paul M. Sweezy, "Demand under Conditions of Oligopoly", *Journal of Political Economy*, Vol. XLVIII, August 1939, reprinted in American Economic Association, *Readings in Price Theory*.
17. R.L. Hall and C.J. Hitch, "Price Theory and Business Behaviour" *Oxford Economic Papers*, No. 2, May, 1939.

oligopoly products are differentiated it is unlikely that when a firm raises its price, all customers would leave it because some customers are intimately attached to it due to product differentiation. As a result, demand curve facing a firm under differentiated oligopoly is not perfectly elastic. On the other hand, under oligopoly without product differentiation, when a firm raises its price, all its customers would leave it so that demand curve facing an oligopolist producing homogeneous product may be perfectly elastic. Further, under oligopoly without product differentiation, there is a greater tendency on the part of the firms to join together and form a collusion, formal or tacit, and, alternatively, to accept one of them as their leader in setting their price. No doubt, kinked demand curve has a special relevance for differentiated oligopoly, but it has also been applied for explaining price and output under oligopoly without product differentiation.

The demand curve facing an oligopolist, according to the kinked demand curve hypothesis, has a 'kink' at the level of the prevailing price. The kink is formed at the prevailing price level because the segment of the demand curve above the prevailing price level is highly elastic and the segment of the demand curve below the prevailing price level is inelastic. A kinked demand curve *dD* with a kink at point *K* has been shown in Fig. 21.5. The prevailing price level is *OP* and the firm is producing and selling the output *OM*. Now, the upper segment *dK* of the demand curve *dD* is relatively elastic and the lower segment *KD* is relatively inelastic. This difference in elasticities is due to the particular competitive reaction pattern assumed by the kinked demand curve hypothesis.

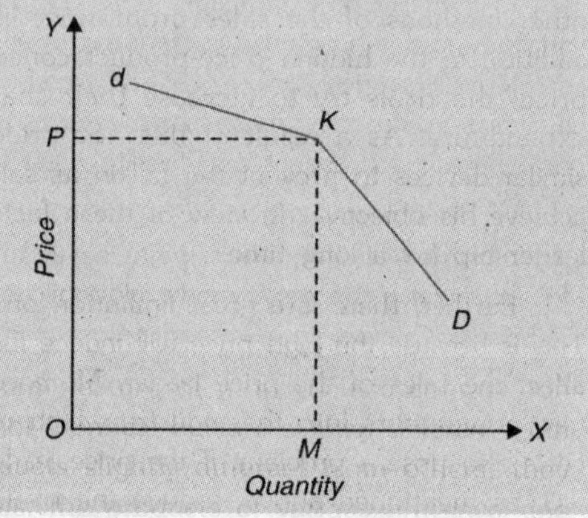

Fig. 21.5. *Kinked Demand Curve under Oligopoly*

The competitive reaction pattern assumed by the kinked demand curve oligopoly theory is as follows:

Each oligopolist believes that if he lowers the price below the prevailing level, his competitors will follow him and will accordingly lower their prices, whereas if he raises the price above the prevailing level, his competitors will not follow his increase in price.

In other words, each oligopolistic firm believes that though its rival firms will not match his increase in price above the prevailing level, they will indeed match its price cut. These two different types of reaction of the competitors to the increase in price on the one hand and to the reduction in price on the other make the portion of the demand curve above the prevailing price level relatively elastic and the lower portion of the demand curve relatively inelastic. This is explained below:

(*a*) Price reduction. If an oligopolist reduces its price below the prevailing price level *OP* in order to increase his sales, his competitors will fear that their customers would go away from them to buy the product from the former oligopolist which has made a price cut. Therefore, in order to retain their customers they will be forced quickly to match the price cut. Because of the competitors quickly following the reduction in price by an oligopolist, he will gain in sales only very little. (His sales will increase not at the expense of his competitors but because of the rise in total quantity demanded due to the reduction in price of the good. In fact, each will gain in sales to the extent of a proportionate share in the increase in total demand). Very small increase in sales of an oligopolist following his reduction in price below the prevailing level means that the demand for him is inelastic below the prevailing price. Thus, the segment *KD* of the demand curve in Fig. 21.5 which lies below the prevailing price *OP* is inelastic showing that very little increase in sales can be obtained by a reduction in price by an oligopolist.

(*b*) Price increase. If an oligopolist raises his price above the pvailing level, there will be a substantial reduction in his sales. This is because as a result of rise in his price, his customers will withdraw from him and will go to his competitors who will welcome the new customers and will gain in sales. These happy competitors will have, therefore, no motivation to match the price rise. The oligopolist who raises his price will be able to retain only those customers who either have a strong preference for his product (if the products are differentiated) or who cannot obtain the desired quantity of the product from the competitors because of their limited productive capacity. Large reduction in sales following an increase in price above the prevailing level by an oligopolist means that demand with respect to increases in price above the existing one is highly elastic. Thus, in Fig. 21.5 the segment *dK* of the demand curve which lies above the current price level *OP* is elastic showing a large fall in sales if a producer raises his price.

It is now evident from above that each oligopolist finds himself placed in such a position that while, on the one hand, he expects his rivals to match his price cuts very quickly, he does not expect his rivals to match his price increases on the other. Given this expected competitive reaction pattern, each oligopolist will have a kinked demand curve *dKD* with the upper segment *dK* being relatively elastic and the lower segment *KD* being relatively inelastic.

Why Price Rigidity Under Oligopoly?

From what has been said above, it is easy to see why an oligopolist confronting a kinked demand curve will have no incentive to raise its price or to lower it. *Since the oligopolist will*

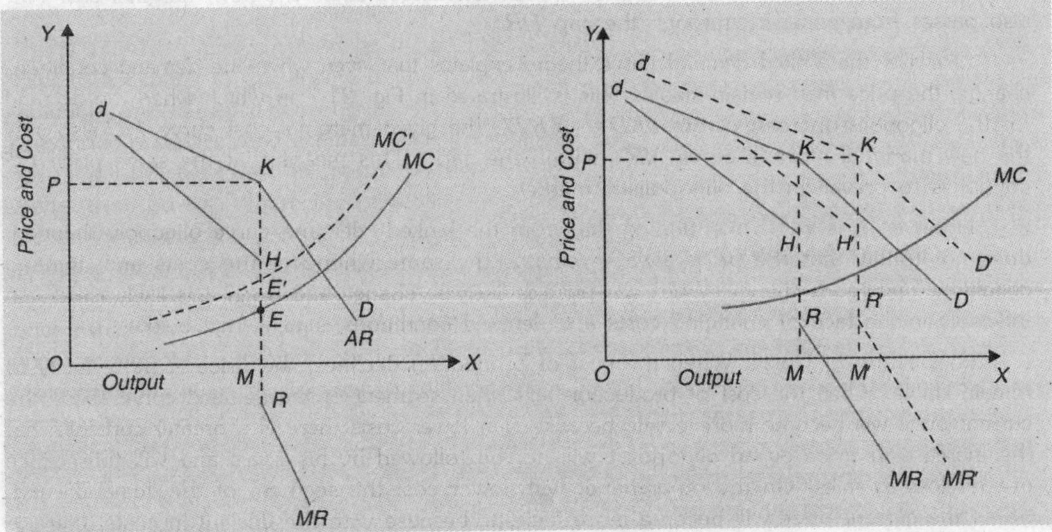

Fig. 21.6. *Changes in costs within limits do not affect the oligopoly price*

Fig. 21.7. *Changes in demand do not affect the oligopoly price*

not gain a large share of the market by reducing his price below the prevailing level, and will have substantial reduction in sales by increasing his price above the prevailing level, he will be extremely reluctant to change the prevailing price. In other words, each oligopolist will adhere to the prevailing price seeing no gain in changing it. Thus, rigid prices are explained in this way by the kinked demand curve theory. In Fig. 21.5, the prevailing price is *OP* at which kink is found in the demand curve *dKD*. The price *P* will tend to remain stable or rigid as every member of the oligopoly will not see any gain in lowering it or in increasing it. It should be noted that if the prevailing price *OP* is greater than average cost, more than normal profits will be made.

Further, it is worth mentioning that the oligopolist confronting a kinked demand curve will be maximising his profits at the current price level. For finding the profit-maximising price-output combination, marginal revenue curve *MR* corresponding to the kinked demand curve *dKD* has been drawn. It is worth mentioning that the marginal revenue curve associated with a kinked demand curve is discontinuous, or in other words, it has a broken vertical portion. The length of the discontinuity depends upon the relative elasticities of two segments *dK* and *KD* of the demand curve at point *K*. The greater the difference in the two elasticities, the greater the length of the discontinuity. In Fig. 21.6 marginal revenue curve *MR* corresponding to the kinked demand curve *dKD* has been drawn which has a discontinuous portion or gap *HR*. Now, if the marginal cost curve of the oligopolist is such that it passes anywhere, say from point *E*, through the discontinuous portion *HR* of the marginal revenue curve *MR*, as shown in Fig. 21.6, the oligopolist will be maximising his profits at the prevailing price level *OP*, that is, he will be in equilibrium at point *E* or at the prevailing price *OP*. *Since the oligopolist is in equilibrium, or in other words, maximising his profits at the prevailing price level, he will have no incentive to change the price.*

Furthermore, even if there are changes in costs, the price will remain stable so long as the marginal cost curve passes through the gap *HR* in the marginal revenue curve. In Fig. 21.6 when the marginal cost curve shifts upward from *MC* to *MC′* (dotted) due to the rise in cost, the equilibrium price and output remain unchanged since the new marginal cost *MC′* also passes from point *E′* through the gap *HR*.

Likewise, the kinked demand curve theory explains that even when the demand conditions change, the price may remain stable. This is illustrated in Fig. 21.7 in which when the demand for the oligopolist increases from *dKD* to *d′K′D′*, the given marginal cost curve *MC* also cuts the new marginal revenue curve *MR′* within the gap. This means that the same price *OP* continues to prevail in the oligopolistic market.

However, it is worth mentioning that from the kinked demand curve oligopoly theory it does not follow that the price always remains the same whenever the costs and demand conditions undergo a change. When the price is likely to change and when it is likely to remain inflexible in the face of changing costs and demand conditions is explained below:

(1) Decline in Costs. When the cost of production declines, the price is more likely to remain stable. When the cost of production falls, then segment of the demand curve above the current price will become more elastic because with lower costs there is a greater certainty that the increase in price by an oligopolist will not be followed by his rivals and will thus cause greater loss in sales. On the other hand, with lower cost the segment of the demand curve below the current price will become more inelastic because with the decline in costs, there is greater certainty that the reduction in price by an oligopolist will be followed by his rivals. With the upper segment becoming more elastic and the lower segment becoming more inelastic than before, the angle *dKD* will become less obtuse and hence the gap in the marginal revenue curve will increase. As a result of the increase in the gap (that is, the length of discontinuity) in the marginal revenue curve, the lower marginal cost curve is likely to pass through this gap showing that the price and output remain the same as before.

(2) Rise in Cost. *If there is a rise in the cost of the oligopolistic industry, the price is not likely to stay rigid.* When there is a rise in the cost of an industry, an oligopolist can reasonably expect that his increase in price will be followed by the others in the industry. Consequently, the segment of the demand curve above the prevailing price will become less elastic and thereby make the angle *dKD* more obtuse and this will narrow down the gap in the

marginal revenue curve. With the smaller gap in the marginal revenue curve, the *higher marginal cost curve is likely to cut it above the upper point H* indicating that the equilibrium price will rise and the equilibrium output will fall. Thus, it follows from the kinked demand curve theory that price is not likely to remain stable in the event of rise in cost.

(3) Decrease in Demand. In case of decrease in demand, the price is very likely to remain inflexible and will not fall. When the demand decreases, it becomes more certain that if one oligopolist initiates the reduction in price, others will follow with the result that the lower segment of the demand curve will become more inelastic. On the other hand, in the face of a decline in demand it is very certain that the increase in price by one oligopolist will never be followed by others. As a result, the upper segment of the demand curve becomes more elastic, that is, it becomes more nearly horizontal. With the increase in the elasticity of the upper segment and the decrease in the elasticity of the lower segment, the gap in the marginal revenue curve becomes wider and therefore it is most likely that the given marginal cost curve will cross the marginal revenue curve inside the gap when the demand curve *dKD* shifts downward. This indicates that the price will remain unchanged in the case of decrease in demand.

(4) Increase in Demand. *When the demand increases, the price is unlikely to remain stable; instead the price is likely to rise.* In the event of increase in demand, an oligopolist can expect that if he initiates the increase in price, his competitors will most probably follow him. Therefore, the upper segment *dK* of the demand curve will become less elastic and the angle *dKD* will become more obtuse. As a result, the gap *HR* in the marginal revenue curve will decrease and if this gap decreases much, it is very likely that the marginal cost curve crosses the marginal revenue curve above the upper point *H*, that is, above the gap, indicating that the price will rise above *OP*.

From above, it is clear that the kinked demand curve analysis of oligopoly explains stability in price in the face of falling costs or declining demand, whereas, price is likely to rise when either the costs rise or demand increases. M.M. Bober, thus rightly writes:

"The kinky demand curve analysis points to the likelihood of price rigidity in oligopoly when a price reduction is in order and of price flexibility when conditions warrant a rise in price. There is hardly any disposition to lower the price when there is decline in demand or in costs, but the price may be raised in response to increased demand or to rising cost."[18]

Critical Apprisal of Kinked Demand Curve Theory

1. We saw above how the kinked demand curve theory of oligopoly provides an explanation of price rigidity under oligopoly. But there is a major drawback in the theory. It only explains why once an oligopoly price has been determined, it would remain rigid or stable, *it does not explain how the price has been determined.* There is nothing in the kinked demand theory which explains how the price which is prevailing is determined. In other words, whereas this theory shows why price tends to stay where it is, it tells us nothing about why the price is where it is. In Fig. 21.8 the kink occurs at the price *OP* because *OP* happens to be the prevailing or established price. The theory does not explain how the price got to be equal to *OP*. Sweezy's kinked demand curve theory does not explain at what level the kink in the demand curve is formed. In Fig. 21.8, we have shown two demand curves *dkD* and *d′K′D′*; the former has a kink at price *OP*, the latter has a kink at price *OP′*. Sweezy's theory does not explain at what price kink will, therefore, be formed and how the price will be determined. Once the price is determined somehow or other, Sweezy theory's explains how it will remain

18. M.M. Bober, *Intermediate Price and Income Theory*.

stable or rigid. Commenting upon kinked demand curve theory Prof. Silberston rightly writes, "The most interesting question is not 'why are prices sticky in the short run?' (if they are), but who decides what the price is to be and on what principles."[19]

However, it may be mentioned that the above criticism applies especially to P.M. Sweezy's version of the kinked demand curve analysis. Hall and Hitch's version of kinked demand curve analysis also explains the determination of oligopoly price. According to Hall and Hitch, equilibrium price is determined by average cost (including normal profits), that is, by the tangency between average cost curve and the demand curve, as shown in Fig. 21.9. However, Hall and Hitch version runs into difficulty when the average cost curve of the various firms in an oligopolistic industry are different.

2. Another shortcoming of the kinked-demand oligopoly theory is that it does not apply

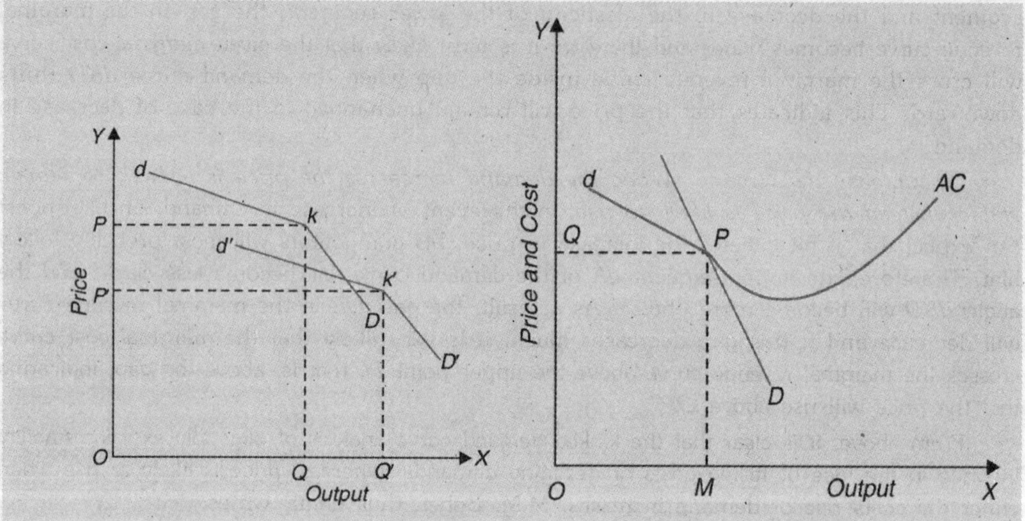

Fig. 21.8. **Fig. 21.9.** *Full-Cost Pricing and Kinked Demand Curve*

to the oligopoly cases of prices leadership and price cartels which account for quite a large part of the oligopolistic markets. When price leadership and price cartels exist in oligopolistic markets there is concerted behaviour in regard to the price changes and hence there is no kink in the demand curve in these cases.

3. Finally, even in the case of pure oligopoly (*i.e.*, oligopoly with homogeneous products), the kinked demand curve theory does not furnish a complete explanation for price rigidity observed in oligopolistic markets. As explained earlier, from the kinked demand curve analysis it follows that prices are likely to remain stable when demand or cost conditions decrease, whereas under pure oligopoly prices are likely to rise in the case of increase in cost or demand.

4. Finally, it has been rightly asserted that explanation of price stability by Sweezy's kinked demand curve theory applies only to depression periods. In periods of depression, demand for the products decreases. As has been explained above, in the context of decreased demand, price in kinked demand curve theory is likely to remain sticky. But in periods of boom and inflation when the demand for the product is high and increasing, the price is likely to rise rather than remaining stable.

In conditions of boom and inflation, the kinked demand curve is of the type shown in Fig. 21.10 by the curve *dCD*. In this, the upper part *dC* of the demand curve is less elastic and the lower part *CD* is highly elastic. This is because under boom and inflationary conditions, it

19. Aubrey Silberston, Price Behaviour of Firms, *Economic Journal*, September 1970.

is expected that when one firm raises its price, its rival firms will follow, and if it cuts its price, they will not follow since the demand for their product is quite good due to boom conditions. Thus, during boom and inflationary conditions, the kinked demand curve is of quite different type from that postulated by Sweezy and Hall and Hitch. In Fig. 21.10 corresponding to the kinked demand curve *dCD*, the marginal revenue curve is *KLHG* with a broken part between *L* and *H*. Because of different types of kink, the marginal revenue curve in Fig. 21.10 is also of different types from the one shown earlier.

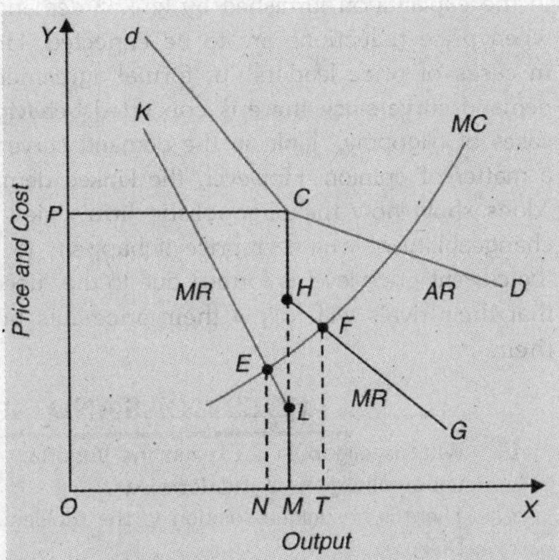

Fig. 21.10. *Kinked Demand Curve during Boom and Inflationary Conditions*

The important implication of this new type of kinked demand curve relevant to the conditions of boom and inflation is that under it price is unlikely to remain stable. Since under such a kinked demand curve, when costs of all firms increase and their marginal cost curves shift upward, there will be greater tendency to pass this increased costs on to the consumers by raising price, since if one firm does it, all are likely to follow it and therefore the quantity demanded of each firm will not decrease much.

Further, the price situation with this type of kinked demand curve is very unstable. As will be seen in Fig. 21.10 marginal cost curve *MC* while it does pass through the gap in the marginal revenue curve, *it cuts marginal revenue curve at two points, E and F.* Therefore, during periods of boom and inflation the price will not remain stable at *OP*, since the profits can be increased both by reducing the output to *ON*, and the raising the output to *OT*. Therefore, the firm (and its competitors too) may raise the price far above the current price *OP* to equate marginal revenue and marginal cost at the lower output *ON*. The firm even in boom conditions may decide to 'go it alone' and cut its price below *OP* so as to raise its output to *OT* and thus equate marginal revenue and marginal cost at higher level of output. We cannot say in advance whether in conditions of boom and inflation price will be raised or lowered but one thing is certain that it will not remain sticky at the current *OP* level.

We therefore, conclude that from Sweezy as well as Hall and Hitch's versions of kinked demand curve theory, it follows that prices are likely to remain stable during depression periods but not during boom and inflationary periods. Our analysis shows that whether we use kinked demand curve of the type postulated by Sweezy as well as Hall and Hitch or an opposite type of the kinked demand curve, prices are unlikely to be stable during the boom periods.

Prof. Stigler's Critique of Kinked Demand Curve and his Empirical Study

Prof. George J. Stigler has made an empirical study of the behaviour of the oligopolies in order to test the theory of kinked demand curve.[20] His empirical study suggests that there does not exist any 'kink' in the demand curve confronting oligopolists. Prof. Stigler has, therefore, rejected the hypothesis of the kinked demand curve under oligopoly. It has been observed by him that in inflationary periods oligopolists do often follow one another's price rises, contrary to what is assumed in the kinked demand theory.

However, it may be pointed out that Prof. Stigler's statistical tests did not involve a sufficiently large number of producers and what might be indicated by a larger sample of

20. Sec George J. Stigler, "The Kinky Oligopoly Demand Curve and Rigid Prices", *Journal of Political Economy*, Vol. LV, October, 1947, reprinted in American Economic Association's *Readings in Price Theory*.

producers is not at all clear from his study. Moreover, it should be noted that Prof. Stigler's empirical study refutes only the hypothesis of kinked demand curve, it does not question the price rigidity under oligopoly. There is considerable empirical evidence found by Prof. Stigler and many others of price rigidity under oligopoly. The point at issue is what is the proper explanation for this price rigidity. Despite Stigler's empirical study, many economists still believe in the explanation furnished by kinked demand curve theory regarding price stability, especially when price reductions are to be expected. However, as mentioned above, it seems clear that in cases of price leadership, formal agreements, price cartels, there cannot exist kink in the demand curve since there is concerted behaviour with respect to price in these cases. In other cases of oligopoly, 'kink' in the demand curve can exist. Whether it actually exists or not is still a matter of opinion. However, the kinked demand curve analysis, as Professor Baumol remarks, "does show how the oligopolistic firm's view of competitive reaction patterns can affect the changeability of whatever price it happens to be charging."[21] It is worth noting that 'kink' at the current price level is formed due to the uncertainty by the oligopolists and their expectations that their rivals will follow their price-cuts but would not follow any increases in prices by them.

QUESTIONS AND PROBLEMS FOR REVIEW

1. What is oligopoly ? Explain the important features of oligopoly. Do you think price and output under oligopoly is indeterminate?
2. There is no unique solution to the problem of determination of price and output under oligopoly. Discuss.
3. What is Collusive Oligopoly ? How are price and output determined under it?
4. What is Cartel ? Explain how a cartel determines price and output of a product to maximise joint profits.
5. Why are cartels generally unstable ? Why is there a tendency on the part of members of cartels to cheat ?
6. Explain Sweezy's kinked demand curve model of oligopoly. How does it explain price rigidity under oligopoly ?
7. What is non-price competition ? What role does it play in oligopolistic market situation ?
8. What alternative objectives to profit maximisation have been proposed which the firms working under oligopoly seek to achieve? Briefly explain them.
9. What are the different types of price leadership that may be established in oligopolistic market situation ? Assuming that there are two firms producing homogeneous products explain how price and output are determined where there is price leadership by
   (1) the lower cost firm, and (2) the dominant firm
10. What is kinked demand curve ? How does it help in explaining price rigidity under oligopoly?
11. Using the kinked demand curve model explain how the increase and reduction in marginal cost need not lead to any change in price or output.
12. What is meant by price rigidity ? Why are prices rigid under oligopoly ? Explain with the help of the kiked demand curve model.
13. What is Prisoner's Dilemma ? How does it help to explain the likelihood of firms opting for sub-optimal solution in oligopoly ?
14. What are the chief difficulties of maintaining price leadership in oligopolistic market situation? Examine the view that price leadership is likely to break down as there is generally a tendency on the part of the rival firms to indulge in *non-price competition* to promote their sales.
15. What is meant by interdependence of firms in oligopoly ? How does it affect price-output equilibrium of a firm ?
16. Explain briefly the various approaches that have been offered to explain the determination of price and output under oligopoly.
17. Explain Prisoner's Dilemma. How does it help to explain that cartels are quite unstable ?

21. William J. Baumol, *Economic Theory and Operations Analysis*, 1961.p.

Non-Price Competiton: Advertising Expenditure

Introduction

Product variation and advertising are the two important instruments of non-price competition by firms. Product variation refers to the changes in some characteristics of the product (for example changing the quality of their product or improving the design of it and providing better service for their products) so as to make their products more appealing to the consumers.

Under monopolistic competition and oligopoly, the firms often compete through product variation and incurring selling costs or advertisement expenditure to increase the demand for their products and thereby increase revenue made. Advertising, salaries paid to staff employed for promotion of sales and other expenses on promotional activities constitute selling costs. Selling cost incurred by the firms in recent years have enormously increased. It has been estimated in recent years that in the USA more than $100 billion are spent on advertising annually. A single company McDonald, famous for its fast food spent as much as $ 2.50 billion on advertising in 1984. For firms working under conditions of monopolistic competition and oligopoly, besides adjustments of price, output and product, the important decision relates to how much selling cost or advertisement expenditure has to be taken so as to achieve the aim of profit maximisation. The first problem that is encountered in connection with selling costs is how they differ from production costs. The other important question which arises is why firms under monopolistic competition and oligopoly incur selling costs and not the firms working under conditions of perfect competition and monopoly. Further, how the firm will decide about the optimum level of selling costs or advertisement expenditure. And, lastly, what is the influence of selling costs on price and output of the product. We shall discuss all these questions concerning selling costs below.

Selling Costs Distinguished from Production Costs

The term "selling costs" is broader than advertisement expenditure. Whereas advertisement expenditure includes costs incurred only on getting the product advertised in newspapers and magazines, radio and television, selling costs include the salaries and wages of salesmen, allowances to retailers for the purpose of getting their product displayed by them, and so many other types of promotional activities, besides advertisement. Chamberlin who introduced the analysis of selling costs in price theory distinguished them from production costs. According to Chamberlin, cost of production includes all those expenses which are incurred to manufacture and provide a product to the consumer to meet his *given* demand or want, while the selling costs are those which are incurred to *change, alter or create the demand for a product.* Costs of production therefore include manufacturing costs, transportation costs, and cost of handling, storing and delivering a product to the consumers, since all of these activities add utilities to a good. And the addition or creation of utilities to satisfy the given wants is called *production* in economics. To quote Chamberlin, "Cost of production includes all expenses which must be met in order to provide the commodity or service, transport it to the buyer, and put it into his hands ready to satisfy his wants. On the other hand, *selling costs include all outlays made in order to secure a demand or a market* for the product The former costs create utilities in order that given demands may be satisfied; the *latter create and shift the demand themselves.* A simple criterion is this : of all the costs incurred in the manufacture and sale of a given product, those which alter the demand curve for it are selling costs, and those which do not are costs of production."[1] The selling costs, according to Chamberlin, include "advertising in its many forms, salaries of salesmen and the expenses of sales departments and sales agencies (except where these agencies actually handle the goods), window displays, and displays and demonstrations of all kinds."[2]

It should be noted that transportation should not be construed as *increasing the demand,* as it apparently appears. This is because the transportation does not really increase the demand; it merely enables the producer to meet the demand of the consumer which is already there whether the transport cost is incurred by the producer or by the consumer himself. Likewise, a high site rent for a shop in a well-located area will increase the sales of the firm but cannot be considered as a part of selling costs, since in this the firm is meeting the given or existing demand for the product more accurately or exactly and not *altering* the demand for the product. By paying a high rent for a shop or a concern in the well-located area, the producer is merely adapting the product or himself more exactly to the given demand and not altering the demand or adapting his customers. Therefore, Chamberlin while drawing the distinction between production costs and selling costs writes that those costs which are "*made to adapt the product to the demand are costs of production; those made to adapt the demand to the product are costs of selling.*"[3]

It should however be noted that the distinction between production costs and selling costs cannot always be sharply made and there are cases where it cannot be said whether product is being adapted to meet the demand, or the demand is being adapted to sell the product. For instance, it is difficult to say whether the extra cost on attractive packaging is production cost or selling cost. However, as far as advertisement expenditure is concerned, there is little doubt about its being selling cost, since purpose of advertisement is to increase or create the demand for the product. Thus Chamberlin's distinction is quite applicable so far as advertisement is concerned. Because *advertising expenditure is the most important and dominant form of selling costs*, we in our analysis below shall use them interchangeably and discuss the various questions concerning selling costs by taking the case of advertisement expenditure.

Importance of Advertising and Other Selling Costs Under Monopolistic Competition and Oligopoly

As has been explained in previous chapters, there is no need for a firm working under perfect competition to undertake advertisement expenditure or to incur other selling costs,

1. Edward, H. Chamberlin, *The Theory of Monopolistic Competition*, 6th edition, p. 123 (italics added)
2. Op. cit. p. 124.
3. Ibid, p. 125.

since, by assumption, the products produced by all firms in the perfectly competitive industry are homogeneous, and an individual firm can sell as much quantity of its product as it likes at the given price. If a perfectly competitive firm advertises for the product, the consumers who are influenced by it may purchase the product from other firms in the industry, since all are selling homogeneous products. Of course, the whole perfectly competitive industry, that is, all firms together or their association may advertise to promote the sales of their product at the expense of the *products of other industries.* Such advertising is known as *promotional advertising*, as compared to competitive advertising with which we are here concerned. In India, there has been advertising by the *Terene* industry producing terylene fabrics for increasing the demand for its product at the cost of other kinds of fabrics. We, therefore conclude that under perfect competition, there can be promotional advertising by the whole industry but not the competitive advertising by individual firms to snatch away the customers from each other.

Under monopoly also, there is no competitive advertising, since, by definition, a monopolist produces a product which has no close substitutes. The monopolist only needs to inform or remind the buyers that a particular product exists and he need not emphasize the competitive nature of its product.Of course, the monopolist may advertise to promote his sales or demand of his product by providing information to the consumers about the existence and nature of his product but it will not be at the expense of its rivals, since no rivals producing close substitutes are there under monopoly. Hence the advertisement by the monopolist is informative and promotional and not competitive.

It is under monopolistic competition and oligopoly with product differentiation that advertisement and other selling costs become important as a competitive weapon at the disposal of a firm to increase its sales at the expense of others. This is because differentiated products produced by different firms under monopolistic competition and differentiated oligopoly are close substitutes of each other. Therefore, each firm under monopolistic competition tries to convince the buyers that its product is better than those of others in the industry. A firm under monopolistic competition and differentiated oligopoly may keep its price and product design constant and seek to increase the demand for its product by increasing the amount of advertisement expenditure and through it persuading the buyers that its brand of the product is of superior quality than others. Thus, this is competitive advertising which is aimed at attracting the customers to their product and weaning them away from the closely related products of the rivals. Thus, "*the fundamental aim of all 'competitive' advertising is to attract the customers' attention and to imprint the name of particular product on his mind' the aim is to persuade the consumer to put his hand in his pocket and buy the product in question...the main aim is to increase the sales of one firm at the expense of others and not to increase the sales of the 'group' as a whole.*"[4] For instance, we all know that all toothpastes are based upon the same chemical formula recommended by the medical science. But the firm producing Colgate through its radio and T.V. commercial programmes has been propagating that the toothpaste of Colgate variety is very much better than others and has special and superior qualities which are absent in other brands of toothpaste. The fundamental aim of Colgate advertisement is not to increase the aggregate demand for toothpaste in the country but to increase the demand for 'Colgate toothpaste' by competing away the buyers from other brands of toothpaste. Similarly, the manufacturers of other brands of toothpaste such as Binaca, Pepsodent, Close Up, etc. are also incurring expenditure on advertisement through various means and trying to convince the buyers that their particular brand of toothpaste

4. Stonier and Hague, op. cit., p. 222.

is better than others. Such competitive advertisement by a firm often proves to be successful in its objective of increasing the demand for a particular brand of the product. Thus, as a result of advertisement demand curve facing an individual firm shifts to the right which indicates that at various prices, a greater quantity of the product can be sold than before.

It follows from above that in the presence of selling costs or advertisement, demand curve for a product cannot be taken as an objective fact given by the tastes or wants of the consumers. A firm can alter or shift the demand curve for its product through its own efforts by incurring advertisement expenditure and other forms of selling costs.

Effect of Selling Costs (Advertising Expenditure) on Demand

As explained above, *the purpose of advertising is to increase the demand, that is, to shift the demand curve for the product to the right.* However, these selling costs or advertising outlays are subject to the varying returns. That is, *equal increments in advertising outlay first yield increasing returns and then eventually diminishing returns in terms of its effect on demand for the product.* In the beginning, increases in advertising outlay will bring about increasing returns in raising demand for the product for two reasons. First, increase in advertising outlay (or selling costs) permits a firm to *repeat many times* the advertisement for the product. And this repetition of advertisement produces favourable effects on demand. "It is well established that repetition is essential if advertising is to make an impact on the consumer's mind. A single advertisement seen once will have at the most a negligible, and probably no effect on the consumer. The outlay for it is wasted. But continued advertising over a period of time and in different media is far more likely to impinge on the consumers' thoughts and consequent consumption choice".[5]

Second reason for occurrence of increasing returns as the advertisement outlay is increased in the beginning is the *economies of large scale* selling operations or advertising outlay. The main advantage is the *specialisation* which is made possible by the large-scale selling or advertising activity. To quote Prof. Hibdon again, "Large-scale activities permit the *use of specialised personnel with greater expertise and effectiveness.* There may also be *economies in the use of advertising media.* Greater total spending permits a shift in the technique and media that are used in the selling effort as well as the use of combinations of media."[6] As a result of the increasing returns from advertising outlay in the beginning, the demand increases more than proportionately to the equal increases in advertising outlay.

Eventually Diminishing Returns to Advertising Expenditure. But as the advertising outlay is stepped up, diminishing returns with respect to its demand raising effect are likely to set in eventually. First, this is because potential buyers differ in tastes, income and wealth. These differences among the potential buyers of the product mean that they will vary in their responses to selling operations or advertising by a firm. Initial advertisements will cause large increases in demand as the more susceptible buyers respond to advertisement. But further increase in advertisements is likely to bring about relatively less increases in demand as they fail to influence other buyers who do not prefer the good so much.

Second reason for the ultimate occurrence of diminishing returns from the increases in advertisement is that the existing buyers may not further increase the demand for the product as a result of more advertising by the firm. This is because *as the consumer buys more of a*

5. James E. Hibdon, *Price and Welfare Theory*, McGraw-Hill, 1969, p. 302.
6. *Op. cit.*, p. 302.

product, its marginal utility to him falls. Further, in order to purchase one good more, he has to give up more of some other goods, his income being limited. As a result, the marginal utility of 'other goods' increases. Thus, on the one hand, the marginal utility of a good declines as it is purchased more under the influence of advertisement, and, on the other hand, the opportunity cost of buying this good increases on account of the rise in the marginal utility of 'other goods'. This makes the existing buyers of product reluctant to buy more units of it when advertising effort by a firm is greatly increased. Thus, this also causes diminishing returns to advertising outlay.

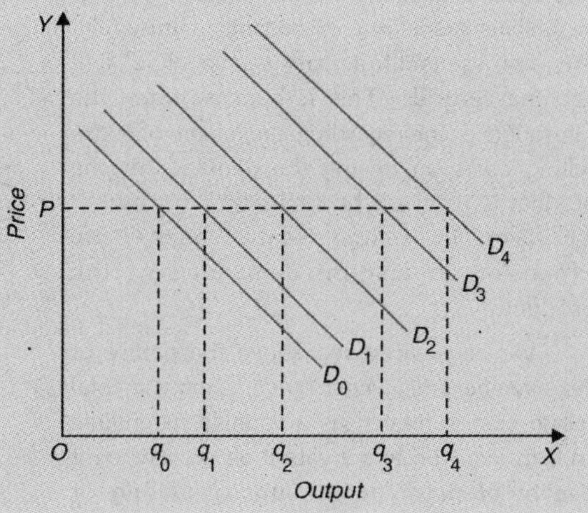

Fig. 22.1. *Increasing and Diminishing Returns to Advertising Expenditure or Selling Costs*

The effect of selling costs on the demand for the product and the varying returns in this connection are illustrated in Fig. 22.1. Demand curve before any advertisement expenditure is undertaken is D_0. Now, equal increments in advertisement expenditure successively bring about rightward shift in the demand curve to D_1, D_2, D_3 and D_4 respectively. We have assumed that the shift in the demand curve is parallel, while in the real world it may not be so. Because in the beginning there are increasing returns and then after a point diminishing returns occur, successive shifts in the demand curve differ in magnitude. At the given price *OP*, as a result of equal increments in advertising outlay, the quantity demanded increases from q_0 to q_1 , q_1 to q_2, q_2 to q_3, and q_3 to q_4. It will be seen from Fig.22.1 that after D_3, diminishing returns to extra advertising outlay occur.

The Curve of Average Selling Cost.

The concept of the curve of average selling cost should be carefully understood. When a firm has to plan what amount of advertising outlay (*i.e.*, selling costs), it should incur we treat the selling cost as a variable magnitude. Thus, with a certain amount of selling costs (advertising outlay) incurred in a period, the average selling cost or advertising cost per unit will depend upon the total output sold as a result of the rightward shift in the demand curve brought about by that amount of selling costs incurred and can be obtained from dividing the amount of advertisement costs incurred by the quantity of output sold. And as a firm plans to increase the amount of selling cost incurred in a period, the average selling cost will change depending, on the one hand, upon the increase in selling costs and, on the other, upon the resultant increase in output demanded (or sold) at a given price.As explained above, it is generally believed that *selling costs* (*advertisement outlay*) is subject to varying returns. In the beginning, increasing returns to selling costs are obtained, that is, equal increases in advertisement outlay cause more than proportionate increase in the amount demanded of the product at the given price. In other words, selling costs per unit of output will fall in the beginning. After a point diminishing returns to selling costs set in, increases in advertisement outlay would cause less than proportionate increases in the amount demanded of the product. In other words, after a point, average selling cost will rise. Hence, average selling cost in the beginning falls due to the increasing returns, reaches the minimum level and then rises due to the diminishing returns. Thus, the curve of average selling cost, like the ordinary average production cost curve, is U-shaped, which is shown in Fig.22.2 by the curve *ASC*.

However, the average selling cost curve *ASC* drawn in Fig. 22.2 should be carefully interpreted. It does not mean how the average selling cost per unit changes as output is increased. But it means the average selling cost per unit *which is required to be undertaken to sell an extra unit of output.* Ultimately, the average selling cost curve *ASC* will become vertical. This is because often the saturation point regarding the effect of extra selling costs on raising the demand for the product is reached, beyond which no further increases in selling costs causes any expansion in amount demanded of the product.

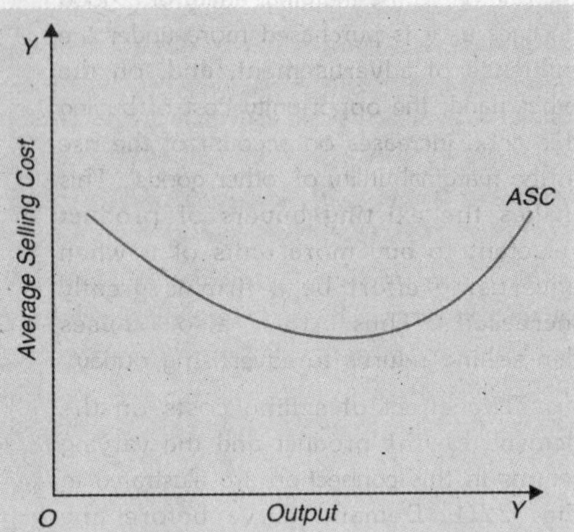

Fig. 22.2. Average selling cost curve when total selling cost is treated as a variable.

We have discussed above the nature of the average selling cost curve when the total selling cost is treated as a variable magnitude and, in fact, the firm treats it as such when it has to plan for an amount of selling or advertisement cost it should incur in a period so as to maximize profits. However, once a firm commits itself to a particular amount of selling costs or advertisement outlay to be incurred in a period, it may regard that cost as a fixed cost during that period. In other words, when *a given fixed amount of total selling cost is decided to be incurred*, then greater the level of output sold, the selling cost per unit would decline. Thus, when a firm commits itself to a given amount of selling costs, it will then treat them as a fixed cost. With a fixed amount of selling costs, average selling cost will fall as more units of output are sold.

OPTIMAL LEVEL OF ADVERTISING

As seen above, advertising not only increases demand for a firm's product, but it also raises the cost of the firm. A firm will undertake advertising only if it leads to the net increase in profits of the firm. A firm will go on increasing its advertisement expenditure if its *marginal contribution to profit (MPC) from an additional unit of output is greater than the increase in advertising cost required to sell an additional unit of* output. The determination of optimal level of advertising is to apply the same marginal decision rule followed by a profit-maximising firm. The optimal level of advertising expenditure is determined at the level at which marginal contribution to profit (*MPC*) of advertising expenditure is equal to the marginal cost of advertising (*MCA*). Thus at the optimal level of advertising expenditure.

$$MPC = MCA$$

Let us elaborate this rule further. Marginal contribution to profit (*MPC*) is the difference between marginal revenue and marginal cost, as usually defined. Marginal revenue is the addition to total revenue earned from producing and selling an additional unit of output $\left(MR = \dfrac{\Delta TR}{\Delta Q}\right)$. Marginal cost is the addition to total cost of production by an extra unit of output produced. The marginal profit contribution (*MPC*) is therefore given by the difference between the marginal revenue (*MR*) and marginal cost of production (*MC*) of an additional unit of output. Thus,

$$MCP = MR - MC$$

On the other hand, marginal cost of advertising is the additional cost of advertisement (*MCA*) required for selling an additional unit of output. That is,

$$MCA = \frac{\Delta A}{\Delta Q}$$

where ΔA is change in cost of advertisement incurred on sale of an additional unit of output (*i.e.* ΔQ).

As stated above, the firm will go increasing its advertisement expenditure until marginal profit contribution (*MPC*) becomes equal to marginal advertisement cost (*MAC*). Thus at optimal or profit-maximising level of advertisement expenditure will be reached at the level where

$$MPC = MCA$$

Now, $MPC = MR - MC$ and

$$MCA = \frac{\Delta A}{\Delta Q}$$

Thus, at the optimal level of advertising

$$MR - MC = \frac{\Delta A}{\Delta Q}$$

Since $MR = \frac{\Delta TR}{\Delta Q}$ and $MC = \frac{\Delta TC}{\Delta Q}$ we can state the condition for optimal level of advertisement expenditure as

$$\frac{\Delta TR}{\Delta Q} - \frac{\Delta TC}{\Delta Q} = \frac{\Delta A}{\Delta Q}$$

or

$$\frac{\Delta TR}{\Delta Q} = \frac{\Delta TC}{\Delta Q} + \frac{\Delta A}{\Delta Q}$$

Thus, if additional cost of advertisement is added to marginal cost of production and calling it as marginal cost of production and sale or *MC**, the condition for optimal level of advertising expenditure can be stated as under :

$$MR = MC^*$$

Thus, in the following analysis we will use this concept of marginal cost which is inclusive of marginal cost of advertisement expenditure. We explain and graphically illustrate the optimal level of advertising and determination of firm's equilibrium output and price in the following two cases:

1. Optimal level of advertising expenditure with price and product variety as given and constant.
2. Optimal level of advertising expenditure when both price and output are variable but product variety remains constant.

Optimum Level of Advertising Outlay (Selling Costs): With Price and Product Variety as Constants

An important question is how much selling costs (advertisement outlay), a firm will undertake as to maximize its profits. In other words, what is the *optimum amount* of advertisement expenditure for a firm. The determination of optimal advertising outlay (selling cost) for the firm can be explained with the average and marginal cost curves. For explaining the amount of advertising expenditure with average and marginal costs, we have to use

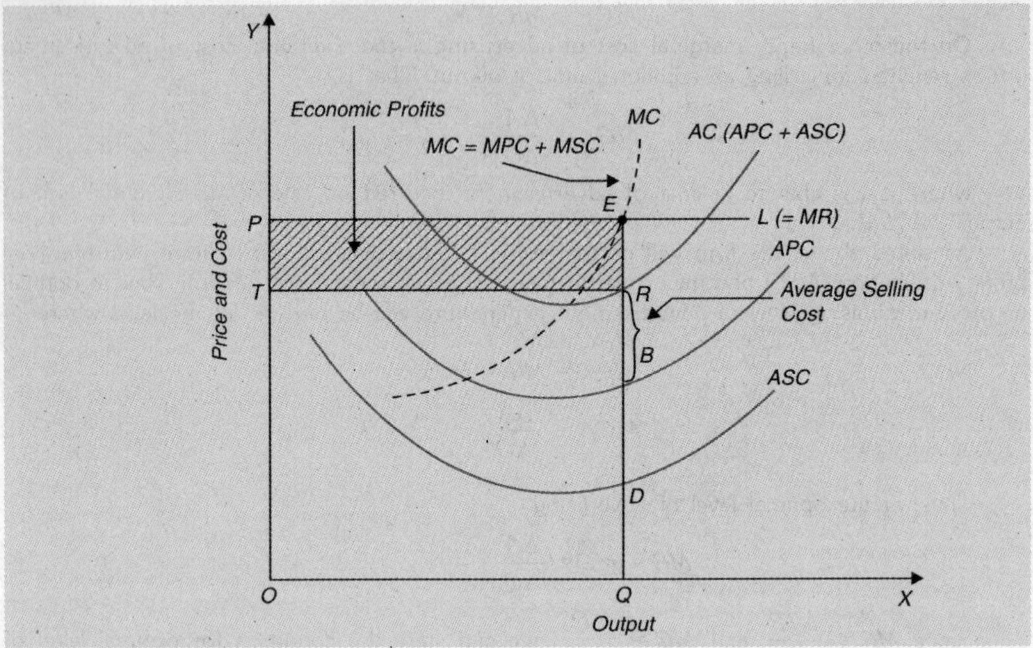

Fig. 22.3. *Optimal Level of Advertising Expenditure with Given Price and Product Variety*

optimal the concept of average selling costs when advertisement outlay is taken to be variable. Consider Fig. 22.3 where *ASC* and *APC* are average selling costs and average production cost curves respectively. Average selling cost curve *ASC* has been superimposed over the average production cost curve *APC* to obtain average total cost curve *AC* (*AC* = *APC* + *ASC*). It should therefore be noted that the vertical distance between the *AC* and *APC* curves measures the average selling cost. *MC* is the marginal curve to the average total cost curve *AC*. We assume that price *OP* has already been fixed by the firm which is kept constant. Further, the nature of the product is also held unchanged and it is only the advertising expenditure which is varied and consequently demand curve shifts to the right and output sold increases.

Since price of the product remains fixed at *OP*, the horizontal line *PL* can be viewed as if it were a marginal revenue curve. This is because through increase in advertisement expenditure, a firm can sell more quantity of the product *without lowering price.* If the firm aims to maximize profits, then it will be in equilibrium regarding advertising outlay where the marginal cost (which is inclusive of both the increase in production cost and selling cost incurred on additional unit of output) is equal to the marginal revenue, *i.e.*, given price *OP*). It will be seen from Fig. 22.3 that marginal cost is equal to marginal revenue (or price) at *OQ* level of output at which profits will be maximized. With *OQ* as the output produced and sold, total profits made by the firm are equal to *PERT* and, as is evident from the figure, average selling cost incurred by the firm in its equilibrium position is equal to *QD* or *BR*. Therefore, the optimal amount of advertisement outlay, incurred by the firm will be equal to (*QD* or *BR*) multiplied by the output *OQ*.

Optimal Level of Advertising Expenditure or Selling Costs when Both Output and Price are Variables

Now, we shall explain the optimal level of advertising expenditure incurred by a monopolistically competitive firm to maximise its profits when it can influence both output and price through its advertising campaigns. In other words, we will now explain the profit-maximising or optimal combination of advertising expenditure, output and price. We shall, however, make our analysis with a two dimensional diagram. It may be emphasized again that advertisement expenditure or selling costs are an important form of *non-price competition*. Advertising represents a method by which a firm can increase the sales of its product and is an alternative to reduction in price of the product for promoting its sales. A firm can increase its sales by lowering the price of its product. But when it thinks price cutting is not prudent, the firm may attempt to promote sales through its advertising campaign. However, through advertisement or other forms of selling costs, a firm can increase both its output and price of its product. It may be noted that cost on advertisement or other forms of sales promotion activities of a firm depends in part also on how much advertising expenses or selling costs are being incurred by the rival firms.

Given the demand for the product of a firm and the amount of advertisement costs incurred by the rival firms, we get a U-shaped average selling cost curve which shows due to the greater effect of advertising on increase in demand and output in the beginning as advertising expenditure is stepped up, the average advertising cost (that is, selling cost per unit of output) falls. But beyond a certain level of advertising expenditure diminishing returns to additional advertising set in causing a rise in selling cost per unit of output. We obtain the average cost curve (*AC*) inclusive of average selling cost *by adding vertically* the average production cost (*APC*) and, average selling cost (*ASC*) curves. Note that the vertical distance between the average total cost curve (*AC*) and average production cost curve (*APC*) increases beyond a point due to the rise in average selling cost following the occurrence of diminishing returns to the increase in advertisement expenditure. The choice of combination of advertising, output and price that maximises the profits of the monopolistically competitive firm is illustrated in Fig. 22.4. We assume that in the absence of selling costs or advertising expenditure the demand for the product of the firm is given by the curve D_0.

On the other hand, in the absence of advertising, *APC* is the average production cost curve which as usual is U-shaped and *MC* is the marginal cost curve associated with it. Prior to any advertising costs the firm is in equilibrium by producing OQ_o level of output and charging price OP_0 for its product. It will seen that in this equilibrium situation prior to any advertising costs, the firm is making zero economic profits since price is equal to average cost.

Now, in order to earn positive economic profits, the firm will attempt to raise demand for its product by launching an advertising campaign to attract customers. As it steps up its advertising expenditure the demand curve for its product will shift to the right. On the other hand, on account of increasing amount of expenditure incurred on advertisement, his average cost curve inclusive of advertising cost per unit will also shift above. It is worth noting that the average selling cost (*i.e.*, selling cost per unit of output) depends in part on the anticipated increase in output following the increase in demand for the product caused by the expansion in advertising expenditure. Since in the present model we are treating selling cost as a variable magnitude, marginal cost curve will also shift upward due to the additional advertising costs incurred as shown by the new higher marginal cost curve *MC′* which includes marginal advertising cost as well.

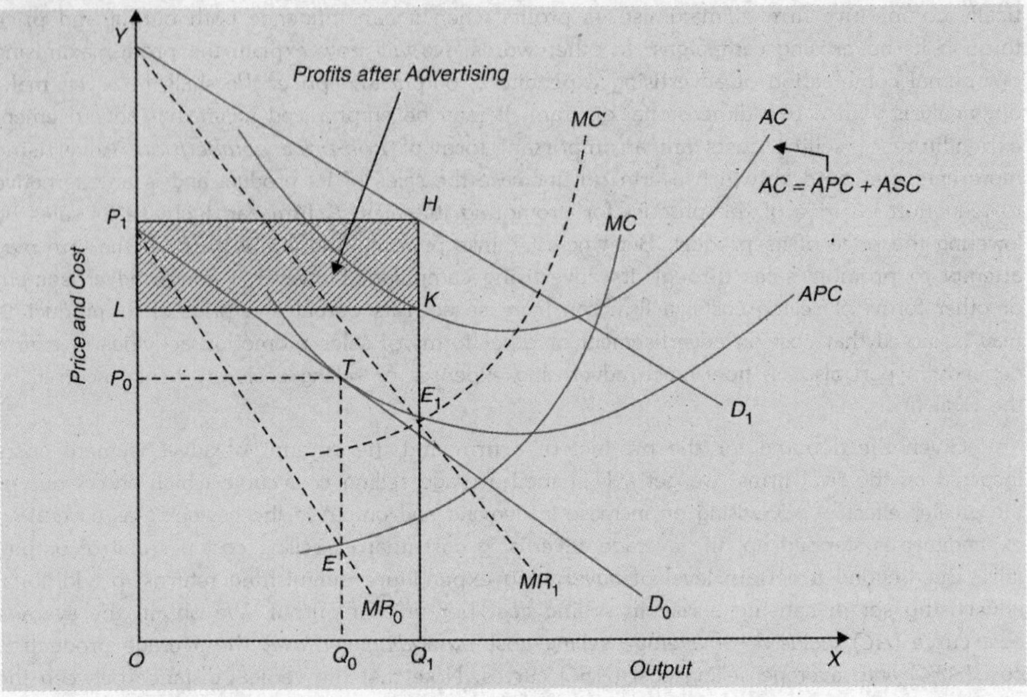

Fig. 22.4. *Optimal Levels of Advertising, Output and Price*

Let us assume that after a certain magnitude of advertising expenditure has been incurred the demand curve for firm's product has shifted up to the level D_1 and the marginal revenue curve corresponding to it has shifted up to the new position MR_1. Now, in order to determine the profit-maximising combination of output, price and advertising cost, the firm will equate marginal cost (inclusive of advertising cost) with marginal revenue corresponding to the demand curve reached after a certain successful advertising campaign. As will *be* observed from Fig. 22.4 that the new marginal cost curve *MC* (inclusive of marginal selling cost) intersects the new MR_1 curve at point E_1 according to which profit maximising output is OQ_1 and price fixed will be equal to OP_1. In this equilibrium position, the firm will be making positive economic profits equal to the area of rectangle P_1HKL. Thus, it is evident that advertising has enabled the firm not only to raise its level of output by increasing demand for its product but also allows it to charge the higher price OP_1. Thus, through successful advertising expenditure the firm has succeeded in increasing economic profits from zero to P_1HKL.

Now, corresponding to the profit-maximising price-output equilibrium situation (output OQ_1 and price OP_1) the optimal advertising expenditure can be easily ascertained from Fig. 22.4. It will be seen from Fig. 22.4 that at profit-maximising output level OQ_1, the average selling cost is equal to E_1B. The total optimal advertising expenditure in this profit-maximising position regarding three variables, namely, output, price and advertising, will therefore be equal to E_1K times the level of output OQ_1.

Long-Run Equilibrium of Firm with Advertising Expenditure

Equilibrium of a monopolistically competitive firm shown in Figure 22.4 is only a short-run equilibrium with regard to optimal advertising expenditure when the firm is making economic profits. These economic profits made possible by an advertising campaign will attract other firms as there is free entry in a monopolistically competitive industry. The new entrants into the industry will produce similar products and also imitate the successful firm's advertising campaign and advertise in the same way to gain sales of their products. As a result of increased advertising by competitors, the first successful firm will find that it has to increase its advertising expenditure to sell a given quantity of its product. That is, it has to send more sales personnel to the market and advertise more frequently to sell a given quantity when there are more rival firms in the market which are producing similar products and doing aggressive advertising to promote their sales. This will push up the selling costs of the firm required to sell a given quantity of its product resulting in an upward shift of the average selling cost curve (*ASC*).

Besides, as more firms producing similar products enter the industry, the demand and marginal revenue curves for the product will shift downward. Thus, the increased selling costs and reduction in demand for the product of the firm will tend to eliminate the economic profits in the long run. It may however, be noted that increased advertising by all the firms to promote sales of their products is likely to lead to an increase in demand for the product in general.

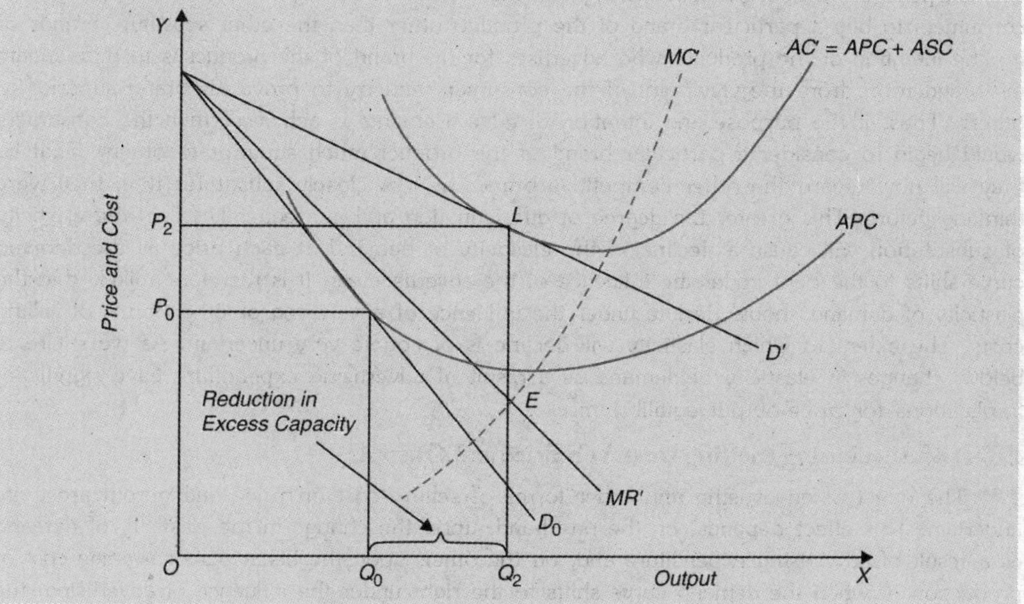

Fig. 22.5. *Long-Run Equilibrium with Advertising under Monopolistic Competition.*

in Figure 22.5 we have shown that the long-equilibrium of the firm with advertising under monopolistic competition has been attained at output level OQ_2, where the demand curve D' and average cost curve inclusive of advertising (selling) costs has been brought to the new tangency position at point *L*. Thus, the firm in this long-run equilibrium position earns zero economic profits. It should be noted that the level of output OQ_2 by the firm in its long-run equilibrium position with advertising is greater than OQ_0 produced in long-run equilibrium without advertising. This implies that excess capacity will be reduced as a result of advertising in the long run. Thus, increased advertising by firms to promote their sales causes an increase in demand for the product in general leading to the reduction in excess capacity in each firm. This helps in lowering average cost of production as the firms increase their size of plants and come closer to the optimum plant with which the product can be produced with minimum possible average cost. However, the consumers do not benefit from this lowering of average production cost because price does not fall due to the fact that whereas average production cost declines, the advertising cost per unit rises as a result of competitive advertising by the rival firms. Thus, whereas, on the one hand, advertising and other selling costs cause increase in demand for the product leading to the expansion in output by the firms, they, on the other hand, tend to raise the price of the product due to the increase in advertising cost per unit of output.

Effect of Advertising (Selling Costs) on Elasticity of Demand

We have seen above that as a result of advertising expenditure demand for the product increases, that is, demand curve shifts to the right. For the sake of convenience, we have assumed that the new demand curves after successive increase in advertising expenditure is undertaken are parallel to the old one, though in actual practice they need not be so. However, in this connection it is useful to consider whether when the demand increases and demand curve shifts to the right, elasticity of demand at each price remains the same, declines or rises. The purpose of competitive advertising or other forms of selling costs are to influence the consumers to buy a particular brand of the product rather than the other substitute brands of it. The intention of the producer who advertises for his brand of the product is to differentiate his brand more from the viewpoint of the consumers and try to prove his brand superior to others. Thus, if the purpose and intention of advertisements is achieved, then the consumers would begin to consider a particular brand of the product much superior to others. That is, they will now regard the other competitive brands as less closely substitutes than they were thinking before. This greater the degree of differentiation and consequently fall in the elasticity of substitution will cause a decline in the elasticity of demand at each price as the demand curve shifts to the right under the influence of the advertisement. It is therefore, likely that the elasticity of demand should decline under the influence of advertising or other forms of selling costs. The extent to which elasticity will decline is of course very uncertain. As we shall see below, changes in elasticity of demand as a result of advertising expenditure have significant implications for price-output equilibrium.

Effect of Advertising (Selling Costs) on Price and Output

The effect of advertising and other forms of selling cost on price and output are quite uncertain. This effect depends, on the one hand, upon the change in the elasticity of demand as a result of advertising expenditure and, on the other, upon the behaviour of average cost of production. If when the demand curve shifts to the right under the influence of advertising, the elasticity of demand at the current price remains the same and *average cost of production is falling* sharply with the expansion in output, then it may be profitable for the firm to set a lower price after advertisement. In this case profit-maximising price will be lower and output larger than those before advertisement. On the other hand, if elasticity of demand declines very much as it shifts to the right as a result of advertisesment, and the average cost of production is rising sharply with the increase in production, then in order to maximize profits in the new situation after advertisement, the firm may raise the price and reduce its level of output. In this case, the advantage of the increase in demand due to advertisement expenditure will be enjoyed in the form of higher price of the product rather than increased sales of the product. But the most likely case to occur is that the elasticity of demand declines after advertisement and the average cost of product is not rising very sharply, and as result of these the firm may find it profitable to raise price of the product somewhat and also increase the output after advertising expenditure is undertaken. Thus, according to Stonier and Hague, "The most probable result for a profit maximising firm will be that the elasticity of demand will fall somewhat at each price, that the volume of demand will increase at each price and that price and output will both increase to some extent as a result of advertising campaign"[7]. And this is the case which we have considered in our analysis of advertising expenditure and depicted in Fig. 22.5. It will be seen from Fig. 22.5 that with successive increments in advertising expenditure price has risen from P_0 to P_2 and also output has increased from Q_0 to Q_2. Thus, in our analysis of Fig. 22.5 both price and output have increased as a result of advertisement outlay.

Evaluation of the Effect of Advertising

The net effect of advertising on consumer's welfare is a highly controversial issue. An eminent economist , J.K. Galbraith regards advertising expenditure as wasteful use of resources. Thus big firms through advertising manipulate the wants and tastes of the consumers and thereby create false needs of the consumers. Besides, they influence the consumers to buy certain varieties of a product at the expense of others while total output of the product does not increase. It is, however, true that advertising diverts resources from other goods to the particular product for which huge advertising expenditure by firms has been made.[8] It is worth noting that as a result of sales promotion through advertising consumers are lilkely to become *more loyal* to certain brand names or product varieties. This reduces the price elasticity of demand for the products of each firm in the long run which indicates that *advertising increases monopoly power* (note that monopoly power is measured by the reciprocal of price elasticity of demand)[9]. Increase in monopoly power also leads to the higher prices being charged by those firms who through successful advertising have established the superiority of their products in the minds of the consumers and thus reducing the price elasticity of demand for them.

However, the effect of advertising on price remains a controversial issue. A recent study of 150 major US industries by *E.W.* Eckard[10] has found that higher than average advertising expenditures relative to sales led to lower rates of increase in prices and higher rates of increase in output during 1963-1977. Thus, according to this study, advertising expenditure seems to increase rather than reduce competition. However, this beneficial effect of advertising has not been generally found by other authors. Contrary to the above view, others have argued that advertising provides information to the consumers and makes them aware of alternatives available to them about which they would otherwise be ignorant. According to this opposite view, advertising tends to *reduce consumer loyality to* particular brands leading to the increase in price elasticity of demand for the products of individual firms.[11] Advocates of advertising point out that it serves a useful social purpose by furnishing information and thereby reduce transaction costs of buying goods.

In their important studies Stigler[12] and Nelson"[13] have defended advertising expenditures

---

7. Stonier Hague, *op.cit.*, p. 226.
8. For a detailed discussion of the impact of advertising on price, output and consumer welfare, see William, Thomas A., "*Journal of Economic Literature*", June 1979, pp. 453-476.
9. Brozen Yale, "Is Advertising a Barrier to Entry?" in Brozen, Yale (Ed), *Advertising and Society*, New York University Press, 1977, pp. 79-109.
10. E.W. Eckard, "Advertising, Concentration Changes and Consumer Welfare", *Review of Economics and Statistics,* May 1988.
11. Scherer, F.M., *Industrial Market Structure and Economic Performance*, 2nd Ed. Houghton Mifflin, 1980, p. 381.
12. George J. Stigler, " The Economics of Informations", *Journal of Political Economy,* June 1961, pp. 213-225.
13. Philip Nelson, "The Economic Consequences of Advertising", *Journal of Business,* April, 1975, pp. 213-241.

by the firms on the ground that it *provides useful information to the consumers* about prices and availabilities of different alternative varieties of the product which *save their cost of search and shopping.* In the absence of advertising, according to them, the consumers are unlikely to find the best price for the product they want to purchase. Without advertising by the firms, it costs a good deal to the consumers on searching for products they want to buy. According to them, advertising leads to the reduction in prices of products and as a result consumers are better off. Besides, Nelson have found that the firms advertising their products have strong incentives to provide *useful and correct* information to consumers. Not only does the advertising reduce search costs of the consumers but also create brand awareness concerning better and inferior quality brands. Nelson distinguishes between what are called *search goods* and *experience goods.* Search goods include non-durable goods such as clothing, footwear, furniture, jewellery etc. The buyers can assess their quality by comparing among different brands and stores. Therefore, according to Nelson, in case of these search goods there is not much scope for befooling the people through misleading advertising.

On the other hand, experience goods are those durable and non-durable goods whose quality can be assessed only by trying them. Examples of experience goods are durable goods such as cars, electronic equipment, instruments and appliances and non-durable goods such as food products, tobacco products, drugs, beer, wine etc. According to Nelson, in case of these experience goods the consumers can be befooled at the first time of their purchasing them. They cannot be repeatedly befooled in their subsequent purchases of these experience goods as consumers come to know about their true quality when try them first time. Therefore, Nelson concludes there is not much scope for misleading advertising of products. The firms, according to him, has a strong incentive to provide useful and truthful information to them.

In our view, however, contrary to the views of Prof. Nelson, the advertising expenditure by big firms in India is quite misleading. For example, both Coca Cola and Pepsi Cola through their heavy advertising campaigns have been claiming about the high quality and of safe nature of their drinks. But it has been found that their drinks actually contain more pesticides which are quite harmful for health of the people. Further, some studies in India have found that advertising by big Indian firms is competitive rather than informational. The firms undertake advertising expenditure to increase the demand for their brand of the product at the expense of others. Since all rival firms have indulged in this competitive advertising the result has been that the big firms only maintain their share of the market.

It follows from above that the effects of advertising are highly controversial and no firm conclusion can be drawn in general about their bad or beneficial effects.

Government Policies Towards Monopoly and Competition

Introduction

People look at monopolies with suspicion and they are considered as undesirable form of market structure. The existence of monopolies in an economy is an important cause of glaring income inequalities and monopolists wield a lot of economic power which they use to exploit both consumers and workers. Economists generally criticise monopolies as they restrict output and raise prices of their products. Thus monopolies and oligopolies not only increase income inequalities but also cause inefficiency in the allocation of resources of a society. In this chapter, we analyse the economic effects of monopolies and imperfect competition represented by oligopolies and what policies government can adopt to reduce their bad effects and to achieve economic efficiency.

THE DRAWBACKS OF MONOPOLIES AND LIMITED COMPETITION

The effect of monopolies and limited competition as in oligopolies is that they lead to economic inefficiency which reduce social welfare. There are four major sources of emergence of economic inefficiency under monopolies and oligopolies. First, *monopolies restrict output* and produce levels of output which are less than what are economically efficient. Second, there exists *managerial slack* under monopoly due to which cost per unit of output is higher. Thirdly, monopolies *spend less on research and development* and therefore, hampers technological progress. Fourth, monopolies and oligopolies often indulge in *rent-seeking activities* to raise or sustain their monopoly profits. We briefly explain below these drawbacks of monopolies and oligopolies.

1. Restriction of Output to Charge Higher Price

Monopolists, like firms working under perfect competitions, aim at maximising profits. But, as seen in the earlier chapters, to maximise profits a monopolist is able to charge higher price by restricting output of the product or service he produces. Given the same demand and cost conditions as prevailing in a competitive industry, the monopolist who maximises his profits at the output level at which his marginal cost equals marginal revenue, produces less than the competitive industry. Thus, by producing less and charging higher price, the monopolist works in an economically inefficient way and causes a loss of consumer welfare. Consider Fig. 23.1 where *DD* is the demand curve for a competitive industry consisting of a large number of firms. *SS* is the short-run supply curve of the competitive industry which is obtained by summing up the marginal cost curves of the firms. The competitive industry is in equilibrium at point *E* at which demand curve and supply curve intersect and produces Q_c quantity of the product and price determined is equal to P_c. Note that under competitive equilibrium price P_c is equal to marginal cost of production at output level Q_c.

Now, with monopolist equating marginal revenue (*MR*) with marginal cost (*MC*) to maximise profits restricts output to Q_m and sets price equal to P_m. Note that when all competitive firms are merged to form a monopoly, supply curve *SS* of the competitive industry will become marginal cost (*MC*) curve of the monopolist . Thus, output under monopoly is lower and price higher than in a competitive industry and this leads to loss of consumer welfare.

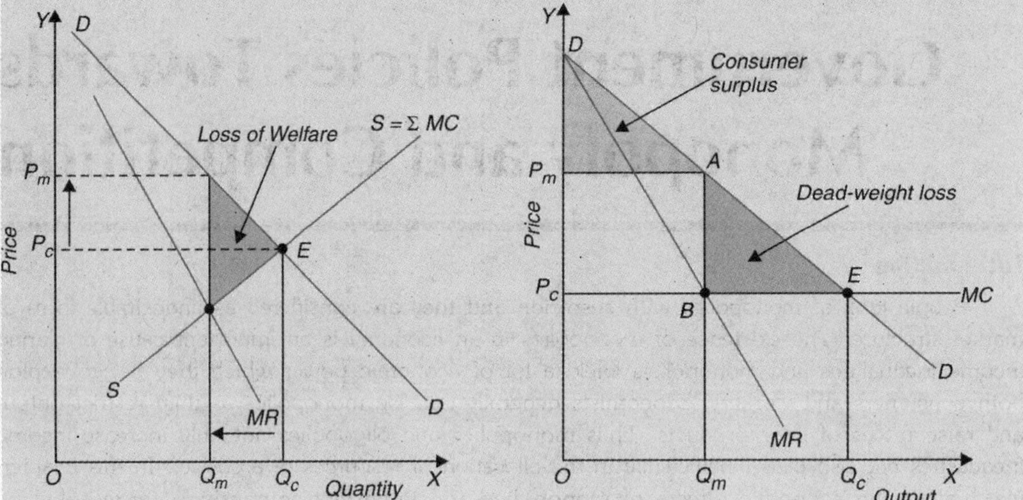

Fig. 23.1. *Monopolist restricts output to raise price*

Fig. 23.2. *Dead-Weight Loss under Monopoly and Reduction in Consumer Surplus*

How monopoly causes loss of consumer welfare can be explained by reinterpreting the demand curve. On this interpretation, demand curve for a product shows *how much money a consumer is willing to pay for an extra unit of the product* as he consumes more quantity of the product. In other words, demand curve which depicts various prices at different quantities of goods purchased measures *marginal benefit* to a consumer of extra units of a product as he purchases more units of it. Since under perfect competition the output level is determined at which demand curve (which reflects marginal benefit) intersects the supply curve (which represents marginal cost curve), under it consumer welfare is maximised. Price paid by the consumers depicting marginal benefit is equal to marginal cost under perfect competition and this ensures maximum welfare. Alternatively, as explained in earlier chapters, allocative economic efficiency is achieved when total surplus (*i.e.*, the sum of consumer surplus and producer surplus, is maximised. Under perfect competition, the sum of consumer surplus and producer surplus is maximised at output level Q_c in Fig. 23.1 at which demand curve *DD* intersects the supply curve *SS*.

On the other hand, by producing level of output at which price exceeds marginal cost, the monopolist reduces social welfare and causes allocative inefficiency. This is explicitly illustrated in Figure 23.2. To keep the analysis simple we assume that marginal cost curve (which is the supply curve under perfect competition) is a horizontal straight line which shows that marginal cost remains constant as output is increased. Under perfect competition as price is equated with marginal cost, output Q_c will be produced. With output Q_c and price P_c, consumer surplus enjoyed by consumers will be EP_cD. On the other hand, the monopolist will equate marginal cost with marginal revenue and will produce lower amount of output Q_m and charge higher price P_m. As a result, consumer surplus is reduced to $AP_m D$ which represents the loss of consumer welfare equal to the area $AE\ P_cP_m$. But this loss of consumer welfare can be broken into two losses. First, the rectangle ABP_cP_m which represents the profits made by the monopolist by restricting output to Q_m and raising price to P_m. But this loss of consumer surplus is not a loss to the society as a whole. It is a transfer of income from the consumers to the monopolist as price of the product is raised and output reduced by the latter. But there is additional loss of consumer surplus equal to the area ABE because of restriction of output from Q_c to Q_m by the monopolist. As will be seen from the segment of demand curve AE in Fig. 23.2 for the units of output from Q_m to Q_c, the consumers are prepared to pay higher price than marginal cost (MC) of these units of output. Thus, this second type of loss of consumer surplus is a complete loss to society as no one in the society has gained a result of this loss suffered by the consumers. Therefore, the loss of consumer surplus equal to the area of triangle ABE is called *dead-weight loss* and represents inefficiency caused by the monopolist.

Managerial Slack

It is generally pointed out that a firm which aims at maximising profits will try to minimise cost as far as possible for producing a given level of output. However, in actual practice it has been found that those firms which enjoy monopoly or face limited competition are able to make a lot of profits and also lack the incentives to keep their cost as low as possible. *The lack of incentives to reduce costs as far as possible due to the absence of pressure of competition is known as 'managerial slack'.* This also leads to inefficiency in production. In the absence of competition it is difficult to know whether or not management of the firms is efficient because it is always claimed by them that they are doing their best to keep their costs as low as possible. For example, before privatisation of telecom services BSNL (Bharat Sanchar Nigam Ltd.) had a monopoly of long distance telephone services and it charged very high prices but was always claiming that its costs were as low as possible. Now that there has been privatisation of Telecom services in India in the past few years with private companies such as Reliance, Tata, Hutch, Airtel have been permitted to provide long-distance telephone services, prices of them have fallen sharply. Now, under the pressure of competition with the private companies, even BSNL has substantially reduced the rates of long-distance calls. That shows there was a lot of managerial slack in BSNL and in fact it was not keeping its costs as low as possible. If it were not so, then how when it has to compete with the private companies it has been able to substantially cut the prices of long-distance calls.

Monopolies do not make Adequate Expenditure on Research and Development

It has often been found that because they do not have to face competition in selling their products, monopolies do not make enough expenditure to develop new products and new and better techniques of production. Since monopolists are able to make a large amount of profits without any effort to make progress in technology, there is lack of incentives on their part to make adequate effort and spend enough expenditure on research and development to develop new technologies which improve productivity and lower costs of production. Of course, there may be some exceptions to this general tendency on the part of monopolies. For example, it has been pointed out that the US telephone company AT & T made important innovations throughout the period when it held almost a monopoly position in providing telephone services in the United States. The invention of laser technology and transistor were two of its important contributions. However, Professor Stiglitz points out that "*greater expenditure on research and development by AT & T was due to the regulation by government.* He writes, AT & T was in a unique position. The prices it charged were set by government regulators and those prices were set to encourage the expenditure of money on research. From this perspective AT & T's research contribution was as much a consequence of government regulatory policy as of anything else."[1]

Rent-Seeking Activities of Monopolies

The last important source of economic inefficiency under monopoly is *their attempt to spend a lot of money in maintaining their monopoly position in the market rather than using their resources or profits for productive purposes.* By maintaining their monopoly position, the monopolists continue making large monopoly profits. It may be noted that since these monopoly profits are over and above the opportunity costs of the capital invested by them and wages for the managerial services performed by the monopolists, they are often referred to as *monopoly rents.* Therefore, *the attempts by the monopolists to maintain or acquire monopoly positions in some industries or in sale of some products or services is referred to as rent-seeking behaviour.*

Sometimes, monopoly position of a firm is the result of protection granted by government. Many developing countries grant a licence to a firm or few firms within their country to produce a product and thus providing a large market power or monopoly power to them which they use to make large profits. In addition, they ban the imports of some goods from abroad so as to prevent any competition from foreign manufacturers. To get these licences and protection from imports from abroad, these firms spend a lot of money for lobbying for them to maintain regulations that restrict competition and yield large profits to them. They liberally contribute to the election expenses of members of parliament and political parties. They even bribe bureaucrats to enforce regulations that favour them. Commenting on these rent-seeking activities, Prof. Stiglitz write "*such activities are socially wasteful. Real resources (including labour times) are used to win favourable rules, not to produce goods and services. There is thus legitimate concern that the willingness of government to restrict competition will encourage firms to spend money on rent-seeking activities rather than on making a better product.*"[2]

Further Disadvantages of Limited Competition

We have seen in the earlier chapters that oligopolies dominate the economy. In these oligopolies, there is limited competition among the few firms that operate to produce either the same or similar product. In oligopolies the output produced is lower than in perfect competition but is more than in monopoly. Though the expenditure on research and development to introduce new products and to discover superior techniques of production to reduce costs is quite intense under oligopoly, but other inefficiences are worse in oligopolies with limited competition. Oligopolistic firms spend more resources on practices to prevent entry of new firms in the industry so as to continue making large profits. An important way to deter entry of potential firms is to issue threat that if they dare to enter, they will reduce price to such a low level that the new entrants will suffer a great monetary loss. To make the threat credible, the existing oligopolistic firms *build excess capacity.* With excess capacity the existing firms can easily expand output to lower price of the product. This convince the potential

1. Joseph E, Stiglitz, *Economics, Second Edition,* p.290.
2. *Op. cit.,* p. 290

entrants that if they enter the industry, the existing firms will lower price to compete them out. To deter entry the existing oligopolistic firms even resort to *predatory pricing. Predatory pricing means the existing firms set price even below cost of production so as to inflict heavy losses on the new entrants.* Unable to bear losses when the new entrants leave the industry, *the existing firms* raise prices so as not only to recover the earlier losses but to ensure high sustained profits in future.

Besides, the oligopolists incur a lot of expenditure on competitive advertising to keep their market share in the product. Further, a large advertising expenditure is incurred to deter entry of potential entrants by influencing the consumers that their products are far better than others. However, the expenditure to deter entry may increase the profits of the existing oligopolistic firms facing limited competition but from the social point of view it involves wasteful expenditure and make consumers worse off. Thus, under oligopoly, firms facing limited competition operate with economic inefficiency.

PUBLIC POLICY TOWARDS MONOPOLY AND COMPETITION

Having discussed the drawbacks of monopolies and oligopolies, we will now explain how government intervenes to influence price charged and quantity produced by the firms working in monopolistic and oligopolistic markets. There are three ways in which government can influence these markets to achieve economic efficiency and to protect the interests of consumers.

1. *Nationalisation or Public Ownership* of the monopolistic and oligopolistic firms.
2. *Regulation of monopolies* so that they should charge such price and produce such quantities of goods which ensure economic efficiency and work in the best interests of public.
3. *To create competitive conditions and discourage monopolistc practices.*

It may be noted that the first two measures have been adopted to deal with monopolies, especially natural monopolies. In case of oligopolies, there is limited competition among the few firms and they often adopt certain business practices to prevent the entry of new firms or they join hand with each other to enter into agreements to promote collusion, formal or tacit. In this respect, the general public policy is to *encourage competition.* When encouraging competition does not work, government *passes legislation to enforce competition.*

We will discuss all the above three types of public policies to deal with monopolies and oligopolies.

Public Policy Towards Natural Monopoly : Nationalisation or Public Ownership

The first public policy approach towards natural monopoly is that government should take it under its ownership and run it as a nationalised enterprise. Before explaining the merits and demerits of public ownership of natural monopoly, it is necessary to clarify the meaning of natural monopoly. *Natural monopoly in an industry is said to exist when there occur economies of scale over a large range of output due to which average cost of production steadly declines and the extent of market demand for a commodity is such that it can support only one big optimum-size firm.* Under these circumstances a large-sized firm enjoying economies of scale and operating with a lower average cost of production can compete away the small-sized firms having higher average costs and can therefore succeed in establishing its monopoly. The examples of industries in which natural monopoly exists is distribution of electricity, water and gas in a city, rail transportation, air transportation, telephone services etc.

Let us first analyse how the working of a natural monopoly leads to economic inefficiency and causes loss of consumer's welfare. This is illustrated in Fig. 23.3 where *DD'* is the demand curve facing the natural monopolist. *ATC* is the average cost curve of the natural monopoly which, as will be seen from Fig. 23.3, is sloping downward throughout due to economies of scale. Marginal cost curve *MC* which shows changes in variable costs as extra units of output are produced is sloping downward. Note that average total cost curve *ATC* is falling throughout due to the economies of scale as more units of output are produced. Under perfect competition output Q_c will be produced at which marginal cost equals price of product P_c. But the natural monopoly maximises its profits by producing output Q_m at which its marginal revenue equals marginal cost and will set price equal to P_m and will make profits equal to $ABKP_m$. Natural monopoly is causing dead-weight loss equal to *ANE* and is, therefore, operating with economic inefficiency.

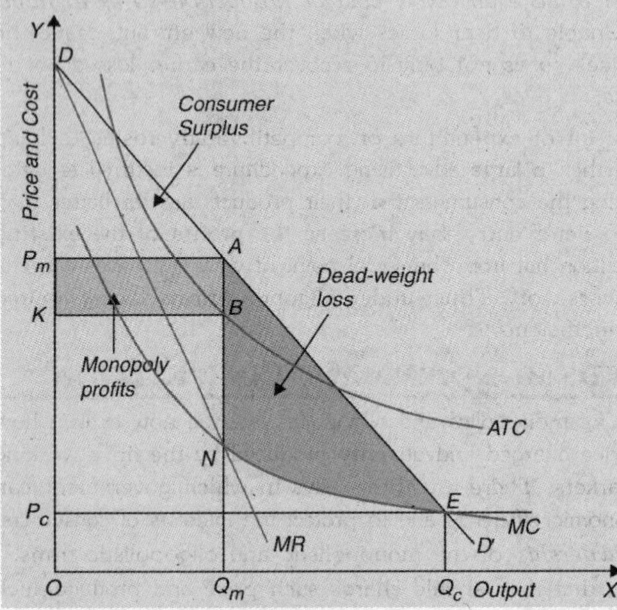

Fig. 23.3. *Profit Maximisation by a Natural Monopoly and its Economic Inefficiency.*

But, as explained above, in the case of natural monopoly because of falling average cost throughout due to economies of scale, competition is ruled out. Under natural monopoly, average cost curve is declining throughout and marginal cost is less than it. Hence if a firm having a natural monopoly is asked to equate marginal cost with price, it will suffer losses as shown by the shaded area $EBSP_c$ in Fig. 23.4. If government wants the natural-monopoly firm to adopt this marginal-cost pricing policy it would have to grant subsidies to the firm equal to the shaded area. To finance subsidies, taxes would have to be imposed on the public. Thus grant of subsidies to the natural monopoly to make it work efficiently will impose costs on the society. Besides, it is very difficult to ascertain the amount of subsidies since the firm may inflate its costs. As a result, instead of subsidising, government may decide to takeover the ownership of the firm having natural monopoly and operate it as a nationalised enterprise. In the UK this policy of nationalisation of natural monopolies in the field of railways, telephones, supply of electricity, gas and water was adopted during the period 1945 to 1951. In India too until recently the natural monopolies belonging to

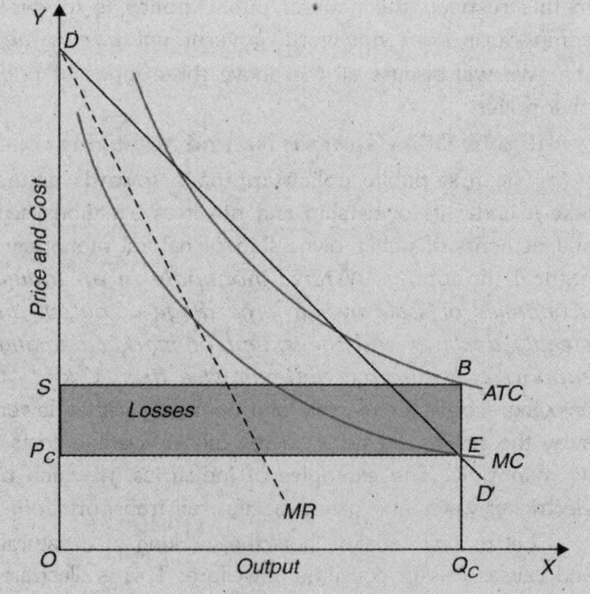

Fig. 23.4. *Natural Monopoly Making Losses on Equating MC with Price under Marginal Cost Pricing.*

railways, post and telegraph, distribution of electricity and water, gas, telephone services have been in public ownership. In the last few years, distribution of electricity in cities like Delhi, Mumbai and Kolkata has been privatised. Also there has been privatisation of Telecom services and air transportation. But railways, post and telegraph are still in public ownership and are operated as nationalised enterprises.

It was expected that, under government ownership, the natural monopolies would not abuse their monopoly power and would neither restrict output, nor charge high prices and thus work in public interest and achieve economic efficiency.

Problems of Nationalised Industries

But public ownership of natural monopolies has not been without problems. First, it has been pointed out that *managers of public owned enterprises lack the incentives to minimise cost.* Managers of a privately owned firms have incentives to minimise costs to make sufficient profits for the owners-shareholders in case of corporations to keep them satisfied. If the managers of a private firm are doing a bad job and not making sufficient profits, they will be fired by the owners of the firm. On the other hand, if bureaucrats who run a government-owned natural monopoly do a bad job, it is consumers and taxpayers who suffer because it is by taxing them that the losses of public-owned enterprises have to be met. The ability of managers of government-owned enterprises to obtain subsidies to cover the losses weaken their incentives to minimise cost. For the same reasons, bureaucrats who manage government-owned companies do not have any incentives to introduce any innovations to cut costs and improve the technology of production.

Besides, it has been found that in running public-sector enterprises governments often yield to temptation to interfere with the working of public sector undertakings to seek goals other than efficient operation. For example, in India, it has been observed that *public sector undertakings have been overstaffed* for sake of generating more employment. In Britain and some other European countries such as Sweden also the experience has been to provide public sector jobs to keep unemployment low, no matter whether extra employees are really required or not.

Further, as a result of incurring losses year after year public sector enterprises in the field of public utilities such as railways, electricity, telephone services etc. their investment plans have been severely constrained. For example in India losses of state electricity boards have been enormous which have adversely affected investment in the power sector. Government enterprises running the public utilities such as railways, electricity have been pressurised to provide some services at below their marginal cost, with the losses so incurred are made up by the profits made in other parts of business. This is often called *cross-subsidisation.* For example, the Indian Railways are required to maintain services on the loss-making routes which are financed by revenue obtained from more profitable routes. Another example of cross-subsidisation is the practice of Post and Telegraph Department of charging the same fee for delivering a piece of mail (e.g. registered letter or a parcel) between any two places within India as a whole or within any two points in a large city like Delhi.

Due to heavy losses made by nationalised or public sector enterprises and their inefficient working, there has been a tendency all over the world (including India) to sell these enterprises to the private sector. This is called *privatisation.* For example, in Delhi electricity distribution has been handed over to BSES (a Reliance Company) and NDPL (a Tata Company) . In Mumbai and Kolkata also, private companies are in charge of distribution of electricity. In Britain, British Telecom, British Gas and nationalised electricity and water companies were sold to the private sector in the 1980s. It has been found that after privatisation, these companies have made large profits and the prices of their shares have risen sharply. However, in order to cut costs, after privatisation these companies have made large cuts in employment and have contributed to growing unemployment in Britain and other European countries.

REGULATION OF NATURAL MONOPOLIES

Another important way in which government can deal with natural monopolies is to regulate their price and output. Privatisation can lead to more operational efficiency and enormous profits earned by the private owners but it cannot solve the basic problem and drawback of natural monopoly that it leads to a large market power enjoyed by private firms which exploits consumers by making enormous profits and causes loss of economic inefficiency. It is therefore necessary to regulate them and put restrictions on their behaviour so that they work in public interest and in economically efficient way. Therefore, even in Britain where previously nationalised industries in the field of public utilities have been privatised, regulatory commissions or committees have been appointed to regulate their behaviour.

Public Interest Theory and Marginal-Cost Pricing

One important theory of regulation is the *public interest theory*. According to public interest theory, the regulation of the firm having natural monopoly should be such as to ensure that it works with economic efficiency, that is, it should fix such price and output of the product or service that maximise the total surplus (sum of consumer surplus and producer surplus). Therefore, according to public interest theory, the regulation requires the firm to adopt *marginal-cost pricing*, as illustrated in Fig. 23.4. It will be seen from this figure that natural monopoly should be so regulated that it should charge price P_c and produce output Q_c at which marginal cost curve *MC* cuts the demand curve *DD'* . However, as explained above, with marginal-cost pricing the natural monopoly makes losses. This is because in a natural monopoly average total cost is falling throughout and marginal cost curve lies below it. Therefore, at output level at which marginal cost (*MC*) curve cuts demand curve and becomes equal to price, the average total cost will exceed price. As a result, with marginal cost equal to price the firm will make losses as shown by the shaded area in Fig. 23.4. Therefore, instead of charging such a low price that equals marginal cost and causes losses to the firm, the monopoly firm will just leave the industry. One response of public policy to this problem is to provide subsidy to the monopolist to compensate him for the losses. But, as pointed out above, to pay subsidy to the monopolist government will levy taxes on the people. However, taxation, as seen in an earlier chapter, involves dead-weight loss and reduce economic efficiency.

The second problem with marginal cost pricing as a regulatory policy is that it does not provide any incentive to reduce costs. Every firm working in a competitive market tries to minimise costs because lower costs mean more profits for it. But in case a of a regulated monopoly the firm knows whenever costs are reduced, the regulator will reduce prices and it will therefore not gain from making efforts to reduce costs. That is why to furnish incentives to reduce costs in actual practice regulators often allow the monopolists to retain some of the profits obtained through reduction in costs. However, this practice represents deviation from marginal-cost pricing.

Average-Cost Pricing

Due to the problems faced in marginal-cost pricing policy, especially when government does not want to give subsidies to the natural monopoly because of its financial costraint, average-cost pricing policy may be adopted. But if it is worthwhile to make investment in a public utility the monopolist must be assured of *fair return on capital*. The fair return on capital represents normal profits which are included in average cost of production. Thus, average-cost pricing policy regulates or fixes price equal to average cost of production which includes fair rate of return on capital invested by the firm. Consider Fig. 23.5. *DD′* is demand curve facing the firm owning a natural monopoly. *ATC* is the average total cost curve which includes fair return on capital invested. *MC* is the marginal cost curve. The regulator following average-cost pricing will set price P_a corresponding to which average total cost curve *ATC* intersects the given demand curve *DD′*. At this regulated price P_a, the firm will produce Q_a quantity of the product. It will be seen from Figure 23.5 that output Q_a is less than the output Q_c at which marginal cost (*MC*) equals price. Therefore, *average-cost pricing leads to the level of output produced being less than the economically efficient output.* As a result, average cost pricing causes *dead-weight loss of welfare* as shown by the shaded area.

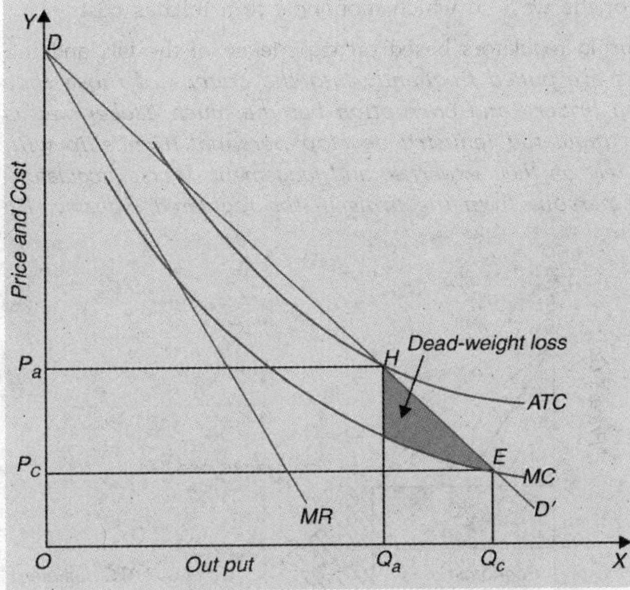

Fig. 23.5. *Average Cost Pricing to Regulate Natural Monopoly*

The second problem facing average cost pricing policy is that under it monopoly firm has no incentive to reduce cost as it knows that if it cuts its costs, the regulatory authority will reduce the price and it will not therefore benefit from making efforts to reduce costs.

The third problem facing average-cost pricing is that since the firms are assured of a fair return on capital, they have a tendency to increase investment in capital as much as possible so as to obtain higher return on capital. This leads to too much investment. Besides, another problem of regulation through average-cost pricing is that firms have no incentives to innovate. This is because technological innovations reduce costs and as a result regualtors reduce price of the product, and therefore firms do not benefit from innovations introduced by them. In recent years, regulatory commissions in both the USA and the UK have realised that unless they reward the firms for introducing innovations, these will not be forthcoming. Therefore, in recent years business firms who by introducing technological innovations succeed in making profits, the regulators have allowed them to retain much of increased profits, at least for few years.

Capturing Regulators

But, the most serious problem of average-cost pricing is that *regulators are often captured by the firms whom they are supposed to regulate.* In contrast to public interest theory, according to capture theory, such regulations are framed that enable the monopolistic firms to maximise their producer surplus. So as a result of regulatory capture, regulatory authorities instead of trying to promote public interest, promote the interests of the monopoly firm. The monopoly firm often bribes the regulators to win them over. The fair return on capital is crucial for calculating average cost and fixing price on that basis. The monopoly firms often through bribe or otherwise succeed in misleading the regulators about true costs and fair return on capital. The managers of a monopoly firm often succeed in inflating their costs by spending a part of firm's revenues on inputs that are not really required. Keeping luxury cars, expensive office suits, lavish international travel, keeping company jets or helicopters, lavish entertainment expenditure are some of the ways in which monopoly firm inflates costs.

Explaining the reasons for capturing regulators based on experience of the UK and the US, Prof. Stiglitz writes, "*regulators are pulled frequently into the cramps of those they regulate. This could happen through bribery and corruption but the much likelier way is just that over time employees of a regulated industry develop personal friendship with the regulators who in turn come to rely on their expertise and judgement. Worse, regulatory agencies (of necessity) tend to hire persons from the firms in the regulated industry. By the same token, regulators who demonstrate an "understanding" of the industry may be rewarded with good jobs in that industry after they leave government service*"[3]. The above reasons apply equally well to India.

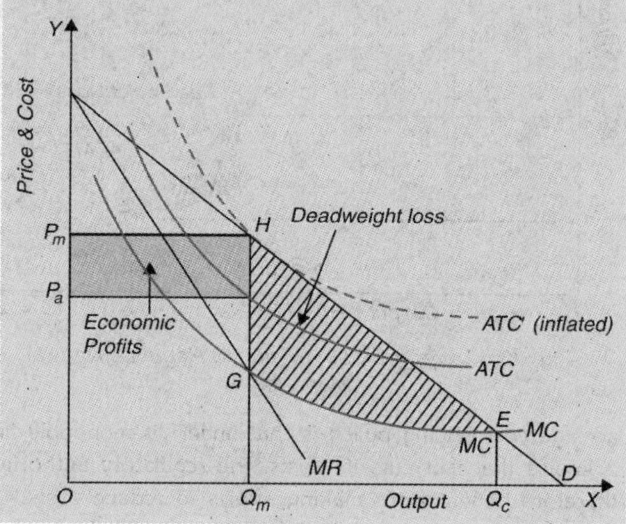

Fig. 23.6. *Outcome when Monopoly Firm Captures Regulator or Inflates Cost.*

When the monopoly firm captures the regulator or succeeds in inflating the cost by misleading the regulator, the outcome is shown in Fig. 23.6. It will be seen from Fig. 23.6 that the firm of natural monopoly is maximising its profits by equating marginal cost (*MC*) with marginal revenue when it produces Q_m and charges P_m price. When the firm captures the regulator it makes the latter to fix price P_m which maximises its economic profits. The economic profits made by the monopoly firm in this situation when it captures regulator are shown by the shaded area in Fig. 23.6.

The same outcome of profit maximising situation for the monopoly firm prevails if it succeeds in inflating its costs by misleading the regulator. With inflated costs, average total cost curve (*ATC*) shifts to the dotted position *ATC* (inflated) which is tangent to the demand curve exactly vertically above the point *G* at which marginal cost equals marginal revenue and monopoly firm maximises its profits by producing output O_m. It will be further observed that with capturing the regulator or succeeding in inflating costs, dead-weight loss has increased to the stripped area *HGE*.

ENCOURAGING COMPETITION

The last way in which government can deal with natural monopoly is to encourage competition between firms, however imperfect competition it may be. This raises question as to how competition can be promoted in the field of natural monopoly when it is generally believed that competition in natural monopoly when average cost is falling over a large relevant range of output, is not viable. Suppose the two firms divide the market for a product of natural monopoly. Thus, we have duopolists competing in this natural monopoly industry. Why is competition not viable between the two ? This is illustrated in Fig. 23.7 where *ATC* is average

3. Joseph E. Stiglitz, *op. cit*, p. 291

total cost curve and DD' is the market demand curve for the product of natural monopoly which the two firms are sharing. If there were one monopolistic firm operating to meet the market demand, its profits would be maximised by producing output Q_m and charging price P_m. Now, when the two firms are sharing the market, suppose each is producing Q_d (half of Q_m) and its cost is AC_d. Now, any one firm can capture the entire market by cutting price below that of its rival firm. By expanding output beyond Q_d, it will be reducing its average cost. Having established its monopoly, it can set its price above AC_d and earn profits without worrying about the entry of any potential rivals trying to capture some of the profits. Potential rivals knows that on the entry by them the existing firm can afford to lower the price since it can enjoy economies of scale by expanding output. This deters the entry of new firms.

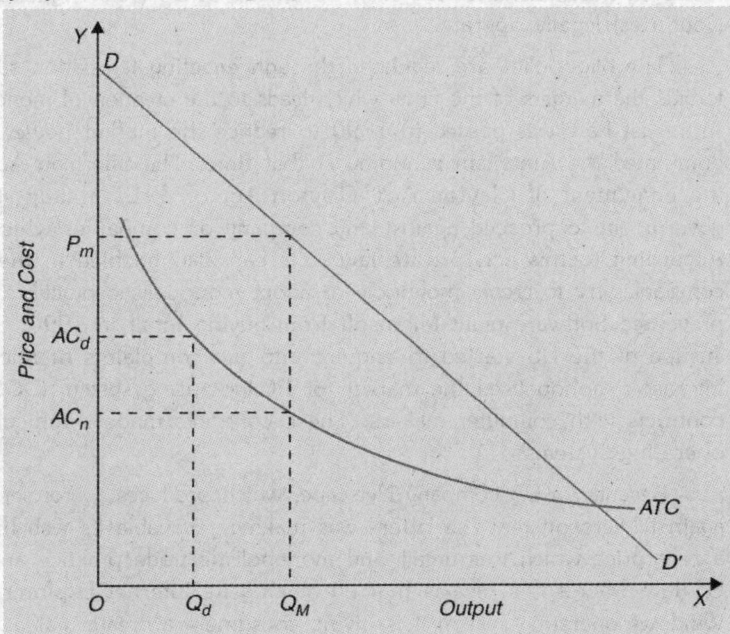

Fig. 23.7. *Natural Monopoly and Need for Competition*

However, in the last three decades, in many countries efforts have been to introduce more competition in the industries of natural monopoly. In Britain bus services were deregulated and competition was promoted by allowing more firms to operate bus services. Competition has been introduced in telephone services in Britain by allowing more firms to use the cables already laid. In India too with the advances in telecom technology and advent of cellular telephones, more firms such as Airtel, Tata Indicom, Reliance have been allowed to provide telephone services. In Britain and India electricity generation has been separated from electricity distribution and more firms have been permitted to compete in generating electricity. Even electricity distribution has been privatised, different private firms have been given licenses to distribute electricity in specific areas.

In the USA and various countries of Europe and India too, airlines have been substantially deregulated and more than one air company has been allowed to compete. Thus, in India, Air Sahara, Jet Airways, Air Decean have been allowed to operate both within India and outside to compete with public sector companies. Increased competition has lowered fares and improved air services. Even there is now competition in the postal services with private courier companies providing the courier service.

But *an important way monopoly firm can be subjected to competition is to allow imports of goods.* When domestic monopolistic companies have to compete with the imported products, they will tend to charge lower prices to remain in business. However, competition from imports is more valid in case of other monopolistic and oligopolistic industries than in case of natural monopolies.

Increasing Competition through Anti-trust Law

In our above analysis, we have explained how public policy has tried to deal with natural monopolies. Government has also intervened to prevent *mergers* of the companies so as to prevent the creation of monopolies and to promote competition between them. When there is oligopoly, that is, there are a few firms in the industry, there is often a tendency among them to merge and form a cartel. A cartel is a collusive agreement among a number of firms aimed at restricting output and achieving larger profits for the member firms. In many countries *formation of cartel is illegal as it leads to monopoly and exploitation of the consumers.* However, international cartels such as famous OPEC (The Organisation of Petroleum Producing Countries) legally operate.

The oligopolies are regulated through enacting legislation such as *Anti-trust Law* which forbids the mergers of the firms which leads to the creation of monopolies. In the USA Sherman Anti-trust Law was passed in 1890 to reduce the market power of 'trusts' (oligopolies) that dominated the American economy at that time. The Sherman Act was amended in 1914 by the enactment of Clayton Act. Clayton Act of 1914 greatly strengthened the powers of government to proceed against any company or companies which try to create monopolies. According to this act, private law suits can also be filed in the courts if any company or companies try to create monopoly or adopt monopolistic practices. It is this Anti-trust law that prevented Software giant Microsoft from buying Intuit in 1994. Similarly, the Department of Justice of the US started to enquire into the complaints of Microsoft competitors that the Microsoft monopolised the market for PC operating system (DOS and Windows) by making contracts with computer makers. These contracts made it difficult for firms producing other operating systems.

Recently, a US company Netscape, which produces a browser called Navigator complained against Microsoft that the latter was making available its web browser 'Internet Explorer' at a zero price which was unfair and monopolistic trade practice and not permissible under the US law. Microsoft's plea is that by making its Internet Explorer free of cost along with its Windows operating system it is giving consumers a greater value. The case is still pending in the court.

The Anti-trust laws provide government various ways in which it can intervene to promote competition. They give power to government to prevent mergers so as to prevent the creation of monopolies. The second, the anti-trust law empowers the government to break up companies to encourage competition. Thus, in the US a famous telecommunication company, AT&T was split up into eight small companies to encourage competition. Thirdly, antitrust laws prevent companies from coordinating their activities in ways that make markets less competitive.

It may be noted that all mergers of companies are not undesirable. Sometimes different firms merge not to reduce competition but to increase efficiency by joint operation and thus lower costs. The recent Indian Competition Act allows mergers of companies if they result in higher efficiency and lower costs but not in restricting competition. Some banks in India have merged in recent years to strengthen their financial position and to improve efficiency.

Thus crucial question is to examine whether formation of mergers of firms is to reduce competition or to improve efficiency and strengthen financial position. If merger is designed to reduce competition it is bad and undesirable, but if it is to improve efficiency and strengthen financial position of the firms without reducing competition it is desirable.

QUESTIONS FOR REVIEW

1. What is meant by managerial slack ? What does it mean when economists say that monopoly output is 'too little' or a monopoly price is "too high"? What benchmark do they use to claim this ?
2. Give reasons for the lack of incentives for the monopoly firm to lower costs as far as possible.
3. Why does a monopolistic firm lack incentives to make adequate expenditure on research and development (R & D) to make advances in technology ?
4. What is a natural monopoly ? Explain why average cost curve of a natural monopoly falls throughout ? What are the consequences of this ?
5. If regulatory authority of a natural monopoly sets price equal to marginal cost, what problem will arise ? How does nationalisation or regulation solve this problem?
6. What is public interest theory of regulation ? What price policy for a natural monopoly does it suggest ?
7. What is regulatory capture hypothesis? What are it consequences ?
8. How oligopolies are regulated so as to prevent them from merging and reducing competition?
9. Explain how competition is not viable in case of natural monopoly. How has government sought to promote competition in this case ?
10. What are the drawbacks of monopolies and limited competition ? Explain why there is need for regulation of monopolies and oligopolies with limited competition.

PART – V

PRICING PRACTICES AND STRATEGIES, MANAGERIAL AND BEHAVIOURAL MODELS OF THE FIRM

- Cost-Plus (or Mark-up) Pricing
- Price Discrimination
- Pricing of Multiple Products
- Transfer Pricing
- Pricing in Non-Profit Enterprises, Ramsey Pricing and Peak-load Pricing
- Sales Maximization Model of Oligopoly Firm
- Managerial Theories of the Firm : Marris and Williamson's Models
- Behavioural Theory of the Firm : Satisficing Model
- Theory of Games and Strategic Behaviour

Cost-Plus (or Mark-Up) Pricing

Adding Mark-Up to Average Cost

So far we have explained those theories of price and output determination under oligopoly which are based on profit maximization assumption. After the marginalist revolution, profit maximisatipn by the firm is generally explained by the marginal analysis, that is, by the use of marginal revenue and marginal cost concepts. An important alternative approach to profit maximisation and marginal analysis is the *cost-plus pricing theory* which does not assume that rational firms seek to maximise profits. It may be pointed out in the beginning that cost-plus cost theory has been given several names. Cost-plus pricing theory is also known as *full-cost pricing* theory, or average cost pricing since in this theory price of a product is fixed on the basis of full average cost, that is, all costs per unit of output which also includes normal profit per unit of output. It is also called *mark-up pricing* theory, since this theory visualises that in order to fix price businessmen add a mark-up to their average cost of production.[1]

Cost-Plus Pricing: Hall and Hitch Version

Hall and Hitch of Oxford University made a root and branch attack on the marginal analysis and on the notion of profits maximization, and put forward the view that business firms in the real world fixed prices on the basis of direct cost (variable cost) per unit of output by adding to it overhead cost per unit and a margin of normal or conventional profits. To quote them, "the way in which businessmen decide what price to charge for their products and what output to produce, casts doubt on the general applicability of conventional analysis of price and output policy in terms of marginal cost and marginal revenue and suggest a mode of entrepreneurial behaviour which current economic doctrine tends to ignore."[2]

As has been mentioned in an earlier chapter, Hall and Hitch made an empirical study of the behaviour of business firms regarding fixation of prices of the products. In this study they interviewed 38 entrepreneurs of whom 33 were manufacturers of various products, 3 were retailers, and 2 were builders. From this empirical study they found, as is clear from the above quotation, that firms for fixing prices do not maximize profits by equating marginal cost with

1. R. L. Hall and C. J. Hitch, Price Theory and Business Behaviour, *Oxford Economic Papers*, Vol. 2, 1939.
2. *Op. cit.*. p. 1

marginal revenue. It is worth mentioning here that they argued not only against marginal analysis of pricing by the firms but also challenged the notion that in fixing prices firms maximise their profits. Profit maximization, according to them, was a wrong way to approach the question of pricing by the business firms. Indeed they pointed out that business firms in the real world only tried to seek a satisfactory profits or, in other words, normal or conventional rate of profit. Thus, according to them, prices are fixed on the basis of full cost that is aveage direct (variable) costs plus average overhead cost plus a satisfactory margin for profit. It should be noted that the average direct cost as well as average overhead cost is calculated on the basis of *expected output* in a period or on the basis of some conventional output.

Many reasons were provided by entrepreneurs as to why they fixed prices on the basis of cost-plus pricing. Firstly, they pointed out that if they fixed prices above average cost which would yield abnormal profits to them, *there was the threat of actual or potential competitors* competing away these profits. Further, they expressed ignorance of the concept of average and marginal revenue and also pointed out the absence of any data regarding marginal revenue and marginal cost. In view of the absence of data regarding *MC* and *MR*, how could they fix price on their basis. Furthermore, according to Hall and Hitch, in fixing prices of their products, entrepreneurs behave according to the moral principle that there is a price that *ought* to be charged and this price is the average cost price which includes normal profit and they think this is the right price that ought to be charged in periods of both good and bad business, that is, in period of both depression and boom. Thus, according to Hall and Hitch, there is not frequent changes in prices. Average-cost or cost-plus pricing, according to them, is the result of (*a*) tacit or open collusion, (*b*) considerations of long-run demand and costs, (*c*) moral conviction of firms and (*d*) uncertain effects of the increases and decreases in price.

They held that oligopolistic firms faced *kinked demand curve* and on account of this they emphasised stickiness of prices in the short run. As has been explained in a previous chapter, kinked demand curve with a kink at the current price, is formed on the assumption that the increase in price by an oligopolist will not be matched by its rivals, while the reduction in price will be immediately followed with the result that part of the demand curve above the current price will be highly elastic, whereas the part of the demand curve below the ruling price will be very much less-elastic.

Hall and Hitch combine cost-plus pricing, that is, average-cost pricing with kinked demand curve analysis. Current price is fixed on the basis of average-cost[3] (as defined above), and a kink in the demand curve is formed at this price. Average-cost pricing together with the kinked demand curve analysis is illustrated in Fig. 24.1. Suppose the firm decides to produce *OM* quantity of the product. This output, as pointed above, is fixed on the basis of expected sales in the period or on some conventional standard. With *OM* as the output, firm then calculates the (1) average direct cost incurred on labour, raw materials, etc. and (2) the average overhead cost

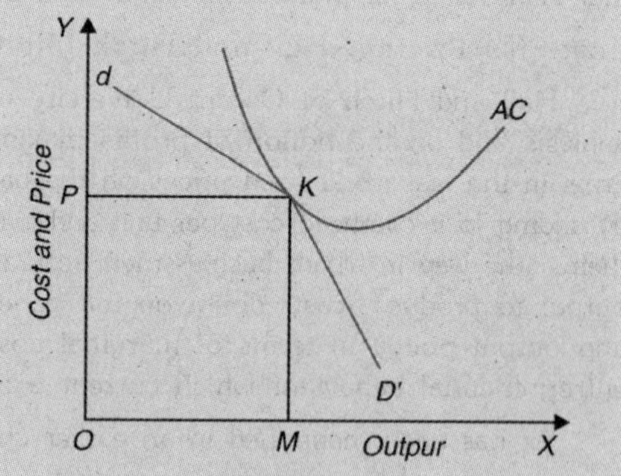

Fig. 24.1. *Average-Cost Pricing and Kinked Demand Curve*

3. As we mentioned in Chapter 21, Sweezy version of kinked demand curve theory of oligopoly cannot explain how the current price came to be what it is. This flaw is not present in Hall and Hitch's version of kinked demand curve analysis.

incurred on capital equipment etc. He then adds to it his normal or conventional margin for profit. Addition of these three items yields full average cost, which let us suppose, is *MK* in Fig. 24.1. He will, therefore, set the price *OP* which is equal to *MK*. It will be noticed that the kink in the demand curve *dD* is formed at this price *OP* or *MK*.

Kinked demand curve analysis as used by Hall and Hitch along with his average-cost pricing theory provides an explanation for the stability or rigidity of prices under oligopoly in the short run. Increases or decreases in demand will usually shift the kink to the right or left but will leave the price unchanged. But Hall and Hitch have mentioned the following two exceptions to this general rule in which case price of the product changes:

(1) If there is a large decrease in demand, and the demand remains at a low level for some time, there is every likelihood that price will be reduced so as to maintain output. According to Hall and Hitch, the explanation for this reduction in price in the context of depressed demand is that one entrepreneur may become panicky and his irrational behaviour forces the others to cut prices.

(2) If the average cost curves of all firms shift by similar amounts on account of changes in factor prices or technology, then this is "likely to lead to a revaluation of the "full cost" price. However, Hall and Hitch point out that "there will be no tendency for price to fall or rise more than the increase in wage and raw material costs."[4]

It should be noted that, given that the average cost curve falls for quite a large range of output, the cost-plus pricing suggests that price of the products will vary inversely with output ; smaller levels of output will involve higher cost per unit and therefore, higher prices will be fixed. But, according to Hall and Hitch, the oligopolists will not produce small outputs and, therefore will not charge higher prices. This is because oligopolists (1) prefer price stability, (2) are prevented by the kink to raise price, and (3) they have propensity to produce larger levels of output or, in the words of Hall and Hitch, they desire to "keep plant running as full as possible, giving rise to a general feeling in favour of price concessions."[5]

Cost-Plus Pricing : Andrew's Version

Price Fixation according to Cost-Plus Principle. Prof. Andrews[6] also propounded a cost-plus principle of price fixation by businessmen. Andrews analysis is similar to that of Hall and Hitch, but there are some differences between the two. An important difference between the two lies in the use of the concept of "*costing margin*" by Andrews. The costing margin is conceived by Andrews as an addition to constant average direct cost and "will normally tend to cover the costs of the indirect factors of production and provide a normal level of net profit."[7] Thus, like the analysis of Hall and Hitch, addition of costing margin to the average variable cost for fixation of price of the product goes against the price fixation on the basis of profit-maximization principle of the traditional theory of value. Thus the concept of costing margin of Andrews is similar to the mark-up of Hall and Hitch, but there is a difference in that whereas Hall and Hitch visualise a *constant or inflexible* mark-up or a margin for overhead cost and normal profit, Andrews discusses at length the circumstances in which there might be some *flexibility* in the costing margin in response to competitive and market forces. As shall be brought out later, the introduction of flexibility in the costing margin brings Andrews' cost-plus or average-cost price theory closer to the price theory based on profit

4. *Op. cit.* p. 32.
5. *Ibid*, p. 28.
6. P.W.S Andrews, *Manufacturing Business*, Macmillan, London, 1949.
7. *Op. cit.* p. 184.

maximisation principle. Another difference between Andrews and Hall and Hitch's versions of cost-plus pricing theory is that while the latter use kinked demand curve along with average cost pricing, the former does not make use of the kinked demand curve hypothesis in his cost-plus pricing theory. Still another important difference between the two is that whereas Hall and Hitch consider that average cost varies with output and average cost curve is U-shaped, Andrews visualises that for a large relevant range of output, average direct (variable) cost remains constant.

Andrews cost-plus pricing theory may be summarised as follows :

(*i*) The price which will be fixed by a business firm will equal *the estimated average direct cost* of production plus a costing margin. In other words, price will be equal to the 'full-cost' per unit of output.

(*ii*) Secondly, Andrews assumes on the basis of empirical investigations that average direct cost (*i.e.,* average variable cost) remains constant over a large range of output, provided the prices of direct factors (*i.e.*, variable factors) remain unchanged. Thus, according to Andrews, *average direct cost curve is a horizontal straight line over a good part,* if the prices of variable factors remain constant.

(*iii*) As said above, the costing margin will cover the cost per unit incurred on the indirect factors of production (*i.e.*, fixed factors) and on the normal rate of profit. Once fixed, the costing margin will remain constant, whatever the level of output. However, costing margin will vary as a result of the permanent changes in the prices of indirect (*i.e.*, fixed) factors of production. As mentioned before, Andrews also visualises changes in the costing margin in response to the competitive and market forces.

(*iv*) Fourthly, Andrews' analysis also suggests that, given the prices of direct factors of production, the price of the product will remain the same whatever the level of output.

(*v*) Lastly, at the price fixed on cost-plus basis, the given product will have a well-defined market and a *firm will sell the amount of the product demanded at that price by the buyers.*

The theory of cost-plus pricing as put forward by Andrews is illustrated in Figure 24.2. Cost curve *AC* in this figure represents the average direct cost (*i.e.*, average variable cost). It will be seen that average direct cost curve *AC* is saucer-shaped, that is, it first falls, then remains constant for quite a large increase in output and then eventually rises. Corresponding to this, *MC* is the marginal cost curve; *MC* curve falls in the beginning and lies below *AC*, then it coincides with *AC* curve and eventually *MC* lies above *AC*. In order to proceed to fix the price, besides average direct cost a business firm has to calculate the total *indirect costs* (*i.e.*, fixed costs) and also the amount of profits it wishes to earn. The total indirect costs plus the amount of profits planned will yield a *fixed sum of money* which will remain constant for fixation of price in the short run. The 'costing margin', according to Andrews, is obtained from this fixed sum of money by dividing it by "some chosen output.

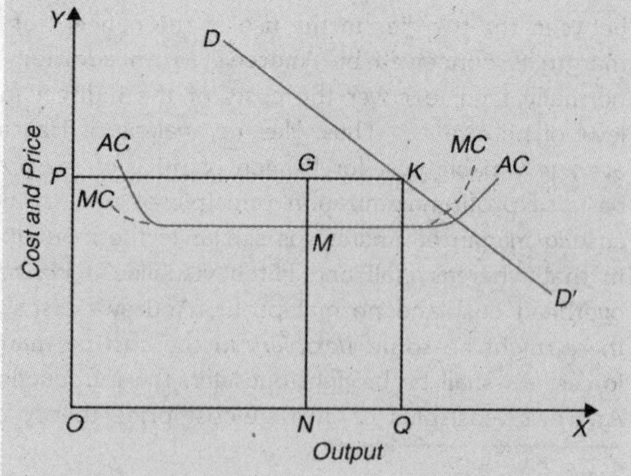

Fig. 24.2. *Price Fixation on the basis of Cost-Plus*

Determination of output for estimating costing margin. The chosen output used for the purpose of estimating costing margin can be determined in several ways. First, it may be fixed on the basis of *capacity output* of the given plant when by capacity output Andrews means the maximum output that can be produced with the given plant. Output can be fixed by a business firm as some percentage of this capacity output. Secondly, the chosen output can be fixed on the basis of *sales of product made in the preceding production period*, or average of sales achieved over a number of previous production periods. Thirdly, the output may be determined on the basis of *expected sales in a future period* for which output is being produced.

If a new firm has to set the price of its product, or if the firm has introduced a new product for which it has to set the price, the above mentioned second way of choosing the output for estimating the costing margin is ruled out and in these circumstances only the first and third methods become relevant. In fact, when the firm is a new one or when an existing firm is introducing a new product, then the first and third methods of choosing output amount to the same thing. This is because the designed capacity of the plant will be determined by the expected sales of the product in the future periods.

In Fig. 24.2, let us assume that the firm has chosen output *ON* for estimating costing margin and for fixing price of the product. Further, suppose that if the given fixed sum of money, representing the total overhead (indirect) costs and the normal level of profits is divided by the chosen output *ON* it yields *MG* amount which will be the costing margin to be added to the average direct cost for determining the price of the product. It will be seen in Figure 24.2 that at *ON* level of output, average direct cost is *NM.* If we add costing margin *MG* to *NM,* we get full-cost equal to *NG.* Thus, the price *OP* will be fixed equal to full cost *NG.* It should be noted that *price OP fixed on the basis of full cost NG will remain unchanged whatever the amount demanded and the actual output produced in the given period.* Now, if the demand for the product is given by the curve DD^1, then it will be seen from the Fig. 24.2 that at price *OP,* quantity *OQ* of the product will be demanded and therefore produced.[8] Now, even if the *demand for the product increases or decreases, the price will remain unaltered at OP, provided the amount demanded lies within the range of constant average direct cost, that is, within its horizontal straight-line portion; and further provided that costing margin remains unaltered. Thus, we see that according to Andrews' version of cost-plus pricing theory also, price will change as a result of the changes in direct and indirect costs of production and not a result of alteration in demand.* Thus, according to cost-plus theory "The price will not be altered in response to changes in demand, but only in response to changes in the prices of the direct and indirect factors.[9]

RECONCILIATION OF COST-PLUS PRICING WITH MARGINAL ANALYSIS

We have elaborately explained the cost-plus pricing theory. In spite of its being based on empirical investigations, cost-plus pricing theory has not found general acceptance among economists. Many have criticised this theory and have defended marginalism and profit maximization.

First, it has been asserted that cost-plus theory does not amount to the refutation of pricing based on the equality of marginal revenue with marginal cost (profit maximisation) and that the cost-plus pricing (or mark-up pricing as it is sometimes called) is *quite consistent with*

8. It should be noted that output *OQ* must lie with the maximum capacity output of the firm if the given demand is to be fully met. However, if *OQ* exceeds the maximum capacity and the firm has accumulated stock of the product from the previous periods, then it can draw upon the stocks to meet the demand.
9. W.J.L. Ryan, *Price Theory*, Macmillan, London, 1958, p. 377.

the pricing based on marginal analysis and profit maximisztion. It has been asserted that costing margin or mark-up is chosen by considering and guessing what the price elasticity of demand for a particular product is. If the elasticity of demand for a product is greater, smaller mark-up is fixed; and if elasticity of demand for the product is less, greater mark-up is fixed. How the cost-plus pricing is consistent and compatible with marginal analysis of pricing is explained below.

We know from our previous analysis of the relationship between price (*P*), elasticity (*e*) and marginal revenue (*MR*) that

$$P = MR\frac{e}{e-1}$$

Since, in equilibrium, $MR = MC$, it follows that

$$P = MC\frac{e}{e-1} \quad \ldots(i)$$

Now, if constant costs prevail, as is generally the case in the real world, and is also assumed generally in cost-plus pricing theory, then marginal cost (*MC*) will be equal to the average variable cost (*AVC*). Therefore, writing *AVC* for *MC* in equation (*i*), we get

$$P = AVC\frac{e}{e-1}$$

or,

$$P = AVC\left(\frac{e-1}{e-1} + \frac{1}{e-1}\right)$$

$$= AVC\left(1 + \frac{1}{e-1}\right)$$

$$P = AVC + AVC\,\frac{1}{e-1}$$

Therefore, Price $P = AVC + \text{Mark-up}$

We, thus see that on the basis of profit maximization assumption, mark-up or costing margin is equal to $AVC\dfrac{1}{e-1}$.

Suppose price elasticity of demand of the product is 5, then mark-up $= AVC\,\dfrac{1}{e-1}$ $= AVC\,\dfrac{1}{5-1} = \dfrac{1}{4}\,AVC$. That is, mark-up fixed will be 25% of *AVC*. Price will be equal to *AVC plus* 25% of *AVC* as mark-up.

It follows from above that pricing fixed on the basis of marginal revenue and marginal cost is consistent with the cost-plus pricing based on adding a mark-up to the average variable cost. Therefore, it is asserted that in cost-plus pricing, it does not necessarily mean that firms are not maximizing profits. Mark-up fixed on the basis of price elasticity of demand amounts to maximising profits. Thus, Prof. Bilas remarks, "*The mark-up will vary from time to time with economic conditions as well as with seasonal changes. These variations bring about changes in the shape of the demand curve and in e. Therefore, when the businessman fixes prices at variable cost plus a mark-up and his mark-up charge is arrived at by a "feel of the market," we know that it is really a guess at the coefficient of price elasticity of demand and that economic theory is not necessarily being contradicted.*[10]

10. R.A. Bilas, *Microeconomic Theory*, second edition, 1971, p. 233.

Similarly, Stonier and Hague write "*If full-cost pricing exists, it does not necessarily mean that firms behave very differently from the way economic theory suggests. Even if there is a widely-held convention in any industry charging 'full cost' prices, about what a 'satisfactory 'profit margin would be, this may well have been arrived at through an understanding, built up over time, of the sort of profit margins that competitive conditions in that industry usually allows.*"[11]

But the whole synthesis established above between cost-plus pricing and marginal analysis of pricing is based upon the view (which has some empirical support too) that mark-up is fixed by taking into account price elasticity of demand for the product. Further, the above conclusion that average-cost pricing and marginal analysis of pricing based on profit maximization amount to the same thing is based upon the assumption that the average variable cost remains constant with changes in output. If average variable cost is not constant but changes with output, marginal cost in equilibrium will not be equal to *AVC* and, therefore, the synthesis established above will not hold good. Secondly, in bringing out the synthesis, it is assumed that mark-up is based on average variable cost (*AVC*) rather than the average total cost. If the mark-up is based on average total cost then the error would be introduced and cost-plus pricing would not maximize profits.

It should be noted that there is little disagreement about the fact that firms in the real world follow average-cost or cost-plus pricing. There are enough empirical studies which support this cost-plus pricing. However, what is contended is that changing the mark-up with changes in the demand and other conditions means that firms are following profit maximising principle in fixing prices, although they may be pricing on the basis of average-cost or cost-plus. In fact, cost-plus pricing can be used whether the aim of the firm is to maximize short-run profits, long-run profits, total revenue from sales. Thus, Professor Hawkins remarks, "There is no reason why short-run profit maximizers, long-run profit maximizers and revenue maximiser should not all use cost-plus as a *means* of setting price. They could all, however, choose different mark-up in order to meet their objectives."[12]

A Critique of Cost-Plus Pricing

An important criticism of cost-plus pricing or full-cost pricing is that *why full-cost pricing is used*, in other words what is the motivation behind cost-plus pricing. To quote Hawkins again, "It is after all not enough just to say that in practice it (cost-plus pricing) is used, since no motivation is implied. And until the motivation is known, there is no way of predicting firms' responses to varying conditions or knowing why they choose any particular size of mark-up."[13]

It may, however, be noted that those who have propounded or supported the cost-plus pricing theory do point out the motivations for fixing full-cost price. One suggestion regarding the motivational aspect of full-cost pricing is that firms are '*satisficers*' and not '*maximizers*' that is, they aim to make a reasonable (or satisfactory) level of profit and not the maximum possible level. Therefore, according to them, margin or mark-up just includes this reasonable and satisfactory level of profit. Another, though a related one, is the suggestion that firms want only a *fair or just rate of profit* and it is immoral and unethical to charge more than a fair rate of profit.

The argument for cost-plus pricing that firms seek merely reasonable or fair rate of profit is thought by many economists to be unconvincing and unrealistic. The critics point out that a good deal of empirical evidence, including even that provided by Hall and Hitch, indicates that

11. Stonier and Hague, *A Textbook of Economic Theory*, 4th edition, 1972, p. 245.
12. Hawkins, *Theory of the Firm*, Macmillan, 1973, pp. 76-77.
13. *Op. cit.*, p. 74.

mark-up varies in response to changing economic conditions[14]. Now, if the firms want merely reasonable, fair or just profits, then why should they raise the mark-up or margin during the boom periods and lower it during the depression periods. Prof. Hawkins rightly asserts "the bulk of the evidence suggests that the size of the 'plus' margin varies; it grows in boom times and it varies with elasticity of demand and barriers to entry. It seems strange that people's concept of a 'fair' profit should generally vary so systematically with the ease of making profits.[15]

However, it should be noted that though the variation in the profit margin does not appear to be consistent with the notion of fair or just profits, but it is consistent with the '*satisficing*' behaviour as suggested by H. A. Simon.[16] According to Simon's satisficing behaviour people set an *aspiration level* regarding profits to be made. And when this aspired level of profit is achieved, they may raise the aspired level of profits which they hope and desire to achieve. This aspired level of profits need not be fixed at the maximum possible level. The point is that the motive of firm using full cost or cost-plus pricing need not be maximising short-run profits.

The second main reason for the use of average-cost or cost-plus pricing by businessmen which has been provided is that we live in a very uncertain world where due to lack of perfect information, demand for a product cannot be correctly predicted for the current month or the current year, let alone for the future years. And, it is asserted that the present price policy may affect the demand for product in the future years. It is further pointed out that in practice it is very difficult to determine what is the profit-maximizing or optimum price in view of the fact that so many variables affect this and firm has to estimate *all the permutations* of all the variables that influence the profit-maximizing (optimum) price.

In view of this Cyert and March[17] in their *Behavioural Theory of the Firm* suggest that for the firms it is better to use cost-plus pricing by applying a standard mark-up as a first approximation which, according to the experience of the firm, works reasonably well. They argue that the firm is then ready to supply whatever is demanded at that cost-plus price. Further, according to them, stocks can be used to cushion the effects of unexpected changes in demand. But, over a period of time, they argue that the firm may decide to change the plus-margin or mark-up in response to changing conditions (booms, slumps, degree of competition, and so on) and by doing experiments with different margins (mark-up), and learning from experience, they would be able to arrive at the proper mark-up. On this view, firms use cost-plus pricing because it is the best that they can do in a very uncertain world where conditions regarding demand, strength of competition, technology etc. are fast changing. Further, according to this view, whether pursuing this cost-plus pricing while varying the mark-up in response to the changing conditions, profits are actually maximized or not depends upon the skill and ability of the firms in making correct responses to the changing conditions.

Further, Machlup, a staunch supporter and defender of profit maximization, argues that the real point at issue is not whether in the real world firms try to maximize profits or not, but that whether the conclusions and predictions regarding firms behaviour derived from profit-maximization assumption are valid (or approximately so) description of the real world. He

14. Besides the study of of Hall and Hitch, Business Behaviour and Price Policy, 1939, other empirical studies which find that mark-up or margin varies are (*i*) A.D. A. Kaplan, J. B. Dirlam and R. P. Lanzilotti, *Pricing in Big Business : A Case Approach*, Brookings Institution, Washington D.C. 1958.(2) B. Fog. *Industrial Pricing Policies*, translated I.A. Bailey, North Holland Publishing Co., Amsterdam, 1960.
15. *Op. cilt.*,p. 75.
16. H. A. Simon, Theories of Decision Making in Economics and Behavioural Sciences, *American Economic Review*, 1959.
17. Cyert and March, *Behaviral Theory of the Firm*, Prentice Hall, 1963, pp. 446.-47.

thinks that profit maximisation does lead us to the correct conclusions and predictions regarding the business behaviour in real world.[18]

Further, it may be pointed out that empirical evidence against profit maximization which is based upon the interviews given by businessmen or the questionnaires which they have filled up are not beyond suspicion because what the people say they are doing may not be what they are doing. There are a good number of difficulties in knowing about the motivations of business firms, entrepreneurs and managers. Often they give contradictory answers to the various questions asked from them regarding profits and price. For instance, Lanzillotti[19], who interviewed a large number of American companies concluded that profit was not their dominant motive. But when the same companies were asked questions about pricing they replied that they did not change prices because it would not increase their long-run profits. This means that in changing prices, long-run profits was the main consideration, although to the question regarding profit motive they replied that profit was not their dominant motive. Likewise, E.A.G. Robinson and Kahn[20], among many others have pointed out that important elements of profit maximization or loss minimization principle actually, entered into the pricing decisions of many of the businessmen investigated by Hall and Hitch.

Another, important criticism against average cost or full-cost pricing has been made by R.F. Kahn who has raised the interesting question on whose *average-cost*, price of a product will be fixed when a large or few firms compete to sell the same or similar product. According to him, if an industry is competitive in some sense, firms will not be able to fix their prices on their own full costs, regardless of the cost of others. Thus, there must be some firms on whose average cost the other firms will base their prices. That firm on the basis of whose cost the other firms in the industry will fix price will emerge as the price leader. Therefore, the theory of cost-plus pricing must consider the possibility of price leadership. Hall and Hitch did not analyse the price leadership satisfactorily while Andrews did not touch the subject. In fact, Andrews lays a much stress on the cosing margin, a firm *has to add* and therefore a firm in Andrews' analysis, according to Silberston pursues "defensive type of price policy, which .... is a policy more appropriate to a price follower than a price leader."[21]

Another reason or motive which has been pointed out for the adoption of average-cost (cost-plus) pricing is that the firms do not charge more than the normal or fair level of profits in order to forestall entry. That is, due to the fear of potential competition from the new firms that may enter the industry, the existing firms will use cost-plus pricing with only normal profits. Another reason which has been given for the use of the cost-plus pricing policy of the firm is that it can ameliorate the problem of uncertain competitors' reactions in oligopoly. The use of cost-plus pricing enables the firms of an industry to have tacit collusion regarding the price to be charged. The various firms in an oligopolistic industry recognizing their interdependence, come to use the same standard mark-up. With the use of same standard mark-up by all the firms in the industry, they can predict each other's reactions to changing conditions such as cost increases. The fact that firms apply a same standard mark-up to their costs, make their prices staying closely in line without any formal price collusion.

18. Machlup, Theories of the Firm : Marginalist, Behavioural, Managerial, *American Economic Review*, March 1967.
19. R. F. Lanzillotti, Pricing Objectives in Large Companies, *American Economic Review*, December 1958. .
20. R. F. Kahn, Oxford Studies in the Price Mechanism, *Economic Journal*, March 1952.
21. Aubrey Silberston, price Behaviour of Firms. *Economic Journal*, 1970

25

CHAPTER

Price Discrimination

MEANING OF PRICE DISCRIMINATION

Price discrimination refers to the practice of a seller of selling the same product at different prices to different buyers. A seller makes price discrimination between different buyers when it is both possible and profitable for him to do so. If the manufacturer of a refrigerator of a given variety sells it at Rs. 5000 to one buyer and at Rs. 5,500 to another buyer (all conditions of sale and delivery being the same in two cases), he is practising price discrimination.

Price discrimination, as defined above, is not a very common phenomenon. It is very difficult to charge different prices for the identical product from the different buyers. More often, the product is slightly differentiated to practise successfully price discrimination. Thus, the concept of price discrimination can be broadened to include the sale of the various varieties of the same good at prices which are not proportional to their marginal costs. Thus, Prof. Stigler defines price discrimination as *"the sales of technically similar products at prices which are not proportional to marginal costs."*[1] On this definition, a seller is practicing price discrimination when he is charging different prices from different buyers for the different varieties of the same good if the differences in prices are not the same as or proportional to the differences in the costs of producing them. For example, if a book costs the publisher Rs. 58 per unit and its deluxe edition Rs. 65 per unit, then he will be practising price discrimination if he sells the ordinary edition at Rs. 70 per unit and the deluxe edition at Rs. 130 per unit. In this case, he is said to be practising price discrimination because the price difference between the two editions (Rs. 130 – 70 = 60) is greater than the cost difference between them (Rs. 65 – 58 = 7).

Though this second case of price discrimination is very relevant, but is more complicated. Therefore, for the purpose of analysis given below, we shall restrict ourselves to the simple case of price discrimination—the sale of the same product at different prices to different

1. G.J. Sitgler, *The Theory of Price*, revised edition 1952, p. 215.

buyers. But the conclusions arrived at in this simple case will be generally valid in case of the more complicated case mentioned above.

Three types of price discrimination may be noted. Price discrimination may be (*a*) *personal*, (*b*) *local*, or (*c*) *according to use or trade*. Price discrimination is personal when a seller charges different prices from different persons. Price discrimination is local when the seller charges different prices from people of different localities or places. For instance, producer may sell a commodity at one price at home and at another price abroad. Discrimination according to use occurs when different prices of a commodity are charged according to the uses to which the commodity is put. For example, the electricity is usually sold at a cheaper rate for domestic uses than for commercial purposes.

Degrees of Price Discrimination

Prof. A.C. Pigou has distinguished between the following three types of price discrimination on another ground : (*i*) price discrimination of the first degree; (*ii*) price discrimination of the second degree; and (*iii*) price discrimination of the third degree.

Price Discrimination of the First Degree. Price discrimination of the first degree is also known as perfect price discrimination because this involves maximum possible exploitation of each buyer in the interest of the seller's profits. *Price discrimination of the first degree is said to occur when the monopolist is able to sell each separate unit of the product at a different price.* Thus under discrimination of the 'first degree' every buyer is forced to pay the price which is equal to the maximum amount he is willing to pay rather than do without the good altogether. In other words, under perfect price discrimination, the seller leaves no consumer's surplus to any buyer. Perfect price discrimination requires that the seller makes a separate bargain with each of his buyers instead of setting just two or a few market prices each of which is available to a good number of buyers. This sort of price discrimination is also marked by the fact that the seller makes *an all or nothing* bargain with each buyer. In this all or nothing bargain, the total amount of money which a buyer is required to pay for a given unit of the good is the maximum amount which he is willing to pay for the unit of the good rather than go without it. Thus, the seller, under discrimination of the first degree, is able to deal individually with each buyer and is able to strike an all or nothing bargain. To sum up, the seller under first-degree price discrimination, charges each buyer the highest price he will pay for each unit of the good he gets, and thus charges a separate price for each such unit. In other words, the seller forces the buyer to pay the maximum amount he is willing to pay for a given quantity of the good by threatening him with the alternative of denying him the good altogether. Perfect price discrimination is depicted in Fig. 25.1.

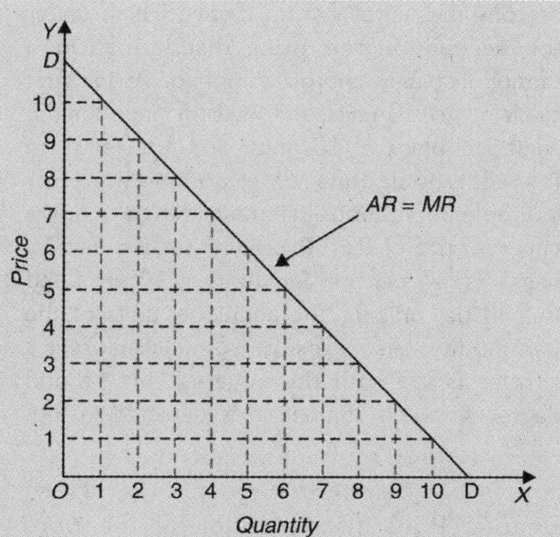

Fig. 25.1. *Price discriminating monopolist of the first degree extracts all the consumer surplus form the buyers*

Now, *the monopolist practising perfect discrimination can extract from the buyer all the surplus which he is getting by threatening him with the alternative of getting none of the good.* Thus, the monopolist, under first-degree price discrimination, will charge from the buyers Rs. 10 for first unit, Rs. 9 for second unit, Rs. 8 for the third unit and so on further units the monopolist will charge the highest price which a buyer is prepared to pay. As a result, the buyer will be left with no consumer's surplus.

An important point about perfect price discrimination is worth noting. *While under simple monopoly,* marginal revenue curve of the seller lies below the demand curve of the buyer, under perfect price discrimination the demand curve of the buyer also becomes the marginal revenue curve of the seller. In the above illustration, the seller gets additional revenue of Rs. 10 from the first unit, that is, the price which he charges for the first unit, Rs. 9 from the second unit, *i.e.,* the price which he charges for the second unit ; Rs. 8 from the third unit, *i.e.,* the price which he charges for the third unit and so on. In other words, Rs. 10, Rs. 9, Rs. 8 and Rs. 7 are the successive marginal revenues of the seller. Under perfect price discrimination each unit of output is sold at a separate price. Each additional unit sold therefore adds to revenue an amount equal to the price for which it is sold. Under perfect price discrimination, the demand curve of the good is, therefore, also the marginal revenue curve of the seller.

Price Discrimination of the Second Degree. Price discrimination of the *second degree* would occur when a monopolist is able to charge *separate prices for different blocks or quantities of a commodity from buyers* and in this way he takes away a part, but not all of consumer surplus from them . Thus, under the second degree price discrimination a monopolist may charge a high price for first block of say 10 units, the medium price for the additional block of 10 units, and a lower price for additional units of a commodity. For example, a monopolist may charge from a buyer a price of Rs. 50 per unit for the first 10 units, Rs. 40 per unit for the next 10 units and Rs. 30 per unit for the additional units of the commodity. As a result, some consumer's surplus is left with the buyers. This second degree price discrimination is depicted in Fig. 25.2.

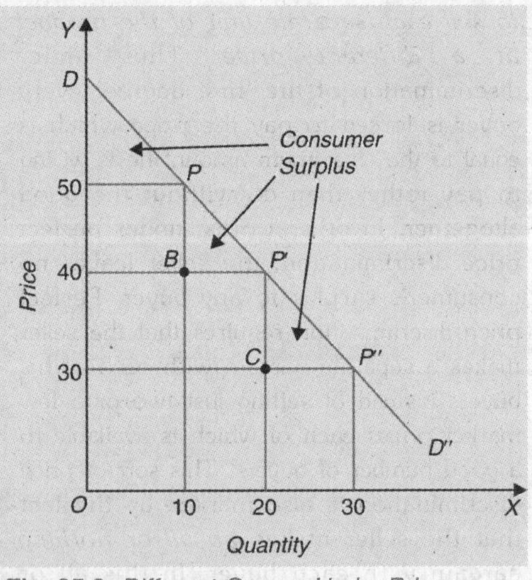

Fig. 25.2. *Different Groups Under Price Discrimination of the Second Degree*

Price Discrimination of the Third Degree. Price discrimination of the *third degree* is said to occur *when the seller divides his buyers into two or more than two sub-markets or groups depending on the demand conditions and charges a different price in each sub-market.* The price charged in each sub-market depends upon the output sold in that sub-market and the demand conditions of that sub-market. Price discrimination of the third degree is most common. A common example of such discrimination is found in the practice of a manufacturer who sells his product at a higher price at home and at a lower price abroad. Again, the third degree price discrimination is found when an electric company sells electric power at a lower price to the households and at a higher price to the manufacturers who use it for industrial purposes. In our analysis of price discrimination made below, we will assume only third degree price discrimination since this is usually more practicable as well as most commonly found in case of the real world.

WHEN IS PRICE DISCRIMINATION POSSIBLE ?

Two fundamental conditions are necessary for the price discrimination to become possible. First, price discrimination can occur only *if it is not possible to transfer any unit of the product from one market to another*. In other words, a seller can practise price discrimination only when he is selling in different markets which are divided in such a way that product sold by him in the cheaper market cannot be resold in the dearer market. Price discrimination by the original seller will break down if his buyers in the cheaper market purchase the product from him and resell it to the buyers of the dearer market. Buyers in the dearer market of the original seller will instead of buying from him will buy the product from the buyers of his cheaper market. Thus, a seller can charge different prices in the two markets when there is no possibility of the product being transferred from the cheaper market to the dearer market.

Second essential condition for price discrimination to occur is that *it should not be possible for the buyers in the dearer market to transfer themselves into the cheaper market to buy the product* or *service at the lower price*. For instance, if a doctor is charging a smaller fee from the poor than from the rich, then his price discrimination will break down if a rich man can pretend to be poor and pay a poor man's charges to the doctor.

It is clear from above that for the price discrimination to become practicable, neither the unit of the good, nor the unit of demand (*i.e.*, buyer) can be transferred from one market to the other. In other words, there should not be any seepage or communication between the two markets. Thus price discrimination depends upon the ability of the seller to keep his two markets quite separate. If he is not able to keep the different markets separate, the price discrimination by him will break down. Price discrimination is possible in the following cases.

1. The Nature of the Commodity. The nature of the commodity or service may be such that there is no possibility of transference from one market to the other. The most usual case is the sale of direct personal services like that of a surgeon or lawyer. The surgeons usually charge different fees from the rich and the poor for the same kind of operation. This is possible for them since the service has to be delivered personally by the surgeon and therefore, it cannot be transferred. Neither is it possible for the rich men to assume to be poor so easily in order to pay the smaller fee.

2. Long Distances or Tariff Barriers. Discrimination often occurs *when the markets are separated by long distances or tariff barriers* so that it is very expensive to transfer goods from a cheaper market to be resold in the dearer market. A monopolist manufacturer at Chennai may sell his product in one town, say Kolkata, at Rs. 20 and in another town, say Delhi, at Rs. 15. If the transport cost between Delhi and Kolkata is greater than Rs. 5 per unit it will not be worthwhile for the buyers in Delhi to transfer the goods to Kolkata on their own. Similarly, if a seller is selling his good in two different markets, say, in a home market which is protected by a tariff and in a foreign market without a tariff, he can take advantage of the tariff barrier and can raise the price of his product in the home market (which is protected by the tariff). As a result, he will be selling the product in the foreign market at a lower price than at home. *This practice of selling the product at cheaper rates abroad than at home is often known as 'dumping'*.

3. Legal Sanction. In some cases there may be *legal sanction for price discrimination.* For example, an electricity company sells electricity at a lower price if it is used for domestic purposes and at a higher price if it is used for commercial purposes. In this case customers are liable to be fined if they use electricity for commercial purposes if the sanction has been granted for domestic purposes only. The same is the case with railways which charge different fares for travelling in First Class, and Second Class compartments. Though the service of

carrying rendered in two classes of compartments slightly differs in each case but the differences in fares are out of proportion to the differences in comforts provided. So this is a clear case of price discrimination by legal sanction. It is unlawful and a criminal offence to travel in the first class with a ticket for the second class.

4. Preferences or Prejudices of the Buyers. Price discrimination may become possible due to *preferences or prejudices of the buyers.* The same good is generally converted into different varieties by providing different packings, different names or labels in order to convince the buyer that certain varieties are superior to others. Different prices are charged for different varieties, although they differ only in name or label. In this way the producers are usually able to break up their market and sell the so-called superior varieties to the rich people at higher prices and the so-called inferior varieties to the poor people. Sometimes there is some actual difference in the various varieties of the good, for instance, generally there is a difference in the paper used and quality of the binding between the deluxe edition and ordinary edition of a book, but the difference in prices of the two kinds of editions is more than proportional to the extra costs incurred on the deluxe edition. So, this is a clear case of price discrimination based on the preferences or prejudices of the various buyers of the product. It is worth quoting Joan Robinson in this connection. "Various brands of a certain article which in fact are almost exactly alike may be sold as different qualities under names and labels which induce rich and snobbish buyers to divide themselves from poor buyers, and in this way the market is split up and the monopolist can sell what is substantially the same thing at several prices.[2]"

Another case of price discrimination falling in this category is that when some people prefer to buy goods in a particular locality at a higher price. For example, if a seller has two shops, one in Connaught Place which is the most fashionable shopping centre in Delhi and another at Sadar Bazar which is very congested and ugly locality in Delhi, he may be selling the same product at a higher price in Connaught Place and at a lower price in Sadar Bazar. It is the fashionable and rich people who usually buy goods in Connaught Place and they will be prepared to pay a higher price rather than go for shopping in the congested and ugly locality of Sadar Bazar.

5. Ignorance and Laziness of Buyers. Price discrimination may become possible due to *ignorance and laziness of buyers.* If a seller is discriminating between two markets but the buyers of the dearer market are quite ignorant of that fact that the seller is selling the product at a lower price in another market, then price discrimination by the seller will persist. Price discrimination will also persist if the buyers of the dearer market are aware of the seller's act of selling the same product at a lower price in another market but due to laziness may not go for shopping in the cheaper market. In these cases if the ignorance is removed or laziness is given up, the price discrimination will break down.

6. Price discrimination may become possible *when several groups of buyers require the same service for clearly differentiated commodities.* For example, railways charge different rates of fare for the transport of cotton and coal. In this case price discrimination is possible since bales of cotton cannot be turned into loads of coal in order to take advantage of the cheaper rate of transport for coal.

Under which Market Structure Price Discrimination is Possible ?

We have seen above those conditions under which price discrimination is possible. Now, the question arises under what market form a seller can practise price discrimination. It is

2. Joan Robinson, *Economics of Imperfect Competition*, pp. 180-81.

obvious that *under perfect or pure competition no seller can charge different prices from different buyers for the same product.* Under perfect or pure competition, there are many sellers selling the homogeneous product. If any seller tries to charge from some buyers a higher price than the prevailing market price, they will refuse to buy from him and will buy the same product at the prevailing price from other sellers. It is worth noting that under conditions of perfect or pure competition price discrimination cannot prevail even if the market can be easily divided into separate parts. This is so because if conditions of perfect or pure competition prevail in each part of the whole market, then sellers will confront a perfectly elastic demand curve in each part and will like to sell the whole of his output in that part of the market in which the highest price prevails. But the attempt by all sellers to do so would force down the price to the competitive level so that a single price will prevail throughout the whole market. But if all sellers under perfect competition, combine or arrive at some understanding, then they can discriminate prices. "*So long as market is perfect it is only if all sellers are combined or are acting in agreement that they can take advantage of the barriers between one part of a market and another to charge different prices for the same thing.*"[3] However, it may be pointed out that if all sellers combine or enter into an agreement regarding price discrimination, perfect competition ceases to exist. We thus see that price discrimination is not possible under perfect competition.

Under monopolistic competition, price discrimination can occur. The degree of price discrimination practised depends upon the degree of imperfection in the market. The monopolistic competition prevails when the product is differentiated and every seller has some attached customers who will not move so readily from one seller to another. Therefore, if monopolistic competition exists and also the market can be divided into different parts by a seller, then price discrimination becomes possible. It should be noted that in this case an individual seller may not produce a single variety of the product but may produce various varieties of his product and thus may break up his market into different parts and charge different prices for different varieties of his good. Price discrimination will occur only if extra prices charged for the so-called superior varieties are not proportional to the extra costs incurred on them.

But *price discrimination is more likely to occur when there is monopoly of the product by a single seller or when there is agreement among the various sellers selling the same product or service.* Monopoly exists when there are no other sellers selling the same good or its close substitutes. Therefore, monopolist is in a position to charge different prices from different buyers for the same good. Price discrimination also usually occurs when there are various sellers selling the same product or same service but there is agreement among them for charging different prices from different groups of buyers. For instance, doctors have generally some understanding with each other to charge higher fees from the rich and lower fees from the poor.

WHEN IS PRICE DISCRIMINATION PROFITABLE ?

We have seen above under what conditions price discrimination is possible. Price discrimination may be possible yet it may not pay the monopolist to discriminate prices in the separate markets. In other words, the monopolist may be able to discriminate prices but it may not be profitable for him to do so. We have to see now under what conditions it is profitable for the monopolist to discriminate prices between the two markets. *Price discrimination is profitable only if price elasticity of demand in one market is different from price elasticity*

3. Joan Robinson, *Economics of Imperfect Competition*, p. 179.

of demand in the other. Therefore, the monopolist will discriminate prices between two markets only when he finds that the price elasticity of demand of his product is different in the different sub-markets. We shall analyse below this condition for the profitability of price discrimination.

(*a*) When Demand Curves in the Separate Markets are Iso-elastic. If demand curves in the two markets are iso-elastic so that at every price the elasticity of demand in the two markets is the same, then it will not pay the monopolist to charge different prices in the two markets. Why? When elasticity of demand is the same in the two markets, it follows from the formula, $MR = AR\frac{e-1}{e}$ that marginal revenues in the two markets *at every price* (*i.e.*, every *AR*) of the good will also be the same. Now, if marginal revenue at every price of the product is the same in the two markets, it will not be profitable for the monopolist to transfer any amount of the good from one market to the other and thus to charge different prices of the good in the two markets.

(*b*) When Elasticity of Demand is Different in Various Markets at the Single Monopoly Price. It will be to the advantage of the monopolist to set different prices if price elasticities of demand in the two markets at the single monopoly price are not the same. In fact, if he wants to maximise profits he must discriminate prices if price elasticities of demand in the two markets *at the single monopoly price* are different. If the producer regards the two markets as one and charges a single monopoly price on the basis of aggregate marginal revenue and marginal cost of the output, he would not be maximising profits if elasticities of demand in the two markets at the single monopoly price are different. If price elasticity of demand is the same in the two markets at the single monopoly price, it will not pay the monopolist to discriminate between the two markets, even if the elasticities are different at other prices.

Suppose on the basis of aggregate marginal revenue and marginal cost, a monopolist fixes a single price (which is called the single monopoly price) and charges the same price in both the markets. If he now finds that price elasticity of demand at this single monopoly price is different he can increase his total profits by discriminating prices between the two markets. How is it profitable for the monopolist to charge different prices in the two markets when price elasticities of demand in them at the single monopoly price are different? This follows from the formula, $MR = AR\frac{e-1}{e}$. When average revenue in both the markets is the same, that is, when the monopolist charges a single monopoly price in both the markets, but price elasticities are different in the two markets, then marginal revenues in the two markets will be different. Suppose the single monopoly price is Rs. 15 and price elasticity of demand in markets *A* and *B* is 2 and 5 respectively. Then,

$$MR \text{ in market A} = AR_a \frac{e_a - 1}{e_a}$$

$$= 15\frac{2-1}{2} = 15 \times \frac{1}{2} = 7.5$$

$$MR \text{ in market } B = AR_b \frac{e_b - 1}{e_b}$$

$$= 15 \times \frac{5-1}{5}$$

$$=15 \times \frac{4}{5} = 12$$

It is thus clear that marginal revenues in the two markets are different when price elasticities of demand at the single monopoly price are different. Further, from the above numerical example, it is evident that the marginal revenue in the market in which price elasticity is higher is greater than the marginal revenue in the market where price eelasticity is lower. Now, it is profitable for the monopolist to transfer some amount of the product from the market *A* where elasticity is less and, therefore, marginal revenue is low to the market *B* where elasticity is higher and, therefore, marginal revenue is larger. In this way, the loss of revenue by reducing sales in market *A* by some marginal units will be smaller than the gain in revenue from increasing sales in market *B* by those units. Thus, in the above example, if one unit of the product is withdrawn from market *A*, the loss in revenue will be Rs. 7.5, while with the addition to sales by one more unit of the product in market *B*, the gain in revenue will be about Rs. 12. It is thus clear that the transference of some units of the product will be profitable, when there is difference in price elasticities of demand and hence in marginal revenues.

It is worth mentioning that when some units of the product are transferred from market *A* to market *B*, price in market *A* will rise and price in the market *B* will fall. This means that the monopolist will now be discriminating prices between the two markets.

But here a relevant question arises: how long will it be profitable for the monopolist to continue shifting his product from the market with lower elasticity of demand to the market with higher elasticity of demand? It is worthwhile for the monopolist to go on transferring units from market *A* (with lower elasticity of demand) to market *B* (with higher elasticity of demand) until the marginal revenues in the two markets become equal. This is because as long as marginal revenue in market *B* is greater than that in market *A*, he will be making addition to revenue in market *B* by selling an additional unit of the product more than the loss he will be incurring in market *A* from reducing sales by one unit. When the marginal revenues in the two markets become equal as a result of transference of some units of output, it will no longer be profitable to shift more units of output from market *A* to market *B*. When the position of equality of the marginal revenues in the two markets is reached, he will be charging different prices in the two markets—a higher price in market *A* with lower elasticity of demand and a lower price in market *B* with a higher elasticity of demand.

PRICE AND OUTPUT EQUILIBRIUM UNDER PRICE DISCRIMINATION

We have explained above the conditions under which price discrimination is possible and profitable. We now turn to analyse the equilibrium of a discriminating monopolist. Under simple monopoly, a single price is charged for the whole output; but under price discrimination the monopolist will charge different prices in different sub-markets. First of all, therefore, the monopolist has to divide his total market into various sub-markets on the basis of differences in price elasticity of demand in them. The monopolist can divide his total market into *several sub-markets* according to the differences in demand elasticity, but for the sake of making our analysis simple we shall explain the case when the total market is divided into *two sub-markets*.

In order to reach the equilibrium position, the discriminating monopolist has to take two decisions: (1) how much total output should be produced; and (2) how the total output should be divided between the two sub-markets and what prices he should charge in the two sub-markets ?

The same marginal principle will guide the decision of the discriminating monopolist to produce a total output as that which guides a perfect competition or a simple monopolist. In other words, the discriminating monopolist will compare the marginal revenue with the marginal cost of output. But he has to find out first the aggregate marginal revenue (*AMR*) of the two sub-markets taken together and then compare this aggregate marginal revenue with the marginal cost of the total output. Aggregate marginal revenue curve is obtained by summing up laterally the marginal revenue curves of the sub-markets. Consider Fig. 25.3. MR_a is the marginal revenue curve in sub-market *A* corresponding to the demand curve D_a. Similarly, MR_b is the marginal revenue curve in sub-market *B* corresponding to the demand curve D_b. Now, the aggregate marginal revenue curve *AMR*, which has been shown in diagram (*iii*) of Fig. 25.3, has been derived by adding up laterally MR_a and MR_b. This aggregate marginal revenue curve depicts the total amount of output that can be sold in the two sub-markets taken together corresponding to each value of the marginal revenue. Marginal cost curve of the monopolist is shown by the curve *MC* in Fig. 25.3 (*iii*).

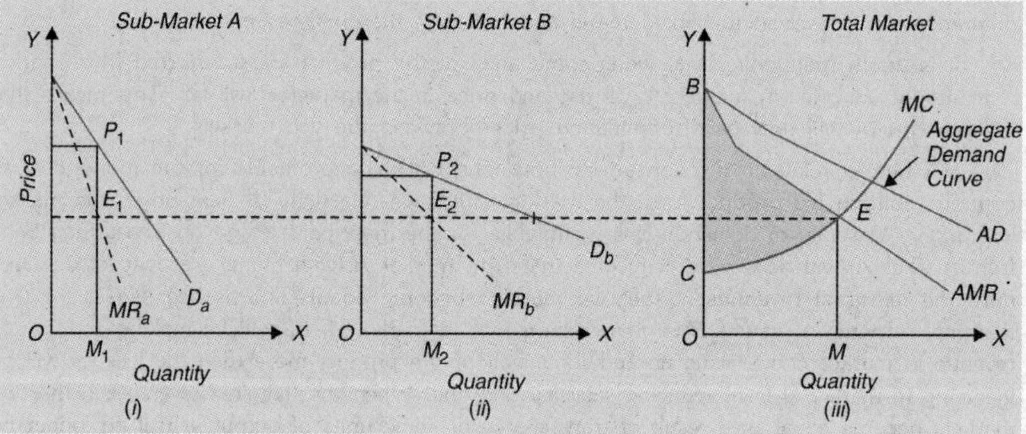

Fig. 25.3. *Determination of Total Output and Different Prices in the Two Markets*

The discriminating monopolist will maximise his profits by producing the level of output at which marginal cost curve *MC* intersects the aggregate marginal revenue curve *AMR*. It will be seen from Fig. 25.3 (*iii*) that profit-maximising output is *OM*, for only at *OM* aggregate marginal revenue (*AMR*) is equal to the marginal cost (*MC*) of the total output. Thus the discriminating monopolist will decide to produce *OM* level of output.

Once the total output to be produced has been determined the next task for the discriminating monopolist is to distribute the total output between the two sub-markets. He will distribute the total output *OM* in such a way that marginal revenues in the two sub-markets are equal. Marginal revenues in the two sub-markets must be equal if the profits are to be maximised. If he is so allocating the output in the two markets that the marginal revenues in the two are not equal, then it will pay him to transfer some amount of output from the sub-market in which the marginal revenue is less to the sub-market in which the marginal revenue is greater. Only when the marginal revenues in the two markets are equal, it will be unprofitable for him to shift any amount from one market to the other.

But for the discriminating monopolist to be in equilibrium it is essential not only that the marginal revenues in the two markets should be the same but that they should also be equal to the marginal cost of the whole output. Equality of marginal revenues in the two markets with marginal cost of the whole output ensures that the amount sold in the two markets will together be equal to the whole output *OM* which has been fixed by equalising aggregate marginal revenue with marginal cost. It will be seen from Fig. 25.3 [diagram (*iii*)] that at equilibrium output OM, marginal cost is ME. Now, the output OM has to be distributed in the two markets in such a way that marginal revenue in them should be equal to the marginal cost ME of the whole output. It is clear from the diagram (*i*) that OM_1 should be sold in sub-market A, because marginal revenue M_1E_1 at amount OM_1 is equal to marginal cost ME. Similarly, OM_2 should be sold in sub-market B, since marginal revenue $M_2 E_2$ at amount OM_2 is equal to the marginal cost ME of the whole output. To conclude, demand and cost conditions being given, the discriminating monopolist will produce total output OM and will sell amount OM_1 in sub-market A and amount OM_2 in sub-market B. It should be carefully noted that the total output OM will be equal to $OM_1 + OM_2$.

Thus, for the discriminating monopolist to be in equilibrium, the following conditions must be fulfilled:

1. $AMR = MC$
2. $MR_1 = MR_2 = MC$

Another important thing to know is what prices will be charged in the two markets. It is clear from the demand curve that amount OM_1 of the good can be sold at price M_1P_1 in sub-market A. Therefore, price M_1P_1 will be set in sub-market A. Likewise, amount OM_2 can be sold at price M_2P_2 in sub-market B. Therefore, price M_2P_2 will be set in sub-market B. Further, *it should be noted that price will be higher in market A where the demand is less elastic than in market B where the demand is more elastic.* Thus, price M_1P_1 is greater than the price M_2P_2. The relation between prices in the two markets and demand elasticities in them can be derived as follows.

We know that the following relationship between price, marginal revenue and price elasticity in a market holds good.

$$MR = \text{Price}\left(\frac{e-1}{e}\right)$$

Therefore, in sub-market A,

$$MR_a = P_a\left(\frac{e_a-1}{e_a}\right) \quad \text{...(}i\text{)}$$

where P_a stands for price, MR_a for marginal revenue and e_a for price elasticity in market A. Likewise, in sub-market B,

$$MR_b = P_b\left(\frac{e_b-1}{e_b}\right) \quad \text{...(}ii\text{)}$$

where P_b stands for price, MR_b for marginal revenue and e_b for price elasticity in market B. Since in equilibrium under price discrimination, $MR_a = MR_b$, from (*i*) and (*ii*) we get

$$P_a\left(\frac{e_a-1}{e_a}\right) = P_b\left(\frac{e_b-1}{e_b}\right)$$

$$\frac{P_a}{P_b} = \frac{\dfrac{e_b-1}{e_b}}{\dfrac{e_a-1}{e_a}} = \frac{\left(1-\dfrac{1}{e_b}\right)}{\left(1-\dfrac{1}{e_a}\right)}$$

Suppose absolute value of price elasticity in market A is equal to 2 and in market B it is equal to 3 then

$$\frac{P_a}{P_b} = \frac{\frac{3-1}{3}}{\frac{2-1}{2}} = \frac{\frac{2}{3}}{\frac{1}{2}}$$

$$= \frac{2}{3} \times \frac{2}{1} = \frac{4}{3}$$

Thus, when elasticities in markets A and B are 2 and 3 respectively, the prices in the two markets will be in the ratio of 4 : 3.

From the foregoing analysis it follows that the following two conditions are required to be satisfied for the equilibrium of a discriminating monopolist :

(1) Aggregate Marginal Revenue (*AMR*) = Marginal Cost (*MC*) of the total output.

(2) $MR_a = MR_b = MC$.

International Price Discrimination and Dumping

A special case of price discrimination occurs when a producer is selling in two markets, one in which he faces perfect competition, while in the other he has a monopoly. The demand curve for the product will be perfectly elastic for him in the market in which he faces perfect competition, while the demand curve will be sloping downward in the market in which he enjoys monopoly position. Such situation might occur when a producer sells his product in his home country in which he has a monopoly and in the world market which is perfectly competitive. Equilibrium in this situation is depicted in Fig. 25.4. In the home market in which the producer has a monopoly, demand curve or the average revenue curve AR^H is sloping downward. So does the marginal revenue curve MR^H. In the international or world market in which he faces perfect competition, the demand for his product is perfectly elastic. The average revenue curve AR^W of the producer in the world market is, therefore, a horizontal straight line and marginal revenue curve MR^W coincides with it. *MC* is the marginal cost curve of output. Aggregate marginal revenue (*AMR*) curve in this case is the composite curve *BFED* which is the lateral summation of MR^H and MR^W. The marginal cost curve *MC* intersects the aggregate marginal revenue curve *BFED* at point *E* and equilibrium output *OM* is determined. The total output *OM* is to be distributed between the home market and the world market in such a way that marginal revenue in each market is equal to each other and to the

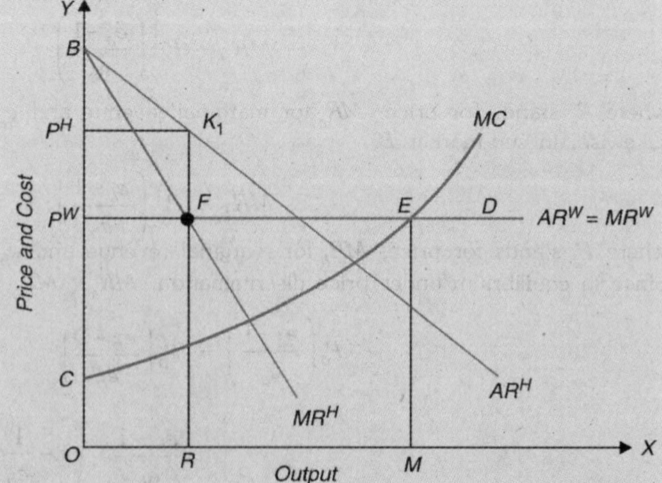

Fig. 25.4. *Equilibrium of the discriminating monopolist when he has a monopoly in the home market and faces perfect competition in the world market.*

marginal cost *ME*. It is clear from Fig. 25.4 that when amount *OR* is sold in the home market, the marginal revenue is *RF* which is equal to marginal cost *ME*. Thus, out of total output *OM*, amount *OR* will be sold in the home market. From the curve AR^H, it is clear that price OP^H will be charged in the home market. Rest of the amount *RM* will be sold in the world market at price OP^W. Area *CEFB* represents the total profits earned by the producer from both the markets. Price in the world market OP^W is lower than the price OP^H in the home market. *When a producer charges a lower price in the world market than in the home market, he is said to be dumping in the international market.*

It is worth mentioning that difference in prices in the world market and home market is due to the differences in price elasticity of demand in them. In the domestic market, elasticity of demand is less and, therefore price charged is higher as compared to the international or world market where elasticity is high (in fact, it is equal to infinity), the price is lower.

Persistent Dumping Vs Predatory Dumping. It may be noted that the type of dumping which we have explained above is called *persistent dumping* by the economists. This persistent dumping is the most usual one and arises when a monopolist pursuing the objective of profit maximization perceives that there exist differences in price elasticity of demand in the domestic market and international market. He therefore finds that he can enlarge his profits by discriminating prices in the two markets. As mentioned above, the elasticity of demand is usually higher in the international market because there is severe competition among countries to sell their products in the world markets and also a relatively larger number of substitutes are available there. Thus, the monopolist maximises profits by charging higher price in the domestic market and lower price in the international market.

There is another type of dumping which is known as *predatory dumping*. Predatory dumping represents unfair method of competition because under it a producer deliberately sells his product in a foreign country at a lower price (even below his cost of production) in order to eliminate competitors and gain control of the foreign market for a short period of time. When the producer succeeds in his ulterior motive of gaining monopoly control of the foreign market, he then exploits the foreign buyers by substantially raising the price of his product and thus maximizing his long-run profits. It is this type of dumping that is severely criticised and opposed.

CASE WHEN OUTPUT OF A COMMODITY IS POSSIBLE UNDER PRICE DISCRIMINATION

It is now proper to discuss whether the total output of the product under price discrimination will be greater than, equal to or smaller than output under simple monopoly in which a single price for the product is charged. There is no single rule in regard to the effect of price discrimination on output. Whether the price discrimination will increase output or reduce output or leave output unchanged depends upon the various conditions.

First of all, there are cases in which no output will be produced at all under simple monopoly. In such cases, output of the product is possible only under price discrimination. The fact that the average revenue under price discrimination is greater than the average revenue under simple monopoly has an important bearing over this question. If the average cost curve of a product lies above the demand curve for it throughout its length, then it will not be profitable for the simple monopolist to produce any output at all. He may find that if he breaks up the market and charges different prices in the various separate markets, it may be profitable for him to produce some output of the product. This is so because the average revenue obtained by discriminating prices in the two separate markets is greater than the average revenue under simple monopoly. The average revenue under price discrimination (*DAR*) may therefore be greater than the average cost, when average revenue under simple monopoly (*SAR*) is less than the average cost. This situation is depicted in Fig. 25.5 in which average cost of output is shown by the *AC* curve. D_1 is the demand curve facing the monopolist in one market and D_2 is the demand curve facing him in the other market. The composite curve *BRT* is the aggregate demand curve (*AD*) or the average revenue curve under simple monopoly (*SAR*).

It is evident from Fig. 25.5 that aggregate demand curve (*AD*) lies below the average cost curve *AC* throughout its length. In other words, average cost is greater than average revenue at all levels of output when a single price is charged for the product. For instance, suppose a simple monopolist decides to produce *OM* level of output, the single price which he will be able to charge from both markets is *MP* which is less than the average cost *MH*. So it will not pay the simple monopolist to produce *OM* output and charge the single price. But it will be profitable for him to produce *OM* output if he discriminates prices in the two markets. Under discrimination he may sell output OM_1 in one market at price M_1P_1 and output OM_2 in the other market at price M_2P_2 ($OM_1 + OM_2 = OM$). By discriminating prices in this way, suppose the average revenue obtained by him is equal to *MP′*. It will be seen from Fig. 25.5. that *MP′* is greater than the average cost *MH* of output *OM*. Thus, whereas it is not profitable for the simple monopolist to produce any output under single price system, it pays him to produce output by discriminating prices in the two markets.

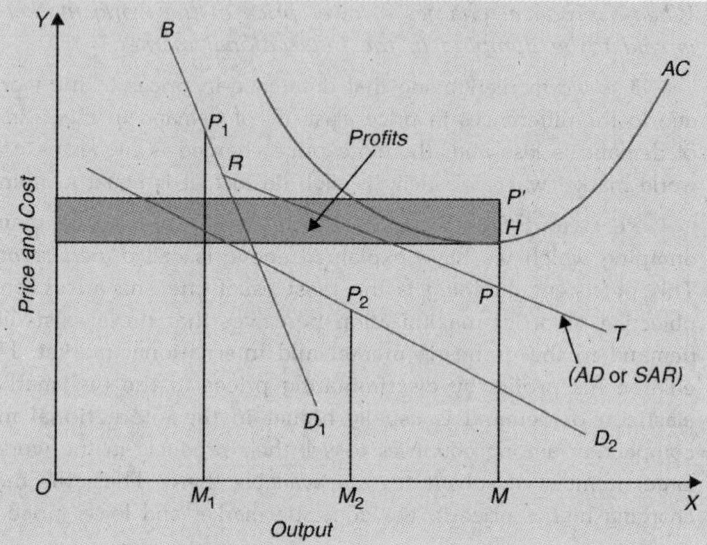

Fig. 25.5. *The Case Where Production is Possible only under Price Discrimination*

We have discussed above the extreme case when there will be no output without price discrimination. In less extreme cases, output under price discrimination can be larger than the output without price discrimination.

PRICE DISCRIMINATION AND SOCIAL WELFARE

Whether price discrimination promotes social welfare or not is difficult to say. Judgement as to whether price discrimination promotes social welfare partly depends upon whether with the adoption of price discrimination, total output of the product increases or not. If we put aside the output effect of price discrimination and consider the *distribution of a given output* in case when price discrimination is being practised, then economist's verdict would be that the price discrimination will adversely affect the social welfare since it will inefficiently allocate the output between the various consumers.

A necessary condition to achieve distributive or consumption efficiency is that marginal rate of substitution (*MRS*) between any two goods must be the same for all consumers consuming the goods. This condition is violated under price discrimination. This is because, under price discrimination, different consumers face different prices and consequently the consumers will not have the same marginal rates of substitution between the goods in their equilibrium positions. In such a case satisfaction or welfare of some consumers can be increased without causing any reduction in the satisfaction or welfare of any other consumer. Thus, *for any given level of output*, the third-degree price discrimination will have an adverse effect on the consumption efficiency, that is, efficiency in the distribution of goods between the consumers and will therefore reduce welfare of the consumers. Thus we conclude that the condition for maximum social welfare that the marginal rate of substitution (MRS) of different consumers between any two goods should be the same, is violated by price discrimination. G.J. Stigler rightly writes : "*given commodities and the buyers money incomes, all buyers can gain by the elimination of price discrimination, for price discrimination prevents them from reaching to the contract curve.*"[4]

But the above argument against price discrimination is based on the assumption that the quantity of commodities produced of the goods is given. The question of their optimum distribution is analysed, by taking the given outputs of the goods. On the other hand, the total output that the monopolist sells in the two markets may increase or decrease as a result of price discrimination. Even monopolist who charges a single price produces less than the efficient or socially optimum output. And when as a result of price discrimination output falls, the inefficiency of monopoly is made even worse. However, when price discrimination leads to the increase in output, the effect of this increase in output on social welfare is positive. *Thus when the price discrimination leads to the increase in output, this extra output made possible by price discrimination has socially beneficial effect flowing from it and which should be put against the possible loss of social welfare due to misallocation of goods between the two individuals.* As we explained above, price discrimination in some cases leads to the increase in output. That is, output of a commodity in some cases is greater under price discrimination than under simple monopoly. Thus, from the point of view of output, especially when a society prefers a greater output to a smaller output, *price discrimination in all those cases where it leads to the increase in output can be held to be promoting social welfare and is, therefore, justified.* We agree with Mrs Joan Robinson when she writes:

"From the point of view of society as a whole, it is impossible to say whether price discrimination is desirable or not. From one point of view, therefore, *price discrimination must be held to be superior to simple monopoly in all those cases in which it leads to an increase of output*, and these cases are likely to be more common. But against this advantage must be set the fact that *price discrimination leads to maldistribution of resources as between different uses*... Before it is possible to say whether discrimination is desirable or not it is necessary to weigh up the benefit from the increase in output against this disadvantage. In those cases in which discrimination will decrease output, it is undesirable on both counts."[5]

We may, however, add that one thing that we can say with certainty is that whether price discrimination leads to rise or fall in output as compared to ordinary monopoly, *the total output under third-degree price-discrimination is less than the efficient or socially optimum output.* This is because monopolist practicing price discrimination or not restricts output from the competitive level.

4. G.J. Stigler, *The theory of Price*, revised edition, pp. 93, 192.
5. John Robinson, *The Economics of Imperfect Competition*, p.206.(italics added)

There is another important reason for which in some cases price discrimination is socially justified. This is the case when under a single uniform price, no output of a commodity is produced and only under price discrimination production of a commodity becomes profitable. Rail transportation is a case in point. It has been observed by many that if railway authorities are not permitted to charge higher fare from the rich people who travel in first or AC class, then it may not be profitable for the authorities to run the railways on a single uniform fare from all, rich and poor.

We have already graphically explained above with the aid of Fig. 25.5 that when aggregate demand curve (*AD*) for a commodity lies below the average cost curve throughout and, therefore, at no level of output average revenue (when single price is charged) is greater than the average cost, the commodity would not be produced at all with a single uniform price, because it is not profitable to do so. When in such cases, price discrimination is practised the average revenue under price discrimination (*DAR*) may become higher than the average cost of production, it becomes worthwhile or profitable to produce a commodity. In those cases, where under single uniform price no production is done and under price discrimination, production becomes possible (to be more exact, becomes profitable), then price discrimination is socially desirable and justified, if the production of that commodity is considered essential and important for the society. In such cases price discrimination leads to the production of goods and services that might otherwise be denied to the consumers.

Price Discrimination and Equity. Finally, price discrimination may be socially justified on grounds of equity. We have discussed above the desirability of price discrimination from the point of view of *efficiency criterion*. As regards *optimum distribution of goods* (that is, distributive efficiency), we have found that price discrimination leads to the maldistribution of the commodities between the individuals and thus violates the criterion of distributive efficiency. But this whole analysis of distributive efficiency is based on the given present distribution of income. If the present distribution of income is not considered equitable, then the mere consumption efficiency is not enough. *Under price discrimination when price is raised for the rich and is lowered for the poor, it has a redistributive effect; the poor are benefited at the expense of the rich.* Therefore, in order to reduce inequalities of personal real incomes, Government often itself practises price discrimination or when it controls prices in the private sector, it may permit or even encourage price discrimination. We thus see that equity criterion may outweigh the efficiency criterion and may make the price discrimination socially justified.

We, therefore, conclude that from the point of view of distributive efficiency and optimum allocation of resources, *given the present distribution of income*, price discrimination is not socially desirable. But from the point of view of expansion in output as well as *for making the distribution of real incomes more equitable*, price discrimination is socially justified. Thus, to pass judgement on the social desirability of a particular case of price discrimination, all these various considerations have to be weighed against each other.

NUMERICAL PROBLEM ON PRICE DISCRIMINATION

Problem 1. *Suppose a discriminating monopolist is selling a product in two separate markets in which demand functions are*

$$P_1 = 12 - Q_1$$

$$P_2 = 20 - Q_2$$

The monopolist's total cost function is

$$TC = 3 + 2Q$$

As an economic adviser you are asked to determine the prices to be charged in the two markets and amount of output to be sold in each market so that profits are maximised. You are also asked to calculate the total profits to be made from the strategy of price discrimination. What advise will you give?

Solution. As profits in case of price discrimination are maximised when $MR_1 = MR_2 = MC$, Therefore, we have to calculate the marginal revenue in the two markets from the given demand functions of the two markets.

Total revenue in market $1 = P_1 Q_1 = 12Q_1 - Q_1^2$ ...(1)

MR_1 in market $1 = \dfrac{\Delta(P_1 Q_1)}{\Delta Q_1} = 12 - 2Q_1$

Total revenue in market $2 = P_2 Q_2 = 20Q_2 - Q_2^2$ . . . (2)

MR_2 in market $2 = \dfrac{\Delta(P_2 Q_2)}{\Delta Q_2} = 20 - 2Q_2$

We can derive the marginal cost from the total cost function

$$TC = 3 + 2Q$$

$$MC = \frac{\Delta TC}{\Delta Q} = 2$$

Profit-maximising amounts of output to be sold in the two markets are determined by applying the equilibrium condition $MR_1 = MR_2 = MC$ and solving the following equations:

$$MR_1 = MC$$
$$12 - 2Q_1 = 2$$
$$2Q_1 = 12 - 2 = 10$$
$$Q_1 = 5$$
$$MR_2 = MC$$
$$20 - 2Q_2 = 2$$
$$2Q_2 = 20 - 2$$
$$Q_2 = 18/2 = 9$$

Substituting these equilibrium outputs, Q_1 and Q_2 in the demand functions, we obtain the profit-maximising prices:

$$P_1 = 12 - Q_1 = 12 - 5 = 7$$
$$P_2 = 20 - Q_2 = 20 - 9 = 11$$

Total profits can be obtained in the usual way.

Total profits
$$\pi = (TR_1 + TR_2) - TC$$
$$= (P_1 Q_1 + P_2 Q_2) - (3 + 2Q)$$
$$= 7\,(5) + 11\,(9) - [3 + 2\,(5 + 9)]$$
$$= (35 + 99) - 31$$
$$= 134 - 31 = 103$$

Problem 2: *An Indian monopoly firm sells its product in the Indian and the US markets. The Indian demand function for the product is $P_i = 100 - Q_i$ and the US demand function for the product is $P_u = 80 - 2Q_u$ where both prices are measured in rupees. The firm's marginal cost of product is Rs. 20 in both countries. If the Indian monopoly firm can prevent any resale what price will it charge in both markets ?*

Solution. Note that in both the markets *inverse demand functions* are given, namely, $P_i = 100 - Q_i$ and $P_u = 80 - 2Q_u$. In order to find the equilibrium output prices in the two markets we have to first find the marginal revenue functions corresponding to the given linear demand functions. Further note that a marginal revenue function is *twice as steep as the slope of the linear demand function*. Therefore,

Marginal revenue in the Indian market is $MR_i = 100 - 2Q_i$

Marginal revenue in the US market is $MR_u = 80 - 4Q_u$

Since resale of the product between one market to another is not possible, the monopolist firm will equate the marginal revenue in each market with the given marginal cost which is equal to 20.

Thus, in India

$$MR_i = 100 - 2Q_i = 20$$
$$2Q_i = 100 - 20 = 80$$
$$Q_i = 80/2 = 40 \text{ units}$$

Similarly, in the US

$$MR_u = 80 - 4Q_u = 20$$
$$4Q_u = 80 - 20 = 60$$
$$Q_u = \frac{60}{4} = 15$$

Now, in order to find the prices charged in the two markets we substitute the equilibrium quantities sold in the two markets in their demand functions. Thus,

Substituting $Q_i = 40$ in the demnad function of India we have

$$P_i = 100 - Q_i$$
$$= 100 - 40 = 60$$

Substituting $Q_u = 15$

in the demand function of the US we have

$$P_u = 80 - 2 \times 15$$
$$= 80 - 30 = 50$$

Thus, price discriminating monopolist charges price of Rs. 60 in India, while he sells it at Rs. 50 in the US.

TWO-PART TARIFF PRICING

Similar to the price discriminating practice, another price practice that is sometimes adopted by the monopolist is two-part tariffs. Two-part tariff policy by the monopolist is an important way.to extract consumer surplus from the buyers of a product or service. Under the two-part tariffs, the monopolist charges *initial fee* for the right to buy a product or service as well as the *specified price* or *usage fee* for each unit purchased by the consumer or buyer of a product or service. The initial fee which is a lump sum payment for right to buy is the first tariff and the specified price or the usage fee to be paid for each unit of the product purchased by the consumer is the second tariff.

Many examples of two-part tariffs pricing practice can be given. First, a telephone company requires its user to pay *a monthly connection fee or rent* and a fee per minute of its use. Golf and tennis clubs often charge an *annual membership fee* as the initial fee as well as the fee for *each round or game* played. Pricing by an amusing park provides another example of two - part tariffs. Management of an amusement park requires its visitors to pay an admission fee and also a fee or price for each ride they take.

It is worth noting again that the purpose of the two-part tariffs pricing by the *monopolist, like* price discrimination, is *to extract as much consumer surplus as possible from the consumers of the product and therefore to maximise his profits.*

To pursue two-part tariffs policy successfully a firm must have a large market power, that is, he must have a sufficient monopoly power to fix price and should know the demand curves of the consumers and further how demands of consumers differ over consumers. Besides, for two-part tariff policy it is necessary that the monopolist must successfully prevent *resales by the buyers*. In what follows we first explain how with two parts tariffs, the monopolist is able to extract consumer surplus from the buyers. The monopolist is able to maximise his profits *by charging usage fee or per unit price equal to marginal cost* and the *initial fee* equal to the entire potential consumer surplus of the buyers. To explain this we assume that demand functions of all consumers are identical as given by demand curve *AD* in Figure 25.6. Now suppose that marginal cost of the monopolist is Rs. 30 and remains constant.

Under the two-part tariffs pricing strategy the monopolist will set price or usage fee of its product equal to marginal cost i.e. Rs. 30 at which a consumer buys 60 units. As price is equal to marginal cost (which is equal to average cost as *MC* remains constant), the monopolist will just cover its costs by charging this usage fee equal to marginal cost. However, under the two -part tariffs policy, the monopolist will also charge *initial membership* or *admission fee* to earn profits. By setting usage price equal to marginal cost it maximises the potential consumer surplus of the buyers of the product or service. Now, the monopolist will set the *initial fee* so as to extract the entire consumer surplus of the buyers. It will be seen from Figure 25.6 that by buying *OQ* (= 60 units) quantity at price *OP* = (Rs. 30 per unit), consumer's surplus is equal to the area *AEP*. To extract this entire consumer surplus *AEP* which is equal to 60 × (90 – 30) × ½ = 1800. Thus the monopolist will charge a lump sum of Rs. 1800 as the initial fee in addition to usage price per unit for the number of units of the product purchased by a buyer. The total profits made by him is equal to the consumer surplus of Rs. 1800 extracted from the consumer for the sale of 60 units of the product.

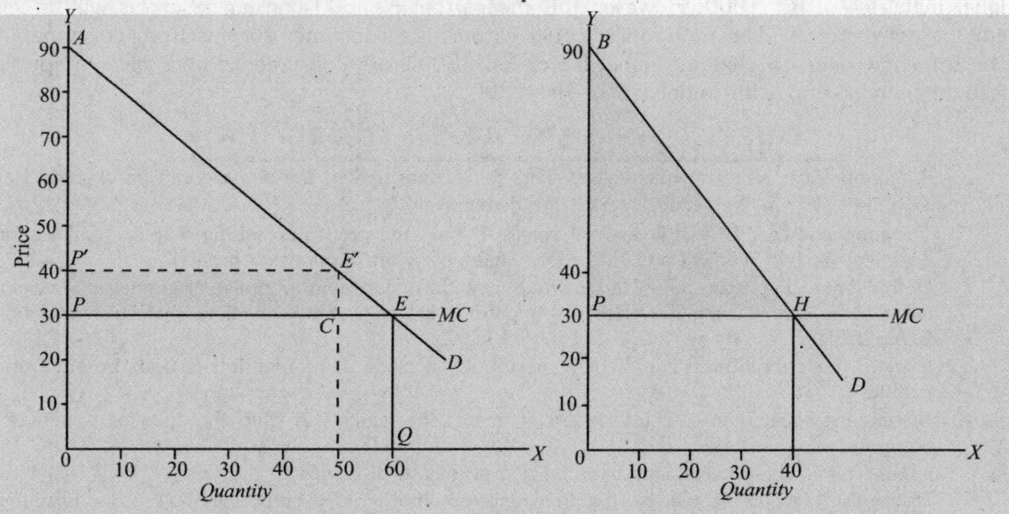

Fig. 25.6. *Two-part Tariff Pricing with a Consumer in the Market*

Fig. 25.7. *Two-part Tariff Pricing with Second Consumer with Different Demand Function*

It may be noted that the profits of the monopolist will be lower at any other price. Suppose he sets price of the product equal to *OP′* (Rs. 40 per unit) which results in lower quantity (50 units) bought by the consumer. With price equal to Rs. 40 or *OP′*, the monopolist will get profits of Rs. 10 more per unit and the gain in profits by charging a higher usage price will increase by 10 × 50 = Rs. 500. But his total profits will fall because of the decline in consumer surplus at the higher price (Rs. 40) . At this higher price of Rs. 40 or *OP′*, the consumer surplus to be extracted from the buyer by charging an initial lump sum will fall. With Rs. 40 (or *OP′*) as the price charged and 50 units of sale, the consumer surplus falls to 50 × (90 – 40) × ½ = Rs. 1250. With this the total profits will be 1250 + 500 = Rs. 1750. Thus at a higher price of Rs. 40 or *OP′*, the total profits fall. In fact, the decline in total profits will be equal to the area of the small triangle *ECE′*. Further, at any price lower than Rs. 30 (or *OP*), the monopolist will incur a loss on each unit of the product sold and this total loss will be greater than the gain in consumer surplus extracted from the buyer by lowering price so that total profits will be less at any price lower than *OP* or Rs. 30 which is equal to marginal cost.

TWO-PART TARIFFS WITH CONSUMERS HAVING DIFFERENT DEMAND FUNCTIONS

Let us now drop the assumption of consumers with identical demand functions. We now consider one consumer A who has a demand function with demand curve *AD* in Fig. 25.7. As seen above, with marginal cost equal to Rs. 30, the firm sets usage price *OP* equal to it and earns total profits of Rs. 1800 which is the consumer surplus extracted from the consumer. Now suppose that the second consumer with the demand curve *BD* in Figure 25.7 can be brought into the market for the product. Setting price *OP* equal to marginal cost of Rs. 30, the consumer *B* buys 40 units of the product and his potential consumer surplus is 40 (90 – 30) ½ = 1200. Now, if the consumer is brought into the market he will be willing to pay Rs. 1200 as the initial fee. It is generally not possible to charge different initial fees from the consumers. Therefore, if the consumer *B* has to be brought into the market, the monopolist has to lower the initial fee to Rs. 1200. Even with this lower initial fee charged from each of the two consumers, the profits of the monopolist will be greater. With lower initial fee of Rs. 1200 equal to the potential consumer surplus of the two consumers the total profits of the monopolist will be Rs. 1200 + 1200 = Rs. 2400 which are greater than the profits of Rs. 1800 if the individual *B* had not been brought into the market by setting a higher initial fee of Rs. 1800. However, this means that Rs. 600 consumer surplus will be left with the consumer A. The monopolist could extract the consumer surplus from consumer *A* if he somehow goes on charging initial fee of Rs. 1800 from consumer *A* and gives a special discount membership with initial fee of Rs. 1200.

QUESTIONS AND PROBLEMS FOR REVIEW

1. A monopolist is able to separate two markets. In one market, the demand can be expressed as $Q_1 = 14 - P_1$. In the second market the demand is $Q_2 = 20 - 2P_2$.
   The monopolist's *MC* (Marginal Cost) equals 4. Find the profit maximising output, its allocation between the two markets and the prices charged. What happens to profit ?
2. Define price discrimination. Under what conditions can a monopolist discriminate between different buyers in fixing the price of his product ? Under what conditions price discrimination is profitable ?
3. Explain the conditions under which monopolistic price discrimination is both possible and profitable.
4. Discuss the equilibrium of a monopolist, if one of the markets in which he operates is perfectly competitive.
   [Hint. This is the situation just like the dumping case discussed in the text.]
5. Distinguish between simple and discriminating monopoly. Show graphically how a discriminating monopolist attains equilibrium.
6. Suppose a monopolist sells his product in the home market and also exports a part of it. The foreign elasticity of demand for its product is below that of the domestic market. If consumer arbitrage between the two markets is impossible, how do the domestic and foreign prices compare ?
7. A firm supplies its product in two markets, demand being more elastic in one than in the other. Assuming that the firm aims to maximise its profits, show how the price and output in each market are determined.
8. A discriminating monopolist finds price elasticity of demand of his product –2.0 in one market and –1.5 in the other. What would be the ratio of prices charged by him in the two markets ?
9. What is Pareto efficiency in the distribution of goods between individuals? Show that price discrimination is not conducive to efficient distribution of goods.
10. When will a monopolist discriminate prices between buyers of his product ? *Is price discrimination socially justified* ?

26
CHAPTER

Pricing of Multiple Products

Introduction

Many firms produce more than one product. In fact, a firm like Hindustan Lever, produces a very large number of different products. This requires to re-examine the model of a firm producing a single product with which we have been concerned so far. As seen in the previous chapters, in the model of a firm producing a single product, it produces the amount of output and fixes a price at which marginal revenue equals marginal cost. A multiproduct firm may produce products with interdependent demands or it may produce products which are interrelated in the production process, that is, they are jointly produced in the same production process. We will explain below both the pricing of multiple products with interdependent demands and the products which are jointly produced.

Pricing of Products with Interdependent Demands

The products produced by a firm with interdependent demands may be interrelated either as substitutes or complements. For example, Maruti Udyog produces a variety of cars with interdependent demands such as Maruti 800, Alto, Zen and Esteem which are substitutes of each other. An increase in price of Zen car will affect the demand for Alto, Maruti 800 and Esteem. In case of substitutes price increase for one good (car in our case) tends to increase the demand for other kinds of car produced by Maruti Udyog. In case of complementary products the increase in price of a product tends to reduce the demand for the other complementary products. For example, power windows, car stereo system, antilocking brakes are complementary to the cars manufactured and sold by the car manufacturing firms. When the price of a car rises and as a result its quantity demanded decreases, the demand for these other complementary products such as car stereo systems, power windows will also decline.

The proper pricing decision by the manager of a multiproduct firm requires that demand inter-dependence between the products produced by it must be taken into account. Instead of setting price of each product separately, the effect of price of each product on the demand for the other products produced by a firm must be taken into account. For setting prices of various products the manager of a firm must aim at maximising total profits for the firm from all products produced by it rather than maximising profits for the individual products in isolation.

In case of products with interdependent demands, manager must consider marginal revenue from the production and sale of each product taking into account the interdependence of demands for the various products. Suppose a firm produces two products, X and Y. The total revenue from the production and sale of these two products can be written as

$$TR = TR_x + TR_y$$

where TR_x and TR_y are total revenues for products X and Y respectively. Assume that demands for products X and Y are interdependent. Keeping in view this interdependence, marginal revenue from these two products is given by

$$MR_x = \frac{dTR_x}{dQ_x} + \frac{dTR_y}{dQ_x} \qquad \text{... (1)}$$

$$MR_y = \frac{dTR_y}{dQ_y} + \frac{dTR_x}{dQ_y} \qquad \text{... (2)}$$

Each of the above two equations for marginal revenue is composed of two parts, Thus. the first term $\frac{dTR_x}{dQ_x}$ in equation (1) marginal revenue from production (and sale) of product X measures the change in revenue from good X caused by a unit increase in its quantity produced and sold. The second part, $\frac{dTR_y}{dQ_x}$ of equation (1) measures demand interdependency between the two products, that is, change in total revenue obtained from sale of a unit of product Y caused by marginal increase (or decrease) in the increase in quantity produced and sold of product X.

Similarly, the equation (2) represents the increase in total revenue from the sale of a marginal increase in product Y and also the increase (or decrease) in product X associated with the marginal increase in product Y.

It is important to note that interdependency terms $\frac{dMR_y}{dQ_x}$ and $\frac{dMR_x}{dQ_y}$ in equations (1) and (2) respectively can be positive, negative or zero depending on the relationship between the two products. If the two products X and Y produced by the multiproduct firm are complements, then the two terms will be positive. In this case increase in sale of one product will lead to the increase in the sale of the other product. On the other hand, if the two products X and Y produced by the firm are substitutes, then the two interdependency terms in equation (1) and (2) will be negative. In this case marginal increase in sale of one product will be associated with the decrease in the quantity sold of the other product. Finally, if there is no interdependence between the two products X and Y, then the two interdependency terms $\frac{dTR_y}{dQ_x}$ and $\frac{dTR_x}{dQ_y}$ in the two equations respectively will be zero.

It follows from above that for optimal decision making for determining price and output of a multiproduct firm with demand interdependence between the products produced by a firm must be considered. Suppose the two products X and Y produced by a firm are complements. In determining profit-maximising output of product X if the manager of the firm does not consider the interdependency term $\frac{dTR_y}{dQ_x}$ which measures the impact of a marginal increase in the quantity of product X on the demand for good Y, then he will be *underestimating* the actual increase in total revenue resulting from the sale of marginal increase in output of product X. This is because increase in revenue from the sale of an additional unit of X is also affected by the associated increase in revenue from product Y caused by the increase in sale of product X due to complementarily between the two products. That is, increase in revenue from additional sale of product X is also affected by the term $\frac{dTR_y}{dQ_x}$ which is positive in case the two products are complements. Thus, the manager of the multiproduct must take into account the demand interdependency effect for determinating the optimum level of output. It follows from equation (1) above that when the interdependency term is taken into account profit-maximising rate of output of product X will be greater in case the two products are complements. In fact, for maximising profits the production of X will be expanded until

$$\frac{dTR_x}{dQ_x} + \frac{dTR_y}{dQ_x} = MC_x$$

where MC_x is the marginal cost of producing an additional unit of product X.

Similarly, in case of substitute goods produced by a multiple-product firm, it can be shown if demand interdependency is not taken into account, it will lead to greater than optimal output of a product being produced by the firm.

Multiple-Product Pricing : Products with Independent Demands

We will now analyse the resource allocation by a firm when it produces products whose demands are unrelated or independent An important reason that impels firms to produce more than one product is to utilise fully their plant and production capacities. When a firm has idle productive capacity as partially used plant facilities and equipment or as under-utilised

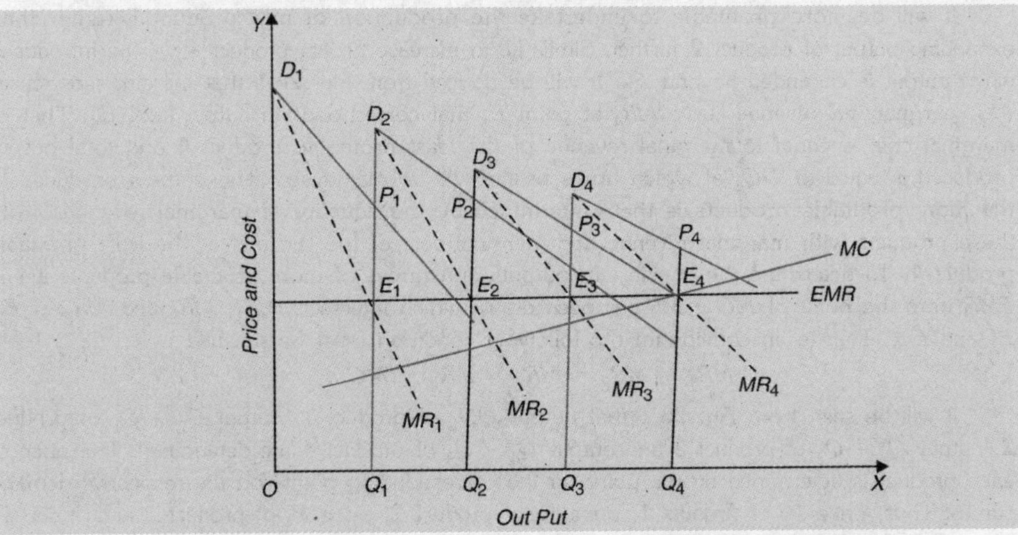

Fig. 26.1. *Multiple-Product Pricing : Products with Independent Demands*

organisational capabilities, it faces a problem of how to make a profitable use of its idle or under-utilised capacities. As long as the addition of new products (or different varieties of a product) may be sold at a price that is greater than its marginal cost, it is profitable to produce them. A range of alternative products which can be produced with the idle capacities and resources should be examined by a firm's manager to choose among them the most profitable products for production. It is assumed in this analysis that the firm's productive resources or capacities can be easily used to produce a variety of products. When a firm has idle capacities, and excess human and organisational resources, different products can be produced with relatively little increase in marginal cost of production.

To begin with a firm will produce the quantity of a single product so that marginal revenue (*MR*) earned from it equals marginal cost (*MC*) of it. If a firm finds that it has idle capacity and unused organisational resources, it will search for adding new products in its production programme. The firm's profits will increase by undertaking the production of new products as long as the marginal revenue from new products exceeds marginal cost of production, Thus, a firm will go on introducing new products (or different varieties or models of the existing product) in order of their profitability until the marginal revenue from the least profitable product becomes equal to the marginal cost of production to the firm. The firm will be maximising its total profits when it is producing the quantity of each product so that marginal revenue from production of different products are equal to each other as well as to the marginal cost of the last unit of the least profitable product produced. The price of each product will then be determined by their respective demand curves and the quantities of them produced. This is illustrated in Fig. 26.1 where D_1, D_2, D_3 and D_4 are the demand curves of four products in order of their profitability. To start with D_1 is the demand curve of a product and its associated marginal revenue is MR_1. When a firm produces output Q_1 of this product, it finds that producing more of it will result in lower price while by undertaking new product 2 whose demand curve is D_2, it can get higher price. Therefore, beyond output Q_1, it will introduce the production of new product 2. When the firm expands its output to the level Q_2, it finds that further increase in its output will lower price while it can obtain higher price and marginal revenue from undertaking the production of new product 3 whose demand curve is represented by D_3.

It will be more profitable to undertake the production of new product 3 rather than expanding output of product 2 further. Similarly, to increase profits product 4 will be introduced when output is expanded beyond Q_3. It will be noticed from Fig. 26.1 that marginal cost curve *MC* cuts marginal revenue curve MR_4 at point E_4 that corresponds to output level Q_4. That is, marginal cost is equal to marginal revenue of the least profitable product 4 and total output produced is equal to OQ_4 at which firm's profits will be maximised. The outputs produced of the more profitable products is then determined by the equality of marginal revenues from these products with marginal revenue and marginal cost of the last unit of the least profitable product 4. To determine the equilibrium outputs and prices of more profitable products a line *EMR* from the point of $MC = MR$ has been drawn which intersects MR_1, MR_2 and MR_3 at E_1, E_2 and E_3. That is, in equilibrium the following condition must be satisfied :

$$MR_1 = MR_2 = MR_3 = \text{MR}_4 = MC.$$

It will be seen from Fig. 26.1 that output OQ_1 of product 1, output $Q_2 - Q_1$ of product 2, output $Q_3 - Q_2$ of product 3 and output $Q_4 - Q_3$ of product 4 are determined. The price of each product is determined by the point on the corresponding points on the respective demand curves. Thus, price P_1 of product 1, price P_2 of product 2, price P_3 of product 3 and price P_4 of product 4 will be set by the firm.

Some important points need to be mentioned with regard to our above analysis of multiple product pricing. First, it will be noticed from Fig. 26.1 that the successive demand curve of the additional product is more elastic and, therefore, price of each extra product is lower than the previous one and marginal cost is higher and as a result, profit per unit declines as additional products are introduced. Second, it will be profitable to expand output by introducing further new products until the price of the last product produced equals marginal cost. Thirdly, it is assumed that the firm's idle or unused production capacity and organisational resources can be suitably adapted to produce the new additional products and marginal cost curve represents any increase in cost that occurs when additional products are produced. Fourth, it is assumed that successive demand curves of additional products are independent of each other. Finally, a firm may produce a product which yields little or no profit so as to offer a full range of products to its customers for attracting new customers or retaining consumers' goodwill.

PRICING OF JOINT PRODUCTS

So far we have been concerned with explaining determination of prices of products that are either related in demand or have independent demands. In the foregoing analysis, it is assumed that products are *technically independent* in the production process. We will now analyse the pricing of joint products which are technically interdependent. Joint products are those which are produced together in the same production process. Products can be jointly produced in fixed proportions or variable proportions. An important example of joint products with fixed proportions is provided by cattle raising to obtain meat and hide. Each carcass of cattle provides a *certain quantity* of meat and hide. There is little one can do to alter the proportions of meat and hide from a cattle. An important example of joint products with variable proportions is provided by petroleum refining which yield products such as petrol, fuel oils and other products. The proportions of these joint products that result from petroleum refining can, within certain limits, be varied by the firm. A manager of a business firm must consider the production interdependence while deciding about optimal prices and outputs of joint products. In what follows we first explain determination of optimal outputs and prices of joint products in fixed proportion and later analyse determination of prices and outputs of joint products with variable proportions.

Joint Products in Fixed Proportions

When joint products are produced in fixed proportion, they should be considered as a *single production package* and all costs are incurred on them as a single package. Since product are produced as a package there is no any other rational way in which the costs can be allocated to individual products of package. For example, costs incurred on raising cattle can not be calculated as to how much cost is incurred on 'meat' and how much on 'hide' as they are jointly produced in the same production process. Although the products are produced jointly, their demands are independent. Figures 26.2 (*a*) and (*b*) illustrate the determination of price and output of joint products in fixed proportion. Let us assume that the two joint products in fixed proportion are product *A* and product *B*. In panel (a) of Fig. 26.2. D_A and D_B are the demand curves of the two products, and MR_A and MR_B are their marginal revenue curves respectively. Total marginal revenue curve (MR_T) of the two products in panel (*a*) of this Fig. 26.2 is obtained by *vertical* summation of the marginal revenue curves MR_A and MR_B of the two products. *MC* is marginal cost of one more unit of the *product package* (*i.e.*, package of the two joint products) and is shown to be rising as the quantity produced of product-package increases.

It will be seen from panel (*a*) of Fig. 26.2 that marginal cost curve *MC* intersects total marginal revenue curve MR_T at point *E* and, therefore, the firm will be maximising profits by producing the units of output Q_0 of the package of joint products. Prices of the two products will be determined by their respective demand curves. It will be seen from panel (*a*) of Fig. 26.2 that with output Q_0 of the package of joint products, equilibrium price of product *A* will be set at P_A and of product *B* will be set at P_B.

It will be observed from panel (*a*) of Fig. 26.2 that marginal revenues MR_A and MR_B of the two products at the profit-maximising level of output Q_0 of package of joint products are positive. Therefore, the equilibrium quantities of the both products would be sold out and there will be *no excess production* of any one of them.

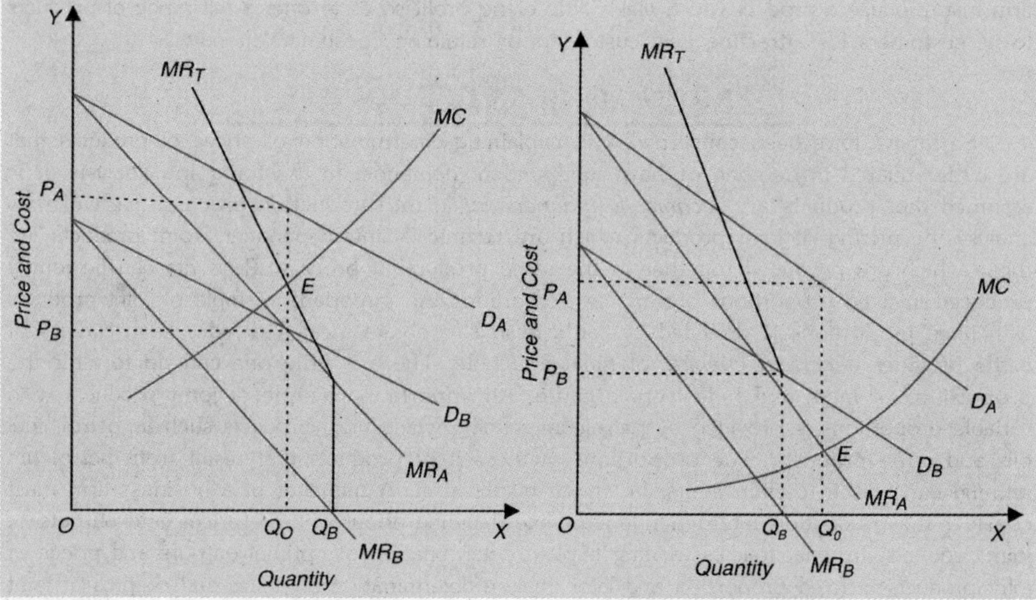

Fig. 26.2. (*a*) *No Excess production of product B*

Fig. 26.2. (*b*) *Excess production of product B*

However, the equilibrium level of output of joint products may occur where marginal revenue (*MR*) of one product may be negative. This is illustrated in panel (*b*) of Fig. 26.2 where equilibrium level of output Q_0 of the joint products is reached to the *right of point* Q_B where marginal revenue of product *B* is negative. This means that in equilibrium excess of output of product *B* equal to Q_BQ_0 will be produced as a part of the package of joint products. This implies that if this excess production of product *B* is sold in the market, the firm's revenue will decline as it will depress its price too much to yield negative marginal revenue. This problem arises because the two products are jointly produced. As such it will be a wise decision on the part of a rational manager not to sell the excess production of product *B* and sell only OQ_B of product *B* at price P_B in the market. (Total revenue from product *B* will be maximum by selling OQ_B quantity of it, the excess output Q_BQ_0 of product B should be withheld from the market and may be destroyed.

Example. Calculating Prices of Joint Products

Suppose a firm is engaged in cattle raising and producing joint products, meat and hides. The demand functions of two products are given as under :

Meat : $P_B = 60 - 0.5\ Q_B$ *and hides :* $P_H = 70 - 2\ Q_H$ *where* P_B *is price of meat and* P_H *is price of hides and* Q_B *and* Q_H *are quantities of the two products respectively.*

Further, suppose that marginal cost of production of joint products of meat and hides is given by

$$MC = 40 + Q$$

How many units of product package be produced and what prices should be set for beef and hides ?

Solution. Let B stand for meat and H stand for hides. In order to determine the profit-maximising level of output of the package of joint products we have to obtain marginal revenues of the two products. Thus,

$$TR_B = P_B Q_B = (60 - 0.5\ Q_B)\ Q_B = 60\ Q_B - 0.5\ Q_B^2$$

$$MR_B = \frac{dTR_B}{dQ_B} = 60 - 1Q_B \quad \text{... (i)}$$

$$TR_H = P_H Q_H = (70 - 2\ Q_H)\ Q_H$$

$$= 70\ Q_H - 2Q_H^2$$

$$MR_H = \frac{dTR_H}{dQ_H} = 70 - 4Q_H \quad \text{... (ii)}$$

Summing up vertically the two marginal revenues, we have

$$MR_T = MR_B + MR_H$$

$$= 60 - 1Q_B + 70 - 4Q_H$$

Since the two are joint products we can write the package of Q_B and Q_H as Q. Therefore

$$MR_T = 130 - 5Q \quad \text{... (iii)}$$

To obtain profit-maximising output of the package of joint products we set

$$MR_T = MC.$$

$$MC = 40 + Q$$

Thus,

$$MR_T = MC$$

$$130 - 5Q = 40 + Q$$

$$6Q = 130 - 40 = 90$$

$$Q^* = \frac{90}{6} = 15$$

or 15 units of the product package.

Substituting the value of equilibrium quantity Q^* in the demand functions of the two products, we have

$$P_B = 60 - 0.5\ (15)$$

$$= 60 - 7.5$$

$$= 52.5$$

$$P_H = 70 - 2Q = 70 - 2(15)$$

$$= 40$$

PRICING OF JOINT PRODUCTS IN VARIABLE PROPORTIONS

We will now analyse the pricing of products which are jointly produced in variable proportions. For example, Hindustan Lever which produces bathing soap such as Lux and also washing powder 'Surf' can decide what proportions of these two products it should produce. Maruti Udyog which produces cars such as Maruti 800, Zen, Alto, Esteem has to decide in what proportions they should be produced. In the real world today the firms are multiple products firms and they produce different products in proportions guided by their cost and demand conditions. Thus, the case of joint products in variable proportions is more common than that of joint products in fixed proportions. When the two products can be produced with similar resources it is then possible to alter the proportions of the products by reallocating resources among them. That is, in case of joint products in variable proportions one product can be substituted for the other. With a given amount of resources or total cost, one product can be produced more by a firm when it reduces the production of another product, that is, one product is substituted for the other. Thus joint products in variable proportions are generally substitutes of each other.

Iso-Cost Curves and Iso-Revenue Lines

In the analysis of pricing of joint products in variable proportions the use of two concepts is made. The first is the concept of Iso-Cost Curve which is also called *product transformation curve.* In fact iso cost curve or product transformation curve represents the production possibility curve for a firm. An iso-cost curve or product transformation curve represents the combinations two products, say, *A* and *B,* that can be produced with a given total cost curve (or the given amount of resources). In Fig. 26.3 an iso-revenue curve *CD* has been drawn that depicts the various combination of two products *A* and *B* that can be produced with a given total cost, say Rs. 5 lakhs. An essential feature of an iso-cost or production transformation curve is that it is *concave* to the origin. This implies that as more of one product *A* is produced, the successively greater quantity of the other product *B* must be given up. The amount of the product *B* that must be given up to produce one more unit of product *A* is called *marginal rate of transformation* (*MRT*) and is measured by the slope of an iso-cost curve at a point on it, that is,

$$MRT_{AB} = \frac{\Delta Q_B}{\Delta Q_A}$$

The iso-cost curve (or production transformation curve) is concave due to the fact that resources are *not perfectly adaptable* to the production of two products *A* and *B*. That is, the productive resources cannot be transferred from one product to another without some loss of productivity.

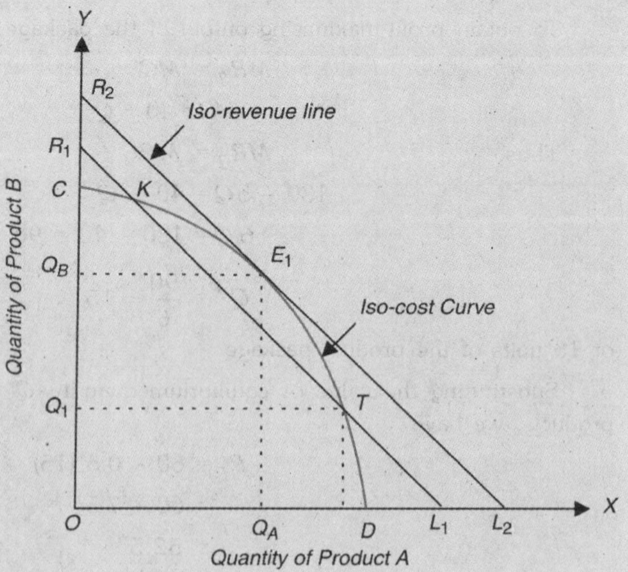

Fig. 26.3. *Joint Production of two products in variable proportions*

Iso-revenue line. The iso-revenue line represents the

combinations of the quantities of two products that yield the same amount of revenue when sold in the market. In Fig. 26.3 R_1L_1, R_2L_2 are the iso-revenue lines. Though each iso-revenue line represents the combinations of two products that yield the same amount of revenue, the higher the iso-revenue line, the greater the amount of revenue obtained from the production and sale of the quantities of two products shown by them.

It may be noted that straight line iso-revenue curves are due to the assumption made that the prices of two products are given and constant for a firm. This implicitly assumes that there exists perfect competition in the product markets. Total revenue is equal to price times the quantity produced and sold of two products.

If production of product B is zero and all given resources of cost-outlay is spent on product A, then the revenue on an iso-revenue line, say, R_1L_1, which will be obtained from selling of product A is

$$TR = OL_1 \times P_A \quad \text{...(1)}$$

On the other hand, if production of product A is zero, then on the given iso-revenue line R_1L_1

$$TR = OR_1 \times P_B \quad \text{...(2)}$$

Since the revenue on each iso-revenue line remains the same on each point, from (1) and (2) we get

$$OL_1 \times P_A = OR_1 \times P_B$$

or

$$\frac{P_A}{P_B} = \frac{OR_1}{OL_1} \quad \text{...(3)}$$

$\frac{OR_1}{OL_1}$ is the slope of the iso-revenue line R_1L_1. Therefore, from equation (3) it follows that ratio of prices of two products is equal to the slope of the iso-revenue line.

Optimum Combination of Two Products in Variable Proportions

Given the level of total cost (incurred on the resources to produce the two products), we will have a given iso-cost curve or product transformation curve. Suppose the level of total cost is such that CD is the iso-cost curve in Fig. 26.4. With a given total cost, the greater the revenue obtained from the production and sale of two products, the greater will be the profits. Therefore, the manager of a firm, who seeks to maximise profits, given the level of total cost, will try to maximise revenue. This implies that the manager will decide to produce the quantities of two products at which the given iso-cost curve is tangent to an iso-revenue line. It will be seen from Fig. 26.4 that the given iso-cost curve CD is tangent to the iso-revenue line R_2L_2 at point E and will, therefore, produce OQ_A of product A and OQ_B of product B. It will be observed from Fig. 26.4 that production of two products on any point (such as K and T) other than the tangency point E will yield lower revenue as they will be at lower iso-revenue line than R_2L_2.

As seen above, the slope of the given iso-cost curve (product transformation curve) CD is defined as marginal rate of transformation (MRT) between the two products and the slope of an iso-revenue line is equal to $\frac{P_A}{P_B}$. Thus, at the optimal tangency point E,

$$MRT_{AB} = \frac{P_A}{P_B}$$

If we know the cost represented by iso-cost line *CD* and the total revenue represented by iso-revenue line R_2L_2 we can calculate the profits made by the firm. Suppose total cost according to iso-cost line *CD* is Rs. 5 lakhs and total revenue according to iso-revenue line R_2L_2 is Rs. 6 lakhs, then profits made by the firm will be equal to one lakh by operating at point *E* and producing OQ_A of product A and OQ_B of product *B*.

Further, since profits are maximised at the tangency point *E*, marginal cost of each product in this optimum situation will be equal to marginal revenue of each product (Note that marginal revenue in the present case of perfect competition will be equal to price).

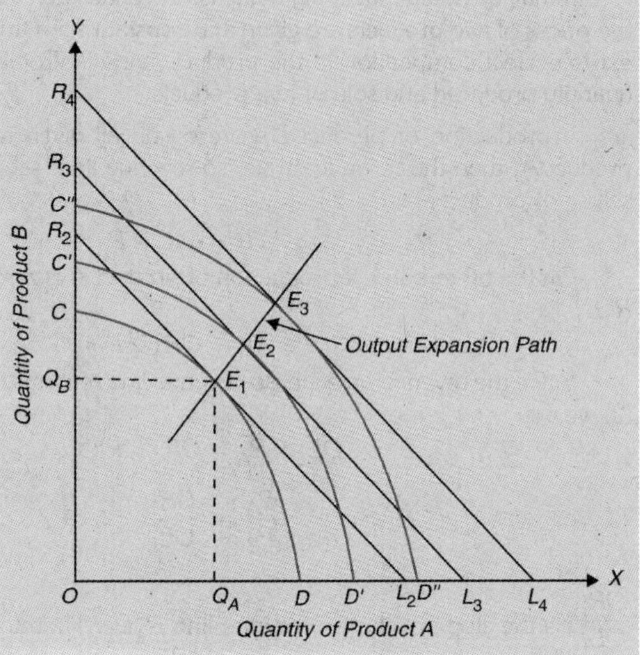

Fig. 26.4. *Output Expansion Path in Case of Joint Production of the Two Products in Variable Proportions*

When the demand for the products increases, the firm will expand their production by employing more resources involving greater total cost. Thus, if total cost increases and iso-cost curve shifts to $C'D'$, the firm will be in equilibrium at point E_2 where the new iso-cost curve $C'D'$ is tangent to the higher iso-revenue line R_3L_3 (Note that prices of two products remain the same and the new iso-revenue line R_3L_3 is parallel to the previous iso-revenue line R_2L_2). With further increase in resources and shift in iso-cost curve to $C''D''$ the firm will expand its production to point E_3. On joining the points E_1, E_2 and E_3 we get output expansion path in case of joint production of two products in variable proportions.

The analysis made above can be expanded further by dropping some of the assumptions. For example, the two products case can be expanded to a more general case of *n-products*. Further, the assumption that prices are constant for the firm and independent of the quantities of products produced by it can be dropped and the firm can be considered to be working under conditions of monopolistic competition or oligopoly in which changes in the quantities of products produced by the firm influence prices of the products. The analysis of such expanded cases of several joint products under conditions of environment of monopolistic competition or oligopoly requires mathematical analysis. However, our analysis of a simple two-product case when for the firm prices of products have been taken to be constant provides us a useful insight for explaining the determination of outputs of several joint products in variable proportions. Further, the technique of linear programming has proved to be very useful in analysing the problems of allocating common productive resources among two or more products to maximise profits.

Besides, the decision to add a new product to a firm's product line or drop the production of an existing product, the manager must take into account its true marginal cost and marginal benefits. If the new product that is being considered for introduction happens to be a close substitute of an existing product, it will affect the sales of the latter and, therefore, the net marginal benefits of adding the former. Similarly, the addition of a new product may affect the marginal cost as it may require new resources for its production and may also affect the costs of producing firm's other products. Thus, the effects on marginal benefits and true marginal costs must be considered by the manager before deciding to add the new product to firm's product line.

Similarly, as explained in the beginning of this chapter, complementarities in demand between two or more products must also be taken into account when deciding about price and output decisions of a multiple product firm.

QUESTIONS FOR REVIEW

1. What is meant by demand interdependence for a multiple product firm? Why a manager of a firm must consider demand interdependence while making price and output decisions?
2. Why do most firms produce multiple products ? Explain the condition for profit maximisation for a multiple product firm.
3. Why are jointly produced products in fixed proportions regarded as a single production package but are treated independently in demand? Explain the appropriate output and pricing strategy in their case.
4. How does a firm determine the optimum level of output and price for the products that are jointly produced in fixed proportions ? When does a firm produce a quantity of a product and then destroys a part of it?
5. Why is the case of products jointly produced in variable proportions more common than the case of joint products produced in fixed proportions? Explain the determination of quantities of joint products in variable proportions using the concepts of production transformation curve and iso-revenue lines.
6. A firm traps and processes rabbits for their fur and hind feet both of which can be sold in the market. Each rabbit yields one pelt and two feet. The demand for pelts (denoted by *P*) and for rabbit feet (denoted by *F*) are given by

   $$P_P = 2.00 - 0.0001\ Q_P$$
   $$P_F = 1.60 - 0.001\ Q_F$$

   The marginal cost of trapping and processing each rabbit is Rs. 60. Determine optimal prices and quantities of pelts and rabbit's feet.
7. A canning company cans pineapples and also sells the pineapple juice that is produced as by-product of peeling and slicing of pineapples. Each 15-pound basket of pineapples yields a 7-pound can of pineapples and a 7-quart can of pineapple juice. The demand functions for canned apples (called as product *A*) and for pineapple juice (called as product *B*) are given by

   $$Q_A = 160 - 10\ P_A$$
   $$Q_B = 100 - 10\ P_B$$

   Marginal cost function of the total pineapple package is given by

   $$MC = 16 + 0.2\ Q$$

   Determine the profit-maximising price and output of pineapples and pineapple juice.

27

CHAPTER

Transfer Pricing

Introduction

The rapid growth of modern large-scale corporate enterprises has been associated with *decentralisation and setting up of semi-autonomous divisions*. The setting up of semi-autonomous divisions of a big corporate enterprise has become necessary because of difficulties of control, communication and coordination among the various operations of production process of a large-scale enterprise. These difficulties of control and coordination tend to raise the costs of the enterprise. Further, it may be noted that semi-autonomous units of a large enterprise often produce intermediate products which are bought by the division which process them into semifinished or finished products. In this context, therefore, the need for *transfer pricing* arises. *Transfer pricing refers to determination of the prices of intermediate products that should be charged by one semi-autonomous division of a big enterprise and purchased by another semi autonomous unit of the same enterprise.* Need for transfer pricing also arises in a large-scale enterprise which is vertically integrated. For example, a steel manufacturing firm may own coal and iron ore mines. Its separate divisions will be engaged in extracting iron ore and coal from which the division manufacturing steel ingots have to buy them to process them for producing steel ingots. Then, the problem of transfer pricing is then to determine what prices the divisions extracting iron-ore and coal charge for them from the division engaged in manufacturing steel ingots. Intermediate pricing requires what amounts of profits be permitted to the divisions producing intermediate products for determining the prices charged by the divisions producing them.

The appropriate pricing of intermediate products is important for the efficient working of the individual divisions of the enterprise as well as of the big enterprise as a whole. This is because the price paid by a division for an intermediate product from another division of the enterprise will affect the output of each division and, therefore, the overall output of the enterprise as a whole. Besides, the transfer prices of the intermediate products paid by one division to another division of the enterprise affects the profitability of the divisions between whom transactions take place and as a result serve as incentives and rewards for the efficient working of various divisions of the enterprise. If transfer prices are set at too a low level, it will adversely affect the profitability of producing the intermediate products, and favourably affect the profitability of the purchasing divisions. This inappropriate transfer pricing serves as a disincentive for the managers and other personnel to improve the efficiency of their divisions. Moreover, such inappropriate transfer pricing is not equitable because the increments in salaries, grant of bonuses and sometimes even the security of jobs of managers and workers employed in a division depend on the profitability of the division. Therefore, it is essential that right transfer prices are fixed so that optimal (*i.e.*, profit-maximising) price and output decisions are made by the enterprise as a whole.

In what follows we assume that an enterprise consists of two divisions : (1) the production division, and (2) marketing division. The production division manufactures an intermediate product which is purchased by marketing division at a transfer price. The marketing division then further processes it and transforms it into a finished product and which it then sells it in the external market which is imperfectly competitive. In what follows we first explain the case when there is no external market for the intermediate product. To simplify the analysis we assume that one unit of the intermediate product is required to be used to produce one unit of the final product which is sold in the external market.

In the next section we will explain price and output determination when there is external market for the intermediate product as well and this external market for the intermediate product is perfectly competitive.

Transfer Pricing with No External Market for the Intermediate Product

Suppose there is no external demand for intermediate product produced by a division of an enterprise or when the division producing the intermediate product can sell it only internally to another division of the enterprise. Since we have assumed that one unit of the intermediate product is required to produce one unit of the final product, the quantity produced of the final product is equal to quantity produced of the intermediate product. Fig. 27.1 illustrates the determination of transfer price and output of the intermediate product and price and output of the final product when there does not exist external market for the intermediate product. D_m is the external demand of the final product of the marketing division and MR_m is the corresponding marginal revenue curve of the final product. MC_m is the marginal cost of the final product processed by the marketing division and MC_p is the marginal cost of intermediate

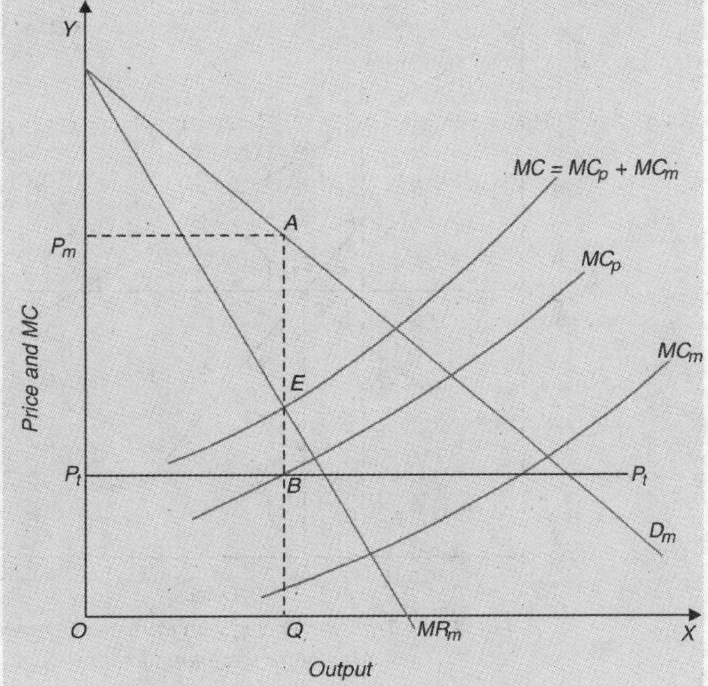

Fig. 27.1. *Determination of Transfer Price of the Intermediate Product with no External Market*

product of the production division. By vertical summation of marginal cost curves MC_m and MC_p we get the total marginal cost MC of the final product.

In order to maximise profits the firm (marketing division) will equate its marginal revenue (MR_m) with its total marginal cost (MC) and, as will be seen from Fig. 27.1, its profit-maximising point is E at which OQ level of output is produced and price P_m of the final product is set. Since by assumption production of one unit of final product requires one unit of intermediate product, the output of the intermediate product by the production division will be equal to the output of the final product. Therefore, the amount OQ of the intermediate product will be produced. *The transfer price for the intermediate product, P_t is set equal to the marginal cost of producing OQ amount of it* which is equal to QB. The transfer price P_t equal to marginal cost of production of output OQ of the intermediate product is a right or appropriate transfer price as by adding it to marginal cost (MC_m) the marketing division equates the combined marginal cost (MC_p + MC_m) with its marginal revenue (MR_m) to maximise the overall profits of the enterprise. As seen above, this causes the top management of the enterprise to decide to produce OQ output of the final product and set price of the final product equal to P_m to maximise overall profits of the enterprise.

Transfer Pricing with External Perfectly Competitive Market for the Intermediate Product

What will be the right transfer prices when there exists *external market* for the intermediate product. We assume that this external market in which the intermediate product is sold is perfectly competitive. With this the division of the enterprise producing the intermediate product and facing the constant price OP_t prevailing in the perfectly competitive external

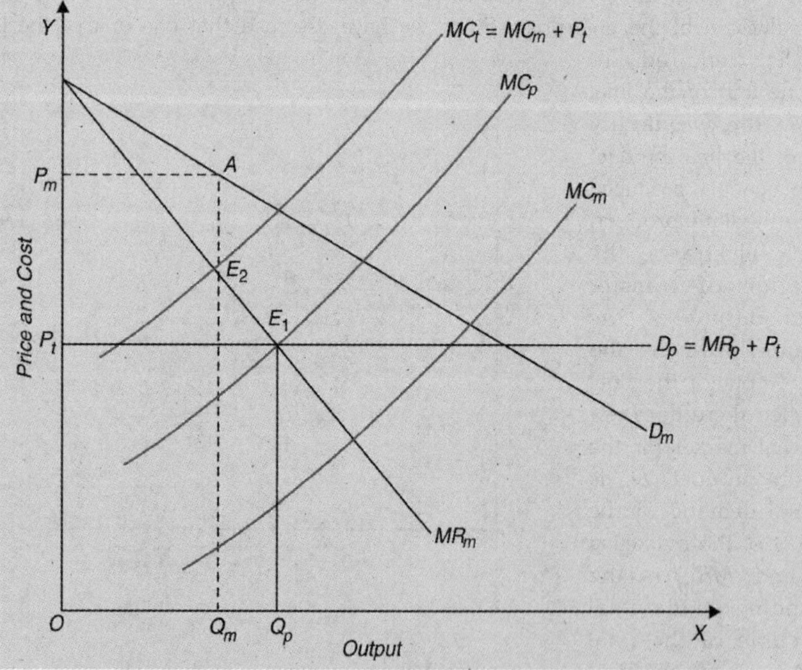

Fig. 27.2. *Transfer Pricing with Perfectly Competitive External Market for the Intermediate Product*

market will equate it with its marginal cost (MC_p) to maximise its profits. It will be seen from Fig. 27.2 that price P_t is equal to marginal cost (MC_p) of the production division at point E_1 and, therefore, it will produce OQ_p of the intermediate product. *This perfectly competitive price of the intermediate product is the right transfer price for the marketing division when there exists external market for the intermediate product.* By adding this transfer price P_t to the marginal cost curve (MC_m) of the marketing division, we obtain the total marginal cost MC_t ($MC_t = MC_m + P_t$). The marketing or assembling division will equate this total marginal cost MC_t with MR_m to maximise its profits and, as will be seen from Fig. 27.2 this happens at point E_2 which corresponds to price P_m and output OQ_m.

It follows from above that of the total output Q_p produced by the production division producing intermediate product, it will sell Q_m units internally to the marketing division and the remaining Q_mQ_p it will sell in the external market. In this way the profits of each unit and the overall profits of the enterprise are maximised.

Transfer Pricing with Imperfectly Competitive External Market

Now we assume that the external market for intermediate product is imperfectly competitive. It may be noted that imperfectly competitive external market exists when the intermediate products are not homogeneous across firms so that the demand curve for an intermediate product is downward sloping and marginal revenue curve lies below it. Transfer pricing with imperfectly competitive external market is illustrated in Fig. 27.3. In panel (*b* of Fig. 27.3 we have drawn the demand (i.e. average revenue) and marginal revenue curves of the intermediate product of the production division of the firm in the *imperfectly competitive external market.* In panel (*a*) of Fig. 27.3 we have shown the net marginal revenue curve (*NMR*) of the intermediate product, internally by the firm's assembling division which sells the *finished product* in the external market. Note that net marginal revenue (*NMR*) of the assembling unit of the firm which produces the finished product is obtained by deducting the

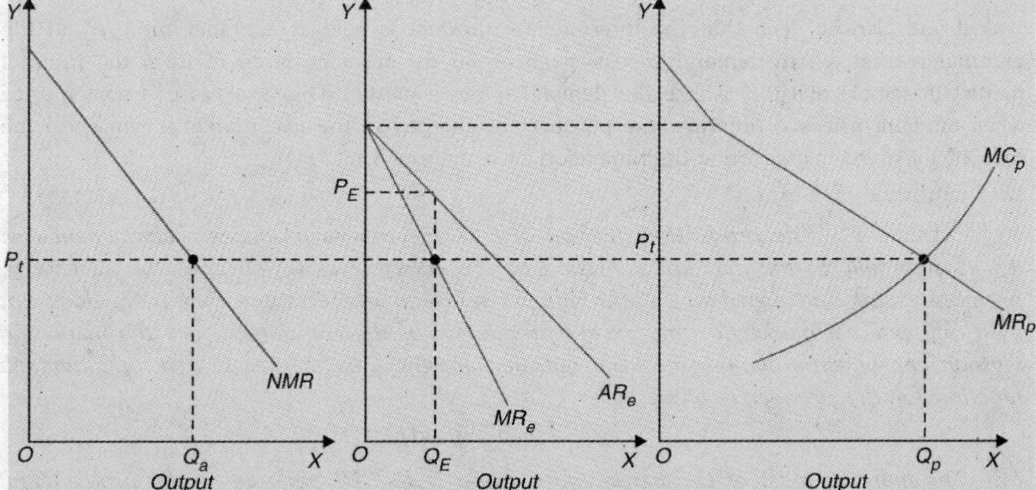

Fig. 27.3. *Transfer Pricing with Imperfectly Competitive External Market*

from the marginal revenue (MR_s) assembling unit

transfer price of the intermediate product (which is equal to marginal cost of production (MC_p) of the production division of the firm) from marginal revenue of the assumbling unit (MR_a).

Thus in panel (*a*) $NMR = MR_a - MC_p$. If marginal cost of production (MC_p) which forms the transfer price is not subtracted from MR_a of the assembling unit, we would be ignoring production division's marginal cost of the intermediate product.

Now, in order to determine profit-maximising output of the intermediate product we have to sum up laterally net marginal revenue curve (*NMR*) of the internal assembling unit of the firm and marginal revenue curve (MR_e) of the intermediate product in the external market. This has been done in panel (*c*) of Fig. 27.3 where lateral summation of *NMR* and MR_e curves yield marginal revenue curve MR_p of the production unit ($MR_p = NMR + MR_e$). It will be seen from panel (*c*) of Fig. 27.3 that marginal cost of production curve MC_p intersects marginal revenue curve MR_p of the intermediate product and accordingly output Q_p of the intermediate product is produced.

Since the price elasticities of demand in the external market and internal market of the assembly division of the firm differs, the division producing the intermediate product will practise price discriminate between these two markets. It will be seen from panel (*c*) that marginal cost of producing profit-maximising total output of the intermediate product Q_p is P_t. Therefore P_t is the transfer price charged from the assembling unit. It will be seen from panel (a) at that with transfer price equal to P_t, the assembling unit will use the quantity Q_a of the intermediate product. Since the assembling unit after further processing the output of intermediate product, will sell it in the external market and its price will be determined by the demand curve of the finished product facing the assembly unit (not shown in panel (*a*) of Fig. 27.3). Further, it will be seen from panel (*b*) that the division of the firm producing intermediate product will sell Q_E of its output in the external market and set higher price P_E in it. The equilibrium of the firm as a whole will be reached when

$$NMR = MR_e = MR_p = MC_p$$

It will be seen from the Fig. 27.3 that output of the intermediate product.

$$Q_p = Q_a + Q_E$$

It will also be seen that the intermediate product is sold at a higher price P_E in the external market where demand is less elastic than the transfer price P_t from the internal market (assembly division) where the demand is more elastic. This analysis of transfer price when different prices of intermediate product are charged in the two market is similar to the case of the third degree price discrimination of a monopolist.

A. Numerical Examples

Example 1 : *The production division of L.G. Electronics produces a component that it sells internally to the marketing division of L.G. Electronics which does the packaging, promotes sales and distributes it through its sales outlets. Assume that there does not exist any external market for any excess production of the component, nor the marketing division can buy the component from outside supplies. The marketing division's demand function for the product is given by*

$$P_m = 100 - 0.001\, Q_m$$

The marginal cost of the marketing division is Rs. 10 per unit of the product and marginal cost of production of the component is given by

$$MC_p = 15 + 0.0010\, Q_p.$$

Find out the profit-maximising quantities of output of marketing and production divisions by L.G. Electronics and optimal transfer price of the component.

Solution :

For maximising profits the marketing division will equate its marginal revenue with the total marginal cost.

The given demand function is

$$P_m = 100 - 0.001\, Q_m$$
$$TR = P_m Q_m = 100\, Q_m - 0.001\, Q_m^{\;2}$$
$$MR_m = \frac{dTR}{dO_m} = 100 - 0.002\, Q_m \qquad \text{...(1)}$$

Total marginal cost (*MC*) of the marketing division is

$$MC = MC_p + MC_m$$
$$= 15 + 0.0010\, Q_p + 10$$
$$= 25 + 0.0010\, Q_p \qquad \text{...(1)}$$

Recognising that $Q_p = Q_m$ and setting $MR_m = MC$ we have

$$100 - 0.002\, Q_m = 25 + 0.0010\, Q_m$$
$$0.002\, Q_m + 0.0010\, Q_m = 100 - 25$$
$$0.0030\, Q_m = 75$$
$$P_t = 75 \times \frac{10000}{30}$$
$$= 25000 \text{ units}$$

Since as per assumption $Q_p = Q_m$

Therefore, $Q_p = 25000$ units.

The optimal transfer price of the component is equal to the marginal cost of production division. Thus, optimal transfer price of the component can be obtained by finding out the marginal cost of output of the component of the production division by substituting the value of output (Q_m) in the MC function of the component.

Thus, transfer price (P_A) = MC_p

$$P_t = 15 + 0.0010\, Q_p$$
$$= 15 + 0.0010\,(25000)$$
$$= 15 + \frac{10 \times 25000}{10000} = 15 + 25$$
$$= \text{Rs. } 40 \text{ per unit.}$$

Example 2 :

J & K Company produces paper and also uses paper to manufacture writing note books. Its production division also sells paper in the external market which is perfectly competitive. The demand function for note books is given by

$$Q_n = 150 - 10P_n$$

The marginal cost function of production of paper and note books are :

$$MC_p = 1 + 0.1Q_p$$
$$MC_n = 0.1Q_n$$

Suppose the price of paper (intermediate product) in the external competitive market is Rs. 6. Determine the optimal levels of output of paper and note books and also the transfer price.

Solution.

Demand function of the final product (*i.e.*, note book) is

$$Q_n = 150 - 10P_n$$
$$10\,P_n = 150 - Q_n$$
$$P_n = 15 - 0.1Q_n$$
$$TR_n = P_n \,.\, Q_n = 15Q_n - 0.1{Q_n}^2$$
$$MR_n = \frac{dTR}{dQ} = 15 - 0.2Q_n$$

Price of paper in the perfectly competitive external market is Rs. 6. To obtain the optimal output level of intermediate product (*i.e.*, paper) we equate marginal cost of producing paper with this price, Rs. 6. Thus

$$MC_p = P_p$$
$$1 + 0.1\,Q_p = 6$$
$$0.1\,Q_p = 6 - 1 = 5$$
$$Q_p = 50$$

To maximise profits, the note book section will equate total marginal cost of producing note book with its marginal revenue. In the present case when there is perfect competition in the external market for the intermediate product (*i.e.*, paper) the transfer price (P_t) will be equal to Rs. 6, that is, price prevailing the external market.

Total marginal cost of producing notebook (MC_t) = $MC_n + P_t$

or $$MC_t = 0.1Q_n + 6$$

Equating total marginal cost of note books MC_t with their marginal revenue (MR_n) we have

$$0.1\,Q_n + 6 = 15 - 0.2Q_n$$
$$0.3Q_n = 9$$
$$Q_n = 9 \times \frac{10}{3} = 30$$

The note book division will produce 30 units of note books. To obtain price of note books we substitute $Q_n = 30$ in the demand function for note books, thus

$$P_n = 15 - 0.1Q_n$$
$$P_n = 15 - 0.1 \times 30$$
$$= 15 - 3 = 12$$

Thus optimal price of note books is Rs. 12 per unit.

It follows from above that production division of paper produces 50 units of paper, and it sells 30 units of it internally to the note-book division at transfer price of Rs. 6 (which is the price prevailing in the perfectly competitive external market) and the remaining 20 units are sold in the external market. 30 units of note books are produced by the note book division and sold at price of Rs. 12 per unit.

Transfer Pricing by International Multinational Corporations

When a division of a domestic company charges a transfer price from the other division of the company in a country, some problems are faced as explained above, for maximisation of profits of the company as a whole. But in case of a multinational corporation which has its subsidiaries operating in several countries, transfer pricing is more complex and has often been used to evade taxes levied by a country. In case of multinational corporation having subsidiaries in the other countries, problems relating to transfer pricing arise because both the components (*i.e.*, intermediate products) and funds (financial payments made) as transfer price for the components supplied by its division in one country to a subsidiary in other country move from one country to another. Different countries have different tax systems and different rates of corporation tax on profits of the companies. In order to evade tax multinational corporations often manipulate transfer price in such a way that lower profits are shown to be earned by the subsidiary company in a country where tax rates are higher. In this way they are able to take away a large amount of funds to the parent country in the form of higher transfer price. For example, in India corporation tax on profits of companies are higher in India than in the USA. Therefore, it has been noticed that some American multinational companies have been charging high transfer prices for the components they are providing to their Indian subsidiaries and therefore these subsidiaries show lower profits earned by them and pay small amount of taxes. A greater amount of profits are drained away to the USA by American multinational companies in the form of higher transfer prices charged and pay lower tax in the USA where corporation tax rates are lower.

A 1986 study on transfer pricing by multinationals operating in Bangladesh concludes that multinational corporations retail a good deal of leeway in setting transfer prices so as to minimise their overall taxes and minimise profits. This is especially true in developing countries since they generally have less effective legal controls on the transfer pricing practices of multinational corporations than developing countries.[1]

In the United States itself Japanese and Canadian multinationals have been charging high transfer prices from US subsidiaries to obtain more profits at the expense of US revenues raised by government from the corporation tax. Thus IRS, the US revenue authority imposed penalty on the Japanese multinational Toyata with systematically charging high transfer price from its US subsidiary for most of the vehicles and components sold in the United States. The effect of these overcharging transfer prices was to transfer profits that would have taxed at higher rates in the United States to Japan where tax rates are much lower. Similarly, in 1994, Japan's tax authorities imposed a heavy penalty of 15 billion yet (equal to about $ 100 million) claiming that Coca Cola charged heavy transfer price for its concentrates and got excessive royalty payments from Coca-Cola Japan, a US subsidiary firm.

It is thus clear from above that manipulation of transfer prices by multinational companies is a very common practice and need to be checked by strict legal action so that multinational companies should work within the bounds of legal and ethical standards of business practice.

For charging of proper transfer price a proposal called "arms-length" test has been put forward. According to arms-length test, the proper transfer price is the price that an unrelated company would pay for the component or intermediate product under the same circumstances. Though there are some difficulties to apply this arms-length test, it is nevertheless a useful way of finding a proper transfer price if competitive environment exists for the sale and purchase of components across countries.

---

1. Quoted by D. Salvatore in *Managerial Economics in a Global Economy,* McGraw-Hill, International Edition, 1993.

Pricing in Non-Profit Enterprises, Ramsey Pricing and Peak-load Pricing

In previous chapters we have seen how private enterprises in a free market economy work to maximise profits. In their price-fixation policy they adopt the rule of equating marginal cost with marginal revenue (*i.e., MC = MR*). When private enterprises, especially if they wield monopoly power, succeed in making monopoly profits by setting higher prices and produce smaller quantities of output cause economic inefficiency in resource allocation. Further, there are some kinds of services such as provision of railway service, electricity, postal service, telephone service, education and health services. These goods and services are called *merit goods as they are socially more beneficial than from private point of view.* These goods ought to be produced on non-profit considerations. The pricing of these goods and services should be done in a manner that ensures allocative efficiency or maximum social welfare rather than maximisation of profits. These merit goods create external benefits which make them socially more useful. It is because of these external benefits that they should not be produced on the basis of profit-maximisation principle.

Three alternative pricing policies have been suggested for non-profit enterprises which may be run by Government or public sector :

1. Marginal Cost Pricing
2. Average Cost Pricing
3 Ramsey Pricing

Ramsey pricing has been proposed when an enterprise produces two or more than two products and services or sells its product in two or more markets and *when common costs are quite large.* In addition to above there is *peak-load pricing* which is often adopted by power distribution companies.

PRICING IN NON-PROFIT ENTERPRISES

Marginal Cost Pricing

We have already discussed marginal cost pricing policy in connection with regulation of monopoly (see Chapter 23). Therefore, we will discuss it here only briefly. Social welfare is maximum or, in other words, economic efficiency in resource allocation is achieved when price is set equal to marginal cost. It has been suggested that non-profit enterprises should pursue marginal cost pricing policy so as to achieve economic efficiency in resource allocation. Consider Fig. 28. 1 where *AD* is demand or average revenue curve for the product of the enterprise. *AC* and *MC* are average cost and marginal cost curves respectively. If this enterprise is run on profit maximisation principle, it will produce Q_0 output and fix price equal to P_0. However, this price is much higher and output much smaller than those required to achieve optimum resource allocation. To ensure efficient or optimum resource allocation, marginal cost pricing requires that price should be fixed at P_1 level and output at Q_1 level. It will be noticed from Fig. 28.1, that even with marginal cost pricing policy firm is making profits equal to P_1RDT which can be ploughed back for investment purposes.

However, marginal-cost pricing does not ensure positive profits when the enterprise is enjoying *very large economies of scale* and as a result *AC* and *MC* curves continue falling as in case of natural monopolies. Marginal cost pricing in this case will lead to losses being made

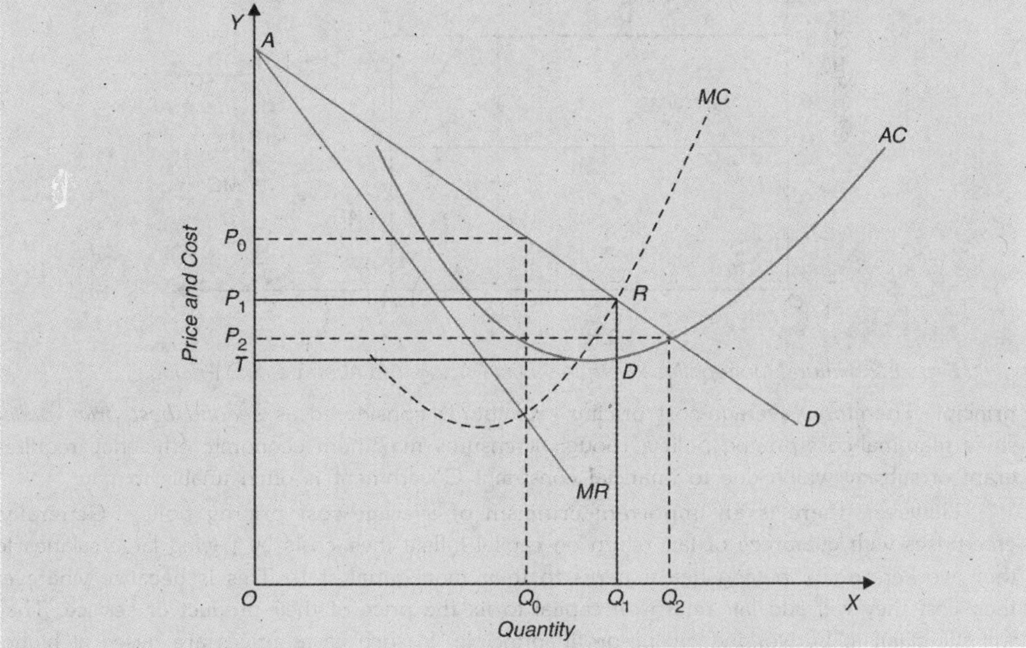

Fig. 28.1. *Non-Profit Enterprises : Marginal Cost Pricing*

by the enterprises. If marginal-cost pricing is pursued in this case, then losses must be met by subsidies paid by the Government. This is evident from Fig. 28.2 where *AC* and *MC* are falling throughout due to the economies of scale. If marginal cost principle is followed, then Q_1 quantity of output will be produced and price P_1 will be charged. As will be seen from Fig. 28.2. with price P_1 and output Q_1, the firm is making losses equal to the area P_1ETH. To induce the enterprise to continue producing the product as it is socially beneficial subsidies equal to P_1ETH should be paid to the enterprise or else the Government should itself undertake the production of the product and meet its losses from the budgetary resources. Thus, in such enterprises where large economies of scale occur marginal-cost pricing is non-viable.

Average Cost Pricing

However, for non-profit enterprises, average-cost pricing is a widely used principle. In this principle, Government does not provide subsidy to keep the enterprise going. In this policy, price is fixed at the level equal to *AC*. However, in this average cost the *fair return on capital* is included. The fair return on capital is cost of capital. In Fig. 28.2, average cost curve *AC* includes fair return capital. Consider Fig 28.2 where *AR* curve is cutting *AC* curve at point S. Accordingly, under average-costpricing principle, price P_2 is fixed and output Q_2 is produced. Though average-cost pricing principle does not aim at maximizing profits and instead it only guarantees fair or normal return on capital, full economic efficiency in resource allocation is not achieved under it. It will be observed from Fig. 28.2 that output under average-cost pricing principle is lower and price higher than under marginal cost

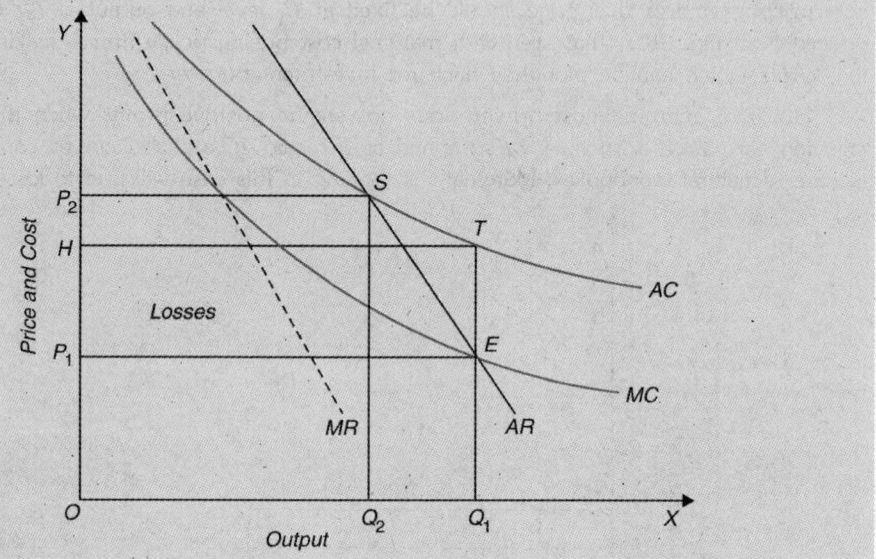

Fig. 28.2. *Natural Monopolies : Marginal cost Pricing and Average cost Pricing.*

principle.Therefore, average-cost pricing principle is considered as *second best price policy* since marginal-cost pricing policy, though it ensures maximum economic efficiency requires grant of subsidy which due to financial constraint Government is often unable to pay.

However, there is an important criticism of average-cost pricing policy. Generally, enterprises with guarantee of fair return on capital inflate their costs by paying large salaries to their workers or by paying heavy perks to their managerial staff. This is because whatever their cost they will add fair return on capital to fix the price of their product or service. They will still claim to be working on 'no-profit' principle. In such cases prices are raised at higher level which causes a lot of economic inefficiency in resource allocation. Besides, average cost principle becomes a tool in the hands of enterprises which seek to cover up their operational inefficiency by declaring higher average cost of production so as to set price at a higher level. The burden of this is borne by the consumers who get the goods or service at a higher price though enterprises claim to be working on no-profit basis. Actually, this is the case in India whereas public enterprises such as railways, postal department have been raising passanger fares, freight charges and postal charges on the pretext of rise in average cost of production which is actually due to their gross operational inefficiencies.

RAMSEY PRICING

Ramsey pricing policy has been suggested in the context of regulating multiproduct monopoly firm or public utility companies such as electric supply company, gas company, railways which have to sell their product in two markets or more, or to two or more classes of customers or users. The problem faced by the enterprises operating in these fields is how to allocate *common costs* incurred on the provision of products to different products or their different buyers in fixing prices of products and services. For example, electric supply company has to incur a lot of expenses on high voltage transmission lines through which electricity is transmitted to residential users for domestic purposes as well as to the commercial and industrial users. The problem is how to allocate among different types of users large expenses incurred on high voltage transmission lines which are common to all types of users. The difficulty arises because common costs by definition cannot be assigned to any specific product or service. Despite these problems many firms extensively use *fully-distributed cost* policy. They decide in an arbitrary manner the distribution of common costs to different products or services or different categories of customers. The price set in this way covers the specific portion of common costs plus costs that are *directly* related to the provision of specific product or service.

Ramsey suggested that though a firm must recover its common costs fully but it is not necessary that the price of each product set at a level high enough to cover an arbitrarily allocated share of common costs. This is because such an arbitrary policy of allocating common costs will result in large economic inefficiency in resource allocation and consequently loss of social welfare. As stated above, for achievement of economic efficiency prices should be fixed at the level of marginal costs. However, marginal costs do not cover fixed common costs as they represent addition to direct costs incurred on providing an extra unit of product or service. *If we rule out grant of subsidies by the Government, no product or service will be supplied even by non-profit enterprise if incremental revenue yielded by a sale of a product or service does not exceed its incremental cost.* Note that incremental cost is whole additional cost which would not be incurred if the product or service is not produced. As long as the revenue from a product exceeds.its incremental cost, the firm will be increasing its profits by supplying the product or service.

However, common cost incurred on providing products or services produced by an enterprise has to be allocated in a rational manner so that minimum possible damage is done to the efficiency in resource allocation. Ramsey suggested such a rational principle for distribution of common costs so that it causes minimum loss of economic efficiency. According to Ramsey pricing principle[1], if a firm provides two or more products or services, *then to cause less loss of efficiency in resource allocation price deviations from marginal costs of products or services should be inversely related to price elasticity of demand.* Thus, if demand for product X is more elastic than demand for product Y, then for least damage to the economic efficiency, price set for product X should be slightly above marginal cost of X and price set for product Y whose demand is relatively inelastic should be set much higher than marginal cost of product Y. Thus, for the enterprise to cover total costs, direct as well as joint or common costs, price of at least one of the two goods must be set above marginal cost. If efficiency in resource allocation is the objective, then Ramsey pricing principle provides '*second best*' pricing scheme that enables the enterprise to at least break even while causing minimum loss to economic efficiency in resource allocation.

Ramsey pricing model can be easily understood from Fig. 28.3 whereas in panel (*a*) demand curve D_x for product X is shown which is relatively more elastic and in panel (*b*) demand curve D_Y for product Y is depicted which is relatively inelastic. It is assumed that marginal cost (MC) is constant for both the products. MC_x, and MC_y are marginal costs curves of products X and Y respectively showing constant marginal costs for both the products. Economically efficient output of X is Q_x and that of product Y is Q_y because with this the

1. F. Ramsey, "A Contribution to Theory of Taxation", *Economic Journal*, 37 (March, 1927), pp. 27-61.

prices equal *MC* of both products. Following Ramsey pricing guidelines price P_x of product *X* whose demand is relatively elastic is set slightly above marginal cost of *X* (MC_x) whereas price P_y set for product *Y* is set much above marginal cost (MC_y) of *Y*. Note that the *shaded area in case of both products depicts the contribution of each product to the recovery of common costs.* It will be seen from the shaded areas in Fig. 28.3. that product *X* whose demand is relatively elastic contributes much less to the recovery of common costs than that by product *Y* whose demand is relatively inelastic. *Fall in quantity demanded and produced of product X from its efficient output Q_x is less because price of product X has been set only slightly above its marginal cost and decline in quantity demanded of product Y from its efficient level Q_y is also less despite price of Y being set much higher than MC_y.* This is because demand for it is relatively inelastic. Making deviations in this way from *MC* which are inversely proportional to their demand elasticities ensures that minimum loss of economic efficiency in resource allocation occurs.

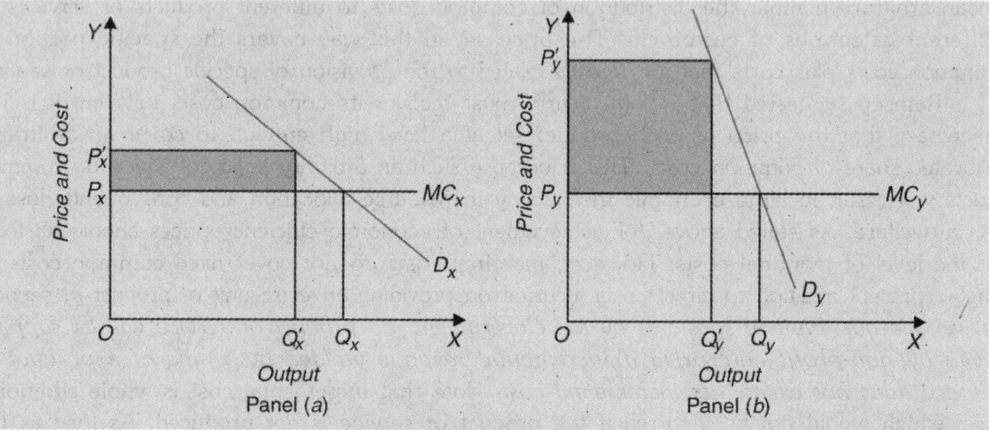

Fig. 28.3. *Ramsey Pricing Model*

Ramsey pricing model has been criticized on the ground that in it prices much above marginal cost are charged from those consumers who have very few alternatives (*i.e.*, have inelastic demand). This is of course true but there is no better alternative to recovery of common costs. If large price deviations from *MC* are made in case of products or services with elastic demand, then there will be large decline in demand as consumers will shift to substitute products and as a result revenue received would not be sufficient to recover common costs. By setting prices above marginal costs (*MC*) which are inversely proportion to the price elasticities of demand, managers of non-profit enterprises can recover common costs while minimising the adverse effect on resource allocation.

PEAK-LOAD PRICING

Now, we shall shed light on an important policy issue. When demand for a commodity or service varies at different periods of time, it has been generally suggested that higher price of a commodity or service be charged for the peak period when demand is greater and lower price be charged for off- peak period when demand is lower. This *dual pricing, that is, higher price for peak period and lower price for off-peak period is known as peak-load pricing.* It may be noted that peak-load pricing is suggested when not only the demand varies between peak and off-peak periods but also cost of production is different in the two time periods. In the peak period when capacity is strained marginal cost is higher as compared to the off-peak period. *Thus, different prices of a commodity for two periods also reflects the different costs of production of the commodity in the two periods.*

Various examples of peak load pricing can be given. In India charges for trunk or STD calls during day time which is the peak period is higher and charges for the off-peak period from 9 P.M. to 6 A.M. are lower. In many countries, electric companies are permitted to charge higher rates during the day time which is the peak period for the use of electricity and lower rates for the night which is off-peak period for the use of electricity. Similarly, air-lines often follow peak-load pricing; in off season they often lower their rates as compared to the peak periods of travel.

It may be noted that *peak-load pricing is generally recommended for regulated monopolies such as electric companies and telephone companies.* As explained above, economic efficiency requires that *marginal-cost pricing principle should be followed. According to marginal cost principle, price of a commodity or service is set equal to the marginal cost of production.* We will therefore explain peak-load pricing in the context of a regulated monopoly. We will analyse it by taking the example of electricity company. The Government *generally appoints a commission to regulate electric company for fixing price for the use of eletricity.* Use of electricity varies a good deal over 24 hours in a day. During the day time when most commercial firms and industries are operating, the use or demand for electricity is the highest, that is, day time is the peak period. On the other hand, during late evening and night, the demand for electricity is lower. Thus there are different demand curves for electricity in the peak and off-peak periods.

Cost of producing electricity also varies over the day. Since production of electricity must be greater during the peak period, *the electric company must have sufficient generating capacity to meet the higher demand for it in this period. As a result, much of the generating capacity required during the peak period remains unutilised during off-peak period.* Thus, marginal cost of producing and supplying electricity during peak hours is higher when capacity is strained and lower during off-peak period when only the most efficient generators are used for producing electricity.

Average Cost Pricing on a Uniform Price Basis : Is it Feasible ?

The case for adoption of peak-load pricing in case of an electric company which is regulated by the Government is illustrated in Fig. 28.4 where D_1D_1 is the demand curve of the electricity in off-peak period and D_2D_2 is the demand curve of the electricity in the peak period. *The regulatory commissions generally follow average-cost pricing under which a single, uniform price or rate is charged in both the peak and off-peak periods.* This average cost is calculated to cover its labour, capital, fuel and other costs plus a fair return on investment. Suppose a uniform price based on this average cost of producing electricity in the two period is fixed at *OP.* It will be

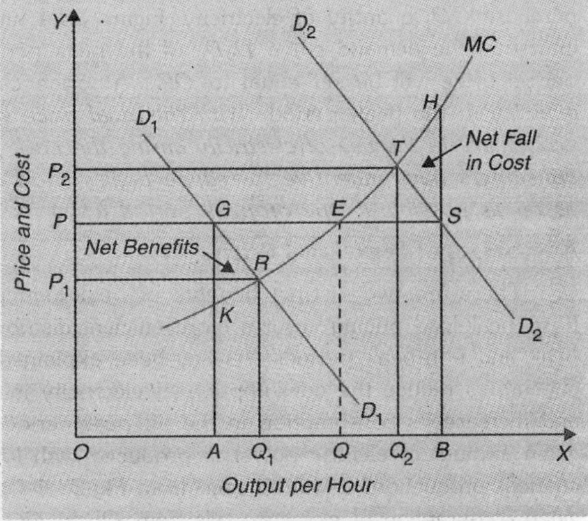

Fig.28.4. *Peak Load Pricing and Its Effect*

seen from Fig. 28.4 that at the single uniform price *OP*, the demand for electricity in the off-peak period is *OA*, while it is *OB* in the peak period. However, during the peak period the company would like to produce *OQ* electricity. This is because at this output, the uniform price *OP* is equal to marginal cost (*MC* = Price) and thus with the *given price OP* it will be maximising its profits by producing *OQ* rate of output. Thus company's rate of production equal to *OQ* during the peak period and quantity demanded of electricity equal to *OB* in this period, *shortage of electricity supply would emerge during the peak period. To* meet this shortage regulatory commission of the electric supply company makes it mandatory for it to produce and supply *OB* quantity of electricity during the peak period. But, as will be observed from Fig.28.4, it is not profitable for the electric company to generate electricity more than *OQ* during the peak period because beyond output *OQ fixed price OP* (= *MR*) is less than marginal cost.

Thus, the interests of the electric company which produces electricity and of the public which uses it clash with each other. It has been observed that *regulated electric companies deliberately resort to black-outs or load shedding quite often during the peak periods.* This shows the reluctance of the companies to generate sufficient electricity at the regulated price to meet the peak-period demand for it. It is because of these pitfalls of uniform-price policy of Public Utility Companies which produce commodities or services such as electricity, telecommunication that in recent years the commissions appointed to regulate these monopolies have recommended peak-load pricing. Which, as explained above, requires different prices to be charged in peak and off-peak periods.

Peak-Load Pricing : Marginal Cost Pricing

It is important to note that to achieve economic efficiency in the use of resources, peak-load pricing policy for regulated public utility companies (which are generally monopolies) follows marginal-cost pricing principle. That is, under peak-load pricing price in each period is set equal to marginal cost of production in that period. Thus, in the cost situation depicted in Fig. 28.4 price in each period will be fixed where marginal cost curve *MC* intersects the demand curves of the peak and off-peak periods. It will be seen from Fig. 28.4 that marginal cost curve *MC* intersects the demand curve D_1D_1 of the off-peak period at point *R* and therefore price set in the off-peak period will be OP_1. At price OP_1, consumers will use or purchase OQ_1 quantity of electricity. Figure 28.4 further reveals that marginal cost curve *MC* intersects the demand curve D_2D_2 of the peak period at point *T* and therefore in the peak period price will be set equal to OP_2. At price OP_2, the consumers will use or buy OQ_2 quantity in the peak period. *With this dual price structure, consumers have incentive to be economical in the use of electricity during the peak period when its price is higher. Secondly, consumers have incentive to reduce peak-period consumption of electricity by shifting it as far as possible to the off-peak period when its price is low.*

Advantages of Peak-Load Pricing

There are two distinct benefits of peak-load pricing as compared to uniform pricing. First, peak-load pricing ensures more efficient distribution of the use of electricity between the peak and non-peak periods. As has been explained above, as a result of peak-load pricing consumers reduce the consumption of electricity in the peak-period when its price is higher and increase its consumption in the off peak-period when its price is lower. Consequently, a given amount of electric power is produced with lower cost than before. This implies more efficient production. It will be seen from Fig.28.4 that with the adoption of peak-load pricing when consumption of electricity falls from *OB* to OQ_2 in the peak period, costs are reduced by the area under the marginal cost curve, that is, area $BHTQ_2$ over this range of output, while benefits, as indicated by the area under the demand curve, fall by the amount equal to the area $BSTQ_2$. It is evident from Fig. 28.4 that there is *net fall in costs* equal to the shaded area *HST*.

Similarly, with the increase in consumption of electric power in the off-peak period from *OA* to OQ_1, there is gain in benefits equal to the area $AGRQ_1$ while there is increase in costs equal to the area $AKRQ_1$ which is less than the gain in benefits. Consequently, there is net *gain in benefits* equal to the shaded area *KGR* in the off-peak period. Note that since we are explaining peak-load pricing in the context of regulated monopoly in which firm makes zero economic profits, the efficiency gain of peak-load pricing will go to the consumers of electricity. This is quite evident from the fact that the peak-load pricing leads to the reduction in total cost of production and given that the total output of electricity remains the same, peak-load pricing will cause the average price of electricity for the consumers to fall.

A second benefit that accrues from peak-load pricing refers to cost saving on account of planning a productive capacity in the long run. In planning for setting up a scale of operations, an electric company must have sufficient generating capacity to meet demand in the peak period. It will be observed from Fig. 28.4 that with peak load pricing quantity demanded of electricity in the peak period falls to OQ_2 under peak-load pricing from *OB* in case of uniform pricing. In view of lower demand in the peak period, the firm has to design a smaller scale of operations under peak-load pricing. Thus, with *peak-load pricing a firm has to install, maintain and house fewer generators to meet the demand in the peak period.* This means a good deal of cost savings which shows another efficiency gain from the peak-load pricing.

Disadvantages. Peak-load pricing is not without disadvantages. Its two disadvantages are worth mentioning. First, some consumers of electricity, especially those businesses whose demand for electricity is wholly or largely in the peak period will be hurt by the higher peak-period price under peak-load pricing policy and also they will not derive any benefits from lower price in the off-peak period. Secondly, a different special type of meter has to be installed to register consumption of electricity separately for the peak and off-peak periods. While these special meters do not cost much more than the meters currently used; the replacement of the existing meters by the new ones however means some increase in one time cost of the firms.

In the opinion of the present author, the disadvantages of peak-load pricing are not very significant as compared to the *substantial gain in efficiency and reduction in cost that result from it.* Therefore, in *recent years, commissions regulating monopolies are increasingly recommending peak-load pricing.*

It may be further noted that we have examined peak-load pricing in the context of regulated monopoly. However, peak-load pricing is applied by the firms working under other forms of market structure when demand in different time periods is different. For instance, hotels in hill stations charge more in summer months when demand is high and charge lower rate during other periods. Similarly, some restaurants charge more at dinner time when demand is high than at lunch. Further, some cinema halls in Delhi charge more in the evening shows than in the afternoon and morning shows. It should be noted that these and other similar case of peak - load pricing do net reflect price discrimination. Instead, these are the adjustments in the rate structure according to market conditions when demand varies systematically over time.

Sales Maximization Model of Oligopoly Firm

Rationale for Sales Maximization Hypothesis

Sales maximization model of oligopoly of firm is another important alternative to profit maximization model. This has been propounded by W. J. Baumol, an American Economist, who challenges the profit maximization assumption regarding business behaviour in these days of manager-dominated corporate form of business organisation and shows how sales maximization is more valid and realistic assumption of business behaviour. Further, we pointed out there that sales maximization was quite consistent with *rationality* assumption about business behaviour. We also noted there that sales maximization model represented one of the managerial theories of the firms because in it the great importance had been given to the managerial role and to his pursuing self-interest in making price, output and advertising policies. Prof. Baumol thinks that *managers are more interested in maximizing sales than profits.*

It should be noted that by sales maximization Baumol does not mean the maximization of the *physical volume* of sales but the maximization of *total revenue from sales*, that is, the dollar value of the sales made. Therefore, his theory is also known as *revenue maximization model.* Further, Prof. Baumol does not ignore profit motive altogether. He argues that there is a *minimum acceptable level of profits* which must be earned by the management so as to finance future growth of the firm through retained profits and also to induce the potential shareholders for subscribing to the share capital of the company. Thus, according to him, management of oligopolistic firms *seeks to maximize sales or, in other words, total revenue subject to this minimum profit constraint.* He thus writes.

"*My hypothesis then is that oligopolists typically seek to maximize their sales subject to a minimum profit constraint. The determination of the minimum just acceptable profit level is a major analytical problem and I shall only suggest here that it is determined by long-run considerations. Profits must be high enough to provide the retained earnings needed to finance current expansion plans and dividends sufficient to make future issue of stocks attractive to potential purchasers. In other words, the firm will aim for that stream of profits which allows for the financing of maximum long-run sales. The business jargon for this is that management seeks to retain earnings in sufficient magnitude to take advantage of all reasonably safe opportunities for growth and to provide a fair return to shareholders*[1]."

With sales maximization subject to minimum profit constraint as the objective of business firms, Baumol explains price-output determination by an oligopolistic firm, advertising expenditure incurred by it, choice of output and input combinations by it, and the effect of changes in overhead costs on the price of products. He draws out the conclusions reached regarding these things in the sales maximization model and how they differ from those of profit maximization model. We explain below all these aspects of Baumol's sales maximization model of oligopoly.

Sales Maximization Model : Price-Output Determination of a Product without Advertising

We first explain Baumol's sales maximization of an oligopoly firm in case when a firm produces a single product and does not undertake any expenditure on advertising or other promotional efforts. We further assume that firm's time horizon is a single period and in this period the firm seeks to maximise its sales revenue subject to a *minimum profit constraint*. The firm does not consider the effect of its price-output decision in the current period on price and output in the subsequent period. Besides, it is assumed that minimum profit constraint is *exogenously* determined by demands and expectations of shareholders and financing institutions of the firm. The firm must achieve this minimum level of profits so as to satisfy the shareholders and to prevent a fall in prices of firm's shares in stock exchange.

It is better to explain graphically price-output determination in Prof. Baumol's sales or total revenue maximization model. Consider Figure 29.1 where the *Y*-axis measures total revenue, total cost and total profits in terms of rupees and the X-axis measures the total output. *TR* and *TC* are respectively total revenue and total cost curves. Since total cost curve *TC* starts from the origin, it means the diagram refers to the long-run cost-revenue situation. *TP* is the total profits curve which first rises and then after a point falls downward. Since total profits are the difference between total revenue and total costs at various levels of output, therefore total profits curve *TP* measures the vertical difference between the *TR* and *TC* curves at various levels of output.

If the firm aims at maximising profits, it will produce *OA* output. This is because corresponding to output, *OA* the highest point of the profit curve *TP* lies. But, as we have seen above, according to Prof. Baumol, the firm does not seek maximisation of profits. On the other hand, if the firm wants to maximise sales (or total revenue), it will fix output at *OC*, level which is greater than *OA*. At output *OC* total sales revenue is CR_2 which is maximum in the diagram[2]. At this total sale revenue maximising output level *OC*, the firm is making total profits equal to *CG* which are less than the maximum, attainable profits *AH*. It will be clear from the figure that total sales revenue maximisation output *OC* is larger than profit-maximising output *OA*. Prof. Baumol contens that the business firms aim at total sales revenue maximization subject to a minimum profit constraint. Now, if *OM* is the minimum total profits which a firm wants to obtain, then *ML* is the minimum profit line.

Now, this minimum profit line *ML* cuts the total profits curve *TP* at point *E*. Therefore, if the firm wants total sales revenue maximisation subject to the minimum profits of *OM*, as has been contended by Prof. Baumol, then it will produce and sell output *OB*. At output *OB*, the

1. W.J. Baumol, On the Theory of Oilgopoly *Economica,* New Series, Vol. 25, 1958.
2. Note that total sales revenue is maximum at the level of output at which $MR = 0$ and price elasticity of demand is equal to unity. This is because at the maximum point of total revenue curve *TR*, its slope is equal to zero. Thus at point $R_2 = \dfrac{dTR}{dQ} = MR = 0$. It is known that corresponding to zero *MR*, price elasticity of demand is equal to unity.

firm will be having total revenue equal to BR_1 which is less than the maximum possible total revenue of CR_2. But the total revenue BR_1 is the maximum obtainable revenue to earn the minimum desirable profits *OM*. It should be noted that the firm can earn minimum profits *OM* even by producing *ON* output (minimum profit line *ML* also cuts the total profits curve *TP* at point *K*). But the total revenue at output *ON* is much less than that at output *OB*. Therefore, given the firm's objective of maximising total revenue subject to the minimum profit constraint, the firm will not produce *ON* output or at point *K*. It will be noticed from the figure that the output *OB* lies in between *OA* and *OC*, that is, it is larger than profit-maximising output *OA* but smaller than the total revenue-maximising output *OC*. Thus, in Prof. Baumol's model, oligopolistic firm will be in equilibrium at output *OB* and will be earning profits *BE* (or *OM*).

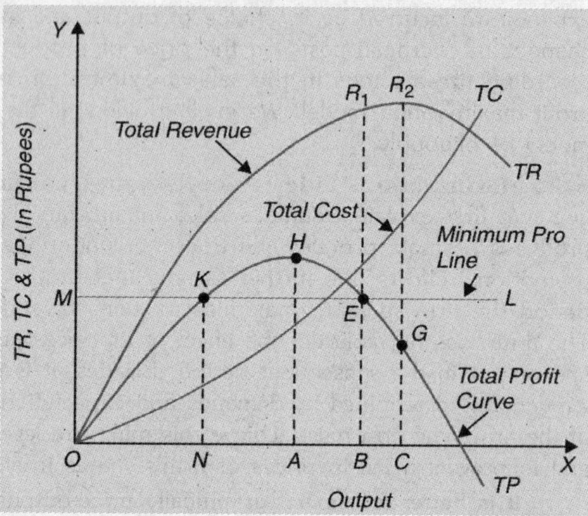

Fig. 29.1. *Prof. Baumol's Sales Maximization Model*

It should be carefully noted that the objective of total revenue (or sales) maximisation subject to the minimum profit constraint leads to a greater output and lower price than does profit maximisation. Price will be lower under revenue maximisation because the output under it, as seen above, is greater and given that demand or average revenue curve is sloping downward, the price will be less when the output is larger. To quote Prof. Baumol "The profit maximizing output *OA* will usually be smaller than the one which yields either type of sales maximum, *OC* or *OB*. This can be proved with the aid of the standard rule that at the point of maximum profit marginal cost must equal marginal revenue. For marginal cost is normally a positive number (we can't usually produce more of a good for nothing). *Hence marginal revenue will also be positive when profits are at a maximum, i.e.*, further increase in output will increase total sales (revenue). Therefore, if at the point of maximum profit the firm earns more profit than the required minimum, it will pay the sales maximizer to lower his price and increase his physical output"[3].

The price charged at output *OB* will be equal to $\frac{\text{Total Revenue}}{\text{Output}}$, that is, $\frac{BR_1}{OB}$.

Now suppose the minimum acceptable profits are equal to *AH* (which are maximum possible profits under the given cost-revenue situation), then even under total revenue maximization objective subject to the minimum profit constraint, the firm will produce the profit maximising output *OA*. But it will produce output *OA* not to maximise profits but to maximise total revenue given the minimum profits constraint *AH*. Now, suppose the minimum acceptable profits for an entrepreneur are larger than *AH*, then it is obvious form the Figure 29.1 that, given the cost-revenue situations depicted in it, he cannot earn profits greater than *AH*. Therefore, the entrepreneur must either lower his minimum acceptable profit level or go out of the industry.

Sales Maximization Model : Optimal Advertising Outlay

We know that firms in oligopolistic market conditions compete not only in terms of price but also in terms of advertising expenditure, product variation and special services offered to

3. William J. Baumol, *Economic Theory and Operations Analysis*, 3rd. ed. pp. 326-27.

the buyers. Advertising expenditure is the chief form of non-price competition. We shall discuss here the question of optimal advertising expenditure to be incurred by an oligopolist and the conclusions reached in this connection will apply equally to the questions of optimal product adjustment and the optimal amount of special services to be provided by an oligopolist when he chooses to maximize sales (total revenue).

The important question in regard to the advertising is how much advertising expenditure a firm will make so as to achieve its objective. How much advertising outlay will be incurred by a firm is greatly influenced by the objective of the firm as to whether it seeks to maximize sales or profits. This optimal advertising expenditure from the viewpoints of both sales maximization and profit maximization is illustrated in Figure 29.2 in which advertising outlay is measured along the X-axis and, total cost, total revenue and total profits on the *Y*-axis. Baumol takes an important assumption in connection with the effect of advertising outlay on total revenue or sales. He assumes, and he quotes empirical evidence for this, that the increase in advertising outlay by a firm *will always raise the physical volume of sales,* though after a point these sales will increase at a diminishing rate. Now, given the price of product, the total revenue (*i.e.* monetary value of the sales) will increase in proportion to the increase in the physical value of sales as a result of the increase in advertising outlay. Therefore, the increase in advertising outlay will always cause the total revenue to increase, though after a point diminishing returns are likely to set in.

In Figure 29.2, *TR* is the total revenue curve which represents the change in total revenue as the advertising outlay is raised, *given the price of the product.* Curve *OD* represents the advertising cost and has been so drawn as to make 45 angle with *X*-axis. This is because we have simply transferred the advertising outlay shown on the *X*-axis to the vertical axis as advertising cost, (for instance *OS* = *SK*). The *other costs* of the firm incurred on fixed and variable factors are taken to be independent of the amount of advertising outlay. Therefore, by adding a fixed amount of other costs (equal to *OT*) to the advertising cost curve *OD*, we obtain the total cost curve *TC*. Finally, by taking out the difference between total revenue curve (*TR*) and total cost curve (*TC*) we draw the total profit curve *PP*′.

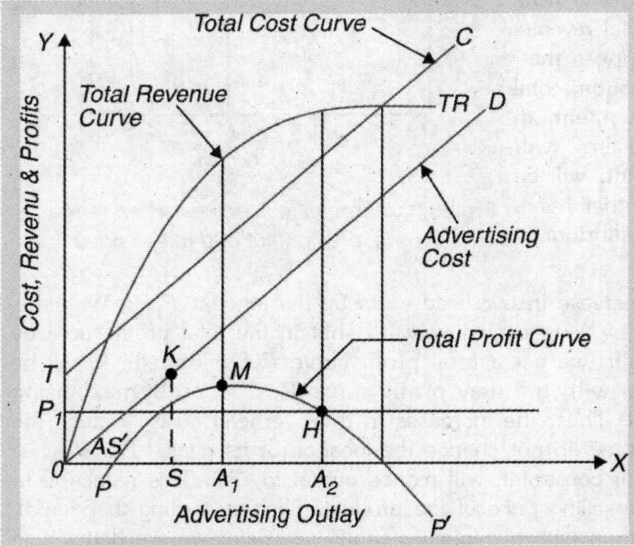

Fig. 29.2. *Optimal Advertising Outlay with Sales Maximization and Profit Maximization.*

Now, it will be seen from Figure 29.2 that if the firm seeks to maximize its profits, it will incur advertising outlay equal to OA_1, at which the profit curve reaches its maximum point *M*. On the other hand, if P_1 is the minimum profit constraint and the firm chooses to maximize its total revenue with P_1 as the minimum profit constraint, it will spend OA_2 on advertisement which is greater than OA_1. We thus see that the objective of constrained revenue maximization leads to a greater level of advertising outlay than the objective of profit maximization. In this connection, it should be noted that here there is no possibility of *unconstrained sales or revenue maximum*, as is there corresponding to output *OC* in the previous Figure 29.1. This is because, unlike a reduction in price, *increase in advertising outlay always raises total revenue or sales* (by assumption). As a result, Baumol concludes that "*it will always pay the sales maximizer to increase his advertising outlay until he is stopped by the profit constraint– until profit have been reduced to the minimum acceptable level. This means that sales maximizer will normally advertise no less than, and usually more than, do profit maximizers.* For, unless the maximum profit level A_1M is not greater than the required minimum P_1 it will be possible to increase advertising some what beyond the profit-maximizing level OA_1 without violating the profit constaint. Moreover, this increase will be desired since, by assumption, it will increase physical sales, and with them, dollar sales will rise proportionately.[4]

Sales Maximization Model : Pricing and Changes in Fixed Costs

An important implication derived from sales maximization hypothesis by Baumol is the effect of changes in fixed or overhead costs on prices of products. Conventional price theory based on profit maximization asserts that so long as overhead costs do not vary with output, the changes in them would not affect prices of the products and nor even outputs produced of the products. But, on the other hand, it has been observed that in actual practice the changes in overhead costs do affect the prices and outputs. Thus, Baumol remarks "This piece of received doctrine is certainly at variance with business practice where an increase in fixed costs is usually the occasion for serious consideration of a price increase."[5]

Now, Baumol asserts that sales maximization hypothesis with its minimum profit constraint can explain and rationalise the change in prices as a result of changes in overhead costs, while profit maximization, as pointed out above, cannot account for it. If a firm chooses to maximize sales with a minimum acceptable profit constraint and is in equilibrium, then the *rise in overhead costs would bring about increase in total costs and as a result the profit of the firm will fall below the minimum acceptable profit level.* In order to prevent this fall in the profit level and to be in equilibrium again, the constrained sales-maximizing firm will reduce the production of the product so as to raise the selling price of the product.

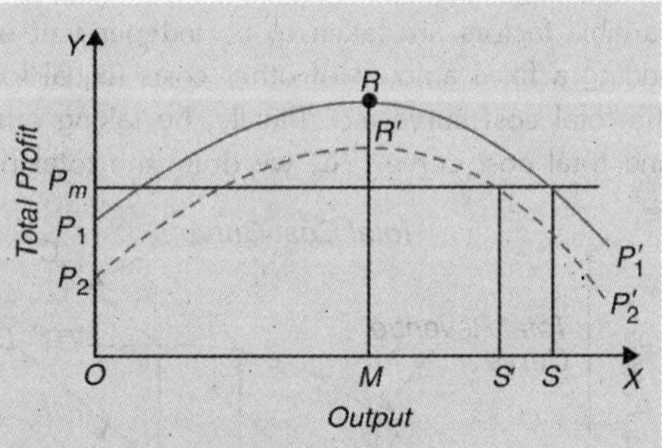

Fig.29.3. *Increase in fixed costs lowers the level of output and raises price*

The argument can be better understood with the help of Figure 29.4 where only total profit curves bereft of total cost and total revenue curves are shown. To begin with, suppose that, given a certain cost and revenue situation, total profit curve is $P_1P'_1$. If OP_m is the minimum profit constraint, then sales-maximizing firm, with OP_m as the minimum profit constraint, will be in equilibrium at output *OS*. On the other hand, profit maximizing firm will be in equilibrium at *OM* output.

Now, suppose that there is an increase in overhead costs by the amount P_1P_2. With this increase in overhead costs, there will be a uniform downward shift in the total profit curve by the amount P_1P_2. Thus, after the shift, we get a total profit curve $P_2P'_2$ (dotted). It will be noticed from Figure. 29.3 that even with the new profit curve $P_2P'_2$, profit-maximising output remains at the same *OM* level. Thus, the increases in the overhead costs "reduce the height of the profit hill uniformly but they do not change the location of its peak. "But a sales-maximizing firm with OP_m as the profit constraint, will reduce output to *OS'*. This reduction in output will permit the firm to raise the selling price of the product. Thus, according to Baumol, with the hypothesis of sales maximization with a minimum profit constraint we are better able

4. *Op. cit.*, p. 262
5. *Op. cit.*, pp. 257-59. (italics added).

to rationalise the businessman's behaviour regarding changes in prices and output in response to changes in overhead costs.

Like the effects of changes in overhead costs on prices and output, sales maximization can also better explain the *impact of corporation income tax on prices and output.* It may be noted that corporation income tax is the tax on the profits of the public limited companies. The analysis of the effect of corporation income tax on the price and output is exactly the same as of change in overhead cost, and P_1P_2 in Figure. 29.4 can be treated as the amount of corporation income tax that has been imposed. According to conventional price theory based on profit maximization, a firm cannot do anything to shift any part of the corporation income or profit tax to the consumer or its employees. Nor a profit-maximizing firm can gain anything by raising the price or changing its output as a result of the imposition of this corporation income tax on a company, provided the rates of the tax are so fixed that the greater the amount of profits earned before tax, the more it retains after the payment of tax. Hence, the output and price of a profit-maximizing firm remain unaltered as a result of the imposition of or changes in corporation income tax. Thus, according to Baumol, "The argument is almost exactly the same as the fixed cost analysis. The corporation tax reduces the height of the total profit curve, but it moves the peak of the curve neither to the right nor to the left."[6]

But if the firm's objective is maximization of sales with a minimum profit constraint, the price will be raised and output reduced when corporation income tax is raised. To quote him, "when taxes are raised, the firm will be motivated to increase its price (and, therefore, to reduce its output) in order to make up its lost profits. The explanation of the shiftability of this apparently unshiftable tax is simple; the sales-maximizing firm will, in effect, have a reserve of profits which it has not claimed it has not maximized profit) but which it can fall-back on when driven to do so by a rise in tax costs, though it can get back to its old profits only by some sacrifice in its sales.[7]

Emphasis on Non-Price Competition in Sales Maximization Moldel

Another important feature of sales-maximization theory of the firm of Baumol is its emphasis on non-price competition in oligopoly as compared with the price competition. It has been observed by many economists that oligopolists are often very much reluctant to use price cutting to promote their sales. Baumol rightly argues that this reluctance on the part of the oligopolists to use price as a competitive weapon should not be explained merely by that they want to live in *quiet life.* This is because when competition under oligopoly does become more intense and vigorous, it may not be in terms of price cutting but in terms of non-price weapons, that is, in the form of more advertising expenditure, product modification, introduction of special services for the customers etc.

This greater propensity to indulge in non-price competition under oligopoly can be better explained with sales-maximization objective rather with the profit maximization objective. This is because as extra expenditure on advertising etc. increases the physical volume of sales, it must also increase the total revenue, whereas the effect of price cutting on the total revenue is doubtful. This is because, "a price reduction is a double-edged sword which, while it serves as an influence to increase total revenue in that it usually adds to the number of units which can be sold, simultaneously works in the opposite direction by reducing the revenue on each unit

6. Op. cit., p. 264
7. *W.J. Baumol, On the Theory of Oligopoly,* p. 266.

sold. In other words, as the economists know so well, depending on whether demand is or is not elastic, price cutting is an uncertain means for increasing dollar sales"[8]. The effect of price cutting on profits is more uncertain because if it fails to raise total revenue, it will most probably reduce profits because the increase in output as a result of reduction in price, will increase total costs. On the other hand, while the profitability of advertising, product modification, improved service is doubtful, their favourable effect on the sales is quite certain. Thus, according to Baumol, "the effect of advertising, improved services, etc. on sales is fairly sure while, very often, their profitability may be quite doubtful. Thus, *sales maximization makes for greater presumption that the businessman will consider non-price competition to be more advantageous alternative.*"[9]

Critical Appraisal of Sales Maximization Model

Implication of sales maximization thsory of Baumol is that price would be lower and output greater under sales maximization than under profit maximization. This is because, total revenue is maximized at the price-output level where marginal revenue is zero, while at the profit-maximizing level of output marginal revenue is positive, given that marginal costs are positive. We have explained above that even under sales maximization with a minimum profit constraint, output will be greater and price lower than under profit maximization objective. If this is true that oligopolists seek to maximize sales or total revenue, then the greater output and lower-price will have a favourable effect on the welfare of the people.

As explained above, another implication of sales maximization objective is that more advertising expenditure will be incurred under it. Further, under sales maximization objective of oligopolists, price is likely to remain sticky and the firms are more likely to indulge in non-price competition. This is what actually happens in oligopolistic market situations in the real world. Another significant implication of Baumol's model is that "there may be a conflict between pricing in the long and short run. In a short-run situation where the scope of expansion in output is limited, revenue would often increase, if prices were raised ; but in the long run it might pay to keep price low in order to compete more effectively for a large share of the market. This price policy to be followed in the short rur would then depend on the expected repercussions of short-run decisions on long-run revenue.[10]

But sales maximization model has not been without its critics. Shepherd[11] has asserted that an oligopolist confronts a kinked demand curve and that if the kink is quite large, total revenue (*i.e.*, sales) and total profits would be maximised at the same level of output. But Hawkins[12] has shown that Shepherd's conclusions are invalid if the oligopolistic firms indulge in any form of non-price competition such as advertising, product variation, improvement in service, etc. and normally in the real world they do so.

An important and convincing criticism against sales maximization model has been made by Hawkins.[13] As has been noted above that, according to Baumol, sales maximizing firm will

8. *Baumol, op. cit., p.* 266.
9. *Ibid, p* 266-67
10. A. Silberston, Price Behaviour of Firms, *Economic Journal*, 1970.
11. W.G. Shepherd, On Sales Maximising and Oligopoly Behaviour, *Economica*, 1962.
12. C.J. Hawkins, 'On the Sales Revenue Maximization Hypothesis, *Journal of Industrial Economics*, April 1970.
13. C.J. Hawkins, "The Revenue Maximization Oligopoly Model", Comment, *American Economic Review*, March 1971.

generally produce and advertise more than the profit-maximizing firm. But Hawkins has shown that this conclusion is generally invalid. According to him, in case of single-product firms, as compared with profit maximizing firm, sales maximizing firm will produce greater, smaller or same output and incur a greater, smaller or same advertising outlay. It all depends upon the responsiveness of demand or total revenue to advertising expenditure as compared with the responsiveness of demand and total revenue to price cuts. As regards multiproduct firms, which are generally found these days in the real world, in the static model, both sales maximization and profit maximization arrive at the same conclusion regarding choice of output and input combination.[14]

But, besides static model, Baumol has also developed a *growth model*[15] of a sales-maximizing firm from which, as has been shown by Williamson, different results follow as compared with profit maximizing firm.

In spite of the above criticism, the present author is of the view that Prof. Baumol's sales maximization model is a significant alternative to profit maximization and brings us closer to reality, for in many cases it explains, as we brought out above in the explanation of the model, the business behaviour in the real world better than profit maximization. Even if in certain cases, sales and profit maximization yield same or similar results, even then by providing interesting insight into managerial motivation in these days of manager-dominated big business corporations as well as by explicitly incorporating advertising and other forms of non-price competition in his model, Baumol has made a significant contribution to our price theory.

Exercise. *A firm faces a demand curve given by $q = 100-2P$. Marginal and average costs for the firm are constant at Rs. 10 per unit. What output levels should the firm produce to (i) maximise profits and (ii) maximise sales revenue ? What are the respective profits at each output level ?*

14. See C.J. Hawkins, On the Sales Revenue Maximization Hypothesis', *Journal of Industrial Economics*, April 1970.
15. See W.J. Baumol's (1) *Business Behaviour, Value and Growth* 1957 (2) On the Theory of Expansion of the Firm, *American Economic Review*, Vol. 52 pp. 1078-87.

Managerial Theories of the Firm : Marris and Willamson's Models

Managerial Models : Separation of Control from Ownership

In recent years, new theories of the firm have been developed which lay stress on the role of managers and their behavioural patterns in deciding about price and output under oligopoly. It has been pointed out that managers do not try to maximize profits but instead pursue other goals. Whether *the firms try to maximize profits also depends upon who controls the business conducted by them.* That is, whether the owner himself or their hired manager controls and directs the business is a very relevant question in this regard. In case of individual proprietorship and partnership, it is the owners themselves who take price and output decisions and perform other entrepreneurial functions. But these days the organizational set up of the firms, especially in case of big firms, is of the nature of joint stock companies or what are also called corporations. In *the case of joint stock companies or corporations we find a separation between ownership and management.* It is the shareholders who are the owners of the joint stock company and bear the risks of business. But price and output decisions are taken by hired managers. Under such a set up, profits of the business go to the shareholders and to the managers usually fixed salaries are paid.

Now, it has been pointed out that it may be expected of the owner-entrepreneurs of individual proprietorship and partnership that they will try to maximize profits since it is in their interest to do so. But hired managers of joint stock companies cannot be expected to try to maximize profits since these profits are not to go to them; they are to go to shareholders. It may be true that when managers are able to earn more profits for shareholders, they may be rewarded by them in some form or the other, but there is great force and truth in the argument regarding managers not maximizing profits. The *incentive to maximize profits is expected to be weaker on the part of persons who are not to get them.*

It is, of course, true that the assumption of profit maximization has made our analysis of firm's behaviour in regard to price and output simple. But whether this assumption is true of the business behaviour in the real world is open to serious doubts. We shall critically examine in this chapter the important managerial theories of the firm which are especially relevant for fixation of price and output under oligopoly.

The important managerial theories of the firm which have been developed in recent years are managerial theories of Williamson and Marris. Like the sales maximization theory of Baumol, managerial theories also do not admit the validity of profit maximization hypothesis regarding the working of the business firms. All these managerial theories lay stress on the role of the manager and his seeking self-interest while making decisions regarding price, output, sales etc. of the corporate firms. Since the managers of corporate firms are motivated by considerations other than the maximization of profits, their decisions regarding price, output etc. are likely to be different from those of the profit-maximizing firm.

It should be noted that Baumol's sales maximization theory, discussed in the previous chapter, is also one type of the managerial theory of the firm. He has argued for the adoption of sales maximization by a firm on the ground that, in his experience, managers always attempt to maximise sales rather than profits and that the prestige and goodwill of a manager depends upon the sales performance of the firm managed by him. Obviously, a manager cannot totally ignore profits because if the firm wants to survive, it must pay acceptable dividends to its existing shareholders and promise good dividends to those who purchase the new shares issued by the firm. Therefore, according to Baumol, managers of the firms aim to maximise sales revenue subject to a minimum profit level.

MARRIS'S MANAGERIAL THEORY OF FIRM

R. Marris[1] has put forward an important theory of the firm according to which managers do not maximise profits but instead, according to him, *they seek to maximise balanced rate of growth* of the firm. *Maximisation of balanced rate of growth of the firm means maximisation of the rate of growth of demand for the products of the firm and rate of growth of capital supply.* If G stands for balanced growth, G_d for the growth rate of demand for the product, G_c for the rate of growth of the capital supply, then the goal of the manager is :

$$\text{Maximise } G = G_d = G_c$$

In seeking to maximise the balanced growth rate, a manager faces the following two constraints :

(1) Managerial Constraint

(2) Financial Constraint

Managerial constraint refers to the strength of the managerial team and their skills. Financial constraint refers to the following three financial ratios :

(i) *ratio of debt* (*D*) *to total assets* (*A*) which is simply called *debt ratio* (*D/A*).

(2) *Liquidity ratio* which is the ratio of liquid assets of the firm to the total assets (L/A).

(3) *Retention ratio* (π_r / π) which refers to the ratio of retained profits to the total profits.

It is important to note that these financial variables determine the job security of the managers. If these financial ratios set by the manger crosses the prudent limits, they expose the firm to the risk of being taken over by others or the managers can be dismissed which can endanger their job security . Therefore, financial constraints are associated with the job security. Managers take into account job security while taking business decisions.

1. R. Marris, A Model of Managerial Enterprise, *Quarterly Journal of Economics* (1963). Also R. Marris, *Theory of Managerial Capitalism*, Macmillan, 1964.

Rationale for Maximising Balanced Growth of the Firm

Now an important question is manager seek to maximise the balanced growth rate of the firm, that is, why do they jointly maximise the rate of growth of demand for firm's products and the growth rate of capital supply. This is because by doing so they maximise their own utility function and the utility function of their owners. Before Marris, it was generally argued by the management theorists that the goals of manager and goals of the owner often cash because the utility functions which they try to maximise greatly differ. The utility function which managers seek to maximise include variables such as salaries, status, job security. On the other hand, utility function which owners seek to maximise include variables such as profits, capital supply, size of output, market share and image or reputation in the public.

According to Marris, despite the difference in the variables in the utility functions of managers and owners, the most of the variables included in both of them are positively correlated with a single variable, namely, the size of the firm. Further, according to him, the size of the firm may be measured by the level of output, capital supply, sales revenue or market share. However, Marris regards steady balanced growth rate over time as the objective of the managers because most of the variables such as sales, output, capital supply, included in their utility function also increase simultaneously so that maximising long-run growth of any variable amounts to maximising long-run growth of others.[2]

It is worth noting that, according to Marris, managers do not maximise the absolute size of the firm but its rate of growth, and the rate of growth of the firm is not the same thing as its absolute size from the viewpoint of managerial utility function. Marris argues that since growth of the firm is compatible with the interests of shareholders who are owners of the firm, there is no need to differentiate between the rate of growth of demand for firm's outputs (G_d) which managers want to maximise and rate of growth of capital supply (G_c) which owners want to maximise because in the state of equilibrium both the rates are equal.

It is clear from above that in Marris's model some variables in the manager's utility function such as salaries, status, power are strongly correlated with the rate of growth of demand for the products, and, therefore, managers' salaries will be higher and they will have more power and esteem, the faster the rate of growth of the firms. Besides, the higher growth of a firm also ensures better job security to the mangers.

Therefore, utility function of managers can be written as

$$U_M = f(G_D, S)$$

U_M = utility of managers

G_D = rate of growth of demand for output of the firm

S = measure of job security of managers

On the other hand, as seen above, utility of owners depend on the growth of capital supply which is positively correlated with the growth of profits.[3] Thus, owners' utility function can be written as

$$U_{owners} = f(G_c)$$

where G_c = rate of growth of capital supply

Following Penrose,[4] Marris thinks that the rate of growth of capital is subject to the

2. See R. Marris, *A Model of Managerial Enterprise, op. cit.*

3. E. Penrose, *The Theory of Growth of the Firm*, Blackwell, 1959.

4. E. Penrose, Op. Cit.

constraint set by the decision making capacity of the managerial team. Besides, according to him, job security of the manager is determined by the weighted average of three financial ratios, namely, (1) debt-asset ratio *(D/A)*, (2) the liquidity ratio *(L/A)*, and (3) profit-retention ratio (π_r / π). These three financial ratios reflect the financial policy of the managers. Further, he is of the opinion that there is a saturation level for job security. Whereas after this saturation level marginal utility from the extra job security is zero, below this level, marginal utility from extra job security is infinite. With this constraint of job security, managerial utility function becomes :

$$U_m = (G_D) \bar{S}$$

where bar (–) on the job security variable S shows it acts as a constraint for utility maximisation of managers. That is, managers maximise their utility, that is, growth of demand for output subject to this job security constraint. Note that financial constraint is reflected in the job security constraint of a manager.

It thus follows from above that in Marris's model, a manager works under two constraints (*i*) managerial constraint set by the decision-making capacity of the managerial team and (*ii*) financial constraint determined by three financial ratios which are reflected in the job security of the managers.

Equilibrium of the Firm

In Marris's model, managers maximise their utility which depends on the rate of growth of demand for the products of the firm subject to the two constraints. It should be noted that in Marris's model, *firms grow by diversification*, that is, by undertaking altogether new products or by producing new designs or models of the existing products. The utility function of the managers is therefore written as :

$$U_M = f(G_D)$$

On the other hand, as seen above, owners try to maximise their own utility which according to Marris depends not on profits but on the rate of growth of capital supply. Thus,

$$U_0 = f(G_c)$$

where U_0 = utility of owners

G_c = rate of growth of capital supply

Now, the firm will reach equilibrium position when it achieves *maximum rate of balanced growth rate* of demand for firms' product and growth rate of firm's supply of capital. Thus, for firm to be in equilibrium, the following condition must be fulfilled :

$$G_D = G_C = \text{maximum}$$

Therefore, in order to show the equilibrium of the firm we have to derive the function for the rate of growth of demand for the products (G_D) and function for the rate of growth of capital supply (G_C).

Rate of Growth of Demand for the Products (G_D). As mentioned above, the rate of growth of demand for products of a firm depends on the rate of diversification, that is, the introduction of the entirely new products per period which are not close substitutes of the competitors or the introduction by the managers per period of products which are close substitutes of existing firms' products. The second important factor on which rate of diversification depends is the proportion of successful new products, denoted by k. The proportion of successful new products depends on the ratio of diversification *(d)*, the price of the product *(p)*, expenditure on advertisement *(A)* and research and development *(R&D)*. Thus, the function for the rate of growth of demand for the firms' products can be written as :

$$G_D = f\,(d,\ k)$$

Where

d = rate of diversification

k = proportion of successful new products

Rate of Growth of Capital Supply (G_c). Marris put forward the view that shareholders (*i.e.*, owners) of the firm pursue the objective of maximising rate of growth of capital supply which is taken as a measure of the growth of size of the firm. Capital supply of a corporate firm is given by summing up fixed assets, inventories, short-term assets and cash reserves. According to Marris, main source of capital supply of a firm is the growth in its profits which depends on profit-retention ratio which is decided by the managers. It may be noted that top managers of a firm cannot fix as high profit retention ratio as they would like. They have to distribute satisfactory dividends to keep shareholders happy and satisfied and also to avoid a fall in the prices of shares. If they do not do so, their job security will be endanagered. Besides profits, growth of capital supply depends on issue of new bonds or borrowing from banks.

Thus, three financial ratios, namely, debt-asset ratio, profit-retention ratio, liquidity ratio which are subjectively decided by managers through the financial coefficient *a*, which, as explained above, determines retained profits and hence determines the rate of growth of capital supply. Marris assumes that the rate of growth of capital supply is proportional to the magnitude of profits. Thus,

$$Q_C = a(\pi)$$

Secondly, tne rate of growth of capital supply depends on the average rate of profits earned by the firms which is denoted by *m*. It is worth noting that Marris takes price of products and its cost per unit as given and average profit margin (*m*) is obtained by deducting the cost per unit, average expenditure per unit on advertising and research and development (R&D) activities from price of the product. Thus,

$$m = P - C - (A) - (R\&D)$$

Since price and cost per unit is assumed to be given and constant by Marris, average profit margin is negatively associated with expenditure on advertising and research and development (R&D). Therefore, the higher the expenditure on advertisement and research and development activities, the lower will be the average rate of profit.

Thirdly, the growth of capital supply depends on the rate of diversification. This is because the magnitude of profits (π) per period which determines the capital supply is also a function of the rate of diversification. The higher the rate of diversification, the greater the rate of growth of capital supply.

Note that profits (π) per period depends on two things : (1) average profit margin (*m*) and the rate of diversification. Thus, profit function can be stated as under :

$$\pi = f(m,d)$$

where π = level of total profits

Substituting this profit function in the function governing supply of capital we have:

$$G_C = \bar{a}\ (\pi)$$

$$G_D = \overline{a}\ [f\ (m,d)]$$

where a is financial security coefficient.

The financial security coefficient is decided upon by the managers exogeneously and is taken to be constant by Marris in the formal model. However, in later stages of his formal model, he relaxes this assumption of constant financial security coefficient (a). However, it is important to note that so long as a is constant, growth of capital supply (G_C) and the magnitude of profits (π) are not competing goals and are positively related. The higher the level of profits means the higher the growth of capital supply.

Given the above functions regarding rate of growth of demand for products and rate of growth of capital supply, the firm is in equilibrium when it is achieving the highest rate of balanced growth. ($G_D = G_C = G$ maximum)

Instrument Variables in Marris's Model

Instrument variables are policy variables which should be manipulated to achieve the objective of the firm. There are three instruments in Marris's model :

(1) the financial security coefficient

(2) rate of diversification

(3) the average profit margin.

An important policy instrument is to choose the value of financial security coefficient. The choice of a financial security coefficient depends on the financial policy of the manager. As seen above, financial security coefficient (a) is the weighted average of three financial ratios, namely, debt asset ratio, liquidity ratio and profit retention ratio. The manager can influence the growth rate by changing its three financial ratios. For instance, if he goes for a larger amount of borrowings and thus opt for high debt-asset ratio, growth of the firm can be accelerated. But a manager has to choose a prudent debt-asset ratio so that there is no risk for the firm to go bankrupt on account of the demands for greater interest payments and repayment of principal sum taken as loan.

Liquidity policy is also very important in its effect on the growth of the firm. Low liquidity ratio means much of the available funds with the firm have been invested to bring about a higher growth of output. But too low liquidity ratio also increases the risk for the firm to go bankrupt. Similarly, profit-retention ratio is also an important policy variable used by a manager. Profits are the most important source of supply of capital. Therefore, the greater the magnitude of retained profits, the greater the supply of capital which would ensure a higher growth of firm. But a higher profit retention ratio means lower dividends for the shareholders which would make them unhappy and would therefore endanger manager's security. Therefore, a manager has to follow a prudent profit retention policy so as to keep the shareholders satisfied and also to avoid the fall in price of shares of the firm.

Further, Marris takes price of the product as given as determined by the oligopolist structure of industry. Hence adjustment in price is not an instrument variable in Marris's model. In Marris's model due to uncertainty of competitors response to changes in price and also imperfect knowledge of rival's strength, managers think it prudent to take the price as given and try to increase the demand for the product by increasing expenditure on advertisement. Marris also assumes that production cost per unit is given and not a policy variable.

The final important instrument variable is the *choice of average profit margin (m)*. Since price and production cost are taken as given by Marris, average profit margin (m) can be affected by changing the level of advertisement (A) and expenditure on research and development (R&D). As mentioned above, the higher the level of expenditure on advertisement and research and development, the lower will be the profit margin, price and cost per unit being given.

It is evident from above that average profit margin in Marris's model is the residual and is negatively correlated with the expenditure on advertisement and research and development. Therefore, *m* is used as a proxy instrument for the policy variables of A and R&D.

EVALUATION OF MARRIS'S MODEL

An important contribution of Marris's model is the inclusion of financial policies in the decision making process by the managers of the firm. This has been done by incorporation of financial constraint as given by *three financial ratios*, namely, debt ratio, liquidity ratio and retention ratio which are set by managers of firms within prudent limits so as to ensure their job security. The fixation of these financial ratios are exogenous to the model and depends on the subjective sub-attitudes of the managers. Some other exogenous factors such as the demands of shareholders influence these financial ratios but the risk attitude of the managers is their prime determinant. However, manager's risk attitude is also governed by the past performance of the firm. If in the past the firm has shown better performance as a result of the present management and profit margin has been rising, the manager will feel encouraged to take more risk.

Marris's managerial model of has ingeneously *found a solution which maximises utility of both the managers and owners*. However, the balanced growth equilibrium of the firm depends on the variables in the various functions of the model which are crucially related to rate of growth of the firm. But the reconciliation of the goals of owners and managers may be true in case of steady growth but are unlikely to be true in condition of recession or sluggish demand.

Further, in this model of maximisation of rate of growth of the firm and maximisation of profits have been treated as conflicting goals. Commenting on this. Koutsoyiannis writes, " The model implies that both managers and owners perceive that the firm cannot simultaneously achieve maximum growth and maximum profits and that owners do in fact prefer the maximisation of the rate of growth, sacrificing some profits. Marris does not justify the preference of owners for capital growth over maximisation of profits."[5]

Besides, Marris in his model assumes the given costs and price structure which is not explained by his model. Further, he fails to explain inter-dependence among oligopolist firms which is an important characteristic of non-collusive oligopoly. This is a great lacuna in Marris's model.

Another shortcoming of Marris's model is his assumption that growth of the firm will continue to grow through diversification, that is through development and introduction of *new products*. He does not realise that introduction new products will be imitated by the rival firms in the long run which will impede the growth of the firms. Besides, he thinks that anything can be sold to the consumers through well-organised market compaings. H. Townsend rightly points out that firms do not enjoy unlimited influence over consumer's demand. If one or two new products introduced by a firm flops in the market, the consumers are unlikely to try other new products of the firm, whatever the publicity."[6]

---

5. A. Koutsoyiannis, *Modern Microeconomics,* (London : MacMillan), 2nd edition 1979, p.368.
6. See H. Townsend, Competition and Big Business Firms; T. M. Rubczynslki (ed). A New Era in Competition (Blackwell, 1973).

Further, Marris considers that the firm grows with introduction of products which have no close substitutes and therefore do not erode the markets of their competitors. This rules out the retaliatory reactions by the rival firms. This is a drawback in Marris's approach because successful new products are imitated by the competitors in the long run. Thus, the introduction of successful new products provide protection from competition only in the short run. In the long run markets for new products are eroded by imitation by the competitors. Koutsoyiannis rightly remarks, "Successful new products thus 'shelter' the firm from competition only in the short run, since in the long run this shelter is eroded by imitation. Secondly, this behaviour create interdependence of oligopolistic firms. Even if prices are assumed as given competition takes the form of new products. This sort of interdependence is not analysed by Marris."[7]

Lastly, another shortcoming of Marris's managerial model is its heavy reliance on the assumption that firms have their own "Research and Development (R&D)' division. In fact, most firms do not have such departments but rely on imitation of the inventions of other firms, or when this is not successful, they pay a royalty for using a patented invention.[8]

WILLIAMSON'S MANAGERIAL THEORY OF THE FIRM

But a full-fledged managerial theory of the firm has been put forward by O. E. Williamson[9] who emphasizes that *managers are motivated by their self-interest and they maximse their own utility function.* Again, the objective of utility maximization by the managers is subject to the constraint that after-tax profits are large enough to pay acceptable dividends to the shareholders and also to pay for economically necessary investments (as opposed to discretionary investment expenditure by the managers).

It may however be pointed out that utility maximization by the self-interest seeking managers, like sales maximization model of Baumol, is possible only in a corporate form of business organisation where there exists separation between ownership and management. Thus, according to Cohen and Cyert, "This separation of ownership and management functions permit the managers of a firm to pursue their own self-interest, subject only to their being able to maintain effective control over the firm. In particular, if profits at any time are at an acceptable level, if the firm shows reasonable rate of growth over time and if sufficient dividends are paid to keep the stockholders happy, then the managers are fairly certain of retaining their power."[10]

Managerial Utility Function. According to Williamson, utility function of the self-seeking managers depends on the following factors:

(1) *The salaries and other forms of monetary compensation* which the managers obtain from the business firms. This is a major factor determining the utility of the managers since salary and other monetary rewards received by the manager from the firm determine his private expenditure and standard of living. However, according to Williamson, salary and other monetary compensations are not the total reward received by the managers from their firms and also these are not the only factor determining the utility of the managers.

(2) The second factor which influences the utility of the managers is *the number of staff under the control of a manager.* The greater the number of staff under the control of a manager, the greater the status and prestige of a manager and also the greater the power

7. A. Koutsoyiannis, *op. cit.*, p. 69.
8. Ibid, p. 369.
9. The important works by O. E. Williamson in which he has developed his managerial theory of the firm are (1) "A Model of Rational Managerial Behaviour" in R. M. Cyert and J. B. March, *A Behavioural Theory of the Firm*, Prentice Hall, 1963. (2) *The Economics of Discretionary Behaviour: Managerial Objectives in a Theory of the Firm*, Markham Publishing Co. Chicago, 1967.
10. Cohen and Cyert, *op. cit.* p. 354.

wielded by him. That is, the greater the number of staff under the control of a manager, the greater the salary and the amount of other monetary rewards . Because of these the number of staff personnel determines the utility which a manager obtains.

Since, according to Williamson, there is a close positive relationship between the number of staff and the manager's salary, he takes a single variable "*monetary expenditure on the staff*" in his formal model of utility maximization by the manager rather than the two separate variables of salary and the number of staff..

(3) Thirdly, the manager's utility depends upon the amount of what Williamson calls "*Management slack*". This management slack consists of those nonessential management perquisites such as lavishly furnished offices, luxurious company cars, large expenses accounts etc. which are not necessary for the efficient and effective operation of the firm. The management slack also enters into the cost of production of the firm.

(4) Finally, utility derived by the manager from his job depends upon the *magnitude of discretionary investment expenditure by the manager*, that is, the amount of resources which the manager can spend according to his discretion. It should be noted that discretionary investment does not include those investment expenditures (such as periodic replacement of capital equipment) which are economically necessary for the survival of the firm. The magnitude of discretionary investment expenditure by a manager indicates the command over resources which he enjoys. By directing the flow of new investment by a firm, the manager determines in an important way the future growth of the firm.

Willianson's Managerial Discretional Model : Concepts of Actual Discretionary and Reported Profits

Before explaining Williamson's formal model of managerial discretion, some concepts of profits used in it are worth nothing. Williamson has distinguished between three concepts of profits : (1) Actual profits (π), (2) Reported profits (π_r) and Minimum profits (π_0)

Actual profits are the difference between total revenue earned less the production costs (*C*) and expenditure on staff (*S*). Thus

$$\pi = R - C - S$$

where R = Total sales revenue

C = Production cost

S = Staff expenditure

Reported profits (π_r) are the difference between actual profits and nonessential managerial expenditure as represented by management slack. Thus

$$\pi_r = \pi - M$$

where M represents management slack

Since $\pi = R - C - S$

$$\pi_r = R - C - S - M$$

Minimum profits (π_0) are the amount of profits (after tax) which are required to be paid as acceptable dividends to satisfy the shareholders who are the owners of the firm. If the shareholders do not get reasonable dividends they may sell their shares and thereby exposing the firm to the risk of being taken over by others, or alternatively they will vote for the dismissal of the top management. Both of these actions by the shareholders will reduce the job security of the top managerial team. Hence managers must give some minimum profits in the from of dividends to keep the shareholders satisfied so as to promote their job security. To meet this objective the reported profits must be large enough to be equal to minimum profit (π_0) plus the tax to be paid to the government. Thus :

$$\pi_r \geq \pi_o + T$$

Discretionary profits (π_D) are the actual profits minus minimum profits and tax to be paid. Thus :

$$\pi_D = \pi - \pi_0 - T$$

where π_D = Discretionary profits
π = Actual profits
π_0 = Minimum profits
T = Tax to be paid to the government

Discretionary profits should be carefully distinguished from *discretionary investment.* Whereas, as seen above, discretionary profits are the amount left after minimum profits (π_0) and tax (T) are deducted from actual profits (π_D) = ($\pi - \pi_0 - T_5$), the discretionary investment equals reported profits minus minimum profits and tax. Thus

Discretionary Investment $I_D = \pi_R - \pi_0 - T$
where π_R = reported profits
π_0 = minimum Profits
T = Tax amount to be paid

Since difference between reported profits (π_R) and actual profits (π) arises due to management slack, discretionary profits can be stated as under :

$$\pi_D = I_D + \text{expenditure due to management slack}$$

Thus, if management slack is zero

$$\pi_R = \pi \quad \text{and} \quad \pi_D = I_D$$

Managerial Utility Maximization

As stated above, Williamson clubs the first two variables, namely (1) salary and other monetary compensations received by the manager and (2) number of staff under his control into a single variable. Utility of a manager in his model is a function of the following three variables :

$$U = U(S, M, I_D)$$

where, U denotes utility function
S stands for monetary expenditure on staff including salaries of managerial team
M stands for management slack
I_D stands for amount of discretionary investment

Maximization of above utility function is subject to the minimum profit constraint. This means level of profits must be such so as to pay satisfactory profit to shareholders and pay for economically necessary investment (not included in discretionary investment).

In Williamson's managerial model, price is regarded as a function of output, the expenditure on staff and a demand shift parameter. Thus,

$$P = P(X, S, e)$$

where, P stands for the price function
X stands for the output level in a period
S stands for the expenditure on staff
e stands for a demand shift parameter

Graphic Representation of Williamson's Managerial Discretionary Model

In order to present a simplified Williamson's managerial model we assume that expenditure on account of managerial slack (M) is zero. Given this, managerial utility function becomes :

$$U_M = f(S, I_D)$$

When management slack (M) is zero, then reported profits equal actual profits, then

$$I_D = \pi - \pi_0 - T$$

Substituting this formulation in managerial utility function we have :

$$U_M = f[S, (\pi - \pi_0 - T)]$$

Thus, we have the following simplified model of managerial function which has to be maximised subject to a constraint. Thus :

$$\text{maximise} : U_m = f[S, (\pi - \pi_0 - T)]$$

$$\text{Subject to: } \pi_r \geq \pi_0 + T$$

In order to find a graphic solution to the model we have to draw utility indifference curves of managers representing their utility function, This has been done in Fig. 30.1 where on the X-axis we measure expenditure on staff (S) and on the Y-axis the amount of discretionary profits. A managerial indifference curve shows various combinations of staff expenditure and discretionary profits which give equal satisfaction to the manager (note that discretionary profits in the present simplified model equal discretionary investment). These indifference curves are convex showing diminishing marginal rate of substitution of staff expenditure for discretionary profits. They do not intersect the axes[11] which means that managers will choose some positive values of both the staff expenditure and discretionary profits.

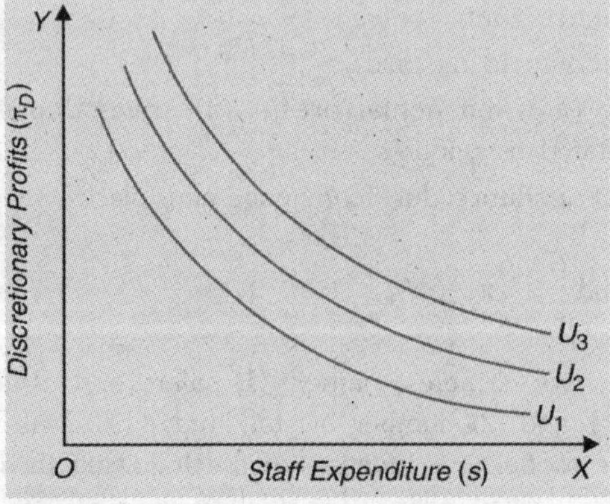

Fig. 30.1. *Utility Indifference Curves of Managers*

In Fig.30.2, we have shown the market relationship between profits and staff expenditure. As the expenditure on staff increases and as a result output expands, discretionary profits increase up to point S_1, and beyond this the discretionary profits start declining. When staff expenditure increases beyond C, discretionary profits become negative. Thus, staff expenditure being less than B and greater than C will not satisfy the minimum profit constraint π_0. In order to find equilibrium position of a manager we bring the indifference curves together with the discretionary profits curve in Fig. 30.3. It will be seen that the manager will maximise its utility at point E, where manager's indifference curve U_3 is tangent to the discretionary profit curve. It will be seen from the figure that in its equilibrium position, the manager will be incurring staff expenditure equal to S^* and making discretionary profits equal to S^*E. It will be further noticed that equilibrium profits will be less than the maximum profits while the staff expenditure will be more than the amount at which discretionary profits are maximum. This is due to managerial utility function according to which an optimum combination of discretionary profits and staff expenditure has to be achieved because both of them enter into managerial utility function. It should be noted that given that indifference curves have a negative slope, the equilibrium will be always be on the

11. Note that non-intersection of indifference curves with the axes implies that corner solutions are ruled out.

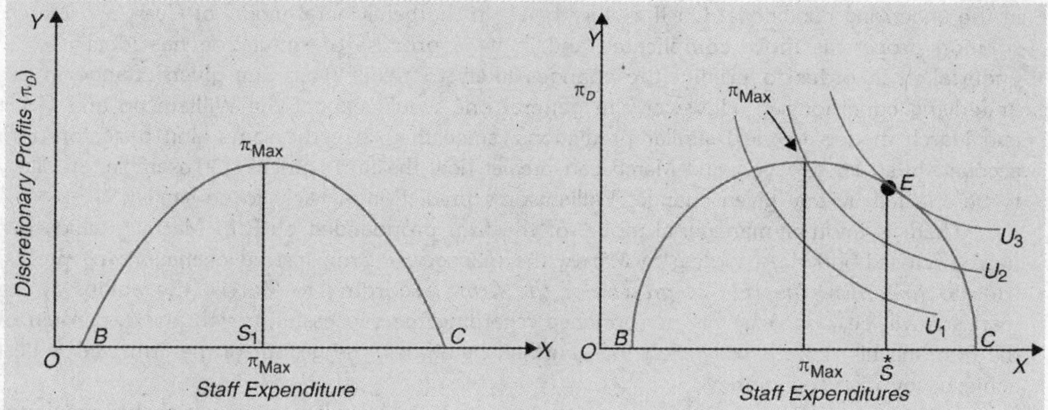

Fig. 30.2. *Dicretionary Profit Curve*

Fig. 30.3. *Equilibrium of Firm in Williamson's Model*

falling portion of the profit staff expenditure curve *BC*. This implies preference of managers for more staff expenditure in Williamson's model

As compared to a profit-maximizing firm, utility-maximizing firm of Williamson's concept has a "*higher staff expenditure and more management slack. No general statement can be made about the relative output levels for the two firms.*[12]

It may be pointed out that under conditions of perfect competition Williamson's utility maximization model retains the result of profit maximization model of the firm. But where competition is weak, that is, under conditions of oligopoly and monopoly, in Williamson's model expenditure on advertising, managerial luxuries (*i.e.*, management slack) will be greater (and therefore more management slack will be absorbed as a cost) and as a result costs of the firm will rise with a upward push to the price. When, under conditions of oligopoly and monopoly, demand weakens, in Williamson's utility maximization model, the expenditure on staff, advertisement, managerial luxuries which are sources of high costs will be reduced and as a result the costs of the firm will decline with a downward push to the price.

It is interesting to compare the predictions of Williamson's model and profit-maximization model of the firm when there is an increase in the profit tax rate or lump sum tax. According to Williamson's model, if the *profit-tax rate* on the firm is increased, there will be increase in the output and staff expenditure of the firm. This is because now that profits have been made less attractive by the imposition of higher tax rate, the manager will try to reduce the reported profits and for this they will increase the expenditure on staff and expand output. In other words, since utility of the manager from profits has been reduced by the higher tax rate on them, they will try to seek utility elsewhere by having more staff and more output.[13] However, if a *lump-sum tax* is imposed on the firm, Williamson's model implies that the firm will reduce its expenditure, particularly on staff. This is because with the imposition of a lump-sum tax, minimum profit constraint is raised and to earn the higher profits, the manager will try to reduce expenditure. On the other hand, a profit-maximising firm will not reduce or increase its expenditure and output whether a lump-sum tax is imposed or the rate of profit tax increased.

A merit of Williamson's model is that, like the profit-maximization model of the firm, in it, given its assumption, *a solution can be found analytically* when there is any given change

12. Cohen and Cyert, *op. cit.*, p. 361.
13. In contrast with Williamson's model, implications of sales maximization model of Baumol in the face of increase in the *profit-tax* rate are different. In Baumol's model, increase in the rate of profit tax will raise the minimum profit constraint, and therefore to obtain higher minimum-level of profits, the firm will try to reduce its expenditure.

in the underlying conditions. On the other hand, in the behavioural model of Cyert and March, solution process is more complicated and in it "a process of simulation has ideally to be undertaken in order to predict the changes likely to result from any given change in the underlying conditions."[14] However, "in general one would expect the Williamson and Cyert and March models to yield similar predictions, since they take the same kind of factors into account. In so far as Cyert and March can predict how the firm's prices, for example, are likely to be affected by any given change, Williamson's prediction is likely to be similar."[15]

There is another managerial model of the firm propounded by R.L. Marris[16] which has been discussed above. According to Marris, the manager of firm, instead of maximizing profits, tries to *maximize the rate of growth of the firm*. According to Marris, the ability of the manager will be judged by his performance regarding the successful growth and expansion of the firm and his rewards will reflect this. Further, he argues, the growth of the firm can be best achieved by diversification.

Comments. Williamson has made various empirical studies from which he concludes that his managerial theory of the firm can better explain the pricing and output under oligopoly than the models based on profit maximization. According to him, reactions of firms to changes in taxation, increase in expenditure on staff and managerial emoluments during periods of boom and drastic cut in these expenditure in recession and changes in compensation of the top executives, staff expenditure in general and managerial emoluments in response to changes in fixed costs can be better explained with his managerial model than the profit maximising model. In our view, however, the available evidence is not sufficient to prove the validity of his model. Besides, the conclusions of Williamson in favour of his managerial discretionary model are based on several implicit assumptions under the *ceteris paribus* clause. These assumptions are not likely to be fulfilled under dynamic conditions of shifts in demand and costs in boom and recession. Further, Williamsons fails to explain pricing and output in those forms of oligopolistic market structure where there is strong rivalry among firms. Williamson model also does not take into account the *interdependence* of firms in oligopoly which is crucial for deciding about price and output under oligopoly.

Williamson in his model lays stress on the managerial discretion in determining not only output and price laid but also the level of staff expenditure and managerial emoluments. Williamson distinguished between desire of manager for discretionary action and the opportunity for managerial discretionary action. He measures the opportunity for managerial discretion by the concentration ratio in the industry (that is, the fewer firms in the industry) and the strength of barriers to the entry in the industry. He argued that the greater the concentration ratio in an industry, the stronger the barriers to the entry, the greater the opportunity for discretionary spending by the managers. Further, the proportionate representation of management on the board is according to Williamson, a measure of desire of manager to act independently of shareholders of the firms. The critics have pointed out that this distinction between desire of management for discretionary behaviour and the opportunity for managerial discretion as drawn by Williamson, is not valid. This is because the greater number of managers on the board, the greater the desire for managerial discretionary behaviour. Thus, according to Koutsoyiannis, "It seems to us that the distinction between the *desire of managers* and the *opportunity of managers* for discretionary behaviour cannot be disentangled."[17]

14. Aubrey Silberston, Price Behaviour of Firms, *Economic Journal*, 1970.
15. Ibid.
16. R.L. Marris, *The Economic Theory of Managerial Capitalism*, Macmillan, London, 1964.
17. Koutsoyiannis, *Modern Microeconomics*, (*London : Macmillan*), Second Edition, 1979 p. 382.

Behavioural Model of the Firm (Satisficing Theory of the Firm)

Introduction

In recent years behavioural approaches to the theory of the firm have been propounded which also do away with the assumption of profit maximisation. Indeed, these behavioural theories visualise that firms do not aim to maximise anything, neither profits, now sales and nor even utility. A distinctive feature of behavioural approach is that instead of hypothesizing about how business firms respond to various situations or how they should respond, it considers how the firms actually behave, that is, how they really take decisions in practice. These decisions relate to price of the product, level of output, sales strategy etc. From the evidence accumulated regarding the actual behaviour or decision-taking of the firms, logical argument has been used to build models regarding the behaviour of big business firms other than those whose actual decision-making processes were studied.

Like Marris's and Williamson's managerial models, the behavioural models also consider a large corporate business firm in which *ownership is separated from management.* It focuses on the organisational problems which arise from *within the internal structure of* these big business organisations and what is their impact on the decision-making process in them.

The advocates of the behavioural approach challenge not only the profit maximisation assumption but also the *omission of element of uncertainty from the conventional theory* of the firm. According to this behavioural approach, under conditions of uncertain demand or cost conditions while taking decisions regarding price, output, sales strategy, it is impossible to know whether profits are being maximised or not; the information required to estimate profits is not there. Most important of all, the advocates of behavioural approach lay stress on the *process of decision making within firms* for predicting decisions regarding price, output, sales, etc. of the firms. The behavioural model of the firm is based on the pioneering works of H.A. Simon[1] starting from his seminal article 'A behavioural Model of Rational Choice'. It was

1. Important works by H. A. Simon, in which he has developed his behavioural theory of the firm are: (1) A Behavioural Model of Rational Choice, *Quartely Journal of Economics,* Feb. 1955. (2) Theories of Decision Making in Economic and Behavioural Sciences, *American Economic Review,* June 1959. (3) *Models of Men,* Willey, New York, 1957.

Simon who first of all put forward the view that the firms instead of maximising profits, normally *satisfice*, that is, seek to have satisfactory performance with regard to profit, market shares, sales etc. Therefore, the behavioural theory is also called '*Satisficing Theory of the Firm*'. However, the behavioural model has been further developed by Cyert and March and Cohen and Cyert. Elaborating the behavioural approach Cohen and Cyert write ;

"*In particular, as one looks closely at the behaviour of actual firms, the justification for the assumption of profit maximisation seems to weaken. When one adds uncertainty to the firm's decision-making process, even defining the meaning of profit maximization becomes difficult to do in an empirically meaningful way. The behavioural theory of the firm takes the position that arguments over motivation are somewhat fruitless. The critical issue is not whether one assumes profit-maximizing instead of satisficing behaviour. Instead, it is fruitful to develop an understanding of the process of decision-making within the firm.*"[2]

The Firm as a Coalition of Group with Conflicting Multiple Goals

A full-scale behavioural theory of the firm has been put forward by Cyert and March[3]. According to them, in these days of large-scale corporate type of business firms, we can no longer consider them as a *single major decision maker* (*i.e.*, the entrepreneur), but instead we should look at them as complex group or complex organisation *composed of various individuals and growths* whose interests may conflict with each other. Cyert and March call this complex organisation or group an *organisational coalition* which may include managers, stock holders, workers, suppliers, bankers customers and so on. They assert that all of these different individuals participate in setting the *goals* of the organisation. To quote them, the concept of a coalition assumes a different type of firm than we have been dealing with .....Hitherto the firm was implicitly regarded as controlled by an entrepreneur and the goals of the entrepreneur were the goals of the organisation. He purchased conformity to these goals by payments in the form of wages to workers, interest to capital sources and profits (when they existed) to himself."[4] According to the behavioural model of Cyert March and Cohen, each group in this business organisation has its own set of *goals or demands* which are conflicting. For example, managers want high salaries and perks, workers want high wages and better pension, good condition of work, the shareholders want large profits and growing capital and so on we explain these conflicting multiple goals below.

Conflicting Multiple Goals : Unlike the conventional theory of the firm with a single-goal of profit maximization, the behavioural theory of the firm does not accept that an organisation has a single goal to achieve. Instead, according to this theory, organisation has many goals. Cyert and March have mentioned five goals which the real-world firms generally possess. These are : (1) *production goal, (2) inventory goal, (3) sales goal, (4) market-share goal and (5) profit goal.* More important, they emphasize that different parts of the organisation have different goals. Goal regarding the level of production represents the demand of the coalition members connected with production, such as workers. Goal regarding the inventory-level of finished goods reflects the demand of those members of organisational coalition who are connected with inventories such as salesmen and customers. Sales goal reflects the demands of those coalition members who are intimately connected with sales such as salesmen and also who regard amount of sales as necessary for survival and stability of organisation.

---

2. P.K.J. Cohen, and R.M. Cyert, *Theory of the Firm,* Prentice-Hall 1965, p. 33, (italics mine).
3. R.M. Cyert and J.C. March, *A Behavioural Theory of the Firm,* Prentice-Hall, 1963.
4. Cohen and Cyert, *op. cit.*, p. 331.

Likewise, market-share goal is affected by those coalition members who are greatly interested in comparative success of the organisation, for example, top-level managers, especially those who look after sales management. Finally, there is the profit goal which firstly meets the demands for accumulating resources so as to distribute them among shareholders as dividends, creditors as interest, and sub-units as increased budgets for them, and secondly it caters to the demands of management who are interested in showing their favourable performance by the amount of profits earned. Profit goal is generally set in terms of aspiration level with respect to the amount of money profits to be made. The profit goal may however be set in the form of return on investment or profit share. It is the profit goal which is intimately connected with the pricing and output decision of a firm.

According to Cyert and March, the business firms are guided by the above five goals while taking decisions regarding price, output and sales strategy. It is worth noting that the above five goals are not mere theoretical hypothesis but have been found to be actually true by empirical investigations by Cyert and March. Further, according to them, all goals must be satisfied, but there is an *implicit order of priority* among them which is reflected in the way search activity takes place. It is also reflected in the speed and manner in which aspiration levels and goals regarding profit, production, sales, market share, and inventories are changed. Variations between firms as regard these latent priorities among the goals are explained, according to Cyert and March, by differences in the bargaining positions of the various members of organisational coalition in different firms.

The Aspiration Level and Satisficing Behaviour

The behavioral model as developed by Cyert, March and Cohen is based on the concept of *aspiration level* put forward by H.A. Simon. Simon points out that the most psychological theories assume that instead of maximising, rational men normally *satisfice*. Applying this to the business decisions, he suggests that instead of maximising profits, the firm aims at satisficing, that is, to achieve satisfactory overall performance of the firm as defined by the aspiration levels of goals set by it. Cyert and March adopt this satisficing behaviour on the basis of aspiration levels of various goals. They focus on explaining how business firms take decisions regarding price, output, sales strategy so as to achieve the satisfactory results in terms of the aspiration level of the goals set by it. Elaborating this viewpoint of the behavioural model, Koutosyiannis writes "The firm is satisficing organization rather than a maximising enterpreneur. The top management responsible for the coordination of the activities of the various members of the firms wishes to attain a satisfactory level of production to attain a satisfactory share of the market to earn a satisfactory level of profits, to divert a satisfactory percentage of the total receipts to research and development or to advertising, to acquire a satisfactory image and so on."[5]

Cyert and March regard the satisficing behaviour as *rational* and lays stress on Simon's concept of *bounded rationality* to justify satisficing behaviour of big corporate firms. The bounded rationality means the prudent behaviour under the given constraints. Satisficing is viewed as the attainment of the aspiration levels of goals which are finally set by the top management and ratified by the board of directors of the corporate firm. It is worth mentioning that goals are not set in terms of maximisation of some relevant magnitudes such as profits, sales, market share etc. but as the achievement of the aspiration levels of the goals set. Thus, the corporate business firms in this model are considered as satisficing organisation rather than the maximizes. Thus, the behavioural model, "redefines rationality. Traditional theory defined the rational firm as the firm that maximises profit (short-run and long-run). The

5. A Koutosyiannis, op. cit. p. 390.

behaviourist school is the only theory that postulates a satisficing behaviour of the firm which is rational given the limited information and limited computational abilities of the managers."

As aspiration level of a firm is based on its goal as well as its past experience, and in fixing it uncertainties are duly taken into account. If the actual performance of the firm reveals that a given aspiration level can be easily achieved, it will be revised upward. On the other hand, if it is found that a given aspiration level is difficult to be achieved, it will be lowered. Simon points out that when the actual performance of a firm falls short of an aspiration level, *'search' activity* is started to find out the ways of better *performance in the* future and therefore achieving the aspiration level.

It may however be noted that according to Simon there is a limit to 'searching activities' which a firm will undertake, because for searching activity must be balanced against its cost. That is why at the same time aspiration level is adjusted downward to a level which is more likely to be achieved. Since the firm limits its searching activity on account of its cost, it does not maximize profits. Therefore, while the firms behaving rationally aim at 'satisficing' rather than 'maximizing'.

Conflicts and their Resolution. According to Cyert and March, there does not prevail perfect harmony among various members of organisational coalition and conflicts among them often arise as regards goals, demands of the various members on the resources of the organisation and therefore organisation should be seen as a *coalition of conflicting interests.* These conflicts among the coalition members are resolved within the firm as a result of persuasion and accommodation of each other's viewpoint.

Further, these conflicts are reconciled by *side payments* which are in various monetary and non-monetary forms. An organisational coalition is viable if the payments made to the various coalition members are adequate to keep them in the organisation. If there are sufficient resources at the disposal of the organisation to meet all the demands of its members, the coalition is feasible one, otherwise not. Of course, since the demands of the members adjust to the actual payments and to their opportunity costs (*i.e.* transfer earnings), there is a *long-run tendency* for the payments and demands to be equal. But in the behavioural theory of Cyert and March, emphasis is laid on the *short-run relation between payments and demands* and on the imperfections in the factor markets.

Organisational Slack

In this connection, a great problem arises when the organisation is not able to accommodate the demands, which may be mutually conflicting and inconsistent, of its members because the available resources are not enough to do so. In this context, Cyert and March introduce the *notion of organisational slack which is the excess of the actual payments to the various coalition members over and above what is required to keep them in the organisation. Thus slack consists in making payments to the various groups of coalition in excess of what is needed for the efficient working of the firm.* To quote Cohen and Cyert, "Because of the frictions in the mutual adjustment of payments and demands, there is ordinarily a disparity between the resources available to the organisation and the payments required to maintain the organisation. The difference between total resources and total necessary payments is called *organisational slack. Slack consists in payments to members of coalition in* excess *of what is required to maintain the organisation.* Many interesting phenomena within the firm occur because slack is typically not zero".[6]

It is worth noting here that in conventional economic theory, organizational slack is zero,

6. *Op, cit,* p. 353.

at least in equilibrium. Cyert and Cohen give various examples of organisational slack which exist in the business firms of the real world. "Many forms of slack typically exist: stock holders are paid higher dividends to keep stockholders (or banks) within the organisation; prices are set lower than necessary to maintain adequate income from customers; wages in excess of those required to maintain labour are paid; executives are provided with services and personal luxuries in excess of those required to keep them; sub-units are permitted to grow without real concern for the relation between additional payments and additional revenues; public services series are provided in excess of those required"[7].

However, according to Cyert, March and Cohen, *organisational slack plays a stability and adaptive role*. When the external environments (*i.e.*, market conditions) are quite favourable, as under conditions of strong boom periods, the organisations secures excess resources which are paid as slack payments to meet the revised demands of those members of coalition whose demand adjusts more rapidly to the better achievement in good times. On the other hand, when the environment becomes less favourable, organisational slack serves as a cushion. In such times, scarcity of resources would tend to reduce the excess payments (*i.e.* organisational slack) to the various coalition members. If this organisational slack did not exist, the dwindling of resources in unfavorable times would have cut into the necessary payments of the members and thereby would have endangered the survival of the organisation. Thus organisational slack provides a pool of emergency resources.

The Process of Decision Making and Price Determination

In this behavioural model, the goals of the firm as set by the top management are implemented through decision making at two levels, one at the level of top management itself and the second at the lower levels of management. Given the goals of the firm, the budgetary resources at the disposal of the firm are allocated among various departments/divisions according to their demands and goals set for them. However, managers of various departments bargain to obtain as large a share as possible from the budgetary resources. The top management retains some funds for use at its discretion at any point of time.

In approving proposals of various departments, two simple criteria are generally followed: the first is the *financial criterion* which examines whether the required funds are available, given the budgetary resources of the organisation. The second is the *improvement criterion* which assesses whether the implementation of the proposal will improve the condition of the organisation.

In the decision making process, the information is required to take appropriate decisions. However, gathering of information is not cost-less and requires budgetary resources. Cyert and March, following Simon, consider that search for information is not *undertaken* according to the marginalist rule, that is, up to the point at which marginal cost of information flow is equal to marginal benefit that would accrue to the firm.

Decision making at lower levels of Management. The decision making process at the lower levels of management is made with various degrees of freedom by departmental managers. With the given share of budget, the departmental managers enjoy considerable discretion in spending funds allotted to them. Besides, there is a lot of decentralisation in taking routine day-to-day decisions which is achieved through delegation of authority within each department or division.

Uncertainty Facing the Firm and its Impact on the Decision-Making Process. Unlike the traditional theory, the behaviourist model of Cyert and March considers the impact of two types of uncertainty. First type of uncertainty arises as a result of changes in consumer's

7. Cohen and Cyert, *op. cit.*, p. 353.

tastes, invention of new methods of production and development of new products. In the behavioural theory this market uncertainty is overcome by business firms by underking only short-term planning and avoiding long-term planning. Thus the behavioral model implies that the firm does not consider long-term consequences of its decussions.

The second type of uncertainty arises out of competitor's reaction to the firm's decision. The behaviourist theory does not consider this type of uncertainty at all. This is because this model assumes that the existing firms have some form of *tacit collusion*. In this way the behaviourist model does not consider the interdepandence among oligopolistic firms which is a prominent feature of oligopolistic market structure. According to Cohen and March, through trade associations meetings, issue of information bulletins by the firms keep their competitors informed about the price, changes in the product and outlays they intend to make in future.

Price and Output Determination in the Behavioural Theory.

What are the implications of this behavioural model for price formation. Cyert and March devised a simplified behavioural model of duopoly when the two duopolistic firms make decisions on price, output and sales strategy. In this model, each duopolistic firm is assumed to have three sets of goal (for profits, production and sales) and three basic decisions with regard to price, output and sales effort to make. In this model each duopolistic firm estimates demand and production cost and fixes its level of output. If this level of output does not yield the aspired level of profits, it then makes searches for ways to reduce costs and also re-estimates demand and, if necessary, lowers its profit goal. The other duopolistic firm also behaves in the same way. Price is fixed at the level of average direct cost (*i.e.*, average variable cost) plus a certain gross profit margin (for example, 20 per cent of the direct cost). Thus, in behavioural model, the cost-plus (*i.e.*, mark-up) pricing rule is followed. Though lower levels of management helps in calculating direct cost, final price decisions are taken by the top management.

The staff at lower level of management learn by experience though they are helped in their task by issuing a blue print containing rules to be followed by them. In the original Cyert and March model, multiple regression analysis was used to examine the extent to which firm's behaviour was sensitive to the variations in the internal parameters of the model. Afterwards Cohen and Cyert[8] produced a model in which simulation process was employed to explain the same general problem.

By taking data on demand, cost, market share, etc. and by using computer simulation, Cohen and Cyert compared the model's prediction with the actual behaviour of duopoly market faced by American Can Company and Continental Can Company. Most of the important moves by the two companies were predicted remarkably well by the model.

In the original behavioural model put forward by Cyert and March it was found that price was highly sensitive (i) to factors which bring about increases and decreases in the magnitude of organisational slack, (ii) to possible reduction of cost on advertisement and other sales promotion measures, and (iii) to adjustment in profit goals after actual profit achievement. For instance, if after the actual achievement, it was found that profits are low, then the organisation will explore the possibilities of reducing costs of production. For bringing about reduction in cost of production, the amount of organisational slack and also the expenditure on sales promotion measures may be cut down. The reduction in cost of production would enable the firm to reduce the price of the product. Further, if the coalition members were prepared to lower the profit goal, then the firm would more readily reduce the price of the product when difficult market situation arises. Thus, in the behavioural theory of the firm as presented by

8. Cohen and Cyert have presented the behavioural theory of the firm in the book "*Theory of the Firm.*" Prentice Hall, 1965.

Cyert and March and also by Cohen and Cyert, close relationship between price, costs and profits has been stressed and price has been found to be highly sensitive to the factors influencing costs. The behavioral theory visualises the adjustment in cost of production and therefore price in response to the varying external market environments, whereas the conventional theory of the firm does not consider any such adjustments in cost of production because in this theory least-cost factor combination is achieved independently of market conditions regarding the product.

Thus, Silbertson in his review article on '*Price Behaviour of Firms' remarks*[9], "The important difference between this type of model (*i.e.*, behavioural model), and more conventional models stems from the fact that this type of model lays emphasis on the process of decision taking, with its continuously changing goals, as the firm learns from its experience and adapts to it. An important corollary of this is that it lays much emphasis on cost reduction, whereas the assumption in conventional models is that for any given output, the least-cost combination of factors has been achieved"[9].

Critical Evaluation of Behavioural Theory

The behaviourist model has made important contributions to the theory of the firm. It has provided a great insight in the process of goal formation and fixation of aspiration levels and also allocation of resources within firm. Its contribution also lies in analysing the stability role of organisation slack for a activity of the firm through changes in slack payments in periods of boom and depression, Further, unlike traditional theory of the firm, the behaviourist theory analyses resource allocation within firm and the decision-making process of a big corporate firm. It highlights the fact that the firm enjoys discretion in decision making and does not take the constraints of market environment as given and impossible to change. Prof. Koutsoyiannis is of the view that traditional theory of the firm and the behavioural theory are comlementary rather than substitutes. To quote him, the traditional theory stressed the role of the market (price) mechanism for the allocation of resources *between* the various sectors of the economy, while the behavioural theory examines the machanism of the resource allocation *within* the firm. Clearly, two theories are complementary rather than substitutes.

Behavioural approach has also been criticised on the ground that it uses a sledge hammer to crack a walnut. The question has been raised as to whether we should really try to construct mirror images of firms, virtually assembling the decision-making process brick by brick for the purpose of predicting their behaviour as the behavioural approach does. Further, it has been asserted that instead of detailed, complicated and simulated model of firm's behaviour, simple model of profit-maximizing firm is sufficient for the prediction of price behaviour of the business firm and its response to increase in taxation in it. The staunch support for profit maximisation has come from Machlup[10]. According to him, "Even if formal accuracy demanded that we accept the maximisation of the decision-maker's total utility as the basic assumption, simplicity and fruitfulness speak for sticking with the postulate of maximisation of money profits for situations in which competition is effective. The question is not whether the firms of the real world will *really* maximise profits, or whether they even *strive* to maximise their money profits, but rather whether the *assumption* that this objective of the theoretical firms in the artificial world of our construction will lead to conclusions very different from those derived from admittedly more 'realistic assumptions'. He further adds, "some of the 'realistic assumption' proposed for inclusion in the theory can affect (by an unknown amount) the magnitude but not the direction of any change that is likely to result from a specified change in conditions".

9. Aubrey, Silberston, Price Behaviour of Firms, *Economic Journal*, 1970.
10. F. Machlup. Theories of the Firm : Marginalist, Behavioural, Managerial, *American Economic Review*, March 1967.

It may however be pointed out that for drawing welfare conclusions from the changes in conditions, we need to know, as has been conceded by Machlup himself not merely the direction of change but also the magnitude. In welfare economics, to quote C.J. Hawkins, "We are interested in predicting more than just the direction of change. We need precise relationships such as '$MC = AR$ for all firms' or 'labour is paid its marginal physical product'. These relationships cannot be derived correctly except by having completely effective (*e.g.* in oligopoly), as Machlup himself concedes, managerial discretion may alter not just the extent of change but also its direction as the Williamson model has clearly demonstrated"[11].

Besides, the simulation approach of the behaviourist theory is only a predictive technique. It does not consider the conditions of entry of new firms in the industry and their effects on behavour of the existing firms.

In this model, it is considered that aspiration level will be adjusted downward whenever the goals, especially of achieving satisfactory rate of profits is not achieved. This rules out the theory of any objective criteria for assessment of satisfactory performance. Therefore, it is not clear in the behavioural theory what is satisfactory and what is unsatisfactory performance.

The behavioural theory has also been critcised on the ground of its belief that the firm behaves in a short-sighted manner as it considers that to overcome uncertainty of market environment the firms undertake only short-term planning. In our view, uncertainty of market environment cannot be successfully tackled by the firm by undertaking only short-term planning. As a matter of fact the business firms need to take a long-rum view of their business decisions and undertake a long-term planning if they want to grow.

A more serious drawback of the theory is that it rules out interdependence among oligopolistic firms by assuming tacit collusion among them. Thus the solution provided by them is quite unstable because collusion can be broken by any firm working contrary to the tacit collusive understanding. The instalitity of solution of behaviourist theory is more when entry of new firms is considered which are not a part of tacity collusion.

QUESTIONS FOR REVIEW

1. What is meant by satisficing behaviour ? Critically examine the view that corporate business firms are satisficers rather than maximizers.
2. The firm is a "Coalition of groups with conflicting goals". Explain the proposition of the behavioural model of the firm.
3. Explain the multiple goals of a corporate business firm. How are these goals formed and who set these goals.
4. What is meant by the aspiration level ? Explain this concept in the context of satisficing behaviour.
5. It is said that behavioural model of the firm redefinses rationality. How is it different from the concept of rationality of the traditional theory of the firm ?
6. Explain the decision making process of the oligopostic firm as conceived in the behavioural theory of the firm. Critically examine how it tables the problem of uncertainty faced by an oligopolistic firm.
7. What is meant by '*organisational slack*. Explain its role in the behavioural theory of the firm.
8. Compare the behavioural theory of the firm with the traditional theory of the firm. Are the two complementary or substitutes ?
9. How are price and output determined in the behavioural model ? Compare it with the marginalist rule of traditional theory of the firm.
10. Critically evaluate the behaviourist theory of the firm. On what grounds has it been criticised?
11. The behavioural theory resolves the core problem of oligopolistic interdependence by assuming tacit collusion of the firm in the industry. Explain and examine critically

11. C.J. Hawkins, *Theory of the Firm*, Macmillan, 1973, p. 73.

Theory of Games and Strategic Behaviour

In the previous few chapters we have discussed those models of oligopoly which explain price and output under oligopoly by assuming objectives other than profit maximization. Another such model is to be found in the application of the theory of games to the oligopoly problem. Professor Neumann and Morgenstern in their book "*The Theory of Games and Economic Behaviour*" which was first published in 1944 provided *a new approach to many problems involving conflicting situations*. The game theory has been applied not only to the oligopoly but also to other economic questions like demand when uncertainty is present. Not only that, the game theory has been applied to the problems of subjects other than economics such as business administration, sociology, psychology, political science, military planning. The theory of games examines the outcome of a situation of interactions between the parties when they have *conflicting* interests. Basically, the game theory seeks to explain what is the rational course of action for an individual who is faced with an uncertain situation, the outcome of which depends not only upon his own actions but also upon the actions of others who too confront the same problem of choosing a rational strategic course of action. We shall describe below how the game theory explains his fundamental question. We shall confine ourselves only to the oligopoly problem. According to professors Neumann and Morgenstern,[1] in an oligopolistic market situation, individual oligopolists is faced with a problem of choosing a rational course of action, which is often called a strategy, keeping in view the possible reactions of his rivals whose reactions in turn would affect him. Thus, he confronts a problem similar to that of the player of any other game.

In a simple form of the game theory, the player has to choose among many possible courses of action which are called strategies. *A strategy is thus a course of action or a policy which a player or a participant in a game will adopt during the play of the game.* There are many possible strategies open to the individual among which he has to choose one at a time. In the case of oligopoly, the various alternative possible strategies which are relevant are: (a) changing the price, (b) changing the level of output, (c) increasing advertisement expenditure,

1. John Von Neumann and Oskar Morgenstern, *Theory of Games and Economic Behaviour,* 3rd ed., New York-Wiley, 1964.

and (d) varying the product. Changing the price may itself be divided into three strategies: (1) lowering the price, (2) raising the price, and (3) keeping the price unchanged. Similarly, the strategy of output may be (1) to increase the level of output, (2) to decrease output, and (3) to keep output constant. Likewise, increasing advertisement expenditure may further be divided into various strategies depending upon the various forms of advertisement, for instance, advertisement on radios, on television, in newspapers, in magazines, through handbills, through posters etc. Likewise, varying the product can be subdivided into various strategies depending upon the nature of the product to be chosen such as whether the colour of the package or the type of the package, or the quality of the product should be changed.

A basic feature of oligopoly is that each firm must take into account of its rival's reactions to its own actions. For example, Maruti Udyog cannot ignore the effect of an increase in price of its product on the prices and profits of its rival firms and how they will respond to its move of rise in price of its product. Thus, it is clear that oligopolistic behaviour has some of the characteristics of a game where a player must know how his move will affect his rival, and how assuming that he is rational, will react to his move.

Game theory highlights that, in an oligopolistic market, *a firm behaves strategically, that is, it adopts strategic decision-making which means that while taking decisions regarding price, output, advertising etc. it takes into account how its rivals will react to its decisions and assuming them to be rational it thinks that they will do their best to promote their interests and take this into account while making decisions.* Game theory sheds new light on some of the important issues faced in explaining decision-making by firms operating in oligopolistic markets. It explains why an individual firm decides to cheat on a cartel agreement. Further, it explains why and how firms operating in oligopolistic markets prevent the entry of new firms in the industry.

Cooperative and Non-Cooperative Games

Games which firms play can be either cooperative or non-cooperative. A game is cooperative if the firms (*i.e*, players in the game) can arrive at an enforceable or binding contract that permits them to adopt a strategy to maximise joint profits. Suppose making of a carpet costs Rs 500 but the buyers value it at Rs 1000. Fixation of price between Rs 500 and 1000 per carpet will yield profits. In this case, two firms producing carpet can cooperate with each other and adopt a joint price strategy to maximise their joint profits rather than competing with each other. *If the two firms can sign a binding contract to share the profits between them from the production and sale of carpets, the game is called a cooperative game.*

On the other hand, a non-cooperative game is one where because of conflict of interests two firms cannot sign a binding contract. In most of the oligopolistic market situations binding contract, that is, contracts that are enforceable cannot be negotiated. Therefore, in oligopoly in most cases we find examples of non-cooperative games. *In a situation of non-cooperative games while the competing firms take each other's actions into account but they take decisions and independently adopt strategies regarding pricing, advertising, product variation to promote their interests.*

It should be noted that a basic difference between a cooperative and non-cooperative game lies in the possibility of negotiating an enforceable contract. In cooperative games, negotiating binding or enforceable contracts are possible, in non-cooperative games they are not. In this chapter while explaining firms' decisions regarding pricing, advertising, we will be concerned mostly with non-cooperative games.

Note that there are games where the players move simultaneously. Each firm chooses a strategy before observing any action or strategy chosen by the rival firms. Not all games are of this type. In some games one player goes first and after which the other player reacts.

DOMINANT STRATEGY

How can firms decide about the optimal choice of a strategy ? Some strategies may be successful (that is, more profitable) if competitors make a *particular* choice, that is, take a particular decision but will not be successful if competitors make *other* choices. On the other hand, *a dominant strategy is one which will be successful or optimal for a firm regardless of what others do, that is, no matter what strategy the rival firms adopt.*

Let us illustrate the dominant strategy in case of duopoly in the choice of whether to '*advertise*' or not. In this case, deciding in favour of advertising by a firm to promote its sales and hence profits or deciding not to advertise are the two strategies. Thus, '*Advertising*' or '*Not Advertising*' are the two strategies between which each firm has to make a choice. We assume there are two firms, *A* and *B* which have to make a choice between the two strategies. The outcome (or profits made) from the various combinations of two strategies chosen by the two firms are presented in the Table 32.1 in the form of payoff matrix. It should be noted that *outcome or profits* made by a firm by adopting a strategy is influenced by the choice of a particular strategy by the rival firm.

Table 32.1 *Matrix for Advertising Game*

		FIRM B	(*in ₹ Crores*)
		Advertising	*Not Advertising*
FIRM A	*Advertising*	A : 10 B : 5	A : 15 B : 0
	Not Advertising	A : 6 B : 8	A : 10 B : 2

It will be seen from the payoff matrix that if *both firms* adopt the strategy of '*Advertising*', the firm A will make profits of 10 crores and firm B will earn profits of 5 crores. If firm A decides to advertise and firm *B* decides not to advertise, profits of firm *A* are 15 crores and of firm *B* are zero. Similarly, if firm *A* decides not to advertise but firm *B* decides in favour of advertising, firm *A* makes profits of 6 crores and *B* of 8 crores. Further, if both firms go in for '*not advertising*' profits of *A* are 10 crores and of *B* are 2 crores.

Now, the question is what strategy each firm should choose. It is assumed that each firm is rational and will adopt a strategy which will ensure it more profits. Let us first consider choices and their outcome available for firm A. If the firm *B* adopts a strategy of '*Advertising*', profits of firm *A* are 10 crores if it also chooses strategy of advertising but only 6 crores if it chooses not to advertise. On the other hand, if firm *B* adopts strategy of '*Not Advertising*', profits of firm *A* are 15 crores if it opts for '*Advertising*' and profits of 10 crores if it also chooses strategy of '*Not Advertising*'.

It is thus clear from the payoff matrix, choice of strategy of '*Advertising*' by firm A is better or optimal since it ensures more profits whether firm B adopts strategy of '*Advertising*' or the strategy of '*Not Advertising*'. Thus, in the present payoff matrix, whatever strategy firm B adopts, for firm A strategy of '*Advertising*' is optimal. *When payoff matrix of a game is such that a choice of one strategy is better regardless of whatever strategy the other firm chooses, the strategy is known as dominant strategy.* In the present case choice of strategy of '*Advertising*' is a dominant strategy for firm A.

From the payoff matrix of the advertising game given in the Table 32.1, the similar conclusion can be drawn for the optimal strategy to be adopted by firm B. Let us state the choices that are open to firm B. If firm A adopts strategy of 'Advertising', the firm B makes profits of 5 crores if it also chooses strategy of 'Advertising' and zero if it chooses strategy of 'Not Advertising'. Thus, choice of strategy of 'Advertising' by firm B is better, if firm A opts for strategy of 'Advertising'. On the other hand, if firm A chooses strategy of 'Not Advertising', profits of firm B are 8 crores, if it chooses strategy of 'Advertising' and 2 crores if it adopts strategy of 'Not Advertising'. Thus, in this case too, choice of strategy of '*Advertising*' by firm B is optimal whatever strategy the firm A adopts. Thus, strategy of 'Advertising' is a dominant strategy for firm B.

Since it is assumed that both firms behave rationally each of them will choose strategy of 'Advertising' and the outcome will be profits of ₹ 10 crores for firm A and ₹ 5 crores for firm B.

It is important to note that all games do not have a dominant strategy for each player. To make it clear we make some changes in the payoff matrix and present them in Table 32.2. The payoff matrix in this table differs from the previous payoff matrix in that profits shown in the bottom right hand corner are different; they are ₹ 20 crores for firm A and ₹ 2 crores for firm B in case both adopt the strategy of 'Not Advertising'.

Table 32.2. *Payoff Matrix for Advertising Game*

		FIRM B	
		Advertising	*Not Advertising*
FIRM A	Advertising	A : 10 B : 5	A : 15 B : 0
	Not Advertising	A : 6 B : 8	A : 20 B : 2

Note. *Numbers in the above table represent profits and are in crores.*

As will be seen from payoff matrix in Table 32.2, if firm *B* chooses strategy of 'Advertising' profits of firm A are ₹ 10 crores if it also opts for strategy of 'Advertising' and are Rs 6 crores if it opts for strategy of 'Not Advertising'. Clearly, choice of strategy of 'Advertising' by firm A yields more profits and is therefore optimal if firm *B* adopts strategy of 'Advertising'. Now, if firm *B* chooses strategy of 'Not Advertising', profits of firm *A* are ₹ 15 crores, if it decides in favour of 'Advertising' strategy and its profits are ₹ 20 crores if it too adopts strategy of 'Not Advertising'. Thus, in this case given that firm *B* chooses strategy of 'Not Advertising' choice of strategy of 'Not Advertising' by firm *A* is optimal.

It follows from above that in the payoff matrix presented in Table 32.2, *optimal strategy for firm A depends on which strategy the firm B adopts.* Choice of strategy of 'Advertising' is optimal for firm *A*, given that the firm *B* adopts the strategy of 'Advertising'. On the other hand, choice of strategy of 'No Advertising' by firm *A* is better, given that the firm *B* adopts strategy of 'Not Advertising'. Thus, in this case there is no dominant strategy for firm *A*. The choice of an optimal strategy by firm *A* in the present case, that is, when dominant strategy does not exist, will be easier if firm *B* adopts a strategy before the firm *A* has to make its choice. But how a firm makes an optimal decision regarding choice of strategy if both firms must choose their strategies simultaneously, that is, at the same time. This is explained below.

Choice of an Optimal Strategy in the Absence of a Dominant Strategy

To decide about the optimal strategy by firm *A* when the choice of strategy by it depends on what strategy the other firm *B* adopts, the *firm A must put itself in firm B's place.* For this the firm A has to know what strategy is the best from firm *B*'s point of view and further that it should assume that the firm *B* is rational and will therefore adopt the best strategy. From the payoff matrix given in Table 32.2, it will be seen that given that the firm *A* chooses strategy of 'Advertising' the firm *B* will make profits equal to ₹ 5 crores if it adopts strategy of 'Advertising' and its profits will be equal to zero if it opts for 'Not Advertising' strategy. Further, if firm *A* chooses strategy of 'Not Advertising' profits of firm *B* will be ₹ 8 crores if it decides to advertise and only ₹ 2 crores if it decides not to advertise. Thus, for firm *B*, strategy of 'Advertising' is better no matter firm *A* adopts strategy of 'Advertising' or 'Not Advertising' and therefore the firm *A* can safely conclude that firm *B* will adopt this strategy of 'Advertising'.

Now, given that *firm B will adopt strategy of 'Advertising'* the firm A will choose its strategy; if it adopts strategy of 'Advertising' its profits will be ₹ 10 crores and if its adopts strategy of 'No Advertising', its profits will be ₹ 6 crores. Thus, given the firm B's strategy of 'Advertising', the optimal strategy of firm A is that of 'Advertising' too. In this way both firms will reach the equilibrium *state by choosing strategy of 'Advertising' and will have no incentive to deviate from* it. It is quite logical outcome of the game because firm A is choosing the best strategy it can, given firm *B*'s strategy, and firm *B* is choosing the best strategy, given firm *A*'s strategy.

Nash Equilibrium

We may refer here to the concept of Nash equilibrium. Nash equilibrium is named after John F. Nash, an American mathematician and economist. We have explained above that in many games we do not have dominant strategies, but still the firms achieve equilibrium in the adoption of their strategies. The application of the concept of Nash equilibrium is quite relevant here. Nash equilibrium is a more general concept of equilibrium that is widely applicable and highly appealing. In the second advertising game whose payoff matrix is given in Table 32.2 and in which firm A has no dominant strategy we reached the conclusion that the equilibrium state is reached when firm A adopts strategy of 'Advertising', *given that the firm B will choose the strategy of 'Advertising'*. That is, firm A is making the best choice, given the choice by its rival firm B and firm B is choosing the best strategy, given the strategy of firm A. Therefore, they have no incentive to change their strategies. Hence, there exists an equilibrium, called Nash equilibrium.

Nash equilibrium describes a set of strategies where each player believes that it is doing the best it can, given the stragey of the other player or players.

In our above example of game 2 of advertising where firm A has no dominant strategy, each firm promotes its own interests and makes a best choice of strategy, given the other firm's strategy. In the above game, both firms *A* and *B* adopt strategy of 'Advertising' which is optimal for them. Since each is doing the best, given other's strategy and no one has a tendency to change it unilaterally, there exists Nash equilibrium. As no one has a tendency to deviate from the Nash equilibrium state, strategies chosen by them *are stable.*

Comparison Between Dominant Strategy and Nash Equilibrium

It is important to compare Nash equilibrium and equilibrium reached where each firm has a dominant strategy. Whereas *a dominant strategy equilibrium describes an optimal or best choice regardless of what strategy the other player adopts*, in Nash equilibrium each player adopts a strategy that is the best or optimal, *given the strategy other player adopts*. However, it may be noted that in some games we do not have Nash equilibrium and that some have more than one Nash equilibrium.

NEUMANN–MORGENSTERN GAME THEORY

There is a fundamental assumption in the Neumann-Morgenstern game theory which is worth mentioning. According to their game theory, *an oligopolist while choosing his strategy will assume that his rivals will adopt a strategy which will be worst for him*, that is, the rivals will adopt the policy which will be most unfavourable to him. That is to say, an oligopolist will adopt the policy of "*playing it safe*". Given this assumption, from among those strategies which provide him with various minimum gains, an oligopolist will select that one which is maximum in those minimum gains.

In order to discuss the solution of oligopoly problem suggested by Neumann-Morgenstern's theory of game, we suppose that an oligopolist knows the complete set of strategies open to him as well as those available to his rivals in the industry. Further, it is assumed that the struggle between the oligopolists is of the nature of "*strictly adversary game*". A strictly adversary game is one in which the outcome which is favourable from the viewpoint of one, is unfavourable to the other. Lastly, we take a *constant-sum game*, in which the outcomes to the two players, *i.e.*, oligopolists always add up to the same constant amount. Thus, in a constant sum game, one player's gain is always another player's loss. Thus, if the constant sum is profits of ₹ 10 which is to be shared between the two sellers, then if A receives ₹ 8, then B will be get ₹ 2, and if A gets ₹ 3, then B will obtain ₹ 7 and so on. In our explanation of the game theory below, we shall describe the behaviour of a pair of duopolists A and B, who compete for a given total profits of ₹ 10. When in a game aggregate of gain (+) and loss (–) is zero, the constant-sum game becomes a *zero sum game*. In the oligopolistic market situation, if advertising compaign launched by a firm for promoting the sales of its product merely causes a *fixed number of consumers* to switch from other brands of the product to his brand without adding to the total demand of the product, it would be an example of a zero sum game.

Maximin and Minimax Strategies

Let us suppose that three strategies are open to *A* and three strategies are open to *B*. It is assumed that the duopolists are able to quantify the outcomes of the various combinations of different strategies. The various different strategies open to the duopolists and the effect on the profits of the various combinations of strategies are depicted in Table 32.3 which is called '*Payoff Matrix*'. The payoff matrix of a game represents the payoffs to each player for each combination of strategies that are chosen. In the Table 32.3 *A*'s strategies such A_1 A_2 and A_3 are represented in a column, and *B*'s strategies such as B_1, B_2 and B_3 are represented in a row. *A*'s payoff matrix in Table 32.3 *shows the amount of profits which accrue to A* as a result of the strategies adopted by him and his rival *B*.

Thus, if *A* adopts strategy A_1 and *B* adopts strategy B_1, then the profits to *A* are ₹ 2. The profits to *B* will be the given constant sum (*i.e.* the profits of ₹ 10) minus the amount of profits which go to *A*. Therefore, in the above case (when *A* adopts strategy A_1 and *B* adopts strategy B_1) the profits of *B* will be ₹ 10 – 2 = ₹ 8. The profits of *B* are not shown in the table though they can be shown in a separate but the same type of table. In the table given above when *A* plays strategy A_1 and *B* plays strategy B_2 the profits to *A* will be ₹ 8. Likewise, if *A* selects strategy A_2 and *B* selects strategy B_3, the profits to *A* will be ₹ 9.

Table 32.3 *A's Payoff Matrix*

		B's Strategies			
		B_1	B_2	B_3	*Row Minima*
	A_1	2	8	1	1
A's Strategies	A_2	4	3	9	3
	A_3	5	6	7	5
Column maxima		5	8	9	

Again, if *A* adopts strategy A_3 and *B* adopts strategy B_1, then the profits to *A* will be ₹ 5. Similarly, each of the other profit figures for *A* in the table corresponds to a particular combination of strategies chosen by *A* and *B*.

Now, given the payoff matrix of the above table, which strategies will be selected by *A* and *B* and what will be the outcome ? Suppose *A* has to choose his strategy before *B* chooses. As pointed out above, *A* will choose his strategy keeping in mind that *B* will adopt the most unfavourable strategy for him, that is, *B* will play that strategy which will provide minimum possible share of profits to *A*. Thus, if *A* decides to choose strategy A_1 then *B* can either choose strategy B_1 or B_2 or B_3. With *A* having adopted strategy A_1, if *B* adopts B_1, the profits to *A* will be ₹ 2; if he adopts B_2 the profits to *A* will be ₹ 8; if he adopts B_3, the profits to *A* will be ₹ 1. It is clear that when *A* has adopted strategy A_1, *B* will cause *A* to get minimum profits (₹ 1) if he plays strategy B_3. Likewise, if *A* decides to select strategy A_2, then *B* would play strategy B_2 and will give in this way minimum possible profits (₹ 3) to A in this case. Again, if A adopts strategy A_3, then *B* will adopt strategy B_1, so as to cause minimum possible profits (₹ 5) to *A* in this case.

It is now obvious that *A* will choose strategy A_3 so that if *B* plays most unfavourable strategy even then he gets profits of ₹ 5 which is greater than theother minimum profits of ₹ 1 and ₹ 3 in case of the selection of strategies A_1 and A_2 respectively. In other words, *A will choose maximum of the minimum profits he gets in three strategies*. For the sake of convenience, minimum profits in each row are written in a new column entitled '*Row Minima*'. Thus while selecting his strategies *A* will look at the column of '*Row Minima*'. A will choose maximum of the row minima, that is, *A* will choose strategy A_3 which gives him maximum (₹ 5) of the minimum profits (₹ 1, 3 and 5). It is clear that *A* will follow *a maximin strategy.*

When *A* has selected strategy A_3 and *B* comes to know of it, then *B* will adopt strategy B_1 because by doing so he will cause minimum possible gains (₹ 5) to *A* and will ensure maximum possible profits to himself. With *A* having adopted strategy A_3, if *B* adopts strategy B_2 or B_3, *A*'s profit will be ₹ 6 or 7 respectively, that is, more than when he adopts strategy B_1. Thus when *A* has selected strategy A_3, *B* will select strategy B_1. With *A* having selected strategy A_3, *B* choosing strategy B_1, A will get profits of ₹ 5 as is seen from his Payoff Matrix in the above table and B will get profits of ₹ 10 – 5 = ₹ 5 (Here, by chance, the shares of the profits of the two are equal, they need not be necessarily equal in all cases.)

Now suppose that *B* has to choose his strategy first before *A* chooses his strategy. While making his choice of a strategy, *B* will also keep in mind that A will adopt the strategy which will be most undesirable for him (*B*). *A*'s worst strategy for *B* will be one which will provide him (*A*) maximum possible profits and therefore reduces the share of profits to *B* to the minimum possible. The same table which shows profits or payoff to *A* can be made use of to explain the strategy to be adopted by *B*.

It will be seen from *A*'s payoff Matrix that if *B* decides to choose strategy B_1, then if *A* chooses strategy A_1, the profits to him will be ₹ 2 (and to B will be ₹ 8); if he chooses strategy A_2 the profits to him will be ₹ 4 (and to B will be ₹ 6); if he chooses strategy A_3, profits to him will be ₹ 5 (to B they will also be ₹ 5). It is thus clear that with B having decided to select strategy B_1, A will choose strategy A_3, because in this way, it will be getting maximum possible profits (₹ 5) and will be rendering the share of profits to B to the minimum possible. Now, if B selects strategy B_2, then A's worst strategy for B will be A_1, in which case share of profits to A will be ₹ 8 as seen from the table, the remaining ₹ 2 will go to B. Likewise, if B selects strategy B_3, A will select strategy A_2 so as to cause maximum possible profits (₹ 9) to him and minimum possible profits (₹ 1) to B.

Given the above reaction pattern of A, what strategy will be selected by B, that is, whether B will adopt strategy B_1 or B_2 or B_3. If he adopts strategy B_1, worst possible for him will be profits to A of ₹ 5 which are maximum in the given column. Similarly, if he adopts strategy B_2 worst possibility for him will be profits to A of ₹ 8 which is maximum in the new column. Further, if B adopts strategy B_3, worst possibility for him will be profits to A of ₹ 9 which is maximum in the column under B_3. In the above table various maxima of the columns have been written in a new row entitled '*Column Maxima*'. The best course of action for B will be to choose *minimum of these maxima of columns*, since by doing so he will ensure minimum possible profits to A and hence maximum possible profits to him. Thus, given the situation as depleted in the above Table 32.3, B will select strategy B_1 which provides to A profits of ₹ 5 which is minimum of the maxima of the column maxima. It follows therefore that B will follow a *minimax strategy*. When B has chosen strategy B_1 and announces it, A will examine his possible strategies and will naturally choose strategy A_3 since it gives him greater possible profits than A_1 or A_2.

We explained above the choice of strategies by A and B separately in two cases, first, when A chooses first before B makes a choice, and secondly when B has to choose first before A's chooses. It has been seen above that, given A's payoff matrix, as shown in the Table 32.3, in both cases A's choice is strategy A_3 and B's choice is strategy B_1. It should be noted that in *the actual game in the real world, neither A nor B has to choose first, they choose simultaneously.* But the foregoing argument nevertheless applies. Given the assumption that each expects worst from his rival, when both have to choose simultaneously, A will look at the row minima of his payoff matrix and will select maximum of the row minima, and B will look at the column maxima of A's payoff-matrix and will choose minimum of the column maxima. Given the A's payoff matrix, A will play *maximin strategy* and B will play *minimax strategy*. Thus even when both choose their strategies simultaneously, A will choose strategy A_3 because it is his maximin strategy and B will choose strategy B_1 because it is his minimax strategy. It is therefore clear that the *result is the same whether A chooses first, B chooses first or both choose simultaneously*.

Equilibrium (Saddle) Point

In payoff matrix in the above table the maximum of the row minima and the minimum of the column maxima are the same, that is, A's maximin strategy coincides with B's minimax strategy. When it happens so, the payoff matrix is said to possess an equilibrium point or, what is also technically called '*saddle point*'. In A's pay off matrix in the Table 32.3, pay-off 5 is an equilibrium or saddle point because the maximum of the row minima is 5 and minimum of the column maxima is also 5. Thus, A by choosing strategy A_3 and B by choosing strategy B_1 are in equilibrium, that is, they will have no incentive to change their strategies. When a payoff-matrix possesses an equilibrium point, then the maximin strategy is the most advantageous strategy open to one firm, *if the other employs a minimax strategy*. Actually, it is because of this coincident pay-off entry 5, in our table above, that the maximin and minimax strategy combination is called an equilibrium point. In other words, when one firm employs a maximin strategy, the other is motivated to employ minimax strategy because that is how it can obtain the largest possible share of the profit. Conversely, if one firm plays minimax strategy, the other is motivated to employ the maximin strategy for the reason just mentioned above. In the words of Prof. Baumol, "*Equilibrium points therefore possess an element of stability in that if one player adopts a strategy consistent with the attainment of such* a *point, the other player is also motivated to do so.*"[2]

It is worth mentioning that when the maximum of row minima is not equal to the minimum of column maxima, that is, when there is no equilibrium or saddle point in the pay-off matrix, then stable equilibrium would not be attained. In such cases, it matters a great deal who plays first and also it is helpful to know rival's strategy in advance. Various methods have been developed to provide solution in such a pay-off matrix which does not contain equilibrium or stable point. One of these methods is to permit the players to employ mixed strategies. A mixed strategy is a combination of two strategies with the probabilities assigned to these strategies. The technique of solving games involving mixed strategies is too complicated and its explanation is therefore not attempted here.

Critical Appraisal of Maximin Strategy

The maximin game theory as applied to the oligopoly problem has been questioned on some grounds. First, the fundamental assumption underlying the game theory, namely, that an oligopolist believes that his rival will do the worst and adopt his strategy keeping this in view has been questioned. It is pointed out that in essence this assumption about the behaviour of the entrepreneur (oligopolist) implies that he minimizes the chance of the maximum loss, that is, his policy is to "play safe". But such behaviour on the part of the oligopolist, it is said, is very pessimistic as well as conservative. In the real world, the entrepreneurs do not adopt such a cautious and pessimistic approach. They seek to increase their profits and share of the market and for that they often take risks. Professors Ferguson and Kreps rightly remark : "The game theory may very well describe the type of the entrepreneur who is primarily intent upon maintaining solvency. It is a much less accurate description of the dynamic businessman who is constantly in quest of profit."[3]

Secondly, it is pointed out that the entrepreneurs in the real world do not possess the amount of knowledge assumed in the game theory. The entrepreneurs do not know even all the various strategies open to them, much less those open to their competitors. Moreover, the real world involves a good deal of uncertainty which has not been incorporated and also cannot be easily incorporated in the game theory.

In the third place, it is said that the oligopoly game is not a strictly adverse game, nor a constant sum game as granted in the theory of games. Contrary to these assumptions, the reduction in price by an oligopolist leads to the increase in the total quantity demanded and not a mere shift of customers from others. Besides, oligopolists do not fight over a lot of profits of a fixed size.

There is another flaw in the game theory. For the game theory to provide a definite solution, both the duopolists must be prudent, that is to say, both should play their maximin or minimax strategies. When one of the duopolists does not possess an adequate knowledge or is not very prudent or is prepared to take risks, then for any of these reasons he will not

2. William J. Baumol, *Economic Theory and Operations Analysis,* PHI, 2nd edition.
3. C.E. Ferguson and J.M. Kreps, *Principles of Economics,* p. 531.

play minimax strategy. If this is so, then the adoption of maximin strategy by others will be unprofitable. In our example above, if B chooses strategy B_2 for any of the above reasons, then the selection of maximin strategy A_3 by A will not give him maximum possible share of the profits. With B having selected non-minimax strategy B_2; A will get maximum possible share of the profits if he plays strategy A_1. It is thus clear that when one of the duopolists is not prudent, the game theory cannot provide a solution. In the words of Professor Baumol "*the prudent maximin strategy is only guaranteed to be good when playing against another prudent man.*"[4]

It is evident from the above criticism that Neumann-Morgenstern game theory does not provide a complete and all agreed solution to the oligopoly problem. To quote Professors Ferguson and Kreps again, "We can reasonably say that while the game theory points out some of the crucial aspects of competitive situations, it is not a model that offers a complete solution to the oligopoly problem".[5]

THE PRISONERS' DILEMMA AND OLIGOPOLY THEORY

The firms working in oligopolistic markets make decisions in the face of uncertainty about how their rivals will react to their moves. As explained above, game theory is a mathematical technique of analysing the behaviour of rival firms with regard to changes in prices, output and advertisement expenditure in the situations of conflicts of interest among individuals or firms. An important game model that has significant implications for the behaviour of the oligopolists is popularly known as prisoner's dilemma. Model of prisoner's dilemma explains how rivals behaving selfishly act contrary to their mutual or common interests. We first explain prisoner's dilemma with an example given originally while propounding this model.

Suppose two persons, Billa and Ranga have been caught for committing a bank robbery. Suppose the prosecution has no enough evidence for their committing the crime. In order to procure confession from them, they are interrogated in two separate rooms so that they cannot communicate with each other. While interrogating each accused, the police offers to Billa "If you confess to the crime (that is, cooperate with the police) while the other keeps silent (*i.e.* does not confess), you will be given imprisonment for only a short period, say, 1 year only but punish the other with 10 years imprisonment. If the other also confesses, then both of you would be sentenced to jail for 5 years". It may however be known that if both prisoners do not confess each can be jailed only for two years. The choices open to each accused are presented in payoff matrix which refers here to years of imprisonment in Table 32.4.

Table 32.4. *Prisoners' Dilemma*

		Ranga's Choice	
		Confesses	*Doesn't confess*
Billa's Choice	Confesses	Ranga : 5 years Billa : 5 years	Ranga : 10 years Billa : 1 year
	Doesn't confess	Ranga : 1 year Billa : 10 years	Ranga : 2 years Billa : 2 years

4. William J. Baumol, *Economic Theory and Operations Analysis*, p. 352.
5. *Op. cit.*, p. 531.

It will be seen that the outcome (*i.e.* length of sentence to each) is determined by the specific strategy, (that is, choice) adopted by each prisoner. The two strategies (choices) refer to (*i*) confess and (*ii*) and does not confess. If both Ranga and Billa confess, each gets 5 years imprisonment. If one confesses, but the other does not, the one who confesses (*i.e.* cooperate with the police) gets a very light punishment, namely, imprisonment for 1 year only and the one who doesn't confess is sentenced for 10 years imprisonment. It will be further seen from the table that if both do not confess (that is, they remain loyal and faithful to each other and do not cooperate with the police), both are sentenced to 2 years imprisonment.

Now, each prisoner faces an uncertainty regarding how the other person will behave, that is, whether or not he will confess. Though each person has to make an independent choice whether to confess or not but *the outcome, i.e. payoff depends on what the other does.*

Now, under these circumstances what choice will be made by the prisoners when they cannot communicate with each other and have to choose between the two alternatives independently. *The model of prisoners' dilemma suggests that both behaving selfishly and working in self-interest confess to the crime and cheat each other.* Since both confess, each will get imprisonment for 5 years. Why do they make this choice and confess can be shown as under. Take Ranga first, most probably, he would confess when he does not know how his co-accused will act. Ranga would reason like this : If I don't confess it is very likely that I will be imprisoned for 10 years as the other prisoner will most probably confess. If I confess, I will get 5 years imprisonment if the other one also confesses, and only one year imprisonment if he does not confess. So in the presence of uncertainty about the other person's choice, and behaving in self-interest, Ranga is likely to confess. Billa too reasoning similarly would confess. As a result, both prisoners would be sentenced for 5 years, though they would have received a lighter sentence of only two years if they had not confessed and remained loyal to each other. However, *it is self-interest which leads each prisoner to confess and prevents them from attaining the best solution* for themselves (2 years imprisonment) if both do not confess to the crime and remain loyal to each other. But the decision of each prisoner in favour of confession is quite rational because each person works in self-interest and tries to make the "*best*" of the "*worst outcomes*" in an uncertain situation.

Prisoners' Dilemma and Instability of a Cartel

The game of prisoners' dilemma is of important relevance to the oligopoly theory. The incentive to cheat by a member of a cartel (*i.e.* in the model of collusive oligopoly), and eventual collapse of cartel agreement is better explained with the model of prisoners' dilemma. Instead of two prisoners we take the two firms *A* and *B* which have entered into a cartel agreement and fixed the price and output each has to produce and sell (*i.e.* share of the market). The choice problem facing each member firm of the cartel is whether to cooperate and abide by the agreement and thus sharing the joint monopoly profits or to cheat the other and try to make higher individual profits. But if both cheat and violate the agreement, the cartel would breakdown and profits would fall to the competitive level. We will show that though both would lose by cheating others but, as seen in case of prisoners dilemma, their selfish behaviour leads them to cheat others. The payoff matrix for two member firms of a cartel from the various combinations of choices to be made by them is presented in Table 32.5.

Table 32.5 *Payoff Matrix for Cartel Members*

		Firm A	
		Cheat	*Cooperate*
Firm *B*	Cheat (lower the price)	A : 5 lakhs B : 5 lakhs	A : 2 lakhs B : 25 lakhs
	Cooperate	A : 25 lakhs B : 2 lakhs	A : 15 lakhs B : 15 lakhs

It will be seen from this table if both firms cooperate and abide by the cartel agreement, they share monopoly profits; 15 lakhs to each of them (right-hand bottom). If both firms cheat, they violate the agreement and profits to each firm fall to the competitive level, ₹ 5 lakhs to each firm (left-hand top). If firm *A* cheats, while firm *B* abides by the agreement, firm *B*s profits drop to low level of ₹ 2 lakhs and *A*'s profits rise to ₹ 25 lakhs (left hand bottom). On the other hand, if firm *B* cheats and firm *A* adheres to the agreement, profits of *A* decline to ₹ 2 lakhs and *B*s profits shoot up to ₹ 25 lakhs (left-hand top).

It is evident from the payoff matrix that from the different choices made by the firms, each firm has a strong incentive to cheat. Under the prevailing circumstances, *A*'s best strategy is to cheat rather than cooperate. The same is true for firm *B* whose best strategy is also to cheat. Again, it is the pursuit of self-interest rather than common interest that prompts the firms to cheat other. Thus both firms will cheat and this will bring about the breakdown of the cartel.

Graphical Illustration: The strong incentive to cheat on the part of cartel members and consequently causing a breakdown of a cartel is graphically illustrated in Figure 32.1 where *DD'* is the market demand curve facing the cartel consisting of two firms *A* and *B*. MC_a and MC_b are the marginal cost curves of the firms *A* and *B* respectively. Summing up horizontally the cost curves we get the combined marginal cost curves MC_{a+b}. The cartel maximises its profits by equating *MR* with MC_{a+b} and accordingly output *OQ* and price *OP* is fixed. The two firms *A* and *B* produce and sell q_a and q_b respectively which is the agreed market share of the two firms (Note that output $OQ = Oq_a + Oq_b$.

It will be seen from panel (1) that, at the price *OP*, if the firm *A* increases its output from q_a to q'_a, it can increase its profits by the shaded area *FKJ*. Similarly, firm *B* also thinks that

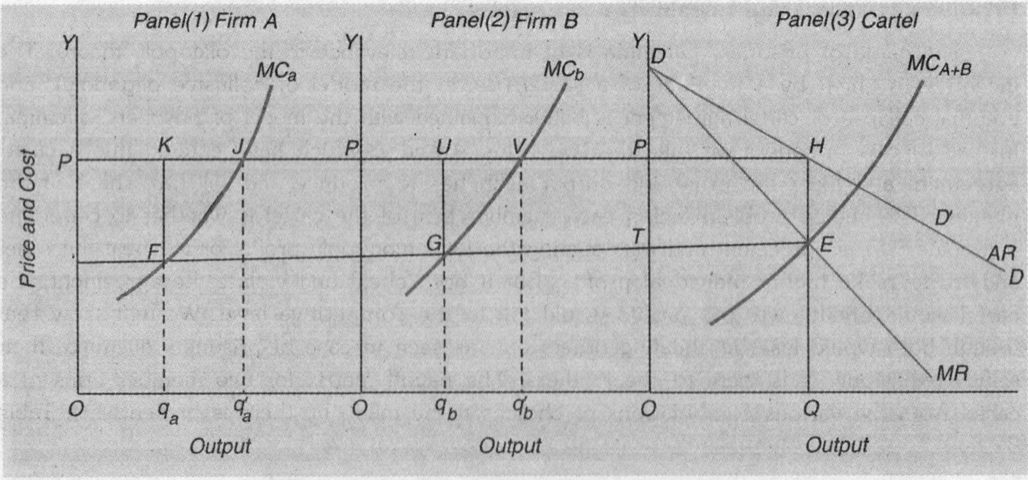

Fig. 32.1. *Instability of Cartel due to Cheating*

given the price OP if it rises its output to q'_b, it can increase its profits by the shaded area by the GUV. Thus, to increase their own profits the firms have incentive to cheat by trying to produce and sell more at the agreed price. It is therefore the working of inner pressures and promotion of self-interest by cartel members that accounts for the instability of cartel arrangements.

REPEATED GAMES AND TIT-FOR-TAT STRATEGY

In our analysis of Prisoner's Dilemma it was assumed that game was played just once. While applying prisoner's dilemma type game to the case of a cartel we concluded that oligopolists like the prisoners lacking trust in each other and behaving selfishly cheated each other. This resulted in bad outcome (*i.e.* lower or no profits) for them. However, the firms facing prisoners' dilemma can increase their profits if they cooperate with each other. But such cooperation is unlikely to occur in a prisoners' dilemma type game played only once. In this game of prisoners' dilemma the players have only single opportunity to play a game (*i.e.* to confess or not). But in the real world oligopolists have to play games repeatedly as they have to set price and output over and over again.

In case of the working of a cartel at every point of time each firm has to decide whether to cheat or not. Behaving selfishly and having no trust in others, all member firms of a cartel cheat (that is, increase their output or undercut price) and as a result make only small profits. However, in case of repeated games the oligopolists may adopt a cooperative behaviour which enables them to earn large profits. Thus, when oligopolists play a repeated game, the analysis of a prisoners' dilemma type game played only once may not be correct.

In the case of a game played repeatedly players come to know how the others react to their moves and this in turn changes their strategic behaviour. Thus, in case of a repeated game, one firm has the opportunity to penalise the other for his previous bad behaviour. In this context it has been suggested that *tit-for-tat strategy* is the optimal strategy that will ensure cooperative behaviour of the players participating in a game[6]. Let us suppose an oligopolist firm *A* adopts a cooperative behaviour and charge a high price. Tit-for-tat strategy means that firm *A* will continue to charge high price so long as its rival firm *B* also continue to do so (*i.e.* adopts cooperative behaviour). But if firm *B* cheats and undercuts its price in a round, then in the next round firm *A* will retaliate and will also set a low price. Thus, the firm *B* knowing that the firm *A* is adopting a tit for tat strategy will have to take into account the possibility of the rival firm *A* retaliating in the next round. In case of repeated game, this tit-for-tat strategy results in cooperative behaviour among oligopolists.

However, whether tit-for-tat strategy will be viable depends on whether the repeated game is played indefinite or finite number of times. Let us first explain the outcome when repeated game is played indefinitely. We assume that there are two oligopolistic firms *A* and *B* and there are two possible strategies, namely, (1) charging a high price, and (2) charging a low price. The firms adopt tit-for-tat strategies. It may be mentioned again that according to tit-for-tat strategy *what one firm does in the current period, the other firm will do in the next period.* In the case of game of prisoners' dilemma which is played only once, if one firm cheats, the retaliation by the other firm in the next period does not arise as the game is over in the first round itself. However, in case of the repeated game, the other player (firm in our case) can penalise the other firm in the next period for any cheating by any player in the current period. It is assumed that a firm knows that its rival firm is adopting tit-for-tat strategy.

6. See R. Axelord, "*The Evolution of Cooperation*" (New York : Basic Books, 1984).

How tit-for-tat strategy is an optimal strategy and will result in cooperative behaviour on the part of the oligopolists is illustrated in payoff matrix given in Table 32.6.

Table 32.6 *Payoff Matrix* (Figures in million rupees)

		Firm B's Strategies	
		Low Price	*High Price*
Firm A's Strategies	Low Price	A's Profits : 10	A's Profits : 100
		B's Profits : 10	B's Profits : –50
	High Price	A's Profits : –50	A's Profits : 50
		B's Profits : 100	B's Profits : 50

If game is *played only once* as in the above case of prisoners' dilemma, both firms will cheat and charge low price and as will be seen from payoff matrix firms will earn profits only ₹ 10 million (see top left-hand box) while if they had cooperated and charged high price, they could have earned ₹ 50 million each (see bottom right hand box). Under tit-for-tat-strategy in case of repeated game played for an indefinite period, suppose firm *A* starts with charging a high price and decides to continue charging the high price so long as the other firm also does likewise. But when the firm *B* cheats, that is, charges a low price, *B*'s profits rises to 100 millions in that round while the firm *A*'s profits have become negative (–50 million). Now, under the tit-for-tat strategy, the firm *A* will retaliate in the next round and set a low price. When both charge low price, profits of each are 10 million (see upper left-hand box of Table 32.6). As the game is repeated indefinitely round after round, the cumulative loss of profits suffered by firm *B* will outweight his gain of profits in one round when it undercut the price. Thus, cheating (*i.e.* undercutting price in the present example) when the rivals are pursuing tit-for-tat strategy is not a profitable proposition. In this way the firms will learn that cooperative behaviour is the best course of action when each firm is pursuing the tit-for-tat strategy. When both cooperate and charge a high price, each firm will earn profits of ₹ 50 million in each round. (See bottom right-hand box in payoff matrix of Table 32.6). Thus, Hal Varian writes, "*The tit-for-tat strategy does very well because it offers an immediate punishment for defection. It is also a forgiving strategy. It punishes the other player only once for each defection. If he falls into line and starts to cooperate, then tit for tat will reward the other player with cooperation. It appears to be a remarkably good mechanism for the efficient outcome in a prisoner's dilemma that will be played an indefinite number of times.*"[7]

Let us now consider the case when the game is repeated a *finite* number of times, say in 10 rounds). Both players know that the game will be played 10 times and also that each is pursuing tit-for-tat strategy. Let us first consider 10th round which by assumption is the last round when the game will be played between the two firms. Whether they will cooperate each charging a high price or they will cheat each other by charging a low price. If firm *B* believes that its rival firm is rational will reason like this: Even knowing that the firm *A* is playing tit-for-tat strategy, the firm *B* will think since 10th round is the last round of playing the game and after that since the game is over, the firm *A* will have no chance to retaliate. Therefore, firm *B* will charge high price for the first 9 rounds but will choose to cheat, that is, will charge low price and make a large profits in the last 10th round (This is shown in the *bottom* left-hand side box of the payoff matrix of Table 32.6).

However, firm *A* will also reason likewise and will charge high price in the first 9 rounds

7. Hal R. Varian, *Intermediate Microeconomics : A Modern Approach* (New York : WW Norton & Co., Fourth Edition, 1997,) p. 487.

but will plan to cheat (charge low price) in the last 10th round and will hope to make a large profits in the last 10th round thinking that firm *B* will have no chance to retaliate thereafter.

Thus, both thinking rationally will decide to choose the low price in the last 10th round and will not cooperate with each other. Hall Varian rightly writes, "Players cooperative because they hope that cooperation will induce further cooperation in the future. But this requires that there will always be the possibility of future play. Since there is no possibility of future play in the last round, no one will cooperate then".[8]

But what about next to the 10th round, that is, the 9th round. Firm *B* will reason that it should charge low price in this next to the last round because in any case there will be no cooperation between the two in the last round. But, of course, the Firm A being equally rational will also reason likewise and will plan to charge low price in the 9th round (*i.e.* next to the last round). The same reasoning can be repeated by both the firms for undercutting price, that is, for charging a low price in the 8th and earlier rounds as well, that is, for the rounds 8th, 7th, 6th etc. till the first round. Thus, when the game is played a *finite* number of times, even while pursuing tit-for-tat strategy the two firms will opt for *non-cooperative behaviour.* Thus, even with tit-for-tat strategy in case of repeated games to be played a *finite* number of times, we are stuck in 'Prisoners' Dilemma' without the outcome of the cooperative behaviour.

But cooperative outcome can come about even in this finite number of time for which the game is to be played if *a firm has a doubt about its competitor's rationality in pursuing tit-for-tat strategy* and its ability to reason out the logical implications of a finite time horizon as explained above. Thus, if competing firms have doubts about whether the other firm is playing tit-for-tat or playing tit-for-tat blindly, this will make cooperative behaviour a good strategy. Besides, in this case of finite number of times the game is to be played cooperative behaviour can be regarded as a good strategy by the competing firms *if the time is long enough and the firms are uncertain about how long will they be competing.* Thus, "Most managers do not know how long they or their firms will be competing with their rivals and this also serves to make cooperative behaviour a good strategy. Although the number of months that the firms compete is probably finite, managers are unlikely to know just what the number is. As a result, the unraveling argument that begins with a clear expectation of undercutting in the last month no longer applies. As with an infinitely repeated game, it will be rational to play tit-for-tat".[9] Thus, in view of the fact that in most oligopolistic markets the game is in fact repeated over a long period and uncertain length of time and managers have doubts about how rationally their competitors behave, in case of repeated game for a finite number of times, the Prisoners' dilemma can have cooperative outcome.[10]

STRATEGIC MOVES

In the earlier sections it has been emphasised that oligopolists must realise that their own profits depend not only on their own decision and behaviour but also on the decision and behaviour of their rivals. This shows the importance of strategic moves by the oligopolists to enhance their profits. By making certain strategic moves an oligopolist can gain competitive advantage in the market. Thomas Schelling of Harvard University who has made an important contribution to the theory of strategic decision making defines the concept of strategic move in

8. Hall R. Varian, op. cit., p. 486.
9. See Pindyek and Rubinfeld, op. cit., p. 466.
10. This result is based on the original research work done by David Kreps, Paul Milgrom, John Roberts, and Roberts Wilson, "Rational Cooperation in the Finitely Repeated Prisoners' Dilemma, *Journal of Economic Theory,* 1982, pp. 245-252."

the following words : "*A strategic move is one that influences the other person's choice in a manner favourable to one's self, by affecting the other person's expectations on how one's self will behave*"[11] For example, if Maruti Udyog threatens to retaliate by cutting the price of their cars to a level that would cause losses to its rival firms which produce Santro and Indica cars if they reduce their prices, this move of Maruti Udyog is a strategic move. This is because this threat is intended to ensure that the rival firms do not cut the prices of their cars.

Threat, Commitment and Credibility

For the strategic move of giving threat to be successful, there must be *commitment* that the firm making a threat will definitely carry it out. *Only when there is commitment to carry out a threat that it becomes credible.* If there is no commitment to carry out the threat, it will be an empty threat and will therefore not have the desired effect on the behaviour of the rivals. If a firm can convince its rival firms that it is committed to a particular move that it is making, then the rivals may cooperate without retaliating because they may think that they would lose more than they would gain from a long period of conflict with the firm making a move.

When a threat is credible is illustrated in the payoff matrix of firms *A* and *B* given in Table 32.7 where the profits of the two firms making different brands of cars are shown when they charge low price or high price for their cars. This payoff matrix shows that charging a high price is a dominant strategy for firm *A*, that is, whatever strategy (whether of charging a high price or low price) the rival firm *B* pursues, the strategy of charging a high price is optimal

Table 32.7 *Payoff Matrix for a Pricing Game* (in lacs)

		Firm *B*	
		Low Price	*High Price*
Firm A	Low Price	20, 20	20, 10
	High Price	30, 40	50, 30

(Note: *The first number in the pair shows profits of firm A, the second number shows profits of firm B*).

for firm *A*. Thus, if firm *B* charges the low price, the firm *A* will earn profits of ₹ 20 lakhs if it charges a low price and ₹ 30 lakhs of it charges a high price. On the other hand, if the firm *B* charges a high price, the firm *A* will earn ₹ 20 lakhs if it charges a low price and ₹ 50 lakhs if it charges a high price. Thus, whether the firm *B* plays a low price strategy or a high price strategy, for firm *A*, high price strategy is the optimal strategy to adopt. It will be seen further from the payoff matrix of Table 32.7, that the firm *A* will charge the high price, the firm B will opt for charging a low price and in this way will earn ₹ 40 lakhs instead of ₹ 30 lakhs if it charges the high price.

Under these circumstances if firm *A* threatens firm *B* that it will charge a low price, this threat will be *incredible* or empty because the firm *B* knows that by charging a low price, the firm *A* will cause its profits to fall to ₹ 20 lakhs. Being an incredible threat the firm *B* will not take it seriously. As explained above, one way to make the threat credible is to make it binding and irreversible. Thus, if a firm threatens to enter a particular market, it can make its threat credible if the potential firm buys a plant rather than lease it or enters into a long-term contract for buying raw materials. This shows that the firm which gives a threat to enter has made an

---

11. Thomas C. Schelling, *The Strategy of Conflict*, (New York : Oxford University Press, 1960). Another important work that discusses strategic moves is by M. Porter, *Competitive Strategy* (New York : Free Press, 1980).

irreversible commitment, and will therefore enter the market, come what may and this makes the threat credible. Take another example. If a firm commits to a price reduction if its rival firm lowers its price, then to make its commitment credible, it can make verbal or written agreement with the customers that it will match any price cut by its rival. On the other hand, if a particular firm has the image that it can easily ignore its particular commitment that it makes, then commitment is not credible and it will not pay much attention to the commitment made.

Another way for a firm to make the threat credible is to *build a reputation of irrationality* for carrying out its threat even if it has to lose some profits or even incur losses. This irrational reputation is developed when a firm has actually carried out its threat several times in the past (even at the expense of its profits). Thus, the threat of a firm with reputation of irrationality is a credible threat and its rivals will take serious note of it. Consider payoff matrix of Table 32.7 again. If the firm *A* is charging a high price and the *firm B is charging the low price,* they are earning profits of ₹ 30 and 40 lakhs respectively (see bottom left-hand corner of Table 32.7). Now, if the firm *A* lowers its price to carry out its threat, then *B* will be induced to charge high price and as a result both firms will be charging high price and firm *A*'s profit will rise to ₹ 50 lakhs, but profits of the firm *B* will fall (see bottom right-hand corner). This is because in case of firm *A* lowering price and with firm *B* also charging a low price each will be making lower profits of ₹ 20 Lakhs. It is due to fall in profits as a result of firm *A* carrying out its threat that firm *B* is induced to charge the high price. It is important to note that though profits of the firm *B* has fallen to ₹ lakhs because under threat from the firm *A* it has decided to cooperate, it is still greater than profits of ₹ 20 lakhs that it would earn if firm *A* had actually carried out its threat and both charged the low price.

In addition to what has been said about credible commitment, it may be noted that *for a threat to be credible, the firm's commitment must be backed up with assets, skills and expertise, financial and technological powers to carry out the commitment.* Besides, a firm's commitments are more credible if it has reputation and a long history of adhering to its commitments.

However, for tit-for-tat strategy to be successful certain conditions must be fulfilled. First, a reasonably *stable set of players* (that is, firms) is required for the successful working of tit-for-tat strategy. If the players (firms) change quite frequently co-operative behaviour between them is not likely to develop. Second, in tit-for-tat strategy for cooperative behaviour to be achieved, there must be *a small number of players* (firms). In case of a large number of competing firms, it is difficult to know what each firm is doing. As a result, cooperation cannot be enforced and generally breaks down when there are many firms confronting each other. Third, for the success of tit for tat strategy to induce cooperative behaviour it is assumed that each firm can quickly detect cheating by others and is able and willing to retaliate if the rivals do cheating. Fourth, *the demand and cost conditions must remain stable* for the success of tit-for-tat strategy. The failure to cooperate is quite often the result of changing demand or cost conditions. Uncertainties about demand or costs make it difficult for the firms to arrive at an implicit understanding of what cooperative behaviour requires. Lastly, as explained above, tit-for-tat strategy to induce cooperative behaviour, *the game is to be played either indefinitely* or for a long *uncertain* number of times.

ENTRY DETERRENCE

The existing firms, especially the monopolists try to prevent the entry of new firms as the entry of new firms reduce the profits of the existing firms. An important strategy for the existing firm to deter the entry of new firms in the market is the threat to lower price and thereby inflict losses on the potential entrant. However, such a threat by the existing firm will work only if it is credible. To illustrate whether threat is credible or not, consider the payoff matrix shown in Table 32.8. From this payoff matrix in Table 32.8, it follows that the threat by the existing firm *A* that if the potential firm *B* enters the market, as explained above, it will

Table 32.8 *Payoff Matrix* *(Profits in lakhs)*

		Firm B (Potential Entrant)	
		Enter	*Stayout*
Firm A	Low Price	4, - 2	6, 0
(Existing Firm)	High Price	7, 2	10, 0

lower the price and impose loss on *B*, is not credible. It will be seen from the payoff matrix of Table 32.8 that before entry of firm *B* the firm A is charging high price and is making profits of ₹ 10 lakhs. (See bottom right-hand corner). Now, on entry by firm *B* in the market, if the existing firm charges a high price, the profits of the existing firm *A* are 7 lakhs and of the new firm *B* are 2 lakhs, and, on the other hand, if the existing firm *A* lowers the price to carry out its threat, the profits of firm A are 4 lakhs[12] and the new firm *B* incurs a loss of 2 lakhs. This shows that despite the entry of new firm *B*, it is profitable for the existing firm to charge a high price and earn profits of ₹ 7 lakhs which are greater than ₹ 4 lakhs in case it lowers the price in accordance with the threat held out. This, shows that threat is *not creditable. Unless the firm is irrational, it will not lower the price on the entry of new firm B.* And since the potential entrant knows this, the threat will not work and will not prevent the firm *B* from entering the market.

To make the threat credible the existing firm has to commit itself to resist the entry of the new firm *B* even at the expense of its profits. One way to make a credible commitment to resist the entry of the potential firm, is the *expansion of its capacity* by the existing firm before it is needed, that is, by *building excess capacity.*[13] Since for building of excess capacity, the existing firm will incur costs, there will be a change in the payoff matrix. The new payoff matrix given in Table 32.9 is the same as in the previous Table 32.8 except that after building

Table 32.9. *Payoff Matrix with Credible Commitment*

		Firm B (*Potential entrant*)	
		Enter	*Stayout*
Firm A	Low Price	4, - 2	6, 0
(Existing firm)	High Price	3, 2	5, 0

excess capacity, firm *A*'s profits are ₹ 3 lakhs if he continues to charge the high price and ₹ 4 lakhs if it lowers the price. The profits of the existing firm *A* are now smaller even with the

12. Note that fall in profits of the existing firm is due to (1) the market will now be shared between the two firms, and (2) lowering of price to deter entry.
13. For an elaborate analysis of the use of excess capacity to prevent entry, see J. Tirole *The Theory of Industrial Organisation* (Cambridge, MA : MIT Press, 1988).

high price charged because of the costs incurred on building new capacity and sharing of the market with the new entrant. On the other hand, in case of low price being charged on the entry of new firm, the profits are the same, namely 4 lakhs as in the previous payoff in Table 32.8. This is because at the low price, the sales of the existing firm will increase resulting in greater revenue and as a result it will be able to utilise a part of the extra capacity built.

Thus, with low price the increase in revenue may cancel out the increase in costs due to the addition of extra capacity and therefore profits of the existing firm *A* remains the same by charging a low price. However, charging a low price by firm *A*, will cause losses of ₹ 2 lakhs to the new entrant (see upper left-hand corner). Thus, *realising that by entering the market, it will suffer a loss, the firm B will not enter the market and stay out.* Thus building of excess capacity before it is needed the existing firm commits itself to lowering price if the firm *B* dares to enter the market and thus makes its threat credible and deters the entry of the potential firm. Having built excess productive capacity, the existing firm *A* will charge a low price and make a profit of ₹ 4 lakhs instead of ₹ 3 lakhs if it charges a high price. Since the new firm *B* on entry will have to sell the product at the low price it will suffer a loss of ₹ 2 lakhs if it entered the market. Therefore, the firm *B* would not enter market and stay out. Thus, the existing firm *A* has succeeded in deterring entry by holding out a credible threat.

An alternative to building excess capacity is *creating a reputation for irrationality* in preventing entry of potential firms in the market even if it causes decline in profits for quite a long time. Thus, when a firm has good reputation for behaving irrationally, then even given the payoff matrix of Table 32.8, it will succeed in deterring entry. The reputation of irrationality of the existing firm creates a credible threat of price warfare if the potential firms enter the industry. As a matter of fact, in the real world it is reputation for irrationality that seems to work for deterring entry.

QUESTIONS FOR REVIEW

1. Distinguish between cooperative game and non-cooperative game. Give examples.
2. Explain a dominant strategy. How is a stable equilibrium reached when a firm pursues its dominant strategy.
3. What is Nash Equilibrium ? Does equilibrium in a prisoners' dilemma game represent Nash Equilibrium ?
4. What is prisoners' dilemma? How is it used to explain the instability of a cartel ?
5. Explain Neumann-Morgenstern theory of game ? On what grounds it has been criticised ?
6. What is a tit-for-tat strategy ? Why is it rational strategy when Prisoners' Dilemma type game is infinitely repeated ?
7. Explain the Prisoners' Dilemma game when it is repeated 15 times and both players are rational. Is tit-for-tat strategy optimal in this case ?
8. What is a "strategic move"? What are the conditions required for strategic move to be successful ?
9. What is a credible threat ? How can a threat be made credible ?
10. How does an incumbent firm succeed in deterring entry into the market by potential competitors ?
11. Can a threat of a price war deter entry by new firms ? What actions might a firm take to make this threat credible ?

PART – VI

Capital Budgeting and Decision Making Under Risk and Uncertainty

- Capital Budgeting : Long-Term Investment Analysis
- Cost of Capital
- Decision Making Under Risk and Uncertainty

Capital Budgeting : Long-Term Investment Analysis

Introduction

Most of the principles of managerial economics discussed so far focus on the analysis of short-run decision making problems of a business firm. For example, deciding about how much price of a product should be fixed, how much quantity of output should be produced so as to maximise profits and similarly how much labour or any other factor be used to minimise cost for a given level of output, or maximise output for a given level of cost are all important short-run decision making problems. In this chapter, however, we will be concerned with the analysis of decisions which have long-run implications for a firm. What new fixed assets, plant and capital equipment be acquired or built up so as to increase the value of the firm and its long-run profitability? Should old capital equipment be replaced by new one embodying the latest technology; should new product be launched to broaden the product line; should a rival firm be taken over to eliminate the competition and expand its outlets. All of these and other similar decisions require long-term investment analysis.

The decisions regarding the above mentioned issues are of crucial importance for determining the long-run profitability of a firm. It should be noted that the *basic objective of a firm is to make those decisions that will increase the value of a firm.* By the value of a firm we mean present value of all future profits or *net cash flows* accruing to the firm. To increase the value of a firm, decisions regarding long-term investment or what is also *capital expenditure* must be made. In this chapter we will first describe issues and problems involved in capital budgeting, that is, analysis of long-term investment projects. Secondly, we will critically examine the various criteria which have been proposed for evaluating capital projects as to whether or not they should be selected for investment. Thirdly, we will explain the choice of investment project from the various alternative projects.

Capital and Investment : Stocks Versus Flows

Investment leads to the increase in the stock of capital. The capital is an important factor of production in the modern economy. But capital has special features which distinguish it from other factors of production. The demand for other factors such as labour depends on their marginal revenue product (*MRP*) in a given period and the price that has to be paid for it. However, capital is a durable factor which can last and go on contributing to the production of goods for several years in future.

Firms sometimes take capital on rent per period for its use just as they hire workers for a monthly wage. But quite frequently the firms directly purchase the capital assets such as plant, factory buildings, machines and incur a lot of investment expenditure. When a firm undertakes investment expenditure for buying a machine or building a factory it has to compare the cost it has to incur *now* (*i.e.* in the present) with the additional profits or revenue it will generate for a number of years in the future. Therefore, while purchasing a capital asset a firm has to estimate how the stream of future profits generated by it is worth today. This problem is not faced while deciding about hiring of labour or purchasing of raw materials. This is because in deciding about hiring labour or purchasing raw materials the firm merely compares their current marginal revenue product (*MRP*) with the wage of workers or the price of raw material, it has to pay. In other words, the element of time does not figure in the calculations by a firm when it hires or purchases labour and raw materials.

Since a capital asset goes on yielding profits or revenue for a firm for several years from now, the firm has to find the present value of the stream of cash flows in the form of profits or revenue and compare it with the cost it has to incur on purchasing or building it. In the calculation of the net present value of capital asset, rate of interest plays a crucial role. Besides, since future flows of profits may be higher or lower than expected, the firms have to take into account the risk and uncertainty involved while making investment in a particular capital asset.

Investment, as mentioned above, is addition to the stock of capital. Measurement of capital as a factor of production is different from that of other factors of production. *Capital is measured as a stock* such as the amount of machines, equipment etc. a firm possesses for production, while other factors of production such as labour and raw materials are measured as *flows* such as the number of labour hours used for production per week, per month etc. It may also be noted that *output of the firm is also measured in terms of flows*, that is, output per week, per month or per year.

Consider the case of a producer who manufactures ceiling fans and has set up a factory equipped with required machines and other capital goods worth Rs 5 crores. He uses labour, copper and steel which are the variable factors to use them along with the capital stock to manufacture ceiling fans. The output of ceiling fans per month is 1000 ceiling fans which are sold at Rs 800 per fan with total sales proceeds per month equal to Rs 800,000. Suppose Re 250 is the variable cost per fan and therefore total variable cost of 1000 fans per month amounts to Rs. 2,50,000. Thus Re. 5,50,000 are the profits made by the producer per month for several months in future. Thus, profits of Rs. 5,50,000 (*i.e.* 8,00,000 – 2,50,000) are also flows which will accrue to the producer per month in future. Thus, capital stock of Rs 5 crores yields to the firm the flow of profit of Rs. 5,50,000 per month.

Now an important question is whether investment made to build the capital stock worth Re 5 crores to yield monthly profits of Rs. 5,50,000 in future is a economically sound decision. To examine this we have to convert the future cash flows of profits into their present value by using market rate of interest and then compare it with the cost of capital built up. If the present value of the flows of money profits for several months in future exceeds the cost of capital stock built up, the investment made will be profitable and would therefore increase the wealth of the firm.

On the other hand, if the present value of future cash flows of profits calculated by discounting at the market rate of interest falls short of the cost of capital investment, it will not pay the firm to undertake to invest in the capital stock. This is because the same monetary funds can be invested in bank's fixed deposits or in purchasing bonds or other interest-bearing financial assets to earn market rate of interest.

It follows from above that evaluating profitability of capital investment in projects we employ the concept of discounted value of the stream of cash flows of profits generated by that capital investment. In what follows we first explain the way in which present discounted value of future cash flows is obtained and then discuss the present value criterion of evaluating a capital investment. We will then compare this criterion with the alternative investment criterion of *Internal Rate of Return* (IRR).

INVESTMENT DECISION

Expectations and Investment. As mentioned above, an important feature of capital is that it yields returns over a period of time. Therefore, investment decision maker must have expectations about how much revenue and profits a particular capital investment will yield over a period of time for which it is used for production of a product or products. Investment in a new plant will yield more profits if the demand for a firm's product increases and its price remains high. The investment in the same plant will yield less revenue and therefore lower profits if in future the economy goes into recession or with development of new products consumers start disliking the product produced with that plant. *Thus, expectations about future earnings from the investment play a crucial role in making investment decision.*

Cost of Investment. Along with expected profits, cost of investment has also to be taken into account while making an investment decision. Investment projects have to be financed. If a firm borrows from financial market to make investment, it will have to pay interest over time. Thus interest on borrowed funds is cost of investment that it decides to make. If instead of borrowing the firm uses its own funds for making investment, there is *opportunity cost* involved. This opportunity cost is the market rate of interest at which it can *lend* its funds to others. The investment will not be undertaken unless it is expected to yield more than the market interest rate.

Capital Budgeting : Meaning

Capital budgeting which is also known *as long-term investment analysis* is the process of planning for investment expenditure on capital projects. Capital or investment projects are those from which returns (or cash flows) are expected to continue beyond one year in future (that is, for several future years). *Expenditure on capital projects, which yield returns beyond one year is called capital expenditure.* Thus, a capital expenditure (or what is also called long-term investment) is defined as an outlay that is expected to generate a stream of future cash flows that accrue to a firm beyond one year. The important examples of capital projects are investment in new factories, machinery, automobiles, trucks, expenditure on research and development, expenditure on advertising campaigns are capital projects as returns from them accrue beyond one year.

Importance of Capital Budgeting

The importance of capital budgeting, that is, planning long-term capital expenditure is that it has a long-term effect on the performance of an enterprise. Capital expenditure affects long-term profitability and leads to the increase in the value of a firm. It indicates such things as when expansion in productive capacity of the firm will take place, what type of products will be produced, what new markets will be entered, where the new plant will be located, what type of technology will be used? It is thus clear that capital budgeting should be carefully done because capital expenditure is both very costly to make and difficult to reverse without incurring heavy costs.

Uncertainty and Capital Expenditure

It is worth mentioning that capital expenditure or long-term investment involves a good deal of uncertainty about its outcome. Since what *state of nature* (*i.e.*, business conditions) will be prevailing in the future is highly uncertain, the outcome of alternative courses of action cannot be known with certainty. Therefore, in making decisions under conditions of uncertainty expected values of each alternative outcome is incorporated into the analysis. Expected values are the weighted averages of the values of all possible outcomes multiplied by the probability of the value of each possible outcome. Under conditions of uncertainty measures of risk based on expected values and other techniques are used to make decisions. Thus, decision making is of particular importance for evaluating alternative investment projects under conditions of uncertainty. However, it may be noted that in our analysis in this chapter we assume that for planning capital expenditure, that is, capital budgeting a manager works under conditions of certainty and possesses full and adequate information about prices, revenue and costs that will be prevailing in future. Therefore, he is in a position to calculate the net cash flows from alternative projects. Decision making under conditions of risk and uncertainty will be studied in a separate chapter.

Classification of Capital Investment Projects

It is useful to classify various capital projects for which long-run investment analysis is needed.

1. *Replacement.* The existing machinery and other capital equipment is worn out by its continuous use for production over a number of years. Therefore, there is a need for its replacement by new machinery and capital equipment. Capital budgeting is required to plan for its replacement.

2. *Cost Reduction.* Some capital projects are undertaken to reduce unit cost of production. Among such capital projects are included the installation of new and *more efficient machinery and equipment* for outdated (*i.e.* obsolete) equipment and machinery so that unit cost of production is reduced. Note that it is *new* equipment and machinery in which improved technology is embodied which makes cost reduction possible.

3. *Output Expansion.* Investment in new capital projects is needed for expansion of productive capacity in response to the increased demand for a firm's *traditional products in the existing markets.*

4. *Expansion by Developing New Products and /or Markets.* Capital expenditure is required for the development of new products in response to changes in tastes of consumers and/or for entering new markets. Note that entering new markets will require additional staff or opening new outlets.

5. *Government Regulations.* There are some investment projects which are required to meet government regulations. Such investment projects include projects for pollution control, projects for health and safety regulation of the government and other legal rules and regulations.

In general, decisions regarding capital expenditure for replacement of worn-out equipment is not difficult to make because the firm is already quite familiar with the nature of existing equipment, its productivity, the operating and maintenance costs required for it. Moreover, the firm knows when it is to be replaced. However, capital expenditure for the reduction of cost by installing *new* machinery and equipment and the output expansion of traditional products are relatively more complex and difficult. Therefore, they require careful and detailed analysis of evaluating the capital projects concerning them and the decisions regarding them are taken by higher level management. But investment projects for producing *new products* and entering *new markets* are very complex and most challenging as they involve a greater degree of risk. However, it may be noted that the projects for production of new products and entering new markets are relatively more important as they are financially highly rewarding in the long run. This is because a firm's established product tends to become outdated over a period of time which lowers its profitability. Similarly, gaining entry into new products or opening new outlets are also more important as traditional markets of a firm soon get shrinked.

It is clear from above that ideas and proposals for undertaking new investment projects are crucial for profitability of a firm in the long run and even for its survival in the future. In well-managed-firms, all employees are provided with incentives so that they should give new ideas about investment but in highly dynamic firms there is a separate division or department known as *'Research and Development (R & D) Department'* which is entrusted with the task of providing proposals for new investment projects. This department is managed by experts in product management, marketing research, industrial engineering etc. and they interact with other departments to discuss proposals for investment in new products, gaining entry into new markets, adoption of new technology for the production of a product. They also discuss strategies to be adopted for the purpose.

For proper capital budgeting, that is, planning for long-term investment there is a need for co-ordination of the operations of the major departments or divisions of a firm. Capital budgeting requires information on sales or demand for the product, costs of production, effects of advertising, and the availability of funds for investment. Therefore, all management divisions of the firm are necessarily involved in it and contribute to the capital budgeting process. Since capital budgeting is crucial for long-run profitability and survival of firm, it is reviewed and guided on continuous basis by *top* management of a firm.

Capital projects are generally very costly and require huge amount of investment funds to finance the capital projects which are taken by the firms from external sources. Further, as mentioned above, it is not easy to reverse the capital projects once the investment is undertaken in them. Thus, if once a cement manufacturing plant has been set up, it is difficult to dismantle it or sell it if market conditions do not sustain any more capacity in cement production. Thus, capital budgeting decision sets the direction or course of a firm for several years to come and if the project does not succeed the firm has to bear heavy losses. The decision regarding price of a product, the amount of advertising may be easily reversed or necessary correction may be made but if decision-making regarding capital projects is not properly done, then the very existence of a firm is threatened.

Steps in Capital Budgeting or Long-term Investment Analysis

If a firm invests in a capital project whose present value is greater than its initial cost, the value of the firm will increase. This increase in the value of the firm as a result of successful capital budgeting will contribute to its future growth. As a result, if capital budgeting by a firm, that is, its planning for long-term investment is more successful in increasing the value of the firm, its future growth rate will be higher which will ensure better profitability of the firm and its share prices. Thus, capital budgeting must be done very carefully so as to achieve the basic objective of the firm, namely, *maximisation of its value* and hence maximisation of its rate of growth. The following six steps are involved in the capital budgeting process.

1. **Determining the cost of the project.** The first step in the budgeting process is to determine the cost of the project, that is, how much cost or capital expenditure will be incurred in undertaking the proposed investment project. This will depend on the prices of new equipment, the quantity of new equipment required (and if it is an imported equipment, the cost of the project will also depend on the foreign exchange rate, customs duties, if any), and expenses on its installation have to be considered for making an estimate of the cost of a project.

2. **Estimating cash flows.** The second step in the budgeting process is to estimate cash flows associated with an investment project. Cash flows generated by an investment project depend on the series of incremental *cash inflows* and *cash outflows* that occur over time when the project is operational. *Cash inflows of a project are incremental revenues generated by the project over a number of years of its operation and cash outflows are incremental costs incurred over a number of years when the project remains operational.* The incremental net cash flows generated by a project are the difference between incremental cash inflows and cash outflows *with and without the project.* How the net cash flows from a project are estimated will be explained below at length.

3. **Measuring riskiness of estimated cash flows.** Since cash flows of investment projects occur in future, varying degrees of risk or uncertainty exist about the values of these flows in the future. The expected values of these flows under conditions of uncertainty can be obtained if the firm has the information about probability distribution of these flows. The estimation of cash flows under varying degrees of risk and uncertainty will be explained in a separate chapter. For now, we assume that a manager has adequate information to estimate cash flows with certainty for deciding whether or not to go in for an investment project.

4. **Determining the appropriate discount rate.** The fourth step in the capital budgeting process is to determine the appropriate discount rate (*i.e.*, the cost of capital) at which future cash flows are to be discounted to obtain the present value of the cash flows in the future.Generally, *opportunity cost of funds* is the appropriate cost of capital. The opportunity cost of funds is the market rate of interest which is used for the purpose of discounting estimates of future cash flows.

5. **Finding present value of future cash flows.** Fifthly, present value of future cash flows are obtained by actually discounting them at the selected discount rate representing the opportunity cost of capital (in many cases, market rate of interest represents the opportunity cost of capital or funds used for investment). It may be noted that present values of both cash inflows and cash outflows during the period of operation of the project are calculated and on that basis the estimates of *net cash flows* are made.

6. **Comparing present value of cash flows with the cost of the project.** Finally, the present value of the estimated net cash flows of a project are compared with the *initial cost of the project* (*i.e.*, initial investment expenditure incurred on the project). If the estimated present value of an investment project exceeds the cost of a project, the project will add to the value of the firm and therefore should be accepted. On the contrary, if the estimated present value of the project is less than the cost of the project it should be rejected.

ESTIMATION OF CASH FLOWS

In the analysis of investment projects, the most important but a very difficult step is the estimation of cash flows generated by a capital project that occur during the life of the project. For projecting cash flows many variables are to be considered and therefore many departments and individuals in the firm are to be consulted. For example, estimates of sales of a product in the future years and its likely price are normally decided by the marketing department of the firm. Note that the managers running marketing department of a firm makes its estimates of future sales and price of the product on the basis of price elasticity of demand and its effect on sales, the state of the economy, trends in tastes of consumers and competitors reaction. It may however be mentioned that *future is highly uncertain*. Therefore, it is very difficult to make accurate future estimates of incremental revenues (*i.e.*, cash inflows) and incremental costs (*i.e.*, cost outflows) associated with a project.

For preparing correct estimates of cash flows some rules or principles should be followed. We discuss below some important rules or principles that should be followed for estimating accurate estimates of cash flows generated by a project in future.

1, First, in estimation of cash flows, it is *net reduction in cost and/or net increment in revenue* associated with a project that should be considered. As stated above, certain capital projects are of cost reducing types. For example, if a proposed project is to replace a machine by a more efficient machine that requires less labour to produce a product the cash flows generated by this new machine should be viewed as net *reduction in operating cost* over a number of years in future. Secondly, a machine project may involve the production of a new product which is of higher quality and, therefore, can be sold at a higher price. The cash flows generated by such machines will be in the form of *net addition to revenue* in the coming years. Further, some projects are of both cost-reducing and revenue-increasing types. For example, a project which involves modernisation and expansion of a plant and equipment embodying superior technology will reduce cost per unit and will also increase productive capacity leading to a higher rate of production and therefore net addition to revenue of the firm. Therefore, in this case, for estimating cash flows the reduction in cost and net increment in revenue in each future year should be taken into account. It needs to be emphasised that both the reduction in cost or increase in revenue generated by a project should be made on the *incremental basis*. This means that cost reduction or revenue expansion due to a project must represent the difference between the cash-flow streams to the firm with and without undertaking of the project.

2. Another important principle for making proper estimates of future cash flows is that *introduction of bias in preparing them* should be avoided. Some members of managerial staff develop vested interests in undertaking some particular projects and, therefore, they tend to overestimate the cash inflows and underestimate the costs, that is, cash outflows. This introduces bias in the estimates of cash flows. Therefore, for obtaining unbiased estimates it is desirable that these are reviewed by some outside experts or the individuals managing finance division of the firm.

3. Thirdly, cash flows should be estimated on an *after-tax basis*. Further, it is important to note that in estimating cash flows of a project, *depreciation should be included* in the incremental revenue accruing over a number of years to the firm as a result of the operation of the project. This is because depreciation is not a *cash expenditure* of the firm. However, since in income tax laws depreciation is allowed as a cost and reduces net taxable income of the firm on which profit or income tax is levied, therefore, while estimating cash flows after taxes, depreciation is first deducted for determining net taxable income, and then it is added to income *after* payment of tax to obtain *cash flows after* tax associated with a particular capital project.

4. The next important rule followed in the estimation of cash flows is that *indirect effects* of the project, both of revenue-increasing or cost-reducing types should be included in them.

For instance, if a division of the firm is planning to undertake investment in a project that will affect the revenue or costs of other divisions, then these external effects should be included in the estimates of cash flows associated with that investment project.

5. Fifthly, *sunk costs* should not be considered for evaluating an investment project. *A sunk cost is an outlay that has already been made and cannot be recovered.* Whether a project should be accepted or rejected, sunk cost has to be borne. Therefore, sunk costs are not taken into account while evaluating capital projects.

6. Another important principle followed in estimating cash flows generated by a project is that *the value of resources used in a capital project should be measured in terms of opportunity costs* for the firm. Opportunity cost is the value of a resource in its next best alternative use. In the analysis of the investment projects, opportunity costs of resources used for a project are the cash flows that these resources would generate if they are not used in the proposed project.

For a typical investment project an investmen is made in year 0, generates a stream of yearly net cash flows over a lifespan of the project. *The net investment in a project is defined as the initial net cash outlay on it in year 0. It consists of a cost of acquiring the new asset plus installation expenses and tax effects.*

Estimating Cash Flows of a Project : An Illustration

It will be useful to give an illustration of estimating cash flows of a project. Let us assume that the proposed project is to install a new machinery which produces a particular product. The engineering department forecasts input-output relationship which tells us which and how much various inputs will be required to produce a given rate of output. The purchase and marketing divisions will predict the costs of inputs and prices of output which will enable them to calculate expected incremental revenues generated by the project and incremental costs of production to be incurred each year in future.

Let us assume that the purchase and installation of machinery requires initial investment of Rs. 150 thousands and has a lifespan of five years. Cash flows each year beginning with the year 2007 are given in Table 33.1. In row 1 of this table *gross sales* of output produced by the machinery (which represents cash inflows in terms of revenues) in each of the five year period are shown. In the second row operating cost of output produced each year is shown that depends, apart from input-output relationship, on the prices of inputs used. The operating costs of production represents the cash outflows each year. Then, in row 3 *depreciation* of machinery is given. It is assumed that the firm follows a *straight-line method* of depreciation which means a constant percentage each year over the life span of the machinery. It is assumed that machinery depreciates at the rate of 20 per cent per annum. The initial investment outlay on machinery being Rs. 150 lakhs, depreciation each year amounts to.Rs. 150 x 20% = Rs. 30 lakhs each year.

The fourth row shows *net profits* after allowing for cost of output and depreciation. Thus, in the first year of operation whereas sales revenue is Rs. 120 lakhs, cost of output and depreciation amount to Rs. 100 + 30 = 130 lakhs. This gives us a negative profits of Rs. 10 lakhs in the year 2007. Similarly, profits or income of the firm before tax is calculated for the next four years. Further, for the sake of simplification it is assumed that the rate of profits or income tax is 50 per cent. Since in the year 2007 there are negative profits or losses, tax on profits will be zero. But in the subsequent years when net profits are positive, 50 per cent of them are paid as profit or income tax. In the sixth row of the table profits or income after tax are given. It is important to understand again that in row 7 we have shown depreciation which has been now added to net profit after tax to obtain net cash flows in row 8. As explained above, depreciation is not a *cash expense* (*i.e.*, cash outflow) but it is exempted from income or profit tax. Therefore, for calculating income tax we have deducted it from gross income or sales revenue. But since it is not cost outflow, we have to add it to net income after tax. Note that *it is net cash flow, shown in row 8, which is available each year for payment of dividend to shareholders and interest on borrowed capital and for ploughing back into investment* in *other capital projects*. Further note that for the purpose of evaluating whether or not a particular capital project should be undertaken, the *present value of the cash flows has to be found out by discounting it*. We shall explain this discounting method at length later in this chapter.

Table 33.1: Estimation of Cash Flows of a Project

(Figures in ₹ lakhs)

	2007	2008	2009	2010	2011
1. Gross Sales (or cash Inflows) (i.e. Revenue)	120	200	240	280	320
2. *Less* : Operating Costs of Production	100	130	160	210	260
3. *Less*: Depreciation	30	30	30	30	30
4. Net Profit (*i.e*, income before tax)	(–)10	40	50	40	30
5. *Less*: Income or Profit Tax	0	20	25	20	15
6. Net Profit after Tax	(–)10	20	25	20	15
7. Plus: Depreciation	30	30	30	30	30
8. Net Cash Flow after Tax	20	50	55	50	45

Discounting and Present Values

People prefer present consumption to future consumption. Therefore, ₹ 100 at hand today is not worth the same as ₹ 100 to be received a year after. In other words, people prefer ₹ 100 today to ₹ 100 to be received after a year. In evaluating investment projects which yield returns or cash flows over a number of years in future, it is imperative to know how much ₹ 100 paid in the future is worth today. In other words, what is the present value of ₹ 100 to be received after one year, after two years, after three years and so forth. How much cash flow of ₹ 100 to be received in a future year is worth today depends on the interest rate at which one can borrow or lend money. Therefore, a future cash flow is discounted at the interest rate to obtain its *present discounted value* (*PDV*) or what is simply called *present value* (*PV*). Suppose you have given a loan of ₹ 100 today to some body at 10 per cent rate of interest. Then after one year you have will receive ₹ 110, that is,

$100 + 100 \times \frac{10}{100}$ or $\left(100 + 100 \quad \frac{1}{10}\right) = 100\,(1 + 0.1) = 110$. This means ₹ 100 today is equivalent to ₹110 a year after, if rate of interest happens to be 10 per cent per annum. In other words, ₹ 110 after a year is worth ₹ 100 today, given 10 per cent rate of interest. Note that in obtaining present discounted values, *interest rate is expressed in proportionate decimal form*, that is, 10% = 0.10. The present value can be found as under

$$100\ (1 + 0.10) = 110$$

$$\text{or} \qquad 100 = \frac{110}{1+0.10} \qquad \text{... (i)}$$

The equation (*i*) shows if ₹ 110 to be paid after a year is discounted at 10 per cent interest rate, we obtain its present value of ₹ 100. To put in general terms, if *r* represents rate of interest, then present value (*PV*) of ₹ 110 to be paid after a year is

$$PV = \frac{110}{1+r}$$

Similarly, if ₹ 110 is to be paid after two years, its present value,

$$PV = \frac{110}{(1+r)^2}$$

Further, if ₹ 110 is to be paid after three years, its present discounted value,

$$PV = \frac{110}{(1+r)^3}$$

and so forth for further future years of payment.

The concept of present discounted value is extensively applied and used in financial matters and to facilitate accounting a table has been prepared which provide present discounted value (*PDV*) of Re. 1 paid after 1 year, 2 years, 3 years, 5 years and so on and this table of present discounted value (*PDV*) is given in Log Tables. We reproduce some parts of it in Table 33.2 so that the students should learn to use them in actual exercises. More details regarding this are given in Appendix B to this chapter. Thus

Table 33.2 PDV of Re. 1 paid in the Future

Interest Rate	1 Year	2 Year	5 Year	10 Year	20 Year
0.01	$0.990	$0.980	$0.951	$0.905	$0.820
0.02	0.980	0.961	0.906	0.820	0.673
0.03	0.971	0.943	0.863	0.744	0.554
0.04	0.962	0.925	0.822	0.676	0.456
0.05	0.952	0.907	0.784	0.614	0.377
0.06	0.943	0.890	0.747	0.558	0.312
0.07	0.935	0.873	0.713	0.508	0.258
0.08	0.926	0.857	0.681	0.463	0.215
0.09	0.917	0.842	0.650	0.422	0.178
0.10	0.909	0.826	0.621	0.386	0.149
0.15	0.870	0.756	0.497	0.247	0.061
0.20	0.833	0.694	0.402	0.162	0.026

If rate of interest (*r*) *is 8 per cent per annum*, then

$$PDV \text{ of Re 1 paid after 1 years} = \frac{1}{1+r} = \frac{1}{1+0.8} = 0.926$$

$$PDV \text{ of Re 1 paid after 2 years} = \frac{1}{(1+r)^2} = \frac{1}{(1+0.8)^2} = 0.857$$

$$PDV \text{ of Re 1 paid after 5 years} = \frac{1}{(1+r)^5} = \frac{1}{(1+0.8)^5} = 0.681$$

If present discounted value of a large number of rupees is to be found we just multiply that number by the *PDV* of Re 1 paid after the given number of years. Thus, if we have to find the present discounted value of ₹ 5000 to be paid after two years with the given rate of interest equal to 8 per cent per annum we can obtain it as under

$$PDV \text{ or } PV \text{ of ₹ 5000 to be paid after 2 years} = 5000 \times \frac{1}{(1+0.8)^2} = 5000 \times 0.857$$

$$= ₹\ 4285$$

Present Value of a Stream of Payments

Quite often investment projects yield a stream of payments or cash flows today and future years. Present value (*PV*) in this case can be calculated by adding the present discounted values of the various amounts paid in various years discounted by the given rate of interest. Two types of payment streams are given in Table 33.3 and we have to find out the present value of these streams of cash flows if rate of interest is 10 per cent.

Table 33.3. *Two Payment Streams*

	Today	1 year	2 years
Payment Stream A :	₹ 500	₹ 500	0
Payment Stream B :	₹ 50	500	500

We have first to find present discounted value (*PDV*) of Re 1 paid in the future by consulting Table 45.1. We present below the present discounted value of the above two payment streams

$$PDV \text{ of stream } A = 500 + \frac{500}{1+r} = 500 + \frac{500}{1+0.10}$$

$$= 500 + \frac{500}{1+0.10} = 500 + 500 \times 0.909$$

$$= 500 + 454.5 = ₹\ 954.5$$

$$PDV \text{ of stream } B = 50 + \frac{500}{1+0.10} + \frac{500}{(1+0.10)^2}$$

$$= 50 + (500 \times 0.909) + (500 \times 0.826)$$

$$= 50 + 454.5 + 413.0 = ₹\ 917.5$$

From above it follows that the first stream *A* is preferred to the second stream *B* at 10 per cent rate of interest because the present value of stream *A* is greater than that of stream *B*.

Now, if rate of interest is 5 percent per annum, then

$$PDV \text{ of stream } A \text{ at 5 per cent interest rate} = 500 + \frac{500}{1+0.05}$$

$$= 500 + 476 = ₹\ 976$$

$$PDV \text{ of stream } B \text{ at 5 per cent rate of interest} = 50 + \frac{500}{1+0.05} + \frac{500}{1+(0.05)^2}$$

$$= 50 + 476 + 453.5 = \text{Rs. } 979.5$$

Thus, at 5 per cent rate of interest, present discounted value (*PDV*) of stream *B* exceeds that of stream *A*. Thus, at 5 percent interest rate, stream *B* is a preferred payment stream. It therefore follows which of the payment stream would a businessman would prefer to receive depend on rate of interest. Besides, it follows from above as *interest rate rises, the present value of a given income stream falls.*

Value of a Bond

A bond is a financial instrument through which corporate firms and government borrow money from the public. The borrower, corporate firm or government, which issues bond agrees to pay the bond holder, that is, who purchases the bond, a stream of money (*i.e.* cash flows). For example, the Indian government's 10 years bond of ₹ 1000 might make a coupon payments of ₹ 100 per year for the next 10 years and then after the expiry of 10 years, the principal amount is paid back. Now, a significant question is what is the value of a bond to you? or ,in other words, how much bond is worth to you today? To know how much bond is worth today which determines how much an individual would pay for the bond, we have to calculate the present value of its payment stream. Thus

$$PDV = \frac{100}{(1+r)} + \frac{100}{(1+r)^2} + \ldots.. + \frac{100}{(1+r)^{10}} + \frac{1000}{(1+r)^{10}}$$

where r is the rate of interest.

As shown above, the present value of a payment stream depends on rate of interest. *As the rate of interest falls, present value (PDV) of a bond with a given payments stream increases. On the other hand, present value of a bond decreases as the interest rate increases.* For example, by applying the above formula we calculate the Present Discounted Value (*PDV*) of cash flows of a 10-year bond paying ₹ 100 annually on a principal sum of ₹ 1000 to be equal to ₹ 1386 when the interest rate is 5 per cent. When the interest rate is 15 per cent per annum, on calculation we find that the same ₹ 1000 bond (i.e., 10 year bond of ₹ 1000 with a coupon annual payment of ₹ 100) is worth (*i.e.* present value) only ₹ 749.

The Effective Yield (i.e .Rate of Return) of a Bond

Bonds of many corporate firms and government are often traded in the bond market and reported by the media. Therefore, what these bonds are worth (that is, their present value) can be known directly by taking a glance at the prices of bonds traded in the market. Though bond prices can be known easily but to determine the effective yield or rate of return on them is bit difficult. *The rate of interest which equates the present discounted value of the bond's payment stream of cash flows with the bond's market price is the effective yield or rate of return on the bond.* In this way the effective yields or rates of return on various bonds can be calculated. We can compare them with the rates of return on other available investment opportunities for the investors.

In the previous section we have explained the equations that show how the present value of bonds depend on the interest rate used to discount the bond's future payment stream. These equations can be rewritten so as to determine effective yield from the bond's value. It is easy to determine interest rate (*i.e.* effective yield) in case of perpetual bond. Thus

$$PV \text{ of a perpetuity with ₹ 100 as the annual money payment} = \frac{100}{r}$$

If market price of a bond (*i.e.* *PV* of bond) is ₹ 1000, then rate of interest r or effective yield can be obtained as under :

$$₹\ 1000 = \frac{100}{r}$$

$$r = \frac{100}{1000} = 0.10 \text{ or } 10 \text{ per cent}$$

Thus 10 per cent is the effective yield of the perpetuity in question.

To find out effective yield of 10 year bond with coupon payment of ₹ 100 per year as given in the previous section is a difficult task as it involves a good deal of calculations. Rewriting the present value equation of 10 year bond with a terminal payment we have

$$PV = \frac{100}{(1+r)} + \frac{100}{(1+r)^2} + \frac{100}{(1+r)^3} + ... + \frac{100}{(1+r)^{10}} + \frac{1000}{(1+r)^{10}}$$

$$\text{or} \quad PV = 100 \times \frac{1}{1+r} + 100 \times \frac{1}{(1+r)^2} + 100 \times \frac{1}{(1+r)^3} + ... 100 \times \frac{1}{(1+r)^{10}} + 1000 \times \frac{1}{(1+r)^{10}}$$

Note that $\frac{1}{(1+r)}$ is the *PDV* of Re 1 after one year; $\frac{1}{(1+r)^2}$ is the *PDV* of Re 1 after two years and so on. Given the price of the 10 year bond (*i.e.* its present value *PV*), we can calculate the value of *r* consistent with bond's price. Some computer programs (even programs on scientific calculators) are available which can greatly help in calculating the rate of interest *r* consistent with the given bond price. The calculation can also be done by using the table of "*PDV* of Re 1 paid in the future" that is, the value of $\frac{1}{1+r}$, $\frac{1}{(1+r)^2}$, $\frac{1}{(1+r)^3}$ etc. as

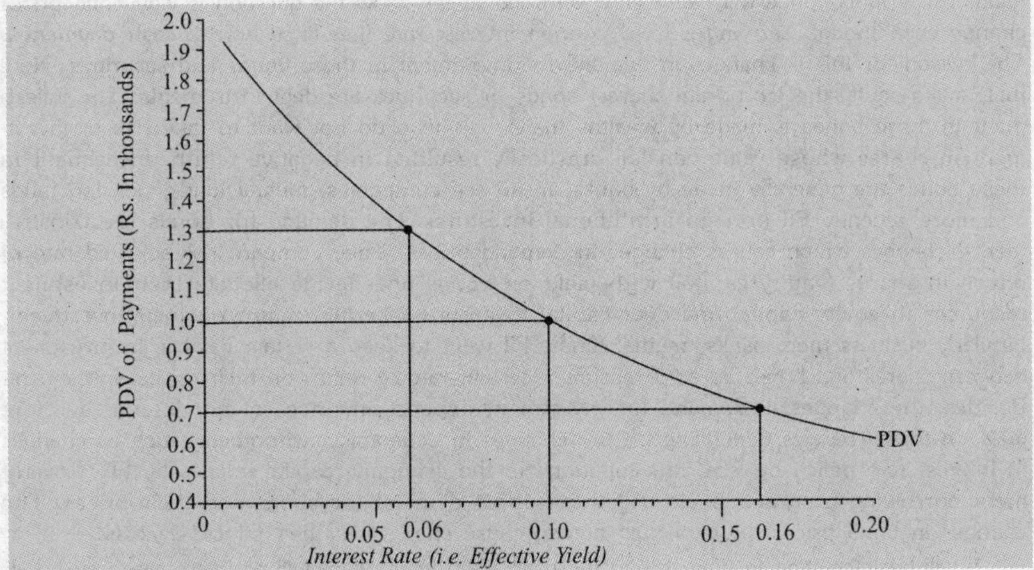

Fig. 33.1. *Effective Yield of a Bond*

explained above. In Figure 33.1 below we have drawn a curve showing interest rate (*i.e.* effective yield) consistent with present value (or market price) 10 year a bond of ₹ 1000 with a coupen. It will be seen from Fig.33.1 that if the price of a bond (*i.e. PV*) is ₹ 1300, the effective yield or rate of return from it is around 6 per cent per annum. If that bond sells at ₹ 700, the effective yield from it will be about Rs 16 per cent per annum.

Effective Yield and Risk

It is a common knowledge that yields from different bonds differ considerably. What are the reasons for the differences in yields (*i.e.* rate of return) from different bonds. Bonds of corporate firms yield more than government bonds. And corporate bonds of some eminent companies such as Reliance, Tata *yield less* than those of financially weak corporate firms. The most important reason for the differences in yields of bonds is that different bonds have different degree of risk. The Indian government is unlikely to default, that is, unlikely to fail in making payments of interest on its bonds and the principal sum borrowed. Therefore, the bonds of Government of India carry less risk and therefore yields on them are relatiely less as compared to the bonds of private corporate firms which can default on interest or principal payments on their bonds. And the bonds issued by the financially strong and reputed private corporate companies such as Reliance and Tata are less likely to default and the yields on their bonds are less as compared to those of the financially weak companies. Thus more risky the investment bond is, the higher must be yield on it. As a matter of fact, the higher yield on a more risky investment is a form of risk premium carried by it. The investors would like to invest in more risky bonds only if they are compensated by higher return or yield. Thus riskier bonds have higher yields.

Why does yield or return on bonds vary ?

Prices of both the corporate bonds and Government securities with a certain fixed coupon interest rate (that is, with a fixed annual coupon payments for a certain maturity period changes in the bond market. The changes in bond prices affect the effective yield or rate return on them. For example if the price a bond of ₹ 1000 carrying 100 annual coupon cash payments, falls, say to ₹ 950, it implies that now purchase of that bond at ₹ 950 will yield ₹ 100 per annum, that is, yield on bond that will now be more than 10 per cent. On the other hand, rise in bond price will cause yield on bond to fall. Now the question is why bond prices change even though carrying a fixed coupon interest rate (i.e. fixed annual cash payments). The reason for this is changes in demand for investment in these bonds and securities. Note that unlike equity (i.e. corporate shares) bonds or securities are debt instruments. The investment in these bonds is made by wealthy individuals who do not want to take risk of investment in shares whose value can fall drastically resulting in negative return. Investment in these bonds are generally made by banks, insurnace companies, mutual funds, pension funds and more recently FII (foreign institutional investors). The demand for bonds (debt instruments) changes which causes changes in demand prices. They compare risk-adjusted rate of return in shares (equity capital) with yield on bonds and decide allocate their investment resources in equity capital and debt capital to ensure a certain return on their investment. Similarly business men, banks, mutual funds, FII want to keep a certain balance in investment between shares and bonds so as to ensure a certain rate of return on their capital investment. Besides, the changes in demand for investment depend on prices of bonds and therefore yield on them changes depending on the changes in economic environment, such as changes in interest rate policy by RBI, rate inflation in the economy, capital inflows by FII, Government borrowing programme etc. All these affect demand for bonds and their prices. The changes in bond prices, as explained above, cause changes in their effective yields.

It will be interesting to note that in the year 2010 in the US yield or interest rate on bonds and securities has been estimated to be near 2 per cent while in India yield on them is presently around 8 per cent. That is why FIIs of the US and other developed economies are pumping more funds into India to purchase equity shares and bonds. This is affecting share prices and bond prices in India.

EVALUATING CAPITAL INVESTMENT PROJECTS

Now we are in a position to evaluate whether an investment project should be accepted or rejected. Further, evaluation of projects is also required to choose among alternative projects when the resources for investment are limited. We explain below the various criteria with which to evaluate capital projects. An economically sound basic rule for capital budgeting is that *those projects should be accepted for making investment that increase the value of the firm.* When the discounted present value of the cash flows generated by a capital project exceeds the initial cost of investment, the project will increase the value of a firm and is therefore worthy of scarce resources being invested in it. Therefore, the net present value analysis forms the basis of decision rules for evaluating investment projects. However, net present value (NPV) method is only one of the four important investment decision criteria which are used in evaluating projects. These investment decision criteria with the exception of payback period method are essentially based on the net present value analysis. The following four methods or criteria for evaluating capital investment projects will be examined below:

1. Payback Period Method
2. Net Present Value Method
3. Rate of Return Method
4. Profitability Index Method

Payback Period Method

A payback period of an investment project is the number of years that it takes for the firm to recover its initial cost of the project. In other words, *payback period is the number of years required for the sum of net cash flows from a project over a period to become equal to the cost of the initial investment outlay on the project.* Consider the estimated net cash flows of the two projects *A* and *B* given in Table 33.4. The initial cost of each of the two projects is ₹ 1,000. It will be seen from Table 33.4 that in case of project *A*, the sum of cash flows in the two years is equal to the initial capital cost of the project. Thus, payback period of project *A* is 2 years. However, in case of project *B*, it is in 3 years that the sum of net cash flows equals the initial investment cost of the project *B*. Thus, payback period of project *B* is 3 years.

Table 33.4. Evaluation with Payback Period Method

Project	*Initial Cost of the project*	*Net Cash Flows* 1	2	3	4	5	*Payback Period*
A	1,000	500	500	1,000	1,000	1,000	2
B	1,000	250	250	500	5,000	10,000	3

Decision rule. If a firm has to decide whether to accept or reject a project without its need to rank it with others, then, according to payback criterion, the decision rule is to compare the project's payback period with a 'cut-off period'. *If a project's payback period is less than or equal to the cut off period, it should be accepted, otherwise rejected.* For example, if a cut-off payback period for a firm is 2 years, then project *A* whose payback period is 2 years should be accepted and project *B* whose payback period is 3 years should be rejected.

If a firm has to choose a project among two or more projects, then the decision rule, according to payback criterion, is that the project with a shortest payback period should be selected. In case of choice between the two projects *A* and *B* whose data of net cash flows are given in Table 33.4, it will be seen that payback period of project *A* is shorter than that of project *B*. Therefore, project A be chosen on the basis of this decision rule.

Limitations. There are two major limitations or drawbacks of the payback period evaluation method. First, in this method no account is taken of the net cash flows generated by projects after the expiry of the payback period. *A* look at Table 33.2 will reveal that even though payback period of project *A* is shorter than that of project *B*, the project *B* has much larger net cash flows of ₹ 5,000 and ₹ 10,000 in the next two years respectively after the payback period and, therefore, it should be preferred to the project *A*, which pays back in two years but have much smaller net cash flows afterwards. Thus, payback period does not consider *all net cash flows generated* by a project.

Secondly, in this evaluation method all net cash flows are given the same weight and therefore, *ignores the time value of money*. It is desirable to understand the meaning of time value of money. An amount of money to be received *in the future* is less valuable to a firm than the same amount of money received *today*. This is because an amount of money received today can be invested in a risk-free security and earn a return or interest from today to any time in future period. The return or interest earned in a risk-free security represents the time value of money. The payback period evaluating method does not discount the net cash flows accruing to a firm in the future to their present values and therefore ignores the time value of money. As a matter of fact, net cash flows of money in the earliest periods are more valuable as they can be reinvested to earn a return. Thus, payback period criterion ignores the possibility of reinvestment of earlier net cash flows. To conclude, using undiscounted future cash flows, this method ignores the possibility of reinvesting. Thus, it is clear that payback period technique is not a sound method of evaluating investment projects.

Net Present Value Criterion : Choice of a Project

An investment project yields a return in the form of a stream of cash flows and it also involves cost to be incurred in the present. For instance, for a project such as investment for purchasing a machine, building a factory, acquiring an educational or technical skill, an individual has to incur costs in the current year. Return from an investment project are obtained as cash flows of income or output in future years. An important decision rule for investment is the net present value criterion. The basis of this criterion or rule is that a unit of a commodity or a rupee in a future year is worth less than a unit of the commodity or rupee this year. Therefore, cash or output flows from a project accruing at different times cannot be simply added to determine whether or not to make investment in the project. The reason for this is that returns in future years have to be discounted at a rate of interest. It is important to note that, as explained above, net cash flows are measured *on after-tax basis* even taking into account the tax saving on account of depreciation and investment allowance (if any) granted by the government. Since profits or net cash flows for each year of project's life is calculated from sales and cost forecasts, the variablity of profits (*i.e.*, net cash flows) year by year is explicitly taken into account.

Let us first explain choice among investment projects when two periods are involved, that is, the present year and the next year. In an investment project, since in the present year cost is incurred, cash flow is negative. The returns start from the next year in the form of increase in income or output, the cash flows are positive in the future years. In the choice of a project a firm is guided by the *principle of maximisation of wealth.* Investment in a project which increases wealth is desirable. Further, as mentioned earlier, while making investment decision, the firm will calculate the net present value of the future cash flows that it expects to obtain from the investment and compare it with the cost of the investment project. The *net present value of a project is the value today of the net cash flows in the future years obtained by discounting them at the market rate of interest minus the cost incurred on the project in the current year.* As explained above the costs incurred on maintenance of a machine or any other type of project have to be substracted from receipts or income flows to obtain the net cash flows for the future years. A project which will yield income only from a year now and has no scrap value, net present value is given by

$$NPV = -C_0 + \frac{R_1}{1+i}$$

where *NPV* denotes the net present value of a project, C_0 is the cost of the investment project in the current year and will therefore be negative, R_1 is the net cash flow in the next year and i is the market rate of interest.

If the net present value of an investment project is positive, this means it increases wealth of the business firm. As the objective of the firm is to maximise its wealth, *it will be desirable to undertake investment in the project if its net present value is positive (i.e. if NPV > 0).* This is a decision rule for deciding about investment in a project.

Net Present Value Rule for Capital Investment Decisions : Multiperiod Case. Many investment projects yields a stream of returns (*i.e.* cash flows) beyond two periods. The net present value rule applies in this case too. However, we have to extend the net present value rule to deal with several years. Return or net cash flow of ₹ 1000 occurring in the third year is worth less than ₹ 1000 occurring in the second year. Likewise, ₹ 1000 accruing in the fourth year is less than ₹1000 accruing in the third year. Therefore, in a multiperiod case the net present value of a project can be obtained as under :

$$NPV = -C + \frac{R_1}{1+i} + \frac{R_2}{(1+i)^2} + \frac{R_3}{(1+i)^3} + \ldots\ldots + \frac{R_n}{(1+i)^n}$$

where *NPV* is the present value of the project, C is the cash flow during the current year (It is negative in case of an investment project as cost has to be incurred on a project in the current year). R_1, R_2, $R_3 \ldots R_n$ are the positive net cash flows in the form of income after first, second, third year and so on.

Net Present Value Criterion : *Approve or undertake any investment project whose net present value is positive and reject any investment project whose net present value is zero or negative.*

Now an important question is at what rate cash flows in future be discounted to arrive at net present value. The market rate of interest is not always the proper discount rate. The discount rate which ought to be used is determined by the alternative uses of the funds available to the firm. Instead of making investment in a particular project, another investment project may be there that generates a different stream of cash flows or profits. Alternatively, a firm may invest in a bond that yields a different rate of return. In fact, for a firm there is the *opportunity cost of capital.* The opportunity cost is the rate of return the firm can earn by investing the available funds in an alternative similar project instead of investment in a particular project. By similar investment project we mean the one which involves the *same risk.* As explained earlier, the making investment in projects with higher risks would require greater return or yield. Therefore, "*the opportunity cost of investing in a project is the return that one could earn from another project or asset of similar riskiness*"[1].

In a later chapter we will explain how a firm makes adjustment for risks involved in various investment projects. In the present analysis we assume that the investment project

1. Robert S. Pindyck and Daniel L Rubinfeld, *Microeconomics,* 3rd ed. Prentice Hall of India, New Delhi, 1995, p-533.

does not involve any risk and uncertainty, that is, the firm is quite certain about the stream of future profits π_1, π_2, π_3 etc. generated by an investment project. Besides, the opportunity cost used to discount the future stream of profits is the *risk-free return*, such as the return that can be earned from investing in government bonds. For example, if the investment project is expected to last for ten years, then the interest rate on a 10 year government bonds can be used to obtaine the net present value (*NPV*) of a project. If the *NPV* of the project is positive (*i.e.* if *NPV* > 0), the yield from the project will exceed the opportunity cost and therefore it is worthwhile to make investment in the project.

The alternative investment criterion such as the internal rate of return criterion and the profitability index criterion have been proposed. But, as we will discuss below, the *NPV* criterion is better than these other investment criteria.

NUMERICAL EXAMPLES

Example 1. *If an investment project costs ₹ 10,000, market rate of interest is 15 per cent per annum and it yields net return of ₹ 16, 100 in the next year. Should the investment in the project be made ?*

Solution. The net present value of this project is given by

$$NPV = -C_0 + \frac{R_1}{1+i}$$

$$NPV = -10,000 + \frac{16,100}{1+0.15}$$

$$= -10,000 + \frac{16,100}{1.15}$$

$$= -10,000 + 16,100 \times \frac{100}{115}$$

$$= -10,000 + 14,000 = ₹4,000$$

Thus, undertaking of this project well increase wealth of the firm by 4000. Therefore, investment in this project should be made.

Example 2. *Suppose a firm is planning to purchase a machine which costs ₹ 20,000 and interest is 10 per cent per annum and anticipated yield from it next year is ₹ 22,000 and at the end of the next year the machine has no salvage or scrap value. Is it worthwhile to approve the project ?*

Solution. Net present value of the machine,

$$NPV = -C_0 + \frac{R_1}{1+i} = -20,000 + \frac{22,000}{1+0.1}$$

$$= -20,000 + \frac{22,000}{1.1}$$

$$= -20,000 + 22000 \times \frac{10}{11} = 0$$

Thus the net present value of the machine is zero. It is not worthwhile to make investment in the machine. However, it may be noted that if the yield from the machine next year exceeds

₹ 22,000, its net present value will become positive and it will then be desirable to purchase it for the production of a commodity. Note that if the yield next year remains ₹ 22,000 but rate of interest falls below 10 per cent, the net present value will again become positive.

Example 3. *Suppose a firm is considering to invest in a project. Its cost this year is Rs. one lakh and its net yield in year one from now is ₹ 1.25 lakh and its scrap value is zero. What is the highest rate of interest at which the project should be undertaken ?*

Solution. To determine the required value of the rate of interest (i), we should make the net present value equal to zero. Thus

$$NPV = -C_0 + \frac{R}{1+i} = 0$$

$$-100{,}000 + \frac{125{,}000}{1+i} = 0$$

$$\frac{125{,}000}{1+i} = 100{,}000$$

or $$100{,}000\ (1 + i) = 125{,}000$$

$$1 + i = \frac{1{,}25{,}000}{100{,}000} = \frac{5}{4}$$

$$i = \frac{5}{4} - 1 = 0.25$$

This means if the rate of interest is 0.25, that is, 25 per cent, the net present value of project is zero. Thus, if the rate of interest falls below 25 per cent, the net present value will become positive. Thus the project should be undertaken for any value of the rate of interest below 25 per cent.

Example 4 : *Suppose a firm is considering to buy a machine today for ₹ 25,000. The use of this machine in the production process of a commodity causes firm's net income to rise by ₹ 15000 in each of the next two years. Assume the rate of interest is 10 per cent and machines has no scrap value. Is it desirable for the firm to purchase the machine ?*

Solution.
$$NPV = -C_0 + \frac{R_1}{1+i} + \frac{R_2}{(1+i)^2}$$

$$= -25000 + \frac{15000}{1+0.1} + \frac{15000}{(1+0.1)^2}$$

$$= -25000 + 15000 \times \frac{10}{11} + 15000 \times \frac{10}{11} \times \frac{10}{11}$$

$$= -25000 + 13636.4 + 12396.7 = 1033.1$$

Thus we find net present value of the machine is positive and therefore it will increase the wealth of the firm by ₹ 1033. It is therefore desirable to make investment in it.

Net Present Value Rule 2 : Choice among Multiple Investment Projects

In our above analysis we have been concerned with explaining a rule regarding whether or not a project should be approved for capital investment. Now, we will discuss the choice by a firm when several projects are available for investment. In this case we need to compare the net present values of the various projects. The project which has the highest present value should be undertaken. The project with the highest net present value will make greatest contribution to the objective of maximising wealth by a firm. Thus, in case of choice among multiple projects we arrive at the following rule. "*If the two or more mutually exclusive projects are available for investment, undertake the project which has the highest net present value.*"

It may be pointed out that we face difficulties in the use of this rule when projects, instead of being mutually exclusive are *interdependent*, that is, undertaking of a project may change the benefits or returns from the other projects. For instance, a project of flood control may increase the benefits or revenue from the project of growing wheat on an agricultural farm. In case of these interdependent projects we have to modify the rule. In this case we should compare not the present values of individual projects but various 'sets' of interdependent projects. Thus, for the choice of a single project from various projects, they must be mutually exclusive, that is, independent of each other.

Let us illustrate this decision rule concerning mutually exclusive multiple projects by giving an example.

Example 5. *Two projects A and B are available to a firm. Cost in the current year and net cash flow in the next year of each is given below. Which project a firm should choose if market rate of interest is 10 per cent per annum ?*

Project	*Cost this year*	*Net cash flow in the next year*
Project A	100 lakh	120 lakh
Project B	150 lakh	180 lakh

Net present (NPV) of Project $A = -C_0 + \frac{R_1}{1+i}$

$$= -100 + \frac{120}{1+0.10} = -100 + 120 \times \frac{10}{11}$$

$$= -100 + 109.09 = 9.09$$

Net present value (NPV) of Project $B = -150 + \frac{180}{1.1}$

$$= -150 + 180 \times \frac{10}{11} = -150 + 163.63 = 13.63$$

Thus, net present value of project B is greater than the net present value of project A. Therefore, the firm which aims at maximising wealth should undertake project B.

Present Value of an Annuity with Perpetual Constant Annual Yield

An interesting case is of annuity with a constant stream of net cash flows for ever (*i.e.* in perpetuity) starting from a year now. As explained above, the present value of such an annuity is given by

$$PV = \frac{R}{i}$$

where R is stream of payments which an investor receives, starting from the next year, i is the rate of interest. This can be proved as follows:-

$$PV = \frac{R}{1+i} + \frac{R}{(1+i)^2} + \frac{R}{(1+i)^3} + \text{...indefinitly}$$

In the above R can be factored out. Therefore,

$$PV = R\left[\frac{1}{1+i} + \frac{1}{(1+i)^2} + \frac{1}{(1+i)^3} + \text{.....}\infty\right] = \frac{R}{i}$$

Let us provide an example.

Suppose a bond yields a sum of ₹ 6,000 per annum indefinitely, starting from a year now. Assuming rate of interest is 12 per cent, its present value is given by

$$PV = \frac{R}{i} = \frac{6000}{0.12} = \frac{6000}{12/100} = 50{,}000$$

This is because if ₹ 50,000 are invested at 12 per cent rate of interest, it will yield ₹ 6,000 every year for ever $\left(50{,}000 \times \frac{12}{100} = 6000\right)$

Effect of Change in Rate of Interest on Net Present Value of an Investment Project

It is important to note that the rate of interest has an important bearing on the present value of an investment project. *The lower the rate of interest, the higher the present value of a project and vice versa.* Thus, in our above example of an annuity, with a constant annual yield of ₹ 6,000 for ever, if the rate of interest falls to 10 per cent, its present value will be

$$NPV = \frac{R}{i} = \frac{6000}{0.10} = 6000 \times \frac{100}{10} = 60{,}000$$

Thus, at a lower rate of interest the present value of the annuity has increased. This not only applies to the case of an annuity with a constant yield indefinitely but also to our earlier examples of present values of investment projects which yield cash flows for a limited number of years and also when annual yields are not constant.

It is also important to note here that cost of an investment project, (for example, purchasing a machine) may not be incurred entirely in the current period, some cost also occurs every year for its maintenance. Therefore, when finding out present value of a project, we need to consider *net cash flows* of the projects. In order to obtain these net cash flows from the extra revenue generated by a project, the cost incurred on it for its maintenance and operation has to be substracted from it. Further, as mentioned above, the projects have some scrap value, therefore when finding out present value of a project, the present value of its scrap value has also to be included in the stream of net cash flows of a machine or any other project.

INTERNAL RATE OF RETURN (IRR) METHOD

Another important method of evaluating investment project is internal rate of return method. This evaluation method is also based on present value of net cash flows generated by a project over its life period. *Internal Rate of Return (IRR) is the rate of discount that equates the present value of net cash flows equal to the initial investment cost of the project.* If R_1, R_2, R_3...R_n represent the net cash flows associated with a project which have an initial investment cost equal to C_0. Internal rate of return (*IRR*) is calculated by setting

$$\frac{R_1}{(1+r)} + \frac{R_2}{(1+r)^2} + \frac{R_3}{(1+r)^3} + \dots \frac{R_n}{(1+r)^n} = C_0$$

or $$\sum_{t=1}^{n} \frac{R_t}{(1+r)^t} = C_0$$

Solving for *r*, we get the internal rate of return.

Decision Rate : According to internal rate of return (*IRR*) method, *if the internal rate of return (r) of a capital project is greater than the cost of capital, investment in the project should be made.* If the internal rate of return (*r*) is less than the cost of capital, the project should be rejected. When the internal rate of return from a project exceeds the cost of capital, it will increase the value of the firm and is therefore, worthwhile to make investment in the project. For instance, if the use of funds costs 12 per cent per annum (that is, cost of capital is 12 per cent per annum) to a firm and if internal rate of return from the project is 15 per cent, the project should be accepted for investment.

It may however be noted that it is not easy to calculate internal rate of return when the life of a project exceeds one year. Fortunately, these days electronic calculators are available with which we can easily calculate internal rate of return from the data. Further, calculations of present values and internal rate of return can be done using personal computers through simple computer programmes.

However, in the absence of calculators and computers, internal rate of return (*IRR*) can be obtained through *trial and error method.* In this trial and error method, a discount rate is arbitrarily selected and the present value of cash flows generated by the project is calculated using the discount rate. If the present value so obtained is higher than the cost of capital to the firm, then a higher discount rate is chosen to evaluate the future cash flows of the project. If with this new higher discount rate, the present value of future cash flows of the project is lower than the initial cost of the project, then in that case repeat the process by reducing the discount rate. This iterative process should be continued until we find the discount rate which make present value of cash flows equal to the cost of the project. *This discount rate at which present value of future cash flows from a project becomes equal to the initial cost of the project to the firm represents the internal rate of return from the capital project.*

Let us illustrate it. *Suppose a firm is considering to invest in a project whose initial investment cost to it equals ₹ 1,000. Net cash flow from this projesct which start coming after a year is ₹ 450 per year for five years. After 5 years the project machine has no salvage value. Firm has to borrow investment funds at 20 percent per annum from a bank. Calculate internal rate of return from the project and give advise whether to accept or reject the project.*

Solution :

$$\frac{R_1}{(a+r)} + \frac{R_2}{(a+r)^2} + \frac{R_3}{(1+r)^3} + \frac{R_4}{(1+r)^4} + \frac{R_5}{(1+r)^5} = C_0$$

$$\frac{450}{(1+r)} + \frac{450}{(1+r)^2} + \frac{450}{(1+r)^3} + \frac{450}{(1+r)^4} + \frac{450}{(1+r)^5} = 1{,}000$$

Using the calculator *r* has been found to be equal to 34.9. Thus, 34.9 per cent is the internal rate of return from the investment in the proposed project. Since, internal rate of return (34.9%) exceeds the cost of capital (*i.e.* cost of borrowed funds) of 20 per cent, the project should be accepted for investment.

Choice Among Several Investment Projects. The method of internal rate of return can also be used to make a choice among several projects. This issue is faced when a firm has limited funds for making investment. To decide about choosing among alternative investment projects on the basis of the criterion of internal rate of return, internal rates of return (*IRR*) are calculated from the cash flows of various available projects. Then, in terms of the magnitudes of internal rate of return of the various projects can be given rank-ordering, from the highest rate of return to the lowest rate of return. Then investment funds should be employed to those projects which yield highest possible rates of return from the given limited available funds.

Comparison of NPV and IRR Methods

When evaluating a single project, the NPV and IRR methods yield the same results. When net present value (NPV) of a project is positive, internal rate of return exceeds the cost of capital and when net present value (NPV) of a project is negative, internal rate of return is less than the cost of capital. This is because when net present value of a project is positive, it implies that the rate at which future cash flows have been discounted to obtain the net present value is greater than the implied rate of return which represents the discount rate which makes the present value of future net cash flows equal to the initial cost of project [2]. In fact, in case of a single project, NPV and IRR are the two sides of the same coin. Therefore, in case of a single investment project, the two evaluation methods always lead to the same accept-reject decision.

However, in case of two or more mutually exclusive projects, that is, when only one out of two or more projects has to be undertaken for investment, the two evaluation criteria can lead to contradictory results. Consider Table 33.5 where values of future net cash flows generated by two projects *A* and *B* are given, and both the net present value (NPV) and internal rate of return (IRR) of the two projects have been calculated. It will be seen from the table that the project *A* has lower net present value (₹ 622) but a higher rate of return (34.9%), whereas project *B* has a higher net present value (675) but a lower internal rate of return (24.2). Thus, on the basis of the net present value (NPV) criterion project *B* should be chosen, while according to internal rate of return (IRR) criterion, project *A* is recommended for investment. So in this case we get inconsistent results from the two evaluation criteria. *The inconsistent results are due to the difference in the rate of return at which annual cash flows are reinvested for the next years.*

Table 33.5. Comparing NPV and IRR Methods

	Net Cash Flows							
Years	*0**	*1*	*2*	*3*	*4*	*5*	*NPV*	*IRR*
Project *A*	1,000	450	450	450	450	450	622	34.9
Project *B*	1,000	– 300	0	600	600	2,000	675	24.2

* *Initial Investment Outlay (i.e., Cost of the Project) in Year 0.*

Whereas under the net present value method, the net cash flows generated by a project are implicitly assumed to be *reinvested at the firm's cost of capital used by the firm for evaluation*, in the IRR method the net cash flows generated by the project are *implicitly assumed to be reinvested at the same higher rate of return earned on the project.* This is somewhat unrealistic assumption because the rate of return on firm's reinvestment of its annual cash flows may not be as high as the cost of capital of the investment in the project under consideration. Therefore, *the net present value (NPV) is considered to be superior or*

2. Note that internal rate of return can also be defined as discount rate which makes net present value (*NPV*) of the project equal to zero (*NPV* = 0).

better than internal rate of return (IRR) criterion in deciding which of the two mutually exclusive projects should be chosen for investment. To conclude, when the two or more projects provides contradictory or inconsistent results on the basis of the two criteria, it is preferable for the firm to choose a project with a higher net present value (NPV) than the one with higher internal rate of return (IRR).

Profitability Index (PI) Method

Another criterion of evaluating investment projects, which is similar to net present value method, is that of profitability index which is also called *benefit-cost ratio.* Profitability index (PI) of a capital project is defined as the ratio of present value of future cash flows from a project to the intial cost of the project. Thus,

$$\text{Profitability Index (PI)} = \frac{\text{Present Value of Future Cash Flows}}{\text{Initial Cost of a Project}}$$

or

$$\text{PI} = \frac{\sum_{t=1}^{n} \frac{R_1}{(1+i)^t}}{C_0}$$

where $\sum_{t=1}^{n} \frac{R_1}{(1+i)^t}$ is the sum of the present value of future cash flows from the project and C_0 is the initial cost of a project.

When profitability index of a project is greater than one, it means it adds more to the value of a firm it costs.

Decision rule. It is clear from above that in the method of profitability index, *a project with profitability index greater than one* (PI > 1) *should be accepted and a project with a profitability index less than one* (PI < 1) *should be rejected.* This means that those projects are accepted for investment which return more than a rupee of discounted cash flows for each rupee cost. Profitability index and net present value criterion always lead to consistent results regarding accept/reject decision when a single independent project is being evaluated. This is because when profitability index is greater than one (PI > 1) implies net present value being positive (NPV > 0) and when profitability index is less than one, it implies net present value being negative (NPV < 0).

However, it may be noted that when choice among alternative projects of unequal size (that is, requiring different amounts of investment outlay) are concerned, the NPV and profitability index (PI) can provide different rankings to the various projects.

The Level of Capital Expenditure and Capital Rationing

Two important decisions are required to be made in the capital budgeting process of a firm. First, if enough funds are available for investment with a firm, it has to determine the level of capital expenditure it will make. Secondly, *if the limited amount of funds are available, how a firm should allocate them among various projects*. Whereas the first type of decision *relates to the determination of the capital expenditure*, the second type of decision-making is called *capital rationing*.

Let us first explain what determines the level of capital expenditure by a firm when there is no constraint on the resources available to it. The level of capital expenditure depends on the internal rate of return (IRR) of the project on the one hand and cost of capital (*i.e.* cost of funds for investment) on the other. In Fig. 33.2 we have drawn histograms representing seven projects. The length of a histogram shows the internal rate of return (*IRR*) of a project, while the width of a histogram represents the *cost of the project*, that is, funds initially required to implement it. The various projects are ranked in order of internal rate of return from them. Thus *IRR* of project *A* is 20%, of project *B* is 18%, of project *C* is 16% and so on. The thick line on the top of the histograms indicates decreasing rate of return of successive investment projects.

MCC curve shows the marginal cost of capital which is shown to be increasing. This is because as the firm borrows more funds, the greater the degree of risk will be borne by the lenders to the firm. This is because as the firm borrows more funds, there is a greater risk of default in its paying back the funds borrowed. Therefore, as a firm borrows more funds a higher rate of interest will be demanded by the lenders. *A project will be undertaken if internal rate return exceeds marginal cost of capital.* Thus, a firm will invest in new projects as long as internal rate of return (IRR) from investment projects is greater than the cost of capital. It will be seen from Fig. 33.2 that given the cost of capital as shown by the curve MCC, the firm will undertake investment in projects *A*, *B*, *C* and *D*. It will not go further as internal rate of return (IRR) on additional projects is less than the cost of capital. It will be seen from Fig. 33.2 that the firm will make total investment or incur capital expenditure equal to ₹ 6 lakhs.

Capital Rationing. However, unconstrained investment funds for a firm are not generally available. Quite often a firm has a limited amount of investment funds. With the given constraint of available funds, it has to decide which projects it should choose for implementation and accordingly allocate or ration capital funds to them.

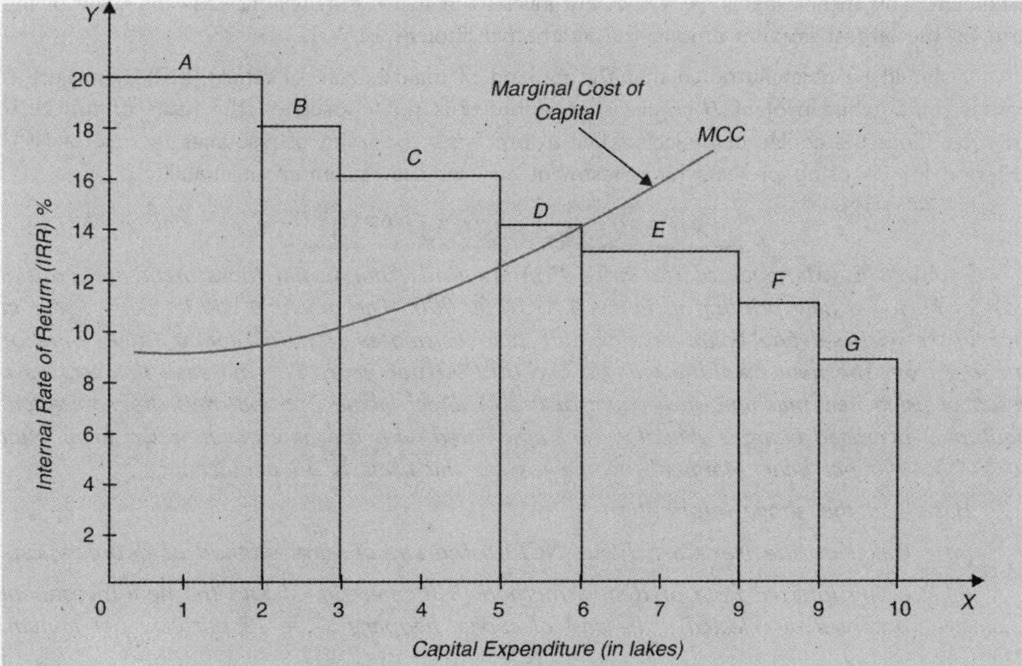

Fig. 33.2. *Determining Capital Expenditure*

Suppose investment funds available for a firm for investment are ₹ 4 lakhs. It will be seen from the Table 33.5 that projects *A*, *B* and *D* cost ₹ 4 lakhs; and projects *A* and *C* also together cost Rs. 4 lakhs; and projects *A* and *B* (which together cost 3 lakhs and therefore

Table 33.6. Capital Rationing

Project	*Initial Cost of Project*	*NPV*	*IRR*	*IRR (Ranking)*
A	2,000,00	10,000	20	1
B	1,000,00	4,000	18	2
C	2,000,00	7,000	16	3
D	1,000,00	2,500	14	4
E	1,000,00	2,000	13	5
F	1,000,00	1,900	11	6
Idle or Unutilised Balance	1,000,00	0	0	7

leave Rs. one lakh unutilised). In this case of choice of projects with a limited resources, the use of criteria of NPV and IRR conflict with each other. This will be easily understood from the data given in Table 33.6.

In this case *optimum choice is one which provides the highest NPV to the firm.* It will be seen from the table that the sum of NPV of the projects *A*, *B* and *D* are ₹ 16,500 (10,000 + 4,000 + 2,500 = ₹ 16,500), the sum of NPV of the projects *A* and *C* is ₹ 17,000 (10,000 + 7,000 = 17,000) and NPV of the projects *A* and *B* (with idle funds of ₹ one lakh is 10,000 + 4,000 + 0 = 14,000). Thus, the NPV of the projects *A* and *C* is the maximum. This means that if ₹ 4 lakh are invested in them, they will increase the value of the firm by the largest amount among the alternative choices.

It should be carefully noted that the ranking of internal rate of return (IRR) of project *C* comes third, while project *B* comes second but it is not chosen on the basis of the NPV criterion. Thus the choice of projects when a firm faces constraint of resources the use of NPV criterion for choosing projects for investment ensures the maximum profitability.

NUMERICAL PROBLEMS

Problem 1. *Manager of Ravindra Printers finds that initial investment (i.e., initial cost of buying a new printing machine is ₹ 10,00,000. The machine will be depreciated in five years with salvage value of zero. He also estimates that increment in revenue or income from the new machine will be ₹ 8,00,000 per year. The increase in costs as a result of using new machine on account of use of direct labour and materials, transportation, additional overhead charges, building rent associated with the new machine would amount to ₹ 4,50,000 per year. Marginal income tax for the firms is 40 per cent.*

Based on the above information :

(a) Calculate the Net Cash Flow (NCF) using straight-line method of depreciation.

(b) Using Internal Rate of Return method (IRR) method, should the new investment project be accepted or rejected if the cost of capital happens to be 12 per cent per annum.

Solution :

(*a*) NCF = Net Income before Tax − Income Tax + Depreciation

Therefore, to calculate Net Cash Flow (NCF), we have to calculate Net Income before Income Tax and Depreciation.

Net Income before Tax = Annual Income (or Revenue) – Incremental Costs – Depreciation

Annual Income or Revenue = ₹ 8,00,000

Incremental Costs = ₹ 4,50,000

Depreciation at the rate of 20% (straight-line method) as the machine's life is 5 years

$$= 10{,}00{,}000 \quad \frac{20}{100} = 2{,}00{,}000$$

Net Income before Tax = 8,00,000 – 4,50,000 – 2,00,000

= ₹ 1,50,000

$$\text{Income Tax} = 1{,}50{,}000 \quad \frac{40}{100} = 60{,}000$$

Net Cash Flow (NCF) = Net Income before Tax – Income Tax + Depreciation

= 1,50,000 – 60,000 + 2,00,000

= ₹ 2,90,000

(*b*) **Rate of Return : IRR Method**

According to IRR method, rate of return is the discount rate at which present value of cash flow will be equal to initial cost of investment.

Thus,

$$\sum_{t=1}^{n} \frac{NCF_t}{(1+r)^t} = C$$

where NCF_t is net cash flow per year, C is the initial cost of investment and r is the rate of return.

As calculated above, NCF = ₹ 2,90,000

Initial Cost (C) = ₹ 10,00,000

n = 5 years

Substituting these values in the formula, we have

$$\sum_{t=1}^{5} \frac{2{,}90{,}000^*}{(1+r)^t} = 10{,}00{,}000$$

$$\text{or} \quad \sum_{t=1}^{5} \frac{1}{(1+r)^t} = \frac{10{,}00{,}000}{2{,}90{,}000} = 3.4483$$

It should be noted that the term $\left[\sum_{t=1}^{5} \frac{1}{(1+r)^t}\right]$ represents the present value of annuity of

---

$$* \sum_{t=1}^{5} \frac{2{,}90{,}000}{(1+r)^t} = \frac{2{,}90{,}000}{1+r} + \frac{2{,}90{,}000}{(1+r)^2} + \frac{2{,}90{,}000}{(1+r)^3} + \frac{2{,}90{,}000}{(1+r)^4} + \frac{2{,}90{,}000}{(1+r)^5}$$

$$= 2{,}90{,}000\left[\frac{1}{1+r} + \frac{1}{(1+r)^2} + \frac{1}{(1+r)^3} + \frac{1}{(1+r)^4} + \frac{1}{(1+r)^5}\right]$$

where r is the rate of discount or return.

Re 1 for five years discounted at the rate of *r*. In order to find out the value of *r* we have to use the table giving the present value of annuity of Re 1 in a future period which is generally called Present Value of Annuity of Re 1 (PVIEA) and is provided in the Log Book (and given in the Appendix – A to this Chapter). Looking at the table giving Present Value of Annuity of Re 1 on the fifth row (indicating 5 years period) it will be seen that figure of 3.4483 lies between 3.5172 and 3.4331 corresponding to 13% and 14% discount rate.[1] This means that the rate of return is greater than 13% but less than 14%. The given cost of capital is 12 per cent. This implies that rate of return is greater than the given cost of capital. Thus, undertaking of the project will add to the value of the firm and should therefore be undertaken.

(c) **NPV Criterion.** According to this, a capital investment project should be accepted if NPV > 0. That is, with the given cost of capital equal to 12%, for capital investment project to be undertaken.

$$NPV = \sum_{t=1}^{5} \frac{NCF_t}{(1+12)^t} - C > 0$$

As calculated above net cash flow (NCF) is ₹ 2,90,000 per year for five years. Thus,

$$NPV = \sum_{t=1}^{5} \frac{2,90,000}{(1+0.12)^t} - 10,00,000$$

$$\sum_{t=1}^{5} \frac{2,90,000}{(1+0.12)^t} = 2,90,000\left[\frac{1}{(1+0.12)} + \frac{1}{(1+0.12)^2} + \frac{1}{(1+0.12)^3} + \frac{1}{(1+0.12)^4} + \frac{1}{(1+0.12)^5}\right]$$

$$= 2,90,000(3.60478)$$

$$= 10,45,386.2$$

$$NPV = 10,45,386.2 - 10,00,000$$

$$= 45,386.2$$

Thus, Net Present Value of the cash flows of the investment project is greater than zero (that is, positive). Therefore, investment in the project should be undertaken as it will increase the value of the firm or shareholders' wealth.

Problem 2. *S. Chand & Co is considering a proposal for investment in a new machine for binding for which it has to incur initial cost of ₹ 25 lacs. It has been estimated by the Company's manager that new binding machine will cause cost-saving in the publication of the books. Because of its cost-saving it has been estimated that it will generate additional net cash flows which are given below over its anticipated life of five years. If S Chand & Co requires return of 15 per cent on the investment project, should the investment in the new binding machine be undertaken ? Use Net Present Value criterion to evaluate the project.*

Year	*Net Cash Flow*
(NCF_t)	
1	6,00,000
2	8,00,000
3	8,00,000
4	6,00.000
5	2,50,000

1. Exact discount rate or interest rate can be obtained through interpolation.

Solution :

$$NPV = \sum_{t=1}^{n} \frac{NCF_t}{(1+0.15)^t} - C^*$$

We calculate the present value of cash flows $\left[\frac{NCF_t}{(1+0.15)^t}\right]$ in the following table by using Table of Present value of Interest Factor (PVIF) given in Appendix B to this Chapter.

Year	*Net Cash Flow* (NCF_t)	*Present Value Interest Factor at 15%* $\left(\frac{1}{(1+0.15)^t}\right)^*$	*Present Value (PV)* *(2) (3)*
(1)	*(2)*	*(3)*	*(4)*
1	6,00,000	0.86957	521,742
2	8,00,000	0.75614	604,912
3	8,00,000	0.65752	526,016
4	6,00,000	0.59175	343,050
5	2,50,000	0.49718	124,295
			Total = 2120,015

Thus, $NPV = \sum_{t=1}^{n} \frac{NCF_t}{(1+0.15)^t} - C = 2120{,}015 - 25{,}00{,}000 = -379985$

Thus, the Net Present Value of the given investment project is negative and should not therefore be undertaken.

QUESTIONS FOR REVIEW

1. Distinguish between investment and stock of capital. What factors determines investment in an economy.
2. What considerations are taken into account by a firm while making investment decision. Explain them.
3. What is meant by capital budgeting ? Why is it of crucial importance ?
4. What general guidelines firms should follow in properly estimating the net cash flows from an investment project ?
5. What is the difference between the profit flow and net cash flow from a capital investment project ? Why do firms use the net cash flow to estimate the net present value of an investment project ?
6. Explain the nature of capital expenditure decision ? How does it involve uncertainty ?
7. What is meant by '*state of nature*' ? What does it imply for capital investment decision ?
8. Capital budgeting decision can make or mar the fortunes of firms. Comment.
9. Explain the rule for calculating present discounted value of a perpetual income stream. What is the worth of a perpetuity paying ₹ 10,000 per year when the rate of interest is 8 per cent per annum.

* The Present Value Interest Factor at 15% is taken from the Log Table which are provided to the students. Present Value Interest Factor at 15% interest rate implies what would be the present value of Re 1 after 1 year, after 2 years, after 3 years and so on at 15 per cent rate of interest.

10. Explain why investment demand curve slopes downward. What factors cause a shift in investment demand curve ?
11. Given the following three projects, which project has the maximum net present value assuming the market rate of interest as 8%.
   (*i*) Project *A* which yields an income of ₹ 200 per year indefinitely into the future.
   (*ii*) Project *B* which yields ₹ 400 per year for two years
   (*iii*) Project *C* which yields ₹ 100 today and ₹ 200 after 2 years
12. For a certain project the anticipated cash flows are ₹ 100 at present and ₹ 125 next year. What is the present value when the interest rate is 10% ? What is the highest rate of interest at which the project should be undertaken ?
13. Calculate the market equilibrium value for the following assets. Assume the market rate of interest is 10%.
   (*i*) A bond that pays ₹ 100 interest per year for two years and is paid off at ₹ 1000 at the end of two years.
   (*ii*) A building that will earn ₹ 100 per year for two years and then will earn ₹ 50 per year indefinitely into the future.
14. What is the internal rate of return on an investment ? Calculate the internal rate of return on an investment yielding ₹ 25,000 after one year and costing ₹ 20,000. Suppose instead that this investment yielded nothing in the first year and ₹ 30,000 after two years, what would be its internal rate of return ?
15. An investment pays ₹ 100 per year for ever starting a year from now. What is its present value if the rate of interest is 10 per cent ? What is its present value if the rate of interest is 20 per cent ?
16. Calculate the market value for an acre of land yielding ₹ 100 per annum, after all expenses, indefinitely into the future. Market rate of interest is 10%.
   (Hints : This is a case of perpetuity)
17. Compare the Net Present Value (NPV) and Internal Rate of Return (IRR) methods of evaluating investment projects. When do they provide contradictory results ? Which method should then be used ?
18. When the Net Present Value (NPV) is greater than zero, what does it imply about internal rate of return ?
19. Why do firms face capital rationing problem ? What investment criterion should the firm use when it faces capital rationing problem ?
20. What is the basic principle underlying capital investment decision (*i.e.*, capital budgeting decision)? Show that capital budgeting is nothing more than the application of the theory of firm to investment project.
   (Hints : According to the theory of firm, a firm produces a rate of output at which marginal revenue equals marginal cost of production. The general principle underlying capital budgeting is the same, namely, a firm undertakes the amount of capital investment at which marginal return from capital project equals marginal cost of capital. For details see the text in the book.)
21. Why is marginal cost of capital schedule or function generally rising for most firms? Explain.
22. Which of the following are capital investment decisions ? Give reasons.
   (i) Replacing old machine by a new machine embodying new technology.
   (ii) Buying 40 per cent common stock (i.e., common shares) of a new competitive firm.
   (iii) Employing additional staff to meet peak-season demand for a product.
   (*iv*) Engaging a security agency at the cost of Rs. 5 lacs per annum to guard factory premises.
   (*v*) Making a plan for higher expenditure on R&D project.
23. What is the *decision rule for investment* in the following methods of project appraisal ?
   1. Payback Period Method 2. NPV Method 3. Inernal Rate of Return Method

Appendix To Chapter 33

Cost Benefit Analysis

Meaning and Significance

In the foregoing chapters we have been mainly concerned with the business decision making by private enterprises which are driven mainly by profit motive. In the selection of investment projects the private firms take into account only the internal direct effects (that is, cash flows accruing to them and the costs they have to incur) and do not take the longer and wider view of their activities from the social point of view. As seen in the previous chapter the private sector firms follow the net present value criterion for acceptance or rejection of investment projects. But public enterprises and non-profit institutions have to take a broader social repercussions of their resource allocation and investment decisions. That is, they take into account both internal (direct) and external (indirect) effects of their business decisions. An analytical model called cost-benefit analysis is used to analyse the wider impact of resource allocation and investment decisions. Properly understood, it is *Social Cost-Benefit* Analysis of investment projects though the word 'social' is often omitted. Thus in social cost-benefit analysis, we estimate both direct and indirect costs of a project to the society and its direct and indirect benefits to the society.Therefore, *cost-benefit analysis is especially used for analysing the desirability of public sector investment programme and is a counter part of which is used to evaluate any investment project by a private enterprise.*

Explaining the essence of cost-benefit analysis Prest and Turvey who are the pioneers of the technique of cost-benefit analysis write, "Cost-benefit analysis is a practical way of assessing the desirability of projects where it is important to take a long view (in the sense of looking at repercussions in the distant future as will as the nearer future) and a wider view (in the sense of allowing for side-effects of many kinds and many persons, industries, regions, etc.), i.e., it implies the enumeration and evaluation of all relevant costs and benefits"[1]. It is important to note that in estimating social costs of a project market prices of resources are not used as they are generally distorted; they are distorted due to the imposition of taxes by the Government or due to the market imperfection or monopoly power of the resource owners. Instead, specially devised prices called *shadow prices* which reflect the opportunity costs or true scarcity values of the resources used.

It is worth noting that public sector enterprises and non-profit institutions face the same problems of resource allocation and investment as the private sector. But in deciding about them while the public sector enterprises take a wider view and consider both internal

1. Prest and Turvey, *Economic Journal,* December, 1975.

and external effects of their decisions, the private sector, guided by profit considerations alone, adopts a narrow view and takes into account only internal effects of their business decisions, disregarding the external effects which may be harmful or beneficial. Thus in cost-benefit analysis we are not concerned with internal benefits and internal costs of an investment project to be undertaken by a private firm. The cost-benefit analysis enumerates and evaluates *all social benefits* and *all social costs* of a project or expenditure programme in contrast to the capital budgeting technique used by private firms which take into account only their private costs and private benefits to judge the desirability of an investment project. Besides, since benefits from an investment project are reaped mostly in in future years and costs are also incurred for a long period in future, it is ***discounted social benefits and discounted social costs that are*** compared to decide about the desirability of a project. However, for discounting social benefits and costs of an investment project, it is *social discount rate* that is often used.

The Use of Cost-Benefit Analysis

As mentioned above, the technique of cost-benefit analysis is particularly used when *a long and wider view* of the effects of a particular project or expenditure programme is needed. As in case of capital budgeting by private firms cost-benefit analysis is generally used in case when the economic effects of a project or an investment expenditure programme or policy change *accrue in future years*. However, unlike the capital budgeting by private firms, the cost-benefit analysis attempts to estimate all direct economic effects as well as indirect spill-over effects.

Cost benefit analysis is used to assess whether a particular project or specific public expenditure programme should be accepted or rejected. In order to do so benefits, both direct and indirect, of the project or specific public expenditure programme and similarly the costs to be incurred on the project over the years are estimated. Then the *present value* of both the benefits and costs over the future years are estimated using an appropriate discount rate from social point of view. It follows from above that cost-benefit analysis is a method of evaluating public projects and expenditure programmes for making decisions regarding the desirability of the projects to be undertaken. Accordingly, it is used to assess big public expenditure schemes such as building dams and airports, controlling diseases (for example, malaria control programme), planning for defence and safety, and spending for health, education and research.

Cost-Benefit Criterion

Having calculated the present values of both benefits and costs at a given social discount rate then the two are compared. If using the given social discount rate *present value of benefits from a project or other investment programme exceeds the present value of costs, the said project or investment programme is accepted for being undertaken.* On the other hand, if present value of benefits is less than the present value of costs, the proposed project or expenditure programme is economically inefficient and should be rejected.

Besides being used to evaluate the economic justification of the entire project or programme, the cost-benefit analysis is used to determine whether the size of project or programme under implementation be increased and if so by what extent. Such decision is usually made by using traditional marginal analysis by estimating additional benefits from the proposed increase in size and additional costs to be made. Thus the objective of public sector decision making whether it is building of an airport or regulating a public utility (such as electricity generation and distribution) is wider than maximising private profits which guides private sector decision. *In making a decision the Government or public enterprise has not only to consider benefits that accrue as revenue to the enterprise but also the external benefits (beneficial externalities) that accrue to other members of the socially.* Likewise, the cost-benefit analysis considers not only the costs that are paid by the enterprise but also the costs (including environment pollution) it inflicts on others by its activity.

General Steps (or Stages) of Cost-Benefit Analysis

There are no simple rules which Government or any public authority should follow to undertake cost-benefit analysis. The following four general stages or steps are involved in conducting cost-benefit analysis.

Let us explain the above stages in some detail of undertaking cost-benefit analysis.

Step 1. In stage 1 we are concerned with assessing whether the proposed investment project or expenditure programm is appropriate from the wider social point of view taking into account all the *externalities* (that is, both beneficial and harmful external effects) of the investment project. Obviously, the project will be considered as appropriate for being undertaken if there are *significant beneficial externalities* so that they exceed the cost of the project. However, the appropriateness of the project depends on the objective function to be maximised. This objective function is set by the Government or in a democracy by the parliament which represents the people.

Step 2. The step or stage - 2 requires identifying and enumerating all external benefits and costs many of which may be intangible such as noise, pollution, beauty and healthly environment. There are both direct and indirect (external) benefits and costs of

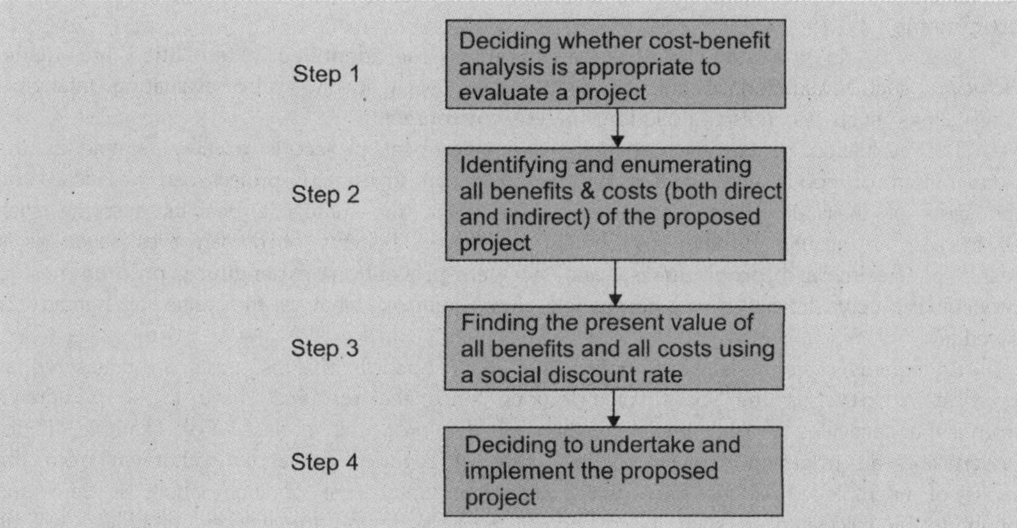

Fig. 33A.1. *Steps (or Stages) of Cost-Benefit Analysis*

an investment project. The direct or internal benefits of a project can be measured by the extra quantity of goods and services produced if the project is undertaken compared to the conditions without it. Thus, the direct benefits of an irrigation project is the quantity of extra crop produced net of extra costs in the form of more labour, seeds and equipment used as compared to the non-irrigated land. On the other hand, direct costs include capital costs incurred on capital equipment, machines installed, land acquired to undertake and implement the project and the operating and maintenance costs incurred over the life span of the project.

In addition to the direct effects of an investment project, there are invariably *indirect or external effects.* These indirect or external beneficial effects are classified into two types, (1) real or technological and (2) the pecuniary effects. The real external benefits may include reduction in costs to be incurred on other Government programmes. For example, the construction of irrigation dam may lead to reduction in flooding and soil erosion which would reduce the Government outlay on flood control and anti-soil erosion programmes. Such real indirect or external benefits are counted in cost-benefit studies.

On the other hand, *indirect (external) pecuniary benefits* are not generally included in the enumeration of benefits and costs in a cost-benefit study. These external pecuniary benefits accrue in the form of increased volume of business or increase in land values as a consequence of undertaking a project. Thus the areas in Delhi which fall near Metro railway routes has caused increase in land values in these areas. Besides, the shops and restaurants which exist in the areas surrounding the metro-lines have found increase in the volume of their business. These indirect or external pecuniary benefits are purely distributional and not counted in cost-benefit studies of Metro-railways.

Similarly, indirect multiplier effects and induced investment effects which result from Government investment projects are also generally not counted (except in some special circumstances) since they would occur whether investment made is by the public sector or private sector. For example, if the objective of Government investment programme is regional development, undertaking a local investment project may induce local investment, create multiplier effect on generation of income and employment resulting in reduction of regional unemployment. Since regional development forms a part of objective function to be maximised, some include them in their cost-benefit studies of regional investment programme.

Steps 3. In the stage 3 the evaluation of the identified externalities are made. However, such evaluation is quite a difficult task as it involves also evaluating intangible externalities such as noise, pollution, green environment.

The evaluation of tangible benefits of an investment project is relatively simple as the extra output of goods and services resulting from an investment project can be valued on the basis of their prevailing market prices. However, the intangible benefits accruing such as increase in beauty, healthy environment and direct benefits of human lives saved as a result of health-care programmes, and accident-prevention expenditure programmes is conceptually very difficult if not impossible. For example, what is the value of human life saved ?

As regards costs, it is worth noting that in cost-benefit analysis, costs are measured as ***opportunity costs*** as the social value forgone since the resources have to be withdrawn from other activities to the implementation of the proposed project.[2] For example, if for undertaking an irrigation project, 50 per cent of required labour is withdrawn from the ranks of unemployed labour force the social opportunity cost of such labour is zero and ought to be calculated as such in cost-benefit analysis though the workers employed will be paid market wages. The same holds in case of *idle land* used for a project. With no alternative use, the opportunity cost of idle land is zero. This is so despite the fact that Government has actually to pay compensation to the landowners for acquiring this idle land. This compensation will affect only the distribution of benefits from the project for use of land and not the social cost of the project.

All the benefits and costs (both internal and external) over the life span of the project have to discounted to obtain their present values. In this connection a difficult decision has

2. See E.J. Mishan, *Cost-Benefit Analysis, An Introduction*, Praeger Publishers, 1971, ph. 7-8.

also to be made about appropriate social discount rate. Besides, constraints placed on cost-benefit analysis have also to be taken into account.

Steps 4. Lastly, in stage 4 on the basis of valuation made in stage-3, decision has to be taken in stage 4 whether to undertake the proposed investment project or it should be rejected. This will be mainly done on the basis of cost-benefit criterion. If the present value of all benefits (both internal and external) exceeds the present value of all costs (both internal and external) of the project, it should be accepted. However, the decision in this regard, especially if the project is in the public sector, political considerations also play a part in making the decision regarding undertaking of the proposed project.

Conclusion

It follows from above that the cost-benefit analysis is a method of evaluating investment project or other public expenditure programme by identifying and evaluating all relevant costs and benefits (both internal and external). A proposed project has to be undertaken, if the present value of all benefits exceeds the present value of all costs. Initially it was developed to evaluate public sector investment project but is now being used by decision making by the private sector as *environment awareness* has greatly increased in recent years because Government imposes taxes on the firms for their harmful externalities and provide subsidies to them if they generate beneficial externalities.

Importance of Cost-Benefit Analysis

Social Cost-benefit analysis is highly significant for development planning in developing countries. The significant benefit of cost-benefit analysis is that it can guide investment decisions, especially for the public sector. Given the constraint of resources, on the basis of cost-benefit analysis, the Government can choose the most beneficial among them. The Government can use the social-cost benefit analysis even for evaluating the effects of private investment projects. This helps the Government for formulating its policies to either support or discourage private investment. The Government can support private investment projects by providing subsidies or provide financial support through financial institutions. The Government can discourage them by imposing taxes if the social costs exceed social benefits of the private investment.

The significance of cost benefit analysis can be better recognised when we consider that alternative method of resource allocation is market mechanism which uses *market prices* of goods and services which do not reflect true social benefits and costs of investment projects. As mentioned above social cost-benefit analysis takes into account wider and broader social benefits and costs incorporating both the *direct and indirect effects* of an investment. To quote Thirwall, "The technique of cost-benefit analysis is recommended for the appraisal of publicly financed projects in order to allocate resources in a way that is most profitable to the society, recognising that the market prices of goods and factors of production do not necessarily reflect their social values and costs respectively and given that the society is concerned with the future level of consumption as well as the present, the level of current saving may be suboptimal."[3]

Ensuring Optimal Use of Scarce Resources. Planning in developing countries requires a lot of investment in infrastructure and heavy industries projects such as building of highways, airports, irrigation dams and canals, power plants, steel plants and communication network. These projects have indirect beneficial effects which are crucial for acceleration of economic growth and generation of employment opportunities. However, these investment projects require not only financial resources which are scarce in

---

3. A.P. Thirwall, *Growth and Development with Special Reference to Developing Economics,* Macmellan, 2004, 7th edition, pp. 373-374.

developing countries but also foreign exchange, skilled or technically trained manpower, a lot of energy resources (such as coal, petroleum oil). The desirability of the investment of these investment projects relating to infrastructure and basic heavy industries cannot be analysed on the basis of market prices of goods and factors. Hence cost-benefit analysis which uses shadow prices reflecting opportunity costs or true scarcity values of resources used in investment projects is essential for optimum use of scarce resources in development planning.

Importance for Planning. Cost benefit analysis is of vital importance in economic planning for growth and employment generation in developing countries. It is on the basis of cost benefit analysis that those investment projects are chosen in a five year plan which help in achieving the objectives of the plan. Since through cost-benefit analysis different investment projects are ranked in accordance with their contribution to the plan objectives relating to GDP growth and employment generation, priorities can be assigned which projects be undertaken in a plan period. Little and Mirrlees consider the appraisal of various investment projects on the basis of cost-benefit analysis as a *sine quo non* of economic planning for development.[4]

Besides, cost-benefit analysis help in promoting social interest rather than any sectional or group interest. If the projects are selected on the basis of social cost benefit analysis, it becomes, difficult for any vested interests or groups of the people to oppose them if they do not suit their narrow interests.[5]

QUESTIONS FOR REVIEW

1. What is cost-benefit analysis ? How does it differ from capital budgeting ?
2. Explain the use of cost-benefit analysis. What types of benefits and costs are included in cost-benefit analysis ?
3. Explain the various steps involved in making cost-benefit analysis of Government's investment project.
4. Explain the cost-benefit criterion which is used to evaluate the desirability of undertaking an investment project by the Government.
5. How are benefits of an investment project yielding benefits over a number of future years are compared with costs incurred over the years ? Explain
6. Explain the importance of cost-benefit analysis for developing countries, especially for planning of projects for growth and employment.

4. I.M.D. Little and Mirrlees, "*Manual of Industrial Projects in Developing Countries*", OECD, 1969.
5. See Stephen A Marglin, *Public Investment Critera*, George Allen & Unwin, London, 1973.

APPENDIX A TO CHAPTER 33

Table 1 : Present Value of an Annuity of Re (PVIFA)

Period	1%	2%	3%	4%	5%	6%	7%	8%	9%	10%	Period
01	.9901	.9804	.9709	.9615	.9524	.9434	.9346	.9259	.9174	.9091	01
02	1.9704	1.9416	1.9135	1.8861	1.8594	1.8334	1.8080	1.7833	1.7591	1.7355	02
03	2.9410	2.8839	2.8286	2.7751	2.7233	2.6730	2.6243	2.5771	2.5313	2.4868	03
04	3.9020	3.8077	3.7171	3.6299	3.5459	3.4651	3.3872	3.3121	3.2397	3.1699	04
05	4.8535	4.7134	4.5797	4.4518	4.3295	4.2123	4.1002	3.9927	3.8896	3.7908	05
06	5.7955	5.6014	5.4172	5.2421	5.0757	4.9173	4.7665	4.6229	4.4859	4.3553	06
07	6.7282	6.4720	6.2302	6.0020	5.7863	5.5824	5.3893	5.2064	5.0329	4.8684	07
08	7.6517	7.3254	7.0196	6.7327	6.4632	6.2093	5.9713	5.7466	5.5348	5.3349	08
09	8.5661	8.1622	7.7861	7.4353	7.1078	6.8017	6.5152	6.2469	5.9852	5.7590	09
10	9.4714	8.9825	8.7302	8.1109	7.7217	7.3601	7.0236	6.7101	6.4176	6.1446	10
11	10.3677	9.7868	9.2526	8.7604	8.3064	7.8868	7.4987	7.1389	6.8052	6.4951	11
12	11.2552	10.5753	9.9589	9.3850	8.8632	8.3838	7.9427	7.5361	7.1601	6.8137	12
13	12.1338	11.3483	10.6349	9.9856	9.3935	8.8527	8.3576	7.9038	7.4869	7.1034	13
14	13.0088	12.1062	11.2960	10.5631	9.8986	9.2950	8.7454	8.2442	7.7860	7.3667	14
15	13.8651	12.8492	11.9379	11.1183	10.3769	9.7122	9.1079	8.5595	8.0607	7.6061	15
16	14.7180	13.5777	12.5610	11.6522	10.8377	10.1059	9.4466	8.8514	8.3126	7.8237	16
17	15.5624	14.2918	13.1660	12.1656	11.2740	10.4772	9.7632	9.1216	8.5435	8.0215	17
18	16.3984	14.9920	13.7534	12.6592	11.6895	10.8276	10.0591	9.3719	8.7556	8.2014	18
19	17.2201	15.2684	14.3237	13.1339	12.0853	11.1581	10.3356	9.6036	8.9501	8.3649	19
20	18.0457	16.3514	14.8774	13.5903	12.4622	11.4699	10.5940	9.8181	9.2185	8.5136	20
21	18.8571	17.0111	15.4149	14.0291	12.8211	11.7640	10.8355	10.0168	9.2922	8.6487	21
22	19.6605	17.6581	15.9368	14.4511	13.1630	12.0416	11.0612	10.2007	9.4424	8.7715	22
23	20.4559	18.2921	16.4435	14.8568	13.4885	12.3033	11.2722	10.3710	9.5802	8.8832	23
24	21.2435	18.9139	16.9355	15.2469	13.7986	12.5503	11.4693	10.5287	9.7066	8.9847	24
25	22.0233	19.5234	17.4181	15.6220	14.9039	12.7833	11.6536	10.6748	9.8226	9.0770	25

APPENDIX A (Continued)

Table 1 : Present Value of an Annuity of $1 (PVIFA)

Period	11%	12%	13%	14%	15%	16%	17%	18%	19%	20%	Period
01	.9009	.8929	.8850	.8772	.8696	.8621	.8547	.8475	.8403	.8333	01
02	1.7125	1.6901	1.6681	1.6467	1.6257	1.6052	1.5852	1.5656	1.5465	1.5278	02
03	2.4437	2.4018	2.3612	2.3216	2.2832	2.2459	2.2096	2.1743	2.1399	2.1065	03
04	3.1024	3.0373	2.9745	2.9137	2.8550	2.7982	2.7432	2.6901	2.6386	2.5887	04
05	3.6959	3.6048	3.5172	3.4331	3.3522	3.2743	3.1993	3.1272	3.0576	2.9906	05
06	4.2305	4.1114	3.9976	3.8887	3.7845	3.6847	3.5892	3.4976	3.4098	3.3255	06
07	4.7122	4.5638	4.4226	4.2883	4.1604	4.0386	3.9224	3.8115	3.7057	3.6046	07
08	5.1461	4.9676	4.7988	4.6389	4.4873	4.3436	4.2072	4.0776	3.9544	3.8372	08
09	5.5370	5.3282	5.1317	4.9464	4.7716	4.6065	4.4506	4.3030	4.1633	4.0310	09
10	5.8892	5.6502	5.4262	5.2161	5.0188	4.8332	4.6586	4.4941	4.3389	4.1925	10
11	6.2065	5.9377	5.6869	5.4527	5.2337	5.0286	4.8364	4.6560	4.4865	4.3271	11
12	6.4924	6.1944	5.9176	5.6603	5.4206	5.1971	4.9884	4.7932	4.6105	4.4392	12
13	6.7499	6.4235	6.1218	5.8424	5.5831	5.3423	5.1183	4.9095	4.7147	4.5327	13
14	6.9819	6.9282	6.3025	6.0021	5.7245	5.4675	5.2293	5.0081	4.8023	4.6106	14
15	7.1909	6.8109	6.4624	6.1422	5.8474	5.5755	5.3242	5.0916	4.8759	4.6755	15
16	7.3792	6.9740	6.6039	6.2651	5.9542	5.6685	5.4053	5.1624	4.9377	4.7296	16
17	7.5488	7.1196	6.7291	6.3729	6.0472	5.7487	5.4746	5.2223	4.9897	4.7746	17
18	7.7016	7.2497	6.8389	6.4674	6.1280	5.8178	5.5339	5.2732	5.0333	4.8122	18
19	7.8393	7.3650	6.9380	6.5504	6.1982	5.8775	5.5845	5.3176	5.0700	4.8435	19
20	7.9633	7.4694	7.0248	6.6231	6.2593	5.9288	5.6278	5.3527	5.1009	4.8696	20
21	8.0751	7.5620	7.1016	6.6870	6.3125	5.9731	5.6648	5.3837	5.1268	4.8913	21
22	8.1757	7.6446	7.1695	6.7429	6.3587	6.0113	5.6964	5.4099	5.1486	4.9094	22
23	8.2664	7.7184	7.2297	6.7921	6.3988	6.0442	5.7234	5.4321	5.1668	4.9245	23
24	8.3481	7.7843	7.2829	6.8351	6.4338	6.0726	5.7465	5.4509	5.1822	4.9371	24
25	8.4217	7.8431	7.3300	6.8729	6.4641	6.0971	5.7662	5.4669	5.1951	4.9476	25

APPENDIX B TO CHAPTER 33

Table I : Present Value of Re 1.00

$$PVIE_{in} = \frac{1}{(1+i)^n}$$

Interest (discount(Rate (i)

Period (n)	1%	2%	3%	4%	5%	6%	7%	8%	9%	11%	12%	14%	15%	16%
1	.9901	.9804.	.9709	.9615	.9524	.9434	.9346	.9259	.9174	.9634	.8929	.8772	.8696	.8621
2	.9803	.9612	.9426	.9246	.9070	.8900	.8734	.8573	.8417	.8364	.7972	.7695	.7561	.7432
3	.9706	.9423	.9151	.8890	.8638	.8396	.8163	.7938	.7722	.7583	.7118	.6750	.6575	.6407
4	.9610	.9238	.8885	.8548	.8227	.7921	.7629	.7350	.7084	.6832	.6355	.5921	.5718	.5523
5	.9215	.9057	.8626	.8219	.7835	.7473	.7130	.6806	.6499	.6219	.5674	.5194	.4972	.4761
6	.9420	.8880	.8375	.7903	.7462	.7050	.6663	.6302	.5963	.5645	.5066	.4556	.4323	.4104
7	.9327	.8706	.8131	.7599	.7107	.6651	.6227	.5835	.5470	.5132	.4523	.3996	.3759	.3538
8	.9235	.8536	.7894	.7307	.6768	.6274	.5820	.5403	.5019	.4565	.4039	.3506	.3269	.3050
9	.9143	.8368	.7664	.7026	.6446	.5919	.5439	.5002	.4604	.4241	.3606	.3075	.2843	.2630
10	.9053	.8203	.7441	.6756	.6139	.5584	.5083	.4632	.4224	.3855	.3220	.2697	.2472	.2267
11	.8963	.8043	.7224	.6496	.5847	.5268	.4751	.4289	.3875	.3505	.2875	.2366	.2149	.1954
12	.8874	.7885	.7014	.6246	.5568	.4970	.4440	.3971	.3555	.3156	.2567	.2076	.1869	.1685
13	.8787	.7730	.6810	.6606	.5303	.4688	.4150	.3677	.3262	.2897	.2292	.1821	.1625	.1452
14	.8700	.7579	.6611	.5775	.5051	.4423	.3878	.3405	.2992	.2533	.2046	.1597	.1413	.1252
15	.8613	.7430	.6419	.5553	.4810	.4173	.3624	.3152	.2745	.2394	.1827	.1401	.1229	.1079
16	.8528	.7284	.6232	.5339	.4581	.3936	.3387	.2919	.2519	.2176	.1631	.1229	.1069	.0930
17	.8444	.7142	.6050	.5134	.4363	.3714	.3166	.2703	.2311	.1975	.1456	.1078	.0929	.0802
18	.8360	.7002	.5874	.4936	.4155	.3503	.2959	.2502	.2120	.1799	.1300	.0946	.0808	.0691
19	.8277	.6864	.5703	.4746	.3957	.3305	.2765	.2317	.1945	.1635	.1161	.0829	.0703	.0596
20	.8195	.6730	.5537	.4564	.3769	.3118	.2584	.2145	.1784	.1436	.1037	.0728	.0611	.0514
21	.8114	.6598	.5375	.4388	.3589	.2942	.2415	.1987	.1637	.1351	.0926	.0638	.0531	.0443
22	.8034	.6468	.5219	.4220	.3418	.2775	.2257	.1839	.1502	.1228	.0826	.0560	.0462	.0382
23	.7954	.6342	.5067	.4057	.3256	.2618	.2109	.1703	.1378	.1117	.0738	.0491	.0402	.0329
24	.7876	.6217	.4919	.3901	.3101	.2470	.1971	.1577	.1264	.1015	.0659	.0431	.0349	.0284
25	.7798	.6095	.4776	.3751	.2953	.2330	.1842	.1460	.1160	.0923	.0588	.0378	.0304	.0245
26	.7720	.5976	.4637	.3607	.2812	.2198	.1722	.1352	.1064	.0839	.0525	.0331	.0264	.0211
27	.7644	.5859	.4502	.3468	.2678	.2074	.1609	.1252	.0976	.0763	.0469	.0291	.0230	.0182
28	.7568	.5744	.4371	.3335	.2551	.1956	.1504	.1159	.0895	.0693	.0419	.0255	.0200	.0157
29	.7493	.5631	.4243	.3207	.2429	.1846	.1406	.1073	.0822	.0630	.0374	.0224	.0174	.0135
30	.7419	.5521	.4120	.3083	.2314	.1741	.1314	.0994	.0754	.0573	.0334	.0196	.0151	.0116
35	.7059	.5000	.3554	.2534	.1813	.1301	.0937	.0676	.0490	.0356	.0189	.0102	.0075	.0055
40	.6717	.4529	.3066	.2083	.1420	.0972	.0668	.0460	.0318	.0221	.0107	.0053	.0037	.0026
45	.6391	.4102	.2644	.1712	.1113	.0727	.0476	.0313	.0207	.0137	.0061	.0027	.0019	.0013
50	.6080	.3715	.2281	.1407	.0872	.0543	.0339	,0213	.0134	.0085	.0035	.0014	.0009	.0006
55	.5785	.3365	.1968	.1157	.0683	.0406	.0242	.0145	.0087	.0053	.0020	.0007	.0005	.0003

Cost of Capital

Introduction

In the long-term investment analysis in the previous chapter we have seen that both in the net present value approach and rate of return approach for deciding to invest in a capital project we have to discount the future cash flows at an appropriate rate of interest. This appropriate rate of interest reflects the cost of capital which the firm has to incur for raising investment funds. In general, *cost of capital is the rate of return* required by lenders and stockholders to lend or invest their funds in the firm. There are three sources of funds for the corporate firm to invest in capital projects.

1. By borrowing from others which is called *debt capital.*
2. By selling common stock to the investors which is called *equity capital.*
3. Using retained earnings (*i.e.*, undistributed profits) of the firm for investment expenditure.

The cost of using retained earnings for investment is the opportunity cost, that is, return foregone which could be obtained by lending or investing outside the firm. Therefore, the cost of using retained earnings is treated at par with the cost of equity capital and is therefore not discussed separately. In what follows we explain how the costs of debt capital and equity capital are estimated.

Cost of Debt Capital

Borrowing money from others is one of the important ways a firm raises funds for investment. The instrument for this is the issue of bonds or debentures which provide lenders annual interest payments and returning the principal sum at maturity. Since the interest payments made by a firm on the borrowed funds are deducted from firm's income to obtain its taxable income, to determine the cost of debt capital adjustment must be made to obtain after-tax cost of it for the firm. For a given rate of interest (i) and the marginal tax rate (t), the firm's cost of debt capital (r_d) is

$$r_d = i(1 - t)$$

For example, if a firm borrows funds at 15 per cent rate of interest and marginal tax rate is 40 per cent, cost of debt capital for it will be

$$r_d = 0.15 \ (1 - 0.40)$$
$$= 0.15 - 0.06$$
$$= 0.09 \text{ or } 9 \text{ per cent}$$

It is evident from above that due to the interest payments being deductible from firm's income to determine its taxable income, the after-tax cost of debt capital is lower than the interest rate charged by the borrowers from the firm. Besides, two other important things are worth mentioning with regard to the cost of debt capital. First, if the firm does not earn profits, its pre-tax and after-tax cost of debt capital will be the same because no marginal tax is payable by the firm. Secondly, since only consideration in measuring cost of capital is the *cost of raising new funds,* we are concerned with marginal cost of capital and not its average cost. This is also because the investment decision requires comparing the rate of return on new projects with cost of raising new capital (that is, marginal cost of capital).

COST OF EQUITY CAPITAL

A firm can raise funds through equity either internally through ploughing back of its retained earnings (*i.e.*, accumulated undistributed profits) or externally through issuing new common stock (that is, equity shares) for sale to the public. *The cost of equity capital is the minimum rate of return that is required by the investors to buy the shares (common equity) of the firm.* Determining the cost of equity capital is more complicated and controversial as compared to the cost of debt capital. Three methods of estimating cost of equity capital have been suggested. They are :

1. *The Risk-Free Rate Plus Risk Premium*
2. *The Dividend Valuation Model*
3. *The Capital Asset Pricing Model*

We explain below in some detail these three methods of estimating cost of equity capital.

Risk-Free Rate Plus Risk Premium

As mentioned above, cost of equity capital is the rate of return that investors require to invest in the common stock (shares) of the firm. Investors in the common stock of the firm are rewarded in two ways. First, they get dividends annually on the shares held by them from the firm. Secondly, they gain from appreciation in the prices of equity shares of the firm. However, investment in the common stock is riskier than investment in debt capital (*i.e.*, bonds or debentures) of the firm which bears fixed rate of interest. This is because whereas bonds have to be paid a fixed rate of interest annually and the principle amount at maturity before any dividends are distributed among the shareholders, the dividends can fluctuate very much depending on the rise and fall of profits of the firm. Besides, the prices of common stock (*i.e.*, shares) of a firm can change very much; they can even fall and thus involve a good deal of loss. Therefore, because of the risk involved in the investment in the common stock of the firm, the shareholders must be rewarded a risk premium over and above risk-free return on capital. The risk involved in investment in common shares of the firm arises because of two factors. First, risk on investment in common stock arises because investors invest in the common stock of a private firm as against investment in *risk-free Government securities.* Return on long-term Government securities is considered as risk-free return as its payment is guaranteed by the Government. Secondly, there is extra risk involved in buying shares rather than bonds of a firm. Since dividends vary with the firm's profits, stocks are riskier than the bonds of the firm. Therefore, they must carry additional premium. Thus, the *cost of equity capital is estimated to be equal to the risk-free rate of return plus a risk premium.* In notational terms :

$$r_e = r_f + r_p$$

where

r_e = cost of equity capital

r_f = risk-free rate of return

r_p = risk premium

The two components of risk mentioned above can be represented by e_1 and e_2 respectively. Thus, the cost of equity is

$$r_e = r_f + e_1 + e_2$$

The first type of risk premium (e_1) is generally estimated by taking the difference between the interest rate on private firm's bonds and the interest rate of Government bonds (*i.e.*, long-term Government securities). The second type of risk premium (e_2) associated with investing in common stock rather than bonds of the firm depends on one's judgement rather than any objective criterion. Financial analysts usually assume that return on a firm's common equity shares is about 3 to 5 per cent points more than the interest rate on firm's bonds. The exact additional return on equity as opposed to firm's bond is calculated by taking the historical difference between the average yield (rate of dividend plus capital gains) on firm's equity capital and average interest rate on firm's bonds.

Let us take an example for estimating cost of equity capital in this method. Suppose the firm's return on equity capital is 4 per cent greater as against return on its bonds. Further suppose that rate of interest on Central Government's securities is 11 per cent and a private firm's bonds bear 14 per cent interest. Therefore, the difference between the risk-free return and yield on private firm's bonds in this case is :

$$0.14 - 0.11 = 0.03$$

The total risk premium in this case is

$$e_p = e_1 + e_2 = 0.03 + 0.04 = 0.07$$

It follows from above that cost of equity capital is

$$r_e = r_f + r_p$$

$$= 0.11 + 0.07 = 0.18 \quad \text{or} \quad 18 \text{ per cent.}$$

It is important to note that dividends paid on equity capital (shares) are not deductible from firm's income. Therefore, no tax adjustment is made in determining the cost of equity capital on account of dividend payments which are not deductible from firm's income.

Discounted Cash Flow Model

The first method of cost of equity capital, namely, "risk-free return plus premium" considers risk involved in investment in shares of common stock of the firm but does not take into account the possibility of *growth in dividend on shares and increase in the price of shares over time.* The discounted cash flow model considers both the increase in dividends and increase in price or value of shares of the firm to determine cost of equity capital. This model is also called '*Dividend Valuation Model*'. It may be noted again that the cost of equity capital is the return on a share of the firm that must be paid to the investors to invest in the firm. *Value or price of a share of common stock of the firm is the present value of all future dividends expected to be paid on a share of the common stock* using the investor's required rate of return (r_e) as the discount rate. If the current dividend (*D*) per share is expected to remain constant indefinitely over time, the present price or value (P) of a share of equity capital of the firm will be

$$P = \sum_{t=1}^{\infty} \frac{D}{(1 + r_e)^t} \quad \text{...(1)}$$

$$P = D\left[\sum_{t=1}^{\infty} \frac{1}{(1 + r_e)^t}\right] \quad \text{...(2)}$$

If it is assumed that dividend on a share remains constant over time and is to be paid indefinitely, then it can be shown that the bracketed term in equation (2) above reduces to $\frac{1}{r_e}$. With this the equation (2) for the price of a share of equity capital becomes

$$P = \frac{D}{r_e} \quad \text{...(3)}$$

That is, *price of a share of equity capital* (*i.e., common stock*) *of a firm is the annual dividend per share divided by the required rate of return* (r_e).

Now, if dividend on a share of the firm is expected to grow annually at the rate g, it can then be proved that price per share of the firm will be

$$P = \frac{D}{r_e - g} \quad \text{...(4)}$$

Solving equation (4) for r_e (that is, required rate of return or cost of equity capital) we have

$$r_e = \frac{D}{P} + g \quad \text{...(5)}$$

This means that the cost of equity capital (r_e), that is, *return required by the investors to invest in the common stock of the firm is equal to the ratio of dividend paid per share* (D) *by the firm and price of its share* (P) plus the expected annual growth rate of dividend payments by the firm. $\frac{D}{P}$ in equation (5) above is often referred to as *dividend yield per share*. It should be noted that g is the *historic growth rate* of dividends paid by the firm in the past which is expected to continue in the future. The growth rate of dividends can also be based on the *forecasts* made by the financial analysis which are based on expected sales, profit margins and competitive strength of the firm and are published in Business Magazines.

Example. Let us illustrate the computation of cost of equity capital according to the Dividend Valuation Model with a numerical example. Suppose a business firm is paying a dividend of 16 per share on its common stock that is currently selling for Rs 200 per share and security analysts forecast that dividend per share will increase at the rate of 5 per cent per year. What will be the cost of equity capital in this case ?

$$r_e = \frac{D}{P} + g$$

$$r_e = \frac{16}{200} + 0.05$$

$$= \frac{2}{25} + 0.05$$

$$= 0.08 + 0.05 = 0.13 \text{ or } 13 \text{ per cent.}$$

Numerical Problem

Suppose the current price of a share of HCL Computers is ₹ 312. The dividend paid per share of the firm in the next year is expected to be ₹ 24 per share. Further, past data reveals that dividend per share has been growing at an average compound annual rate of 8 per cent over the past 8 years and it is expected that this growth rate in dividend will be maintained in the future too. Using this information, calculate the cost of equity capital by dividend valuation method.

Solution

According to *discounted cash flow method* which is also called dividend valuation method, cost of equity capital is

$$r_e = \frac{D}{P} + g$$

where D = annual dividend per share

g = the annual growth rate in the dividend per share

P = the current price of the share.

Substituting the values of D, g and P in the above formula, we have

$$r_e = \frac{24}{312} + 0.08$$

$$= 0.077 + 0.08 = 0.157 \text{ or } 15.7\%$$

Capital Asset Pricing Model (CAPM)

For determining cost of capital, this is a very important method developed during 1970s and 1980s and is extensively used by the modern financial analysts. To determine the cost of equity capital, this model takes into consideration not only the risk differential between the risk-free Government securities and the shares of common stock but also the risk differential between the common stock and the *average common stock* of all firms in the market taken together, or, broad-based market portfolio of shares of various firms.

The risk differential between the common stock and Government's securities is given by $r_m - r_f$, where r_m stands for the return on the average common stock and r_f for the return on risk-free Government securities.

On the other hand, relative risk differential between the common stock of a firm and the common stock of all firms measured by a risk index, called *beta coefficient* (β). This β-coefficient is the ratio of the variability of return on the common stock of a firm and the variability in the average return on the common stock of all firms. This β-coefficient is obtained by regressing the average return on all capital stock (or a representative basket of stocks) on the return on a share of the common stock of a firm, say a firm J. This is represented by k_i^J. Thus,

$$k_i^J = a + \beta k_i^m$$

where k_i^J = return on a share of a common stock of a firm J in the ith period.

k_i^m = the average return on all common stocks of all firms in the ith period.

If the β-coefficient for the stock of a firm is estimated to be equal to 1, this means that the return on common stock of a firm varies in proportion to the return on all stocks. This implies average risk of investment in the common stock of a firm. The greater the value of β-coefficient for the stock of a firm, the greater the variability in the return on the common stock of the firm which therefore means higher risk for the investors. Thus, if β-coefficient for the common stock of a firm is equal to 2, it means the variation in return on the common stock of a firm is twice that of the variation in return on the total stock of all firms and this shows higher risky stock of that firm for investment purposes. On the other hand, if the value of β-coefficient is less than 1, say it is equal to 0.5, this will indicate lower risky stock of the firm as in this case 1 per cent variation in the total stock of all firms will be associated with a $\frac{1}{2}$ per cent variation in the return on the stock of that firm.

From the above analysis it follows that in the capital asset pricing model (CAPM), the cost of equity capital is given by

$$r_e = r_f + (r_m - r_f)\,\beta$$

where

r_e = the cost of equity capital of a firm

r_f = the risk-free return (*i.e.*, return on Government securities)

r_m = return on the common stock of a firm

β = Beta-coefficient

Numerical Problem

Suppose the common stock of the Indian firm 'Reliance Petroleum' has a beta (β) coefficient of 0.8 and present risk-free rate of return is 9 per cent. If the expected return on the investment in the common stock on the market as a whole is 15 per cent, using Capital Asset Pricing Model (CAPM), calculate the cost of equity capital of the Reliance Petroleum.

Solution.

According to Capital Asset Pricing Model (CAPM), the cost of equity capital is

$$r_e = r_f + (r_m - r_f)\,\beta$$

Substituting the values of r_f, = 9, r_m = 15% and β = 0.8 in the above formula, we have

$$r_c = 9 + (15.0 - 9.0)\,0.8$$
$$= 9 + (6 \times 0.8)$$
$$= 9 + 4.8 = 13.8\%$$

Overall Cost of Capital or Composite Cost of Capital

The cost of capital is calculated in order to compare it with the benefits or rate of return expected to be obtained from the proposed capital expenditure projects (that is, long-term investment proposals). As we know that the purpose of capital or long-term investment expenditure is to determine which proposed capital project should be actually undertaken by the firm. If the expected return from a capital project exceeds the cost of capital, it is undertaken by the firm. It is wofth mentioning that capital expenditure whose cost is measured and compared with the return expected to be obtained relates to the proposed *new or marginal* capital expenditure project for which funds are to be raised. In other words, we are concerned with *the marginal cost of capital*. Thus, for evaluating new capital expenditure projects, *historical cost* of capital (that is, costs of capital incurred in the earlier periods) is not used. Instead, as mentioned above, we use marginal cost of capital for evaluating long-term investment projects.

It is also worth-mentioning that typically a firm's capital structure consists of both debt capital and equity capital in certain proportions. Usually, a firm plans for a *target capital structure* consisting of both debt capital and equity capital. Therefore, the firm calculates the cost of each component of capital (that is, cost of debt capital and that of equity capital) which it has to incur for raising funds in the *next year* for financing proposed capital expenditure projects.

It should be noted that for each *individual project* the firm does not actually specify the proportions of funds to be raised through debt and equity but it is generally assumed that each capital project is financed with the proportions of debt and equity capital as contained in the firm's overall target capital structure. Therefore, the cost of capital to be used in evaluating capital expenditure projects is not only based on cost of capital incurred on raising funds for financing new or marginal capital expenditure project but also consists of the same proportions of debt and equity capital as those contained in the firm's target capital structure. Thus, the overall cost of capital or what is also called *composite cost of capital is the weighted average of the cost of debt capital* (r_d) *and the cost of equity capital* (r_e) *where weights used are the proportions of debt capital and equity capital in the firm's target capital structure.*

Let w_d represent the proportion of debt capital and w_e the proportion of equity capital in the firm's target capital structure. Thus, the *overall cost of capital which is also called weighted or composite cost of capital* (r_c) *is*

$$r_c = w_d\, r_d + w_e\, r_e$$

where

r_c = overall cost of capital

w_d = the proportion of debt capital in the firm's capital structure

r_d = the cost of debt capital

w_e = the proportion of equity capital in the firm's capital structure

r_e = the cost of equity capital

Differences in Capital Structumre and the Risk

There are differences in the capital structure of different firms. Firms belonging to manufacturing industries usually prefer a capital structure which has a smaller proportion of debt capital and larger proportion of equity capital, say 30 per cent debt capital and 70 per cent equity capital. On the other hand, firms belonging to public utilities such as electric supply companies, water supply companies, firms providing telephone services generally have a higher ratio of debt capital as compared to that of equity capital. This difference in capital structure arises because of preference for risk-bearing on the part of owners or managers of firms and also because of the nature of industry or business in which they happen to be working. It should be noted that a capital structure heavily inclined towards debt means greater risk because in this a firm commits itself to a *fixed interest rate and payments of the principal amount at maturity in time.* As a result, risk of default arises with serious consequences when the firm is not making sufficient profit. Therefore, manufacturing companies which face competition in the market have lower proportion of debt capital as they cannot afford to bear greater risk involved in the high proportion of debt capital.

On the other hand, companies operating in public utilities usually have a monopoly position in the market and product they supply is generally a necessity which enable them to exercise greater control over the price which ensure reasonably stable flow of revenue and profits. As a result of this, risk involved is reduced very much and therefore capital structure of firms operating in public utilities have generally a higher proportion of debt capital.

NUMERICAL PROBLEMS

Problem 1. *Suppose Satyam Computers has a target capital structure of 60 per cent equity and 40 per cent debt. Over the next year it plans to raise ₹ 200 crores partly by selling bonds at the after-tax cost of 8 per cent and partly by issuing new equity at ₹ 350 per share at the cost of 12 per cent per share. Find out the overall cost of capital.*

Solution

In order to maintain the target capital structure, of ₹ 200 crores it will raise 60 per cent of it through issuing new equity shares at the cost of 12 per cent per share and 40 per cent of it through selling bonds at the cost of 8 per cent. It should be noted that no adjustment on account of interest payments is required as cost of debt capital given is after-tax cost of debt capital. Thus, the overall cost of capital is

$$r_c = w_d\, r_d + w_e\, r_e$$

Substituting the value of w_e equal to 60 per cent (*i.e.*, 0.60), r_e equal to 12, w_d equal to 40 per cent (*i.e.*, 0.40), r_d equal to 8, we have

$$r_c = 0.60 \times 12 + 0.40 \times 8$$
$$= 7.20 + 3.20 = 10.4$$

Thus, the overall cost of capital is 10.4 per cent which will be used to evaluate all capital expenditure projects to decide whether or not to undertake a project.

Problem 2. *Suppose a computer firm Wipro has a current capital structure of 75 per cent equity and 25 per debt and financial managers of Wipro do not want to change its capital structure. The firm plans to finance in the next year 100 crores capital budget through using retained earnings at the capital cost of 12 per cent per share and by issuing long-term bonds at 11 per cent interest rate. Further assume that 35 per cent is the marginal tax rate. Calculate the weighted or overall cost of capital.*

Solution

Note that financing capital budget through using retained earnings is treated at par with raising funds by externally selling common shares in the market. Further note that in this problem cost of debt capital is not directly given. Instead, interest rate on the bonds issue is given. Since interest payments are deductible from income to arrive at taxable income adjustment has to be made on this count to estimate the true cost of debt capital.

With 35 per cent rate of income tax, after-tax cost of debt capital will be

$$r_d = r_i\,(1 - t)$$
$$r_d = 11\,(1 - 0.35) = 11 \times 0.65 = 7.15$$
$$r_c = w_e\, r_e + w_d\, r_d$$
$$w_e = 75 \text{ per cent, that is, } 0.75$$
$$r_e = 12 \text{ per cent}$$
$$w_d = 25 \text{ per cent, that is, } 0.25$$
$$r_d = r_i\,(1 - t)$$
$$r_c = w_e\, r_e + w_d \,.\, r_i\,(1 - t)$$
$$= 0.75 \times 12 + 0.25 \times 7.15$$
$$= 9 + 1.79 = 10.79$$

Problem 3. *Suppose the return on Government securities is 9 per cent and a bond* *of a firm yields 12 per cent. Calculate (1) total risk premium, (2) cost of equity capital of the firm.*

Solution.

The component of risk premium p_1 is given by the excess of the rate of interest on a firm's bonds (which is 12 per cent in the problem) over the risk-free interest on Government's bonds (*i.e.*, 9 per cent).

Thus, $p_1 = 12 - 9 = 3\%$

The second component of risk in buying firm's common stock (*i.e.*, common shares) rather than bonds is generally assumed to be equal to 4 percentage points greater than the return on bonds.

Thus, total risk premium is

$$r_p = p_1 + p_2 = (12 - 9) + 4 = 7 \text{ per cent}$$

Cost of equity capital, $r_e = r_f + p_1 + p_2$

$$= 9 + 3 + 4 = 16\%$$

Problem 4. *The current price of common stock of a firm is Rs 2.40. The firm has just paid a dividend of 8 paise per share this year and expects that its dividend will grow in future at a constant rate of 12 per cent per year. Calculate the firm's cost of equity capital using discounted cash flow method (i.e., Dividend Valuation Method).*

Solution.

Dividend per share (D) = 8 paise

Price of share = ₹ 2.40 = 240 paise

$g = 12\%$ or 0.12

Cost of equity capital $(r_e) = \dfrac{D}{P} + g$

$$= \frac{8}{240} + 0.12$$

$$= \frac{1}{30} + 0.12$$

$$= 0.033 + 0.12 = 0.153 \quad \text{or} \quad 15.3\%$$

Problem 5. *Suppose shares of HCL Computer Company are sold in the market at ₹ 200 per share. The company declares its dividend of ₹ 12 per share. Security analysts estimate that the annual growth of dividend of the company will be 8 per cent. What will be the cost of equity capital for this company ?*

Solution.

Cost of capital is the required rate of return by the investors

$P =$ ₹ 200 per share

$g = 8\%$ or 0.08

Thus, $r_e = \dfrac{12}{200} + 0.08$

$$= \frac{6}{100} + 0.08$$

$$= 0.06 + 0.08 = 0.14 \quad \text{or} \quad 14\%$$

Problem 6. *Suppose Telco Company has a beta coefficient showing variability of return on its common stock has been estimated to be equal to 0.8. Rate of interest on Government bonds is 9 per cent and the average return on the common stock on the market as a whole is 12 per cent. Find out the cost of equity capital for Telco using Capital Asset Pricing Model (CAPM).*

Solution

Cost of equity capital $(r_e) = r_f + \beta\ (r_m - r_f)$

where r_f = is risk-free return. This is equal to 9%

r_m = is the return on the average stock on the market as a whole which is equal to 12 per cent

$\beta = 0.8$

Substituting these values in the CAPM model, we have

$$r_e = 9 + 0.8\ (12 - 9)$$
$$= 9 + 2.4 = 11.4\%$$

QUESTIONS FOR REVIEW

1. What is meant by cost of capital ? Mention the two important components of the overall cost of capital.
2. Distinguish between cost of debt capital and cost of equity capital. Why is debt capital usually cheaper than equity capital ?
3. How do you expect the cost of capital will change ?
   (*i*) If market rate of interest rises.
   (*ii*) If the firm changes its capital structure by raising the proportion of debt capital.
   (*iii*) If the marginal rate of tax on the income of the companies is raised.
4. Debt capital is usually cheaper than equity capital. Why then the firms do not exclusively rely on debt financing of their investment projects ?
5. Why are Government securities taken to be risk-free ? What is used as risk-free rate ?
6. What additional risks do the shareholders of a firm face in comparison with the holders of Government securities ?
7. Why do different firms choose different debt-equity ratio ?
8. What is the relationship between the firm's net cost of debt capital with marginal income tax rate ?
9. Why do firms have substantially different capital structure ? Why do firms in the public utility undertakings have generally higher debt component in their capital structure ?
10. What is meant by composite cost of capital ? What are its two constituents ?
11. If a firm borrows funds at 15 per cent rate of interest and pays a marginal income tax rate of 35 per cent, calculate the cost of debt capital.

Decision Making Under Risk and Uncertainty

Introduction

So far in our analysis of decision making we have assumed that while taking decisions the consumers and firms do not face any uncertainty. For example, it has been assumed that the consumer knows with certainty about the present and future prices of goods and the managers of firms know with certainty the present and future demand and cost conditions facing them. Though this assumption of certainty about the situations and their outcomes facing consumers, investors and managers is not entirely correct but it is good enough to make reasonably correct predictions about the outcomes of the decisions made.

However, the real world is full of uncertainty and due to this choices or decisions made by the individuals and firms involve risk. For example, many individuals borrow to buy or build a house, factory or a car etc. and plan to pay for them out of their future incomes. But, as is quite well known, future incomes of the people are quite uncertain. Their future income of the people may go up, but they can also go down and they are therefore unable to pay back the loans. Besides, people have often to choose how much risk to bear. The persons who want to invest their savings have to decide whether to keep their savings in Saving Accounts or banks' fixed deposits or invest in shares of some companies or in mutual funds. Investment of savings in shares or equity-based mutual funds involves higher risk as the value of the shares can go down. To make a choice among these alternatives we need to measure the risk so as to compare the riskiness of alternative choices. Further, when a firm launches a new product it is not certain whether it will be liked by the people and will therefore have sufficient demand to yield a profit for them. In this uncertain economic environment we need to measure the risk involved in various outcomes of the decision.

In what follows we first explain the concept of risk and how to measure it. We will then explain the different preferences towards risk. Risk is considered to be undesirable. Many individuals are risk averse and like to avoid risks, but some others are willing to bear risk if it yields them sufficient return. In the end we will explain the ways such as diversification, insurance, gathering of information by which risk can be reduced.

The Concept of Risk

The risk refers to a situation when the outcome of a decision is uncertain but when the probability of each possible outcome is known or can be estimated. The analysis of decision making and choice involving risk or uncertainty requires that the individual knows all the possible outcomes and also have some idea of the probability of occurrence of each possible outcome. For example, in tossing a coin there is equal of 50-50 chance of getting either a head or tail. Likewise, when an individual invests in the shares of a company, the probability of outcome (that is, how much dividend it will be yield and how much its price will rise in a year) can be estimated from the past experience. The outcome can vary a good deal. *The greater the variability of possible outcome, the greater the risk involved in making the investment decision.* Therefore, in the theory of choice or decision making under uncertainty it is necessary to know the meaning of probability of outcome and its variability.

It is important to mention the distinction between risk and uncertainty. *The uncertainty refers to the situation when there is more than one possible outcome of a decision but where the probability of occurrence of each particular outcome is not known or even cannot be estimated.* This may be due to lack of sufficient past information or the great instability of the variables involved that determine the outcome. In some extreme cases even outcomes themselves are not known. For example, in case of drilling for exploration of oil in an *unproven field,* investor does not know either the probability of oil being struck or the possible output of oil from it. Though the distinction between risk and uncertainty is theoretically significant the two terms are generally used interchangeably in decision making analysis.

In decision making involving risk or uncertainty the three terms are quite often used. They are : (*i*) *strategy,* (*ii*) *state of nature* and (*iii*) *outcome.* A strategy refers to one of several alternative courses of action or plans that can be implemented to achieve the desired goal. For example, a manager may be considering the following three strategies aimed at increasing profits of the firm.

(i) building a new technologically more efficient plant so as to reduce the cost of production.

(ii) launching of a new advertising and marketing campaign to increase sales.

(iii) redesigning of the product so as to lower the cost of production and to increase in demand for it by getting greater consumer acceptance.

A state of nature refers to the conditions that prevail in future and which have a significant effect on the success or failure of the strategy. For example, in case of building a technologically superior plant the different states of nature that may exist in some future years are (a) boom, (b) recession, or (c) normal conditions. It is worthwhile to note that the decision maker has little or no control over the state of nature. For example, whether economic conditions of boom or recession will exist in future is beyond the control of the decision maker.

Finally, outcome refers to the results which are usually in the form of profit that come about as a result of implementation of a strategy. A *payoff matrix* lists the outcomes associated with combinations of each strategy and state of nature. It is important to note that *risk refers to the amount of variability in the outcome as a result of the adoption of a particular strategy.*

Measuring Risk : Probability of an Outcome

We have seen above that risk refers to the situation when there is more than one possible outcome of a decision and the probability of each outcome is either known or can be estimated.

Therefore, to measure the degree of risk we need to know the probability of each possible outcome of a decision. *The probability means the likelihood of occurring of an event.* Thus, if possibility of an outcome occurring is 1/4 or 0.25, this means that there is 1 chance in 4 or 25 per cent chance for the outcome to occur. For example, suppose a person is considering to invest in a company which is engaged in the new exploration of offshore oil. If the exploration is successful, the price of company's stock will rise to ₹ 50 per share and if its exploration meets with a failure, the company's stock will fall to ₹ 10 per share. Given these two possible outcomes, namely, ₹ 50 per share price and ₹ 10 per share price, if the past information reveals that the chance of oil exploration being successful is $\frac{1}{4}$ or 25 per cent and chance of its failure is $\frac{3}{4}$, then we say the probability of success of oil exploration is 25 per cent and the probability of its failure is 75 per cent (The success and failure are the two possible outcomes). Thus *probability is a number that indicates the likelihood of an event or outcome occurring.*

These are two concepts of probability depending on how it is measured. The first is the *frequency concept of probability.* If past information or data is available regarding occurrence of outcomes or events, the probability is defined as the proportion of times an outcome occurs if the situation is repeated in the long run over and over again. In general, if a situation is repeated over a large number of times, say *M*, and if outcome, say *X*, occurs *m* times, then

$$P(X) = \frac{m}{M}$$

Thus, in our example if we know from the past data of oil exploration that rate of success is 25 per cent, then the probability of getting success is 1/4 or 0.25. The measurement of probability based on the past experience is generally known as the *objective measure of probability.*

But in many cases there are no similar past situations which help us in measuring probability. In that case the *concept of subjective probability* is used. The subjective probability is an individual's personal view about the chance of an outcome to occur and is based on his personal judgement, experience or knowledge about the subject and not on the frequency with which outcome actually took place in the past. Obviously, when probability is subjectively determined and not based on the past data, the different individuals will attach different probabilities to the occurrence of various outcomes and therefore they will make different choices. In whatever way the probability is arrived at, it helps us to measure two important concepts, namely, *expected value and variability of outcome.* With the use of these two concepts we compare the profitability of various strategies involving risk and uncertainty which helps us to make a choice among them. We explain below the meaning of these two concepts.

Measuring Risk with Probability Distribution

As explained above, the probability of an outcome is the likelihood that an event will occur. *Probability distribution describes the occurrence of all possible outcomes of an event and the probability of occurrence of each outcome.* It is worth noting that the sum of probabilities of all possible outcomes must equal *unity* because probabilities of all outcomes together must equal certainty. Thus, in Table 35.1 we give *all possible cash flows* that will occur from an investment project A in the *next year* and the probabilities of their occurrence.

It will be seen from Table 35.1 that there are five possible cash flows in the next year depending on the state of the economy which is determined by general economic conditions, nature of competition in the industry to which the firm belongs. If all conditions are favourable for the firm, its cash flow will be 70 lakhs whose probability is 0.1 or 10 per cent. On the other hand, if all conditions are unfavourable for the firm, its cash flow from the investment project will be ₹ 30 lakhs whose probability of occurrence is also 0.1 or 10 per cent. One of the other three cash flows will occur if some factors work in favour of the firm's project A and others unfavourable to it. The data of various alternative cash flows and their probabilities given in Table 35.1 are shown as bar diagram in Fig. 35.1 with cash flows measured on the *X*-axis. In it the length of the bar shows the probability of the particular cash flows. The probability distribution shows that there is 10 per cent probability that all determining conditions work in favour of the investment project which yields cash flow of ₹ 70 lakhs in the next year. Similarly, there is 10 per cent probability that all conditions will be unfavourable and yields cash flow of ₹ 30 lakhs in the next year. It is more probable that some conditions will be favourable and others unfavourable for firm's project so that intermediate cash flows such as ₹ 40 lakhs, 50 lakhs and ₹ 60 lakhs would occur.

Table 35.1 *Probability Distribution*

Cash flows (in ₹ Lakh) (X_i)	*Probability* (P_i)	*Expected Value* (P_iX_i)
30	0.1	3
40	0.2	8
50	0.4	20
60	0.2	12
70	0.1	7
		$\Sigma P_iX_i = 50$
	$E(X)$ or $\bar{X} = 50$	

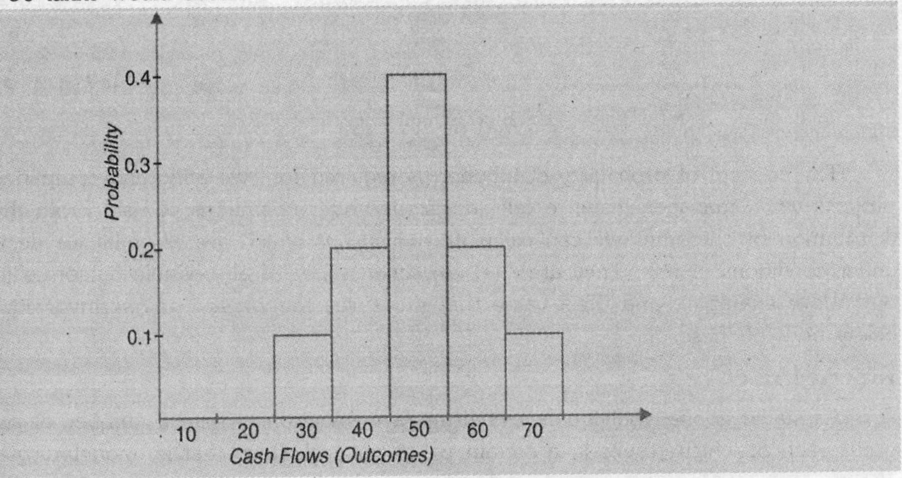

Fig. 35.1 : *Cash Flows from Investment Project A*

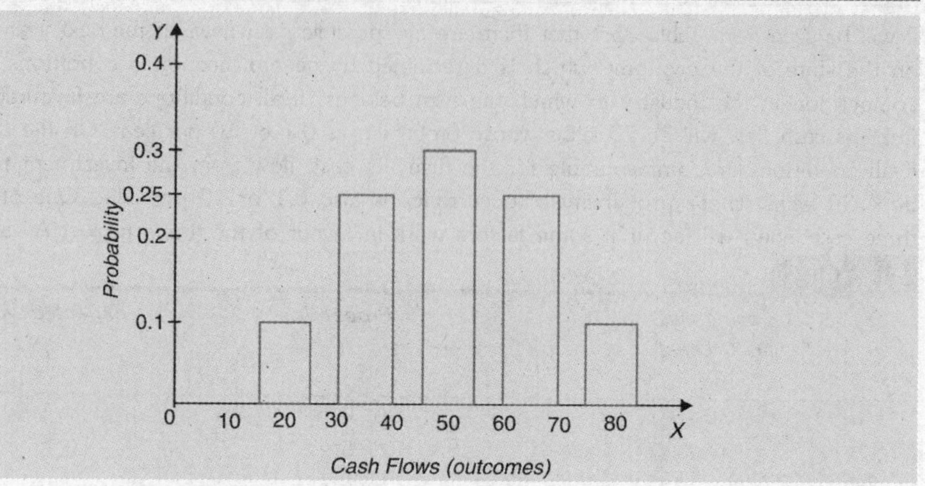

Fig. 35.2 : *Cash Flows from Investment Project B*

In Table 35.2 we give the cash flows that will occur in the next year and their associated probabilities from an investment project *B*. We have depicted these cash flows through bar diagram in Figure 35.2. It will be seen that cash flows from investment project *B* are more dispersed as compared to the cash flows from investment project *A*.

Table 35.2 *Cash Flows from Investment Project B*

Cash Flows (in ₹ Lakhs) (X_i)	Probability (P_i)	(P_iX_i)
20	0.10	2
35	0.25	8.75
50	0.30	15
65	0.25	16.25
80	0.10	8
		$\Sigma P_iX_i = 50$
	$E(X)$ or $\bar{X} = 50$	

The concept of probability distribution is required for evaluating and comparing investment projects when managers have to take decisions under conditions of risk. From the probability distribution of outcomes we can calculate two values which are essential for decision making under conditions of risk. They are : (1) *expected value* of all possible outcomes (cash-flows in our above example), and (2) a value that measures the *degree of risk* involved. We explain below both of these.

Expected Value

As stated above, individuals and firms face situations where a number of outcomes can occur each of which results in a certain payoff or cash flow, that is, monetary gain or loss. *If the probability of each outcome is known* we can find out the expected monetary value in this uncertain situation (that is, when a variety of outcomes can occur). *The expected monetary value is the weighted average of payoffs of all possible outcomes with the probability of each outcome used as weights.* Thus the expected value of an uncertain income is the average payoff of the various outcomes. For example, it investment in offshore oil exploration, there are two possible outcomes, namely, the success of the project yielding a payoff of ₹ 50 per share with a probability of 0.25 and the failure yielding a payoff ₹ 10 per share with a probability of 0.75. Thus in this case, expected value of investment per share

$$= 0.25 \times 50 + 0.75 \times 10$$

$$= 12.5 + 7.5$$

$$= ₹\ 20$$

In general terms if there are two possible outcomes with payoffs of X_1 and X_2. and the probability of each possible outcome denoted by P_1 and P_2, then the expected value of investment is given by

$$E(X) \text{ or } \bar{X} = P_1X_1 + P_2X_2$$

Similarly if there are n possible outcomes, then the expected value is

$$E(X) \text{ or } \bar{X} = P_1X_1 + P_2X_2 + P_2X_3 \ldots\ldots P_nX_n$$

or in condense form, expected value in case of n possible outcomes with their associated probabilities can be written as

$$E(X) = \sum_{i=1}^{n} P_iX_i$$

In the data given in Table 35.1 regarding 5 possible cash flows from an investment project, the expected value is obtained by multiplying the possible cash flows with their associated probabilities and then adding them. This we have done in the last column of Table 35.1 whose sum yields 50. Thus

$$E(X) \text{ or } \bar{X} = (0.1 \times 30) + (0.2 \times 40) + (0.4 \times 50) + (0.2 \times 60) + (0.1 \times 70)$$

$$= 3 + 8 + 20 + 12 + 7 = 50$$

Risk and Probability Distribution

In addition to the expected value, the probability distribution of outcomes also helps us in measuring risk involved in a project. In fact, *the variability of outcomes measures the degree of risk involved in any choice of a project or strategy from the various alternative projects or strategies*. In economics and finance, risk is the measured by the extent of dispersion (*i.e.* deviation) of possible outcomes from the expected value. The greater the variability or dispersion of payoff of various outcomes from the expected value of payoff means the greater risk involved. *The variability of outcomes may be measured by the average deviation of actual values of payoffs of various outcomes from the expected value of payoff with probability of each being used as weights*. Let X_1 and X_2 are the payoffs of two outcomes and the probability of each is P_1 and P_2, then the average deviation (V) as a measure of risk is given by

$$V = P_1[X_1 - E(X_1)] + P_2\,[X_2 - E(X_2)]$$

However, the most widely used measure of dispersion or variability is the standard deviation. The standard deviation (d or σ) is defined as the square root of the weighted average of the squared deviation of all possible outcomes from the expected value with probabilities of various possible outcomes used as weights. Thus, in case of three possible outcomes

$$\sigma = \sqrt{P_1(X_1 - E(X))^2 + P_2[X_2 - E(X)]^2 + P_3[X_3 - E(X)]^2}$$

Where σ is standard deviation and X_1, X_2, X_3 are outcomes and $E(X)$ is the expected value of outcomes.

In general terms, when there are n outcomes, standard deviation (σ) of outcomes is given by

$$\sigma = \sum_{i=1}^{n} \sqrt{(X_i - E(X))^2 P_i}$$

Since expected value $E(X)$ is also written as $\bar{X}$, the standard deviation is also written as

$$\sigma = \sum_{i=1}^{n} \sqrt{(X_i - \bar{X})^2 P_i}$$

Standard Deviation and Probability Distribution

What is the implication of standard deviation of 50 in the probability distribution of outcomes of Table 35.1. It is worth mentioning that probability distribution of outcomes is assumed to be one of *standard normal distribution* which is symetric around the expected value and also there is 50 per cent possibility that outcome will be above the expected value and there is 50 per cent possibility that outcome will be less than 50. The probability of a *particular outcome* occurring depends on *how many standard deviations it is* away from the expected value (*i.e.* mean value). According to normal curve theory (which will be explained fully in a later section), about 68 per cent of all possible outcomes will lie within 1 standard deviation on either side (*i.e.* $\bar{X} \pm 1\sigma$).

In other words, there is about 34 per cent chance that outcome will be above 1 standard deviation from the expected value and about 34 per cent chance that outcome will lie below 1 standard deviation from the expected value. In the probability distribution given in Table 35.3, the expected value of all five outcomes is ₹ 50 lakhs and standard deviation is

$$\sigma = \sum_{i=1}^{n} \sqrt{(X_i - \bar{X})^2 P_i} = \sqrt{120} = 10.95$$

Table 35.3: Calculation of Standard Deviation of Outcomes as given in Table 35.1.

Cash Flow (Outcome) (X)	*Probability (P)*	$X - \bar{X}$	$(X - \bar{X})^2$	$(X - \bar{X})^2 P_i$
30	0.1	-20	400	40
40	0.2	-10	100	20
50	0.4	0	0	0
60	0.2	10	100	20
70	0.1	20	400	40
$\bar{X} = 50$				120

$$\sigma = \sqrt{120} = 10.95$$

It follows from above that there is around 68 per cent probability that the outcome (cash flow in our example) will lie between $\bar{X} \pm 1\sigma$ or 50 ± 10.95, that is, between 60.95 and

39.05. In other words, that there is about 34 per cent chance that outcome (cash flow) will be between 50 and 60.95 and about 34 per cent chance that the outcome (cash flow) will be between 50 and 39.05. This only means that there is about 16 per cent probability (50 – 34 = 16)* that cash flow will be more than 60.95 and similarly 16 per cent probability that it will be less than 39.05.

Further, the two standard deviations are equal to 2 10.95 = 21.9. With probability distribution of the standard normal curve, it means that there is around 95 per cent possibility that the outcome will lie between $\bar{X} \pm 2\sigma$ (in our example 50 ± 21.9, that, is between 71.9 and 28.1 lakh rupees). Likewise there is 99.74 per cent probability (*i.e.* almost certain) that the outcome (cash flow) will lie within $50 \pm 3\sigma$ or 50 ± 32.85.

Now, take the investment project *B* whose outcomes are more dispersed. We calculate the standard deviation of outcomes (cash flows) of this project *B* in Table 35.4 as under.

Table 35.4 : *Calculating Standard Deviation of Investment Project B*

X_i	P_i	$X_i - \bar{X}$ $\bar{X} = 50$	$(X_i - \bar{X})^2$	$(X_i - \bar{X})^2 P_i$
20	0.10	-30	900	90
35	0.25	-15	225	56.25
50	0.30	0	0	0
65	0.25	+15	225	56.25
80	0.10	+30	900	90

$\bar{X}=50$

$$\sum_{i=1}^{n}(X_i-\bar{X})^2.P_i = 292.5$$

$$\sigma \text{ or } sd = \sum_{i=1}^{n}\sqrt{(X_i-\bar{X})^2.P_i} = \sqrt{292.5} = 17.10$$

Thus we find that whereas the expected values of cash flows of the two investment projects are equal, the degree of risk as measured by standard deviation involved in project *B* is greater. Therefore, if managers or business firms are *averse to risk* (*i.e.* risk averter), they will choose investment project *B.* We will explain later in detail the problem of choice of an investment project from the various available alternative projects when both the expected values and degrees of risk differ.

Continuous Probability Distribution and Normal Curve

In our above example of measuring probabilities with normal distribution we have considered 5 possible outcomes of the two investment projects. This is a step-like probability distribution of cash flows which is known as *discrete probability distribution* of cash flows. However, it is quite likely that other outcomes in between these fives and beyond them will occur. In that case we will have a *continuous distribution of outcomes.* In case of continuous distribution bars representing the outcomes become thinner and thinner and approaches a vertical line in the limit. This continuous probability distribution is represented by a bell-shaped curve, known as a normal curve as shown in Figure 35.3. Where two probability distribution curves are shown.

* Note that there is 50 per cent chance that the cash flows will be above the expected value which is here also equal to 50, and 50 per cent chance that it will be below the expected value (50).

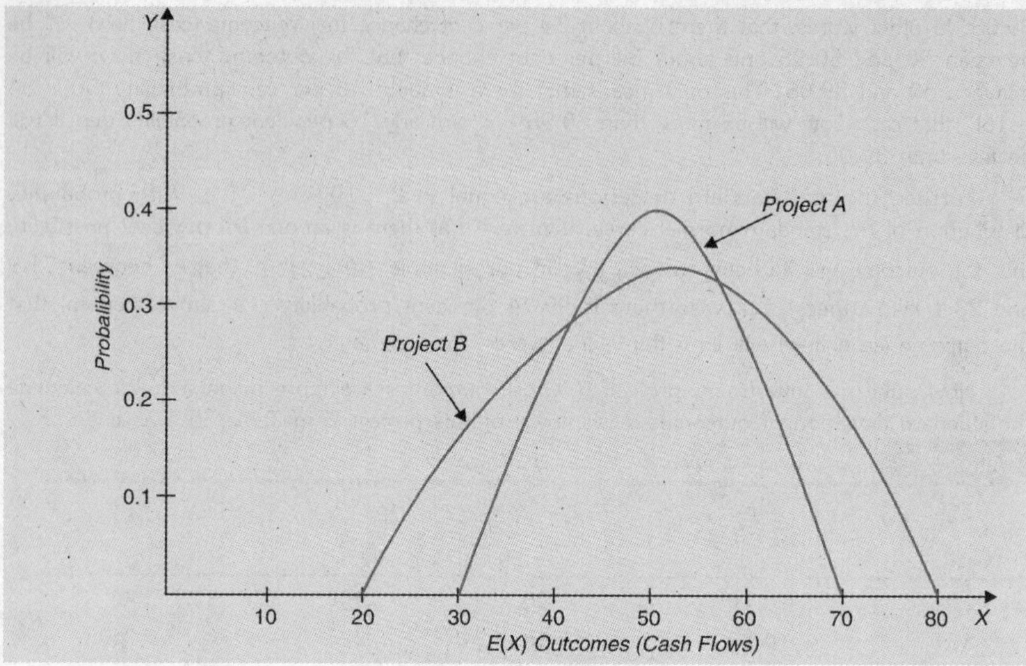

Fig. 35.3: *Continuous Probability Distribution of Cash Flows of Project A*

This curve of normal distribution is symmetrical about the expected value of distribution. The area under a normal curve represents the total probability of one. According to the normal curve theory 68.26 per cent of the total area under the normal curve lies within plus or minus one standard deviation (*i.e.* $\pm 1\sigma$) from its zero mean and 95.44 per cent lies of the area within $\pm 2\sigma$ and 99.74 per cent of the area lies within $\pm 3\sigma$

It will be seen from Figure 35.3 that the probability distribution of investment project A is tighter (*i.e.* less despersed) from its expected value as compared to that of investment project, B. It may be noted that in our above analysis we have mentioned the possibility of outcome (cash flow) lying within $\pm 1\sigma$, $\pm 2\sigma$ and $\pm 3\sigma$ from the expected vlaue.

Measuring Probability of an Outcome Lying within a Particular Range

Assuming that outcomes are normally distributed, we can determine or measure the probability a particular outcome (cash flow in our example) lying within a specific range. For this purpose subtract the expected value of the probability distribution of outcomes from the particular outcome and divide the result by the standard deviation of the given probability distribution of outcomes. The value so obtained is generally denoted by *Z*. Thus

$$Z = \frac{X - \overline{X}}{\sigma}$$

where *Z* is the number of standard deviations from the mean (*i.e.* expected value). *X* is value of the variable in question (such as cash flows in our above examples and $\overline{X}$ is the expected value of the variable.

For example, in case of probability distribution of cash flows given in Table 35.1 we are interested to know what will be the probability of cash flow of ₹ 62 lakhs from the project

A will be within range of ₹ 50 lakhs and ₹ 60 lakhs. Assuming that cash flows are approximately normally distributed with expected value equal to ₹ 50 lakhs and standard deviation of 10.59. We first find the value of *Z* as under

$$Z = \frac{62-50}{10.95} = \frac{12}{10.95} = 1.09$$

This means that the cash flow of ₹ 62 lakhs is 1.09 *standard deviation more than the expected value* (₹ 50 lakhs). Now looking at Table *C* (given at the appendix to this book) relating to the *area under the standard normal curve,* for the value of $Z = 1.09$ we go down the column *Z* upto 1.0 and then move horizontally along it until we are exactly below the column 0.09 so as to have 1.09 we obtain the value of 0.3621, that is, 36.21 per cent. This means that the area under the normal distribution curve between the expected value and 1.09 standard deviation to the right of the expected value (*i.e.* mean value) is 36.21. Thus the probability that cash flow of ₹ 62 lakhs from investment project *A* lying between 50 and 62 lakhs is 36.21 per cent.

Since the standard normal curve is symmetrical about its mean we will get the same probability of 36.21 per cent for the cash flow to be between 38 lakhs and 50 lakhs (expected value). This is because in this case

$$Z = \frac{38-50}{10.95} = 1.09$$

The probability of any other cash flow from the project falling in any other specific range can be found out.

The Coefficient of Variation

The Relative Measure of Risk. When the expected values of the two projects are equal or very close to each other, the standard deviation is an appropriate measure of riskiness of the projects. However, when the expected values of the investment projects are quite different, the standard deviation will not provide us a proper measure of risk. This is because standard deviation is an absolute measure of the degree of risk. To compare the two projects with divergent expected values, we make use of coefficient of variation which is a relative measure of risk. *The coefficient of variation measures risk relative to the expected values of the projects.* That is, the coefficient of variation measures *risk per rupee of the expected value.* As such it is relative measure that can be used to compare the relative riskiness of the two or more projects.

The coefficient of variation is obtained from dividing the standard distribution of probability distribution by the expected value (*i.e.* mean). Thus coefficient of variation, $V = \frac{\sigma}{\overline{R}}$.

where σ is the standard deviation of the probability distribution and $\overline{R}$ is the expected value or mean.

Let us take an example. The expected values of the two projects and their standard deviations are given below:

Table 35.5 *Standard Deviation and Coefficient of Variation*

	Expected Value	*Standard Deviation*
Project A	250	60
Project B	125	40

As compared to project *B*, project *A* has greater expected value and higher standard deviation indicating higher absolute risk as compared to project *B*. In order to compare them it is proper to use the coefficient of variation for measuring relative riskiness of the two projects.

$$V_A = \frac{\sigma_A}{\bar{R}_A} = \frac{60}{250} = 0.24$$

$$V_B = \frac{\sigma_B}{\bar{R}_B} = \frac{40}{125} = 0.32$$

Thus, though standard deviation is greater for project *A*, the coefficient of variation is smaller than that of project *B*. This means relative risk of project *A* that is, risk per rupee of expected value is smaller as compared to the project *B*. Therefore, since the expected value of project *A* is greater and its relative risk is small, the manager will decide to invest in this project.

DECISION MAKING UNDER RISK

Having described the risk and the ways of measuring it we are now in a position to explain how a rational individual will make a choice among various alternative courses of action, for example among various investment strategies involving risk. Since individuals have different preferences for risk taking, these preferences should be known and their effect on decision making have to be evaluated for the choice of a decision involving risk and uncertainity. Different individuals respond to the same risky situation differently. As mentioned above, some individuals are risk averse and some are risk-seekers. Thus the choice of a course of action also depends on the individual's attitude toward risk. For making a rational decision, the following three things should be determined.

1. The expected values of payoffs associated with various outcomes be calculated.

2. The degree of risk of various strategies be measured by estimating the standard deviation of the average deviation of payoffs of various outcomes from the expected value.

3. Information about the decision maker regarding his preference toward risk be obtained.

Let us illustrate decision making involving risk. Suppose an individual is considering two types of investment, say *A* and *B*. Further suppose that each type of investment requires an initial cost of ₹ 1 lakh and have a life of 5 years. The monetary return on these two types of investment depends on the *rate of inflation* (which is the state of nature) in the next five years. However, rate of inflation is not known and therefore investment decision involves risk and uncertainty. On the basis of the forecasts of economists, the probability of no inflation is 0.20, the probability of moderate inflation is 0.50, and the probability of high inflation is 0.30. The outcomes or payoffs are the net present value of profits for the next five years. The data regarding outcomes for different states of nature (*i.e.* different rates of inflation) for both types of investment are given in Table 35.6. Note that three outcomes (or monetary returns) from two types of investment depend on the rate of inflation, that is, the state of nature.

The analysis of the choice of an investment by an individual can be made by calculating and comparing their expected values and the degree of risk involved as measured by the standard deviation which indicate the variability of outcomes and therefore the amount of risk involved. We evaluate the two types of investment out of which an individual has to choose one.

Table 35.6 Probability Distribution and Expected Return on Investments.

State of Nature	Probability (P_i)	Outcome (Monetary Return) X_i
	Investment Project A	
No Inflation	0.20	150
Moderate Inflation	0.50	200
High Inflation	0.30	400
	Investment Project B	
No Inflation	0.20	200
Moderate Inflation	0.50	240
High Inflation	0.30	300

Investment Project A

Expected Value, $E(X) = P_1 . X_1 + P_2 . X_2 + P_3 . X_3$

$$= 0.20\ (150) + 0.50\ (200) + 0.30\ (400)$$

$$= 250$$

$$Sd = \sqrt{P_1[X_1 - E(X)]^2 + P_2[X_2 - E(X)]^2 + P_3[X_3 - E(X)]^2}$$

$$= \sqrt{0.20(150-250)^2 + 0.50(200-250)^2 + 0.30(400-250)^2}$$

$$= \sqrt{0.20(-100)^2 + 0.50(-50)^2 + 0.30(150)^2} = \sqrt{10000}$$

$$= 100$$

Investment Project B

Expected Value, $E(X) = P_1 . X_1 + P_2 . X_2 + P_3 . X_3$

$$E(X) = 0.20(200) + 0.50(240) + 0.30(300)$$

$$= 250$$

$$Sd = \sqrt{0.20(200-250)^2 + 0.50(240-250)^2 + 0.30(300-250)^2} = \sqrt{1300}$$

$$= 36.05$$

It will be seen from above that expected return from investment project *A* and the *B* are equal (as both are equal to 250) but investment project *A* involves greater risk as compared to investment *B* (*Sd.* of *A* is 100 while *Sd.* of *B* is 36.0). Therefore, if manager or a business man is risk averter, as is generally the case, be will choose project *B*. It is thus clear that decision making involving risk depends not only on the expected value but also on the degree of risk involved and the individual's attitude toward risk.

It may be noted that the analysis of *decision making by an individual involving risk and uncertainty is useful not only for deciding about investments but also analysing choice among any activity involving risk and uncertainty.* Thus choice between different courses of action (*i.e.* strategies) that differ in both expected value and riskiness we need to analyse the individuals preference towards risk. We explain below the different preferences of individuals toward risk and their impact on the decision-making involving risk and uncertainty.

ATTITUDE TOWARD RISK

We analysed the problem of investment choice to describe how people makes a choice among alternative investments involving different degree of risk involved. But the underlying principles of making a choice in risk and uncertain situation, namely expected return and the degree of risk involved apply equally well to other choices. In this section we focus on examining individual's choices in the face of risk. In the theory of consumer's behaviour we saw that in making choices among commodity bundles when there is no risk and uncertainty, the consumer maximises his utility. We will analyse below how an individual maximises his expected utility when risk or uncertainty is present.

People's preferences toward risk greatly differ. Most individuals generally prefer the less risky situation (that is, the situation with less variability in outcomes). In other words, most individuals seek to minimise risk and are called *risk averter* or *risk averse.* However, some individuals prefer risk and are therefore called *risk-seekers* or *risk lovers.* Some other individuals are indifferent toward risk and are called *risk-neutral.* But it is important to note that these different preferences toward risk depend on whether for an individual *marginal utility of money diminishes or increases or remains constant his income or wealth increases.* As shall be explained below, *for a risk averse individual marginal utility of money diminishes* as he has more money, while *for a risk-seeker marginal utility of money increases as money with him increases.* In case of *risk-neutral individual marginal utility of money remains constant as he has more money.*

Risk Averter. To explain the preference toward risk and the choice of an individual involving risk and uncertainty we will consider a single composite commodity, namely, money income. An individual's money income represents the market basket of goods that he can buy. It is assumed that the individual knows the probabilities of making or gaining money income in different situations. But the outcomes or payoffs are measured in terms of utility[1] rather than rupees.

In Fig. 35.4 we have drawn a curve *OU* showing utility function of money income of an individual who is risk-averse whereas money income has been measured on the *X*-axis and utility from money income has been measured on the *Y*-axis. It will be seen from this figure that utility function of the individual who is risk averter is *concave* toward the income axis (*i.e.*, *X*-axis) indicating that the utility from increase in money income increases but at a diminishing rate (*i.e.*, slope of the utility function decreases). This implies that in this concave utility function depicted in Fig. 35.4 marginal utility of money of an individual decreases as his money income decreases and therefore it represents the case of risk-averse individual. We will now explain the choice by a risk-averse individual whose utility function is concave when he faces a risky and uncertain situation. Suppose an individual is currently employed on a fixed monthly salary basis of ₹ 20,000. There is no uncertainty about the income from this present job on a the fixed salary basis and hence no risk. Now, suppose that the individual is considering to join a new job of a salesman on a *commission basis.* This new job involves risk because his income in this case is not certain. This is because if he proves to be a successful salesman his income

1. Neumann and Mrgenstern in their important contribution. *"The Theory of Games and Economic Behaviour"* suggested a way of measuring utility in quantitative terms in situations involving risk and uncertainty. They construct index numbers, termed as *N-M Index Numbers,* to measure utility. However, to simplify our analysis we just assume that utility can be measured in some units.

may increase to ₹ 30 thousand per month but if he does not happen to be a good salesman his income may go down to ₹ 10 thousand per month. Suppose in this new job there is 50-50 chance of either earning ₹ 30 thousands or ₹ 10 thousands (that is, each has a probability of 0.5). When there is uncertainty, the individual does not know the actual utility from making a particular choice.

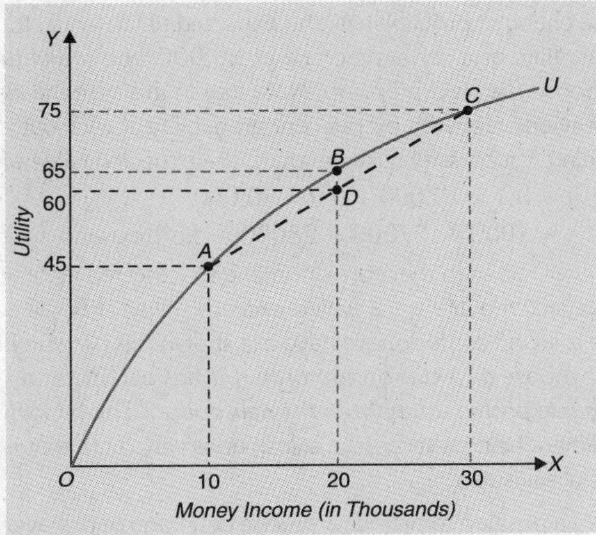

Fig. 35.4. *Utility Function of a Risk Averter*

But given the probabilities of alternative outcomes, we can calculate his expected utility. Whether the individual will choose the new risky job or retain the present salaried job with *a certain* income can be known by comparing the expected utility from the new risky job with the utility of the current job. It will be seen from the utility function curve *OU* in Fig. 35.4 that the utility of money income of ₹ 20,000 with *certainty* is ₹ 65. Further, in case of new risky job if he is proved to be a successful salesman and his income rises to ₹ 30 thousands, his utility from ₹ 30 thousands is 75, and if he fails as a good salesman, his income falls to ₹ 10 thousands which yields him utility of 45. (Note that in the new risky job, the expected income is also 20,000 which is given by $E(X) = 0.5 \times 10{,}000 + 0.5 \times 30{,}000 =$ ₹ 20,000). Given that the probability of success or failure as a salesman is 0.5, the expected utility of the new job is given by

$$\begin{aligned} E(U) &= 0.5\,U(10{,}000) + 0.5\,U(30{,}000) \\ &= 0.5 \times 45 + 0.5 \times 75 \\ &= 22.5 + 37.5 \\ &= 60.0 \end{aligned}$$

Thus with the present job with a fixed salary of ₹ 20,000 with no uncertainty his utility is 65, whereas the expected utility of the new job as salesman on commission basis is 60 at point *D* in Fig. 35.4 corresponding to the expected income of ₹ 20,000. Since the expected utility of the new risky job is less than the utility of the present job with a *certain* income, he will reject the offer of new job involving risk.

Let us change the data suppose the individual's subjective probability of proving to be a successful salesman is 90 per cent (*i.e.*, probability of being a successful salesman is 0.9), then given the above income data and utility function (as shown in Fig. 35.4), the expected utility from joining the new job of a salesman on a commission basis is:

$$E(U) = 0.1U(10{,}000) + 0.9\,U(30{,}000)$$
$$= 0.1 \times 45 + 0.9 \times 75$$
$$= 4.5 + 67.5 = 72$$

Now, in these changed probabilities, the expected utility (equal to 72) of a riskier choice is greater than the utility of a certain income of 20,000, *the individual even though he is risk-averse will choose the riskier option*. Note that in this case the *expected value* is much greater than the previous case with 50 per cent probability of each outcome. Now with 90 per cent chances of being a successful business man, the expected value of the outcome is:

$$E(V) = 0.1 \times 10{,}000 + 0.9 \times 30{,}000$$
$$= 1000 + 27000 = 28000 \text{ or } 28 \text{ thousand}$$

In Fig. 35.4, it will be seen that corresponding to expected income from a new job equal to 28 thousand, expected utility is 72 which exceeds utility of 65 of certain income of ₹ 20 thousand (In order to avoid confusion we have not shown this point in Fig. 35.4). To conclude *a risk averter will choose a riskier option only if it has a sufficiently large expected value and therefore higher expected utility from the new option*. This happens only if the individual's subjective probability of being a successful salesman is very high, that is, he is more confident of being a successful salesman.

We are now in a position to provide a precise definition of risk-averse individual. Precisely speaking, *a person who prefers a certain given income to a risky job with the same expected income is called risk averter or risk-averse*. Risk aversion is the most common attitude toward risk.

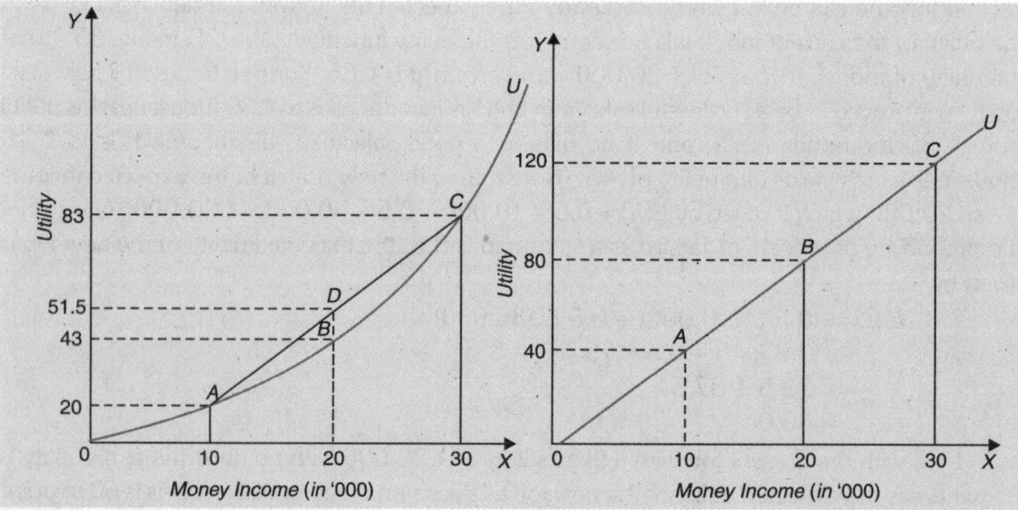

Fig. 35.5. *Utility Function of a Risk-Seeker*

Fig. 35.6. *Utility Function of a Risk Neutral*

Risk Lover. On the other hand, *a person is risk-seeker or risk-lover who prefers a risky job with the expected income equal to a certain income*. In case of a risk-loving individual, marginal utility of income to the individual increases as his money income increases as shown by the *convex* total utility function curve *OU* in Fig. 35.5. Suppose this risk-seeking individual has a present job with a certain income of ₹ 20 thousands. It will be seen from Fig. 35.5 that the utility of ₹ 20 thousands is 43 units to this individual. Now, if he is offered a risky job with his income of ₹ 30 thousands if he happens to be highly efficient and ₹ 10 thousands if he happens to be not so efficient in the new job with the equal probability of 0.5 in these two jobs, then the expected utility from the new job is given by

$$E(U) = 0.5\, U\,(10{,}000) + 0.5\, U\,(30{,}000)$$

It will be seen from Fig. 35.5 that the utility of ₹ 10 thousand to this individual is 20 while utility of ₹ 30 thousands to him is 83. Therefore,

$$E(U) = 0.5\,(20) + 0.5\,(83)$$

$$= 10 + 41.5$$

$$= 51.5$$

Since the expected utility from the new risky job is 51.5 which is *greater* than the utility of 43 from the present job with a certain income of ₹ 20 thousand, the *risk-loving individual will prefer the new risky job even though the expected income in the new risky job is also ₹ 20,000* as (0.5 × 10,000) + 0.5 (30,000) = ₹ 20,000).

As mentioned above, most of the individuals are risk averse but there is a good deal of evidence of people who are risk seekers. It is risk-loving individuals who indulge in gambling, buy lotteries, engage in criminal activities such as robberies, big frauds even at risk of getting heavy punishment if caught.

Risk-Neutral. *A person is called risk neutral, if he is indifferent between a certain given income and an uncertain income with the same expected value.* An individual will be risk neutral if his marginal utility of money income remains constant with the increase in his money. The total utility function of a risk neutral person is shown in Fig. 35.6. It will be seen from this figure that utility of a *certain* income of ₹ 20 thousands is 80. Now, in a risky job when income increases to ₹ 30 thousands if he proves to be a successful salesman, the utility of ₹ 30 thousands is 120 units to him.

On the other hand, if in a new risky job, he proves to be a bad salesman, his income goes down to ₹ 10,000 whose utility to the individual is 40 units. We assume that there is equal probability of high and low income in the new risky job. Note that expected value of income in the new job with an uncertain income is 2,000 as (0.5 × 10,000 + 0.5 (30,000) = 20,000. The expected utility of the new risky job is given by

$$E(U) = 0.5\, U\,(10{,}000) + 0.5\, U\,(30{,}000).$$

$$= 0.5\,(40) + 0.5\,(120)$$

$$= 20 + 60$$

$$= 80$$

It is seen from above that in case of risk-neutral person expected utility of an uncertain income with the same expected value (₹ 20,000 in the present case), is equal to utility of an assured or a certain income of the same amount. That is, risk-neutral person is indifferent between them.

INSURANCE AND RISK PREMIUM

Our foregoing analysis shows why most people buy insurance when they are faced with a risky and uncertain situation. As mentioned above, most people are risk averters and therefore they buy insurance to avoid risk. Now an important question is how much money or premium a risk-averse individual will pay to the insurance company to avoid risk and uncertainty facing him. Suppose the individual buys a house which yields him income of ₹ 30 thousands per month. But if the house catches fire and due to the damage caused, his income from it falls to ₹ 10 thousands per month and thus he suffers a loss of income. For the sake of simplifying analysis suppose there is 50 per cent chance of the house catching fire. Then the expect value of income in this risky and uncertain situation is

$$E(X) = 0.5 \times 30{,}000 + 0.5 \times 10{,}000$$
$$= 15{,}000 + 5{,}000$$
$$= 20{,}000$$

The utility function *OU* with a diminishing marginal utility of money income of a risk-averse individual is shown in Fig. 35.7. With money income of ₹ 30 thousands, his utility is 75 and with his lower income of 10 thousands his utility is 45. Given that there is probability of 0.5 for each outcome, expected utility of the two outcomes is given by

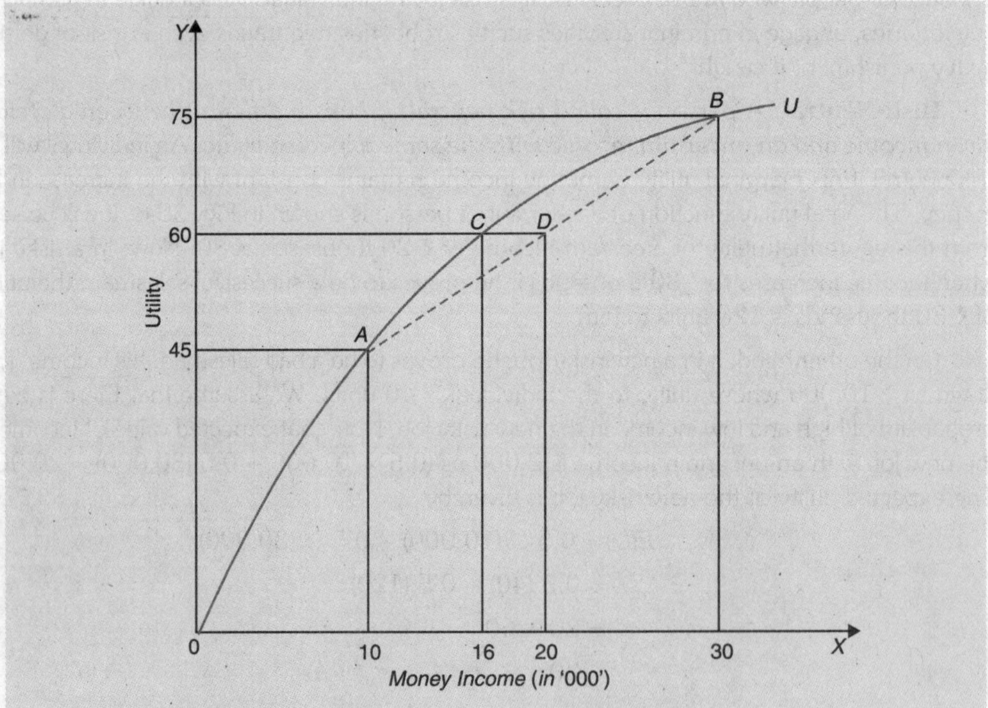

Fig. 35.7. *Insurance and Risk Premium*

$$E(U) = 0.5\,U(30{,}000) + 0.5\,U(10{,}000)$$
$$= 0.5 \times 75 + 0.5 \times 45$$
$$= 37.5 + 22.5$$
$$= 60$$

It will be seen from Fig. 35.7 that we have drawn a straight line *AB* joining the utilities of 75 and 45. It is on this straight line *AB* that the amount of expected utility will be corresponding to the expected value of income in the present risky and uncertain situation. It will be seen from Fig.35.7 that on this straight line *AB* and corresponding to the expected value of income of ₹ 20 thousands, the expected utility is 60 which corresponds to point *D* on the straight line *AB*. But it will be seen from the individual's utility function *OU*, that utility of 60 is associated with *an assured and certain income* of ₹16 thousands. Thus the individual with an uncertain income of ₹ 20 thousands will be willing to forego ₹ 4 thousands (or *DC*) to get a certain or guaranteed income of ₹ 16 thousands as the expected utility of uncertain expected income of ₹ 20 thousands is equal to the utility of a certain income of ₹ 16 thousands. This means that if the individual gives up ₹ 4 thousands (20 – 16 = 4) from his uncertain expected income he will get the same utility of 60 as with a certain income of ₹ 16 thousands. ₹ 4 thousands equal to distance *DC* is called the *risk premium*. Therefore, *the risk premium is the maximum amount of money that a risk-averse individual will be willing to pay to avoid the risk*. By paying the risk premium the individual can insure himself against a large loss from a fire and to get an assured or certain income.

It is clear from above way people buy insurance for fire, accident, ill health and even life.

MANAGEMENT OF RISK : REDUCING RISK

We have seen above that though some individuals are risk-seekers, most of the individuals are risk-averse and try to reduce risk or uncertainty they face. There are three methods by which individuals or consumers can reduce risk. They are :

1. Diversification
2. Insurance
3. Gathering more Information.

We discuss below these methods.

Diversification

An important way of reducing risk is diversification, that is, spreading the risks. For example, an investor can reduce risk involved in investment by investing his investible funds in a number of independent projects rather than in a single project. There is a famous saying for safe investment, "Do not put all your eggs in one basket." Thus, for reducing risk in investing in stock market is to purchase shares of many companies at the same time. If the investment projects are not closely related, then risk can be reduced by investing in a number of them, that is, by diversifying the investment portfolio. If there is inverse or negative relation between two activities, that is, when one's demand is strong, the other's demand is weak, diversification will help in reducing risk involved in investment or activity.

As mentioned above, a person can reduce risk by investing his funds in the stock of a number of companies rather than investing in the stock of a single company as the stocks of different companies are not generally positively related. In recent years, investment in *mutual funds* are preferred as they enable small investors to invest in a large number of unrelated companies. It is however important to note that risk cannot be entirely eliminated by diversification of investment in stocks of a number of companies. This is because in case of a recession the share prices of all companies tend to fall. Therefore, diversification can greatly help in reducing risk, it cannot eliminate it completely. Risks of *systemic nature* are non-diversifiable and have to be borne. However, as long as you can allocate your investible funds or effort in a number of activities whose outcomes are not closely positively related, risks can be reduced to some extent.

Insurance

Insurance is another important method of reducing risk. We have explained above that risk averse individuals are willing to give up some income to avoid risk. *The maximum price which an individual is willing to forego or pay for insurance is called risk premium.* Therefore, if the cost of insurance is equal to the amount of *risk premium* which they are prepared to give up to assure themselves a certain income in a risky and uncertain situation, they will buy the insurance policy. For example, if an individual owns a house worth ₹ 20 lakhs and faces a probability of 0.01 i.e., one per cent chance of his house getting burnt down, then the expected value of loss is $\frac{1}{100} \times 20{,}000{,}00 = 20{,}000$. If a fire insurance policy is offered to the house owner for ₹ 20,000, he will definitely buy it. Such an insurance premium is fairly priced as it is equal to the expected loss that may assure to the individual in case his house is burnt down due to catching fire. In fact, a risk averse individual may be willing to pay more than this depending on the degree of his risk-aversion as measured by the risk premium he is prepared to pay.

The individuals generally buy insurance from the companies which specialize in the insurance business. These insurance companies work on the basis of *a law of large numbers*. The insurance companies not only insure against the loss suffered by the individuals but also earn profits for them. For example, from the past information, the insurance companies know that I per cent houses will catch fire. To provide insurance cover they pool a large number of policies. It insures against the expected loss to 100 policy holders, they will actually pay the loss to one policy holder if the probability of houses catching fire is one percent. They fix such an amount of insurance premium that they are not only able to compensate the loss to the individuals but also earn profits for themselves.

Gathering More Information

Collecting more accurate information is one important way by which individuals can reduce risk while making a choice under conditions of uncertainty. More information will enable them to increase expected value and utility. With more information about the new good which a person wants to purchase or a new job he is offered will reduce the possibility of suffering a loss. For example, for buying a car or refrigerator of a company many individuals seek information from friends, read review of the car or refrigerators of the company in the newspapers or television to know how frequently a particular brand is likely to break down and requires repairs more often. By gathering information he can reduce the possibility of making a wrong decision.

RISK SEEKER AND THE GAMBLING

Now, we explain how a risk lover responds to a fair gamble. It may be noted that a risk lover is one who prefers a gamble with the same expected value of income to the equivalent income with certainty. In Figure 35.8 the utility curve of a risk lover has been drawn and, as it will be seen, it is *convex*. The convexity of the utility curve implies that marginal utility of money income of the person increases as his income increases. Now, suppose that present income of the individual is ₹ 3,000 and is offered a gamble with 50:50 chance of winning or losing ₹ 1,000. Therefore, if he wins, his money income will rise to ₹ 4,000, and if he loses his income will fall to ₹ 2,000. The expected money value of the gamble will therefore be equal to 1/2(4000) + 1/2(2000) = ₹ 3,000. And the expected utility from the expected value of income of ₹ 3,000, as it will be seen from Figure 35.8 will be M_2D or OU_2 which is more than utility M_2C or OU_1 of income of ₹ 3,000 with certainty.

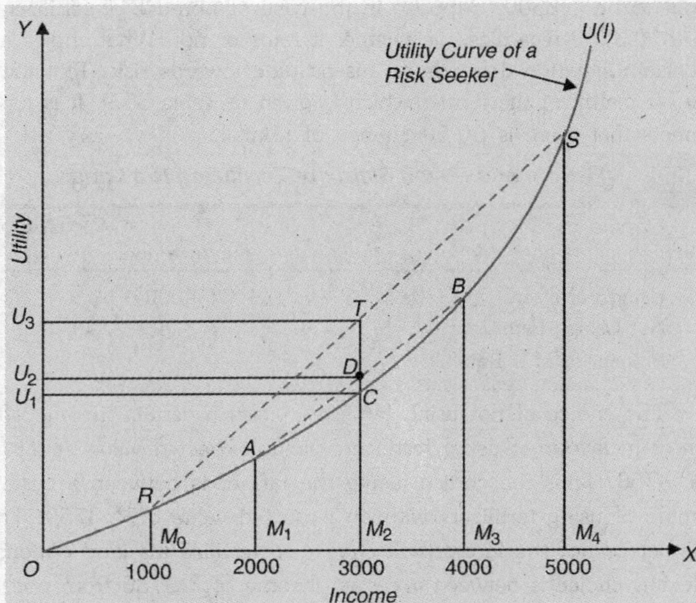

Fig. 35.8. *The Utility Curve of a Risk-Lover and his Preference for Gambling.*

Since his expected utility from the gamble is greater than that from his income with certainty, he will accept the gamble. Further, it can be shown that risk lover, a person whose marginal utility of money increases with increase in his income, will prefer a gamble having greater risk, that is, the gamble which has a larger variability of outcome to a gamble with less risk (that is, with smaller variability of outcome). Suppose a person with increasing marginal utility of income is offered two fair gambles: One with 50:50 chance of winning or losing ₹ 1,000 and the other with a 50:50 chance of winning or losing ₹ 1500 as outcome of the gamble. Given his present income of ₹ 3,000, the expected value of the two gambles is the same.

$E(V)$ of the Gamble I = 1/2 (4000) + 1/2 (2000) = 3000

$E(V)$ of the Gamble II = 1/2 (5000) + 1/2 (1000) = 3000

However, it will be seen from Figure 35.8 that the expected utility of the two gambles differs; the expected utility of the second gamble, as will be seen from the straight-line segment *RS*, is equal to M_2T or OU_3 which is greater than M_2D or OU_2 of the first gamble with less variability (or risk) of outcome. It therefore follows that the risk lover will prefer the second gamble with greater risk and variability of outcome.

An Application: Farmer's Gambling Against Nature

We will now provide an interesting and useful application of choice under risk and uncertainty to the case of a farmer who in the absence of irrigation has to face an uncertain situation regarding outcome of his use of fertilizer which yields higher output only in the presence of water, the availability of which, in the absence of irrigation, depends on the rain. If the farmer fertilizers his land and nature is kind and there is good and timely rainfall, he will reap a bumper crop. One the contrary, if it does not rain, his output (and therefore his income) will be low because the use of fertilizers in the absence of water is likely to burn his seed and damage his soil. If the farmer does not use fertilizers, he will have a moderate but a certain income. Thus the farmer for deciding whether or not to fertilize the land is playing a game against nature. Let us illustrate it with a numerical example. Suppose if our farmer uses fertilizer, his income rises to ₹ 5,000 but only if there is a good rainfall. And if it does not rain, his output or income will be small because in the absence of water, the use of fertilizers may destroy much of his seed and also cause damage to his soil. Let his output or income in this case comes about to be ₹ 2500. Suppose in the case of non-use of fertilizers, he has a moderate output worth ₹ 3750 regardless of whether it rains or not. What choice a farmer will make under this uncertain situation depends on his attitude towards risk. To know this we have constructed a pay off matrix of the farmer which is given in Table 35.9. It is further assumed that the farmer expects that there is 50:50 chance of rainfall.

Table 35.9. ***Farmer's Payoff Matrix of Fertilizing His Land***

Choice	*Outcome*	
	Rain	*No. Rain*
Using Fertilizers	₹ 5000	₹ 2500
Not Using Fertilizers	₹ 3750	₹ 3750
Probability of a Rainfall	0.5	0.5

The choice of not using fertilizers yields a certain income of ₹ 3750. The choice by the farmer in favour of using fertilizers yields expected value equal to 1/2 (5000) + 1/2 (2500) = ₹ 3750. Thus the choice facing the farmer is between a certain income of ₹ 3750 and a gamble of using fertilizers with an expected value of ₹ 3750. This is quite a fair game. But whether or not the farmer will choose to fertilize his land depends upon his attitude towards risk. His choice is between a certain income of ₹ 3750 from not using fertilizers and a gamble of using the fertilizers the expected money value of which also equals ₹ 3750. If the farmer is risk averter, he will choose not to fertilize the land, that is, he will not gamble. On the other hand, if a farmer is risk lover, as depicted in Figure 35.8 he will fertilize the land that is, he will gamble. Of course, if he is a risk neutral, he will be indifferent between the two choices.

RISK-RETURN TRADE-OFF AND CHOICE OF A PORTFOLIO

For measuring risk premium on a risky investment and for analysis of choice of a portfolio of assets by individuals or firms we require to explain the concept of risk-return trade-off

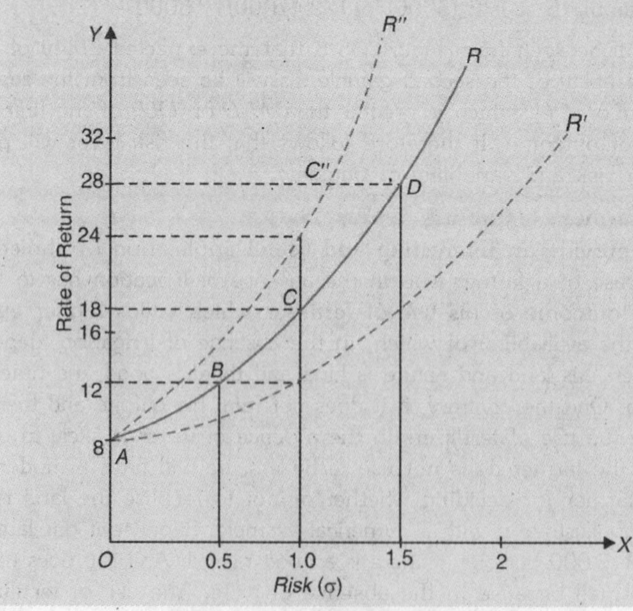

Fig. 35.9. *Risk-Return Trade off*

function. The concept of risk-return trade-off function can be better explained with Fig. 35.9 where on the X-axis, we measure risk in terms of standard deviation (σ) of probability distribution, and rate of return as per cent of investment is measured along the Y-axis. An upward sloping solid curve AR has been drawn from point A.Point A represents risk-free return of 8 per cent. This AR curve represents the risk-return trade off function of an individual or a firm and shows that 4 per cent extra return over and above risk-free return of 8 per cent is required to compensate him for the degree of risk given by $\sigma = 0.5$ (Note that 12 – 8 = 4).

Here 8 per cent is a risk-free return as corresponding to it standard deviation (σ),which measures the level of risk, is zero. *The difference between the required rate of return on a risky investment and the return on risk-free investment is called risk premium.* Thus in the trade-off curve AR rate of return of 4 per cent is required on an investment with a risk of σ = 0.5. Similarly, as will be seen from AR trade off curve in Figure 35.9 that to compensate the individual for undertaking an investment with a risk of $\sigma = 1.0$, return of 18 per cent is required (that is , risk premium on this investment is 10 per cent, 18 – 8 = 10). 28 per cent rate of return is required or expected on risky investment with $\sigma = 1.5$.

For a *more risk-averse manager* the higher rate of return is required for a risky investment with a given standard deviation. Therefore, for a more risk-averse manager risk-return trade-off curve will be steeper than AR curve. Thus, with a more risk-averse manager, a steeper risk return trade-off curve AR' (dotted) has been drawn. With AR' risk-return trade off curve to compensate for risky investment with $\sigma = 1.0$, 24 per cent return is required, that is, his risk premium is 16 per cent as compared to 10 per cent of the previous manager.

Similarly, for a less risk-averse manager trade-off curve will be less steep such as AR'' (dotted). A manager with trade off curve AR'', to compensate him for risky investment with $\sigma = 1.0$, return of 12 per cent is required, (that is, 4 per cent risk premium is needed for a risk of $\sigma = 1.0$.

In the next chapter we will explain how to modify capital budgeting of a firm by using risk-premium to get risk-adjusted discount rate which is used to find net present value of stream of cash flows from investment project which yields return in a number of future years, In the present chapter we use the risk-return trade off curve for analysing the choice of an investment portfolio.

The Choice of an Investment Portfolio

As explained above, the firms try to reduce risk by diversification. Towards that end the firms produce different types of products, that is, invest in different lines of business. Similarly, investors choose a portfolio of assets to reduce overall risk of their investment. We have explained above how risk is measured by standard deviation and risk-return trade off curve is obtained. Now, the investors choose a risky portfolio of assets if they provide them adequate return.

To explain the choice of an optimum portfolio we need another concept generally called *a budget frontier* which represents the combinations of risk and return that are obtainable with the given available funds from mixed portfolios of two assets, say, shares of Reliance Industries and Tata Steel.

Suppose the expected returns from these assets are 20 percent and 10 per cent respectively. If a portion W_i of the given available funds are invested in Reliance Industries and the remaining funds W_t are invested in Tata Steel, the expected return of the portfolio of these two assets is given by

$$r_p = W_i r_i + W_t . r_t \qquad ...(1)$$

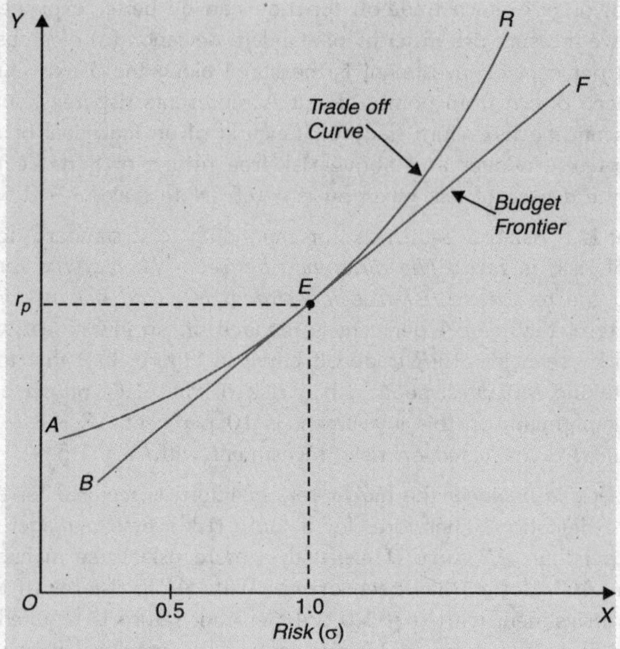

Fig. 35.10. *Choice of an Investment Portfolio*

where r_p = expected return of the portfolio of two assets.

r_i = the expected return of investment in Reliance Industries

r_t = the expected return from Tata Steel.

W_i = the proportion of the given funds invested in Reliance Industries

W_t = the remaining portion of the given funds invested in Tata Steel.

Note that $W_i + W_t = 1$ and different portfolios or combinations of two assets will involve different degrees of risk (σ) and also yield different return. Note that rate of return from a portfolio is the weightage average of the returns from the two assets as given by equation (1). It is worth noting that any linear weighted combinations of returns from two assets with the given returns, r_i and r_t shows the rate of return from a postfolio of these two assets. We draw in Figure 35.10 such a budget frontier *BF* which shows the continuations or portfolios of two assets which are obtainable with the given funds. It will be seen from Figure 35.10 that budget frontier *BF* is tangent to the trade-off function curve *AR* at point *E* which represents the optimum portfolio of two assets which yield return of r_p and involve a risk (σ) of 1.0. The combination of two assets represented by *E* is an optimally diversified portfolio containing a mix of the two assets.

If the rate of return on shares of Reliance Industries is 20 per cent and return on Tata Steel shares is 10 per cent. Suppose in the optimum portfolio, the individual spends 40 per cent of its investible funds on shares of Reliance Industries and the remaining 60 per cent on shares of Tata Steel, the rate of return on the portfolio can be calculated as follows

$$r_p = W_r \; r_i + W_t \, r_t$$
$$= 0.40 \times 20 + 0.60 \times 10$$
$$= 8 + 6 = 14$$

Thus rate of return of the portfolio of the two assets is 14 per cent.

SOME NUMERICAL PROBLEMS

Problem 1. *An investor has to choose between two investment projects A and B, each requires an initial outlay of ₹ 10 lakhs. The present value of possible cash flows from them and their associate probabilities are given below.*

	Investment Project A (in ₹ lakhs)		*Investment Project B (in ₹ lakhs)*		
Cash Flow	*40*	*60*	*30*	*50*	*70*
Probability	*0.6*	*0.4*	*0.4*	*0.3*	*0.3*

(a) Calculate the expected value of each investment project. (b) Calculate the level of risk of each investment project. (c) In which project the firm should undertake investment.

Solution:

(*a*) Expected value of project *A*

$$E(X) \text{ of Project } A = X_1 P_1 + X_2 P_2$$
$$= 40 \times 0.6 + 60 \times 0.4$$
$$= 24.0 + 24.0$$
$$= 48$$

$$E(X) \text{ of Project } B = X_1 P_1 + X_2 P_2 + X_3 . P_3$$
$$= 30 \times 0.4 + 50 \times 0.3 + 70 \times 0.3$$
$$= 12.0 + 15.0 + 21.0$$
$$= 48$$

The expected value of projects *A* and *B* are both equal to 48. Since each project costs ₹ 10 lakhs, the expected value of profits of each will be 38 lakhs.

(*b*) We can measure risk by calculating the standard deviation of each probability distribution.

$$\sigma \text{ of } A = \sqrt{\sum_{i=1}^{n} [X_i - E(X_i)]^2 P_i}$$

$$= \sqrt{[X_1 - E(X_1)]^2 P_1 + [X_2 - E(X_2)]^2 P_2}$$

$$= \sqrt{(40-48)^2 .0.6 + (60-48)^2 0.4}$$

$$= \sqrt{(-8)^2 .0.6 + (12)^2 \times 0.4}$$

$$= \sqrt{64 \times 0.6 + 144 \times 0.4}$$

$$= \sqrt{38.4 + 57.6}$$

$$= \sqrt{96} = 9.79$$

$$\sigma \text{ of } B = \sqrt{(30-48)^2 \times 0.4 + (50-48)^2 \times 0.3 + (70-48)^2 \times 0.3}$$

$$= \sqrt{(-18)^2 \times 0.4 + (2)^2 \times 0.3 + (22)^2 \times 0.3}$$

$$= \sqrt{324 \times 0.4 + 4 \times 0.3 + 484 \times 0.3}$$

$$= \sqrt{129.6 + 1.2 + 145.2}$$

$$= \sqrt{276} = 16.6$$

It follows from the values of standard deviations that investment in project B is more risky.

(*c*) Since expected value of cash flows of each investment is the same but investment project B is more risky, the firm will undertake investment in project A.

Problem 2. *A manager of a firm is faced with the problem in which of the two products A and B he should invest. The market studies estimate the following net present values of all future profits under three possible states of the economy.*

State of the Economy	*Investment in Product A*		*Investment in Product B*	
	Probability	*Profit*	*Probability*	*Profit*
Boom	0.2	50	0.2	30
Normal	0.5	20	0.4	20
Recession	0.3	0	0.4	10

The manager's utility function for money is : $U = 100\,M - M^2$ where M stands for money profits.

(a) Determine whether manager is risk-averse, risk neutral or risk, seeker.

(b) If manager's objective is to maximise money profits irrespective of risk, in which product he should invest?

(c) What is the relative level of risk involved in each investment?

(d) If the manager's objective were to maximise utility in which product he should invest ?

Solution:

(*a*) To determine whether manager is risk-seeker, risk neutral or risk averter, we find the marginal utility of money from the given utility function of money of the manager. Thus

$$U = 100\,M - M^2 \quad ...(1)$$

Taking the first derivative of (1), which will indicate the marginal utility of money, we have

$$\frac{dU}{dM} = 100 - 2M \quad ...(2)$$

Taking the second derivative

$$\frac{d^2U}{dM^2} = -2$$

The negative value of the second derivative implies that marginal utility of money for the manager diminishes. Therefore he is a risk averter

(*b*) To find investment in which product will yield him more profits we find the expected values of money profits for investment in the two products.

Investment in Product A

State of the Economy	P_i	π_i	$P\pi_i$	$\pi - \bar{\pi}$	$(\pi - \bar{\pi})^2$	$(\pi - \bar{\pi})^2 \cdot P_i$
Boom	0.2	50	10	30	900	180
Normal	0.5	20	10	0	0	0
Recession	0.3	0	0	-20	400	120
			$\bar{\pi} = 20$			300

Expect profits from A = 20

$$\text{Standard deviation } (\sigma) \text{ of } A = \sqrt{\sum_{i=1}^{n} = (\pi_i - \bar{\pi})^2 . P_i}$$

$$= \sqrt{300} = 17.32$$

$$\text{Relative risk is obtained by coefficiation of variation} = \frac{\sigma}{\bar{\pi}} = \frac{17.32}{20} = 0.866$$

Investment in Product B

State of the Economy	P_i	π_i	$P\pi_i$	$\pi_i - \bar{\pi}$ $(\bar{\pi} = 18)$	$(\pi_i - \bar{\pi})^2$	$(\pi_i - \bar{\pi})^2 \cdot P_i$
Boom	0.2	30	6	+12	144	28.8
Normal	0.4	20	8	+2	4	1.6
Recession	0.4	10	4	-8	64	25.6

$$\bar{\pi} = 18 \qquad \Sigma(\pi_i - \bar{\pi})^2 . P_i = 56.0$$

$$E(\pi) = 18$$

$$\sigma = \sqrt{\sum_{i=1}^{n} (\pi_i - \pi)^2 . P_i} = \sqrt{56} = 7.48$$

$$\text{Coefficient of Variation} = \frac{7.48}{18} = .41$$

It follows from above that if manager's objective is to maximise profits, he will choose to invest in product A as expected value of profits for it (20) is greater as compared to expected value of profits for product B.

(c) Relative risk is measured by coefficient of variation (V) which in the present case will indicate standard deviation per rupee of profits. Coefficient of variation of investment in product

$$A = \frac{\sigma}{\bar{\pi}} = \frac{17.32}{20} = 0.866$$

$$\text{Coefficient of variation of investment in product } B = \frac{7.48}{18} = 0.41$$

Thus investment in product A involves more risk, though it yields higher expected money profits.

(*d*) To find expected utility we first calculate utilities of money profits and then multiply them by their associated probabilities. For calculating utilities obtained from money profits, we use the given utility function $U = 100\ M - M^2$.

Calculating Expected Utility from Investment in A

π_i	U_i	P_i	P_iU_i
50	$100\ 50 - (50)^2 = 2500$	0.2	500
20	$100\ 20 - (20)^2 = 1600$	0.5	800
0	0	0.3	0
			$\Sigma\ P_iU_i = 1300$

Calculating Expected Utility from Investment in B

π_i	U_i	P_i	P_iU_i
30	$100\ 30 - (30)^2 = 2100$	0.2	420
20	$100\ 20 - (20)^2 = 1600$	0.4	640
10	$100\ 10 - (10)^2 = 900$	0.4	360
			$\Sigma\ P_iU_i = 1420$

Thus, if manager's objective is to maximise utility, he will invest in product *A*

Problem 3. *A manager of a soft-drink company has to decide which of the two advertisement strategies to promote sales and profits of the company : (1) Giving advertisement on various TV Channels, (2) Giving advertisements in various national newspapers. The marketing division of the company has estimated the following possible sales and their probabilities of each advertising strategy.*

Strategy I (Ads. on TV)		*Strategy II* (Ads. in Newspapers)	
Sales (₹ lakhs)	*Probability*	*Sales (₹ lakhs)*	*Probability*
80	*0.2*	*80*	*0.3*
100	*0.3*	*120*	*0.4*
120	*0.3*	*160*	*0.3*
140	*0.2*		

It is known that 50 per cent of the sales of the company constitutes profits of the company

(*a*) *Calculate the expected value of monetary profits for the two alternative sales promotion strategy*

(*b*) *Calculate the level of risk for each sales promotion strategy*

(*c*) *Which sales promotion strategy the manager should choose?*

Solution:

Let X stand for profits and $\overline{X}$ stand for expected value of profits. Taking into account that 50 per cent of sales are profits we calculate below the expected value of monetary profits of the alternative promotion strategies.

Strategy I (Ads. on TV)

Profits (X_i)	Probability (P_i)	$X_i P_i$	$(X_i - \bar{X})$	$(X_i - \bar{X})^2$	$(X_i - \bar{X}) P_i$
40	0.2	8	−15	225	45.0
50	0.3	15	−5	25	7.5
60	0.3	18	+5	25	7.5
70	0.2	14	+15	225	45.0

$$\bar{X} \text{ or } \Sigma X_i P_i = 55 \text{ and } \sigma = \sum_{i=1}^{n} (X_i - \bar{X})^2 . P_i = \sqrt{105} = 10.25$$

$$\text{Coff. of variation} = \frac{10.25}{55} = 0.186$$

Strategy II (Ads. in Newspapers)

Profits (X_i)	Probability (P_i)	$X_i P_i$	$(X_i - \bar{X})$	$(X_i - \bar{X})^2$	$(X_i - \bar{X})^2 P_i$
40	0.3	12	−20	400	120
60	0.4	24	0	0	0
80	0.3	24	+20	400	120

$$\bar{X} = 60 \text{ and } \sigma = \sqrt{\sum_{i=1}^{n} (X_i - \bar{X})^2 . P_i} = \sqrt{240} = 15.49$$

$$\text{Coff. of variation} = \frac{15.49}{60} = 0.258$$

Thus, it will be seen from above that strategy II has a higher expected value of monetary profits but is more risky than strategy I on the basis of coefficient of variation. The manager who is risk neutral or risk seeker will go in for sales promotion strategy II. However, if the manager is risk-averse, it cant be said which strategy he will choose as it depends on the utility function of the manager which is not given in the question.

Problem 4. *An oil drilling company offers the opportunity of investing ₹ 5,000 with 20 per cent probability of return of ₹ 20,000 if oil-drilling operation is successful (that is, if oil is struck) and if it is a failure (that is, oil is not found), the individual loses ₹ 5,000.*

(a) Calculate expected monetary value of return on investment.

(b) The utility schedules of three individuals A, B and C are given. What is the expected utility for each of these individuals ? Who will invest in this oil-drilling operations ?

Money →	– ₹ 5000	0	₹ 5000	₹ 10,000	₹ 15,000	₹ 20,000
Utility of A	–5	0	4	7	9	10
Utility of B	–5	0	5	10	15	20
Utility of C	–5	0	6	13	21	30

Solution:

Expected monetary return $E(X) = \sum_{i=1}^{n} P_i X_i$

$$= 0.20 \times 20{,}000 + 0.80 \times -5000$$
$$= 4000 - 4000$$
$$= 0$$

(Note that if there is 20 per cent probability of being successful, there will be 80 per cent probability of its failure)

Now consulting the given utility schedule we find that for individual *A* utility of return of ₹ 20,000 is 10 and utility of loss of ₹ 5,000 for him is –5. Thus

$$E(U) \text{ of } A = 0.20\,(10) + 0.80\,(-5)$$
$$= 2.0 - 4.0 = -2$$

Similarly,

$$E(U) \text{ of } B = 0.2\,(20) + 0.8\,(-5)$$
$$= 4.0 - 4.0 = 0$$
$$E(U) \text{ of } C = 0.2\,(30) + 0.8\,(-5)$$
$$= 6.0 - 4.0 = +2.0$$

It will be seen from expected utility of the three individuals that for individual *C*, the expected utility from investment in drilling operations is positive. Therefore, only individual *C* will invest in the project. It is worth noting that as revealed by the given utility schedule for individual *C*, his marginal utility of money increases and therefore he is risk seeker. The utility functions of *A* reveals that he is risk averter, and that of *B* reveals that he is risk neutral.

QUESTIONS FOR REVIEW

1. What is meant by risk ? How does it differ from uncertainty ?
2. Define the terms : (1) strategy, (2) state of nature, and (3) outcome. How are they related to the decision-making under risk and uncertainty.
3. What is meant by risk and uncertainty ? Why are these concepts important in the theory of consumer choice ?
4. How does the process of utility maximisation by an individual differ in the case of risk or uncertainity from the case of certainty.
5. How is risk measured ? In this connection explain the concepts of expected value, variance and standard deviation, and coefficient of variation.
6. Explain the process of decision making in a situation involving risk and uncertainty. Is maximisation of the expected value valid criterion for decision making in a risky economic situation.
7. What is meant by risk aversion, risk seeking and risk neutrality ? How are these concepts related to the individual's utility function of money income.

8. What is risk premium ? How is it measured ?
9. Why do people buy insurance ? Explain
10. How can risk be reduced by businessmen ?
11. What is meant by when it is said that a person is risk averse ? Why are most people risk averse while some are risk lovers ?
12. How is risk measured through probability distribution of outcomes. Explain standard deviation and coefficient of variation as measures of risk.
13. Distinguish between discrete and continuous probability distribution. How is probability distribution useful in risk analysis ?
14. Why do some people indulge in gambling as it may bring heavy losses to them ? Illustrate graphically.

Decision Making Under Risk and Uncertainty (Continued)

Our above analysis of decision making regarding the choice of an investment project under conditions of risk is confined to *one period* only. However, the risk analysis is more important when an investment plan is for a period of a number of years. So we now try to explain how to assess a capital investment proposal subject to risk in which an initial capital investment yields a stream of cash flows as a return over a number of future years. In an earlier chapter we have analysed capital budgeting but in that analysis risk was not considered explicitly. We will now explain capital budgeting (*i.e.* long term investment analysis) incorporating risk factors in the analysis.

Capital Budgeting Under Conditions of Risk

The first steps in this investment appraisal is to obtain net present value (*NPV*) of expected values of the cash inflows in future years. For investment project that yields return in the form of cash inflows for three years, the net present value can be expressed as follows :

$$\text{NVP} = \frac{R_1}{1+r} + \frac{R_2}{(1+r)^2} + \frac{R_3}{(1+r)^3} - C_0$$

or in more generalised expression

$$\text{NPV} = \sum_{t=1}^{n} \frac{R_t}{(1+r)^t} - C_0$$

where NPV = Expected net present value

R_t = Expected values of annual cash inflows

C_0 = Initial investment expenditure

r = risk-free interest rate (*i.e.*, cost of capital)

Note that in the above formula of expected net present value (NPV) of annual cash inflows are discounted at the risk-free interest rate. We will explain below the methods which are used to calculate expected net present value at a discount rate that includes a risk premium.

Risk-Adjusted Discount Rate

One method which is commonly used for deciding about long-term investment subject to risk is employing risk-adjusted discount rate for estimating net present value of the long-term investment. Risk-adjusted rate is obtained by adding the risk premuim (*RP*) to the risk-free interest rate (*r*). Thus,

$$k = r + RP$$

where,

k = Risk adjusted discount rate
r = Risk-free interest rate
RP = Risk premium

It is at this risk adjusted discount rate (*k*) that cash inflows from investment project are discounted to calculate the net present value of annual cash inflows. The risk-premium represents the *additional return* that is required over and above risk-free interest rate that is necessary to be paid to a manager or investor to compensate him for additional-risk.

We can adjust the net present value of the cash inflows from an investment project subject to risk by using the following formula.

$$NPV \text{ of investment project} = \sum_{t=1}^{n} \frac{R_t}{(1+k)^t} - C_0 .$$

Where R_t represents the annual net cash flow (or return) from the investment project and k is risk adjusted discount rate which is equal to risk-free interest rate (*r*) plus risk premium (*PR*), that is, $k = r + PR$ and C_0 is the initial investment outlay.

It must be emphasised that obtaining a risk-adjusted discount rate is largely a matter of a manager's judgement and is determined subjectively. Different managers will arrive at different risk-adjusted discount rates. Besides, the amount of risk-adjusted discount rate k depends on the risk involved in an investment project. The higher the risk, the greater the risk premuim. It is important to note that decision whether to accept or reject an investment project depends on the risk-adjusted discount rate. Let us illustrate it through an example. Suppose the risk-free interest rate is 8 per cent and a given investment project involves an average risk with risk premium equal to 2, then the risk-adjusted discount rate for the project will be 10 per cent. Suppose the project costs ₹ 4,90,000 and is expected to yield annual cash inflow of ₹ 2,90,00 for two years only, then the *NPV* of the project with 10 percent adjusted discount rate can be calculated as follows :

$$NPV = \frac{R_1}{(1+k)} + \frac{R_2}{(1+k)^2} - C_o$$

$$= \frac{2,90,000}{(1+0.10)} + \frac{2,90,000}{(1+0.10)^2} - 4,90,000$$

$$= \frac{2,90,000}{1.10} + \frac{2,90,000}{1.21} - 4,90,000$$

$$= (263636 + 239669) - 4,90,000$$

$$= 503305 - 4,90,000$$

$$= + 13305$$

Thus at the average risk premium of 2 per cent, the investment project is profitable and will add to the value of the firm and will therefore be accepted.

However, if manager thinks that the investment project is of above average risk with risk premium of 5 per cent, then risk adjusted discount rate will be 8 + 5 = 13 per cent . With 13 per cent as the adjusted discount rate, we calculate the net present value (*NPV*) to see whether the project should be accepted or rejected.

Thus,

$$NPV = \frac{2,90,000}{1+0.13} + \frac{2,90,000}{(1+0.13)^2} - 4,90,000$$

$$= 256637 + 227094 - 490,000$$

$$= -6,268$$

Since the net present value of the project is negative at 13 per cent discount rate, the manager will reject it. Thus, the assessment of the project's risk by a manager will affect its profitability and determines whether the manager will accept it or reject it.

It may be noted that a manager will use different discount rates for projects relating to different divisions of the firm depending on the amount of risk involved in each case. For example, the manager is considering the investment in two projects, one which concerns the development of a new product and the other the replacement of old inefficient capital equipment. The risks involved in these two cases will be different.

Certainty-Equivalent Approach

In the approach of using risk-adjusted discount rates to incorporate risk in the valuation model we *modify the denominator* of the formula of calculating *NPV*. On the other hand, in certainty equivalent approach, we *modify the numerator* of the NPV model, while using risk-free discount rate in the denominator of the model. As mentioned above, managers of business firms or business owners themselves are risk- averter; they prefer a smaller cash flow that is certain (i.e. risk free) to the one that involves risk. To incorporate this the risky cash flow is adjusted by reducing it by some amount or multiplied by a smaller number than 1 to arrive at certainty equivalent cash flow. This adjustment factor. is therefore called *certainty equivalent factor*.

We write below the net present value model incorporating the certainty equivalent factor

$$NPV = \sum_{t=1}^{n} \frac{\alpha R_t}{(1+r)^t} - C_0$$

where R_t is the annual cash flow obtained from an investment project, r is the risk-free interest rate used as a discount rate, α is the certainty equivalent factor. The certainty equivalent factor or coefficient is the ratio of equivalent certain amount to the expected risk amount, Thus

$$\alpha = \frac{\text{Equivalent Certain Amount}}{\text{Expected Risky Amount}}$$

$$= \frac{R_t^*}{R_t}$$

R_t^* is certainty equivalent factor, while R_t is the expected cash return for a year. It is important to note that for getting certain equivalent factor the manager must tell how much certain return form a project is equivalent in terms of utility to him to the expected risky return from a project. The value of certainty equivalent factor varies form 0 to 1 for a risk-averse manager or a business man. A value of 0 as a certainty equivalent factor implies that the project is too risky for the manager to decide for investment in it. On the other hand, value of certainty equivalent equal to one means that the project is considered to be risk free by the manager or business man. Within the range 0 to 1, the smaller the value of certainty equivalent the larger is the risk assigned to the project by the manager. For instance, if a manager or an investor considers the risk-free (*i.e.* certain) amount of ₹ 1,00,000 equivalent to the expected net risky cash return of ₹ 1,25,000, then the certainty equivalent coefficient is found as under :

$$\alpha = \frac{1,00,000}{1,25,000} = 0.8$$

A Numerical Example

Suppose an investor is considering to invest in a project which yields return of ₹ 1,25,000 for the next five years and whose initial cost is ₹ 2,50,000 given that risk free interest is 10 per cent and his certainty equivalent is 0.8. Find out the net present value of the investment project.

$$NPV = \sum_{t=1}^{5} \frac{\alpha R_t}{(1+r)^t} - C_o$$

$$= \sum_{t=1}^{5} \frac{0.8(1,25,000)}{(1+0.10)^t} - 250,000$$

$$= 100,000\left(\frac{1}{1.10}\right)^t - 250,000$$

$$= 100,000\ (3.7908) - 250,000$$

$$= 379,080 - 250,000$$

$$= 129,080$$

Thus, the net present value is positive and the project should be accepted[1]. If the project is considered as more risky so that its certainty equivalent coefficient 0.4, its net present value is calculated as follows :

$$NPV = \sum_{t=1}^{5} \frac{\alpha R_t}{(1+r)^t} - C_o$$

$$= \sum_{t=1}^{5} \frac{0.4(125,000)}{(1+0.10)^t} - 250,000$$

$$= 50,000\left(\frac{1}{1.10}\right)^t - 250,000$$

$$= 50,000\ (3.7908) - 250,000$$

$$= 189,540 - 250,000$$

$$= -\ 60460$$

---

1. The *interest factor for* $\sum_{t=1}^{5} \frac{1}{1.10}$ being equal to 3.7908 has been obtained from the log Table relating to *Present Value of Annuity Rs.* 1 *(PVIFi,n)* by moving horizontally to 10 per cent and then moving down to 5 (i.e. number of periods)

Though like the risk- adjusted discount rate, the certainty equivalent coefficient is subjectively determined. It is considered as superior to the former because it explicity introduces the manager's attitude towards risk. However, business men generally prefer Risk Adjusted Discount Rate (*RADR*) and is therefore more frequiently used by them. This is because it is very much easier to make a rough estimate of risk-adjusted discount rate as cost of capital than to estimate each year's cash flow certainty equivalent factor.

It may be further noted that if risk increases over the time span, then it is appropriate to use the constant risk-adjusted discount rate(k). However, in cases when risk does not increase with time using a constant risk-adjusted discount rate will penalise longer term projects that do not involve increase in risk with time.

DECISION TREE APPROACH TO DECISION MAKING UNDER RISK

Managerial decision making under risk in the real world is more complex than they the ones analysed above. An important approach of analysing this more complex decision making involving risk is the use of decision trees. Decision making involving risk in the real world is done in various stages with later decisions depend on the outcomes of the earlier decisions and events. *A decision tree depicts the sequence of possible choice of strategies or alternative courses of action and the expected outcomes under each set of circumstances known as states of nature.* As the sequence of decisions and their expected outcomes are graphically shown as branches of a tree, this method is called decision tree approach. The construction of trees begin with the initial choice of a strategy or course of action and moves forward through a series of decisions and their outcomes shown as branches until all possible decisions and events have been shown. We will explain the decision tree approach in connection with (1) investment decision problem and (2) the price decision problem.

In a decision tree, decision nodes (depicted as boxes) are used to depict the point where decision maker must decide which strategy from the available ones or which course of action from the alternative ones to choose. Besides, in the decision tree, there are states of nature nodes depicted as circles which show possible state of nature.

In Figure 36.1 we have depicted the decision tree for deciding whether to make investment

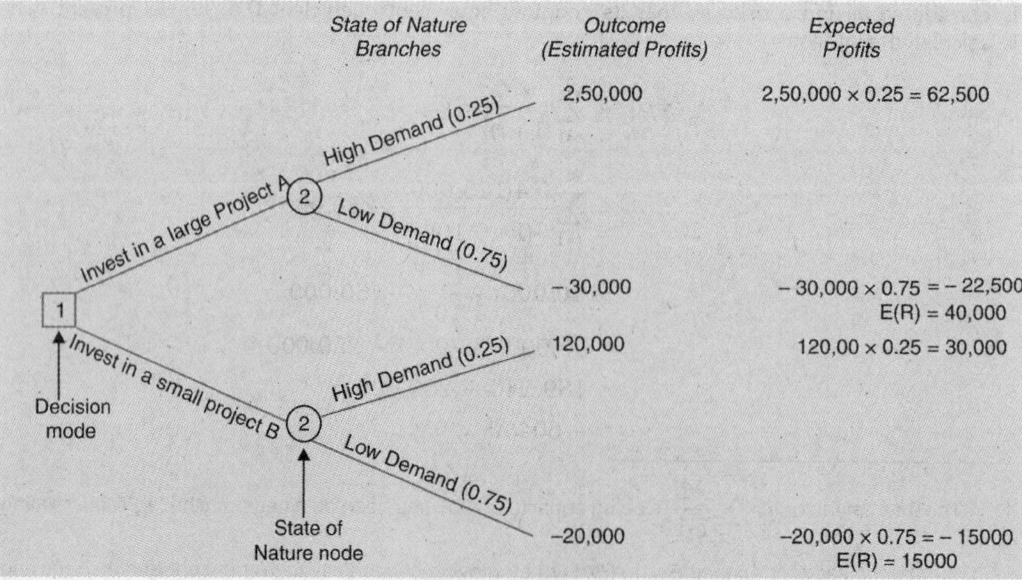

Fig. 36.1. *Decision Tree Model: Choice of an Investment Project.*

in a large project or small project. At decision node there are two decisions branches where the investor has to choose among alternative investment proposals (a) to invest in a large profit and (*b*) to invest in a small project. At the state of nature nodes there are two states of nature branches which depict outcome of each alternative decisions. These states of nature are (*i*) high demand and (*ii*) low demand. The high demand of the product of the large project has a 0.25 probability and yields positive monetary profits of 2,50,000. The low demand of the product of the large project has a 0.75 probability which yields negative profits of ₹ 30,000 (Note that the sum of probability is equal to one (0.25 + 0.75 = 1) The outcomes (*i.e.* estimated profits) of the project are shown at the end of the branch.

On the other hand, investment in a small project, a high demand with a probability of 0.25 is estimated to yield monetary profits of ₹ 120,000 and investment in the small project in case of low demand which has a probability of 0.75 yields a loss of ₹ 20,000. These outcomes (profits or losses) are shown at the end of the branches.

Lastly, we have to calculate the expected values of the profits of the two investment projects. As before, we calculate these expected values by multiplying the estimated profits by their probabilities. Thus in case of large investment project A, the expected value of profits of this project in case of high demand is 0.25 x 250,000 = ₹ 62,500 and in case of low demand is 0.75 *X* 30,000 = –22,500. Thus, the total expected value of profits from investment project A is 62,500 – 22,500 = ₹ 40,000.

On the other hand, in case of investment in small project B, if the demand happens to be high and probability of its occurrence is 0.25, estimated profits yielded by it are equal to ₹ 120,000, the expected value of profits is therefore 120,000 × 0.25 = 30,000 and in case of low demand with probability equal to 0.75 losses are equal to ₹ 20,000 and the expected value of losses is equal to 20,000 × 0.75 = – ₹ 15000. Thus the total expected value of profits is 30,000 – 15,000 = ₹ 15,000.

We thus see from above and as shown in the last column of the decision tree in Fig. 36.1 that the expected value of profits of project *A* exceeds that of project *B*. Therefore, the manager will decide to understake investment in project *A*.

In actual world decisions are much more complex than the one illustrated in Fig. 36.1. The actual world decision tree have multiperiod decision points in a sequential manner. We illustrate below a more complex decision tree model relating to the choice of a price strategy.

Decision Tree :Choice of a Price Strategy

As mentioned above, managerial decisions involving risk are often made in stages wherein the subsequent decisions and events depend on the outcome of earlier decisions. We have illustrated above a simplified model of decision tree regarding choice of an investment project involving risk. Another important decision which managers of business firms have to take relates to the choice of a price strategy, that is, whether to set a high price or low price of its product. This is shown at the decision point represented by a box. Then the issue is how the rival firms will react to the pricing decision of a firm; whether the competitive firm will also choose a high price strategy or they will choose a low price strategy in response to the decision of one firm. The construction of a decision tree begins on the left-hand side box (1) which represents the decision point. The two branches originating from this decision point are two alternative price strategies; one of high price, say of ₹ 250 per unit. The second branch represents low price strategy, say of ₹ 175 per unit. The second stage is how the competitors will react to each of these two price strategies of a firm ; they set a high price or low price. The probability of each reaction of competitors is also given in brackets. As will be seen from

Figure 36.2, there are two branches of price reaction, each of a competitive firm, that is, two branches from high price and two from low price decisions of a firm. Further, the sum of probabilities of two branches originating from a circle showing an event is equal to 1.

Then there is a third stage in a sequence representing the *state of nature* (that is, the economic circumstances prevailing in the economy). There are three types of states of nature, namely, (1) boom, (2) normal and (3) recessionary conditions, each with a given probability

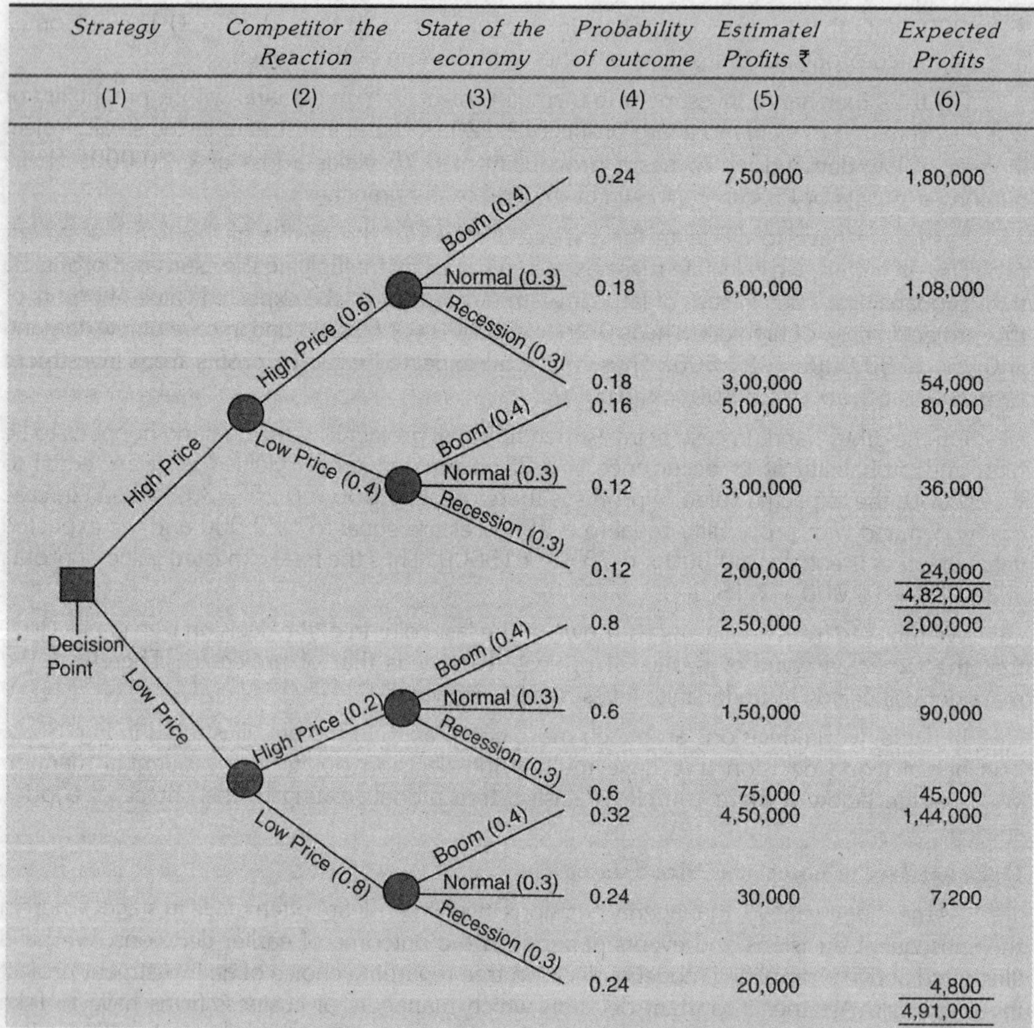

Fig. 36.2. *Decision Tree : Choosing Pricing Strategy.*

of occurrence. Thus at the top there are three branches showing charging high price in reaction to the high price strategy of a firm under boom (with probability of 0.4), normal condition (with probability of occurrence equal to 0.3) and (3) recessionary conditions (with a probability of occurrence equal to 0.3) The sum of these probabilities must also be equal to unity (0.4 + 0.3 + 0.3 = 1).

Similarly, charging a low price by the competitors in response to the high price strategy of the firm can occur under three states of nature, that is, boom, normal and recessionary conditions with probabilities of occurrence whose sum, as will be seen from Figure 36.2, must also be equal to unity. Thus there are six branches of a tree originating from a decision of high price strategy of the firm. Likewise there are six branches of a tree if in the beginning the firm decides to set a low price of its product. The price response of the competitors (*i.e.* whether they will choose a high price or low price) in reaction to the firm's low price strategy can also occur in three states of nature (boom, normal and recession), each with a probability of occurrence. The sum of the probabilities of these three states of nature must be equal to one as in the above case. Thus there will be 12 branches showing competitors response to the firm's two price strategies under three types of state of nature.

Corresponding to each response there will be different outcome in the form of estimated money profits. It is worth noting that probability of occurrence of each outcome is the *joint probability* which is obtained by multiplying the probability of each state of nature with the probability of a particular price response of the competitors of the firm. Thus at the top branch of relating to choice of a high price strategy by a firm, the probability reaction of the competitors charging a high price as well is 0.6 and the *probability of occurrence of boom* is 0.4 and therefore the joint probability of an outcome in terms of estimated profits equal to ₹ 7,50,000 is 0.6 × 0.4 = 0.24. Similarly, the competitors reaction of high price with a probability 0.6 and the *normal state of the economy* with the probability of its occurrence equal to 0.3, the joint probability is 0.6 × 0.3 = 0.18 and its outcome is profits of ₹ 600,000 and so on for other combinations of probability of competitors response and probability of the occurrence of a particular state of the economy, we can calculate the joint probability and see what is the outcome in terms of estimated money profits in each case. The estimated money profits of 12 outcomes are recorded in section 5 of Figure 36.2.

Expected Value of Profits. Lastly, we calculate the *expected value of profits* for each of 12 outcomes. There are 6 outcomes originating from each of the two alternative price strategies which may be chosen by the firm in question. *The expected value of profits for each outcome can be obtained by multiplying the joint probability with its estimated profits*. Thus, at the top most branch the joint probability is 0.24 and its outcome is 750,000. By multiplying them we get ₹ 180,000 (0.24 × 750,000 = 180,000). In this way in case of six possible outcomes associated with high price strategy of a firm we calculate the total expected value of profits. It will be seen from Figure 36.2 that total expected value of profits from choosing a high price strategy is ₹ 482,000. Likewise, we calculate the expected value of 6 outcomes emanating in response to the choice of a low price strategy by the firm by multiplying the joint probability with outcome (i.e. estimated profits). Thus by multiplying 0.8 with ₹ 250,000 we get ₹ 200,000, multiplying 0.6 with 150,000 we get ₹ 90,000 and so on. Thus, as will be seen from Figure 36.2, the total expected value of profits of choosing a low price strategy by the firm has been found to be equal to ₹ 4,91,000. Thus, assessing that the firm has already factored in the difference in risk involved in estimating the value of profits of the two price strategies, the firm will choose a low price strategy as its expected value of profits exceeds the expected value of profits of the high price strategy.

DECISION MAKING UNDER UNCERTAINTY

As explained above, *uncertainty exists when there are more than one outcome of a decision and the probability of the occurrence of each particular outcome is not known*. Therefore, decision making under uncertainty is quite subjective. Under these circumstances what is the appropriate criterion for choosing among the alternative courses of action. However, a number of rules or criteria for making decisions under uncertainty are available if a decision maker knows the various states of nature and estimates of the profits or returns from adopting each strategy or course of action. The two important decision criteria for making decisions under uncertainty are : The (1) maximin criterion and (2) the minimax regret criterion.[1] We explain below these two criteria.

Maximin Criterion. According to the maximin criterion, the decision maker should find out the worst possible outcomes of various strategies (*i.e.* possible alternative courses of action) under all states of nature and choose the strategy or course of action that yields the maximum payoff from these worst possible outcomes. An example will clarify this criterion. Suppose a manager is considering (1) to make investment in the product or (2) not to invest in the product. The demand for the product will determine whether the investment in the product will be a success or a failure. The success will provide him positive profits and the failure will yield losses (*i.e.* negative profits). The two states of nature are : (*a*) the success of investment in the product and (*b*) the failure of the investment in the product. In Table 36.1 we give payoffs in the two alternative decisions regarding whether or not to invest in the product Due to uncertainty of outcomes, that is, whether there will be a success or failure, probability of each outcome is not given. Because probability of success or failure of investment cannot be known, we cannot estimate the expected value of payoffs of the outcomes. Hence the maximin criterion is used[2].

Table 36.1 *Payoffs of Alternative Decisions*

Course of Action	*State of Nature*		*Minimum*
	Success	*Failure*	
Invest	Rs 500,000	–250,000	–250,000
Do not invest	0	0	0

To use the maximin criterion, the manager has to determine the worst possible outcome of each course of action. There are two alternative courses of action relating to the investment problem being considered : (1) Invest in the product ; (2) do not invest in the product shown as rows in Table 36.1. Besides, there are two states of nature, namely, success and failure shown as columns in Table 36.1.

It will be seen from Table 36.1 that for decision to make investment in the product, the worst possible outcome is loss of ₹ 250,000 and in case of deciding not to invest in the product has obviously payoff in case of success is zero and in case of failure is zero as well. That is, the worst possible outcome in case of not deciding to invest is 0. The worst possible outcomes of the two alternative decisions are given in the last column of Table 36.1. If the manager follows the maximin criterion, he will choose the *maximum (i.e. best) of these worst outcomes* (i.e. maximin outcome). As will be seen from the last column of Table 36.1, decision '*not to invest*' which has the maximum (best) payoff of the two worst outcomes. This is because 0 is greater than –250,000, that is, no profit, no loss is better than a loss of ₹ 250,000.

---

1. Luce and Raiffa in their important contribution, *'Games and Decisions* have offered various other criteria, for example,Hurwics Criterion, Principle of Insufficient Reason. For details see his above mentioned work.

2. John Von Neumann and Oskar Morgenstern in their theory of games explains that the best strategy for a firm under oligopoly where the behaviour of rivals is quite uncertain to predict is that it is prudent on the part of a firm to follow maximin criterion. See their, '*Theory of Games and Economic Behaviour*' (New York : Wiley 1964).

This maximin criterion is criticised on the ground that it is a very conservative decision rule for decision making under uncertainty. This is because this rule concentrates on the worst possible outcomes of each of the various strategies and recommends the choice of the best among them. This maximin criterion assumes that the decision maker has a pessimistic outlook of the economic world and does not want to bear any risk. However, this maximin criterion is useful in those cases where firm's managers have a strong aversion to risk. For example, a small firm which is struggling to survive, it will be prudent to avoid risk of loss. Besides, the use of maximin criterion is helpful in case of oligopoly where the various firms are inter- dependent, that is, decision of one firm significantly affects the others. Under these circumstances, if an oligopolistic firm wants to play safe, it will follow a maximin criterion in deciding about choice of its price and advertisement strategies.

The Minimax Regret Criterion. Another important criterion to choose, under uncertain circumstances, a strategy or decision among the alternatives available is a minimax regret criterion. According to this, a manager should choose the strategy that minimises the maximum regret of the wrong decision or strategy that may be chosen for a given actual state of nature. Note that regret in this connection means the loss that is incurred if wrong decision is taken or inappropriate strategy is chosen. The regret associated with the choice of one of the alternative strategies *measures the difference between the maximum possible payoff that could have been received and the actual payoff that is received under the same specific state of nature.* The reason for measuring regret in this way is that if the firm's manager had chosen the best strategy that yields the maximum profits *for a specific state of nature* that has actully occurred, then there would have been no regret. But if the manager chooses any other strategy, the regret is the difference between the payoff from the best strategy and the payoff from the strategy actually chosen under the same state of the nature that has actually occurred.

In this criterion the manager has first to find out the maximum value of regret for each strategy under various states of nature and then select the one that has the minimum value of regret among them. We can illustrate this minimax regret criterion with the above example of whether to invest or not to invest in the product. To use minimax regret criterion the manager of the firm has to construct a minimum regret matrix of the payoffs of the various strategies in different states of nature, In our example, there are two alternative strategies, namely, invest in the product and do not invest in the product. In Table 36.2 we have given the same data relating to payoff of the two strategies or decisions of making investment in the product or not as given in Table 36.1. To make the investment decision, the decision maker constructs

Table 36.2

	(A) Payoff Matrix		*(B) Regret Matrix*		
Decision	*State of Nature*		*State of Nature*		*Value of*
	Success	*Failure*	*Success*	*Failure*	*of regret*
Invest	500,000	-250,000	0	250,000	250,000
Do not invest	0	0	500,000	0	500,000

regret matrix in Table 36.2(*B*). Given that the state of nature of 'success' actually occurs, then the best strategy is to invest which yields maximum payoff of ₹ 500,000. Therefore, if the decision maker had actually chosen to invest in this specific state of nature, then there is no regret and therefore we record 0 in regret matrix in Table 36.2(*B*). If the decision maker chooses 'not to invest' and gets payoff equal to 0, then in the state of nature of success that has actually occurred, the value of regent is equal to 500,000. This is because he failed to avail the opportunity of earning ₹ 500,000, by deciding not to invest Value of his regret is equal to

₹ 500,000 which we record against the decision not to invest in the column of state of nature of success in the regret matrix of Table 36.2 (*B*).

Now assume that the state of nature of failure has actually occurred, then the best strategy would be 'not to invest' as though it yields zero profits, the alternative decision of investing in the product would bring losses equal to ₹ 250,000 in case of state of failure. Thus in the state of failure, the decision of the manager not to invest has zero value of regret while choice of investing in the product involves regret value of ₹ 250,000.

Having constructed the regret matrix with maximum regret value for each investment decision (*i.e.* strategy), the manager should choose the investment decision or strategy with minimum regret value. It will be seen from last column of Table 36.2 (*B*) that for the decision of investing in the product has the minimum regret value of ₹ 250,000. Thus the best strategy for the manager will be to invest in the product under the given uncertain circumstances.

As in case of Maximin stategy, minimax regret criterion is criticised as highly subjective. However, Minimax regret criterion is considered superior to maximin criterion as this considers opportunity costs of alternative investment decisions or strategies.

QUESTIONS FOR REVIEW

1. What is meant by risk-adjusted discount rate ? How is it useful in capital budgeting under conditions of risk ?
2. Explain briefly valuation model of a firm. How is risk incorporated in the valuation model of a firm ?
3. Explain the certainty equivalent coefficient. How is it used for incorporating risk in the valuation model of a firm (i.e. capital budgeting by a firm) ? Compare it with risk-adjusted discount rate.
4. Critically examine maximin criterion for decision making under uncertainty. Why is this criterion highly subjective ?
5. Explain minimax regret criterion for decision making under uncertainty. Under what conditions then the use of this criterion is appropriate ?
6. Explain the decision tree approach for decision making under risk. Using decision tree approach depict the choice between three plant sizes, the three possible ways competitors will react under each of the three different states of nature ? How is the estimated return from each outcome calculated ?
7. The manager of Kawality Ice Cream is to decide between the two investment projects. Project A is the investment in the introduction of high quality ice cream and the investment B in the introduction of bottles of cold milk. The two investment projects yield the following net cash flows and the initial investment expenditure.

Net Cash Flows (in ₹)

Investment Projects	Year 1	Year 2	Years 3	Initial investment Expenditure (₹)
A	50,000	70,000	40,000	120,000
B	40,000	80,000	50,000	110,000

(*a*) Calculate the net present value (*NPV*) of each project with risk-free discount rate of 8 per cent.

(*b*) Which of the investment projects the manager should choose if the risk premium is 4 per cent on project *A* and 6 per cent on project B.

Solution: The *NPV* of projects *A* and *B* at 8 per cent risk-free rate of discount

$$NPV_A = \frac{R_1}{(1+r)} + \frac{R_2}{(1+r)^2} + \frac{R_3}{(1+r)^3} - C_0$$

$$= \frac{50,000}{1+0.08} + \frac{70,000}{(1+0.08)^2} + \frac{40,000}{(1+0.08)^3} - 120,000$$

$$= \frac{50,000}{1.0800} + \frac{70,000}{1.1664} + \frac{40,000}{1.2597}$$

$$= 46296.3 + 60013.7 + 31753.6 - 120,000$$

$$= 138063.6 - 120,000 = 18,063.6$$

$$NPV_B = \frac{40,000}{1+0.08} + \frac{80,000}{(1+0.08)^2} + \frac{50,000}{(1+0.08)^3} - 110,000$$

$$= \frac{40,000}{1.0800} + \frac{80,000}{1.1664} + \frac{50,000}{1.2597} - 110,000$$

$$= 37037.0 + 68587.1 + 39691.9 - 110,000$$

$$= 145316 - 110,000$$

$$= 35316$$

(*b*) With a risk premium of 4 per cent on project *A*, the risk-adjusted discount rate is 8 + 4 = 12 per cent. Thus, the risk-adjusted net present value of project *A* is

$$NPV_A = \frac{50,000}{1.12} + \frac{70,000}{(1.12)^2} + \frac{40,000}{(1.12)^3} - 120,000$$

$$= \frac{50,000}{1.12} + \frac{70,000}{1.2544} + \frac{40,000}{1.4049} - 120,000$$

$$= 44643 + 55803 + 28472 - 120,000$$

$$= 128918 - 120,000$$

$$= 8918$$

The risk premium for project *B* is 6 per cent, the risk-adjusted discount rate is 8 + 6 = 14 per cent

$$NPV_B = \frac{40,000}{1+0.14} + \frac{80,000}{(1+0.14)^2} + \frac{50,000}{(1+0.14)^3} - 110,000$$

$$= \frac{40,000}{1.14} + \frac{80,000}{(1.14)^2} + \frac{50,000}{(1.14)^3} - 110,000$$

$$= \frac{40,000}{1.14} + \frac{80,000}{1.2996} + \frac{50,000}{1.4815} - 110,000$$

$$= 35087.7 + 61557.4 + 33795.7 - 110,000$$

$$= 13,0440 - 110,000$$

$$= 20,440$$

The above results show that though project *B* is more risky than project *A* it will be chosen by the manager since its risk-adjusted net present value is higher as compared to that of project *A*.

PART - VII

MACROECONOMICS FOR MANAGEMENT

- Macroeconomics: Issues and Concepts
- Macroeconomic Aggregates : Aggregate Consumption, Gross Domestic Saving and Capital Formation
- Determination of National Income: Keynes's Simple Two Sector Model
- Determination of National Income with Government and Foreign Trade: Three Sector and Four Sector Models
- Consumption and Investment Demand
- Money Supply, Money Demand and Money Market Equilibrium
- The IS-LM Curve Model (Synthesis of Monetary and Real Factors)
- International Economic Linkages and Mundell-Fleming Model
- Inflation: Nature and Causes
- Analysis of Business Cycles
- Economic Stabilisation: Fiscal Policy
- Economic Stabilisation: Monetary Policy
- Monetary Policy and Economic Growth with Special Reference to India
- Role of Fiscal Policy in Economic Development: Taxation
- Role of Fiscal Policy: Government Borrowing for Financing Development

37

CHAPTER

Macroeconomics: Issues and Concepts

In the first volume of this book we have studied microeconomics which is concerned with the behaviour of individual consumers, factor owners, firms and individual industries and markets. It is through their interaction that microeconomic theory explains how prices of products and factors are determined and how resources are allocated among various products. In microeconomic theory it is assumed that full employment of resources such as labour and capital prevails and it analyses how they are allocated among different products. Further, it explains whether resource allocation achieved is economically efficient. In this second volume we will study macroeconomic theory and its applications to the formulation of economic policies. In this chapter we shall briefly explain what macroeconomics is about and why the English economist J.M. Keynes laid stress on macroeconomic analysis as a separate study from microeconomic analysis. Besides, we shall explain the various issues that are studied in macroeconomics. In the end we shall briefly explain the various post-keynesian developments in macroeconomics.

What is Macroeconomics?

Whereas microeconomics deals with the analysis of small individual units of an economy such as individual consumers, individual firms, individual industries and markets and explains how prices of products and factors are determined. On the basis of these prices microeconomics explains how resources are allocated among various products and how income distribution among factors is determined. On the other hand, *macroeconomics is concerned with the analysis of the behaviour of the economic system in totality. Thus, macroeconomics studies how the large aggregates such as total employment, national product or national income of an economy and the general price level are determined. Macroeconomics is therefore a study of aggregates. Besides, macroeconomics explains how the productive capacity and national income of the country increase over time in the long run.*

Professor Gardner Ackley makes the distinction between macroeconomics and microeconomics more clearly when he says, "macroeconomics concerns itself with such variables as the aggregate volume of the output of an economy, with the extent to which its resources are employed, with the size of the national income, with the 'general price level'. Microeconomics, on the other hand, deals with the division of total output among industries, products and firms and the allocation of resources among competing uses. It considers problem of income distribution. Its interest is in relative prices of particular goods and services."[1]

It is evident from above that the subject matter of macroeconomics is to explain what *determines the level of total economic activity* (that is, the size of the national income and employment) and fluctuations (*i.e.*, ups and downs) in it in the short run. It also explains what causes the general price level to rise and determines the rate of inflation in the economy. Besides, modern macroeconomics analyses those factors which determine the increase in productive capacity and national income in the long run. The problem of increasing productive capacity and national income over time in the long run is called the problem of *economic growth*. Thus, what determines rate of growth of an economy is also the concern of macroeconomics.

Thus, why is national income higher today than it was in 1950? Why does rate of unemployment in a free market economy go up in a period and falls in another period? Why do some countries have high rates of inflation, while others maintain price stability? What causes alternating periods of depression and boom (generally described as business cycles)? Why should government intervene in the economy and what policy it should adopt to check inflation, control business cycles, raise level of national income, reduce unemployment and restore equilibrium in the balance of payments are some of the important questions which macroeconomics attempts to answer.

The Origin of Macroeconomics: Keneysian Revolution

The Great Depression. Beginning in late 1929, capitalist economies of the world experienced a severe depression which created a lot of involuntary unemployment and also a sharp fall in their GDP. This depression was caused by drastic decline in private investment. For example, in the United States in 1929, 1.5 million workers were unemployed. After four years in 1933 this unemployment of labour rose to 13 million people out of labour force of 51 million, that is, around 25 per cent of labour force became unemployed. The similar situation prevailed in Britain and other capitalist countries. This depression spurred a great deal of controversy among economists about the causes of this depression and the policies to overcome it and restore full employment. It was at this time that a noted British economist J.M. Keynes (1883-1946) challenged the view of classical economists who applied microeconomic models to explain depression and involuntary unemployment. By emphasising that the prevailing depression and large-scale involuntary unemployment was due to lack of aggregate effective demand resulting from a fall in private investment he laid the foundation of modern macroeconomics. In his theory he showed that economy was not-self-correcting and therefore there was a need for the government to intervene and take appropriate fiscal measures to restore full employment in the economy.

Classical and neoclassical economists[2] assumed that full-employment of labour and other resources always prevailed in the economy and concentrated mainly upon explaining how the resources were allocated to the production of various goods and services and how the relative prices of products and factors were determined. It is mainly because of their full-employment assumption that they concentrated on the problem of determination of prices, outputs and resource employment in the individual industries. They believed that if there were departures from full employment, a free market economy would automatically work in a way that would restore full employment of resources. They argued that involuntary unemployment and underutilisation of the productive capacity could not occur in capitalist economies if market

1. Gardner Ackley, *Macroeconomic Theory*, 1961, p. 4
2. Note that Keynes called all those economists who preceded him as classical economists. Thus, neoclassical economists are included in the term classical economists as used by Keynes.

mechanism were allowed to work freely without any interference by the trade unions. Thus, according to them, even when deficiency of aggregate demand arises as it happens during the times of recession or depression, prices and wages would change in such a way that employment, output and national income would not decline. The belief of classical economists that full-employment of labour and capital stock will always exist was based on *Say's Law of Markets*. According to Say's Law, *supply creates its own demand* and therefore, the problem of lack of demand for supply of goods and services does not arise. Factors which produce goods and services for supply in the market get rewards (wages, interest and rent) for their contributions to the production of goods and services produced. Thus, incomes earned become expenditure made on goods and services. Therefore, the problem of deficiency of demand does not arise. They thus could not provide adequate explanation of the occurrence of huge unemployment that prevailed during depression of 1930s in the capitalist economies. What is worse, the classical economists, particularly A.C. Pigou tried to apply the economic laws that hold good in the case of an individual industry to the case of the behaviour of the whole economic system and macroeconomic variables.

However, the classical model was not found to be true as the depression appeared to be not self-correcting. During the Great Depression of 1930s unemployed remained at a high level for nearly 10 years. At that time, an eminent British economist A.C. Pigou asserted that involuntary unemployment existing at the time of depression in the 1930s was due to the obstacles put up by trade unions and government and further that this involuntary unemployment could be eliminated and employment expanded by cutting down wages. A noted British economist J.M. Keynes challenged this classical viewpoint during the early nineteen thirties when severe depression took place in the capitalist countries such as Britain and the U.S.A. While the cut in wages may expand employment in an individual industry, the reduction in wages throughout the economy will result in fall in incomes of the working classes and is likely to cause decrease in the level of aggregate demand. The fall in aggregate demand will tend to lower the level of employment rather than expand it.

Though there were pre-Keynesian theories of business cycles and the general price level that were "macro" in nature, but it was J.M. Keynes who laid stress on macroeconomic analysis and put forward a general theory of income and employment in his revolutionary book, "*A General Theory of Employment, Interest and Money*" published in 1936. Keynes' theory made a genuine break from the classical and neo-classical economics and produced such a fundamental and drastic change in economic thinking that his macroeconomic analysis has earned the names '*Keynesian Revolution*' and '*New Economics*'. Keynes in his analysis made a frontal attack on the classical '*Say's Law of Markets*' which was the basis of full-employment assumption of classical view that involuntary unemployment could not prevail in a free private enterprise economy. He showed how the equilibrium level of national income and employment was determined by aggregate demand and aggregate supply and further that due to lack of aggregate effective demand equilibrium level of income and employment might well be established at far less than full-employment level in a free-market capitalist economy. This causes involuntary unemployment of labour on the one hand and excess productive capacity (*i.e.* under-utilisation of the existing capital stock) on the other. His macroeconomic model reveals how consumption function, investment function, liquidity preference function, conceived in aggregate terms, interact to determine the level of national income and employment.

Further, the fall in employment in the Great Depression of 1930s and emergence of huge unemployment of labour which in some countries went up to 25 per cent of labour force gives unmistakable evidence that aggregate demand is not always large enough to ensure full-employment of labour and full use of productive capacity.

After Keynes, there has been significant developments in macroeconomics. Apart from what determines the level of employment of labour and use of productive capacity, modern macroeconomics is concerned with many more issues such as the problems of inflation, economic growth, business cycles, stagflation and the balance of payments and the exchange rate. The analysis of these six major issues describes the scope of macroeconomics. We shall be explaining all these six issues of macroeconomics in detail in later chapters. Here we shall explain only briefly what these problems are.

THE MAJOR ISSUES IN MACROECONOMICS

As explained above, Keynes in his book *'Theory of Employment, Interest and Money'* explained how levels of income and employment were determined in a free market economy. During the Second World War period, he extended his macro-theory to explain inflation. However, after Keynes, economists have further developed and extended macroeconomics. We briefly explain below the main issues of macroeconomics.

Employment and Unemployment. The first major issue in macroeconomics is to explain what determines the level of employment and national income in an economy and therefore what causes involuntary unemployment. Why is level of national income and employment very low in times of depression as in 1930s in various capitalist countries of the world. This will explain the cause of huge unemployment that emerged in these countries. As mentioned above, classical economists denied that there could be involuntary unemployment of labour and other resources for a long time. They thought that with changes in wages and prices, unemployment would be automatically removed and full employment established. But this did not appear to be so at the time of depression in the thirties and after. Keynes explained that level of employment and national income is determined by aggregate demand and aggregate supply. With aggregate supply curve remaining unchanged in the short run, it is the deficiency of aggregate demand that cause underemployment equilibrium with the appearance of involuntary unemployment. According to him, it is the changes in private investment that causes fluctuations in aggregate demand and is therefore, responsible for the problems of cyclical unemployment. We will explain Keynes's theory of employment and income and its various aspects in detail in the subsequent chapters.

Determination of National Income (or GNP). National income is the value of all final goods and services produced in a country in a year. Level of national income or what is called Gross National Product (GNP) shows the performance of the economy in a year and determines the *overall living standards of the people* of a country. The higher the per capita national income, the greater the amounts of goods and services available for consumption per individual on an average. Given the technology used for production, the magnitude of employment goes hand-in-hand with the change in size of national income. The fluctuations in economic activity primarily manifest themselves in changes in national income and employment. When all resources in an economy are being employed for production, the size of national income generated is called *potential GNP* or full-employment level of income. In a free market economy, the changes in aggregate demand cause divergence of national income from the level of potential GNP in the short run.

It is important to note that in a developing country such as India it is not a mere level of aggregate demand that determines national income. In it the *supply-side* factors such as availability of physical capital, human capital (skills and education of people), material resources, the technology used for production in agriculture and industries play a more important role in the determination of national income.

General Price Level and Inflation. Another macroeconomic issue is to explain the problem of inflation. Inflation has been a major problem faced by both the developed and developing countries in the last fifty years. Classical economists thought that it was the quantity of money in the economy that determined the general price level in the economy and, according to them, rate of inflation depended on the growth of money supply in the economy. Keynes criticised the '*Quantity Theory of Money*' and showed that expansion in money supply did not always lead to inflation or rise in price level. Keynes who before the Second World War explained that involuntary unemployment and depression were due to the deficiency of aggregate demand, during the war period when prices rose very high he explained in a booklet '*How to Pay for War*' that just as unemployment and depression were caused by the deficiency of aggregate demand, inflation was due to the excessive aggregate demand. Thus, Keynes put forward what is now called *demand-pull theory of inflation*. After Keynes, theory of inflation has been further developed and many theories of inflation depending upon various causes have been put forward. *Cost-push* and *structuralist* theories of inflation have been put forward. To analyse the problem of inflation is an important issue of macroeconomics.

Business Cycles. Throughout history market economies have experienced what are called business cycles. Business cycles refer to fluctuations in output and employment with alternating periods of boom and recession. In boom periods both output and employment are at high levels, whereas in recession periods both output and employment fall and as a consequence large unemployment come to exist in the economy. When these recessions are extremely severe, they are called depressions. What are the causes of these business cycles or ups and downs in market economies is an important macroeconomic issue which has been highly controversial. The objective of macroeconomic policy is to achieve economic stability with equilibrium at full employment level of output and income. We shall discuss various theories of business cycles and also monetary and fiscal policies to control business cycles and achieve economic stability.

Stagflation. How to control business cycles and achieve economic stability has been a very difficult problem for the economies to solve ? But during the decade of 1970s and in some later times in the subsequent decades market economies have experienced a still more intricate problem which has been described as stagflation. While in business cycles, recession or depression is accompanied by high unemployment and falling prices, *in the seventies recession or stagnation was accompanied by not only high unemployment but also rapid inflation*. Since in that period high unemployment and recession (or stagnation) co-existed with high inflation, this problem was given the name stagflation. This stagflation could not be explained with the Keynesian theory which focuses on the demand side. Therefore, a new economic thought which is called *Supply-side Economics* emerged which explained stagflation by laying stress on the supply-side of economic activity. Stagflation is an important issue of modern macroeconomics. Stagflation along with supply-side economics will be explained at length in a separate chapter.

Economic Growth. Another important issue in macroeconomics is to explain what determines economic growth in a country. Economic growth means *sustained* increase in national income (GNP) or per capita income over a sufficiently long period of time. Given the availability of natural resources, economic growth of a country depends on the growth of physical capital, human capital and progress in technology. The growth of all these factors requires saving and investment. The growth rate can therefore the stepped up by raising the rates of saving and investment. However, the expansion in these factors determines the increase in productive capacity. To ensure full use of the rising productive capacity aggregate to demand for output must be increasing sufficiently.

Theory of economic growth or what is simply called *growth economics* which has been recently developed a good deal is an important branch of macroeconomics. The problem of growth is a long-run problem and Keynes did not deal with it. In fact, Keynes is said to have once remarked that "in the long run we are all dead". It was Harrod[3] and Domar[4] who extended the Keynesian analysis to the long-run problem of growth with stability. They laid stress on the dual role of investment—one of *income-generating*, which Keynes considered, and the second of *capacity-creating* which Keynes ignored because of his preoccupation with the short run. In view of the fact that an investment adds to the productive capacity (*i.e.*, capital stock), then if growth with stability (*i.e.*, without stagnation or inflation) is to be achieved, income or demand must be increasing at a rate large enough to ensure the full utilisation of the increasing capacity. Thus, macroeconomic models of Harrod and Domar have explained the rate of growth of income that must take place if the steady growth of the economy is to be achieved. These days growth economics has been further developed and extended a good deal and new theories of growth have been put forward by Solow, Meade, Kaldor and Joan Robinson.

It is important to note that in the context of developing countries, *economic growth* has been distinguished from *economic development*. Economic development is a more inclusive concept than economic growth. Economic development is generally understood to mean that apart from increase in national income or per capita income, poverty, unemployment and inequality must also be declining in the growth process. Besides, according to Amartya Sen, winner of Nobel Price in economics, freedom to improve the quality of life of the poor, their freedom from undernourishment, freedom from illiteracy, freedom from illness are essential requirements of economic development. *It is the building up capabilities of the poor and enlargement of the opportunities to gain freedom in these respects* that Amartya Sen calls development[5]. The macroeconomics for developing countries must therefore concern itself with not only economic growth but also economic development.

Since the above growth theories apply particularly to the present-day developed economies, special theories which explain the causes of underdevelopment and poverty in less developed countries (LDCs) and which also suggest strategies for initiating and accelerating growth in them have also been propounded. These special growth theories relating to less developed countries (LDCs) are generally known as *Economics of Development*.

Balance of Payments and Exchange Rate. Balance of payments is the record of economic transactions of the residents of a country with the rest of the world during a period. The aim to prepare such a record is to present an account of all receipts on account of goods exported, services rendered and capital received by the residents of a country and the payments made for goods imported, services received and capital transferred to other countries by residents of a country. There may be deficit or surplus in balance of payments. Both create problems for an economy. An important effect is that the transactions in balance of payment are influenced by the exchange rate. The exchange rate is the rate at which a country's currency is exchanged for foreign currencies. The instability in exchange rate has been a major problem in recent years which has given rise to serious balance of payments problems. During the two years 1997 and 1998, currencies of many East Asian Countries and Japan rapidly depreciated in terms of US dollar. This created the situation of economic crisis which also affected other economies of the world. Both interrelated problems of balance of payments and instability of foreign exchange rate will be analysed in a separate part of this book.

THE ROLE OF GOVERNMENT IN THE MACROECONOMY

In modern macroeconomics, the intervention by the government to influence economic activity is well recognised. It is now widely believed that instability is inherent in a free-market economy and further that there is no any self-correcting mechanism to ensure stability at full employment level and sustained economic growth. There are three types of economic policy that are used by the government to influence the working of macroeconomy.

3. R.F. Harrod, *Towards a Dynamic Economics*, (1948).
4. E.D. Domar, Expansion and Employment, *American Economic Review* (March 1947).
5. Amartya Sen, *Development as Freedom*, Oxford University Press, 2000.

1. Fiscal Policy 2. Monetary Policy 3. Growth Policies

We will discuss these three policy instruments in detail in the subsequent chapters. However, we briefly explain them below and indicate what they are concerned with.

Fiscal Policy.

An important way the government affects the economy is through the adoption of appropriate fiscal policy. The fiscal policy refers to taxation and expenditure decisions of the government. Before Keynes it was believed that the government budget should preferably be balanced, that is, revenue collected through taxes should be equal to the expenditure made by the government. Keynes showed that balanced budget is not good under all circumstances. He advocated that at times of depression, *deficit budget* should be made to get the economy out of it and to eliminate involuntary unemployment. In case of deficit budget the government expenditure exceeds revenue collected through taxes. The budget deficit arises when the government increases its expenditure without raising taxes or it arises when taxes are reduced without cutting back on expenditure. Therefore, the policy of deficit budget represents expansionary fiscal policy. The budget deficit raises aggregate demand and leads to the increase in national income and employment.

To meet the budget deficit, the government borrows from the banks and the public and pays interest to them. This raises debt burden of the government. The borrowing by the government increases the demand for loanable funds and leads to rise in rate of interest. The higher interest rate discourages private investment. It is therefore claimed that government borrowing to finance budget deficit *crowds out* some private investment so that net effect of budget deficit on expansion of output and employment is small. We will explain in detail in a subsequent chapters how far this crowding-out effect is significant.

However, to avoid borrowing and rise in public debt, the alternative way to finance the budget deficit is printing of money by the government. The danger of financing budget deficit through printing of money is that it may lead to inflation in the economy. The implications of different ways of financing budget deficit will be discussed in detail in a later chapter.

On the contrary, when there is high inflation in the economy the government can check it by reducing its expenditure or raising taxes and in this way make a surplus budget. This will tend to reduce aggregate demand which will help in controlling inflation. Thus fiscal policy is an important instrument used by the government to change the level of of aggregate demand and thereby affect income, employment and prices.

Monetary Policy

Monetary policy is another important instrument which the government (or Central Bank of the country) uses to achieve the objectives of price stability, full-employment and economic growth. Monetary policy refers to the policies regarding growth of money supply, availability of credit and interest or cost of credit. Monetary policy is an important tool of controlling inflation in the economy. It is generally believed that large expansion in money supply causes rise in price level. To check inflation *tight monetary policy is* adopted wherein rate of interest is raised and availability of credit is reduced. When interest rate rises, businessmen and households find it more costly to borrow. This discourages demand for credit and leads to the contraction of money supply in the economy. Besides, to discourage the creation of excess credit by the banks for investment and consumption purposes, cash reserve ratio is raised or Government bonds and securities are sold to the banks and the public. The decrease in credit for investment and consumption will cause decline in aggregate demand which will exert downward pressure on prices.

On the contrary to get the economy out of recession expansionary monetary policy is adopted. The increase in money supply lowers the rate of interest. The credit from banks becomes cheaper which encourages investment. At lower interest rate households also tend to borrow more for consumption. As a result, aggregate demand in the economy increases which raises levels of output and employment. However, it may be noted that Keynes was not optimistic about the efficacy of monetary policy to tackle the problem of depression and unemployment. He argued that demand for money at the time of depression is highly interest-elastic and therefore expansion in money supply will not lead to lowering of interest rate significantly. Besides, according to him, investment demand is not much interest-elastic so that even smaller interest rate will not stimulate investment.

In a developing country such as India the right monetary policy can play a useful role for achieving the objectives of higher economic growth with price stability. For example, in India the Reserve Bank of India ensures that while genuine demand for credit for investment by firms must be met, the excessive growth in money supply and credit should be avoided. The Reserve Bank of India has been often adjusting its monetary policy to suit the changing economic situation.

Growth Policies

Many economists doubt the efficacy of fiscal and monetary policies to eliminate the fluctuations in the economic activity through *demand management* (that is, influencing the level of aggregate demand). A school of economic thought known as *supply-side economics* argues that focus of government policy should shift from demand management to stimulation of aggregate supply of output. For example, in the seventies when the USA and Britain experienced the problem of *stagflation*, some economists suggested that instead of demand management the government should reduce taxes to increase the incentives to work, save and invest more. More labour supply and more investment will increase the supply of goods and services. As a result, price level will fall and at the same time output will rise. The policies to reduce inflation through expansion in supply of output are generally described as *supply-side policies*.

Besides, for promotion of growth, especially in developing countries, the government adopts appropriate fiscal and monetary policies. It is generally believed that higher economic growth in the developing countries will lead to the reduction in poverty and unemployment. To raise the rate of saving and investment the government must take appropriate fiscal and monetary measures. Recently, it has been found that policy of moderate taxes generates more revenue through greater tax complianice and at the same time it provides incentives to save and invest more. In developing countries in order to speed up economic growth the government should increase its expenditure on infrastructure such as irrigation projects,x roads and highways, power, telecommunication, ports etc. Besides, as has been emphasised by Amartya Sen, for accelerating growth and removal of poverty the government must invest more in social sector consisting of education, health, literacy. It is important to note that a developing country cannot rely on private sector investment alone which is governed and guided by profit motive. Therefore, to supplement the private sector investment the government itself should directly undertake investment to promote and accelerate economic growth.

INFLATION AND PRICE INDICES: WPI AND CPI

We have explained above that inflation has been one of the important problems facing the economies of the world. Precisely stated, inflation is the rate of change of general price level during a period of time. And the general price level in a period is the result of inflation in the past. Through rate of inflation economists measure the *cost of living* in an economy. Let us explain how rate of inflation is measured. Suppose P_{t-1} represents the price level on 31st March 2005 and P_t represents the price level on 31st Mach 2006. Then the rate of inflation in year 2005-06 well be equal to

$$\pi = \frac{P_t - P_{t-1}}{P_{t-1}}$$

where π represents rate of inflation. Suppose Consumer price index (CPI) on March 31 , 2005 which was 250, it rose to 275 on March 31, 2006, rate of inflation in 2005-06 will be

$$\pi = \frac{275-250}{250} \times 100 = \frac{25}{250} \times 100 = 10\%$$

Thus rate of inflation during 2005-06 will be 10 per cent. This is called *point-to-point inflation* rate. There are 52 weeks in a year, average of price indexes of 52 weeks of a year (say 2005) can be calculated to compare the average of price indexes of 52 weeks of year 2006 and find the inflation rate on the basis of average weekly price levels of a year. In both these ways rate of inflation in different years is measured and compared. We now explain in detail how inflation is measured with the help of various price indices.

Measuring Inflation with Price Indices

Having explained the meaning of inflation we will now explain how inflation rate is measured. As inflation means rate of change in average or general price level over a period time we need to explain how the prices of various individual goods are aggregated to obtain the measure of general price level. This is done through construction of price index numbers. There are a number of price indices that are prepared to assess the changes in price level (i.e. inflation). The following types of price indices are generally used:

1. The Consumer Price Index Number (CPI)
2. The Wholesale Price Index (WPI)
3. GDP Deflator

In India inflation is generally measured by changes in wholesale price index (WPI), while in the developed countries such as US it is consumer price index (CPI) that is used for this purpose. We explain below all these three price indices.

Consumer Price Index (CPI)

The Consumer Price Index (CPI) is used to measure *cost of living* of the people and is based on *retail prices* of the selected goods constituting the consumption basket of a particular group of consumers. For instance, in India CPI is prepared for (1) industrial workers (CPI-IW) and for its preparation retail prices of those goods are selected which generally form the consumption basket of industrial workers. Second, consumer price index for agricultural labour (CPI-AL) is prepared and this includes the retail prices of consumer goods that constitutes the consumption basket of agricultural labour. Third, CPI for urban non-manual employees (CPI-UNME) is constructed to measure retail prices of those consumer goods and services purchased by urban non-manual employees.

Method of Constructing Consumer Price Index (CPI)

We now proceed to explain the method used for constructing consumer price index (CPI). The first step is to *choose the basket of consumer goods and services* that is generally purchased by a specific group of consumers, for example, industrial workers.

The second step in the construction of CPI is to select the base year. In India at present the year 2001 is selected as the base year for the construction CPI for industrial workers. It is the retail prices in the base year with which retail prices of the current year are compared that enable us to obtain the relative price.

The third step is collecting the retail prices for the current year of various goods included in the consumption basket of the specific group of consumers. The price data from different centres or locations in the country is gathered for this purpose. The fourth step involves choosing weights to be given to the prices of different items in the consumption basket of the specific group of consumers. If simple average prices of various items of consumption are used, it would mean treating all items equally for the specific group. However, this is not realistic as consumers spend different amounts on various items. Therefore, different weights are assigned to different items in consumers' basket of goods. The weight assigned to an item is the proportion of expenditure on an item to the consumers' total expenditure on the consumption basket. It is calculated as follows:

Expenditure on an item in the base year = $P_i^0 Q_i^0$

Superscript '0' in the above expression stands for the base year P_i stands for price of an item and Q_i for the quantity of the item. The total expenditure of all items in the consumption basket in the base year is give by:

$$\text{Total expenditure} = \sum_{i=1}^{n} P_i^0 Q_i^0$$

Thus weight assigned to an item is given by

$$W_i = \frac{P_i^0 Q_i^0}{\sum_{i=1}^{n} P_i^0 Q_i^0} \qquad \text{. . . (1)}$$

Suppose expenditure on a commodity of a household, say rice, in a week is ₹ 500 (i.e., $P_i^0 Q_i^0$ = ₹ 500 and total expenditure on all items in its consumption basket is ₹1500 (i.e. $\sum_{i=1}^{n} P_i^0 Q_i^0$ = ₹ 1500), then weight to be assign to the item 'rice' will be 500 ÷ 1500 = 0.33).

As said above, a consumer price index expresses the current price relative to its price in the base period. Thus the consumer price index for a period t is given by

$$CPI_t = \frac{P^t}{P^0} \times 100 \qquad \text{. . . (2)}$$

Thus, if price of rice in the base year is ₹ 5 per kg and the price in the current period t is ₹ 9 per kg. then

$$CPI_t = \frac{9}{5} \times 100 = 180$$

This means the price of rice in the current period has risen by 80 per cent.

But the expression $\frac{P_t}{P_0}$ is price index of and individual item. A general consumer price index is *weighted average* of various items in the consumption basket. Therefore, general consumer price index is written as

$$CPI = \sum W_i \left(\frac{P_i^t}{P_i^0} \right) \times 100 \qquad \text{. . . (3)}$$

Substituting the value of W_i in (3)

We have

$$CPI_i = \sum \left(\frac{P_i^0 Q_i^0}{\Sigma P_i^0 Q_i^0} \right) \left(\frac{P_i^t}{P_i^0} \right) \times 100$$

Simplifying

$$CPI = \frac{\sum Q_i^0 . P_i^t}{\sum Q_i^0 . P_i^0} \times 100 \qquad \text{. . . (4)}$$

The expression (4) of consumer price index is known as *Laspeyre's index* as in it takes base year's quantity while finding weighted average of the relative prices of different items.

As example will make clear the process of calculating CPI. This is done in the following table.

Table 37.1. Calculating CPI

Item	Quantity Q_i^0	Price in 2001 P_i^0	Expenditure in 2001, $P_i^0Q_i^0$	Price in the Current Period (2012)	Expenditure in the current period $P_i^t.Q_i^t$
Rice	25 kg	₹ 5/kg	₹ 125	₹ 10/kg	250
Pulses	5 kg	₹ 10/kg	₹ 50	₹ 25/kg	125
Clothing	5 m	₹ 20/m	₹ 100	₹ 50/m	250
Housing	1 room set	₹ 500 per one room set	₹ 500	₹ 800	800

$\sum P_i^0Q_i^0 = 775$ $\sum P_i^t.Q_i^0 = 1425$

This implies that price in 2012 is 84 per cent higher compared to the base year 2001.

$$CPI = \frac{\sum P_i^t Q_i^0}{\sum P_i^0 Q_i^0} \times 100 = \frac{1425}{775} \times 100 = 184$$

Wholesale Price Index (WPI)

While consumer price index is based on retail prices of a few consumer goods making up the consumption basket of a specific group of consumers, wholesale price (WPI) is constructed to measure the *average wholesale prices of all commodities* produced and/or transacted in the economy. Two things must be noted in this regard. First, wholesale price index (WPI) measures wholesale prices of commodities, and not their retail prices. Second, it is based on all commodities produced and/or transacted in the economy. Thus it includes not only consumer goods but also raw materials used in industrial production such as coal, cotton, steel and capital goods such as machines, tractors, pump sets and other equipment. However, WPI does not cover the prices of services such as health, education, transport communication.

The commodities included in the construction of WPI are classified into the following three categories.

1. Primary articles such as food, non-food and minerals
2. Manufactured goods
3. Fuel, power, light and lubricants

In India at present wholesale price index is prepared with 2004-05 as the base year as the base year. Movements in WPI over a period of time is used to measure inflation rate. Since WPI is based on changes in prices of all commodities, from change in inflation rate it can be ascertained which particular group of commodities, for example, whether changes in prices of food products or manufactured goods or of fuel and power are responsible for rise in general price level.

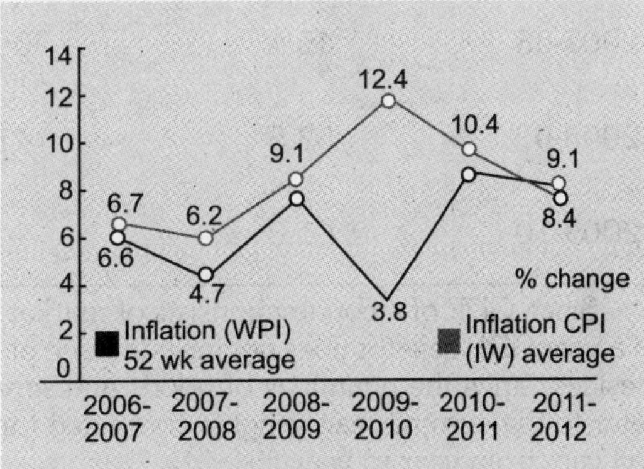

Fig. 37.1. India's Inflation rate based on CPI (IW) and WPI

The method of constructing WPI is the same used in case of CPI. *The WPI is the weighted average of wholesale prices of all commodities.* The weights to various commodities are assigned on the basis of relative values of different commodities to the total value of commodities produced and/or transacted in the economy. For preparing WPI, price data is collected from all important wholesale markets or centres in the country like that of construction of CPI, Laspeyre's formula is used to construct WPI, namely, base-year's values of commodities produced or transacted are used as weights in its preparation. Thus

$$WPI = \frac{\sum P_i^t Q_i^0}{\sum P_i^0 Q_i^0} \times 100$$

The above formula indicates the percentage change in the price level of commodities in period *t* compared to the base year. If wholesale price index for the year 2011 is 198 with base year 2004-05, then it implies that in 2011 general wholesale price level is 98 per cent higher than in 2004-05. We have depicted in Fig. 37.1 infaltion rate in India since 2006-07 both in terms of CPI and WPI.

GDP Deflator

As a measure of changes in price level or inflation rate GDP deflator is important because besides all goods it also includes *all services* that go to make up the Gross Domestic Product (GDP). It shows the relation between nominal GDP and real GDP as the two differ because of the changes in prices of commodities and services over a period of time. It may be noted that nominal GDP is the value of GDP at *current prices*, while real GDP is the value of GDP at constant prices (i.e. prices of a certain year taken as the base year).

$$\text{Thus, GDP Deflator} = \frac{\text{Naminal GDP}}{\text{Real GDP}} \times 100$$

Table. 37.1B. GDP Deflator

Year	GDP at current prices (in lakh crore)	GDP at constant prices (2004-05 = 100) (in lakh crore)	GDP Deflator $\frac{\text{GDP at current prices}}{\text{GDP at 2004-05 prices}} \times 100$
2004-05	29.5	29.5	$\frac{29.5}{29.5} \times 100 = 100$
2005-06	33.6	32.3	$\frac{33.6}{32.3} \times 100 = 104.0$
2006-07	39.2	35.4	$\frac{39.2}{35.4} \times 100 = 110.7$
2007-08	45.6	36.8	$\frac{45.6}{36.8} \times 100 = 123.9$
2008-09	52.5	41.4	$\frac{52.5}{41.4} \times 100 = 126.8$
2009-10	61.0	44.6	$\frac{61.0}{44.6} \times 100 = 136.7$

Since GDP of a country consists of market value of all *final* goods and services produced in a year,GDP deflator does not include value of *intermediate goods* to avoid double counting. Besides, since the quantities of goods and services in both the nominal GDP and real GDP refer to the current year, weights computed for the construction of WPI will not be fixed but will vary from year to year.

It needs to be emphasized that since GDP deflator measures the changes in prices of goods and services produced domestically, it does not capture the changes in prices of goods imported from abroad, such as patrol and petroleum products.

The calculation of GDP deflator in India is illustrated in the following table where we have calculated it from India's GDP at current prices and GDP at constant prices with 2004-05 as the base year. The last column in this table shows GDP deflator.

In India the wholesale price Index (WPI) of all commodities with base year 1993-94 price level at the end of fiscal year is used to measure rate of inflation and is widely reported in the media. Since the wholesale price index does not truly indicate the cost of living, separate consumer price index (CPI) for agricultural labourers and consumer price index (CPI) for industrial workers (with base 1982 = 100) at the end of fiscal year) are constructed to measure rate of inflation. In constructing the consumer price index (CPI) the price of a *basket* of goods which a typical consumer industrial worker or agricultural labourer as the case may be are taken into account. We will explain the nature and causes of inflation in a separate chapter.

EMPLOYMENT AND UNEMPLOYMENT

An important macroeconomic aggregate is the level of employment in the economy is What determines the level of employment in the economy and what causes involuntary unemployment is important issue in macroeconomics. *Involuntary unemployment is defined as the situation when in the country there are a large number of workers who are willing to work at the current wage rates but are unable to get employment*. In times of depression, the level of employment in the economy declines very much with the result that a large number of persons become involuntarily unemployed

Say's Law and Employment

Classical economists were of the view that there was always full employment in a free-market economy. According to them, if there are lapses from the full employment level, then some forces would work automatically to restore full employment. Their view was based upon their faith in *Say's Law of Markets*. According to Say's law, *supply creats its own demand*. This implies that there can be no problem of deficiency of aggregate demand. Thus there is always enough expenditure or aggregate demand to purchase the total output produced with full-employment of resources. In other words, the classical economists neglected the problem of deficiency of demand for purchasing goods produced at full-employment level of resources. Even when deficiency of aggregate demand arises, according to them, *prices and wages would adjust quickly in such a way that real production, employment and income will be restored automatically to full employment level*.

J.B. Say was the famous French economist of the 19th century. Say's Law is based on the fact that every production of goods also creates incomes for the factors of production equal to the value of goods produced by them. Incomes earned by the factors are spent on purchasing goods produced. In other words, production of goods creates purchasing power for itself. Therefore, Say's law is expressed as "*supply creates its own demand*", that is, the supply of goods produced creates demand for it equal to its own value. As a result, the problem of general overproduction and unemployment of resources do not arise. In this way, in Say's law, the possibility of lack of aggregate demand had been ignored.

We thus see that according to Say's law, aggregate demand for goods will always be adequate so as to ensure that all resources are fully employed. The factors which participate in productive activity and earn incomes from it, spend a good part of their incomes on consumer goods and save some part of them. But, according to classical economists, savings by the individuals are automatically spent on investment or capital goods. Therefore, since saving becomes another form of expenditure (that is, investment expenditure), in classical theory the whole income is spent, partly on consumption and partly on investment. There is thus no reason for any leakage in the income stream and therefore supply creates its own demand.

According to classical theory, it is changes in rate of interest which makes investment equal to saving. When savings of the people increase, rate of interest declines. As a result of fall in the rate of interest, demand for investment increases and in this way investment expenditure becomes equal to the increased savings. Hence, according to classical economists, it is changes in the interest rate that bring about equality between saving and investment and therefore Say's law applies in spite of savings by the people. This guarantees full employment of resources in the economy. In terms of circular flow of income we can say that it is changes in the rate of interest due to which the withdrawal of some money from the income stream as a result of savings automatically comes back to it in the form of investment expenditure and therefore income flow continues unchanged and supply goes on creating its own demand.

Flexibility in Prices and Wages and Full Employment:

Classical economists also proved the validity of the assumption of full employment with another reasoning. According to them, especially the then living British Classical economist, A.C. Pigou, if changes in rate of interest somehow fail to bring about equality between savings and investment and as a result deficiency of aggregate demand or expenditure arises, even then the problem of overproduction and involuntary unemployment will not arise. This is because they thought that the deficiency of aggregate demand would be made up by changes in the price level. When, due to the increase in savings by the people, the consumption expenditure of the people declines, it will affect the prices of products. As a result of fall in aggregate expenditure or demand, prices of products would decline and at reduced prices their quantity demanded will increase. As a result, all the quantity produced of goods will be sold out at lower prices.

Thus, Classical economists thought that a *free-market capitalist economy works in a self-correcting manner* and when aggregate expenditure on goods or aggregate demand for them declines, then various sellers and producers will reduce prices of their products so as to avoid the excessive accumulation of stocks of goods with them. Hence, according to them, when aggregate demand declines due to investment expenditure falling short of saving, the prices of products will decline, and at lower prices more output will be demanded and produced, the level of employment remaining unaffected. Further, to make their business profitable *producers will have to reduce the prices of the factors of production such as labour. With a fall in wages of labour, all labourers who are willing to work at the new prevailing wages will get employment.*

Involuntary Unemployment. If some workers do not want to work at lower wages, they will not get any job or employment and will therefore remain unemployed. But, according to Classical economists, those workers who do not want to work at lower wages and thus remain unemployed are only *voluntarily unemployed*. This voluntary unemployment is not real unemployment. According to the classical thought, it is *involuntary unemployment* which is not possible in a free-market capitalist economy. All those labourers who want to work at the prevailing wage rate determined by market forces will get employment.

During the period 1929-33 when there was a great depression in capitalist economies, eminent classical economist A.C. Pigou suggested a cut in wage rates in order to remove huge and widespread unemployment prevailing at that time. According to him, the cause of depression and unemployment was that the Government and trade unions of workers were preventing the free working of the capitalist economy and were artificially keeping the wage rates at high levels. He expressed the view that if wage rates were cut down, the demand for labour would increase so that all would get employment. It was at this time that J.M. Keynes challenged the classical theory and put forward a new theory of income and employment. *He brought about a basic change in economic thought regarding the determination of income and employment. Therefore, it is often said that Keynes brought about a revolution in economic theory.* Keynes made a genuine break and a basic departure from the Classical economics. His macro-economic theory is therefore called *Keynesian Revolution.*

Keynes on Employment and Unemployment

Towards the close of the nineteen twenties and early nineteen thirties (1929-33) free-market capitalist economies experienced severe depression rendering a large number of workers unemployed. For example, in the USA unemployment of labour increased from 3.2 per cent in 1929 to 25 per cent of labour force in 1933 and national income declined by 30 per cent during this period. This huge unemployment of labour persisted for a long time and full employment did not get automatically restored. Therefore, it became evident that there was something wrong with Classical economics which believed in self-correcting nature of a free market economy to eliminate involuntary unemployment. It was at this time that the English economist John Maynard Keynes challenged the classical theory of full employment, especially Say's law and Pigou's proposal to cut down wages to restore full employment. He put forth a new theory in his book "*A General Theory of Employment, Interest and Money*". Keynes laid a great stress on macro-economic analysis. He showed how incorrect was the view that involuntary unemployment could not prevail in a free-market capitalist economy.

Keynes challenged the correctness of Say's law that supply creates its own demand. He also criticised Pigou's view that a general cut in wages during depression and unemployment would restore full employment in the economy. As explained above, according to Say's law, every supply or production creates its own demand. Therefore, problems of demand deficiency and unemployment do not arise. It is, of course, true that supply creates demand for goods because the various factors which are employed in a productive activity earned incomes from it, which are spent on goods. But the incomes earn by the various factors of production are not wholly spent on the output of goods produced. A part of the income that is saved does not create demand. If entrepreneurs do not invest equal to the desired savings by the people, then aggregate demand which consists of demand for consumer goods and capital goods, will not be enough to purchase available supply of output. If aggregate demand is not sufficient to purchase the entire supply of goods, the producers would be unable to sell their whole output. As a result, their *inventories of goods will increase beyond their desired level*. This will cause the producers to reduce their level of production giving rise to unemployment in the economy.

Keynes showed that there was no guarantee that investment expenditure by entrepreneurs would be equal to the desired savings by the people. Saving and investment are generally made by two different classes of the people. While savings are done by individuals and households, investment expenditure is made by entrepreneurs. Further, while savings depend on various subjective factors such as willingness to save for old age, for periods of sickness and unemployment, for education and marriage of their children, for amassing wealth to leave behind a large estate etc. Apart from these subjective factors savings depend on level of prices, rate of inflation, rate of interest, taxation policy of the Government, distribution of income and wealth in the society and expectations of future income. On the other hand, investment by the entrepreneurs are determined by rate of interest and expected rate of profits in the short run and progress in technology and growth in population in the long run. Therefore, it is not likely that investment will be automatically equal to savings at full-employment level of income and output. As a result, problem of demand deficiency arises which causes involuntary unemployment.

Keynes also challenged the classical viewpoint regarding the impact of all-round cut in money wages on output and employment of labour. According to him, *while in case of the analysis of price and output determination of an individual industry, it is justified to assume that a cut in wages by the industry would not significantly affect the demand for the product of that industry because most of the demand for the product of that industry comes from the workers and persons employed in other industries*. However, to assume that aggregate demand for output of *all industries* will remain unchanged when a *simultaneous cut in wages in all industries together* is made is not valid. In other words, to apply the result of micro analysis of the determination of price, output and employment in an individual industry to the economy as a whole is quite misleading and invalid. This is because *wages are not only costs for the individual industries, they also constitute incomes of the workers and these incomes determine the demand for the products of various industries.* When all-round cut in wages is made in all industries, it will reduce aggregate demand for the products because workers would have now less incomes and therefore would spend less on goods and services. With reduced demand for the products of industries smaller output will be produced. As a result, smaller amount of labour will be demanded and employed. Thus, elaborating Keynesian view Stonier and Hague write, "When there is general unemployment, a general cut in wages in all industries cannot be assumed to leave demand unchanged for a part of that demand results from spending out of wages. It is thus quite clear that a general cut in wages will merely cause a reduction and will not in itself remove unemployment."[6]

Keynes explained that level employment was determined by aggregate demand and aggregate supply. He further showed that equilibrium level of income and employment could well be established at less than full-employment level of national income. Thus, according to him, lack of aggregate demand can cause involuntary unemployment of labour and unutilised productive capacity. In a later chapter we will explain in detail how, according to Keynes, levels of national income and employment are determined.

Involuntary Unemployment and Labour Market Equilibrium: Keynes's View

Let us explain through labour market equilibrium how Keynes explain the emergence of cyclical involuntary un-employment. As stated above, *involuntary unemployment refers to those workers who are seeking work or willing to work at the prevailing wage rate but are unable to get jobs.* According to Keynes, this involuntary unemployment happens to prevail in an economy on a large scale in times of depression due to fall in aggregate demand for goods and services. Classical economists thought that at times of recession wages and prices would fall to eliminate involuntary unemployment and ensure full employment. Keynes challenged this Classical viewpoint on two grounds. First, he pointed out that *money wages are rigid downward and fail to adjust even when there exists involuntary unemploy-ment due to lack of aggregate demand for output.* Secondly, even if money wages are flexible downward or there is all-round cut in money wages, involunt-ary unemployment will not be removed as aggregate demand will fall due to all-round redu-ction in wages.

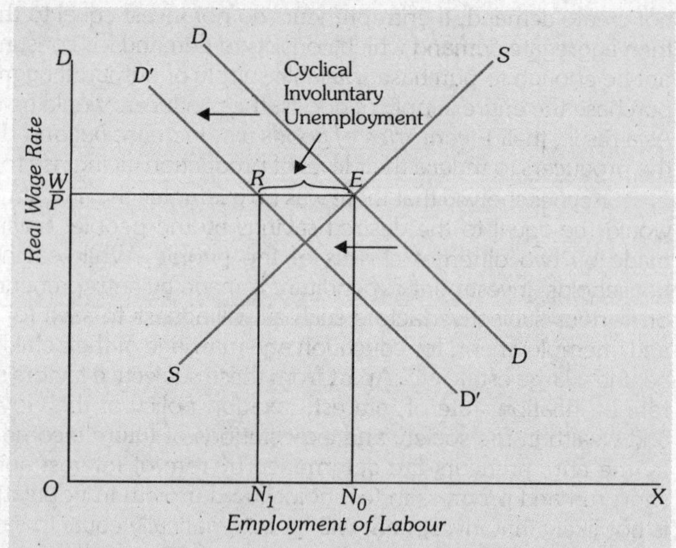

Fig. 37.1. *Labour Market Equilibrium and Involuntary Unemployment with Downward Rigidity of Money Wage Rate*

Consider Figure 37.1 where we have shown labour market equilibrium. *DD* is the demand curve of labour which is sloping downward to the light. This shows that at lower real wage rates more labour is demanded and employed and vice versa. *SS* is the supply curve of labour which is sloping upward to the right. This shows that at higher real wages more labour is supplied and vice versa. These demand and supply curves of labour intersect at point *E* at

6. Stonier A.W. and Hague, D.C. *A Textbook of Economic Theory*, Fourth Edition, 1997, p. 397

which real wage rate $\frac{W}{P}$ and labour employment of ON_0 are determined. At the real wage rate $\frac{W}{P}$, all those who are willing to work and supply their labour services are employed. Thus, at this labour market equilibrium, there is full employment of labour and involuntary unemployment does not prevail.

Now suppose aggregate demand for output of goods and services declines, as it happens in times of recession. *Demand for labour is a derived demand*. Decline in aggregate demand for output causes demand curve of labour to shift to the left to $D'D'$ in Fig. 37.1. Now, at the given real wage rate, $\frac{W}{P}$, the quantity ON_1 labour will be demanded, whereas supply of labour at this wage rate remains ON_0. Thus, *RE* number of workers will be rendered unemployed who are willing to work at the prevailing wage rate but their services are not demanded by the producers.

According to classical economists, this involuntary unemployment cannot persist for long. The excess supply of labour and competition among unemployed workers will bring down the money wage rate and at lower wage rate more labour will be demanded and employed. Besides, in recession prices of goods will also fall due to excess of supply of goods over the demand for them. In this way, according to classical economists, due to downward adjustment in wages as well as prices of goods involuntary unemployment of labour will be eliminated and full employment will be restored.

Rigid Money Wages. However, Keynes contended that *money wages are rigid* downward and do not fall and as a result involuntary unemployment continues to prevail. There are a number of reasons for rigidity of money wages. First, workers strongly resist a reduction in money wages. Second, there is usually a wage contract between workers (or their trade unions) with the employers for a period of two to three years during which wage rates cannot be changed. Thirdly, there are minimum wages fixed by the government below which employers are not permitted to pay wages to the workers. Lastly, employers themselves may not be interested in reducing wages, as lower wages are likely to reduce efficiency or productivity of labour. Thus, if in Figure 37.1, wages remain rigid at $\frac{W}{P}$ despite the leftward shift in the demand curve of labour to $D'D'$, involuntary unemployment would continue to exist.

All Round Cut in Wages and Employment. However, Keynes argued that even if there is all-round cut in wages during the period of recession caused by lack of effective demand, this will not ensure elimination of involuntary unemployment. This is because *wages are not only costs of production for firms and industries but are also incomes of workers.* In case of all-round cut in wages, incomes of the working class, which constitutes a majority in a society, will fall which will work to reduce consumption demand for output. Reduction in consumption will lower aggregate demand which will therefore further deepen the depression and result in more involuntary unemployment rather than removing it.

UNEMPLOYMENT IN DEVELOPING COUNTRIES

As stated above, Keynesian theory is mainly concerned with cyclical unemployment which emerges in the developed capitalist countries, especially in times of depression. During the period 1929-33, the developed capitalist economies suffered from severe depression which caused huge magnitude of unemployment. Keynes analysed this type of cyclical unemployment and explained that it was caused by deficiency of aggregate demand. That is, unemployment in advanced developed countries generally arises in a short period, say two to three years, in recessionary phase of business cycles due to deficiency of aggregate demand. When the economy recovers from recession in these advanced countries the cyclical unemployment disappears and as a result full employment comes to prevail. On the other hand, the nature of unemployment in developing countries is quite different, *it is of chronic and long-term nature,* which is the result of the operation of structural factors, namely, the rate of capital formation relative to growth of labour force has not been large enough to absorb increases in workers in productive employment. Besides, extreme unequal distribution of land resulting in lack of access to land and other assets to a vast majority of workers and use of capital-intensive technology in industries have accentuated the problem of unemployment and under-employment in developing countries. We explain below the important factors responsible for the existence of unemployment in developing countries such as India.

1. Lack of Adequate Capital and other Assets Relative to Labour Force. It is now recognised that the chronic unemployment and under-employment in less developed countries such as India are not due to the lack of aggregate effective demand which, according to J.M. Keynes, was responsible for unemployment in developed countries in times of depression. Rather it is stated to be due to the lack of land, capital and other complementary resources in relation to the total population and labour force. In the phenomenon examined by Keynes, not only labour force but also capital equipment were unemployed due to the deficiency of aggregate effective demand. In other words, in the Keynesian scheme, both the labour force and capital equipment were crying out for full employment which could be achieved by raising the level of aggregate monetary expenditure. Thus, according to Joan Robinson: "Keynes' theory has little to say, directly, to the under-developed countries, for it was framed entirely in the context of an advanced industrialised economy, with highly developed financial institutions and a sophisticated business class. The unemployment that concerned Keynes was accompanied by under-utilisation of capacity already in existence. It had resulted from a fall in effective demand. The unemployment of under-developed economies arises because capacity and effective demand never have been great enough"[7].

Thus, the standard explantation for the existence of labour surplus or unemployment and under-employment in less developing countries like India is that as compared with the magnitude of population and labour force there is limited availability of capital or complementary resources which include land, factories, machines, tools and implements–the means with which labour produces. Now, if the population grows faster than the stock of capital of a country, the entire addition to the labour force cannot be absorbed in productive employment because not enough instruments of production are there to employ them. Since in less developed countries, the stock of capital has not been growing at a rate fast enough to keep pace with the growth of labour force, the ability to offer productive employment is very limited. This has resulted in surplus labour which is manifested in the existence of huge magnitude of under-employment or disguised unemployment and open unemployment in both the rural and urban areas.

2. Use of Capital Intensive Techniques. Apart from lack of capital relative to labour force, another important factor responsible for slow growth of employment has been the use of capital-intensive techniques of production, even in consumer goods industries where alternative labour-intensive techniques are available. Even before 1991, under the industrial policy resolution 1956, the development of consumer goods industries were left open for the private sector. However, private sector prefers to invest in highly capital-intensive plants and equipment on the basis of technology developed in labour-scarce Western countries. It is argued by them the alternative labour-intensive techniques have low productivity and low-surplus-generating capacity. However, the important reason for the use of capital-intensive techniques has been the availability of cheap capital. Even firms in modern small industry sector which were expected to generate large employment opportunities have tended to use capital-intensive techniques of production. Thus, Prof. J.C. Sandesara of the 'Institute of Economic Growth' *states, "the availability of cheap capital has tended to encourage the modern small-scale industries sector to over-capitalise and use more capital-intensive methods of*

7. Joan Robinson, *Economic Philospghy*, p. 119

production and thus reduce employment potential"[8].

In agriculture, reckless mechanisation of various agricultural operations despite the existence of surplus labour has reduced the employment-augmenting effect of new high-yielding technology involving the use of HYV seeds, fertilisers and pesticides. This has prevented the generation of enough employment opportunities in rural areas.

Now, a pertinent question is why capital-intensive techniques are used in industries despite the condition of labour-abundance in the economy. First reason is the *relatively low price of capital*. Relatively low price of capital has caused by (*a*) lower rate of interest, (*b*) liberal depreciation allowance on capital investment permitted in the taxation system of the country, (*c*) relatively cheap capital equipment imported from abroad. Second, higher wages of labour in the organised sector relative to their productivity under pressure from trade unions. Thirdly, rigid labour laws also discourage the employment of labour. It is difficult to retrench labour even when it is not required in case an industrial unit becomes sick and proposes to close down or exit.

Fourthly, Research and Development (R & D) activity has not been adequately directed to discover and identify labour-intensive appropriate techniques to be used in industries which, though labour-intensive, have also reasonably good productivity.

3. Inequitable Distribution of Land. Another cause of unemployment prevailing in the developing countries like India is inequitable distribution of land so that many agricultural households have *no adequate access to land* which is an important asset for agricultural production and employment. Sub-division of land holdings under the pressure of rapid population growth since 1951 has further reduced access to land for several agricultural households. As a result many persons who were self-employed in agriculture have become landless agricultural labourers who suffer from acute unemployment and under-employment.

4. Rigid Protective Labour Legislation. Another reason for the slow growth of employment in the organised sector has been the existence of unduly rigid protective labour legislation which makes it very difficult to retrench a worker who has been employed for 240 days. Labour-legislation is so much rigid that it is even difficult to close down the unit and quit the industry. Thus, this excessively protective labour-legislation induces private entrepreneurs to prefer the maximum use of capital in place of labour.

Employment opportunities in the economy can be increased at a greater rate by stepping up capital accumulation (i.e. investment). Higher rate of capital formation will increase the rate of both economic growth and employment. However, higher rate of capital formation through essential for generation of employment opportunities is not sufficient. For adequate expansion in employment opportunities and thereby to eliminate unemployment in addition to rapid capital formation, the steps should be taken to promote the use of labour-intensive (or less capital-intensive) techniques in the industrial and agricultural sectors of the economy.

BALANCE OF PAYMENTS

In the modern world, there is hardly any country which is self-sufficient in the sense that it produces all the goods and services it needs. Every country imports from other countries the goods that cannot be produced at all in the country or can be produced only at an unduly high cost as compared to the foreign supplies. Similarly, a country exports to other countries the commodities which those countries prefer to buy from abroad rather than producing at home.

8. J.C. Sandesara, *Small-scale Enterprises in Industrial Development. The Indian Experience* (1998), Sage Publications, Delhi.

Besides trade of goods and services, there are *flows of capital*. Foreign capital flows are in the form of portfolio investment by forigen institutional investors or in the form of foreign direct investment. *The balance of payments is a systematic record of all economic transactions of residents of a country with the rest of the world during a given period of time.*

This record is so prepared as to measure the various components of a country's external economic transactions. Thus, the aim is to present an account of all receipts and payments on account of goods exported, services rendered and capital received by the residents of a country, and goods imported, services received and capital transferred by residents of the country. The main purpose of keeping these records is to know the international economic position of a country which helps the Government in making decisions on monetary and fiscal policies on the one hand, and trade and payments policies on the other.

Balance of Trade and Balance of Payments. Balance of trade and balance of payments are two related terms but they should be carefully distinguished from each other because they do not have exactly the same meaning. *Balance of trade refers to the difference in values of imports and exports of commodities only, i.e., visible items only.* Movement of goods between countries is known as visible trade because the movement of goods is open and and visible and can be verified by the custom officials.

During a given period of time, the exports and imports may be exactly equal, in which case the *balance of trade is said to be in balance.* But this is not necessary because those who export and import are not necessarily the same persons. If the value of exports exceeds the value of imports, the country is said to have an *export surplus.* On the other hand, if the value of its imports exceeds the value of its exports, the country is said to have a *deficit balance of trade.*

Distinction between Current Account and Capital Account. The distinction between the current account and capital account of the balance of payment may be noted. The current account deals with payment for *currently produced goods and services*. It includes also interest earned or paid on claims and also gifts and donations. *The capital account, on the other hand, deals with capital receipts and payments of debts and claims.* The current account of the balance of payments affects the level of national income directly. For instance, when India sells its currently produced goods and services to foreign countries, the producers of those goods get income from abroad. In other words, current account receipts have the effect of increasing the flow of income in the country. On the other hand, when India imports goods and services from foreign countries and pays them money which could have been used to demand goods and services within the country money flows out to foreign countries. Thus, current account payments to foreigners involve reduction in the flow of income within the country and constitute a leakage. Thus, the current account of the balance of payments has a direct effect on the level of income in a country. The capital account, however, does not have such a *direct effect* on the level of income; it *influences the volume of assets which a country holds.*

Balance of Payments on Current Account

Balance of payments on current account is more comprehensive in scope than balance of trade. It includes not only imports and exports of goods which are visible items but also *invisible items* such as foreign travel, transportation (shipping, air transport etc.), insurance, tourism, software services, investment income (e.g. interest on investments), transfer payments i.e. remittances from abroad, donations, gifts, etc.

A country, say India, has to make payments to the other countries not only for its imports of merchandise but also for tourists travelling abroad, insurance and shipping services rendered by other countries. Further, it has to pay the royalties to foreign firms, expenditure of Indians in foreign countries, interest and dividends on foreign investment in India. These are debit items for India, since the transactions involve *payments made to the rest of the world*. In the same way, foreign countries import goods from India, make use of Indian films and so on, for all of which they make payments to India. An important item which has recently emerged as an item of invisible exports is *software service exports* which has become a good foreign exchange earner for us. These are the credit items for India as *we receive payments from abroad*. Balance of payments on current account thus gives a comprehensive picture of all such transactions including imports and exports of goods as well as of services.

The Table 37.1 (given below) gives the position of India's balance of payments on current account for six years 2006-07 to 2011-12. The data regarding both visible and invisible items of current account are given in this table. The visible items are exports and imports of goods and the invisible items of balance of payments on current account are trade in services such as travel, transportation and insurance, interest on loans given and other investment income, private and official transfers. Both visible and invisible items together make up the *Current Account*. Interest on loans, tourist expenditure, banking and insurance charges, etc., are similar to visible trade since receipts from selling such services to the foreigners are very similar in their effects to receipts from sales of goods; both provide income to the people who produce goods and services.

Table 37.1C. ***India's Balance of Payments on Current Account*** ***(in Billion US $)***

S.No. Items	2008-09	2009-10	2010-11	2011-12	2012-13	2013-14	2014-15
1. Exports	189.0	182.4	256.2	309.8	306.6	318.6	316.5
2. Imports	307.6	300.6	383.5	499.5	502.3	466.2	461.5
3. **Trade Balance**	–118.6	–118.2	–127.3	–189.8	–195.7	–147.6	–144.5
	(–9.8)	(–8.7)	(–7.8)	(–10.1)	N.A	N.A	NA
4. **Invisibles (Net)**	89.9	80.0	79.3	111.6	107.5	115.2	118.1
(*i*). Non-factor Services	49.6	36.0	44.1	64.1	72.9	73.0	76.6
(*ii*). Income	–4.0	–8.0	–17.9	–16.0	–21.5	–23.0	–24.1
(*iii*). Private Transfers	44.6	52.0	53.1	63.5	64.0	65.3	65.7
5. **Goods and Services Balance**	–69.0	–82.2	– 83.2	–125.7	–	–	–
6. **Current Account Balance (Net)**	**–28.7**	**–38.2**	**–48.1**	**–78.2**	**–88.2**	**–32.4**	**–26.8**
	(–2.4)	**(–2.8)**	**(–2.7)**	**(–4.2)**	**–4.7)**	**(–1.7)**	**(–1.3)**

Source : RBI

Note : *Figures in brackets show per cent of GDP at market prices.*

It will be noted from Table 37.1 above that the most important item in the balance of payments on current account is balance of trade which refers to imports and exports of goods. In the Table 37.1 balance of trade does not balance, and shows a deficit in all the six years. In the years 2011-12 and 2012-13, trade deficit substantially increased. Trade deficit was over 10 per cent of GDP in these two years. In fact, it is huge trade deficit in these two years that caused huge current account deficit of over 4 per cent of India's GDP. Economic slowdown in advanced countries and its spill over effects in Emerging Market Economies coupled with rising crude oil and gold prices were responsible for sharp increase in trade deficit in these two years.

As regards invisible account of the current account of BOP (which includes trade in services, income from investment made by the Indians abroad private transfers mainly remittances from Indians abroad) there has been surplus throughout (see Table 37.1) which has worked to offset the deficit in trade balance resulting in lower overall deficit on current account. For the two years 2011-12 and 2012-13 the current account deficit was 4.2% and 4.7% of GDP respectively which was quite high. Contrary to popular perception, deficit on current account is not always bad provided it is within reasonable limits and can be easily met by non-debt capital inflows. In fact, *deficit on current account represents the extent of absorption of capital inflows in India during a year*. However, due to global financial crisis in 2008-09, there was first slowdown and then decrease in exports, there was a large deficit of 2.4 of per cent of GDP on current account which could not be met by capital inflows as they were quite meagre as a result of global financial crisis. Therefore, to finance the deficit in current account deficit we had to withdraw US $ 20 billion from our foreign exchange reserves in 2008-09. Again in the two years, 2011-12 and 2012-13 the current account deficit (CAD) had been quite large. However, in the years, 2013-14 and 2014-15, current acount balance of payments situation improved substantially and in 2013-14 and 2014-15 current account deficit was 1.7% and 1.3% of GDP respectively.

It is important to note that high current account deficit (CAD) tends to weaken the rupee by raising the demand for dollars. In 2011-12, the current account deficit was 4.2 per cent of GDP and since capital inflows in this year was not sufficient to finance current account deficit, RBI had to withdraw 12.8 billion US dollars from its foreign exchange reserves to meet the demand for US dollars. In the year 2012-13, also the current account deficit was even higher at around 4.7 per cent of GDP. But capital inflows were quite large which were enough to meet the deficit on current account. However, the current account balance situation in 2013-14, 2014-15 and 2015-16 improved a lot, so that with net capital inflows India succeeded in adding to foreign exchange reserves in these years. The current account deficit poses a great challenge to the macroeconomic management of the economy. *The dependence on risky volatile capital inflows through FIIs to meet current account deficit is unsustainable* as these capital funds can go back when global situation worsens causing a good deal of risk for Indian investors as stock market crashes when there are large capital outflows. Thanks to government's liberal foreign direct investment (FDI) policy, capital inflows through FDI, which are a more stable source, has substantially increased during the last two years, 2014-15 and 2015-16.

Large Invisible Surpluses of Current Account. The balance of payments profile of current account reveals important trends. In the recent years deficits in the trade account have been made up by the large invisible surpluses resulting in a small deficit in current account balance. *The robust growth in invisibles is due to large inflows of private transfers and non-factor services.* Buoyant inflows of private transfers have been one of the main factors contributing to remarkable growth in invisibles. The current high level of private transfers which comprise largely inflows of remittances from Indians working abroad have made India the highest global recipient of remittances. The bulk of these remittances come in from expatriates in the USA and the Middle East. Invisible surplus of India was $ 115.2 billion in 2013-14 and $ 118 billion in 2014-15.

In addition to private transfers, the contribution of *non-factor services* to the invisible account has also been increasing steadily since 2001-02. This contribution has increased further in the recent years. Among the non-factor services enhancing the invisible surplus is the *buoyant earnings from software services.* The high skill intensity of the Indian work force has given a decisive comparative advantage to Indian software services exports and has helped the country in carving out a niche in the global market for software services and IT-enabled services. Besides, in recent years, India has emerged as one of most preferred destination of outsourcing IT-enabled services from advanced economies. While software services exports more than trebled between 1998-99 and 2003-04, exports of IT -enabled and business process outsourcing (BPO) services have increased significantly in recent years.

India's current account deficit (CAD) with the exception of two years, 2011-12 and 2012-13 has remained within manageable limits in past several years and has been financed largely by capital flows. There is increase in Balance of Payments vulnerability when there is a sudden shock and reversal of capital flows as occurred in 2008-09 due to global financial crisis is 2008, especially when sizeable flows occur due to changes in volatile portfolio investment by FIIS. The priority has therefore been to reduce CAD through improving trade balances. Efforts have been made to promote exports by diversifying the export commodity basket and export destinations. One way to limit imports is to bring prices up to international levels so that users see the full cost. The fall in crude oil prices in the years 2014-15 and 2015-16 has helped to lower current account deficit. To discourage the imports of gold which has played a significant role in causing trade deficit, customs duty on the import of gold has been raised from 4% to 6%.

Further, emphasis has continued on facilitating remittances and encouraging software exports that have been responsible for the surplus on the invisible account. In recent years, this surplus has lowered the impact of widening trade deficit in CAD significantly. The two components together met nearly two-thirds of the trade deficit that was more than 10 per cent of GDP in 2011-12.

Balance of Payments on Capital Account

In the balance of payments on capital account given in Table 37.2 important items are net borrowings from foreign countries, non resident deposits and foreign investment, both direct and portfolio. The foreign borrowings take two forms: (*i*) *External assistance* which means capital flows from foreign countries at *concessional* rates *of interest*; (*ii*) *Commercial borrowings* under which the Indian Government and the private corporate sector borrow funds from world money markets at *the market rates of interest*. The *non-resident deposits* which are another important item in capital account. These are the deposits made by non-resident Indians (NRI) who keep their surplus funds with Indian Banks. Another important item in balance of payments on capital account is *foreign investment* by foreign companies in India. There are two types of foreign investment. First is *portfolio investment* under which foreign institutional investors (FIIs) *purchase shares (equity) and bonds* of Indian companies and Government securities. The second is *foreign direct investment* (FDI) under which foreign companies set up plants and factories on their own or in collaboration with the Indian companies or invest in their private equity capital.

Table 37.2 ***India's Balance of Payments on Capital Account*** ***(in Billion US $)***

	2009-10	2010-11	2011-12	2012-13	2013-14	2014-15
External Assistance (Net)	2.9	4.94	2.3	0.98	1.0	1.7
External Commercial Borrowing (Net)	2.0	12.16	10.3	8.5	11.8	1.6
Non-Resident Deposits (Net)	2.9	3.24	11.9	14.8	38.9	14.1
Foreign Investment (Net)	50.4	42.13	39.2	46.7	26.4	73.5
of which						
(*i*) FDI net	18.0	11.36	22.1	19.8	21.6	31.3
(*ii*) Portfolio Investment (Net)	32.4	30.29	17.2	26.9	4.8	42.2
Other capital flows (Net)	–13.1	–12.48	–7.0	–5.1	–10.8	1.0
Capital Account Balance (Net)*	**51.6**	**61.1**	**65.3**	**91.9**	**47.9**	88.2
Use of Exchange Reserves	–13.4	–13.1	+12.8	–3.8	–15.5	–61.4

Source: RBI. Use of Reserves (– indicates increase of reserves, + indicates decrease of foreign exchange reserves (on BOP Basis)

* *Also includes errors and omissions*

Capital inflows in the capital account can be classified into *debt creating* and *non-debt creating* Foreign investment (both direct and portfolio) represents non-debt creating capital inflows, whereas external assistance (i.e. concessional loans taken from abroad), external commercial borrowing (ECB) and non-resident deposits are debt-creating capital inflows.

The Table 37.2 gives the position of India's balance of payments on capital account for six years 2008-09, 2009-10, 2010-11, 2011-12, 2012-2013, 2013-14 and 2014-15. It will be seen from Table 37.2 that during 2014-15, there was net foreign investment of 73.5 billion US dollars with foreign direct investment equal to $31.3 billion and portfolio investment of $42.2 billion. When all items of balance of payments on capital account are taken into account we had *a surplus* of 88.2 billion US dollars in 2014-15. Taking into current account deficit of $ 26.6 billion in year 2014-15 there was accretion to our foreign exchange reserves by $ 61.4 billion in 2014-15.

Global financial crisis affected our capital account balance as there was **reversal of capital flows after Sept. 2008** with the result that we used $ 20.1 billion of our foreign exchange reserves in 2008-09 to meet our current account deficit resulting in *decrease* of our foreign exchange reserves.

The balance of payments situation improved further in 2015-16 as due to fall in crude oil prices, current account deficit declined to around 1.3 per of GDP and capital flows on account of both as foreign direct investment (FDI) and portfolio investment by FIIs increased substantially. However, India is now (July 2016) is in a better position to cope with any reversal of capital flows as our foreign exchange reserves have reached record level of around $365 billion. Therefore India has come out well even after Brexit (i.e. Britain exiting EU) which was predicted to cause large capital outflows from India causing stock-market crisis.

Capital flows are driven by both pull factors such as economic fundamentals of recipient countries and push factors such as policy stance of source countries. The capital flows have implications for exchange rate management, overall macroeconomic and financial stability including liquidity conditions. Capital account management therefore needs to emphasize promoting foreign direct investment (FDI) and reducing dependence on volatile portfolio capital flows. This would ensure that to the extent current account deficit is bridged through capital surplus, it would be through stable and growth enhancing direct investment flows. In the prevailing international financial architecture, reserves are the first line of defense against the volatile capital flows. In this context, the decline in reserves as a fraction of GDP, while not an immediate source of concern for India need to be watched closely.

Determinants of Balance of Payments

It may be further noted that when there is a deficit in the current account, it has to be financed either by *using foreign exchange reserves* with Reserve Bank of Bank, if any, or by *capital inflows* (in the form of foreign assistance, commercial borrowing from abroad, non-residental deposits). There are several variables which determine the balance of payments position of a country, viz., national income at home and abroad, the prices of goods and factors, the supply of money, the rate of interest, etc. all of which determine exports, imports, and demand and supply of foreign currency. At the back of these variables lie the supply factors, production function, the state of technology, tastes, distribution of income, economic conditions, the state of expectations, etc. If there is a change in any of these variables and there are no appropriate changes in other variables, disequilibrium will be the result.

The main cause of disequilibrium in the balance of payments arises from imbalance between exports and imports of goods and services, that is, deficit or surplus in balance of trade. When for one reason or another exports of goods and services, of a country are smaller than their imports, disequilibrium in the balance of payments is the likely result. Exports may be small due to the lack of exportable surplus which in turn results from low production or the exports may be small because of the higher costs and prices of exportable goods and severe competition in the world markets. Important causes of lower exports are the inflation or rising prices in the country or appreciation of exchange rate. When the prices of goods are high in the country, its exports are discouraged and imports encouraged. If it is not matched by other items in the balance of payments, disequilibrium in the balance of payments emerges.

Does Balance of Payments must always balance?

It is often said that balance of payments must always balance. What does it mean ? The individuals and business firms of an economy have to pay for the imports from abroad. If exports are not sufficient to pay for the imports, then how the balance of payments will be in balance. For example, the balance of payments on current account of India had been in deficit for most of the years till 2014-15. Deficit on current account implies that the residents of a country are spending more on imports of goods and services than the incomes they are earning from exports of goods and services. For the overall balance of payments to be in balance, this deficit in the current account of the balance of payments must by financed by selling capital assets such as shares and bonds of companies or other assets such as gold or foreign exchange reserves of a country or by borrowing from abroad. Both by selling assets or by borrowing from abroad, foreign capital flows into the country as has been happening in the last several years in India. These foreign capital inflows are shown in the capital account of the balance of payments which must be in surplus or there must be sufficient foreign exchange reserves to finance the deficit in the current account. Thus

$$\text{current account} + \text{capital account surplus and use of foreign exchange reserves} = 0. \qquad \ldots (i)$$

The above fact has an important lesson that must be borne in mind. If a country has no foreign currency reserves or it has no assets to sell to pay for the imports and if no body is willing to lend to it, it will have to cut down its imports which will reduce productive activity in the economy and adversely affect economic growth of the country. Such a crisis situation arose in India in 1991 when our foreign exchange reserves had fallen to a very low level and no one was willing to lend to us or give us aid. In fact, due to loss of confidence of foreign investors, *capital outflows* were taking place. Therefore, in 1991 India had to mortgage and sell gold to Bank of England and Central Bank of Japan to get the necessary foreign exchange to pay for the needed imports. We had to accept the pre-conditions of IMF for providing us assistance to tide over the crisis. It is interesting to note this was done under the guidance of Dr. Manmohan Singh, who was then the Finance Minister.

GLOBALISATION, CAPITAL FLOWS AND BALANCE OF PAYMENTS

Let us first explain what is meant by globalisation. Globalisation refers to the increased openness of an economy to the international trade, capital flows (both portfolio and foreign direct investment, FDI), transfer of technology and free movement of labour or people. Thus **globalisation means the integration of economies of the world resulting from free flows of trade, capital, labour (or people) and technology between countries.** The term globalisation signifies new international economic order which envisages the following:

(*a*) free flow of trade of goods and services between different countires of the world.

(*b*) free flow of capital among countires.

(*c*) free flow of technology among different countries of the world.

(*d*) free movement of labor or people internationally.

The growing interaction between different countries of the world has made the idea of globalisation increasingly popular in recent years.

The globalization of the Indian economy has an important consequence with regard to capital flows into the economy. Suppose India faces given prices of its imports and a given demand for its exports of goods and services. Under these circumstances, if domestic rate of interest is higher as compared to what exists abroad, then, given the mobility of capital, foreign capital will flow into the Indian economy to a very large extent. This principle can be expressed as follows.

$$BP = NX(Y_d, Y_f, R) + CF(i_f - i_d) \qquad \ldots (ii)$$

where *BP* = balance of payments, *NX* is net exports (*i.e.* exports–imports which is also called trade balance). *CF* stands for surplus in the capital account of the balance of payments, that is, capital flows. i_f represents rate of interest in foreign market and i_d represents rate of interest in the domestic economy.

The above equation reveals that trade balance (*NX*) is a function of level of domestic income (Y_d) and foreign income (Y_f) and real rate of exchange (*R*). An increase in the domestic income due to higher industrial growth or fall in real exchange rate of rupee will adversely affect the trade balance (*NX*) by increasing imports. $i_f - i_d$ in equation (*ii*) measures interest rate differential between the foreign country and domestic economy on which *i.e.* net capital flows depend. Further, the above equation (*ii*) show-s that higher interest rate in India as compared to that in the foreign country such as the United States will cause large capital inflows into India. Such capital inflows have actually taken place in India in recent years. Due to large capital inflows into the Indian economy our foreign exchange reserves crossed 100 billions US dollars in December 2003, reached 170 billion US \$ in December 2006 and further increased to 247 billion US \$ dollars in September 2007, and to 300 billion US \$ in Sept. 2008. Due to reversal of capital flows, there was decline in our reserves in 2008-09 and in March 2009, they stood at US \$252 billion. From the second half of 2009-10 there has been reversal of capital flows and capital inflows into Indian economy have occurred on a large scale since then, India's foreign exchange reverse rose to \$292 billion in the end-March 2013. Our foreign exchange reserves further rose to \$360 billion is end-March 2016. The sharp reduction in crude oil prices and commodity prices has helped India to reduce its foreign trade and current account deficit. Besides, liberal foreign investment policy has caused large capital inflows leading to the increase in our foreign exchange reserves.

Globalisation has both advantages and disadvantages. It is through globalisation and openness of an economy that foreign trade of a country increases which promotes economic growth. Trade between countries help them to specialise in the production of goods and services according to their factor endowments and comparative efficiency. Besides, globalisation helps in the transfer of technology from the developed countries to the developing countries. Globalisation also promotes capital flows between countries which in general are welcome. Capital inflow in the form of foreign direct investment (FDI) adds to the productive capacity of a country by increasing capital accumulation. Capital inflows in the form of portfolio investment by FIIs (Foreign Institutional Investors), which are invested in buying equity shares and corporate and Government bonds lead to the development of financial markets. Besides, capital flows provide foreign exchange which can be used to meet the current account deficit which generally emerges in a developing country such as India due to large imports of fuel, machines and industrial raw materials required for industrial growth of the economy.

However, the global financial crisis of 2007-09 which originated in the sub-prime housing loan market in the US and enveloped the entire world has clearly brought out the adverse impact of globalisation. It adversely affected growth of exports of developing countries such as India which brought about large current account deficit. It also caused capital outflows from them which led to the stock market crash. When capital flows are large and volatile they hurt macroeconomic stability. Large capital inflows as they occurred in India in 2010 lead to appreciation of exchange rate of the national currency (Rupee in case of India) which adversely affects growth of our exports and encourage imports. As a result they widen current account deficit.

Owing to these adverse effects of globalisation each country decides about the extent of openneses of its economy with which it is quite comfortable by imposing some restrictions on their foreign trade, especially in financial services. Besides, because of the adverse effects of large capital inflows, some countries are trying to control them by imposing taxes on capital inflows. However, in case of India size of capital inflows are currently (2016) within our absorptive capacity. Therefore, we need not put any restrictions on capital inflows.

When there is, current account deficit of India it is financed by surplus in capital account. Thus in the years 2012-13, 2013-14, and 2014-15 it was financed by capital inflows. Thus there has been gainful absorption of foreign capital inflows. If India wants to continue to grow at a high rate of 8% to 9% there will be deficit in current account of BoP since growth in our exports cannot keep pace with our higher growth in imports due to rapid increase in our industrial activity. Current account deficit is a matter of concern only if stable capital inflows are not adequate to finance the current account deficit. It will be seen from Table 37.1 and 37.2 that from 2012-13 to 2014-15 our capital surplus [i.e. capital account (net)] exceeded our current account deficit, with the result that *there was addition to our foreign exchange reserves* (see last row of Table 37.2). Note that minus (–) sign in the use of reserves for various years implies that instead of using foreign exchange reserves in these years we added to our foreign exchange reserves. In the year 2008-09 when there was global financial crisis which caused not only negative growth in our exports but also large capital outflows from the Indian economy with the result that capital surplus in 2008-09 was quite small and fell short of our current account deficit which was quite large in this year. As a result, we withdrew $20 billion from our foreign exchange reserves to meet the current account deficit in 2008-09. Hence the plus sign before US $ 20 in 2008-09. However, after 2009-10 with the exception of the year 2011-12 there has been revival of large capital inflows with the result that our surplus on capital account (net) was $65.3 billion in 2011-12, $92 billion in 2012-13 and $88 billion in 2014-15. Therefore, after meeting deficit in current account we instead of withdrawing from our foreign exchange reserves added to them in these years. This means India successfully tackled global financial crisis and its consequences. However, in the year 2011-12 our capital inflows were not sufficient to fully meet the current account deficit (CAD) with the result that we had to withdraw $12.8 billion from our foreign exchange reserves. Therefore, there is plus sign before $12.8 billion for the use of foreign exchange reserves. For the last, four years (2012-2016) as our capital account surplus exceeded current account deficit (CAD) we added to our foreign exchange reserves. Our foreign exchange reserves are estimated to be $ 365 billion at the end of June 2016. It may be further noted that capital inflows into India through foreign direct investment have increased in recent years and therefore our current account deficit are being financed by both capital inflows as a result of foreign direct investment (FDI) and portfolio capital investment by FIIs. It in volatility of capital flows by FIIs that affect our foreign exchange rate stability, stock market prices, price stability, and thus create a good deal of macroeconomic instability.

Macroeconomic Aggregates: Aggregate Consumption, Gross Domestic Saving and Capital Formation

Having explained the various macroeconomic issues and concepts we will now study the various macro-economic aggregates which are often used to explain the working of an economy and assess its performance. The important macro-economic aggregates are: (1) aggregate consumption, (2) Gross Domestic Saving (GDS). (3) Gross Domestic Capital Formation (GDCF), In this chapter, we will explain their meaning and how they have changed in India. In the next chapter, we will explain national income aggregates and how they are measured.

AGGREGATE CONSUMPTION

Aggregate consumption is an important macro-economic aggregate which deserves detailed explanation. In fact, the standard of living of the people of a country depends on their consumption per capita which leads to the satisfaction of their wants. Aggregate consumption is an important component of aggregate demand which plays an important role in determining national income of a country. The other two components of aggregate demand are aggregate investment (i.e., gross domestic capital formation or GDP) and net exports (NX), that is, exports – imports. When in a year, growth in aggregate consumption is relatively greater than increases in aggregate investment and net exports, the growth in national income that occurs is said to be ***consumption-led growth***. On the other hand, in a year when role of increase in aggregate investment or gross capital formation is relatively more in causing expansion in national income, it is said to be *investment-led* growth. In exports-oriented economies where growth in exports play a relatively more important role in expansion of national product, it is said to be ***export-led growth***. We shall first explain the concept of aggregate consumption. Aggregate consumption is divided into two categories:

1. Private Final Consumption Expenditure (PFCE)
2. Government Final Consumption Expenditure (GFCE)

We explain below both of these consumption categories.

Private Final Consumption Expenditure (PFCE)

Private Final Consumption Expenditure (PFCF) is the money expenditure made by resident households and non-profit institutions (such as charitable organisations) on purchases of goods and services for satisfaction of their wants. Apart from the purchases of goods and services from market, private final consumption expenditure includes the value of foodgrains and other goods produced by the farmers for their self-consumption and not sold in the market. Besides, private final consumption expenditure includes *imputed value* of rent of self occupied houses by the households themselves. Further, it also includes *wages and salaries in kind* and money *value of gifts* received by the households.

PFCE is divided into three sub-categories on the basis of duration of the use of various goods and services.

1. Expenditure on *durable consumer goods* such as automobiles, televisions, referigerators, washing machines. They continue to be used for more than a year which is generally taken to be the accounting period.
2. Expenditure on *non-durable consumer goods* such as foodgrains, milk, clothing, tooth pastes, bathing soaps etc. They are consumed or used up within a year.
3. Expenditure by households on *services* such as those of teachers, lawyers, doctors, barbers etc. These services are intangibles and are used by by households at time and place when they are provided.

Government's Final Consumption Expenditure (GFCE)

The government (Central, State and local authorities) provides collective services to the people for satisfaction of their collective wants. The government consists of (a) *Administrative Departments* and (b) *government enterprises* Administrative departments which are also called *general government* (of the centre, states and local bodies) provides services such as defence, law and order, social and community services such as education, health care, sanitation.

As for government enterprises, they may be departmental enterprises such as railways, post and telegraph or non-departmental enterprises such as steel authority of India, LIC, ONGC, State Bank of India, MTNL. Both department and non-departmental enterprises produce goods and services which cover their cost of production and are also intended to make some reasonable profits. Therefore, in national income accounts, they are treated in the same way as private corporate companies.

As for general government (i.e. Government administrative departments), the collective services such as defence, law and order, health care provided by it are *not sold* by it to the households and *by* ***convention these services are valued at the costs incurred***. These costs include (1) value of *goods and services* purchased by the government for use by its employees for providing collective services and these represent *intermediate consumption,* and (2) *wages and salaries* (i.e., compensation of employees paid to government employees who are engaged in providing these services, (3) the costs incurred by the government on account of *consumption of fixed capital* for providing the services.

By summing up the data of the above three to categories of general government (administrative departments) we get Government's final consumption expenditure.

Government's Transfer Payments. It is worth noting that in addition to making expenditure on goods and services, government also makes a lot of expenditure on transfer payments. Main examples of these transfer payments are social security benefits, unemployment allowance, old age pension, interest on public debt paid to the people by the government. Against these transfer payments to the people government does not get any service in exchange in the current period.

They are therefore not counted in estimation of national income. Besides, the recipients of these transfer payments will either spend them on their consumption or use them for investment. If we count these transfer payments as a separate part of GNP we will be making the mistake of double counting.

OTHER COMPONENTS OF AGGREGATE EXPENDITURE OR AGGREGATE DEMAND

Besides private final consumption expenditure (PFCE) and government final consumption expenditure (GFCE), the two other components of aggregate expenditure are: (1) ***Gross Capital Formation*** also known as investment expenditure which comprises gross fixed capital formation (GFCE), change in stock (i.e. inventories), of goods, and (2) **net exports** which represent the difference between exports and imports of goods. The shares of different components of aggregate expenditure in Gross Domestic Product (GDP) of India at constant (2011-12) prices are shown in Table 38.1. It will be seen from this table that the private final consumption expenditure (PFCE) at constant (2011-12) prices comprises around 55.5 to 56 per cent of GDP (at constant 2011-12 prices), while government final consumption (GFCE) account for about 10 per cent of GDP.

Table 38.1: ***The Percentage Share of Various Components of Aggregate Expenditure in GDP at Constant (2011-12) Prices***

Type of Expenditure	2013-14	2014-15	2015-16
Private Final Consumption Expenditure (PFCE)	56.1	55.6	55.5
Govt. Final Consumption Expenditure (GFCE)	9.9	10.4	9.9
Gross Fixed Capital Formation (GFCE)	33.0	32.3	31.2.
Change in Stock (CIS)	1.6	1.8	1.8
Valuables	1.5	1.6	1.5
Exports of Goods & Services	25.1	23.8	20.9
Less Imports of Goods & Services	26.9	25.2	30.9
Discrepencies	–0.4	–0.3	1.9
GDP at Constant (2011-12) Prices (in ₹ crore)	9,839,434	10,552,151	11,350,249

Source: CSO

The other important component of aggregate expenditure is gross *fixed* capital formation (that is, gross fixed investment expenditure) which was 33 per cent of GDP in 2013-14 but fell to 32.3 per cent in 2014-15 and further to 31.2 per cent in 2015-16 whereas change in stock (i.e. inventory investment) has been around 1.6% to 1.8% of GDP in these years. Finally, exports of goods and services as will be seen from Table 38.1 whose share in GDP was 25 per cent in 2013-14 declined to 20.9 per cent in 2015-16, while share of imports increased from 26.9 per cent of GDP in 2013-14 to 30.9 per cent at constant (2011-12) prices. This means *net exports* as percentage of GDP at constant prices fell in 2015-16.

The last item, namely, *discrepencies* for the year 2015-16 is very large (1.9 per cent of GDP at constant prices) represents the unaccounted part of expenditure approach to GDP from the "value added approach" for measuring GDP in India. These large discrepencies in GDP estimation for 2015-16 has been a matter of severe controversy and many have challenged the estimates of real GDP growth rate of 7.6 per cent for the year 2015-16.

GROSS DOMESTIC SAVING (GDS)

It may be noted that higher GDP growth rate in India since 2003 has been caused by the acceleration in gross domestic saving (GDS) and gross capital formation (GCF). Gross domestic saving rate at current market prices which was 23.6 per cent of GDP rose to the peak level of 36.8 per cent in 2007-08 and caused higher capital formation rate and plus 9 per cent growth in GDP for three successive years (2005-06, 2006-07 and 2007-08). As will be seen from Table 38.2, gross domestic saving rate (GDS) declined to 34.6 per cent of GDP in 2011-12 and further to 33 per cent in 2013-14 and 2014-15. A glance at this table will reveal that this is due to decline in public saving from 1.5 per cent of GDP in 2011-12 to 1.2 per cent in 2014-15 and the fall in household saving rate from 23.6 per cent of GDP in 2011-12 to 19.1 per cent in 2014-15. It will be seen from Table 38.2 that it is only the saving rate of private corporate sector rose from 9.5 per cent of GDP in 2011-12 to 12.7 per cent to 2014-15.

The chief source of financing domestic capital formation is gross domestic saving. Apart from the funds kept on account of consumption of fixed capital to acquire new capital goods, the savings by households, corporate firms and government are used to finance domestic capital formation. Besides, *net capital transfers* from the rest of the world are also used to finance domestic capital formation.

Central Statistical organisation (CSO) of India which is entrusted with the task of estimating national income accounts, classifies domestic savings into three categories: (1) Domestic savings by private sector which is further divided into (a) households savings and (b) corporate sector savings (2) Public sector savings. The gross domestic saving and its components at *current market prices* as a percentage of GDP in case of India for the last four years 2011-12 to 2014-15 are shown in Table 38.2.

Table 38.2: ***India's Gross Domestic Saving and Gross Domestic Capital Formation at Current Market Prices as Per Cent of GDP at Current Market Prices***

Item	2011-12	2012-13	2013-14	2014-15
Gross Domestic Saving	34.6	33.8	33.0	33.0
Public Saving	1.5	1.4	1.3	1.2
Private Corporate Sector	9.5	10.0	10.8	12.7
House hold Saving	23.6	22.4	20.9	19.1
Physical*	16.3	15.1	13.3	11.4
Financial	7.4	7.4	7.7	7.7
Gross Domestic Capital Formation (GDCF)	39.0	38.6	34.7	34.2
Public Sector	7.5	7.2	7.1	7.4
Private Sector	29.1	28.3	26.1	25.2
Valuables	2.9	2.8	1.4	1.5
Saving-Investment Gap	–4.4	–4.8	–1.7	–1.2
Net Capital Inflow	4.4	4.8	1.7	1.2

Source: CSO

*Household physical savings include valuables of household.

GROSS DOMESTIC CAPITAL FORMATION (GDCF)

Gross domestic capital formation is another important macro-economic aggregate because the growth of the economy depends on it to a good extent. Gross domestic capital formation is also referred to as *aggregate investment* and represents the addition to the stock of physical capital goods such as factories, machines, plants and equipment which are meant for use in future production of goods and services. Thus, capital formation in a year increases *productive capacity* of an economy and therefore its *potential growth* in future. Given the sufficient demand, created productive capacity will be fully utilised which will ensure that higher growth will be actually achieved. The nationals of a country also make investment abroad by purchasing fixed assets in foreign countries. The foreign investments by the nationals of a country are *excluded* to arrive at the estimate of gross domestic capital formation.

It may be noted that some capital goods such as machinery and equipment are imported from abroad to build up the domestic stock of capital. Thus domestic capital formation has some imported components. It may be further noted that ratio of gross domestic capital formation is greater than ratio of gross domestic saving to GDP as a part of domestic capital formation has been financed by capital inflows from abroad. Gross domestic capital formation is divided into the following three categories :

(1) **Gross fixed capital formation (GFCF)** which consists of (a) addition to machinery and equipment in both the public and private sectors. (This is generally referred to as *business fixed investment*) and (b) construction of new houses (*i.e.*, residential houses), new buildings and offices and this is referred to as *residential investment*. From the viewpoint of economic growth, it is fixed capital formation that is of more importance as it represents increase in productive capacity and therefore determines future potential growth rate of the economy.

(2) **Inventory investment** which represents addition to the stocks of goods in a year. When inventories of goods decline, there is a negative inventory investment.

(3) **Investment in Valuables.** In a year the people make investment in precious metals such as gold, diamonds, platinum and jewellery. Investment in these valuables is unproductive from social point of view. In recent years in India demand for gold for investment purposes has substantially increased and a large quantity of gold has been imported from abroad. The large quantity of imports of gold from abroad has been an important factor responsible for our current account deficits.

By summing up the data of the above three items we get gross domestic capital formation (GDCF) of a year. Changes in real gross domestic capital formation in India at current market prices for the four years period (2011-12 to 2014-15) are shown in Table 38.2. It is worthwhile to note that real gross domestic capital formation (GDCF) at current market prices had shown a rising trend from 2001-02 to 2007-08 and caused higher growth in GDP. The GDCF as per cent of GDP at current market prices rose from 23.6 per cent in 2001-02 to 32.8 per cent in 2004-05 and reached at the peak level of 38.1 per cent in 2007-08. In 2008-09, due to global recession which adversely affected our exports, gross capital formations rate came down to 34.3% of GDP due to adverse investment sentiments and flight of foreign capital. As a result of fiscal stimulus measures adopted by the Government gross capital formation at current market prices as a percentage of GDP rose to 36.3 per cent in 2009-10 and 36.5 per cent in 2010-11in the old series.

As mentioned above from 2011-12 onwards CSO has calculated new series of national income and capital formation data with some changes in methodology. We have shown the Gross Fixed capital fromation data according to the new series in

Table 38.3: *Gross Fixed Capial Formation (GFCF) as per cent of GDP at Current Market Prices (New Series)*

Item	2011-12	2012-13	2013-14	2014-15	2015-16
Gross Fixed Capital Formation (GFCF)	34.3	33.4	31.6	30.8	29.3
Public Sector	7.3	7.0	7.1	7.5	–
Private Corporate Sector	11.2	11.8	11.7	12.3	–
Household Sector	15.7	14.6	12.9	11.0	–
Change in Stock	1.9	1.5	1.6	1.8	1.7

Source: CSO. Note that while in Table 38.2 GFCF is at *constant* (2011-12) market prices, in Table 38.3 the data is at *current* market prices.

Table 38.3. It will be seen from this table that in tandem with gross domestic saving at current market prices which declined from 34.6 per cent of GDP in 2011-12 to 33 per cent in 2014-15, gross fixed capital formation (GFCF), also known as fixed investment, fell from 34.3 per cent in 2011-12 to 30.8 per cent in 2014-15 and further to 29.3 per cent in 2015-16 at current market prices. This is due to sharp fall in investment by the household sector in fixed assets from 15.7 per cent in GDP in 2011-12 to 11 per cent in 2014-15. The fall in fixed investment by public sectors and household sector was partly made up by increase in fixed investment by the corporate sector which rose from 11.2 per cent of GDP in 2011-12 to 12.5 per cent at current in 2014-15. Thus, as in seen from Table 38.2 whereas gross saving of the private corporate significantly increased from 9.5 per cent of GDP at current market prices is 2011-12 to 12.7 per cent in 2014-15 (i.e. 3.2 per centage points increase), the gross fixed capital formation (GFCF) by the corporate sector increased from 11.2 per cent of GDP at current market prices in 2011-12 to 12.3 per cent in 2014-15 (i.e. only 1.1 per centage point increase). Thus fixed investment by the private corporate sector did not increase equal to the increase in its savings i.e. its retained profits. This has been partly due to the shrinkage in demand for our exports due to global slowdown in these years. Besides, due to the various scams that took place during UPA regime which led to the policy paralysis in the government caused great uncertainities and adversely affected the investment sentiments of the corporate world.

Saving-Investment Gap

The saving-investment gap, reflecting the gap between gross domestic savings and gross capital formation, increased significantly for the economy in the years 2011-12 and 2012-13. A sudden drop in the gross saving rate by 5.8 per centage points between 2007-08 and 2011-12 caused by decline in saving rate by all three segments, namely, household, private corporate sector and public section sector, the saving-investment gap as per cent of GDP rose from a negative –1.3 per cent 2007-08 to –2.3 in 2008-09, –2.8 per cent 2009-10 and 2010-11 and to a huge amount of –4.4 per cent of GDP in 2011-12 and –4.8% of GDP_{MP} in 2012-13. From Table 38.2 which gives the data of gross domestic savings (GDS) at current market prices according to new series, saving-investment gap declined shorply to –1.7 per cent of GDP_{MP} in 2013-14and further to 1.2 per cent of GDP in 2014-15. It may be noted that the saving-investment gap in an open economy implies current account deficit (CAD) which requires capital inflows to finance it. If these capital inflows are of portfolio type they are quite volatile and changes in them lead to lot of macroeconomic instability.

It is worth mentioning that, small saving-investment gap implies that gross capital formation or investment in India has been substantially financed by internal resources, that is, by domestic savings. The gross domestic saving (GDS) which as per cent of GDP at market prices was 23.6 in 2001-02 rose to 32.4 per cent in 2004-05 and further to 36.8 per cent in 2007-08 and due to increase in Government consumption expenditure as a part of fiscal stimulus, GDS fell to 32.0% of GDP in 2008-09 but rose to 33.7 per cent of GDP in 2009-10 and 2010-11 and again fell to 31.3 per cent of GDP in 2011-12 (in the old series with 2004-05 as the base).

However, it may be noted that in the short run, when there is excess capacity in the economy increase in consumption demand promotes growth in GDP. When there is already unutilized productive capacity, firms are not likely to make more investment in these circumstances, it is increase in consumption demand that will ensure more utilisation of inventories and fuller utilisation of capacity. But in the long run, it is increase in investment or gross capital formation that determine growth in GDP because investment in a year adds to the productive capacity of an economy that yields higher growth in future, It is because of increase in gross domestic investment (GDCF) from 23.6% in 2001-02 to 38.1% of GDP in 2007-08 that brought about over 9% growth of GDP from 2005-06 to 2007-08 in India. Thus in the long run increase in gross domestic capital formation or gross investment rate is the main driver of economic growth.

ROLE OF CAPITAL FORMATION IN ECONOMIC GROWTH

Capital plays a vital role in the modern productive system. Production without capital is hard for us even to imagine. Nature cannot furnish goods and materials to man unless he has the tools and machinery for manufacturing, mining, fishing, etc. If man has to work with his hands on barren soil, productivity would be very low indeed. Even in the primitive stage, man used some tools and implements to assist him in the work of production. Primitive man made use of elementary tools like bow and arrow for hunting and fishing net for catching fishes. With the growth of technology and specialisation, capital has become more complex and is of superior and advanced type. More goods can be produced with the aid of capital. In fact, higher productivity of the modern economy like that of U.S.A. is to a greater extent due to the extensive use of capital, *i.e.*, machinery, tools or implements in the production process. Capital adds greatly to the productivity of workers and hence of the economy as a whole. Because of its important role in raising productivity, capital occupies a central position in the process of economic development. In fact, capital accumulation is the very core of economic development.

Capital goods are man-made instruments of production and ***increase*** the ***productive capacity*** of the economy. Therefore, accumulation of capital goods every year greatly increases the national product or income. Capital accumulation is necessary to provide people with tools and implements of production. If the population goes on increasing and no net capital accumulation takes place, then the growing population would not be able to get necessary tools, instruments, machines and other means of production with the result that their capacity to produce would be seriously affected.

Thus, capital accumulation makes possible the use of *indirect or roundabout methods of production* which greatly increase the productivity of the workers. Under these indirect or roundabout methods of production, workers instead of working with bare hands, work with the aid of more productive tools, instruments and machinery. Under these indirect or roundabout methods some labourers and other productive resources are first employed in producing capital goods and then with the help of these capital goods other workers produce consumer goods. The greater the extent to which the methods of production would be indirect or roundabout, the greater their productivity and efficiency. But, as we have seen above, for the use of indirect or roundabout methods of production capital has to be accumulated. Therefore, we see that capital accumulation makes the use of indirect or roundabout methods of production possible and thereby greatly increases the national product and is helpful in bringing about rapid economic growth. Moreover, productivity of the workers depends upon the amount of capital per worker. The greater the quantity of capital per worker, the greater the productivity and efficiency of the worker.

From the viewpoint of economic growth capital formation is important also because it make large scale production and greater degree of specialisation possible. Thus, with capital accumulation the *advantages of large-scale production and specialisation* are obtained. The advantage of large-scale production and specialisation is that they greatly increase output and productivity and thereby bring down the *cost of production per unit*. Without adequate capital accumulation neither the scale of production can be increased nor greater specialisation and division of labour in the production process is possible. Hence, capital accumulation by increasing the scale of production and specialisation increases the production and productivity in the economy and thereby promotes economic growth.

Another important economic role of capital formation is the *creation of employment opportunities* in the country. Capital formation creates employment at two stages. First, when the capital is produced, some workers have to be employed to make capital like machinery, factories, dams, irrigation works, etc. Secondly, more men have to be employed when built-up capital is used for producing further goods. In other words, many workers have to be engaged to produce goods with the help of machines, factories etc. Thus, one sees that employment will increase as capital formation is stepped up in the economy. Now. if the population grows faster than the increase in the stock of capital the entire addition to the labour force cannot be absorbed in productive employment because not enough instruments of production will be there to employ them. This results in unemployment. The rate of capital formation must be kept sufficiently high so that, employment opportunities are enlarged to absorb the additions to the working force of the country as a result of population growth. In India in the past the stock of capital has not been growing at a fast enough rate so as to keep pace with the growth of population. That is why there is huge unemployment and underemployment in both the urban and rural areas. The fundamental solution to this problem of unemployment and underemployment is to speed up the rate of capital formation so as to enlarge employment opportunities.

Another contribution of capital accumulation is that it makes the *technological progress of the economy* possible. Different technologies need different types of capital goods. Therefore, when new, superior and better technology is discovered, its use can be made for production only if that technology is embodied in new capital goods, that is, if capital goods according to that technology are made. Therefore, without capital accumulation, not much technical progress can be made. If there is no capital accumulation, then the various new inventions or discoveries will remain unused for production. It is, therefore, clear that capital accumulation promotes technical progress and thereby accelerates the economic growth of the country.

Technological Change and Capital Formation

Capital formation and technological change are intimately related. What factors cause sustained growth of national income and per capita income is an important issue that has been the concern of economists. Capital accumulation, growth in labour force and technological progress contribute to the growth of an economy. American economist R.M. Solow[1] used the aggregate production function that relates the level of output to the levels of various

1 R.M. Solow, "Technical Change and Aggregate Production Function, *Review of Economics and Statistics*, Aug. 1957.

inputs such as growth of capital, labour and technological progress over time. Solow used the following production function:

$$Y = A(t)F(K, L) \quad \ldots (1)$$

where Y stands for output, K for capital and L for labour. The term $A(t)$ represents technological change which is taken to depend merely on time, that is, as time passes, $A(t)$ increases showing that over time technological progress enables more output to be produced with the given quantities of capital and labour. With such specification of production function technological progress does not cause any change in the relative marginal productivities of capital and labour, that is, such technological progress brings about equal increases in the productivities of the two factors and is said to be Hicks' neutral in the sense that it favours neither capital nor labour.

But the important thing to note *in the production function given above is that it represents technological progress which is* ***exogenous and disembodied***. By exogenous technological progress we mean it comes from outside the model and, therefore, the term $A(t)$ is shown outside the production function. Disembodied technological change raises the productivity of both old and new machines (i.e., capital goods) and does not depend on the rate of new investment. The disembedied technological changes is *purely organisational in nature* which permits more output to be produced from the given inputs without any new investment. That is, disembodied technological change causes a shift in the production function without disturbing capital-labour ratio. It is through organisational changes that disembedied technological change enables more output to be produced with existing inputs being used more effectively.

On the other hand, in *the* ***embodied technological change***, *the increase in investment or capital accumulation is regarded as the vehicle of technological progress*. Technological progress increases the productivity of new machines built in a period compared with old machines built in the previous periods. This implies that embodied technological change does not cause increase in the productivity of machines already in existence. About embodied technological change. Halm and Malthew in their review of the theory of economic growth write, "Technological change is embodied in new machines. Machines unalterably embody the technology of their date of construction. Machines built in different dates are therefore qualitatively dissimilar and cannot in the general case be aggregated into a single measure of capital. A separate production function is needed for each vintage. Total output is the sum of output of all vintages of capital in use."[2]

Production function of embodied technology can be written as

$$Y_t = F(K_t, L_t, A_t) \quad \ldots (2)$$

where output Y_t depends on the amount of capital (K_t), labour (L_t) and the level of technology (A_t). Note that in the production function (2), the term A_t for technology appears inside the production function as one of the endogenous inputs.

It is important to note that in the production function (2), the relationship between output and technology differs from the relationship between output and other inputs, capital and labour. This can be better understood by considering this production function in case of an individual firm which can be stated as under:

$$Y_{it} = F(K_{it}, L_{it}, A_t) \quad \ldots (3)$$

The production function (3) of the individual firm shows that output of an individual firm depends not only on its own level of capital (K_{it}) and labour (L_{it}) but also on the economy-wide level of technology. Expressing the production function in this way, the technological progress in the economy will increase the productivity of *all* firms including the firm whose production

2 E.H. Halm, and R.C. Malthew, "Theory of Economic, Growth", *A Survey of Economic Growth*, Vol. 74, 1964.

function (3) is given above. *In this formulation of production function, the technology is assumed to progress endogenously instead of being an exogenous change*. Thus, *in the concept of embodied technology, production function depends on the investment in new capital*. Technological progress fosters inventions and makes improvements in machines. Thus new improved technology is embodied in investment in new machines.

Human Capital and Education

Gross domestic product of a country depends on not only the amount of labour (i.e. work-hours) used for producing goods and services but also on its productivity. One of the important factors that determines productivity of worker is human capital, that is, education. In the modern economics, the concept of capital is not confined to physical capital such as machines, tractors, capital equipment etc. that raises productivity of labour but also includes what is called human capital. *By human capital we mean the skills and knowledge that workers acquire through education and training*. This human capital, that is, knowledge and skills, are accumulated by human beings through education during the time they spend in primary and secondary schools and upto graduation and post graduation in colleges or universities. Besides, specialised professional education such as engineering, computer training, management education and others raises greatly the productivity of workers. Therefore, accumulation of human capital is generally called *investment in people*.

Human capital though less tangible than physical capital, is similar to it in many ways. First, like physical capital, accumulation of human capital increases the ability of a country to produce more goods and services. Second, like physical capital, human capital is a produced factor of production. Producing human capital requires investment in inputs such as student time, teachers, books and libraries, college buildings. Thirdly, like the physical capital, the accumulation of human capital increases the productivity of workers and therefore causes their wages to rise. Fourthly, like the accumulation of physical capital, the accumulation of human capital requires the sacrifice of some present consumption so as to have more consumption in future.

DETERMINANTS OF CAPITAL FORMATION

Saving is essential for capital formation. But, in a modern monetary economy, savings do not directly and automatically result in the production of capital goods. Savings must be invested in order to have capital goods. In a modern economy where savings and investment are done mainly by two different classes of people, there must be certain means or mechanism whereby savings of the people are obtained and mobilised in order to give them to businessmen or entrepreneurs to invest in capital goods. Therefore, in the modern free-market economy, the process of capital formation consists of the following three stages:

(*i*) An increase in the rate of real savings so that resources that would have been devoted to the production of consumption goods should be released for the purpose of capital formation.

(*ii*) Existence of a good financial system so that the available resources are obtained by private investors for capital formation.

(*iii*) The act of investment itself so that resources are actually used for the production of capital goods.

Rate of Saving

Savings in India are classified into three groups:

1. Household Savings;
2. Corporate Savings; and

3. Government Savings.

We discuss below these categories of savings and the factors determining them.

Household Savings

Household savings comprise savings of all households and individuals, both rural and urban, and non-corporate business undertakings, partnerships and non-profitable institutions like charitable trusts. Households save when they do not spend all their incomes on consumer goods. When individuals or households save, they release resources from the production of consumer goods. Resources (workers, capital, natural resources, materials, etc.) thus released are made available for the production of capital goods. The level of savings in a country depends upon *the power to save and the will to save*. The savings of the households are either in the form of *financial assets* like bank deposits, shares, bonds, provident fund, life insurance policies, national saving certificates etc, or in the form of *physical assets* such as various capital goods, houses, etc.

1. **Level of per capita inocme and distribution of income.** The power to save or saving capacity of an economy mainly depends upon the level of per capita income and *the distribution of national income*. The greater the level of per capita income, the greater will be the amount of savings. The countries having higher levels of per capita income can save more than those with low levels of income. Keynes emphasized that it is level of disposable income that determines saving. As income rises both consumption and saving increase. Further, according to Keynes, average propensity to consume declines as income increases and therefore saving rate rises at higher levels of income. After Keynes, Milton Friedman laid stress on *permanent income* which is a reflection of wealth (both physical and human wealth) possessed by him. After Keynes, level of income has been considered as the most important factor determining saving in an economy. Further, the greater the inequalities of income, the greater will be the amount of savings in the economy. If the national income is equally distributed, much of the income will be consumed and a little would be saved. On the contrary, if national income is unequally distributed, a larger amount of savings will be done by richer people. People save during working years so that they can consume enough in the years of retirement. And interest rate affects the saving for retirement.

Apart from the power to save, the total amount of savings depends upon the will to save. Various personal, family, or national considerations induce the people to save. People save in order to provide against old age and unforeseen contengencies. Some people desire to save a large sum to start their own business or to expand the existing business. Moreover, people want to make provision for education, marriages and a good start in business for their children.

2. **Interest Rate.** Interest rate is another factor that determines supply of savings in the economy. The rise in interest rate generally brings about increase in supply of savings, though this effect is not significant. *The effect of rise in interest rate has income effect as well as substitution effect.* A rise in rate of interest increases income of the individual and therefore makes him better off. This induces him to consume more in the present. This is the income effect which tends to reduce savings. But the rise in interest rate also increases return on savings. This induces him to postpone consumption because every sacrifice of consumption (i.e. savings) will mean more consumption in the next period due to higher interest earned. This is substitution effect which tends to increase savings. Thus the substitution effect and income effect of rise in interest rate work in opposite direction. Therefore, net effect of rise in interest rate on saving is quite uncertain. Either of the two effects may dominate. As a result, higher interest rate may cause

more or less savings. However, empirical evidence shows that substitution effect outweights the income effect. As a result, there is a small net positive effect of higher interest rate on savings.[3]

Thus, a rise in the rate of interest induces the individual to save more. In this way, we can determine the saving of an individual at different rates of interest. The higher the rate of interest, the greater is the supply of saving by him. By summing up the savings of various individuals at various rates of interest we can obtain market supply curve of savings, which will slope upward showing positive relationship between rate of interest and savings. It may be noted that in case of some individuals who have a target of having a certain fixed level of income or consumption in future, a higher rate of interest will enable them to earn that fixed income by saving and lending less in this year. That is, for these individuals supply curve of saving will be backward sloping. Therefore, if those individuals who save and lend more at higher rates of interest predominate, the overall supply curve of savings slopes upward. The, empirical evidence in the United States shows that a rise in interest rate has only a small positive effect on the rate of saving. However, empirical evidence in India shows that there is significant positive relationship between interest rate and saving. Therefore, the elasticity of supply curve of saving in India is quite high.

3. **Social Security Provisions.** Social security measures adopted by the government such as state pension, unemployment allowance, free health care lower savings. Generous pension scheme reduces the need for saving for the retirement years. Similarly, the provision of free health care through the National Health Service also reduces the need for savings to meet the medical expenses. It has been pointed by some economists that low saving rate of the UK and USA is mainly due to the comprehensive social security system in these countries.

4. **Taxation System.** Taxes also affect savings by individuals. In India and other countries income tax is the main direct tax levied on individuals' incomes including interest and dividend income. It has been pointed out that income tax discourages saving. For people who keep their savings in bank deposits or use them for buying bonds and shares, tax on interest and dividends reduce after-tax return from them. "*The tax on interest income substantially reduces the future payoff from current saving and as a result reduces the incentives for people to save*"[4]. According to N.G. Mankiw, "*Low rate of saving in the United States is at least partly attributable to tax laws that discourage savings*"[5].

5. **Rate of Inflation.** Another important factor which determines the household saving in the country is the price situation. In the economy when there is high inflation rate or prices are continuously rising, value of money declines. The rise in prices or the fall in the value of money has an a adverse effect on the savings in the economy. When the value of money is declining every year due to the rise in prices, it is not profitable to save money and, therefore, propensity to save diminishes. Besides, inflation or rise in prices reduces the capacity to save of the people because a greater part of income has to be spent on essential consumption due to the rise in prices.

6. **Bequest Motive.** An important factor that determines saving of a society is bequest motive. In order to leave behind a good amount of wealth for their children some rich people save during their life. If high inheritance taxes are levied, they would discourage saving on this account. Since bequest motive is an important reason for savings by individuals,

---

3. For the evidence about the United States See J. Stiglitz, *Economics*, p. 166. But as reported by C. Rangarajan Indian experience shows that there is significant positive relationship between saving and interest rate. See his "Monetary Policy Revisited", Published in his book, *Indian Economy, Essays on Money and Finance,* UBSPD, 1998, p.24.
4. See J. Stiglitz, *op. cit p.* 176.
5. N. Gregory Mankiw, *Principles of Economics*, Second Edition, 2001, *P.* 566

especially the wealthy people, the lower inheritance taxes will have a large effect on increasing the saving rate of the economy.

7. **Precautionary Motive.** The people save for the unforeseen contingencies such as illness and periods of unemployment to protect themselves against these emergencies for which these is no insurance coverage.

8. **Purchasing Power of Assets.** The real value, that is, purchasing power of assets such as shares, bonds, houses possessed by the people also influence savings of the people. If the prices of these assets rise, people feel better off than before. This induces them to consume more and therefore save less. It has been found that when prices of assets rise, people even get more loans from the banks and spend them for consumption purposes.

Savings of all individuals in a society constitute aggregate savings of the economy. At any time, some individuals who are in working life save and others who are old and leading a retired life dissave. The retired people withdraw money from their bank accounts and/or sell shares and bonds to supplement income from their pension and other social security schemes. In determination of aggregate savings, *demographic factors* also play a role. A more slowly growing population has a proportionately larger population of old and retired people and this depresses aggregate saving rate of the economy.

9. **Growth rate of per capita income.** In addition to the current level of per capita income, *growth rate of per capita income* as emphasised by life cycle theory of consumption and saving is also an important determinant of household saving. If income per capita is not growing the task of raising the marginal rate of saving is likely to be difficult because more saving in this case has to be achieved by curtailing present consumption. If per capita income is rising due to increase in productivity it becomes possible to save relatively more out of increment in income and thereby rate of saving can be increased white increasing absolute consumption at the same time. It is noteworthy that the growth in per capita income can occur if investment in physical capital and human capital or its productivity increases. A higher rate of saving ensures higher rate of investment and thereby generates higher growth in per capita income. But the reverse is also true; a higher growth rate in per capita makes it possible to raise the rate of saving by keeping marginal rate of saving higher than average rate of saving.

10. **Policies to restrain growth in consumption.** To increase the rate of saving deliberate policies to restrain the growth of consumption have also been adopted. For example in India prior to mid 1980's industrial licensing was actively used to ensure that there was no more investment in luxury durable consumer goods like automobiles, colour TVs, air conditioners, referigerators except in small scale sectors and existing factories. Heavy excise duties were levelled on consumer goods, especially durable ones to discourage their production. Besides, to restrain the consumption of durable consumers goods heavy tariffs were levied on imports of such goods or imports of such goods were prohibited. It may however be noted that policies of using physical controls and detailed industrial licensing obstructed the rate of industrial growth. Therefore, in India with implementation of economic reforms since 1991 in the five year plans output projections for the plan periods were based on consumption requirements of the people and physical controls on the production and consumption of goods were liberalised to step up economic growth.

11. **Interest rate Policy.** To promote savings policy of following positive real interest rate has been suggested by several economists. Positive real rate of interest has been suggested for raising household savings. Real rate of interest rate is nominal rate of interest rate minus rate of inflation. Advocates of the policy of real rate of interest argue that negative real interest rate will divert savings to informal financial markets, unproductive investment (such as gold,

jewellery, luxurious houses) and will cause flight of capital from the country. Therefore, for promoting savings nominal rate of interest should be kept above rate of inflation. Positive real rate of interest also ensures efficient utilisation of resources, particularly scarce capital. Thus, rise in positive real rate of interest causes the *financial savings* of households to increase.

Public Savings

Public Savings are another source of savings. In Government savings are included the surplus of revenue obtained through taxes and surpluses from public undertakings over and above the current expenditure of the Government. Given the current consumption expenditure of the Government, the greater the revenue collected from taxes and the profits earned from public enterprises, the greater the Government or public savings. It is worth noting that all revenue earned from taxes, etc. does not constitute the public savings because a good part of the tax revenue is spent on current consumption expenditure of the Government such as civil administration, defence and other unproductive services. That part of income or revenue of the Government which is over and above the expenditure on civil administration, defence and other current consumption is called the public savings. The Government savings are used for public investment spending on building of factories, roads, irrigation facilities, and other various types of industries started in the public sector.

In India public savings of both Centre and State governments was around 2.9 per cent of GDP at market price in 1970-71, it reached its peak of 4.9 per cent of GDP in 1976-77 and started declining thereafter and in 1989-90, it fell to 1.6 per cent of G.D.P. The decline in *budgetary savings* of government as distinguished from those of public enterprises was relatively much higher. It is note worthy that trends in fiscal deficit determine the performance in public savings. The public savings increased to 2.0 per cent of GDP in 1995-96, the year in which revenue deficit was at the lowest mark in the nineties. Subsequently, with the increase in revenue deficit, public savings declined and even became negative. In 2001-02 and 2002-03 public saving was – 2.0 and –0.7 per cent of GDP respectively. Had the household savings not increased during this period, this would have led to the decline in gross domestic saving (GDS) and would have adversely affected investment and economic growth in the economy. However, after 2002-03 public sector savings became positive and rose to 3.6 per cent in 2006-07 and 5.0 per cent in 2007-08 but after this it started declining and was estimated at 1.2 per cent of GDP in 2014-15 at current market prices.

The huge combined fiscal deficit of the centre and the states which presently (2014-15) constitutes around 8 per cent of Gross Domestic Product is adversely affecting saving and investment in the economy and therefore the rate of economic growth of the Indian economy. To quote Shankar Acharya, a former economic advisor to the Ministry of Finance "It is quite interesting how the deterioration of about 3 per cent points of GDP in the consolidated revenue deficit between 1995-96 to 1998-99 is reflected strongly in the worsening of aggregate savings and investment ratios over the period. It would be hard to find more telling evidence of the adverse impact of fiscal deficit on savings and investment. Another way to look at this is that if the fiscal deficit deterioration from1995-96 to 2000-01 had not occurred, saving and investment might well have been higher by around 3 per cent points of GDP in recent years"[6]

The above analysis underlines the importance of measures to reduce fiscal deficit, particularly revenue deficit, if rate of saving and investment in the Indian economy is to be raised to accelerate the rate of economic growth. For this purpose base of taxation must be widened by withdrawing the several exemptions in income and wealth taxes as suggested

6. Shankar Acharya, "Macroeconomic Management in the Nineties", *Economic and Political Weekly*, April, 20, 2000, p.1525.

by various committees.[7] Besides, the subsidies must be well targeted so that only the poor should take advantage of them and the remaining subsidies must be phased out. Further, to reduce revenue deficit, non-plan non-essential government expenditure must be reduced along with the reforms in the taxation system. However, care should be taken to avoid any cut in Government expenditure on education and health which promotes accumulation of human capital and have a beneficial effect on economic growth.

It may be pointed out that savings may be either voluntary or forced. Voluntary savings are those which people make of their own free will. As explained abvoe, voluntary savings depend upon the power to save and will to save of the people. On the other hand, taxes by the Government represent forced savings.

Private Corporate Savings

Furthermore savings may be done not only by households and Government but also by corporate business enterprises. Business enterprises save when they do not distribute whole of their profits but retain a part of them in the form of undistributed profits. They then use these undistributed profits for investment in real capital. In advanced countries like U.S.A. and England, these corporate savings form the largest part of the total savings. In U.S.A. England, corporate savings, *i.e.*, undistributed profits constitute about 50% to 60% of the total annual domestic savings. Note that *savings of unincorporated business enterprises are included in household savings*. Savings of corporate sector in India are shown separately in Table 38.1. It will be seen from this table that the corporate sector, which operates in the organised sector, though contribute significantly to gross National Product their saving makes only a small contribution to gross domestic savings. The corporate savings which contributed on an annual average of 2.0 per cent of GDP to gross domestic saving rose to 4.9 per cent of GDP in 1996-97. Thereafter, it declined to 3.7 per cent of GDP in 1998-99 but rose to 4.7 per cent in 2003-04. Since 2004-05 these has been a significant increase in corporate sector saving which rose to 7.5% in 2005-06, to 8 per cent in 2006-07 and reached the peak level to 9.4 per cent of GDP in 2007-08 before falling to 7.4% in 2008-09. Since 2010-11, private corporate sector savings has substantially increased; it rose to 10.8 per cent of GDP in 2013-14 and further to 12.7% in 2014-15. Liberalisation regime initiated in India since 1991 providing for reduction in tariff rates on imported raw materials, reduction in corporate tax, and excise duties resulted in higher corporate saving in 1995-96 and 1996-97. These liberal policies have continued thereafter. The increase in corporate saving in these years (since 2004-05) is attributed to the low interest rate policy pursued by the RBI to boost investment, large increase in profitability of the corporate sector, policy of payment of lower dividends to the shareholders, reduction in corporate income tax, various tax exemptions to increase investment and ensure fuller utilisation of productive capacity.

Financial System

Next step in the process of capital formation is that the savings of households must be mobilised and transferred to businessmen or entrepreneurs who require them for investment. In the capital market, funds are supplied by the individual investors (who may buy securities or shares issued by the companies). Banks, investment trusts, life insurance companies, finance corporations, are other financial institutions which mobilise savings for investment purposes. In India, there is also unorganised capital market constituting indigenous bankers and money-lenders. If the rate of capital formation in the private sector is to be stepped up, the development of sound capital market and financial system

7. Recently Kelkar Committee has recommended reforms in taxation system on these lines.

is very necessary. Well-developed financial system (both capital market and banking system) will ensure that the savings of the society will be mobilised and transferred to the entrepreneurs or businessmen who require them for investment.

Investment

For savings to result in capital formation and economic growth they must be invested. Further, for investment of savings to take place, there must be a good number of honest and dynamic entrepreneurs in a country who are willing to take risks and bear uncertainty of production.

Marginal Efficiency of Capital and Rate of Interest. Given that a country has got enough good and venturesome entrepreneurs, investment will be made by them only if there is sufficient *inducement to invest*. Inducement to invest depends on *marginal efficiency of capital*, (*i.e.*, expected rate of return or profit) on the one hand, and real rate of interest on the other. If expectations about profit are quite bright, that is, when entrepreneurs expect large profits from investment, marginal efficiency of capital or investment will be higher and investment will be made on a large scale. If profits are expected to be low, investment made will also be small. Keynes laid greater emphasis on expectations of entrepreneurs in determining marginal efficiency of capital and, therefore, changes in expectations regarding earnings or future profits will cause an upword shift in the investment demand curve. The other factor, according to Keynes, that determine investment is rate of interest. It is generally believed that at a lower real rate of interest, investment is more and at a higher real rate of interest, investment is less. In other words, it means that when credit is cheaper, businessmen will borrow more funds for undertaking investment projects. On the other hand, a higher rate of interest will discourage investment in those projects return from which is lower.

Of the two determinants of inducement to investment, namely, marginal efficiency of capital and the rate of interest, it is the former which is of greater importance. Marginal efficiency of capital depends upon the *cost or supply price of capital* as well as the *expectations of profits*. Fluctuations in investment are mainly due to the changes in expectations regarding profits. But it is *the size of market* (*i.e.*, level of demand for goods) which ultimately determines the scope for profitable investment. Thus primary factor which determines the level of investment or capital formation in an economy is the *size of market* for goods. Demand for capital equipment like machinery depends upon the demand for goods it helps to produce. The inducement to invest is limited by the size of the market *i.e.* the demand for the goods. The greater the size of the market, the greater will be the inducement to invest. The small size of the market will discourage the entrepreneurs to make investment. Many poor developing countries have a small market and this is a great hurdle in the way of capital formation in these countries.

Animal Spirits and Investment. J.M. Keynes who emphasised that marginal efficiency of capital played a crucial role in determining investment also laid stress on animal spirits of entrepreneurs for causing fluctuations in investment. By animal spirits, Keynes means the ***waves of optimism and pessimism*** which quite often grip business class and greatly affect their investment behaviour. Keynes attributed the drastic fall in private investment in the 1930s to the collapse of marginal efficiency of capital which was caused by wave of pessimism among the business class about profit earnings in future which resulted in stock market crash in England. Even in India lack of confidence among business class resulting from their animal spirits has been responsible for slowdown of private investment from 1997 to 2000, and again in 2008-09 and 2011-12 and 2012-13.

Availability of Infrastructure. Private investment is also affected by the availability of infrastructure such as power, good roads and means of transport, good means of communication, good ports, etc. Investment in the Indian economy is often impeded by lack of good infrastructure. It has therefore been suggested that *public investment in infrastructure not only generates demand for the industrial products but also leads* to the expansion of infrastructural facilities such as power, ports, roads etc. Thus, in the Indian context public investment helps to solve both the supply-side and demand-side problems of private sector investment. Therefore, in India the greater public investment *crowds* in private investment rather than *crowding it out*.

Taxation Policies. Taxation policies of the Government also affect investment behaviour of the corporate sector. High corporate taxes discourage private investment. For example, high corporation income tax, tax on dividend distribution, high excise duties and tariffs adversely affect corporate sector investment by lowering the profitability of investment. Threfore, to increase corporate investment, investment-friendly taxation policies need to be adopted.

Availability of Credit. Apart from internal savings, the corporate sector gets investment funds from the capital market and banks. To meet their needs for working capital, they rely on bank credit. Therefore, to ensure greater private investment adequate credit facilities must be made available.

Stock Market Situation. Besides, corporate sector raises its equity capital from the stock market. Therefore, the working of stock markets must be improved and made fair and transparent so that people should have confidence in fair dealings at the stock market. For instance, stock market crash in 1992 engineered by Harshad Mehta and later by Ketan Parikh and scams involving UTI had badly shaken the confidence of small investors who withdrew from the market. Again when share prices crashed (BSE which was around 21000 in Jan. 2008 fell below 8000 in Dec. 2008 due to aggressive sale of shares by FIIs as a result of financial crisis in the US, investors lost confidence about making profits on their investment. This created difficulties for private corporate sector for raising investment funds from the stock market through issue of equity capital.

National Income Aggregates (GDP & GNP) and their Measurement

NATIONAL INCOME AND NATIONAL PRODUCT

An important thing to understand in macroeconomics is how national income of a country is related to national product, that is, to the value of final goods and services produced in a country in a year. In fact, in an economy with no government and no foreign trade *national income and national product are the same thing from two different viewpoints*. The sum of all incomes of the people of a country is called national income. This national income is greatly related to the national product. In fact in a two sector economy without the government and its imposition of indirect taxes and grant of subsidies and also assuming no depreciation national income and national product are one and the same thing. The incomes which different people of the society get are obtained by them for their contribution of labour, land, capital and entrepreneurial services to the national production. Hence the income which the labourers get are wages for the productive services which they lend to the various firms which undertake the work of production. Similarly, the owners of land get income as rent because of their contribution of land to the productive firms; the capitalists get interest for lending their money capital to the entrepreneurs for undertaking any work of production or business. The entrepreneurs get profits for starting and organising the work of production and bearing risk and uncertainty involved in it. It is thus clear that the different individuals of a country obtain their income either as wages of their labour, or as interest on their money capital, or as rent for their land, or as profits for their enterprise. The sum of incomes obtained as wages, rent, interest and profits is the national income of the country.

Various households obtain their income from the productive firms or businesses which utilise their labour, land, capital and other services for the production of goods and services. The incomes earned by the various households and individuals from the work of production are in fact costs of production of the goods produced. The total value of all final goods and services produced by various productive firms or businesses in a year is known as national product. Therefore, the national product of a country can be estimated by multiplying the total output of final goods and services with their market prices.

Hence the total national product in terms of rupees or value, which is produced by various productive firms in a year, will be distributed among the various productive factors which have contributed to its production. Therefore, out of this national production (in value terms) wages will be paid to those households which have sold their labour to the productive firms. Out of this total value of the national product, land owners would get rent for the contribution of the services of land and capitalists would get interest for lending money capital to the productive firms. After the payment of wages, rent, interest, what is left is the profits of the entrepreneurs who set up productive firms, organise their work and bear risk and uncertainty and because of these services they get profits. It is thus clear the national product (value of total output of final goods and services in a year of a country) is distributed among wages, rents, interests and profits. As we have stated above, the sum of total wages, total interest, total rents and total profits is national income. Hence national product will be equal to the national income. The above conclusion that in a two-sector economy national income equals national product can be expressed in the form of the following equation :

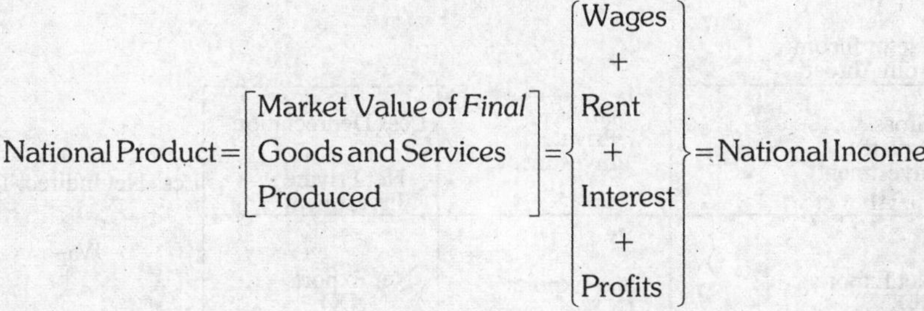

From the above analysis it is evident that in an economy with no government and no foreign trade national income and national product are one and the same thing. Professor J.R. Hicks rightly writes, "*The value of the net social product of the community and the sum of the incomes of its members are exactly equal. The net social product and the social income are one and the same thing.*"[1]

It needs to be emphasised that the above conclusion regarding equality of national product and national income is valid only in our simple two sector economy where we have assumed no depreciation funds are kept and also no role of government (and therefore no indirect taxes collected by it and no subsidies granted by it). In case of a real economy, firms keep a part of some value created as depreciation allowance which therefore do not become a part of the income of the factors. When role of government is brought into our analysis, a part of the value of output is taken away by the government as indirect taxes and therefore the incomes of factor owners are reduced to that extent. Thus, only in the absence of depreciation funds and net indirect taxes, national product will be equal to national income. In our simple economy we assume away these depreciation funds and net indirect taxes levied by the government on business firms to emphasise the point that national income does not come out of thin air, it is in fact generated by the production of goods and services. Therefore, growth in national income can be achieved by the increase in production of goods and services.

NATIONAL INCOME AGGREGATES

There are various concepts of national income which we explain below and spell out how they are different from each other.

Gross Domestic Product (GDP)

This is the basic national accounting measure of the total output or aggregate supply of goods and services. *Gross Domestic Product is defined as the total market value of all final goods and services produced in a year in the domestic territory of a country.* Two things must be noted in

1. J.R Hicks, *Social Framework*

regard to gross domestic product. First, it measures the market value of annual output. In other words, GDP is a *monetary measure*. There is no other way of adding up the different sorts of goods and services produced in a year except in terms of their money prices. But in order to know accurately the changes in physical output over time, the figure for gross domestic product is adjusted for price changes.

Secondly, for calculating gross domestic product (GDP) accurately, *all goods and services produced in any given year must be counted once, and not more than once*. Most of the goods go through a series of production stages before reaching a market. As a result, parts or components of many goods are bought and sold many times. Hence to avoid double counting the parts of goods that are sold and resold, gross domestic product includes the market value of only *final goods* and ignores transactions involving intermediate goods.

Net Factor Income from Abroad			
Gross Private Investment (I)	Gross Private Investment (I)	Less Depreciation	
		Net Private Investment	Less Net Indirect Taxes
Net Exports (NX)	Net Exports (NX)	Net Exports (NX)	Wages + Profits Saving + Interest + Rent
Government Purchases (G)	Government Purchases	Government Purchases (G)	
Consumption Expenditure (C)	Consumption Expenditure (C)	Consumption Expenditure (C)	
GNP_{MP}	GDP_{MP}	NDP_{MP}	NDP_{FC}

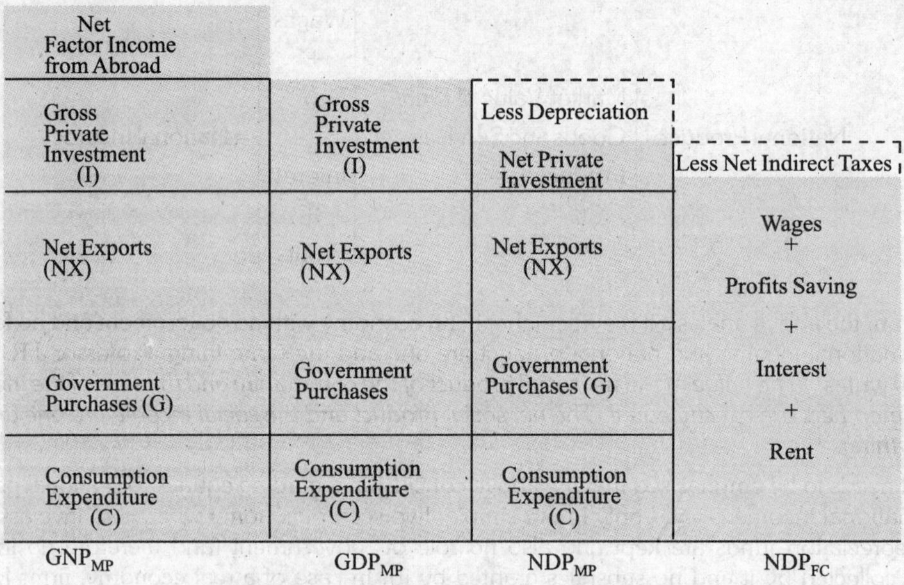

Fig. 38A.1. *Various Concepts of National Product*

Final Goods and Intermediate Goods. What do we mean by *final goods*? Final goods are those goods which are purchased for final use and not for resale or further processing. Intermediate goods, on the other hand, are those goods which are purchased for further processing or for resale. The sale of intermediate goods is excluded from gross national product. Why? Because the value of final goods includes the value of all intermediate goods used in their production. The inclusion of intermediate goods would involve double counting and will therefore give an exaggerated estimate of gross domestic product. An example will clarify this point. Suppose in our economy only two things are being produced, raw cotton worth ₹ 1000 and cotton cloth worth ₹ 2000. Now what will be the measure of gross national product? For finding it, if we add up the sales value of cloth and cotton, there is clearly an element of *double counting* in the sense that we have added the value of cotton *twice*—one as the sales value of cotton and secondly when we added to it the value of cloth. Actually, the value of cloth includes also the value of cotton which having been used in the production of cloth should not be added second time.

Further, it is worth noting that Gross Domestic Product (GDP) includes only *currently produced* goods and services in a year. It is a *flow measure* of output of goods and services per time period, say in a year. In it only *final goods and services produced in a particular year* are included. Market transactions involving goods produced in previous periods such as old houses, cars, factories built earlier are not included in GDP of the current year. Similarly, purchase and sale of assets such as stock and bonds do not involve current production of goods and are therefore excluded from GDP of the year.

Lastly, Gross Domestic Product (GDP) refers to the value of *final* goods and services currently produced by *producers in the domestic territory of a country in a year.* These producers may be national or non-national companies. Thus, many foreign companies such as Pepsi Cola and Coca Cola have set up plants in India. They are owned by non-nationals but work to produce goods and services within the domestic territory of India and generate incomes for the Indian people employed in them. These foreign companies can only send back profits earned by them to their own countries.

Gross domestic product has the following components:

1. Value of *final consumer goods and services* produced in a year and consumed by the households which is referred to as *consumption* (*C*) by households.
2. Value of *new capital goods produced and addition to the inventories of goods* in a year such as raw materials, unfinished goods and consumer goods produced but not sold during a year. This is called *Gross Investment* (*I*) or Gross Capital formation on (GCF).
3. Value of output of General Government which is taken to be equal to the value of *purchases of goods and services by the Government* which we denote by *G*.
4. Net Exports (NX) which is equal to value of goods *exported* (X) minus the value of goods *imported* (*M*), that is, $NX = X - M$.

Thus, we obtain Gross Domestic Product (GDP) at market prices by adding up the above four components.

$$GDP = C + I + G + NX$$

where $NX = X - M$

Gross Domestic Product (GDP) is graphically shown by the second bar in Fig. 38A.1.

Note that the above concept of GDP is calculated using *market prices* of goods. It is worthwhile to note that in India in the new series of national income accounts (with 2011-12 as the base) *rate of economic growth is measured in terms of Gross Domestic Product at Market Prices* (GDP_{MP}), *while earlier it was measured in terms of GDP at factor cost.*

Gross National Product (GNP)

Another important concept of national income is gross national product (GNP). *Gross national product is the money value of all final goods and services produced in the domestic territory of a country but also includes net factor income earned from abroad.* Thus difference between gross domestic product (GDP) and gross national product (GNP) at market prices arises due to the existence of '*net factor income from abroad*'. Gross domestic product does not include net factor income from abroad, whereas gross national product includes it. Therefore,

$$GNP_{MP} = GDP_{MP} + \text{net factor income from abroad}$$

It should however be noted that net factor income from abroad should not be confused with income from *net exports* which are a part of both gross national product (GNP) and gross domestic product (GDP). *Net exports equal total exports minus imports*. Gross exports are the total value of domestically produced goods and services sold to foreign buyers in a year and are therefore a part of Gross Domestic Product (GDP) and not a factor income from abroad. On the other hand, imports are the value of imported goods and services purchased by the domestic buyers from abroad and not produced inside the country. Therefore, imports do not form a part of GDP or GNP. In national income accounting, we subtract the value of imports from the value of exports to arrive at net exports which are a part of GDP and therefore also of GNP. Thus, earnings from net exports are quite distinct from net factor income from abroad.

Thus, we can obtain Gross National Product (GNP) by adding to Net Income from Abroad to the four items of Gross Domestic Product listed above. Thus,

$$GNP_{MP} = C + I + G + NX + \text{Net Income from abroad}$$

where $NX = X - M$

We have graphically depicted GDP_{MP} by second bar in Fig. 38A.1.

We explain below net factor income from abroad.

Net Factor Income From Abroad: Now, what does net factor income from abroad stand for? The sum of factor incomes such as wages and salaries (*i.e.*, compensation of employees), rent, interest and profits generated within the domestic territory of a country in a year is called *domestic factor income*. It includes factor incomes generated both by residents and non-nationals working in the domestic territory of a country. For example, non-residents (*i.e.*, foreigners) work in the domestic territory of India and earn wages and salaries. Besides, foreign individuals and companies from the USA, Great Britain and other countries have acquired property such as factories, offices, buildings in India and have also acquired financial assets such as bonds and shares of Indian companies. This generates incomes in the form of rent, interest and dividends to them. In addition to this, foreign residents—individuals and companies—have set up industrial plants and factories producing goods and services from which they earn profits. The factor incomes have to be paid to non-residents (i.e., foreigners) who work in the domestic territory of a country.

On the other hand, some normal residents of India go abroad and work in the territories of other countries and earn wages and salaries. Likewise, some resident Indian individuals and corporate companies have acquired assets such as buildings, factories, commercial space, and have also invested in bonds, bank deposits of foreign countries and thus receive rent, interest and dividends. Some Indian companies have set up factories abroad and earn profits. Thus, some nationals of India receive factor incomes from abroad.

Now, the *net factor income from abroad is the difference between factor incomes such as wages, rent, interest and profits received from abroad by normal residents of India for rendering factor services in other countries minus such factor incomes paid to the foreign residents for factor services rendered by them in the domestic territory of India.*

Gross Domestic Product at Factor Cost (GDP_{FC})

The concept of Gross Domestic Product at factor cost (GDP_{FC}) is distinguished from Gross Domestic Product at market prices (GDP_{MP}). Gross Domestic Product at factor costs (GDP_{FC}) measures the *sum total of factor incomes earned* by suppliers for the *services of their* factors which they provide for the production of goods and services in a year. Market prices of goods and services are raised by the inclusion of various indirect taxes (such as excise duty, sales tax, service tax) levied by the government but are reduced by the subsidies paid by the government on the production of goods and services. Therefore, to derive Gross Domestic Product at factor cost (GDP_{FC}), gross domestic product at market prices (GDP_{MP}) is adjusted by *substracting indirect taxes net of subsidies*. Thus,

$$GDP_{FC} = GDP_{MP} - \text{Indirect taxes} + \text{Subsidies}$$

$GDP_{FC} = GDP_{MP} -$ Net Indirect Taxes where net indirect taxes are excess of indirect taxes over subsidies

Net National Product (NNP) or Net National Income at Market Prices (NNI_{MP})

The other important concept of national income is that of net national product (NNP). In the production of gross national product of a year, we consume or use up some fixed capital *i.e.*, equipment, machinery, etc. The capital goods, like machinery, wear out or fall in value as a result of its consumption or use in the production process during a year. This *consumption of fixed capital* or fall in the value of fixed capital due to wear and tear during a year is called *depreciation*. When charges for depreciation are deducted from the gross national product we get net national product. Clearly, net national product it means the *market value of all final goods and services* produced in the domestic territory of a country including net factor income from abroad in a year after providing for depreciation. Therefore, it is also called *'net national income at market prices'*. Therefore,

Net National Product at Market Prices (NNP_{MP}) = Gross National Product – Depreciation

Similarly, Net Domestic Product at market prices (NDP_{MP}) is obtained by deducting depreciation from Gross Domestic Product at market prices (GDP_{MP}). Thus

$NDP_{MP} = GDP_{MP} - \text{Depreciation}$

Net National Product at Factor Cost (NNP_{FC})

Net National Product at factor cost which means the sum of all *incomes earned* by suppliers of factors of production for their contribution of land, labour, capital and entrepreneurial ability which go into the year's net production. In other words, national income (or net national product at factor cost) shows how much it costs society in terms of economic resources to produce net output. The difference between net national product at factor cost and net national product at market prices arises from the fact that *indirect taxes* and *subsidies* cause market prices of output to be different from the factor incomes earned from producing it. Suppose for instance, a metre of mill cloth sold for ₹ 200 includes ₹ 25 on account of the excise and the sales tax. In this case, while the market price of the cloth is ₹ 200 a metre, the factors engaged in its production and distribution would receive ₹ 175 a metre. The value of cloth at factor cost would thus be equal to its value at market price less the indirect taxes on it. On the other hand, a subsidy causes the market price to be less than the factor cost. Suppose handloom cloth is subsidised at the rate of ₹ 10 per metre and it sells at ₹ 90 per metre. Then while the consumer pays ₹ 90 per metre, the factors engaged in the production and distribution of such cloth will receive ₹ 100 per metre (₹ 90 + 10 = ₹ 100). The value of handloom cloth at factor cost would thus be equal to its market price plus the subsidies paid on it. It follows, therefore, that the national income (or national income at factor cost) is equal to net national product minus indirect taxes plus subsidies. Net National Product at factor cost (NNP_{FC}) is also called national income (NI).

Net National Product at Factor Cost = Net National Product at Market Prices – Indirect Taxes + Subsidies

Net of indirect taxes and subsidies is also called Net Indirect Taxes. Therefore,

National Income = Net National Product at market prices – Net Indirect Taxes

Net National Product at factor cost or $NNP_{FC} = NNP_{MP}$ – Net Indirect Taxes

Personal Income (PI)

Personal Income is the sum of all *incomes actually received* by all individuals or households during a given year. National income, that is, total *incomes earned* and personal income, that is, total *incomes received* must be different because some incomes which are earned such as social security contributions, corporate income taxes and undistributed corporate profits are not actually received by households, and conversely, some incomes which are received by them like transfer payments are not currently earned (examples of transfer payments are old-age pensions, unemployment compensation, relief payments, interest payments on the public debt, etc.). Obviously, in moving from national income as an indicator of income earned to personal income as an indicator of income actually received, we must *subtract* from national income those three types of income which are *earned but not received* and *add* those incomes which are *received but currently not earned*. Therefore,

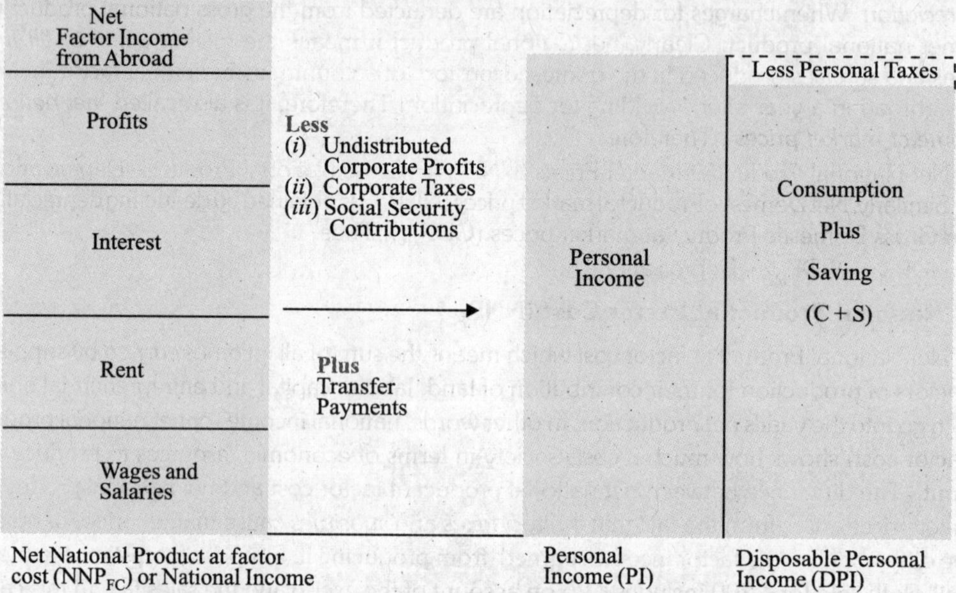

Fig. 38A.2. *From National Income (NNP_{FC}) to Disposable Income*

Personal Income = National Income (NNP_{FC})– Social Security Contributions – Corporate Income Taxes – Undistributed Corporate Profits + Transfer Payments.

Disposable Personal Income (DPI)

Even whole of the incomes which are actually received by the people are *not available to them for consumption*. This is because governments levy some personal taxes such as income tax, personal property taxes. Therefore, after a part of personal income is paid to government in the form of *personal taxes* like income tax, personal property taxes, etc., what remains of personal income is called *disposable personal income*. Therefore,

Disposable Personal Income = Personal Income – Personal Taxes.

Disposable Personal Income can be either consumed or saved. Hence,

Disposable Personal Income = Consumption + Saving.

How do we get personal income and disposable income from national income is illustrated in Fig. 38A.2.

ITEMS THAT ARE EXCLUDED FROM GNP AND GDP

As has been explained above, GNP or GDP is the total market value of all final goods and services produced in a year. But in the real world many transactions occur which though involve final goods and services but they have to be excluded from the measurement of Gross National Product. In addition to this, there are certain non-market activities and illegal transactions whose true value cannot be measured easily. Therefore, they are also excluded from the measurement of Gross National Product. We explain below some of the activities and transactions which are excluded while estimating GNP of a country.

1. **Buying and Selling of Securities.** The sale of securities such as shares and bonds of business firms are not included in the measurement of Gross National Product. The sale and purchase of shares and bonds involve only transfer of ownership rights of the assets. No new assets are created in the transaction and they are therefore excluded while measuring the value of national product.

2. **Government Transfer Payments.** Transfer payments by the government such as unemployment benefits, old age pension, interest on public debt are the payments for which no goods or services are provided in exchange by the recipients in the current year. Therefore, the government transfer payments are excluded from the value of GNP.

3. **Private Transfer Payments.** Examples of private transfer payments are pocket money given by the parents to their children, gifts by elders to the young ones, etc. These payments also involve only transfer of money from one individual to another and are not the rewards for the contribution of the recipients to the production of goods and services in a year. They are therefore not included in the estimation of national product.

4. **Sale of Used Goods.** In the estimation of gross national product we also do not count the sale and purchase of used goods such as sale of old cars, second hand air conditioners, old houses, etc. This is because GNP measures the value of final goods and services produced *in a given year*. Since old or second hand goods were produced in the earlier years, their value is excluded while measuring value of output of the current year.

5. **Non-Market Goods and Services.** GNP generally measures those goods and services which are sold and bought in the market. Therefore, vegetables grown by some households in their backyards instead of buying them from the market, the works such as repairing of electricity fault by the house owners themselves etc. are not included in the measurement of GNP. In this connection a widely quoted example of non-market transaction is housewife's services rendered to her husband and other members of the family. Since the housewives are not paid for their services, they are not included in the measurement of GNP.

However, exception to the above rule must be mentioned. In the developing countries a large number of farmers use a good part of food grains and other agricultural products produced by them for their self-consumption and are not brought in the market for sale. If we exclude them from the measurement of GNP, we will be greatly reducing the value of GNP of the developing countries. *Therefore, in developing countries, the value of the agricultural products used for self-consumption by the farmers is counted in the estimation of GNP.* The value of the output used for self-consumption is obtained by valuing them at the prevailing market prices.

6. **Illegal Activities and Transactions.** Incomes earned from illegal activities such as smuggling, gambling, drug trafficking, prostitution, sale of illegal arms etc. are not counted in the estimation of GNP. This is because it is difficult to know the exact value of the transactions involving these illegal activities. These illegal activities are done in what is called ***'underground economy'*** and are unreported or unaccounted because they are unlawful and also involve evasion of taxes.

7. **The Value of Leisure.** Leisure is regarded as a normal economic good. The other things being equal, more leisure a person has, the greater his satisfaction. When people become richer, they prefer to have more leisure and reduce their work effort. The reduction in work effort leads

of the fall in GNP. However, this does not mean that people's welfare will decrease as a result of more leisure and less GNP. Though more leisure increases the welfare of the people, it is difficult to measure its true value. Therefore, the value of leisure enjoyed by the residents is excluded from the measurement of GNP.

MEASUREMENT OF NATIONAL INCOME

Since *factor incomes* arise from the production of goods and services, and since incomes are spent on goods and services produced, three alternative methods of measuring national income are possible.

1. Value Added Method

This is also called *production method*. In this method, the contribution of each productive enterprise and sector to the addition in value by them in the production of goods and services is measured. *Value added by an enterprise is the value of goods or services* produced minus the *value of inputs* used for their production. Value of inputs used is also called *intermediate consumption*. Under this method, the economy is divided into different industrial sectors such as agriculture, fishing, mining, construction, manufacturing, trade and commerce, transport, communication and other services. It is important to mention here that in India since 2014-15 there have been significant changes in value-added method to measure national income. We describe here the new value-added method. In this method, first, the gross value added at basic price (GVA) by each productive enterprise as well as by each industry or sector is estimated. Measuring gross value added at basic price (GVA_{BP}) by each industry requires first to find out the value of output. By basic market prices we mean the market prices which do not incorporate the impact of *indirect taxes* (i.e. taxes on products including import duties) and *subsidies* on these prices. Value of output of an enterprise or industry is found out by multiplying the physical output with basic prices of the goods produced. It should be noted that value of output produced is equal to the *sales* of output plus the change in stock. Thus

$$\text{Value of output by an enterprise} = \text{Sales} + \text{Change in stock}$$

Then in order to arrive at the *gross value added (GVA) by an enterprise* we have to subtract the intermediate consumption (which is the value of inputs such as raw materials, fuels purchased from other enterprises) from the value of output of an enterprise. Thus

$$GVA_{BP} = \text{Value of output} - \text{Intermediate Consumption}$$

Summing up the gross values added at (ΣGVA_{BP}) of all productive enterprises of an industry or sector gives us the gross value added at basic market prices of each industry or sector. *We then add up gross values added at basic prices by all industries and sectors to get* gross value added of the economy

Thus, ΣGVA_{BP} of all sectors = GVA_{BP} of the economy as a whole

Gross value added at basic prices (GVA_{BP}) is a basic measure of national income and is reported separately by CSO in the new value-added method adopted in India since 2014-15.

GVA_{BP} and GDP_{MP}

In the new value-added method used in India, Gross Domestic Product at market prices (GDP_{MP}) is obtained by *adding* indirect taxes (i.e. taxes on products including import duties) and *subtracting* the subsidies. Thus

$$GDP_{MP} = GVA_{BP} + \text{Indirect taxes} - \text{Subsidies}$$

[Note the difference from the old value added method used to measure national income in which the sum of GVA_{MP} (Gross value added market prices) of all productive enterprises of all industries and sectors equal GDP_{MP}. Thus in old methodology $\Sigma GVA_{MP} = GDP_{MP}$]

Now by deducting depreciation (i.e. consumption of fixed capital from GDP_{MP} we get *Net Domestic Product at market prices* (NDP_{MP})).

This method of calculating national income can be used where there exists a census of production for the year. In many countries, the data of production of only important industries are known. Hence this method is employed along with other methods to arrive at the national income. In India both value added method and expenditure methods are used to measure national income. The one great advantage of this method is that it reveals the relative importance of the different sectors of the economy by showing their respective contributions to the national income.

Precautions. The following precautions should be taken while measuring national income of a country through value added method:

1. *Imputed rent values* of self-occupied houses should be included in the value of output. Though these payments are not made to others, their values can be easily estimated from prevailing values in the market.
2. Sale and purchase of *second-hand goods* should not be included in measuring value of output of a year because their values were counted in the year of output of the year of their production. Of course, commission or brokerage earned in their sale and purchase has to be included because this is a new service rendered in the current year.
3. *Value of production for self-consumption* is to be counted while measuring national income. In this method, the production for self-consumption should be valued at the prevailing market prices.
4. *Value of services of housewives* are *not included* because it is not easy to find out correctly the value of their services.
5. Value of intermediate goods *must not be counted* while measuring value added because this will amount to double counting.

2. Income Method

This method approaches national income from distribution side. In other words, this method measures national income at the phase of distribution and appears as income paid and or received by individuals of the country. Thus, under this method, *national income is obtained by summing up the incomes of all individuals of a country*. Individuals earn incomes by contributing their own services and the services of their property such as land and capital to the national production. Therefore, national income is calculated by adding up the rent of land, wages and salaries of employees, interest on capital, profits of entrepreneurs (including undistributed corporate profits) and incomes of self-employed people. This method of estimating national income has the great advantage of indicating the distribution of national income among different income groups such as landlords, owners of capital, workers, entrepreneurs. Measurement of national income through income method involves the following main steps:

1. Like the value added method, the first step in income method is also to *identify* the productive enterprises and then *classify* them into various industrial sectors such as agriculture, fishing, forestry, manufacturing, transport, trade and commerce, banking, etc.

2. The second step is to classify *the factor payments*. The factor payments are classified into the following groups:

1. *Compensation of employees* which includes wages and salaries, employers' contribution to social security schemes.
2. *Ren.*
3. *Interest*
4. *Profits*: Profits are divided into three subgroups:
   (*i*) Dividends

(*ii*) Undistributed profits
(*iii*) Corporate income tax

5. *Mixed income of the self-employed*:

In India as in other developing countries there is fifth category of factor income which is termed as *mixed income of self-employed*. In India a good number of people are engaged in household industries, in family farms and other unorganised enterprises. Because of self-employment nature of the business it is difficult to separate wages for the work done by the self-employed from the surplus or profits made by them. Therefore, the incomes earned by them are mix of wages, rent, interest and profit and are, therefore, called *mixed income of the self-employed*.

3. The third step is to *measure factor payments*. Income paid out by each enterprise can be estimated by gathering information about the number of units of each factor employed and the income paid out to each unit of every factor. Price paid out to each factor multiplied by the number of units of each factor employed would give us the factor's income.

4. The *adding up of factor payments* by all enterprises belonging to an industrial sector would give us the incomes paid out to various factors by a *particular* industrial sector.

5. By summing up the incomes paid out by *all industrial sectors* we will obtain domestic factor income which is also called *net domestic product at factor cost* (NDP_{FC}).

6. Finally, by adding net factor income earned from abroad to domestic factor income or NDP_{FC} we get net national product at factor cost (NNP_{FC}) which is also called *national income*.

Income approach to measurement of national income is shown through bar diagrams in Fig. 38A.3

Precautions. While estimating national income through income method the following precautions should be taken:

1. *Transfer payments* are not included in estimating national income through this method. This is because these payments are not received for any services provided in the *current year*.

2. *Imputed rent* of self-occupied houses are included in national income as these houses provide services to those who occupy them and its value can be easily estimated from the market value data.

3. *Illegal money* such as *hawala money, money earned through smuggling* etc. are not included as they cannot be easily estimated.

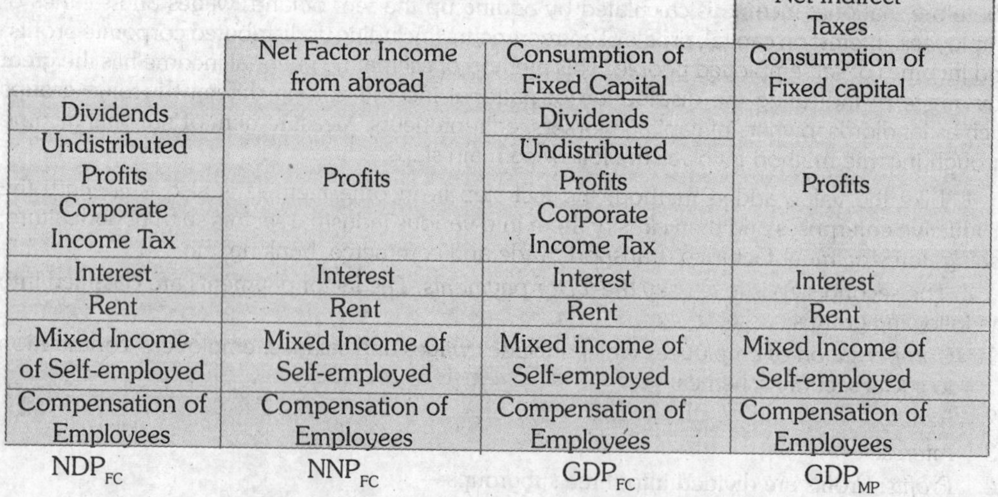

			Net Indirect Taxes
	Net Factor Income from abroad	Consumption of Fixed Capital	Consumption of Fixed capital
Dividends	Profits	Dividends	Profits
Undistributed Profits		Undistributed Profits	
Corporate Income Tax		Corporate Income Tax	
Interest	Interest	Interest	Interest
Rent	Rent	Rent	Rent
Mixed Income of Self-employed	Mixed Income of Self-employed	Mixed income of Self-employed	Mixed Income of Self-employed
Compensation of Employees	Compensation of Employees	Compensation of Employees	Compensation of Employees
NDP_{FC}	NNP_{FC}	GDP_{FC}	GDP_{MP}

Fig. 38A.3. *Income Approach to National Income*

4. *Windfall gains* such as prizes won, lotteries are also not included while estimating national income as they do not represent receipts for any contribution to any current productive activity.

5. Corporate profit tax (that is, tax on income of the companies) should not be separately included as it has already been included as a part of profits.

6. *Death duties, gift tax, wealth tax, tax on lotteries*, etc., are paid from past savings or wealth and not from current income. Therefore, they should not be treated as a part of national income of a year.

7. The receipts from the *sale of second-hand goods* should not be treated as a part of national income. This is because the sale of second-hand goods does not create new flows of goods and services in the current year.

8. Income equal to the *value of production used for self-consumption* used by farmers and others should be estimated and included in the measure of national income.

3. Expenditure Method

Expenditure method arrives at national income by adding up all expenditures made on goods and services during a year. Income can be spent either on consumer goods or capital goods. Again, expenditure can be made by private individuals and households or by government and business enterprises. Further, people of foreign countries spend on the goods and services which a country exports to them. Similarly, people of a country spend on imports of goods and services from other countries. We add up the following types of expenditure by households, government and by productive enterprises to obtain national income.

1. Expenditure on consumer goods and services by individuals and households. This is called *final private consumption expenditure*, and is denoted by *C*.
2. Government's expenditure on goods and services to satisfy collective wants. This is called *government's final consumption expenditure*, and is denoted by *G*.
3. The expenditure by productive enterprises on capital goods and inventories or stocks. This is called *gross domestic capital formation*, or gross domestic investment and is denoted by *I* or GDCF. Gross domestic capital formation is divided into two parts:
   (*i*) Gross fixed capital formation (*ii*) Addition to the stocks or inventories of goods
4. The expenditure made by foreigners on goods and services of a country exported to other countries which are called *exports* and are denoted by X. We deduct from exports (*X*) the expenditure by people, enterprises and government of a country on imports (*M*) of goods and services from other countries. That is, we have to estimate net exports (that is, exports –imports) or (*X* – *M*).

Thus, we add up the above four types of expenditure to get final expenditure on gross domestic product at market prices (GDP_{MP}). Thus,

GDP_{MP} = Private final consumption expenditure + Government's final consumption expenditure + Gross domestic capital formation + Exports – Imports

$$GDP_{MP} = C + G + I + (X - M)$$
$$= C + G + I + NX$$

On deducting consumption of fixed capital (*i.e.*, depreciation) from gross domestic product at market prices (GDP_{MP}) we get net domestic product at market prices (NDP_{MP}).

In this method, we then subtract net indirect taxes (that is, indirect taxes – subsidies) to arrive at net domestic product at factor cost (NDP_{FC}),

Lastly, we add 'net factor income from abroad' to obtain net national product at factor cost (NNP_{FC}), which is called *national income*.

Thus,

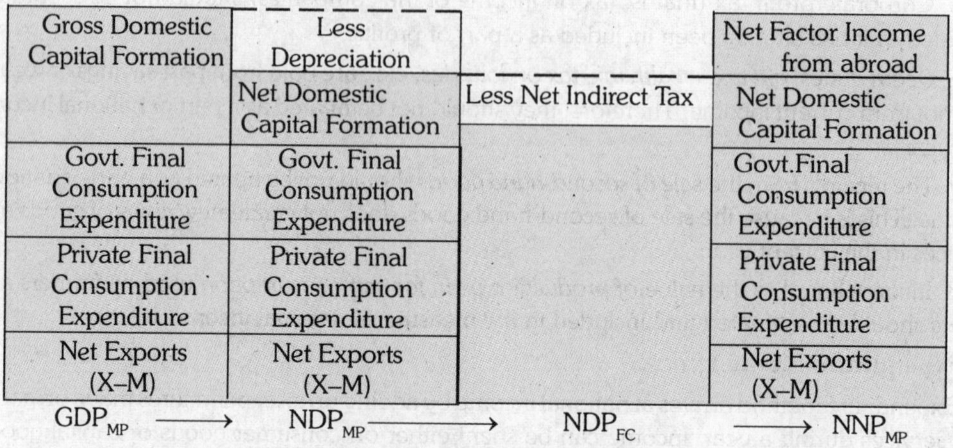

Gross Domestic Capital Formation	Less Depreciation		Net Factor Income from abroad
	Net Domestic Capital Formation	Less Net Indirect Tax	Net Domestic Capital Formation
Govt. Final Consumption Expenditure	Govt. Final Consumption Expenditure		Govt.Final Consumption Expenditure
Private Final Consumption Expenditure	Private Final Consumption Expenditure		Private Final Consumption Expenditure
Net Exports (X–M)	Net Exports (X–M)		Net Exports (X–M)

$GDP_{MP} \longrightarrow NDP_{MP} \longrightarrow NDP_{FC} \longrightarrow NNP_{MP}$

Fig. 38A.4. *Expenditure Approach to National Income Concepts*

$NNP_{FC} = GDP_{MP}$ – Consumption of Fixed capital – Net Indirect taxes + Net Factor Income from Abroad.

Expenditure approach to national income is shown through bar diagram in Fig. 38A.4.

(**Note:** To any concept of the domestic product, if we add *'Net Income from Abroad'* we will get corresponding National Product)

Precautions. While estimating Gross Domestic Product through expenditure method or measuring final expenditure on Gross National Product, the following precautions should be taken:

1. *Second-hand goods*: The expenditure made on second-hand goods should not be included because this does not contribute to the current year production of goods and services.

2. *Purchase of shares and bonds*. Expenditure on purchase of old shares and bonds from other people and from business enterprises should not be included while estimating Gross Domestic Product through expenditure method. This is because bonds and shares are mere financial claims and do not represent expenditure on currently produced goods and services.

3. *Expenditure on transfer payments* by government such as unemployment benefits, old-age pension should also not be included because no goods or productive services are produced in exchange by the recipients of these payments.

4. *Expenditure on intermediate goods* such as fertilisers and seeds by the farmers and wool, cotton and yarn by manufacturers of garments should also be excluded. This is because we have to avoid double counting. Therefore, for estimating Gross Domestic Product we have to include only *expenditure on final goods* and services.

NATIONAL INCOME AND ECONOMIC WELFARE

National income, or GNP, as explained in the last chapter, measures the value of aggregate output of goods and services produced in a year. Since goods and services satisfy the wants of the people, national income or GNP has often been used as a measure of satisfaction or economic welfare of the people. The greater the magnitude of national income, the greater the level of economic welfare. Besides, economic progress or what is now generally called *economic* growth has been measured in terms of increase in national income (that is, increase in GNP or NNP) in terms of total or per capita income. In recent years doubts have been expressed about the validity of national income or gross national product (GNP) as a measure and index of economic welfare.

Net Economic Welfare. It has been asserted by several modern economists that national income as it is usually defined is not a satisfactory measure of economic welfare. According to them, in order to obtain a true measure of economic welfare, some adjustments both in the form of additions and subtractions have to be made in the aggregate of national income. National income, as it is usually conceived and measured, includes some things that do not increase welfare of the people. Therefore, such things ought to be excluded in order to get a true measure of economic welfare. This true measure of economic welfare is now often called "*Net Economic Welfare*" or simply *NEW*. On the other hand, the usual concept of national income excludes some goods and services which increase satisfaction of the people and therefore ought to be included in any good index of Net Economic Welfare.

As regards the things that ought to be added to obtain the index of Net Economic Welfare (NEW), the first important thing is the *value of satisfaction that people derive from leisure*. The usual concept of national income (or GNP) does not attach any significance to the amount of leisure people enjoy. However, the individuals derive satisfaction not only from the consumption of goods and services but also from leisure they have. Therefore, for constructing any index of net economic welfare, the value of leisure which the people enjoy must also be included. For example, if the average working hours are reduced, this is likely to reduce national production or national income but may raise welfare of the people by enabling them to enjoy more leisure.

The other important items that ought to be added to obtain a true measure of welfare are the *non-marketed personal services* (that is, the personal services which are not sold and purchased in the market) which also greatly raise the satisfaction and welfare of the people. For instance, services rendered by the housewives to the family members greatly add to their welfare but they are not recorded in national income accounting. Likewise, personal services rendered by the individuals to themselves such as gardening, painting one's own house significantly raise their welfare but do not get registered in the national income or GNP. Hence in order to get any true index of economic welfare, the value of non-market activities such as personal services which increase welfare ought to be incorporated.

As regards the items that have to be deducted from the national income, mention may be made of those harmful effects which result from increase in output. As is well known, the production of modern industries pollutes the environment such as polluting air, water and calmness which significantly reduce welfare of the people. Though modern industrialization has greatly increased national income of the countries but by causing *air pollution, water pollution and noise* has tended to reduce the welfare of the people. Therefore, for preparing a measure of net welfare, negative values ought to be assigned to the *environment pollution* that results from the production of goods and services. The various forms of pollution of environment have often been referred to as *costs of economic growth*, which like other costs, have to be deducted to obtain the index of net economic welfare.

Apart from environment pollution, certain other deductions on account of wasteful and non-productive expenditure such as government expenditure on police and law courts so as to maintain law and order and on defence to protect the country from external aggression. These have been called ***"regrettable costs"***, because economists consider them regrettable necessities expenditure on which does not lead to increase in welfare of the people. Hence expenditure on them should be excluded from GNP to arrive at the measure of net economic welfare.

To sum up, the measure of and Net Economic Welfare (NEW) can be derived from Gross National Product (GNP) as follows:

Real GNP
– Depreciation
+ Value of leisure
+ Value of non-market activities (*i.e.*, services of housewives and personal services)
– Environment pollution
– Regrettable costs
= Net Economic Welfare

But it is worth-mentioning that even the measure of Net Economic Welfare (NEW) as defined above does not truly indicate the welfare enjoyed by the people. There are other things which play a significant role in determining welfare of a nation and which do not get registered in national income or in Net Economic Welfare. Thus, *composition of national output* as between wage goods and luxuries and also the *distribution of goods between individuals* determine welfare to a great extent. If with the increase in total national income and per capita income, the rich are getting richer and the poor getting poorer, then this growth in national income and per capita income cannot be said to promote welfare. Professor Hicks rightly remarks, "the national income only measure the total volume of goods and services at the disposal of the community during the year; it can tell us nothing, for example, about the way in which the national income is divided up between rich and poor."

Thus growth of GDP or NDP does not truly indicate increase in welfare or well-being as growth of GDP may be very high but is unequally distributed or its benefits are not shared by all. For instance, in India despite high growth in GDP Tendulkar Committee on poverty found that 37 per cent of the Indian population lived below the poverty line in 2004-05. Further, a recent survey has shown that more than 30 per cent of Children in India are underweight or malnourished. This is deposite the average growth rate of over 8 per cent in GDP since 2003-04. In the past high growth in GDP was thought to promote general welfare as it would generate adequate employment opportunities and reduction in the incidence of poverty. But what we have witnessed in India is jobless growth and perpetuation of acute problem of poverty despite high growth in GDP. Of course, some more employment opportunities and have been created, some people have been pulled out from poverty through the growth process, but there is no significant progress in various social indicators such as nourishment of children, infant mortality rate, adequate growth in gainful employment opportunities and reduction in poverty. Thus writing about high GDP growth rate achieved in the nineties (1991-2002), Profs. Jean Dreze and Amartya Sen wrote "The potential benefits of accelerated economic growth in the nineties appear to have diluted by severe imbalance in the growth process, growing inequalities and continued state inertia in crucial social fields of elimination of depreviation requires not merely more economic growth but also direct public action in social fields".[2]

To conclude in our view increase in welfare of the people should not be judged from the *growth in GDP alone* but also the changes in other indicators such as fall in unemployment, reduction in poverty and inequalities of income. Indeed, the concept of *economic development*, as distant from economic growth, involves apart from GDP growth improvement in these other indicators of welfare.[3]

2. *Jean Dreze and Amartya Sen "Indian Development and Participation" 2002, p. 329*
3. *Ibid.*

Further national income and per capita income are also not true measures of welfare because they do not consider the *composition of output*. A country's national income and per capita income may be very high but the well-being of the people may be very low because the national output consists of a larger quantity of war materials. This is a very important factor because it is well known fact that various countries are spending quite a large part of national budgets on the manufacture of war materials, and the greater the expenditure on the defence forces, the smaller will be the actual well-being of the people, given the size of national and per capita income.

Similarly, the well-being of the people also depends upon composition of national product especially the *relative proportions of wage-goods (necessities) and luxuries* in the national product. It may be noted that in a country if luxuries are being produced in relatively greater quantities than the wage-goods, then in that case while the few rich will be rolling in luxuries, the poor will be deprived of even sufficient quantities of necessities of life. Likewise, national and per capita income do not accurately reflect improvements in the quality of products. This is a shortcoming because improvements in the quality of products affect the economic welfare of the people as much as the increase in quantities of goods.

Lastly, the increase in national income does not truly indicate the increase in welfare of the people because it does not take into account *how the national income is being produced and how the increase in it* has been brought about. If increase in national income has been brought about by making workers work longer hours which impair their health and efficiency, then this increase in national income will not promote welfare but will adversely affect it. Similarly, if the increase in national income has been obtained by introducing labour-saving machinery throwing out a large number of workers out of employment, this growth in national income which increases unemployment cannot therefore lead to the increase in social welfare.

SOME EXAMPLES OF NATIONAL INCOME CALCULATION

We solve below some numerical problems of calculation of national income by three methods, namely, expenditure method, income method and value added method.

Problem 1. *Calculate (1) GDP at market prices and (2) national income from the following information.*

	₹
Personal consumption expenditure	***6,500***
Indirect taxes less subsidies	***150***
State government consumption and investment expenditure	***500***
Central government consumption and investment expenditure	***2,000***
Change in business inventories	***100***
Gross private domestic fixed investment	***1,200***
Exports	***900***
Net factor payments to rest of the world	***100***
Imports	***1,200***
Depreciation	***200***

Solution.

(*i*) GDP_{MP} = (Private Consumption Expenditure + Gross private investment (both fixed and inventories) + Gov. Expenditure (both State and Central) + Net exports (X–M))

$= 6500 + (1200 + 100) + (500 + 2000) + (900 - 1200)$
$= 6500 + 1300 + 2500 - 300$
$= 10,000$

(*ii*) ***National Income***. National income is net national product at factor cost (NNP_{FC}). Therefore, to find out *net domestic product at factor cost* we have to deduct depreciation and net indirect taxes from GDP_{MP} and to get *national* income we have to deduct net factor payments to the rest of the world. Thus

NI or $NNP_{FC} = GDP_{MP}$–Depreciation–net Indirect taxes (*i.e.*, indirect taxes less subsidies) – net factor payments to the rest of the world.

$NI = 10,000 - 200 - 150 - 100$
$= 9550$

Problem 2. *Calculate the national income and personal disposable income from the following information*:

	₹
GDP_{MP}	***6,000***
Receipts of factor income from the rest of the world	***150***
Payments of factor income to the rest of the world	***225***
Depreciation	***800***
Indirect taxes minus subsidies	***700***
Corporate Profits	***1,200***
Dividend	***600***
Transfer payments to persons	***1,300***
Personal Taxes	***1,500***

Solution.

(*i*) National Income is Net National Product at factor cost

NI or NNP_{FC} $= GDP_{MP}$ – Depreciation – Net Indirect taxes + Net Factor income from abroad
$= 6000 - 800 - 700 + (150 - 225)$
$= 6000 - 1500 - 75$
$= 6000 - 1575$
$= 4425$

(*ii*) Personal Disposable income = National Income – Retained Corporate Profits + Transfer Payments to Persons – Personal taxes

PDI $= 4425 - (1200 - 600) + 1300 - 1500$
$= 4425 - 600 + 1300 - 1500$
$= 3625$

(Note: Retained corporate profits equal corporate profits minus dividends paid to shareholders)

Problem 3. *Calculate (1) Net Domestic Product at market Prices and (2) National Income from the following data of all the enterprises in an economy. Use new value added method adopted in India.*

		₹ in Crore
(i)	***Subsidies***	**10**
(ii)	***Sales***	**1000**
(iii)	***Closing stock***	**100**
(iv)	***Indirect taxes***	**50**
(v)	***Intermediate Consumption***	**300**
(vi)	***Opening stock***	**200**
(vii)	***Consumption of fixed capital***	**150**
(viii)	***Net factor income from abroad***	**10**

Solution.

NDP_{MP} and National Income can be obtained through *value added method*. We first find out the value of output of the economy

Value of output = Sales + Change in Stock
= 1000 + (Closing Stock – Opening Stock)
= 1000 + (100 – 200)
= 900 crore

The Net Value Added at basic prices (NVA_{BP})
= Value of total output – Intermediate Consumption – Consumption of fixed capital
= 900 – 300 – 150
= 450 crore

NDP_{MP} = NVA_{BP} + Indirect taxes – Subsidies
= 450 + 50 – 10 = 490

National Income (NNP_{FC}) = NDP_{MP} – Net Indirect taxes + Net factor income from abroad
= 490 – 40 + 10
= 460 crore

Problem 4. *On the basis of the following data about the economy which consists of only two firms, find out:*

(*a*) *Gross Value Added at basic prices*

(*b*) *Gross Domestic Product at market prices and factor cost*

		₹ in Crore
(i)	***Sales by firm A***	**200**
(ii)	***Purchases from B by firm A***	**80**
(iii)	***Purchases from A by firm B***	**120**
(iv)	***Sales by firm B***	**400**
(v)	***Closing stock of firm A***	**40**
(vi)	***Closing stock of firm B***	**70**
(vii)	***Opening stock of firm A***	**50**
(viii)	***Opening stock of firm B***	**90**
(ix)	***Subsidies to the two firms***	**10**
(x)	***Indirect taxes paid by both firms***	**60**

Solution:

Firms	Value of Output	Intermediate cost	Gross Value added
Firm A:	Sales = 200 Change in stock = 40 – 50 = –10 Total Value of output = 200 – 10 = 190	Purchases From B = 80	190 – 80 = 110
Firm B:	Sales = 400 Change in stock = 70 – 90 = –20 Total Value of Output = 400 + (–20) = 380	Purchases From A = 120	380 – 120 = 260

ΣGVA at basic prices = 110 + 260 = 370

Gross domestic product at market prices (GDP_{MP}) = GVA_{BP} + Indirect taxes – Subsidies

= 370 + 60 – 10 = 420

Gross domestic product at factor cost (GDP_{FC}) = GDP_{MP} – Indirect taxes + Subsidies

= 420 – 60 + 10

= 370 crore

Problem 5. *Calculate Gross Domestic Product at Market Prices and Net National Product at Factor Cost and Gross Domestic Product at Factor Cost from the following data:*

		₹ in Crore
(i)	Net indirect taxes	38
(ii)	Consumption of fixed capital	34
(iii)	Net factor income from abroad	(–) 3
(iv)	Rent	100
(v)	Profit	125
(vi)	Interest	20
(vii)	Mixed Income of self employed	120
(viii)	Wages and salaries	170
(ix)	Employers' contribution to social security schemes	30

Solution.

Note that (*viii*) wages and salaries and (*ix*) Employer's contribution to social security schemes together constitute compensation of employees.

Net national product at factor cost (NNP_{FC}) = Wages and salaries + Employers' contribution to social security schemes + Rent + Profit + Interest + Mixed Income of Self employed + Net factor income from abroad

= 170 + 30 + 100 + 125 + 20 + 120 – 3

= 562 crore

GDP_{MP} = NNP_{FC} + Net Indirect taxes + Consumption of fixed capital – Net factor income from abroad

= 562 + 38 + 34 – (– 3)

$= 562 + 38 + 34 + 3$

$= 637$ crore

$GDP_{FC} = GDP_{MP}$ – Net Indirect Taxes

$= 637 - 38 = 599$ crore

Problem 6. *Calculate gross domestic product at market prices (GDP_{MP}), gross domestic product at factor cost (GDP_{FC}) and net national product at factor cost (NNP_{FC}) from the following data:*

		₹ *in Crore*
(i)	***Private final consumption expenditure***	**290**
(ii)	***Government's final consumption expenditure***	**50**
(iii)	***Subsidies***	**20**
(iv)	***Gross domestic fixed capital formation***	**105**
(v)	***Indirect taxes***	**70**
(vi)	***Depreciation (i.e., Consumption of Fixed Capital)***	**45**
(vii)	***Net factor income from abroad***	**(–) 5**
(viii)	***Net addition to stock***	**15**
(ix)	***Net exports***	**(–) 5**

Solution.

Gross domestic product at market prices (GDP_{MP}) = Private final consumption expenditure + Government's final consumption expenditure + Gross domestic fixed capital formation + Change in stock + Net exports

$= 290 + 50 + (105 + 15) + (-5)$

$= 290 + 50 + 105 + 15 - 5$

$= 455$ crore

$GDP_{FC} = GDP_{MP}$ – Net Indirect Taxes

$= 455$ – (Indirect Taxes – Subsidies)

$= 455 - (70 - 20) = 405$ crore

$NNP_{MP} = GDP_{MP}$ – Depreciation

$= 455 - 45$

$= 410$ crore

$NDP_{FC} = NDP_{MP}$ – Indirect taxes + Subsides

$= 410 - 70 + 20$

$= 360$ crore

$NNP_{FC} = NDP_{FC}$ + Net factor income from abroad

$= 360 + (-5)$

$= 360 - 5$

$= 355$ crore

QUESTIONS FOR REVIEW

1. Explain how national income is related to national product. Are they two sides of the same coin?
2. Explain the concept of Gross Domestic Product at Market Prices (GDP_{MP}). What are its components?
3. Distinguish between Gross Domestic Product at Market Prices (GDP_{MP}) and Gross Domestic Product at Factor Cost (GDP_{FC}). Which concept is currently used to measure economic growth in India?

4. Explain how national income is measured through (a) income method and (b) expenditure method?
5. What is meant by Gross Value Added (GVA) at basic prices? Explain how Gross Domestic Product at market prices (GDP_{MP}) is measured through value added method in India?
6. Explain the difficulties of measuring national income in developing countries like India.
7. Explain why national income or GNP does not indicate welfare of the society.
8. What is meant by *net economic welfare*? How is it derived or obtained from the estimate of GNP?
9. *On the basis of the following data about an economy which consists of only two firms, find out:*
   (a) *Value added by Firms A and B.*
   (b) *Gross domestic product at market prices.*

		₹ in Crore
(i)	***Exports by Firm A***	**40**
(ii)	***Imports by Firm A***	**100**
(iii)	***Sales to households by Firm A***	**180**
(iv)	***Sales to Firm B by Firm A***	**80**
(v)	***Sales to Firm A by Firm B***	**60**
(vi)	***Sales to households by Firm B***	**120**

(**Hint.** Note that value of exports by firm A will be a part of value of output, whereas imports by it will be a part of intermediate cost of production.)

10. *From the following data calculate Gross National Product and Net National Product at market prices by (i) income method, and (ii) expenditure method.*

		₹ in Crore
(i)	***Mixed income of self-employed***	**400**
(ii)	***Compensation of employees***	**500**
(iii)	***Private final consumption expenditure***	**900**
(iv)	***Net factor income from abroad***	**(–)20**
(v)	***Net Indirect taxes***	**100**
(vi)	***Consumption of fixed capital***	**120**
(vii)	***Net domestic capital formation***	**280**
(viii)	***Net Exports***	**(–)30**
(ix)	***Profits***	**350**
(x)	***Rent***	**100**
(xi)	***Interest***	**150**
(xii)	***Government final consumption expenditure***	

(**Ans.** GNP_{MP} = 1700 crore and NNP_{MP} = 1580 crore)

Appendix to Chapter 38A

GDP Growth and its Sources in the Indian Economy

GROWTH OF GDP IN INDIA

Until recently in India, economic growth was measured in terms of gross domestic product (GDP) at factor cost at constant prices. Before, 2011-12 in India to measure rate of economic growth at constant prices, market prices of 2004-05 were taken as the base for measuring GDP at factor cost at constant prices. We have explained in detail the concept of gross domestic product (GDP) and its related national income aggregates in the previous chapter. It is suffice it state here that the *gross domestic product* (GDP) is the market value of *final goods and services* produced in a year in an economy. In 2014-15, following the international practice, CSO has started measuring economic growth in terms of gross domestic product at constant market prices (GDP_{MP}) with 2012-13 prices as the base. Besides, it has increased its coverage by including output of some industrial enterprises which were not included earlier. Therefore, data of national income and its growth according the new series beginning from 2011-12 are not strictly comparable with earlier ones. The word 'domestic' in GDP indicates that it does not include '*net factor income from abroad*'. Besides, gross domestic product at market prices (GDP_{MP}) is distinguised from gross domestic product at factor cost (GDP_{FC}). Gross domestic product at market prices (GDP_{MP}) is obtained by adding *indirect taxes net of subsidies* to GVA at basic prices, that is, while GDP_{MP} includes the impact of indirect taxes and subsidies in GDP_{FC} they are excluded. By gross value added at *basic prices*, we mean the prices which were originally used in measuring value added of various enterprises of different sectors. Therefore, economic growth in India is now measured by increase in GDP at constant market pries in a year (with 2011-12 prices as the base).

Starting from the year 2004–05, growth of GDP at market prices is given in Table 38AA.1.

Table 38AA.1: Rate of GDP Growth in India

Year	GDP Growth Rate	Growth in GVA at Basic Prices
2004–05	7	-
2005–06	9.5	-
2006–07	9.6	-
2007–08	9.5	-
2008–09	6.7	-

(*Contd*)

Table 38AA.1: (Contd)

Year	GDP Growth Rate	Growth in GVA at Basic Prices
2009–10	8.9	-
2010–11	6.9	-
2011–12	6.7	-
2012–13	5.6	5.4
2013–14	6.6	6.3
2014–15	7.2	7.1
2015–16	7.6	7.3

Source: CSO

Note: Up to the year 2011-12, growth rate is measured in terms of GDP at factor cost in old series, *whereas in the last four years, growth is measured in terms of increase in GDP at market prices with 2011-12 as the base in the new series.*

It is important to note that prior to 1980, India's growth rate was stuck at 3.5 per cent per annum when public sector played a leading role in India's economic development and India followed Mahalanobis strategy of development which gave high priority to basic heavy industries and import substituting industrialisation. Due to partial liberlisation of industrial policy and relaxation of controls and encouragement to export promotion, India achieved 5.6 per cent annual growth in GDP during the eighties of the last century.

After economic reforms initiated in 1991, growth in Gross Domestic Product (GDP) has greatly picked up, especially after 2002-03. In fact for three years, 2005-06, 2006-07 and 2007-08, India achieved GDP growth rate of over 9 per cent plus as seen from the Fig. 38AA.1. It will be seen that while in 2004-05, the growth rate of GDP at factor cost was 7.5 per cent, it rose to 9.5 per cent in 2005-06, 9.6 per cent in 2006-07 and 9.5 per cent in 2007-08, that is, 9% plus growth rate in three successive years in a row. In 2008-09, when there was world-wide slowdown due to global financial crisis of 2008, India achieved 6.7 per cent growth rate of GDP at factor cost, mainly due to decline in our growth in exports. Though lower growth rate of 6.7% was less than 9% plus growth rate of the previous three years, it was considered to be quite high by international standards. Indeed, since 2005-06, India's growth rate has been the second fastest in the world, next only to China and it is now estimated by both IMF and World Bank that from 2015-16 onwards India's GDP growth will exceed that of China.

In 2009-10, growth rate of GDP rose to 8.9 per cent but in 2010-11, it again fell to 6.9 per cent. For the year 2011-12, CSO put the growth rate of GDP at 6.7 per cent. Partly due to global slowdown and partly due to *policy paralysis* in the last years of UPA government, the lower GDP growth rates of 5.6 per cent at constant (2011–12) prices in 2012–13 and 6.6 per cent in 2013–14 were achieved. However, with the change in central government in 2014–15, the growth rate has risen to 7.2 per cent in 2014–15 and further to 7.6 per cent in 2015–16. With this India has overtaken China and has become the *fastest growing economy of the world.*

As we have seen in the previous chapter, the growth rate depends upon rate of saving and investment and capital-output ratio. The fall in growth rate of GDP in 2011-12 was mainly due to *decline in gross fixed capital formation* (GFCF) which is another name for gross fixed investment. GFCF (*i.e.*, gross fixed investment) fell to 31.7 per cent of GDP in 2009-10 and 30.4 per cent 2010-11 and slightly rose to 31.8 per cent of GDP in 2011-12 and to 30.6% of GDP in 2012-13 while it was 33.0 per cent in the year, 2007-08. There are various reasons for this fall in investment in the years, 2010-11 to 2013-14. First, in order to fight higher rate of inflation, Reserve Bank of India raised its repo interest rate at which it lends to commercial banks to 8.5 per cent. This prompted commercial banks to raise their lending rates of interest. These higher interest rates and rise in other input costs induced business firms to defer investment. Secondly, various scams were revealed for which officials of the Ministries got involved. This created uncertainty and fear among the high officials which resulted in *policy paralysis* which hurt the investment activity. Thirdly, high persistent inflation, especially of food items, during 2010-11, 2011-12 and 2012-13 reduced the purchasing power of the people which adversely affected the demand for industrial goods. The manufacturing sector which accounts for 80 per cent of India's industrial output slowed down considerably in 2011-12. As will be seen from Table 38AA.2 manufacturing sector (both organised and unorganised) was estimated to grow at 2.7 per cent in 2011-12 compared to 9.7 per cent 2010-11 and 11.3 per cent in 2009-10. Estimated growth in mining in 2011-12 was – 0.6 per cent, down from 4.9% in the previous year. Estimated growth in construction in 2011-12 was 5.6 per cent, down from 10.2 per cent last year. Besides, estimated growth in agriculture in 2011-12 wis 3.6%, down from 7.9% in previous year. Contribution of different sectors to GDP growth is depicted Table 38AA.2.

Table 38AA.2: Sources of Growth of GDP: Supply Side

Industry	2007-08	08-09	09-10	10-11	11-12	12-13	13-14	14-15	15-16
A. Agriculture, forestry & fishing	5.8	0.1	0.8	7.9	3.6	1.2	3.7	1.1	1.2
B. Industry	9.6	3.7	8.3	7.8	2.6	2.3	4.5	5.9	NA
2. Mining & quarrying	3.7	2.1	5.9	4.9	–0.6	–0.2	5.4	2.3	7.4
3. Manufacturing	10.3	4.3	11.3	9.7	2.7	6.2	5.3	6.8	9.3
(i) Registered	10.1	5.9	11.7	7.8	2.6	–	–	–	–
(ii) Unregistered	10.7	1.3	5.4	7.1	3.0	–	–	–	–
4. Electricity, gas & water supply, etc	8.3	4.6	6.2	5.2	6.5	4.0	4.8	9.6	6.6
5. Construction	10.8	5.3	6.7	10.2	5.6	–4.3	2.5	4.5	3.9
C. Services	10.4	9.3	9.7	9.2	7.8	8.0	9.1	10.6	9.2
6. Trade, hotels, Transport & Communications	10.1					9.6	11.1	8.4	9.0
7. Financing, insurance, real estate & professional services	12.0	12.0	9.7	10.1	11.7	8.8	7.9	13.7	10.3
8. Public administration, defence and other services	6.9	12.5	11.7	4.3	6.0	4.9	7.9	9.0	6.6
9. Total Gross Domestic Product	9.3	6.7	8.6	8.9	6.7	5.6	6.6	7.2	7.6

Source: CSO

Contribution to GDP Growth: Supply-side

From the supply side, overall GDP growth originates from (A) the primary sector consisting of agriculture, forestry and fishing, (B) the industrial sector consisting of (i) mining and quarrying (ii) manufacturing and (iii) electricity, gas and water supply etc. and (iv) construction (C) services which consist of (1) trade and hotels, and (2) transport, storage and communications, (3) financing, insurance, real estate and professional services and (4) public administration, defence and other services.

An important question is to understand how much different sectors of the economy contribute to the growth of GDP (*i.e.*, supply side of production). This is revealed by Table 38AA.2. For example, in 2014-15, there was 7.2 per cent growth in GDP. This growth in GDP in 2014-15 occurred as a result of 1.1 per cent growth rate in agriculture, 5.9 per growth in industry and 10.6 per cent growth in services. It will be seen from Table 38AA.2 that slowdown in GDP growth rate in 2008-09 was due to very low growth rate in industry (3.7 per cent) and agriculture (0.1 per cent), while services registered a high growth rate of 9.3 per cent. An important fact revealed by Table 38AA.2 is that the *services sector which now constitutes about 58 per cent in India's GDP is the major source of growth in GDP*. It will be seen from Table 38AA.2 that in the five years period (2006-07 to 2011-12), the growth rate of services sector has been more than 9 per cent per annum. It is therefore often said that from the supply-side viewpoint Indian economic growth is largely driven by services sector or in India, there has been *services-led growth*.

GROWTH OF GDP: DEMAND SIDE

In our above analysis, we have explained the growth of India's GDP from the supply-side, that is, how much contribution to growth of GDP is made by growth of output in (*a*) agriculture, (*b*) industry and (*c*) services sector. Economists are also interested in knowing the demand-side growth of GDP, that is, how much increase in GDP at constant market prices in a year has been due to (1) increase in private final consumption Expenditure (PFCE), (2) increase in Government Final Consumption Expenditure (GFCE), (3) how much it has been due to increase in investment expenditure (*i.e.*, capital formation, and (4) how much is due to increase in net exports. **Note that the sum of these four items constitutes aggregate demand in the economy.**

It is important to note that from the *demand-side perspective* unlike countries of East Asia during their high growth phase or China in recent times, GDP growth in India in the post-reform period until 2003-04 (except the year 2001-02) had been driven mostly by increase in private final consumption expenditure (PFCE) growth. It was therefore called *consumption-led growth*. But during the Tenth Plan Period (2002-07) there had been a significant change in pattern of economic growth. It was investment (that is, Gross Capital Formation) rather than PFCE (Private Final Consumption Expenditure) that had been the main source or driver of GDP_{mp} growth in

Table 38AA.3: Growth in GDP and its Components at Constant Market Prices (per cent), 2007-08 to 2015-16

	2007-08	2008-09	2009-10	2010-11	2011-12	2012-13	2013-14	2014-15	2015-16
1. Total final consumption expenditure	**9.4**	**7.7**	**8.4**	**8.1**	**8.1**	**4.9**	**6.5**	**7.6**	**NA**
1.1 Private final consumption expenditure	9.4	7.2	7.4	8.6	8.0	5.5	6.8	6.2	7.4
1.2 Government final consumption expenditure	9.6	10.4	13.9	5.9	8.6	1.7	–0.4	12.8	2.2
2. Gross capital formation	**18.1**	**–5.2**	**17.3**	**15.2**	**0.5**	**2.6**	**4.0**	**NA**	**NA**
2.1 Gross fixed capital formation	16.2	3.5	7.7	14.0	4.4	–0.3	3.4	4.9	3.9
2.2 Changes in stocks	31.3	–51.4	67.7	29.7	–30.6	–6.2	–18.6	20.3	–
2.3 Valuables	2.9	26.9	57.6	32.4	6.6	3.3	–42.2	18.4	13.3
3. Exports	**5.9**	**14.6**	**–4.7**	**19.7**	**15.3**	**6.7**	**7.3**	**1.7**	**–5.2**
4. Less imports	**10.2**	**22.7**	**–2.1**	**15.8**	**21.5**	**6.9**	**8.4**	**0.8**	**–2.5**
5. Growth in GDP at 2004-05 market prices	**9.8**	**6.7**	**8.6**	**8.9**	**6.7**	**5.6**	**6.6**	**7.2**	**7.6**

Note : Note that in this Table 38AA.3 the growth figures till 2011-12 are at **2004-05 market prices** and from 2012-13 to 2015-16 they are based on 2011-12 prices as the base. NA stands for Not Available.

Source : CSO.

India. Therefore, during the Tenth Plan period (2002-07) there was investment-led growth in India. In 2008-09 due to global financial crisis there was slowdown in economic growth as a result of slow growth in aggregate demand, especially demand for exports and capital formation (i.e., investment expenditure). To prevent the greater fall in GDP growth Government adopted fiscal stimulus measures to boost both consumption demand and investment demand. It will be seen from Table 38AA.3 that in 2008-09, and 2009-10 while *increase* in private consumption dipped to 7.2% and 7.4 per cent respectively over the previous years, the increase in consumption expenditure by the Government of 10.4 per cent in 2008-09 and 13.9 per cent in 2009-10 as a result of fiscal stimulus was main driver of economic growth. It is worthwhile to look at the fact that when developed countries such as the USA, UK, Germany, Japan, Spain faltered, India's GDP still grew at 6.7 per cent in 2008-09 and 8.6 per cent in 2009-10 and 8.9 per cent in 2010-11.

However, it may be noted that in the short run, when there is underutilisation of capacity in the economy increase in consumption demand will promote growth of GDP. When there is already unutilized productive capacity, firms are not likely to make more investment in these circumstances, it is increase in consumption demand that will ensure fuller utilisation of inventories and fuller utilisation of capacity. But in the long run, it is increase in investment or fixed capital formation that determine growth in GDP because investment in a year adds to the productive capacity of an economy that yields higher growth in future. It is because of increase in Gross Domestic Capital Formation (GDCF) from 23.6% in 2001-02 to 38.1% of GDP in 2007-08 that brought about over 9% growth of GDP from 2005-06 to 2007-08 was achieved in India. Thus in the long run increase in investment rate is the main driver of economic growth.

The acceleration in trend growth rate of the Indian economy since around 2003-04 came about due to significant improvement in our domestic investment (capital formation) and saving rate) as is seen from Table 38AA.3. The most important contribution to demand growth during the Tenth Five Year Plan period (2002-07) had come from investment or Gross Capital formation (GCF) while the contribution of net exports (i.e., exports–imports) to GDP growth had been either negative or negligible. The contribution of gross capital formation from 2003-04 to 2007-08 to growth of GDP had been higher than that of consumption. As noted above, therefore it is often said that during the 10th plan period (2002-07), there was investment-led growth in India. However, this pattern changed in 2008-09. In 2008-09 when the growth on the demand side was driven by consumption (private consumption and government consumption expenditure taken together).

Under the impact of global financial crisis and consequently slowdown of the Indian economy it was initially expected that the contribution of *private consumption* to aggregate growth would decline dramatically in 2008-09. But during 2008-09 Government implemented fiscal stimulus packages involving huge increase in public expenditure and cut in taxes to sustain growth momentum. These led to higher growth in private consumption. Besides, implementation of 6th Pay Commission during 2008-09 also greatly added to disposable income of the people which caused increase in private consumption. Further, under the fiscal stimulation programme Government's consumption expenditure was also raised to keep the growth momentum and therefore the contribution of Government consumption expenditure to GDP growth also rose to 10.4 per cent in 2008-09 and 13.9 per cent in 2009-10 as against 9.6 per cent in 2007-08 at constant (2004-05) market prices. It is important to observe from Table 38AA.3 the *growth* of gross capital formation and net exports to GDP growth in 2008-09 was negative. It is thus evident that contributions to GDP growth by key demand-side aggregates do indicate that in 2008-09, slowdown in demand and therefore growth rate is largely explained by decline in investment expenditure or gross capital formation and net exports.

Growth in GDP at constant market prices and of its components for four years 2012-13, 2013-14, 2014-15 and 2015-16 according to new series (2011-12 as the base), is given in last four columns of Table 38AA.3. It will be seen from this table that there has been increasing trend in private final consumption expenditure, which grew significantly and its growth rate of 7.4 per cent in 2015-16 almost equals the growth rate of GDP in this year. The government final consumption expenditure which recorded 13.9 per cent growth in 2009-10, 8.6 per cent in 2011-12 and 12.8 per cent in 2014-15 could not keep its momentum and registered growth of only 2.2 per cent in 2015-16 (R.E)

As regards growth in fixed capital formation, also known as fixed investment expenditure, and reflects addition to the productive capacity has remained depressed; it registered annual growth rate of 3.4 per cent in 2013-14, 4.9 per cent in 2014-15 and 3.9 per cent in 2015-16(RE), Besides, due to sluggish global demand for India's exports, the negative growth in exports during 2014-15 and 2015-16 acted as a drag on GDP growth.

It therefore follows from above that it is due to the growth of Private Final Consumption expenditure (PFCE) that India succeeded in achieving a fairly rapid growth in recent years and has overtaken China and has emerged as the fastest growing economy of the world. Further, it can be said that relatively speaking it is *growth in domestic private consumption* demand that has been the driver of India's GDP growth with both private and government consumption expenditure growing in strength.

INDIA'S GROWTH PERFORMANCE SINCE 2003

Since 2003 India has emerged as one of the fastest growing economies of the world. In fact, next to China, India's growth rate from 2003-04 to 2013-14 has been highest in the world. This is often referred to as India's growth miracle. Before 1980s, India's average growth rate stuck at around 3.6 per cent per annum which Late Prof. Raj Krishna called Hindu rate of growth. In the nineteen eighties, Indias average rate of economic growth rose to 5.6 per cent per annum and further in the 1990s and uptill 2002-03 (*i.e.* in 12 years period). India's average growth rate went up to 6.2% per annum under liberalisation and globalisation of the Indian economy. But from 2004-05 to 2007-08 India's average annual growth rate of GDP rose to over 9 per cent per annum. In 2008-09 while the advanced developed countries were experiencing recession (i.e., negative growth). India succeeded in achieving 6.7 per cent growth rate which further rose to 8.6% in both 2009-10 and 8.9% in 2010-11.

Now, the question is how do we account for such a high growth rate in GDP from 2003-04 to 2010-11 in India. Growth depends mainly on rate of saving and investment (or in other words, on rate of capital formation), and improvement in technology or capital-output ratio. In India, such as in other emerging economies, China, Singapore, Indonesia and South Korea, it is increase in rate of saving and investment (*i.e.*, rate of capital formation) that brought about a sharp growth in GDP. Rates of domestic gross saving and capital formation and GDP growth since 2002-03 are given in Table 38AA.4 Prior to 2003-04 rate of gross domestic saving in India was around 24 to 26% of GDP. But, as will be seen from the Table 38AA.4, from 2004-05 to 2007-08 (that is, prior to global financial crisis) gross domestic saving rate rose to 36.8 per cent of GDP in 2007-08 which pulled up the rate of investment or capital formation. As a result, *average* growth rate of GDP for the five years period (2004-08) rose to over 9 per cent. With this, India became the second fastest growing economy of the world next only to China.

Table 38AA.4: Rate of Domestic Saving and Fixed Capital Formation, from 2002-03 to 2011-12 (Old Series)

as % of GDP

	2002-03	04-05	05-06	06-07	07-08	08-09	09-10	10-11	11-12
Gross Domestic Saving (GDS)	26.6	32.4	33.4	34.6	36.8	32.0	33.7	33.7	30.1
Household Saving	23.1	23.6	23.5	23.2	22.4	23.6	25.2	23.5	22.3
Private Corporate Sector Saving	4.1	6.6	7.5	7.9	9.4	7.4	8.4	7.9	7.2
Public saving	–0.7	2.3	2.4	3.6	5.0	1.0	0.2	2.6	1.3
Gross Fixed Capital formation (GFCF)	24.1	28.7	30.3	31.3	32.9	32.3	31.7	31.7	30.6
GDP_{mp}	–	8.3	9.3	9.6	9.3	6.7	8.6	8.9	6.7

Source : CSO data after 2004-05 are based on national income series with 2004-05 as the base. GDP growth rates for 2009-10, 2010-11 and 2011-12 are revised estimates.

In keeping with the higher saving rate from 2003-04 onwards, *rate of fixed capital formation* (GFCF) rose from 24.8 per cent in 2003-04 to about 33 per cent of GDP in 2007-08 (see 5th row in the Table 38AA.4). This higher growth rate of fixed capital formation, caused 9 per cent plus average growth in GDP during 2004-05 to 2007-08. In 2008-09 global financial crisis (2007-09) and consequently global meltdown caused fall in saving rate to 32.0% of GDP in 2008-09 but it rose again to 33.7 in both 2009-10 and 2010-11 before falling to 30.1% of GDP in 2011-12. This was due to the substantial increase in consumption expenditure under the fiscal stimulus measures to keep the growth momentum which caused drop in public saving rate to 1.0 per cent of GDP in 2008-09 as compared to 5.0 per cent in 2007-08. This financial crisis which caused negative growth of India's export in 2008-09 slowed down the rate of economic growth in 2008-09 to 6.7 per cent.

However, while advanced developed countries of the US, Japan and European countries experienced worst ever recession since the Great depression of 1930s. India was successful in attaining the growth rate of 6.7 per cent in 2008-09. With the saving rate going up to 33.7 per cent and gross capital formation rate to 36.5 per cent of GDP in 2009-10 and revival of positive growth in exports in the second half of 2009-10, rate of growth of GDP rose to 8.6 % in 2009-10. In 2010-11 also with domestic saving rate equal to 33.7 per cent which along with capital inflows raised gross capital formation around 36.5 per cent and as a result rate of GDP growth rose to 8.9 per raised in 2010-11 (RE). However, for the reasons explained below in 2011-12, growth rate of GDP fell further to 6.7 per cent, lowest in nine years. In 2012-13 growth rate in GDP fell further to 5.6 per cent.

Reasons for Substantial Rise in Saving Rate from 2003-04 to 2007-08

Now, what has caused saving rate in India to rise substantially since 2004. Components of saving rate are : (1) household savings, (2) private corporate sector saving and (3) public saving. It can be seen from Table 38AA.4 that while household savings had stuck at around 23.5 per cent of GDP from 2002-03 to 2011-12 and therefore it cannot explain remarkable rise in overall saving rate in the Indian economy since 2004. It is the private corporate sector which registered a substantial rise in saving rate from 4.1 per cent of GDP in 2002-03 to 9.4 per cent of GDP in 2007-08, that is, the private corporate sector saving more than doubled in the five-year period. After dipping to 7.4 per cent of GDP in 2008-09, the year of global crisis, private sector saving again rose to 8.4 per cent in 2009-10 and around 8 per cent 2010-11. It is this significant increase in corporate sector saving that resulted in higher rate of fixed capital formation which contributed to a big jump in annual growth rate to over 8 per cent in these years.

Besides, large increase in **public saving** since 2003 also contributed a lot to the increase in the overall saving rate and capital formation from 2003-04 to 2007-08. After 2007-08 due to fiscal stimulus, public saving and its contribution to capital formation or investment declined in the Indian economy. The public sector saving which was negative prior to 2003-04 turned positive and rose to 5 per cent of GDP in 2007-08. (See 4th row in Table 38AA.4). Thus private corporate sector and public savings together increased by around 10 per cent from 2003-04 to 2007-08, which brought about higher rate of overall saving and capital formation and ensured higher rate of economic growth. It will be seen from Table 38AA.4 that fixed capital formation which was 24.1% of GDP in 2002-03 rose to about 33% of GDP in 2007-08. No wonder that with such a high rise in fixed capital formation that the average growth rate GDP during the period 2003-08 rose to over 9%.

How do we explain the large increase in saving of the private corporate sector? It is primarily due to the increase in profitability of private corporate sector as measured by the ratio of *profit after tax (PAT) to sales, which rose from 3.6% to 8% in the six years period, 2003-09*[1]. Besides the rise in profitability of the private corporate sector, the companies also *reduced dividend rate* from half of profits to 1/4 the of them. That is, the corporate companies retained (i.e. saved) a greater amount of profits for their expansion or capital formation. Thus, the profits of the private corporate sector not only increased faster on account of higher economic growth but also the companies distributed less of them as dividends that resulted in substantial increase of corporate sector saving.

As regards the public savings, they rose from negative rate in 2003-04 to 5 per cent of GDP in 2007-08. It occurred due to increase in tax revenue, especially from the corporate sector. Thus, revenue from corporate tax rose from 1.9 per cent of GDP to 3.6 per cent during this period. Indeed, as a result of it since 2004 *overall tax–GDP* ratio rose from 8.9 per cent in 2003-04 to 11.9 per cent in 2007-08. This better tax performance along with Government control of its public expenditure under the Fiscal Responsibility Budget Management (FRBM) Act resulted in the fall in Central government's fiscal deficit to 2.5 per cent of GDP in 2007-08. Thus, the improved performance of both the private corporate sector and the public sector in the liberalisation era, especially during the period from 2003-04 to 2007-08, became the significant driver of faster economic growth of the Indian economy.

It may be further noted that rapid growth of some new sectors such as Telecom and IT which hardly existed before 2000 contributed a good deal to rapid economic growth since 2004. Besides, low interest rate policy of the Reserve Bank of India until 2008 made borrowing from the banks cheaper which created large demand for *consumer durables* such as cars, electronics and housing. This ensured relatively higher growth of consumer durables since 2003-04.

Slowdown in the Indian Economy in 2011-12 and 2012-13

It may be noted that situation regarding *saving in the two years (2011-12 and 2012-13)* deteriorated, which adversely affected its potential growth rate. Saving as per cent of GDP fell to 31.3 in 2011-12 as against 36.8 per cent in the year 2007-08 (according to old series). This slowdown in saving rate prevented the Indian economy to grow at a faster pace. Saving rate remained depressed with 33.8 per cent in 2012–13 and 33 per cent in 2013–14. As explained above, high saving rate had allowed India to domestically finance a major part of its investment and slowdown in savings lowered the *potential* growth rate.

It may be noted that slowdown in savings in recent years has been seen in all three segments, household saving, private corporate saving and public saving (see Table 38AA.4). The fall in household savings has been due to high inflation. Because of high inflation the households had to spend more on consumer goods to maintain their usual standard of living

1. Sumant Sinha, Decoding the Saving Rate Miracle, *The Economic Times*, Oct. 22, 2010.

which resulted in reduction of their savings. Besides, high inflation caused the real rate of interest earned on investment in bank deposits and other forms of financial savings that caused fall in financial savings of the households who instead used their savings to buy gold, silver, real estate as hedge against inflation. This adversely affected productive investment.

It is worth mentioning that the poor recovery in the US and European countries and uncertainty caused by Eurozone sovereign debt crisis, it was difficult to get sustained capital inflows to finance investment. It was therefore necessary to increase domestic saving to finance increase in investment for attaining higher rate of economic growth.

As, at times of global recession in 2008-09, in India there was fiscal and monetary space, timely stimulus allowed the economy to recover fairly quickly to a growth of 8.9 per cent in 2009-10 but dropped to 6.9 per cent in 2010–11, 6.7 per cent per cent in 2011-12 and further to 5.6% in 2012-13 (revised estimate). A number of factors, both global and domestic, led to a *slowdown* of the Indian economy.

It may however be noted that slowdown in economic growth was not confined to India alone during this period. There had been a general slowdown in the global economy which was passing through a rather prolonged phase of uncertainty. The recovery from the global crisis of 2008-09 in the advanced economies had been slow and uneven, with a decisive resolution of sovereign debt problem of the Eurozone area had yet to be achieved. Having achieved a GDP growth of 5.1 per cent in 2010, the rate of growth in the global economy declined to 3.8 per cent in 2011 and is declined further to 3.3 per cent in 2012, as per the World Economic Outlook released by the IMF in October 2012. The rate of growth of developed economies declined from 3.0 per cent in 2010 to 1.6 per cent in 2011 and is expected to decline further to 1.3 per cent in 2012. Even the emerging economies slowed down during this period, partly as a result of the slowdown in their export markets. China's growth declined from 10.4 per cent in 2010 to 9.3 per cent in 2011 and is expected to be 7.8 per cent in 2012. Brazil's growth dipped from 7.5 per cent in 2010 to 2.8 per cent in 2011 and is expected to be 0.7 per cent in 2012 as shown in Fig. 38AA.1.

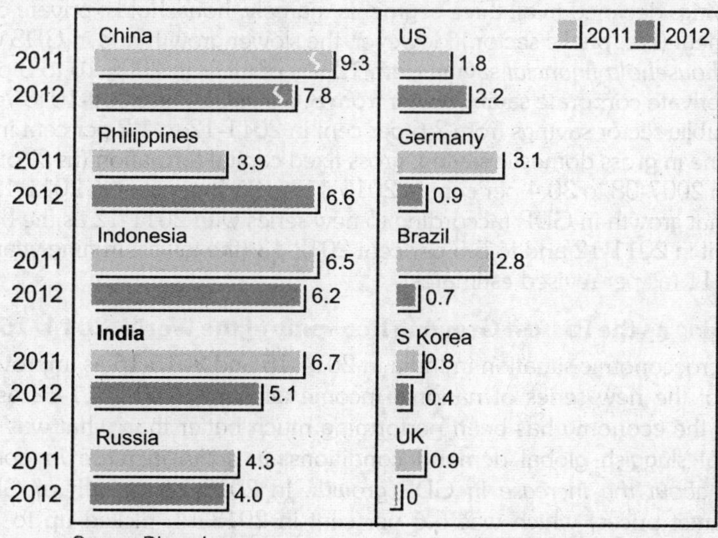

Fig. 38AA.1. *Growth Rates in Major Countries of the World in 2011 and 2012*

The slowdown in growth rate in India is 2011-12 and 2012-13 can be explained in terms of both global and domestic factors. First, the slowdown in growth in developed economies and near recessionary conditions in Europe resulted not only in *lower growth* of *international trade but also lower capital flows.* As a result, the growth rate of India's exports declined which contributed to the decline in overall growth rate and also caused problem of current account deficit (CAD). Besides, fall in capital inflows not only resulted in lower investment in the Indian economy but also made the problem of financing Current Account Deficit (CAD) difficult.

Further, international price of crude oil remained high which led to the increase in fuel subsidy bill of the Indian government and drained away resources from public investment. This also adversely affected economic growth. Besides, high crude oil prices led to the widening of India's trade and current account deficits which caused sharp depreciation of rupee which adversely affected the sentiments of foreign investors.

Turning to the domestic factors, higher borrowing costs for the corporate sector due to high RBI's repro rate, the rate at which Reserve Bank lends to the commercial banks, discouraged investment by the corporate sector harming economic growth. The Reserve Bank of India continued to follow a relatively tight monetary policy to control inflation although there was some relaxation by it in lowering Cash Reserve ratio (CRR) and reducing repo rate by 0.50 per cent in April 2012 and 0.25 per cent in the end of January 2013. As a result of this tight monetary policy of RBI, the cost of borrowing remained at an elevated level and this had an impact on investment and growth in the Indian economy, particularly that of the industrial sector. The erratic power supply due to coal shortage caused delays in implementation of investment projects which made their financing more difficult and investors more cautious. Difficulties in clearances of various investment projects also resulted in lower investment. Further due to various scams and corruption charges against several ministers and bureaucrats, caused *policy paralysis* which made investors hesitant to make investment.

Besides, rainfall in the monsoon season of 2012-13 had been below normal particularly in the key months of June and July, 2012. This affected sowing and resulted in a lower growth rate of agriculture and allied sectors. But for the most important factor causing fall in growth rate, as seen above, has been fall in saving and investment rates both by the public and private sectors. Worrisome for the economy's long-term growth rate gross domestic saving (GDS) rate fell sharply to 31.3 per cent of GDP is 2011-12 (which is lowest since 2005-06) as against 33.7 per cent in 2010-11. Savings declined in all three segments, namely, households, private corporate sector and Government (i.e., public sector.) However, the slower growth rate in GDS was mainly due to *decline in household financial* saving from 12.9% of GDP in 2009-10 to 8 per cent of GDP in 2011-12, private corporate saving sector from 8.4% of GDP in 2009-10 to 7.3% in 2011-12 and that of public sector savings from 2.6 per cent in 2011-12 to 1.2 per cent in 2012-13. As a result of decline in gross domestic saving, gross fixed capital formation (as % of GDP) fell from 33 per cent in 2007-08 to 30.4 per cent in 2010-11, to 31.8 per cent in 2011-12 and 2012-13. No wonder that growth in GDP (according to new series with 2011-12 as the base) fell sharply to 6.7 per cent in 2011-12 and to 5.6 per cent 2012-13 (the lowest in nine years) from 8.9 per cent in 2010-11 (as per revised estimates).

India Emerging as the Fastest Growing Economy of the World, 2014–15 and 2015–16

The macroeconomic situation in India in 2014-15 and 2015-16 as improved significantly. The release of the new series of national income accounts with 2011-12 as the base year revealed that the economy has been performing much better than what was thought earlier. In the face of sluggish global demand conditions, *it is the increase in domestic demand that brought about the increase in* GDP *growth*. In 2013-14, growth of GDP at constant (2011-12 market prices) which was 6.6 per cent in 2013-14, picked up to 7.3 per cent in 2014-15 and further to 7.6 per cent in 2015-16 (See Table 38AA.1). Most of the buoyancy in domestic demand can be traced to increase in consumption expenditure, especially Private Final Consumption Expenditure (PFCE). It can be seen from Table 38AA.3 that *private final consumption expenditure* at constant market prices increased by 6.8 per cent in 2013-14, 6.2 per cent in 2014-15 and 7.4% in 2015-16 while *Government final consumption expenditure* increased by 12.8 per cent in 2014-15 but declined to 2.2% increase in 2015-16.

India's growth story is expected to dominate the headlines in the years to come as both the World Bank and the IMF are predicting that from 1915-16 onwards India will overtake China to become the fastest growing economy of the world. The World Bank in its report in 2015 estimated that India would achieve 7.5 per cent growth in 2015-16 while China's growth will be be around 6.8 percent to 7 per cent. Further, according to IMF's latest forecasts, india's growth rate will be 7.5 per cent in 2016 and 2017. India's GDP growth at market prices was 7.2 per cent in 2014-15 and 7.6 per cent in 1915-16. In our view, with around 31.0% as the present (2015-16) saving rate and with capital inflow of around 2 per cent, investment or capital formation will be around 33 per cent. With capital-output ratio estimated to be equal to 4, the growth rate of 8 per cent in 2016–17 is quite feasible.

As regards demand side, domestic demand is likely to get a boost as 7th Pay Commission recommended enhanced salaries and pensions to be paid during 2016-17. Besides, the Indian government has taken a number of economic reforms and is planning several more which has boosted investment sentiments of both the domestic and foreign investors. This is expected to have a positive impact on investment and economic growth. Besides, investment proposals by investors are getting quick clearance by the government.

Further, an important factor that will boost *growth will be provided by lower oil prices and increasing monetary easing* by RBI made possible by fall in inflation rate. Decline in oil prices will reduce substantially the government expenditure on subsidies, thus releasing funds for investment. Stimulating effects of tax cuts made in the budgets for 2014-15 and 2015-16, declining oil prices will add to spending power of households, thereby boosting consumption and growth. "Oil is also a significant input in production and its declining prices will shore up profit margins and hence balance sheets of the coparate sector."[2]. Similarly, IMF says, "Growth in India will benefit from recent policy reforms, a consequent pick-up in investment and lower oil prices will raise real disposable incomes particularly among poor households" IMF report further says that inflationary pressures in the Indian economy are likely to ease gradually on account of lower credit prices and improved utilisation of production capacity will prevent overheating in the medium term. Reviewing global growth outlook in its '*World Economic Outlook*' on April 2016, IMF says, "**India remains a *bright spot* with strong growth and rising real incomes**".

A few years ago, no one had imagined that India would overtake countries like China, Japan, South Korea to become the fastest growing economy of the world. Till now, China has been the fastest growing economy of the world. Now, both World Bank and IMF have estimated that beginning from the year 2015 (2015-16), India will overtake China and become the fastest growing economy of the World. In 2015 China's GDP grew at 6.9 per cent while India's GDP growth rate was 7.3 per cent. But China's growth rate is projected by IMF to slip to 6.5 per cent in 1916, to 6.2 per cent in 2017 whereas India's growth rate will rise to 7.5 per cent in 2016, to 7.9 per cent in 2017 (see Table 38AA.5). It will be seen from Table 38AA.5 that growth rate in Advanced Economies such as US, UK, Japan, Soviet Russia is far behind that of India. The same is the case of growth rate in Indonesia, Brazil, Mexico, and South Africa which is much less than that of India.

Table 38AA.5 *Projection GDP Growth Rate in Some Developed and Developing Countries*

	GDP growth rate (Per cent)		
	2015	2016	2017
Global growth rate	3.1	3.2	3.5
Advanced Economies	1.9	1.9	2.0
United States	2.4	2.4	2.5
Euro area	1.6	1.5	1.6
Germany	1.5	1.5	1.6
France	1.1	1.1	1.3

(Contd)

2. GOI, *Economic Survey* Vol. I, 2014-15, p.70.

Table 38AA.5 *(Contd)*

	GDP growth rate (Per cent)		
	2015	2016	2017
Italy	0.8	1.0	1.1
Spain	3.2	2.6	2.3
Japan	0.5	0.5	–0.1
United Kingdom	2.2	1.9	2.2
Canada	1.2	1.5	1.9
Emerging Market and Developing Countries			
Russia	–3.7	–1.8	0.8
China	6.9	6.5	6.2
India	7.3	7.5	7.5
Brazil	–3.8	–3.8	00
Mexico	2.5	2.4	2.6
Saudi Arabia	3.4	1.2	1.9
Algeria	2.7	2.3	3.5
South Africa	1.3	0.6	1.2

Source : IMF, *World Economic Outlook*, April 16, 2016.

India's Economic survey 2014-15 has provided a graph which is given below comparing the growth rate of india and China. With the exception of few years, China's growth rate has been much higher since 1981 but from 2015, India's growth rate has gone above that of China.

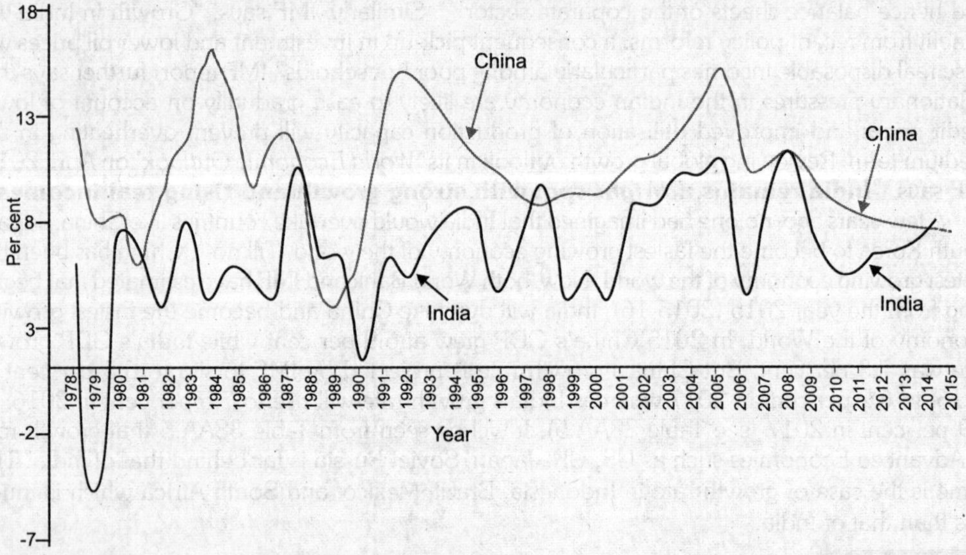

Fig. 38AA.2. *Real GDP Growth: India and China*

Determination of National Income : Keynes's Simple Two Sector Model

Keynes's Income-Expenditure Approach

We have explained in the previous chapter how national income is measured. In the present chapter we will explain how national income is determined in a simple two sector Keynesian model. It is worth noting here that the Keynesian theory of determination of national income is relevant in the context of the short run only since the stock of capital, techniques of production, efficiency of labour, the size of population, forms of business organisation have been assumed to remain constant in this theory. Further, in his model of income determination *Keynes assumed that price level in the economy remains unchanged.* Therefore, in the Keynesian theory which deals with the short run, the level of income of the country will change as a result of changes in the level of labour employment. Capital stock, level of technology, labour efficiency, the size of population remaining unchanged. We also saw in an earlier chapter that national income was the same thing as national product. In fact, national income and national product represent the value of aggregate output from two different points of view. Further, the level of employment in the economy depends on the level of national income or product. Given the stock of capital and level of technology, as more goods and services are produced, more labour is employed and more incomes are generated. In fact, in the Keynesian model income and employment go together.

Keynesian theory of income determination can be explained by assuming two sectors in the economy, namely, households and business firms. Keynes focussed on this simple two sector model of determination of national income and derived conclusions regarding policy formulation from this basic model. Analysis of determination of national income will be extended in the next chapter to incorporate Government and foreign trade. We start with the analysis of determination of national income by *taking a simple two-sector economy with a fixed price level*.

Aggregate Expenditure and Demand (with a Fixed Price Level)

Aggregate demand is the total expenditure which at given fixed prices all households and business firms want to make on goods and services in a period at various levels of national income. Though J.M. Keynes used the term aggregate demand assuming price level to remain constant, in modern macroeconomics in the analysis of determination of national income the term *aggregate expenditure* is generally used. *The terms of aggregate demand and aggregate supply are now generally used in the model with flexible price level*. In this chapter however we use the term aggregate demand and aggregate expenditure interchangeably but assume that price level remains constant. In a two-sector economy, aggregate expenditure *AE* represents aggregate demand which consists of two components: First, there is consumption expenditure by households and, secondly, there is a demand for and expenditure on capital goods by business firms, which is called investment expenditure. Thus, by aggregate demand we mean how much expenditure the households and the entrepreneurs are undertaking on consumption and investment. Therefore,

Aggregate Expenditure or Aggregate Demand = Consumption expenditure + Investment expenditure

$$AE \text{ or } AD = C + I$$

where expenditure or AD stands for aggregate demand, C for consumption expenditure and I for investment expenditure.

Consumption Expenditure

As for consumption demand, it depends upon the propensity to consume of the community and the level of current national income. Given the propensity to consume, as income increases, consumption expenditure will also increase. In other words, given the propensity to consume, consumption demand is a function of income. Consumption function can take more than one form. The most common form of short-run consumption function is

$$C = a + bY$$

where a is the intercept term of the function and represents *autonomous* consumption expenditure where b represents the slope of the function.

Consider Fig 39.1 in which national income is measured along the X-axis and consumption expenditure (C) is shown on the Y-axis. In this figure, a straight line OZ which makes 45° angle with the X-axis has been drawn. The straight line OZ forms 45° angle with the X-axis represents the reference income line to measure the difference between consumption and level of income. This is often called *income line*. On a point on this 45 line in Figure 39.1 consumption expenditure will equal the current level of national income. In this figure a curve C has also been drawn which represents consumption function, $C = a + bY$ of the community. This curve of consumption function slopes upward from left to right, which shows that as income increases, the amount of consumption expenditure also increases. As income line OZ makes 45° angle with the X-axis, *the gap between the consumption function curve C and the income line OZ represents the saving of the community*. The reason for this is that a part of the income is consumed and a part is saved, *i.e.*, National Income = Consumption + Saving. This is also written as $Y = C + S$, where Y represents income, C consumption and S saving. It will be seen from Fig. 39.1 that the gap between the consumption function curve C and the income line OZ goes on increasing as income increases. In other words, *the amount of saving or saving gap increases as income increases.*

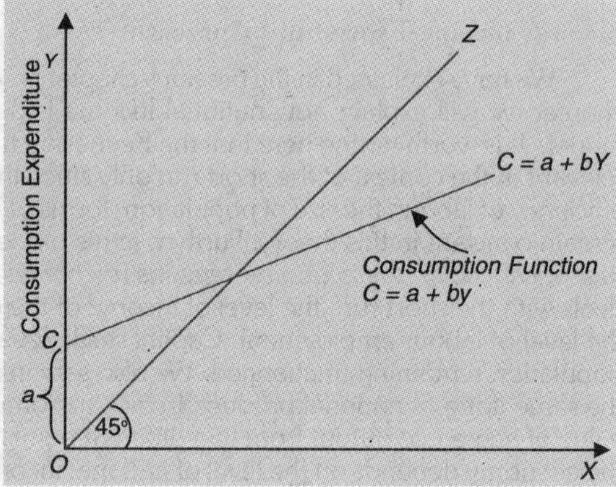

Fig. 39.1. *Consumption Function*

It is worth mentioning that in the short run consumption function does not change. This is because the propensity to consume, that is, the whole consumption function curve C depends upon the tastes, preferences, the income distribution in the society, the population level, etc, which do not undergo any change in the short run. However, in addition to current income level, consumption expenditure depends on the rate of interest, stock of wealth, fiscal policy or taxation by the government, the general price level. The impact of changes in these other factors is shown by *shift of the consumption function curve* upward or downward as the case may be. For example if rate of interest rises, the people will save more and therefore consume less at each level of current income. As a result, the consumption function curve will *shift* downward. We will explain these determinants of consumption function in detail in a late chapter. An important thing to note about consumption function is its slope which measures *marginal propensity to consume*. Marginal propensity to consume means the increase in consumption resulting from increase in income. Thus, $MPC = \frac{\Delta C}{\Delta Y}$ It may noted that while Keynes emphasised the level of current income as the important determinent of consumption some other economists think that it is permanent income or life-time income that determines consumption in a period.

Investment Demand

The other component of the aggregate demand is investment which is a crucial factor in the determination of equilibrium level of national income. Investment demand depends upon two factors : (1) marginal efficiency of capital and (2) rate of interest. Of these two factors, rate of interest is comparatively stable and does not frequently change in the short run. Therefore, the fluctuations in the level of investment demand chiefly depend upon the changes in the marginal efficiency of capital. *The marginal efficiency of capital means the expected rate of return or profit which the business community hopes to get from the investment in capital assets*. Marginal efficiency of capital depends upon the replacement cost of the capital goods on the one hand, and profit expectations of entrepreneurs on the other. Profit expectations are more important because they often change even in the short run and cause fluctuations in investment. If the level of national income and employment is desired to be raised in market economy, then steps should be taken which will raise the expectations of the entrepreneurs (i.e., business firm) regarding profit earning from investment.

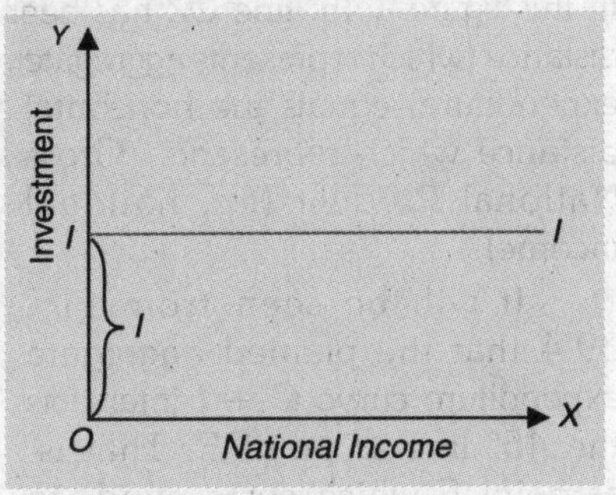

Fig. 39.2. *Autonomous Investment*

In any particular period there will be a level of investment expenditure which, according to Keynes, depends on marginal efficiency of capital and the rate of interest but is *exogenously* determined independent of the level of national income in the simple Keynesian model. In other words, there will be a given definite demand for investment independent of the level of income. Thus, in the simple Keynesian model of income determination, investment is not taken to a be function of income. In other words, in Keynes's model investment is treated as *autonomous, that is, investment does not change with a change in the level of income.*

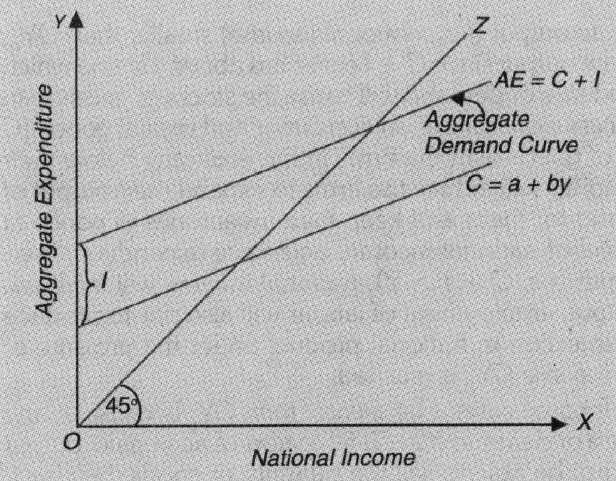

Fig. 39.3. *Aggregate Demand or Expenditure Curve*

This type of investment is shown in Figure 39.2. This is the assumption which Keynes made and in this chapter we will also do likewise. In actual practice when the level of income rises, the demand for goods will also rise and this will favourably affect the expectations of the entrepreneurs regarding making of profits. Rise in the profit expectations will raise the marginal efficiency of capital which in turn will increase the level of investment. But it is quite clear that investment demand does not directly depend upon income; it is only affected *indirectly* by changes in income. Therefore, in our figure 39.3 we have taken a given amount of investment demand independent of the level of income and added it to consumption function curve to get aggregate expenditure curve $C + I$. This aggregate expenditure (*AE*) curve ($C+I$) is also called aggregate demand (*AD*) curve with a fixed price level. The distance between the C curve and the $C + I$ curve is the same throughout and therefore $C + I$ curve is parallel to the C curve which indicates that the level of investment is constant and does not change with the change in national income. Note that aggregate expenditure curve $C + I$ is interpreted as *planned or desired* expenditure on goods and services by both households and business firms.

Determination of Equilibrium Level of National Income

Equilibrium in economics signifies when there is no tendency to change in a variable. A level of national income is in equilibrium when aggregate expenditure on consumption and investment equals aggregate output of consumer and capital goods. Thus level of national income is determined by the equilibrium in the *goods market*. Equilibrium in the goods market is reached at the point at which planned or desired aggregate expenditure ($C + I$) is equal to aggregate output (*i.e.* national product). The national product, as seen before, is the same thing as national income. Fig. 39.3 illustrates the determination of national income in a market economy. In this figure a 45° line *OZ* has been drawn which implies that on any point of it the vertical distance (which represents aggregate expenditure) equals the horizontal distance which represents Gross National Product (*i.e.* national income).

It will be seen from Fig. 39.4 that the plained aggregate expenditure curve $C + I$ intersects the 45° line at point *E*. That is, at point *E* which corresponds to the income level OY_0 planned aggregate expenditure ($C + I$) equals aggregate output. Therefore, *E* is the equilibrium point and *OY* represents the equilibrium level of national income. Now, income cannot be in equilibrium at levels *smaller than* OY_0. This is because at any level of aggregate output (*i.e.*, national income) smaller than OY_0, planned aggregate demand exceeds aggregate output since $C + I$ curve lies above 45° line which depicts aggregate output. This excess expenditure or demand will cause the stocks of goods with business firms to fall greatly. That is, the excess expenditure on consumer and capital goods ($C + I$) will lead to the decline in inventories of goods with the firms in the economy below their desired levels. This unintended fall in inventories will induce the firms to expand their output of goods and services to meet the extra demand for them and keep their inventories of goods at the desired levels. Thus when at a given level of national income, aggregate expenditure (i.e., aggregate demand) exceeds aggregate output (*i.e.* $C + I > Y$), national income will increase. With this increase in national income or output, employment of labour will also rise to produce the increment in output. This process of expansion in national product under the pressure of excess demand will continue until national income OY_0 is reached.

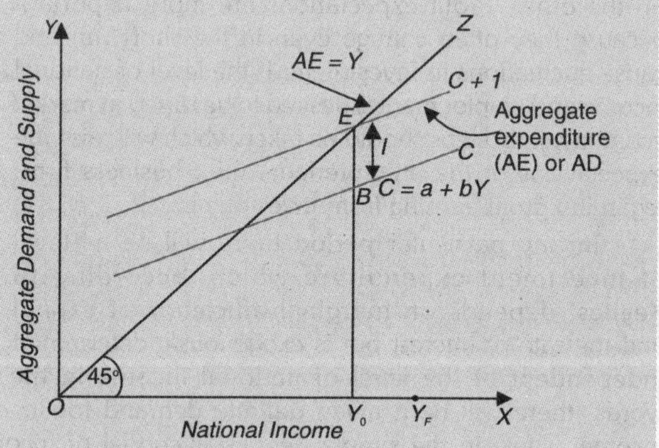

Fig. 39.4. *Determination of National Income ; Simple Two Sector Keynesian Model*

On the contrary, the level of national income cannot be *greater than* OY_0 because at any level greater than OY_0, aggregate expenditure or demand ($C + I$) falls short of aggregate output (*i.e.* $C + I < Y$). As a result, the firms will not be able to sell the quantity of goods they have produced and will therefore cause the increase in inventories of goods with the firms beyond the desired levels. To this situation of the unintended increase in inventories of goods, the firms will respond by cutting down production to keep their inventories at the desired levels. Thus, deficiency in aggregate demand (i.e. planned aggregate expenditure) relative to the aggregate supply of output will lead to the fall in national income and output until the level OY_0 is reached where planned aggregate expenditure $(C + I)$ is equal to the value of aggregate output OY_0. Thus, OY_0 is the equilibrium level of national income.

Principle of Effective Demand

We have seen above that the equilibrium level of national income is determined by aggregate demand. Consider Fig. 39.4 where it will be seen that aggregate demand (*AD*) curve with a fixed price level which in fact represents aggregate expenditure $C + I$ *shows varying levels of aggregate demand or expenditure at various levels of national income. Aggregate demand is not equal to national product at all levels of national income. The particular aggregate demand which is equal to national income (or national product) and therefore determines the equilibrium national income is called effective demand.* In other words, effective demand is that level of aggregate demand which becomes effective in determining equilibrium level of income because it is equal to aggregate supply of output. Remember that aggregate supply of output with a given price level is the same thing as national product or real national income. This is called *Keynesian principle of effective demand.* In Fig. 39.4, the effective demand is equal to Y_0E. Note that the level of national income OY_0 which has been determined equals the effective demand Y_0E $(OY = Y_0E)$.

There are several other points on the aggregate demand or expenditure curve $(C + I)$ but what distinguishes effective demand from all these points is that at this point aggregate demand is equal to national income. On all other points aggregate demand is either more or less than national income. Thus, the level of national income is determined by and equal to effective demand. In a two sector Keynesian model, we can express the principle of effective demand in symbolic terms as under:

$$Y_0 = AD^*$$
$$AD^* = C^* + I$$
$$Y_0 = AD^* = C^* + I$$

where
Y_0 = Equilibrium National income
AD^* = Effective demand
C^* = Effective consumption demand
I = Investment

Note that star marks on *AD* and *C* shows the aggregate demand and consumption demand which become effective.

It is thus clear that national income and employment in the short run are determined by effective demand. The higher the level of effective demand, the greater are the levels of national income and employment and vice-versa. *Unemployment is due to deficiency of aggregate effective demand and the basic remedy to remove this unemployment is to raise the level of aggregate effective demand.* The classical economists believed that aggregate effective demand was always large enough to ensure full-employment. But Keynes proved that it was not so and that is why the problem of cyclical unemployment was common in the free-market capitalist economies.

Equilibrium is not Necessarily Established at Full-Employment Level

The most important contention of J.M. Keynes in his now famous work "*General Theory of Employment, Interest and Money*" was that in a free market economy it is not necessary that the equilibrium level of income is established at the level of full employment. This view of Keynes was quite contrary to the views of the classical economists who believed that the economy always tended towards full-employment. Keynes refuted this important idea of the classical economics. To understand the Keynesian viewpoint consider Fig. 39.5. Suppose the full-employment level of labour corresponds to the level of national income equal to OY_F. Thus OY_F represents the level of income at which there is full-employment in the economy. But, as seen above, the equilibrium level of income is not established at OY_F but at OY_0 at which some number of labour will be unemployed. Thus equilibrium at OY_0 at less than full employment level of national is known as *under-employment equilibrium*. It is worth noting that in the situation depicted in Fig. 39.5, the equilibrium level of national income will be established at full-employment level only when investment demand is sufficiently large to fill the saving gap between income and consumption at the full-employment level of income OY_F. It will be seen from Fig. 39.5, that corresponding to the full-employment level of income OY_F, RH is the desired or planned savings of the community. Therefore, if the equilibrium is to be established at OY_F level, then planned investment must be equal to RH. But the prevailing planned investment expenditure is only equal to BE which is less than RH. With RH as the level of investment and the consumption function curve C as the level of consumption demand, $C + I'$ curve would represent the level of aggregate demand. This $C + I'$ curve intersects the aggregate supply curve OZ at point R and therefore determines equilibrium level of national income equal to OY_F at which labour will be fully employed.

But there is no guarantee that the investment demand will be equal to the saving gap corresponding to full-employment level of income. There are various reasons for this. First, the people who save are not necessarily those who make investment; while it is the general public

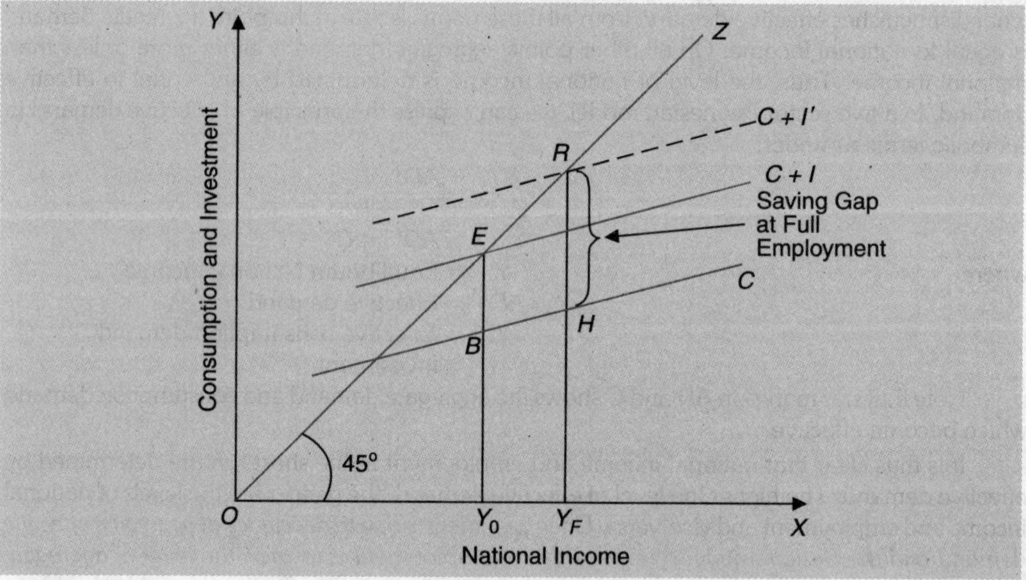

Fig. 39.5. *Under-employment Equilibrium due to Insufficiency of Investment Expenditure*

which save but only few people constituting the entrepreneurial class undertakes investment. Secondly, the factors which determine saving are quite different from those which determine investment. While the people save for providing for the education, marriages of their children and also for contingency purposes such as diseases and unemployment periods. They also save in order to acquire durable goods such as houses, gold and jewellery. They also save to accumulate sufficient funds for their old age. But the level of investment depends upon marginal efficiency of capital and rate of interest in the short run and on the level of population, technological progress in the long run. Therefore, it is not essential that planned investment expenditure should be equal to the amount of planned or desired savings by the people at full-employment level. If due to the adverse changes in the profit expectations of the entrepreneurs, level of planned investment falls, the equilibrium level of national income will also decline.

It is also worth noting that if aggregate expenditure ($C + I$) increases beyond the $C + I'$ in Fig. 39.5 it will mean that the economy is spending and demanding more than it can produce. The result of this will be rise in prices of the commodities. In other words, if the planned investment expenditure in any year is greater than HR, then the inflationary process will start. In this situation, national income will rise beyond OY_F only in money terms but not in real terms.

DETERMINATION OF NATIONAL INCOME: ALGEBRAIC ANALYSIS

A study of how the level of national income is determined will become more clear by using simple mathematics. As has been explained above, the level of national income is in equilibrium at which aggregate demand equals aggregate supply of output. In a simple model of income determination in which we do not consider the impact of Government expenditure and taxation and also exports and imports, the national income is the sum of consumption expenditure (C) and investment expenditure, that is,

$$Y = C + I$$

where Y stands for the level of national income.

Suppose the consumption function is of the following form :

$$C = a + bY$$

a is the intercept term in the consumption function and therefore represents the autonomous consumption expenditure which does not vary with income. b is a constant which represents the marginal propensity to consume ($MPC = \Delta C/\Delta Y$). Thus total consumption demand is equal to the sum of autonomous consumption expenditure (a) and the induced consumption expenditure (bY).

Now, suppose that investment expenditure equals I_a. This investment I_a is autonomous because this does not depend on national income. Thus, we get the following three equations for the determination of the equilibrium level of national income.

$$Y = C + I \quad \text{...(i)}$$

$$C = a + bY \quad \text{...(ii)}$$

$$I = I_a \quad \text{...(iii)}$$

Substituting the values of C and I in equation (i) we have

$$Y = a + bY + I_a \quad \text{...(iv)}$$

$$Y - bY = a + I_a$$

$$Y(1 - b) = a + I_a$$

$$Y = \frac{1}{1-b}(a + I_a) \quad \text{...(v)}$$

The equation (v) shows the equilibrium level of national income when aggregated expenditure equals national income. The equation (v) reveals that in equilibrium autonomous consumption and autonomous investment ($a + I_a$) *generates so much expenditure or aggregate demand which is equal to aggregate income generated by the production of goods and services. From the equation (v) it also follows that the equilibrium level of national income can be known from multiplying the elements of autonomous expenditure (that is,* $a + I_a$*) by the term* $\frac{1}{1-b}$ *which is equal to the value of multiplier.*

Further, it also follows that equilibrium level of income is higher, the greater the marginal propensity to consume (*i.e.* b) and autonomous investment (I_a)

Illustration of Equilibrium Level of Income with Numerical Examples

A few numerical examples will make it clear how the equilibrium level of national income is determined.

Problem 1. *Suppose in an economy, autonomous investment (I) is ₹ 600 crores and the following consumption function is given:*

$$C = 200 + 0.8Y$$

Given the above, find out the equilibrium level of income.

Solution. The equilibrium level of income is

$$Y = C + I \quad \text{...(i)}$$

$$C = 200 + 0.8Y$$

$$I = 600$$

Putting the values of C and I in the equilibrium equation (i) we have

$$Y = 200 + 0.8Y + 600$$

$$(Y - 0.8Y) = 200 + 600$$

$$Y(1 - 0.8) = 800$$

or $$Y = \frac{800}{0.2} = \frac{800}{\frac{2}{10}} = ₹ 4000.$$

Alternative Method. We can directly use equation (v) above using multiplier and autonomous items (i.e., autonomous consumption and autonomous investment) to obtain equilibrium national income. The multiplier is given by $\frac{1}{1-b}$ where b = *MPC*. Autonomous consumption in the present problem is 200 crore and autonomous investment is ₹ 600 crore. Thus

$$Y = \frac{1}{1-b}(200 + 600)$$

$$= \frac{1}{1-0.8}(800)$$

$$= 5\ (800) = ₹ 4000$$

Problem 2. *Suppose the consumption function of an economy is C = 0.8 Y. Planned investment by entrepreneurs for a year is ₹. 500 crores. Find out what will be the equilibrium level of income.*

Solution :

$$Y = C + I \quad \text{...(i)}$$

$$C = 0.8Y$$

$$I = ₹\ 500 \text{ crores}$$

Substituting the values of C and I in (i) we have

$$Y = 0.8Y + 500$$

$$Y - 0.8Y = 500$$

$$Y(1 - 0.8) = 500$$

$$0.2 = 500$$

$$Y = 500 \times \frac{10}{2} = ₹\ 2500 \text{ crores.}$$

Using Alternative Method:

$$Y = \frac{1}{1-b}(a + I_a) = 5(0 + 500) = ₹\ 2500$$

Note that given the value of *MPC* or *b* equal to 0.8, the value of multiplier $\left(i.e., \frac{1}{1-b}\right)$ equals 5.

Problem 3. *Suppose the consumption of an economy is given by*

$$C = 20 + 0.6Y$$

The following investment function is given :

$$I = 10 + 0.2Y$$

What will be the equilibrium level of national income?

Solution. Note that in this problem, investment varies with income. However, this will not change our method of determining equilibrium level of income.

$$Y = C + I \quad \text{...(i)}$$

$$C = 20 + 0.6Y$$

$$I = 10 + 0.2Y$$

Substituting the values of *C* and *I* in (*i*) we have

$$Y = 20 + 0.6Y + 10 + 0.2Y$$

$$Y = 30 + 0.8Y$$

$$Y - 0.8Y = 30$$

$$Y(1 - 0.8Y) = 30$$

$$0.2Y = 30$$

$$Y = 30 \times \frac{10}{2} = 150$$

Thus, we find that the equilibrium level of income to be equal to 150.

Problem 4. *The following consumption function of an economy is given :*

40 + 0.8Y where Y is national income

If the planned level of investment in a year equals ₹ 75 crores, what will be the equilibrium level of national income and consumption ?

Solution : Equilibrium level of national income is determined where

$$Y = C + I \quad \text{...(i)}$$

Now,
$$C = 40 + 0.8\,Y$$

$$I = 75$$

$$Y = 40 + 0.8Y + 75$$

$$Y - 0.8Y = 40 + 75 = 115$$

$$0.2Y = 115$$

$$Y = 110 \times \frac{10}{2} = 575$$

$$C = 40 + 0.8\,Y$$

Substituting the value of *Y* we have

$$C = 40 + 0.8 \times 575$$

$$= 40 + 460 = 500$$

Problem 5. *For an economy following consumption function is given :*

$$C = 60 + 0.75\,Y.$$

(a) If investment in a year is ₹ 35 crores what will be the equilibrium level of income or output?

(b) If full-employment level of income (i.e. level of potential output) is ₹ 460 crores what investment is required to be undertaken to ensure equilibrium at full-employment.

Solution : (*a*)

$$Y = C + I$$
$$Y = 60 + 0.75Y + 35$$
$$Y - 0.75Y = 60 + 35 = 95$$
$$Y(1 - 0.75) = 95$$
$$0.25Y = 95$$
$$Y = 95 \times \frac{100}{25} = 380$$

(*b*) To ensure full-employment equilibrium, investment should be equal to the saving gap at full-employment income. With the given full-employment income equal to ₹ 460, the saving gap at full employment level is

$$S_F = Y_F - C_F = Y_F - (60 + 0.75Y_F)$$
$$= 460 - 60 - (0.75 \times 460)$$
$$= 400 - 345 = 55$$

Thus, investment required for full-employment equilibrium is 55 crore.

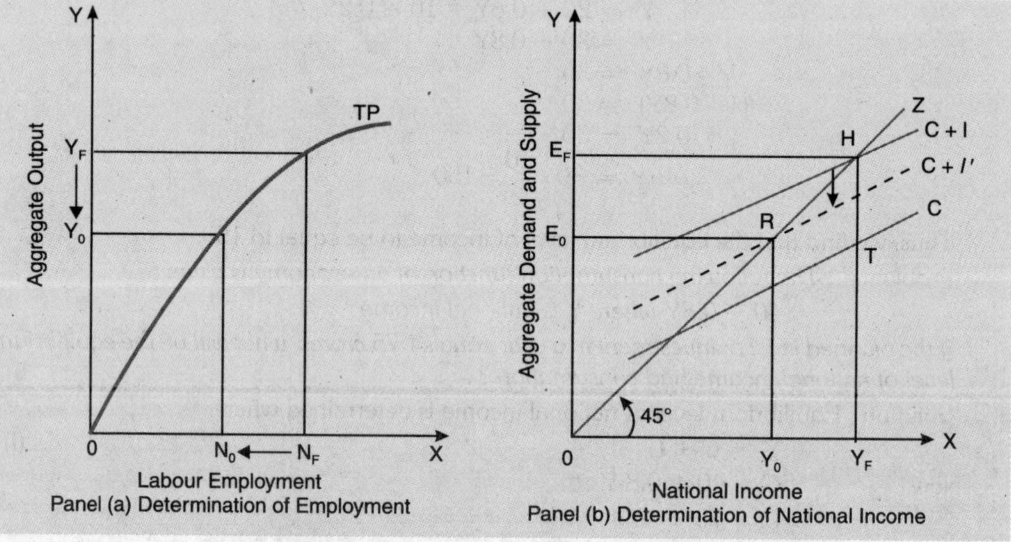

Fig. 39.6. *The Emergence of Involuntary Unemployment*

National Income and Employment

In the foregoing analysis we have explained the determination of level of national income. In fact, the levels of national income and employment are determined jointly. In the Keynesian model level of employment depends on the level of national income, that is, aggregate output. When more output of goods and services are produced, more labour is employed. Thus in the Keynesian theory, employment is a function of income. Relationship between income and labour employment is given by production function showing diminishing returns to labour. This production function can be stated as under :

$$Y = f(N, \bar{K}, \bar{T})$$

According to above function, given the capital stock and technology, the greater the level of national output (*i.e.* income, *Y*), the greater will be the number of workers (*N*) employed. As explained above in detail that, according to Keynesian theory, levels of national income is determined by aggregate effective demand. In a closed economy with no intervention by the government, aggregate demand consists of consumption demand and investment demand. According to Keynes, in the short run consumption function is stable and it is investment demand which is highly volatile as it depends on profit expectations of business men. Equilibrium at full employment level of income is determined when investment expenditure fills the saving gap at full employment level of national income.

Consider Fig. 39.6 where in panel (b) determination of national income is shown through *Keynesian cross,* that is, through intersection of aggregate demand curve with the 45° line from the origin. According to Keynes, equilibrium at full-employment level of income OY_F will be determined if planned investment expenditure by entrepreneurs is equal to planned saving HT at full-employment level of national income OY_F. Total expenditure (i.e., aggregate demand) and output produced are both equal to OE_F corresponding to full-employment equilibrium point H, ($OE_F = OY_F$). In the left-side panel (*a*) where production function curve TP has been drawn, we have measured employment of labour on the X-axis and aggregate output (or national income) on the Y-axis. It will be seen from this left-side panel (*a*) that output OY_F is produced by employing ON_F amount of labour. We assume that ON_F represents the full employment of labour, that is, all workers who want to work at the prevailing wage rate are getting employment. With this full employment of labour, national income equal to OY_F is being generated ($OY_F = ON_F$).

Now, Keynes argued that if somehow or the other profit expectation of entrepreneurs become dim, this would cause a fall in the expected rate of return resulting in reduction in planned investment expenditure. With the fall in investment expenditure, aggregate demand curve shifts downward to the dotted position $C + I'$ which intersects 45° line at point R. As a results new equilibrium level of national income OY_0 is determined ($OY_0 = OE_0$).

It will be seen from left-side panel (a) that aggregate output (i.e., national product) OE_0 is produced by employing ON_0 amount of labour. Thus, as a result of fall in aggregate demand, N_0N_F number of workers are rendered unemployed. N_0N_F workers will be involuntarily unemployed. According to Keynes, there is no any mechanism which should automatically eliminate this involuntary unemployment.

DETERMINATION OF NATIONAL INCOME : SAVING-INVESTMENT APPROACH

We have seen how equilibrium level of national income is determined through income-expenditure approach. The equilibrium level of national income is established at the point where aggregate demand or expenditure curve intersects the 45° line. But there is an alternative method for the explanation of the determination of national income. This alternative method explains the determination of national income by planned saving and investment.

Look at the income-expenditure Fig. 39.4 again. In this figure, at the equilibrium level of national income OY_0, planned investment equals planned saving. Both are equal to BE. Given the aggregate expenditure curve $C + I$, the amount of *desired or planned saving* at income *greater than* OY_0 exceeds planned investment and *for income less than* OY_0 planned investment exceeds planned saving. It is obvious that planned saving and investment are equal only at the equilibrium level of national income and when planned saving and investment are not equal, the national income will not be in equilibrium. Let us see why it is so and how national income is determined by *planned* or *desired* saving and investment. In Figure 39.7 we have drawn *planned* saving curve SS and planned investment, as determined by marginal efficiency of capital and rate of interest, is equal to OI which remains constant in the period under consideration

When at a certain level of national income, planned investment by the entrepreneurs is more than intended saving by the people, this would mean that aggregate expenditure is greater than aggregate supply of output. This will lead to the decline in inventories below the desired level. This would induce the firms to increase production, raising the level of income and employment. The result will be that national output will be increased on account of which national income will go up. Further, when at any level of income, planned investment is less than planned saving, It means that aggregate expenditure is less than aggregate output. As a result, the entrepreneurs will not be able to sell their entire output at given prices. The result will be that output will be reduced which will result in the reduction of national income.

Thus, when, at any level of national income, planned investment expenditure of the entrepreneurs is less than the desired or planned savings of the people, the national income will decrease. It will come down to the level at which investment spending is just equal to the planned savings by the community. But, when at any level of national income, planned investment expenditure on the part of the entrepreneurs is equal to intended savings of the people, it means that aggregate expenditure is equal to the total, aggregate output and therefore the national income will be in equilibrium. Hence, equilibrium level of national income will be determined at the level at which the amount of planned investment by the entrepreneurs is equal to the amount of desired savings by the people.

We can explain the determination of national income through saving and investment in another way. *Saving represents withdrawal of some money from the income stream. On the other hand, investment represents injection of money into the income stream.* Now, if planned investment is greater than planned saving, it means that more money has been put into the income stream than has been taken out of it. As a result, income stream, i.e., flow of national income would expand. On the contrary, if planned investment is less than desired saving, it means that less amount of money has been put into the income stream than has been taken out of it. The result would be that national income would decrease. But when planned investment is just equal to desired saving, it would mean that as much money has been put into the income stream as has been taken out of it. The result will be that national income will neither increase nor decrease, i.e., it will be in equilibrium. It is thus clear that the equilibrium level of national income will be determined at the level at which the planned investment is equal to planned saving.

The determination of national income by planned investment and saving is illustrated in Fig. 39.7. In this figure, national income is shown along the *X*-axis. *SS* is the saving curve which shows desired saving at different levels of income, *II* curve shows planned investment demand i.e., planned investment. The *II* investment curve has been drawn parallel to the *X*-axis. This is done on the assumption that in any year depending on the marginal efficiency of capital and rate of interest the entrepreneurs plan to invest a certain amount of money. This implies that we assume that investment is independent of changes in income, that is, investment does not change with income.

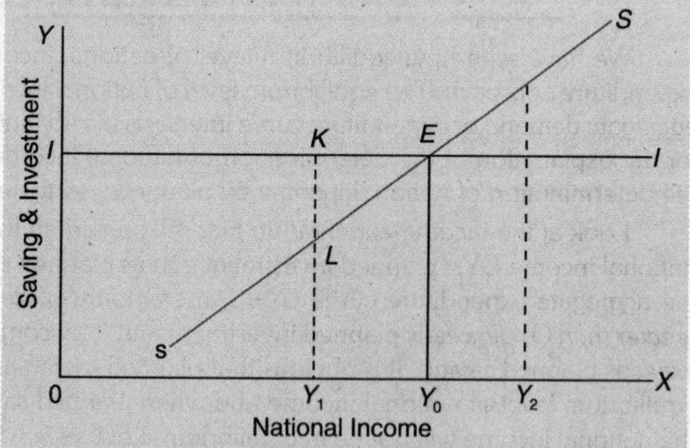

Fig. 39.7. *Determination of National Income : Saving-Investment Approach*

The saving curve *SS* and the investment curve *II* intersect each other at *E*. That is, the planned investment and planned saving are equal at the OY_0 level of income. Hence, OY_0 is the equilibrium level of income. It will be seen from the Fig. 39.7 that at the level of income less than OY_0, (for example if it is OY_1), the amount of intended investment is more than intended savings. This implies that stocks of goods with the firms will fall greatly below the level what the entrepreneurs had planned. In other words, inventories of goods with the firms will fall below their desired level. This will induce the firms to expand production. As a result, national income will rise and this adjustment process will continue until the income level OY_0 is reached at which planned investment expenditure equals planned saving by the households. On the contrary, if national income is greater than OY_0, say OY_2, in Fig. 39.7, it will be seen from the figure that planned saving exceeds planned investment. This implies that at national income greater than OY_0 planned aggregate expenditure will be less than the aggregate output (i.e. national product or national income). As a result, the producers will not be able to sell all the goods produced by them. This will cause accumulation of inventories of goods in excess of their desired levels. This will induce the firms to cut back on production of goods leading to the decline in national product or income. The aggregate production will continue falling until equilibrium national income OY_0 is reached. At the level of OY_0 income, planned investment and planned savings are equal, so that there is neither the tendency for income to increase, nor to decrease. Hence, national income OY is determined. It is thus clear that national income is determined by planned investment and saving.

Synthesis between the Two Approaches

The determination of national income has been explained above by two methods, namely, income expenditure approach and saving-investment approach. The equilibrium level of national income is determined where two conditions are fulfilled:

(i) Aggregate Demand = Aggregate output or national income.

(ii) Planned Investment = planned Savings.

As has been explained above, the equality between aggregate demand and aggregate supply and equality between intended investment and intended saving in reality mean the same thing. This is illustrated in Fig. 39.8. It will be seen in this figure that aggregate demand curve $C + I$ intersects 45° aggregate supply curve OZ at point Q and thereby determines national income equal to OY. In the lower part of this diagram we have drawn planned savings curve SS and planned investment curve II. It is worthwhile to note that saving curve SS has been derived from the consumption function curve C and measures the gap between income and consumption at various levels of income. Further, investment curve II drawn in the lower part of the figure represents the difference between consumption function curve C and aggregate demand curve $C + I$. This difference is the amount of planned investment assumed in this figure. We thus see that both saving and investment curves drawn in the lower part are embedded in the upper part showing aggregate expenditure and income. It is because of this that planned saving and planned investment curves also determine the same level of national income OY which is determined through the equality of aggregate expenditure $(C + I)$ and aggregate output.

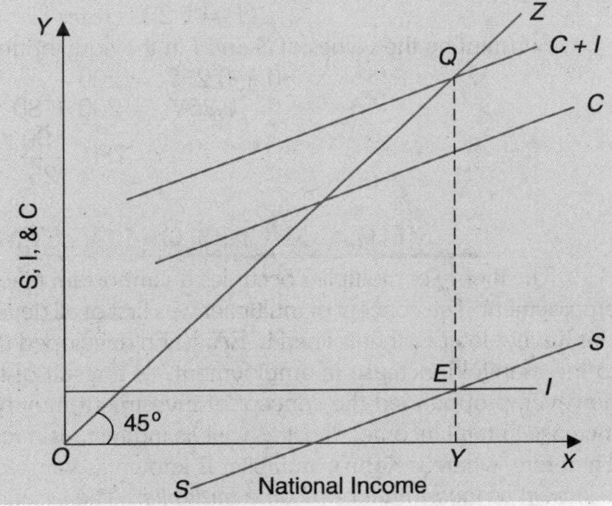

Fig. 39.8. *Synthesis between Income and Expenditure Approach and Saving-Investment Approach*

Saving-Investment Approach : Algebraic Analysis

That the level of national income is determined by the equality of planned saving and planned investment can be derived from the equilibrium condition explained above that level of income is equal to effective demand.

That is,

$$Y = AE \qquad \text{. . . }(i)$$

Now in our simple economy, aggregate demand (*AD*) is equal to the sum of consumption expenditure and investment expenditure. Thus

$$AE = C + I$$

or $$Y = C + I \qquad \text{. . . }(ii)$$

Since $$C = Y - S$$

Substituting $Y - S$ for C in equation (ii) we have

$$Y = Y - S + I$$

$$Y - Y + S = I$$

or $$S = I$$

Thus, we reach at the alternative condition of equilibrium of national income, namely, planned saving be equal to planned investment.

Numerical Problem on Saving-Investment Approach

Problem 5. *Suppose the level of autonomous investment in an economy is 200 crores. The following saving function is given :*

$$S = -80 + 0.25Y$$

Find the equilibrium level of income.

Solution. According to the saving-investment approach, the level of income is in equilibrium at which

$$S = I \qquad \text{...}(i)$$

Given, $S = -80 + 0.25Y$, and

I = ₹ 200 crores

Substituting the values of S and I in the equilibrium equation we have

$$-80 + 0.25Y = 200$$

$$0.25Y = 200 + 80 = 280$$

$$Y = 280 \times \frac{100}{25} = 1120 \text{ crores}$$

THE CONCEPT OF INVESTMENT MULTIPLIER

The theory of multiplier occupies an important place in the modern theory of income and employment. The concept of multiplier was first of all developed by F.A. Kahn in the early 1930s. But Keynes later further refined it. F.A. Kahn developed the concept of multiplier with reference to the manifold increase in employment, as a result of initial increase in investment. Keynes, however, propounded the concept of investment multiplier with reference to the much larger increase in total income, direct as well as indirect, as a result of original increase in investment. Therefore, whereas Kahn's multiplier is known as `*employment multiplier*', Keynes's multiplier is known as *investment or income multiplier*. The essence of multiplier is that total increase in income, output or employment is manifold the original increase in investment. For example, if investment equal to ₹ 100 crores is made, then the income will not rise by ₹ 100 crores only but a multiple of it. If as a result of investment of ₹ 100 crores, national income increases by ₹ 300 crores, multiplier is equal to 3. If as a result of investment of ₹ 100 crores, total national income increases by ₹ 400 crores, multiplier is 4. The *investment multiplier is, therefore, the ratio of increment in income to the increment in investment.* If ΔI stands for increment in investment and ΔY stands for the resultant increase in income, then multiplier $k = \frac{\Delta Y}{\Delta I}$ where k stands for multiplier.

The Working of Multiplier

Now, the question is why the increase in income is many times more than the initial increase in investment. It is easy to explain this. Suppose Government undertakes investment expenditure equal to ₹ 100 crores on some public works, say the construction of rural roads. For this Government will pay wages to the labourers engaged, prices for the materials to the suppliers and remunerations to other factors who make contribution to the work of road-building. The total cost will amount to ₹ 100 crores. This will increase incomes of the people equal to ₹ 100 crores. But this is not all. The people who receive ₹ 100 crores will spend a good part of them on consumer goods. Suppose marginal propensity to consume of the people is 4/5 or 0.8%. Then out of ₹ 100 crores they will spend ₹ $100 \times \frac{4}{5}$ = ₹ 80 crores on consumer goods, which would increase incomes of those people who supply consumer goods equal to ₹ 80 crores. But those who receive these ₹ 80 crores will also in turn spend these incomes, depending upon their marginal propensity to consume. If their marginal propensity to consume is also 4/5, then they will spend $80 \times \frac{4}{5} =$ ₹ 64 crores on consumer goods. (This can also be obtained from $100 \times \left(\frac{4}{5}\right)^2$ .Thus, this will further increase incomes of some other people equal to ₹ 64 crores.

In this way, the chain of consumption expenditure would continue and income of the people will go on increasing. But every additional increase in income will be progressively less since a part of the income received will be saved. Thus, we see that the income will not increase by only ₹ 100 crores, which was initially invested in the construction of roads, but by many times more.

Derivation of Investment Multiplier

How much increase in national income will take place as a result of an initial increase in investment can be expressed in the following mathematical form :

Increase in income, Or

$$\Delta Y = 100 + 100 \times 4/5 + 100(4/5)^2 + 100(4/5)^3 + 100(4/5)^4 \ldots 100\,(4/5)^n$$

$$= 100[1 + (4/5) + (4/5)^2 + (4/5)^3 + (4/5)^4 \ldots (4/5)^n$$

Since the above series is one of geometric progression, increase in income (ΔY)

$$= 100 \frac{1}{1-4/5} = 100 \times \frac{1}{1/5} \qquad \ldots (i)$$

$$= 100 \times 5 = 500$$

Thus, ΔY = ₹ 500

It is thus clear from above that if the marginal propensity to consume is 4/5, the investment of ₹ 100 crores leads to the increase in national income by ₹ 500 crores. Therefore, multiplier here is equal to 5.

If b stands for marginal propensity to consume, ΔI for change in investment, then above geometric progression series can be written in the following general form

$$\Delta Y = \Delta I + \Delta I \times b + \Delta I(b)^2 + \Delta I(b)^3$$

or

$$\Delta Y = \Delta I \left(\frac{1}{1-b}\right) \qquad \ldots (ii)$$

$$\frac{\Delta Y}{\Delta I} = \frac{1}{1-b} \qquad \text{. . . } (iii)$$

$\frac{\Delta Y}{\Delta I}$ measures the size of the multiplier which is generally denoted by k and b stands for marginal propensity to consume. Therefore,

$$\text{Size of multiplier or } k = \frac{1}{1-MPC}$$

It is clear from above that the size of multiplier depends upon the marginal propensity to consume of the community. The multiplier is the reciprocal of one minus marginal propensity to consume. However, we can express multiplier in a simpler form. As we know that saving is equal to income minus consumption, one minus marginal propensity to consume will be equal to marginal propensity to save, that is, 1 – *MPC* = *MPS*. Therefore, multiplier,

$$k = \frac{1}{1-MPC} = \frac{1}{MPS} \qquad \text{... } (iv)$$

The equation (*ii*) above provides us with the relation between change in income (ΔY) and change in investment (ΔI). By using this relation we can obtain the increase in national income which will take place as a result of any increase in investment.

Derivation of Multiplier : Alternative Method

The multiplier can be derived algebraically as follows:

Writing the equation for the equilibrium level of income we have

$$Y = C + I \qquad \text{...(1)}$$

As in the multiplier analysis we are concerned with changes in income induced by changes in investment, rewriting the equation (1) in terms of changes in the variables we have

$$\Delta Y = \Delta C + \Delta I \qquad \text{...(2)}$$

In the simple Keynesian model of income determination, change in investment is considered to be autonomous or independent of changes in income while changes in consumption are function of changes in income.

In the consumption function,

$$C = a + bY$$

where a is a constant term, b is marginal propensity to consume which is also assumed to remain constant. Therefore, change in consumption can occur only if there is change in income. Thus

$$\Delta C = b\Delta Y \qquad \text{...(3)}$$

Substituting (3) into (2) we have

$$\Delta Y = b\Delta Y + \Delta I$$

$$\Delta Y - b\Delta Y = \Delta I$$

$$\Delta Y (1 - b) = \Delta I$$

$$\Delta Y = \frac{1}{1-b}\Delta I \qquad \text{...(4)}$$

or

$$\frac{\Delta Y}{\Delta I} = \frac{1}{1-b} \qquad \text{...(5)}$$

As b stands for marginal propensity to consume

$$\frac{\Delta Y}{\Delta I} = \frac{1}{1-MPC} = \frac{1}{MPS}$$

This is the same formula of multiplier as obtained earlier. Note that the value of multiplier $\frac{\Delta Y}{\Delta I}$ will remain constant as long as marginal propensity to consume remains the same.

Calculating the Size or Value of Multiplier

If the marginal propensity to consume of a community is equal to $\frac{2}{3}$, we can find out the size of multiplier as under:

$$\text{Multiplier, } k = \frac{1}{1-MPC}$$

$$= \frac{1}{1-\frac{2}{3}} = \frac{1}{\frac{1}{3}} = 3$$

Likewise, if the marginal propensity to consume is equal to $\frac{1}{2}$ or 0.5, then the multiplier:

$$= \frac{1}{1-\frac{1}{2}} = \frac{1}{\frac{1}{2}} = 2$$

Two Limiting Cases of the Value of Multiplier. There are two limiting cases of the multiplier. One limiting case occurs when the marginal propensity to consume is equal to one, that is, when the whole of the increment in income is consumed and nothing is saved. In this case, the size of multiplier will be equal to infinity, that is, a small increase in investment will bring about a very large increase in income and employment so that full employment is reached and even the process goes beyond that. "In such circumstances, the Government would need to employ only one road builder to raise income indefinitely, causing first full employment and then a limitless spiral of inflation."[1] However, this is unlikely to occur since marginal propensity to consume in the real world is less than one. The other limiting case occurs when marginal propensity to consume is equal to zero, that is, when nothing out of the increment in income is consumed, and the whole increment in income is saved. In this case, the value of the multiplier will be equal to one. That is, in this case, the increment in income will be equal to the original increase in investment and not a multiple of it. But in actual practice the marginal propensity to consume is less than one but more than zero . $\left(1 > \frac{\Delta C}{\Delta Y} > 0\right)$. Therefore, *the value of the multiplier is greater than one but less than infinity*.

Assumptions of Multiplier Theory

In our above explanation of multiplier, we have made many simplifying assumptions. First, we have assumed that the *marginal propensity to consume remains constant throughout* as the income increases in various rounds of consumption expenditure. However, the marginal propensity to consume may differ in various rounds of consumption expenditure. But this constancy of marginal propensity to consume is a realistic assumption, since all available empirical evidence shows that marginal propensity to consume is very stable in the short run. Secondly, we have assumed that there is a net increase in investment in a period and no further indirect effects on investment in that period occur or if they occur they have been taken into account so that there is a given net increase in investment. Further, we have assumed that *there is no any time-lag* between the increase in investment and the resultant increment in income. That is, increment in income takes place instantaneously as a result of increment in investment.

1. Stonier and Hague, A Textbook of Economic Theory, 4th edition, 1972.

J.M. Keynes ignored the time-lag in the process of income generation and therefore his multiplier is also called *instantaneous multiplier*. In recent years, the importance of time lag has been recognised and concept of dynamic multiplier has been developed on that basis. But in an elementary study as the present one the time lags will be ignored as was done by Keynes.

Another important assumption in the theory of multiplier is that excess capacity exists in the consumer goods industries so that when the demand for them increases, more amounts of consumer goods can be produced to meet this demand. If there is no excess capacity in consumer goods industries, the increase in demand as a result of some original increase in investment will bring about rise in prices rather than increases in real income, output and employment. As we shall see later, Keynes's multiplier was evolved in the context of advanced capitalist economies which were in grip of depression. In times of depression and there did exist excess capacity in the consumer goods industries due to lack of aggregate demand. The Keynesian multiplier effect is very small in developing countries like India when there is not much excess capacity in consumer goods industries.

In our above analysis of the multiplier process we have taken a closed economy, that is, we have not taken into account imports and exports. If ours were an open economy, then a part of the increment in consumption expenditure would have been made on imports of goods from abroad. This would have caused increment in income in foreign countries rather than within the country. This will reduce the value of the multiplier. *Imports are important leakage from the multiplier process* and we have ignored them in our above analysis for the purpose of simplicity.

Multiplier Works both in Money Terms and Real Terms

It is worth noting that multiplier not only works in money terms but also in real terms. In other words, multiple increment in income as a result of a given net increase in investment does not only take place in money terms but also in terms of real output, that is, in terms of goods and services. When incomes increase as a result of investment and these increments in income are spent on consumer goods, the output of consumer goods is increased to meet the extra demand brought about by increased incomes. Therefore, real income or output, increases by the same amount as the increment in money incomes, since *the prices of goods have been assumed to be constant*. Of course, we have assumed, as has been mentioned above, that there exists excess productive capacity in the consumer goods industries so that when the demand for consumer goods increases, their production can be easily increased to meet this demand. However, if due to some bottlenecks output of goods cannot be increased in response to increasing demand, prices will rise and as result the real multiplier effect will be small.

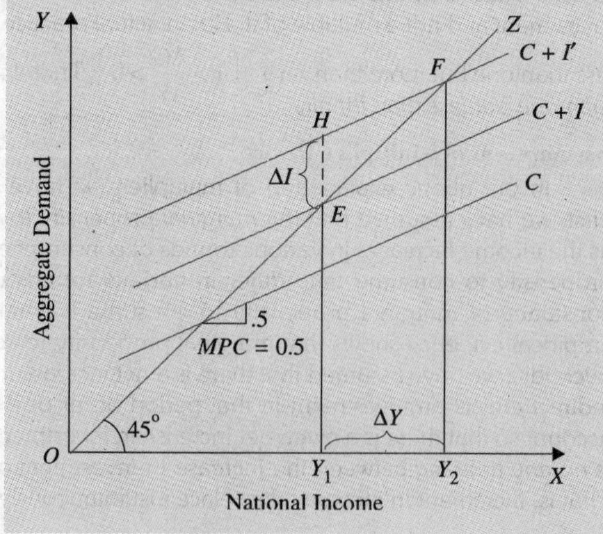

Fig. 39.9. *Keynes's Income or investment Multiplier*

Diagrammatic Illustration of Multiplier

We have already explained that the level of national income is determined by the equilibrium between aggregate demand and aggregate supply. In other words, the level of national income is fixed at the level where $C + I$ curve intersects the 45° income curve. With such a diagram we can explain the multiplier. The multiplier is illustrated in

Fig. 39.9. In this figure C represents marginal propensity to consume. Marginal propensity to consume has been here assumed to be equal to $\frac{1}{2}$ i.e., 0.5. Therefore, the slope of the curve *C* of marginal propensity to consume curve *C* has been taken to be equal to 0.5. $C + I$ represents aggregate demand curve. It will be seen from Fig. 39.9 that the aggregate demand curve $C + I$ which intersects the 45° line at point *E* so that the level of income equal to OY_1 is determined. If investment increases by the amount *EH* we can then find out how much increment in income will occur as a result of this. As a consequence of increase in investment by *EH*, the aggregate demand curve shifts upward to the new position $C + I'$. This new aggregate demand curve $C + I'$ intersects the 45° income line at point *F* so that the equilibrium level of income increases to OY_2. Hence as a result of net increase in investment equal to *EH*, the income has increased by Y_1Y_2. It will be seen from the figure that Y_1Y_2 is greater than *EH*. On measuring, it will be found that Y_1Y_2 is twice the length of *EH*. This is as it is expected because the marginal propensity to consume is here equal to $\frac{1}{2}$ and therefore the size of multiplier will be equal to 2.

The multiplier can be illustrated through saving-investment diagram also. In a previous chapter we explained the determination of national income also through planned saving the investment. Therefore, the multiplier can also be explained with the help of saving-investment diagram, as has been shown in Fig. 39.10. In this figure *SS* is the saving curve indicating that as the level of income increases, the community plans to save more. Slope of planned saving curve *SS* has been taken to be equal to 0.5, that is, $MPS = 0.5$ or $\frac{1}{2}$. *II* is the investment curve showing the level of investment planned to be undertaken by the investors in the community. The investment has been taken to be a constant amount and autonomous of changes in income. This investment level *OI* has been determined the marginal efficiency of capital and the rate of interest. Investment being autonomous of income means that it does not change with the level of income. Keynes treated investment as autonomous of income and we will here follow him. It will be seen from Fig. 39.2 that when investment increases from *OI* to *OI'*, the equilibrium level of national income increase from OY_1 to OY_2 (*i.e.* $\Delta Y = Y_1Y_2$). Thus

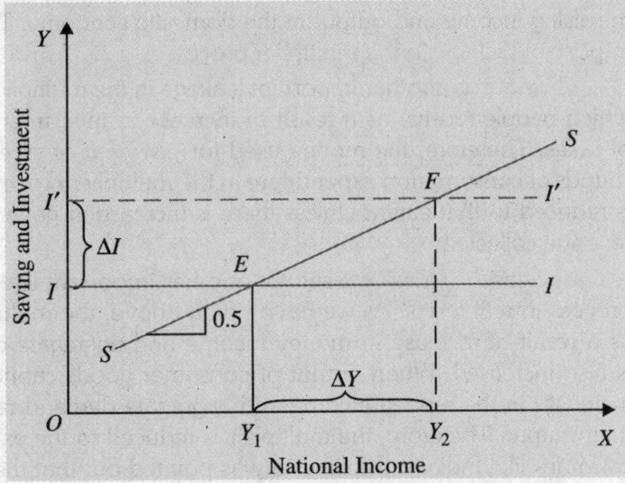

Fig. 39.10. *Multiplier Explained with the Aid of Savings-Investment Approach*

$$\text{Multiplier } \frac{\Delta Y}{\Delta I} = \frac{Y_1Y_2}{II'} = 2$$

Since marginal propensity to save is here equal to 0.5 the multiplier on the basis of our above formula, namely, $K = \frac{1}{MPS} = \frac{1}{0.5}$ will be equal to 2.

Leakages in the Multiplier Process

We have seen above that as a result of increase in investment, the level of income increases by a multiple of it. In our above analysis, saving is a leakage in the multiplier process. Had there been no saving and as a result marginal propensity to consume was equal to 1, the multiplier would have been equal to infinity. In that case as a result of some initial increase in investment, income would go on rising indefinitely. Since marginal propensity to consume is actually less than one, some saving does take place. Therefore, multiplier in actual practice is less than infinity. But besides saving, there are other leakage in the process of income generation which reduces the size of the multiplier. Therefore, the increase in income as a result of some increase in investment will be less than warranted by the size of the multiplier measured by the given marginal propensity to consume.

Payment of Debt. The first leakage in the multiplier process occurs when people, especially business men, make payment of old debts rather than spending their increase in income on consumer goods. This reduces the size of the multiplier.

Secondly, if the people *hold a part of their increment in income as idle cash balances* and do not use it for consumption, they also constitute leakage in the multiplier process and reduces the size of multiplier.

Thirdly, in an open economy as is usually the case, a part of increment in income will also be spent on the imports of consumer goods. The proportion of increment in income spent on the imports of consumer goods will generate income in foreign countries and will not help in raising income and output in the domestic economy. Therefore, imports constitute another important leakage in the multiplier process.

Taxation is another important leakage in the multiplier process. The increments in income which people receive as a result of increase in investment are also in part used for payment of taxes. Therefore, the money used for payment of taxes does not appear in the successive rounds of consumption expenditure in the multiplier process, and therefore the size of multiplier is reduced to that extent Unless there is increase in government expenditure equal to the tax revenue collected.

Increase in Prices constitutes another important leakage in the working of the multiplier process in real terms. As we have noted above, the multiplier works in real terms only when as a result of increase in money income and aggregate demand, output of consumer goods is also increased. When output of consumer goods cannot be easily increased, a part of the increases in the money income and aggregate demand raises prices of the goods rather than their output. Therefore, the multiplier is reduced to the extent of price inflation. In developing countries like India in the fifties it was pointed out that there was not much excess capacity in many consumer goods industries, especially in wage-goods industries. Therefore, when income and demand increase as a result of increase in investment, it generally raises the prices of these goods rather than their output and therefore weakens the working of the multiplier in real terms. Thus, it was often asserted that Keynesian theory of multiplier was not very much relevant to the conditions of developing countries like India.[2] However, what was true in the fifties is not true in the present-day economic conditions in India and other developing countries. Today after over six decades of economic development there is greater responsiveness of industrial output to increase in demand resulting from increase in investment. As a result, at present Keynes's multiplier does work in real terms in developing countries like India to a good extent. Of course, due to various leakages mentioned above, the size of multiplier is not as high as warranted by the high propensity to consume in India and other developing countries.

2. See V.K.R.V. Rao, investment, Income and the Multiplier in an Underdeveloped Economy printed in A.N. Agarwala and S.P. Singh (edited), The Economics of Underdevelopment, Oxford, 1958.

Importance of the Concept of Multiplier

Multiplier is one of the most important concepts developed by J.M. Keynes to explain the determination of income and employment in an economy. The theory of multiplier has been used to explain the cumulative upward and downward swings of the trade cycles that occur in a free-enterprise capitalist economy. When investment in an economy rises, it has a multiple and cumulative effect on national income, output and employment. As a result, economy experiences rapid upward movement. On the other hand, when due to some reasons, especially due to the adverse change in the expectations of the business class, investment falls, then backward working of the multiplier causes a multiple and cumulative fall in income, output and employment and as a result the economy rapidly moves on downswing of the trade cycle. Thus, Keynesian theory of multiplier helps a good deal in explaining the movements of trade cycles or fluctuations in the economy.

The theory of multiplier has also a great practical importance in the field of fiscal policy to be pursued by the Government to get out of the depression and achieve the state of full employment. To get rid of depression and remove unemployment, Government investment in public works was recommended even before Keynes. But it was thought that the increase in income will be limited to the amount of investment undertaken in these public works. But the importance of public works is enhanced when it is realised that the total effect on income, output and employment as a result of some initial investment has a multiplier effect. Thus, Keynes recommended Government investment in public works to solve the problem of depression and unemployment. The public investment in public works such as road building, construction of hospitals, schools, irrigation facilities will raise aggregate demand by a multiple amount. The multiple increase in income and demand will also encourage the increase in private investment. Thus, the deficiency in private investment which leads to the state of depression and underemployment equilibrium will now be made up and a state of full employment will be restored. If the multiplier had not worked, the income and demand would have risen as a result of some public investment but not as much as they rise with the multiplier effect. Inspired by the Keynesian theory of multiplier, expansionary fiscal policy of increase in Government expenditure and reduction in income has have been adopted by President John Kenedy and present president George W. Bush in the United State of America to remove involuntary unemployment and depreciation. This had a great success in removing unemployment and, depression and, therefore, Keynesian theory of multiplier was vindicated and as a result people's belief in it increased.

Numerical Problems on Multiplier

Problem 1. *Suppose the level of autonomous investment in an economy is ₹ 200 crores and consumption function of the economy is :*

$$C = 80 + 0.75Y$$

(a) What will be the equilibrium level of income?

(b) What will be the increase in national income if investment increases by ₹ 25 crores.

Solution. (*a*) For equilibrium level of income,

$$Y = C + I \qquad \text{...}(i)$$

where

$$C = 80 + 0.75$$

$$I = 200 \text{ crores}$$

Substituting the values of C and I in (*i*) we have

$$Y = 80 + 0.75Y + 200$$

$$(Y - 0.75Y) = 80 + 200 = 280$$

$$0.25Y = 280$$

$$Y = 280 \times \frac{100}{25} = 1120$$

Equilibrium level of income is therefore equal to 1120 crores.

(*b*) How much increase in income will occur as a result of increase in investment by ₹ 25 crores depends on the size of multiplier. The size of multiple is determined by the value of marginal propensely to consume. In the given consumption function ($C = 80 + 0.75Y$) marginal propensity to consume is equal to 0.75 or $\frac{3}{4}$. Thus,

$$\text{multiplier } (k) = \frac{1}{1-MPC} = \frac{1}{1-\frac{3}{4}} = 4$$

$$\Delta Y = \Delta I \times k$$

$$\Delta Y = 25 \times 4 = 100 \text{ crores}$$

Thus, with increase in investment by ₹ 25 crores, national income will rise by 100 crores.

Problem 2. *What increase in investment is needed to raise income by ₹ 4000 if MPC is 0.75. How much will there be increase in consumption and saving due to this increase in income?*

Solution :

$$\text{Multiplier, } k = \frac{\Delta Y}{\Delta I}$$

or $$\Delta I = \frac{\Delta Y}{\Delta k} \quad \ldots (i)$$

Multipler, $$K = \frac{1}{1-\text{MPC}}$$

Given $$MPC = 0.75$$

in $$k = \frac{1}{1-0.75} = 4$$

Given $$\Delta Y = 4{,}000$$

Substituting the values of ΔY and k in equation (i) we have

$$\Delta I = \frac{4000}{4} = ₹\,1000$$

Thus investment should rise by ₹ 1000 to achieve ₹ 4000 increment in income.

Now, $$\Delta C = \Delta Y \times MPC$$

$$= 4000 \times 0.75 = ₹\,3000$$

$$\Delta S = \Delta Y - \Delta C$$

$$= 4000 - 3000 = 1000$$

WHAT CAUSES DEPRESSION OR RECESSION : ROLE OF MULTIPLIER

During 1929-33, capitalist economies of the world found themselves in the grip of depression. Such was the severity of this depression that in the United States, the rate of unemployment rose from 3.2 per cent in 1929 to 25% of the labour force in 1933. Besides, there was a drastic decline in Gross National Product (GNP) which fell from 315 billion dollars in 1929 to 222 billion dollars in 1933, that is, national income declined by 30 per cent during these four years period. This reflects a dismal picture of the American economy during the period of Great Depression. In England as well as in other European countries also such a grave situation of severe recession and huge unemployment prevailed during this period. Before 1929-33 and even after it, recessions have occurred in these economies but they have not been as severe as that took place during 1929-33.

Classical economists had no valid explanation of such a severe depression and large-scale cyclical unemployment of labour. A.C. Pigou and other economists of his view attributed this situation to the high wage rates kept by trade unions and Government. Pigou, therefore, suggested all-round cut in wages to increase employment and to remove depression and unemployment. However, this solution of the problem was neither logically sound nor practical to be implemented. Keynes challenged this view of the classical economists and put forward a different explanation of depression and cyclical unemployment which was accepted by many as logical and correct. He explained his viewpoint in his now noted work, '*General Theory of Employment, Interest, and Money*'. He not only gave a sound and valid explanation of depression and its associated problem of cyclical unemployment but also suggested effective policy measures to cure them.

According to Keynes, the cause of depression and cyclical unemployment in the industrialised capitalist countries was sharp decline in private investment due to the adverse business expectations about profit making. There was a wave of pessimism prevailing among investors. The decline in private investment due to fall in marginal efficiency of capital (that is, expected rate of return) caused a fall in aggregate demand and resulted in less than full-employment equilibrium. Consequently, level of output and employment fell drastically and involuntary unemployment came to prevail on a large scale. The involuntary unemployment that prevails in times of recession/depression is called cyclical unemployment and, as we have seen above, according to Keynes, it is due to deficiency of aggregate demand.

Large fluctuations in investment, according to Keynes, is due to the uncertain basis of profit expectations on which investment decisions are made. To quote him, "*We have to admit that our basis of knowledge for estimating the yield ten years hence of a Railway, a copper mine, a textile factory, the goodwill of a patent medicine ... amounts to little and sometimes to nothing.*"[3] In view of this uncertainty of future. Keynes stressed that investment decisions were greatly

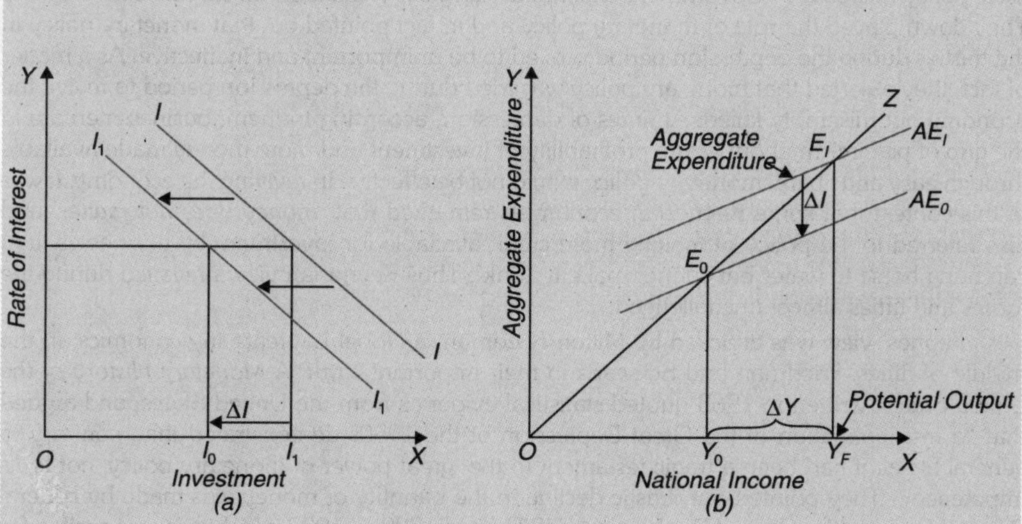

Fig. 39.11. *What Causes Depression and Cyclical Unemployment : Keynes's Explanation.*

influenced by how optimistic or pessimistic investors feel. He used the term *animal spirits* to describe these pessimistic or optimistic expectations of the investors about profit earning from

3. J.M. Keynes, The Genral Theory of Employment, Interest and Money, pp. 149-150.

investment projects. The term animal spirits implies that there may be no good or intelligent basis for expectations on which investors base their decisions. Thus the cause of depression or cyclical involuntary unemployment is the deficiency of aggregate demand due to fall in private investment that results from adverse business expectations and loss of confidence of the investors.

It will be useful to explain through a diagram how a fall in investment causes a decline in level of output and employment and results in depression. This is illustrated in Fig. 39.11. It will be seen from Figure 39.11 (*a*) that due to adverse profit expectations or pessimism of investors, investment demand curve shifts to the left from *II* to *I'I'*. With this it will be seen that investment falls from I_1 to I_0 at a given rate of interest. This fall in investment demand by I_1I_0 causes a downward shift in the aggregate expenditure curve from *AE* to AE_0 (See Fig. 39.11 (*b*). As a result, the equilibrium between aggregated expenditure and aggregate output which was initially at full employment level Y_F (which corresponds to point E_1 where the aggregate expenditure curve intersects 45° line) falls to the new equilibrium level of income OY_0. Therefore, the *cause of depression is deficiency of aggregate demand.* It should also be noted, that the decline in the level of GNP or national income following the fall in investment and aggregate demand will also result in decrease in level of employment in the economy and cause the emergence of large-scale unemployment.

It is also important to note that with help of *his theory of multiplier* Keynes showed that the fall in the level of national income was much greater than that of decline in investment. This can be known by comparing decline in investment demand (ΔI) and fall in national income. (ΔY) in Figure 39.11 (*b*).

Explaining Great Depression (1929-33) : Monetarist View

We have explained above Keynes' view that great depression of 1929-33 was caused by fall in investment caused by the drastic fall in the profit expectations of business class. The decline in investment, according to him, caused aggregate demand to fall which along with the reverse working of multiplier caused conditions of depression (*i.e.* high rate of unemployment, substantial decrease in GNP and fall in prices) Keynes and his followers emphasise the role of fiscal policy (increase in Government expenditure and cut in taxation) to stimulate investment. They down played the role of monetary policy and in fact pointed out that monetary policy in the thirties during the depression period proved to be unimportant and ineffective. As a matter of fact, they asserted that monetary policy was tried during the depression period to revive the economy but miserably failed. At times of depression, according to them, businessmen are in the grip of pessimism about future profitability of investment and more money made available through easy and liberal monetary policy would not be effective in reviving the economy. It was in this context that some Keynesian economists remarked that '*money does not matter*' and also referred to the policy of making more credit available for investment by businesses 'you can bring horse to water but cannot make it drink'. Thus Keynesian view prevailed during the forties and fifties almost unchallenged.

Keynes' view was attacked by Milton Friedman, a Nobel Laureate in economics, in the middle of fifties. Friedman and Schwartz in their important work '*A Monetary History of the United States*' written in 1963 quoted statistical evidence from the United States, and argued that "a re-examination of the Great Depression of the 1930s demonstrated that, contrary to general belief, it had been a tragic testament to the great power of monetary policy, not to its impotence'[4] They pointed out drastic decline in the quantity of money was made by Federal Reserve System (the Central Banks of the USA) from 1929 to 1933 which was responsible for severe depression in the American economy. They argued that the failure of the federal Reserve system to prevent bank failures and the drastic decrease in money supply during 1930-1933

4. Freidman and Schwartaz, Monetary History of the United States, 1963, p. 300.

increased the intensity of depression. To quote them, "The US Federal Reserve System, could have prevented the *decline of one-third* in the quantity of money that occurred from 1929 to 1933. Had it done so, the evidence indicated, the depression would have been far milder and briefer"[5].

We thus see that Freidman and other monetarists emphasise monetary policy in causing depression. In fact, they go to the other extreme view '*money alone matters*'. However, in our view in recent recession during 2000-2003.the Fed Reserve System made successive cuts in rate of interest more than 7 times to revive the American economy without any success. For stimulating investment and growth, it cut the rate of interest even below 1 per cent, the lowest in the last 50 years but failed in its objective to overcome recession. Even in India Reserve Bank also lowered the bank rate, several times during 1998 – 2003 and reduced it to 6 per cent - the lowest in forty years to bring about industrial recovery but it had also not much effect. In the case of the USA, the signs of recovery in the first quarter of 2003-04 seems to have been the result of drastic reduction in taxation to the extent of 3.5 billion dollars and huge increase in defence expenditure for war in Iraq. Both of these are fiscal policies suggested by Keynesians that seems to have worked to start a recovery in the American economy.

To conclude, in the view of present author the truth lies in between the two extreme views of Keynes and Friedman. Therefore, modern economists give importance to both fiscal and monetary policies for influencing investment and growth in GNP. Both can be complements to each other. Thus, both profit expectations of entrepreneurs and cost and availability of credit play a significant role in determining national income, employment and price level in the economy.

It many however be noted that in the recent global financial crisis in 2008 that resulted in severe recession in USA, UK and other European countries it is Keynesian policy of *fiscal stimulus* (that is, increase in Government expenditure to stimulate aggregate demand) to lift the economy out of recession was adopted with great success as in most of these countries (including the USA) experienced recovery during 2009-10. On the other hand, monetary policy measures adopted in the USA and other countries, as predicted by Keynes, failed to increase consumption and investment demand. This shows Friedman's view of effectiveness of monetary policy to fight recession proved wrong. The failure to increase liquidity in the banking system and soften interest rate to revive the economy by the Federal Reserve during 1927-33. Milton Friedman had argued that Great Depression in the US during the early thirties would have been stopped in its tracks by the Federal Reserve simply by providing banks with enough liquidity which would have ensured adequate increase in the money supply. In the US, during 2007-09 Federal Reserve had injected large liquidity in the American banking system and lowered its key interest rate to almost zero and still the recession in the US deepened further. It has now become evident that preventing recession through monetary policy measures is not so easy as believed by Friedman and other monetarists. Monetary policy alone has proved to be ineffective to get rid of recession as Keynes had asserted during the thirties and laid stress on fiscal policy of large-scale deficit spending by the Government. It is the Keynesian policies of increasing Government expenditure and reducing taxes not only in the US but also in other countries including India that were adopted to overcome recession or prevent slowdown in the economies. In India to prevent slowdown by boosting investment and consumption demand we have not relied on monetary policy alone but have also provided fiscal stimulus to prevent slowdown is the Indian economy. As regards effectiveness of monetary policy in preventing recession or slowdown is concerned the remarks of Paul Krugman, a Nobel Prize winner for economics for the year 2008 are worth quoting. He writes, "It turns out, however, that preventing depression is not that easy after all. Under Bernanke's leadership, the Fed has been supplying liquidity like an engine crew trying to put out a five-alarm fire, and the money supply has been rising rapidly

5. Friedman and Schwartz, op. cit.

yet credit remains scarce and the economy is still in free fall.... Friedman's claim that monetary policy could have prevented the Great depression was an attempt to refute the analysis of John Maynard Keynes, who argued that monetary policy is ineffective under depression conditions and that fiscal policy – large-scale deficit spending by the government – is needed to fight mass unemployment. The failure of monetary policy in the current crisis shows that Keynes had it right the first time. And Keynesian thinking lies behind Obama's plan to rescue the economy".[3]

POLICY IMPLICATIONS OF KEYNES'S THEORY OF EMPLOYMENT AND INCOME

Keynes's theory has important policy implications for raising the level of employment and income in the economy. When the equilibrium of the economy is at less than full-employment level and as a consequence there is depression or recession in the economy and with it huge unemployment of labour prevails. According to Keynes, this occurs due to lack of aggregate effective demand. There are two types of policies which may be adopted to overcome this situation of recession and unemployment. They are (1) monetary policy and (2) fiscal policy. Under monetary policy, through expansion in money supply rate of interest can be lowered which will encourage private investment. With the increase in private investment, aggregate demand will increase (that is, aggregate demand curve will shift upward) which will raise the equilibrium level of employment. As a result, the economy will be lifted out of necessionary conditions and unemployment will be removed.

However, Keynes had serious doubts about the effectiveness of monetary policy. He was of the view that in times of depression rate of interest is already very low and at this liquidity preference curve of the community (that is, the curve of demand for money to hold) is *absolutely elastic, that is, it is of horizontal shape*. Therefore, in this situation when money supply is increased, rate of interest will not fall. Thus, with no fall in the rate of interest, private investment will not pick up further.

Importance of Fiscal Policy

In view of ineffectiveness of monetary policy, Keynes laid stress on the role of fiscal policy in curing recession/depression and removing involuntary unemployment. Under the fiscal policy, a major measure is the *increase in expenditure by the Government on several types of public works* in times of depression. The increase in Government expenditure will cause an upward shift in the aggregate demand curve. This increase in aggregate demand will bring about increase in employment and output. If the increase in Government expenditure and as a result rise in aggregate demand is sufficient, it will help in achieving equilibrium at full-employment level. As a result, depression and involuntary unemployment will be eliminated. It is worth noting that in this regard Keynes put forward a theory of multiplier which strengthened the case for raising Government expenditure on public works in times of depression or when large-scale unemployment prevailed in the economy. We shall discuss the theory of multiplier at length in later chapter. Briefly, theory of multiplier implies that increase in Government expenditure will raise aggregate demand and therefore output and employment not by the amount of increase in Government expenditure but by a multiple of it.

Another important measure of fiscal policy to raise employment and output is the *reduction in taxes*. When rates of personal taxes such as income tax are reduced, disposable income of the people increases which brings about rise in their demand for consumption. The rise in consumption demand pushes up aggregate demand curve and helps in removing recession and unemployment. It may be noted that on the recommendations of Keynesian

3. Paul Krugman, Fighting off Depression, New York Times News Service, Feb. 2009.

economists American President John Kennedy made a drastic cut in income taxes in 1964. This had a great success as output and employment in the USA increased significantly and, as a result, recession and unemployment were removed. Cut in personal taxes to boost aggregate demand has also been applied in later years in the USA as well as in Great Britain. Recently in 2003, the President of the USA Geoge W. Bush made a $ 3.5 billion cut in taxes to revive the American economy. Again in 2007-09, to revive the American economy out of severe recession both Bush and Obama adopted a fiscal stimulus package involving increase in public expenditure and cut in taxes.

In the end, it is important to note that modern economists though agree with Keynes' view about the effectiveness of fiscal policy in curing recession, they do not entirely agree with Keynes' view about the ineffectiveness of monetary policy. It may be noted that, according to the modern Keynesians and others, liquidity preference curve of the community is fairly elastic even in times of recession which implies that expansion in money supply will cause a decline in interest rate and will therefore stimulate private investment. Further, according to them, investment demand curve is also fairly elastic which implies that fall in interest rate will have significant impact on private investment. Thus, according to a majority of modern economists, both monetary and fiscal policies are important instruments whereby aggregate demand of the economy can be changed. We shall discuss in detail the roles of monetary and fiscal policies for attaining economic stabilisation in later chapters.

QUESTIONS FOR REVIEW

1. Explain how equilibrium level of national income is determined by level of effective demand in a simple two-sector Keynesian model. Is this equilibrium necessarily established at full employment level ?
2. Explain the equilibrium of national income by consumption and investment. When will the equilibrium be established at full-employment ?
3. Explain Keynes' income-expenditure approach to the determination of national income. Why can this equilibrium be reached below full-employment level ?
4. Define planned (desired) saving and planned (desired) investment. Explain how equilibrium level of national income is determined by planned saving and planned investment. Why is this equilibrium not always attained at full-employment level ?
5. What do you understand by the equilibrium level of national income. Explain that both saving–investment approach and aggregate demand–aggregate supply approach yield the same level of equilibrium.
6. Explain the Keynesian concept of aggregate demand. How is the Keynesian aggregate demand function different from the classical demand function.
7. Given the saving function $S = -10 + 0.2y$ and autonomous investment, $I =$ ₹ 50 crore.
   (*i*) Find the equilibrium level of income.
   (*ii*) Find the level of consumption.
   (*iii*) If investment increases permanently by ₹ 5 crores, what will be the new levels of income and consumption
8. Explain Keynes's theory of employment spell out the reason for under-employment equilibrium in the Keynesian model.
9. The logical starting point of Keynes's theory of employment is the principle of aggregate effective demand. Explain how Keynes explains the emergence of involuntary unemployment in a free market economy.
10. What is investment multiplier ? How is it, related to marginal propensity to consume.
11. Explain Keynes's theory of multiplier. What are the leakages that may occur in the working of multiplier process in an economy.
12. Explain how Keynes and monetarists explained the depression that gripped the Capitalist economies during 1929-33.

Determination of National Income with Government and Foreign Trade : Three Sector and Four Sector Models

Introduction

We carry our analysis of determination of national income further in this chapter. Having explained the Keynesian two sector model of determination of national income in the previous chapter, we will explain in this chapter the determination of national income in the three sector and four sector models. The three sector model incorporates the role of government with its expenditure and taxation in the determination of national income. In the a four sector model we add the foreign trade in our analysis of determination of national income and discuss how exports and imports affect national income of a country.

DETERMINATION OF NATIONAL INCOME : THREE SECTOR MODEL

Government Expenditure and National Income

In our analysis of two sector model we have explained how the equilibrium level of national income is determined by the consumption function and autonomous investment demand. In our analysis we did not take into account the role of Government expenditure in the determination of national income. However, in all economies today including the free-market capitalist economies such as those of U.S.A., Britain, Japan, the Government expenditure on goods and services plays an important role in the determination of national income and therefore it should also be included in the analysis of income determination. It is important to note here that the magnitude of Government expenditure on such things as highways, public parks, education, health services is governed by the consideration of promoting social welfare, employment and growth in the economy and does not depend on the level of income of the economy. Therefore, in the simple Keynesian model of income determination, the Government expenditure is treated as *autonomous expenditure*. We further assume for the moment that Government spends on goods and services but imposes no taxes. We denote Government expenditure by *G*. Thus in the three sector economy when we take into account the income generating effects of Government expenditure, we get the following equation for the equilibrium level of national income.

$$Y = C + I + G$$

where Y is national income or output and $C + I + G$ represents the level of aggregate demand including Government expenditure, G.

Since consumption function $C = a + bY$ where b stands for marginal propensity to consume and a for autonomous consumption expenditure, we can rewrite the equilibrium level of national income as under :

$$Y = a + bY + I + G$$
$$Y - bY = a + I + G$$
$$Y(1 - b) = a + I + G$$
$$Y = \frac{1}{1-b}(a + I + G)$$

Thus it is clear that the *equilibrium level of income (when impact of Government expenditure is also considered) is equal to the sum of three types of fixed autonomous expenditure*, namely, autonomous consumption, autonomous investment and Government expenditure $(a + I + G)$ multiplied by the value of the multiplier $[1/(1 - b)]$.

Graphic Illustration

The impact of Government expenditure on goods and services on the equilibrium level of national income is illustrated in Fig. 40.1. C is equal to $a + by$ is the consumption function curve on which we have added the autonomous investment equal to I and the autonomous Government expenditure on goods and services (G) to get the aggregate expenditure (or aggregate demand) curve $C + I + G$. With this, the equilibrium national income OY_2 is determined at the level at which the aggregate expenditure curve $(C + I + G)$ interesets the 45° line, that is, aggregate demand $(C + I + G)$ equals aggregate supply of output at OY_2. The reason for the determination of equilibrium level of income at OY_2 when Government expenditure is included in the aggregate demand curve is the same as stated earlier.

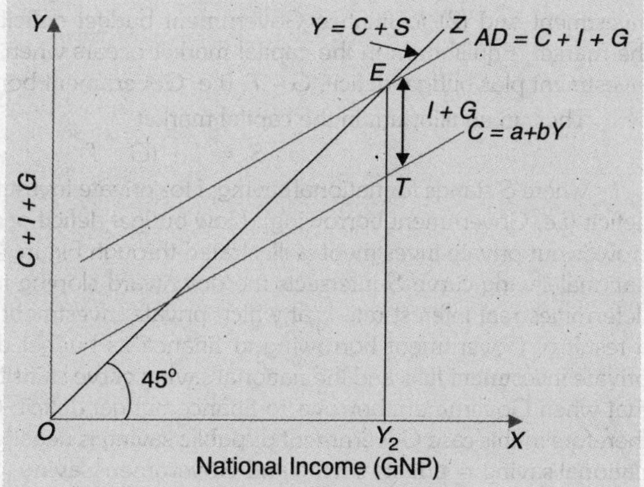

Fig. 40.1. *Determination of National Income : The Three Sector Model*

It will be observed from Fig. 40.1 that at a level of national income less than OY_2 aggregate expenditure $C + I + G$ exceeds aggregate supply. This implies *unintended decline in the inventories* of goods with the firms which will induce them to expand the level of aggregate output to the level OY_2. On the contrary, at the level of national income greater than OY_2, the aggregate expenditure is less than aggregate supply of output. *This deficiency of demand for goods will cause unintended accumulation of inventories.* The firms would respond to this by cutting back production of goods which will lead to the reduction of national income to OY_2.

It is important to note that in the presence of Government expenditure, national income is determined at the level at which the saving gap is equal to the sum of private investment and Government expenditure $(I + G)$. It will be seen from Fig. 40.1 that at OY_2 equilibrium level of national income (GNP), the saving gap is TE which is equal to the sum of private investment and government expenditure. It may be further noted that just as investment expenditure has a multiplier effect on increase in income Government expenditure too has a multiplier effect on increase in income and its value is equal to $\frac{1}{1-b}$ where b is marginal propensity to consume.

Government Expenditure, Budget Deficit and Capital Market

We have explained above how the government expenditure affects the product market by bringing about increase in aggregate demand. Now, an important question is how the Government expenditure is financed. Imposition of taxes is an important way of financing Government expenditure. But taxes reduce aggregate demand in the product market by lowering disposable income of the community and thereby causing a decline in its consumption expenditure. Therefore, if Government expenditure equals tax revenue collected ($G = T$), then Government has a balanced budget and much of the expansionary effect of government expenditure is offset by taxes levied. If Government increases its expenditure without raising taxes, (*i.e.* $G > T$), then it has a *budget deficit* which has a large expansionary effect on the product market and, as seen above, leads to increase in national income (*GDP*). This deficit budget can be financed by borrowing from the market. But borrowing by the Government to finance its deficit affects the capital market. This is because borrowing by the Government will compete with private investors for the saving of the public. As a result of borrowing by the Government from the market, less saving is available for private investment. When the Government runs a deficit, national saving has two uses : (1) to finance private investment and (2) to finance Government budget deficit which is met by borrowing from the market. Equilibrium in the capital market occurs when national saving is equal to private investment plus budget deficit, $G - T$, (i.e. Government borrowing).

Thus, in equilibrium in the capital market

$$S = I + (G - T)$$

where S stands for national saving, I for private investment, and ($G - T$) stands for budget deficit (*i.e.* Government borrowing). How budget deficit or Government borrowing reduces or crowds out private investment is illustrated through Figure 40A.1 where to begin with vertical national saving curve S intersects the downward sloping investment curve II at point E_0 and determines real interest rate r_0 at which private investment is equal to I_0 takes place. Now, as a result of Government borrowing to finance its budget deficit ($G - T$) saving available for private investment falls and the national saving curve shifts to the left[1] to the new position. Note that when Government borrows to finance budget deficit, Government is said to dissave and therefore in this case Government or public saving is negative ($G - T = -S_g$). Note further that national saving = private saving and Government saving ($S = S_p + S_g$). The capital market is now in equilibrium at point E_1 and rate of interest rises to r_1. At this higher interest rate r_1, private investment falls to I_1. Thus, borrowing by the Government to finance its budget deficit has led to *crowding out of private investment*. As mentional above, a part of national saving is used to finance private investment and a part to finance budget deficit of the Government.

It is worth noting that when Government expenditure is fully matched by increase in taxes (*i.e.* $G = T$) we have a balanced budget but, as will be explained later, it will still have a expansionary effect on national income, though, the multiplier effect of a balanced budget is equal to one. However, since in case of balanced budget increase in Government expenditure is matched by increase in taxes which reduces disposable income $Y_d = Y - T$. And reduction in the disposable income (Y_d) leads to decrease in both consumption and saving ($Y_d = C + S$). The decrease in saving will cause rate of interest to rise and thereby crowds out private investment.

Further, when the Government has a *budget surplus* (i.e. $T > G$), it has a *positive saving* which will lead to the increase in national saving and make more funds available for private sector to borrow. This will cause real rate of interest to fall. As a result, higher private investment will occur in case of surplus budget.

1. Note that budget deficit or borrowing by the Government is also viewed as Government Dissaving

It is worth noting that in our above analysis Government expenditure has been treated as consumption expenditure on goods and services purchased to satisfy collective wants. However, this is strictly true in case of a purely free-market economy such as that of the US where the Government is not a major investor. But in case of India's mixed economy the Government is an important investor and a good part of its borrowing is used for investment purposes, especially for investment in infrastructure projects such as power, transport, highways, roads, ports etc. Such Government borrowing for investment purposes cannot be considered as consumption expenditure or *dissaving*. Therefore, it has a large expansionary effect on national income with a usual multiplier effect. Viewed as such Government borrowing for investment, especially for infrastructure projects in developing countries, may *crowd in* private investment rather than *crowding it out*. This is so because lack of adequate infrastructure hinders private investment.

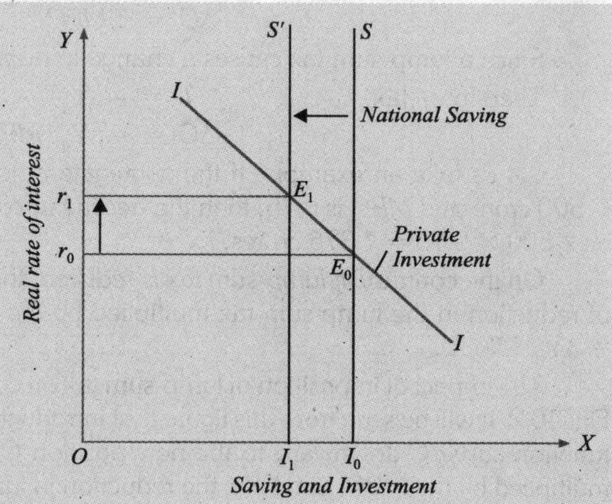

Fig. 40A.1. *Effect of Budget Deficit and Government Borrowing on Capital Market*

Determination of National Income with Government Expenditure and a Lump Sum Tax

Now, in a three sector model we analyse the impact of Government expenditure when to finance this expenditure the government levies a lump sum tax. Note that a lump-sum tax does not vary with income. In this case if government expenditure equals revenue from lump-sum tax, its budget will be in *balance*. On the other hand, if government expenditure exceeds tax revenue, there will be a *budget deficit*. Further, if tax revenue is more than its expenditure, government will have a *surplus budget*. We are thus concerned here with the impact of government expenditure and taxation together on the determination of national income. Let us assume *the government follows a balanced budget policy* in which case government expenditure equals tax revenue from lump-sum tax. Let us assume that there are no *transfer payments* made by the government.

The simplest kind of a tax is the *lump-sum tax* in which a given fixed amount of revenue is collected irrespective of the level of income. Suppose government has decided to raise extra ₹ 500 crore by way of imposing lump-sum tax on the public. Every one will have to pay the fixed amount out of his income as his share of lump sum tax. In the aggregate, the disposable income of the economy will be reduced by this fixed amount of lump-sum tax *i.e.*, (500 crore) whatever the level of national income (GNP). Consequently, people will consume less after the levy of lump-sum tax. A lump-sum tax of ₹ 500 crores imposed by the Government will reduce the disposable income by the same amount, that is, by ₹ 500 crores. As a result, the people will consume less (and also save less) at each level of national income (GNP). However, it is worth mentioning that *consumption will not fall by the full amount of the tax* because a part of the reduction in disposable income due to the tax was being consumed and a part of it was being saved prior to taxation. Therefore, reduction in disposable income due to the lump-sum tax will partly cause a decline in consumption and partly a decline in saving. As a result, the amount by which consumption will fall due to the imposition of lump-sum tax will be equal to the amount of tax multiplied by the marginal propensity to consume. If ΔY_d stands for change in disposable income, *T* for lump-sum tax imposed and *MPC* for marginal propensity to consume, then the decline in consumption ($-\Delta C$) due to the imposition of lump-sum tax is given by

$$-\Delta C = T.MPC$$

Since a lump-sum tax causes a change in disposable income (Y_d)

Therefore tax, $T = -\Delta Y_d$

$$-\Delta C = -\Delta Y_d . MPC$$

Let us take an example. If the aggregate amount collected by way of lump-sum tax is ₹ 500 crore and *MPC* is 0.75, then the decline in consumption ($-\Delta C$)due to lump-sum tax will be ₹ 500 × 0.75 = ₹ 375 crores.

On the contrary, *if lump-sum tax is reduced*, the consumption will increase by the amount of reduction in the lump-sum tax multiplied by the marginal propensity to consume ($+\Delta C = + \Delta Y_d . MPC$).

The impact of imposition of lump-sum tax on consumption function is graphically shown in Fig. 40.2. It will be seen from this figure that introduction of lump-sum tax shifts the consumption function curve *C* downward to the new position *C′* by the amount given by the tax amount multiplied by the *MPC*. Similarly, the reduction in lump-sum income tax shifts the consumption function curve upward to *C″*.

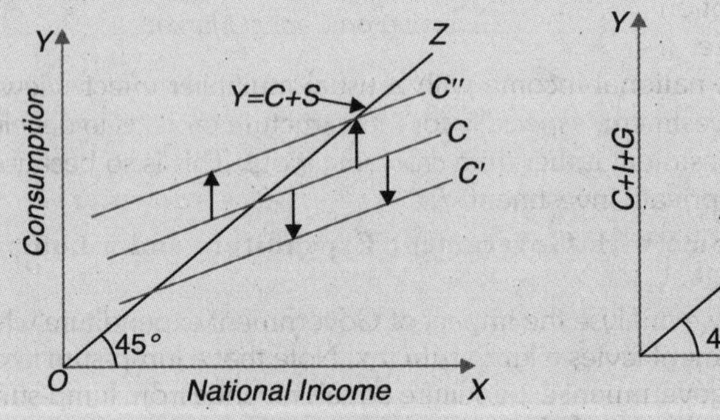

Fig. 40.2. *Effect of Lump-Sum Tax on Consumption Function*

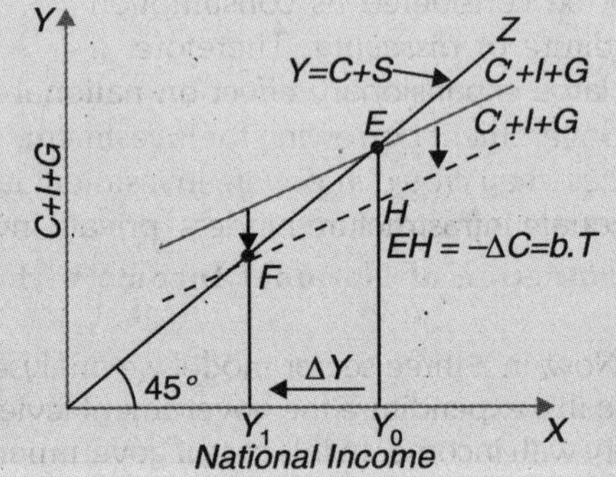

Fig. 40.3. *Effect of imposition of Lump-Sum Tax on National Income*

Fig. 40.3 shows the effect of imposition of lump-sum tax on the equilibrium level of national income (GNP). It will be observed from Fig. 40.3 that due to lump-sum tax equal to *T*, and consequently downward shift in aggregate expenditure curve to the lower new dotted position $C' + I + G$, the equilibrium level of national income falls from OY_0 to OY_1. An important point worth mentioning is that the fall in the level of income ($-\Delta Y$) is not equal to the amount of tax (*T*) collected but by a multiple of it, tax multiplier being equal to $\frac{-b}{1-b}$ where *b* stands for marginal propensity to consume. Thus, $\frac{-b}{1-b}$ or $\frac{-MPC}{1-MPC}$ is lump-sum *tax multiplier*. We will explain this tax multiplier in detail later in this chapter.

It will be seen from Fig. 40.2 that if Government reduces lump sum income tax, the consumption function curve shifts upward to the new position C″. From this it follows that *reduction in tax by the government will increase the disposaible income of the society and raise consumption demand. The rise in consumption demand will raise the equilibrium level of income by a multiple amount depending on the marginal propensity to consume.*

Three sector model with the above specifications can be developed as follows :

$$Y = AE = C + \bar{I} + \bar{G}$$

or $$Y = C + \bar{I} + \bar{G} \quad ...(i)$$

Now, consumption function can be stated as :

$$C = a + b\,Y_d$$

Where a is constant autonomous consumption expenditure, Y_d is disposable income. In this three sector model with lump-sum tax and no transfer payments, consumption function can be written as

$$C = a + b\,(Y - T)$$

where T = lump-sum tax

or $C = a + bY - bT$

Substituting the value of C in income equation (*i*) we have

$$Y = a + b\,Y - bT + \bar{I} + \overline{G}$$

$$Y - bY = a - bT + \bar{I} + \overline{G}$$

$$Y(1 - b) = a - bT + \bar{I} + \overline{G}$$

$$Y = \frac{1}{1-b}\left(a - bT + \bar{I} + \overline{G}\right) \quad ...(ii)$$

The equation (*ii*) furnishes us the equilibrium level of national income in the three sector economy when there is both government expenditure and lump sum tax. Therefore, for an economy if the data regarding consumption function, investment, Government expenditure and lump-sum tax are given we can compute the equilibrium level of national income. A numerical example will clarify the determination of equilibrium level of income in this case.

Numerical Example

Problem. *The following data characterises the macroeconomic conditions of a hypothetical economy*

$$C = 50 + 0.8\,Y_d$$

$$I = 100$$

$$G = T = 75$$

where C, I, and Y_d are consumption, investment and disposable income respectively.

Calculate equilibrium income of the economy. What is the value of multiplier?

Solution: Note that since $G = T$, budget of the Government is balanced.

$$Y = C + I + G$$

$$C = a + bY_d = a + b(Y - T)$$

Substituting the values of C, I and G we have :

$$Y = 50 + 0.8\,(Y - 75) + 100 + 75$$

$$= 50 + 0.8Y - 60 + 100 + 75$$

$$Y = 165 + 0.8Y$$

$$Y - 0.8Y = 165$$

$$Y\,(1 - 0.8) = 165$$

$$0.2\,Y = 165$$

$$Y = 165 \times \frac{10}{2} = 825$$

Thus, equilibrium level of income is 825.

In the present case $G = T$, there is a balanced budget.

Value of balanced budget multiplier $= \dfrac{1}{1-b} + \dfrac{-b}{1-b}$

$$= \frac{1}{1-0.8} + \frac{-0.8}{1-0.8}$$

$$= \frac{1}{0.2} + \frac{-0.8}{0.2} = 5 - 4 = 1$$

Determination of National Income in the Three Sector Economy with Lump-Sum Tax and Transfer Payments

We have explained above the determination of national income in the three sector economy when government expenditure is financed by imposition of lump sum tax. We now extend our model to include transfer payments and see how they affect determination of national income. *Transfer payments are payments to the people by the government for which it receives no service or goods in return from them*. Transfer payments are made by the government to promote social welfare. Unemployment allowance, poverty relief grants, social security contributions, old age pension are some important examples of transfer payments. Transfer payments are antithesis of tax. Whereas tax reduces disposable income of the people, transfer payments increase their disposable income.

Transfer payments may be autonomous of tax or they may be financed by imposition of a lump sum tax. If, like the government expenditure on goods and services, transfer payments are financed through tax, then transfer payments become a part of government expenditure (G) and imposition of additional tax to finance transfer payments become a part of total lump sum tax (T) which reduces disposable income. Therefore, in this case when transfer payments are financed through additional taxes, the analysis of income determination is similar to the model of income determination with government expenditure and lump sum tax explained above. However, the inclusion of transfer payments which are of autonomous type makes the analysis of income determination somewhat different. We describe it below.

Since transfer payments increase the disposable income of the people, they will increase their consumption expenditure depending on their propensity to consume. Thus

$$C = a + bY_d$$

$$Y_d = Y - T + TR$$

where T is lump sum tax and TR is transfer payments

$$\therefore \quad C = a + b(Y - T + TR)$$

$$Y = C + I + G$$

$$= a + b(Y - T + TR) + I + G$$

$$Y = a + bY - bT + bTR + I + G$$

$$Y - bY = a - bT + bTR + I + G$$

$$Y = \frac{1}{1-b}(a - bT + bTR + I + G) \qquad \text{... (ii)}$$

Government Expenditure Multiplier and Transfer Payments Multiplier

It is important to note that the multiplier of government expenditure on goods and services is different from transfer payments multiplier. This is because whereas Government expenditure on goods and services raises aggregate demand directly by its full amount, the transfer payments raises consumption demand by bTR, that is, *less than the full amount* depending on the marginal propensity to consume. Let us illustrate it by using income equation (*ii*).Suppose government expenditure increases by ΔG. Then, increased income is

$$Y + \Delta Y = \frac{1}{1-b}(a - bT + bTR + I + G + \Delta G) \qquad \text{...(iii)}$$

Subtracting equation (*ii*) from equation (*iii*) we have

$$\Delta Y = \frac{1}{1-b}(\Delta G)$$

or

$$\frac{\Delta Y}{\Delta G} = \frac{1}{1-b}$$

Thus, **Government expenditure multiplier,** $\frac{\Delta Y}{\Delta G}=\frac{1}{1-b}$.

If instead of increase in government expenditure on goods and services, government increases transfer payments by ΔTR we will get the following income equation

$$Y + \Delta Y = \frac{1}{1-b}(a-bT+bTR+b\Delta TR+I+G) \quad ... (iv)$$

Subtracting equation (*ii*) from equation (*iv*) we have

$$\Delta Y = \frac{1}{1-b}b\Delta TR$$

or

$$\frac{\Delta Y}{\Delta TR} = \frac{b}{1-b}$$

Thus, **transfer payments multiplier,** $\frac{\Delta Y}{\Delta TR}=\frac{b}{1-b}$

Taking the difference between the Government expenditure multiplier and transfer payments multiplier we have

$$\frac{1}{1-b}-\frac{b}{1-b}=\frac{1-b}{1-b} = 1$$

It follows from above that the difference between Government expenditure multiplier and transfer payments multipiler is equal to one.

Numerical Example

Problem. *Suppose the structural model of an economy is given below :*

$$C = 100 + 0.75\,Y_d$$
$$I = 200$$
$$G = T = 100$$
$$TR = 50$$

where G is government expenditure on goods and services, T is lump sum tax and TR are transfer payments

(1) *Find the equilibrium level of income*

(2) *Calculate Government expenditure multiplier and transfer payments multiplier. What is the difference between the two ?*

(3) *If full-employment level of income is 1,600 crores, how much government expenditure be increased to attain full employment ?*

Solution :

$$Y = C + I + G$$
$$= a + bY_d + I + G$$

Disposable income $Y_d = Y - T + TR$

Therefore, $Y = a + b\,(Y - T + TR) + I + G$

Substituting the values of various parameters and variables we have

$$Y = 100 + 0.75\,(Y - 100 + 50) + 200 + 100$$
$$= 100 + 0.75Y - 75 + 37.5 + 200 + 100$$

$$Y - 0.75Y = 100 - 75 + 37.5 + 200 + 100$$
$$Y(1 - 0.75) = 362.5$$
$$0.25\,Y = 362.5$$
$$Y = 362.5 \times \frac{100}{25} = 1450$$

Thus, equilibrium income is 1450 crores

(2) Government expenditure multiplier $(G_m) = \frac{1}{1-b} = \frac{1}{1-0.75} = \frac{1}{0.25} = 4$

Transfer payments multiplier $(TR_m) = \frac{b}{1-b} = \frac{0.75}{1-0.75} = \frac{0.75}{0.25} = 3$

The difference between G_m and TR_m is $4 - 3 = 1$

(3) The equilibrium income of ₹ 1,450 crores falls short of full-employment income of 1,600 crores by 1,600 – 1,450 = 150 crores. ΔG required to achieve full employment income is given by

$$\Delta Y = G_m \times \Delta G \quad \Delta G = \frac{\Delta Y}{G_m}$$

or
$$= \frac{150}{4} = 37.5 \text{ crore}$$

Proportional Income Tax and Equilibrium Level of National Income

Now, instead of lump sum tax, if Government levies proportional income tax how it will affect the consumption function curve and the equilibrium level of income. With proportional income tax, a *fixed percentage* of income is collected as tax, irrespective of the level of income. If an income tax at the rate of 25 per cent of income is levied regardless of the level of income, it will be an example of a proportional income tax. As in case of lump-sum tax, the introduction of proportional income tax will reduce the disposable income. This will bring about decline in the amount of consumption and saving at each level of real national income. However, in case of proportional income tax consumption will not fall by the same amount at each level of income but instead it will fall by the *same percentage of the level of income*. Therefore, as a result of proportional income tax, the consumption function curve rotates downward (with point *a* as a pivot) to the right, so that the fall in amount of consumption varies but fall as a pecentage of income level remains the same. This is shown in fig. 40.4 where the vertical distance between the consumption function curve *C* before tax and the consumption function curve *C*′ after tax is equal to the fall in consumption due to the proportional income tax. It is however worth noting that in case of proportional income tax at *each level of real national income, consumption falls by the tax revenue multiplied by the marginal propnesity to consume.*

In Fig. 40.5 we have shown the effect of proportional income tax on the equilibrium level of national income tax. As a result of imposition of proportional income tax, the aggregate demand curve $C + I + G$ rotates downward due to the downward rotation of consumption function curve. It will be seen from Fig. 40.5 that due to imposition of prooprotional income tax, the equilibrium level of national income falls from OY_0 to OY_1. It may be noted that other things remaining the same, the higher rate of proportional income tax, the greater the fall in consumption and, therefore, the greater the decline in equilibrium level of national income.

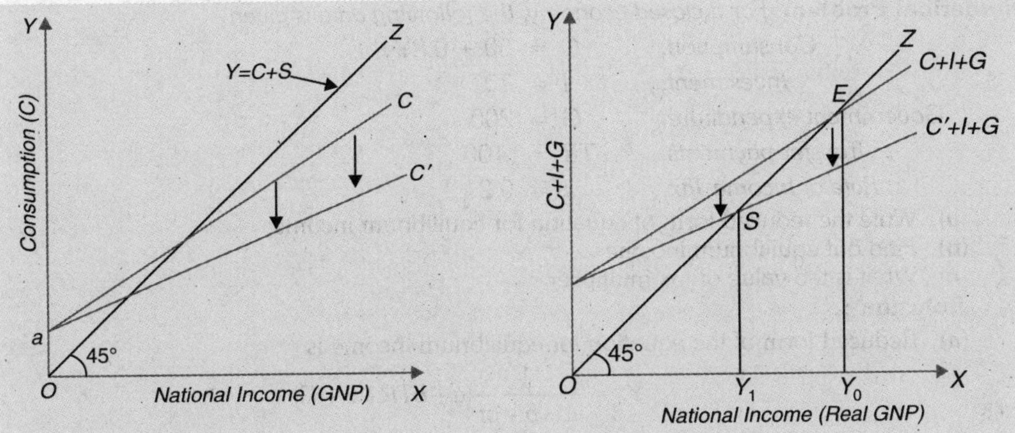

Fig. 40.4. Effect of Proportional Income Tax on Consumption Function

Fig. 40.5. Effect of Proportional Income Tax on Aggregate Demand and National Income

THREE SECTOR MODEL FURTHER EXTENDED
(Incorporating Proportional Income Tax)

So far in our above analysis of determination of equilibrium national income in a three sector economy we have assumed autonomous constant investment, apart from consumption function of households and Government expenditure on goods and services and transfer payments. In the further extension of the model we also include *proportional income tax*, that is, a tax levied as a fixed percentage or proportion of income irrespective the level of income. Mathematically proportional income tax is therefore expressed as tY where t is the rate or proportion of income which is payable as a tax. In a real economy proportional income tax may be imposed along with any lump sum tax. Thus, the total tax (T) can be expressed as

$$T = \overline{T} + tY$$

where

$\overline{T}$ = constant autonomous lump-sum tax

t = rate or proportion of income tax

Y = Income

Equilibrium income,
$$Y = C + I + G \quad ...(i)$$

where
$$C = a + bY_d$$
$$= a + b\,(Y - \overline{T} - tY + TR)$$

Substituting the consumption function in equation (*i*) for equilibrium income we have

$$Y = a + b\,(Y - \overline{T}) - tY + TR) + I + G$$
$$= a + b\,Y - b\,\overline{T} - btY + bTR + I + G$$
$$Y - b\,Y + btY = a - b\,\overline{T} + bTR + I + G$$
$$Y\,(1 - b + bt) = a - b\overline{T} + bTR + I + G$$
$$Y = \frac{1}{1-b+bt}\left(a - b\overline{T} + bTR + I + G\right) \quad ...(ii)$$

Note that $\frac{1}{1-b+bt}$ represents tax multiplier when tax is a proportion of income.

Tax multiplier can also be expressed as $\frac{1}{1-b(1-t)}$.

Numerical Problem. *For a closed economy, the following data is given*

Consumption,	$C = 50 + 0.8Y_d$
Investment,	$I = 70$
Government expenditure,	$G = 200$
Transfer payments,	$TR = 100$
Rate of Income Tax,	$t = 0.2$

(*a*) Write the reduced form of equation for equilibrium income
(*b*) Find out equilibrium income
(c) What is the value of tax multiplier ?

Solution :

(*a*) Reduced form of the equation for equilibrium income is

$$Y = \frac{1}{1-b+bt}(a + bTR + I + G)$$

(*b*) Substituting the values of parameters in the above equation for equilibrium income we have

$$Y = \frac{1}{1-0.8+0.8\times 0.2}(50 + 0.8 \times 100 + 70 + 200)$$

$$= \frac{1}{1-0.64}(50 + 80 + 70 + 200)$$

$$= \frac{1}{0.36}(400)$$

Thus, the equilibrium income is 1111

$$\text{Value of tax multiplier} = \frac{1}{1-b+bt} = \frac{1}{1-0.8+0.8\times 0.2}$$

$$= \frac{1}{1-0.64} = \frac{1}{0.36}$$

$$= \frac{100}{36} = 2.77$$

THE LUMP SUM TAX MULTIPLIER: FURTHER EXPLAINED

We have explained the multiplier effect of change in Government expenditure on goods and services and of change in transfer payments (*TR*) on the equilibrium level of income. We will now explain the multiplier effect of *change in tax*. Reduction in taxes has often been used by the policy makers to increase aggregate demand of the economy and thereby to lift the economy out of recession. For example, in 1964 John F Kennedy, the president of the United States made a substantial cut in personal and corporate taxes to stimulate expenditure on consumption and investment to bring about expansion in income and employment in the economy. This policy of cut in taxes to revive the American economy had a grand success. There was a large growth in Gross Domestic Product (GDP) of the United States in 1964 and 1965. There was a substantial fall in unemployment as a result of the policy of cut in taxes.

Recently when George Bush was elected president in 2001 the American economy found itself in the grip of recession. He also made a drastic cut in income tax to stimulate aggregate demand so as to overcome recession. Again this policy of tax cut was greatly successful and the American economy recovered in 2003-04.

The change in lump sum income tax and proportional income tax affect equilibrium income differently, but both have a multiplier effect on equilibrium income. We have already explained the effect of lump-sum income tax and proportional income tax on the equilibrium level of income. We are now concerned with analysing the effect of change in lump sum tax and proportional income tax. For the sake of simplicity and convenience we explain the multiplier effect of lump sum income tax. Note that while a cut in tax will have a positive effect on equilibrium income, increase in tax will reduce equilibrium income.

Suppose the government *increases lump-sum income tax* by ΔT we are interested to know its multiplier effect on income. As found above, in the three sector economy with Government expenditure and lump-sum tax :

$$Y = \frac{1}{1-b}(a - bT + I + G) \quad ...(1)$$

where T is lump sum income tax. Now, a decrease in lump-sum income tax by ΔT will cause a change in income (that is, ΔY). Increase in tax will reduce the disposable income and therefore the consumption demand. As a result of increase in tax, consumption demand will decrease by the change in lump-sum tax times the marginal propensity consume, that is, $\Delta Y = b\Delta T$. Let us incorporate change in the lump-sum tax (ΔT) in the three sector equation (1) for equilibrium income and see how much change in income (ΔY) it brings about. Thus

$$Y + \Delta Y = \frac{1}{1-b}[a - b(T + \Delta T) + I + G]$$

$$Y + \Delta Y = \frac{1}{1-b}(a - bT - b\Delta T + I + G) \quad ...(2)$$

Now subtracting equation (1) from equation (2) we have

$$\Delta Y = \frac{1}{1-b}(-b\Delta T)$$

Dividing both sides by ΔT we have

$$\frac{\Delta Y}{\Delta T} = \frac{-b}{1-b} \quad ...(3)$$

$\frac{\Delta Y}{\Delta T}$ is the expression for lump-sum tax multiplier. It will be seen that increase in tax by ΔT will *reduce* equilibrium income by a multiple. For example, if marginal propensity to consume is 0.75, then the lump-sum tax multiplier is

$$\frac{\Delta Y}{\Delta T} = \frac{-b}{1-b} = \frac{-0.75}{1-0.75} = \frac{-0.75}{0.25} = -3$$

This means that, given *MPC* or *b* equal to 0.75, increase in lump-sum tax by Re. 1 will cause a decline in equilibrium income by 3.

Note that we can similarly prove that a *cut in lump-sum tax will raise* the equilibrium income through the tax multiplier. Therefore, in case of *reduction in lump-sum income tax*, the lump-sum tax multiplier is

$$\frac{\Delta Y}{\Delta T} = \frac{b}{1-b}$$

With 0.75 as marginal propensity to consume, the lump-sum tax multiplier of cut in tax is,

$$\frac{\Delta Y}{\Delta T} = \frac{0.75}{1-0.75} = \frac{0.75}{0.25} = 3.$$

BALANCED BUDGET MULTIPLIER

We now analyse the impact of balanced budget of the government. In case of a balanced budget, the government's expenditure is equal to its tax revenue, that is, $G = T$ and therefore when the government increases its expenditure by ΔG, then it also raises taxes to get more tax revenue (ΔT) so that $\Delta T = \Delta G$. The effect of a balanced budget on the equilibrium income is described by the *balanced budget multiplier* which is also called *balanced budget theorem*. According to this, the *balanced budget multiplier is always equal to one*. That is, balanced budget is not fiscally neutral, it also has an expansionary effect on the economy. We prove it below by assuming a lump sum tax.

In order to analyse the effect of a balanced budget multiplier, we reproduce below the equation for equilibrium income for a three sector economy.

$$Y = \frac{1}{1-b}\left(a - b\overline{T} + I + G\right) \quad \text{... (1)}$$

where $\overline{T}$ is constant lump sum tax levied by the government.

Let us incorporate increase in government expenditure (ΔG) fully financed by additional lump sum tax (ΔT), that is, $\Delta G = \Delta T$. By doing so we get

$$Y + \Delta Y = \frac{1}{1-b}\left[a - b(\overline{T} + \Delta T) + I + G + \Delta G\right] \quad \text{...(2)}$$

Subtracting equation (1) from equation (2) we have

$$\Delta Y = \frac{1}{1-b}(-b\Delta T + \Delta G)$$

Since in a balanced budget, $\Delta T = \Delta G$

$$\Delta Y = \frac{1}{1-b}(-b\Delta G + \Delta G)$$

$$\Delta Y(1 - b) = \Delta G(1 - b)$$

or

$$\Delta Y = \Delta G \quad \text{...(3)}$$

Dividing both sides of the above equation by ΔG we have

$$\frac{\Delta Y}{\Delta G} = \frac{\Delta G}{\Delta G} = 1$$

Thus, balanced budget multiplier is equal to one. This implies that when $\Delta G = \Delta T$ and budget is therefore balanced, national income increases by the same amount as the increase in government expenditure. That is, even balanced budget has an expansionary effect and its multiplier is equal to one.

Alternative Proof

That the balanced budget multiplier is equal to one can be proved in an alternative way. Balance budget multiplier is the sum of government expenditure multiplier and lu mp-sum tax multiplier.

Government expenditure multiplier (G_m) = $\frac{1}{1-b}$ where b stands for marginal propensity to consume

$$\text{Lump-sum tax multiplier } (T_m) = \frac{-b}{1-b}$$

$$\text{Balanced budget multiplier} = G_m + T_m$$

$$= \frac{1}{1-b} + \frac{-b}{1-b}$$

$$= \frac{1-b}{1-b} = 1$$

Thus, the balanced budget multiplier is equal to one.

NUMERICAL EXAMPLES

Problem. *Suppose we have an economy characterised by the following functions :*

$$C = 100 + 0.8\, Y_d$$
$$\bar{I} = 100$$
$$\bar{G} = 100$$
$$\bar{T} = 100 \qquad \textit{(Figures are in crores)}$$

(a) Find the equilibrium level of income.

(b) How much increase in income will take place if government expenditure on goods and services increases by ₹ 60 crores.

(c) Find the tax multiplier and balanced budget multiplier

(d) Find the equilibrium level of national income if $T = \bar{T} + tY = 100 + 0.25Y$.

Solution :

(a) Equilibrium $\quad Y = C + \bar{I} + \bar{G}$

$$Y = a + bY_d + \bar{I} + \bar{G}$$

Therefore, $\quad Y = a + b(Y - \bar{T}) + \bar{I} + \bar{G}$

Substituting the values of a, b, $\bar{T}$, $\bar{I}$ and $\bar{G}$ we have

$$Y = 100 + 0.8\,(Y - 100) + 100 + 100$$
$$= 100 + 0.8Y - 80 + 100 + 100$$
$$Y - 0.8\,Y = 220$$
$$Y\,(1 - 0.8) = 220$$
$$0.2Y = 220$$
$$Y = 220 \times \frac{10}{2} = 1100$$

(b) Government expenditure multiplier $(G_m) = \frac{1}{1-b} = \frac{1}{1-0.8} = 5$

Increase in national income can be obtained by multiplying the increase in government expenditure (*i.e.*, by 60 crores) with the increase in Government expenditure multiplier. Thus

$$\Delta Y = G_m \cdot \Delta G$$
$$= 5 \times 60 = 300$$

(c) Tax multiplier, $\quad T_m = \frac{-b}{1-b} = \frac{-0.8}{1-b} = \frac{-0.8}{1-0.8} = \frac{-0.8}{0.2}$

$$= -4$$

Balanced Budget Multiplier $= G_m + T_m$

$$= 5 + (-4)$$
$$= 1$$

(d) The equilibrium level of national income when $T = 100 + 0.25Y$

$$Y = \frac{1}{1-b+bt}\left(a - b\bar{T} + \bar{I} + \bar{G}\right)$$

$bt = 0.8 \times 0.25 = 0.2$. Now, substituting the values of b, a, $\bar{T}$, $\bar{I}$ and $\bar{G}$ in the above formula of equilibrium income we have

$$= \frac{1}{1-0.8+0.2}(100-0.80\times100+100+100)$$

$$= \frac{1}{1-0.6}(100-80+100+100)$$

$$= \frac{1}{0.4}(220)$$

$$= 2.5\ (220) = 550$$

DETERMINATION OF NATIONAL INCOME IN AN OPEN ECONOMY: FOUR SECTOR MODEL

Foreign Trade and National Income

In the four sector model of determination of national income, we add the foreign trade sector to the three sectors, namely, households, firms, and Government. Foreign trade, that is, volume of exports and imports of a country also affects the level of national income of a country. We now extend the Keynesian model of determination of national income by including the effect of exports and imports of a country on the generation of income. For example, the exports of India represent the foreign demand and generates income for the Indian people. On the other hand, imports represent the demand for foreign goods by the Indians and generate incomes for the people of other countries. Therefore, imports tend to reduce the domestic aggregate expenditure. It therefore follows that national income will depend on the net exports, that is, exports minus imports $(X - M)$ where X stands for exports and M for imports. The exports and imports of a country depend to a great extent on the level of economic activity (that is, the level of output and income of the country). Thus, when the growth of industrial output in India is rapid, it will generate greater demand for imported materials. On the other hand, the higher industrial growth would also cause our exports to rise provided there is demand for our goods abroad. However, in the Keynesian model of income determination, exports and imports are considered as autonomous, that is, independent of income, being determined outside the model. Further, as mentioned above, the increase or decrease in aggregate expenditure or demand due to exports and imports depends on the net exports, that is, $X–M$ which we may write as NX. If the net exports are positive, there will be addition to the aggregate demand or expenditure of a country. On the other hand, if the net exports are negative, there will be decrease in aggregate expenditure.

When we include net exports (NX) in our analysis we get the following equation for the equilibrium level of income.

$$Y = C + I + G + (X - M)$$

where

$$C = a + b\,(Y–T)$$

$$Y = a + bY - bT + I + G + NX$$

or

$$Y(1 - b) = a - bT + I + G + NX$$

$$Y = \frac{1}{1-b}\ (a - bT + I + G + NX)$$

Thus, in an open economy the equilibrium level of income is the sum of all fixed autonomous expenditures (*i.e.*, $a - bT + I + G + NX$) times the value of multiplier $[1/1 - b]$. It is worth noting that in the four sector model, national income is determined at the level at which saving gap between consumption and income is equal to the sum of investment, Government expenditure and net exports. (that is, $I + G + NX$). That is, in an open economy, equilibrium level of national income is reached at the level at which :

$$S = I + G + NX$$

Graphic Illustration. In Fig. 40.6, we have depicted the determination of national income when there are positive net exports (that is, when exports exceed imports, $X - M > 0$. To obtain the aggregate demand curve incorporating the positive net exports (NX) we add the $I + G + NX$ to the consumption function curve C to get the higher aggregate demand curve $C + I + G + NX$ which intersects the 45° line at point R and determines a level of income OY_3. It will be seen that saving gap at OY_3 level of national income is RT which is equal to the given sum of $I + G + NX$.

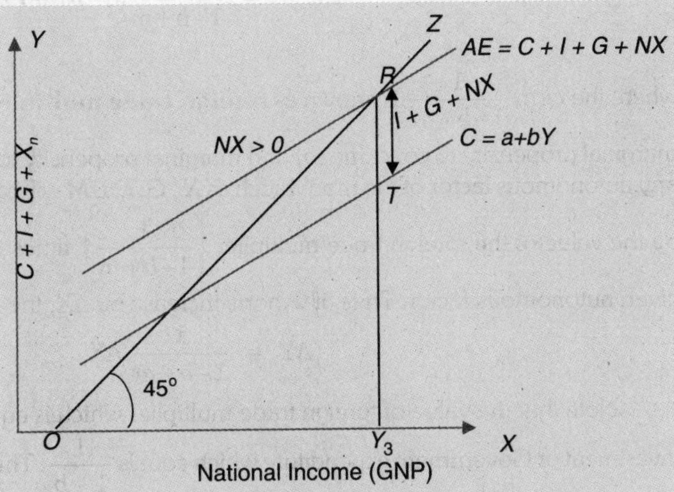

Fig. 40.6. *Determination of National Income in an Open Economy with Foreign Trade : Four Sector Model*

If the net exports NX are negative, that is, imports exceed exports, $X - M < 0$, the aggregate demand curve incorporating net exports would lie at a lower level than $C + I + G$ curve and determine a lower level of income.

Foreign Trade Multiplier

So far in our analysis of four sector model of income determination we have assumed that both exports and imports are constant autonomous items, that is, independent of income. In our later chapters concerning the external sector we shall explain in detail what are the factors that determine exports and imports of a country. In the model of income determination while exports are regarded as constant autonomous factor *determined exogenously* (that is, $X = \overline{X}$), imports are treated as function of two variables, namely, (1) autonomous imports (*i.e.* independent of income), and (2) level of income. Thus, import function used in the model can be written as

$$M = \overline{M} + mY$$

where $\overline{M}$ represents autonomous imports, mY represents imports dependent on level of income (Y) and m is marginal propensity to import. Given the marginal propensity to import (m), as income increases, mY will increase.

By incorporating the above import function we can derive the complete four sector model of income determination as follows

$$Y = C + I + G + (X - M) \quad \ldots(i)$$

where $C = a + b\,(Y - T)$

and $M = \overline{M} + mY$

Substituting the consumption function and import function in the income equation ... (*i*)

we have

$$Y = a + b\,(Y - T) + I + G + [X - (\overline{M} + mY)]$$

$$= a + bY + I + G + X - \overline{M} - mY$$

$$Y - bY + mY = a - bT + I + G + X - \overline{M}$$

$$Y(1 - b + m) = a - bT + I + G + X - \overline{M}$$

$$Y = \frac{1}{1-b+m}(a - bT + I + G + X - \overline{M})$$

where the term $\frac{1}{1-b+m}$ is known as **foreign trade multiplier** whose value is determined by marginal propensity to consume (b) and marginal propensity to import (m). Note that change in any autonomous factor of the model such as X, G, I, a, $\overline{M}$ will cause a change in national income by the value of the foreign trade multiplier $\left(\frac{1}{1-b+m}\right)$ times the change in the amount of the given autonomous factor. Thus, if exports increase by ΔX, the national income will increase by

$$\Delta Y = \frac{1}{1-b+m}.\Delta X$$

Note that the value of foreign trade multiplier which is equal to $\frac{1}{1-b+m}$ is less than the investment or Government expenditure which equals $\frac{1}{1-b}$. This is because imports are leakages from the domestic income stream and therefor does not cause increase in gross domestic income of a country. On the contrary, expenditure on imports lead to the increase in incomes of foreign countries (Taking any values of be (*i.e.*, *MPC*) and *m* (*i.e.*, propensity to imports) and compare the values of $\frac{1}{1-b}$ and $\frac{1}{1-b+m}$)

Incorporating Proportional Income Tax in the Four Sector Model

If in the above four sector model of income determination proportional income tax is incorporated, then only the term of foreign trade multiplier will change, the other terms of the model remaining the same. Thus, if income tax is of form $T = \overline{T} + tY$ where T is constant lump-sum, t is the proportion of income that is taken as tax. With incorporation of proporational income tax, the value of foreign trade multiplier becomes :

$$= \frac{1}{1-b(1-t)+m}$$

or

$$= \frac{1}{1-b+bt+m}$$

where t is the proportional income tax rate.

With this proportional income tax, the above equilibrium income equation can be written as

$$Y = \frac{1}{1-b(1-t)+m}(a - bT + I + G + X - \overline{M})$$

TRADE BALANCE (NET EXPORTS) AND INTERNATIONAL CAPITAL FLOWS

In an open economy as in the closed economy product markets and capital markets are closely related. To know this relationship let us consider the equilibrium level of national income in an open economy which is :

1. Note that national saving $Y - C - G$ is the sum of private saving $(Y - T - C)$ and Government saving $(T - G)$. Thus $Y - T - C + T - G = Y - C - G$.

$$Y = C + I + G + (X - M) \quad \ldots \text{(i)}$$

where $X - M$ are net exports (NX)

Therefore, rearranging the above equation and writing NX for $X - M$ we have

$$Y - C - G = I + NX \quad \ldots (1)$$

Now $Y–C–G$ represents national saving[1] which we represent by S.

Writting S for national saving ($Y–C–G$) in equation (2) we have

$$S = I + NX \quad \ldots (2)$$

or

$$S - I = NX \quad \ldots (3)$$

From equation (3) it is evident that difference between domestic saving and domestic investment ($S - I$) equals net exports (NX). *Since difference between domestic saving and investment ($S - I$) represents capital flows*, equation (3) reveals that capital flows between an economy and the foreign ones are related to net exports (NX) which are also called *trade balance*. If for a country domestic saving exceeds domestic investment ($S > I$), then the country would have *positive* net *capital outflows* which means residents of the country would be lending or investing abroad more than the foreigners would be lending or investing in the country concerned. The equation (3) above shows that these *positive net capital outflows* imply that they will be equal to *positive net exports* (NX), that is, the country will be exporting more than it will be importing. Foreigners will need financial loans to buy that country's more goods and services than they are exporting to it. This has been the relationship with Japan and the US. Japan has a trade surplus (i.e. positive net exports) with the US and to enable the US to buy more Japanese goods than Japan is importing from it, it has been lending to the US which has been running a trade deficit, that is, there has been net capital outflows from Japan to the US.

Now, when domestic saving of a country is less than the domestic investment ($S < I$ or $S - I$ is negative), the equation (3) above reveals that the net exports (NX) will be negative (i.e., the country has a trade deficit) and, therefore, there will *net capital-inflow*. The net capital inflow implies that the country will be borrowing from abroad or receiving foreign investment. The country having negative net exports or deficit trade balance requires foreign capital funds either through borrowing from foreigners or foreign investment so as to enable it to import more goods and services than it is exporting them. For example, in India we have a *deficit in the current account of balance of payments* (which has the same meaning as the concept of trade balance but comprise both goods and services) for several years now so that foriegn savings or capital inflows have contributed to the increase in investment in India. However the share of capital inflows (foriegn savings) as a per cent of its GDP in India are relatively small.

It follows from above that *international flows of capital to finance investment and international flow of goods and services are two sides of the same coin.*

NUMERICAL PROBLEMS

Problem 1. *An economy is characterised by the following equations:*

C (Consumption)	$= 60 + 0.9Y_d$
I (Investment)	$= 10$
G (Government expenditure)	$= 10$
T (Tax)	$= 0$
X (Exports)	$= 20$
M (Imports)	$= 10 + 0.05\,Y$

(a) *What is the equilibrium income?*

(b) *Calculate trade balance.*

(c) *What is the value of foreign trade multiplier ?*

Solution : (a) *National Income*

$$\begin{aligned} Y &= C + I + G + Nx \\ &= (60 + 0.9\,Y_d) + 10 + 10 + 20 - (10 + 0.05Y) \\ &= 60 + 0.9\,(Y - T) + 10 + 10 + 20 - 10 - 0.05Y \\ &= 60 + 0.9Y - 0 + 30 - 0.05Y \\ Y &= 90 + .85Y \\ Y - 0.85Y &= 90 \\ 0.15Y &= 90 \\ Y &= 90 \times \frac{100}{15} = 600 \end{aligned}$$

(*b*) *Trade Balance* $= X - M$

$$= 20 - (10 + 0.05Y)$$

Substituting the value of Y we have

$$\text{Trade balance} = 20 - \left(10 + \frac{5}{100} \times 600\right)$$

$$= 20 - 10 - 30 = -20$$

Trade balance is in deficit.

(*c*) *Value of foreign trade multiplier* $= \dfrac{1}{1 - b + m}$

Where b is marginal propensity to consume, and m is marginal propensity to import.

$$\text{Foreign trade multiplier} = \frac{1}{1 - 0.9 + 0.05}$$

$$= \frac{1}{1 - 0.85} = \frac{1}{0.15}$$

$$= \frac{100}{15} = 6.66$$

Problem 2. *Behavioural and structural equations of an economy are given below :*

$$\begin{aligned} C &= 100 + b(Y - 50 - tY) \\ I &= 50 \\ G &= 50 \\ X &= 10 \\ M &= 5 + 0.1Y \end{aligned}$$

The marginal propensity to consume (b) is equal to 0.8 and proportional income tax rate, t = 0.25.

(*a*) *Find the equilibrium national income*

(*b*) *Find foreign trade multiplier*

(*c*) *Find equilibrium value of imports*

(*d*) *If equilibrium national income falls short of full-employment income by ₹ 50, how much government should increase its expenditure to attain full-employment.*

Solution :

(*a*) Reduced form of the equation for equilibrium income is

$$Y = \frac{1}{1 - b(1 - t) + m}(a - bT + I + G + X - \bar{M})$$

Substituting the values of the variables and parameters we have

$$Y = \frac{1}{1 - 0.8(1 - 0.25) + 0.1}(100 - 50 \times 0.8 + 50 + 50 + 10 - 5)$$

$$Y = \frac{1}{1-0.8+0.2+0.1}(100-40+50+50+10-5)$$

$$= \frac{1}{0.5}(165)$$

$$= 2\ (165) = 330$$

(*b*) Foreign trade multiplier

$$= \frac{1}{1-b(1-t)+tm}$$

$$= \frac{1}{1-0.8(1-0.25)+0.1}$$

$$= \frac{1}{1-0.8+0.2+0.1}$$

$$= \frac{1}{0.5} = 2$$

(*c*) Equilibrium value of imports can be obtained by substituting the equilibrium income (330) in the import function. Thus

$$M = 5 + 0.1Y$$

$$= 5 + 0.1 \times 330$$

$$= 38$$

(*d*) Required increase in Government expenditure to attain ₹ 50 increase in income can be obtained as under

$$\Delta Y = \text{Foreign Trade multiplier} \times \Delta G$$

$$\Delta Y = 2 \times DG$$

Or

$$\Delta G = \frac{\Delta Y}{2} = \frac{50}{2} = 25$$

QUESTIONS FOR REVIEW

1. How does Government expenditure on goods and services affect level of national income? Has it a multiplier effect? What is the value of government expenditure multiplier.

2. Show that with Government expenditure in a three sector economy (households, firms and Government) equilibrium of national income is established at the level where sum of investment and Government expenditure ($I + G$) is equal to the amount of saving.

3. Show how the increase in Government expenditure without raising taxes (*i.e.*, incurring budget deficit) affects national income, real rate of interest and private investment, Illustrate diagrammatically.

4. It is often asserted that budget deficit crowds out private investment. Do you agree? Explain.

5. Show what will be the effect of cut in government expenditure without reduction in taxes (creating budget surplus in this way) affect equilibrium national income, real rate of interest and private investment in the economy.

[**Hints.** A cut in government expenditure without reducing taxes leads to increase in public saving (*i.e.*, $T–G$ increases). This causes a shift in national saving curve to the right and leads to the fall in rate of interest and increases in private investment.

6. Show how does a cut in taxes without being balanced by cut in government expenditure affect real interest rate and investment.

7. What is effect of a balanced budget (*i.e.*, increasing government expenditure matched by increase in equal amount of taxes) on national income, real interest rate and investment.

8. Explain how balanced budget has an expansionary effect. What is value of balanced budget multiplier? Explain.

9. How does cut in direct taxes lead to increase in national income? What is the size of lump-sum tax multiplier?

10. Assuming full-employment in an economy balanced budget *increase* in taxes and Government expenditure will reduce consumption and investment and raise the real interest rate? Explain.

11. Assuming full-employment prevails in an economy, increased government expenditure matched by taxes crowds out private investment.

12. When the government runs a budget deficit, how capital market is affected?

13. What are the components of aggregate expenditure in an open economy. With Government spending on goods and services show that equilibrium level of national income in an open economy is established at the level at which $I + G + NX$ equals saving.

14. Explain foreign trade multiplier (the open economy multiplier). What it its value? Why is it smaller than closed economy expenditure multiplier?

15. You are given the following information about an economy.

Consumption function	$C = 80 + 0.8\,Y$
Investment function	$I = 80$
Government fspending	$G = 60$
Net Taxes	$T = 60$
Exports	$X = 20$
Imports	$M = 0.2\,Y_d$

(*i*) What is the current account balance for this economy

(*ii*) What is the value of the open economy multiplier?

(**Note** : Since in this question no data of '*invisibles*' are given current account balance equals *trade balance*).

16. You are given the following information about an economy –

Consumption function, $C = 1000 + 0.5\,(Y - T)$

Investment, $I =$ ₹ 2,000 crores.

Government expenditure = ₹ 1,000 crores

Taxes = ₹ 1,000 crores

(*i*) Find the equilibrium level of GDP without taxes.

(*ii*) Find the equilibrium level of GDP with taxes.

(*iii*) Use your answers in (*i*) and (*ii*) above to calculate the tax multiplier.

(*iv*) Explain the working of the tax multiplier intuitively.

[**Hints.** Find the equilibrium level of GDP (*i.e.*, national income Y), first by laking $T = 0$ and then find the equilibrium GDP *i.e.*, (Y) by taking $T = 1000$. Then tax multiplier is $\frac{\Delta Y}{\Delta T}$. Note that $\Delta T = 1000$.)

17. Explain the relationship between the trade deficit and the inflow of foreign capital.

18. International flow of capital to finance investment and international flow of goods and services are two sides of the same coin. Explain.

19. Show that saving-investment gap in an economy is equals to current account deficit (CAD). How is it finances?

Consumption and Investment Demand

Introduction

In the previous chapter we have explained how the level of national income is determined. In the present chapter and the succeeding ones we shall study the various factors which determine the levels of national income and employment. As we have seen, in the Keynesian two-sector model the level of income or employment is determined by the level of aggregate demand; the greater the aggregate demand, the greater the level of income and employment and *vice versa*. Keynes was not interested in the factors determining the aggregate supply since he was concerned with the short run and utilisation of the existing productive capacity. In the simple two-sector Keynesian model aggregate demand consists of two parts—consumption demand and investment demand. In this chapter we will explain both consumption demand and investment demand and the factors which determine them.

The Concept of Consumption Function

As the demand for a good depends upon its price, similarly consumption of a community depends upon the level of income. In other words, consumption is a function of income. *The consumption function relates the amount of consumption to the level of income.* When the income of a community rises, consumption also rises. How much consumption rises in response to a given increase in income depends upon the marginal propensity to consume. It should be borne in mind that the consumption function is the whole schedule which describes the amounts of consumption at various levels of income. We give below such a schedule of consumption function.

Consumption function should be carefully distinguished from the *amount of consumption*. By consumption function we mean the whole schedule which shows consumption at various levels of income, whereas amount of consumption means the amount consumed at a specific level of income. The schedule given in Table 41.1 and the consumption function curve *CC* drawn in Fig. 41.1 reflect the consumption function of a community, *i.e.*, they indicate how the consumption changes in response to the change in income.

Table 41.1. Consumption Function : Average and Marginal Propensity to Consume

Income (₹ *in crore*) Y	*Consumption* (₹ *in crore*) C	*Average Propensity to Consume (APC)* $\frac{C}{Y}$	*Marginal Propensity to Consume (MPC)* $\frac{\Delta C}{\Delta Y}$
1000	950	$\frac{950}{1000}=0.950$	–
1100	1020	$\frac{1020}{1100}=0.927$	$\frac{70}{100}=0.70$
1200	1090	$\frac{1090}{1200}=0.906$	$\frac{70}{100}=0.70$
1300	1160	$\frac{1160}{1300}=0.892$	$\frac{70}{100}=0.70$
1400	1230	$\frac{1230}{1400}=0.878$	$\frac{70}{100}=0.70$
1500	1300	$\frac{1370}{1500}=0.867$	$\frac{70}{100}=0.70$
1600	1370	$\frac{1370}{1600}=0.856$	$\frac{70}{100}=0.70$

Consumption demand depends on income and propensity to consume. Propensity to consume depends on various factors such as price level, interest rate, stock of wealth and several subjective factors. Since Keynes was concerned with short-run consumption function he assumed price level, interest rate, stock of wealth etc. remain constant in his theory of consumption. Thus with these factors being assumed constant in the short run, Keynesian consumption function considers consumption as a function of income. Thus, according to Keynes,

$$C = a + bY \quad \text{. . . (1)}$$

where a and b are constants. While a is intercept term of the consumption function, b stands for the slope of the consumption function and therefore represents marginal propensity to consume. In Table 41.1 above it will be seen that while *APC* is falling, *MPC* is constant and therefore represents Keynes's consumption function as described by equation (1) above. Keynes's consumption function is also represented by *CC'* curve in Fig. 41.1 in which *APC* falls as income rises but *MPC* remains constant.

In Fig. 41.1, a line *OZ* making 45° angle with the *X*-axis has been drawn. Because line *OZ* makes 45° angle with the *X*-axis, every point on it is equidistant from both the *X*-axis and *Y*-axis. Therefore, if consumption function curve coincides with 45° line *OZ*, it would imply that the amount of consumption is equal to the income at every level of income. In this case, with the increase in income, consumption would also increase by the same amount. However, in actual practice consumption increases less than the increase in income. Therefore, in actual practice the curve depicting the consumption function will deviate from the 45° line. If we represent the above consumption schedule by a curve, we would get the propensity to consume curve such as *CC* in Fig. 41.1.

It is evident from this figure that the consumption function curve *CC* deviates from the 45° line *OZ*. At lower levels of income, the consumption function curve *CC* lies above the *OZ* line, signifying that at these lower levels of income consumption is greater than the income. It is so because at lower levels of income, a nation may draw upon its accumulated savings to maintain its consumption standard or it may borrow from others. As income increases, consumption also increases and at the income level OY_0, consumption is equal to income. Beyond this, with the increase in income, consumption increases but less than the increase in income and, therefore, consumption function curve CC lies below the 45° line OZ beyond Y_0.

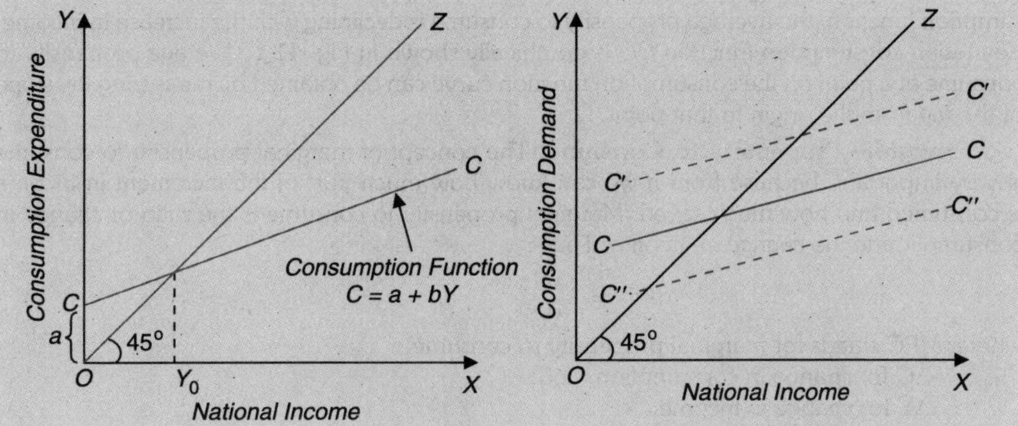

Fig. 41.1. *Keynesian Linear Consumption Function* **Fig. 41.2.** *Shift in Consumption Function*

An important point to be noted here is that beyond the level of income OY_0, the gap between consumption and income is widening. The difference between consumption and income represents savings. Therefore, *with the increase in income, saving gap widens* and as we shall see later, this has a significant implication in macroeconomics.

It is useful to point out here that when the consumption function of a community changes, the whole consumption function curve changes or shifts. When propensity to consume increases, it means that at various levels of income more is consumed than before. Therefore, as a result of increase in propensity to consume of the community, the whole consumption function curve shifts upward as has been shown by the upper curve $C' C'$ in Fig. 41.2. On the contrary, when the propensity to consume of the community decreases, the whole consumption function curve shifts downward signifying that at various levels of income, less is consumed than before.

Average and Marginal Propensity to Consume

There are two important concepts of propensity to consume, the one being average propensity to consume and the other marginal propensity to consume. They should be carefully distinguished, for they are equal in some cases but different in others. Consider Table 41.1, where we have calculated the average and marginal propensity to consume in columns 3 and 4. As seen above, consumption changes as income changes. Now, how much consumption changes in response to a given change in income depends upon the average and marginal propensity to consume. Thus, propensity to consume of a community can be known by the average and marginal propensity to consume. **Average propensity to consume is the ratio of the amount of consumption to total income.** Therefore, average propensity to consume is calculated by dividing the amount of consumption by the total income. Thus,

$$APC = \frac{C}{Y},$$

where APC stands for average propensity to consume
C for amount of consumption, and
Y for level of income.

In Table 41.1 it will be seen that at the level of income ₹ 1000 crore, consumption expenditure is equal to ₹ 950 crore. Therefore, average propensity to consume is here equal to $\frac{950}{1000}$ = 0.95. Likewise, when the income rises to ₹ 1100 crore, consumption rises to ₹ 1020 crore. Therefore, the average propensity to consume will be $\frac{1020}{1100}$ = 0.933. In this schedule of consumption function, the average propensity to consume is declining with the increase in income. Keynesian consumption function *CC* is graphically shown in Fig. 41.1. Average propensity to consume at a point on the consumption function curve can be obtained by measuring the slope of the ray from the origin to that point.

Marginal Propensity to Consume. The concept of marginal propensity to consume is very important, because from it we can know how much part of the increment in income is consumed and how much saved. Marginal propensity to consume is the ratio of *change* in consumption to the *change* in income. Thus :

$$MPC = \frac{\Delta C}{\Delta Y}$$

where, *MPC* stands for marginal propensity to consume,

ΔC for change in consumption, and

ΔY for change in income.

Marginal propensity to consume needs to be carefully distinguished from average propensity to consume. **Whereas average propensity to consume is the ratio of total consumption to total income, i.e., $\frac{C}{Y}$, the marginal propensity to consume is the ratio of change in consumption to the change in income, i.e. $\frac{\Delta C}{\Delta Y}$.**

The concept of marginal propensity to consume can be easily understood with the aid of Table 41.1, in column 4 of which we have calculated the marginal propensity to consume at various levels of income. In this schedule when income rises from ₹ 1000 crore to ₹ 1100 crore, the consumption increases from ₹ 950 crore to ₹ 1020 crore. Here the increment in income is ₹ 100 crore and the increment in consumption is ₹ 70 crore. Therefore, marginal propensity to consume which is $\frac{\Delta C}{\Delta Y}$ is here equal to $\frac{70}{100}$ or 0.7. Similarly, when national income rises from ₹ 1100 to ₹ 1200 crore and as a result consumption increases from ₹ 1020 crore to ₹ 1090 crore, the marginal propensity to consume is again equal to $\frac{70}{100}$ or 0.7. Therefore, it may be noted that *MPC* in Figure 41.1 depicting Keynesian consumption function remains constant as slope of the consumption function curve *CC* remains the same.

KEYNES'S THEORY OF CONSUMPTION

Keynes in his "*General Theory*", published in 1936, laid the foundations of modern macro-economics. The concept of consumption function plays an important role in Keynes' theory of income and employment. Keynes mentioned several subjective and objective factors which determine consumption of a society. However, according to Keynes, of all the factors it is the *current level of income* that determines the consumption of an individual and also of society. Since Keynes laid stress on the *absolute size of income* as a determinant of consumption, his theory of consumption is also known as **absolute income theory of consumption.** Further, Keynes put forward a ***psychological law of consumption,*** according to which, as income increases consumption increases but by less than the increase in income. In other words, marginal propensity to consume is less than one. That is,

$$1 > \frac{\Delta C}{\Delta Y} > 0$$

While Keynes recognized that many subjective and objective factors including interest rate and wealth influenced the level of consumption expenditure, he emphasised that it is the current level of income on which the consumption spending of an individual and the society depends. To quote him: "*The amount of aggregate consumption depends mainly on the amount of aggregate income. The fundamental psychological law, upon which we are entitled to depend with great confidence both a priori from our knowledge of human nature and from the detailed facts of experience is that men (and women, too) are disposed, as a rule and on an average, to increase their consumption as their income increases, but not by as much as the increase in their income.*"[1]

In the above statement about consumption behaviour, Keynes makes three points. First, he suggests that consumption expenditure depends mainly on absolute income of the current period, that is, consumption is a positive function of the absolute level of current income. The more income in a period one has, the more is likely to be his consumption expenditure in that period. In other words, in any period the rich people tend to consume more than the poor people do. Secondly, *Keynes points out that consumption expenditure does not have a proportional relationship with income.* According to him, as the income increases, a smaller proportion of income is consumed. The proportion of consumption to income is called average propensity to consume (*APC*). Thus, Keynes argues that *average propensity to consume (APC) falls as income increases.*

The third feature of Keynes's Consumption function is that *as income of individuals increases their consumption increases but not as much as the increase in their income, that is, marginal propensity to consume (MPC) is less than one.* This feature of his consumption theory has been called as *psychological law of consumption*. As we will explain later, Keynes's theory of multiplier is based on this law that *MPC* is less than one.

The Keynes' consumption function can be expressed in the following form :

$$C = a + bY_d$$

where C is consumption expenditure and Y_d is the real disposable income which equals gross national income minus taxes, a and b are constants, where a is the intercept term, that is, the amount of consumption expenditure at zero level of income. Thus, *a is autonomous consumption*. The parameter b is the marginal propensity to consume (*MPC*) which measures the increase in consumption spending in response to per unit increase in disposable income, that is, $b = MPC = \frac{\Delta C}{\Delta Y}$. The behaviour of consumption expenditure as perceived by Keynes implies that the marginal propensity to consume is less than average propensity to consume ($MPC < APC$). This is because as income increases, consumption does not rise proportionately and as income falls, consumption does not fall proportionately because people protect their consumption standards by not reducing their consumption proportionately to the reduction in their income. Implication of the proposition that $MPC < APC$ as income rises is that the ratio of consumption demand to income falls. This can be seen from Fig. 41.3 where the slope of consumption function line *CC′* is *MPC* which remains constant and the slope of lines such as *OA* and *OB* from the origin to points *A* and *B* on the consumption function line *CC′* which measures *APC*, that is, ratio *C/Y* at these points is falling.

In Fig. 41.3 we have shown a Keynesian consumption function with an intercept term. In this form of consumption function, though marginal propensity to consume ($\Delta C/\Delta Y$) is constant, average propensity to consume is declining with the increase in income as indicated by the slopes of the lines drawn from the origin to different points on consumption function curve *CC*.

1. J.M. Keynes, *The General Theory of Employment, Interest and Money* (New York : Harcourt), First Edition, 1936, p. 96.

The decline in average propensity to consume as income increases implies that the *proportion of income that is saved increases with the increase in national income of the country.*

The assumption of diminishing average propensity to consume is a significant part of Keynesian theory of income and employment. This implies that as income increases, a progressively larger proportion of national income would be saved. Therefore, to achieve and maintain equilibrium at full-employment level of income, increasing proportion of national income is needed to be invested. If sufficient investment opportunities are not available, the economy would then run into trouble and in that case it would not be possible to maintain full employment because aggregate demand will fall short of full-employment output. On the basis of this increasing proportion of saving with the increase in income and, consequently, the emergence of the problem of demand deficiency, some Keynesian economists based the theory of *secular stagnation* on the declining propensity to consume.

Important Features of Keynes's Consumption Function

In macroeconomics, Keynes's consumption function plays a highly important role. Therefore, it is essential to state its important features. The following are the important features of Keynes's consumption function:

1. First, *absolute level of current income is the important factor that determines consumption* of the community. Increase in national income causes an increase in consumption. On the other hand, classical economists thought that it was rate of interest that primarily determined saving and consumption of a community. A rise in rate of interest induces the people to save more and thus to reduce their level of consumption. According to Keynes, though rate of interest is one of the factors that determine consumption of the community, he did not consider it a very important determinant of it. By considering level of *current absolute income* as the most important factor determining consumption and saving, Keynes made a significant contribution to the macroeconomic theory.

2. The second important feature of Keynes' consumption function is that *marginal propensity to consume is less than one* but greater than zero ($0 < MPC < 1$). As has been explained above, the feature of Keynes's consumption function that marginal propensity to consume is less than one is known as Keynes's psychological law of consumption. According to this law, as income increases, consumption increases but not as much as the increase in income. We will explain in a later chapter that Keynes's theory of multiplier is based on the marginal propensity to consume being less than one but greater than zero.

3. In Keynes consumption function, namely, $C = a + bY$, *as income increases, average propensity to consume (APC) falls.* Keynes was of the view that rich people relatively save a higher proportion of their income at higher levels of income so that average propensity to consume (*APC*), that is, proportion of total consumption to national income, falls as national income rises.

4. Another important feature of consumption function as put forward by Keynes is that *it remains stable in the short run.* Consumption function, according to Keynes, depends on various institutional factors such as distribution of income and wealth and psychological factors such as willingness to save. Since there cannot be much changes in these institutional and psychological factors in the short run, consumption function remains stable in the short run, that is, it does not shift upward or downward. Therefore, Keynes in his theory explains the determination of income and employment in the short run by considering consumption function to be stable.

CONSUMPTION FUNCTION PUZZLE: KEYNES'S CONSUMPTION FUNCTION AND KUZNETS' FINDINGS

Empirical studies of long-term times series data of the US economy for the period 1869-1938 made by the noted American economist Kuznets estimated a consumption function which contradicted Keynes's consumption function which was found to be correct on the basis of cross-section studies of household budget data and short-term time series data. *This contradiction between Kuznets's empirical findings and Keynes's consumption function has been called consumption function puzzle.* Efforts have been made by several economists to resolve this puzzle and new theories of consumption function have been put forward to resolve the conflict between Keynes's consumption function and Kuznets's findings. These alternative theories of consumption function will be discussed later in this chapter.

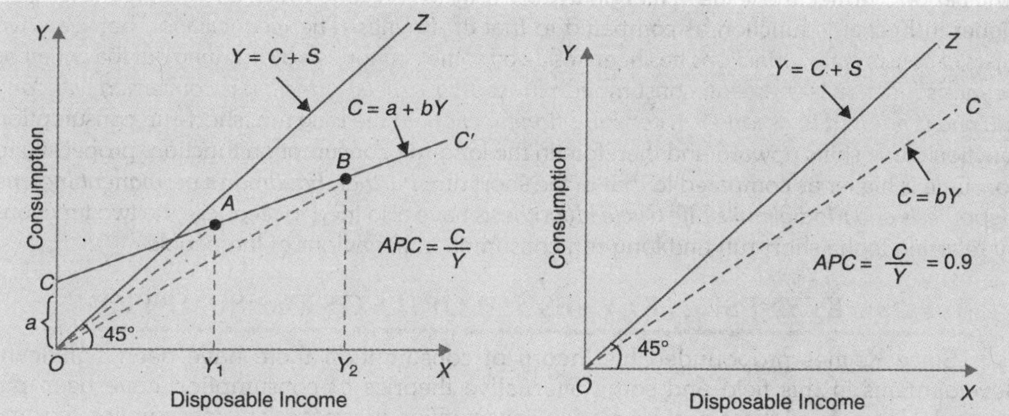

Fig. 41.3. *Keynes's Consumption Function: Falling Average Propensity to Consume*

Fig. 41.4. *Kuznets's Consumption Function: Constant APC*

To compare the Keynes's and Kuznets's consumption functions, it will be useful to write them in algebraic form and graphically represent them. Keynes's consumption function can be algebraically written as below:

$$C = a + bY \qquad ...(1)$$

where *a* is a positive intercept term which is also called *autonomous consumption* as it does not vary with income. The constant *a* shows that even when income is zero, a certain consumption is present. This is possible when in any year a community can live either on its past savings or borrow from other communities. Keynes's consumption function is shown in Fig. 41.3.

Secondly, *b* in the consumption function represents marginal propensity to consume $\left(\frac{\Delta C}{\Delta Y}\right)$.

The above mentioned Keynes's consumption function ($C = a + bY$) shows that average propensity to consume $\left(\frac{C}{Y}\right)$ falls as income increases. This can be known by comparing slopes of the rays *OA* and *OB* at income levels Y_1 and Y_2 respectively in Fig. 41.3.

Kuznets's Consumption Function

On the other hand, Kuznets found that consumption function is of the following form:

$$C = bY \qquad ...(2)$$

In Kuznets's consumption function there is no intercept term (that is, autonomous consumption). This is shown in Fig. 41.4 where it will be seen that Kuznets's consumption function curve starts from the origin and is very near to 45° line depicting that the propensity to consume (*b*) is very high. From his empirical study Kuznets estimated that average propensity to consume was nearly 0.9. Besides, by dividing the entire period (1869-1933) into three overlaping 30 years sub-periods Kuznets found that the proportion of consumption to income (that is, average propensity to consume) was nearly the same and equal to about 0.87 in all the three sub-periods. Thus Kuznets concluded that there was no tendency for the average propensity to consume to decline as disposable income rises. Thus, rounding off Kuznets's estimated propensity to consume is equal to 0.9. His consumption function presented in equation (2) can be rewritten as

$$C = 0.9\,Y \qquad ...(3)$$

From the above discussion it follows that implication of Keynes's consumption function ($C = a + bY$) and Kuznets's consumption function ($C = bY$) are different. *Whereas in Keynes's consumption function APC falls as income rises, in Kuznets's function it remains constant over a long period.* Further, the value of marginal propensity to consume which is less than one is much higher in Kuznets's function as compared to that of Keynes. The reconciliation between two types of consumption functions has been made by some economists by pointing out that whereas Keynes's function is short-run consumption function, *Kuznets's function is concerned with long run and is referred to as long-run consumption function.* In the long run, short-run consumption function curve shifts upward and therefore in the long-run consumption function, propensity to consume is higher as compared to that in the short run. *Further, Friedman's permanent Income Hypothesis and Modigliani's Life Cycle Hypothesis* have also tried to reconcile the two functions by referring to the short-run and long-run consumption behaviour of the people.

POST-KEYNESIAN KEYNES THEORIES OF CONSUMPTION

Since Keynes propounded his theory of consumption there have been significant developments in this field and some alternative theories of consumption have been put forward. However, all these post-Keynesian consumption theories relate consumption to *some form of income*. First J.S. Duesenberry expressed the view that consumption expenditure of the individuals depends not on their own absolute income but on their income *relative* to the incomes of others. Therefore, his theory is also called '*Relative Income Theory of Consumption*'. Second, Modigliani and Ando put forward a theory known as '*Life Cycle Theory of Consumption*' according to which, individuals plan their consumption profile for their whole lifetime which depends not so much on their current income but on their expectations of whole lifetime income.

Further, a famous American economist, Milton Friedman, advanced an hypothesis regarding consumption behaviour called *permanent income hypothesis* according to which consumption of individuals depend on their *permanent* income rather than their current level income. We discuss below briefly these three post-keynesian theories of consumption.

Life-Cycle Theory of Consumption.

In Keynes's theory of consumption function, consumption expenditure in a period depends mainly on *current income*. After Keynes some economists such as Franco Modigliani and Milton Friedman pointed out that individuals while making their consumption decisions take into account not only the current income which was emphasised by Keynes but also the income they expect to receive in the future. Therefore, the consumption theories of Franco Modigliani and Milton Friedman, both are Nobel Laureates, have been called *Future-Oriented Consumption Theories* by Joseph Stiglitz.[2]

Consumption theory put forward by Modigliani and Ando is called *Life-Cycle Theory of Consumption*[3] as they lays stress that in deciding about consumption out of income in the working years of their life individuals attempt to save for the post-retirement period. Their motive for doing so is to smooth out or even their consumption in their entire life span. That is, they save from the income of working period of their life so that they will not have to cut down consumption level after they retire.

The life-cycle theory assumes that an individual in early years of his life earn no income and is maintained by his parents or other relatives. In the middle period of his life he works and earns income. Though in the middle period of his life he spends a good deal on consumption of his own and his family members, on balance he earns more than he consumes and therefore

2. See J. Stglitz, *Economies*, 2002, p. 634
3. Ando A. Franco Modigliani, The Life Cycle Hypothesis of Saving : Aggregate Implications and Tests, *American Economic Review*, March 1963, pp. 55-84.

saves a part of his income. **His motive of saving is to accumulate assets or wealth, which yields him enough income so as to maintain satisfactory standard of consumption in later years of his life after he retires.**

According to life-cycle theory consumption in any *period is not the function of current income of that period but of the whole lifetime expected income.* Thus, in life cycle hypothesis the individual is assumed to plan a pattern of consumption expenditure based on expected income in his entire lifetime. If is further assumed that individual maintains a more or less constant or slightly increasing level of consumption. However, this level of consumption is limited by his expectations of lifetime income. A typical individual in this theory in his early years of life spends on consumption either by borrowing from others or spending the assets bequeathed by his parents. It is in his main working years of his lifetime that he consumes less than the income he earns and therefore makes net positive savings. **He invests these savings in assets, that is, accumulates wealth which he consumes in the future years.** He will accumulate enough wealth or assets in his working years of his life to maintain what he considers satisfactory standard of living even after he retires from work. In his lifetime after retirement he again dissaves, that is, consumes more than his income in these later years of his life but is able to maintain or even slightly increase his consumption in the lifetime after retirement.

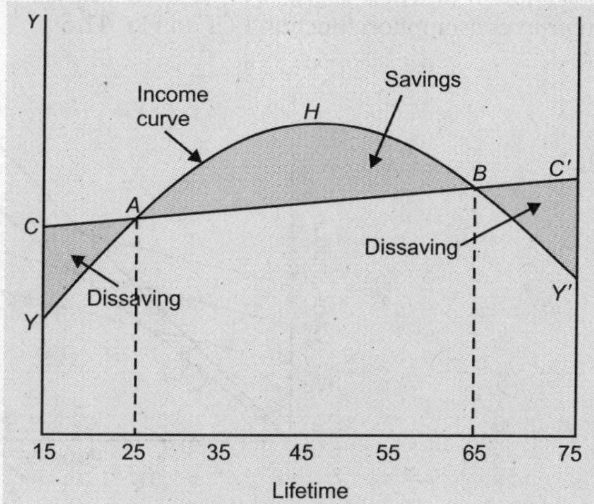

Fig. 41.5. *Life Cycle Theory of Consumption*

Life cycle hypothesis has been depicted in Fig. 41.5. It is assumed that a typical individual knows exactly at what age he will die. In Fig. 41.5 it is taken that the individual would die at the age of 75 years. That is, 75 years is his expected lifetime. If an individual does not want to leave any assets for his children then in the life cycle theory net savings in the entire lifetime will by zero, that is, the savings done by the individual in the working years of his life will be equal to the dissavings made by him in his early years of life before he is able to earn income as well as the dissavings which he makes after retirement. It is also assumed for the sake of simplicity that interest paid on his assets is zero. The curve *YY'* shows income pattern of the whole lifetime of the individual whereas *CC'* is the curve of consumption which is assumed to be slightly increasing as the individual grows old. It is assumed that our individual enters into labour force (*i.e.*, working life) at the age of 15 years. It will be noticed from Fig. 41.5 that up to the age of 25 years his income, though increasing, is less than his consumption, that is, he will be dissaving during the first 13 years of his working life. To finance his excess consumption over his income, he may be borrowing from others.

In the final stage of his life cycle when the individual has retired from work his earnings from work is very little or nil while he spends a good deal on his consumption, it is income from his past savings or accumulated assets that enables him to maintain satisfactory standard of consumption over his whole life cycle.

Some important conclusions follow from life cycle theory of consumption. The fundamental idea of the life cycle hypothesis is that people make their consumption plans for their entire lifetime and further that they make lifetime consumption plans on the basis of their expectations of lifetime income. *Thus in life cycle model consumption is not a function of current* but of expected life-time income. Besides, according to life cycle hypothesis, consumption of an individual also depends on wealth held by him which he accumulates during working years of life by investing his saving. In fact, wealth is used to balance income streams over his entire life.

The life cycle theory can explain the puzzle that arose from the empirical fundings of consumption function by Kuznets, namely, that *APC* is constant, that is, increase in consumption is proportional to increase in income. According life cycle hypothesis, like Keynes's consumption function theory, the relationship between consumption and income is non-proportional, that is, *APC* falls as income rises as will be seen from consumption function curve *CC′* in Figure 41.5 which has an *intercept. The intercept of the consumption function of life saving hypothesis measures the wealth effect.* However, the intercept of such short-run consumption function is not constant. As wealth increases and the intercept rises, the short-run consumption shifts upward as shown in Fig. 41.6 where as a result of increase in wealth, consumption curve CF_1 shifts to CF_2 and further increase in wealth it shifts uprivard to CF_3. Through the shifting of short-run consumption function curve such as from CF_1 to CF_2 and then to CF_3 we can trace out the long-run consumption function *LCF* in Fig. 41.6

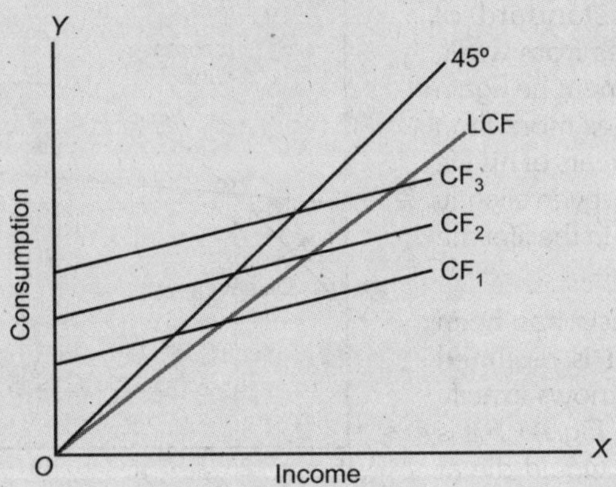

Fig. 41.6. *Shift in Short-run Consumption Function as a Result of Increase In Wealth*

If the ratios of wealth and labour income to the disposable income are relatively constant over time life cycle hypothesis about consumption is in conformity with the findings arrived at by Kuznets from the long-run time series data that long-run consumption – Income relation such as *LCF* in Fig. 41.6 is proportional with average propensity to consume being relatively stable at around 0.9. This, according to life cycle hypothesis, shows that while the short-run consumption function like that of Keynesian one shows non-proportional relationship between income and consumption (*i.e. APC* falling with increase in income). The long-run consumption function is in accordance with Kuznets's finding that there is proportional relationship between consumption and income in the long run with *APC* as stable. In this way life cycle hypothesis has succeeded in resolving the difference between Keynes's view and Kuznets's findings. While Keynes was concerned with short-run consumption function, Kuznets's findings were about long-run consumption function.

Critique, Although life cycle theory has provided an explanation of various puzzles about consumption function, it is not without critics. Gardner Ackley has criticized the assumption of life cycle hypothesis that in making consumption plans, households have "a definite and conscious vision." According to Ackley, the possession of this long-term vision on the part of households sounds unrealistic. Further, according to him, to assume that a household has complete knowledge of "family's future size, including the life expectancy of each member, entire lifetime profile of income of each member, the extent of credit available in the future, emergencies, opportunities and social pressure which have a bearing on consumption spending" is quite unrealistic.

Life cycle theory has also been criticized that it fails to recognize the importance of *liquidity constraints* in determining the response of consumption to income. According to critics, even if a household has a concrete vision of future income, the opportunities to borrow from the capital markets for quite a long period on the basis of expected future income, as has been visualised by life cycle hypothesis, are very little. This creates the liquidity constraints for deciding about consumption plans. As a result, the consumption becomes highly responsive to current income which is quite contrary to the life cycle hypothesis.

Duesenberry's Relative Income Theory of Consumption

Duesenberry's theory is based on two relative income hypotheses. First, he lays stress on *relative incomes of individuals* rather than their absolute incomes as determinant of their consumption, that is, consumption behaviour of individuals is interdependent. Second, according to him, consumption of individuals does not depend on their current income *but on certain previous reached income levels.* That is, consumption-income relation of individuals is *irreversible over time*.

Demonstration Effect, Duesenberry's first statement implies that consumption of individuals are not so much concerned with the absolute level of their income as with their relative position in the income distribution in a society, that is, consumption behaviour of an individual is governed not by level of his absolute income but his income relative to the incomes of other individuals in the society. This tendency of an individual arises to keep up with other individuals' consumption standard, or what is called, to "keep up with the Joneses". This is called by Duesenberry as *demonstration effect.*

According to this hypothesis of Duesenberry, if incomes all individuals in society increases by the *same percentage*, then their relative incomes would remain the same though their absolute incomes would have increased. According to Duesenburry, because relative income of each individual in a society remains the same, *every one will be spending the same proportion of his income on consumption as he was doing before the increase in his absolute income.* That is, the *average propensity to consume* (*APC*) will *remain the same* despite the increase in absolute incomes of individuals if the relative incomes of individuals remain the same. That *APC* remains the same as the community's income increases conforms to the time-series empirical findings such as that of Kuznets. This conclusion of Duesenburry's relative income theory of consumption differs from the Keynesian theory, of consumption, according to which, as seen above, as absolute income of a community increases, it will devote a *smaller proportion of its income to consumption expenditure, that is, its APC will decline.*

Duesenberry's demonstration effect also shows that a person with a given income *would devote a larger proportion of his income to consumption* if he is living in a community or area where that income is considered relatively low. This is due to the working of demonstration effect. On the other hard, a person will spend a *lower proportion of his income* if he is living in a community in which that income is considered relatively high. This is because in this later case demonstration effect will not be working.

Ratchet Effect. Duesenberry's second hypothesis of irreversibility of consumption-income relation over time suggests that when incomes of individuals or households falls from a previously attained levels their consumption does not fall to that extent. According to Duesenberry, individuals show resistance to lowering their consumption level once attained. This is called *ratchet effect.* This is partly due to the demonstration effect explained above. People do not want to show to their neighbour that they do not afford to maintain their previous high standard of living. Further, this is also partly due to the fact that people become accustomed to their previous high level of consumption and it is quite hard and difficult to reduce their consumption expenditure when their income has fallen. They try to maintain their earlier consumption level by reducing their savings. Therefore, the fall in their income, as during the period of recession or depression, does not result in decrease in their consumption expenditure very much as one would conclude from the cross-section family budget studies. Thus, it is because of the ratchet effect that decrease in income of individuals will have less than proportionate effect on consumption.

That is, *MPC* is less than APC.

It follows from above that through demonstration and ratchet effects Duesenberry's relative income hypothesis provides a convincing explanation for why aggregate short-run *consumption function of the community may be flatler* than the family budget studies would suggest. It is because, he emphasises, it is relative income rather than absolute income which determines consumption expenditure of the households. Further, *it also follows from Duesenberry's relative income hypothesis that short-run aggregate consumption function of the community is linear rather than curved.* As explained above, if in the short run the level of income increases, the proportion of consumption expenditure does not increase much due to the operation of demonstration effect and with the fall in income the proportion of consumption expenditure to income is not likely to decrease much due to ratchet effect. It is worth that Duesenberry's theory assumes that income distribution in a society does not change much in the short run which is in conformity with the real world situation.

Permanent Consumption Theory

Like Modigliani, Milton Friedman[4] also thinks that expectations about future income affect current consumption in a period. According to Friedman, income of an individual consists of permanent income and temporary or transitory income.

$$Y = Y_p + Y_t$$

$$C = C_P + C_t$$

where Y stands for income, Y_p for permanent income, Y_t for temporary or transitory income, C for consumption, C_p for permanent consumption and C_t for temporary or transitory income. It is worth emphasizing that Friedman thinks that permanent income is viewed to be earned by both *human and non-human capital of the individual.* Income from human capital is expected income earned from human labour by individuals and income from non-human capital or wealth is the expected earnings from physical assets held by them.

He points out that people save in good years so that they have not to curtail consumption in bad years. In other words, in Friedman's view consumption of individuals or households depends on *permanent income* in contrast to *current income* level as emphasised by Keynes. **By permanent income he means average long-run income.** Therefore, Friedman's theory is known as *permanent consumption hypothesis*. According to this view, *temporary changes* in income such as bonus received in a year, or large capital gains received due to rise in prices of shares or real estate would not have much effect on consumption compared to the permanent changes in income, that is, changes in long-run average income. According to Friedman, temporary or transitory changes in income will have little effect on consumption while permanent changes in income will have large effect on consumption. Thus, according to Friedman's permanent consumption theory, if households could predict their future income level, they will adjust their consumption levels according to their permanent or average long-run income.

As mentioned above, Friedman is of the view that both income and consumption of an individual should be divided into two parts—*permanent and transitory*. Permanent income is the part of income that an individual expects to go on receiving over time in future. On the other hand, according to him, there is transitory income which occurs accidently or by chance. These transitory incomes may occur due to bad purchases of commodities or assets which yield him losses which therefore represents negative income or they be the result of favourable chance purchases or winning of lotteries which therefore yield positive income.

Corresponding to the concept of permanent income there is a notion of permanent consumption. Permanent consumption is the consumption expenditure which an individual expects he will be making over time in future. The crucial point which Friedman makes is that

4. Milton Friedman, A *Theory of Consumption*, Princeton University Press, 1957.

permanent consumption of individuals depends on permanent income rather than current income as believed by J.M. Keynes. Besides, according to Friedman, permanent income is *very much a reflection of the capital value or wealth* and this wealth consists of capital value of principal assets possessed by an individual and his *human capital* (*i.e.* his earning ability depending on the knowledge and skills possessed). According to Friedman, *consumption is proportional to permanent income and can be stated as under :*

$$C = kY_p$$

Thus, Friedman's consumption theory is summed up in the following equation:

$$C_p = k\,(i, w, u)Y_p$$

This proportion (k) of permanent income that is consumed depends on rate of interest (i), desire to accumulate wealth (w) and individuals' desire for immediate current consumption (u). Thus, according to Friedman, permanent consumption is function of rate of interest (i), the ratio of non-human (*i.e.* physical wealth) to income (w) and the preference of individuals for immediate or current consumption as against his willingness to accumulate assets or wealth. According to Friedman, higher rate of interest would induce people to save more and thus reducing his consumption expenditure. Besides, proportion of individuals' consumption to their permanent income depends to a great deal on their assets or wealth, that is, w in the above function. The greater the wealth, or assets of an individual, the higher his consumption expenditure. Lastly, the proportion (k) of consumption expenditure to permanent income depends on individual's desire for immediate or current consumption as against his willingness to add to his wealth or assets and is denoted by u.

Milton Friedman emphasises that consumption of individuals is affected by changes in individuals' wealth which is a stock variable in contrast to the current income which is a flow variable. Friedman's permanent consumption theory suggests that individuals' consumption depends on how well-off they are and that is better measured by their wealth. Individuals' wealth changes when the value of their assets such as prices of stock, shares and real estate change. When their prices rise, people enjoy capital gains which make them wealthier and as a result their consumption out of a given income rises. With this the consumption functions curve shifts above. Commenting on the future-oriented theories of consumption and saving of Modigliani and Friedman, Joseph Stiglitz writes, **"Both Modigliani and Friedman stressed that individuals generally try to stabilise their consumption using savings to smooth consumption so that it does not fluctuate dramatically from year to year. They also stressed that individuals will be forward-looking, basing current consumption decisions on their expectations about future income"**[5].

Implications. There are three important implications of the above two future-oriented theories of consumption and saving, namely, life cycle theory of Modigliani and permanent income theory of Friedman. First important implication is that *changes in expectations about future income* affect the current consumption of individuals even though their current income has not changed. Consider the case when an economy is currently experiening recession, as had been the case in 2008-09 caused by global financial crisis and global meltdown, people became quite pessimistic about their future income prospects which led them to curtail consumption and save more even though their current income did not change. This causes the consumption function curve to shift downward.

Another implication is that one-time or transitory changes in income will cause only a small change in consumption. Suppose a person has a windfall gain of ₹ 10 lakhs in a year due to his winning a lottery. Given his marginal propensity to consume equal to 0.8, the Keynesian consumption function predicts that his consumption will increase by ₹ 8 lakhs and the remaining ₹ 2 lakhs will be saved by him in that year. On the other hand, the future-oriented theories of both Modigliani and Freidman predict that the consumption of extra income gained by the lottery

5. Stiglitiz, *op. cit.*, p.634

winner during a year *will be spread over his lifetime or over a long period of time*. Similarly, a more important case from the viewpoint of economic policy is the *temporary reduction in the direct tax* at the time of recession by the government to boost consumption demand as had been done by the US government in 2007-08 and 2008-09 to fight recession will have only limited effect on consumption. The above two future-oriented theories, especially that of Friedman, predict that contrary to the prediction of the Keynesian model the temporary reduction in direct taxes will be much less effective in boosting consumption demand as due to uncertain economic prospects much of the income gained through temporary tax reduction will be saved. The evidence from the US shows this has in fact been the case.

The third related implication of the future-oriented theories is that since changes in income that individuals expect to be only temporary will have only small effect on consumption spending, marginal propensity to consume will be lower and the multiplier effect of such changes in incomes will be smaller.

To conclude, leaving aside the cases of transitory changes in income and the concern of the forward-looking people to ensure same consumption standard in the future, the Keynesian theory of consumption is right in visualising that individuals' consumption spending is more dependent on current income. To quote Stiglitz, "**The permanent income and life-cycle saving hypotheses contain large elements of truth. Families do save for their retirement and they do smooth their consumption between good years and bad. Even so, *households spending appear to be more depended on current income than either future-oriented theory would saggest*"**[6].

DETERMINANTS OF CONSUMPTION DEMAND

The important question is on what factors does the propensity to consume of a community or consumption demand depend. In other words, what are the factors that determine the level and position of the propensity to consume or the consumption function. Apart from such subjective factors such as unforeseen contingencies (*e.g.* illness, unemployment period) and future needs for education and marriage of their children. Consumption demand depends on the following factors:

(1) Changes in the General Price Level : Real Balance Effect. The general price level is an important factor which influences the consumption of a community. When the general price level increases or, in other words, when inflation occurs, the consumption function shifts downward. This is because the rise in the general price level, real value (that is, purchasing power) of people's money balances and financial assets with fixed monetary values decline. This causes a downward shift in the consumption function. This is called *real balance effect*. Similarly, when the general price level falls, real value of money balances and financial assets increase. This will induce people to consume relatively more out of their current income. This will cause an upward shift in the consumption function.

(2) Fiscal Policy. Fiscal policy of the Government, especially taxation policy, affects the propensity to consume of the country. By levying excise duties, sales tax, the Government can cut down the consumption and thereby increase savings of the community. Likewise, when the Government reduces taxes, consumption of the people increases and this raises the propensity to consume. Rationing and price control by the Government also affects the propensity to consume, as was witnessed during the Second World War. In the modern times, pursuing of the welfare state policy by the Government under which progressive taxes have been levied on the rich people and the revenue obtained from them have been spent to provide many social security benefits and amenities to the poor people, has tended to raise the consumption function.

6. Stiglitz, *op.* cit. p. 335 (italics added)

(3) Rate of Interest. Rate of interest also affects the propensity to consume and save. It is generally believed that higher rate of interest induces the people to save more and this results in reducing their propensity to consume. But this is not true in the case of all the people. Some individuals are of such a type who want a certain fixed income in the future. And when the rate of interest rises these individuals consume more and save less because with higher rate of interest they can obtain the given fixed income with lesser savings. Therefore, when the rate of interest rises such individuals save less than before. Thus, it cannot be said with certainty whether with the changes in the rate of interest the propensity to consume of the whole community will change or not.

(4) Stock of Wealth. The stock of wealth owned by the households in the economy is also an important factor that determines propensity to consume. In wealth we include not only real assets such as land, houses, automobiles but also *financial assets* such as cash balances, saving and fixed deposits with banks, stocks and bonds possessed by households. The greater the amount of wealth accumulated by households in the economy, the greater is generally the propensity to consume (*i.e.* the greater the amount of consumption out of any level of current income). The important motive of the people to save is to accumulate wealth. Generally speaking, the greater the wealth which people have accumulated, the weaker is the incentive to save further. In other words, the other things remaining the same, the increase in wealth generally causes an upward shift in the consumption function and decrease in wealth causes a downward shift in the consumption function.

An important example which is often cited to emphasise the importance of wealth as a determinant of consumption is the stock market crash of 1929 in England (*i.e.* drastic fall in share prices) which substantially reduced the financial wealth of the households overnight resulting in shifting the consumption function downward.

(5) Credit Conditions and Consumer Indebtedness. The availability of easy credit causes an increase in consumption and shifts the consumption function upward. It is now a common experience in India that in recent years lowering of lending interest rates by Indian banks on loans for houses, cars, computers and other durable consumer goods has greatly increased the consumption of the people and shifted consumption function upward. On the other hand, tightening of credit produces an opposite effect, that is, causes a downward shift in the consumption function. Furthermore, the recent increase in facilities of Credit Cards by banks and their acceptance by sellers of consumer goods have also worked to shift the consumption function upward in India.

Similarly, the level of consumer indebtedness also greatly affects the propensity to consume of the people. If the households are heavily indebted, say 25 to 30 per cent of their current, they are committed to save (*i.e.* consume less) to that extent so that they are able to pay their installments of previous credit taken. Thus, the greater the degree of indebtedness of households in the economy, the higher will be the consumption function curve and *vice versa*.

(6) Income Distribution. Lastly, distribution of income in a society also determines the level of consumption function. If national income is more unequally distributed, the lower will be the propensity to consume. This is because propensity to consume of the rich is relatively less as compared to that of the poor. Therefore, if inequalities in income distribution increase, this reduces the consumption out of any given level of national income and thus causes a downward shift in the consumption function.

(7) Windfall Gains and Losses. Windfall gains and losses also affect the propensity to consume. When the prices of the shares go up, the shareholders begin to think themselves better off and this raises their consumption. On the other hand, when the prices of the shares go down, the shareholders have to suffer sudden losses and they begin to think themselves relatively poorer than before. This induces them to reduce their consumption. We thus see that the windfall gains and losses affect the propensity to consume.

(8) Change in Expectations. Changes in the expectations of the people also influence the propensity to consume. When people expect that war will break out in the near future and they expect prices to go up, then they will try to spend more on goods so as to meet the needs of the immediate future. This raises the consumption function in the current period. On the other hand, when people expect the prices to fall they reduce their current consumption so that they should spend more when the prices actually fall.

We have explained above various subjective and objective factors which taken together determine the consumption function of a community. It is worth noting that propensity to consume does not generally change in the short run, because it depends more on psychological and institutional factors which change only in the long run. *The institutional factors which determine the distribution of income in the society are important forces determining the consumption function.* And these institutional factors do not change in the short run. Therefore, Keynes was of the view that consumption function remains stable in the short run.

INVESTMENT DEMAND

Since consumption function is more or less stable in short run, investment demand is of crucial importance in the determination of income and employment. The greater level of investment, the greater the level of income and employment. According to Keynes, the equilibrium of free market economy is generally not established at the level of full employment, primarily because investment demand is insufficient to fill up the saving gap corresponding to the level of full employment. Therefore, *underemployment equilibrium*, on which Keynes laid a great stress, is due to the lack of investment demand as compared to the amount of saving at full-employment level of income. On the other hand, as Keynes later showed, when investment demand is more than the magnitude of saving at full-employment level of income, there emerges an *inflationary gap* in the economy which brings about the rise in general price level. We thus see that investment demand plays a vital role in the determination of national income, employment and prices in the country.

Meaning of Investment

It is useful to make the meaning of investment clear. When a person buys shares, bonds or debentures of a public limited company from the market, it is generally said that he has made investment. But this is not the real investment which determines income and employment in the country and with which we are here concerned. Buying of existing shares and bonds by an individual is merely a financial investment. When one individual purchase the shares or bonds, some other one would sell them. Thus, the purchase and sale of the shares merely represents the change in the ownership of assets which already exists rather the creation of new capital assets. It is the new addition, to the stock of physical capital such as plant, machines, trucks, new factories and so on that creates income and employment. Therefore, *by real investment we mean the addition to the stock of physical capital.* Thus, in economics, investment means the new expenditure incurred on addition of capital goods such as machines, buildings, equipment, tools, etc. The addition to the stock of physical capital, *i.e.*, net investment raises the level of aggregate demand which brings about addition to the level of income and employment in the economy. Keynes and many other economists also include the increase in the *inventories* of consumer goods in the capital of the country and therefore in the investment.

Autonomous Investment and Induced Investment

After Keynes two types of investments have been distinguished. One is *autonomous investment* and the second is *induced investment*. By autonomous investment we mean the investment which does not change with the changes in the income level and is therefore independent of income. Keynes thought that the level of investment depends upon marginal efficiency of capital and the rate of interest. He thought changes in income level will not affect investment. This view of Keynes is based upon his preoccupation with short-run problem. He was of the opinion that changes in income level will affect investment only in the long run. Therefore, considering that this was the short run problem he treated investment as independent of the changes in the income level. In fact the distinction between autonomous investment and induced investment has been made by post-Keynesian economists. *Autonomous investment refers to the investment which does not depend upon changes in the income level.* This autonomous investment generally takes place in houses, roads, public undertakings and in other types of economic infrastructure such as power, transport and communication. This *autonomous investment depends more on population growth and technical progress than on the level of income.* Most of the investment undertaken by Government is of the autonomous nature. The investment undertaken by Government in various development projects to accelerate economic growth of the country is of autonomous type. The autonomous investment is depicted in Fig. 41.7 where it will be seen that whatever the level of nation income, investment remains the same at I_a. Therefore the autonomous investment curve is a horizontal straight line.

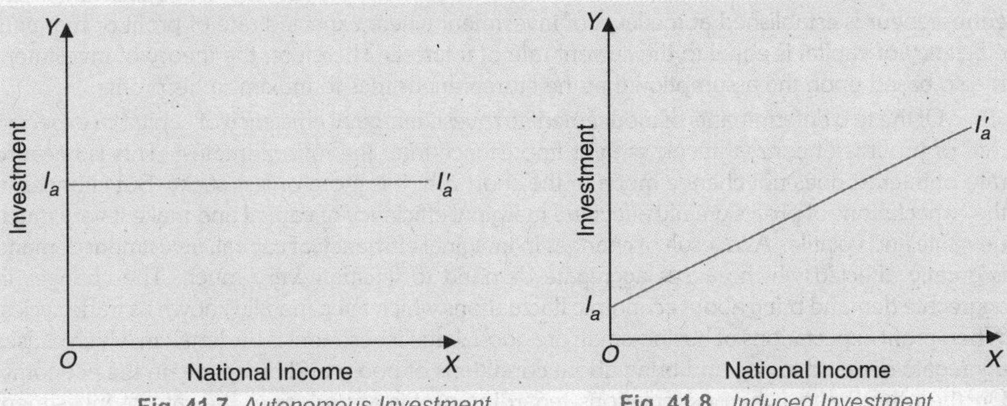

Fig. 41.7. *Autonomous Investment* **Fig. 41.8.** *Induced Investment*

On the other hand, induced investment is that investment which is affected by the changes in the level of income. The greater the level of income, the larger will be the consumption of the community. In order to produce more consumer goods, more investment has to be made in capital goods so that greater output of consumer goods becomes possible. Keynes regarded rate of interest as a factor determining induced investment but the empirical evidence gathered so far suggests that induced investment depends more on income than on the rate of interest. Induced investment is shown in Fig. 41.8 where it will be seen that with the increase in national income, induced involvement is increasing. Increase in national income implies that demand for output of goods and services increases. To produce greater output, more capital goods are required to produce them. To have more capital goods more investment has to be undertaken. This induced investment is undertaken both in fixed capital assets and in inventories. The essence of induced investment is that greater income and therefore greater aggregate demand affects the level of investment in the economy. The induced investment underlines the concept of the principle of accelerator, which is highly useful in explaining the occurrence of trade cycles.

DETERMINANTS OF INVESTMENT

Inducement to invest or investment demand depends upon two factors: (1) expected rate of profits to which Keynes gives the name *Marginal Efficiency of Capital,* and (2) the rate of interest. It can be easily shown that investment is determined by expected rate of profit and the rate of interest. A person having an amount of savings has two alternatives before him. Either he should invest his savings in machines, factories, etc., or he can lend his savings to others on a certain rate of interest. If investment undertaken in machines or factories is expected to fetch 25% rate of profit, while the current rate of interest is only 15%, then it is obvious that the person would invest his savings in machinery or factory.

It follows from above, if investment is to be profitable then the expected rate of profit must not be less than the current market rate of interest. If the expected rate of profit is greater than the market rate of interest, new investment will take place. If an entrepreneur does not invest his own savings but has to borrow from others, then it becomes much clear that the expected rate of profit from investment in any capital asset must not be less than the rate of interest he has to pay. For instance, if an entrepreneur borrows funds from others at 15% rate of interest, then the investment proposed to be undertaken will actually be undertaken only if the expected rate of profit from it is more than 15 per cent. We thus see that investment depends upon marginal efficiency of capital on the one hand and the rate of interest on the other. Investment will be undertaken in any given form of capital asset so long as expected rate of profit or marginal efficiency of capital falls to the level of the current market rate of interest. The equilibrium of the entrepreneur is established at the level of investment where expected rate of profit or marginal efficiency of capital is equal to the current rate of interest. Therefore, the theory of investment is also based upon the assumption that the entrepreneur tries to maximize his profits.

Of the two determinants of inducement to invest, marginal efficiency of capital or expected rate of profit is of comparatively greater importance than the rate of interest. This is because rate of interest does not change much in the short run; it is more or less sticky. But changes in the expectations of profits greatly affect the marginal efficiency of capital and make it very much unstable and volatile. As a result of changes in imaginal efficiency of capital, investment demand is greatly affected which causes aggregate demand to fluctuate very much. The changes in aggregate demand bring about economic fluctuations which are generally known as trade cycles. When profit expectations of businessmen are good, large investment is undertaken which causes aggregate demand to rise and bring about conditions of boom and prosperity in the economy. On the other hand, when expectations regarding profits are adverse, the rate of investment falls which causes decline in aggregate demand and brings about depression, unemployment and excess productive capacity in the economy. Thus, the changes in the marginal efficiency of capital play a crucial role in causing changes in the investment level and economic activity.

We have read in the theory of interest that, according to Keynes, the rate of interest is determined by liquidity preference and the supply of money. The greater the liquidity preference, the greater the rate of interest. Given the liquidity preference curve, the greater the supply of money, the lower will be the rate of interest. We have already studied how the rate of interest is determined. We explain below in detail the concept of marginal efficiency of capital and describe the factors on which it depends.

Marginal Efficiency of Capital

As has been pointed out above, the concept of marginal efficiency of capital refers to the rate of profit expected to be made from investment in certain capital assets. The rate of profit expected from an extra unit of a capital asset is known as marginal efficiency of capital. Now, the question is how the marginal efficiency of capital is measured. Suppose an entrepreneur invests money in a certain machinery, how will he estimate the expected rate of profit from it? To estimate the marginal efficiency of capital, the entrepreneur will first take into consideration how much price he has to pay for the particular capital asset. The price which he has to pay for the particular capital asset is called its *supply price* or *cost of capital*. The second thing which he will consider is that how much yield he expects to obtain from investment from that particular capital asset. A capital asset continues to produce goods and yield income over a long period of time. Therefore, an entrepreneur has to estimate the prospective yield from a capital asset over his whole life period. Thus, the supply price and the prospective yields of capital asset determine the marginal efficiency of capital. By deducting the supply price from the prospective yield during whole life of a capital asset the entrepreneur can estimate the expected rate of profit or marginal efficiency of capital. Keynes has defined the marginal efficiency of capital in the following words: "I define the marginal efficiency of capital as being equal to that rate of discount which would make the present value of the series of annuities given by the returns expected from the capital asset during its life just equal to its supply price." Thus, according to Keynes, marginal efficiency of capital is the rate of discount which renders the prospective yields from a capital asset over its whole life period equal to the supply price of that asset. Therefore, we can obtain the marginal efficiency of capital in the following way:

$$\text{Supply Price} = \text{Discounted Prospective Yields}$$

$$C = \frac{R_1}{1+r} + \frac{R_2}{(1+r)^2} + \frac{R_3}{(1+r)^3} \cdots\cdots + \frac{R_n}{(1+r)^n}$$

In the above formula, C stands for Supply Price or Replacement Cost and R_1, R_2, R_3, R_n *etc.*, represent the annual prospective yields from the capital asset, r is that rate of discount which renders the annual prospective yields equal to the supply price of the capital asset. Thus r represents the expected rate of profit or marginal efficiency of capital.

The measurement of marginal efficiency of capital can be illustrated by an arithmetical example. Suppose it costs ₹ 3000 to invest in a certain machinery and the life of the machinery is two years, that is, after two years it becomes quite useless, having no value. Suppose further that in the first year the machinery is expected to yield income of ₹ 1100 and in the second year ₹ 2420. By substituting these values in the above formula, we can calculate the value of r, that is, the marginal efficiency of capital:

$$\text{Supply Price} = \text{Discounted Prospective Yields}$$

$$C = \frac{R_1}{1+r} + \frac{R_2}{(1+r)^2}$$

$$3{,}000 = \frac{1{,}100}{1+r} + \frac{2{,}420}{(1+r)^2}$$

On calculating the value of r in the above equation it is found to be equal to 10. In other words, marginal efficiency of capital here is equal to 10 per cent. If we put the value of r, that is, 10 in the above equation, we obtain the following:

$$3{,}000 = \frac{1{,}100}{1.10} + \frac{2{,}420}{(1.10)^2}$$

$$= 1{,}000 + 2{,}000 = 3{,}000$$

Marginal Efficiency of Capital in General. We have explained above the marginal efficiency of a *particular type* of capital asset. But we also require to know the marginal efficiency of capital *in general.* It is the marginal efficiency of capital in general that will indicate the scope for investment opportunities at a particular time in any economy. *At a particular time in an economy the marginal efficiency of that particular capital asset which yields the greatest rate of profit is called the marginal efficiency of capital in general.* In other words, marginal efficiency of capital in general is the greatest of all the marginal efficiencies of various types of capital assets which could be produced but have not yet been produced. Thus, marginal efficiency of capital in general represents the highest expected rate of return to community from an extra unit of capital asset which yields the maximum profit which could be produced.

Keeping in view the existing stock of a capital asset, we can always calculate the marginal efficiency of any particular capital asset. The marginal efficiency of capital will vary when more is invested in a given particular capital asset. In any period of time marginal efficiency of capital from any type of capital asset will decline as more investment is undertaken in it. In other words, marginal efficiency of a particular type of capital asset will be sloping downward as the stock of capital increases. The main reason for the decline in marginal efficiency of capital with the increase in investment in it is that the prospective yields from capital asset fall as more units are installed and used for production of a good. Prospective yields decline because when more quantity of good is produced with the greater amount of a capital asset prices of goods decline. The second reason for the decline in the marginal efficiency of capital is that the supply price of the capital asset may rise because the increase in demand for it will bring about increase in its cost of production.

Rate of Interest and Investment Demand Curve

We have explained above how the marginal efficiency of capital is estimated. We can represent diminishing marginal efficiency of capital in general by a curve which will slope downward. This has been done in Fig. 41.9. in which along the X-axis investment in capital assets is measured and along the Y-axis marginal efficiency of capital in general is shown. It will be seen from the figure that when investment in capital asset is equal to OI_1, marginal efficiency of capital is i_1. When the investment is increased to OI_2, marginal efficiency of capital falls to i_2. Likewise, when investment rises to OI_3, marginal efficiency of capital further diminishes to i_3.

We have seen above that inducement to investment depends upon the marginal efficiency of capital and the rate of interest. With the given particular rate of interest and given the curve of marginal efficiency of capital in general we can show what will be the equilibrium

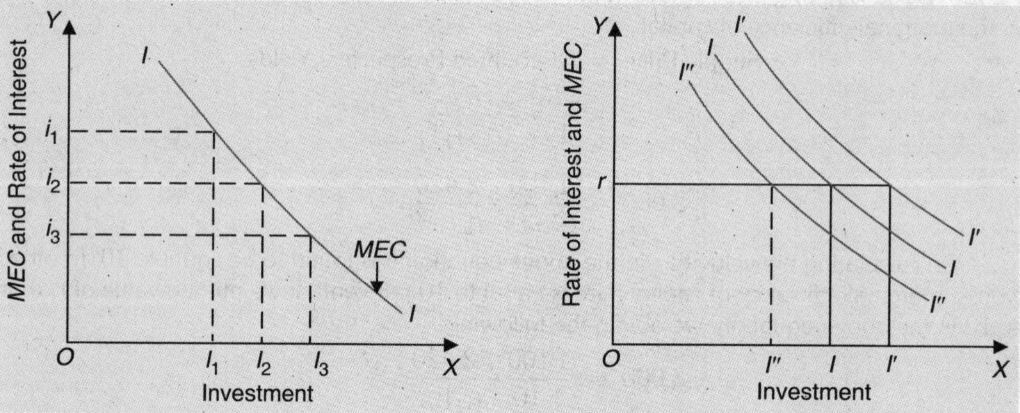

Fig. 41.9 *Investment Demand Curve*

Fig. 41.10. *Shift in Investment Demand Curve due to Changes in Marginal Efficiency of Capital*

level of investment in the economy. If in Fig. 41.9 along the Y-axis, rate of interest is also shown, then level of investment can be easily determined. The equilibrium level of investment will be established at the point where marginal efficiency of capital becomes equal to the given current rate of interest. Thus, if the rate of interest is i_1, then OI_1 investment will be undertaken since at OI_1 level of investment, marginal efficiency of capital is equal to the rate of interest i_1. If the rate of interest falls to i_2, investment in the capital assets will rise to OI_2 since at OI_2 level of investment the new rate of interest i_2 is equal to the marginal efficiency of capital. Thus, we see that the curve of marginal efficiency of capital in general shows the demand for investment or inducement to invest at various rates of interest. Hence marginal efficiency of capital curve represents the investment demand curve. This investment demand curve shows how much investment will be undertaken by the entrepreneurs at various rates of interest. If the investment demand curve is less elastic, then investment demand will not increase much with the fall in the rate of interest.

But if the investment demand curve or marginal efficiency of capital curve is very much elastic, then the changes in the rate of interest will bring about large changes in investment demand.

It follows from above that rate of interest, along with the marginal efficiency of investment, determines the volume of investment. If the rate of interest is higher than the marginal efficiency of investment, it will not be profitable to invest in a new physical asset. This is because we assume that the aim of the individual investor is to maximise his money profits. Two courses of action are open to an investor: either he can use his money to buy additional physical assets, (*i.e.*, he can invest in the Keynesian sense of the term), or else he can lend his money to others at a certain rate of interest. Now, if marginal efficiency of investment is lower than the current rate of interest, it is more profitable to lend one's money rather than use it for investing in new capital assets. On the other hand, if marginal efficiency of investment is higher than the rate of interest, it is better to invest more. At the point, where marginal efficiency of investment equals the current rate of interest, we have the equilibrium level of the rate of investment.

It follows, therefore, that the rate of investment also depends on the rate of interest. If it is interest elastic a low rate of interest tends to stimulate investment. But it may fail to do so, if marginal efficiency of investment is already lower than the rate of interest (as may well happen during a depression). Of the two determinants of the rate of investment, marginal efficiency of capital (investment) is more volatile than the rate of interest.

Investment is highly volatile and fluctuates greatly. It is fluctuations in investment that is mainly responsible for fluctuations in aggregate demand. We have seen above that investment demand depends on rate of interest and marginal efficiency of capital, that is, expected rate of profit on investment. Now, an important question is what are the factors that determine marginal efficiency of capital which determines investment demand. We discuss these factors below:

Business Expectations and Shift in Investment Demand Curve.

We have studied above that the marginal efficiency of capital depends upon the supply price of capital on the one hand and prospective yields on the other. It is important to note here that the prospective yields are greatly affected by the expectations of the entrepreneurial class regarding the profit making. These expectations generally change very frequently. Indeed, it is the profit expectations of the entrepreneur that determine the level of investment. When the expectations of the entrepreneur regarding profit making become dim, the marginal efficiency of capital declines and as a result demand for investment falls. The occurrence of depression is mainly due to the pessimistic expectations of the entrepreneurial class regarding profit making. On the contrary, when the expectations of the entrepreneurs regarding profit opportunities increase, their inducement to invest rises. As a result of the increases in investment, aggregate demand in the economy increases and levels of income and employment increase. We thus see that profit expectations of entrepreneurs greatly affect investment demand and consequently the level of income and employment.

Short-term and Long-run Business Expectations. We have explained above that, according to Keynes, marginal efficiency of capital along with rate of interest determines the level of investment and therefore of the levels of income and employment. A significant contribution of Keynes is that he emphasized the important role that business expectations play in determing the prospective yield from assets on which marginal efficiency of capital and therefore the level of investment depends. He drew distinctions between *short-term expectations and long-term expectations*. Keynes thought that prospective yields of capital assets depended on partly *existing facts* which we can assume to be known with a fair degree of certainty and partly on *future events* which can be predicted with a degree of uncertainty and involves greater risk. It is the existing facts which are known almost with certainty that determine short-term expectations. The short-term business expectations about prospective yields from investment depend on (*i*) the *existing stock of capital assets and* (*ii*) the *strength of consumer demand* for goods which require a good deal of those assets for their production. The investors think that the *current consumption demand will continue in immediate future* too and base their expectations of prospective yield from investment in capital assets on it.

As regards the state of *long-term expectations*, Keynes emphasized *future changes in the stock of capital assets* and *changes* in the level of aggregate demand during the entire future life of the assets whose prospective yields are being estimated. Businessmen acquiring new assets which have long life for production of goods are more concerned with long-run forces on which future earnings from capital assets depend. It is these long-run forces which make long-run expectations about future yields that make them quite uncertain. Changes in these long-term expectations make investment quite volatile. Therefore, Keynes gave great importance to the state of investors' confidence for determining investment.

It should be carefully noted that when the expectations regarding profit-earning change, the whole curve of the marginal efficiency of capital will shift. If profit expectations fall, the marginal efficiency of capital curve, that is, investment demand curve will shift downward to left, as shown by the shift of the curve from *II* to *I″ I″* in Fig. 41.10. On the other hand, when the profit expectations of the entrepreneurial class become better than before, the marginal efficiency of capital curve will shift upward to the right, as shown by the marginal efficiency of capital curve *I″I″*. Downward shift in the marginal efficiency of capital curve indicates that at the given rate of interest, less investment will be undertaken than before. And upward shift in the marginal efficiency of capital curve indicates that more will be invested at the given rate of interest than before. In Fig. 41.10 when in the beginning, investment demand curve, that is, marginal efficiency of capital curve is represented by *II*, at the rate of interest *r*, demand for investment is *OI*. As a result of downward shift in the marginal efficiency of capital cost curve to *I″ I″*, investment demand at the rate of interest *r* falls to *OI″*. When marginal efficiency capital curve shifts upward to *I′ I″*, investment demand at the given rate of interest *r* rises to *OI′*.

Animal Spirits and Expectations. The Keynes theory gives importance to profit expectations of business for determining marginal efficiency of capital in the economy. It is worth mentioning here the concept of **animal spirits of Keynes**. Keynes pointed out that it was not possible to make accurate calculations about the future profitability of investment. He believed that the *swings of optimism and pessimism of the business class* were more important driving forces in the stock market that determine investment. It is these swings of optimism and pessimism about future profitability of investment which he referred to as *animal spirits*. According to Keynes, it is these animal spirits rather than economic *fundamentals* that determine investment by business firms.

However, marginal efficiency of capital or investment by a business firm depends to a large extent on the demand it anticipates for its product. For the economy as a whole the marginal efficiency of investment (*i.e.*, expected net return on investment) depends significantly on the consumption expenditure of households on the products produced in the economy. As studied above in this chapter, apart from income, consumption expenditure on goods and services depends on several factors such as propensity to save of the people, price level, rate of interest, stock of wealth, taxation policy of the government. Changes in these factors would cause a change in consumption of households and demand for the products. As a result, expected rate of return on investment *i.e.* MEI will change.

Marginal efficiency of capital or investment which depends on prospective yields from investment in capital goods which are used in the production of certain products depends on expected demand for these products. The prospective yields also depend on expected monetary and fiscal policies of the government in the future and stock market situation etc. Changes in them will change the marginal efficiency of investment and result in shift in investment demand curve.

Both monetary and fiscal policy measures affect investment. In what follows we first analyse the effect of discretionary monetary policy and then of discretionary fiscal policy.

Monetary Policy and Investment

Both monetary policy and discretionary fiscal policy affect investment. As explained above, interest rate measures the cost of capital and along with marginal efficiency of capital (*i.e.* expected rate of return on investment) determines the level of investment. It is primarily through its *effect on interest rate* that monetary policy affects investment decisions. Besides interest rate, investment also depends on the *availability of funds or credit*, especially from the banks. The easy monetary policy which aims at lowering interest rate and increasing the availability of credit will lead to more investment. It may be noted that under easy monetary policy the Central Bank lowers the bank rate and cash reserve ratio. The lowering of bank rate sends a signal to the banks to reduce their lending rates. The lowering of cash-reserve ratio (CRR) leads to the more liquidity or extra cash reserves with banks. This not only increases the availability of more credit for investment by businessmen but also puts downward pressure on lending interest rates as a result of increase in the supply of lendable funds with the banks. In India, Reserve Bank of India often lowers a ***repo rate*** (which is an interest rate charged by RBI for borrowing by commercial banks at times of need for a very short period, even for a day) to ensure lowering of lending rates by banks and thereby to stimulate private investment. At a lower interest rate, given the schedule of marginal efficiency of capital, more investment will be undertaken by business firms. The Central Bank can also undertake open market operations to increase availability of bank credit for investment. For this purpose it buys government securities from the banks and pays rupee funds to them. This raises money supply in the economy which not only makes more funds available for lending to businessmen but also tends to lower interest rates.

Keynes and his early followers believed that monetary policy is not very effective for increasing private investment. This view was based on the assumption that during the period of depression rate of interest was already very low and at this low interest rate there is *liquidity trap* in the demand curve for money. Under these conditions, they thought the expansion in money supply by the banks would not lower interest rate. Besides, they believed that investment demand is relatively inelastic so that even lowering of interest rate will not cause much increase in investment. However, later empirical evidence shows that at relevant rates of interest demand for money is quite elastic (that is, liquidity rap does not exist at the generally prevailing interest rates). As a result, expansionary monetary policy lowers interest rate and thereby stimulates private investment. Besides, later empirical evidence also shows that investment demand schedule is quite elastic and therefore lowering of interest rate and more availability of funds lead to more investment. Therefore, the modern Keynesians have veered round to the view that discretionary easy monetary policy can be effective in raising private investment to get rid of recession in the economy and to promote economic growth.

One modification in our above analysis of the impact of monetary policy on investment which is required is the *incorporation of distinction between nominal interest rate and real interest rate.* As explained earlier, it is the real interest rate that is relevant for investment decisions. Therefore, monetary policy must affect the real interest rate if it has to stimulate private investment. However, it is worth noting that in both the Keynesian and monetarist theories expected inflation depends primarily on the inflation prevailing in the recent past and further that it changes slowly over time. Under these conditions changes in monetary rate of interest will mean changes in real interest rate for all practical purposes. In view of this, our above analysis of the effect of monetary policy on investment remains unchanged.

Fiscal Policy and Investment

We now turn to explain the effect of fiscal policy on investment. It is generally believed that there is *adverse effect* of expansionary fiscal policy on private investment. According to this view, though increase in government spending financed by borrowing would bring about increases in aggregate demand for goods and services, it would raise interest rate. Borrowing by the government would raise the demand for funds or money in the market which, given the supply of money, would cause interest rate to rise. The higher interest rate would lower private investment. Thus, it is asserted that expansionary fiscal policy ***crowds out private investment.*** Another route through which adverse effect of expansionary fiscal policy is brought out is that the increase in aggregate demand as a result of expansionary fiscal policy in terms of either increase in government expenditure or cut in taxes would raise aggregate demand and lead to increase in national income. However, the increase in national income brought about by increase in aggregate demand would bring about increase in transactions demand for money which, given the supply of money, would cause interest rate to rise and lower private investment. The reduction or crowding out of private investment would offset a part of the initial expansionary effect on aggregate demand brought about by increase in government expenditure or reduction in taxation. If investment demand is highly elastic, the decrease in private investment resulting from the rise in interest rate will be quite substantial.

However, in view of the present author even if there is significant crowding-out effect on private investment of expansionary fiscal policy, it can be avoided if as a part of expansionary fiscal policy, tax policy of providing *investment tax credit* (*i.e.*, investment rebate) to the business firms is adopted. Under investment tax credit policy, a deduction from business income or profits equal to a certain percentage of investment made is allowed. As this lowers the tax liability of the firm, policy of investment tax credit stimulates investment and consequently there is no any *net adverse effect* of expansionary fiscal policy on private investment.

Further, in our view, the crowding-out effect of expansionary fiscal policy has been exaggerated by the critics of Keynes. As a matter of fact, when government raises its expenditure or cuts personal income tax, aggregate demand for goods and services increases which raises expectations of increased sales and revenue of the business firms. This improves profitability or marginal efficiency of investment. This is more valid at times of depression when private investment declines due to lack of demand for goods and services. Thus when expected profitability or marginal efficiency of capital rises due to expectations of increase in aggregate demand resulting from expansionary fiscal policy, investment demand curve shifts to the right and businessmen invest more at any given rate of interest. This can more than offset any adverse effect on private investment due to rise in interest.

Further, according to *investment theory based on acceleration principle* investment depends on expected changes in output or national income. Thus, even in the absence of investment tax credit expansionary fiscal policy that increases national output or national income through its beneficial effect on aggregate demand will stimulate private investment through accelerator principle.

In the context of a developing country like India the expansionary fiscal policy even when increased government expenditure is financed by borrowing can have beneficial effect on private investment, especially when the economy is experiencing recession or slowdown in economic growth. If in such a situation the government increases its expenditure and spends money on *infrastructure projects,* it will have a favourable effect on private investment as the latter is often constrained by lack of adequate infrastructure facilities. Thus, in developing countries if government borrowing is used to spend more on infrastructure projects, it generally crowds in private investment rather than crowding it out. Besides, when manufacturing industries in developing countries experience recessionary conditions due to sluggish demand, as happened in India during the period 1997 to 2002, and again in 2008-09, increase in public expenditure will lead to increase in aggregate demand through its multiplier effect and thereby improve the demand conditions for increase in private investment.

It follows from above that it is not necessarily true that expansionary fiscal policy crowds out private investment. The expansion in public expenditure can have a beneficial effect on private investment.

QUESTION FOR REVIEW

1. What is consumption function? Explain the various factors that determine consumption demand in the economy.
2. Distinguish between average propensity to consume (APC) and marginal propensity to consume (MPC). In Keynes's consumption function ($C = a + bY$) how do they change with increase in income?
3. Explain the concept of Keynes's consumption function. What factors cause shift in consumption function?
4. Distinguish between Keynes's consumption and Kuznets"s consumption function. How have these two functions been reconciled?
5. Explain the Duesenberry's relative income theory of consumption. How does it differ from Keynes's consumption function theory?
6. Explain the concepts of demonstration effect and ratchet effect. How do they ensure that proportion of consumption to income (*i.e.* average propensity to consume) remains the same as absolute income of the community increases.
7. Explain how Duesenberry's relative income hypothesis shows that short-run consumption function in *linear* rather than *curved*.
8. Explain the essential features of the life cycle theory of consumption. How does it resolve the puzzle that emerged between Kuznets's empirical findings of proportional consumption function (*i.e.* APC remains constant with the increase in income) and Keynes's theory of non-proportional relationship between consumption and income (*i.e.* APC falls as income increases).
9. Show how according to Duesenberry's relative income hypothesis, while short-run consumption function shows APC falls as income increases, long-run consumption function shows APC remains constant with increase in income.
10. How does life cycle hypothesis resolve the apparent contradiction between Keynes's short-run consumption function which suggests a non-proportional relation between consumption and income and Kuznets's findings on the basis of long-run data that suggests relationship between consumption and income is proportional?
11. Explain the permanent income theory of consumption. Compare Friedman's permanent income hypothesis with (1) Keynes's theory of consumption and (2) life cycle theory of consumption.
12. Distinguish between autonomous investment and induced investment. What are the factors that, according to Keynes, determine inducement to invest?
13. What is marginal efficiency of capital? On what factors does it depend?
14. Explain Keynesian theory of investment. How does Keynes explain fluctuations in investment in the short run?
15. What are *animal spirits*? How do they affect investment?
16. What is investment? Explain the factors that determine it.
17. Distinguish between short-sun and long-run business expectations. Explain how business expectations cause fluctuations in investment.
18. How does expansionary fiscal policy affect investment? In the Indian context is it correct to say that expansionary fiscal policy of increasing goyesument expenditure by borrowing will crowd out private investment?
19. Explain how easy monetary policy affect private investment. Why did Keynes think that easy monetary policy is ineffective to revive the economy from recession or depression?

Money Supply, Money Demand and Money Market Equilibrium

Money supply plays a crucial role in the determination of price level and interest rate. In the present chapter we shall explain what determines the money supply in an economy. In economic analysis it is generally presumed that money supply is determined by the policy of Central Bank of a country and the Government. However, this is not fully correct as in the determination of money supply, besides Central Bank and Government, the public and commercial banks also play an important role. There are various measures of money supply depending upon which types of deposits of banks and other financial institutions are included in it. We will explain various measures of money supply later in this chapter.

Importance of Money Supply

Growth of money supply is an important factor not only for acceleration of the process of economic development but also for the achievement of price stability in the economy. What constitutes the money supply and what factors causes variation and growth in money supply will be explained in the present chapter. There must be controlled expansion of money supply if the objective of development with stability is to be achieved. A healthy growth of an economy requires that there should be neither inflation nor deflation. Inflation is the greatest headache of a developing economy. A mild inflation arising out of the creation of money by deficit financing may stimulate investment by raising profit expectations and extracting forced savings. But a runaway inflation is highly detrimental to economic growth. The developing economies have to face the problem of inadequacy of resources in initial stages of development and it can make up this deficiency by deficit financing. But it has to be kept strictly within safe limits. Thus, increase in money supply affects vitally the rate of economic growth. In fact, it is now regarded as a legitimate instrument of economic growth. Kept within proper limits it can accelerate economic growth but exceeding of the limits will retard it. Thus, management of money supply is essential in the interest of steady economic growth.

THE CONCEPT OF MONEY SUPPLY AND ITS MEASUREMENT

By money supply we mean the total stock of monetary media of exchange available to a society for use in connection with the economic activity of the country. According to the standard concept of money supply, it is composed of the following two elements :

1. Currency with the public,
2. Demand deposits with the public.

Before explaining these two components of money supply two things must be noted with regard to the money supply in the economy. First, the money supply refers to the total sum of money available to the public in the economy *at a point of time*. That is, money supply is a *stock concept* in sharp contrast to the national income which is a flow representing the value of goods and services produced *per unit of time*, usually taken as a year. Secondly, money supply always refers to the amount of money *held by the public*. In the term public are included households, firms and institutions other than banks and the government. The rationale behind considering money supply as held by the public is to separate the producers of money from those who use money to fulfil their various types of demand for money. Since the Government and the banks produce or create money for the use by the public, the money (cash reserves) held by them are not used for transaction and speculative purposes and are excluded from the standard measures of money supply. This *separation of producers of money from the users of money is important from the viewpoint of both monetary theory and policy.*[1]

Let us explain the two components of money supply at some length.

Currency with the Public

In order to arrive at the total currency with the public in India we add the following items:

1. Currency notes in circulation issued by the Reserve Bank of India.
2. The number of rupee notes and coins in circulation.
3. Small coins in circulation.

It is worth noting that *cash reserves* with the banks has to be deducted from the value of the above three items of currency in order to arrive at the total currency with the public. This is because cash reserves with the banks must remain with them and cannot therefore be used for making payments for goods or by any commercial banks' transactions. It may further be noted that these days paper currency issued by Reserve Bank of India (RBI) are not fully backed by the reserves of gold and silver, nor it is considered necessary to do so. Full backing of paper currency by reserves of gold prevailed in the past when gold standard or silver standard type of monetary system existed. According to the modern economic thinking the magnitude of currency issued should be determined by the monetary needs of the economy and not by the available reserves of gold and silver. As mentioned in the last chapter, as in other developed countries, since 1957 Reserve Bank of India follows Minimum Reserve System of issuing currency. Under this system, minimum reserves of ₹ 200 crores of gold and other approved securities (such as dollars, pound sterling, etc.) have to be kept and against this any amount of currency can be issued depending on the monetary requirements of the economy.

As stated earlier, RBI is not bound to convert notes into equal value of gold or silver. In the present times currency is inconvertible. The word written on the note, say 100 rupee notes and signed by the governor of RBI that 'I promise to pay the bearer a sum of 100 rupees' is only a legacy of the past and does not imply its convertibility into gold or silver. Another important thing to note is that paper currency or coins are *fiat money*, which means that currency notes and metallic coins serve as money on the bases of the *fiat* (*i.e.* order) of the Government. In other words, on the authority of the Government no one can refuse to accept them in payment for the transaction made. That is why they are called *legal tender*.

Demand Deposits with the Public

The other important component of money supply are demand deposits of the public with the banks. These demand deposits held by the public are also called *bank money* or

1. S. B. Gupta, *Monetary Economics : Institutions, Theory and Policy*, S. Chand & Co., New Delhi, 3rd Edition, 1997, p. 272.

deposit money. Deposits with the banks are broadly divided into two types: demand deposits and time deposits. Demand deposits in the banks are those deposits which can be withdrawn by drawing claques on them. Through cheques these deposits can be transferred to others for making payments from whom goods and services have been purchased. Thus, cheques make these demand deposits as a medium of exchange and therefore make them to serve as money. It may be noted that demand deposits are *fiduciary money proper*. Fiduciary money is one which functions as money on the basis of *trust of* the persons who make payment rather than on the basis of the authority of Government. Thus, despite the fact that demand deposits and cheques through which they are operated are not legal tender, they functions as money on the basis of the trust commanded by those who draw cheques on them. They are money as they are generally acceptable as medium of payment.

Bank deposits are created when people deposits currency with them. But far more important is that banks themselves create deposits when they give advances to businessmen and others. On the basis of small cash reserves of currency, they are able to create a much larger amount of demand deposits through a system called *fractional reserve system* which will be explained later in detail.

In the developed countries such as USA and Great Britain deposit money accounted for over 80 per cent of the total money supply, currency being a relatively small part of it. This is because banking system has greatly developed there and also people have developed banking habits. On the other hand, in the developing countries banking has not developed sufficiently and also people have not acquired banking habits and they prefer to make transactions in currency. However in India after 50 years of independence and economic development the proportion of bank deposits in the money supply has risen to about 50 per cent.

FOUR MEASURES OF MONEY SUPPLY

Several definitions of money supply have been given and therefore various measures of money supply based on them have been estimated. First, different components of money supply have been distinguished on the basis of the different functions that money perform. For example, demand deposits, credit card and currency are used by the people primarily as a medium of exchange for buying goods and services and making other transactions. Obviously, they are money because they are used as a medium of exchange and are generally referred to as M_1. Another measure of money supply is M_3 which includes both M_1 and time deposits held by the public in the banks. Time deposits are money that people hold as store of value.

The main reason why money supply is classified into various measures on the basis of its functions is that effective predictions can be made about the likely affects on the economy of changes in the different components of money supply. For example, if M_1 is increasing fastly it can be reasonably expected that people are planning to make a large number of transactions. On the other hand, if time-deposits component of money-supply measure M_3 which serves as a store of value is increasing rapidly, it can be validly concluded that people are planning to save more and accordingly consume less. Therefore, it is believed that for monetary analysis and policy formulation, a single measure of money supply is not only inadequate but may be misleading too. Hence various measures of money supply are prepared to meet the needs of monetary analysis and policy formulation.

Recently in India as well as in some developed countries, four concepts of money supply have been distinguished. The definition of money supply given above represents a narrow measure of money supply and is generally described as M_1. From April 1977, the Reserve Bank of India has adopted four concepts of money supply in its analysis of the quantum of and variations in money supply. These four concepts of measures of money supply are explained below.

Money Supply M_1 or Narrow Money

This is the narrow measure of money supply and is composed of the following items:

$$M_1 = C + DD + OD$$

where C = Currency with the public

DD = Demand deposits with the public in the Commercial and Cooperative Banks.

OD = Other deposits held by the public with Reserve Bank of India.

The money supply is the most liquid measure of money supply as the money included in it can be easily used as a medium of exchange, that is, as a means of making payments for transactions.

Currency with the public (C) in the above measure of money supply consists of the following

(i) Notes in circulation.
(ii) Circulation of rupee coins as well as small coins
(iii) Cash reserves on hand with all banks.

Note that in measuring demand deposits with the public in the banks (*i.e.*, DD), inter-bank deposits, that is, deposits held by a bank in other banks are excluded from this measure.

From the other deposits with Reserve Bank of India (*i.e.*, *OD*) deposits held by the Central and State Governments and a few others such as RBI Employees Pension and Provident Funds are excluded. However, these other deposits of Reserve Bank of India include the following items.

(i) Deposits of Institutions such UTI, IDBI, IFCI, NABARD etc.
(ii) Demand deposits of foreign Central Banks and Foreign Governments.
(iii) Demand deposits of IMF and World Bank.

It may be noted that other deposits of Reserve Bank of India constitute a very small proportion (less than one per cent).

Money Supply M_2

M_2 is a broader concept of money supply in India than M_1. In addition to the three items of M_1, the concept of money supply M_2 includes savings deposits with the post office savings banks. Thus,

$M_2 = M_1$ + Savings deposits with the post office savings banks.

The reason why money supply M_2 has been distinguished from M_1 is that saving deposits with post office savings banks are not as liquid as demand deposits with Commercial and Co-operative Banks as they are not chequable accounts. However, saving deposits with post offices are more liquid than time deposits with the banks.

Money Supply M_3 or Broad Money

M_3 is a broad concept of money supply. In addition to the items of money supply included in measure M_1, in money supply M_3 time deposits with the banks are also included. Thus

$$M_3 = M_1 + \text{Time Deposits with the banks.}$$

It is generally thought that time deposits serve as store of value and represent savings of the people and are not liquid as they cannot be withdrawn through drawing cheque on them. However, since loans from the banks can be easily obtained against these time deposits, they can be used if found necessary for transaction purposes in this way. Further, they can be withdrawn at any time by forgoing some interest earned on them.

It may be noted that recently M_3 has become a popular measure of money supply. The working group on monetary reforms under the chairmanship of Late Prof. Sukhamoy Chakravarty recommended its use for monetary planning of the economy and setting target of the growth of money supply in terms of M_3. Therefore, recently RBI in its analysis of growth of money supply and its effects on the economy has shifted to the use of M_3 measure of money supply. In the terminology of money supply employed by the Reserve Bank of India till April 1977, this M_3 was called *Aggregate Monetary Resources* (AMR).

Money Supply M_4

The measure M_4 of money supply includes not only all the items of M_3 described above but also the total deposits with the post office savings organisation. However, this excludes contributions made by the public to the national saving certificates. Thus,

$M_4 = M_3$ + *Total Deposits with Post Office Savings Organisation*.

Let us summarise the four concepts of money supply as used by Reserve Bank of India in the following tabular form:

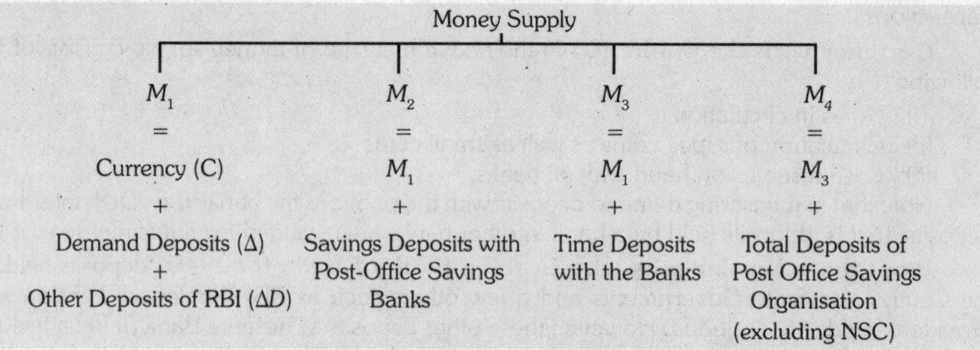

DETERMINATION OF MONEY SUPPLY : MONEY MULTIPLIER THEORY

In order to explain the determinants of money supply in an economy we shall use M_1 concept of money supply which is the most fundamental concept of money supply. We shall denote it simply by M rather than M_1. As seen above this concept of money supply is composed of currency held by the public (C_p) and demand deposits with the banks (D). Thus

$$M = C_p + D \quad \text{...(1)}$$

where M = Total money supply with the public

C_p = Currency with the public

D = Demand deposits held by the public

The two important determinants of money supply as described in (1) are (*a*) the amounts of high-powered money which is also called *Reserve Money* by the Reserve Bank of India and (*b*) the size of money multiplier. We explain below the role of these two factors in the determination of money supply in the economy.

1. High-Powered Money (H)

The high-powered money which we denote by H consists of the currency (notes and coins) issued by the Government and the Reserve Bank of India. A part of the currency issued is held by the public, which we designate as C_p and a part is held by the banks as reserves which we designate as R. A part of these currency reserves of the banks is held by them in their own cash vaults and a part is deposited in the Reserve Bank of India in the Reserve Accounts which banks hold with RBI. Accordingly, the high-powered money can be obtained as sum of currency held by the public and the part held by the banks as reserves. Thus

$$H = C_p + R \quad \text{...(2)}$$

where H = the amount of high-powered money

C_p = Currency held by the public

R = Cash Reserves of currency with the banks.

It is worth noting that Reserve Bank of India and Government are *producers of the high-powered money* and the commercial banks do not have any role in producing this high-powered money (H). However, commercial banks are *producers of demand deposits* which are also used as money like currency. But for producing demand deposits or credit, banks have to keep with themselves cash *reserves of currency* which have been denoted by R in equation (2) above. Since these cash reserves with the banks serve as a basis for the multiple creation of demand deposits which constitute an important part of total money supply in the economy, it provides high poweredness to the currency issued by Reserve Bank and Government. A glance at equations (1) and (2) above will reveal that the difference in the two equations, one describing the total money supply and the other high-powered money is that whereas in the former, demand deposits (D) are added to the currency held by the public, in the later it is cash reserves (R) of the banks that are added to the currency held by the public. In fact, it is against these cash reserves (R) that banks are able to create a multiple expansion of credit or demand deposits due to which there is large expansion in money supply in the economy.

The theory of determination of money supply is based on the supply of and demand for high-powered money. Some economists therefore call it *'The H Theory of Money Supply*[2]. However, it is more popularly called *'Money-multiplier Theory of Money Supply'* because it explains the determination of money supply as a certain multiple of the high-powered money. How the high-powered money (H) is related to the total money supply is graphically depicted in Fig. 42.1. *The base of this figure shows the supply of high-powered money (H), while the top of the figure shows the total stock of money supply.* It will be seen that the total stock of money supply (that is, the top) is determined by a multiple of the high-powered money (H). It will be further seen that whereas currency held by the public (C_p) uses the same amount of high-powered money, that is, there is one-to-one relationship between currency held by the public and the money supply. In sharp contrast to this, bank deposits (D) are a multiple of the cash reserves (R) of the banks which are part of the supply of high-powered money. That is, one rupee of high-powered money kept as bank reserves gives rise to much more amount of demand deposits. Thus, the relationship between money supply and the high-powered money is determined by the money multiplier. The money multiplier which we denote by m is the ratio of total money supply (M) to the stock of high-powered money, that is, $m = \frac{M}{H}$. The size or value of money multiplier depends on the preference of the public to hold currency relative to deposits in banks (that is, ratio of currency to to bank deposits which we denote by K) and banks' desired cash reserves ratio to deposits which we call r. We explain below the precise multiplier relationship between high-powered money and the total stock of money supply.

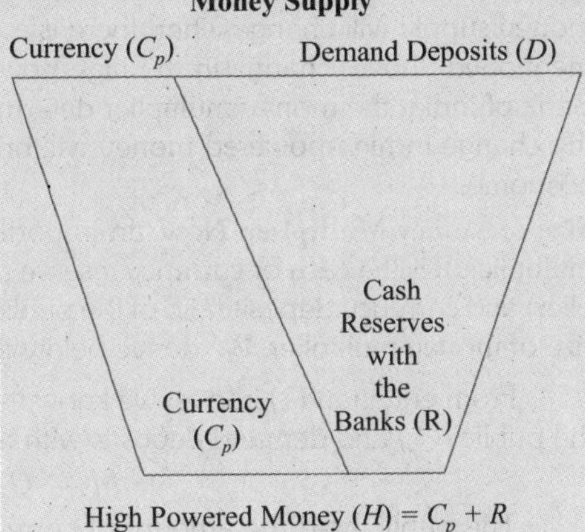

Fig. 42.1. *The High Powered Money and the Stock of Total Money Supply*

It follows from above that if there is increase in currency held by the public which is a part of the high powered money with demand deposits remaining unchanged, there will be a direct increase in the money supply in the economy because this currency constitutes a part of

2. See S.B. Gupta, *Monetary Economics: Institutions Theory and Policy*, 3rd Edition, 1992, S. Chand & Co., New Delhi.

the money supply. If instead currency reserves held by the banks increase, this will not change the money supply immediately but will set in motion a process of multiple creation of demand deposits of the public in the banks through the working of money multiplier as will be explained below. Although banks use these currency reserves held by the public which constitutes a part of the high-powered money to give more loans to the businessmen and thus create more demand deposits themsolves they do not affect either the amount of currency or the composition of high-powered money. The *amount of high-powered money is fixed by RBI considering the prevailing economic situation and needs of the economy. Thus, changes in high-powered money are the result of decisions of Reserve Bank of India or the Government which own and controls it.*

2. Money Multiplier

As stated above, money multiplier is the degree to which money supply is expanded as a result of the increase in high-powered money. Thus

$$m = \frac{N}{H}$$

Rearranging we have, $M = H.m$ ...(3)

Thus money supply is determined by the size of money multiplier (m) and the amount of high-powered money (H). If we know the value of money multiplier we can predict how much money supply will change when there is a change in the amount of high-powered money. As mentioned above, change in the high-powered money is decided and controlled by Reserve Bank of India, the money multiplier determines the extent to which decision by RBI regarding the change in high-powered money will bring about change in the total money supply in the economy.

Size of Money Multiplier. Now, an important question is what determines the size of money multiplier. It is the cash or currency reserve ratio r of the banks (which determines deposit multiplier) and currency-deposit ratio of the public (which we denote by k) which together determines size of money multiplier. We derive below the expression for the size of multiplier.

From equation (1) above, we know that total money supply (M) consists of currency with the public (C_p) and demand deposits with the banks. Thus

$$M = C_p + D \quad \text{...(1)}$$

The public hold the amount of currency in a certain ratio of demand deposits with the banks. Let this currency-deposit ratio be devoted by k,

$$C_p = kD$$

Substituting kD for C_p in equation (1) we have

$$M = kD + D = (k + 1)D \quad \text{...(2)}$$

Now take equation which defines high powered money (H) as

$$H = C_p + R \quad \text{...(3)}$$

where R represents cash or currency reserves which banks keep as a certain ratio of their deposits with the Central Bank and is called cash-reserve ratio and is denoted by r. Thus

$$R = rD$$

Now substituting rD for R and kD for C_p in equation (3) we have

$$H = kD + rD$$

$$H = (k + r)\,D \quad \text{...(4)}$$

Now, money multiplier is ratio of total money supply to the high powered money, therefore, we divide equation (1) by equation (4), to get the value of multiplier, which we denote by m. Thus

$$m = \frac{M}{H} = \frac{(k+1)D}{(k+r)D} = \frac{k+1}{k+r}$$

or, Money multiplier(m) $= \frac{M}{H} = \frac{1+k}{r+k}$

or Money Supply $M = H\frac{1+k}{r+k}$ ...(4)

where r = Cash-reserve ratio of the banks

k = Currency-deposit ratio of the public.

From above it follows that money supply is determined by the by the amount of high powered money (H) and the size of money multiplier which equals $\frac{1+k}{r+k}$ where k is the currency deposit ratio of the public and r is the case reserve ratio of the banks. This cash reserve ratio (r) of banks determines the magnitude of deposit multiplier.

From the equation (4) expressing the determinants of money supply, it follows that *money supply will increase* :

1. When the supply of high-powered money (which is also called *base money* or *reserve money*) H increases;
2. When the currency-deposit ratio (k)[4] of the public decreases; and
3. When the cash-reserve ratio of the banks is reduced.

Cash Reserve Ratio and the Deposit Multiplier. In a later chapter we will see that because of *fractional reserve system*, with a small increase in cash reserves with the banks, they are able to create a multiple increase in total demand deposits which are an important part of money supply. The ratio of change in total deposits to a change in reserves is called the *deposit multiplier* which depends on cash reserve ratio. The value of deposit multiplier is the reciprocal of cash reserve ratio, $\left(d_m = \frac{1}{r}\right)$ where dm stands for deposit multiplier. If cash reserve ratio is 10 per cent of deposits, then $d_m = \frac{1}{0.10} = 10.$. Thus deposit multiplier of 10 shows that for every ₹ 100 increase in cash reserves with the banks, there will be expansion in demand deposits of the banks by ₹ 1000 assuming that no leakage of cash to the public occurs during the process of deposit expansion by the banks.

Currency-Deposit Ratio and Multiplier. However, in the real world, with the increase in reserves of the banks, demand deposits and money supply do not increase to the full extent of deposit multiplier. This is for two reasons. First, the public does not hold all its money balances in the form of demand deposits with the banks. When as a result of increase in cash reserves, banks start increasing demand deposits, the people may also like to have some more currency with them as money balances. This means during the process of creation of demand deposits by banks, some currency is leaked out from the banks to the people. This drainage of currency to the people in the real world reduces the magnitude of expansion of demand deposit and therefore the size of money multiplier. Suppose the cash reserve ratio is 10 per cent and cash or currency of ` 100 is deposited in a bank $A$. The bank $A$ will lend out ` 90 and therefore create demand deposits of ` 90 and so the process will continue as the

3. It will be noticed that in the equation $M = H\frac{1+k}{r+k'}k$ appears both in the numerator and denominator. While in the numerator k is added to unity, in the denominator it is added to fraction. Mathematically, it means that a fall in k will affect the denominator relatively more than the numerator. Therefore, with fall in k, the value of multiplier term $\frac{1+k}{r+k'}$, will increase. Thus, with *decrease* in k, the money supply will *increase* and *vice versa*.

borrowers use these deposits for payment through cheques to others who deposit them in another bank B. However, if borrower of bank A withdraw ₹ 10 in cash from the bank and issue cheques of the remaining borrowed amount of ₹ 80, then bank B will have only ₹ 80 as new deposits instead of ₹ 90 which it would have if cash of ₹ 10 was not withdrawn by the borrower. With these new deposits of ₹ 80, bank B will create demand deposits of ₹ 72, that is, it will lend out ₹ 72 and keep ₹ 8 as reserves with it $\left(80 \times \frac{10}{100} = 8\right)$. The drainage of currency may occur during all the subsequent stages of deposit expansion in the banking system. The greater the leakage of currency, the lower will be the money multiplier. We thus see the currency-deposit ratio, which we denote by k is an important determinant of the actual value of money multiplier.

It is important to note that deposit multiplier works both ways, positively when cash reserves with banks increase, and negatively when the cash reserves with the banks decline. That is, when there is a decrease in currency reserves with the banks, there will be multiple contraction in demand deposits with the banks.

Excess Reserves. In the explanation of the expansion of demand deposits or deposit multiplier we have assumed that banks do not keep currency reserves in excess of the required cash reserve ratio. The ratio r in the deposit multiplier is the *required cash reserve ratio* fixed by Reserve Bank of India. However, banks may like to keep with themselves some excess reserves, the amount of which depend on the extent of liquidity (*i.e.* availability of cash with them) and profitability of making investment and rate of interest on loans advanced to business firms. Therefore, the *desired reserve ratio* is greater than the statutory minimum required reserve ratio. Obviously, the holding of excess reserves by the banks also reduce the value of deposit multiplier.

Conclusion

Theory of determination of money supply explains how a given supply of high-powered money (which is also called *monetary base or reserve money*), leads to multiple expansion in money supply through the working of money multiplier. We have seen above how a small increase in reserves of currency with the banks leads to a multiple expansion in demand deposits by the banks through the process of deposit multiplier and thus causes growth of money supply in the economy. Deposit multiplier measures how much increase in demand deposits (or money supply) occur as a result of a given increase in cash or currency, reserves with the banks depending on the required cash reserve ratio (r) if there are no cash drainage from the banking system. But in the real world drainage of currency does take place which reduce the extent of expansion of money supply following the increase in cash reserves with the banks. Therefore, *the deposit multiplier exaggerates the actual increase in money supply from a given increase in cash reserves with the banks.* In contrast, money multiplier takes into account these leakages of currency from the banking system and therefore measures actual increase in money supply when the cash reserves with the banks increase. *The money multiplier can be defined as increase in money supply for every rupee increase in cash reserves (or high powered money), drainage of currency having been taken into account. Therefore, money multiplier is less than the deposit multiplier.*

It is worth noting that rapid growth in money supply in India has been due to the increase in high-powered money H, or what is also called Reserve Money. Lastly Reserve Bank of India the money multiplier remaining almost constant.

The money supply in a country can be changed by Reserve Bank of India by undertaking open market operations, changing minimum required currency reserve-deposit ratio, and by varying the bank rate. The main source of growth in money supply in India is creation of credit by RBI for Government for financing its budget deficit and thus creating high-powered money. Further, though the required currency reserve-deposit ratio of banks can be easily varied by RBI, the actual currency reserve-deposit ratio cannot be so easily varied as reserves maintained by banks not only depend on minimum required cash reserve ratio but also on their willingness to hold excess reserves.

Lastly[5], an important noteworthy point is that though money multiplier does not show much variation in the long run, it can change significantly in the short run causing large variations in money supply. This unpredictable variation in money multiplier in the short run affecting money supply in the economy prevents the Central Bank of a country from controlling exactly and precisely the money supply in the economy.

FACTORS DETERMINING MONEY SUPPLY : RBI'S ANALYSIS

In its analysis of factors determining money supply in India and sources of variation in it, Reserve Bank of India does not follow any explicit theory of money supply such as money multiplier theory explained above. It provides only purely *accounting or ex-post analysis* of variations in money supply and the factors or sources causing these variations. Although Reserve Bank provides figures of the high powered money in its analysis, it virtually clubs high powered money with the ordinary money to calculate the total money supply in the country and therefore does not give due importance to the high powered money as an important factor causing variation in money supply in the economy. Further, Reserve Bank also does not lay emphasis on the two behavioural ratios, namely, desired currency-deposit ratio (k) of the public and desired cash reserve ratio (r) of the banks as determinants of money supply, though it provides *ex-post* or realised figures of these ratios. We explain below Reserve Bank's analysis of sources of variation in money supply.

Reserve Bank of India classifies factors determining money supply into the following categories:

(*a*) Government borrowing from the banking system;
(*b*) Borrowing of the private or commercial sector from the banking system;
(*c*) Changes in net foreign assets held by the Reserve Bank of India caused by changes in balance of payments position; and
(*d*) Government's currency liabilities to the public.

Bank Credit to the Government. When the Government expenditure exceeds government revenue and there is deficit in government's budget, then it resorts to borrowing from the Reserve Bank of India which creates new currency notes for the purpose. This creation of new currency for financing the deficit of the Central Government Budget is known as *monetistion of deficit*. It was previously called deficit financing. Monetisation of deficit is an important source of change in money supply in the economy. It may noted here that since 1995, a good part of budget deficit is financed through open market operations by RBI by selling Government securities to the banks. This is done to neutralise the monetary impact of large accumulation of net foreign exchange assets with RBI caused by *capital inflows* on a large scale. Therefore, there has been a decline in RBI's credit to the Government in the last about 10 years.

The Government also borrows from the ordinary commercial banks. When banks lend money to the Government, they create credit. For instance, for purchase of foodgrains by the Food Corporation of India, the banks gives a large amount of loan to the Government. The creation of deposits by the banks when they create credit for the Government leads to the increase in money supply in the economy.

Bank Credit to the Commercial or Private Sector. The private sector also borrows from the banking system when its own resources are less than its total expenditure. This also adds to the money supply with the public because when banks lend, they create credit. This also affects the money supply in the same manner as the Government borrowing from the

4. Note that Reserve Bank of India calls the high-powered money as *Reserve Money* (RM).

banking system. There is, however, an important difference. Whereas Government can borrow more or less compulsorily from Reserve Bank of India, the private sector cannot do so from the commercial banks.

Changes in Net Foreign Exchange Assets. Changes in the foreign exchange assets held by the Reserve Bank can also bring about a change in the money supply. The change in the net foreign assets may be caused by balance of payment situation. Suppose the balance of payments is adverse or unfavourable and therefore available foreign exchange is less than the country needs to pay for its imports, both visible and invisible. In order to meet this adverse balance of trade the country will have to dispose of some of its foreign exchange assets. If there is a net adverse balance of payments, rupees would flow into the Reserve Bank which pays out foreign exchange. This would have the effect of reducing the *Reserve Money* (*i.e.* the high powered money) in India and the contraction of the money supply with the public. Opposite result would follow when there is a net surplus in the balance of payments of a country.

It follows from above that a deficit in the balance of payments on current account decreases the supply of rupee currency (that is, high powered or reserve money) in the economy and thereby causes contraction in money supply with the public. On the contrary, a surplus in the balance of payments will increase the foreign exchange assets and thereby will lead to the expansion in reserve money and money supply in the economy. It may also be noted that to meet the deficit on the balance of payments on current account foreign exchange reserves or assets may also come through either foreign aid, or external commercial banks (ECB) or deposits in Indian banks by NRI or foreign direct investment (FDI) and portfolio investment by FIIs made by foreign companies in India. For example, in recent years there has been a large-scale inflow of foreign exchange through investment made by foreign companies and NRI deposits in India. As a result, our foreign exchange reserves have substantially gone up, which have resulted in the issue and expansion of rupee currency in circulation. In August 2004 foreign exchange reserves had risen to US $ 119 billion. But RBI *neutralised its monetary impact* by moping up liquidity of the banks through open market operations by selling them Government securities. This is called *sterlisation* of inflows of foreign exchange. Further, to deal with the problem of excess liquidity of the Indian banks caused by the rise in foreign exchange reserves, and with a view to check rise in inflation rate Reserve Bank of India in April 2004 entered into an agreement with the Central Government to sterlise the monetary impact of these reserves. With this agreement, *Market Stabilisation* Scheme (MSS) has been started. Under this scheme the Central Government has issued Market Stabilisation Bonds. These bonds have been sold by RBI to commercial banks to mop up excess liquidity of ₹ 60,000 crores in 2004-05. But these ₹ 60,000 crores were kept apart in special deposits with RBI and was not to be used ordinarily by the Government.

It should be noted that if the foreign exchange reserves are used to import goods in short supply, it will help in lowering inflation rate for two reasons. First, this will reduce rupee currency in circulation which will cause reduction in money supply in the economy. Contraction in money supply will help in controlling inflation through reducing aggregate demand. Secondly, the imports of goods will increase aggregate supply of goods in the economy which will tend to lower prices.

(*d*) **Government's Currency Liabilities to the Public.** Changes in money supply in the economy are also brought about by Government's currency liabilities to the public. Coins and one-rupee notes represent Government's currency liabilities to the public. On 31st march 2004-05, there were outstanding balances of Government currency liabilities of ₹ 7291 crores as compared to ₹ 7071 crores on March 31, 2003. If Government's currency liabilities increase, the money supply also increases.

BUDGET DEFICIT AND MONEY SUPPLY

A budget deficit is also an important source of expansion of money supply in the economy. There are two possible links between budget deficit and growth in money supply. First, when following an expansionary fiscal policy the government raises its expenditure without financed by extra taxation and thereby causing a budget deficit, it will tend to raise interest rate. This happens when budget deficit is financed through borrowing from the market. As a result, demand for money or loanable funds increases which, given the supply of money, causes interest rate to rise. Rise in interest rate tends to reduce or crowd out private investment. If the Central Bank is following the policy of a fixed interest rate target, when the government resorts to borrowing to finance the budget deficit, then to prevent the rise in interest rate the Central Bank will take steps to increase the money supply in the economy.

The second link between budget deficit and expansion in money supply is direct. This occurs when the Central Bank itself purchases government securities when the government resorts to borrowing.[6] The Central Bank is said to *monetise* budget deficit when it purchases government securities as it prints new notes for the purpose and gives it to the government for meeting public expenditure. In some countries such as the US, Federal Reserve (which is the Central Bank of the USA) enjoys a good deal of independence from the Treasury (*i.e.*, the Government) and voluntarily decides when and how much to purchase government securities to finance its budget deficit.

Central Bank's Dilemma

The Central Bank of a country faces a dilemma in deciding whether or not to monetise budget deficit. If the central Bank does not monetise budget deficit to meet its increased expenditure, the government will borrow from the market and in the absence of any accomodating monetary policy this will tend to raise interest rate and thereby *reduce or crowd out private investment.* Referring to the policy of Federal Reserve of the United States, Dornbusch, Fischer and Startz write, " There is accordingly a temptation for the Federal Reserve to prevent crowding out by buying government securities thereby increasing the money supply and hence allows an expansion in income without a rise in interest rates"[6]

But the policy of monetisation of budget deficit by the Central Bank involves a risk. If the economy is working near full employment level, that is, at near full production capacity, monetisation of budget deficit will cause inflation in the economy. However, if the economy is in the grip of a severe depression, the risk of causing inflation through monetisation of budget deficit and consequent growth in money supply is not much there.

It follows from above that in any particular case the Central Bank, if it enjoys freedom from the Government, has to judge whether it should adopt accomodatory monetary policy to achieve its goal of *interest-targeting* or *allow fiscal expansion through monetisation of budget deficit accompanied by the tight monetary policy to check inflation*. It is the latter course of action that was adopted by Reserve Bank of India before 1995 when government's fiscal deficit was high and a good part of it was monetised by it.

MONEY SUPPLY AND THE OPEN ECONOMY

The transactions of an open economy also affects the growth of money supply in it. In the open economy there is free flow of goods and services through trade with foreign countries. Besides, in the open economy there are flows of capital between countries. The impact of transactions of an open economy on the money supply can be letter understood from national income identity of an open economy. National income of the open economy is written as

$$Y = C + I + G + NX \quad ...(1)$$

or

$$NX = Y - (C + I + G) \quad ...(2)$$

where NX stands for net exports or trade balance. In the trade balance if we also include exports and imports of services (*i.e.*, invisibles), then NX can be taken as current account balance.

5. It is important to note that when government borrows from the market, it does so through sale of its securities (i.e. bonds)
6. Dornbusch, Fischer, and Startz, *op.cit.* 9th edition, 2004, p.275

The current account balance (*NX*) can be either positive or negative. If in equation (2) above aggregate expenditure ($C + I + G$) exceeds national output (Y), current account balance or *NX* will be negative, that is, imports will be greater than exports. In other words, there will be deficit in current account of the balance of payments. On the other hand, if aggregate expenditure is less than national income [$(C + I + G) < Y$], there will be surplus in current account balance of payments. This implies our exports will be greater than imports.

Now, if in a year there is deficit in current account, that is, *NX* is negative, it means our demand for foreign exchange, say the US dollars, for imports of goods and services will exceed the supply of foreign exchange. This situation is depicted in Fig. 42.2 where the curve *DD* represents demand curve for foreign exchange (US $) and *SS* is the supply curve of foreign exchange (US $) at exchange rate (₹ per US dollar) is *OR* and *LK* represents deficit in current account.

If the economy is under flexible exchange rate regime and the Central Bank of the country does not intervene at all, the exchange rate will change to *OR′* and as a result deficit in current account balance will be eliminated and equilibrium restored at the new exchange rate. If there is such a situation, there is no impact on the money supply. However, if the Central Bank wants to maintain the exchange rate at *OR*, then current account deficit equal to *LK* has to be met. If there are no capital inflows, then to maintain the exchange rate at *OR*, the Central Bank of the country has to supply foreign exchange equal to *LK* out of the reserves held by it. But when the Central Bank (RBI in case of India) pays out foreign exchange from its reserves, *it will receive money (i.e., rupees in India) from importers of goods and services in return for foreign exchange paid to them to meet the deficit*. Thus some money (say Indian rupees) will flow into the Central Bank and thus withdrawn from circulation. As a result of Central Bank intervention to meet the current account deficit and to maintain the exchange rate money supply in the economy decreases. It is important to note that the Central Bank of the country cannot go on supplying foreign exchange reserves, year after year, for a long time because foreign exchange assets with the Central Bank are available in limited amount.

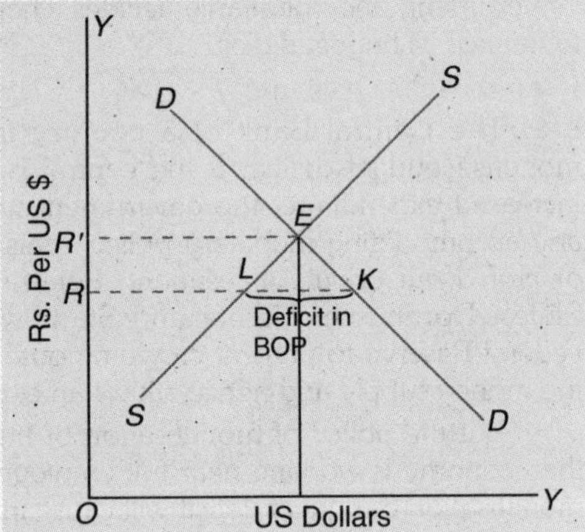

Fig. 42.2. *Deficit in Balance of Payments and Foreign Exchange Market*

The above analysis of contraction in money supply as a result of use of foreign exchange reserves to meet the current account deficit is based on the two assumptions. First, it is assumed that there are no capital flows to meet the deficit in current account balance. Second, it is assumed the exchange rate is not allowed to change as result of inbalance between demand and supply of foreign exchange due to current account deficit.

Capital inflows. However, if there are sufficient net capital inflows accruing from the capital account of balance of payments, then deficit in current account (*i.e.*, negative *NX*) can be met by these capital inflows. In this case there will be no impact of deficit in current account balance of payments on money supply in the economy.

Now take the opposite case of surplus in current account balance (*i.e.*, when *NX* is positive). This implies that the supply of foreign exchange exceeds demand for it. In the absence of capital outflows this excess supply of foreign exchange will have to by purchased by the Central Bank if exchange rate is to be maintained. The Central Bank (RBI) will print new notes to pay for the purchase of foreign exchange. This will lead to the increase in money supply in the economy.

However, if exchange rate is allowed to change, as the case under flexible exchange rate system, the exchange rate will adjust to bring supply and demand for foreign exchange in equilibrium.

Overall Balance of Payments and Capital Inflows

When in an open economy with flexible exchange rate regime there is *deficit in overall balance of payments* (*i.e.*, on both current and capital accounts), it means that capital inflows are insufficient to bridge the gap in the balance of payments, then, in case of India, this has to met with use of foreign exchange reserves by the Reserve Bank of India. When Reserve Bank of India pays foreign exchange (*e.g.* US $) to finance the deficit in overall balance of payments, it get rupees in return. Thus rupee currency flows into the RBI. As a result, money supply (rupee currency) in the economy will decline. However, an explained above, under flexible, rate system, if RBI does not intervene, the deficit in overall balance of payments will cause rupee to depreciate.

Now suppose there is *surplus in overall balance of payment* as capital inflows exceed the deficit in current account. The large capital inflows can occur due to heavy foreign direct investment (FDI) and portfolio investment by foreign institutional investors (FII) as it happened in some years in India, especially in 2006-07 and 2007-08 and in May 2010. In the absence of intervention by RBI under the flexible exchange rate system, these large capital inflows will cause appreciation of Indian Rupee. In fact, though RBI has been intervening in foreign exchange market from time to time, its intervention has been only limited. As a result, between Oct. 2006 and Oct 2007, rupee appreciated by 15 per cent. By making our exports relatively expensive the appreciation of rupee adversly affects our exports and therefore growth in GNP and employment. Besides, appreciation of rupee makes imports relatively cheaper and leads to large imports of goods and materials and thereby harms our domestic manufacturing industries.

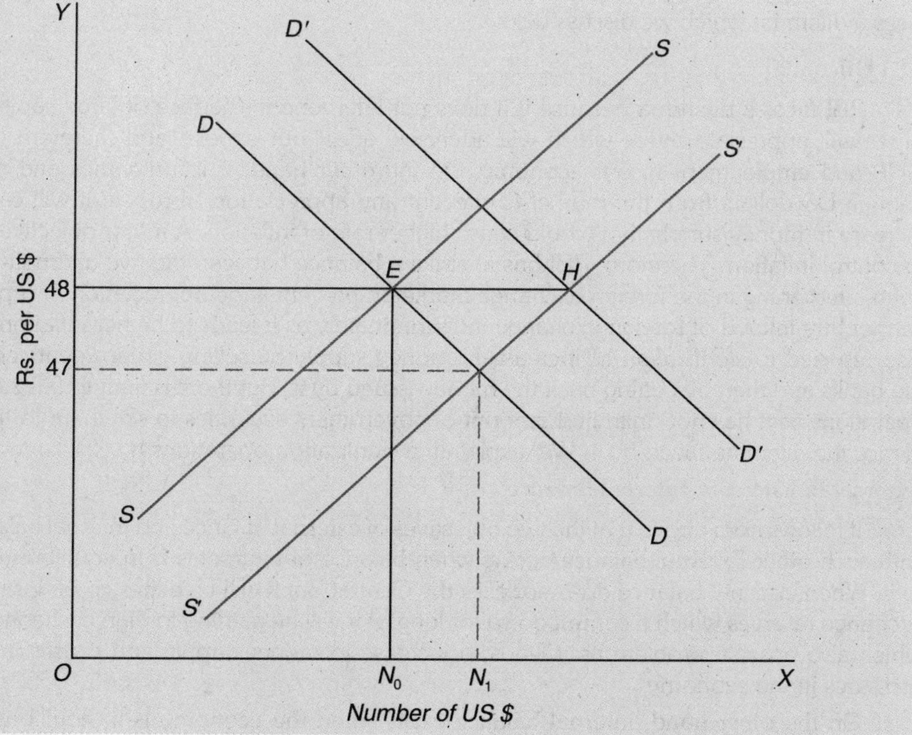

Fig. 42.3. Capital Inflows and Appreciation of Rupee

To prevent the high appreciation of the Indian Rupee RBI has been purchasing US dollars from the foreign exchange market from time to time. When RBI purchases dollars from the foreign exchange market, it pays rupees to the sellers of foreign exchange. To do so more rupee currency is printed by RBI to pay for US dollars purchased by it. In this way more rupee currency (*i.e.*, high–powered money) comes into existence in the economy. Thus intervention by RBI to prevent appreciation of rupee results in increase in money supply in the economy.

The effect of large capital inflows and its effect on appreciation of currency and money supply in the Indian economy is illustrated in Fig. 42.3 where exchange rate of rupee for US dollars (₹ per US $) is measured on the Y-axis and number of US dollars are measured on the X-axis.

Initially the equilibrium between demand for and supply of dollars in the Indian foreign exchange market and equilibrium exchange rate is ₹ 48 per US $. As a result of large capital inflows supply curve of US dollars shifts to the right to *S'S'*. With this, at the existing exchange rate of ₹ 48 per US dollar, *EH* is the increase in capital inflows. Now, if under a variable exchange rate regime as it exists today the exchange rate is allowed to adjust freely, rupee will rise to ₹ 47 per US dollar. If Reserve Bank wants to manage it and tries to maintain it at ₹ 48 per US dollar it will have to buy US dollars equal to *EH* from the market. By buying US dollars equal to *EH* it will cause the demand curve for US dollars to shift to the right to the new position *D'D'* and the new equilibrium is at point *H* which corresponds to ₹ 48 per US dollar.

But for buying US dollars equal to *EH*, RBI will have to print new rupee currency to pay for US dollars. Thus more high power money (*i.e.*, rupee currency) would come into circulation in the Indian economy. Thus RBI did not intervene sufficiently to prevent the appreciation of rupee between Oct. 2006 and Oct. 2007. This is because such intervention leads to the increase in money supply that is likely to cause inflation in the Indian economy. Therefore, RBI intervened only to a small degree and let the rupee to appreciate to some extent. In fact, RBI faces a dilemma which we discuss below.

RBI Dilemma

RBI faces a dilemma because if it does not intervene in the face of large capital inflows rupee will appreciate much which will adversely affect our exports and therefore growth of GNP and employment in our economy. On the other hand, if it intervenes and purchases enough US dollars from the market to prevent any appreciation of rupee, it will cause large increase in money supply that would cause higher rate of inflation. A major objective of RBI is to control inflation. Therefore, RBI has to strike a balance between the two alternatives. It has been intervening in the foreign exchange market to prevent large appreciation of rupee. But it cannot buy inflows of foreign exchange indiscriminately as it leads to higher inflation. RBI has also resorted to *sterilization* of increase in money supply by selling government securities to the banks and thereby getting back the money issued by it. But there is limit to this sterilization operations as it has not unlimited amount of government securities to sell them to the banks. Hence the dilemma faced by it. We explain the sterilization operations by RBI later.

External Balance and Internal Balance

It follows from above that the two objectives of external balance and internal balance clash with each other External balance occurs when balance of payments is in equilibrium or close to it. When external balance does not exist the Central Bank will be either go on losing foreign exchange reserves which it cannot do so for long or it will be gaining foreign exchange reserves which also poses a problem as it leads to increase in money supply and causes inflationary pressures in the economy.

On the other hand, internal balance exists when the economy is in equilibrium at full employment or full productive capacity level without any inflationary pressures. Thus, to ensure internal balance requires that money supply should not be allowed to increase much. Since the two require different types of policy measure by the Central Bank, they clash with each other. Hence, the dilemma faced by the Central Bank.

Sterilization by the Central Bank

Sterilization provides a way out of the problem of clash between the goals of external balance and internal balance. *Sterilization refers to the action by the Central Bank of a country to offset or cancel the impact of its foreign exchange market intervention on the money supply through open market operations.* The sterilization measures can be used both to offset the reduction in money supply when in case of current account deficit the Central Bank of the country sells foreign exchange in the market and also when the Central Banks offsets the effect of increase in money supply when it buys foreign exchange from the market in case of surplus in balance of payments or when large capital inflows are coming into the economy.

Let us first explain sterlisation operation by the Central Bank in case of deficit in current account of the balance of payments. As seen above, the deficit in current account balance requires that the Central Bank to sell foreign exchange from its reserves to prevent the depreciation of domestic currency (that is, to maintain the exchange rate constant). The sale of foreign exchange in foreign exchange market by the Central Bank causes money supply in the economy to decrease that has deflationary effect on the economy. To avoid this adverse effect, the Central Bank buys government securities (*i.e.,* bonds) through open market operations. When it does so the Central Bank prints domestic currency to pay for the bonds it purchases. In this way money supply in the economy increases which offsets the decrease in money supply brought about by the Central Bank when it sells foreign exchange to prevent the depreciation of the domestic currency. Thus, provided it has enough foreign exchange assets, with sterilization operations by the Central Bank *persistent* deficit in balance of payments is possible because it *insulates* the money supply changes in the domestic economy from the Central Bank intervention in the foreign exchange market.

Sterilization Operations in Case of Surplus in Balance of Payments or Large Capital Inflows. Now, we take up the opposite case when there is surplus in balance of payments or when large capital inflows are taking place. This situation requires that Central Bank intervenes in the foreign exchange market and buys foreign exchange inflows from the market to maintain the foreign exchange rate or to prevent the appreciation of domestic currency. As mentioned above, in the two years (2006 - 08) due to large net capital inflows in the Indian economy there was a quite large appreciation of the Indian rupee against US dollar that produced undesirable effects. Therefore, Reserve Bank intervened in the foreign exchange market by buying US dollars to prevent too much appreciation of the Indian rupee. The purchase of foreign exchange (US dollars) from the foreign exchange market by the Reserve Bank led to the increase in money supply in the Indian economy that caused inflationary pressures. To sterilize the effect of this increase in money supply RBI undertook open market operations by *selling* government securities to the banks which paid rupees to it. In this way some rupee currency had been withdrawn from the economy. In this way inflationary pressures created by the original increase in money supply through intervention in foreign exchange market have been offset.

MONEY MARKET EQUILIBRIUM

We have explained in the above factors which determine supply of money and demand for money. In the previous chapter we have discussed various theories of demand for money. In this chapter we will explain how money market equilibrium comes about. *Money market is in equilibrium when at a rate of interest demand for and supply of money are equal.* It is worth noting that in the money market people increase or decrease the money they hold by selling short-term bonds that carry a fixed rate of interest. These bonds may be of corporate companies, generally called corporate bonds or debentures or may be securities of government, which are called treasury bills.

Money as a Financial Asset

The wealth of a household and a business firm consists of tangible assets such as a house, commercial property and the value of financial assets. Financial assets include (1) *stocks*, that is, equity shares of corporate firms (*i.e.* public limited companies), (2) *bonds* which carry a fixed rate of interest and (3) *money*. *Money is a financial asset.* We have seen in a previous chapter as to why people demand money. It is important to note that money is different from income or wealth. In macroeconomics demand for money has a narrower meaning. *Demand for money is a part of wealth of the people which they want* to hold in the form of money rather than other assets. What part of their wealth people want to hold in the form of money determines the demand for money to hold.

Transactions and Speculative Demand for Moeny

In the previous chapter we have explained the various theories of demand for money. Broadly speaking, people demand money for two purposes : (1) Transactions demand for money (2) Speculative demand for money. When the number of transactions in the economy increases, demand for money increases. The most important factor determining the volume of transactions is the level of national income or aggregate output. In a modern economy most goods are produced in the various stages of production. Money is required to buy raw materials for production, to make payment of wages to labour and so forth. A larger stock of money is therefore required to undertake more transactions.

As explained in the previous chapter, a society keeps a certain proportion of national income in the form of money to carry out various transactions. The greater the level of national income, the higher the demand for money, given the proportion of income which a society keeps in the form of money. Thus

$$M_T^d = kY \qquad \ldots(i)$$

where $M_T{}^d$ stands for transaction demand for money, Y is the level of national income and k is the proportion of national income which is kept in the form of money. The constant proportion k does not have to be unity because one unit of money is used more than once for exchanging goods and services produced. The number of times a unit of money is used for buying goods and services is called *income velocity of money*. Thus, $V = \frac{Y}{M}$ where V stands for income velocity of money. It is worth noting that low income velocity of money implies that demand for money is a higher fraction of income. This indicates that individuals and business organisations keep their money stock for a longer period of time with themselves or in demand deposits with the banks and do not *quickly* use their money holdings for transaction purposes.

On the other hand, a high income velocity of money implies that demand for money is a smaller fraction of income. This means that individuals and firms quickly use their money stock for purposes of buying goods and services and do not keep it for a longer period with them or in their banks.

Speculative Demand for Money. Keynes in his book '*The General Theory*' emphasised that individuals demand money to hold for speculative purpose. Money demand for speculative purpose means that individuals want to hold money to take advantages of the 'changes in future rate of interest, that is, changes in bond prices'. At any given time households or individuals want to keep a certain portfolio of assets consisting of both real and financial assets. When people decide how much money to hold with them for speculative purposes, they make a *portfolio choice*. At a time some people would like to hold more money and therefore will sell bonds or other assets. Some people may like to hold more bonds or other assets in their portfolio and to achieve this they would withdraw money from demand deposits to buy the bonds and other assets.

Cost of Holding Money and Profolio Choice

The money held by the people in their wallets or in demand deposits with the banks do not earn any interest[7]. Instead of holding money in their wallets or demand deposits, they can buy government bonds or corporate bonds and earn higher nominal rate of interest. The cost of holding money as an asset arises from the fact that money earns no interest or very low interest. Thus, *interest rate on government or corporate bonds is the opportunity cost of holding money*. The assets other than money such as government bonds or corporate bonds earn higher rate of return. But keeping money and other assets in investment portfolio have advantages and disadvantages. The advantage of holding money as an asset is that it can be easily and quickly used to purchase goods and services. Its disadvantage, as mentioned just above, is that it earns no interest or very low interest. On the other hand, other assets such as bonds cannot be directly or quickly used for transaction purposes and when they are sold to convert them into money for being used for these purposes, they involve costs such as brokerage fees apart from time and efforts involved in their sale.

Portfolio choice. Deciding about how much money to hold as an asset is deciding about a portfolio choice. This portoflio choice depends on individuals' assessment of advantages and disadvantages of holding money as an asset as compared to other financial assets. At a given interest rate on bonds, an individual or household decides about an investment portfolio after weighing their advantages and costs. If rate of interest on bonds rises, bonds would become more attractive than money. In this case, the holding of money will decline and that of bonds will increase in the portfolio.

Demand for Money and Interest Rate

It is evident from above analysis that demand for money as an asset, that is, for speculative purposes depends on rate of interest on bonds, which is the opportunity cost of holding money. If rate of interest is higher, the people would demand less money to hold for speculative purposes. This is because at a higher rate of interest they would go in for holding more bonds or other financial assets in their investment portfolio. On the other bond, at a lower rate of interest on bonds, they would demand more money to hold.

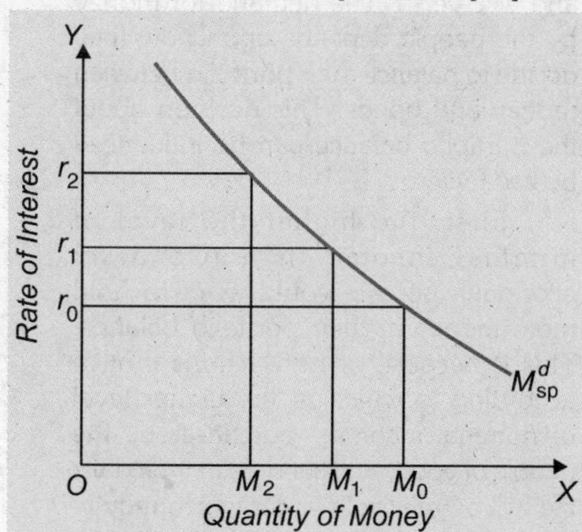

Fig. 42.4. *Speculative Demand for Money and Rate of Interest*

Thus, demand for money to hold for speculative purposes, that is, as an asset is negatively related to rate of interest. Therefore, demand curve for money for speculative purposes slopes downward. This indicates at a higher rate of interest, less money is held as an asset and at a lower interest rate, more money is held as an asset. Demand for money to hold for speculative purposes is drawn as M^d_{sp} in Figure 42.4.

Mathematically, we can express the demand for money to hold for speculative purposes as follows :

$$M^d_{sp.} = f(i) = hi \qquad \ldots(ii)$$

7. Demand deposits may earn very low interest rate.

where h is the sensitivity of money demand to hold as an asset to changes in rate of interest (i).

Total Demand for Money. Demand for money to hold comes from transactions and speculative purposes[8]. Therefore, total demand for money to hold depends on level of income and rate of interest. Thus, by adding demand for money equations (*i*) and (*ii*) we have

$$M^d = M_T^d + M_{sp}^d$$

$$M^d = kY - hi \qquad \ldots(iii)$$

Two things are worth noting in the money demand equation (*iii*). First, demand for money to hold depends on level of income and rate of interest. The higher the income (Y), the greater will be demand for money. Secondly, demand for money is negatively related to rate of interest (i). At a given level of income, the higher the rate of interest, the lower will be demand for money. In Figure 42.5 demand for money curve M_{d1} has been drawn at the given level of income Y_1. At the given level of income Y_1, if rate of interest rises we move up the money demand curve M_{d1} indicating that quantity of money demanded will decrease, and if rate of interest falls, the quantity of money demanded will increase

As with the increase in income, demand for money for transaction purposes increases at all rates of interest, the rise in level of national income will cause a shift of M_d curve to the right. Thus, if level of income increases from Y_1 to Y_2, money demand curve shifts to the right from M_{d1} to M_{d2} in Fig. 42.5.

The Demand for Money in a Two Asset Economy : Portfolio Choice

In order to explain the demand for money and interest-rate determination. Kenyes assumed a simplified economy where there are two assets which people can keep in their portfolio balance. These two assets are : (1) money in the form of currency and demand deposits in the banks which earn no interest and (2) long term bonds. It is important to note that rate of interest and bond prices are inversely related. When bond prices go up, rate of interest rises and vice versa. The demand for money by the people depends upon how they decide to balance their portfolio between money and bonds. This decision about the portfolio balance can be influenced by two factors.

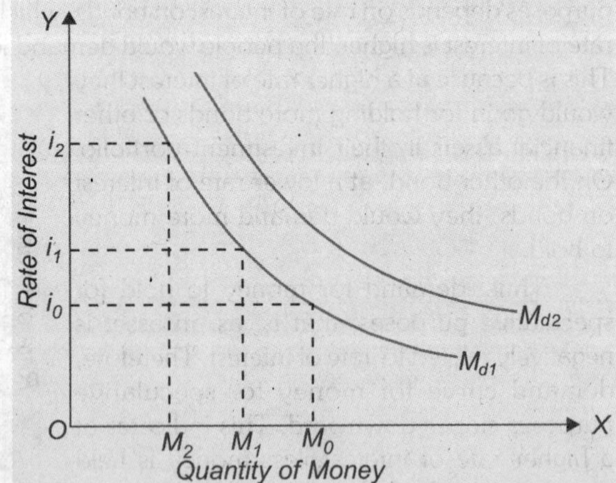

Fig. 42.5. *Demand for Money, Rate of Interest and Level of Income*

First, the higher the level of nominal income in a two asset economy, people would want to hold more money in their portfolio balance. This is because of transactions motive according to which at the higher level of nominal income, purchases by the people of goods and services in their daily life will be relatively larger which require more money to be kept for transaction purposes.

Second, the higher the nominal rate of interest, the lower the demand for money for speculative motive. This is firstly because a higher nominal rate of interest implies a higher opportunity cost for holding money. At a higher rate of interest holders of money can earn more

8. For simplicity sake we include demand for money for precautionary motive in the transaction motive for holding money.

incomes by holding bonds instead of money. Secondly, if the current rate of interest is higher than what is expected in the future, the people would like to hold more bonds and less money in their portfolio. On the other hand, if the current rate of interest is low (in other words, if the bond prices are currently high), the people will be reluctant to hold larger quantity of bonds and instead they could hold more money in their portfolio for the fear that bond prices would fall in the future causing capital losses to them.

It follows from above that quantity of money demanded increases with the fall in the rate of interest or with the increase in level of nominal income. At a given level of nominal income, we can draw a money demand curve showing the quantity of money demanded at various rates of interest. As demand for money is inversely related to the rate of interest, the money demand curve at a given level of income, say Y_1 will be downward-sloping as is shown by the curve Md_1 in Figure 42.5. When the level of money income increases, suppose from Y_1 to Y_2, the curve of demand for money shifts upward to the new position M_{d2} as shown in Fig. 42.5.

The Supply of Money

Money is an important factor which is used as a medium of exchange for undertaking transactions and for holding as an asset. Money can perform these functions if it is kept scarce, that is, supply of money at a given point of time is fixed and over time it is increased at a limited rate. Therefore, the Central Bank of a country (in case of India Reserve Bank of India) is given the right to control the supply of money in the economy. The money supply is fixed by the policy actions of the Central Bank of country, Through open market operations changes in cost reserve ratio (CRR) of banks Central Bank of a country can influence the creation of bank credit which constitutes an important part of the money supply of the country. Besides, the extent to which the Central Bank of the country absorbs foreign exchange reserves, also affects the supply of money in the economy. When the Reserve Bank of India buys more foreign exchange from the market, it issues new money to make payments for purchase of foreign exchange from the market. However, it is assumed that money supply does not vary with either level of income or rate of interest[9] unless Reserve Bank decides to change it. In Fig. 42.6 we have therefore drawn a vertical supply curve of money with measuring interest rate on the Y-axis. If the Central Bank of the country decides to increase money supply and fixes it at M_2, money supply curve shifts to the right from MS_1 to MS_2 as shown in Figure 42.6. On the other hand, if the Central Bank decides to reduce the money supply in the economy money supply curve will shift to the left.

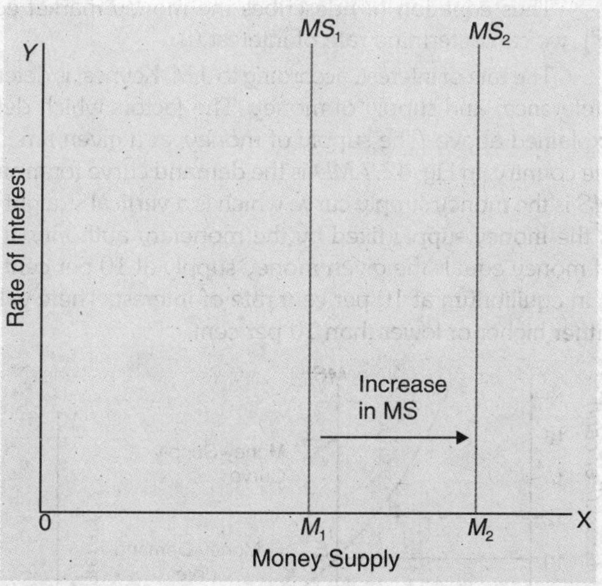

Fig. 42.6. *Money Supply is Independent of rate of Interest.*

9. It may be noted that rate of interest can influence the decisions of banks to create credit and can therefore affect *to some extent* the money supply in the economy. We however assume that interest induced changes in money supply are undone by Reserve Bank of India by taking appropriate policy measures.

MONEY MARKET EQUILIBRIUM : DETERMINATION OF RATE OF INTEREST

Once the Central Bank of a country fixes the money supply in the economy, households and business firms can make individual decisions regarding how much money to hold. But the *total money supply will be unaffected* by their decisions to hold more or less money to fulfil transaction and speculative purposes. *Money market is in equilibrium at a rate of interest when demand for money is equal to the fixed money supply*. Thus money market is in equilibrium when

$$MS = MD$$

As explained above, money demand (*MD*) is determined by the level of income and rate of interest. Assuming that money demand is a linear function we can write it as

$$MD = kY - hi$$

Thus, money market is in equilibrium when

$$MS = kY - hi$$

or $$i = \frac{1}{h}(Ky - MS) \qquad \ldots(iv)$$

Thus equation (*iv*) describes the money market equilibrium. Given the level of income (*Y*), we can determine rate of interest (*i*).

The rate of interest, according to J.M. Keynes, is determined by demand for money (liquidity preference) and supply of money. The factors which determine demand for money has been explained above. The supply of money, at a given time, is fixed by the monetary authority of the country. In Fig. 42.7 *MD* is the demand curve for money at a given level of nominal income. *MS* is the money supply curve which is a vertical straight line showing that 200 crores of rupees is the money supply fixed by the monetary authority. It will be seen that quantity demanded of money equals the given money supply at 10 per cent rate of interest. So the money market is in equilibrium at 10 per cent rate of interest. There will be disequilibrium if rate of interest is either higher or lower than 10 per cent.

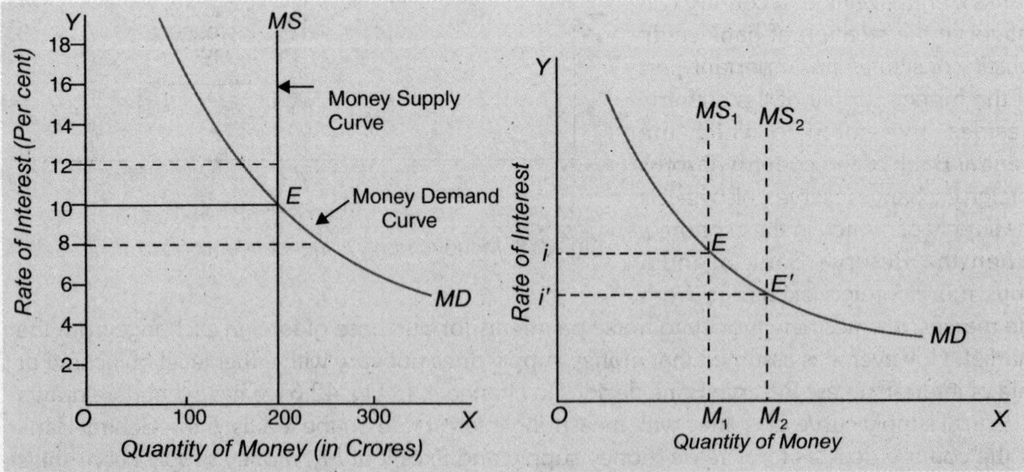

Fig. 42.7. *Money Market Equilibrium*

Fig. 42.8. *Effect of increase in Money Supply on the Rate of Interest*

Suppose the rate of interest is 12 per cent. It will be seen from Fig. 42.7 that at 12 per cent rate of interest, the given supply of money exceeds the demand for money. The excess supply of money reflects the fact that people do not want to hold as much money in their portfolio as the monetary authority has made it available to them. The people holding assets in the present two-asset economy would react to this excess money supply with them by buying bonds and thus replace some of money in their portfolios with bonds. Since the *total money supply* at a given moment remains fixed, it cannot be reduced by buying bonds by individuals. But the bonds-buying spree would lead to the rise in prices of bonds. The rise in bond prices means the fall in the rate of interest. As will be seen from the Fig. 42.7, with the fall in the interest rate from 12 per cent to 10 per cent, quantity demand of money has increased to be once again equal to the given supply of money and the excess supply of money is entirely eliminated and money market equilibrium is restored.

On the other hand, if the rate of interest is lower than the equilibrium rate of 10 per cent, say it is 8 per cent, then as will be seen from Fig. 42.7 there will emerge *excess demand for money*. As a reaction to this excess demand for money, people would like to sell bonds in order to obtain a greater quantity of money for holding at the lower rate of interest. The stock of money remaining fixed, the attempt by the people to hold more money balances at a rate of interest lower than the equilibrium level through sale of bonds will only cause the bond prices to fall. The fall in bond prices implies the rise in the rate of interest. Thus, the process started as a reaction to the excess demand for money at an interest rate below the equilibrium level will end up with the rise in the interest rate to the equilibrium level.

Effect of an Increase in the Money Supply

Let us now examine the effect of increase in money supply on the rate of interest. In Fig. 42.8, *MD* is the demand for money for satisfying various motives. To begin with, OM_1 is the quantity of money available. Rate of interest will be determined where the demand for money is in balance or equal to the fixed supply of money OM_1. It is clear from Fig. 42.8 that demand for money is equal to OM_1 quantity of money at *i* rate of interest. Hence *i* is the equilibrium rate of interest. Assuming no change in expectations and nominal income, an increase in the quantity of money (through buying securities by the Central Bank of the country from the open market), will lower the rate of interest. In Fig. 42.8, when the quantity of money increases from OM_1 to OM_2 the rate of interest falls from *i* to *i'* because the new quantity of money OM_2 is in balance with the demand for money at *i'* rate of interest. In this case we move down on the curve. Thus, given the money demand curve or curve of liquidity preference, an increase in the supply of money brings down the rate of interest.

Let us see how increase in money supply leads to the fall in the rate of interest. With initial equilibrium at *i*, when the money supply is expanded from M_1 to M_2, there emerges excess supply of money at the initial *i* rate of interest. The people would react to this excess quantity of money supplied by buying bonds. As a result, the bond prices will go up which implies that the rate of interest will decline. This is how the increase in money supply leads to the fall in rate of interest.

Effect of Increase in Money Demand

The position of money demand curve depends upon two factors: (1) the level of nominal income, (2) the expectations about the changes in bond prices in the future which implies changes in rate of interest in future. As has been explained above, a money demand curve is drawn by assuming a certain level of nominal income. With the increase in nominal income, money demand for transactions motive increases causing an upward shift in the money demand curve.

Shift in money demand curve (or what Keynes called liquidity preference curve) can also be caused by changes in the expectations of the people regarding changes in bond prices or movements in the rate of interest in the future. If some changes in events lead the people on balance to expect a higher rate of interest in the future than they had previously supposed, the money demand or liquidity preference for speculative motive will increase which will bring about an upward shift in the money demand curve or liquidity preference curve and this will raise the rate of interest.

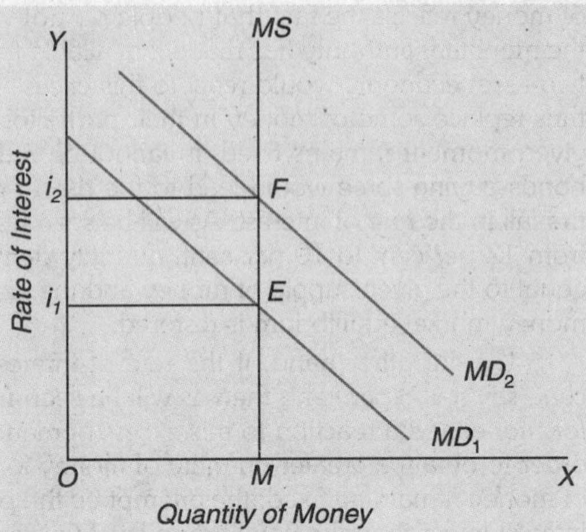

Fig. 42.9. *Effect of Increase in Demand for Money on the Rate of Interest*

In Fig 42.9 assuming that the quantity of money remains unchanged at *M*, the shift in the money demand curve from MD_1 to MD_2, the rate of interest rises from i_1 to i_2 because *at* i_2, the new demand for money is in equilibrium with the supply of money *OM*. It is worth noting that when the money demand curve shifts from MD_1 to MD_2, the amount of money held does not increase; it remains *OM* as before. Only the rate of interest rises from i_1 to i_2 to equilibrate the new liquidity preference or money demand with the available quantity of money *OM*.

Critical Apraisal

Thus we see that *Keynes explained interest in terms of purely monetary forces and not in terms of real forces like productivity of capital and supply of saving which formed the foundation-stones of both classical and loanable fund theories.* According to him, demand for money for speculative motive together with the supply of money determines the rate of interest. He agreed that the marginal revenue product of capital tends to become equal to the rate of interest but the rate of interest is not determined by marginal revenue product of capital. Moreover, according to him, interest is not a reward for saving or thriftiness or waiting but for parting with liquidity. Keynes asserted that it is not the rate of interest which equalises saving with investment. But this equality is brought about through changes in the level of income.

According to Keynes, rate of interest is determined by liquidity preference (*i.e.* demand for money) and supply of money. However, as we have seen, liquidity preference, especially demand for money for transactions motive depends on level of income. Now, when income increases, liquidity preference curve (that is, money demand curve) will shift to the right and, given the supply of money, new equilibrium rate of interest will be obtained. Thus, at different levels of income there will be different money demand curves. As a result, at different levels of income, there will be different equilibrium rates of interest. Thus, we cannot know the rate of interest unless we know the liquidity preference curve, and also we cannot know the liquidity preference curve unless we know the level of income. According to different levels of income, there will be different demand curves for money and therefore different rates of interest, given the supply of money. In this way we can derive *LM* curve which indicates various combinations of interest rate and income at which money market is in equilibrium. We will explain in detail in a later chapter the derivation of *LM* curve.

Thus, Keynes's analysis at the most helps us to obtain *LM* curve which shows what will be the rate of interest at different levels of income and not any unique or particular rate of interest. Thus, the Keynesian theory, like the classical theory, is indeterminate. "In the Keynesian case the supply and demand for money curves cannot give the rate of interest unless we already know the income level, in the classical case the demand and supply schedules for saving offer no solution until the income is known. Precisely the same is true of loanable funds theory. Keynes' criticism of the classical and lonable funds theories applies equally to his now theory[10].

10. A. H. Hansen, *Guide to Keynes*. p. 141

QUESTION FOR REVIEW

1. Explain the concept of money supply. What are the factors responsible for the rapid increase in money supply.
2. Explain the four measures of money supply. Which money supply measures are often used?
3. Distinguish between broad money by and narrow money. Which concept is more relevent in the discussion of causes of inflation in the economy.
4. Explain high-powered money supply theory of money supply.
5. What is money multiplier. Explain its role in the determination of money supply in the economy.
6. Explain the impact of budget deficit on the supply of money in the economy. Explain the Central Bank's dilemma in this connection?
7. Explain the impact of (1) deficit in balance of payments, and (2) large capital inflows on the money supply in the open economy. Explain sterilization operations by the central Bank of the country in each case.
8. Explain the Reserve Bank's dilemma in the face of large capital inflows in the Indian economy?
9. How money supply in the economy is affected by open economy.
10. Explain how supply of money depends upon the high powered money, the currency deposit ratio and cash reserve ratio.
11. What is meant by steralisation operations by RBI ? For what purpose they are used ? Explain

The IS-LM Curve Model

(Synthesis of Monetary and Real Factors)

THE GOODS MARKET AND MONEY MARKET : LINKS BETWEEN THEM

Keynes in his analysis of national income explains that national income is determined at the level where aggregate demand (i.e., aggregate expenditure) for consumption and investment goods (C + I) equals aggregate output. In other words, in Keynes' simple model the level of national income is shown to be determined by the *goods market equilibrium*. In this simple analysis of equlibirum in the goods market Keynes considers investment to be determined by the rate of interest along with the marginal efficiency of capital and is shown to be independent of the level of national income. The rate of interest, according to Keynes, is determined by money market equilibrium by the demand for and supply of money. In this Keynes' model, changes in rate of interest either due to change in money supply or change in demand for money will affect the determination of national income and output in the goods market through causing changes in the level of investment. In this way changes in money market equilibrium influence the determination of national income and output in the goods market. However, there is apparently one flaw in the Keynesian analysis which has been pointed out by some economists and has been a subject of a good deal of controversy. It has been asserted that in the Keynesian model whereas the changes in rate of interest in the money market affect investment and therefore the level of income and output in the goods market, *there is seemingly no inverse influence of changes in goods market i.e., (investment and income)* on the money market equilibrium.

It has been shown by J.R. Hicks and others that with greater insights into the Keynesian theory one finds that the changes in income caused by changes in investment or propensity to consume in the goods market also influence the determination of interest in the money market. According to him, the level of income which depends on the investment and consumption demand determines the transactions demand for money which affects the rate of interest. Hicks, Hansen, Lerner and Johnson have put forward a complete and integrated model based on the Keynesian framework wherein the variables such as investment, national income, rate of interest, demand for and supply of money are interrelated and mutually interdependent and can be represented by the two curves called the *IS* and *LM* curves. This extended Keynesian model is therefore known as *IS-LM* curve model. In this model they have shown how the level of national income and rate of interest are jointly determined by the simultaneous equilibrium in the two interdependent goods and money markets. Now, this *IS-LM* curve model has become a standard tool of macroeconomics and the effects of monetary and fiscal policies are discussed using this *IS* and *LM* curves model.

GOODS MARKET EQUILIBRIUM : THE DERIVATION OF THE *IS* CURVE

The *IS-LM* curve model emphasises the interaction between the goods and money markets. The goods market is in equilibrium when aggregate demand is equal to income. The aggregate demand is determined by consumption demand and investment demand. In the Keynesian model of goods market equilibrium we also now introduce the rate of interest as an important determinant of investment. With this introduction of interest as a determinant of investment, the latter now becomes an endogenous variable in the model. When the rate of interest falls the level of investment increases and vice versa. Thus, changes in the rate of interest affect aggregate demand or aggregate expenditure by causing changes in the investment demand. When the rate of interest falls, it lowers the cost of investment projects and thereby raises the profitability

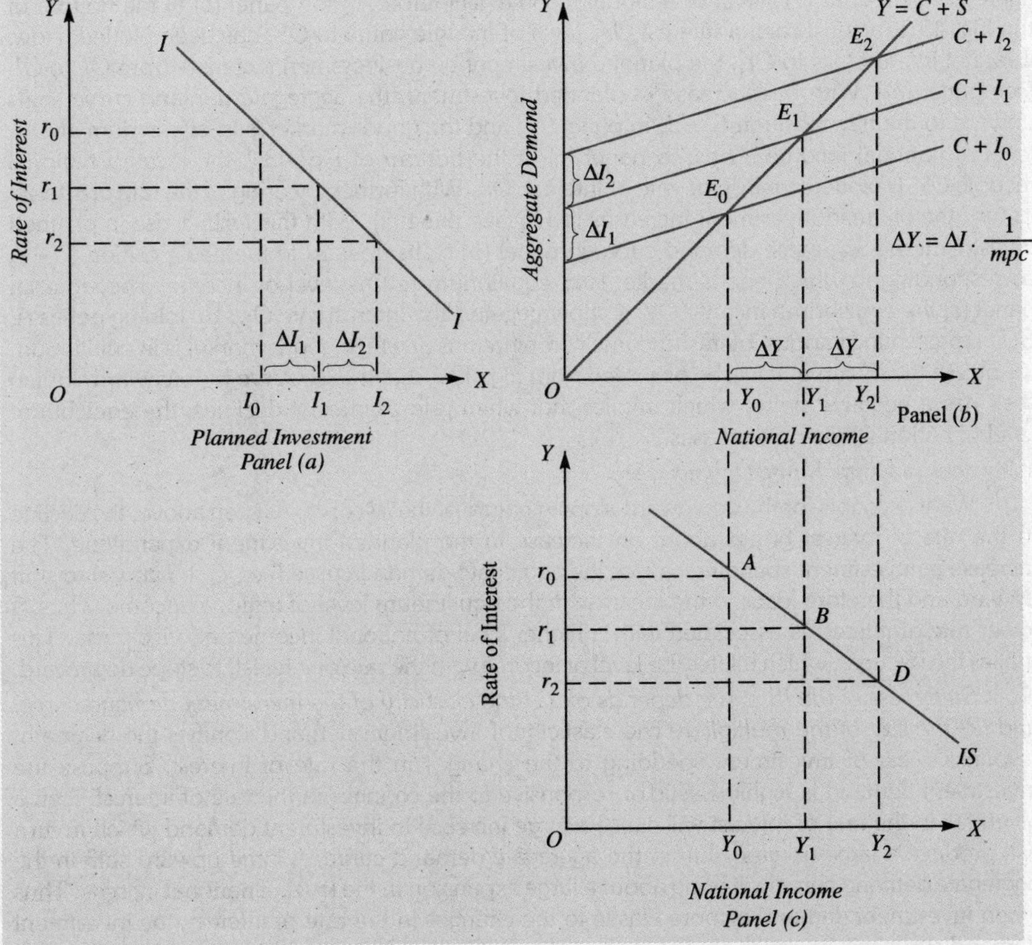

Fig. 43.1. *Derivation of IS Curve : Linking Rate of Interest with National Income through Investment and Aggregate Demand*

of investment. The businessmen will therefore undertake greater investment at a lower rate of interest. The increase in investment demand will bring about increase in aggregate demand which in turn will raise the equilibrium level of income. *In the derivation of the IS Curve we seek to find out the equilibrium level of national income as determined by the equilibrium in goods market by a level of investment determined by a given rate of interest. Thus IS curve relates different equilibrium levels of national income with various rates of interest.* As explained above, with a fall in the rate of interest, the planned investment will increase which will cause an upward shift in aggregate demand function ($C + I$) resulting in goods market equilibrium at a higher level of national income.

The lower the rate of interest, the higher will be the equilibrium level of national income. Thus, the *IS* curve is the locus of those combinations of rate of interest and the level of national income at *which goods market is in equilibrium*. How the *IS* curve is derived is illustrated in Fig. 43.1. In panel (a) of Fig. 43.1 the relationship between rate of interest and planned investment is depicted by the investment demand curve *II*. It will be seen from panel (*a*) that at rate of interest Or_0 the planned investment is equal to OI_0. With OI_0 as the amount of planned investment, the aggregate demand curve is $C + I_0$ which, as will be seen in panel (*b*) of Fig. 43.1, equals aggregate output at OY_0 level of national income. Therefore, in the panel (*c*) at the bottom of the Fig. 43.1, against rate of interest Or_0, level of income equal to OY_0 has been plotted. Now, if rate of interest falls to Or_1, the planned investment by businessmen increases from OI_0 to OI_1 [see panel (*a*)]. With this increase in planned investment, the aggregate demand curve shifts upward to the new position $C + I_1$ in panel (*b*), and the goods market is in equilibrium at OY_1 level of national income. Thus, in panel (c) at the bottom of Fig. 43.1 the level of national income OY_1 is plotted against the rate of interest, Or_1. With further lowering of the rate of interest to Or_2, the planned investment increases to OI_2 (see panel *a*). With this further rise in planned investment the aggregate demand curve in panel (*b*) shifts upward to the new position $C + I_2$ corresponding to which goods market is in equilibrium at OY_2 level of income. Therefore, in panel (*c*) the equilibrium income OY_2 is shown against the interest rate Or_2. By joining points *A*, *B*, *D* representing various interest-income combinations at which goods market is in equilibrium we obtain the *IS* curve. It will be observed from Fig. 43.1 that the *IS* Curve is downward sloping (*i.e.*, has a negative slope) which implies that when rate of interest declines, the equilibrium level of national income increases.

Why does *IS* Curve Slope Downward?

What accounts for the downward-sloping nature of the *IS* curve. As seen above, the decline in the rate of interest brings about an increase in the planned investment expenditure. The increase in investment spending causes the aggregate demand curve (i.e., $C + I$ curve) to shift upward and therefore leads to the increase in the equilibrium level of national income. Thus, a lower rate of interest is associated with a higher level of national income and vice-versa. This makes the *IS* curve, which relates the level of income with the rate of interest, to slope downward.

Steepness of the IS curve depends on (1) the elasticity of the investment demand curve, and (2) the size of the multiplier. The elasticity of investment demand signifies the degree of responsiveness of investment spending to the changes in the rate of interest. Suppose the investment demand is highly elastic or responsive to the changes in the rate of interest, then a given fall in the rate of interest will cause a large increase in investment demand which in turn will produce a large upward shift in the aggregate demand curve. A large upward shift in the aggregate demand curve will bring about a large expansion in the level of national income. Thus when investment demand is more elastic to the changes in the rate of interest, the investment demand curve will be relatively flat (or less steep). On the contrary, when investment demand is not much sensitive or is less elastic to the changes in the rate of interest, the *IS* curve will be relatively more steep.

The steepness of the *IS* curve also depends on the magnitude of the multiplier. As has been explained in a previous chapter the value of multiplier depends on the marginal propensity to consume (*mpc*). It may be noted that the higher the marginal propensity to consume, the aggregate demand ($C + I$) curve will be more steep and the magnitude of multiplier will be large. In case of a higher marginal propensity to consume (*mpc*) and therefore a higher value of multiplier, a given increment in investment demand caused by a given fall in the rate of interest will help to bring about a greater increase in equilibrium level of income. Thus, the higher the value of multiplier, the greater will be the rise in equilibrium income produced by a given fall in the rate of interest and this makes the *IS* curve flatter. On the other hand, the smaller the value of multiplier due to lower marginal propensity to consume, the smaller will be the increase in equilibrium level of income following a given increment in investment caused by a given fall in the rate of interest. Thus, in case of smaller size of multiplier the *IS* curve will be more steep.

Shift in *IS* Curve

It is important to understand what determines the position of the *IS* curve and what causes shifts in it. It is the level of autonomous expenditure which determines the position of the *IS* curve and changes in the autonomous expenditure cause a shift in it. *By autonomous expenditure we mean the expenditure, be it investment expenditure, the Government spending or consumption expenditure which does not depend on the level of income.* The government expenditure is an important type of autonomous expenditure. Note that the Government expenditure which is determined by several factors as well as by the policies of the Government, does not depend on the level of income and the rate of interest. Similarly, some consumption expenditure has to be made if individuals have to survive even by borrowing from others or by spending their savings made in the past year. Such consumption expenditure is a sort of autonomous expenditure and changes in it do not depend on the changes in income.

Further, autonomous changes in investment can also occur. In the goods market equilibrium of the simple Keynesian model the investment expenditure is treated as autonomous or independent of the level of income and therefore does not vary as the level of income increases. However, in the complete Keynesian model, the investment spending is thought to be determined by the rate of interest along with marginal efficiency of investment. Following this complete Keynesian model, in the derivation of the *IS* curve we consider the level of investment and changes in it as determined by the rate of interest along with marginal efficiency of capital. However, there can be changes in investment spending autonomous or independent of the changes in rate of interest and the level of income. For instance, growing population requires more investment in house construction, school buildings, roads, etc., which does not depend on changes in level of income or rate of interest. Further, autonomous changes in investment spending can also take place when new innovations come about, that is, when there is progress in technology and new machines, equipment, tools etc., have to be built embodying the new technology. Besides, Government expenditure is also of autonomous type as it does not depend on the level of income in the economy. As is well-known government increases its expenditure for the purpose of promoting social welfare and accelerating economic growth. Increase in Government expenditure and autonomous increase in investment and consumption will cause a rightward shift in the *IS* curve.

MONEY MARKET EQUILIBRIUM : DERIVATION OF *LM* CURVE

The *LM* curve can be derived from the Keynesian theory from its analysis of money market equilibrium. According to Keynes, demand for money to hold depends upon transactions motive and speculative motive. It is the money held for transactions motive which is a function of income. The greater the level of income, the greater the amount of money held for transactions motive and therefore higher the level of money demand curve.

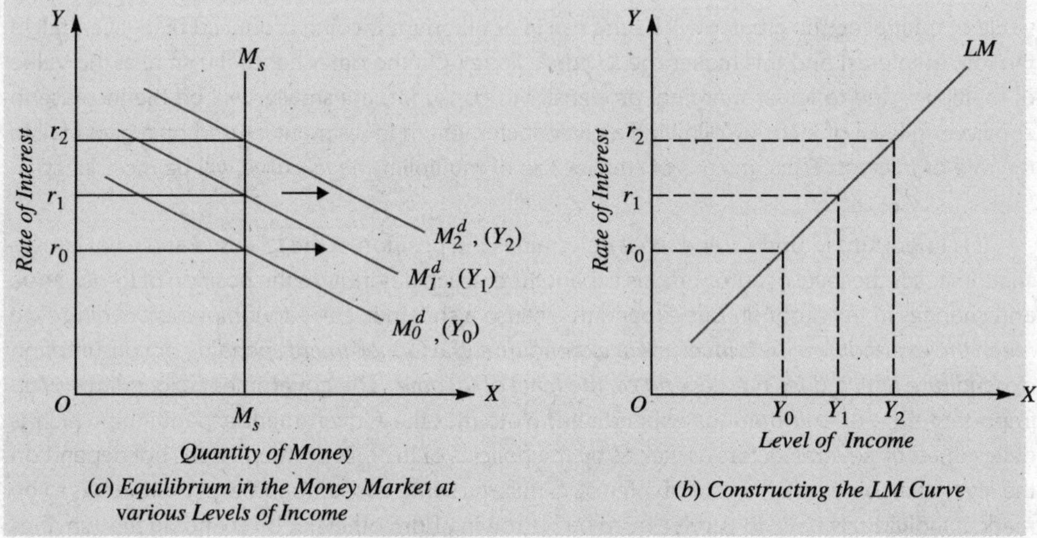

Fig. 43.2. *Derivation of LM Curve*

The demand for money depends on the level of income because they have to finance their expenditure, that is, their transactions of buying goods and services. The demand for money also depends on the rate of interest which is the cost of holding money. This is because by holding money rather than lending it and buying other financial assets, one has to forgo interest.

Thus demand for money (M^d) can be expressed as:

$$M^d = L(Y, r)$$

where M^d stands for demand for money, *Y* for real income and *r* for rate of interest. Thus, we can draw a family of money demand curves at various levels of income. Now, the intersection of these various money demand curves corresponding to different income levels with the supply curve of money fixed by the monetary authority would gives us the *LM* curve. The *LM* curve relates the level of income with the rate of interest which is determined by money-market equilibrium corresponding to different levels of demand for money. The *LM* curve tells what the various rates of interest will be (given the quantity of money and the family of demand curves for money) at different levels of income. But the money demand curve or what Keynes calls the liquidity preference curve alone cannot tell us what exactly the rate of interest will be. In Fig. 43.2 (*a*) and (*b*) we have derived the *LM* curve from a family of demand curves for money. As income inicreases, money demand curve shifts outward and therefore the rate of interest which equates supply of money with demand for money rises. In Fig. 43.2 (*b*) we measure income on the *X*-axis and plot the income level corresponding to the various interest rates determined at those income levels through money market equilibrium by the equality of demand for and the supply of money in Fig. 43.2 (*a*).

Slope of *LM* Curve

It will be noticed from Fig. 43.2 (*b*) that the *LM* curve slopes upward to the right. This is because with higher levels of income, demand curve for money (M^d) is higher and consequently the money-market equilibrium, that is, the equality of the given money supply with money demand curve occurs at a higher rate of interest. This implies that rate of interest varies directly with income. It is important to know the factors on which the slope of the *LM* curve depends. There are two factors on which the slope of the *LM* curve depends. First, *the responsiveness of demand for money (i.e., liquidity preference) to the changes in income.* As the income increases, say from Y_0 to Y_1, the demand curve for money shifts from M_0^d to $M^d{}_1$, that is, with an increase in income, demand for money would increase for being held for transactions motive, M_t^d or $L_1 = f(Y)$ where M_t^d or L_1 is the demand for money for transactions purposes. This extra demand for money would disturb the money market equilibrium and for the equilibrium to be restored the rate of interest will rise to the level where the given money supply curve intersects the new demand curve corresponding to the higher income level. It is worth noting that in the new equilibrium position, *with the given stock of money supply,* money held under the transactions motive will increase whereas the money held for speculative motive will decline. The greater the extent to which demand for money for transactions motive increases with the increase in income, the greater the decline in the supply of money available for speculative motive and, given the demand for money for speculative motive, the higher the rise in the rate of interest and consequently the steeper the *LM* curve. $r = f(M^S{}_2, L_2)$ where r is the rate of interest, $M^s{}_2$ is the stock of money available for speculative motive and L_2 is the money demand for speculative motive.

The second factor which determines the slope of the *LM* curve is the *elasticity or responsiveness of demand for money (i.e., liquidity preference for speculative motive) to the changes in rate of interest.* The lower the elasticity of liquidity preference for speculative motive with respect to the changes in the rate of interest, the steeper will be the *LM* curve. On the other hand, if the elasticity of liquidity preference (money demand-function) to the changes in the rate of interest is high, the *LM* curve will be flatter or less steep.

Shifts in the *LM* Curve

Another important thing to know about the *IS-LM* curve model is that what brings about shifts in the *LM* curve or, in other words, what determines the position of the *LM* curve. As seen above, a *LM* curve is drawn by keeping the stock of money supply fixed. Therefore, when the money supply increases, given the money demand function, it will lower the rate of interest at the given level of income. This is because with income fixed, the rate of interest must fall so that demand for money for speculative and transactions motive increases to become equal to the greater money supply. This will cause the *LM* curve to shift outward to the right.

The other factor which causes a shift in the LM curve is the change in liquidity preference (money demand function) for a given level of income. If the liquidity preference function for a given level of income shifts upward, this, given the stock of money, will lead to the rise in the rate of interest for a given level of income. This will bring about a shift in the *LM* curve to the left.

It therefore follows from above that *increase in the money demand function causes the* *LM* curve to shfit to the left. Similarly, on the contrary, if the money demand function for a given level of income declines, it will lower the rate of interest for a given level of income and will therefore shift the *LM* curve to the right.

The *LM* Curve : The Essential Features

From our analysis of the *LM* curve, we arrive at its following essential features:

1. The *LM* curve is a schedule that describes the combinations of rate of interest and level of income *at which money market is in equilibrium.*

2. The *LM* curve slopes upward to the right.
3. The *LM* curve is flatter if the interest elasticity of demand for money is high. On the contrary, the *LM* curve is steep if the interest elasticity demand for money is low.
4. The *LM* curve shifts to the right when the stock of money supply is increased and it shifts to the left if the stock of money supply is reduced.
5. The *LM* curve shifts to the left if there is an increase in the money demand function which raises the quantity of money demanded at the given interest rate and income level. On the other hand, the *LM* curve shifts to the right if there is a decrease in the money demand function which lowers the amount of money demanded at given levels of interest rate and income.

SIMULTANEOUS EQUILIBRIUM OF THE GOODS MARKET AND MONEY MARKET

The *IS* and the *LM* curves relate the two variables: (*a*) income and (*b*) the rate of interest. Income and the rate of interest are therefore determined together at the point of intersection of these two curves, *i.e.*, *E* in Fig. 43.3. The equilibrium rate of interest thus determined is Or_2 and the level of income determined is OY_2. At this point income and the rate of interest stand in relation to each other such that (1) the goods market is in equilibrium, that is, the aggregate demand equals the level of aggregate output, and (2) the demand for money is in equilibrium with the supply of money (*i.e.*, the desired amount of money is equal to the actual supply of money). It should be noted that *LM* curve has been drawn by keeping the supply of money fixed.

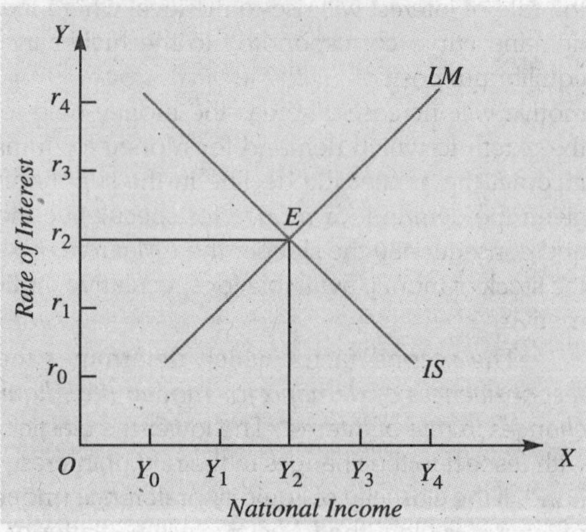

Fig. 43.3. *The IS and LM Curves Combined: The Joint Determination of the Interest Rate and the Income Level*

Thus, the *IS-LM* curve model is based on: (1) the investment-demand function, (2) the consumption function, (3) the money demand function, and (4) the quantity of money. *We see, therefore, that according to the IS-LM curve model both the real factors, namely, saving and investment, productivity of capital and propensity to consume and save, and the monetary factors, that is, the demand for money (liquidity preference) and supply of money play a part in the joint determination of the rate of interest and the level of income. Any change in these factors will cause a shift in IS or LM curve and will therefore change the equilibrium levels of the rate of interest and income.*

The *IS-LM* curve model explained above has succeeded in integrating the theory of money with the theory of income determination. And by doing so, as we shall see below, it has succeeded in synthesising the monerary and fiscal policies. Further, with the *IS-LM* curve analysis, we are better able to explain the effect of changes in certain important economic variables such as desire to save, the supply of money, investment, demand for money on the rate of interest and level of income.

Effect of Changes in Supply of Money on the Rate of Interest and Income Level

Let us first consider what will happen if the supply of money is increased by the action of the Central Bank. Given the liquidity preference schedule, with the increase in the supply of money, more money will be available for speculative motive at a given level of income which will cause the interest rate to fall. As a result, the *LM* curve will shift to the right. With this rightward shift in the *LM* curve, in the new equilibrium position, rate of interest will be lower and the level of income greater than before. This is shown in Fig. 43.4 where with a given supply of money, *LM* and *IS* curves intersect at point *E*. With the increase in the supply of money, *LM* curve shifts to the right to the position *LM′*, and with *IS* schedule remaining unchanged, new equilibrium is at point *G* corresponding to which rate of interest is lower and level of income greater than at

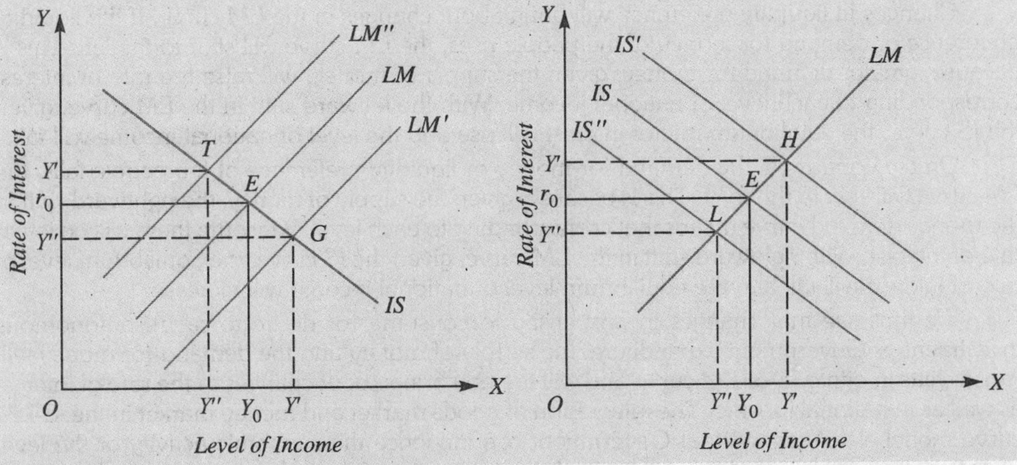

Fig. 43.4. *Impact of Change in Supply of Money* **Fig. 43.5.** *Impact of Change in Propensity to Save*

E. Now, suppose that instead of increasing the supply of money, Central Bank of the country takes steps to reduce the supply of money. With the reduction in the supply of money, less money will be available for speculative motive at each level of income and, as a result, the *LM* curve will shift to the left of *E*, and the *IS* curve remaining unchanged, in the new equilibrium position (as shown by point *T* in Fig. 43.4) the rate of interest will be higher and the level of income smaller than before.

Changes in the Desire to Save or Propensity to Consume

Let us consider what happens to the rate of interest when desire to save or in other words, propensity to consume changes. When people's desire to save falls, that is, when propensity to consume rises, the aggregate demand ($C + I$) curve will shift upward and, therefore, level of national income will rise at each rate of interest. As a result, the *IS′* curve will shift outward to the right. In Fig. 43.5 suppose with a certain given fall in the desire to save (or increase in the propensity to consume), the *IS* curve shifts rightward to the higher position *IS′*. With *LM* curve remaining unchanged, the new equilibrium position will be established at *H* corresponding to which rate of interest as well as level of income will be greater than at *E*. Thus, *a fall in the desire to save has led to the increase in both rate of interest and level of income.* On the other hand, if the desire to save rises, that is, if the propensity to consume falls, aggregate demand ($C + I$) curve will shift downward which will cause the level of national income to fall for each rate of interest and as a result the *IS* curve will shift to the left. With this, and *LM* curve remaining unchanged, the new equilibrium position will be reached to the left of *E*, say at point *L* (as shown in Fig. 43.5) corresponding to which both rate of interest and level of national income will be smaller than at *E*.

Changes in Autonomous Investment and Government Expenditure

Changes in autonomous investment and Government expenditure will also shift the *IS* curve. If either there is increase in autonomous private investment or Government steps up its expenditure, aggregate demand for goods will increase and this will bring about increase in national income through the multiplier process. This will shift *IS* schedule to the right, and given the *LM* curve, the rate of interest as well as the level of income will rise. On the contrary, if somehow private investment expenditure falls or the Government reduces its expenditure, the *IS* curve will shift to the left and, given the *LM* curve, both the rate of interest and the level of income will fall.

Changes in Demand for Money or Liquidity Preference

Changes in liquidity preference will bring about changes in the *LM* curve. If the liquidity preference or demand for money of the people rises, the *LM* curve will shift to the left. This is because, greater demand for money, given the supply of money, will raise the rate of interest corresponding to each level of national income. With the leftward shift in the *LM* curve, given the *IS* curve, the equilibrium rate of interest will rise and the level of national income will fall.

On the contrary, if the demand for money or liquidity preference of the people falls, the *LM* curve will shift to the right. This is because, given the supply of money, the rightward shift in the money demand curve means that corresponding to each level of income there will be lower rate of interest. With rightward shift in the *LM* curve, given the *IS* curve, the equilibrium level of rate of interest will fall and the equilibrium level of national income will increase.

We thus see that changes in propensity to consume (or desire to save), autonomous investment or Government expenditure, the supply of money and the demand for money will cause shifts in either *IS* or *LM* curve and will thereby bring about changes in the rate of interest as well as in national income. The integration of goods market and money market in the *IS-LM* curve model clearly shows that Government can influence the economic activity or the level of national income through monetary *and fiscal measures*. Through adopting an appropriate monetary policy (*i.e.*, changing the supply of money) the Government can shift the *LM* curve and through pursuing an appropriate fiscal policy (expenditure and taxation policy) the Government can shift the *IS* curve. Thus both monetary and fiscal policies can play a useful role in regulating the level of economic activity in the country.

The Critique of the *IS-LM* Model

The *IS-LM* model makes a significant advance in explaining the simultaneous determination of the rate of interest and the level of national income. It represents a more general, inclusive and realistic approach to the determination of interest rate and level of income. Further, the *IS-LM* model succeeds in integrating and synthesising fiscal with monetary policies, and theory of income determination with the theory of money. But the *IS-LM* model is not without limitations. Firstly, it is based on the assumption that the rate of interest is quite flexible, that is, free to vary and not rigidly fixed by the Central Bank of a country. If the rate of interest is quite inflexible, then the appropriate adjustment explained above will not take place. Secondly, the model is also based upon the *assumption that investment is interest-elastic,* that is, investment varies with the rate of interest. If investment is interest-inelastic, then the *IS-LM* model breaks down since the required adjustments do not occur. Thirdly, Don Patinkin[1] and Milton Friedman have circiticised the *IS-LM* model as being too artificial and over-simplified. In their view, division of the economy into two sectors – monetary and real – is artificial and unrealistic. According to them, monetary and real sectors are quite interwoven and act and react on each other. Further, Patinkin has pointed out that the *IS-LM* model has ignored the possibility of changes in the price level of commodities. According to him the various economic variables such as supply of money, propensity to consume or save, investment and the demand for money not only influence the rate of interest and the level of national income but also the prices of commodities and services. Patinkin has suggested a more integrated and general equilibrium approach which involves the simultaneous determination of not only the rate of interest and the level of income but also of the prices of commodities and services.

1. Don Patinkin, Money, Interest and Prices, Harper and Row, 1965.

IS-LM CURVE MODEL : EXPLAINING ROLES OF GOERNMENT'S FISCAL AND MONETARY POLICIES

With the help of *IS-LM* curve model we can explain how the *intervention by the Government* with proper fiscal and monetary policies can influence the level of economic activity, that is, inocme and employment level. We explain below the impact of changes in fiscal and monetary policy on the economy in the *IS-LM* model.

Role of Fiscal Policy

Let us first explain how *IS-LM* model shows the effect of increase in Government expenditure on level of income. This is illustrated in Fig. 43.6. As explained above, increase in Government expenditure which is of autonomous nature raises aggregate demand for goods and services and thereby causes an outward shift in *IS* curve, as is shown in Fig. 43.6 where increase in Government expenditure leads to the shift in *IS* curve from IS_1 to IS_2. Note that the horizontal distance between the two *IS* curves is equal to $\Delta G \times \frac{1}{1-MPC}$ which shows the increase in income that occurs in Keynes's multiplier model. It will be seen from Fig. 43.6 that with the *LM* curve remaining unchanged, the new IS_2 curve intersects *LM* curve at point *B*. Thus, in *IS-LM* model with the increase in Government expenditure (ΔG), the equilibrium moves from point *E* to *B* and with this the rate of interest rises from r_1 to r_2 and income level rises from Y_1 to Y_2. Thus, *IS-LM* model shows that expanoinary fiscal policy of increase in Government expenditure raises both the level of income and rate of interest.

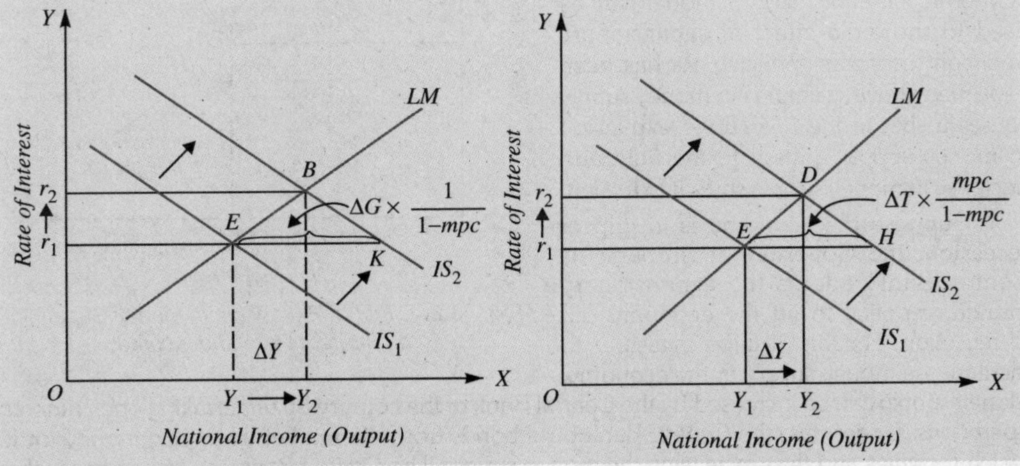

Fig. 43.6. *Impact of Increase in Government Expenditure on Interest Rate and Income*

Fig. 43.7. *Effect of Cut in Taxes*

It is worth noting that in the *IS-LM* model increase in national income by Y_1Y_2 in Fig. 43.6 is less than *EK* which would occur in Keynes's model. This is because Keynes in his simple multiplier model assumes that investment is fixed and autonomous, whereas *IS-LM* model takes into account the fall in private investment due to the rise in interest rate that takes place with the increase in Government expenditure. That is, increase in Government expenditure crowds out some private investment.

Likewise, it can be illustrated that the reduction in Government expenditure will cause a rightward shift in the *IS* curve, and given the *LM* curve unchanged, will lead to the fall in both rate of interest and level of income. It should be noted that Government often cuts expenditure to control inflation in the economy.

Reduction in Taxes. An alternative measure of *expansionary fiscal policy* which may be adopted is the reduction in taxes which through increase in disposable income of the people raises consumption demand of the people. As a result, cut in taxes causes a shift in the *IS* curve to the right as is shown in Fig. 43.7, from IS_1 to IS_2. It may however noted that in the Keynesian multiplier model, the horizontal shift in the IS curve is determined by the value of *tax multiplier* which is equal to $\Delta T \times \frac{MPC}{1-MPC}$ and causes level of income to increase by *EH* in Fig. 43.7. However, in the *IS-LM* model, with the shift of the *IS* curve from IS_1 to IS_2 following the reduction in taxes, the economy moves from equilibrium point *E* to *D* and as is evident from Fig. 43.7, rate of interest rises from r_1 to r_2 and level of income increases from Y_1 to Y_2.

On the other hand, if the Government intervences in the economy to *reduce inflationary pressures, it will raise the rates of personal taxes to reduce disposable income of the people. Rise in personal taxes will lead to the decrease in aggregate demand.* Decrease in aggregate demand will help in controlling inflation. This case can also be shown by *IS-LM* curve model.

Role of Monetary Policy

Through making appropriate changes in monetary policy the Government can influence the level of economic activity. Monetary policy may also be expansionary or contractionary depending on the prevailing economic situation. *IS-LM* model can be used to show the effect of expansionary and tight monetary policies. As has been explained above, a change in money supply causes a shift in the *LM* curve; expansion in money supply shifts it to the right and decrease in money supply shifts it to the left.

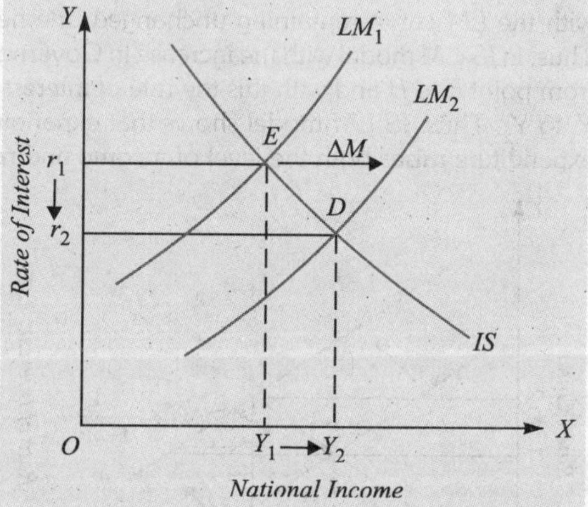

Fig. 43.8. *Effect of Expansion in Money Supply on Interest Rate and Income*

Suppose the economy is in grip of recession, the Government (through its Central Bank) adopts the expansionary monetary policy to lift the economy out of recession. For this, it takes measures to increase the money supply in the economy. Money supply can be increased by the Central Bank of the country by *undertaking open market operations.* Under this, the Central Bank buys bonds from the market by paying money for it which it creates and thus increasing the money supply. The Central Bank can also increase the money supply in the economy by lowering the *cash reserve ratio* (CRR) of the banks which will release new money for the banks. Banks can lend the new money so released to business men.

The increase in money supply, state of liquidity preference or demand for money remaining unchanged, will lead to the fall in rate of interest. At a lower interest there will be more investment by businessmen. More investment will cause aggregate demand and income to rise. This implies that with expansion in money supply *LM* curve will shift to the right as is shown in Fig. 43.8. As a result, the economy will move from equilibrium point *E* to *D* and with this the rate of interest will fall from r_1 to r_2 and national income will increase from Y_1 to Y_2. Thus, *IS-LM* model shows the expansion in money supply lowers interest rate and raises income. We have also indicated what is called monetary transmission mechanism, that is, how *IS-LM* curve model shows the expansion in money supply leads to the increase in aggregate demand for goods and services. We have thus seen that increase in money supply lowers the rate of interest which then stimulates more investment demand. Investment demand through multiplier process leads to a greater increase in aggregate demand and national inocme.

If the economy suffers from inflation, the Government will like to check it. Then its Central Bank should adopt tight or contractionary monetary policy. That is, it should reduce the money supply. *The Central Bank of a country can reduce money supply through open market operation by selling bonds in the market in exchange for money from those who buy the bonds.* To fight inflation the Central Bank of the country can also reduce money supply by rasing the cash reserve ratio (CRR). The higher cash reserve ratio implies that banks have to keep more cash balances with the Central Bank and as result, money supply in the economy decreases. Now, the *IS-LM* model can be used to show, as we have seen above in case of expansionary monetary policy, *that reduction in money supply will cause a leftward shift in LM curve and will lead to the rise in interest rate and fall in the level.of national income*. This is shown in Fig. 43.9 where as a result of reduction in money supply which causes a shift in *LM* curve from LM_0 to LM_1 and raises interest rate in from r_0 to r_1. The rise in interest causes investment demand to decline which results in decline in aggregate demand. This will help in reducing inflation.

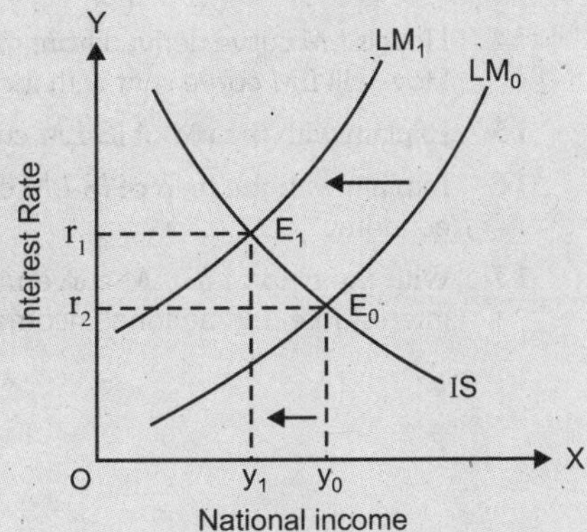

Fig. 43.9. *Contractionary monetary policy causes rate of interest to rise and national income to fall*

QUESTIONS FOR REVIEW

1. What is *IS* curve ? How is it derived from goods market equilibrium ?
2. Define *IS* curve. What are the factors that determine the slope or steepness of *IS* Curve ?
3. What is *LM* curve ? How is it derived from money market equilibrium ? On factors does its slope and position depend ?
4. How do the product and money markets interact to determine the short-run equilibrium level of national income and the rate of interest ?
5. Using IS-LM model analyse the impact of expansion in money supply on the equilibrium level of income and rate of interest.
6. How do the product and money markets interact to determine the short-run equilibrium level of national income and the rate of interest ?
7. Using IS-LM model analyse the impact of an decrease in money supply on the equilibrium level of income and rate of interest. How will this help in controlling.
8. What do the *IS* and *LM* curves signify ? Using them show how the desire to save more affect national income and rate of interest.
9. What is crowding out effect of Government's fiscal policy ? Is it very significant ? What role does interest elasticity of investment play in determining the slope of *IS* curve ?
10. Explain and show graphically how product market is in equilibrium along *IS* curve.
11. Explain *IS* and *LM* curves. What is the role of these two curves in simultaneous determination of equilibrium rate of interest and level of income ?
12. (*a*) Derive *IS* curve for an economy. What are the factors which determine slope of the *IS* curve?

    (*b*) Show how *IS* curve will change as a result of increase in Government expenditure.

13. Why does *IS* curve slope downward ? How is *IS* curve related to investment multiplier in the Keynesian income theory ? What are the factors which cause a shift in *IS* curve ?
14. How is *LM* curve derived from money market equilibrium ? Why does *LM* curve slope upward? How will *LM* curve shfit with increase in money supply in the economy ?
15. Explain with the aid of *IS-LM* curves role of monetary policy for stabilisation of the economy.
16. Explain with the help of *IS-LM* curve model role of fiscal policy in overcoming recession in the economy.
17. With the help of *IS-LM* curve model show how the increase in demand for money will affect interest rate and national income.

Appendix to Chapter 43

The IS-LM Model : Algebraic Analysis

In the foregeing chapter we have explained the *IS-LM* curve model with graphs. In this section we make algebraic analysis *IS-LM* curves model. We first derive the equations for IS and *LM* curves and then combine them to show how level of national income and rate of interest are jointly determined through the simultaneous equilibrium of goods and money markets. This algebraic analysis of *IS-LM* model provides additional insights into how fiscal and monetary policy instruments affect national income and rate of interest.

The Derivation of Equation for IS Curve : Algebraic Method

The IS curve is derived from goods market equilibrium. The *IS* curve shows the combinations of levels of income and interest at which goods market is in equilibrium, that is, at which aggregate demand equals income. Aggregate demand, as explained earlier, consists of consumption demand investment demand, government expenditure on goods and services and net exports. Consumption demand is function of disposable income. Disposable income is level of income minus taxes ($Y_d = Y - T$) where Y_d stands for disposable income and T for taxes. However, in a two sector model where we do not incorporate taxation by the government, $Y_d = Y$.

Investment depends on rate of interest. With a given level of income, a higher rate of interest reduces investment demand and a lower rate of interest leads to more investment, that is, investment is negatively related to rate of interest. Thus

$$I = \bar{I} - di$$

Where d stands for sensitivity of investment to changes in rate or interest.

Therefore, we have the following equation for aggregate demand (*AD*)

$$AD = C + I + G + NX \qquad \ldots (1)$$

where $C = a + bY$ (Consumption function)

$I = \bar{I} - di$ (Investment function)

Where $\bar{I}$ is autonomous investment, that is, independent of income and rate of interest

G is government expenditure on goods and services and NX is net exports, that is, exports – imports.

Product market is in equilibrium when

$$Y = AD = C(Y) + I(i) + G + NX \quad \text{...(2)}$$

or

$$Y = (a + bY) + (\bar{I} - di) + G + NX$$

$$Y - bY = a + \bar{I} - di + G + NX$$

$$Y(1 - b) = a + \bar{I} - di + G + NX$$

$$Y = \frac{1}{1-b}(a + \bar{I} + G + NX) - \frac{di}{1-b} \quad \text{...(3)}$$

The above equation (3) describes *IS* curve. Terms in the brackets are all automous expenditure and are independent of both income and rate of interest. If we denote all these autonomous items by $\bar{A}$, then equation (3) for *IS* can be written as

$$Y = \frac{1}{1-b}(\bar{A}) - \frac{1}{1-b}(di)$$

or

$$Y = \frac{1}{1-b}(\bar{A} - di) \quad \text{...(4)}$$

$\frac{1}{1-b}$ is the income multiplier and *b* is marginal propensity to consume. Given the marginal propensity to consume (*b*) and the value of automous expenditure, we can obtain value of *Y* at different rates of interest to draw an *IS* curve. It is worth noting that the value of automous ($\bar{A}$) determines the intercept of the *IS* curve, *d* in the term *di* in equation (3) shows the sensitivity of investment to the changes in rate of interest and determines the slope of *IS* curve. Since fall in interest rate increases investment spending, it will raise aggregate demand and thus the equilibrium level of income. Besides, the slope of the *IS* curve depends on the size of income multiplier.

NUMERICAL PROBLEMS ON *IS* CURVE : TWO SECTOR MODEL

Problem 1. *The following equations describe an economy :*

$C = 10 + 0.5Y$ *(Consumption function)*

$I = 190 - 20\,i$ *(Investment function)*

Derive the equations for IS curve and represent it graphically

Solution.

IS curve describes the equation for product market equilibrium at various combinations of level of income and rate of interest.

$$Y = AD = C + I$$

Thus, *Y*

$$= 10 + 0.5Y + 190 - 20\,i$$

$$Y - 0.5Y = 200 - 20\,i$$

$$Y(1 - 0.5) = 200 - 20\,i$$

$$\frac{1}{2}Y = 200 - 20\,i$$

$$Y = 400 - 40\,i$$

Thus, *IS* curve is : $Y = 400 - 40\,i$

Alternative Method

Alternative way to get *IS* curve is to directly use *IS* curve equation and fill in it the values of various parameters and variables.

The equation for *IS* curve is given by :

$$Y = \frac{1}{1-b}(\bar{A} - di)$$

where $\bar{A} = a + \bar{I}$ (*i.e.* the sum of autonomous consumption (a) and investment expenditure ($\bar{I}$), b is marginal propensity to consume, d is sensitivity of investment to changes in rate of interest. Y and i are level of income and rate of interest respectively.

Substituting the values of various parameters we have the following *IS* equation :

$$Y = \frac{1}{1-0.5}[(10+190)-20i]$$

$$= \frac{1}{0.5}(200-20i)$$

$$= 400 - 40i$$

or equation for *IS* curve : $Y = 400 - 40i$

Graphic Representation : We can represent the *IS* equation graphically by taking some values of interest and calculate the level of income using the *IS* equation.

Suppose rate of interest is 5 per cent. Substituting this value of interest in *IS* equation we have

$$Y = 400 - 40i$$
$$= 400 - 40 \times 5$$
$$= 400 - 200 = 200$$

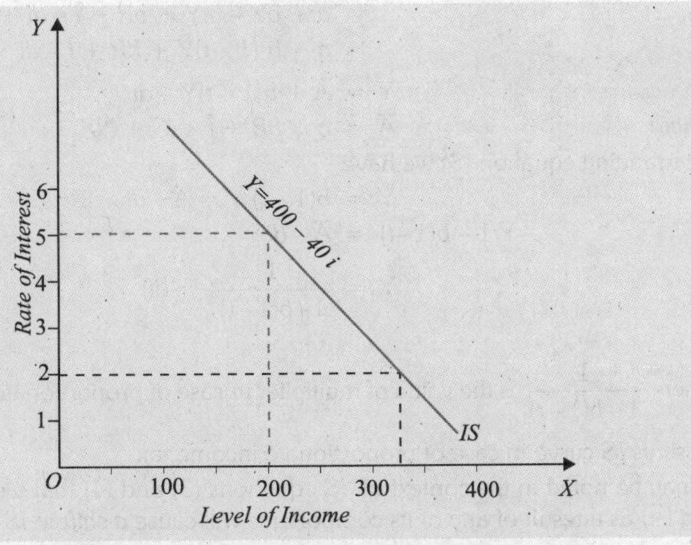

Fig. 43A.1. *Graphic Representation of IS Curve*

Thus, at 5 per cent rate of interest level of income is 200,

Now, suppose rate of interest is 2, then the level of income,

$$Y = 400 - 40 \times 2$$
$$= 400 - 80 = 320$$

At 2 per cent rate of interest, level of income is 320.

We have now two combinations of interest and income. We can plot these and obtain *IS* curve. This is done in Figure 43A.1

***IS* Curve : Three Sector Model with Taxation and Transfer Payments**

In the last section we have derived the *IS* curve taking government expenditure G on goods and services without considering taxation and transfer payments by it. In fact the concept of consumption function conceives consumption as a function of disposable income and is therefore written as

$$C = a + bY_D \qquad \text{. . . (1)}$$

Now, disposable income Y_D is obtained from deducting tax and adding transfer payments by the government. Thus

$$Y_D = Y - T + R$$

where T is tax revenue and R is the transfer payments by the government. Whereas a tax reduces disposable income, transfer payment raises it.

Further, whereas transfer payments are assumed as lump sum amount, tax can be lump sum tax or levied as proportion of income. If we assume proportionate income tax, then,

$$T = tY$$

where t is the proportion of income which is taken away by way of tax. . . . (2)

Let us derive *IS* equation incorporating proportionate income tax and lump sum transfer payments.

$$Y = AD = C + I + G + NX$$

$$Y = a + bY_D + I + G + NX$$

$$= a + b\,(Y - tY + R) + \bar{I} - di + G + NX$$

$$= a + bY - btY + bR + \bar{I} - di + G + NX$$

$$= a + b\,(1 - t)Y + bR + \bar{I} - di + G + NX$$

$$Y = \bar{A} + b(1 - t)Y - di \qquad \text{. . .(3)}$$

where $\bar{A} = a + bR + \bar{I} + G + NX$

Rearranging equation (3) we have

$$Y = b(1 - t)\,Y = \bar{A} - di$$

or $Y/1 - b(1 - t) = \bar{A} - di$

$$Y = \frac{1}{1-b(1-t)}(\bar{A} - di) \qquad \text{. . . (4)}$$

where $\frac{1}{1-b(1-t)}$ is the value of multiplier in case of proportionate income tax. Equation (4) represents *IS* curve in case of proportionate income tax.

It may be noted in the context of *IS* equations (3) and (4) that a change in autonomous spending ($\bar{A}$) as a result of any of its components will cause *a shift* in *IS* curve.

NUMERICAL PROBLEMS ON THE *IS* CURVE : THREE SECTOR MODEL (With Taxation)

Problem 1. *The following equations describe an economy*

$$C = 100 + 0.75\,Y_d$$

$$I = 50 - 25i$$

$$T = G = 50$$

where C is aggregate consumption, Y_d is disposable income, I is aggregate investment, T is taxes, G is government purchases and i is the interest rate. Derive the *IS* curve for the economy.

Solution. $Y = C + I + G$

Now, $C = 100 + 0.75\, Y_d = 100 + 0.75\, (Y - T)$

$$C = 100 + 0.75\, (Y - 50)$$

$$I = 50 - 25\, i$$

$$G = 50$$

$$T = 50$$

$$Y = 100 + 0.75\, (Y - 50) + 50 - 25i + 50$$

$$Y = 200 + 0.75\, Y - 0.75 \times 50 - 25i$$

$$Y - 0.75Y = 200 - 37.5 - 25i$$

$$Y\,(1 - 0.75) = 162.5 - 25i$$

$$\frac{1}{4}Y = 162.5 - 25i$$

$$Y = 650 - 100\, i$$

IS equation is : $Y = 650 - 100\, i$

DERIVATION OF EQUATION FOR *LM* CURVE : ALGEBRAIC ANALYSIS

Having derived algebraically equation for *IS* curve we now turn to the derivation of equation for *LM* curve. It will be recalled that *LM* curve is a curve that shows combinations of interest rates and levels of income at which money market is in equilibrium, that is, at which demand for money equals supply of money. We explain the derivation of *LM* curve in two steps. First, we show how money demand depends on interest rate and level of income. It is worth noting that in their demand for money people care more about the purchasing power of money, that is, people's demand is for *real money balances* rather than nominal money balances. Real money balances are given by $\frac{M}{P}$ where M stands for nominal money demand and P for price level.

The demand for real money balances depends on the level of real income and interest rate. Thus $M_d = L(Y, i)$. As explained earlier, demand for real money balances increases with the rise in level of income and decreases with rise in rate of interest. Let us assume that money demand function is linear. Then

$$L(Y, i) = kY - hi \qquad k,\ h > 0 \qquad \ldots (5)$$

Parameter k represents how much demand for real money balances increases when level of income rises. Parameter h represents how much demand for real money balances decreases when rate of interest rises. The equilibrium in the money market is established where demand for real money balances equals supply of real money balances and is given by

$$\frac{M}{P} = kY - hi \qquad \ldots (6)$$

Money supply (M) is set by the central bank of a country and we assume it to remain constant for a period. Besides, we assume the price level (P) to remain constant.

Solving the equation (6) for interest rate we have

$$i = \frac{1}{h}\left(kY - \frac{M}{P}\right) \qquad \ldots (7)$$

The above equation (7) describes the equation for *LM* curve. To be precise it gives us the equilibrium interest rate for any given value of level of income (*Y*) and real money balances. In drawing *LM* curve, real money balances are assumed to be constant. Thus *LM* curve describes money market equilibrium for different values of income and rate of interest, given a fixed value of real money balances $\left(\frac{M}{P}\right)$. Thus, given the real money balances $\left(\frac{M}{P}\right)$, we can obtain a rate of interest for different values of income.

Let us state some conclusions about *LM* curve as given by equation (7). First, since in equation (7) for *LM* curve, the coefficient (*k*) of income (*Y*) is positive, *LM* curve will slope upward. That is, higher income requires higher interest rate for money market to be in equilibrium, given the supply of real money balances. Second, since the coefficient of real money balances is negative, the expansion in real money balances will cause a shift in the *LM* curve to be right, and decrease in the real money balances will shift *LM* curve to the left.

From the coefficient of income *k*/*h*, we can know whether *LM* curve is steep or flat. If demand for money is not much sensitive to level of income, then *k* will be small. Therefore, in case of small *k* (*i.e.* low sensitivity of interest with respect to changes in income), small change in interest rate is required to offset a small increase in money demand caused by a given *increase in income*.

NUMERICAL PROBLEMS

Problem 1. *Given the following data about the monetary sector of the economy :*

$$M_d = 0.4Y - 80\,i$$
$$M_s = 1200 \text{ crores.}$$

where M_d is demand for money, Y is level of income, i is rate of interest and M_s is the supply of money

1. *Derive the equation for LM function*
2. *Give the economic interpretation of the LM curve. Draw LM curve from the above data*

Solution.

For money market to be in equilibrium

$$M_d = M_s$$
$$0.4\,Y - 80\,i = 1200$$
$$80\,i = 0.4\,Y - 1200$$
$$i = \frac{0.4Y}{80} - \frac{1200}{80}$$
$$i = \frac{1}{200}Y - 15$$

Thus we get the following *LM* function :

$$i = \frac{1}{200}Y - 15 \qquad \ldots (i)$$

Alternatively, *LM* equation or function can also be stated as :

$$Y = 200\,i + 3000 \qquad \ldots (ii)$$

LM curve means what would be rate of interest when money market is in equilibrium, given the level of income. Thus, if level of national income is ₹ 4000 crores, then using *LM* equation (*i*) we have

$$i = \frac{1}{200} \times 4000 - 15$$

$$= 20 - 15 = 5\%$$

Thus, at income of ₹ 4000 crores, rate of interest will be 5 per cent when money market is in equilibrium.

Now, if level of income is ₹ 4400 crores, equilibrium rate of interest will be

$$i = \frac{1}{200} Y - 15$$

$$= \frac{1}{200} \times 4400 - 15$$

$$= 22 - 15 = 7\%$$

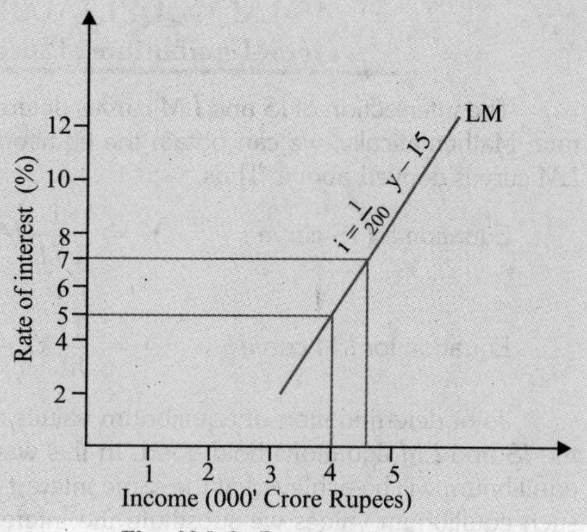

Fig. 43A.2. *Drawing LM Curve*

With two combinations of interest rate and income level when money market is in equilibrium we can draw *LM* curve as shown in 43A.2.

Problem 2. *The following data is given for the monetary sector of the economy.*

Transaction demand for money, $M_t = 0.5Y$. Speculative demand for money, $M_{sp} = 105 - 1500\, i$

Money supply $M_s = 150$

Derive LM equation from the above data

Solution. Total demand function for money can be obtained by adding up the transactions demand for money (M_t) and speculative demand for money (M_{sp}). Thus

$$M_d = M_t + M_{sp}$$

$$M_d = 0.5Y + 105 - 1500\, i$$

In money market equilibrium

$$M_d = M_s$$

$$0.5Y + 105 - 1500i = 150$$

$$1500\, i = 0.5Y + 105 - 150$$

$$i = \frac{0.5Y}{1500} - \frac{45}{1500}$$

$$= \frac{1}{3000} Y - \frac{3}{100}$$

Thus, *LM* equation is :

$$i = \frac{1}{3000} Y - \frac{3}{100}$$

Alternatively, *LM* equation can be written as

$$Y = 3000i + \frac{3}{100} \times 3000$$

$$Y = 3000\, i + 90$$

IS-LM MODEL : ALGEBRAIC ANALYSIS (Joint Equilibrium of Income and Interest Rate)

The intersection of *IS* and *LM* curves determines joint equilibrium of income and interest rate. Mathematically, we can obtain the equilibrium values by using the equations of *IS* and *LM* curves derived above. Thus,

Equation for *IS* curve : $$Y = \frac{1}{1-b}(\bar{A} - di) \qquad \ldots (i)$$

Equation for *LM* curve : $$i = \frac{1}{h}\left(kY - \frac{M}{p}\right) \qquad \ldots (ii)$$

Joint determination of equilibrium values of income and interest rate requires that both the *IS* and *LM* equations hold good. In this way both the goods market and money market equilibrium will be achieved at the same interest and income levels in the two markets. To find such equilibrium values we substitute the interest rate from the *LM* equation (*ii*) into the *IS* equation (*i*). Doing so we have

$$Y = \frac{1}{1-b}\left[\bar{A} - \frac{d}{h}\left(kY - \frac{M}{P}\right)\right]$$

$$Y = \frac{1}{1-b}\left[\bar{A} - \frac{d}{h}(kY) + \frac{d}{h}\left(\frac{M}{P}\right)\right] \qquad \ldots (iii)$$

The equation shows that the equilibrium level of income depends on exogenously given autonomous variables ($\bar{A}$) such as automous consumption, autonomous investment, government expenditure on goods and services, and the real money supply $\left(\frac{M}{P}\right)$ and further on the size of multiplier $\left(\frac{1}{1-b}\right)$. It will be noticed from equation (*iii*) that higher the autonomous expenditure, the higher the level of equilibrium income. Further, the greater the real money supply, the higher the level of national income.

NUMERICAL PROBLEMS ON IS-LM MODEL

Problem – 1. *For an economy the following functions are given :*

$$C = 100 + 0.8\,y$$
$$S = -100 + 0.2\,y$$
$$I = 120 - 5\,i$$
$$M^s = 120$$
$$M^d = 0.2y - 5i$$

Find out (1) IS equation, (2) LM equation, (3) equilibrium level of income and interest rate

Solution.

IS curve : $$Y = \left[\frac{1}{1-b}(a + \bar{I}) - di\right]$$

where $b = MPC$, a and $\bar{I}$ are autonomous consumption and autonomous investment respectively, d is sensitivity of investment demand to changes in rate of interest (i).

Substituting the values of various parameters we have

$$Y = \frac{1}{1-0.8}[(100+120)-5i]$$

$$= \frac{1}{0.2}=(220-5i)$$

$$Y = 5(220-5i)$$

$$Y = 1100-25i$$

Thus *IS* curve is :

$$Y = 1100-25i \qquad \ldots \text{(i)}$$

Derivation of *LM* Equation :

For money market equilibrium

$$M^d = M^s$$

$$0.2Y-5i = 120$$

$$5i = 0.2Y-120$$

$$i = \frac{0.2}{5}Y-24$$

LM curve is :

$$i = \frac{0.2}{5}Y-24 \qquad \ldots \text{(ii)}$$

Substituting the value of *i* in the *IS* equation (*i*) we have

$$Y = 1000-25\left(\frac{0.2}{5}Y-24\right)$$

$$= 1100-(1Y-600)$$

$$Y = 1100-Y+600$$

$$2Y = 1700$$

$$Y = \frac{1700}{2} = 850$$

Thus the equilibrium level of income is 850. To obtain the equilibrium rate of interest we substitute the value of *Y* in *LM* equation (*iii*) obtained above we have

$$i = \frac{0.2}{5}(850)-24$$

$$= \frac{1}{25}(850)-24$$

$$= 34-24 = 10$$

Thus equilibrium rate of interest is 10 per cent.

Problem 2. *Consider the following economy :*

$$C = 100\ 0.8\,Y_d$$

$$I = 50-25i$$

$$G = T = 50$$

$$\frac{M^s}{P} = 200$$

$$M^d = Y - 25\,i$$

1. *Derive the equation for IS and LM curves.*
2. *Calculate the equilibrium levels of output and interest.*

Solution :

$$Y = C + I + G$$

Substituting the values of C, *I* and G we have

$$Y = 100 + 0.8\,Y_d + 50 - 25\,i + 50$$
$$Y = 100 + 0.8\,(Y\text{–}T) + 50 - 25i + 50$$

or
$$Y = 100 + 0.8\,(Y\text{–}50) + 50 - 25\,i + 50$$
$$Y = 200 + 0.8Y - 40 - 25\,i$$
$$= 160 + 0.8Y - 25i$$
$$(Y - 0.8Y) = 160 - 25\,i$$
$$Y\,(1\text{–}0.8) = 160 - 25\,i$$
$$0.2Y = 160 - 25\,i$$
$$Y = 800 - 125\,i$$

IS curve is :
$$Y = 800 - 125\,i \quad \ldots (i)$$

Money Market Equilibrium : Money market is in equilibrium when $M^d = \dfrac{M^s}{P}$

Thus, in equilibrium

$$M^d = \frac{M^S}{P}$$
$$Y = 25\,i = 200$$
$$Y = 200 + 25\,i$$

Thus, *LM* curve is :
$$Y = 200 + 25\,i \quad \ldots (iii)$$

Since in equilibrium *IS* and *LM* curves intersect (or *IS* = *LM*) we have

$$200 + 25i = 800 - 125i$$
$$150\,i = 800 - 200 = 600$$
$$i = \frac{600}{150} = 4$$

Thus equilibrium rate of interest is 4%

Substituting the value of *i* in *IS* equation (*i*) we have :

$$Y = 800 - 125 \times 4$$
$$= 800 - 400 = 400$$

Thus, the equilibrium rate of interest is 4 per cent and equilibrium level of income is 200

Problem 3. *Consider an economy with the following features*

Consumption, $C = 100 + 0.9\,Y_d$

Income tax, $t = \dfrac{1}{3}Y$

Investment, $I = 600 - 30\,i$

Government expenditure, $G = 300$

Transaction demand money for $M_d = 0.4Y$

Speculative demand for money, $M_2 = -50\,i$

Nominal money supply $\overline{M} = 1040$

Price level = 2

(where Y_d *stands for disposable income, and i for rate of interest)*

Derive the IS and LM equations and fund out the equilibrium levels of income and rate of interest.

Solution :

(i) Obtaining *IS* equation :

$$Y = C + I + G$$
$$= 100 + 0.9\,Y_d + 600 - 30i + 100$$
$$= 100 + 0.9\left(Y - \frac{1}{3}Y\right) + 600 - 30i + 300$$
$$= 1000 + 0.9y - 0.3y - 30\,i$$
$$Y - 0.9y + 0.3Y = 1000 - 30\,i$$
$$Y(1 - 0.9 + 0.3) = 1000 - 30\,i$$
$$0.4Y = 1000 - 30\,i$$
$$Y = 1000 \times \frac{10}{4} - \left(30 \times \frac{10}{4}\right)i$$
$$= 2500 - 75i$$

Thus *IS* equation is : $Y = 2500 - 75\,i$ . . . (i)

(*i*) Obtaining *LM* equation :

For money market equilibrium :

$$M^d = M^S$$
$$M^d = M_1 + M_2$$
$$= 0.4y - 50i$$

Real money supply, $M^S = \dfrac{\bar{M}}{P} = \dfrac{1040}{2} = 520$

Therefore, $0.4Y - 50i = 520$

$$0.4Y = 520 + 50i$$
$$Y = 520 \times \frac{10}{4} + (50 \times \frac{10}{4})i$$
$$= 1300 + 125i$$

LM function is : $1300 + 125i$

In equilibrium $IS = LM$

$$2500 - 75\,i = 1300 + 125\,i \quad \text{. . . (ii)}$$
$$125i + 75i = 2500 - 1300$$
$$200i = 1200$$

Therefore, interest, $i = \dfrac{1200}{200} = 6\%$

Substituting the value of $i = 6$ in *IS* equation we have

$$Y = 2500 - 75 \times 6$$
$$= 2500 - 450$$
$$= 2050$$

Thus, equilibrium income is 2050 and equilibrium interest is 6 %.

Problem 4. (Four Sector Model) : *The major macro aggregates for an economy are given as follows :*

Consumption, $C = 60 + 0.8Y_d$ (Y_d *is disposable income)*

Investment $I = 100 - 5i$

% Interest rate $i = 6$

Government expenditure, $G = 76$

Lump-sum Tax, $T = 15$

Transfer payments, $TR = 60$

Exports $X = 70$

Imports $M = 12 + 0.2Y$

1. *Derive the IS curve using the above data*
2. *Calculate equilibrium level of income*
3. *Calculate foreign trade multiplier*

Solution :

$$Y = C + I + G + X - M \qquad \text{. . . (i)}$$

and $$Y_d = Y - T + TR$$

Substituting the values of variables in equation (i) we have

$$Y = 60 + 0.8\,(Y - 15 + 60) + 100 - 5i + 76 + 70 - (12 + 0.2Y)$$

$$= 60 + 0.8Y + 0.8 \text{X} 45 + 100 + 76 + 70 - 12 - 0.2Y - 5i$$

$$Y - 0.8Y + 0.2Y = (60 + 36 + 100 + 76 + 58) - 5i$$

$$Y\,(1 - 0.8 + 0.2)\,Y = 330 - 5\,i$$

$$0.4Y = 330 - 5i$$

or $$\frac{2}{5}Y = 330 - 5i$$

$$Y = 330 \times \frac{5}{2} - \frac{5}{2} \times 5i$$

$$Y = 825 - 12.5\,i$$

(*i*) Equation for *IS* curve is : $Y = 825 - 12.5\,i$

(*ii*) Equilibrium level of income when rate of interest is 6 per cent

$$Y = 825 - 12.5 \times 6$$

$$= 825 - 75 = 750$$

(*iii*) Foreign trade multiplier $\dfrac{1}{1 - b + m}$

where $b = MPC = 0.8$

m = marginal profensity to import = 0.2

Thus, foreign trade multiplier $\dfrac{1}{1 - 0.8 + 0.2} = \dfrac{1}{0.4} = \dfrac{5}{2} = 2.5$

Problem 5. *The follow data are given for an an economy*

Consumption : $C = 40 + 0.75y$

Investment : $I = 140 - 10i$

Government expenditure : $G = 100$

Lump sum tax $T = 80$

Money demand, $M^d = 0.2\,Y - 5i$

Money supply, $M^S = 85$

(i. is % interest rate; other figures in ₹ crores)

(a) *Find out the equilibrium income, Y and interest rate i*

(b) *Suppose the government increases its expenditure on education and health services by ₹ 65 crores what would be its effect on equilibrium income and rate of interest ?*

Solution. In order to obtain equilibrium income, we have to find out first the equations for *IS* and *LM* curves.

$$Y = C + I + G$$

where $C = 40 + 0.75\,Y_d$ and $I = 140 - 10\,i$ and $G = 100$

Therefore,

$$\begin{aligned} Y &= 40 + 0.75\,Y_d + 140 - 10\,i + 100 \\ &= 40 + 0.75\,(Y - 80) + 140 - 10\,i + 100 \\ &= 40 + 0.75Y - 60 + 140 - 10\,i + 100 \\ Y - 0.75\,Y &= 220 - 10\,i \\ 0.25\,Y &= 220 - 10\,i \\ \frac{1}{4}Y &= 220 - 10\,i \\ Y &= 880 - 40\,i \end{aligned}$$

Thus *IS* equation : $Y = 880 - 40i$ . . . (*i*)

To obtain *LM* function, we equate demand for money with supply of money.

$$\begin{aligned} M^d &= M^S \\ 0.2Y - 5i &= 85 \\ 5i &= 0.2Y - 85 \\ i &= \frac{0.2}{5}Y - 17 \end{aligned}$$

Thus, *LM* function is

$$i = 0.04\,Y - 17 \quad \text{. . . (ii)}$$

Substituting the value of *i* in the *IS* function equation (*i*) we have

$$\begin{aligned} Y &= 880 - 40\,(0.04\,Y - 17) \\ &= 880 - 1.6Y + 680 \\ Y + 1.6Y &= 880 + 680 \\ 2.6Y &= 1560 \\ Y &= 1560 \times \frac{10}{26} = 600 \end{aligned}$$

Thus, equilibrium level of national income is 600 crores

Substituting the value of 600 for *Y* in *IS* equation (i) we have

$$\begin{aligned} 600 &= 880 - 40\,i \\ 40\,i &= 880 - 600 = 280 \\ i &= \frac{280}{40} = 7 \end{aligned}$$

The equilibrium rate of interest is 7 per cent.

(*b*) With the increase in Government expenditure by ₹ 65 crores

New Income, $Y' = C + I + G + \Delta G$

$$Y' = 40 + 0.75\,(Y'-80) + 140 - 10\,i + 100 + 65$$

$$= 40 + 0.75Y' - 60 + 140 - 10\,i + 100 + 65$$

$$Y' - 0.75\,Y' = 285 - 10\,i$$

$$Y'(1-0.75) = 285 - 10\,i$$

$$\frac{1}{4}Y' = 285 - 10i$$

$$Y' = 1140 - 40i$$

New equation for *IS* curve is = $Y' = 1140 - 40i$

Substituting the value of *i* from *LM* function equation (*ii*) we have

$$Y' = 1140 - 40(0.04\,Y' - 17)$$

$$Y' = 1140 - 1.6Y' + 680$$

$$Y' + 1.6Y' = 1820$$

$$Y'(1 + 1.6) = 1820$$

$$2.6Y' = 1820$$

$$Y' = 1820 \times \frac{10}{26} = 700$$

Now, substituting the value of *Y* in the *LM* equation (*ii*) we have

New interest $i = 0.04\,(700) - 17$

$= 28.00 - 17 = 11 = 11$

Thus, the new equilibrium income is 700 crores and interest rate is 11 per cent

---

* The students can check this with the general equation for *IS* curve, that is, $Y = \frac{1}{1-b+m}(\bar{A} - di)$ where A is the sum of automous factors, that is, $\bar{A} = a + bTR - bT + \bar{I} + \bar{G} + \bar{X} - \bar{M}$ and $\frac{1}{1-b+m}$ is foreign trade multiplier

Aggregate Demand and Aggregate Supply: Flexible Prices Model

Introduction to AD-AS Flexible Price Model

Keynes in his theory of income and employment assumed that price level remained constant. As explained in the previous chapters Keynes in his macroeconomic analysis used these concepts which related aggregate demand and supply to the levels of national income. Concerned as he was with the problem of an economy under the grip of depression characterised by demand deficiency and excess capacity in the economy he assumed the price level to remain constant.

On the other hand, classical economists thought national output or income was determined by real factors such as capital stock, state of technology, labour supply and in no way affected by the general price level which was determined by the quantity of money. This classical doctrine is generally referred to as **classical dichotomy**. The *AD-AS* model with flexible price level highlights the breakdown of **classical dichotomy** as it explains how real national income and price level are jointly determined in *AD-AS* model with flexible prices. The aggregate demand and aggregates supply model with flexible price level, which is generally referred to as *AD-AS* model, is used to explain fluctuations in aggregate output, price level and rate of inflation in the economy.

In what follows we explain the concepts of aggregate demand and aggregate supply with flexible price level and analyse how the interaction between the two determines jointly aggregate output (*i.e.* real GDP) and general price level.

Aggregate Demand (AD)

Let us first explain aggregate demand. ***Aggregate demand** is the total desired quantity of goods and services that are bought by consumer households, private investors, government and foreigners at each possible price level, other things being held constant.* Thus aggregate demand is not any quantity demanded at a particular price level but is a whole schedule of total output demanded at various price levels and is represented by a curve. The aggregate demand has four components: consumption demand, private investment demand, Government purchases of goods and services and net exports. *Thus, aggregate demand curve depicts the total output of goods and services which households, firms, and Government are willing to buy at each possible price level.*

Thus aggregate demand curve shows the relationship between the total quantity demanded of goods and services and general price level. It is worth noting that aggregate demand curve (*AD*) differs from the ordinary demand curve of an individual commodity with which we are concerned in microeconomics though both slope downward to the light. In case of a demand curve of an individual commodity when price of a commodity rises, it will tend to be substituted by other commodities which are its close substitutes resulting in fall in the quantity demanded of the commodity at a higher price. Thus, the slope of demand curve of an individual commodity depends mainly on the possibility of substitution between the commodities. On the other hand, as we shall see below, the slope of aggregate demand curve depends on factors totally different from those that cause demand curve of an individual commodity to slope downward. We have drawn an *AD* curve in Figure 43A.1 where on the horizontal axis we measure level of aggregate output and on the vertical axis we measure the ge neral price level. As will be seen from Figure 43A.1 aggregate demand curve *AD* slopes downward to the right.

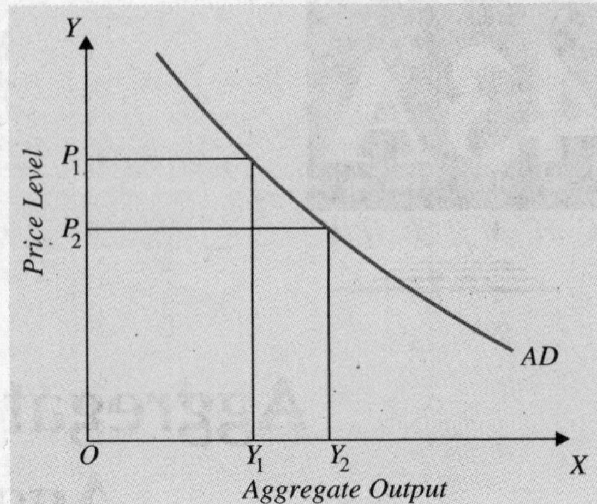

Fig. 43A.1. *Aggregate Demand Curve with Varying Price Level*

It is important to note that the *AD-AS* model with flexible price level is unlike that of market demand-supply model of microeconomic theory. When we consider demand and supply in a particular market, say for cotton cloth, rise in its price will cause increase in its quantity supplied but in doing so resources will be withdrawn from other goods. Such reallocation of resources between products and consequently rise in output of one product and fall in that of the other is not considered in macroeconomics where we are concerned with determination of aggregate output, total employment of resources in the economy as a whole. Similarly, in macroecnomic model of aggregate demand and aggregate supply we study the determination of general price level and does not explain the relative prices of various products.

In what follows we will explain in detail the concepts of aggregate demand (*AD*) and aggregate supply (*AS*) curves *with flexible prices* and their likely shape and factors determining them. We will also explain less than full-employment equilibrium and problem of stagflation with this Keynesian Flexible Prices *AD-AS* model.

Why does Aggregate Demand Curve Slope Downward?

Like the demand curve of an individual commodity aggregate demand curve showing graphically the relationship between total spending and price level slopes downward to the right. This means that at higher price levels, the total spending or quantity of aggregate output purchased or demanded is less and at lower price level the total spending or total purchases of aggregate output of goods is greater.

This is depicted in Figure 43A.1. Aggregate output demanded per period of time is measured along the X-axis, and the general price level along the Y-axis. It should be carefully understood why aggregate demand for output or total spending falls at higher aggregate price level and increases at lower price levels, or, in other words, why aggregate demand (*AD*) curve slopes downward. The following factors are responsible for this.

Real Balance Effect. First, the changes in the general price level affect the real value or *purchasing power of money balances and monetary assets* with fixed nominal values (such as bank deposits, bonds, etc.) held by the people. With the rise in the general price level, the real value of these monetary assets will fall making people feel poorer than before. This induces them to consume less and therefore lead to the decline in quantity of output purchased by them. Conversely, if the price level falls, the real value of their monetary assets increases inducing them to buy more. This is called *real balance effect* of the change in the price level.

Rate of Interest Effect. Secondly, another important reason for the downward sloping nature of aggregate demand curve is *the effect of change in general price level on the rate of interest and through it on investment demand.* At a higher price level, the people will require more money for conducting a given amount of transactions. This will lead to the increase in the demand for money for making transactions. Given the money supply, the increase in demand for money will cause the rate of interest to go up. At a higher rate of interest, demand for investment in new capital goods (*i.e.* plant, machinery and equipment) will decrease. On the contrary, if aggregate price level falls, demand for money for transaction purposes will decline and, the money supply being given, this will lead to the fall in the rate of interest. At the lower rate of interest, investment demand will increase. To conclude, *the investment demand and the general price level are also inversely related.*

Foreign Trade Effect. Thirdly, changes in the price level also causes a change in *foreign demand for goods*. This is called *foreign trade effect of the change in price level.* If a general price level in India falls, its exports will become cheaper leading to their increase. On the other hand, the lower price level in India will induce India people to buy India goods instead of imported ones. Thus, fall in general price level in India will lead to more exports and lesser imports causing expansion in aggregate demand for Indian goods. On the contrary, a rise in price level in India will lead to decline in its exports (*i.e.* foreign demand for Indian goods) and increase in its imports. Thus, rise in price level, that is, inflation will cause a decline in net exports.

To sum up, the quantity of aggregate demand for consumption, investment and net exports increases with a fall in the price level and declines with a rise in the price level. This means that aggregate demand curve showing relationship between aggregate output demanded and the general price level slopes downward to the right as is shown in Figure 43A.1.

DERIVING AGGREGATE DEMAND CURVE WITH IS-LM MODEL

In a previous chapter we have used Keynesian IS-LM model as propounded by Hicks and Hansen to explain how national income and rate of interest are determined, treating price level as fixed. We can now use IS-LM model to derive aggregate demand curve with variable price level. It is this aggregate demand curve with variable price level that with intersection of aggregate supply curve determines the level of national income and the general price level. In the *AS-AD* model, aggregate demand curve describes the relationship between the price level and aggregate output demanded. Note that the in macroeconomic equilibrium the aggregate effective demand for output equals national income or *GDP*. Viewed in this way aggregate demand curve shows the relationship between the price level and the level of national income. As seen before, this aggregate demand curve with variable price level slopes downward to the right. How this is derived from IS-LM model is depicted in Fig. 43A.2.

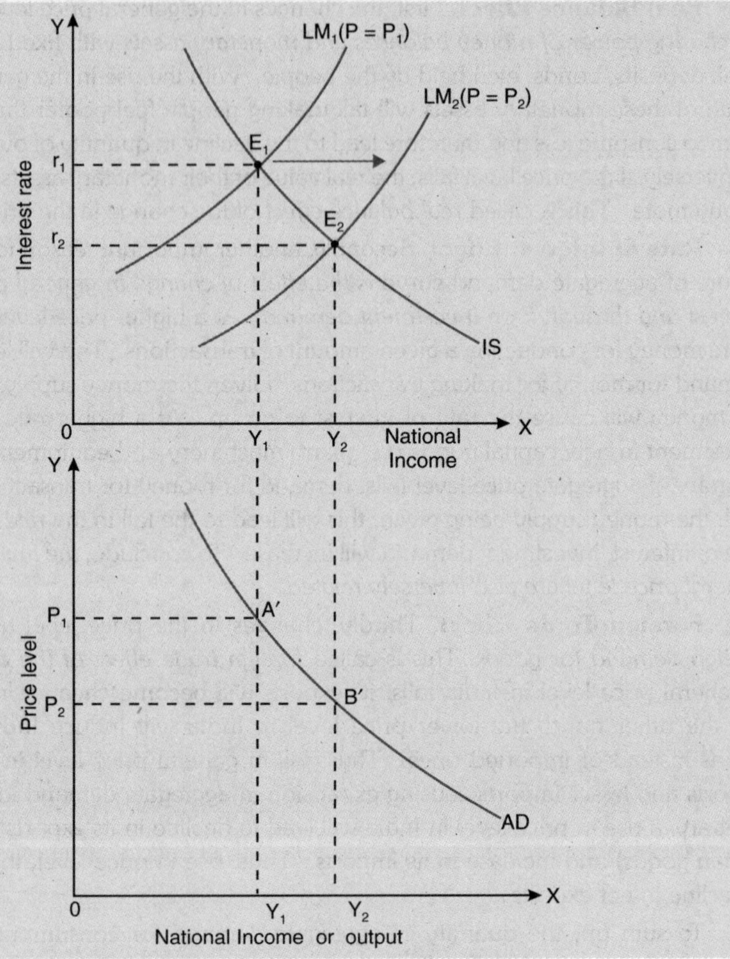

Fig. 43A.2. *Deriving Aggregate Demand Curve with IS-LM Model*

For any given money supply when price level falls the supply of *real money balances* increases. The increase in real money balances causes a shift in the *LM* curve to the right as shown in the upper panel of Fig. 43A.2. With price level equal to P_1, LM_1 is the *LM* curve and its intersection with the given *IS* curve determines Y_1 level of national income or output. With the fall in price level to P_2 ($P_2 < P_1$), *LM* curve shifts to the right to LM_2 position and its intersection with the given *IS* curve determines Y_2 level of national income or output. Thus, with this rightward shift in the *LM* curve from LM_1 to LM_2 as a result of fall in price level, equilibrium national income (output) which was Y_1 with LM_1 curve with price level equal to P_1 has risen to Y_2 with LM_2 curve at a lower price level P_2. Accordingly, in the panel at the bottom of Fig. 43A.2 we have plotted national income or output level Y_1 against price level P_1 and higher national output level Y_2 against the lower level P_2. With this we get the downward-sloping aggregate demand curve *AD*. Note that along with this aggregate demand curve *AD* both goods market and money market are in equilibrium as it has been derived from IS-LM model.

Factors Causing Shift in Aggregate Demand Curve

Now, what will bring about a shift in the aggregate demand curve. This can also be known from the results of *IS-LM* model. The factors which cause a shift in either *IS* or *LM* curve (with a given price level) will bring about a shift in the aggregate demand curve. As we know changes in money supply or government expenditure or taxes bring about a change in the short-run macroeconomic equilibrium as explained by *IS-LM* model, they will also shift the aggregate demand curve. This is shown in Fig. 43A.3.

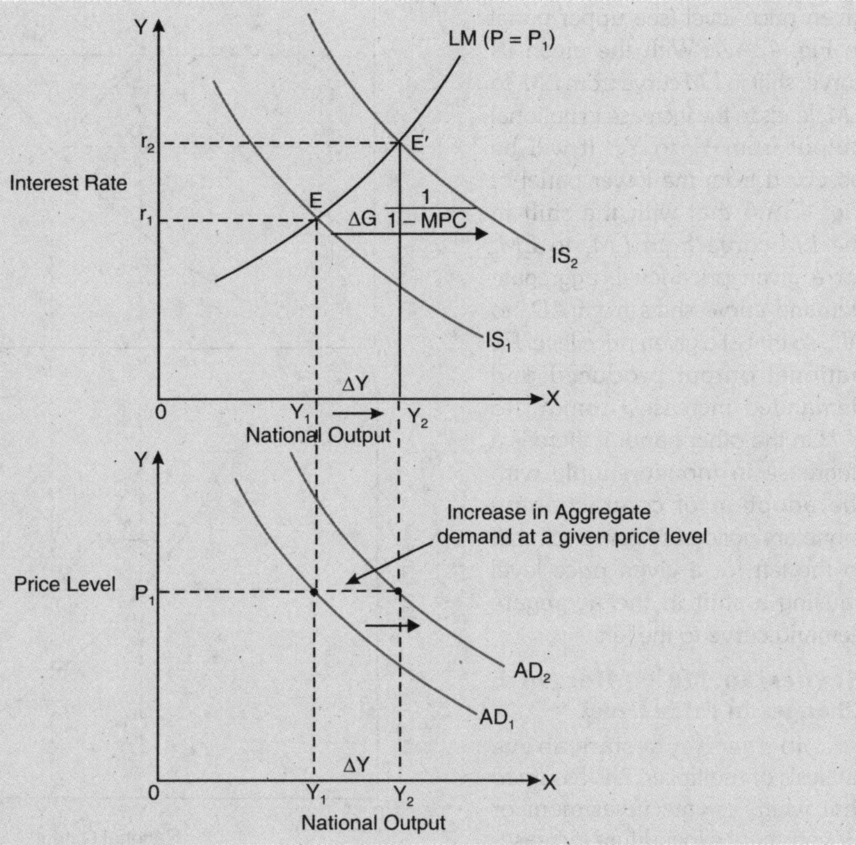

Fig. 43A.3. *Shift in Aggregate demand Curve due to Increase in Government Expenditure*

For example, expansionary fiscal policy which involves increase in government expenditure or reduction in taxes will cause a shift in the *IS* curve to the right in the *IS-LM* model for a given price level. This expansionary fiscal policy will cause increase in the national income (output) at a given price level and therefore lead to a shift in the aggregate demand curve to the right as shown in the lower panel of Fig. 43A.3. It may however be noted that increase in national income or output (i.e., ΔY) will not be equal to the increase in government expenditure times the multiplier, that is $\Delta G \bar{X} \dfrac{1}{1 - MPC}$ but, as will be seen from the upper part of Fig. 43A.3, increase in income (ΔY) is less than this. This is because with the shift in the *IS* curve to the right its new equilibrium with the given *LM* curve is reached at a lower level of national income or output. Similarly, if there is a *decrease* in government expenditure or increase in taxes, this will cause a shift in the *IS* curve to the left at a given price level in the *IS-LM* model and will lead to the decrease in national income or output for a given price level. As a result, aggregate demand curve will shift to the left.

Changes in Money Supply and Shift in Aggregate Demand Curve

Changes in money supply in the IS-LM model affects national income or output by causing shifts the *LM* curve for a given price level. For example, when Central Bank of a country adopts an expansionary monetary policy and accordingly there is increase in money supply, LM curve shifts to the right from LM_1 to LM_2 for a given price level (see upper panel in Fig. 43A.4. With the given IS curve, shift in LM curve from LM_1 to LM_2 leads to the increase in national output from Y_1 to Y_2. It will be observed from the lower panel of Fig. 43A.4 that with the shift in the LM curve from LM_1 to LM_2 for a given price level, aggregate demand curve shifts from AD_1 to AD_2 so that at a given price level P_1, national output produced and demanded increases from Y_1 to Y_2. On the other hand, if there is a decrease in money supply with the adoption of contractionary monetary policy, LM curve will shift to the left for a given price level causing a shift in the aggregate demand curve to the left.

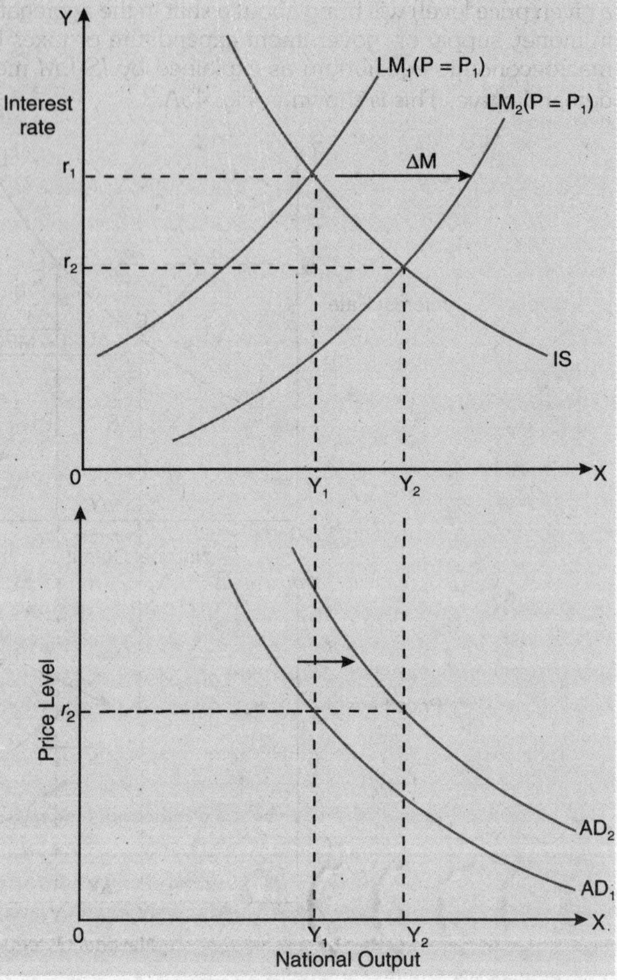

Figure 43A.4. *Shift in Aggregate Demand Curve due to Expansion in Money Supply*

Keynesian Multiplier with Changes in Price Level

In the Keynesian above analysis of multiplier, it is assumed that when private investment or Government expenditure increases price level remains constant and the firms are willing to supply more output at a given price. How much national income or GNP increases as a result of any autonomous expenditure such as government expenditure, investment expenditure, net exports is determined by a shift in aggregate demand curve by the size of simple Keynesian multiplier when price level is fixed. This implies a horizontal short-run supply curve. However, as studied above, short-run aggregate supply curve slopes upward as the firms are willing to supply additional output in the short run only at a higher price level. With short-run aggregate supply curve sloping upward, a rightward shift in aggregate demand curve raises new equilibrium GNP level not equal to the horizontal shift in the aggregate demand curve but less than it. Consequently, the size of multiplier in case of flexible price level is smaller than that of simple Keynesian multiplier with a given fixed price level. This is because a part of expansionary effect on GNP of the increase in autonomous government expenditure is offset by rise in the price level.

The multiplier effect in case of upward-sloping short-run aggregate supply curve is shown in Fig. 43A.5. To begin with, in the top panel of Fig. 43A.5 aggregate expenditure curve AE_0 intersects 45° line at point B and determines Y_0 equilibrium level of GNP. In the panel at the bottom of Fig. 43A.5 the corresponding aggregate demand curve AD_0 and the short-run

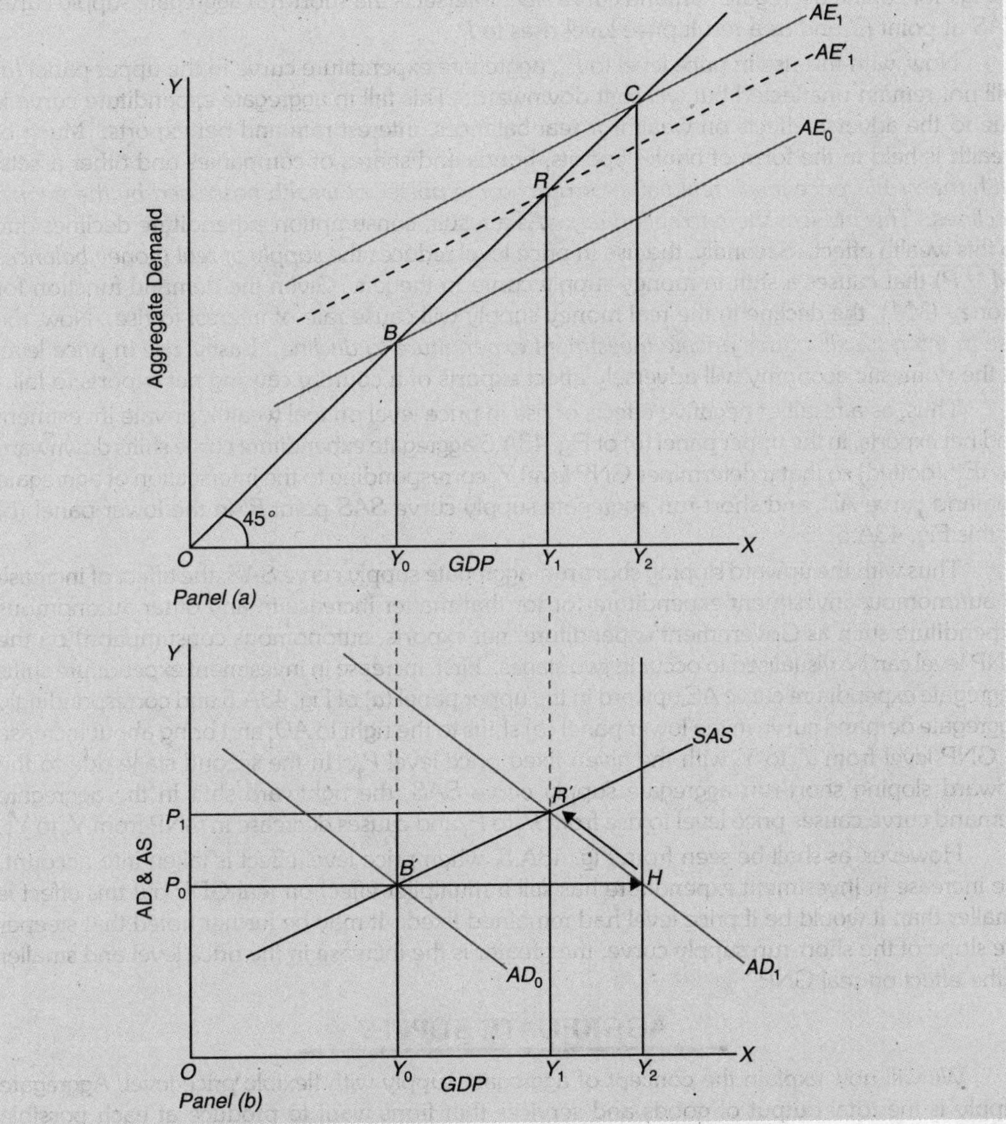

Fig. 43A.5. *Multipler Effect with Changes in Price Level*

aggregate supply curve *SAS* to intersect at *B′* at the above determined GNP level Y_0. Now suppose autonomous investment expenditure (which is independent of changes in price level) increases by ΔI. As a result, aggregate expenditure curve *AE* shifts upward to AE_1 and determines new equilibrium GNP level equal to Y_2. In the lower panel (*b*), due to the upward shift in aggregate expenditure curve, aggregate demand curve shifts rightward from AD_0 to AD_1. The horizontal shift in the aggregate demand curve *at a given price level* is determined by the increase in investment expenditure multiplied by the simple Keynesian multiplier (*B′H* or

$Y_0Y_1 = \Delta I \dfrac{1}{1-MPC}$)

But given the upward-sloping short-un aggregate supply curve *SAS* with new aggregate demand curve AD_1, price level does not remain fixed. As will be seen from the lower panel (*b*)

of Fig. 43A.5, the aggregate demand curve AD_1, intersects the short-run aggregate supply curve *SAS* at point *R′* and as a result price level rises to P_1.

Now, with this rise in price level to P_1, aggregate expenditure curve in the upper panel (*a*) will not remain unaffected but will shift downward. This fall in aggregate expenditure curve is due to the adverse effects on wealth or real balances, interest rate and net exports. Much of wealth is held in the form of bank deposits, bonds and shares of companies and other assets. *With the rise in price level, real value or purchasing power of wealth possessed by the people declines. This induces them to spend less.* As a result, consumption expenditure declines due to this wealth effect. Secondly, the rise in price level reduces the *supply of real money balances* (M^s/P) that causes a shift in money supply curve to the left. Given the demand function for money (M^d), the decline in the real money supply will cause rate of interest to rise. Now, *the rise in interest will induce private investment expenditure to decline*. Lastly, rise in price level in the domestic economy will adversely affect exports of a country causing net exports to fall.

Thus, as a result of negative effects of rise in price level on real wealth, private investment and net exports, in the upper panel (*a*) of Fig. 43A.5 aggregate expenditure curve shifts downward to AE_1' (dotted) so that it determines GNP level Y_1 corresponding to the intersection of aggregate demand curve AD_1 and short-run aggregate supply curve *SAS* point *R′* in the lower panel (*b*) of this Fig. 43A.5.

Thus with the upward sloping short-run-aggregate supply curve *SAS*, the effect of increase in autonomous investment expenditure (or for that matter increase in any other autonomous expenditure such as Government expenditure, net exports, autonomous consumption) on the GNP level can be visualised to occur in two stages. First, increase in investment expenditure shifts aggregate expenditure curve *AE* upward in the upper panel (*a*) of Fig. 43A.5 and correspondingly aggregate demand curve in the lower panel (*b*) shifts to the right to AD_1 and bring about increase in GNP level from Y_0 to Y_2 with the given fixed price level P_1. In the second stage due to the upward sloping short-run aggregate supply curve *SAS*, the rightward shift in the aggregate demand curve causes price level to rise from P_0 to P_1 and causes decrease in GNP from Y_2 to Y_1.

However, as shall be seen from Fig. 43A.5, when price level effect is taken into account, the increase in investment expenditure has still a multiplier effect on real GDP but this effect is smaller than it would be if price level had remained fixed. It may be further noted that steeper the slope of the short-run supply curve, the greater is the increase in the price level and smaller is the effect on real GNP.

AGGREGATE SUPPLY

We will now explain the concept of aggregate supply with flexible price level. Aggregate supply is the total output of goods and services that firms want to produce at each possible price level. Thus, like aggregate demand, aggregate supply is the whole schedule of total quantities of aggregate output that firms in the economy are willing to produce at each possible price level and is represented by an aggregate supply curve. It is worth noting that aggregate supply is the outcome of the decisions of all producers in the economy to hire workers and buy other inputs for production of goods and services for selling them to consumers, other producers, government as well as for exporting them to other countries. It may be noted while drawing aggregate supply curve that depicts relationship been quantities of aggregate output that are produced for sale in the market by the firms in the economy at various price levels, all other factors that affect aggregate supply are held constant.

Short-run Aggregate Supply Curve

In the model of determination of general price level, the concept of aggregate supply curve which relates aggregate supply of output with price level is used. In this sense, *aggregate supply curve shows the various amounts of aggregate output which the producers in the economy are willing to produce and sell in the market at various price levels.* There is a lot of disagreement among economists about the shape of aggregate supply curve. The classical economists assumed that there normally prevailed full employment of resources in the economy. According to them, if at any time there is deviation from this full employment level, the wages, interest and prices quickly and automatically adjust or change to restore equilibrium at the full employment level. Thus, in the classical theory, the aggregate supply curve of output is perfectly inelastic (*i.e.* a vertical straight line) at the output level corresponding to full-employment level of resources. This aggregate supply curve relating aggregate supply with price level of the classical theory of income and employment is shown in Figure 43A.6. by *AS* curve.

As mentioned above, Keynes considered the situation of economic depression when the economy was operating before the level of full employment of resources. He further believed that in such a situation money wage rates were sticky *i.e.* remain constant. He further assumed that average and margined products of labour remain constant when more of it is employed following the increase in aggregate demand. With these assumptions, more aggregate output is produced and supplied at the given price level in response to increase in aggregate demand. But when full employment of labour and capital stock is attained and aggregate demand further increases, aggregate supply of output being unable to increase any more, it is the price level that will rise in response to the increase in aggregate demand.

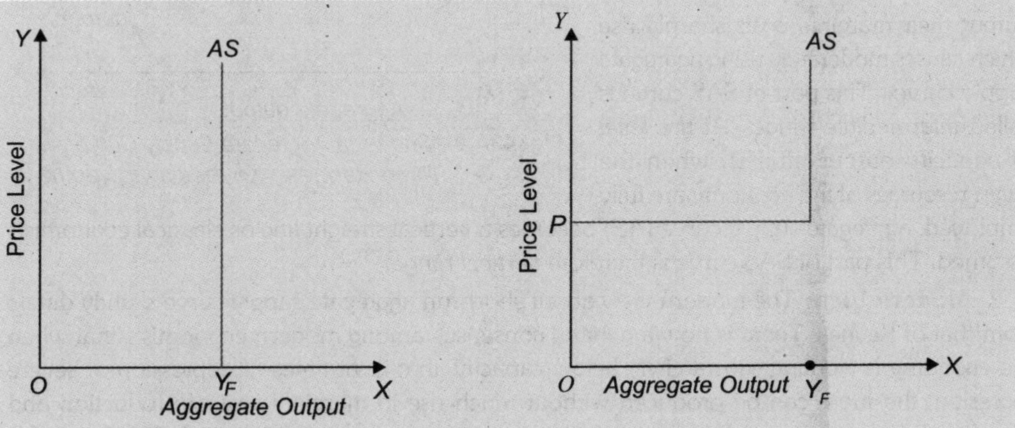

Fig. 43A.6. *Aggregate Supply Curve: Classical View*

Fig. 43A.7. *Keynes's short-run Aggregate Supply Curve*

The Keynes's aggregate supply curve depicting the relationship between price level and the aggregate production (supply) *during the period of depression and involuntary unemployment* when there is a lot of excess capacity in the economy is shown in Figure 43A.7 where it will be seen that aggregate supply is a horizontal straight line (*i.e.* perfectly elastic) up to the level of full employment, showing thereby that in response to increase in aggregate demand more is produced and supplied at the same price level *OP*. Since output of goods and services cannot be increased beyond the full-employment level, Keynes's aggregate supply curve becomes vertical at it.

It may however be noted that Keynes recoganised that as the aggregate supply approaches close to the full-employment level the cost of output per unit tends to rise due to the rise in wage rate and also due to diminishing returns to extra factors employed. But, according to Keynes, the rise in price level before full employment or less than capacity output will not be much.

It is evident from above that shape of aggregate supply curve is a highly controversial issue. As mentioned above, aggregate supply curve indicates the total output which the producers are willing and able to sell at different price levels. It is important to note that as the average price level rises above the current marginal cost of production, producers find it profitable to expand output. When the economy is working substantially below capacity, that is at times of depression or severe recession, the more can be produced without much rise in marginal cost of production and therefore the short-run aggregate supply curve is horizontal or flat. This part of aggregate supply curve is called Keynesian range. With the given stock of capital (*i.e.* plant and equipment) when output is expanded the diminishing returns and rising marginal costs occur which ultimately cause the short-run aggregate supply curve to slope upward gently. But as the firms in the economy approach near their capacity output their marginal costs sharply rise which causes moderately rising aggregate supply curve. This part of SAS curve is called *intermediate range*. At *the level of capacity output*, that is, when the given resources of the economy are fully employed, aggregate supply curve (*AS*) becomes a vertical straight line as classical economists assumed. This part of SAS curve is therefore *vertical range*.

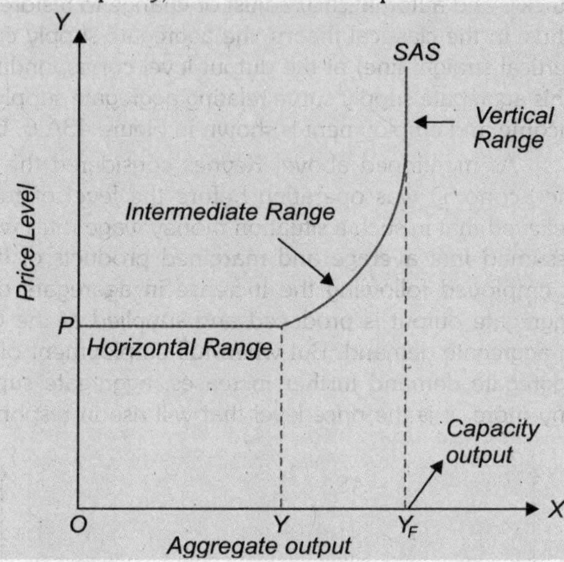

Fig. 43A.8. *Short-run Aggregate Supply Curve with Three Ranges : Keynes's viewpoint*

Modern View. The modern view about short-run aggregate supply curve slightly differs from that of Keynes. There is now a general consensus among modern economists that when the economy is working substantially below capacity, that is, at times of depression or severe recession, the more can be produced without much rise in marginal cost of production and therefore the aggregate supply curve is *nearly flat* rather than perfectly horizontal. This first range is therefore called *nearly flat range*. With the given stock of capital (*i.e.* plant and equipment) when output is expanded beyond this range the diminishing returns and rising marginal costs occur which cause the aggregate supply curve to slope upward gently. Thus there is a part of gently rising short-run aggregate supply curve which represents *intermediate range* of short run aggregate supply curve just as in case of Keynes's viewpoint. But as the firms in the economy approach near their capacity output their marginal costs rise sharply which cause sharply rising aggregate supply curve. Beyond the level of capacity-output, that is, when the given resources of the economy are fully employed, short-run aggregate supply curve (*SAS*) becomes a *highly steep curve rather than becoming vertical*. This is because, unlike the view of Keynes, modern economists think that there is some scope of increasing aggregate output beyond the so called full employment level by reduction in frictional and structural unemployment and by inducing work force to work over time.

Thus the short-run aggregate supply curve has three segments or ranges-: (1) the *nearly flat range*, (2) the *intermediate upward-sloping range*, and (3) *the highly steep range*. This aggregate supply curve having three distinct segments is shown in Figure 43A.9.

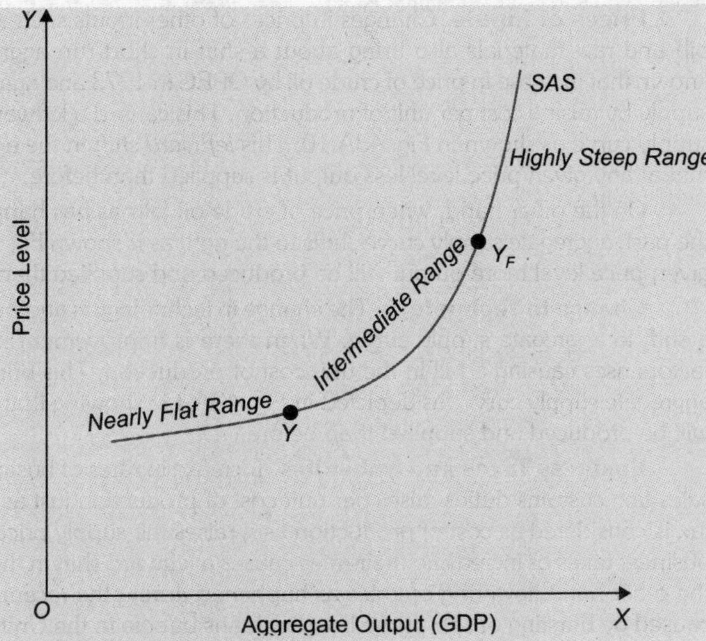

Fig. 43A.9 *Short-run Aggregate Supply Curve with Three Ranges*

Shifts in Short-run Aggregate Supply Curve

In explaining the upward-sloping nature of short-run aggregate supply we stated that aggregate supply curve depicts the relationship between price level and aggregate output (i.e. real GDP), *other factors* such as wages, input prices, technology and indirect taxes that determine aggregate supply being held constant. Now, it is the *changes* in these other determining factors that cause a *shift* in the aggregate supply curve. We explain below the factors that cause a shift in aggregate supply curve.

Changes in Wage Rate. Change in wage rate of workers is an important factor that causes a shift in short-run aggregate supply curve. For example, when wage rate of workers increases, they cause a leftward shift in short-run aggregate supply curve. This is because increase in wages raises cost per unit of output. With a given price of output, higher wage rate means profit per unit of output will decline. As production becomes less profitable, it is likely that the firms will cut back on production and supply less output. Now when wage rate of workers increases, it causes a leftward shift in short-run aggregate supply curve as shown in Fig. 43A.10.

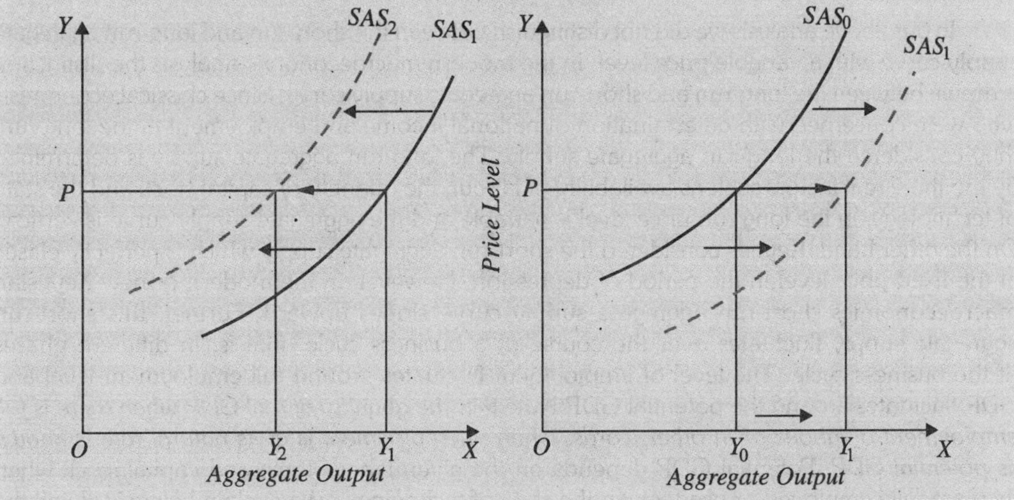

Fig. 43A.10. *Leftward Shift in Aggregate Supply Curve*

Fig. 43A.11. *Rightward Shift in Aggregate Supply Curve*

Prices of Inputs. Changes in prices of other inputs such as energy (for example, crude oil) and raw materials also bring about a shift in short-run aggregate supply curve. It is well known that increase in price of crude oil by OPEC in 1973 and again in 1979 affected aggregate supply by raising cost per unit of production. This caused a leftward shift in short-run aggregate supply curve as shown in Fig. 43A.10. This *leftward shift* in the aggregate supply curve implies that at any given price level less output is supplied than before.

On the other hand, when price of crude oil falls as has happened at several occasions in the past, aggregate supply curve shifts to the right as is shown Fig. 43A.11 indicating that at any given price level more output will be produced and supplied than before.

Change in Technology. The change in technology is another important factor that causes a shift in aggregate supply curve. When there is improvement in technology, productivity of factors rises causing a fall in the unit cost of production. This brings about a rightward shift in aggregate supply curve (as depicted in Fig. 43A.11) showing that at any given price level more will be produced and supplied than before.

Business Taxes and Subsidies. Increase in rates of business taxes such as excise duty, sales tax, customs duties raises per unit cost of production just as rise in wage rate. (Note that tax is considered as cost of production as it raises the supply price of output). Thus, by levying business taxes or increasing their rates causes a leftward shift in the aggregate supply curve. On the other hand, lowering of taxes as happened during the recent global slowdown (2007-09), caused by bursting of sub-prime housing loans bubble in the United States, will cause a shift in the aggregate supply curve to the right. Provision of subsidies on products of various industries also causes a shift in the aggregate supply curve to the right.

Available Supply of Resources. Lastly, a very important factor determining the position of aggregate supply curve is the available quantity of resources. When the available supplies of resources such as labour and capital increase, the short-run aggregate supply curve will shift to the right. As labour force grows and supply of capital is increased through investment, the short-run short-run aggregate supply curve will shift to the right implying that more output will be produced for sale at any given price level.

LONG-RUN AGGREGATE SUPPLY CURVE

In our above analysis we did not distinguish between the short-run and long-run aggregate supply curve with a variable price level. In the modern macroeconomic analysis the distinction is drawn between the long-run and short-run aggregate supply curve. Since classical economists who were concerned with determination of national income and employment in the long run, they considered the long-run aggregate supply. The long-run aggregate supply is determined by the three real factors such as availability of labour, the quantity of capital stock and the state of technology. In the long run price level is variable and the aggregate supply curve is vertical. On the other hand, Keynes considered the short-run aggregate supply which is perfectly elastic at the fixed price level in the period of depression. However, in the modern or new Keynsian macroeconomics short-run aggregate supply curve slopes upward. Further, this short-run aggregate supply fluctuates over the course of a business cycle, that is, in different phases of the business cycle. The level of employment fluctuates around full employment level and GDP fluctuates around the potential GDP. Note *that the quantity of real GDP when there is full employment of labour or in other words, when unemployment is at its natural rate is known as potential GDP*. Potential GDP depends on the given labour force and capital stock when they are fully employed or used, given the state of technology. We explain below in detail the concept of long-run aggregate supply and short-run aggregate supply.

The long-run aggregate supply of output or real GDP depends on three factors (1) the quantity of available labour (2) the stock of capital and (3) the state of technology. The aggregate production function which describes the influence of these three factors is written as :

$$Y = F(L, K, T)$$

Where Y is the quantity of aggregate output or real GDP, L is the quantity of labour, K is the stock of capital and T is the state of technology. At any given time, the stock of capital and state of technology are given and fixed. Though at any time population of a country is fixed but the quantity of labour is variable; it depends on the preferences between work and leisure of the people on the one hand and the decisions of the firms about the demand for labour on the other. People supply labour only if wage rate which is reward for their work effort is sufficient to overcome their preference for leisure. The higher the wage rate, the greater is the quantity of labour supplied. On the other hand, the firms demand labour if it is profitable to use it for production. The lower the wage rate, which is the cost of labour, the greater is the quantity of labour used. The equilibrium wage rate and the quantity of labour employed are determined by labour market equilibrium. The labour market is in equilibrium at the wage rate at which the quantity of labour demanded equals the quantity of labour supplied. *At this equilibrium wage rate, all those who are willing to supply their labour are is fact demanded and employed. Therefore, at this equilibrium wage rate, full employment of labour is said to prevail.*

However, even at full employment, there are always some workers searching for jobs and some firms are looking for workers to offer them employment. This is because of two factors, frictional and structural. Every week some workers leave their old jobs and search for new better jobs more suited to their skills and ability. But due to lack of information, it takes time to find the new jobs even through these are available. This represents what is called *frictional unemployment*. Second, every week or month some industries are declining due to technological changes in technology or preferences of the people for goods while others are expanding. In this case while some people are laid off from the declining industries but sometime is required before they acquire new skills and training needed for employment in the expanding industries. Therefore, for some time they remain unemployed though job vacancies for them exist. This second type of unemployment is called *structural unemployment*.

Thus, at any time some frictional and structural unemployment inevitably exist in a free market economy. Therefore, in modern macroeconomics, the amount of frictional and structural unemployment is called the *natural rate of unemployment.* Around 4 to 5 per cent of labour force in the developed free-market economies represents the natural rate of unemployment. And full employment is said exist in spite of the existence of frictional and structural unemployment. As mentioned above, the quantity of real GDP produced and supplied when there is full employment (that is, when there exists only natural rate of unemployment) is called potential GDP. It may be noted again that potential GDP depends on full employment of labour, the full use of the existing stock of capital and the available technology.

The long-run aggregate supply describes the relationship between the quantity of real GDP and the price level in the long run when real GDP equals potential GDP. The long-run aggregate supply curve is a vertical line (at potential GDP level) as shown by *LAS* in Figure 43A.12. The long-run aggregate supply is vertical because potential GDP does not vary with price level, that is, it is independent of the price level. For example, when aggregate demand curve is AD_2, price level is at 160 (WPI) and when aggregate demand falls and aggregate demand curve shifts to the left to AD_1 and determines price level equal to 130 (WPI), aggregate output remains unchanged at potential GDP equal to $\overline{Y}$ The reason for the independence of potential GDP from the price level is that the movement along the long-run aggregate supply curve involves not only the change in price level of goods but also prices of factor inputs such as wages of labour etc. For example, when there is 5 per cent decrease in the prices of goods and services, this is matched by the same (*i.e.* 5 per cent) decline in wage rate and other factor prices so that relative prices and real wage rate remain unchanged. This explains why it is profitable to produce the same quantity of real GDP at lower price level of goods and services. When price level of goods and services falls, the cost also falls as wage rate and other factor prices fall by the same percentage. Therefore, aggregate supply of output (*i.e.* real GDP) in the long run also remains constant at potential GDP level.

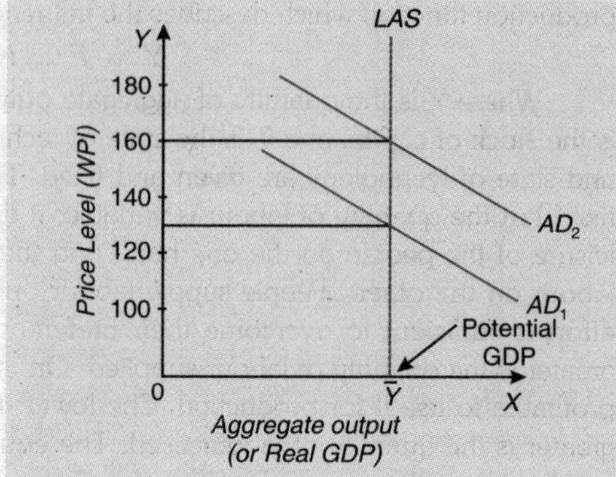

Figure 43A.12. *Long-Run Aggregate Supply Curve*

It is evident from above that long-run aggregate supply curve is the same as the classical aggregate supply curve.

Changes in Long-run Aggregate Supply Curve

We have seen above that long-run aggregate supply curve is a vertical straight line at the level of potential GDP. Changes in price level bring about a movement along the long-run aggregate supply, but the quantity of aggregate supply remains fixed at the level of potential GDP. It is changes in potential GDP that causes a shift in the long-run aggregate supply curve. The following factors cause a change in potential GDP resulting in a shift in the long-run aggregate supply curve.

1. The change in the full-employment quantity of labour.
2. Change in the stock of capital.
3. Progress in technology.

Increase in Labour Force. Labour is an important resource of production. Over time, given the capital stock and the state of technology potential GDP will increase as full-employment quantity of labour force increases. Therefore, the increase in the full-employment quantity of labour force causes a shift in the long-run aggregate supply curve to the right as shown in Figure 43A.13. It may be noted that changes in labour employment over the business cycle cause fluctuations in real GDP. But these changes in real GDP that take place over the business cycle are not changes in potential GDP. As mentioned above, changes in potential GDP also occur due to changes in labour force and stock of capital, and improvement in technology.

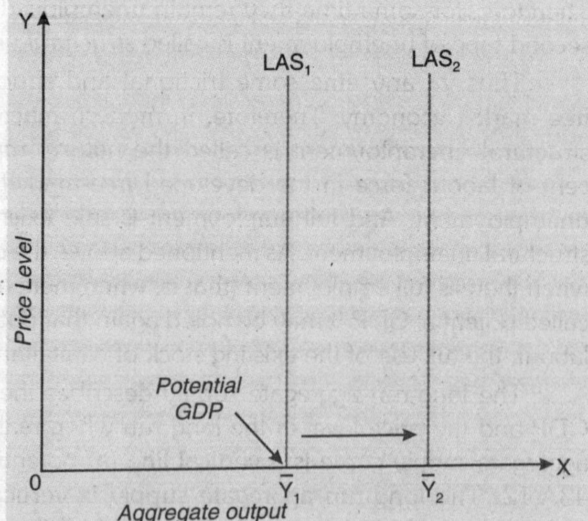

Fig. 43A.13. *Increase in Labour Force, Capital Stock and Progress in Technology Increase potential GDP and shift LAS curve to the right.*

Growth in the Stock of Capital. The stock of capi tal in an economy determines the productive capacity of the economy. The larger the stock of capital in the economy, the more productive is the labour force of the economy and the greater is its potential GDP. The higher per capita output and potential GDP of the American economy as compared to those of the Indian economy are mainly due to the greater stock of capital in the United States. Note that in the capital stock the modern economists include not only physical capital but also human capital. Human capital means the acquired skills, education and training of the workers. Like the increase in labour force, growth in capital stock also brings about increase in potential GDP and causes a shift in the long-run aggregate supply curve (*LAS*) to the right.

Progress in Technology. Progress in technology enables firms to produce more from the given resources. Empirical research studies have shown that technological progress is by far the most important source of increase in GDP over the past two centuries. It is due to advances in technology that a modern worker, both in industry and agriculture produces many times more output than the worker in the olden times. Thus, even with the fixed quantities of labour and capital, progress in technology raises potential GDP and causes in shift in the long run aggregate supply curve to the right.

Change in Money Wages and Other Resource Prices. It is worthwhile to note that changes in money wages and other factor prices such as *the price of oil affect the short-run aggregates supply curve but do not affect the long-run aggregate supply curve*. This is because along the long-run aggregate supply curve any change in the money wage rate or other resource prices bring about an equal percentage change in the price level so that *relative prices* and *real* wage rate remain constant. Since the relative prices remain the same, the firms do not have any incentive to increase or reduce their production and therefore potential GDP and long-run aggregate supply curve remain constant. However, changes in money wage rate and other resource prices affect firms' cost of production and therefore cause a shift in short-run aggregate supply curve. For example, when money wage rate and other resource prices rise, firms' costs go up and therefore they will be willing to supply smaller quantity of output at each price level. As a result, short-run aggregate supply curve shifts to the left.

Relation of Short-Run Aggregate Supply Curve with Long-Run Aggregate Supply Curve

In macroeconomics short run is defined as the period during which aggregate output has fallen either below potential GDP or has risen above potential GDP. Accordingly, in the short run, the rate of unemployment either increases above the natural rate of unemployment or falls below the natural rate of unemployment. Thus short-run aggregate supply curve describes the relationship between the aggregate output (*i.e.* real GDP) produced and the price level in the short run when money wage rate and other factor prices remain constant. The *short-run aggregate supply curve (SAS) slopes upward to the right and intersects the long-run aggregate supply curve at the current and expected price level*. Consider Figure 43A.14. If the current and expected price level is P_1, then on this basis the contracts about wage rate and other resource prices would have been reached. Therefore, the short-run aggregate supply curve will intersect the vertical long-run aggregate supply curve (*LAS*) at the current and

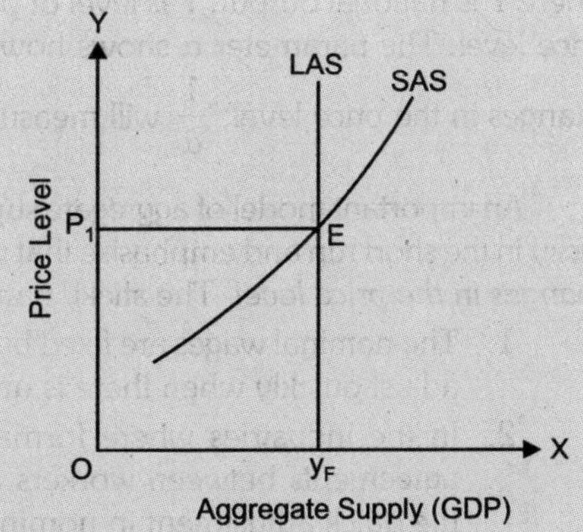

Fig. 43A.14. *Relation between Short-run Aggregate Supply Curve and Long-run Aggregate Supply curve*

expected price level. Now, if the actual price level rises, wages and other factor prices remaining constant, it will become profitable for the firms to expand production resulting in the increase in short-run aggregate supply of output. With this, the real GDP will increase beyond potential GDP and the economy will move rightward along the short-run aggregate supply curve *SAS* in Fig. 43A.14. On the other hand, with the current long-run price equal to P_1, if price level falls, wages and other resource prices remaining the same, the firms will not be able to cover the higher marginal costs of producing a large output $\overline{Y}_1$ and will therefore cut back on production. As a result, the economy will move leftward along the short-run aggregate supply curve *SAS*. With this, real GDP falls below the potential GDP level.

It is evident from above why short-run aggregate supply curve (*SAS*) slopes upward. The firms produce the output that maximises profits, if the price level of goods and services rises while the wage rates and other resource costs per unit remain the same, it pays the firms to expand production. Thus more real GDP is produced and supplied at a higher price level.

Let us briefly distinguish between the movement along the short-run aggregate supply curve (*SAS*) and the movement along the long-run aggregate supply curve (*LAS*). When the price level rises, with money wage rate and other resource prices remaining the same, it is profitable to produce more goods and services which bring about increase in the quantity of real GDP produced and supplied. As a result, there is a movement along the short-run aggregate supply curve (*SAS*) as shown in Figure 43A.14 by the upward-sloping arrow. On the other hand, when the price level rises and *also there is the same percentage rise in wage rate and other resource prices*, relative prices of goods and services remaining unchanged it is not profitable to produce more output of goods and services. As a result, real GDP remains equal to the potential GDP and there is a movement along the long-run aggregate supply curve (*LAS*) as shown by vertical arrow mark in Fig. 43A.14.

DERIVATION OF SHORT-RUN AGGREGATE SUPPLY CURVE : THE STICKY WAGE MODEL

We have studied above that while the long-run supply curve (LAS) is a vertical straight line at the level of potential GNP (or at the natural rate of unemployment), the short-run aggregate supply curve (SAS) slopes upward to the right. There are three models of aggregate supply but all of them depends on the following short-run aggregate supply equation.

$$Y = \overline{Y} + \alpha (P - P^e), \quad \alpha > 0$$

where Y is national output, $\overline{Y}$ is level of potential GNP, P is the price level and P^e is the expected price level. The parameter α shows how much output changes in response to the unexpected changes in the price level. $\frac{1}{\alpha}$ will measure the slope of the short-run aggregate supply curve.

An important model of aggregate supply curve assumes that nominal (*i.e.* money) wages are sticky in the short run and emphasise that nominal wages are *slow in adjustment to the unexpected changes in the price level.* The sticky nature of nominal wages is due to the following reasons :

1. The nominal wages are fixed by long-term contracts. Therefore, nominal wages cannot adjust quickly when there is unexpected change in the price level.
2. In the industries where formal labour contracts do not prevail, there are implicit agreements between workers and employers about nominal wages. These prevent the quick adjustment in nominal wages when economic conditions warrant.
3. Wages also depend on social norms and notions of equity. These also prevent changes in wages in the short run.

The above factors account for stickiness of nominal wages in the short run. Recall that short-run aggregate supply curve shows how the quantity of aggregate output (*i.e.* real GDP) changes in the short run when the actual price level deviates from the expected price level. As the actual price level rises in the short run, more quantity of the aggregate output (*i.e.* real GDP) is produced and supplied. That is, the short-run aggregate supply slopes upward to the right. Now, what accounts for the upward-sloping nature of the short-run aggregate supply curve. Since the nominal wages are sticky in the short run, a rise in the actual price level in the short run lowers the real wage rate of workers. The lower real wage induces the firms to employ more labour. The increase in labour employment will lead to the increase in aggregate output (*i.e.* real GDP). Thus, when actual price level increases above the expected price level in the short

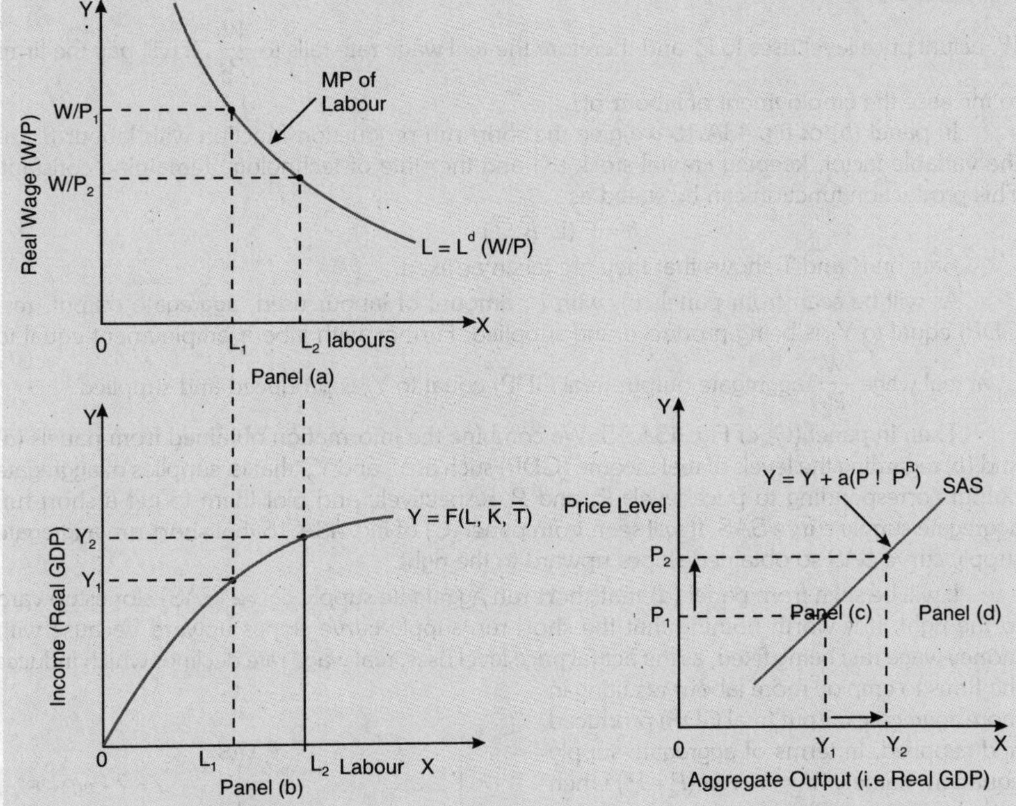

Fig. 43A.15. *Deriving Short-run Aggregate Supply Curve : Stickly Wage Model*

run, the quantity of aggregate output or real GDP increases. That is, short-run aggregate supply curve slopes upward to the right. It is worthwhile to note that the greater quantity of aggregate output could be produced and supplied in the short run only at a higher actual price because of employment of more labour in the short run, quantity of capital and the state of technology remaining the same, leads to the rise in marginal cost of production of the firms. Therefore, higher price of output is required to cover this higher marginal cost of production as expansion in aggregate output takes place in the short run.

How the short-run aggregate supply curve is derived in the sticky wage model is illustrated in figure 43A.15. In panel (*a*) of this figure we show the determination of labour employment through demand for labour function. This labour demand function of labour is given by marginal product curve and can be stated as under.

$$L = L^d\left(\frac{W}{P}\right)$$

where L is demand for employment of labour and $\frac{W}{P}$ is the real wage rate. With W as the nominal wage rate and P as the price level. It will be seen from panel (*a*) that given the nominal wage equal to W, when price level is P_1, the real wage equals $\frac{W}{P_1}$. At this real wage $\frac{W}{P_1}$, the firms employ L_1 amount of labour. This is because at L_1 amount of labour employed, the real wage rate $\frac{W}{P_1}$ is equal to marginal product of labour. If, with nominal wage remaining stuck at W, actual price level rises to P_2 and therefore the real wage rate falls to $\frac{W}{P_2}$, it will pay the firms to increase the employment of labour of L_2.

In panel (*b*) of fig. 43A.15 we give the short-run production function with labour (L) as the variable factor, keeping capital stock (K) and the state of technology remaining constant. This production function can be stated as

$$Y = F(L, \overline{K}, \overline{T})$$

Bars on K and T shows that they are taken as fixed.

As will be seen from panel (*b*), with L_1 amount of labour used, aggregate output (real GDP) equal to Y_1 is being produced and supplied. Further, with labour employment equal to L_2 at real wage $\frac{W}{P_2}$ aggregate output (real GDP) equal to Y_2 is produced and supplied.

Then in panel (*C*) of Fig. 43A.15. We combine the information obtained from panels (*a*) and (*b*) regarding the levels of real income (GDP) such as Y_1 and Y_2, that is, supplies of aggregate output corresponding to price levels P_1 and P_2 respectively and plot them to get a short-run aggregate supply curve *SAS*. It will seen from panel (*C*) of Fig. 43A.15 that short-run aggregate supply curve *SAS* so obtained slopes upward to the right.

It will be seen from panel (*d*) that short-run aggregate supply curve (*SAS*) slopes upward to the right. It is worth nothing that the short-run supply curve slopes upward because with money wage rate being fixed, as the actual price level rises, real wage rate declines which induces the firms to employ more labour resulting in more aggregate output (real GDP) produced and supplied. In terms of aggregate supply equation, namely, $Y = \overline{Y} + \alpha\,(P - P^e)$ when actual price level (P) deviates from expected price level (P^e) which formed the basis of fixation of nominal wages (W), the real wage rate $\left(\frac{W}{P}\right)$ will fall below the target wage rate and will therefore raise the amount of labour employed and aggregate output produced.

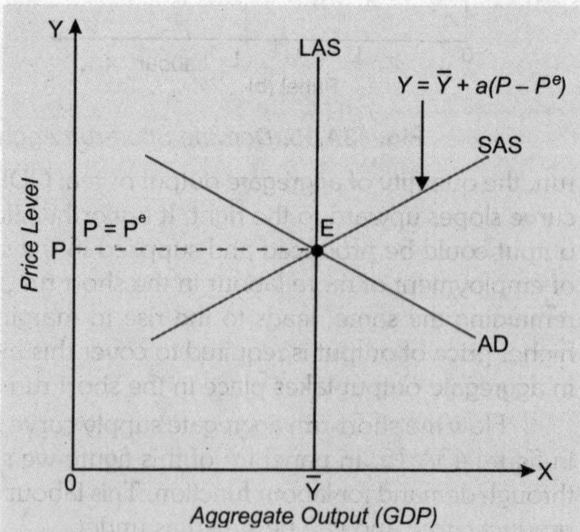

Fig. 43A.16. *Short-Run and Long-Run Aggregate Supply Curve*

Short-run and Long-run Aggregate Supply Curve

Note that when actual price level (P) equals the expected price level (P^e), $P - P^e$ in the aggregate supply equation $Y = \overline{Y} + \alpha\,(P - P^e)$ will be zero and therefore aggregate output (or real GDP) will be equal to potential GDP ($\bar{Y}$). Therefore, when the actual price level and the expected price level are equal, the short-run aggregate supply (*SAS*) curve will intersect the long-run aggregate supply curve (*LAS*) at the level of current real price level as shown by point *E* in Figure 43A.16. When the actual price level rises above the expected price level ($P > P^e$ or $P - P^e > 0$). the real wage rate will fall and consequently more labour will be employed resulting in more aggregate output. With this we will move towards right form *E* on short-run supply curve *SAS*. This implies that the level of unemployment will fall below the natural rate of unemployment.

On the other hand, when actual price level falls below the expected price level ($P < P^e$ or $P - P^e < 0$) real wage rate will rise above the target wage rate. This will induce the firms to reduce the quantity of labour employed resulting in smaller aggregate output produced. As a result, with the initial equilibrium at point *E*, the economy will be move to the left of point *E*. With this, real GDP will be below the potential GDP ($\bar{Y}$) and rate of unemployment well rise above the natural rate of unemployment.

MACROECONOMIC EQUILIBRIUM: AS-AD FLEXIBLE PRICE MODEL

Having explained the concepts of aggregate demand and aggregate supply with variable price level. Now we shall explain how macro equilibrium is reached between the aggregate supply and aggregate demand to determine the amount of real GDP and the price level. As there is difference between the long-run and the short run aggregate supply curves, the long-run equilibrium differs from the short-run macroeconomic equilibrium. while long-run equilibrium is the state toward which the economy is moving short-run equilibrium is the actual state of the economy in the short run as it fluctuates around potential GDP. The purpose of AS-AD model is to explain how the various events, fiscal and monetary policies bring about changes in real GDP and the price level. We explain below both the short-run and long-run macroeconomic equilibrium.

Short-run Macroeconomic Equilibrium

Short-run macroeconomic equilibrium occurs at the price level at which aggregate output demanded equals aggregate supply of output. That is, short-run equilibrium is reached at the price level at which aggregate demand curve *AD* intersects the short-run aggregate supply curve *SAS*. This is shown in fig. 43A.17 where *AD* is the aggregate demand curve and *SAS* is the aggregate supply curve. It will be seen that the short-run macroeconomic equilibrium occurs at point *E* at which the price level is P_0 and the real GDP is Y_0. If price level is different from P_0, the economy will not be in equilibrium. Suppose, for example, price level is P_2, the quantity of the real GDP demanded P_2 is less than the quantity P_2B of real GDP supplied. This means the firms will not be able to sell all

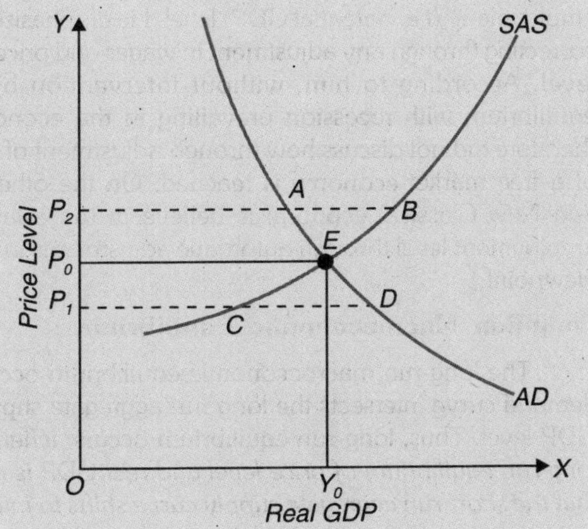

Fig. 43A.17. *Short-run Macroeconomic Equilibrium: Joint Determination of GDP and Price Level*

their output. As a result ,unintended inventories well pile up and firms will cut both production and prices. The process of cutting production and prices will continue until the equilibrium price level P_0 is reached and real GDP produced and sold is Y_0.

Now suppose that price level is P_1. It will be seen from Fig. 43A.17 that at price level P_1 the quantity of aggregate output demanded (P_1D) exceeds the aggregate supply (P_1C). Thus at the price level P_1, the people will not be able to get all the goods and resources they want to buy. As a result, inventories of goods with the firms will decrease below the desired level. This will induce firms to increase production and raise prices. The production and price level will rise until price level P_0 is reached and real GDP produced is Y_0 which meets the demands of the people fully at the price level P_0. Thus, the price level P_0 and real GDP equal to Y_0 represents the short-run macroeconomic equilibrium.

It is worthwhile to note that in the short-run the money wage rate is fixed. *It does not adjust to bring macro equilibrium at full-employment level of real GDP.* Thus, in the short run macro equilibrium can be attained with real GDP less than or greater than potential GDP (*i.e.* the level of GDP at which there is full employment of labour) depending on the level of aggregate demand. It is only in the long run when money wage rate adjusts that equilibrium is restored at potential GDP.

Further, it may be noted that fluctuations in the economy occur due to changes in the factors that cause changes in either aggregate demand or aggregate supply. For example, changes in money supply, the government expenditure, taxes, investment demand by business firms or consumption demand of households will bring about changes in aggregate demand and cause shift in the short-run macroeconomic equilibrium. On the other hand, changes in money wage rate and other resource prices such as oil price stock will cause a shift in aggregate supply curve and bring about a change in the short-run macroeconomic equilibrium

Keynes's View about Short-run Equilibrium

It is important to note that, according to Keynes, the short-run equilibrium at less than full-employment level when there prevails recession in the economy comes into existence due to deficiency of aggregate demand caused by a fall in private investment by the business class. He argued that unless the Government intervenes in the economy through adoption of expansionary fiscal policy (that is, increasing its expenditure and cutting taxes) and finance its budget deficit through deficit financing, a free market economy cannot be brought into equilibrium at full employment. (*i.e.* potential GDP) level. He emphasized that a free market economy was not self-correcting through any adjustment in wages and prices to restore equilibrium at full employment level. According to him, without intervention by the Government, under-employment equilibrium with recession prevailing in the economy will persist in the long run. Keynes therefore did not discuss how through adjustment of wages and prices the long-run equilibrium of a free market economy is reached. On the other hand, classical economists, monetarists and New Classical economists believe in the establishment of long-run equilibrium at full employment level through automatic adjustments in wages and prices. We explain below their viewpoint.

Long-Run Macroeconomic Equilibrium

The long-run macroeconomic equilibrium occurs at the price level where the aggregate demand curve intersects the long run aggregate supply curve which is vertical at the potential GDP level. Thus, long-run equilibrium occurs *when real* GDP *equals potential* GDP. *But this long-run equilibrium of price level and real* GDP *is reached when money wage rate adjusts so that the short-run aggregate supply curve shifts to intersect the long-run aggregate supply curve (LAS) at the point at which aggregate demand curve intersects the latter. The long-run macro equilibrium and how it is reached is illustrated in Figure 43A.18 & 43A.19. From Fig. 43A.18 it will be seen that the short-run aggregate supply curve* SAS_0 *intersects the given aggregate demand curve AD at point E and determines the price level equal to* P_0 *and real GDP equal to* Y_0 *in the short run. Thus in this short-run macroeconomic equilbrium, real GDP which is equal to* Y_0 *is less than the potential GDP (remember that the potential GDP corresponds to full employment level of labour, with the given stock of capital and the given state of technology). The difference* $Y_0\bar{Y}$ *between the short-run equilibrium GDP and the potential GDP is called recessionary gap which exists because at the short-run equilibrium price level* P_0 *aggregate demand is not sufficient for the purchase of potential GDP. Besides, the production of less than potential GDP implies that in the short-run equilibrium, there will exist cyclical unemployment, that is, the rate of unemployment will exceed the natural rate of unemployment.*

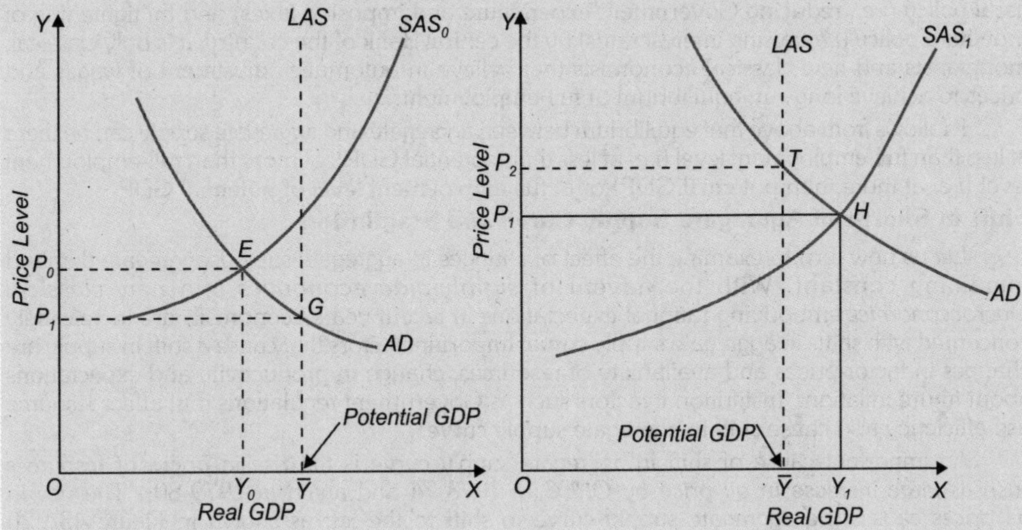

Fig. 43A.18. *Short-run Equilibrium at less than Full-employment (or Potential GDP).*

Fig. 43A.19. *Short run Equilibrium at more than Employment Level with Inflation.*

If money wage rate is flexible as classical economists, monetarists and new classical economists think they are, then in the short-run equilibrium at point *E* with more than natural rate of unemployment, money wage rate will fall. As a result, short-run aggregate supply curve (*SAS*) will shift to the right. This rightward shift in the short-run aggregate supply curve will continue until it intersects the long-run aggregate supply curve (*LAS*) at point G (see Figure 43A.18) where the given aggregate demand cuts the latter. At the new equilibrium point G price level has fallen to P_1 and aggregate quantity of output demanded has increased to the potential GDP level $\bar{Y}$. Point G in Figure 43A.18 represents the long-run equilibrium at full-employment level, that is, the level at which only natural rate of unemployment prevails.

Let us consider the opposite case when the short-run equilibrium is initially at more than potential GDP, that is, above full employment level. Suppose initially with aggregate demand curve *AD* and the short-run aggregate supply curve SAS_1, the short-run equilibrium is at point *H* at which the price level is P_1 and real GDP is Y_1 which is greater than potential GDP equal to $\bar{Y}$. (see Fig. 43A.19).

Now, the question may be asked how real GDP has risen to the level which is more than the potential GDP. The answer is that even beyond potential GDP, real GDP rises as labour-employment increases by reduction in rate of unemployment more than the natural rate and the given capital stock is utilised more intensively. The amount $\bar{Y}Y_1$ by which real GDP which is equal to Y_1 exceeds potential GDP $\bar{Y}$) represents the *inflationary gap* as this gap creates inflationary pressures in the economy.

When equilibrium of the economy is established at more than full-employment or potential GDP level, unemployment falls below the natural level of unemployment, shortage of labour will emerge which will push up wages. With the rise in money wages short-run aggregate supply curve SAS will shifts to the left and this process of rise in wages and leftward shift in short run aggregate supply curve *SAS* will continue until it intersects the long-run aggregate supply *LAS* at point *T* (in Fig. 43A.19) at which long-run equilibrium is established.

Again, it may be noted that, according to Keynes, equilibrium at more than full employment when inflation prevails in the economy comes into existence due to the excess of aggregate demand over aggregate supply cannot be automatically corrected through adjustment in wages and prices. He rightly argued that inflation in the economy can be overcome by *demand management policy*, that is, by reducing aggregate demand through contractionary fiscal policy (*i.e.*, reducing Government expenditure and imposing taxes) and by tightening of monetary policy (*i.e.* raising interest rates) by the central Bank of the country. It is only classical, monetarists and new classical economists that believe in automatic adjustment of wages and prices to achieve long-run equilibrium at full-employment.

It follows from above that equilibrium between aggregate and aggregate supply can be there at less than full-employment level (*i.e.* at less than potential GDP), at more than full-employment level (*i.e.* at more than potential GDP) or at full employment level of potential GDP.

Shift in Short-run Aggregate Supply Curve and Stagflation

Let us now turn to examine the effect of changes in aggregate supply, aggregate demand remaining constant. With the advent of *supply-side economics and new classical macroeconomics* embodying rational expectations in recent years economists are increasingly concerned with shifts in aggregate supply curve. Important factors that cause a shift in supply are changes in factor-prices and availability of resources, change in productivity and expectations about future inflation. Institutional factors such as Government regulations that affect resource use efficiency also cause shift in aggregate supply curve.

An important cause of shift in aggregate supply curve is the *rise in prices of resources such as large increase in oil price by OPEC* in 1973-74 and again in 1979-80. The rise in oil prices causes the aggregate supply curve to shift to the left as shown in Figure 43A.20 where due to the higher per unit resource cost aggregate supply curve has shifted leftward from SAS_0 to SAS_1. The aggregate demand curve *AD* remaining constant, with the leftward shift in aggregate supply curve from AS_0 to AS_1, leads to the new macro-economic equilibrium being established at *T*, at which price level is higher and aggregate output smaller than before.

The emergence of rise in price level or inflation due to the leftward shift in aggregate supply curve is called *cost-push inflation*. There is important differences between deman pull inflation cost-push inflation. *Whereas in case of demand-pull inflation, price rises along with rise in GDP, in case of cost-push inflation price level rises but GDP declines.*

Thus, in Fig. 43A.20 leftward shift in the *SAS* curve leads to rise in the price level from P_0 to P_1, while national output falls from Y_0 to Y_1. *When both inflation and recession occur simultaneously, economists call this situation as stagflation.* We thus see that increase in costs or resource prices are both inflationary and recessionary. It may be noted that stagflation is also said to occur when instead of absolute fall in aggregate output there is *slowdown in economic growth rate* when inflation rate remains steadly high and also unemployment levels are quite high. It is evident from

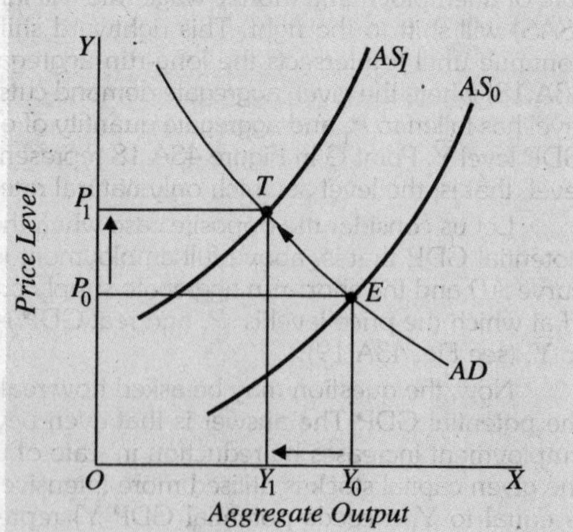

Fig. 43A.20. *Emergence of stagflation due to leftward shift in aggregate supply curve*

above that stagflation occurs as a result of supply shock, that is, rise in price of essential inputs such as crude oil which causes a shift in the short-run aggregate supply curve to the left. Given the aggregate demand curve, the new equilibrium is reached at a higher price level (*i.e.* inflation) and at the same time reduced aggregate output (*i.e.* GDP) which generates unemployment in the economy.

We have explained above stagflation as a result of sharp rise in price of crude oil effected by restriction of oil output by callusive agreement of OPEC. In India stagflation can arise when there is decline in agricultural output due to failure of monsoon. The decline in agricultural output causes *food inflation* which in turn leads to rise in wages of workers which cause a shift in the short-run aggregate supply curve to the left. Besides, drastic decline in agricultural output also leads to the rise in prices of raw materials provided by agricultural sector to industries. The rise in wages and raw material prices for industries shifts aggregate supply curve to the left causing both inflation and reduction in output.

Solution. To solve the problem of stagflation is a difficult task. In the seventies when the problem of stagflation was first faced efforts were made to solve it through demand management policies. However, when to reduce inflation, steps were taken to reduce aggregate demand by cutting expenditure, the result was decline in aggregate output which further worsened the unemployment problem. On the other hand, when to reduce unemployment attempt was made to increase aggregate expenditure through expansionary fiscal and monetary policies the result was acceleration in inflation.

The proper solution of stagflation is to shift the short-run aggregate supply curve to the right by reducing cost through raising productivity levels. The productivity in both industry and agriculture can be raised through technological improvements and more capital accumulation. Besides rightward shift in short-run aggregate supply can be made by reducing indirect taxes such as excise duties, sales tax, customs duties not only on final products but also on essential inputs used in the production of commodities. Stagflation can also be tackled if through imports of goods, short-run aggregate supply curve is shifted to the right.

QUESTIONS FOR REVIEW

1. Briefly explain AS–AD model of determination of national product. With this model explain the impact of (1) increase in aggregate demand and (2) decrease in aggregate supply on price level and aggregate output.
2. Derive the aggregate demand curve (with varying price level). Why does it slope downward? Show the effect of an increase in nominal money stock on aggregate demand curve.
3. Compare the Keynesian and Classical aggregate supply curve. Briefly explain their policy implications.
4. With AS–AD model explain the multiplier effect of increase in Government expenditure on private investment when (1) price level remains constant and (2) when price level rises.
5. What is stagflation? Explain with AS–AD model what can cause stagflation.
6. Distinguish between short-run aggregate supply and long-run aggregate supply. What are the factors that cause shift in them?
7. Derive a short-run aggregate supply curve when nominal wages are stricky. Give reasons for the stickiness of nominal wages.
8. With AS–AD model explain economic fluctuations in the economy. Explain the impact of increase and decrease in aggregate demand on GDP and price level in the economy.
9. What is meant by stagflation ? How is it caused ? What measures can be adopted to tackle it ?
10. How according to classical monetarists long-run equilibrium is established at potential GDP when due to deficiency of aggregate demand short-run equilibrium is at less than full employment ? How do Keynes and new Keynesian economists refute this classical viewpoint ?
11. What is inflation ? What factors, according to Keynes, can cause inflation in the economy.

International Economic Linkages and Mundell-Fleming Model

International Economic Linkages: Flows of Trade and Capital

Different economies of the world are linked together through two channels: (1) through trade in goods and services; (2) movement of finance or capital across countries. It is because of these international linkages that both the higher economic growth and recession in the U.S.A. make a substantial difference to income and output in other countries such as India, Mexico, Japan and vice versa as the latter have both the trade and financial relations with the former. For example, recession in the United States that reduces the incomes of the American people affects their demand for imported goods and would affect India's exports to the United States. Besides, if the Central Bank of America lowers interest rate below that prevailing in India, this will increase capital outflows from the United States to India as has been witnessed in 2003 to 2007. Dollar inflows into India will affect the foreign exchange rate of rupee and also the reserves of foreign exchange with Reserve Bank of India. It will be recalled that reserves of foreign exchange with RBI determine the money supply in India.

It is quite evident from above that in this age of globalisation when the economies of the world have been integrated through flows of trade and capital, growth and recession in one economy have world-wide repercussions. International linkages in the area of financial and capital movements have acquired crucial importance in modern times. The households, banks or corporate firms, say of the USA, can hold assets such as government bonds, corporate bonds, equity (i.e. share capital) of companies not only of their own country but also those of foreign countries. In most countries of the world today (India included) there are no restrictions on holding of financial assets such as corporate bonds, equity capital (i.e. corporate shares) and physical assets abroad. As a matter of fact, portfolio managers of the banks or large corporations shop around the world for parking their funds in the assets of the countries which offer them most attractive yields. It is through shifting of their assets by rich households, banks or corporate firms that link financial markets around the world. This mobility of capital or finance to search for better yield around the world affects income and employment, exchange rates and interest rates at home and abroad.

As mentioned above, households, institutional investors, banks and corporate firms search around the world for the highest return (of course, adjusted for risk). As a result, returns or yields in capital markets in various open economies get linked together. For example, if rates of interest or return on equity capital in India rise relatively to those in the USA, the US investors would try to lend or invest their capital in India to take advantage of higher returns. On the other hand, the borrowers would turn to the USA to borrow funds from the US financial markets to take advantage of lower rates of interest.

National Income and Trade Balance in the Open Economy

An important difference between the open economy and the closed economy is that in an open economy, the aggregate expenditure in any year need not be equal to its output of goods and services. This is because a country can spend more than the income it earns from production of goods and services. It can do so by borrowing from abroad. On the contrary, a country can spend less than the value of goods and services it produces because it can lend the difference to foreigners. To understand it fully recall the national income accounting explained in an earlier chapter.

It will be recalled that the economy's gross domestic output (GDP) can be divided into the four components :

$$Y = C + I + G + NX \qquad \text{... (1)}$$

where C stands for consumption expenditure, I for investment, G for government purchases of domestic goods and services and NX for net exports. NX is the difference between expenditure on exports (EX) and expenditure on imports (IM). Thus, net exports (NX) = $EX - IM$. The net exports is also known as belance of trade.

From the national income accounts identity given in equation (1) above we can know the relationship between net exports, gross national product and aggregate domestic expenditure. To do so we rearrange the equation (1) above as under :

$$NX = Y - (C + I + G) \qquad \text{... (2)}$$

where $(C + I + G)$ represents aggregate domestic expenditure and Y represents gross domestic product (GDP). The equation (2) shows that if Gross Domestic Product (Y) exceeds aggregate domestic expenditure $(C + I + G)$, net exports (NX) are positive, that is, we are exporting more than we are importing. On the other hand, if a country's Gross Domestic Product is less than aggregate domestic expenditure, it will be importing more than it is exporting and therefore its net exports will be negative.

SAVING, INVESTMENT AND INTERNATIONAL FLOWS OF GOODS AND CAPITAL

We have seen that saving and investment play an important role in determining the level of national income and employment in an economy in the short run. Besides, saving and investment are crucial to the long-run economic growth of a country. It is therefore important to know how saving and investment are related to the international flows of goods and capital. This can be shown by rearranging the national income accounts identity. Let us first rewrite the national income identity.

$$Y = C + I + G + NX \qquad \text{... (1)}$$

Rearranging we have

$$Y - C - G = I + NX \qquad \text{... (2)}$$

Since saving is the part of national income (Y) that is left after expenditure on consumption by households and Government purchases of goods and services[1], $Y - C - G$ in (2) above represents saving (S) of the economy. Note that national saving $Y - C - G$ is the sum of private saving which is equal to $Y - T - C$ (where T represents taxes) and public saving which is equal to $T - G$. Thus national saving = Private Saving + Public Saving

or $$S = (Y - T - C) + (T - G)$$
$$= Y - C - G$$

writing S for Y – C – G in national income identity in (2) above we have

$$S = I + NX \quad \text{... (3)}$$

Subtracting I from both sides of equation (3) we have

$$S - I = NX \quad \text{... (4)}$$

The national income accounts identity of the open economy presented in (4) above shows that economy's net exports (NX) must always be equal to the difference between domestic saving and investment ($S - I$). This difference between domestic saving and investment represents net capital outflow. The equation (4) above shows that net capital outflow equals net exports. Net capital outflow is also called *net foreign investment* by some economists. Thus the equation (4) indicates that if domestic saving (S) exceeds investment (I), that is, if net capital outflow is positive, the economy will be lending or investing the excess saving abroad. If, on the other hand, domestic investment in the economy is greater than its saving, that is, if capital outflow is negative, that is, if there is *net capital inflow* it means that it will be receiving net investment funds from abroad. Thus net capital outflow, that is, the difference between saving and investment of the economy ($S - I$) equals the difference between the amounts the residents of country will be lending or investing abroad and the amount that the foreigners will be lending or investing in that country.[2]

Thus the net capital flow represents the international flow of funds to finance investment in a country. It follows from above that the difference between national saving and domestic investment, that is, net capital outflows always equals the net exports. It may be noted that *net exports is also called trade balance* because it represents to what extent trade in goods and services of a country departs from the equality of imports and exports. Thus

Net Capital Outflow ($S - I$) = Trade Balance

From our above analysis we arrive at the following conclusions :

(1) If saving exceeds domestic investment ($S > I$) for an economy it follows from above that net exports (NX) or trade balance will be positive. In other words, in this case the country will be running a *trade surplus*. This case implies that the residents of the country would be lending or investing abroad. That is, net capital outflow will be positive.

(2) If domestic saving is less than domestic investment ($S < I$ or $S - I < 0$) of a country, its net exports will be negative, that is, the country will be running a *trade deficit. In this case there will be capital inflows to finance the extra imports.*

(3) Thirdly, if saving equals investment ($S = I$ or $S - I = 0$), the net exports (NX) will be zero, that is, the country will have a *balanced trade.*

It follows from the above identity of national income accounts of an open economy ($S - I = NX$) that the *international flow of capital and international flow of goods and services are the two sides of the same coin*. It may however be noted that international flows of capital can take many forms. First, foreigners can lend to a country when it has excess of imports over

1. All Government expenditure on goods and services is treated as consumption expenditure. Though this is strictly true of the capitalist developed economies, it is not true of developing countries like India where Government undertakes a lot of investment expenditure.
2. It will be interesting to note that for the three years (2002 – 2003, 2003 – 2004 and 2004 – 2005) India's Gross Saving exceeded Gross Domestic Investment, which means we lended or invested the excess saving abroad in these years.

exports. Secondly, the foreign can buy domestic assets such as the American firms buying shares in the Indian Stock Exchange or buying physical assets in India. By buying assets of another country, the foreigners are making investment and providing financial funds to the country.

THE GOODS MARKET AND IS CURVE IN THE OPEN ECONOMY

The analysis of determination of national income, employment and rate of interest in open economies is also made in the framework of *IS –LM* model with a few changes. In particular, *IS* curve in the open economy contains a new term of net *exports (NX)*.

An important change in the *IS-LM* model applicable to an open economy is that in it *domestic spending* does not determine level of national income and output. Instead, it is *spending on domestic goods* that determines level of national income and employment in an open economy. A part of spending by domestic residents is done on imports from foreign countries and the rest on domestically produced goods and services. Besides, a part of spending on domestic goods is by foreigners to whom we export goods. Thus, net exports which means exports minus imports together with spending by domestic residents on domestic goods constitute aggregate demand for or spending on domestic goods. Thus, goods market equilibrium in an open economy is represented by the following equation:

$$Y = C + I + G + NX$$

or

$$Y = C + I + G + (X-M)$$

Where NX or $(X-M)$ represents next exports. The above equation states that equilibrium level of national income is equal to the sum of consumption demand (C), investment demand (I), government purchases of goods and services (G) and net exports (NX). Consumption expenditure (C) depends on disposable income or Y-T, investment depends negatively on interest rate, G is autonomous government expenditure and net exports, among others, depends on exchange rate (e).

Incorporating the above in the *IS* equation we have the following *IS* curve for an open economy :

$$IS \text{ curve} : Y = C\,(Y-T) + I\,(r) + G + NX\,(e)$$

where r represents rate of interest e represents nominal exchange rate

Net Exports (*NX*). The term net exports (NX) needs further elaboration. Net exports, as mentioned above, represents the excess of exports over imports, depend on domestic income (Y) which affects spending on imports and therefore net exports. Besides, net exports depend on (1) foreign income (Y_f) which affects foreign demand for our exports and (2) the real exchange rate which we denote by R. Depreciation in real exchange rate will increase our exports and reduce our imports and as a result improves our trade balance as demand shifts from foreign goods to the domestically produced goods. It may be noted that the exchange rate is the ratio of price of foreign goods (P_f) to price of goods at home (P) is $\frac{P_f}{P}$. If e is the nominal exchange rate (that is, ratio of prices of domestic and foreign currencies), then the real exchange rate R equals $e.\ \frac{P_f}{P}$. Now, depreciation of national currency will lower the prices of its exports and raise the prices of its imports. This will tend to increase exports and reduce imports and thereby tend to improve trade balance. The net exports or trade balance can be represented as under:

$$NX = X - M$$

$$NX = X\,(Y_f, R) - M(Y,R)$$

$$NX = NX\,(Y, Y_f, R)$$

It follows from the last equation that net exports depend on (1) domestic income or output (Y), which determines imports; (2) foreign income (Y_f) which determines demand for our exports; and (3) real exchange rate (R) which determines prices of our exports and imports. Three important results follow from the equation for net exports.

1. *A rise in our domestic income, other things remaining the same, will raise our spending on imports and hence adversely affect trade deficit.*

2. *A rise in foreign income, say of the USA, other things remaining the same, will increase our exports and improve our trade balance. As a result, aggregate demand will increase in our country with a favourable effect on our national income, output and employment.*

3. *A depreciation in real exchange rate of our currency will increase our exports and reduce our imports with a favourable effect on national output and employment.*

MACRO-ECONOMIC EQUILIBRIUM IN AN OPEN ECONOMY WITHOUT CAPITAL FLOWS : IS-LM MODEL

IS – LM curve model involves the determination of national income and rate of interest through joint equilibrium of goods market and money market. Since in an open economy a part of increase in income is spent on imports rather than on domestically produced goods, *IS* curve of an open economy is steeper than that of a closed economy. This means that for a given reduction in interest rate, a smaller increase in output and income is required to restore equilibrium in the goods market.

Besides, as explained above, *IS* curve of the open economy also includes net exports (*NX*) as a component of aggregate demand for goods. The real exchange rate of the national currency, which determines the prices of exports and imports and thereby determine net exports also affects the open economy *IS* curve. Fore example, depreciation of real exchange rate of the national currency which raise exports and lowers imports results in increase in net exports and will therefore cause an outward shift in the *IS* curve to the right. Similarly, increase in foreign income which will raise foreign spending on our goods will lead to the increase in net exports, which is a component of aggregate demand, will also cause a shift in the IS curve to the right.

LM curve which represents money market equilibrium at various rates of interest and level of income is represented by the following equation:

$$\frac{M}{P} = L(r, Y)$$

where $\frac{M}{P}$ stands for supply of real money balances, and $L(r, Y)$ for demand for money which is determined by rate of interest (r) and level of income (Y).

The intersection of open-economy *IS* and *LM* curves determine jointly the income and rate of interest in the

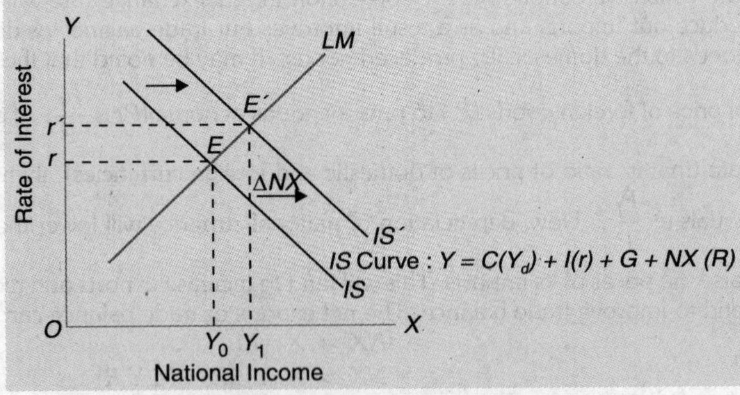

Fig. 44.1. *Determination of National Income in the Open Economy without Cappital Flows through IS and LM Curves*

open economy. This is shown in Figure 44.1. It will be seen that open economy *IS* and *LM* curves interested at joint *E* and determine Y_0 equilibrium level of income and *r* equilibrium rate of interest.

Impact of Increase in Net Exports (NX). Since equilibrium level of income in the open economy depends on foreign income (Y_f) and real exchange rate (*R*), changes in foreign income or real exchange rate will affect equilibrium level of income. For example, if foreign income increases, it will raise the foreign spending on domestic goods or, in other words, it will increase our net exports. The increase in net exports (*NX*) will cause a shift of *IS* curve to the right. This is shown in Fig. 44.1 where as a result of increase in foreign income, say of the United States, which is our important trade partner. *IS* curve shifts from *IS* to *IS´* With this it will be seen that equilibrium level of income has risen to Y_1 and rate of interest to *r*′. It should be noted that increase in income also implies increase in output and employment.

On the other hand, if there is recession in foreign economies, as was the case of American economy during 2001-03, it will reduce their imports and thereby reduce foreign demand for our exports. This will cause a leftward shift in the *IS* curve. As a result, our level of income and output will fall. Besides, rate of interest will also decline.

Effect of Depreciation on Exchange Rate

Let us now see how depreciation in real exchange rate of the national currency, say Indian rupee, affects our national income. This can also be explained with the help of Fig. 44.1 As explained above, depreciation in exchange rate encourages exports and discourages imports and thereby leads to increase in net exports. Since net exports increase at each level of income, *IS* curve shifts to the right, say to *IS*′ in Fig. 44.1. Thus, as a result of depreciation in real exchange rate, equilibrium level of income will increase.

Conclusion: In the Table 44.1 given below, we summarise the effects of changes in domestic spending, foreign income and depreciation in real exchange rate on domestic income and net exports. It may be noted that + sign indicates increase and – sign indicates decrease. It will be seen from this table that *increase in domestic spending leads to increase in domestic income and decrease in net exports*. Increase in domestic spending leads to greater aggregate demand for goods and services and have therefore favourable

Table 44.1. Effects of changes in domestic spending, foreign income and real domestic income and net exports

	Increase in Domestic Spending	*Depreciation in Exchange Rate*	*Increase in Foreign Income*
Domestic Income	+	+	+
Net Exports	–	+	+

effect on the level of domestic income. Since a part of increase in domestic spending is made on imports of goods from abroad, it increases imports and, given the exports, will cause a decrease in net exports of the economy.

Increase in foreign income causes an increase in foreign demand for our goods (i.e. exports) which are a component of aggregate demand and has therefore a favourbale effect on the level of domestic income. Likewise, as increase in foreign income leads to more exports and, given the imports, will cause an increase in net exports.

Lastly, as explained above, since depreciation in real exchange rate causes increase in exports and decrease in imports, it leads to increase in net exports. Increase in net exports raises aggregate demand for goods and has, therefore, a favourable effect on domestic income.

THE MUNDELL - FLEMING MODEL

One of the important fact about the world economy today is the high degree of integration or linkage among financial or capital markets. As mentioned above, households, banks or corporations of different countries search around the world for the highest return (of course, adjusted for risk). As a result, returns or yields in capital markets in different countries get linked together. For example, if rates of interest or return on equity capital in India rise relative to those in the USA, the US investors would try to lend or invest their capital in India to take advantage of higher returns. On the other hand, the borrowers would turn to the USA to borrow funds from the US financial markets to take advantage of lower rates of return.

The tendency for the rates of return on capital to become equal in financial markets of different countries as a result of perfect mobility of capital was formalised in a model in the 1960s by Robert Mundell, now a professor at Columbia University and the Late Marcus Fleming, an economist at the IMF. They assume (1) **a small open economy** (2) tax rates are the same everywhere, (3) *foreign investors do not face political risk (i.e. the fear of nationalism of foreign assets, restrictions of transfer of assets, risk of default by foreign governments)*. Under these conditions and with perfect mobility of capital investors or foreign asset holders would try to invest in the asset in any country that yields the highest return. This would force rates of return on assets to become equal everywhere in the international capital markets because no one would invest at a lower return. It may however be noted that perfect equlisation of returns in different countries is crucially dependent on the twin assumptions of perfect mobility of capital and fixed foreign or world interest rate for an economy. In fact, as mentioned above, Mundell-Fleming model assumes a small open economy which is incapable of influencing world interest rate. Besides, it assumes perfect capital mobility. "*Capital is perfectly mobile internationally when investors can purchase assets in any country they choose, quickly with low transaction costs, and in unlimited amounts.* When capital is perfectly mobile, asset holders are willing and able to move large amounts of funds across borders in search of the highest return or lowest borrowing costs"[3] The assumption of a small open economy with perfect capital mobility plays an important role in Mundell-Fleming model. The assumption of a small open economy implies that the economy can borrow or lend as much as it likes in world financial markets without affecting rate of interest. Thus, for a small open economy, rate of interest is determined by the world interest rate. Mathematically, we can state this assumption as

$$r = r_f$$

where r stands for domestic interest rate in the economy and r_f is the world rate of interest. It is the perfect mobility of capital that makes domestic interest rate (r) equal to the world interest rate. If due to some event or economic policy domestic interest rate happens to be lower than the world interest rate, the capital outflows would drive the domestic interest rate back to the world interest rate. On the other hand, if some event or policy causes domestic interest to exceed world interest rate, then the capital inflows would bring down the domestic interest rate to the level of world interest rate. Hence the equation $r = r_f$ represents that internationd flow of capital quickly brings the domestic interest rate equal to the world interest rate.

The Mundell-Fleming model, with domestic interest rate determined by the world interest rate, focuses on the role of exchange rate in the determination of national income in the short run. Another important aspect of Mundell-Fleming model is that behaviour of

3. R. Dornbusch, S Fischer, R. Startz, Macroeconomics, TATA McGrawhill, 2002, P.282.

the economy depends on whether it adopts the fixed exchange rate system or flexible exchange rate system. In what follows we first explain below Mundell-Fleming model when the economy operate under the fixed exchange rate system and then analyse the model when the economy has adopted the flexible exchange rate system.

The Mundell-Fleming model of a small open economy with perfect capital mobility can be described by the following equations for *IS* and *IM* curves

IS equation: $Y = C\,(Y - T) + I(r_f) + G + NX(R)$

LM equation: $\frac{M}{P} = L\,(r_f, Y)$

The *IS* equation describes the goods marks equilibrium and the second *LM* equation describes money market equilibrium. *G* and *T* are the variables determined by fiscal policy, *M* is the monetary policy variable and they are important exogenous variables. The price *P* and world interest rate (r_f) are the other exogenously given variables. The interest rate being given, the intersection of *IS* and *LM* curves determine the level of national income at which both the goods market and money market are in equilibrium. Besides, in case of the variable exchange rate system, the equilibrium of the two markets also determine the exchange rate.

However, Mundell – Fleming Model is based on some conditions which do not prevail in the real world. First, there are tax differences among countries which hinder the mobility of capital in response to interest-rate differentials among countries. Secondly, exchange rates between different currencies can change, sometimes considerably, which affect return in dollars on foreign investment. Finally, countries adopt measures to restrict capital outflows or simply default in making payments. These are some of the reasons due to which interest rates in different countries are not equal.

Mundell-Fleming Model of the Small Open Economy with a Fixed Exchange Rate Regime : Impact of Monetary Policy

An important result of the Mundell–Fleming linkage model under fixed exchange rate regime is that a central bank of a country cannot pursue an independent monetary policy. Under perfect mobility, a very small difference in interest rates in different countries would cause infinite capital flows that would bring about changes in balance of payments. These changes in balance of payments will affect exchange rate between different national currencies which would eliminate interest rate differential. Take an example. Suppose Central Bank of a country tightens its monetary policy so as to raise interest rate in the economy. When with the adoption of this policy interst rate rises in the economy, foreigners will shift their investible funds to this country so as to take advantage of the higher interest rate. With a huge inflow of capital, foreign exchange rate of the domestic currency will rise, that is, the currency of the country that adopts a higher interest rate monetary policy will appreciate. This appreciation of the currency will discourage exports and encourage imports which would have an adverse effect on balance of payments. This will force the Central Bank of the country which is committed to maintain the exchange rate at the fixed level to intervene to prevent the appreciation of exchange rate of the national currency.

To prevent the currency from appreciation, the Central Bank will buy the foreign currency, say US dollar. This will lead to the increase in foreign exchange reserves with the Central Bank which will issue more national currency against the increase in foreign exchange reserves. As a result, money supply in the economy will expand causing the rate of interest to fall. Thus, with the perfect mobility of capital and given a fixed exchange rate, domestic interest rate has been pushed back to the initial level. To quote Dornbusch and Fischer again, *"Under fixed exchange rates and perfect capital mobility, a country cannot move out of line with those prevailing in the world market. Any attempt at independent monetary policy leads to capital flows and need to intervene until interest rates are back in line with those in the world market*"[4].

It follows from above that, given a higher degree of capital mobility across countries, interest rates cannot be very much different. The differences in interest rates beyond a point will bring about capital flows across countries that will tend to provide world level yield in all of them.

Expansionary Monetary Policy Under Fixed Exchange Rate and Perfect Capital Mobility. Let us now analyse the effect of monetary expansion under the fixed exchange rate regime using *IS-LM* model. Consider Fig. 44.2 where in panel (a) we have drawn the *IS* and *LM* curves as well as the horizontal straight line *BP*. The horizontal line *BP*= 0 at domestic interest rate *i* equal to foreign interest rate i_f ($i=i_f$) shows that the country has neither deficit nor surplus in its balance of payments, that is, its balance of payments is in equilibrium. At any other interest rate massive capital flows will occur which will cause disequilibrium in the balance of payments and will force the Central Bank to intervene to maintain the exchange rate.

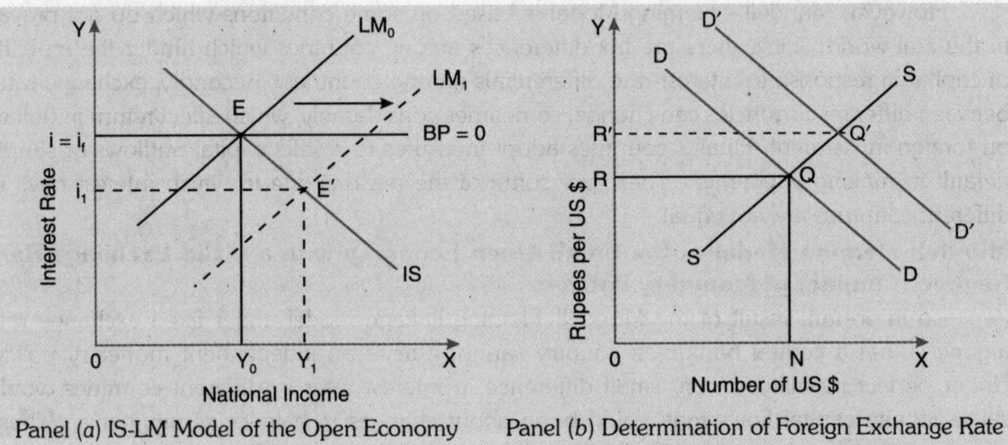

Panel (*a*) IS-LM Model of the Open Economy Panel (*b*) Determination of Foreign Exchange Rate

Fig. 44.2. *Effect of Monetary Expansion Under the Fixed Exchange Rate Regime and Perfect Capital Mobility*

To illustrate this we consider that Government adopts a policy of monetary expansion. Let the economy in panel (a) of Fig. 44.2 is initially in equilibrium at point *E* where the given *IS-LM* curves intersect at *E* which determines domestic rate of interest *i* which is equal to foreign rate of interest i_f. With monetary expansion, *LM* curve shifts to the right and as a result the economy moves to the new equilibrium position *E*′ where domestic rate of interest has fallen to i_1. However *E*′ is not the *final* equilibrium situation. This is because at point *E*′ the rate of interest has fallen to i_1 which is lower than the world interest rate (i_f). This will cause *capital outflows* from the domestic economy, which will exert a pressure on the exchange rate of domestic currency to *depreciate*. This is because these capital outflows of the of US dollars will cause demand for US dollars to increase, and given the supply curve, will cause exchange rate of rupee to depreiate. Determination of foreign exchange rate is shown in panel (*b*) of Fig. 44.2 where initially demand curve *DD* and supply curve *SS* of US dollars determine

4. Dornbusch and Fischer, op. cit. p.285

exchange rate equal to *OR* (*i.e.* number of rupees per US dollar). When as a result of expansion in money supply, *LM* curve shifts to the right to the new position LM_1 and consequently domestic rate of interest falls to i_1 (panel (*a*) of Fig. 44.2), there will be large capital outflows (i.e., outflows of US $). These dollar outflows will lead to the increase in demand for US dollars in foreign exchange market. This is because to send US dollars abroad the rupees have to be first converted into US dollars. This can be done through foreign exchange market where the demand for US dollars will increase when there are capital outflows. Therefore in panel (b) of Fig. 44.2 as a result of capital outflows demand curve of US dollars shifts to the right to *D 'D '* and given the supply curve SS of US dollars, the exchange rate (rupees per US dollar) falls to *R'* (that is, more rupees per US dollar). This means Indian rupee will depreciate. To maintain the exchange rate, the Central Bank of the country will intervene; it will sell foreign currency reserves in the foreign exchange market. With the sales of US dollars, the foreign currency assets with Reserve Bank will decline on the basis of which rupee currency is issued. Therefore the supply of domestic money supply in the economy will decrease. As a result of this reduction in domestic money supply, *LM* curve will shift back to the left [see panel (a) of Fig. 44.2]. This process of contraction in money supply and consequent shifting back of *LM* curve to the left will continue until the initial equilibrium at *E* is reached again. As a matter of fact, with perfect capital mobility, the economy is not likely to reach at the new equilibrium joint *E´*. This is because the response of capital flows is so large and quick that the Central Bank will be forced to reverse quickly the initial expansion in money supply before the new equilibrium at *E´* is reached.

Contraction in Money Supply Under fixed Exchange Rate System

Conversely, if the Central Bank adopts the policy of contraction in money supply, *LM* curve will shift to the left of the initial equilibrium point *E*. Given the *IS* curve the new equilibrium will be reached at a higher domestic rate of interest as compared to foreign interest rate. This will induce massive capital inflows which will increase the demand for domestic currency and as a result domestic currency will appreciate. To maintain the exchange rate, the Central Bank will buy the foreign currency and give the domestic currency in exchange. As a result, central bank will be forced to expand the money supply and this monetary expansion will cause shift in *LM* curve back to the right so that ultimately the domestic economy returns to the initial equilibrium situation .

Conclusion. From the foregoing analysis of Mundell-Fleming model under the fixed exchange rate regime, it follows that when capital mobility is perfect, interest rates in the home country cannot deviate from those prevailing abroad. It is quite evident from above that *with perfect mobility of capital, under fixed exchange rate regime, monetary policy in a small open economy is quite ineffective to influence the levels of national income (output) and employment.* Any attempt by the central bank of the country to reduce interest rate by expansion in money supply would lead to massive outflows of capital tending to cause depreciation of the home currency. The Central Bank, which is under obligation to maintain the exchange rate at a fixed level, would buy the domestic currency in exchange for foreign currency. This will result in reduction in money supply to its original level with the home economy again attaining equilibrium at the initial level. This shows under fixed exchange rate regime, the *Central bank of a country cannot undertake an independent monetary policy.*

Mundell-Fleming Model : Role of Expansionary Fiscal Policy under Fixed Exchange Rate System

While expansionary monetary policy under fixed rate regime is quite ineffective to affect national income and output, fiscal policy is highly effective, given the perfect mobility of capital. To show this through open economy *IS-LM* model, consider Fig. 44.3. Suppose adopting expansionary fiscal policy Government increases its expenditure with money supply remaininingunchanged. It will be seen from panel (a) that increase in government expenditure causes shift in the *IS* curve to the right to the new position *IS* ′. As will be seen from panel (a) the new equilibrium is at *H* and as a result both the interest rate and level of national income (output) have risen. However, point *H* is not the final equilibrium. The higher domestic rate of interest *as compared to the world interest rate* (i_f) *will cause capital inflows into the economy*. These capital inflows will bring about appreciation in exchange rate of national currency.

The determination of foreign exchange rate is illustrated in panel (*b*) of Fig. 44.3 where demand curve *DD* and supply Curve *SS* of US dollars intersect at point Q and determine *R* the exchange rate between US dollar and rupee in terms of rupees per US dollar. It will be observed from panel (*b*) that as a result of capital inflows, supply curve of foreign exchange (*i.e.* US dollars) shifts to the right from *SS* to *S′S′* . The new supply curve *S′S′* of US dollars intersects the demand curve for US dollar at point *Q′* and determines the higher new foreign exchange rate *R′* (i.e., less rupees per US dollar). This implies that there is appreciation of rupee as fewer rupees are required to exchange for a US dollar. To maintain the exchange rate at *R* the Central Bank will have to buy *QT* dollars from the foreign exchange market. When the Central Bank buys US dollars it will pay rupees to the sellers of these dollars. For this payment the Central Bank will have to print new rupee notes. Thus to maintain the exchange rate at *R* the Central Bank has to expand the money supply (i.e. supply of rupees) in the domestic economy which will cause a shift the *LM* curve in panel(a) of Fig. 44.3 to the right and will lead to the increase in national income further and fall in interest rate. It will be seen from panel (*a*) of Figure 44.3 that when money supply is increased so much that *LM* curve shifts to the new position *LM′* and domestic rate of interest falls back to the original level so that it is again equal to the world interest rate ($i = i_f$). Thus, in this case, with endogenous expansion in money supply to maintain the exchange rate, interest rate effectively remains fixed at a given level. Fiscal expansion leads to increase in national income by Y_1Y_3, equal to the Keynesian multiplier effect.

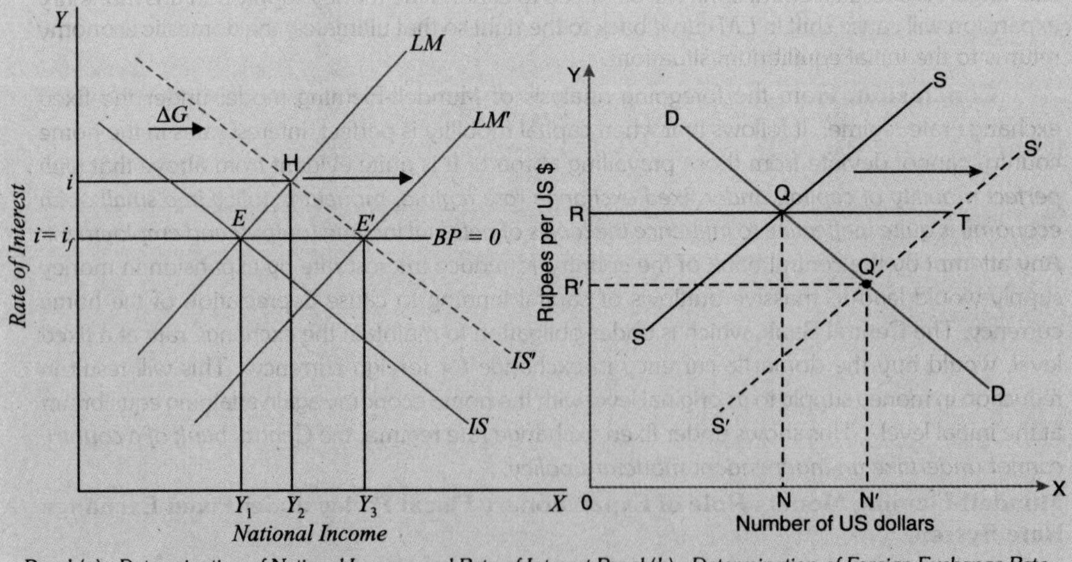

Panel (*a*) : *Determination of National Income and Rate of Interest* Panel (*b*) : *Determination of Foreign Exchange Rate*

Fig. 44.3. *Effect of Expansionery Fiscal Policy in a Small Open Economy under Fixed Exchange Rate with Perfect Capital Mobility*

Conclussion

The upshot of the above analysis is that the *commitment to maintain a fixed exchange rate makes the changes in money supply endogenous*. This is because the Central Bank through its intervention has to sell or buy the foreign exchange as the case may be to maintain the exchange rate at the fixed level. The Central Bank under the fixed exchange rate system with perfect capital mobility *cannot conduct an independent monetary policy* to achieve domestic economic stability. However, *government can use expansionary fiscal policy to raise the level of national income and employment*.

MUNDELL-FLEMING MODEL FOR A SMALL OPEN ECONOMY UNDER FLEXIBLE EXCHANGE RATES

We now use Mundell-Fleming Model to explain how monetary and fiscal policies in a small open economy work when there is completely flexible exchange rate regime and perfect capital mobility. It is assumed that domestic prices remain fixed while exchange rate is fully flexible. It is important to note that under flexible exchange rate regime, the Central Bank does not intervene in the market for foreign exchange. The exchange rate adjusts itself to bring demand for and supply of foreign exchange in equilibrium. Therefore, *under flexible exchange rate system and without the intervention of the Central Bank, balance of payments must always be in equilibrium*, that is, there is neither any deficit nor any surplus. This implies that any current account deficit must be financed by private capital inflows. On the contrary, any current account surplus must be balanced by capital outflows. It is worth noting again that it is adjustments in foreign exchange rate under flexible exchange rate system that guarantees that sum of current and capital accounts of blance of payments is zero

A second *important consequence of fully flexible exchange rate regime is that under it the Central Bank can pursue its independent monetary policy*, that is, it can expand or contract the money supply at will according to its assessment of the needs of the domestic economy. Since under flexible exchange rates, there is no obligation for the Central Bank to intervene there is no any link between the balance of payments and the money supply in the economy.

In Mundell-Fleming model the assumption of perfect capital mobility ensures that at only one interest rate which is equal to world interest rate ($i = i_f$) the balance of payments is zero, that is, in equilibrium ($BP = 0$). At any rate of interest other than this causes a change in the real exchange rate through its effect on capital flows for the domestic economy. Assuming that domestic and foreign prices of goods (p and p_f) remain constant, decline in the domestic interest rate below the world interest rate (*i.e.* i_f) will cause unlimited capital outflows and bring about depreciation in the exchange rate. As explained above, exchange rate is a determinant of net exports (*NX*) which in the open economy affects aggregate demand and therefore determines level of income in the open-economy *IS* curve (*IS* curve : $Y = Y(Y, i) + NX(Y, Y_f, R)$ where R stands for the real exchange rate and *NX* for net exports). Now, depreciation in the exchange rate following capital outflows when $i < i_f$ will raises exports and reduce imports and will cause increase in net exports (*NX*). The increase in net exports will shift the *IS* curve to the right and thereby affect national income and output.

On the contrary, if $i > i_f$, there will be unlimited capital inflows causing appreciation in the exchange rate which will reduce exports and increase imports and will thus lead to the reduction in net exports (*NX*). The reduction in net exports (*NX*) as a result of appreciation in the exchange rate causes a shift in the *IS* curve to the left and will therefore affect national income and output.

In the small open economy with international linkages in terms of trade of goods and capital flows, our open economy model under flexible exchange rate regime consists of the following three equations.

$$IS \text{ curve: } Y = A(Y, i) + NX(Y, Y_f, R) \quad \ldots(i)$$

$$BP = NX(Y, Y_f, R) + CF(i - i_f) \quad \ldots(ii)$$

$$i = i_f \quad \ldots(iii)$$

where *CF* stands for capital flows.

With this Mundell-Fleming linkage model of a small open economy under flexible exchange rate regime we explain below the effect on national income (output), interest rate and exchange rate of the following factors and policies.

1. Exogenous increase in exports
2. Fiscal policy
3. Monetary policy

Exogenous Increase in Net Exports under Flexible Exchange Rate

The effect of exogenous increase in exports, say due to the increase in world demand for our goods, is shown in Fig. 44.4 Initially, the economy is in equilibrium at point *E* with national output equal to Y_0 and interest rate *i* which is equal to world interest rate i_f $(i=i_f)$. When there is exogenous increase in our net exports, *IS* curve shifts to the right to *IS'*.

Now, new *IS'* curve interests *LM* curve at point *E´* where both goods and money markets clear. It may be noted that at this new equilibrium point, *E´*, national income increases to Y_1. The increase in national income also induces the rise in equilibrium interest rate above the world interest rate i_f. This higher domestic interest rate will lead to the capital inflows which will exert pressure on the exchange rate. These capitals inflows, as seen above, will cause the domestic currency to appreciate. The appreciation in exchange rate will make our exports relatively expensive and imports cheaper than before. As a result, demand shifts away from domestic goods and as a result net exports (*NX*) decline.

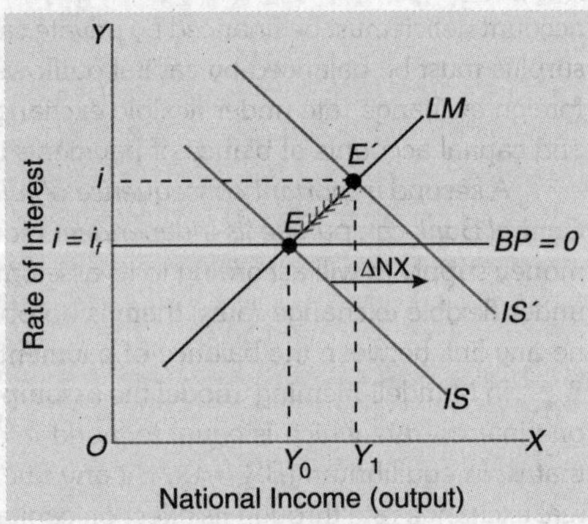

Fig. 44.4. *Effect of Exogenous Increase in Exports*

In Fig. 44.4, the appreciation of exchange rate and consequently decline in net exports will cause a shift in the *IS* curve back to the left. The capital inflows will continue and net exports will go on declining as a result of appreciation of domestic currency until *IS* curve shifts back to the original level *IS* and equilibrium level of national income and output is restored at OY_0 level which is consistent with monetary equilibrium at the world rate of interest.

Conclusion. It follows from above that under conditions of perfect capital mobility, increase in exports of a small open economy has no lasting effect on the equilibrium level of national income and output. Increase in net exports (NX) causes interest rate to rise through increase in level of national income. This induces capital inflows which result in appreciation of the exchange rate and reduces net exports. This cancels out the effect on national income of the initial exogenous increase in exports of a country.

Effect of Expansionary Fiscal Policy in a Small Open Economy under Flexible Exchange Rate

We can use the Mundell-Fleming linkage model to analyse the effect of expansionary fiscal policy in a small open economy under flexible exchange rate system. Expansionary fiscal policy has the same effect as that of exogenous increase in exports explained above. Under expansionary fiscal policy either government expenditure is increased or taxes are reduced. This fiscal expansion leads to the increase in aggregate demand and causes a shift in the *IS* curve to the right. This, given the *LM* curve, induces the interest rate to rise and invites capital inflows into the economy. These capital inflows result in appreciation of the exchange rate. This appreciation of the exchange rate induced by higher interest rate leads to reduction in exports and increase in imports. As a result, there is reduction in net exports which completely offsets the impact of fiscal expansion on national income and output.

We arrive at an important conclusion from our above analysis. *Real disturbances such as exogenous increase in exports or expansion in government expenditure or a tax cut does not affect equilibrium level of income in a small open economy under flexible exchange rate system with perfect capital mobility.* We have seen above that under the fixed exchange rate regime, expansionary fiscal policy in a small open economy is highly effective in increasing the level of national income. However, *under flexible exchange rate system with conditions of perfect capital mobility, equilibrium level of aggregate income or output remains unaffected as a result of expansionary fiscal policy*. Under flexible exchange rate fiscal expansion causes appreciation of exchange rate which causes exports to decrease and imports to increase and thus leads to a shift in the composition of domestic demand towards foreign goods and away from domestic goods.

Mundell-Fleming Model : Expansionary Monetary Policy in a Small Open Economy under Flexble Exchange Rates

In sharp contrast to the expansionary fiscal policy, in Mundell-Fleming model expansionary monetary policy under flexible exchange rate regime is highly effective in raising the level of national income or output. This favourable affect of expansion in money supply on the level of national output comes through its causing depreciation in exchange rate of domestic currency. Consider Fig. 44.5 where to begin with *IS* and *LM* curves interest at point *E* and determine level of national income Y_0 and rate of interest *i*, ($i = i_f$). Now, suppose there is increase in the nominal quantity of money supply *M*. Since we are assuming that prices of goods remain constant, increase in money will bring about increase in real money balances, $\frac{M}{P}$ As a result *LM* curve shifts to the right to the new position *LM*´. With this at the equilibrium point *E*, there will be excess supply of real money balances. To restore equilibrium, rate of interest will have to fall or aggregate income will have to rise. The new *LM*´ curve interesects the original *IS* curve at new point *E*´. At the new point *E*´, whereas goods and money markets are in equilibrium (at the initial exchange rate), rate of interest has fallen below the world interest rate i_f. This will cause capital outflows

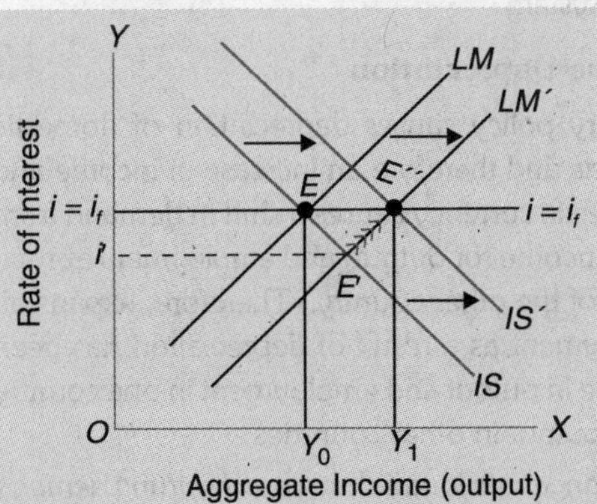

Fig. 44.5. *Mundell Fleming Model : Effect of Expansion in Money Supply on Level of Income or Output in a Small Open Economy under Flexible Exchange Rate System*

from the country. These capital outflows will increase the demand for foreign exchange (say *US* dollars) and lead to the depreciation of the domestic currency. The depreciation of domestic currency will make exports of the country relatively cheaper and its imports relatively expensive than before. This will lead to the increase in exports and reduction in imports of the country resulting in larger net exports (*NX*). Increase in net exports (*NX*), which is a component of aggregate demand, will cause *IS* curve to shift to the right. Thus point E' is really not a final equilibrium point as adjustment process is not complete at point E'. *IS* curve will continue shifting to the right until the joint equilibrium of goods market and money market is established at the rate of interest which is equal to the world interest rate. In Fig. 44.5. such equilibrium is reached at point E'' at which new LM' and IS' curves interesect and determine rate of interest $i = i_f$. It will be seen from Fig. 44.5 that at the new final equilibrium point E'', level of national income (or aggregate output) Y_1 is greater than the initial income Y_0.

Comparison. It is interesting to compare in case of a small open economy the impact of expansion in money supply under flexible rate system with that under fixed exchange rate regine. Under the fixed exchange rate regime the expansionary monetary policy is quite ineffective in raising national income or aggregate output. Any attempt to increase money supply lowers rate of interest below the world interest rate which causes unlimited capital outflows. These capital outflows lead to the reversal of increase in money supply so that finally the equilibrium of the economy is restored at the initial level of income or output.

On the other hand, under flexible exchange rate system where Central Bank does not intervene, increase in money supply, as seen above, is not *reversed* in the foreign exchange market. Capital outflows that take place in the foreign exchange market following the fall in the rate of interest below the world rate of interest leads to depreciation of domestic currency. This depreciation causes exports to increase and imports to decline resulting in increase in net exports (*NX*). Consequently, expansion in income or output actually occurs assuming fixed prices. Thus, ability of the Central Bank to control money supply under flexible exchange rate is an important effect of the flexible exchange rate system.

Beggar Thy Neighbour Policy and Competitive Depreciation

We have seen above expansionary monetary policy causes depreciation of domestic currency and thereby leads to increase in net exports and therefore an increase in income and employment in the economy. Depreciation of domestic currency causes a shift in demand from foreign goods towards domestic goods. As a result, income (or output) and employment abroad decline. That is, one country gains at the expense of the other country. Therefore, expansion in net exports and therefore in income and employment as a result of depreciation has been called *beggar thy-neighbour policy*. That is, increase in output and employment in one country takes place by creating unemployment and loss of output in other countries.

It follows from above that *depreciation in exchange rate is mainly a way of shifting demand from foreign goods towards domestic goods rather than increasing the level of world demand.* Exchange rate adjustment can play an important role in promoting economic stability at full employment level when different countries find themselves in different phases of business cycles. That is, some are in boom phases and experiencing over full employment while others are in recession phase of business cycles. In this case, if the countries experiencing recession depreciate their domestic currencies, they will shift foreign demand to their domestic products. In this way this will remove divergence from full employment in each country.

However, it has been witnessed that business cycles are highly synchronised such as world-wide depression in the early 1930s and consequence of oil shack of 1973 and also recently in 2001-03, exchange rate adjustment will not contribute much towards achieving world-wide full employment conditions. For example, if level of total world demand is deficient, then depreciation in exchange rate by various countries will affect only the distribution of given world demand among countries and will not help in increasing the level of world demand for goods and services. In other words, exchange rate adjustments by various countries experience recessionary conditions are merely policies of beggar thy-neighbour variety. Of course, from the angle of an individual country depreciation of domestic currency shifts foreign demand to itself and is able to increase its output and employment. But, if one country can raise its output and employment by depreciating its currency, others can also do so. This leads to *competitive depreciation by different countries* for attracting world demand for their goods at the expense of others.

Appendix to Chapter 44

Foreign Capital Flows and their Impact on Macroeconomic Stability

VOLATILITY OF CAPITAL FLOWS INTO INDIA: ITS IMPACT

As explained in the previous chapter capital flows in the form of foreign direct investment (FDI) and portfolio investment by FII play not only an important role in economic growth of the country but also are badly needed to finance the deficit in current account of our balance of payments. However, volatility of capital flows creates a lot of macroeconomic instability in the Indian economy. This volatility creates sometimes boom in stock market and some times crash in it. Capital inflows cause appreciation of exchange rate of rupee and thereby adversely affect our exports and through creating excess liquidity they add to inflationary pressures in the economy. On the other hand, capital outflows cause depreciation of rupee and thereby encourage exports but make our imports costlier.

Volatile capital movements have influenced the domestic stock price movements, exchange rate and domestic liquidity conditions significantly in the past. In 2009-10, the and current account deficit widened to 2.8 per cent of GDP in 2010-11 and it is estimated at 3.6 percent of GDP in 2011-12. Volatile capital flows have been a potential source of instability for emerging market economies (EMEs). Costs of volatility of the capital flows could magnify for an economy during periods of both too little and too much of capital flows, unless they are managed judiciously. India, in recent years, had to manage phases of capital flows characterised by large net inflows as well as sudden outflows in the midst of a global crisis. *A judicious mix of flexible exchange rate, sterilisation of the impact of inflows on domestic liquidity, cautious approach to liberalisation of the capital account and the cushion of foreign exchange reserves has been used to deal with the adverse ramifications of capital flows.*

Volatility of capital flows is caused mainly by investment by FIIs. In India it is the inflows and outflows of portfolio capital by FIIs that have caused a lot of macroeconomic instability in the Indian economy. The total *net* FII flows to India in 2009 stood at US $ 18.51 billion. These flows grew remarkably in 2010 and India received FII investment worth US $ 39.71 billion in 2010 which was the highest in the last decade. These inflows were largely driven by equity inflows which remained buoyant on the back of strong domestic macroeconomic fundamentals and high GDP growth. FIIs had been quite active in the debt segment as well in 2010. However, against the high net FII inflows of the year 2010, the flows during the year 2011 were quite low. During the first ten months (Jan.-Oct.) of the calender year 2011 India received only $ 4.66 billion against US $ 39.47 billion during 2010. FII investment in India during 2007-11 is given below in Table 44A.1.

Table 44A.1 FII Investment in India

Segment	2007	2008	2009	2010	2011*
Equity	17.65	–11.97	16.87	29.36	0.39
Debt	2.34	2.63	1.64	10.11	4.27
Total	19.99	–9.34	18.51	39.47	4.66

Source: MOF *Mid-year review* 2011-12

* Investment upto Oct. 31, 2011

Capital Inflows and Economic Instability

While capital inflows during 2009 remained moderate, in 2010 there was a return of another phase of surge in capital flows to India in response to global search for higher yields in an environment of easy liquidity conditions in advanced economies and the prospect of relatively higher return on investment in India in view of its superior growth outlook. The Indian economy grew at 8.4 per cent during 2010-11 which is the second highest growth rate in the world, next only to China. While stronger growth could help in absorbing higher magnitude of foreign capital within the limits of sustainable current account deficit, excess capital inflows would entail the risk of exerting *appreciation pressure on the exchange rate of the rupee*, which in turn could weaken the competitive advantage of Indian exports. Sterilised intervention by RBI could limit the pressure on appreciation of the rupee on account of capital inflows, but may lead to a higher interest rate environment. *Unsterilised intervention* by the RBI that could relieve the pressure on both exchange rate and interest rate, however would involve excess liquidity creation in the economy. In an environment of high inflation, this could only increase the inflationary situation further.

High inflation would also adversely impact export competitiveness through appreciation of the real effective exchange rate (REER), which would further widen the current account deficit. Excess capital inflows, thus, would continue to pose challenges for the country's exchange rate, interest rate and inflation environment and through these channels, may at times also weaken the beneficial impact of capital flows on economic growth. Unlike the pre-global crisis period, international perception now seems to have changed significantly *in terms of support for use of soft capital controls to deal with excessive capital flows*. In the case of emerging market economies (EMEs), surges in capital flows into them have contributed to asset price build up, along with exchange rate appreciation. Given the complications, asset price build-up could pose problem for monetary policy and potential risks to financial stability. Therefore, management of capital flows into India would need to strike a balance between the objectives of growth and financial stability.

Stronger recovery in India in 2009-10 and 2010-11, ahead of the global recovery along with positive sentiments of global investors about India's growth prospects, encouraged a revival in capital flows into India during 2009-10. The turnaround was mainly driven by large capital inflows under profitfolio investment by FIIs and short-term trade credits. As a result *net* capital flows into India at US $53.4 billion (3.8% of GDP were much higher during 2009-10 as compared to US $6.8 billion (0.5 per cent of GDP) in 2008-09. The strong domestic demand for goods in India, unlike many other emerging markets which depend on exports to the West where consumer confidence is waning, was an added attraction. Net equity inflows hit $ 23-25 billion in 2010-11, while net debt flows will also be significantly higher. Globally, with debt investment yields so low, money continues to be allocated to equities and gold. And within the equity universe, emerging markets, especially India, witnessed increased capital inflows and many new investors in 2009-10 and 2010-11.

The fact that when a country witnesses a volatile capital inflows comprising short-term capital flows while stable capital flows represented by FDI slows down, country faces an acute problem of economic instability. This forced Brazil with an emerging economy to go in for capital controls in April 2011 to ensure economic stability. The too much inflows of volatile capital in Brazil threatened to fuel an *asset bubble.* Surprisingly enough, the champion of free flow of capital, International Monetary Fund conceded in April 2011 that governments can resort to capital controls when they have to prevent economic destabilisation.

Now, the pertinent question where does India, a prominent emerging market economy, stand ? It is a very different situation. The emerging economies of Brazil, Russia, India and China – normally known as BRICs for their uniform opportunities in the past – are beginning to diverge. Inflation is a common theme running across these countries. So are slowing domestic growth and investment opportunities, but not the current account deficit. That throws up a peculiar problem for Indian policy makers who need the foreign capital flows to keep the economy growing by financing its current account deficit. But we also need to prevent rise in inflation due to large capital inflows. This requires fine-tuning *capital flows management.* We cannot resort to controlling capital inflows whether through FDI or FII for we need them to finance our current account deficit which is now of a significant size. For India it is a big problem to rely on volatile capital inflows by FIIs for financing our current account deficit. What we need are *stable and long term* capital flows of foreign direct investment.

Capital Outflows and Economic Instability

There was capital flight from the Indian markets in Feb, 2011 but it returned to India in April and there was *net inflow of capital* of US $3.1 billion by FIIs in April-July 15, 2011 bringing boom in the Indian stock and bond market and also led to appreciation of rupee to some extent. However, from Aug. 2011 there had again been outlow of capital due to worsening of sovereign debt crisis of European countries and slowdown of the US economy. This caused Bombay Stock Exchange Index (SENSEX) to fall heavily from over 18000 to 16200 on September 24, 2011 and further to 15500 in Mid-December 2011, Besides, this capital outflow led to a large depreciation of rupee from September 2011. The Indian Rupee which was around ₹ 44 to a US dollar in July 2011 fell to nearly ₹ 52 to a US dollar on Nov. 22, 2011 and further to ₹ 53.7 to a US dollar in mid-December 2011. The sharp-depreciation of the Indian rupee caused by capital outflows from Sept. 2011 proved to be highly harmful for the Indian economy. To prevent excessive depreciation of the Indian rupee the RBI used its foreign exchange reserves to sell US dollars in foreign exchange market. This caused decline in foreign exchange reserves which are needed to cover imports of goods and services needed for industrial growth. Further, lack of adequate foreign exchange reserves with the RBI will lead to the loss of confidence among foreign investors about the ability of the country to pay back the loans from foreign financial institutions. Besides, weakening of the rupee is likely to cause losses to the foreign investors who repatriate their profits to their home countries. This will discourage inflows of foreign direct investment needed for economic growth of the country. To attract capital inflows Reserve Bank of India also relaxed norms for external commercial borrowing and removed the cap on NRI deposits in Indian banks. It is evident from above the that capital outflows create a lot of macroeconomic instability and therefore they need to be prudently managed. As mentioned above, India faces a different problem from other emerging economies as it has to contend with a large deficit on current account balance which during the year 2011-12 may go up to 3.6 % of GDP or more for which we need foreign exchange. In this context it is not advisable for India to impose any control on foreign capital inflows. Our foreign exchange reserves stood at around US $272 billion at end-January 2012 and if monthly deficit on current account goes on occurring at the present rate, due to small capital outflows we may find it difficult to meet our current account deficit and as a result we will have to use some of our foreign exchange reserves for this purpose.

Further, of late there is another adverse situation that is developing is the falling cover of our exchange reserves for our imports which means the number of months of imports that our foreign exchange reserves can finance. After touching a peak of being able to Finance 16.5 months imports in February 2010, it fell to 8 months in Feb. 2012.

However, things go on changing dramatically depending on the global economic and financial situation. When there are large capital outflows causing depreciation of rupee as it occured in Sept.-Dec. 2011, there is need for intervention by RBI to sell US dollars from its foreign exchange resourves to check excess depreciation of rupee. On the other hand, when there is excess capital inflows causing appreciation of exchange rate of rupee, the RBI can intervene and buy or absorb some foreign exchange (*i.e.* dollars) coming into the country.

Composition of Capital Flows: A Problem

But the problem for India is more of the adverse nature of the composition of capital flows. In the recent past *capital flows are more of portfolio route by FIIs* which was the largest component of total capital flow in FY 2010-11 (see Figure 44A.1). The difficult problem posed by these volatile capital flows, as mentioned above, is that they are being used to finance widening deficit in current account balance. Foreign direct investment (FDI) which prior to 2010 was the largest component of capital inflows has declined in 2010-11 (see Fig. 44A.1). As will be seen from Fig. 44A.1 the NRI deposits also have slowed down in 2010-11. Even the external commercial borrowing (ECB) has also not risen much in 2010-11 as compared to 2009-10. Because of these the Reserve Bank has to use its policy regarding management of capital flows and foreign exchange rate more proactively than adopt a mere reactive policy in this regard. Even though with the use of proper foreign exchange rate policy the RBI can encourage imports to fight inflation. But it has refrained from doing so. The extent of the RBI intervention in the foreign exchange market has been much less in the last two years. Exchange rate policy has not been used to promote exports or to encourage imports to fight inflation.

It is due to the lack proactive policy of management of capital flows and foreign exchange rate that there is a lot of macroeconomic instability in the Indian economy. When capital outflows by FIIs occur we face a problem of crash in Indian stock market and depreciation of exchange rate of rupee as it occurred during Sept.-Dec. 2011. By increasing the costs of imports (including crude oil) this results in rise in inflation which adds to the problem of ongoing inflation unless they are offset by fall in international commodity prices.

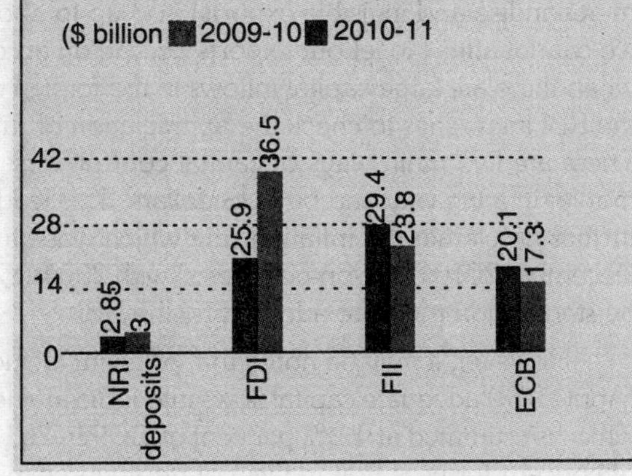

Fig. 44A.1. *Compostion of Capital flows in 2009-10 and 2010-11*

On the other hand, when there is excess capital inflows beyond our absorptive capacity as occurred during April-July 2011 this leads to the appreciation of rupee which makes our exports less competitive and increases excess liquidity in the economy. Intervention by the RBI in such a situation is called for but it has been hesitant to intervene. Explaining this non-intervention Dr. D. Subba Rao, the present Governor of the RBI, states, "*If this resultant liquidity is left unsterilised, it fuels inflationary pressures. If the resultant liquidity is sterilized, it puts upward pressure on interest rates which, apart from hurting competitiveness, also encourages further flows*". This is arguing for unfettered free market in foreign exchange and no controls over the capital flows.

This indicates the RBI should be more watchfal of the movement of capital flows and foreign exchange rate of rupee and should actively intervene in forex market to ensure exchange rate stability and to encourage stable long-run capital flows into the Indian economy.

Macroeconomic Instability. It follows from above that the capital flows, if not regulated properly, can lead to macroeconomic instability. They cause changes in foreign exchange rate which affect exports and imports and therefore the balance of payments of a country. They also lead to the changes in foreign currency assets of Reserve Bank of India bringing about changes in money supply and thus causing price instability. Thus large capital inflows, if not regulated properly, cause inflation in the economy by bringing about expansion in money supply. Besides, as seen above, the large capital inflows of portfolio type affect stock market prices; when they come into the country, they generate boom in the stock market but when there is reversal of these flows, they cause crash in the stock market.

Controlling Capital Inflows

It may be noted that the central banks of the US and Japan have reduced their interest rate to almost zero and bought government securities from the market to pump more money into the market. From Nov. 2010 to June 2011 the US Federal Reserve pumped in $ 600 billion in the US economy which led to capital outflow from the US economy to the emerging economies and caused depreciation of US dollar. Besides, their Central Banks have given loans to their FIIs which are investing in India, and other emerging economies. This has created surplus liquidity in the financial system of some emerging economecs such as Brazil. Besides, the depreciation of the US dollar will make its products cheaper which will boost its earnings from exports. These funds are being brought by FIIs into the emerging economies like Brazil, China and India where growth prospects are very bright and rates of return on capital are quite high. Besides, capital inflows will cause appreciation of rupee which will affect our GDP growth. This is because exports at present are not a negligible part of our GDP. Goods and services put together (that is, both merchandise and invisible exports) add up to about 22 per cent of our GDP. This implies that we cannot afford to let our exports decline on account of appreciation of our rupee. Therefore, when there are large capital inflows in the foreign exchange market is absolutely necessary that the RBI intervenes to check the appreciation of rupee rather than go on waiting and watching. There are two main ways of capital control. First, the RBI intervenes in the foreign exchange market in a big way and buy US dollars. This leads to the expansion in money supply that will further accelerate the inflation rate which was at the uncomfortable level of 8.53 per cent in December 2010 (year-on-year basis) with 2004-05 as the base. But this inflation can be checked by *sterilization measure* adopted by the RBI.

However, it may be noted that problem facing India at present is quite different. At present (April 2013) adequate capital flows into India are necessary for meeting its current account deficit which is estimated at 4.2% per cent of GDP in 2011-12 and 5% of GDP in 2012-13. The matter of concern for us is that in view of decline in capital inflows through foreign direct investment (FDI) we are meeting our large current deficit with portfolio capital inflows by FIIs which are quite volatile and when there is reversal of these inflows it creates problems for the Indian economy. For instance, after a surge of these portfolio capital inflows prior to August 2011, there was again reversal of these flows from September 2011 onwards which put pressure on stock market prices and exchange rate of rupee. Therefore, what is needed for India is to encourage capital inflows through foreign direct investment to build infrastructure facilities and to meet to a large extent the country's current account deficit through these stable FDI inflows. However, at present in view of large current account deficit *there is no need for India for imposing any control on inflows of portfolio capital*, but Reserve Bank of India should prevent the adverse consequences of its volatility through its timely intervention in foreign exchange market.

At present, if adequate capital flows through FDI and FIIs rotues into India do not occur, it will be difficult to finance our increasing current account deficit. In these circumstances we will have to draw upon our mearge foreign exchange reserves ($ 296 billion in March 2013) to finance our current account deficit. Our foreign exchange reserves are already sufficient to finance only 8 months of our imports.

Inflation: Nature and Causes

Meaning

Having discussed the relationship between quantity of money and price level in the previous chapter, we are now in a position to explain the nature and causes of inflation. By inflation we mean *a general rise in prices*. To be more correct, inflation is a persistent rise in the general price level rather than a once-for-all rise in it. On the other hand, *deflation represents persistently failing prices*. These days all the economies of the world, underdeveloped as well as developed, suffer from inflation. Inflation or persistently rising prices is a major problem in world today. Rate of inflation during the seventies and eighties was very high as compared to the rates of inflation experienced earlier during peace periods. Since the late nineties, rate of inflation in several countries (including India) has declined. However, in some countries, it still remain very high.

Causes of Inflation

Let us understand how the inflation originates or what causes it. Depending upon the specific causes, four types of inflation have been distinguished: (1) *Demand-pull inflation* (2) Excessive growth in money supply (3) *Cost-push inflation*, (4) *Structural inflation*. An important cause of inflation is the excessive growth of money supply in the economy. We will explain this cause in *Monetarist Theory of Inflation*. We will explain and discuss below these four types of inflation. At the end of this discussion, we will explain how inflation in the developing countries like India can be explained.

DEMAND-PULL INFLATION

This represents a situation where the basic factor at work is the increase in aggregate demand for output either from the government or the entrepreneurs or the households. The result is that the pressure of demand is such that it cannot be met by the currently available supply of output. If, for example, in a situation of full employment, the government expenditure or private investment goes up, this is bound to generate an inflationary pressures in the economy. Keynes explained that inflation arises when there occurs an *inflationary gap* in the economy which comes to exist when aggregate demand exceeds aggregate supply at full employment level of output. Basically, inflation is caused by a situation whereby the pressure of aggregate demand for goods and services exceeds the available supply of output (both being counted at the prices ruling at the beginning of a period). In such a situation, the rise in price level is the natural consequence. Now, this imbalance between aggregate demand and supply may be the result of more than one force at work. As we know aggregate demand is the sum of consumers' spending on consumer goods and services, government spending on consumer goods and services and net investment being contemplated by the entrepreneurs. The ordinary functioning of an economy should result in distributing and spending income in such a manner that aggregate demand for output is equivalent to the cost of producing total output including profits and taxes. At times, however, the government, the entrepreneurs or the households may attempt to secure a larger part of output than would thus accrue to them. If other sectors are not prepared to acquiesce in this increase in the share of output used by any one sector, all of the sectors together will be trying to get more of the national output than production has provided. This is the basic cause for inflation to start. *When aggregate demand for all purposes—consumption, investment and government, expenditure—exceeds the supply of goods at current prices, there is a rise in prices.*

To illustrate the above point, let us assume that the government adopts expansionary fiscal policy under which it increases its expenditure on education, health, defence and finances this extra expenditure by borrowing from Reserve Bank of India which prints new notes for this purpose. This will lead to increase in aggregate demand $(C + I + G)$. If aggregate supply of output does not increase or increases by a relatively less amount in the short run, this will cause demand-pull inflation in the economy, that is, general rise in price level from one period to another.

If the government is insistent on securing additional resources, it will get them in one way or another—by issuing currency or by borrowing from the central bank or from commercial banks. If other sectors, particularly the active sectors—entrepreneurs and wage earners—are unwilling to contract their investment or consumption by the amount of these additional resources used by the government, an inflationary process will be initiated. Similarly, an inflationary process will be initiated if entrepreneurs wish to use more of national output than the ordinary functioning of the economy provides (through savings out of profits and savings lent to them or invested by the public) while other sectors do not wilingly reduce their demands for resources to the extent that entrepreneurs want to use them more.

It is important to note that Keynes in his booklet *How to Pay for the War* published during the Second World War explained inflation in terms of excess demand for goods relative to the aggregate supply of their output. His notion of the *inflationary gap* which he put forward in his booklet represented excess of aggregate demand over full-employment output. This inflationary gap, according to him, leads to the rise in prices. Thus Keynes explained inflation in terms of demand-pull forces. Therefore, the theory of demand-pull inflation is associated with the name of Keynes. Since beyond full-employment level of aggregate supply, output cannot increase in response to increase in demand this results in rise in prices under the pressure of excess demand.

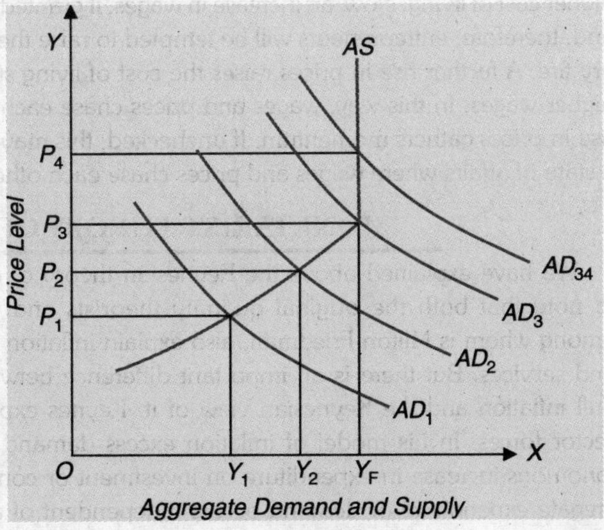

Fig. 45.1. *Demand-Pull Inflation*

Demand-pull inflation can be illustrated with aggregate demand and supply curves. Consider Fig. 45.1 in which aggregate demand and aggregate supply are measured along the X-axis and general price level along the Y-axis. Curve AS represents the aggregate supply which rises upward in the beginning but when full-employment level of aggregate supply OY_F is reached, aggregate supply curve AS takes a vertical shape. This is because after the level of full employment, supply of output cannot be increased. When aggregate demand curve is AD_1, the equilibrium is at less than full-employment level where price level OP_1 is determined. Now, if the aggregate demand increases to AD_2, price level rises to OP_2 due to the emergence of excess of demand at price level OP_1. It will be noticed that here the rise in price level has also brought about increase in aggregate output supplied from OY_1 to OY_2. If the aggregate demand further increases to AD_3, the price level rises to OP_3 under the pressure of more demand. But since the aggregate supply curve is yet sloping upward, increase in aggregate demand from AD_2 to AD_3 has caused the increase in output from OY_2 to OY_F. If aggregate demand further increases, say to AD_4, only price level rises to OP_4 with output remaining constant at YF. OY_F is the full-employment level of output and aggregate supply curve is perfectly inelastic at Y_F.

Demand-Pull Inflation and Wage Price Spiral

If the total claims on output exceed the available supply of output, prices will rise. The rise in prices provides the necessary mechanism whereby the real resources being currently used by inactive sectors are reduced so that they should be used by the more active sectors. If, for example, the initiative for the inflationary pressure comes from the government demand for more resources, the only way that the government can have more resources is by the consumers and private entrepreneurs having less of them (assuming that all the resources are fully employed already). If they are not willing to reduce their claims on resources voluntarily, the prices will rise and the result will be that the value of spending by these sectors will be reduced and to that extent resources will be made available for use by the government.

But that will not be the end of the story. A rise in prices reduces the real consumption of the wage earners. They will, therefore, press for higher money wages to compensate them for the higher cost of living. Now, an increase in wages, if granted, will raise the prime cost of production and, therefore, entrepreneurs will be tempted to raise the prices. This adds fuel to the inflationary fire. A further rise in prices raises the cost of living still further and the workers ask for still higher wages. In this way, wages and prices chase each other and the process of inflationary rise in prices gathers momentum. If unchecked, this may lead to *hyper-inflation* which signifies a state of affairs where wages and prices chase each other at a very quick speed.

MONETARIST THEORY OF INFLATION

We have explained above the Keynesian theory of demand-pull inflation. It is important to note that both the original quantity theorists and the modern monetarists, prominent among whom is Milton Friedman, also explain inflation in terms of excess demand for goods and services. But there is an important difference between the monetarist view of demand-pull inflation and the Keynesian view of it. Keynes explained inflation as arising out of real sector forces. In his model of inflation excess demand comes into being as a result of *autonomous* increase in expenditure on investment or consumption, that is, the increase in aggregate expenditure or demand occurs independent of any increase in the supply of money.

On the other hand, monetarists explain the emergence of excess demand and the resultant rise in prices on account of the increase in money supply in the economy. To quote Friedman, "*Inflation is always and everywhere a monetary phenomenon*........ and can be produced only by a more rapid increase in the quantity of money than in output.[1]

Friedman holds that when money supply is increased in the economy, then there emerges an excess supply of real money balances with the public over the demand for money. This disturbs the equilibrium. In order to restore the equilibrium, the public will reduce the money balances by increasing expenditure on goods and services. Thus, according to Friedman and other modern quantity theorists, the excess supply of real monetary balances results in the increase in aggregate demand for goods and services. If there is no proportionate increase in output, then extra money supply leads to excess demand for goods and services. This causes inflation or rise in prices. The whole argument can be presented in the following scheme:

$$M^S > kPY \rightarrow AD\uparrow \rightarrow P\uparrow \qquad \ldots (1)$$

M^S stands for quantity of money and P for the price level. Therefore, $\frac{M^S}{P}$ represents real cash balances.

Y stands for national income and k for the ratio of income which people want to keep in cash balances. Hence kY represents demand for cash balances (*i.e.*, demand for money)

AD represents aggregate demand for or aggregate expenditure on goods and services which is composed of consumption demand (C) and investment demand (I).

In the above scheme it will be seen that when the supply of money (M^S) is increased, it creates excess supply of real cash balances. This is expressed by $M^S > kPY$. This excess supply of real money balances leads to ($\rightarrow$) the rise ($\uparrow$) in aggregate demand (AD). Then increase ($\uparrow$) in aggregate demand (AD) leads to ($\rightarrow$) the rise ($\uparrow$) in prices (P).

Friedman's monetarist theory of inflation can be better explained with quantity equation $\left(P = \frac{MV}{Y} = \frac{M}{Y} \cdot \frac{1}{k}\right)$. Writing in percentage form which is written as below taking V or k as constant

$$\frac{\Delta P}{P} = \frac{\Delta M^S}{M^S} - \frac{\Delta Y}{Y} \qquad \ldots (2)$$

$\frac{\Delta P}{P}$ is the rate of inflation, $\frac{\Delta M^S}{M^S}$ is the rate of growth of money supply and $\frac{\Delta Y}{Y}$ is the rate of growth of output. Thus, according to equation (2), rate of inflation $\left(\frac{\Delta P}{P}\right)$ is determined by growth of money supply $\left(\frac{\Delta M^S}{M}\right)$ and rate of growth of output $\left(\frac{\Delta Y}{Y}\right)$, with velocity of circulation (V) or k remaining constant. *Friedman and other monetarists claim that inflation is predominantly a monetary phenomenon* which implies that changes in velocity and output are small.

It thus follows that when money supply increases, it causes disturbance in the equilibrium, that is, $M^S > kPY$. According to Friedman and other monetarists, the reaction of the people would be to spend the excess money supply on goods and services so as to bring money sup-

1. Milton Friedman, The Role of Monetary Policy, *American Economic Review*, 1968, March 1-17.

ply in equilibrium with the demand for money. This leads to the increase in aggregate demand or expenditure on goods and services which, k remaining constant, will lead to the increase in *nominal* national income (PY). They further argue that the real national income or aggregate output (*i.e.*, Y in the demand for money function stated above) remains stable at full employment level in the long run due to the flexibility of wages. Therefore, according to Friedman and his followers (modern monetarists), in the long run, the increase in nominal national income (PY) brought about by the expansion in money supply and resultant increase in aggregate demand will cause a proportional increase in the price level. However, in the short run, like Keynesians, they believe that the economy may be working at less than full employment, that is, in the short run there may prevail excess capacity and unemployment of labour so that expansion in money supply and consequent increase in nominal income partly induces expansion in real income (Y) and partly results in rise in the price level as shown in Fig. 45.2. To what extent price level increases depends upon the elasticity of supply or aggregate output. It will be seen from Fig. 45.2 that effect of increase in money supply from M_0 to M_1 and resultant increase in aggregate demand curve for goods and services from AD_0 to AD_1 is split up into the rise in price level (from P_0 to P_1) and the increase in real income or aggregate output (from Y_0 to Y_1).

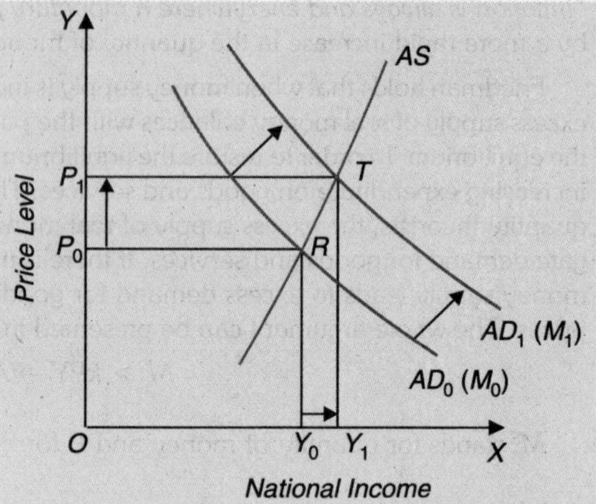

Fig. 45.2. *The Effect of expansion in money supply in the short run is split up into price rise and increase in Real National Income: Friedman's Monetarist Approach.*

It should be noted that Friedman and other modern quantity theorists believe that in the short run full-employment of labour and other resources, may not prevail due to recessionary conditions and, therefore, they admit the possibilities of increase in output. But they emphasise that when the growth in money supply is greater than the growth in output, the result is excess demand for goods and services which causes rise in prices or demand-pull inflation.

It follows from above that both Friedman and Keynesians explain inflation in terms of excess demand for goods and services. Whereas Keynesians explain the emergence of excess demand due to the increase in *autonomous expenditure*, independent of any increase in money supply. Friedman explains that inflation is caused by *proportionately greater increase in money supply than the increase in aggregate output.* In both views inflation is of demand-pull variety.

Money and Sustained Inflation

Many economists believe in the monetarist view of inflation. Increase in money shifts the aggregate demand curve to the right and if the economy is operating at full capacity (i.e. along the vertical part of the aggregate supply curve), the upward shift in aggregate demand curve will cause price level to rise. A big drawback of this approach is that it assumes that supply of output does not increase sufficiently to counter this effect of expansion in money supply on aggregate demand. In this context there is a need to distinguish between a *one-time increase* in the price level and *sustained inflation* which occurs when the general price level continues to rise over a long period of time. It is generally believed by most of the economists that whatever be the initial cause of inflation (demand-pull, cost-push or inflationary expectations), for the price level to continue rising, period after period, it must be *accommodated* by expansion in money supply. *Sustained inflation is therefore considered as a purely monetary phenomenon.* It is not possible for the price level to continue rising if the money supply remains constant. The increase in money supply continues shifting the aggregate demand curve to the right; if aggregate supply does not increase sufficiently to match the increase in aggregate demand, price level will continue rising.

Sustained inflation can be better understood when Government increases its expenditure without raising taxes. This leads to the increase in aggregate demand which, *aggregate supply remaining constant*, will cause a rise in price level. It is important to know what happens when the price level rises. The higher price level raises the demand for money to rise for transaction purposes. With supply of money remaining constant, the greater demand for money causes interest rate to rise. The rise in interest rate *crowds out* private investment. If the Central Bank of a country wants to prevent the fall in the private investment, it will expand the money supply to keep the interest constant. But this expansion in money supply through its effect on aggregate demand will cause the price level to rise further if increase in more supply of output is not possible. This further rise in price level will again cause greater demand for money leading to higher interest rate. And the Central Bank, if it is committed to keep the interest rate constant so that private investment does not decline, it will further expand the money supply which will cause further inflation. This process could lead to *hyper inflation* which represents *a rapid* and *continuous rise in price level*, period after period. The historical experience shows this hyperinflation in some countries when the Central Bank or Government of these countries kept pumping in more and more money either to finance the persistent budget deficit of the government year after year or to prevent the interest rate to rise. However, as mentioned above, hyperinflation disrupts the payment system and people's loss of credibility of the currency. This leads to a deep crisis in the economy. If hyper inflation is to be avoided, then the process of rapid expansion in money supply must be halted.

Inflationary Expectations

Inflationary expectations are an important cause of inflation. The expectations of future prices play a significant role in decision-making by firms regarding price and output. If a firm expects that its rival firms will raise their prices, it may also raise its own price in anticipation. Suppose inflation has been occurring at a rate of 8 per cent per annum in the past, a firm will expect this inflation rate to continue in future too and therefore it will raise its price by 8 per cent. If every firm expects that other firm will raise their prices by 8 per cent, every one will raise its prices by 8 per cent. As a result, inflation rate of about 8 per cent will occur. This is how inflationary expectations cause inflation. Elaborating on this, Case and Fair write, "Expectations can lead to an inertia that makes it difficult to stop an inflationary spiral. If prices have been rising and if people's expectations are *adaptive*, that is, if they form their expectations on the basis of past pricing behaviour – that firm may continue raising prices even if demand is slowing."[1a] Therefore, to check inflation, steps should be taken to break the inflationary expectations.

COST-PUSH INFLATION

We can visualise situations where even though there is no increase in aggregate demand, prices may still rise. This may happen if there is increase in costs independent of any increase in aggregate demand. Three such autonomous increases in costs which generate cost-push inflation have been suggested. They are:

1. Wage-push inflation

1a. Karl E. Case, and Race C. Fair, *Principles of Economics*, Pearson Education, 6th Edition, 2002,

2. Profit push inflation
3. Increase in prices raw materials, especially energy inputs such as rise in crude oil prices.

It may be noted that rise in prices of raw materials, especially of energy inputs (petrolium products) which have a cost push effect are also called *supply shocks*. We discuss these below:

Wage-Push Inflation. It has been suggested that the growth of powerful trade union is responsible for the spread of inflation, especially in the industrialized countries. When trade unions push for higher wages which are not justifiable either on grounds of a prior rise in productivity or of cost of living they produce a cost-push effect. The employers in a situation of high demand and employment are more agreeable to concede to these wage claims because they hope to pass on these rises in costs to the consumers in the form of hike in prices. If this happens we have cost-push inflation. It may be noted that as a result of cost-push effect of higher wages, aggregate supply curve of output shifts to the left and, given the aggregate demand curve, this results in higher price of output.

Profit-Push Inflation. Besides the increase in wages of labour without any increase in its productivity, there is another factor responsible for cost-push inflation. This is the *increase in the profit margin by* the firms working under monopolistic or oligopolistic conditions and as a result charging higher prices from the consumers. In the former case when the cause of cost-push inflation is the rise in wages it is called *wage-push inflation* and in the latter case when the cause of cost-push inflation is the rise in profit margins, it is called *profit-push inflation*. The increase in profit margins also produces a cost-push effect and results in shift in the aggregate supply curve to the left.

Rise in Raw material Prices or Oil Price Shock. In addition to the rise in wage rate of labour and increase in profit margins, in the seventies the other supply-shocks causing increase in marginal cost of production became more prominent in bringing about cost-push inflation. During the seventies, rise in prices of raw materials, especially energy inputs (hike in crude oil price made by OPEC resulting in rise in prices of petroleum products). The sharp rise in world oil prices during 1973-75 and again in 1979-80 produced significant supply shocks resulting in cost-push inflation.

The cost-push inflation can also be illustrated with the aggregate demand and supply curves. Consider Fig. 45.3, where aggregate supply and demand are measured along the X-axis and price level along the Y-axis. *AD* is the aggregate demand curve and AS_1 and AS_2 curves are aggregate supply curves. Now, when wages increase, and as a result cost of production rises, the aggregate supply curve would shift upward to the left. As will be seen in Fig. 45.3 when there is an upward shift in the aggregate supply curve from AS_1 to AS_2 due to the rise in wages, price level rises from OP_1 to OP_2. Thus, in this case when aggregate demand curve remains the same, price level rises due to rise wages which has caused leftward shift in the supply curve. *An important feature of cost-push inflation is that this causes not only rise in price level but brings about a fall in aggregate output.* Thus in Fig. 45.3 when price level rises from OP_1 to OP_2, aggregate output falls from OY_1 to OY_2.

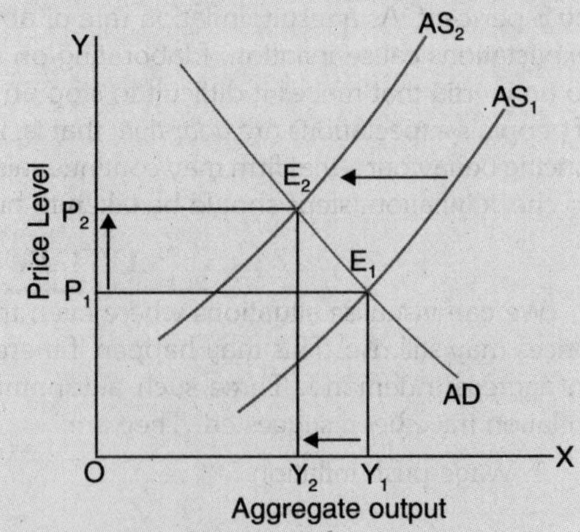

Fig. 45.3. *Cost-Push Inflation*

Indirect Effect of Increase in oil prices or other raw material prices. In addition to the direct effect of oil price shocks and increase in other raw material prices, there are indirect effects of such supply shocks which cause further rise in rate of inflation. It may be noted that an aggregate supply curve is drawn assuming given price level expectations over time. When a certain event occurs, the workers will revise their price expectations. Now, when due to increase in raw material prices or oil price shock price level of output has risen as a result of cost-push effect, the workers would revise upward their expectations of price level. With this, the expected real wage rate $\left(\frac{W}{P}\right)$ will decline and therefore less labour will be supplied at a given money wage rate. Thus, in Fig. 45.3 with the increase in expected price level, aggregate supply curve will further shift to the left as a result of this *indirect effect* through the upward revision of expected price level. As a result of this indirect effect, the price level will rise above P_2 in Fig. 45.3

Interaction between Demand-Pull and Cost-Push Inflation.

Many economists think inflation in the economy is generally caused by the interaction of the demand-pull and cost-push factors. The inflation may be started in the first instance either by cost-push factors or by demand pull factors both work and interact to cause sustained inflation over time. Thus, according to Machlup, "there cannot be a thing as cost push inflation because without an increase in purchasing power and demand, cost increases will lead to unemployment and depression, not to inflation"[2] Likewise, Cairncross writes, "there is no need to pretend that demand and cost inflation do not interact or that excess demand does not aggravate wage inflation, of course it does."[3]

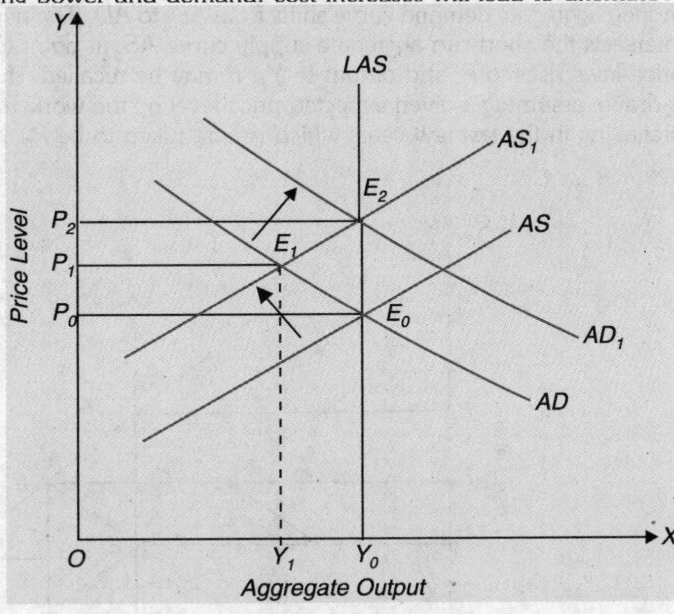

Fig. 45.4. *Interaction of Cost-Push and Demand-Pull Inflation*

We will explain this interaction, first with inflationary process starts with cost push factor and then secondly when inflation begin with shift in aggregate demand. In both cases rate of inflation over time is the result of interaction of demand-pull and cost-push factors.

1. Let us consider the Figure 45.4 where to begin with aggregate demand curve *AD* and aggregate supply curve *AS* intersect at point E_0 and determine price level P_0 and output

2. Fritz Machlup, "Another View of Cost-Push and Demand-Pull Inflation" in *Review of Economics and Statistics* Vol. 42. 1960.
3. Alec Cairncross *Inflation, Growth and International Trade,* George Allen and Unwin, 1975.

level Y_0. Further suppose that Y_0 is the full capacity (*i.e.*, full-employment) level of output and therefore long-run aggregate supply curve *LAS* is vertical at Y_0 level of output. Suppose there is increase in oil prices which causes shifts in aggregate supply curve to the left from *AS* to AS_1. As a result, price level rises to P_1 but output falls from Y_0 to Y_1. With decline in output unemployment will also increase. This is a cost-push inflation which has caused a recessionary conditions in the economy. The Government and Central Bank are likely to adopt expansionary monetary and fiscal policies in order to avoid recession. Consequent to the adoption of expansionary policies, (for example, increase in money supply or increase in Government expenditure or reduction in taxes), aggregate demand curve will shift to the right, say to AD_1, which intersects AS_1 curve and *LAS* curve at point E_2. Though as a result of this accommodatary policy while output level has increased to the original full-capacity level Y_0, price level has further risen to P_2 level. This later rise in price level from P_1 to P_2 is the result of demand-pull Inflation. It is thus clear that both cost-push and demand -pull inflation interact to cause inflation in the economy.

2. Let us now explain inflationary process which starts with demand-pull inflation in the first instance. Consider Figure 45.5. where to begin with aggregate demand curve AD_0 and aggregate supply curve AS_0 intersect at E_0 and determine level of price P_0 and aggregate output Y_0. Assume long-run aggregate supply curve *LAS* also passes through point E_0 so that equilibrium level of output Y_0 also represents full-employment level of output (that is, at Y_0 only natural unemployment exists) and price level P_0 also represents long-run equilibrium price level.

Now suppose due to increase in Government expenditure financed by creation of new money aggregate demand curve shifts from AD_0 to AD_1. The new aggregate demand curve AD_1 intersects the short-run aggregate supply curve AS_0 at point E_1. As a result, in the short run price level rises to P_1 and output to Y_1. It may be recalled, short-run aggregate supply curve is drawn assuming a given expected price level by the workers which is usually the price level prevailing in the last few years which is here taken to be P_0. Now that as a result of increase

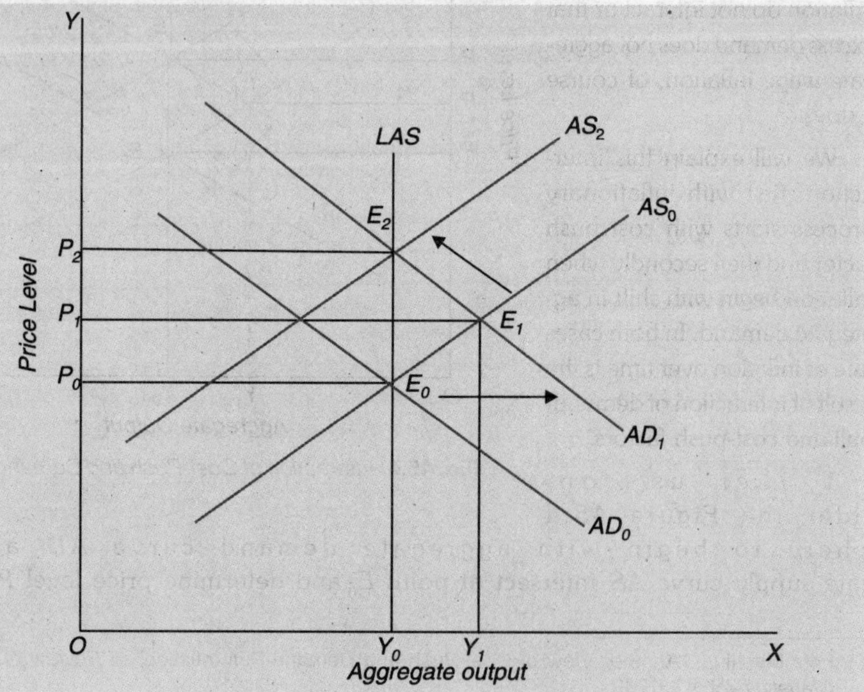

Fig. 45.5. *Interaction betwen Demand-Pull and Cost-Push Inflation*

in aggregate demand price level has actually risen to P_1, workers' real wages would decline. Therefore, in order to restore their real wages, they would demand higher money wages. When their demand for higher wages are conceded to, short-run aggregate supply curve will shift to the left. With this leftward shift in the aggregate supply curve, price level will rise further. In this way *wage-price spiral* will go on operating until short-run aggregate supply curve shifts to the level AS_2 and together with aggregate demand curve AD_1 determine a long-run equilibrium at point E_2. It will be seen that both demand-pull inflation and cost-push inflation have operated together to raise price level from P_0 to P_2.

To conclude, demand-pull inflation and cost-push inflation are intertwined and operate together to determine rate of inflation over time. *It is difficult to say in actual practice what part of inflation is due to demand-pull factors and what due to cost-push factors*, though, as seen above, theoretically speaking, we can distinguish between demand-pull and cost-push inflation.

STRUCTURALIST THEORY OF INFLATION

But there is another important theory of inflation known as *structuralist inflation* which explains inflation in the developing-countries in a slightly different way. The structuralists argue that increase in investment expenditure and the expansion of money supply to finance it are the only proximate and not the ultimate factors responsible for inflation in the developing countries. According to them, one should go deeper into the question as to why aggregate output, especially of foodgrains, has not been increasing sufficiently in the developing countries to match the increase in demand brought about by the increase in investment expenditure, and money supply. Further, they argue why investment expenditure has not been fully financed by voluntary savings and as a result excessive deficit financing has been done.[4]

Structural theory of inflation has been put forward as an explanation of inflation in the developing countries especially of Latin America. The well-known economists, Myrdal and Streeten who have proposed this theory have analysed inflation in these developing countries in terms of structural features of their economies. Recently Kirkpatrick and Nixon have generalised this structural theory of inflation as an explanation of inflation prevailing in all developing countries.[5]

Myrdal and Streeten have argued that it is not correct to apply the highly aggregative demand-supply model for explaining inflation in the developing countries.[6] According to them, there is a lack of balanced integrated structure in them where substitution possibilities between consumption and production and inter-sectoral flows of resources between different sectors of the economy are not quite smooth and quick so that the inflation in them can not be reasonably explained in terms of aggregate demand and aggregate supply. In this connection it is noteworthy that Prof. V.N. Pandit of Delhi School of Economics has also felt the need for distinguishing price behaviour in the Indian agricultural sector from that in the manufacturing sector.[7]

Thus, it has been argued by the exponents of structural theory of inflation that economies of the developing countries of Latin America and India are structurally underdeveloped as well as highly fragmented due to the existence of market imperfections and structural rigidies

4. G.Myrdal, *Asian Drama, An Enquiry into the Poverty of Nations*, 1968, Penguin Books.
5. The expansionary monetary and fiscal policies adopted in response to recessionary conditions are called *accomodating polcies.*
6. P. Streeten, *The Frontiers of Development Studies*, 1972, London, MacMillan.
7. See V.N. Pandit, "An Analysis of Inflation in India, 1950-75, *Indian Economic Review*, Vol. 22, 1978

of various types. The result of these structural imbalances and rigidies is that whereas in some sectors of these developing countries, we find shortages of supply relative to demand, in others under-utilisation of resources and excess capacity exist due to lack of demand. According to structuralists, these structural features of the developing countries make the aggregate demand-supply model of inflation inapplicable to them. They therefore argue for analysing disaggregative and sectoral demand-supply imbalances to explain inflation in the developing countries. They mention various sectoral constraints or bottlenecks which generate the sectoral imbalances and lead to rise in prices. Therefore, to explain the origin and propagation of inflation in the developing countries, the forces which generate these bottlenecks or imbalances of various types in the process of economic development need to be analysed. A study of these bottlenecks is therefore essential for explaining inflation in the developing countries. These bottlenecks are of three types : (1) Agricultural bottlenecks which make supply of agricultural products inelastic, (2) resources constraint or Government budget constraint, and (3) foreign exchange bottleneck. Let us explain briefly how these structural bottlenecks cause inflation in the developing countries.

Agricultural Bottlenecks. The first and foremost bottlenecks faced by the developing countries relate to agriculture and they prevent supply of food grains to increase adequately. Of special mention of the structural factors are disparities in land ownership, defective land tanure system which act as disincentives for raising agricultural production in response to increasing demand for them arising from increase in people's incomes, growth in population and urbanisation. Besides, use of backward agricultural technology also hampers agricultural growth. Thus, in order to control inflation, these bottlenecks have to be removed so that agricultural output grows rapidly to meet the increasing demand for it in the process of economic development.

Resources Gap or Government's Budget Constraint. Another important bottleneck mentioned by structuralists relate to the lack of resources for financing economic development. In the developing countries planned efforts are being made by the Government to industrialise their economies. This requires large resources to finance public sector investment in various industries. For example, in India, huge amount of resources were used for investment in basic heavy industries started in the public sector. But socio-economic and political structure of these coun tries is such that it is not possible for the Government to raise enough resources through taxation, borrowing from the public, surplus generation in the public sector enterprises for investment in the projects of economic development. Revenue raising from taxation has been relatively very small due to low tax base, large scale tax evasion, inefficient and corrupt tax administration. Consequently, the government has been forced to resort to excessive deficit financing (that is, creation of new currency) which has caused excessive growth in money supply relative to increase in output year after year and has therefore resulted in inflation in the developing countries. Though rapid growth of money supply is the proximate cause of inflation, it is not the proper and adequate explanation of inflation in these economies. For proper explanation of inflation one should go deeper and enquire into the operation of structural forces which has caused excessive growth in money supply in these developing economies. Besides, resources gap in the private sector due to inadequate voluntary savings and under-development of the capital market have led to their larger borrowings from the banking system which has created excessive bank credit for it. This has greatly countributed to the growth of money supply in the developing countries and has caused rise in prices. Thus, Kirkpatrick and Nixon write, "the increase in the supply of money was a permissive factor which allowed the inflationary spiral to manifest itself and become cumulative—it was a system of the structural rigidities which give rise to the inflationary pressures rather than the cause of inflation itself."[8]

---

8. C. Kirkpatrick and F., Nixon, Inflation and Stabilisation policy in LDC's in N. Gemmel (ed.), *Surveys in Development Economics*, 1987 Basil, Blackwell.

Foreign Exchange Bottleneck. The other important bottleneck which the developing countries have to encounter is the shortage of foreign exchange for financing needed imports for development. In the developing countries ambitious programme of industrialisation is being undertaken. Industrialisation requires heavy imports of capital goods, essential raw materials and in some cases, as in India, even foodgrains have been imported. Besides, imports of oil on a large scale are being made. On account of all these imports, import expenditure of the developing countries has been rapidly increasing. On the other hand, due to lack of export surplus, restrictions imposed by the developing countries, relatively low competitiveness of exports, the growth of exports of the developed countries has been sluggish. As a result of sluggish exports and mounting imports, the developing countries have been facing balance of payment difficulties and shortage of foreign exchange which at times has assumed crisis proportions. This has affected the price level in two ways. First, due to foreign exchange shortage domestic availability of goods in short-supply could not be increased which led to the rise in their prices. Secondly, in Latin American countries as well as in India and Pakistan, to solve the problem of foreign exchange shortage through encouraging exports and reducing imports devaluation in the national currencies had to be made. But this devaluation caused rise in prices of imported goods and materials which further raised the prices of other goods as well due to cascading effect. This brought about cost-push inflation in their economies.

Physical Infrastructural Bottlenecks. Further, the structuralists point out various *bottlenecks* such as lack of infrastructural facilities *i.e.*, lack of power, transport and fuel which stands in the way of adequate growth in output. At present in India, there is acute shortage of these infrastructural inputs which are hampering growth of output. Sluggish growth of output on the one hand, and excessive growth of money supply on the other have caused what is now called *stagflation*, that is inflation which exists along with stagnation or slow economic growth.

According to the structuralist school of thought, the *above bottlenecks and constraints are rooted in the social, political and economic structure of these countries*. Therefore, in its view a broad-based strategy of development which aims to bring about social, institutional and structural changes in these economies is needed to bring about economic growth without inflation. Further, many structuralists argue for giving higher priority to agriculture in the strategy of development if price stability is to be ensured. Thus, we see that structuralist view is greatly relevant for explaining inflation in the developing countries and for the adoption of measures to control it. Let us further elaborate the causes of inflation in the developing countries.

INFLATION IN DEVELOPING COUNTRIES: DEMAND-PULL OR COST-PUSH INFLATION

Now, the question arises as to which theory of inflation can explain inflation in developing countries. Of course, the rise in prices has come about as a result of excess of aggregate demand over aggregate supply. In other words, inflation in the developing countries is mainly of demand-pull variety. However, how this excess demand for goods and services has been caused is issue at dispute. In our view both the Keynesian and Friedman's views are relevant to explain the emergence of excess demand for goods. To promote rapid economic growth a hunge investment expenditure has been made in India in successive development plans. If this increase in investment expenditure had been financed by raising resources through taxation, Government borrowings from the public, profits of public undertakings, then the increase in investment expenditure would have been matched by increase in savings with the result that excess demand for goods had not arisen. As a matter of fact, a good deal of increase in investment expenditure has been financed by deficit financing *i.e.*, through creating of new money by the central bank. Besides, the increase in private investment expenditure has also been financed to a good extent by expansion of credit or demand deposits by the commercial banks. This increase in investment expenditure for promoting economic growth has been made possible by the expansion in money supply, which as emphasized by Friedman and other monetarists, causes prices to rise through creating excess demand for goods and services. Thus, it is hard to distinguish whether it is increase in investment expenditure as such or expansion in money supply to finance it which has caused demand-pull inflation in the face of slow growth of output of goods, especially foodgrains and other essential consumer goods. Indeed, both have played a part in causing inflationary situation in India.

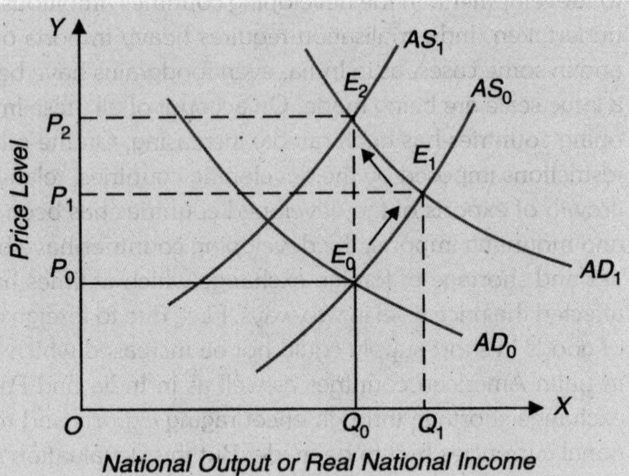

Fig. 45.6. *Rise in General Price Level as a Result of Joint Impact of Demand-Pull and Cost-Push Factors*

What has caused the inflationary pressures in India's developing economy? To think that only demand-pull factors or excess demand generated by huge budget deficits and huge growth in money supply are responsible for the problem of inflation facing the Indian economy would not be fully correct. As a matter of fact, both types of factors, namely, demand-pull and cost push factors have operated to cause inflation in India, which crossed the two-digit figure in some years. As a result of rapid growth in Government expenditure without corresponding increase in mobilisation of resources, the Government has resorted to heavy deficit financing (*i.e.*, the creation of new money). This has further created the conditions of excess demand in the economy which have led to the rise in general price level. Besides, the increase in petroleum prices, many times during the last few years, the hike in administered prices of steel, cement, coal, fertilizers, increase in indirect taxes on several commodities, increase in railway fares and freights have all led to the *cost-push inflation* or what is also called *supply-side inflation*.

Now, when due to the demand pull inflation, the general price-level rises, the demand for rise in wages and dearness allowance are made by the working classes and they have to be conceded to in view of the rising cost of living. The rise in wages and dearness allowance of the workers raises the cost of production. The increases in cost of production due higher wages and dearness allowance also cause the aggregate supply curve shift to the left and brings about cost-push or supply side inflation. Thus there has been persistent rise in prices under the combined impact of demand-pull factors caused by the large budget deficits and cost-push factors due to the hike in administrated prices of petroleum, steel, cement, coal etc., and increase in indirect taxes on commodities such as sugar, cloth, cooking gas, soaps, cold-drink, etc.

Let us illustrate graphically how the operation of the various demand-pull and cost-push factors resulting in persistent rise in general price level. Consider Fig. 45.6, where AD_0 represents aggregate demand curve and AS_0 the aggregate supply curve and the two intersect at point E_0 and the price level P_0 is determined. With huge budget deficits and large expansion in money supply generating conditions of excess demand cause upward shift in the aggregate demand curve to AD_1. The general price level rises to P_1 corresponding to the new equilibrium point E_1. Now, the increase in cost of production brought about by either independently of the rise in price caused by increase in aggregate demand or by rise in wages and dearness allowances induced by the demand-pull inflation in the first instance, aggregate supply curve shifts to the left to AS_1. With this the price level further rises to P_2 under the influence of cost push factors. The price equilibrium moves from E_0 to E_1 and then to E_2. This process of joint operation of demand-pull and cost-push factors has been going on year after year and is responsible for the persistent rise in prices in the Indian economy. Therefore, to check and moderate this inflationary process not only the budget deficits have to be drastically cut but also steps should be taken to prevent the increase in cost of production by avoiding the frequent hike in administered prices and indirect taxes.

Is Monetarist Theory a Valid Explanation of Inflation. Does the classical quantity theory of money or Friedman modern monetarist theory of inflation appy to India quite well. *In our view it is not true that inflation in India is a purely monetary phenomenon*, though rapid growth is money supply in the past has contributed to the inflation in India. However, recent experience shows that despite relatively higher growth in money supply during the last 8 years rate of inflation remained at low level. It will be seen from Table 45.1 that whereas rate of growth money supply has been quite high (it has varied from 14 per cent a year to 21 per cent a year, but rate of inflation has been relatively low. This shows that growth in money supply alone is not the cause of inflation. Even after adjusting for rate of GDP growth rate during the period 1995-2007 there still remains a large gap between money supply growth and rate of inflation. Taking the Indian time series data of whole sale price index number and the money supply, when whole sale price index number data was regressed on money supply and GDP (*i.e.*, aggregate output), the coefficient of money supply was found to be around 0.5 and of aggregate output to be around 0.45. This shows there is no one-to-one relationship between money supply and price level and further that the growth of output (*i.e.*, supply side factor, also plays an important role in determing inflation in India's growing economy; this disproves strict quantity theory of money.)

Table 45.1. Growth in Money Supply and Rate of Inflation in India (1995–2005)

Year	Growth in Money Supply M_3	Rate of inflation based on WPI	Rate of Inflation based on CPI	Growth rate in GDP
1955–96	13.6	4.4	8.9	6.5
1996–97	16.2	5.4	10.0	4.8
1997–98	18.0	4.5	8.3	7.8
1998–99	19.4	5.3	8.9	7.3
1999–2000	14.6	6.5	4.8	6.1
2000–2001	16.8	4.9	2.5	4.4
2001–2002	14.1	1.6	5.2	5.8
2002–2003	14.8	6.5	4.1	4.0
2003-2004	16.8	4.6	3.5	8.5
2004-2005	12.3	5.1	4.2	7.5
2005-2006	17.0	4.1	5.0	9.2
2006-2007	21.1	6.7	6.9	9.4
2007-08	21.4	4.7	6.2	9.3
2008-09	19.3	8.1	9.1	6.7
2009-10	16.8	3.8	12.4	8.6
2010-11	16.0	9.6	10.4	9.3
2011-12	15.6	8.9	8.4	6.2
2012-13	11.2	7.6	10.0	5.0

INFLATION AND INTEREST RATE : THE FISHER EFFECT

Interest rate is an important macroeconomic variable as it dermines saving and investment in the economy that play an important rate in the determination of national income and employment. Through its effect on saving and investment, interest links the present with the future. It is therefore important to understand the relation between interest rate and inflation. To understand the relation between interest rate and inflation, it is necessary to know the distinction between *nominal interest rate and real interest rate*. Nominal interest rate is the stated interest rate which a bank provides to its depositors on the saving account and the fixed deposits of different maturity periods. Nominal interest is also the agreed nominal rate at which the lenders lend money to the borrowers. If your bank gives you 8 per cent interest rate on the fixed deposit of one year, then 8 per cent is the nominal interest rate.

On the other hand, real interest rate means how fast the purchasing power of your deposits in the *bank increases over a year*. The rate of increase in purchasing power of your money deposits over time depends not only on the nominal interest rate but also on the inflation rate that takes place over time. For example, if nominal interest rate on a fixed deposit for a year is 8 per cent and inflation rate in the year is 5 per cent, then 5 per cent of purchasing power of nominal interest rate has been wiped out by infaltion. Therefore, in this case 8 per cent minus 5 per cent, that is, 3 per cent is the *increase in purchasing power of your deposits* and therefore represents the real rate of interest.

Thus real interest rate can be obtained from nominal interest rate by adjusting for inflation rate that takes place in a year. Thus relationship among the real rate of interest, nominal rate of interest and inflation rate can be stated as under.

Real interest rate = nominal interest rate – inflation rate.

If we denote real interest rate by r, nominal interest rate by i and inflation rate by π, then

$$r = i - \pi \qquad \ldots (i)$$

Fisher Equation and Effect

An important principle of Classical theory is that money is neutral, that is, it does not affect the real variables. Changes in money supply determine only the changes in price level or rate of inflation in the economy. This principle has an important application in the determination of relation between nominal interest rate, real interest rate and inflation rate.

Rearranging the equation (i) we have

Nominal interest rate = real interest rate + rate of inflation

In symbolic terms,

$$i = r + \pi \qquad \ldots (ii)$$

The above equation (2) shows that change in nominal interest rate (i) can occur due to the reasons : (1) changes in real interest rate, and (2) changes in rate of inflation. The relationship between nominal interest rate, real interest rate and inflation rate described in equation (2), namely, *nominal interest rate is the sum of real interest rate and inflation rate is called Fisher Equation* after the economist. Irving Fisher (1867 – 1947) who first of all stated this relation.

The viewing nominal interest rate as the sum of real interest rate and inflation rate is quite useful as entirely different forces determine the real interest rate and the inflation state which together determine the nominal interest rate. As has been studied earlier, according to classical theory, real interest rate is determined by saving and investment (or, according to neo-classical theory, demand for and supply of loanable funds), rate of inflation is determined by rate of growth of money supply. According to Classical theory, rate of inflation is determined by rate of growth of money supply. Growth of many supply does not influence real interest rate. As a matter of fact, real interest rate is a real variable, and, as stated above, according to the important classical principle of monetary neutrality, changes in money supply do not affect the real variables.

Fisher Effect. An important macroeconomic issue is how nominal interest rate adjusts to change in inflation rate which in turn is determined by growth of money supply. When Central Bank of a country increases money supply in the economy, it will cause rate of inflation to rise. Since nominal interest rate is the sum of real interest rate and rate of inflation, rise in inflation rate will raise the nominal interest rate, real interest rate remaining unchanged. In fact there is one-for-one adjustment of nominal interest rate to changes in inflation rate. *Adjustment of nominal interest rate to changes in inflation rate is called Fisher effect.* Let us take an example. Suppose on your fixed deposit for a year your bank pays you 8 per cent. Further suppose inflation rate in the economy is 5 per cent per annum. Writing them in Fisher equation we have

$$i = r + \pi$$

$$8 = 3 + 5$$

Now, if as a result of higher growth of money supply rate of inflation rises to 6 per cent per annum, then given the real interest rate as 3 per cent, nominal interest rate will rise to 9 per cent. This is because

$$9 = 3 + 6$$

If follows from above nominal interest rate adjusts to change in rate of inflation. The higher the rate of inflation, the higher will be the nominal interest rate.

The historical experience shows that nominal interest rate and rate of inflation are closely associated in recent years. Chile and Brazel have experienced high rates of inflation. In recent years Chile experienced an annual inflation rate of around 30 per cent with nominal interest rate of 45 per cent. Brazil experienced a still higher inflation rate and in it inflation rate and nominal interest rate were about 45 per cent *per month*.

EFFECTS OF INFLATION

Inflation is a very unpopular happening in an economy. Opinion surveys conduced in India, the U.S.A. and other countries reveal that inflation is the most important concern of the people as it badly affects their standard of living. The political fortunes of many political leaders (Prime Ministers and Presidents) and Governments in India and abroad have been determined by how far they have succeeded in tackling the problem of inflation. So much so that some American presidental candidates called '*inflation as enemy number one*'. Same is the case in India where inflation is the most hotly debated issue during the general elections for the Parliament and Assemblies. A high rate of inflation makes the life of the poor very miserable. It is, therefore, described as anti-poor. It redistributes income and wealth in favour of some and greatly harms others. By making the rich richer and the poor poorer, it militates against social justice. Besides, inflation lowers national output and employment and impedes long-run economic growth, especially in developing countries like India. We shall discuss below all these effects of inflation.

Anticipated and Unanticipated Inflation

The difference between anticipated inflation and unanticipated inflation is of crucial importance as the effects of inflation, especially its redistributive effect, depend on whether it is anticipated or not. If rate of inflation is anticipated, then people take steps to make suitable adjustments in their contracts to avoid the adverse effects which inflation could bring to them. For example, if a worker correctly anticipates the rate of inflation in a particular year to be equal to 10 per cent and if his present wage rate is ₹ 5000 per month, he can enter into contract with the employer that to compensate for the 10 per cent rise in prices his money wage per month next year be raised by 10 per cent so that next year he gets ₹ 5500 per month. In this way he has been able to prevent the erosion of his real income with the automatic revision of his money wage depending on the anticipated rate of inflation.

Take another example. You lend ₹ 10,000 to a person at a rate of 10 per cent per annum. After a year you will receive ₹ 11,000. But if it is anticipated that during the year there will be 8 per cent rate of inflation, then 8 per cent of your income will be offset by the rise in prices that would occur so that you will get only 2 *per cent real rate of interest*. Therefore, in order to receive 10 per cent real rate of interest, in view of 8 per cent anticipated inflation rate you must demand 18 per cent nominal rate of interest.

Cost of Unanticipated Inflation. Unanticipated inflation has a more substantial and harmful effect as compared to the cost of anticipated inflation rate. The significant effect of unanticipated inflation is that it *arbitrarily re-distributes wealth* among individuals. Consider the value of assets fixed in nominal terms. Between 1995 and 2006, price level in India rose by about 100 per cent. This implies that those who held *claims on assets fixed in nominal terms in 1996*, their real value in terms of purchasing power would have declined significantly. Thus, a person who bought government bound of 10 years maturely with a face value of ₹ 1000 bearing 8 per cent nominal interest rate in 1996 will find that ₹ 1000 he gets bank in 2006 has far less value than when he purchased the bond in 1996.

Similarly, unanticipated inflation harms the individuals, who retire on pensions fixed in rupee terms. After some years of inflation, the real value or purchasing power of the fixed nominal pension will greatly decline and will therefore reduce his standard of living in his old age. Thus inflation hurts individuals with fixed pensions. Workers and the private firms often agree on fixed nominal pension payable to the workers after retirement. Workers are greatly harmed when inflation is higher than anticipated. Likewise, higher than anticipated inflation rate hurts the creditors who give loans to the others and get back the principal amount after the stipulated period. Thus *inflation redistributes wealth in favour of debtors*. On the other hand, effects of unanticipated inflation are unavoidable because in this case you do not know what would be the rise in the price level. That is, unanticipated inflation catches you by surprise.

Effects of Inflation in General

In what follows we shall examine the *effects of inflation in general, especially unanticipated.* The effects of inflation can be divided into three categories:

1. Effect on real income;
2. Effect on distribution of income and wealth;
3. Effect on output; and
4. Effect on long-run economic growth.

Inflation Erodes Real Incomes of the People. To examine the effect of inflation it is important to note the difference between money income and real income. It is the change in the general price level that creates the crucial difference between the two. Money income or what is also called nominal income means the income such as wages, interest, rent *received in terms of rupees*. On the other hand, *real income* implies the amount of goods and services which you can buy. In other words, real income means the purchasing power of your income. If your money or nominal income increases at a lower rate than the rate of rise in the general price level (*i.e.*, the rate of inflation), you will be able to buy less goods and services, that is, your real income will decline. Real income will rise only if nominal income rises faster than the rate of inflation. For illustration, take the case of workers who enter into contract with their employer at an agreed wage rate of ₹ 5000 per month for the period, say 5 years. Now, suppose the rate of inflation is 10 per cent per annum. This means after a year, with money wage rate of ₹ 5,000 workers will be able to buy less goods and services. That is, their real income will decrease and therefore their standard of living will fall.

Take another example. Suppose you deposit your saving of ₹ 100 in a saving account which carries 5 per cent rate of interest. After a year you will receive ₹ 105. However, if during that year rate of inflation has been 12 per cent, you will be a loser in real terms. In fact your real interest-income will be negative as, with 12 per cent rate of inflation, ₹ 105 after a year will buy less goods and services than what you can purchase with ₹ 100 today.

The above two examples clearly show that inflation reduces the purchasing power of money and thereby adversely affects real income of the people.

Effect on Distribution of Income and Wealth

An important effect of inflation in that it redistributes income and wealth in favour of some at the cost of others. Inflation adversely affects those who receive relatively fixed incomes and benefits businessmen, producers, traders and others who enjoy flexible incomes. Inflation brings windfall profits for the producers and traders. Thus, all do not lose as a result of inflation, rather some gain from it. We examine below how inflation redistributes income and wealth and thereby harms some people and benefits others.

Creditors and Debtors. Unanticipated inflation harms creditors and benefits debtors and in this way redistributes income in favour of the latter. As explained above, value of money declines due to inflation. For creditors (including financial institutions such as banks and insurance companies) who enter into agreement with the borrowers to provide loans at fixed nominal rate of interest, the real value of money in terms of goods and services which they will receive at the end of the period would be much less if during the period prices rise sharply. Thus, the debtors or borrowers gain because they would return the loan-money when its real value has declined greatly due to the unexpected rapid rate of inflation.

Fixed Income Groups. Those who get fixed incomes stand to lose from inflation. Workers and salaried people who earn fixed wages and salaries are hit hard by unanticipated inflation. These people often enter into contract with the employers regarding wages or salaries fixed in nominal terms. When inflation occurs, the purchasing power of their nominal incomes falls greatly causing a decline in their levels of living. Thus, when inflation persists for some years there are demands for revision of wages and salaries. It may be mentioned that now-a-days workers and other salaried people get dearness allowances to compensate them for the rise in cost of living due to inflation. However, these dearness allowances do not fully neutralise the rise in price level and therefore they also demand revision of wages and pay scales.

Pensioners. They also come in the category of the people who get income in fixed nominal terms. For the people who retired in 1984 with the monthly pension of Rs. 2000, the real value of their pension in Oct. 1998 would been reduced to one third as compared to 1984 as there has been more than 300 per cent rise in the price level during this period. It may also be noted that in order to reduce the hardship of the pensioners, some dearness allowance is also provided on pension. But effects of inflation on the real value of their pension are only partly offset in this way.

Businessmen : Producers and Traders. Businessmen, that is, entrepreneurs and traders, stand to gain by inflation. During periods of inflation, the prices of goods produced by entrepreneurs rise relatively faster than the cost of production because wages lag behind the rise in prices of goods. Consequently, *inflation increases the profits of businessmen*. The value of the inventories or stocks of goods and materials kept by the entrepreneurs and traders increases due to rise in prices of goods which brings about an increase in their profits.

Wealth Holders of Cash, Bonds and Debentures. Inflation also adversely affects wealth holders who hold their wealth in the form of cash money, demand deposits, saving and fixed deposits and interest-bearing bonds and debentures. These wealth holders are severely hurt by inflation as inflation reduces the real value of their wealth. Saving and demand deposits, bonds and debentures represent assets whose value is fixed in terms of money. The rise in prices reduces the purchasing power of these fixed-value money assets such as saving and time deposits, bonds and debentures which bear a fixed nominal rate of interest.

Inflation, therefore reduces the real rate of interest earned by them. Consequently, it has been observed that during periods of rapid inflation people try to convert their holdings of money and near money into goods and physical property so as to avoid the loss due to inflation. It may also be noted that if inflation is anticipated and all expect equal rates of inflation the nominal rates of interest are adjusted upward so as to obtain targeted real rate of interest. Thus, if creditors want real rate of interest equal to 10 per cent and anticipate rate of inflation is equal to 8 per cent, they will try to have nominal rate of interest fixed at 18 per cent. This is known as **Fisher effect** *which states that market or nominal rate of interest is equal to the real rate of interest (based on productivity of capital and rate of time preference) plus the anticipated rate of inflation*. Thus nominal rate of inflation includes what is called *inflation premium* to prevent the erosion of purchasing power due to inflation.

Effect on Output. There is a good deal of uncertainty and also disagreement as to whether inflation will adversely or favourably affect national output. The effect of inflation on output also depends on whether it has been caused by demand-pull or cost-push factors. Further, the effect of inflation on output depends on whether it is moderate or very rapid or whether it is anticipated or unanticipated. Let us examine the likely effects of inflation in each of these cases.

Demand-pull Inflation and Output. Till recently a large number of economists favoured a mild or modest inflation and they argued that rising prices are caused by increase in aggregate demand which are accompanied by expansion in output. Indeed, according to them, rising prices create a tonic effect on the level of investment and employment of labour and other resources by raising the marginal efficiency of capital (*i.e.*, expected rate of profits). We know the level of output and employment depend on aggregate demand, given the aggregate supply curve. For instance, in Fig. 45.1, aggregate supply curve slopes upward up to full-employment aggregate output level Y_F and beyond it, it becomes vertical. If in Fig. 45.1 in the beginning aggregate demand curve is AD_1 and in equilibrium aggregate output is OY_1 and price level is P_1, the economy. The level of aggregate output Y_1 is far below the full-employment level of output Y_F. Now, if aggregate demand increases to AD_2, the price level level rises to P_2 and output rises to Y_2. Even if aggregate demand further increases upto AD_3, aggregate output increases to Y_F and is accompanied by rise in the price level to P_3. Thus, in until the full-employment output Y_F is reached, increase in aggregate demand causes moderate inflation and also raises aggregate output and employment. It is only when aggregate demand increases beyond full-employment output that it leads to a higher rate of inflation without affecting output. Thus, so far as economy finds itself in in equilibrium before full-employment in view of the rising aggregate supply curve *AS*, moderate inflation has to be tolerated if higher levels of output and employment are to be achieved. Therefore, some economists have argued that there exists trade-off between output and inflation or between employment and inflation. Some inflation has to be accepted if you want higher output (and therefore less unemployment). However, this viewpoint has been criticised in recent years and it has been asserted that any trade-off between rate of inflation and output (or unemployment) is only a short-run phenomenon and there is no such trade-off in the long run.

Cost-Push Inflation and Output. But, as seen above, the economic events in recent years have thrown up another type of inflation which is generally described as cost-push the effective inflation which is caused by leftward shift in the aggregate supply curve due to rise in prices of crucial inputs such as petroleum oil, wages of labour etc. In the cost-push inflation, rise in price level is associated with a fall in aggregate output as will be seen from Fig. 45.3. In the early years of 1970s and again in 1979–80 when oil price shock given by *OPEC* created cost-push inflation, prices rose but at the same time output fell and unemployment went up. Such a situation has been described as *stagflation* which implies occurrence of inflation with static or lower output and higher unemployment.

From the above it is clear that there is no necessary relationship between inflation and output. Inflation may come about with either a higher or a lower level of output and employment. To quote Samuelson, "*Today, macroeconomists believe that there is no necessary relationship between prices and output. An increase in aggregate demand will increase both prices and output, but a supply shock shifting up aggregate supply curve will raise prices and lower output.*"[9]

EFFECTS OF INFLATION ON LONG-RUN ECONOMIC GROWTH

Some Economists have argued that inflation of a creeping or mild variety has a tonic effect on the long-run economic growth. In their support they give the example of today's industralised countries in the Eighteenth and Nineteenth Centuries when the rate of growth of output had been more rapid during long periods of inflation witnessed in these countries. The driving force in the process of economic growth, according to them, has been *high profit margins* created by inflation. They argue that wages lag behind the rise in general price level and thus creating higher profit margins for businessmen and industrialists. This tends to increase the profit share in national income. The businessmen and industrialists who receive profits as income belong to the upper income brackets whose propensity to save is higher as compared to the workers. As a result, savings go up which ensures higher rate of investment. With greater rate of investment more accumulation of capital is made possible. More rapid capital accumulation generates a higher rate of long-run economic growth.

Looking at the problem from an alternative angle, with wages lagging behind rise in prices, inflation causes a large shift of resources away from the production of consumer goods for the wage earners to the production of capital goods. The higher rate of expansion in capital stock raises the growth of productive capacity of the economy productivity of labour. This generates rapid economic growth.

Bad Effect of Inflation on Economic Growth

However, it is now widely recognised that, far from encouraging savings and generating higher rate of economic growth, inflation slows down the rate of capital accumulation. There are several reasons responsible for this. First, as seen above, when due to rapid inflation value of money is declining, people will not like to keep money with themselves and will, therefore, be eager to spend it before its value goes down heavily. This raises their consumption demand and therefore lowers their saving. Besides, people find that the rapid inflation will erode the real value of their savings. This discourages them to save. Thus, *inflation or rapid rise in prices serves as a disincentive to save*. Further, as a consequence of the rise in prices, a relatively greater part of the income of the people is spent on consumption to maintain their level of living and therefore little is left to be saved. Thus, not only does inflation reduce the willingness to save, it also slashes their ability to save.

Secondly, *inflation or rising prices lead to unproductive form of investment* in gold, jewellery, real estate, construction of houses etc. These unproductive forms of wealth do not add to the productive capacity of the economy and are quite useless from the viewpoint of economic growth. Thus, inflation may lead to more investment but much of this is of unproductive type.

9. Samuelson, P.A. & Nordhaus, W.D., *Economics,* Fourteenth edition, McGraw-Hill, 1992

In this way economic surplus is frittered away in unproductive investment.

Thirdly, a highly undesirable consequence of inflation, especially in developing countries, is that *it accentuates the problem of poverty in these countries which is against inclusive growth*. It is often said inflation is enemy number one of the poor people. Due to rising prices poor people are not able to meet their basic needs and maintain minimum subsistence level of consumption. Thus inflation sends many people to live below the poverty line with the result that the number of people living below the poverty line increases. Besides, due to inflation, consumption of a large number of poor people is reduced much below what may be regarded as *productive consumption*, that is, essential consumption required to maintain health and productive efficiency. In India, rapid inflation in recent years is as much responsible for the mounting number of people below the poverty line as the lack of employment opportunities.

Fourthly, *inflation adversely affects balance of payments* and thereby hampers economic growth, especially in the developing countries. When prices of domestic goods rise due to inflation, they cannot compete abroad and as a consequence exports of a country are discouraged. On the other hand, when domestic prices rise relatively to prices of foreign goods, imports of foreign goods increase. Thus, falling exports and rising imports create disequilibrium in the balance of payments which may, in the long run, result, in a foreign exchange crisis. The shortage of foreign exchange prevents the country to import even essential materials and capital goods needed for industrial growth of the economy. The Indian experience during 1988–92 when foreign exchange reserves declined to abysmally low level and created an economic crisis in the country, shows the validity of this argument.

There is no agreement among economists whether or not moderate or mild inflation encourages saving and therefore ensures higher rate of capital accumulation and economic growth. However, there is complete unanimity that a very rapid inflation or what is often called hyperinflation discourages saving and hinders economic growth. However, barring the special case of hyperinflation, whether or not saving is encouraged by inflation depends on whether there exists *wage lag*. While there is sufficient evidence in the industrialised countries such as the U.S.A. Great Britain, France etc., about the existence of wage lag in the period before the World War II, in the period after this there is no solid evidence of it. In the present wages quickly catch up with the rising prices. Indeed, there is evidence in some developed countries that the share of profits in national income has declined and that of wages has gone up during the post World War II period. Therefore, "To the extent that rate of long-run economic growth depends on the rate of capital accumulation, a major basis for the conclusion that inflation promotes rapid economic growth is undermined given that *wages no longer lag during inflation as they apparently did in time of past.*"[10]

However, it may be noted that in the developing countries like India where labour is mostly unorganised and trade unions of labour are not strong and further there is a lack of information which causes wages lagging behind prices during periods of inflation. This itself will cause greater proportion of national income going to profits and other business incomes which should ensure higher saving rate. However, in India, businessmen are prone to make unproductive investment in speculative activities, gold, jewellery, real estate and palatial houses whose prices rise rapidly during periods of inflation. Such kind of investment is not only counter-productive and anti-growth but is repugnant to social justice as it further accentuates inequalities in the distribution of income and wealth.

It follows from above that rising prices as a goal of monetary policy are full of disastrous consequences for the economy and the people and therefore cannot be recommended as a desirable

10. E.' Shapiro, Macroeconomic Analysis, Fourth Edition, 1978, p.443.

goal for the economic policy. Rising prices often get out of hand and hyperinflation might set in which will shake the confidence of the people in the monetary and fiscal system of the country.

MEASURES TO CONTROL INFLATION

Measures to Control Demand-Pull Demand

As has been explained above, inflation occurs due to the emergence of excess demand for goods and services relative to their supply of output at the prevailing prices. Inflation of this type is called *demand-pull inflation*. Various fiscal and monetary measures can be adopted to check this inflation. We discuss below the efficacy of the various policy measures to check demand-pull inflation which is caused by excess aggregate demand.

1. Fiscal Policy: Reducing Fiscal Deficit

The budget deals with how a Government raises its revenue and spends it. If the total revenue raised by the Government through taxation, fees, surpluses from public undertakings is less than the expenditure it incurs on buying goods and services to meet its requirements of defence, civil administration and various welfare and developmental activities, there emerges a fiscal deficit. It may be noted here that the budget of the government has two parts: (1) *Revenue Budget*, (2) *Capital Budget*. In the revenue budget on the receipts side revenue raised through taxes, interests, fees, surpluses from public undertakings are given and on the expenditure side consumption expenditure by the government on goods and services required to meet the needs of defence, civil administration, education and health services, subsidies on food, fertilizers and exports, and interest payments on the loans taken by it in the previous years are important items. In the capital budget, the main items of receipts are market borrowings by the government from the Banks and other financial institutions, foreign aid, small savings (*i.e.*, Provident Fund, National Savings Schemes etc.). The important items of expenditure in the capital budget are defence, funding of public enterprises for developmental purposes, especially those relating to infrastructure projects and loans to states and union territories.

Fiscal deficit can be financed in two ways. First, borrowing by the government from thje central bank (RBI in case of India) against its own securities. This leads to the creation of more money supply and therefore gives rise to inflationary pressures in the economy. For some years ago, this was called deficit financing which was held to be the main cause of demand-pull inflation in India. Now, we call it *monetisation of fiscal deficit*. However, in recent years fiscal deficit in India is financed mainly through borrowing by the Government through sale of its bonds which are generally purchased by banks, insurance companies, mutual funds and corporate firms. The increase in government expenditure made possible by borrowing without being matched by extra taxation causes aggregate demand to increase. The net increase in Government expenditure leads to multiple increase in aggregate demand through *Government expenditure* multiplier.

In the opinion of many economists, the expansion in aggregate expenditure caused by fiscal deficit leads to the excess aggregate demand and inflationary pressures in the economy, especially when aggregate supply of output is inelastic. To some extent increase in aggregate demand may not generate demand-pull inflation because if the aggregate output increases, especially of essential consumer goods such as foodgrains, cloth, the extra demand arising out of increase in expenditure would be matched by extra supply of output.

But when increase in expenditure occurs and the economy is already utilising its production capacity fully or working near to it, this leads to demand-pull inflation. Therefore, to tackle the problem of demand-pull inflation fiscal deficit should be reduced. In its recommendation for India, IMF has suggested that fiscal deficit must be reduced to 3 per cent of GDP if inflation has to be kept under check.

To reduce fiscal deficit the Government can mobilise more resources through taxes, both direct and indirect. In India there is a lot of scope for raising resources through taxation. In both personal and corporate income taxes, there are a large number of unnecessary exemptions which lower the effective rate of income tax. Thus it has been found that though there is 33 per cent tax on corporate income but because of several exemptions which have outlived their utility, effective rate of corporate income tax in India is only about 24 per cent. Thus with withdrawal of these exemptions can lead to significant increase in revenue of the Government. Besides, improving efficiency of tax-collecting administration tax evasion which occurs on a large scale in India and generate a lot of black money can *yield* large revenue for the Government. On the other hand, it can reduce fiscal deficit by curtailing its wasteful and inessential expenditure, especially subsidies to the non-poor people. In India, it is often argued that there is a large scope for pruning down non-plan expenditure on defence, police and general administration and on subsidies being provided on food, fertilizers and fuel oil. Though it is easy to suggest cutting down of Government expenditure, it is difficult to implement it in practice. However, in our view, there is a large-scale inefficiency in resource use and also a lot of corruption involved in the spending by the Government expenditure which can be curtailed to a good extent. Thus, both by greater resource mobilisation on the one hand and pruning down of wasteful and inessential Government expenditure on the other, the fiscal deficit can be reduced.

2. Monetary Policy to Control Inflation : Monetary Tightening

Monetary policy refers to the adoption of suitable policy regarding *interest rate* and the *availability of credit*. Monetary policy is important measure for reducing aggregate demand to control inflation. As an instrument of demand management, monetary policy can work in two ways. First, it can affect the *cost of credit* and second, it can influence the *credit availability* for private business firms. Let us first consider the cost of credit. The higher the rate of interest, the greater the cost of borrowing from the banks by the business firms. As anti-inflationary measure, the rate of interest has to be raised to discourage businessmen to borrow more so that less bank credit is created. In the fifties and early sixties, the cheap credit policy (*i.e.*, lower interest rates) was recommended on the ground that lower rate of interest will promote more private investment which is an important factor determining economic growth. Keeping in view this consideration, cheap money policy was adopted in India upto 1972 and accordingly bank rate was kept low.

The dear money policy (that is, *higher interest rate policy* has been often used in India to curb the inflationary pressures in the Indian economy. In India, bank rate has not been generally used to check inflation. Instruments like *repo rate* and *reverse repo* rate have often been used to manage aggregate demand. Repo rate is the interest rate at which Reserve Bank of India lends funds to the commercial bank *for a short period*. To curb inflation *repo rate* is raised. Hike in repo rate raises the cost of funds for the banks which will, if they do not have excess reserves, raise their *lending rates*. The higher lending rates will lower the demand for bank credit for investment and for purchases of cars (auto loans and housing (housing loans). Under these circumstances to mobilise funds banks raise their deposit rates. The higher rate of interest on saving and fixed deposits will induce more savings by the households and help in cutting down aggregate consumption expenditure. Besides, higher rates of interest will discourage more investment in inventories and consumer durables and will help in reducing aggregate demand. However, rise in repo rate will lead to the decline in credit growth if *monetary transmission mechanism* works. This will happen only if banks are short of liquid funds. If the banks have excess liquid reserves with them they would not raise their lending rates when the RBI raises repo rate. Therefore, for monetary transmission mechanism to work liquidity with the banks must be curtailed. This can be done by the RBI by raising Cash Reserve ratio (CRR) and by *open market operation* through sale of Government securities.

It is noteworthy that a recent monetary theory emphasizes that it is the changes in the ***credit availability*** rather than ***cost of credit*** (*i.e.*, rate of interest) that is a more effective instrument of regulating aggregate demand. There are several methods by which credit availability can be reduced. Firstly, it is through *open market operations* that the central bank of a country can reduce the availability of credit in the economy. Under open market operations, the Reserve Bank sells Government securities. Those, especially banks, who buy these securities will make payment for them in terms of cash reserves. With their reduced cash reserves, their capacity to lend money to the business firms will be curtailed. This will tend to reduce the supply of credit or loanable funds by the banks which in turn would tend to reduce aggregate demand.

However, in India open market operations do not play a significant role as an instrument of credit control to fight against inflationary situation. This is because market for Government securities is narrow as well as captive. General public do not buy more than a fraction of Government securities. It is the institutions such as commercial banks, LIC, GIC and Provident Funds which are required by law to invest a certain proportion of their funds in buying Government securities. However, the RBI can reduce the liquidity with the banks by selling Government securities to them through open market operations.

In India, it is the ***Cash Reserve Ratio (CRR)*** which can be effectively used to curb inflation. By law banks have to keep a certain proportion of cash money as reserves against their deposits. This is called cash reserve ratio. To reduce liquidity with the banks and thereby to contract credit availability Reserve Bank can raise this ratio. In recent years to squeeze credit for checking inflation, cash reserve ratio in India has been raised from time to time.

Another instrument with Reserve Bank of India for affecting credit availability is the ***Statutory Liquidity Ratio*** (SLR). According to statutory liquidity ratio, in addition to *CRR*, banks have to keep a certain minimum proportion of their deposits in the form of specified liquid assets. And the most important specified liquid asset for this purpose is the Government securities. To mop up extra liquid assets with banks which may lead to undue expansion in credit availability for the business class, the Reserve Bank has often raised statutory liquidity ratio.

Limitations of Tight Monetary Policy

However, tight monetary policy for controlling inflation is not without its limitations. First, monetary transmission mechanism may be weak and raising of short-term interest rates by the RBI may not actually lead to the restriction of bank credit. First, the banks may have surplus liquidity (i.e., cash reserves) with them and therefore they may not follow tight monetary policy and raise their lending rates. As a result, supply of credit by banks will not be restricted. Secondly, if the economic environment is such that boom conditions prevail in the economy and aggregate demand for products is quite high, demand for credit may not be much affected by higher lending rates. As emphasized by J.M. Keynes investment is determined more by marginal efficiency of capital (that is, expected rate of return) rather than rate of interest. Thirdly, at present in India corporate firms are more easily able to borrow from foreign capital markets (i.e., external commercial borrowing, ECB) especially when rates of interest in the US, European zone and Japan are extremely low. Therefore, unless this debt-capital inflow (i.e. ECB) is checked RBI's monetary policy may not be effective to check the supply of credit to control inflation in the economy.

Thirdly, when the stock market prices are rising and aggregate demand is quite high, the corporate sector is able to raise funds itself more easily from the capital market. This will also offset the impact of tight monetary policy of the RBI to control inflation. Fourthly, if adequate internal funds are available with the corporate firms as a result of *retained profit earnings* by the companies they can use them to finance their expansion plans and thereby add to the aggregate expenditure or demand. This will also nullify the tight monetary policy of the RBI to curb inflation.

It may be noted that in recent years to control inflation the Reserve Bank of India raised its *repo rate* 13 times from March 2010 to Nov. 2011 (from 4.75% in March 2010 to 8.50% in Nov. 2011) but inflation as measured by the WPI remained at an elevated level. It was estimated at 10 per cent (YoY) in September 2011, 9.73% in Oct. 2011 and 9.11 per cent in Nov. 2011. After Nov. 2011, WPI inflation declined because of dip in food inflation due partly to the base effect and partly to easing of supply position of some food articles. Thus tight monetary policy failed to check inflation despite 3.75 per centage points increase in repo rate. The RBI explained failure of its tight monetary policy to curb inflation by pointing out to *large fiscal deficit* of the Government in 2011-12. Due to large fiscal deficit, aggregate demand was increasing which was feeding inflation in the Indian economy. According to the RBI, unless fiscal deficit is brought down by the Government, tight monetary policy alone will not succeed in checking inflation. Besides, the RBI blamed supply-side factors responsible for food inflation which has contributed to overall rise in WPI inflation.

Lastly, if inflation in the economy has originated from the **supply-side factors**, for example, if production of foodgrains and other essential food articles such as milk, vegitables, fruits etc. in a year declines or does not increase adequately to meet the growing demand for them due to certain supply-side bottlenecks, this will cause the demand supply imbalances leading to the rise in inflation. Such supply-side inflation cannot be checked by raising interest rates under the tight monetary policy. This happened in 2009-10 when due to the shortage of monsoon rainfall, drop in agricultural production was expected, inflationary pressures emerged in the Indian economy raising food-inflation to around 20 per cent in December 2009. This food inflation continued to prevail at double digit level till November 2010. Tight monetary policy which is aimed at management of aggregate demand rather than augmentation of supply is ineffective in tackling this supply-side inflation as in case of food inflation in 2010. Likewise, in 2010-11 and 2011-12 shortage of protein-based food products such as pulses, milk, fruits and vegetables, eggs, meat and fish, contributed a good deal to the persistence of food inflation. It is only after Oct. 2011 when there was a drop in food-inflation, that headline WPI inflation also declined. Similarly, supply-side inflation arises when prices of petroleum products rise which is passed on to the domestic consumers and cannot be tackled with use of tight monetary policy. In addition to fuel, if output growth in *core industries* such as steel, cement, coal declined as they did during 2011-12 in India they create supply-side bottlenecks in various industries leading to supply-side inflation.

Now to control food inflation what is required to take long-term measures to augment supply of foodgrains and other food articles by raising agricultural productivity by undertaking appropriate technological changes and land-reform measures. In the short run to control food inflation what is needed is to release food stocks through public distribution system (PDS) which should be properly monitorad to check black-market. Besides, to control rise in food prices in the short run release of food stocks for sale in the open market should be made. However, this pre-supposes enough food stocks with the Government. Further, to check food-inflation foodgrains, pulses, oilseeds and other feed articles in shor-supply can be imported.

It may however be noted that when inflationary expectations arise as a result of emergence of shortage of supply of some essential commodities there is tendency on the part of traders to hoard stocks of goods in short supply for speculative purposes. To discourage such speculative hoarding of goods in short supply monetary policy of hgih interest rates can be helpful. Besides, as will be explained below, selective credit controls of monetary policy can also be used to check excessive hoarding of foodgrains, oil-seeds and other essential commodities.

Selective Credit Controls

Important anti-inflationary measure in India is the use of selective credit controls. The methods of credit control described above are known as ***quantitative or general methods*** as they are meant to control the cost and availability of credit in general. Thus, bank rate policy, repo and reverse repo rate, open market operations and variation in cash reserves ratio expand or contract the availability of credit for all purposes. On the other hand, selective credit controls are meant to regulate the ***flow of credit for particular or specific purposes***. Whereas the general credit controls seek to regulate the total available quantity of credit (through changes in the high powered money) and the cost of credit, the *selective credit control seeks to change the distribution or allocation of credit between its various uses*. These selective credit controls are also known as ***Qualitative Credit Controls***. The selective credit controls have both the positive and negative aspects. In its positive aspect, measures are taken to stimulate the greater flow of credit to some particular sectors considered as important. Thus, in India, agriculture, small and marginal farmers, small artisans, small-scale industries are the priority sectors to which greater flow of bank credit has been sought to be encouraged by the Reserve Bank of India. In its negative aspect, several measures are taken to restrict the credit flowing into some specific activities or sectors which are regarded as undesirable or harmful from the social point of view. The selective credit controls generally used in India was **changes in the minimum margin for lending by banks** against the stocks of specific goods kept or against other types of securities.

In India, in the past the selective credit controls were used by the Reserve Bank to prevent speculative hoarding of essential commodities so as to check the rise in prices of these commodities. The selective credit controls in India were used in case of foodgrains, oilseeds, vegetable oils, cotton, sugar, gur and Khandsari. It may be noted that the Reserve Bank of India has the power to vary the minimum margin requirements against the security of stocks of commodities. While lending advances to businessmen, the commercial banks leave a margin of the value of stock kept as security to be financed by the businessmen from their own sources and lend money equal to the remaining amount of the value of the stock. This minimum requirement of the value of the stock left to be financed by the borrowers themselves is known as margin. Suppose the margin fixed for a stock of particular commodity is 60 per cent. In this case, the businessmen can borrow up to the value of 40 per cent of the stock of that commodity and the remaining 60 per cent of the value of stock will be financed by he businessman himself. Now, if the Reserve Bank raises the margin to 70 per cent, then he can borrow from the bank to the extent of 30 per cent of the value of the stock of that commodity. This will lead to the contraction of credit for holding the stock of the commodity by the businessman. If the businessmen are not able to finance the holding of 10 per cent extra stock of the commodity, they will be forced to sell that in the market and thus raising market supply of the commodity. This will lower the prices, other things remaining the same.

Some conditions are necessary for the successful operations of selective credit controls of commodities. First, they should be accompanied by general credit control measures. This is because the clever businessmen can obtain credit from the banks by offering other securities and use the funds so obtained to finance the speculative holdings of the stocks of sensitive commodities. Therefore, if the selective credit controls are to succeed in preventing the rise in prices of sensitive commodities, they have to be accompanied by general credit controls aimed at reducing the capacity of banks to lend money. It also follows from above that end-use or purpose of all credit ought to be taken into account by the banks and credit advanced accordingly if selective credit controls are to be effective. In India the selective credit controls have been in operation since 1956 to check the rise in prices of sensitive commodities. But in recent years, the RBI has stopped using selective credit control measures to check inflation in India.

The success of the selective credit controls also depends upon the extent to which the funds from *non-bank sources* (*i.e.*, from their own funds and also from the unregulated money market) is available to the businessmen. When the bank credit for a particular purpose is reduced, the businessmen can use their own funds or borrow from non-regulated money markets for speculative holding of inventories. In India today the businessmen have large quantities of black money with them which they generally use for speculative holding of foodgrains and other sensitive commodities and in this way succeed in defeating the purpose of selective control of credit to contain inflation.

Supply-side Inflation in India

In case of India, demand-supply imbalances in certain commodities was found to be widening in recent years (2008-09, 2009-10) causing significant swings in their prices. Barning a few edible oils and pulses, *India has so far met the bulk of its food demand through domestic production. For wheat and sugar, India has occasionally resorted to imports, though generally it is an exporter of these commodities.*

In the case of *edible oils*, the demand has far outstripped the domestic supply and the deficit is met through imports, the share of imports being around 35 per cent of the total consumption. *Pulses production* has also lagged behind the demand resulting in dependence on imports to the extent of 14-15 per cent. *In the case of commodities like crude oil, where the import dependence is more than 80 per cent, while full pass through of international prices to domestic prices has implications for inflation* in the short-run, it will contribute to price stability by alleviating the pressure on the fiscal situation (that is, they will help in reducing fiscal deficit). The deregulation of petroleum products besides contributing to improve the fiscal situation could also *promote energy efficiency and conservation.*

The increase in inflation in India in certain commodities, especially food items in recent years has been on account of structural factors, which has created supply-side bottlenecks. *As the growth in food production has been lower than the overall growth in population the net availability of food has come down*, which gets partly reflected in sustained increase in prices. Moreover as the economy exhibits stronger inclusive growth, the resultant increase in income of the population at large would lead to shift in the pattern of demand and consumption of food items like pulses, milk and sugar could increase which would exert pressure on prices of these products for which supply response may lag behind the growing demand.

Tackling Supply-side Inflation

The identification of sources of inflation is important for the conduct of monetary policy. Tightening of monetary policy in the face of demand pressures could yield desirable results by reducing money supply or bank credit which will reduce the level of aggregate demand. However, *when the inflationary pressures are dominated by adverse supply shocks, monetary policy could be less effective in containing* price pressures. Supply shocks, however, generally tend to alter relative prices, and in certain conditions, relative price trends could necessitate monetary policy actions, as had been the case for India in the last quarter of 2009-10.

In case of inflation arising on account of shortage of supply, the latter can also be raised by importing goods in short supply. In India, to check the rise in prices of foodgrains, edible oils, sugar etc., the Government has often taken steps to increase imports of goods in short supply to enlarge their available supplies. Thus, when inflation is of the type of *supply-side inflation*, imports are increased to augment the domestic supplies of goods. To increase imports of goods in short supply, the Government can reduce customs duties on them so that their imports become cheaper and therefore their imports help in containing inflation. For example, in 2008-09 the Indian Government removed customs duties on imports of wheat and rice and reduced them on oilseeds, steel etc. to increase their supplies in India. Besides, to increase the domestic supplies the government can ban the exports of some commodities for some time.

At times of inflationary expectations, there is a tendency on the part of businessmen to hoard goods for speculative purposes. The attempt by the Government to import goods in short supply would compel the hoarders to release their hoarded stocks. This will have a favourable impact on prices of these goods. However, when international prices of commodities are high, their imports cannot be very helpful for tackling domestic inflation. This was the case in 2009-10 when commodities such as sugar, wheat, oil seeds could not be imported sufficiently to augment domestic supplies because of their high world prices.

Fiscal and Administrative Measures Tackle Supply-Side Inflation in 2009-10

Since the inflationary situation during 2009-10 largely emerged from the supply side constraints the government took a number of short and medium-term fiscal and administrative measures to improve domestic availability of essential commodities and thereby moderate the pressure on inflation. These included (1) reduction of import duty to zero for select food items like rice, wheat, pulses, edible oils, sugar and maize; (2) additional allocation of foodgrains for sale through public distribution system (PDS); (3) allocation of wheat for release by the Food Corporation of India (FCI) in the open market (4) ban on export of non-basmati rice, edible oils and pulses, (5) distribution of imported pulses and edible oils thorough PDS at subsidised rates and (6) increase in Minimum Support Prices of key agricultural commodities to augment production.

QUESTIONS FOR REVIEW

1. Define demand-pull inflation. How, is it caused by the Government's insistence of keeping the market rate of interest low so as to stimulate investment.
2. What are the main factors that cause cost-push inflation ? Suggest measures to control cost-push inflation ?
3. Distinguish between demand-pull inflation and cost-push inflation. How are they often intertwined ?
4. Inflation may originate because of cost-push but it cannot be sustained for long unless it is supported by demand-pull inflation.
5. Inflation in the less developed countries can be explained in terms of the structural features of these economies
6. Inflation is inevitable in an economy attempting to grow rapidly in the presence of structural bottlenecks, Discuss.
7. An inflationary process may begin on the supply side but it will not continue for long unless there is increase in demand. Discuss.

8. Distinguish between demand-pull and cost-push inflation. How can demand-pull inflation be controlled?
9. Inflation is a purely monetary phenomenon. Explain your viewpoint making use of Fisher's equation of exchange.
10. Define inflation. Explain its effects on (*a*) creditors and deletors (b) persons of fixed income group.
11. Explain the effects of inflation on output and distribution of income.
12. How does inflation distort the pattern of production and distribution in an economy?
13. Define inflation. What measures would you suggest to control it?
14. What are the main causes of inflation in India? Which policies of government has helped to check rise in prices ?
15. State the Fisher's equation describing the relation between real rate of interest, inflation rate and nominal interest rate. What is the effect of inflation rate on real rate of interest and nominal rate of interest.
16. What is Fisher effect ? Show how nominal interest rate depends on inflation rate.
17. What is supply-side inflation ? How can it be controlled ?

    Explain the limitations of monetary policy to contain supply-side inflation.
18. Explain the roles of fiscal and monetary policies to check inflation.
19. Distinguish between selective credit controls and quantitative credit controls. Explain the role of selective credit controls to contain inflation.

Analysis of Business Cycles

Introduction

Many free enterprise capitalist countries such as USA and Great Britain have registered rapid economic growth during the last two centuries. But economic growth in these countries has not followed steady and smooth upward trend. There has been a long-run upward trend in Gross National Product (GNP), but periodically there have been large short-run fluctuations in economic activity, that is, changes in output, income, employment and prices around this long-term trend. The period of high income, output and employment has been called the period of *expansion, upswing* or *prosperity*, and the period of low income, output and employment has been described as *contraction*, *recession*, *downswing* or *depression*. The economic history of the free market capitalist countries has shown that the period of economic prosperity or expansion alternates with the period of contraction or recession. *These alternating periods of expansion and contraction in economic activity has been* called business cycles. They are also known as *trade cycles*. J.M. Keynes writes, "A trade cycle is composed of periods of good trade characterised by rising prices and low unemployment percentages with periods of bad trade characterised by falling prices and high unemployment percentages."[1]

A noteworthy feature about these fluctuations in economic activity is that they are recurrent and have been occurring periodically in a more or less regular fashion. Therefore, these fluctuations have been called business cycles. It may be noted that calling these fluctuations as `cycles' mean they are periodic and occur regularly, though perfect regularity has not been observed. The duration of a business cycle has not been of the same length; it has varied from a minimum of two years to a maximum of ten to twelve years, though in the past it was often assumed that fluctuations of output and other economic indicators around the trend showed repetitive and regular pattern of alternating periods of expansion and contraction. However, actually there has been no clear evidence of very regular cycles of the same definite duration. Some business cycles have been very short lasting for only two to three years, while others have lasted for several years. Further, in some cycles there have been large swings away from trend and in others these swings have been of moderate nature.

1. J.M. Keynes, *The General Theory of Employment, Interest and Money*, 1936

A significant point worth noting about business cycles is that they have been very costly in the economic sense of the word. During a period of recession or depression many workers lose their jobs and as a result large-scale unemployment, which causes loss of output that could have been produced with full-employment of resources, come to prevail in the economy. Besides, during depression many businessmen go bankrupt and suffer huge losses. Depression causes a lot of human sufferings and lowers the levels of living of the people. Fluctuations in economic activity creates a lot of uncertainty in the economy which causes anxiety to the individuals about their future income and employment opportunities and involve a great risk for long-run investment in projects. Who does not remember the great havoc caused by the great depression of the early thirties of the present century? Even boom when it is accompanied by inflation has its social costs. Inflation erodes the real incomes of the people and makes life miserable for the poor people. Inflation distorts allocation of resources by drawing away scarce resources from productive uses to unproductive ones. Inflation redistributes income in favour of the richer sections and also when inflation rate is high, it impedes economic growth. About the harmful effects of the business cycles Crowther writes, "On the one hand, there is the misery and shame of unemployment with all the individual poverty and social disturbances that it may create. "On the other hand, there is the loss of wealth represented by so much wasted and idle labour and capital."[2]

Phases of Business Cycles

Business cycles have shown distinct phases the study of which is useful to understand their underlying causes. These phases have been called by different names by different economists. Generally, the following phases of business cycles have been distinguished :

1. Expansion (Boom, Upswing or Prosperity)
2. Peak (upper turning point)
3. Contraction (Downswing, Recession or Depression)
4. Trough (lower turning point)

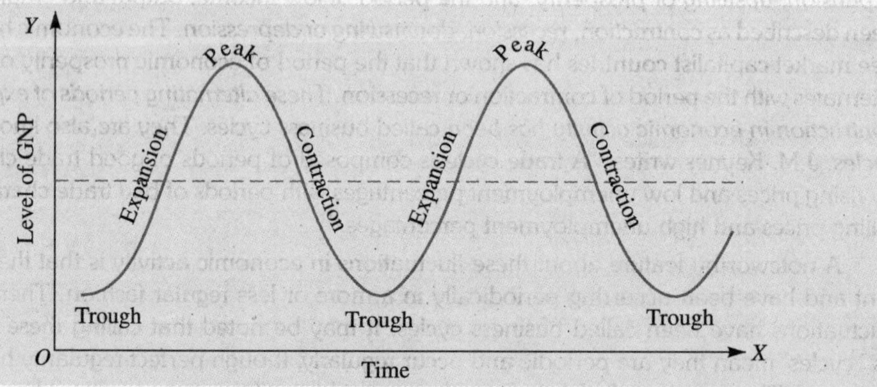

Fig. 46.1 *Four Phases of Business Cycles without Growth Trend*

The four phases of business cycles have been shown in Fig. 46.1 where we start from trough or depression when the level of economic activity *i.e.*, level of production and employment is at the lowest level. With the revival of economic activity the economy moves into the expansion phase, but due to the causes explained below, the expansion cannot continue indefinitely, and after reaching peak, contraction or downswing starts. When the contraction gathers momentum, we have a depression. The downswing continues till the lowest turning point which is also called trough is reached. In this way cycle is complete. However, after remaining at the trough for some time the economy revives and again the new cycle starts. Haberler

2. G. Crowther, *An Outline of Money*, (London 1962), p. 192

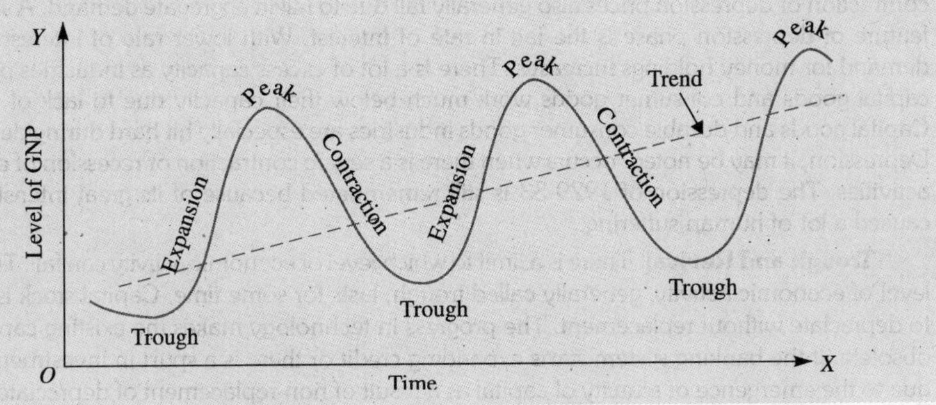

Fig. 46.2. *Cycles with Trend (i.e, Growth)*

in his important work[3] on business cycles has named the four phases of business cycles as (1) Upswing, (2) Upper turning point, (3) Downswing, and (4) Lower turning point.

There are two types of patterns of cyclic changes. One pattern is shown in Fig. 46.1 where fluctuations occur around a stable equilibrium position as shown by the horizontal line. It is a case of dynamic stability which depicts change but without growth or trend. The second pattern of cyclical fluctuations is shown in Fig. 46.2 where cyclical changes in economic activity take place around a growth path (i.e., rising trend). J.R. Hicks in his model of business cycles explains such a pattern of fluctuations with long-run rising trend in economic activity by imposing factors such as autonomous investment due to population growth and technological progress causing economic growth on the otherwise stationary state. We briefly explain below various phases of business cycles.

Expansion and Prosperity. In its expansion phase, both output and employment increase till we have full-employment of resources and production is at the highest possible level with the given productive resources. There is no involuntary unemployment and whatever unemployment prevails is only of frictional and structural types. Thus, when expansion gathers momentum and we have prosperity, the gap between potential GNP and actual GNP is zero, that is, the level of production is at the maximum production level. A good amount of net investment is occurring and demand for durable consumer goods is also high. Prices also generally rise during the expansion phase but due to high level of economic activity people enjoy a high standard of living.

Then something may occur, whether banks start reducing credit or profit expectations change adversely and businessmen become pessimistic about future state of the economy that bring an end to the expansion or prosperity phase. As shall be explained below, economists differ regarding the possible causes of the end of prosperity and start of downswing in economic activity. Monetarists have argued that contraction in bank credit may cause downswing. Keynes have argued that sudden collapse of expected rate of profit (which he calls marginal efficiency of capital, MEC) caused by adverse changes in expectations of entrepreneurs lowers investment in the economy. This fall in investment, according to him, causes downswing in economic activity.

Contraction and Depression. As stated above, expansion or prosperity is followed by contraction or depression. During contraction, not only there is a fall in GNP but also level of employment is reduced. As a result, involuntary unemployment appears on a large scale. Investment also decreases causing further fall in consumption of goods and services. At times of

3. See G Haberler, Prosperity and Depression, *A Theoretical Analysis of Cyclical Movements*, Harward University Press, 1960.

contraction or depression prices also generally fall due to fall in aggregate demand. A significant feature of depression phase is the fall in rate of interest. With lower rate of interest people's demand for money holdings increases. There is a lot of excess capacity as industries producing capital goods and consumer goods work much below their capacity due to lack of demand. Capital goods and durable consumer goods industries are especially hit hard during depression. Depression, it may be noted, occurs when there is a severe contraction or recession of economic activities. The depression of 1929-33 is still remembered because of its great intensity which caused a lot of human suffering.

Trough and Revival. There is a limit to which level of economic activity can fall. The lowest level of economic activity, generally called trough, lasts for some time. Capital stock is allowed to depreciate without replacement. The progress in technology makes the existing capital stock obsolete. If the banking system starts expanding credit or there is a spurt in investment activity due to the emergence of scarcity of capital as a result of non-replacement of depreciated capital and also because of new technology coming into existence requiring new types of machines and other capital goods. The stimulation of investment brings about the revival or recovery of the economy. The recovery is the turning point from depression into expansion. As investment rises, this causes induced increase in consumption. As a result industries start producing more and excess capacity is now put into full use due to the revival of aggregate demand. Employment of labour increases and rate of unemployment falls. With this the cycle is complete.

Features of Business Cycles

Though different business cycles differ in duration and intensity they have some common features which we explain below:

1. Business cycles occur *periodically*. Though they do not show same regularity, they have some distinct phases such as expansion, peak, contraction or depression and trough. Further the duration of cycles varies a good deal from minimum of two years to a maximum of ten to twelve years.
2. Secondly, business cycles are *Synchronic*. That is, they do not cause changes in any single industry or sector but are of all embracing character. For example, depression or contraction occur simultaneously in all industries or sectors of the economy. Recession passes from one industry to another and chain reaction continues till the whole economy is in the grip of recession. Similar process is at work in the expansion phase, prosperity spreads through various linkages of input-output relations or demand relations between various industries and sectors.
3. Thirdly, it has been observed that fluctuations occur not only in level of production but also simultaneously in other variables such as employment, investment, consumption, rate of interest and price level.
4. Another important feature of business cycles is that investment and consumption of durable consumer goods such as cars, houses, refrigerators are affected most by the cyclical fluctuations. As stressed by J.M. Keynes, investment is greatly volatile and unstable as it depends on profit expectations of private entrepreneurs. These expectations of entrepreneurs change quite often making investment quite unstable. Since *consumption of durable consumer goods* can be deferred, it also fluctuates greatly during the course of business cycles.
5. An important feature of business cycles is that consumption of *non-durable goods and* services does not vary much during different phases of business cycles. Past data of business cycles reveal that households maintain a great stability in consumption of non-durable goods.

6. The immediate impact of depression and expansion is on the *inventories of goods*. When depression sets in, the inventories start accumulating beyond the desired level. This leads to cut in production of goods. On the contrary, when recovery starts, the inventories go below the desired level. This encourages businessmen to place more orders for goods whose production picks up and stimulates investment in capital goods.
7. Another important feature of business cycles is *profits fluctuate more than any other type of income*. The occurrence of business cycles causes a lot of uncertainty for businessmen and makes it difficult to forecast the economic conditions. During the depression period profits may even become negative and many businesses go bankrupt. In a free market economy profits are justified on the ground that they are necessary payments if the entrepreneurs are to be induced to bear uncertainty.
8. Lastly, business cycles are *international in character*. That is, once started in one country they spread to other countries through trade relations between them. For example, if there is a recession in the USA, which is a large importer of goods from other countries, will cause a fall in demand for imports from other countries whose exports would be adversely affected causing recession in them too. Depression of 1930s in USA and Great Britain engulfed the entire capital world.

THEORIES OF BUSINESS CYCLES

We have explained above the various phases and common features of business cycles. Now, an important question is what causes business cycles. Several theories of business cycles have been propounded from time to time. Each of these theories spells out the factors which cause business cycles. Before explaining the modern theories of business cycles we first explain below important *earlier* theories of business cycles as they too contain important elements whose study is essential for proper understanding of the causes of business cycles.

Hawtrey's Monetary Theory of Business Cycles

An old monetary theory of business cycles was put forward by Hawtrey.[4] His monetary theory of business cycles relates to the economy which is under gold standard. It will be remembered that economy is said be under gold standard when either money in circulation consists of gold coins or when paper notes are fully backed by gold reserves in the banking system. According to Hawtrey, increases in the quantity of money raises the availability of bank credit for investment. Thus, by increasing the supply of credit expansion in money supply causes rate of interest to fall. The lower rate of interest induces businessmen to borrow more for investment in capital goods and also for investment in keeping more inventories of goods. Thus, Hawtrey argues that lower rate of interest will lead to the expansion of goods and services as a result of more investment in capital goods and inventories. Higher output, income and employment caused by more investment induces more spending on consumer goods. Thus, as a result of more investment made possible by increased supply of bank credit economy moves into the expansion phase. The process of expansion continues for some time. Increases in aggregate demand brought about by more investment also causes prices to rise. Rising prices lead to the increase in output in two ways. First, when prices begin to rise businessmen think they would rise further which induces them to invest more and produce more because prospects of making profits increase with the rise in prices. Secondly, the rising prices reduces the real value of idle money balances with the people which induces them to spend more on goods and services. In this way rising prices sustain expansion for some time.

However, according to Hawtrey, the expansion process must end. He argued that rise in incomes during the expansion phase induces more expenditure on domestically produced goods

4. R.G. Hawtrey, *Good and Bad Trade*, Constable and Co., London, 1913.

as well as more on imports of foreign goods. He further assumes that domestic output and income expand faster than foreign output. As a result, imports of a country increase more than its exports causing *trade deficit* with other countries. If exchange rate remains fixed, trade deficit means there will be *outflow of gold* to settle its balance of payments deficit. Since the country is on gold standard, outflow of gold will cause reduction in money supply in the economy. The decrease in money supply will reduce the availability of bank credit. Reduction in the supply of bank credit will cause the rate of interest to rise. Rising interest rate will reduce investment in physical capital goods. Reduction in investment will cause the process of contraction to set in. As a result of reduced order for inventories, producers will cut production which will lower income and consumption of goods and services. In this state of reduced demand for goods and services, prices of goods will fall. Once the prices begin to fall businessmen begin to expect that they will fall further. In response to it traders will cut order of goods still causing further fall in output. The fall in prices also causes real value of money balances to rise which induce people to hold larger money holdings with them. In this way contraction process gathers momentum as demand for goods start declining faster and with this economy plunges into depression.

But after a lapse of some time depression will also come to an end and the economy will start to recover. This happens because in the contraction process imports fall drastically due to decrease in income and consumption of households, whereas exports do not fall much. As a result, *trade surplus* emerges which causes *inflow of gold*. The inflow of gold would lead to the expansion of money supply and consequently availability of bank credit for investment will increase. With this, the economy will recover from depression and move into the expansion phase. Thus, the cycle is complete. The process, according to Hawtrey, will go on being repeated regularly.

Critical Appraisal. Hawtrey maintains that the economy under gold standard and fixed exchange rate system makes his model of business cycles self-generating as there is built-in tendency for the money supply to change with the emergence of trade deficit and trade surplus which cause movements of gold between countries and affect money supply in them. Changes in money supply influence economic activity in a cyclical fashion. However, Hawtrey's monetary theory does not apply to the present-day economies which have abandoned gold standard in 1930s. However, Hawtrey's theory still retains its importance because it shows how changes in money supply affects economic activity through changes in price level and rate of interest. In modern monetary theories of trade cycles this relation between money supply and rate of interest plays an important role in determining the level of economic activity.

Under-Consumption Theory

Under-consumption theory of business cycles is a very old one which dates back to the 1930s. Malthus and Sismodi criticised Say's Law which states *supply creates its own demand* and argued that consumption of goods and services could be too small to generate sufficient demand for goods and services produced. They attribute over-production of goods due to lack of consumption demand for them. This over-production causes piling up of inventories of goods which results in recession.

Under-consumption theory as propounded by Sismodi and Hobson was not a theory of recurring business cycles. They made an attempt to explain how a free enterprise economy could enter a long-run economic slowdown. A crucial aspect of Sismodi and Hobson's under-consumption theory is the distinction they made between the rich and the poor. According to them, the rich sections in the society receive a large part of their income from returns on financial assets and real property owned by them. Further, they assume that the rich have a large propensity to save, that is, they save a relatively large proportion of their income and therefore, consume a relatively smaller proportion of their income. On the other hand, less well-off people in a society obtain most of their income from work, that is, wages from labour and have a lower propensity to save. Therefore, these less well-off people spend a relatively less proportion of their income consumer goods and services. In their theory, they further assume that during the expansion process, the incomes of the rich people increase relatively more than the wage-income. Thus, during the expansion phase, income distribution changes in favour of the rich with the result that average propensity to save falls, that is, in the expansion process saving increases and therefore consumption demand declines.[5]

According to Sismodi and Hobson, increase in saving during the expansion phase leads to more investment expenditure on capital goods and after some time lag, the greater stock of capital goods enables the economy to produce more consumer goods and services. But since society's propensity to consume continues to fall, consumption demand is not enough to absorb the increased production of consumer goods. In this way, lack of demand for consumer goods or what is called under-consumption emerges in the economy which halts the expansion of the economy. Further, since supply or production of goods increases relatively more as compared to the consumption demand for them, the prices fall. Prices continue falling and go even below the average cost of production bring losses to the business firms. Thus, when under-consumption appears, production of goods becomes unprofitable. Firms cut their production resulting in recession or contraction in economic activity.

Karl Marx and Under-Consumption. It is worth mentioning that Karl Marx, the philosopher of scientific socialism had also predicted the collapse of the capitalist system due to the emergence of under-consumption. He predicted that capitalism would move periodically through expansion and contraction with each peak higher than its previous peak and each crash (*i.e.*, depression) deeper than the last. Ultimately, according to Marx, in a state of acute depression when the cup of misery of working class is full, they will overthrow the capitalist class which exploits them and in this way the new era of socialism or communism would come into existence.

Like other under-consumption theorists, Marx argues that driving force behind business cycles is ever increasing income inequalities and concentration of wealth and economic power in the hands of the few capitalists who own the means of production. As a result, the poor workers lack income to purchase goods produced by the capitalist class resulting in under-consumption or over-production. With the capitalist producers lacking market for their goods, capitalist economy plunges into depression. Then the search for ways of opening of new markets is started. Even wars between capitalist countries take place to capture other countries to find new markets for their products. With the discovery of new methods of production of finding new markets, the economy recovers from depression and the new upswing starts.

Critical Appraisal. The view that income inequalities increase with growth or expansion of the economy and further that this causes recession or stagnation is widely accepted. Therefore, even many modern economies suggest that if growth is to be sustained (that is, if recession or stagnation is to be avoided), then consumption demand must be increasing sufficiently to absorb the increasing production of goods. For this deliberate efforts should be made to reduce inequalities in income distribution. Further, under-consumption theory rightly states that income redistribution schemes will reduce the amplitude of business cycles.

Besides, the suggested behaviour of average propensity to save and consume of the property owners and wage earners in this theory have been found to be consistent with the observed phenomena. Even in the theory of economic development the difference in average propensity to save (APS) of the property owners and workers has been widely used.

5. J.A. Hobson, *The Economics of Unemployment, London: Allen & Union Ltd.*, 1922.

It is clear from above that under-consumption theory contains some important elements, especially the emergence of the lack of consumption demand as the cause of recession but it is regarded as too simple. There are many features other than growing income inequalities which are responsible for causing recession or trade cycles. Although under-consumption theory concentrate on a significant variable, it leaves too much unexplained.

Over-Investment Theory of Business Cycles

It has been observed that over time investment varies more than that of total output of final goods and services and consumption. This has led economists to investigate the causes of variation in investment and how it is responsible for business cycles. Two versions of over-investment theory have been put forward. One theory offered by Hayek emphasises monetary forces in causing fluctuations in investment. The second version of over-investment theory has been developed by Knut Wickshell which emphasises spurts of investment brought about by innovation. We explain below both these versions of over-investment theory. It is worth noting that in both the versions of this theory distinction between natural rate of interest and money rate of interest plays an important role. Natural rate of interest is defined as the rate at which saving equals investment and this equilibrium interest rate reflects marginal revenue product of capital or rate of return on capital. On the other hand, money rate of interest is the rate at which banks give loans to the businessmen.

Hayek's Monetary Version of Over-investment Theory. Hayek[6] suggests that it is monetary forces which cause fluctuations in investment which are prime cause of business cycles. In this respect Hayek's theory is similar to Hawtrey's monetary theory except that it does not involve inflow and outflow of gold causing changes in money supply in the economy.

To begin with, let us assume that the economy is in recession and businessmen's demand for bank credit is therefore very low. Thus, lower demand for bank credit in times of recession pushes down the money rate of interest below the natural rate. This means that businessmen will be able to borrow funds, that is, bank credit at a rate of interest which is below the expected rate of return in investment projects. This induces them to invest more by undertaking new investment projects. In this way, investment expenditure on new capital goods increases. This causes investment to exceed saving by the amount of newly created bank credit. With the spurt in investment expenditure, the expansion of the economy begins. Increase in investment causes income and employment to rise which induces more consumption expenditure. As a result, production of consumer goods increases. According to Hawtrey, the competition between capital goods and consumer goods industries for scarce resources causes their prices to rise which in turn push up the prices of goods and services.

But this process of expansion cannot go on indefinitely because the excess reserves with the banks come to an end which force the banks not to give further loans for investment, while demand for bank credit goes on increasing. Thus, the inelastic supply of credit from the banks and mounting demand for it cause the money rate of interest to go above the natural rate of interest. This makes further investment unprofitable. But at this point of time there has been over-investment in the sense that savings fall short of what is required to finance the desired investment. When no more bank credit is available for investment, there is decline in investment which causes both income and consumption to fall and in this way expansion comes to an end and the economy experiences downswing in economic activity.

However, after a lapse of some time the fall in demand for bank credit lowers the money rate of interest which goes below the natural rate of interest. This again gives boost to investment activity and as a result recession ends. In this way alternating periods of expansion and contraction occur periodically.

---

6. F.A. Hayek, *Monetary Theory and Trade Cycle,* New York Harcourt Brace, 1933 and also *'Profits, Interest and Investment,* London Routledge, 1935.

Wicksell's Over-investment Theory. Over-investment theory developed by Wicksell[7] is of non-monetary type. Instead of focusing on monetary factors it attributes cyclical fluctuations to spurts of investment caused by new innovations introduced by entrepreneurs themselves. The introduction of new innovations or opening of new markets make some investment projects profitable by either reducing cost or raising demand for the products. The expansion in investment is made possible because of the availability of bank credit at a lower money rate of interest. The expansion in economic activity ceases when investment exceeds saving. Again it may be noted that there is over-investment because the level of saving is insufficient to finance the desired level of investment. The end of investment expenditure causes the economy to go into recession. However, another set of innovations occurs or more new markets are found which stimulates investment. Thus, when investment picks up as a result of new innovations, the economy revives and moves into the expansion phase once again.

Appraisal. Though the over-investment theory does not offer an adequate explanation of business cycles, it contains an important element that fluctuations in investment are the prime cause of business cycles. However, it does not offer a valid explanation as to why changes in investment take place quite often. Many exponents of this theory point to the behaviour of banking system that causes diverges between money rate of interest and natural rate of interest. However, as Keynes later on emphasised, investment fluctuates quite often because of changes in profit expectations of entrepreneurs which depends on several economic and political factors operating in the economy. Thus, the theory fails to offer adequate explanation of business cycles.

KEYNES'S THEORY OF BUSINESS CYCLES

J.M. Keynes in his seminal work *General Theory of Employment, Interest and Money* made an important contribution to the analysis of the causes of business cycles. According to Keynes's theory, in the short run, the level of income, output or employment is determined by the level of aggregate effective demand. In a free private enterprise, the entrepreneurs will produce that much of goods as can be sold profitably. Now, if the aggregate demand is large, that is, if the expenditure on goods and services is large, the entrepreneurs will be able to sell profitably a large quantity of goods and therefore they will produce more. In order to produce more they will employ a larger amount of resources, both men and materials. In short, a higher level of aggregate demand will result in greater output, income and employment. On the other hand, if the level of aggregate demand is low, smaller amount of goods and services can be sold profitably. This means, that the total quantity of national output produced will be small. And a small output can be produced with a small amount of resources. As a result, there will be unemployment of resources, both labour and capital. Hence, *the changes in the level of aggregate effective demand will bring about fluctuations in the level of income, output and employment.* Thus, according to Keynes, the fluctuations in economic activity are due to the fluctuations in aggregate effective demand. Fall in aggregate effective demand will create the conditions of recession or depression. If the aggregate demand is increasing, economic expansion will take place.

Now the question arises : What causes fluctuations in aggregate demand? The aggregate demand is composed of demand for consumption goods and demand for investment goods. Thus aggregate demand depends on the total expenditure of the consumers on consumption goods and entrepreneurs on investment goods. Propensity to consume being more or less stable in the short run, fluctuations in aggregate demand depend primarily upon the fluctuations in investment demand. Keynes shows that the fundamental cause of fluctuations in ag-

7. Knut Wicksell, *Interest and Prices,* London : Macmillan, 1936.

gregate demand and hence in fluctuations in economic activity is the fluctuations in investment demand. *Investment demand is very unstable and volatile and brings about business cycles in the economy.*

Let us start from the phase of economic expansion to explain Keynes's theory of business cycles. We first explain how in Keynesian theory expansion comes to end and recession or depression sets in. During an economic expansion two factors eventually work to cause investment to fall. First, during the expansion phase increase in demand for capital goods due to large-scale investment activity leads to the rise in prices of capital goods due to rising marginal cost of their production. Higher prices of capital goods raise the cost of investment projects and thereby reduce marginal efficiency of capital (that is, expected rate of return). Secondly, as income rises during expansion phase, the demand for money increases which raises interest rate. Higher interest rate makes some potential, projects unprofitable. Thus, fall in marginal efficiency of capital on the one hand and rise in interest rate on the other cause decline in investment demand. Declining trend of investment, according to Keynes, raises doubts about the *prospective yield on capital goods* which is more important factor determining marginal efficiency of capital than cost of investment projects and rate of interest. When among businessmen pessimism sets in about future profitability of investment projects stock prices tumble. The crash in stock prices worsens the situation and causes investment to fall even more. Besides, fall in prices of shares reduces wealth of households. Wealth, according to Keynes, is an important factor determing consumption. Thus, the decline in stock prices reduces autonomous consumption demand of households. With the fall in both investment and consumption demand aggregate demand declines which result in accumulation of unintended inventories with the firms. This induces the firms to cut production of goods.

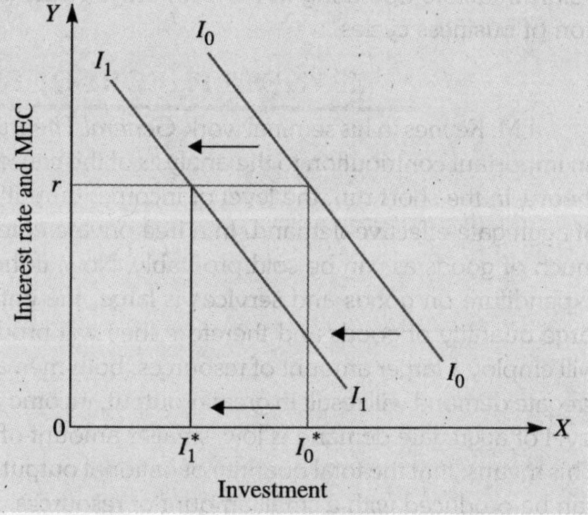

Fig. 46.3. *A Decline in Investment Expenditure due to Fall in Marginal Efficiency of Capital*

It follows from above that besides the rise in cost of capital goods and rise in rate of interest towards the end of the expansion phase, it is the fall in expected prospective yield that reduces the marginal efficiency of capital and causes investment demand to fall. This induces a wave of pessimistic expectations among businessmen and speculators. These pessimistic expectations cause stock prices to tumble which work like adding fuel to the fire. They cause a further fall in the marginal efficiency of capital. *The turning point from expansion to contraction is thus caused by a sudden collapse in marginal efficiency of capital.* In terms of graph, a sudden fall in the marginal efficiency of capital causes on leftward shift in the investment demand curve, for example from I_0I_0 to I_1I_1 in Figure 46.3 resulting in decline in investment from I_0* to I_1* at the given rate of interest. Note that decrease in investment does not automatically decrease in rate of interest to offset the fall in the marginal efficiency of capital.

However, additional factor that makes Keynes's business cycle theory potent is the working of multiplier which was an important discovery of J.M. Keynes. According to Keynes, a decrease in investment expenditure causes a decline in income which in turn reduces consumption expenditure. The reduction in consumption expenditure further reduces income and this process of reduction in income continues further. The total fall in income (ΔY) due to an initial decline in investment (ΔI) will be equal to $\Delta I \times \frac{1}{1-MPC}$ where $\frac{1}{1-MPC}$ is the value of multiplier. If marginal propensity to consume is 0.75, the multiplier will be equal to 4. Thus, a decline in investment by 100 crores will lead to the decline in income by 400 crores. Note that multiplier here works in reverse. Thus, the multiplier process magnifies the effect of decline in investment expenditure on aggregate demand and income and further deepens the depression. As income and output are falling rapidly under the multiplier effect, the employment also goes tumbling down. Thus, the Keynes theory of income multiplier plays a significant role in causing magnified changes in income, output and employment following a reduction in investment.

It is important to note that, in Keynes's views, wages and prices are not flexible enough to offset the decline in investment expenditure and thereby restore full employment. This is in sharp contrast to the classical theory where changes in wages and prices ensure continuous full employment. In Keynes model wages and prices are "sticky" downward which implies that though wages and prices do not remain constant but when demand falls wages and prices will fall but not sufficient to restore full employment in the economy.

Since wage and price flexibility does not ensure the recovery of the economy out of the state of depression, Keynes thinks that marginal efficiency of capital must rise to stimulate investment. During depression investment falls to a very low level, capital stock begins to wear out and requires replacement. Further, some existing capital equipment becomes technologically obsolete and has to be abandoned. This generates demand for replacement investment. A long period of time is necessary for existing capital to depreciate because most capital goods are durable as well as irreversible. By durability of capital goods we mean that they last for a long time and by irreversibility we mean that they cannot be used for purposes other than those for which they are meant.

Thus, just as the collapse of marginal efficiency of capital is the main cause of the upper turning point, similarly the lower turning point, *i.e.*, change from recession to recovery is due to the revival of the marginal efficiency of capital, that is, expected rate of profit. Restoration of business confidence is the most important, yet the most difficult factor to achieve. Even if the rate of interest is reduced, the investment will not increase. This is because of the fact that in the absence of confidence the profitability of investment may remain so low that no practicable reduction in the rate of interest will stimulate investment. The interval which will elapse between the upper turning point and the start of recovery is conditioned by two factors: (*i*) the time necessary for wearing out of durable capital assets, and (*ii*) the time required to absorb the excess stocks of goods left over from the boom. Just as the expected rate of profit was pushed down by the growing abundance of capital during the period of boom, similarly as the stocks of capital goods are depleted and there grows a scarcity of capital goods, then the expected rate of profit rises thereby inducing the businessmen to invest more. When the level of investment increases, income increases by a magnified amount due to the multiplier effect. So the cumulative process starts upward.

Thus, over time as depreciation of capital stock occurs without replacement and also some existing capital equipment becomes technologically obsolete, the size of capital stock declines. New investment must be undertaken even to produce reduced depression level of output. Thus with the emergence of scarcity of capital, marginal efficiency of capital rises which boosts investment. Once investment increases, it induces further rise in income and consumption demand through the multiplier process. Now, the multiplier works to magnify the effect of increase in investment on raising aggregate demand. The mood of business men changes from pessimism to optimism which drives up stock prices. All these factors work to lift the economy out of depression and puts it on the road to prosperity.

However, it is noteworthy that the recovery process from depression takes a very long time. Keynes argued that Government should not wait for long for the natural recovery to occur. This is because persistence of depression creates a lot of human sufferings. He, therefore, advocated for the active intervention by the Government to raise aggregate through fiscal policy, that is, stepping up its expenditure or reducing taxes. Thus, he argued for the adoption of policy of deficit budget to boost aggregate demand so that economy is lifted out of depression.

It may be noted that Keynes' business cycle theory is self-generating. In it the economy passes through a long phase of expansion. But eventually some forces automatically work for example, the growing abundance of capital stock, which reduces marginal efficiency of capital. Pessimisin overtakes businessmen. This causes reduction in investment which is responsible for bringing about downswing in the economy. The idea that it is the fluctuations in investment that bring about the fluctuations in the level of economic activity is an important contribution made by Keynes. Of course, even before Keynes, it was believed that the fluctuations in the investment demand have something to do with the business cycles, but a systematic exposition was lacking. Keynes propounded a definite relationship between a change in investment and the resulting change in income and employment. This relationship is embodied in his famous theory of multiplier.

The Critical Appraisal of Keynes's Theory

J.M. Keynes has made three important contributions to the business cycle theory. First, it is fluctuations in investment that cause changes in aggregate demand which bring about changes in economic activity (*i.e.*, income, output, and employment). Secondly, fluctuations in investment demand are caused by changes in expectations of businessmen regarding making of profits (that is, marginal efficiency of capital). Thirdly, Keynes put forward an important theory of multiplier which tells us how changes in investment bring about magnified changes in the level of income and employment.

But the Keynesian theory of multiplier alone does not offer a full and satisfactory explanation of the trade cycles. A basic feature of the trade cycle is its cumulative character both on the upswing as well as on the downswing *i.e.*, once economic activity starts rising or falling, it gathers momentum and for a time feeds on itself. Thus, what we have to explain is the cumulative character of economic fluctuations. The theory of multiplier alone does not prove adequate for this task. For example, suppose that investment rises by 100 rupees and that the magnitude of multiplier is 4. From the theory of multiplier we know that national income will rise by 400 and if multiplier is the only force at work, that will be the end of the matter, with the economy reaching a new stable equilibrium at a higher level of national income. But in real life this is not likely to be so, for a rise in income produced by a given rise in investment will have further repercussions in the economy. This reaction is described in the *principle of the accelerator.* According to the principle of acceleration, a change in national income will tend to induce changes in the rate of investment. *While multiplier refers to the change in income as a result of change in investment, the acceleration principle describes the relationship between a change in investment as a result of change in income.*

In the above example, when income has risen by 400 rupees, people's spending power has risen by an equivalent amount. This will induce them to spend more on goods and services. When the demand for goods rises, initially this will be met by overworking the existing plant and machinery. All this leads to an increase in profits with the result that businessmen will be induced to expand their productive capacity and will instal new plants, *i.e.*, they will invest more than before. Thus, *a rise in income leads to a further induced increase in investment.* The accelerator describes this relation between an increase in income and the resulting increase in investment. Thus, Samuelson combined the accelerator principle with the multiplier and showed that the interaction between the two can bring about cyclical fluctuations in economic activity.

SAMUELSON'S MODEL OF BUSINESS CYCLES : INTERACTION BETWEEN MULTIPLIER AND ACCELERATOR

We have briefly explained above the Keynes made an important contribution to the understanding of the cyclical fluctuations by pointing out that it is the ups and downs in investment demand, depending as it is on the profit expectations of the entrepreneurs, that causes changes in aggregate demand which affect the levels of income, output and employment. Further, by putting forward the theory of multiplier, Keynes has shown how the effect of increase and decrease in investment on output and employment get magnified when multiplier is working during either the upswing or downswing of a business cycle. However, Keynes did not explain the cyclical and cumulative nature of the fluctuations in economic activity. This is because Keynes did not give any importance to the accelerator in his explanation of business cycles. Samuelson in his seminal paper[8] convincingly showed that it is the interaction between the multiplier and accelerator that gives rise to cyclical fluctuations in economic activity. The multiplier alone cannot adequately explain the cyclical and cumulative nature of the economic fluctuations. An autonomous increase in the level of investment raises income by a magnified amount depending upon the value of the multiplier. This increase in income further induces the increases in investment through the acceleration effect. The increase in income brings about increase in aggregate demand for goods and services. To produce more goods we require more capital goods for which extra investment is undertaken. Thus the relationship between investment and income is one of mutual interaction; investment affects income which in turn affects investment demand and in this process income and employment fluctuate in a cyclical manner.

We have shown below in Fig. 46.4 how income and output will increase by even larger amount when accelerator is combined with the Keynesian multiplier.

where ΔI_a = Increase in Autonomous Investment

ΔY = Increase in Income.

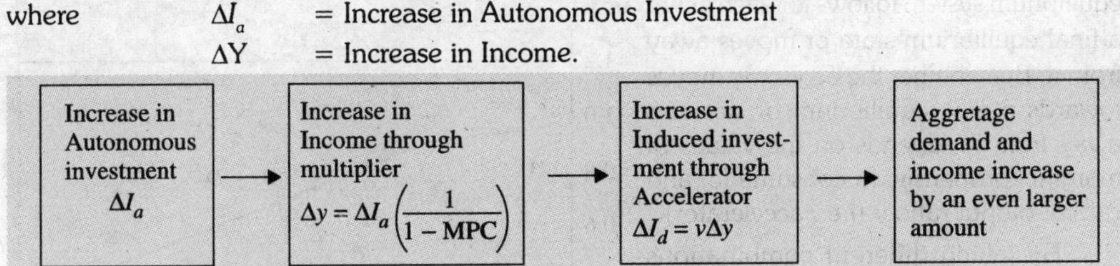

Fig. 46.4. *Combining Accelerator with Keynesian Multiplier*

$\frac{1}{1-MPC}$ = Size of Multiplier where MPC = Marginal Propensity to Consume.

ΔI_d = Increase in Induced Investment

v = Size of accelerator.

Fluctuations in investment are the main cause of instability in a free private-enterprise economy. This instability further increases due to the interaction of the multiplier and accelerator. The changes in any component of aggregate demand produce a multiplier effect whose magnitude depends upon the marginal propensity to consume. When consumption, income and output increase under the influence of multiplier effect, they induce further changes in investment and the extent of this induced investment in capital goods industries depends on the capital-output ratio, that is, the interaction between the multiplier and accelerator without any external shocks can give rise to the business cycles whose pattern differs depending upon

8. Samuelson, P.A. "*Interaction* Between the Multiplier Analysis and the Principle of Acceleration" in *Review of Economic Statistics,* May 1939, p. 751.

the magnitudes of the marginal propensity to consume and capital-output ratio. The model of interaction between multiplier and accelerator can be mathematically represented as under:

$$Y_t = C_t + I_t \quad \text{...(i)}$$

$$C_t = C_a + c\,(Y_{t-1}) \quad \text{...(ii)}$$

$$I_t = I_a + v\,(Y_{t-1} - Y_{t-2}) \quad \text{...(iii)}$$

Where Y_t, C_t, I_t stand for income, consumption and investment respectively for a period t, C_a stands for autonomous consumption, I_a for autonomous investment, c for marginal propensity to consume and v for the capital-output ratio or accelerator.

From the above equations it is evident that consumption in a period t is a function of income of the previous period Y_{t-1}. That is, one period lag has been assumed for income to determine the consumption of a period. As regards induced investment in period t, it is taken to be the function of the change in income in the previous period. This means that there is two periods gap for changes in income to determine induced investment. In the equation (*iii*) above, induced investment equals $v(Y_{t-1} - Y_{t-2})$ or $v(\Delta Y_{t-1})$. Substituting equations (*ii*) and (*iii*) in equation (*i*) we have the following income equation which states how changes in income are dependent on the values of marginal propensity to consume (c) and capital-output ratio v (*i.e.*, accelerator).

$$Yt = C_a + c(Y_{t-1}) + I_a + v\,(Y_{t-1} - Y_{t-2}) \quad \text{...(iv)}$$

In static equilibrium, the level of income determined will be:

$$Y = C_a + cY + I$$

This is due to the fact that in static equilibrium, given the data of the determining factors, the equilibrium level of income remains uncharged, that is, in this case, $Y_t = Y_{t-1} = Y_{t-2} = Y_{t-n}$ so that period lags have no influence at all and accelerator is reduced to zero. Thus, in a dynamic state when autonomous investment changes, the equation (*iv*) describes the path which a dis-equilibrium system follows to reach either a final equilibrium state or moves away from it. But whether the economy moves towards a new equilibrium or deviates away from it depends on the values of marginal propensity to consume (c) and capital-output ratio v (*i.e.*, accelerator).

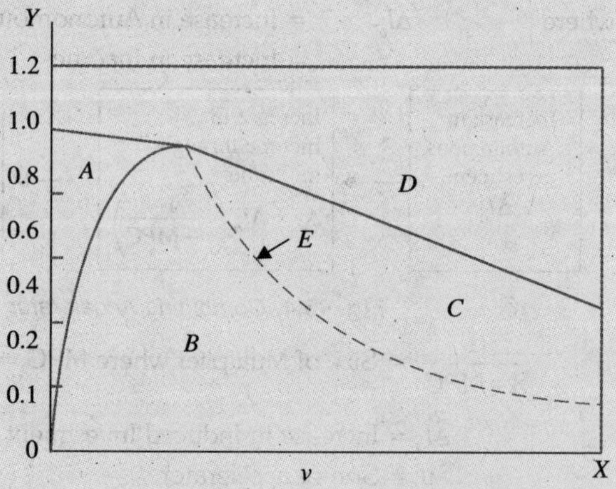

Fig. 46.5. *Combination of c & v*

By taking different combinations of the values of marginal propensity to consume (c) and capital-output ratio (v), Samuelson has described different paths which the economy will follow. The various combinations of the values of marginal propensity to consume and capital-output ratio (which respectively determine the magnitudes of multiplier and accelerator) are shown in Fig. 46.5. The four paths or patterns of movements which the economic activity (as measured by gross national product or income) can have depending upon various combinations of the values of marginal propensity to consume (c) and capital-output ratio (v) are depicted in Fig. 46.6. When the combinations of the value of marginal propensity to consume (c) and capital-output ratio (v) lie within the region marked A, with a change in autonomous investment, the gross national product or income moves upward or downward at a decreasing rate and finally reaches a new equilibrium as is shown in panel (a) of Fig. 46.6. If the values of c and v are such that they lie within the region B, the change in autonomous investment or autonomous consumption will generate fluctuations in income which follow the pattern of a series of damped cycles whose amplitudes go on declining until the cycles disappear as is shown in panel (*b*) of Fig. 46.6.

The region *C* in Fig. 46.6 represents the combinations of *c* and *v* which are relatively high as compared to the region *B* and determine such values of multiplier and accelerator that bring about explosive cycles, that is, the fluctuations of income with successively greater and greater amplitude. The situation is depicted in panel (*c*) of Fig. 46.6 which shows that the system tends to explode and diverges greatly from the equilibrium level. The region *D* provides the combinations of *c* and *v* which cause income to move upward or downward at an increasing rate which has somehow to be restrained if the cyclical movements are to occur. This is depicted in panel (*d*) of Fig. 46.6. Like the values of multiplier and accelerator of region *C*, their values in region *D* cause the system to explode and diverge from the equilibrium state by an increasing amount.

In a special case when values of *C* and *V* (and therefore the magnitudes of multiplier and accelerator) lie in region *E*, they produce fluctuations in income of constant amplitude as is shown in panel (*e*) of Fig. 46.6.

It follows from above that region *A* and *B* are alike, they after a disturbance caused by a change in autonomous investment or consumption finally bring about stable equilibrium in the system. On the other hand, the values of *c* and *v* and therefore the magnitudes of multiplier and accelerator of region *C* and *D* resemble each other but are such that they cause great instability in the system as both of these values cause successively greater divergence from the equilibrium level and the system tends to explode. The case of region *E* lies in between the two as the combinations of values of *c* and *v* in it are such that cause cyclical movements of income which neither move toward nor away from the equilibrium.

It is worth noting that all the above five cases do not give rise to cyclical fluctuations or business cycles. *It is only combinations of c and v lying in regions B, C and E that produce*

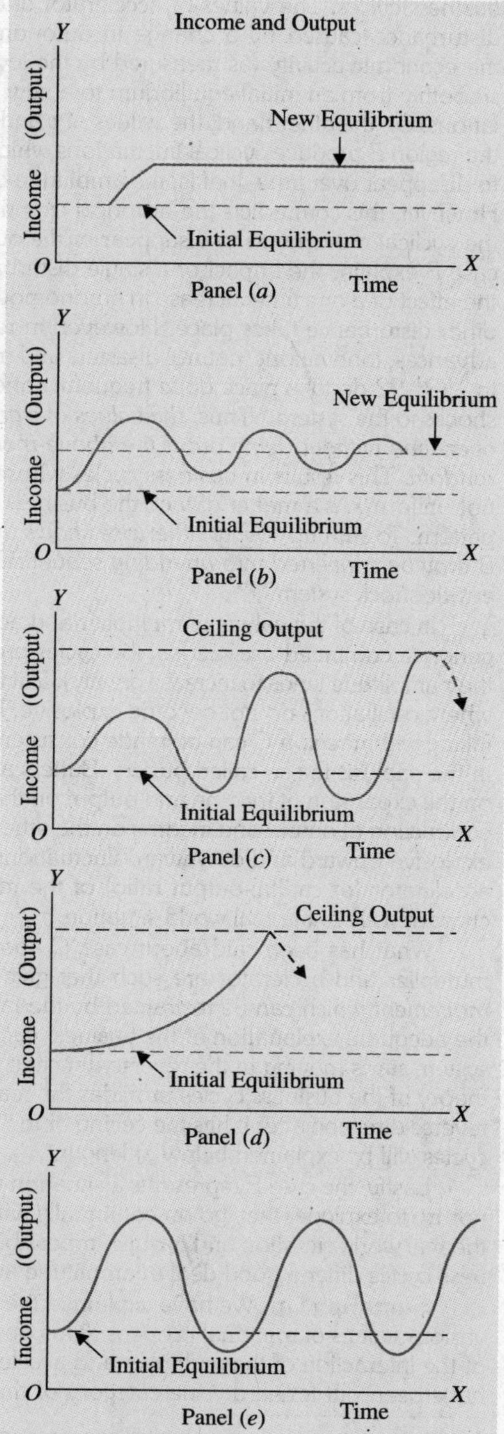

Fig. 46.6. *Interaction between Multiplier and Accelerator : Different Patterns of Income (output) movements for various values of c and v*

business cycles. The values of accelerator and multiplier in the region *A* are such that with a disturbance caused by a change in autonomous investment or autonomous consumption, the economic activity (as measured by the level of income or Gross National Product) moves smoothly from an initial equilibrium to a new equilibrium with no cyclical fluctuations or oscillations. On the other hand, the values of *c* and *v* (and therefore of multiplier and accelerator) of the region *B* produce cyclical fluctuations which are of the type of *damped oscillations* that tend to disappear over time, that is, the amplitude of the cycles shrinks to zero over a period of time. However, this contradicts the historical experience which reveals that there is no tendency for the cyclical movements to disappear or die out over time. However, it is worth noting that the case *B* explains the impact of a single disturbance on income and employment. For example, the effect of a one time increase in autonomous investment goes on diminishing over time if no other disturbance takes place. However, in reality, further disturbances such as technological advances, innovations, natural disasters and man-made disasters such as security scam in India in 1991-92 do take place quite frequently and at random intervals and in a way they provide shocks to the system.[9] Thus, *the values of c and v of region B can generate cyclical fluctuations over time without dying out if the above-mentioned disturbances are occurring frequently at random*. This results in business cycles whose duration and amplitude are quite irregular and not uniform. As a matter of fact, the business cycles in the real world also reveal such irregular pattern. To sum up, "*what otherwise shows up as a tendency for the cycle to disappear in case B may be converted into unending sequence* of cycles by the addition of randomly disturbed erratic shock system."[10]

In case of the values of multiplier and accelerator falling within the region *C*, though they generate continued oscillations, the cycles produced by them tend to become `*explosive*' (*i.e.* their amplitude tends to increase greatly). But they are not consistent with the real world situation where oscillations do not become explosive. However, the values of multiplier and accelerator falling within region *C* can be made consistent with the actual world situation by incorporating in the analysis the so called buffers. Buffers are the factors which impose upper limit or ceiling on the expansion of income and output on the one hand or impose a lower limit or floor on the contraction of output and income on the other. With the inclusion of these buffers the otherwise explosive upward and downward fluctuations arising out of values of multiplier (or *MPC*) and accelerator (or capital-output ratio) of the region *C* can become limited cyclical fluctuations, characteristic of the real world situation.

What has been said about case *C* above also applies to region *D* where the values of multiplier and acclerator are such that give rise to *directly explosive upward or downward movement* which can be restrained by the factors determining the ceiling and floor. However, the adequate explanation of the business cycles in this case would require the reasons why the system starts moving in the reverse direction, say, after striking the ceiling. Hicks in his famous theory of the business cycles provides the reasons which cause movement of the system in the reverse direction after it hits the ceiling or the floor as the case may be. Hicks theory of business cycles will be explained below at length.

Lastly, the case E represents a situation where the business cycles neither try to disappear, nor try to explode, they go on continually with a *constant amplitude.* This however contradicts the real world situation and is quite impossible. This is because in the real world situation, business cycles differ a good deal in amplitude and duration.

Summing Up. We have explained the interaction of multiplier and accelerator in case of various values of marginal propensity to consume (*c*) and capital-output ratio (*v*). On the basis of the interaction of the multiplier and accelerator the two categories of business cycle theories have been put forward. One category of these business cycle theories assumes the values of

9. The concept of erratic shocks has been put forward by Nobel Prize winner in economics R. Frisch "Propagation Problems and Impulse Problems in Dynamic Economics" in *Economic Essays in Honour of Gustav Cassel.* Allen and Unwin, 1993, pp. 171-205.
10. Shapiro Edward, *Macroeconomic Analysis,* Forth Edition, 1978, p. 378

multiplier and accelerator which generate explosive cycles. For example, Hicks' theory of business cycles falls in this category. On the other hand, Hansen has propounded a business cycle theory based on the interaction of multiplier with a *weak* accelerator which produces only damped oscillations. Further, as indicated above, the interaction theories have been modified either by incorporating in the analysis erratic shocks or random disturbances or by including so called buffers which check the upward movement of income and output by imposing ceiling of expansion and checking a downward movement by imposing a floor on the contraction of output. One of the famous theories of business cycles based on the interaction of multiplier and accelerator which also incorporate buffers in his analysis of fluctuations is that put forward by the noted English economist J.R. Hicks. We discuss below his theory of business cycles in detail.

Table 46.1. A Multiplier-Acceleration Interaction Model

Period	*Autonomous Investment*	*Induced Consumption (c = 2/3)*	*Induced Investment (v = 2)*	*Change in Income from the base period t*
1	2	3	4	5
	₹ in Crores	*₹ in Crores*	*₹ in Crores*	*₹ in Crores*
t	0	0	0	0
t + 1	10	0	0	10
t + 2	10	6.7	13.4	30.1
t + 3	10	20.0	26.6	56.6
t + 4	10	37.8	35.6	83.4
t + 5	10	55.6	35.6	101.2
t + 6	10	67.6	23.8	101.2
t + 7	10	67.6	0.2	67.8
t + 8	10	51.8	−10.0	51.8
t + 9	10	34.6	−10.0	33.8
t + 10	10	23.0	−10.0	23.0
t + 11	10	15.4	−10.0	15.4
t + 12	10	10.2	−10.0	10.2
t + 13	10	6.8	−6.8	10.0
t + 14	10	6.6	0.2	16.8

A Numerical Example of the Interaction of the Multiplier and Accelerator

How the interaction between the multiplier and accelerator gives rise to the cyclical movements in economic activity (as measured by income or output) will become clear from Table 46.1. In formulating this table we have assumed that marginal propensity to consume (*c*) being equal to 2/3 or 0.66 and capital-output ratio (*v*) or accelerator being equal to 2. Further, one period time lag has been assumed which implies that an increase in income in a period induces the increase in consumption in the next period. It is assumed that initially in period *t* + 1, autonomous investment is of ₹ 10 crores. In period *t* + 3, with autonomous investment being maintained constant at ₹ 10 crores, the deviation of total income in the period *t* + 3 as compared to the base period will be equal to 10 + 20 + 26.6 = ₹ 56.6 crores. Similarly, the changes in induced consumption and induced investment and hence in income brought about by the initial increase in autonomous investment of ₹ 10 crores which is maintained throughout, can be found out. It will be seen from column 5 of the Table 13.1 that there are large fluctuations in income. Under the influence of the interaction between the multiplier and accelerator, the income increases up to the period *t* + 6. In other words, period up to *t* + 6 represents the expansion phase or upswing of the business cycle. Therefore, the period *t* + 6 is the upper turning point of the business cycle beyond which the contraction phase or downswing of the business cycle begins. It will be further observed that beyond the period *t* + 13, income again starts rising, that is, *recovery from the depression begins.*

Thus, $t + 13$ represents the lower turning point of the business cycle. In this way we see that the interaction between the multiplier and accelerator can give rise to the cyclical movements of the economic activity and its various phases. It is worth mentioning that we have taken particular values of marginal propensity to consume (which determine the size of the multiplier) and capital-output ratio (which determines the size of the accelerator). The other values of multiplier and accelerator that have been explained above would give rise to the different patterns of fluctuations.

HICKS' THEORY OF BUSINESS CYCLES

Hicks[11] put forward a complete theory of business cycles based on the interaction between the multiplier and accelerator by choosing certain values of marginal propensity to consume (c) and capital-output ratio (v) which he thinks are representative of the real world situation. According to Hicks, the values of marginal propensity to consume and capital-output ratio fall in either region C or D of Fig. 46.5. As seen above, in case values of these parameters lie in the region C, they produce *cyclical movements* (*i.e.*, oscillations) whose amplitude increases over time and if they fall in region D they produce an *explosive upward movement* of income or output without oscillations. To explain business cycles of the real world which do not tend to explode, Hicks has incorporated in his analysis the role of buffers. On the one hand, *he introduces output ceiling* when all the given resources are fully employed and prevent income and output to go beyond it, and, on the other hand, he visualises a *floor or the lower limit* below which income and output cannot go because some autonomous investment is always taking place.

Another important features of Hicks' theory is that business cycles in the economy occur in the background of economic growth (*i.e.*, the rising trend of real income of output over time). In other words, cyclical fluctuations in real output of goods and services take place *above and below this rising line of trend* or growth of income and output. Thus in his theory he explains business cycles along with an equilibrium rate of growth. In Hicks's theory of long-run equilibrium growth that is determined by rate of increase of autonomous investment over time and, therefore, long-run equilibrium growth of income is determined by the autonomous investment and the magnitudes of multiplier and accelerator. Hicks assumes that autonomous investment, depending as it is on technological progress, innovations and population growth, grows at a constant rate. With further assumptions of stable multiplier and accelerator, equilibrium income will grow at the same rate as autonomous investment. It follows therefore that the failure of actual output to increase along the equilibrium growth path, some times to move above it and some times to move below it determines the business cycles.

Hick's Theory of business cycles has been explained with the help of the Fig. 46.7. In this figure, *AA* line represents autonomous investment. Autonomous investment is that investment which is not induced by changes in income and is made by entrepreneur as a result of technological progress or innovations or population growth. Hicks assumes that autonomous investment grows annually at a constant rate given by the slope of the line *AA*. Given the marginal propensity to consume, the simple multiplier is determined. Then the magnitude of multiplier and autonomous investment together determine the equilibrium path of income shown by the line *LL*. Hicks calls this the floor line as this sets the lower limits below which income (output) cannot fall because of a given rate of growth of autonomous investment and the given size of the multiplier. But induced investment has not yet been taken into account. If national income grows from one year to the next, as it would move along the line *LL*, there is some amount of induced investment via accelerator. The line *EE* shows the equilibrium growth path of national income determined by autonomous investment and the combined effect of the multiplier and

11. Hicks, J.R., A *Contribution to the Theory of Trade Cycles*, Oxford University Press, p. 50.

accelerator. *FF* is the full employment ceiling. It is a line that shows the maximum national output at any period of time when all the available resources of the economy are fully employed. Given the constant growth of autonomous investment, the magnitude of multiplier and the induced investment determined by the accelerator, the economy will be moving along the *equilibrium growth* path line *EE*. Thus starting from point *E*, the economy will be in equilibrium moving along the path *EE* determined by the combined effect of multiplier and accelerator and the growing level of the autonomous investment.

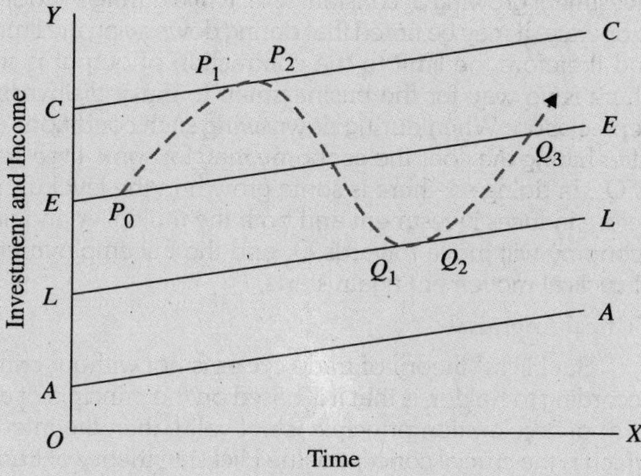

Fig. 46.7. *The Hicks' Model of Business Cycles*

Suppose when the economy reaches point P_0 along the path *EE*, there is an *external shock*—say an outburst of investment due to certain innovation or jump in governmental investment. When the economy experiences such an outburst of autonomous investment it pushes the economy above the equilibrium growth path *EE* after point P_0. The rise in autonomous investment due to external shock *causes national income to increase at a greater rate than that shown* by the slope of *EE*. This greater increase in national income will cause further increase in induced investment through acceleration effect. This increase in induced investment causes national income to increase by a magnified amount through multiplier. So under the combined effect of multiplier and accelerator, national income or output will rapidly expand along the path from P_0 to P_1. Movement from P_0 to P_1 represents the upswing or expansion phase of the business cycle. But this expansion must stop at P_1 because this is the full employment output ceiling. The limited human and material resources of the economy do not permit a greater expansion of national income than shown by the ceiling line *CC*. Therefore, when point P_1 is reached the rapid growth of national income must come to an end. Prof. Hicks assumes that the full employment ceiling grows at the same rate as autonomous investment. Therefore, *CC* slopes gently unlike the very steep slope of the line from P_0 to P_1. When point P_1 is reached the economy must grow at the same rate as the usual growth in autonomous investment.

For a short time the economy may crawl along the full employment ceiling *CC*. But because national income has ceased to increase at the rapid rate, the induced investment via accelerator falls off to the level consistent with the modest rate of growth determined by the constant rate of growth of autonomous investment. But the economy cannot crawl along its full employment ceiling for a long time. The sharp decline in growth of income and consumption when the economy strikes the ceiling causes a sharp decline in induced investment. Thus with the sharp decline in induced investment when national income and hence consumption ceases to increase rapidly, the contraction in the level of the income and business actually must begin. Once the downswing starts, the accelerator works in the reverse direction. That is, since the change in income is now negative the inducement to invest must begin to decrease. Thus there is slackening off at point P_2 and national income starts moving toward equilibrium growth path *EE*. This movement from P_2 downward therefore represents the downswing or contraction phase of the business cycle. In this downswing investment falls off rapidly and therefore multiplier works in the reverse direction. The fall in national income and output resulting from the sharp fall in induced investment will not stop on touching the level *EE* but will go further down. The economy must consequently move all the way down from point P_2 to point Q_1. But at point Q_1 the floor has been reached.

Whereas the upswing was limited by the output ceiling set by the full employment of available resources, in the downswing the national income cannot fall below the level of output represented by the floor. This is because the floor level is determined by simple multiplier and autonomous investment growing at constant rate, while during the downswing after a point accelerator ceases to operate. It may be noted that during downswing the limit to negative investment (disinvestment) and therefore the limit to the contraction of output is set by the depreciation of capital stock. There is no way for the businessmen to make disinvestment at a desired rate higher than the depreciation. When during downswing such conditions arise, accelerator becomes inoperative. After hitting the floor the economy may for some time crawl along the floor through the path Q_1 to Q_2. In doing so, there is some growth in the level of national income. This rate of growth as before induces investment and both the multiplier and accelerator come into operation and the economy will move towards Q_3 and the full employment ceiling *CC*. This is how the upswing of cyclical movement again starts.

Critical Appraisal

But Hicks' theory of trade cycles is not without critics. A major weakness of Hicks' theory, according to Kaldor, is that it is based on the principle of acceleration in its rigid form.[12] If the rigid form of acceleration principle is not valid, then the interaction of the multiplier and accelerator which is the crucial concept of the Hicksian theory of trade cycles is not valid. Thus Duesenberry writes, "the basic concept of multiplier-accelerator interaction is important one but we cannot really accept to explain observed cycles by a mechanical application of that concept."[13] and, according to him, Hicks in his business cycle theory actually tries to do so.

It may be noted that Kaldor puts forward a theory of business cycles which does not make use of the rigid or strict form of the acceleration principle. In his trade cycle theory Kaldor provides for investment being *directly related* to the level of income and *inversely related* to the stock of capital. Thus Kaldor's approach which is also supported by Goodwin abandons the rigid and inflexible relation of investment to changes in income (output) as implied by the rigid acceleration principle [*i.e.*, $I_t = I_a + v\,(Y_{t-1} - Y_{t-2})$] and instead has used the following form of the investment function

$$I_t = I_a + gY_{t-1} - jK_t$$

where It stands for investment in period *t*, I_a for autonomous investment, Y_{t-1} for income in the previous period, K_t for the stock of capital, and *g* and *j* are constants.

A look at the above investment function used by Kaldor will reveal that investment is directly related to the income and inversely related to the stock of capital. Thus in Kaldor-Good win investment function, the increase in income, the capital stock remaining constant, will cause an increase in investment which will enlarge the stock of capital. On the other hand, according to this new investment function, if capital stock increases, output or income remaining constant, investment will fall due to its being negatively related to capital stock. Thus, Kaldor-Goodwin approach to investment while gives up the rigid acceleration principle but still retains the basic idea of investment related to income because in this approach investment will cause the capital stock to expand towards the stock of capital as desired for the production of output of the preceding year.

However, despite the shortcomings of Hicks' theory of business cycles, this is a valuable contribution to the theory of business cycles. Even its critics such as Kaldor though indicating some of its weaknesses acknowledge its merit. Thus Kaldor writes that Hicks's theory of trade cycles provides us many brilliant and original pieces of analysis''. Duesenberry considers it as an "ingenious piece of work".

12. See Kaldor N., "Hicks on the Trade Cycles" in *Economic Journal,* Dec. 1951, pp. 833-478
13. Duesenberry, J.S. "Hicks on the Trend and Cycles" in *Quarterly Journal of Economics,* August 1950, pp. 464-76.

Economic Stabilisation: Fiscal Policy

Introduction: Macroeconomic Policy and Stabilisation

The economy does not always work smoothly. There often occur fluctuations in the level of economic activity. At times the economy finds itself in the grip of recession when levels of national income, output and employment are far below their full potential levels. During recession, there is a lot of idle or unutilised productive capacity, that is, available machines and factories are not working to their full capacity. As a result, unemployment of labour increases along with the existence of excess capital stock. On the other hand, at times the economy is `*overheated*' which means inflation (*i.e.* rising prices) occurs in the economy. Thus, in a free market economy there is a lot of economic instability. The classical economists believed that an automatic mechanism works to restore stability in the economy; recession would cure itself and inflation will be automatically controlled. However, the empirical evidence during the 1930s when severe depression took place in the Western capitalist economies and also the evidence of post Second World II period amply shows that no such automatic mechanism works to bring about stability in the economy. That is why Keynes argued for intervention by the Government to cure depression and inflation by adopting appropriate tools of macroeconomic policy. *The two important tools of macroeconomic policy are fiscal policy and monetary policy*. According to Keynes, monetary policy was ineffective to lift the economy out of depression. He emphasized the role of fiscal policy as an effective tool of stabilising the economy. However, in view of the modern economists both fiscal and monetary policies play a useful role in stabilising the economy. In the present chapter we shall dwell upon the role of fiscal policy for stabilising the economy and will discuss the role of monetary policy in bringing about stabilisation in the next chapter.

Goals of Macroeconomic Policy

Stabilising the economy at a higher level of employment and national output is not the only goal of macroeconomic policy. Ensuring price stability is its another goal. Both inflation, (that is, rising prices) and deflation (that is, falling prices) have bad economic consequences. It is therefore desirable to achieve price stability. Similarly, every nation wants to raise the level of living of its people which can be attained through bringing about economic growth which in turn depends on raising the rates of saving and investment and accumulating capital. Macroeconomic policies can play a useful role in raising the rate of saving and investment and therefore ensure rapid economic growth. Thus, three important goals or objectives of macroeconomic policy (both fiscal and monetary) are follows:

1. Economic stability at a high level of output and employment.
2. Price stability.
3. Economic growth.

In the present chapter we shall confine ourselves to the discussion of the role of fiscal policy in achieving economic stability at full employment level and in controlling inflation and deflation and thus attaining price stability. The role of monetary policy for encouraging economic growth will be discussed at length in a later chapter.

DISCRETIONARY FISCAL POLICY FOR STABILISATION

Fiscal policy is an important instrument to stabilise the economy, that is, to overcome recession and control inflation in the economy. Fiscal policy is of two kinds: *Discretionary fiscal policy and Non-discretionary fiscal policy of automatic stabilisers.* By discretionary policy we mean deliberate change in the Government expenditure and taxes to influence the level of national output and prices. Fiscal policy generally aims at managing aggregate demand for goods and services. On the other hand, non-discretionary fiscal policy of automatic stabilisers is a built-in tax or expenditure mechanism that automatically increases aggregate demand when recession occurs and reduces aggregate demand when there is inflation in the economy without any special deliberate actions on the part of the Government. In this section we shall confine ourselves to the discussion of discretionary fiscal policy.

At the time of recession the Government increases its expenditure or cuts down taxes or adopts a combination of both. On the other hand, to control inflation the Government cuts down its expenditure or raises taxes. In other words, *to cure recession expansionary fiscal policy and to control inflation contractionary fiscal policy is adopted.* It is worth mentioning that fiscal policy aims at changing aggregate demand by suitable changes in Government spending and taxes. Thus, *fiscal policy is mainly a policy of demand management.* It should be further noted that when the Government adopts expansionary fiscal policy to cure recession, it raises its expenditure without raising taxes or cuts down taxes without changing expenditure or increases expenditure and cuts down taxes as well. With the adoption of any of these types of expansionary fiscal policy Government's budget will have a deficit. Thus expansionary fiscal policy to cure recession and unemployment is a deficit budget policy. If, on the other hand, to control inflation, Government reduces its expenditure or increases taxes or adopts a combination of the two, it will be planning for a budget surplus. *Thus policy of budget surplus, or at least reducing budget deficit is adopted to remedy inflation.* In what follows we will discuss fiscal policy first to cure recession and then to control inflation.

Fiscal Policy to Cure Recession

As we know, the recession in an economy occurs when aggregate demand decreases due to a fall in private investment. Private investment may fall when businessmen become highly pessimistic about making profits in future, resulting in decline in marginal efficiency of investment. As a result of fall in private investment expenditure, aggregate demand curve shifts down creating a deflationary or recessionary gap. It is the task of fiscal policy to close this gap by increasing Government expenditure, or reducing taxes. Thus there are two fiscal methods to get the economy out of recession.

(*a*) Increase in Government Expenditure

(*b*) Reduction of Taxes.

We discuss below both these methods.

(*a*) **Increase in Government Expenditure to Cure Recession.** For a discretionary fiscal policy to cure depression, the increase in Government expenditure is an important tool.

Government may increase expenditure by starting public works, such as building roads, dams, ports, telecommunication links, irrigation works, electrification of new areas etc. For undertaking all these public works, Government buys various types of goods and materials and employs workers. The effect of this increase in expenditure is both direct and indirect. The direct effect is the increase in incomes of those who sell materials and supply labour for these projects. The output of these public works also goes up together with the increase in incomes. Not only that, Keynes showed that increase in Government expenditure also has an *indirect effect* in the form of the working of a multiplier. Those who get more incomes spend them further on consumer goods depending on their marginal propensity to consume. As during the period of recession there exists *excess capacity* in the consumer goods industries, the increase in demand for them brings about expansion in their output which further generates employment and incomes for the unemployed workers and so the new incomes are spent and respent further and the process of multiplier goes on working till it exhausts itself.

How large should be the increase in expenditure so that equilibrium is established at full employment or potential level of output. This depends on the magnitude of GNP gap caused by deflationary gap on the one hand and the size of multiplier on the other. It may be recalled that the size of the multiplier depends on the marginal propensity to consume. The impact of increase in Government expenditure in a recessionary condition is illustrated in Fig. 47.1. Suppose to begin with the economy is operating at full-employment or potential level of output Y_F with aggregate demand curve $C + I_2 + G_2$ intersecting 45° line at point E_2. Now, due to some adverse happening (say due to the crash in the stock market), investor's expectations of making profits from investment projects become dim causing a decline in investment. With the decline in investment, say equal to E_2B, aggregate demand curve will shift down to the new position $C + I_1 + G_1$ which will bring the economy to the new equilibrium position at

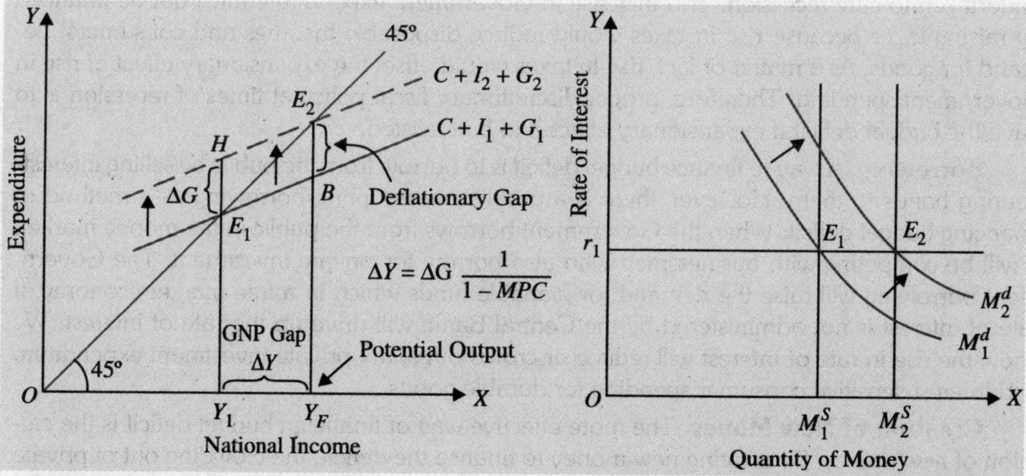

Fig. 47.1. *Increase in Government Expenditure to Cure Recession*

Fig. 47.2. *Expansion in Money Supply to Keep the Rate of Interest Unchanged*

point E_1 and thereby determine Y_1 level of output or income. The fall in output will create involuntary unemployment of labour and also excess capacity (*i.e.*, idle capital stock) will come to exist in the economy. Thus emergence of deflationary gap equal to E_2B and the reverse working of the multiplier has brought about conditions of recession in the economy. It will be observed from Fig. 47.1 that, to overcome recession if the Government increases its expenditure by E_1H, the aggregate demand curve will shift upward to original position $C + I_2 + G_2$ and as a result the equilibrium level of income will increase to the full-employment or potential level of output Y_F and in this way the economy would be lifted out of depression. Note that the increase

(ΔY) in national income or output by Y_1Y_F is not only equal to the increase in Government expenditure by ΔG or E_1H but a multiple of it depending on the marginal propensity to consume. Thus, increase in national income is equal to $\Delta G \times \frac{1}{1-MPC}$ where $\frac{1}{1-MPC}$ is the value of multiplier.

It may also be further noted that increase in Government expenditure without raising taxes (and therefore the policy of deficit budgeting) will fully succeed in curing recession if rate of interest remains unchanged. With the increase in Government expenditure and resultant increase in output and employment demand for money for transactions purposes is likely to increase as is shown in Fig. 47.2 where demand for money curve shifts to right from $M_1{}^d$ to $M_2{}^d$ as a result of increase in transactions demand for money. Money supply remaining constant, with increase in demand for money rate of interest is likely to rise which will adversely affect the private investment. The decline in private investment will tend to offset the expansionary effect of rise in Government expenditure. Therefore, if fiscal policy of increase in Government expenditure (or of deficit budgeting) is to succeed in overcoming recession, the Central Bank of the country should also pursue expansionary monetary policy and take steps to increase the money supply so that increase in Government expenditure does not lead to the rise in rate of interest. It will be noticed from Fig. 47.2 that if money supply is increased from $M_1{}^S$ to $M_2{}^S$, the rate of interest does not rise despite the increase in demand for money. With rate of interest remaining unchanged, private investment will not be adversely affected and increase in Government expenditure will have full effect on raising national income and employment.

Financing Increase In Government Expenditures and Budget Deficit

An important question is how to finance the increase in Government expenditure which is undertaken to cure recession. This increase in Government expenditure must not be financed by raising taxes because rise in taxes would reduce disposable incomes and consumers' demand for goods. As a matter of fact, rise in taxes would offset the expansionary effect of rise in Government spending. Therefore, proper discretionary fiscal policy at times of recession is to have the budget deficit if expansionary effect is to be realisted.

Borrowing. A way to finance budget deficit is to borrow from the public by selling interest-bearing bonds to them. However, there is a problem in adopting borrowing as a method of financing budget deficit. When the Government borrows from the public in the money market, it will be competing with businessmen who also borrow for private investment. The Government borrowing will raise the demand for loanable funds which in a free market economy, if rate of interest is not administered by the Central Bank, will drive up the rate of interest. We know the rise in rate of interest will reduce or crowd out some private investment expenditure and interest-sensitive consumer spending for durable goods.

Creation of New Money. The more effective way of financing budget deficit is the creation of new money. By creating new money to finance the deficit, the crowding out of private investment can be avoided and full expansionary effect of rise in Government expenditure can be realised. Thus, creation of new money for financing budget deficit or what is called *monetisation of budget deficit* has a greater expansionary effect than that of borrowing by the Government.

(*b*) **Reduction in Taxes to Overcome Recession.** Alternative fiscal policy measure to overcome recession and to achieve expansion in output and employment is reduction of taxes. The reduction in taxes increases the disposable income of the society and causes the increase in consumption spending by the people. If tax reduction of Rs. 200 crores is made by the Finance Minister, it will lead to Rs. 150 crores in consumption, assuming marginal propensity to consume is 0.75 or 3/4. Thus reduction in taxes will cause an upward shift in the consumption function. If along with the reduction in taxes, the Government expenditure is kept unchanged, aggregate demand curve $C + I + G$ will shift upward due to rise in consumption function curve. This will have an expansionary effect and the economy will be lifted out of recession, and national income and employment will increase and as a result unemployment will be reduced. Note that reduction in taxes, with Government expenditure remaining constant, will also result in budget deficit which will have to be financed either by borrowing or creation of new money.

It is worth noting that *reduction in taxes has only an indirect effect on expansion and output* through causing a rise in consumption function. But, like the increase in government expenditure, the increase in consumption achieved through reduction in taxes will have a multiplier multiplier effect on increasing income, output and employment. As we have shown in a previous chapter the increase in income due to tax multiplier as a result of tax reduction, is given by

$$\Delta T \times \frac{MPC}{1-MPC} \text{ or } \Delta C \times \frac{1}{1-MPC}$$

The effect of reduction in taxes in curing recession and in causing expansion in income and output can be graphically shown by figure such as Fig. 47.1. In case of reduction in taxes, instead of increase in Government expenditure G, it is increase in consumption C which will cause upward shift in the aggregate demand curve $(C + I + G)$ and will result in, through the working of multiplier, a higher level of equilibrium national income.

There are some instances in the history of the capitalist world, especially U.S.A. when taxes were reduced to stimulate the economy. In 1964, the President Kennedy reduced personal and business taxes by about $12 billion to give a boost to the American economy when there was high unemployment and lower capacity utilisation in the American economy. This tax cut was quite successful in reducing unemployment substantially and expanding national income through full utilisation of excess capacity. Again, over the period 1981-84, President Reagan made a very large tax reduction to get out of recession and to achieve expansion in national income to reduce unemployment. There is some debate whether President Reagan's tax cut alone had positive effect on national income as some economists attribute the recovery in that period to the monetary expansion that took place. However, tax reduction by President Reagan did play a significant role for bringing about the recovery.

Fiscal Policy Option: Increase in Government Expenditure or Reduction in Taxes

Is it better to use Government expenditure or changes in taxes to stabilise the economy at full employment and potential-level of output. The answer depends to a great extent upon one's view regarding the role of public sector. Those who think that public sector should play a significant role in the economy to meet various failures of a free market system will recommend the increase in Government expenditure during recession on public works to achieve expansion in output and employment. On the other hand, those economists who think that public sector is inefficient and involves waste of scarce resources would advocate for reduction in taxes to stimulate the economy.

The choice between tax reduction and increase in Government expenditure depends on the basis of another factor, namely, the magnitude of the effect of expenditure multiplier and tax multiplier. The value of tax multiplier is less than the Government expenditure multiplier. Ignoring the signs of the multipliers, it should be noted that whereas expenditure multiplier is equal to $\frac{1}{1-MPC}$, the tax multiplier equals $\frac{MPC}{1-MPC}$ or $MPC \times \frac{1}{1-MPC}$ which is less than $\frac{1}{1-MPC}$. Suppose marginal propensity to consume is 0.75 or 3/4 so that value of expenditure multiplier is 4. Increase in Government expenditure by ₹ 100 crores will raise national output by ₹ 400 crores. On the other hand, reduction in taxes by ₹ 100 crores will increase income and output by $100\times\frac{MPC}{1-MPC}=100\times\frac{3/4}{1-3/4}=$ ₹ 300 crores. Thus, the effect of reduction in taxes by an equal amount as the increase in Government expenditure has a smaller impact on national income than that of increase in Government expenditure. This difference in the effects of the two methods of expanding output has implications for the size of the Government deficit. If we want to achieve expansion in income by the same amount, we need to cut taxes by more than we would need to increase Government expenditure because the size of the tax multiplier is less than that of expenditure multiplier. In other words, in case we adopt the policy of tax reduction, to achieve expansion by a given amount the budget deficit planned will to have to be much greater.

However, the size of expenditure multiplier relative to the size of the tax multiplier is not the sole deciding factor for the choice of a policy option. For example, reduction in taxes are greatly welcomed by the people as it directly increases their disposable incomes. Further, it is individual or households who themselves decide how to spend their extra disposable income made possible by a tax cut, while in case of increase in expenditure the Government decides how to spend it.

Fiscal Policy to Control Inflation

When due to large increases in consumption demand by the households or investment expenditure by the entrepreneurs, or bigger budget deficit caused by too large an increase in Government expenditure, aggregate demand increases beyond what the economy can potentially produce by fully employing its given resources, it gives rise to the situation of *excess demand* which results in inflationary pressures in the economy. This inflationary situation can also arise if too large an increase in money supply in the economy occurs. In these circumstances *inflationary gap* occurs which tend to bring about rise in prices. If successful steps to check the emergence of exceeds demand or close the inflationary gap are not taken, the economy will experience a period of inflation or rising prices. For the last some decades, problem of demand-pull inflation has been faced by both the developed and developing countries of the world[1]. An alternative way of looking at inflation is to view it from the angle of business cycles. After recovery from recession, when during upswing an economy finds itself in conditions of boom and become overheated prices start rising rapidly. Under such circumstances anticyclical fiscal policy calls for reduction in aggregate demand. Thus, *fiscal policy measures to control inflation are* (1) *reducing Government expenditure and* (2) *increasing taxes*. If in the beginning the Government is having balanced budget, then increasing taxes while keeping Government expenditure constant will yield budget surplus. The creation of budget surplus will cause downward shift in the aggregate demand curve and will therefore help in easing pressure on prices. If there is a balanced budget to begin with and the Government reduces its expenditure, say on defence, subsidies, transfer payments, while keeping taxes constant, this will also create budget surplus and result in removing excess demand in the economy.

It is important to mention that in the developing countries like India, the main factor responsible for inflationary pressures *is heavy budget deficit* of the Government for the last several years resulting in excess demand conditions. Rate of inflation can be reduced not necessarily by planning for budget surplus which is in fact impracticable but by *trying to take steps to reduce budget deficits*.[2] It has been estimated that the aim should be to reduce fiscal deficit 2 to 3 per cent of GNP to achieve price stability in the Indian economy.

---

1. It is worth noting that in the mid nineties in the developed countries inflation has become very moderate which is currently at the rate of about 4 per cent per annum.
2. There is some difference in the meaning of *budget deficit and fiscal deficit*. However, we shall not go into this issue and will be treating them to be of the same meaning.

How the reduction in Government expenditure will help in checking inflation is shown in Fig. 47.3. It will be seen from this figure that an aggregate demand curve $C + I + G_1$ intersects 45° line at point E and determines equilibrium national income at full-employment level of income Y_F. However, if due to excessive Government expenditure and a large budget deficit, the aggregate demand curve curve shifts upward to $C + I + G_2$, this will determine Y_2 level of income which is greater than full employment or potential output level Y_F. Since output cannot increase beyond Y_F, income will rise only in money terms through rise in prices, real income or output remaining unchanged. To put in other words, while the economy does not have labour, capital and other resources sufficient to produce Y_2 level of income or output, the households, businessmen and Government are demanding Y_2 level of output. This excess demand pushes up the price level so that level of only *nominal income* increases, real income or output remaining constant. It is thus clear that with the increase in aggregate demand beyond the full-employment level of output to $C + I + G_2$ causes excess demand equal to EA to emerge in the economy. It is this excess demand EA relative to full-employment output Y_F which causes the price level to rise and thus creates inflationary situation in the economy. This excess demand EA at full-employment level has therefore been called inflationary gap. *The task of fiscal policy is to close this inflationary gap by reducing Government expenditure or raising taxes.* With equilibrium at point H and nominal income equal to Y_2, if Government expenditure equal to HB (which is equal to inflationary gap AE) is reduced, aggregate demand curve will shift downward to $C + I + G_1$ which will restore the equilibrium at the full-employment level Y_F. The reduction in Government expenditure equal to HB through the operation of multiplier will result in a multiple decline in the level of national income or output. It will be seen from Fig. 47.3 that the decrease in Government expenditure by HB has led to a much bigger decline in output by Y_2Y_F. Ideally Government expenditure should cut down its expenditure on non-development or unproductive heads such as defence, unnecessary subsidies. It may however be noted that in India to control inflation the Government has been reducing *capital expenditure* which is mainly of development nature and has therefore been validly criticised.

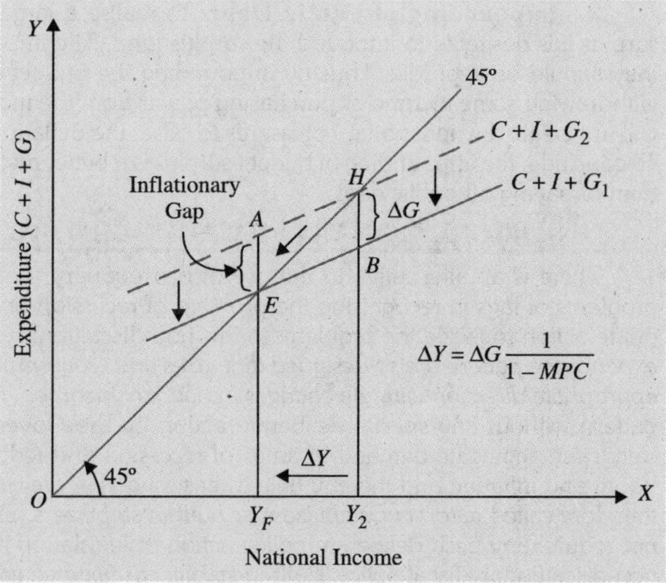

Fig. 47.3. *Reducing Expenditure to Check Inflation*

Raising Taxes to Control Inflation. *As an alternative to reduction in Government expenditure, the taxes can be increased to reduce aggregate demand.* For this purpose especially personal direct taxes such as income tax, wealth tax, corporate tax can be raised. The hike in taxes reduces the disposable incomes of the people and thereby force them to reduce their consumption demand. Note that in Fig. 47.3 as a result of hike in personal taxes it is the decrease in consumption-demand (C) component which will cause the aggregate demand curve $C + I + G_2$ to shift downward. Since, as shown above, the magnitude of tax multiplier is smaller than the expenditure multiplier, the tax revenue will be raised by a greater amount to achieve contraction in national income by Y_2Y_F.

Disposing of Budget Surplus. We have seen above to control demand-pull inflation, the Government either reduces its expenditure or raises taxes to lower aggregate demand for goods and services. Reduction in expenditure or hike in taxes results in decrease in budget deficits (if occurring before such steps) or in the emergence of budget surplus if the Government was having balanced budget prior to the adoption of anti-inflationary fiscal policy measures. Let us assume that anti-inflationary fiscal policy results in budget surplus. Anti-inflationary impact of budget surplus depends to a good extent on how the Government disposes of this budget surplus. There are two ways in which budget surplus can be disposed of: (1) reducing or retiring public debt and (2) impounding public debt.

We examine below the anti-inflationary effects of these two ways of disposing of the budget surplus

1. Retiring Public Debt. The budget surplus created by anti-inflationary policy can be used by the Government to pay back the outstanding debt. However, using budget surplus for retiring public debt will weaken its anti-inflationary effect. In paying off the debt held by the public, the Government will be returning the money to the public which it has collected through taxes. Further, this will also add to the money supply with the public. The general public will spend a part of the money so received which will raise consumption demand. Besides, retiring of public debt will result in the expansion of money supply in the money market which will tend to lower the rate of interest. The lower rate of interest will stimulate consumption and investment demand while anti-inflationary policy requires that they should be reduced.

2. Impounding of Public Debt. To realise a large anti-inflationary effect of budget surplus it is desirable to impound the surplus fund. The impounding surplus funds means that they should be kept idle. Thus by impounding the budget surplus, the Government shall be withdrawing some income or purchasing power from the income-expenditure stream and thus will not create any inflationary pressures to offset the deflationary impact of the budget surplus. To conclude, the impounding of budget surplus is a better method of disposing of budget surplus than of paying off public debt.

NON-DISCRETIONARY FISCAL POLICY: AUTOMATIC STABILIZERS

There is an alternative to the use of discretionary fiscal policy which generally involves problems of lags in recognising the problem of recession or inflation and lag of taking appropriate action to tackle the problem. In this non-discretionary fiscal policy, *the tax structure and expenditure pattern are so designed that taxes and Government spending vary automatically in appropriate direction with the changes in national income.* That is, these taxes and expenditure pattern without any special deliberate action by the Government and Parliament automatically raise aggregate demand in times of recession and reduce aggregate demand in times of boom and inflation and thereby help in ensuring economic stability. These fiscal measures are therefore called *automatic stabilizers or built-in stabilizers.* Since these automatic stabilizers do not require any fresh deliberate policy action or legislation by the government, they represent non-discretionary fiscal policy. Built-in-stability of tax revenue and Government expenditure of transfer payments and subsidies is created because they vary with national income. These taxes and expenditure automatically bring about appropriate changes in aggregate demand and reduce the impact of recession and inflation that might occur in an economy at some times. This means that because of the existence of these automatic or built-in stabilizers recession and inflation will be shorter and less intense than otherwise be the case. Important automatic fiscal stabilisers are personal income taxes, corporate income taxes, transfer payments such as unemployment compensation, welfare benefits, corporate dividends.

We discuss below these taxes, revenue from which varies directly with the change in national income.

Personal Income Taxes. The tax rate structure is so designed that revenue from these taxes directly varies with income. Moreover, personal income taxes have progressive rates; the higher rates are charged from the upper income brackets. As a result, when national income increases during expansion and inflation, increasing percentage of the people's income are paid to the Government. Thus, through causing a decline in their disposable income these taxes automatically reduce people's consumption and therefore aggregate demand. This decline in aggregate demand because of imposition of progressive personal income taxes tends to check inflation from becoming more severe. On the other hand, when national income declines at times of recession, the tax revenue declines as well which prevents aggregate demand from falling by the same proportion as the decline in income.

Corporate Income Taxes. Companies, or corporations as they are called now, also pay a percentage of their profits as tax to the Government. Like personal income taxes, corporate income tax rate is also generally higher at higher levels of corporate profits. As recession and inflation affect corporate taxes greatly, they have a powerful stabilising effect on aggregate demand; the revenue from them rises greatly during inflation and boom which tends to reduce aggregate demand, and revenue from them falls greatly during recession which tends to offset the decline in aggregate demand.

Transfer Payments: Unemployment Compensation and Welfare Benefits. When there is recession and as a result unemployment increases, the Government has to spend more on compensation for unemployment and other welfare programmes such as food stamps, rent-subsidies, subsidies to farmers. This hike in Government expenditure tends to make recession short-lived and less intense. On the other hand, when at times of boom and inflation national income increases and therefore unemployment falls, the Government curtails its programme of social benefits which result in lowering Government expenditure. The smaller spending by the Government helps to control inflation.

Corporate Dividend Policy. With economic fluctuations, corporate profits also rise and fall. However, corporations do not so quickly increase or reduce dividends in tune with fluctuations in profits and follow a *fairly stable dividend policy*. This permits the individuals to spend more during recession and spend less than would have the case if dividends were lowered in time of recession and raised in conditions of boom and inflation. Thus, fairly stable dividends tend to cushion a recession and curb inflation by stabilising consumption expenditure.

Conclusion

It follows from above that automatic stabilisers reduce the intensity of business fluctuations, that is, both recession and inflation. However, the automatic or built-in stabilizers cannot alone correct the recession and inflation significantly. According to an estimate made for the U.S.A., automatic stabilizers have been able to reduce fluctuations in national income only by one-third. Therefore, the role of discretionary fiscal policy, namely, deliberate and explicit changes in tax rates and amount of Government expenditure are required to cure recession and curb inflation.

CROWDING OUT AND EFFECTIVENESS OF FISCAL POLICY

The critics of Keynesian theory has pointed out that expansionary effect of fiscal policy is not as much large as keynesian economists suggest. In the Keynesian theory it is asserted that when Government increases its expenditure without raising taxes or when it reduces taxes without changing expenditure, it will have a large expansionary effect on national income. In other words, deficit budget would lead to the large increase in aggregate demand and thereby help to expand national output and income. However, it has been pointed that the above analysis of effect of expansionary fiscal policy of budget deficit ignores the effect of increase in Government expenditure or budget deficit on private investment. It has been argued that increase in Government expenditure or creation of budget deficit adversely affects private investment which offsets to a good extent the expansionary effect of budget deficit. This adverse effect comes about as increase in Government expenditure or reduction in taxes causes rate of interest to go up. There are two ways in which rise in rate of interest is explained. First, within the framework of

Keynesian theory increase in Government expenditure leads to the rise in national output which raises the transactions demand for money. Given the supply of money in the economy, the increase in transactions demand for money will cause the rate of interest to go up. Secondly, in order to finance its budget deficit the Government will borrow funds from the market. This will raise the demand for loanable funds which will bring about rise in the rate of interest.

Whatever the mechanism the budget deficit or increase in Government expenditure to achieve expansion in national income and output will cause the rate of interest to go up. The rise in the rate of interest will discourage private investment. As we know from the theory of investment, at a higher rate of interest, private investment declines. Thus, *increase in Government expenditure or fiscal policy of budget deficit crowds out private investment.* This fall in private investment as a result of the rise in rate of interest will offset or cancel out a part of the expansionary effect of increase in Government expenditure. The magnitude of this crowding out effect depends on the elasticity of the investment demand. If investment demand is more elastic, the decrease in private investment consequent to the rise in rate of interest will be quite substantial and will greatly offset the expansionary effect of the increase in Government expenditure. On the contrary, if investment demand is relatively inelastic, the rise in rate of interest will lead to only a small decline in private investment and therefore crowding out effect will be relatively small.

It, therefore, follows that the magnitude of crowding out weakens the effectiveness of fiscal policy. The crowding out effect of expansionary fiscal policy and its effect on national output and employment is graphically shown in Fig. 47.4. and 47.5. To begin with the economy is in equilibrium at Y_1 level of income where aggregate demand curve $C + I_1 + G_1$ intersects the 45° line and determines Y_1 level of income. Let us assume that this is much below the potential or full-employment level of output. Suppose in order to raise the level of national income and output, the Government raises its expenditure from G_1 to G_2 so that the aggregate demand curve shifts upward to the new position $C + I_1 + G_2$ which intersects the 45° line at point E_3. With increase in Government expenditure national income will rise by $\Delta G \times$ multiplier, that is, by

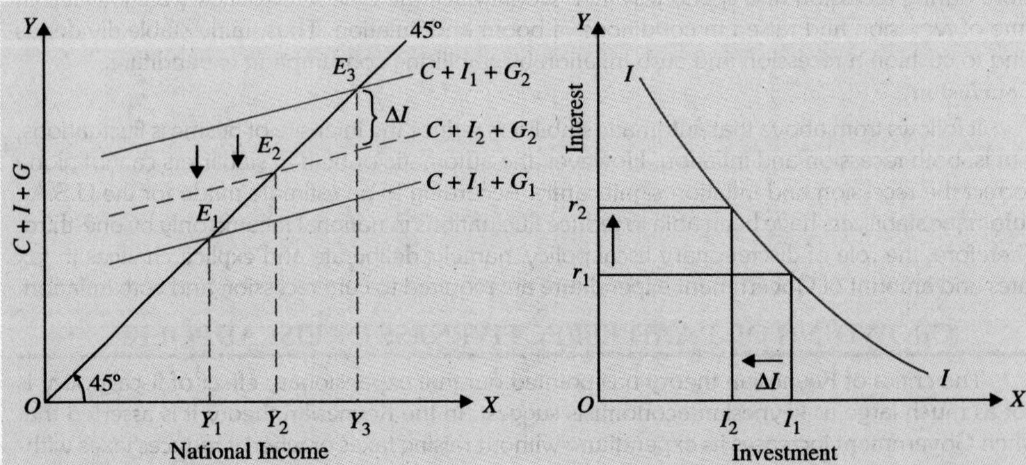

Fig. 47.4. *Effect of Crowding Out on National Output or Income*

Fig. 47.5. *Crowding Out of Private Investment*

$\Delta G \times \left(\frac{1}{1-MPC}\right)$. In the absence of crowding out effect, national income will rise to Y_3. This change in national income, ΔY or by Y_1Y_3 is equal to the increase in Government expenditure (G) times the value of multiplier $\frac{1}{1-MPC}$. However, as explained above, the increase in

Government expenditure or the creation of budget deficit causes the rate of interest to rise, say from r_1 to r_2 (See Figure 47.5). It will be seen from Fig. 47.5 that with the rise in interest from r_1 to r_2, private investment decreases from I_1 to I_2. Now, with the decline in private investment expenditure, aggregate demand curve in Fig. 47.4 shifts below to the new lower position $C + I_2 + G_2$ (dotted) and as a result new equilibrium is reached at Y_2 level of income. Thus, net result of increase in Government expenditure (ΔG) and crowding out of private investment equal to I_1I_2 or ΔI is the expansion in national income equal to only Y_1Y_2 which is relatively very small as compared to the rise in income by Y_1Y_3 in the absence of crowding out effect. Thus, the crowding out effect has weakened the expansionary effect of fiscal policy.

However, in view of this author crowding out effect has been blown out of all proportions by the critics of Keynes. As a matter of fact, when Government raises its expenditure, it leads to a large increase in aggregate demand for several goods and services through working of the multiplier. This rising aggregate demand improves investment climate by raising expectations of making profits by the private sector. As a result, the investment demand curve *II* shown in Fig. 47.5 will shift outward to the right showing that at each rate of interest more private investment will be forthcoming. Thus, while negative crowding out effect takes place as a result of moving upward along the given investment demand curve, there is positive effect of increase in aggregate demand on private investment which occurs as a result of rightward shift in the investment demand curve. Thus, we see that crowding out effect is a highly controversial issue of macro-economics.

QUESTIONS FOR REVIEW

1. What is meant by fiscal policy? Why did Keynes argue for the adoption of proper fiscal policy as an instrument of demand management to get out of depression.
2. Explain the various objectives of fiscal policy in the advanced developed economies.
3. Explain the role of fiscal policy in overcoming recession and in achieving economic stability at full-employment level.
4. What is meant by discretionary fiscal policy? How does it differ from the fiscal policy of automatic stabilizers? Explain the effectiveness of discretionary fiscal policy in curing recession and attaining equilibrium at full employment level.
5. Expansionary fiscal policy and expansionary monetary policy are complementary with each other.
6. What is effective demand ? How will it change if the Government covers its entire expenditure by (*a*) raising tax or (*b*) printing more currency.
7. Explain fiscal policy measures to control inflation. How far do you think they can be effective?
8. In an inflationary situation, the task of fiscal policy is to close the inflationary gap by reducing government expenditure or raising taxes. Discuss.
9. What is balanced budget multiplier ? Explain that even balanced budget multiplier has an expansionary effect.
10. Derive mathematically to show that the balanced budget multiplier is equal to one.
11. What is meant by crowding out effect ? Show how the expansionary effect of fiscal policy is reduced by the crowding out effect.
12. Increase in government expenditure, especially financed by borrowing from the open market, crowds out private investment. Discuss.
13. How does mechanism of crowding out of private investment work? Does it always occur ?"
14. How is private investment affected if increase in Government spending is financed by sale of Government bonds ? Do you think borrowing from the Central Bank to finance budget deficit is preferable if desired expansionary effect is to be realised ?

Economic Stabilisation: Monetary Policy

Introduction

Monetary policy is another important instrument with which objectives of macroeconomic policy can be achieved. It is worth noting that it is the Central Bank of a country which formulates and implements the monetary policy in a country. In some countries such as India the Central Bank (the Reserve Bank is the Central Bank of India) works on behalf of the Government and acts according to its directions and broad guidelines. However, in some countries such as the USA the Central Bank (*i.e.*, Federal Reserve Bank System) enjoys an independent status and pursues its independent policy. Like the fiscal policy the broad objectives of monetary policy are to establish equilibrium at full-employment level of output, to ensure price stability and to promote economic growth of the economy. Monetary policy is concerned with changing the supply of money stock and rate of interest for the purpose of stabilizing the economy at full-employment or potential output level by influencing the level of aggregate demand. More specifically, at times of recession monetary policy involves the adoption of some monetary tools which tend the increase the money supply and lower interest rates so as to stimulate aggregate demand in the economy. On the other hand, at times of inflation, monetary policy seeks to contract the aggregate spending by tightening the money supply or raising the rate of interest.

It may however be noted that in a developing country such as India, in addition to achieving equilibrium at full employment or potential output level, monetary policy has also to promote and encourage economic growth both in the industrial and agricultural sectors of the economy. Thus, in the context of developing countries the following three are the important goals or objectives of monetary policy:

(1) to ensure economic stability at full-employment or potential level of output;

(2) to achieve price stability by controlling inflation and deflation; and

(3) to promote and encourage economic growth in the economy.

In line with the above goals of monetary policy it has often been asserted by Governors of Reserve Bank of India that *growth with price stability is the goal of monetary policy of the Reserve Bank of India*. The role of monetary policy in achieving economic stability at a higher level of output and employment will be discussed below and its role in promoting economic growth in developing country with special reference to India will be explained and critically examined at length in a later chapter.

Tools of Monetary Policy

There are four major tools or instruments of monetary policy which can be used to achieve economic and price stability by influencing aggregate demand or spending in the economy. They are :

1. Open market operations;
2. Changing the bank rate;
3. Changing the cash reserve ratio; and
4. Undertaking selective credit controls.

How these three tools of monetary policy work to influence aggregate spending and economic activity has been explained in a previous chapter. We shall explain how these various tools can be used for formulating a proper monetary policy to influence levels of aggregate output, employment and prices in the economy. In times of recession or depression, *expansionary monetary policy* or what is also called *easy money policy* is adopted which raises aggregate demand and thus stimulates the economy. On the other hand, in times of inflation and excessive expansion, *contractionary monetary policy* or what is also called *tight money policy* is adopted to control inflation and achieve price stability through reducing aggregate demand in the economy. We discuss below both these policies.

EXPANSIONARY MONETARY POLICY TO CURE RECESSION OR DEPRESSION

When the economy is faced with recession or involuntary cyclical unemployment, which comes about due to fall in aggregate demand, the central bank intervenes to cure such a situation. Central Bank takes steps to expand the money supply in the economy and/or lower the rate of interest with a view to increase the aggregate demand which will help in stimulating the economy. The following three monetary policy measures are adopted as a part of an expansionary monetary policy to measures are adopted as a part of an expansionary monetary policy to cure recession and to establish the equilibrium of national income at full employment level of output.

1. The central bank undertakes open market operations and *buys securities in the open market*. Buying of securities by the central bank, from the public, chiefly from commercial banks will lead to the increase in reserves of the banks or amount of currency with the general public. With greater reserves, commercial banks can issue more credit to the investors and businessmen for undertaking more investment. More private investment will cause aggregate demand curve to shift upward. Thus buying of securities will have an expansionary effect.

2. The Central Bank *may lower the bank rate or what is also called discount rate*, which is the rate of interest charged by the central bank of country on its loans to commercial banks. At a lower bank rate, the commercial banks will be induced to borrow more from the central bank and will be able to issue more credit at the lower rate of interest to businessmen and investors. This will not only make credit cheaper but also increase the availability of credit or money supply in the economy. The expansion in credit or money supply will increase the investment demand which will tend to raise aggregate output and income.

3. Thirdly, the *central bank may reduce the Cash Reserve Ratio (CRR) to be kept by the commercial banks*. In countries like India, this is a more effective and direct way of expanding credit and increasing money supply in the economy by the central bank. With lower reserve

requirements, a large amount of funds is released for providing loans to businessmen and investors. As a result, credit expands and investment increases in the economy which has an expansionary effect on output and employment. In April 1996, when *Reserve Bank* lowered the CRR from 14 per cent to 13 per cent, it was estimated that this would release funds equal to ₹ 5,000 crores for the banks and thereby would significantly increase their lending capacity.

Similar to the Cash Reserve Ratio (CRR), in India there is another monetary instrument, namely *Statutory Liquidity Ratio* (SLR) used by the Reserve Bank to change the lending capacity and therefore credit availability in the economy. As explained in a previous chapter, according to Statutory Liquidity Ration, in addition to the Cash Reserve Ratio (CRR) banks have to keep a certain minimum proportion of their deposits in the form of some specified liquid assets such as Government securities. To increase the lendable resources of the banks, Reserve Bank can lower this Statutory Liquidity Ratio (SLR). Thus, when Reserve Bank of India lowers statutory liquidity Ratio (SLR), the credit availability for the private sector will increase.

It may be noted that the use of all the above tools of monetary policy leads to an increase in reserves or liquid resources with the banks. Such reserves are the basis on which banks expand their credit by lending, the increase in reserves raises the money supply in the economy, Thus, *appropriate monetary policy at times of recession or depression can increase the availability of credit and also lower the cost of credit.* This leads to more private investment spending which has an expansionary effect on the economy.

How Expansionary Monetary Policy Works: Keynesian View

Now, it is important to understand how expansionary monetary policy works to cause increase in output and employment and thus help the economy to recover from recession. In the Keynes' theory rate of interest is determined by the demand for and supply of money. According to Keynesian theory, expansion in money supply causes the rate of interest to fall . An this fall in the rate of interest will encourage businessmen to borrow more for investment spending. As is well known, *rate of interest is the opportunity cost of funds invested for purchasing capital goods.* As rate of interest falls, it becomes profitable to invest more in producing or buying capital goods. Thus, fall in the rate of interest raises the investment expenditure which is an important componet of aggregate demand. The increase in aggregate demand causes expansion in aggregate output, national income and employment. How, according to Keynesian view, expansion in money supply can help to cure recession is illustrated in Fig. 48.1. In apanel (*a*) of Fig. 48.1 it will be seen that when as a result of some measures taken by the central bank, the money supply increases from M_1 to M_2, the rate of interest falls from r_1 to r_2. It will be seen from panel (*b*) that with this fall in rate of interest, investment increases from I_1 to I_2. Now, in panel (*c*), it is shown how the increase in investment expenditure from I_1 to I_2 shifts the aggregate demand curve ($C + I_1 + G$) upward so that the new aggregate demand curve $C + I_2 + G$ intersects the 40° line at point E_2 and thus establishes equilibrium at full-employment output level Y_F. It may be noted that with the given increase in investment how much aggregate output or national income will increase depends on the size of income multiplier which is determined by marginal propensity to consume. The greater the size of multiplier, the greater the impact of increment in investment on expansion of output and income.

From above, it is clear that monetary policy can play an important role in stimulating the economy and ensuring stability at full employment level. But it is work mentioning that there are sever weak links in the full chain of increase in money supply achieving a significant expansion in economic activity. In fact, *Keynes himself was of the view that in times of depression, monetary policy will be ineffective in revisiion the economy and therefore he laid stress on the adoption of fiscal policy to overcome depression.*

The first weak link in the above argument of expansionary monetary policy relates to the elasticity of money-demand (*i.e.*, liquidity preference) curve M^d in panel (*a*) of Fig. 48.1. As shall be explained at length below, if demand for money curve M^d is nearly flat (*i.e.*, highly elastic), the increase in money supply by the central bank will not greatly affect the rate of interest and consequently further steps of significant expansion in investment and aggregate demand will not be realized. Besides, even of significant expansion in investment and aggregate demand will not be realised. Besides, even if money demand curve is elastic and, therefore, expansion of money supply lowers the rate of interest significantly, the investment may not rise much. This is because if the investment demand curve is steep or inelastic, that is, investment is not sensitive to the changes in rate of interest, the fall in the rate of interest will fail to cause any significant increase in investment. As a result, aggregate demand curve will not change much and expansionary effect on output and employment will not be realised.

Further, the effect of increase in investment on output and employment depends on the size of multiplier. If there are several leakage in the multiplier process, even increase in investment may not bring about much change in output and employment. Thus, because of

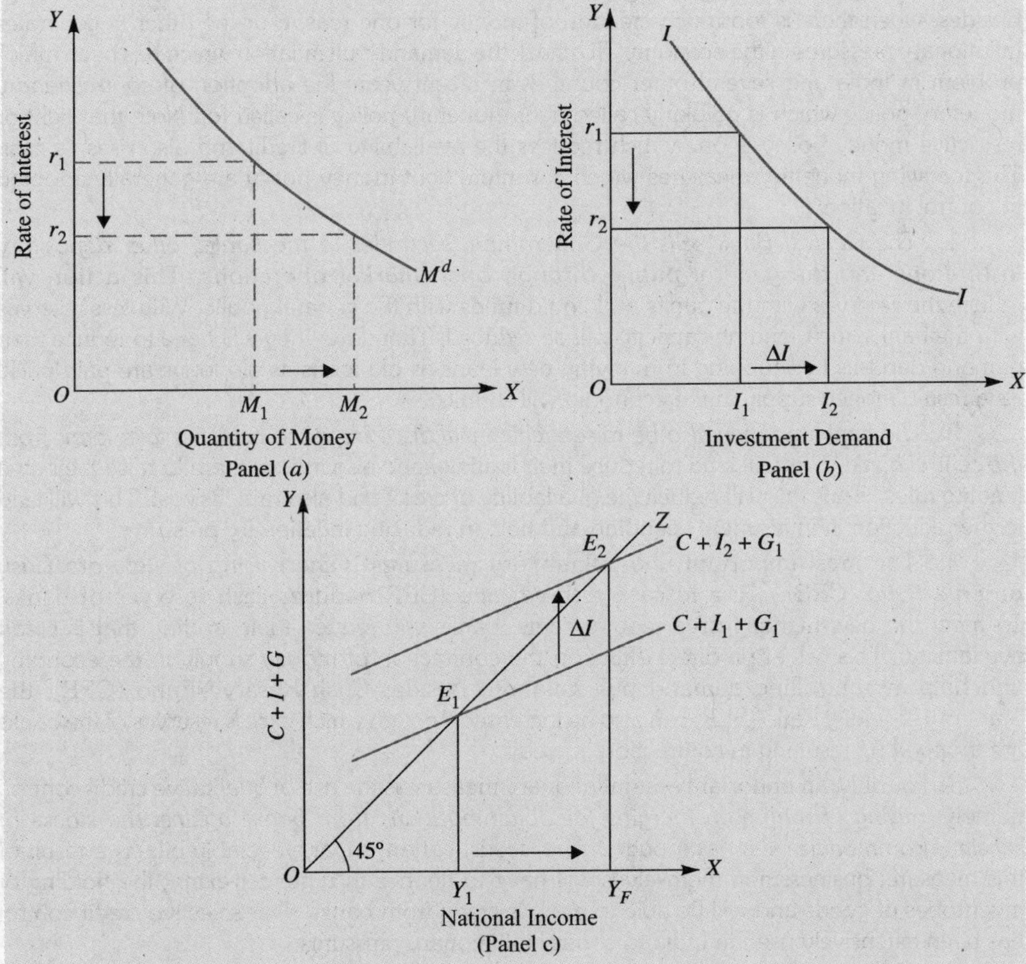

Fig. 48.1. *How Expansionary Monetary Policy Works : Keynesian View*

several weak links in the process or chain in expansion in money supply bringing about expansion, Keynes remarked that *there are many a slip between the cup and the lip*. Therefore, for all these reasons (especially because of the liquidity trap in the demand for money curve at lower rates of interest). Keynes was of the view that monetary policy is not an effective instrument in bringing about revival of the economy from the depressed state.

It may however be noted that modern Keynesians do not share the pessimistic view of the effectiveness of monetary policy. They think that liquidity preference curve is not flat and further that investment demand is fairly sensitive to the changes in the rates of interest. Therefore, *modern Keynesians equally advocate for the adoption of discretionary monetary policy as for the discretionary fiscal policy to get rid of recession.*

TIGHT MONETARY POLICY TO CONTROL INFLATION

When aggregate demand rises sharply due to large consumption and investment expenditure or more imprantly, due to the large increase in Government expenditure relative to its revenue resulting in huge budge deficits, a demand-pull inflation occurs in the economy. Besides, when there is too much creation of money for one reason or the other, it generates inflationary pressures in the economy. To check the demand-pull inflation which has been major problem in India and several other countries in recent years the adoption of *contractionary* monetary policy which is polularly called tight monetary policy is called for. Note that tight or restrictive money policy is one which reduces the availability of credit and also rises its cost. The following monetary measures which constitute tight money policy are generally adopted to control inflation:

1. *The Central Bank sells the Government securities to the banks, other depository institutions and the general public through open market operations.* This action will reduce the reserves with the banks and liquid funds with the general public. With less reserves with the banks, their lending capacity will be reduced. Therefore, they will have to reduce their demand deposits by refraning from giving new loans as old loans as old loans are paid back. As a result, money supply in the economy will shrink.

2. *The bank rate may also be raised which will discourage the banks to take loans from the central bank.* This will tend to reduce their liquidity and also induce them to raise their own lending rates. Thus this will reduce the availability of credit and also raise its cost. This will lead to the reduction in investment spending and help in reducing inflationary pressures.

3. The most important anti-inflationary measures is the *raising of statutory Cash Reserve Ratio (CRR)*. Rise in cash reserve ratio (CRR) reduces cash reserves of banks. To meet the new higher resrve requirements, banks will reduce their lending that is credit availability. This will are a direct effect on the contraction of money supply in the economy and help in controlling demand pull inflation. Besides Cash Reserve Ratio (CRR), the Statutory Liquidity Ratio (SLR) can also be increased through which excess reserves of the banks are mopped up resulting in contraction in credit.

4. Fourthly, an important anti-inflationary measure is the use of qualitative credit control, namely, *raising of minimum margins for obtaining loans from banks against the stocks of sensitive commodities* such as foodgrains, oilseeds, cotton, sugar, vegetable oil. As a result of this measure, businessmen themselves will have to finance to a greater extent the holding of inventories of goods and will be able to get less credit from banks. This selective credit control has been extensively used in India to control inflationary pressures.

How the Tight Monetary Policy Works : Keynesian View

It is important to understand how tight monetary policy works to check inflation. As explained above, tight monetary policy seeks to reduce the money supply through contraction of credit in the economy and also raising the cost of credit, that is lending rates of interest. The reduction in money supply itself raises the rate of interest. The higher interest rate reduces investment spending which results in lowering of aggregate demand curve ($C + I + G$). The decrease in aggregate demand tends to restrain demand pull inflation. How tight money policy helps in checking inflation is graphically shown in Fig. 48.2. Let us assume that full-employment level of national income is Y_F as depicted in panel (*c*) of Fig. 48.2. Now, if due to a large budget deficit and excessive creation of money supply, aggregate demand curve shifts to $C + I_2 + G_2$; inflationary gap of E_1H comes to exist at full-employment level. That is, the sum of consumption expenditure, private investment spending and Government expenditure exceeds the full-employment level of output by E_1H. This creates a demand-pull inflation causing rise in prices. Though with aggregate demand curve $C + I_2 + G_2$ equilibrium reaches at point E_2 and as a result national income increases but only in money terms ; real income or output level remaining constant at OY_F.

Now, it will be seen from panel (*a*) that if tight money policy succeeds in reducing money supply from M_2 to M_1 the rate of interest will rise from r_1 to r_2. Panel (*b*) of Fig. 48.2 shows that at a higher interest rate r_2, private investment falls from I_2 to I_1. This reduction in investment expenditure shifts aggregate demand curve $C + I_2 + G_2$ downward to $C + I_1 + G_1$ and in this

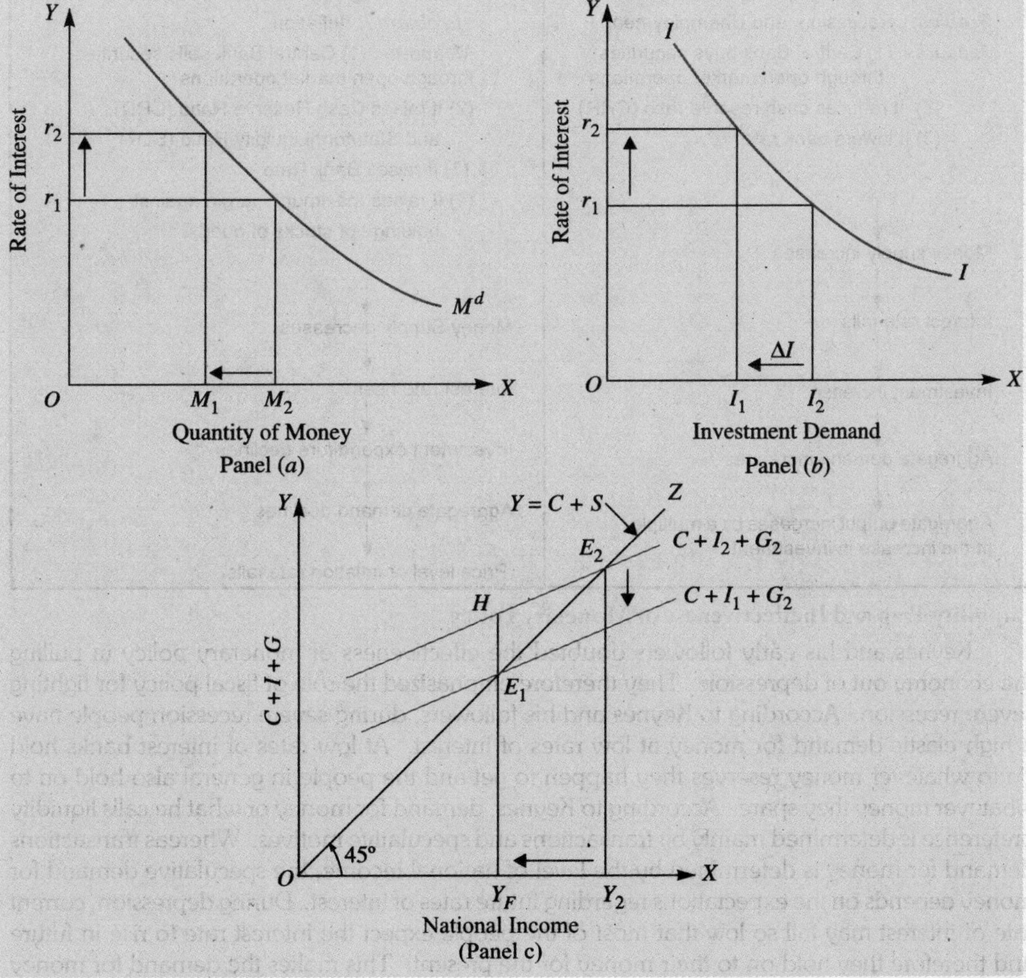

Fig. 48.2. *How Anti-inflationary Monetary Policy Works : Keynesian View*

way inflationary gap is closed and equilibrium at full-employment output level Y_F is once again established. In our figure it has been assumed that contraction of money supply from M_2 to M_2 and as a result rise in rate of interest form r_1 to r_2 is sufficient to reduce investment expenditure equal to $I_2 - 1_2$ which is equal to inflationary gap and in this way macroeconomic equilibrium without any inflationary pressure is established at output leave Y_F.

It should be further remembered that in our analysis of the successful working of the tight monetary policy it is assumed that demand for money curve (*i.e.*, liquidity preference curve) is fairly steep so as to push up the rate of interest from r_1 to r_2 and further that investment demand curve *II* in panel (*b*) of Fig. 48.2 is fairly elastic so that rise in rate of interest from r_1 to r_2 is sufficient to reduce investment by $I_2 - I_1$ or ΔI. If these conditions regarding the shapes of the money demand curve and investment demand curve represent the real world situation, then tight monetary policy will succeed in controlling inflation and ensuring price stability.

To sum up, Keynesian view of how expansionary and contractionary (tight) monetary policies work to achieve the twin goals of price stability and equilibrium at full-employment level of output is shown in the accompanying box.

Monetary Policy: Keynesian View

Expansionary Monetary Policy	Tight Monetary Policy
Problem : Recession and Unemployment	***Problem*** : Inflation
Measures: (1) Central Bank buys securities through open market operations (2) It reduces cash reserve ratio (CRR) (3) It lowers bank rate	***Measures***: (1) Central Bank sells securities through open market operations (2) It raises Cash Reserve Ratio (CRR) and Statutory Liquidity Ratio (SLR) (3) It raises Bank Rate (4) It raises maximum margin against holding of stocks of goods.
↓ Money supply increases	↓ Money Supply decreases
↓ Interest rate falls	↓ Interest rate rises
↓ Investment increase	↓ Investment expenditure declines
↓ Aggregate demand increases	↓ Aggregate demand declines
↓ Aggregate output increases by a multiple of the increase in investment	↓ Price level or inflation rate falls

Liquidity Trap and Ineffectiveness of Monetary Policy

Keynes and his early followers doubted the effectiveness of monetary policy in pulling the economy out of depression. They therefore emphasized the role of fiscal policy for fighting severe recession. According to Keynes and his followers, during severe recession people have a high elastic demand for money at low rates of interest. At low rates of interest banks hold on to whatever money reserves they happen to get and the people in general also hold on to whatever money they spare. According to Keynes, demand for money or what he calls liquidity preference is determined mainly by transactions and speculative motives. Whereas transactions demand for money is determined by the level of national income, the speculative demand for money depends on the expectations regarding future rates of interest. During depression, current rate of interest may fall so low that most of the people expect the interest rate to rise in future and therefore they hold on to their money for the present. This makes the demand for money absolutely elastic at a low rate of interest as is shown in Fig. 48.3. It will be seen from Fig. 48.3

that at a low rate of interest r_0 demand curve for money M^d is absolutely elastic showing people demand or hold on to all the increases in money supply beyond MS_1 for speculative purposes and not invest in bonds. Under these circumstances the economy is said to have fallen in a liquidity trap. A liquidity trap occurs when under conditions of depression the economy finds itself in a situation where people hold all the increments in the stock of money and money demand curve M^d takes a horizontal shape.

Suppose during a recession, stock of money is equal to MS_1 and money demand curve is given by M^d. The interaction between these two determines r_0 rate of interest. Suppose now, to pull the economy out of recession, the stock of money supply is expanded to MS_2. A glance at Fig. 48.3 reveals that expansion in money supply from MS_1 to MS_2 does not lower the rate of interest as the economy is operating in the rage of liquidity tap. Now, Fig. 48.4 shows that with the rate of interest remaining unchanged at r_0, the level of investment does not rise. With level of investment remaining the same, there is no increase in aggregate demand and the economy remains in a state of depression. Thus, under these circumstances Keynes and his early followers contended that expansionary monetary policy did not help the economy in staging a recovery from recession.

It may, However, he noted that the concept of liquidity trap is not supported by empirical studies. The empirical studies show that demand for money (liquidity preference) never becomes

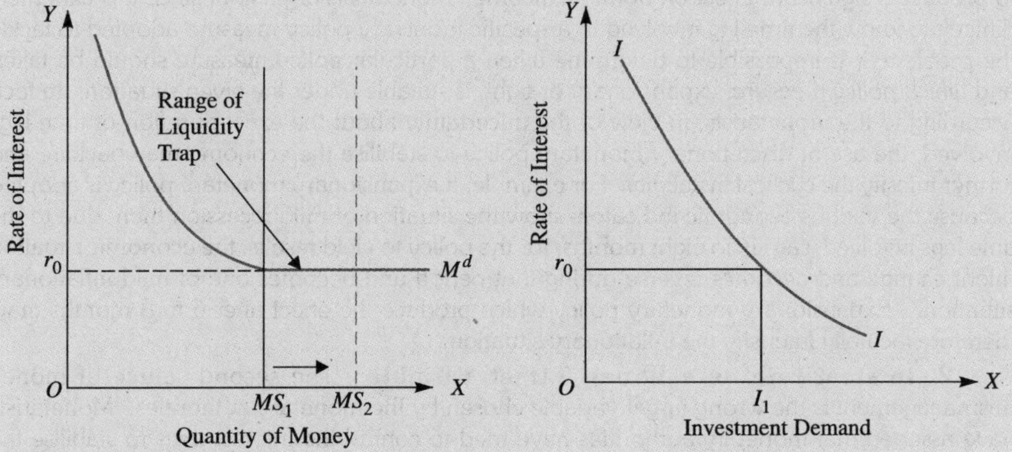

Fig. 48.3. *Liquidity Trap and Increase in Money Supply* ***Fig. 48.4.*** *Investment Demand*

flat and instead it falls throughout. Therefore, modern Keynesians and toehr economists now believe that monetary policy can play a useful role in stabilising the economy at full employment level. However, as shall be discussed below, it is the *monetarists* led by Friedman who do not favour discretionary monetary policy to check cyclical instability.

MONETARY POLICY: MONETARIST VIEW

Though most of the modern economists regard both fiscal and monetary policies as important tools for stabilising the economy there is a group of economists known as *monetarists* led by Friedman who thick that changes in money supply are the key determinants in the level of economic activity and the price level. They contend that demand curve for money is quite steep and the investment demand curve is quite elastic so that when there is a change in money supply, it significantly affects the investment demand and therefore the equilibrium level of nominal income.

However, surprisingly, enough, the most monetarists do not advocate the use of discretionary monetary policy, namely, an expansionary or easy money policy, to lift the economy out of recession and tight monetary policy to check inflationary boom and thereby correct the `downs' and `ups' of the business cycles. In fact, *Friedman, the chief exponent of monetarism, contends that, historically, far from stabilishing the economy, discretionary changes in money supply or rates of interest have a destabilising effect on the economy.* On the basis of his study of monetary history of United States, he contends that faulty decision regrading changes in money supply, made by the monetary authorities, are responsible for a lot of instability that prevailed during the period of his study. Thus, according to monetarists, *it is not the presence of certain inherent destabilising factors in a free-market economy but the monetary mismanagement* by the discretionary monetary policies which is the root cause of economic instability that has been existing in the free market economies.

Source of Monetary Mismanagement

According to monetarists, there are two important sources of monetary mismanagement. (1) *variable time lags* concerning the effect of money supply on the nominal income and (2) *treating interest rate as the target of monetary policy* for influencing investment demand for stabilising the economy. We examine below both these sources of monetary mismanagement.

1. Variable Time Lags. First there is a problem of variable long time lags that occur for changes in money supply to bring about desirable effect on nominal income. From his empirical studies Friedman concludes that it takes six months to two years for the changes in money supply to produce a significant effect on nominal income. Monetarists argue that since it is extremely difficult to know the time lag involved in a specific monetary policy measure adopted to tackle the problem, it is impossible to determine *when* a particular policy measure should be taken and *which policy measure*, expansionary or tight, is suitable under the given situation. In fact, according to the monetarists, in view of the uncertainty about the exact duration of time lags involved, the use of discretionary monetary policy to stabilise the economy may backfire and further intesify the cyclical instability. For example, if expansionary monetary policy is adopted because the various economic indicators show the situation of mild recession then, due to the time lags involved, say six to eight months, for the policy to yield results, the economic situation might change and becomes reverse during that period and becomes one of mild inflationary situation. Expansionary monetary policy which produce the effect after 6 to 8 months may, therefore, acutally intensify the inflationary situation.

2. Interest rate as a Wrong Target Variable. The second source of money mismanagement is the wrong target variable chosen by the monetary authorities. Monetarists have asserted that monetary authorities have tried to control the interest rates to stabilise the economy. It has been argued that Central Bank cannot simultaneously stabilise both the interest rate and money supply. By controlling the interest rate it has actually destabilised the economy. For example, if the economy is recovering from recession and is presently approaching full employment with aggregate demand, output, employment and prices all registering a rise, the transactions demand for money will increase. This increase in transactions demand for money will cause the rate of interest to rise. But if the monetary authorities have chosen to stabilise the interest rate, they would adopt tight monetary policy to prevent the interest rate from going up. Demand when the economy is recovering from recession, and will again cause the recessionary omy unstable. Similarly, when the economy is going into recession, it will result in lowering aggregate output and prices. This fall in aggregate output and prices will cause a decline in the transactions demand for money. And the decrease in transactions demand will lead to the fall in interest rate. To prevent this fall in interest rate, if money supply is increased, it will generate stability in the economy rather than removing it.

Monetary Rule : Monetary Policy Prescription

From the above analysis it follows that monetarists are not in favour of stabilising the interest rate they advocate for the *adoption of a rule rather than pursuing discretionary monetary policy* to stabilize the economy. They prescribe a *rule for the growth of the money supply* to achieve economic grow with stability. According to the monetary rule suggested by Friedman, *money supply should be allowed to grow at the rate equal to the rate of growth of output.* If the economy is expected to growth annually at the rate of 3, 4 or 5 per cent, money supply should also grow at this rate. The growth of output of an economy will absorb the extra money supply created as per this rule, without generating inflationary or recessionary conditions, and will thus ensure stability in the economy. To quote Ritter and Silber, "such a rule would eliminate the major cause of instability in the economy—the capricious and unpredictable impact of counter cyclical monetary policy. As long as the money supply grows at a constant rate each year, be it 3, 4 or 5 per cent, any decline into recession will be temporary. The liquidity provided by a constantly growing money supply will cause the aggregate demand to expand. Similarly, if the supply of money does not rise at a ore than average rate, any inflationary increase in spending will burn itself out for lack of fuel."[1]

Monetary rule has been criticised by the Keynesian economists. They have argued that monetary rule will have a destabilising effect. Given that the velocity of money (*V*) is unstable or variable, increase in money supply (*M*), according to this rule, may not ensure growth of aggregate demand (which, according to monetarist theory, is equal to *MV*) equal to the rate of growth of output in a year which is difficult to predict. Thus, money supply increase may sometimes exceed the growth of output and sometimes fall short of it and as result may cuase sometimes demand-pull inflation and sometimes necessary conditions. Thus, according to Keynesian economists, policy of monetary rule does not guarantee economic stability and it may itself create economic instability.

THE POLICY OF QUANTITATIVE EASING (QE)

We have explained above the conventional monetary policy to bring stability in the economy. Now, in 2008 there was a severe economic crisis caused by bursting of housing buble in the U.S.A. Prior to 2008, when the prices of houses were rising the Americans had made excessive investment in houses financed by sub-prime housing loans given on a large scale by the American banks at a low rates of interest. The American banks sold these sub-prime mortgaged housing loans to other financial institutions which converted them into securities that were traded in the market. In 2007-08 when the prices of houses declined sharply, the people who had got the sub-prime housing loans from the banks started defaulting on paying interest and the principal amount. This caused serious financial crises as the prices of securities based on sub-prime mortgage housing loans fell almost to zero. As a result, the banks and financial institutions such as Lehman Brothers, Citi Bank which had made large investment in them came to the brink of bankruptcy. In July 2008, Lehman Brothers declared itself bankrupt. This caused great panic which ultimately result in severe recession in the US economy which had world-wide repercussions. The recession in the US economy was so severe that its growth rate came down to almost zero and unemployment shot up to 10 per cent of labour force.

It is to tackle such severe recessionary conditions the *non-conventional monetary policy* of quantitative easing (QE) was adopted by the Federal Reserve (which is the Central Bank of the US). The interest rates were then so low that the conventional monetary policy of lowering interest rates had lost its ability to stimulate the economy. Therefore, non-conventional monetary policy of quantitative easing (QE) was adopted by the Federal Reserve keeping near zero rate of interest. Under the quantitative easing (QE) the Federal Reserve purchased bonds (both treasury bonds and private corporate bonds) and other financial assets on a large scale and *to purchase*

1. L.S. Ritter and W.L. Silber, Money 5th ed., Basic Books Publishers, 1984, pp. 141-142.

them created new money. In this way, the Federal Reserve pumped a large liquidity (*i.e.*, cash) into the banking system and has continued this policy for several years now since 2008, though the scale of purchase of bonds has slowed down in recent years.

Now, selling bonds and other financial assets to Federal Reserve and getting a lot of cash allowed American Commercial banks to provide loans to business firms and investors at low rate of interest to make more investment and thus increasing spending in the economy. It was hoped that more investment and spending would help the economy to get out of recession. Thus, quantitative easing (QE) was expected to stimulate the US economy and recover from recessionary conditions.

It may be noted that with the Federal Reserve purchasing bonds from the market on a large scale, their supply in the market was reduced which drived up the bond prices. Higher bond prices mean the yield from them declines and therefore investors are discouraged to buy them. The investors or business firms which got loans from the banks not only invested some money in building new factories or expanding their existing capacities but also used them to buy back their own stock or shares with the intention to shore up their prices. Since return on more investment in the US was very low, a good amount of US dollars created through quantitative easing also flowed into the emerging economies, especially India and China where returns from investment in shares and bonds were quite high. The inflows of capital (*i.e.*, US dollars) in India and China caused share prices in these countries to shoot up. In this way, American foreign institutional investors (FIIs) made a good amount of profits in investing in India and China.

With the policy of pumping a lot of liquidity into the banks which gave liberal loans at very low interest rates has succeeded in reviving the American economy whose annual GDP growth has on average reached 2.5 per cent and unemployment rate has also declined to 5 per cent labour force (June 2015). However, the recovery of the American economy is fragile. The Federal Reserve has quite often decided to withdraw completely the quantitative easing policy and raise rate of interest but each time it has postponed the implementation of its decision. It may be noted that when quantitative easing (QE) policy is completely withdrawn and rate of interest raised by the Federal Reserve, there will be *outflows of capital* (*i.e.*, dollars) by FIIs from India. When this happens the share prices in India will fall sharply, the Indian rupee would depreciate and thus creating a lot of economic instability in the Indian economy. This economic instability will also be seen in other emerging economies.

QUESTIONS FOR REVIEW

1. What is meant by monetary policy? Briefly explain the instruments of monetary policy.
2. Expaling the objectives of monetary policy.
3. Explain monetary policy measures that should be adopted for curing recession (or depression) and reviving the economy. How does expansionary monetary policy work? How does Keynesian view in this regard differe the onetarist view?
4. What are the factors that determine the effectiveness of monetary policy in reviving the economy from recession. Why Keynes thought that monetary policy was ineffective in reviving the economy from depression?
5. What is liquidity trap? How does it make the expansionary monetary policy ineffective in reviving the economy from recession?
6. Explain the main instruments of monetary policy that can be adopted to control inflation in the economy.
7. Explain the mechanism through which tight monetary policy works to check inflation. Illustrate diagrammatically.

8. Descritionary monetary policy can play an important role in stabilising the economy at full employment. Discuss.
9. Explain the views of Friedman and his follower modern monetarists regarding monetary policy as a tool of economic stabilisation. In this connection also comment on the monetarist view that interest rate is a wrong target variable of proper monetary policy.
10. What is meant by 'time lags'? How do they affect the efficiency of monetary policy to stabilise the economy?
11. What are the instruments of monetary policy? Explain the role of changes in bank rate and open market operations in controlling trade cycles.
12. "Monetary policy for its success depends on fiscal policy." Explain and critically examine this statement.

Monetary Policy and Economic Growth with Special Reference to India

Introduction

Monetary policy is concerned with the measures taken to regulate the supply of money, the cost and availability of credit in the economy. Further, it also deals with the distribution of credit between uses and users and also with both the lending and borrowing rates of interest of the banks. In developed countries the monetary policy has been usefully used for overcoming depression and inflation as an anti-cyclical policy. However, in developing countries it has also to play a significant role in promoting economic growth with price stability. As Prof. R. Prebisch writes, "The time has come to formulate a monetary policy which meets the requirements of economic development, which fits into its framework perfectly." Further, along with encouraging economic growth, the monetary policy has also to ensure price stability, because the excessive inflation not only has adverse distribution effect but hinders economic growth also.

It is important to understand the distinction between *objectives* or *goals*, *targets* and *instruments* of monetary policy. Whereas goals of monetary policy refer to its objectives which, as mentioned above, may be price stability, full employment or economic growth, *targets refer to the variables such as supply of money or bank credit, interest rates which are sought to be changed through the instruments of monetary policy so as to attain these objectives*. The various instruments of monetary policy are changes in the supply of currency, variations in bank rate and other interest rates, open market operations, selective credit controls, and variations in cash reserve requirements of banks. We have explained these instruments in detail in a previous chapter.

Repo Rate and Reverse Repo Rate

It may be noted that in recent years in India changes in bank rate are not used both for the purpose of achieving price stability and for promoting economic growth. In India a new mechanism called *liquidity adjustment facility* (LAF) has been introduced by RBI to adjust liquidity in the banking system on a daily basis. Under the liquidity adjustment mechanism two interest rates are announced by RBI. First is the *repo rate* of interest at which RBI lends funds for overnight to the banks when they need. When RBI raises repo rate, the cost of borrowing funds from RBI for the banks rises and in turn they raise their own lending rates of interest and thereby making bank credit costlier. The opposite happens when RBI lowers repo rate of interest.

The second interest rate under liquidity adjustment facility (LAF) is the *reverse repo rate*. Reverse repo rate is interest rate at which banks park their surplus funds for overnight with RBI. That is, reverse repo rate is the interest rate at which banks lend to RBI for overnight.

Both repo rate and reverse repo rates are conducted on daily basis. RBI keeps two windows; repo window and reverse repo window. At repo window banks come to borrow at repo rate from RBI when they are in need of liquid funds for lending purposes. On the other hand, at reverse repo window, banks approach RBI to park their surplus funds for a short-period (of course, on day to day basis) to earn some interest. Since both repo and reverse repo rate operations are conducted on daily basis, banks can renew their position daily and decide accordingly as to how much they borrow from RBI for every day or how much they park their surplus funds with RBI. Thus when there are tight liquidity conditions banks approach repo window of LAF to borrow funds from RBI on day-to-day basis. On the other hand, when there are excess liquid funds with the banks, they park these surplus funds with RBI at reverse repo interest rate.

We shall first explain below the objectives or goals of monetary policy in a developing economy with special reference to those adopted by Reserve Bank of India. After having explained the objectives we shall explain role of monetary policy in promoting economic growth in a developing country like India. In the end we will explain monetary policy of reserve Bank of India in different periods of planned development, especially its recent monetary policy stance.

OBJECTIVES OF MONETARY POLICY OF RESERVE BANK OF INDIA

Before explaining in detail the monetary measures undertaken by RBI to regulate credit and growth of money supply, it is important to explain the objectives of monetary policy pursued by RBI in formulation of its policy. Since monetary policy is one instrument of economic policy, its objectives cannot be different from those of overall economic policy. The three important objectives of monetary policy are:

1. ensuring *price stability,* that is, containing inflation.
2. to encourage *economic* growth.
3. to ensure *stability of exchange rate of the rupee,* that is, exchange rate of rupee with the US dollar, pound sterling and other foreign currencies.

Let us explain below these objectives in some detail.

Price Stability or Control of Inflation

It may be noted that each instrument of economic policy is better suited to achieve a particular objective. Monetary policy is better suited to the achievement of price stability, that is, containing inflation. To quote C. Rangarajan, a former Governor of Reserve Bank of India, "Faced with multiple objectives that are equally relevant and desirable, there is always the problem of assigning to each instrument the most appropriate target or objective. Of the various objectives, *price stability is perhaps the one that can be pursued most effectively by monetary policy.* In a developing country like ours, acceleration of investment activity in the context of supply shocks in the agricultural sector tends to be accompanied by pressures on prices and, therefore, monetary policy has much to contribute in the short-run management."[1]

Thus, achieving price stability has remained the dominant objective of monetary policy of Reserve Bank of India. It may however be noted that price stability does not mean absolutely

1. C. Rangarajan, *"Issues in Monetary Management"* printed in *Indian Economy : Essays on Money and Finance,* 1998, p. 6.

no change in price level at all. In a developing economy like ours, where structural changes take place during the process of economic growth some changes in relative prices do occur that generally put upward pressure on prices. Therefore, some changes in price level or, in other words, a certain rate of inflation is inevitable in a developing economy. Thus, *price stability means reasonable rate of inflation.* A high degree of inflation has adverse effects on the economy. First, inflation raises the cost of living of the people and hurts the poor most. Therefore, inflation has been described as enemy No. 1 of the poor. Inflation sends many people below the poverty line. Secondly, inflation makes exports costlier and, therefore, discourages them. On the other hand, due to higher prices at home people are induced to import goods to a large extent. Thus, inflation has an adverse effect on the balance of payments. Emphasising the importance of price stability from the viewpoint of India's balance of payments, Prof. Rangarajan writes, "*The increasing openness of the economy, the need to service external debt and the necessity to improve the share of our exports in a highly competitive external environment require that the domestic price level not be allowed to rise unduly, particularly since our major trading partners have had notable success in recent years in achieving price stability.*[2]

Thirdly, when due to a higher rate of inflation value of money is rapidly falling, people do not have much incentive to save. This lowers the rate of saving on which investment and economic growth depend. Instead, a high rate of inflation encourages people to invest their savings in the unproductive physical assets such as gold, silver, jewellery, real estate etc.

An expert committee on monetary reforms headed by Late Prof. S. Chakravarty suggested 4 per cent rate of inflation as a reasonable rate of inflation and recommended that monetary policy by RBI should be so formulated that ensures that rate of inflation does not exceed 4 per cent per annum.

Economic Growth

Promoting economic growth is another important objective of the monetary policy in developing countries. In the past Reserve Bank has often been criticised that it pursued the objective of controlling inflation and achieving price stability and neglected the objective of promoting economic growth. Monetary policy can promote economic growth through ensuring adequate availability of credit and lower cost of credit. There are two types of credit requirements of businesses. First, they have to finance their requirements of working capital and for importing needed raw materials and machines from abroad. Secondly, they need credit for financing investment in projects for building fixed capital. Easy availability of credit at low interest rate stimulates investment and thereby quickens economic growth.

However, during the seventies, eighties and the first half of nineties of the 20th century, Reserve Bank followed a tight monetary policy under which Cash Reserve Ratio (CRR) and Statutory Liquidity Ratio (SLR) were continually raised to restrict the availability of credit for private sector. Besides, lending rates of interest were kept at high levels which discouraged private investment. This tight monetary policy worked against promoting growth.

Price Stability Vs Economic Growth. However, in the opinion of Prof. Rangarajan, there is no conflict between the objectives of price stability and growth. Price stability, according to him, is a means to ensure economic growth. To quote him, "*It is price stability which provides the appropriate environment under which growth can occur and social justice can be ensured.*" In our opinion, this may be true in the long run but in the short run there exists *trade off between growth and inflation.* To ensure higher economic growth the adequate expansion of money supply and greater availability of credit at a lower rate of interest is needed. But large expansion in money supply and bank credit leads to the increase in aggregate demand which tends to cause a higher rate of inflation. This raises the issue of what is *acceptable trade off*

2. *Op. cit.*, p. 7.

between growth and inflation, that is, what rate of inflation is acceptable to promote growth through appropriate monetary policy. Expert Committee on monetary policy headed by Late Prof. Chakravarty suggested a target of 4 per cent as "the acceptable rise in prices". According to it, the growth of money supply and availability of credit should be so regulated that rate of inflation does not exceed 4 per cent per annum. However, C. Rangarajan, former Governor of Reserve Bank fixed a higher target, namely, 5 to 6 per cent rate of inflation in the context of objective of achieving 6 to 7 per cent rate of economic growth. To quote him, "keeping the price and growth objectives in view the money supply growth should be so regulated that inflation rate comes down initially to 6 to 7 per cent and eventually to 5 to 6 per cent. That indeed must be the goal of monetary policy."[3]

Exchange Rate Stability

It may be noted that in the context of the openness of the economy and floating exchange rate system, as is the case of the Indian economy today, the objective of achieving higher rate of economic growth through monetary measures may also conflict with objective of exchange rate stability, that is, value of rupee in terms of the US dollar and other foreign currencies. Whereas prevention of the depreciation of rupee requires tightening of monetary policy, that is, raising of interest rate and reducing liquidity of the banking system so that banks restrict their credit supply, the promotion of growth objective requires lower lending rates of interest and greater availability of credit for encouraging private investment. It is this dilemma of conflicting objectives of achieving higher economic growth or exchange rate stability that has often been faced in India.

Until 1991, India followed fixed exchange rate system and only occasionally devalued the rupee with the permission of IMF. The policies of floating exchange rate and increasing openness and globalisation of the Indian economy, adopted since 1991 have made the exchange rate of rupee quite volatile. The changes in capital inflows and capital outflows and changes in demand for and supply of foreign exchange, particularly US dollar, arising from the imports and exports cause great fluctuations in the foreign exchange rate of rupee. In order to prevent large depreciation and appreciation of foreign exchange rate Reserve Bank has to take suitable monetary measures to ensure foreign exchange rate stability. Owing to the fixed exchange rate system prior to 1991 the concern about foreign exchange rate had not played a significant role in the formulation of monetary policy.

Today, the exchange rate of rupee is determined by demand for and supply of foreign exchange (say, US dollar). When there is mismatch between demand for and supply of foreign exchange, external value of rupee changes. For instance, in November-December 2011 there was sharp depreciation of Indian rupee as against US dollar with the value of rupee falling from ₹ 48 per US dollar in August 2011 to ₹ 53.70 per US dollar on Dec. 15, 2011 caused by the increase in demand for dollars from (1) the corporate sector for financing their imports, (2) Foreign Institutional Investors (FII) who wanted to take out their dollars from India (*i.e.*, capital outflow) to the US due to uncertainty caused by Eurozone sovereign debt crisis, and (3) increase in demand for US dollar by the Indian banks on the instructions of the public sector undertakings for financing necessary imports from abroad. Since export earnings and capital inflows which determine the supply of dollars did not rise adequately, mismatch between demand and supply of dollars had arisen causing the depreciation of rupee as against the US dollar.

Thus when there is large current account deficit (CAD) that exceeds the comfortable level (which in India is estimated at around 2.5 per cent of GDP) it tends to depreciate the Indian rupee. In 2011-12 and 2012-13 there was current account deficit of 4.2% and 4.7% of GDP respectively. This is too high a current account deficit which put downward pressure on the exchange rate of Indian rupee. The depreciation of rupee raises the costs

3. C. Rangarajan, "*The Changing Context of Monetary Policy*". Address at 31st Convocation of the Indian Statistical Institute, March 31, 1997.

of imports which adds to the inflationary pressures in the Indian economy. Therefore, reducing current account deficit to the comfortable level is not only essential for exchange rate stability but also for controlling inflation and achieving price stability. Thus, according to D. Subbarao, the then governor of RBI, the widening current account deficit in the last two years (2011-12 and 2012-13) emerged as a major constraint for easing of monetary policy as by causing lower lending interest rates and large availability of funds with banks it will lead to more imports which will add to the current account deficit.

To arrest the fall in value of rupee Reserve Bank took several measures. RBI raised bank rate and repo rate and thus sending signals to the banks to raise their lending rates. Besides, it also raised cash reserve ratio (CRR) to reduce the liquidity in the banking system. First, Reserve Bank intervented by selling some dollars from its foreign exchange reserves in the foreign exchange market. This increased the supply of US dollars in the foreign exchange market and helped in arresting the fall in the foreign exchange rate of rupee. Besides, it eased the norms for foreign commercial borrowing (ECB) by the corporate firms to meet their requirements of US dollars for importing necessary raw materials and other inputs. Further, it removed the ceiling on interest rates on Non-resident Indian (NRI) deposits so that interest rates on them rise and capital inflows are attracted. As result of these measures, the exchange rate of rupee rose to ₹ 48.70 to a US dollar in February 2012. However, it again fell to ₹ 51 to a US dollar in the first week of April 2012.

The higher interest rates in India as a result of tight money policy also discouraged foreign institutional investors and Indian corporates to invest abroad. This also worked to reduce the demand for dollars which tended to prevent the fall in the value of the rupee.

On the contrary, when rupee appreciates, it raises the prices of Indian exports and make them uncompetitive. As a result, growth of exports is discouraged. This situation emerged during 2003-04. Due to the huge inflows of foreign exchange rate into India, supply of US $ increased substantially. As a result, value of US $ fell and the Indian rupee appreciated. Exchange rate of rupee per US $ which had gone down to about ₹ 48 per US $ rose to around ₹ 43.50 per US $ in the early 2004. In order to prevent the appreciation of Indian rupee RBI intervened and started buying US dollars from the market. As a result of this, demand for US $ in the market increased bringing about rise in the value of US dollar in terms of rupees or in other words, value of rupee in terms of US $ started falling. Thus, with the invention of RBI, value of rupee was stablised at a reasonable level.

It is clear from above that in the context of flexible exchange rate system, Reserve Bank has to intervene frequently to achieve stability of exchange rate at a reasonable level.

ROLE OF MONETARY POLICY IN ECONOMIC GROWTH

Economic growth implies the expansion in productive capacity or capital stock in the economy so that increases in real national output or income are attained. As is well known, economic growth can be speeded up by accelerating the rate of savings and investment in the economy. This requires the following steps:

(*a*) Increase in the aggregate rate of savings in the economy.

(*b*) Mobilisation of these savings so that they are made available for the purpose of investment and production.

(*c*) Increase in the rate of investment.

(*d*) Allocation of investment funds for productive purposes and priority sectors of the economy.

Proper monetary policy can help in producing favourable effects on the above requirements of economic growth. We explain below appropriate monetary policy measures to promote economic growth in developing countries.

Monetary Policy and Savings

Several monetary measures can be adopted to raise the aggregate rate of saving. First, a high interest rate policy can promote savings. In the fifties and sixties of the 20th century it was widely believed that interest rate reflected the price of capital and since capital was scarce in developing countries, the real interest rates should be kept at higher levels to promote saving so that capital accumulation is speeded up. However, this argument in favour of higher real interest rates in developing countries was based upon the belief that *savings were positively elastic or sensitive to the interest rate.*

It is worthwhile to mention the opposite viewpoint regarding interest rate policy which has gained large support in recent years. According to this view (emphasised by Keynes in his monetary theory), rate of interest represents the cost of investment, and lower the rate of interest, the greater will be inducement to invest. However, Keynes was of the view that investment was not much sensitive or elastic to lower rate of interest Dr. K.N.Raj argued that *since investment is an important factor determining economic growth in developing countries, it should be promoted by lowering the interest rate.* However, in our view, this is to look at demand-side of the investment problem. This is because whereas inducement to invest may be promoted by lowering the interest rate, the adequate amount of savings or resources needed to finance larger investment may not be forthcoming at lower interest rate.

Further, a low interest rate policy in developing countries like India is likely to promote not only more investment in inventories and purchases of luxury consumer goods such as cars, air-conditioners, luxury houses rather than investment in fixed capital goods but also induce savers to invest in unproductive assets such as gold, silver, jewellery and real estate. In our view, therefore in a developing economy to promote savings rate of interest must be high enough to ensure reasonable return to savers. For this purpose, nominal rate of interest must be at least 5 per cent higher than the current rate of inflation in the economy to provide incentives to the people to save. That is, *real interest rate* should not be less than 5 per cent. That is, if annual rate of inflation in the economy is 7 per cent, nominal interest rate should be 12 per cent so as to ensure 5 per cent real rate of interest per annum. It may be noted in recent years (2011-12 and 2012-13) in India low deposit rates offerred to the public by banks in India prompted the people to invest their savings in unproductive assets such as gold, jewellery, real estate. *This led to the fall in financial saving* required for productive investment. This has led the then finance minister Mr Chidambaram to announce issuing of *inflation-indexed bonds* on which nominal rate of interest will automatically rise with the increase in inflation rate.

In this connection it is worth while to mention the Indian experience in recent years that contradicts the view that savings are insensitive to interest rate. In year 2009-10 and 2010-11 when rates of interest on fixed deposits in banks were around 6 to 7 per cent per annum growth of bank deposits declined and were lower than the growth in demand for credit. In fact, due to lower (even negative) real rates of interest on bank deposits, people invested their savings in buying gold, silver, jewellery and real estate. Beside, in recent years, 2009-10, 2010-11 and 2011-12 a higher rate of inflation eroded the real return on saving, which led to drop in national saving rate to 30 per cent of GDP in 2012-13 as against 36 per cent of GDP in 2007-08. This adversely affected rate of capital formation which fell to around 35 per cent in 2011-12 as against 38 per cent of GDP reached in 2007-08. This led to lowering of growth rate to 6.7 per cent in 2011-12 and 5.1 per cent in 2012-13 from 9.5 per cent in 2007-08.

If follows from above that savings for financing investment cannot be taken for granted. Savers must be ensured reasonable return so as to induce them to save more so that large resources are made available for investment in fixed capital stock. If monetary policy in a developing country is to promote economic growth it must aim at raising the rate of saving. For this purpose, it must ensure *reasonable real rate of interest* to provide incentives for saving.

Therefore, with the rise in rate of inflation nominal rate of interest should also be raised to keep incentives for saving intact.

Besides, the monetary policy can play a strategic role in increasing national savings by promoting the expansion of banking facilities and other financial intermediaries in the developing countries, especially in their rural areas. With more bank branches in under-banked and under-developed regions, the people who consume away their surplus incomes, will be induced to save them in the form of bank deposits which are quite safe as a store of value. The commercial banking encourages thrift or propensity to save by offering a return on savings in the form of interest rate on bank deposits. It also induces more savings by providing outlets for fruitful investment of the savings by the people who would have otherwise put them to unproductive or wasteful uses such as buying land, real estate, gold and jewellery. But to tap and raise savings sufficiently and to prevent its unproductive use banks and other financial institutions need to be numerous and dispersed throughout the economy in both the urban and rural areas. Speaking from the development experience of various countries. Prof. Lewis, a development economist, has emphasised that the volume of savings depends partly upon how widespread banking and other financial institutions are. To quote him, "*if the saving institutions are placed under the individual's nose, people save more than if the nearest saving institutions is some distance away.*"[4]

Thus growth in saving in the form of bank deposits will be greater if banking facilities are vastly expanded in the country. Similarly, with the expansion of other financial institutions, the people will feel induced to save more for buying financial assets. It is generally agreed that the rapid expansion of banking facilities after the nationalisation of major commercial banks in 1969 promoted by the Reserve Bank of India has contributed considerably to the growth of aggregate savings. While the aggregate saving rate has gone up from 16.5 per cent in 1969-70 to 22.7 per cent in 1982-83, bank deposits which accounted for 8.7 per cent of total domestic savings in 1969-70, accounted for 22.5 per cent of these savings in 1982-83. The number of commercial banks offices increased from 8,262 in July 1969 to 44,521 in 1984 and to 62,350 in 1995. Although it is difficult to establish a precise quantitative relationship between expansion of bank branches and savings in the form of bank deposits, its significant contribution to the promotion of savings cannot be denied. Therefore, the future branch expansion policy must fully take into account the untapped saving potential of under-banked and under-developed regions.

It may be noted that in order to facilitate mobilisation of an increasing proportion of savings by the banking system it is essential to maintain a reasonable price stability. For, as Dr. Manmohan Singh, when he was Governor of Reserve Bank of India, pointed out, "*it is only, under conditions of reasonable price stability that people will have less attraction for savings in the form of physical assets such as gold, real estate and excessive accumulation of inventories.*" Further, according to him, if banks are to mobilise adequate amount of savings in the form of bank deposits, interest rates on bank deposits must remain positive in real terms. That is, the nominal rate of interest be maintained at a higher level than the rate of inflation. If through excessive rise in nominal prices, real rate of interest becomes negative, people will be discouraged to save.

Monetary Policy and Investment

Monetary policy has an important role to play in boosting up the level of investment by making available savings or resources mobilised by banks for purposes of investment and production. The banks fulfil this task by offering bank credit for investment to business and industry.

Cost of Credit. It may be noted that Keynesian theory of monetary policy emphasises that the effect of a change in the supply of money on the level of production and investment operates through the changes in the rate of interest. The increase in the supply of money by

4. Arthur Lewis, *Theory of Economic Growth*. George Allien and Unwin, 1960.

the monetary authority will cause the market rate of interest to fall. At lower rate of interest, the entrepreneurs will be induced to invest more. Accordingly, Keynesian monetary theory has been described as "*cost of credit*" theory. However, Keynes himself and several economists after him believed that this effect of changes in money supply on investment which operates through rate of interest was not very vigorous. It had been asserted that investment in fixed capital was interest inelastic. That is why Keynes did not have much faith in the effectiveness of monetary policy and instead emphasised the role of fiscal policy in influencing the level of economic activity. However, it is now generally believed by the economists that since interest is important cost of investment, investment demand is fairly interest elastic. Therefore, to promote investment easy monetary policy should be adopted provided the economy is not facing the inflationary pressures.

It may be noted that in the post-reform period from 1996 to 2006 in India, persistently soft interest rate policy had been adopted to promote private investment so as to revive the industrial sector whose growth slowed down from 1996-97 to 2002-03. Following the soft-interest rate policy of Reserve Bank of India prime lending rates of interest of commercial banks which varied between 15 to 16 per cent prior 1996, were reduced over a period of time to 10 to 11 per cent in 2003-04. Again when in September 2008, global financial crisis occurred as a result of bust of housing bubble in the US there had been worldwide slowdown. Reserve Bank of India in October 2008 reduced its repo rate of interest from 9 per cent in August 2008 to 7 per cent in October 2008 and further to 4.75 per cent on March 4, 2009 to promote private investment so as to prevent sharp economic slowdown in India.

However, the soft interest rate policy does not always, especially during recession, achieve much success in stimulating private investment. This is because when there are sluggish demand conditions, the existing fixed capital is underutilised, and it is not profitable to make more investment for expanding fixed capital stock. Private enterprises are therefore not willing to make further investment despite lower interest rates. It is for such economic conditions that it has been said that '*you can bring the horse to water but you cannot make it drink*'. Therefore, in our view, the favourable effect of lower interest rate on investment has been exaggerated. As Keynes emphasised it is the *prospective yield from investment which plays a crucial role in determining investment*. Unless the private business class expects to earn sufficient profits, they will not increase their investment. Unless the expectations of the business class about profit making are raised or what he called *animal spirits* of entrepreneurs are revived, private investment will not increase. The profit expectations can be raised by government by increasing its own expenditure, especially on infrastructure projects which through its multiplier effect will raise the aggregate demand for goods and services. Besides, through its fiscal policy the government can provide liberal depreciation allowance in calculating tax liability. This will raise the internal rate of return. However, the profit expectations of businessmen depend on demand for goods produced by the capital assets in which they plan to invest. Thus, "*the only way in which businessmen can be persuaded to invest more is if they genuinely believe that the demand for the output of the assets will be there when they have been acquired ..... Consequently, the better way of increasing prospective yield is to increase demand either by increasing consumption demand or by increasing government expenditure*".[5]

Availability of Credit

It is noteworthy that a recent monetary theory emphasises the *credit-availability effect* on investment of the changes in the supply of money. According to this, lowering cash reserve ratio for the banks causes expansion in the money supply with the banks which directly enlarges the

5. Stonier and Hague, A *Textbook of Economic Theory*, 5th Edition, Pearson Education, Ltd. 1980, p.539

availability of bank credit for investment purposes and thereby raises the level of investment in the economy of the business firms are willing to make investment. On the contrary, increase in cash reserve ratio will directly reduce the availability of credit and hence tend to decrease investment in the economy. The credit availability of bank can be increased by lowering the cash reserve ratio (CRR) and statutory liquidity ratio (SLR) of the banks by RBI.

Friedman's View and Effectiveness of Monetary Policy

It is worthwhile to mention here the views of Friedman regarding monetary policy for the effectiveness of increasing liquidity in the banking system and softening of interest rate to revive economic growth. Milton Friedman had argued that Great Depression in the US during the early thirties would have been stopped in its tracks by the Federal Reserve simply by providing banks with enough liquidity which would have ensured adequate increase in the money supply. In the US, during the recent period of financial crisis, 2007-09, Federal Reserve injected large liquidity in the American banking system and lowered its key interest rate to almost zero and still the recession in the US deepened further. It has now become evident that preventing recession is not so easy through easy monetary policy as believed by Friedman and other monetarists. Monetary policy alone has proved to be ineffective to get rid of recession as Keynes had asserted during the thirties and laid stress on fiscal policy of large-scale deficit spending by the government. It is the Keynesian policies of increasing Government expenditure and reducing taxes not only in the US but also in other countries including India that were adopted to overcome recession or prevent slowdown in the economies.

In India also in 2008-09 and 2009-10 for preventing slowdown by boosting investment and consumption demand we did not rely on monetary policy alone but also provided fiscal stimulus to prevent slowdown is the Indian economy. As regards effectiveness of monetary policy in preventing recession or slowdown in economic growth is concerned the remarks of Paul Krugman, a Nobel Prize winner for economics for the year 2008 are worth quoting. He writes, "*It turns out, however, that preventing depression is not that easy after all. Under Bernanke's leadership, the Fed has been supplying liquidity like an engine crew trying to put out a five-alarm fire, and the money supply has been rising rapidly yet credit remains scarce and the economy is still in free fall .... Friedman's claim that monetary policy could have prevented the Great depression was an attempt to refute the analysis of John Maynard Keynes, who argued that monetary policy is ineffective under depression conditions and that fiscal policy – large-scale deficit spending by the government – is needed to fight mass unemployment. The failure of monetary policy in the current crisis shows that Keynes had it right the first time. And Keynesian thinking lies behind Obama's plan to rescue the economy*".[6]

We have seen above that private investment is *mainly determined* by the aggregate demand for products and availability of credit rather than cost of credit (i.e., rate of interest). Of course, lowering of rate of interest or cost of credit plays a role in increasing private investment, but not a dominant role. We are now in a position to spell out the role of monetary policy in promoting investment in a developing country like India. Further, in this context it is noteworthy that in developing countries, government or public investment plays a crucial role in the development of their economies. Therefore, monetary policy requires to promote not only private investment but also public investment by making available adequate amount of credit.

Monetary Policy and Public Investment. Let us first explain the promotion of public investment through monetary policy. Monetary policy has to ensure that the banking system contributes to the financing of the planned public investment. For this a good part of bank deposits

6. Paul Krugman, Fighting of Depression, *New York Times*, News Service, Feb. 2009.

mobilised by the banks has to be invested in government and other approved securities so that the government should be able to finance its planned investment, especially in infrastructure. At present in India, there is lack of infrastructure such as power, roads, highways, ports, irrigation facilities which is obstructing economic growth. Besides, at some times private industry faces demand recession. In this situation public investment is an ideal tool to develop infrastructure and to increase the demand for industrial products through the operation of multiplier. This will stimulate private investment. Thus a developing country such as ours, policy of raising public investment will *crowd in* private investment rather than *crowding it out*. In India a new instrument of monetary policy has been designed to secure larger resources from the banking system for financing public investment. This instrument has been described as *statutory liquidity ratio* (SLR). According to this, *in addition to cash reserve requirements* banks in India are required to keep a minimum proportion of its total demand and time deposits in the form of specified liquid assets. And the most important specified liquid asset for this purposes is the investment in government securities.

Thus, in a pre-reform period (i.e., before 1991) when public sector played a more crucial role in promoting investment statutory liquidity ratio (SLR) was raised to a high level of 38.5 per cent. That is, banks had to invest in government securities to the extent of 38.5 per cent of their demand and time deposits. Since the economic reforms of liberalisation and privatisation that were started in 1991 private sector has been assigned a greater role in economic development, statutory liquidity ratio (SLR) has been reduced to 25 per cent so that more bank credit be made available for private investment. To raise the lendable resources of the banks, cash reserve ratio of the banks has been kept at a low level.

RELATION BETWEEN MONETARY POLICY AND FISCAL POLICY

Monetary policy in a planned economy of India cannot be framed independently of fiscal policy for achieving growth with price stability are the objectives of both these policies. In India the Reserve Bank of India has often adopted accommodative monetary policy to government's fiscal policy. *Prior to 1991 when economic reforms were initiated the basic goal of monetary policy was to neutralise the impact of large fiscal deficits of the government.* To boost public sector investment for accelerating economic growth there was large increase in government expenditure under various Five Year plans which was financed by borrowing by the government and deficit financing (i.e., monetatisation of budget deficit). Both government borrowing from the market and deficit financing leads to the increase in aggregate demand and have therefore potential for causing inflation. Therefore, to ensure adequate funds to meet the borrowing requirements of the government the statuary liquidity ratio (SLR) of the banks was raised to the maximum limit of 38.5 per cent. That is, banks were to buy government securities to this extent.

Besides to check inflation, cash reserve ratio (CRR) of banks was raised to a high level of 15 per cent. The high cash reserve leaves less funds with the banks to lend to the private commercial sector. In this way large expansion of credit for private sector was prevented. To quote C. Rangarajan the former Governor of the Reserve Bank of India, "Until the overall reforms process was initiated in 1991 the basic goal of monetary management took the form of compensatory increase in the cash reserve ratio (CRR) for banks, controls on the growth of commercial credit (mainly to the private enterprises sector) and adjustments of administered interest rates. The fixation of CRR and SLR at their maximum levels *crowded out* credit for the commercial sector. Thus, even when money supply was growing at a rapid rate, private sector could not get the needed credit for financing industry and trade". Explaining the monetary policy adopted prior to reform process of 1991, Dr. Y.V. Reddy, also a former Governor of the Reserve Bank of India writes, "given the command and controlled nature of the Indian economy, the RBI had to resort to direct instruments like interest rate regulation selective credit control and cash reserve ratio (CRR) as major policy instruments. *These instruments were used to neutralise the monetary impact of the government's budgetary operations*".

In the recent post-reforms period also, accommodative nature of monetary policy to the government's fiscal policy may be noted. In October 2008, a severe global financial crisis gripped the world economy following from the bankruptsy of Lehman's brothers in the US. This affected the growth of our exports and also led to the capital outflows from the Indian economy leading to the depreciation of the Indian economy and crash in Indian stock market. As a result, industrial and overall growth of the Indian economy started declining. To check the economic slowdown the government increased its expenditure, especially on infrastructure projects, and cut indirect taxes such as excise duty service tax to boost private sector investment and expenditure. To supplement and accommodate government expansionary policy, the Reserve Bank reversed its earlier tight monetary policy in October 2008 and to boost private sector investment it reduced its repo rate from 9 per cent in July 2008 to 7.5 per cent in October 2008 and further to 4.75 per cent in March 2009. Similarly, RBI reduced cash reserve ratio (CRR) from 9 per cent in July 2008 to 6.5 per cent in October 2008 and further to 5 per cent in March 2009 to make more funds available with banks to buy government securities to finance its borrowing and also to the private sector for expanding investment.

Thus, the RBI's monetary policy has been accommodatory in the sense that it provided support to government's fiscal stimulus package to promote investment and growth. When in the later half of 2009-10 inflation rate again started rising the RBI began the process of withdrawing from the accommodative monetary policy stance in October 2009 and started tightening its monetary policy to fight inflation. Again in 2015, when inflation as measured by consumer price index (CPI) has been brought under control (CPI inflation was estimated to be around 5 per cent in March 2015), to support government's expansionary fiscal policy to boost economic growth, RBI reduced its repo rate three times in 2015 (upto June) each by 25 basis points so that banks should reduce their lending rates and private investment is picked up.

QUESTIONS FOR REVIEW

1. Discuss the objectives of monetary policy in a developing economy.
2. What is meant by price stability ? "Of the various objectives price stability is perhaps the one that can be pursued most effectively by monetary policy" (C. Rangarajan). Discuss.
3. "The objective of achieving price stability through monetary policy clashes with its objective of economic growth". Do you agree ? Discuss.
4. "Both the large depreciation and appreciation of rupee is bad." Explain the measures that have been taken by RBI from time to time to ensure exchange rate stability.
5. Explain the role of monetary policy to promote economic growth in the economy.
6. Explain the role of monetary policy in promoting saving and investment in developing countries.
7. Explain the role of monetary policy in ensuring price stability in a developing economy. What tools of monetary have been used by Reserve Bank to control inflation in the Indian economy and with what success ?
8. Explain monetary policy of Reserve Bank of India before 1996. Was it targeted only at controlling inflation in the Indian economy ?

9. From October 2008 to January 2009 Reserve Bank of India followed easy monetary policy to promote private investment and revive the Indian economy from recession. Explain, what monetary steps it had taken in this direction and how far they succeeded in raising investment.
10. What are repo rate and reverse repo rate ? How are they used to regulate liquidity in the Indian economy ?
11. Monetary policy faces the ticklish problem of trade-off between inflation and growth. Has RBI successfully tackled this problem since 1996 ? Explain.
12. To get rid of recession, monetary policy is ineffective and fiscal policy can be successfully used to revive the economy. In the light of this Keynes's view, comment on the success of policies adopted in the US and India to tackle recession/slowdown during 2007-09.
13. Despite raising repo rate 13 times from January 2010 to November 2011, by the Reserve Bank of India, inflation remained at the elevated level of above 9 per cent year-on-year basis. Discuss why this dare monetary policy failed to check inflation.
14. Explain, 'growth vs. inflation' dilemma faced by the Reserve Bank of India in the conduct of its tight monetary policy.

50 CHAPTER

Role of Fiscal Policy in Economic Development: Taxation

Introduction

In this chapter, we shall explain the role of fiscal policy for mobilising resources for economic growth and for achieving the objectives of equity and stability. Fiscal policy is concerned with the various sources of public revenue and pattern of government expenditure. Today, since government plays a crucial role in the working of an economy, understanding of role of fiscal policy for mobilising resources to spend up investment or capital formation is of great importance.

The government announces its fiscal policy in its annual budget. Fiscal policy relates to how the government raises its revenue and how it spends it. What new taxes are levied, what changes in the existing tax rates are made, how much expenditure government wants to spend on defence, education, health, capital formation, economic infrastructure are all proposed in the budget.

Classical economists were of the view that sound budget should always be balanced, that is, government expenditure should equal government revenue. They thought that deficit budget meant more borrowing by the government to meet the increased expenditure. According to them, this increases public debt which raises the burden on future generations. However, after Keynesian revolution role of budget has underwent a basic change. Today budget is not regarded as a mere *instrument for raising revenue for the government. Instead, budget is an important tool of economic policy to achieve certain objectives*. At times of recession, there is a need to increase aggregate demand. To overcome recession, the government should increase its expenditure and lower taxes and make a deficit budget. This will help to raise aggregate demand and achieve equilibrium at full-employment. On the contrary, at times of severe inflation government has to reduce its expenditure and increase direct taxes so as to eliminate excess demand. Thus, balanced budgets are no longer considered as sacred. Whether government budget should be balanced, deficit or surplus depends on the prevailing economic situation and the objectives of economic policy. Thus, after Keynesian revolution budget making has acquired a functional role of maintaining economic stability at full-employment level. Later, promoting steady growth in the long run also became the objective of fiscal policy both in the developed and developing countries. Therefore, *the present view of budget making is not one of mere resource raising for the government but one of serving as an instrument for promoting full employment, price stability and steady economic growth*. This view of budget making as a tool for performing some economic functions or achieving certain economic policy objectives has been called as *Function Finance*.

Objectives of Fiscal Policy in India

In a developing country such as India, taxation, government expenditure and borrowing have to play a very important role in accelerating economic development. In fact, fiscal policy is a powerful instrument in the hands of the government by means of which it can achieve the objectives of economic growth. Rapid economic growth is needed to solve the problem of poverty and unemployment. There are several peculiar characteristics of a developing country which necessitate the adoption of a special fiscal policy to accelerate investment which ensures a rapid economic growth. There are vast and diverse resources, human and material, which are lying underutilised in a developing country. Such countries have weak infrastructure, *i.e*, they lack adequate means of transport and communications, roads, ports, highways, irrigation and power. They also lack technical know-how. Indian population is increasing at a rapid rate which necessitates rapid economic growth to meet the requirements of the rapidly-growing population. Above all, there are acute problems of mass poverty and unemployment which for their solution require a high rate of investment to bring about rapid economic growth. In order to tackle these problems, a suitable fiscal and taxation policy is called for.

In developing countries like India, budget has to play a more important role. The developing countries face a more difficult problem of how to generate a higher economic growth so as to tackle the problems of poverty and unemployment. Therefore, fiscal policy has to play a special role of promoting economic growth in the developing countries like India so as to tackle the twin problems of poverty and unemployment. Besides, India has been facing the problem of *inflation* from time to time. Inflation adversely affects economic growth and hurts the poor most. Therefore, besides accelerating economic growth, fiscal policy has to control inflation and thus to ensure price stability. Besides, fiscal policy has to reduce large inequalities of income distribution and to ensure just distribution of fruits of economic growth. Thus the fiscal policy in a developing country such as ours has to "strike a fine balance among three mutually reinforcing objectives of growth, stability and equity." Further, for developing countries more economic growth is not enough, the budgetary policies should be so designed so as to ensure removal of poverty and unemployment. Therefore, the function of fiscal policy has not only to raise resources for development and to achieve optimum allocation of resources, but also has to promote fair distribution of income and expansion in employment opportunities. This is the functional view of public finance in the context of the developing countries.

The principal objectives of fiscal policy in a developing economy such as ours are:

1. to mobilise resources for accelerating investment, especially for the public sector;
2. to promote economic growth in the private sector by providing incentives to save and invest;
3. to restrain inflationary forces in the economy in order to ensure price stability; and
4. to ensure equitable distribution of income and wealth so that fruits of economic growth are fairly distributed, that is, to achieve **inclusive growth**.

In the Indian economy, the government has to play a very active role in promoting economic growth and fiscal policy is an important instrument that the state must use. In a democratic society, there is an inherent dislike for direct (physical) controls and regulation by the state. The entrepreneurs would not like to be ordered about to produce this or that, how much to produce or where to produce. Fiscal incentives in the form of tax concessions, rebates or subsidies are, therefore, preferable. Similarly, the consumers would not like to be told directly to curtail their consumption or to consume this and not to consume that. Taxation of commodities and services whose consumption is to be discouraged is therefore preferable. Hence, a democratic state must rely on indirect methods of control and regulation and this is done through fiscal and monetary policies. Thus, in democratic countries, fiscal policy is a powerful and least undesirable weapon on which government can rely for promoting investment and economic growth.

Capital formation is of strategic importance for bringing about rapid economic growth. It is, therefore, necessary to achieve a higher ratio of savings to national income. In early days of capitalism, payment of low wages and the existence of inequalities of income helped capital formation in the present-day developed countries. But no democratic country can adopt this method in modern times; the effort rather is to raise wages and reduce inequalities of income and wealth. Under a regime of socialist dictatorship such as that prevailed in erstwhile Soviet Russia capital formation was brought about by ruthlessly curtailing consumption and keeping down the standards of living. But in modern democracies with every adult person having a right to vote very low levels of living for a long time is not feasible. *Hence the state must rely on instruments of fiscal policy to mobilise resources for economic development*. Taxation can be used to to raise collective savings for public investment and also at the same time to promote private investment. A well-conceived scheme of taxation is an important way of raising ratio of savings to national income which is one of the crucial determinants of the rate of economic growth. However, is a liberal mixed economy such as ours the task of fiscal policy is not only to raise saving ratio for acceleration of growth but also to improve investment eliminate for private sector so that higher rate of investment be achieved. As Nurkse says, "*public finance assumes a new significance in the face of the problem of capital formation in underdeveloped countries.*"[1]

On the expenditure side, there is positive need for public investment, especially in those spheres of economic activity where the private investments are not easily attracted, for example, the development of power resources, roads and highway, ports and airports, means of transport and communications, basic heavy industries, social infrastructure such as education and research, public health etc. Such investments are very often the very foundations of rapid economic advance. Thus, the role of fiscal policy for mobilising resources for public investment in physical infrastructure, and education and health is of crucial importance in accelerating the pace of economic growth in developing countries.

As mentioned above, capital formation is an important determinant of economic growth. For accelerating the rate of capital formation, savings and investment rate in the economy has to be stepped up. For this purpose, savings have to be mobilised and channelled into productive investment. The alternative means other than fiscal policy available to promote savings and investment in the developing countries are not very effective in mobilising enough resources for investment and capital formation.

Fiscal policy has also to promote *voluntary savings*. There exist large inequalities of income in these countries and this should ensure a large voluntary savings by the richer sections of the society. But the richer sections in them indulge in conspicious consumption such as building of luxury houses, indulging in five star culture, buying air-conditioners and such other things and, therefore, the volume of their voluntary savings is inadequate. This propensity to indulge in conspicuous consumption is reinforced by demonstration effect which is operating strongly these days due to the development of better communication system and superior means of advertisement. Further, rich people tend to invest their rising incomes on unproductive investment such as gold and jewellery, real estate etc., which yield high profits due to their appreciation. In view

1. Ragnar Nurkse, *Problems of Capital Formation in Underdeveloped Countries.*

of these, without proper fiscal policy savings cannot be made available for raising significantly the rate of capital formation.

Direct Taxes and Mobilisation of Resources

Fiscal policy, if properly designed, is an efficient and equitable way of mobilising resources for augmenting public investment. Through it not only collective public savings can be raised for financing public investment but also at the same time private savings and investment can be encouraged. In fact *taxation may be the most effective means of increasing the total volume of savings and investments in an economy where the propensity to consume is normally high.* Further, the fiscal policy can be so devised that not only the objective of rapid capital accumulation or growth, but also other objectives of economic policy such as equitable distribution of income and wealth, price stability and promotion of employment opportunities can be achieved.

Now the question arises what should be the taxation structure of a developing economy which will mobilise the potential economic surplus to the maximum, that is, what kinds of taxes be levied, how much progressive should be their rates and what should be the exemptions and concessions in various taxes. This is, however, a highly controversial issue. It has been suggested that an appropriate tax which would mobilise resources or mop up economic surplus is the progressive income tax. Income tax is imposed not only on the incomes of individuals but also on the profits of the corporate companies. Thus there is *personal income tax* and *corporate income tax* (that is, tax on net profits earned by corporate companies). *In India and the other developing countries income has been regarded as a good base for direct taxation.* And the imposition of highly progressive income tax not only mops up relatively greater amount of resources but also tend to reduce inequalities of income. However, a progressive income tax with a high marginal rates of taxes adversely affects private saving and investment and also raises the propensity to evade the tax. In view of this, two proposals have been put forward to make the income tax both as an effective instrument of resource mobilisation for the public sector and of providing incentives to save and invest. First, Prof. Kaldor of Cambridge University, who in 1956 was invited by government of India to suggest reforms in the Indian tax system for mobilising resources for development, suggested that whereas the marginal rate of income tax be reduced to, say, 45 to 50 per cent, expenditure tax be levied to discourage the people belonging to upper income brackets from dissipating their income in conspicuous consumption. According to him, this will also reduce the tendency to evade income tax on the one hand and promote private savings on the other. The second proposal to reform the income tax put forward by others is that whereas marginal rates of income tax be kept high but some exemptions for approved forms of saving and investment be allowed to the individuals. This will channel individual savings along desired lines and at the same time mobilise resources for development.

Recently supply-side economics has pointed out that increase in income tax rate beyond a point will lead to reduction in tax revenue because of adverse effect on incentives to work, save and invest. In this connection, the concept of Laffer curve has been suggested. According to the Laffer curve concept put forward by an American economist Arthur Laffer raising income tax rate beyond a point will yield lower tax revenue. This is because higher income tax rates adversely affect incentives to work, save and investment and are therefore counter-productive. Thus higher income tax rates beyond a certain point causes reduction in supply of labour and capital and lead to lower national income and tax revenue. A Laffer curve is shown in Figure 50.1 where along the *X*-axis income tax rate is measured and along the *Y*-axis tax revenue is measured. It will be seen from this figure that as rate of income tax is increased, in the beginning tax revenue rises but after the tax rate t_3, further increases in tax rate yields lower tax revenue. At tax rate t_3, tax revenue revenue $t_3 H$ is maximum. Empirical studies have found that tax rate in the range of 30 to 35 per cent is optimal from the viewpoint of maximum tax revenue.

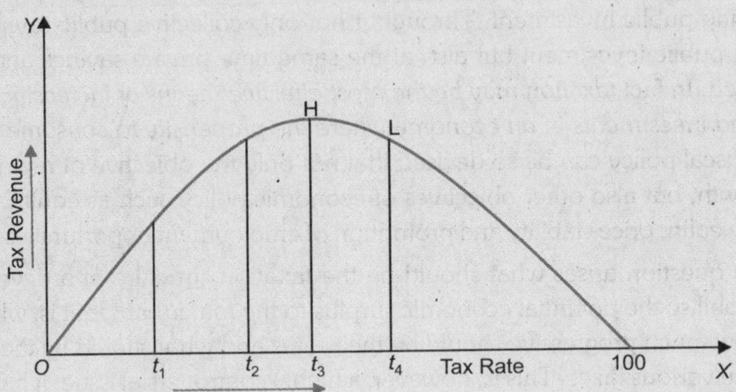

Fig. 50.1. Laffer curve depicting relationship between income tax rate and tax revenue

Apart from the income tax on individuals and companies, the imposition of other direct taxes such as capital gains tax, wealth tax, gift tax, and estate duty are also needed to mobilise sufficient resources for capital formation. Unlike income tax, these capital taxes do not have any adverse effects on incentives to save and invest.[2] They are also important instruments of reducing inequalities of income and wealth. Because of these advantages, Professor Kaldor in his report of taxation reforms in India recommended the imposition of these capital taxes and this recommendation was accepted and the annual wealth tax and gift tax were levied in 1957 with estate duty having been already introduced in 1954.

Agricultural Taxation and Resource Mobilisation. A good part of national income in India and other developing countries originates in the agricultural sector which has substantial economic surplus which can be tapped for capital formation. This economic surplus mainly goes to rich farmers, landlords, merchants and other intermediaries and, in the absence of suitable taxation on agriculture, this is used for conspicuous consumption and for investing in unproductive activities such as buying gold, jewellery, real estate. Thus, according to Professor Kaldor, "*the taxation of agriculture by one means or another has a critical role to play in the acceleration of economic development.*"[3] Further, owing to economic growth in general and agricultural development in particular income of the agricultural class and therefore economic surplus enormously increases and therefore need to be mopped up for further development. Besides, the agricultural sector has to be taxed not only because it has a potential surplus but also to achieve maximum utilisation of land through devising a system of land taxation which would penalise poor use of good land. In this regard, a progressive land tax "the effective rates of taxation of which vary with the total value of landholdings of the family unit" may be suitable one. Besides this, progressive agricultural income tax with appropriate exemption may be levied to tap resources from affluent sections of the agricultural sector.

2. See, S. Gulati, *Capital Taxation in India,* Orient Longman, 1957.
3. N. Kaldor, The Role of Taxation in Economic Development, in E.A.G. Robinson (ed.), *Problems in Economic Development,* 1965, p. 177.

It may be noted that as compared to the non-agricultural sector, agricultural sector in India and other developing countries is quite under-taxed. Land revenue which was at one time the greatest source of revenue for government has now become an insignificant yielder of revenue. In the context of India, Agricultural Taxation Committee under the Chairmanship of Dr. K.N. Raj recommended Agricultural Holdings Tax (AHT) which was to be imposed at a progressive rate on the rateable value of an agricultural holdings of ₹ 5000 and above. It was expected to yield annually ₹ 200 crores. However, Agricultural Holdings Tax was found to be difficult to assess and administer. In our view, a *graded surcharge on the existing land revenue* will be far easier to assess and administer and make land revenue a more elastic source of revenue. In 2002, Kelkar Committe on tax reforms also recommended imposition of tax on agricultural income, proceeds from which were to be distributed among the states. But this was vehemently opposed by the members of the ruling party. However, it may be noted that in India agricultural taxation is a state subject and there is lack of political will on the part of the state governments to raise the level of land taxation in a country. But if sufficient resources are to be mobilised for development, the level of agricultural taxation has to be raised.

Role of Taxation in Promoting Private Saving and Investment

It is worth mentioning that in a mixed economy such as ours, there is need to raise not only the public savings and investment but also to promote private saving and investment so that the overall rate of saving and investment in the economy is stepped up. This implies that taxation measures should not impair incentives to save and invest of the people. Therefore, a developing economy encounters a crucial dilemma in augmenting larger resources for public investment on the one hand and to promote private savings and investment on the other. Thus, according to Prof. Heller, "Tax Policy faces a basic dilemma in its role as a an instrument of capital formation for economic development. On the one hand, high levels of taxes are necessary to finance that part of the development which falls in the government share and to mobilise for investment the private resources that might otherwise be dissipated. On the other hand, the lower the taxes the greater will be the inducement to private investment. The dilemma is worsened by the fact that those taxes which are most effective in capturing a large share of the gains from economic development for further capital formation are the ones most likely to affect the returns from private investment. *Only way of the dilemma may be to combine high rates of taxation in general, with preferential treatment for categories of desired development activity.*"

However, the empirical evidence of the last 20 years of tax reforms in India confirms the *Laffer curve* concept that increase in tax rate beyond a point causes total tax revenue to fall. Therefore, in our view, moderate rates of tax on income with preferential treatment of some desired development activities such as building of infrastructure can ensure higher private saving and investment. Private savings can be promoted in several other ways. First, interest on several types of private savings such as bank deposits, investment in units of Unit Trust of India and National Savings Certificates, and other approved forms of saving be exempted from taxation to a reasonable extent. This will encourage private savings through raising the rate of return on savings as the savers would earn some interest income free of income tax. Secondly, voluntary savings in certain selective lines such as voluntary contributions to provident fund, life insurance premium, certain specific units (of UTI) and National Savings Certificates be substantially exempted from income tax. This will also stimulate private savings by raising the rate of return on these savings. For, people will not only earn rate of interest or dividend but will save a good amount of income tax on these approved forms of savings.

Thirdly, as noted above, if very high progressivity in tax rates is avoided (that is, if rates of income taxes do not increase much with the increase in income) private saving and investment will be boosted up. The Laffer curve concept shows that the policy of moderate progressivity in tax rates will not only help to maintain incentives to save and investment but will also yield more revenue to the government. In view of the present author, the lower marginal rates of taxes will place more disposable income in the hands of higher income brackets which will tend to raise their conspicuous consumption, especially when goods catering to their frivolous wants are available in abundance these days through both domestic production and imports. As mentioned above, this is reinforced by the international demonstration effect which exercises a strong influence on the consumption behaviour of the richer sections of the Indian society. The increase in consumption can be discouraged by levying expenditure tax as proposed by Nicholas Kaldor.

Besides private savings, private investment can be directly encouraged through taxation. Firstly, in order to stimulate private investment, the *retained profits* which are reinvested by the business firms instead of distributing them among the shareholders can be exempted from taxation or taxed at preferential rates. Secondly, to boost private investment *liberal depreciation and investment allowances* can also to be allowed to the business firms which will be used for purposes of investment in new plant, equipment and machinery. Further, **subsidies on investment**, that is, tax break or tax rebate can also be provided by the government which generally prove to be a very effective way of promoting private investment.

Another important fiscal method of stimulating private investment in developing countries is *granting of tax holidays or relief from tax on the profits of new enterprises* for some specified period of time. Further, indirect taxes can also be manipulated in a variety of ways to promote private investment in certain selected fields of industrial activity. Thus exemption or lowering of sales tax or excise duties on some domestically produced important raw materials or lowering of import duties on raw materials and capital goods from abroad can provide a boost to private investment. Likewise, reduction of export duties may also bring about a healthy effect on investment outlook.

It needs to be stressed that various incentives to promote private savings and investment will prove effectively only if they are kept as simple, transparent, certain and stable as far as possible. A complicated schemes of incentives with frequent and arbitrary changes are likely to defeat the very purpose of these incentive schemes. Prof. Prest rightly points out, "*If the main purpose of investment incentives is to raise the long-term level of investment rather than offset cyclical downturns and this clearly is the case in underdeveloped countries ... the emphasis should be on the stability of these tax arrangements rather than their variability.*"[4]

It is important to note that private investment depends upon several factors such as size of the market, cost of inputs, availability of infrastructure facilities such as power, coal, oil, transport, availability of technical know-how. Tax incentives will prove effective only if conditions regarding these other factors are not unfavourable. Further, unless there is an efficient and competent system of tax administration it is very likely that incentives become tax loopholes. The businessmen in the developing countries tend to take advantages of these tax exemptions on bogus basis without fulfilling and carrying out the underlying intent of such concessions. An honest and efficient administrative machinery, therefore, remains the basic precondition for the purposeful use of incentives.[5]

4. See A.R. Prest, Fiscal Measures and Capital Accumulation in Agarwala and Singh (ed.), *Accelerating Investment in Developing Countries,* Oxford University Press.
5. A.R. Prest. *op. cit., p.* 445.

In India there has been revenue deficit throughout since 1980-81 which as per cent of GDP increased from 3.4 in 1990-91 to 4.4 in 2001-02 and to 5.2 per cent in 2009-10 but declined to 3.4 per cent 2010-11. It is important to note that *revenue deficit of the government indicates public disavings*. This shows that far from contributing to resources for investment and capital formation receipts from tax and non-tax revenue have not been sufficient to meet Central government current (*i.e.*, consumption) expenditure. As a result, borrowed funds (*i.e.*, capital receipts) have been used to finance the current government expenditure. Thus revenue deficit has been a great impediment to economic growth. This is because resources which could have been used to step up investment expenditure have been used to meet revenue expenditure.

Recognising this lacuna in India's fiscal system. Fiscal Responsibility Budget Management Act (FRBMA) was passed in 2003 which prescribed reduction of revenue deficit to zero by 2008-09. Accordingly, effort was made to raise more resources through taxation so as to achieve the target of zero revenue deficit by 2008-09. As percentage of GDP revenue deficit declined to 2.5% in 2005-06, to 1.9 per cent in 2006-07 and to 1.1 per cent in 2007-08. But during 2008-09 to meet the slowdown in the Indian economy and keep the growth momentum following global financial crisis, the government had to raise its expenditure and cut customs duties and excise duties to give *fiscal stimulus*. Consequently *revenue deficit* rose to 4.5 per cent of GDP in 2008-09. 5.2 per cent of GDP in 2009-10 but fell to 3.2 per cent in 2010-11. Accordingly, due to increase in government expenditure and cut in taxes to fight global meltdown following global financial crisis, gross fiscal deficit which had been reduced to 2.5 per cent of GDP in 2007-08 rose to 6.0 per cent in 2008-09 and 6.5 per cent of GDP in 2009-10 and was estimated at 4.8 in 2010-11 but at again went up to 5.7 per cent in 2011-12. For 2012-13 it has been contained at 5.2 per cent of GDP(RE). The target set for 2013-14 is 4.8% of GDP.

Merits of Direct Taxes for Resource Mobilisation. As seen above, as an instrument of resource mobilisation for development direct taxes enjoy several advantages. (1) They raise resources in a non-inflationary way. Indeed, by reducing disposable incomes of the people direct taxes tend to check inflation by curtailing consumption demand. (2) If they are made progressive, they help to reduce inequalities of income and wealth, and thus help in achieving the equity objective, and (3) Progressive direct taxes discourage conspicuous and non-necessary consumption and thereby enlarge economic surplus. But the direct taxation of income and wealth has its own limits. The coverage of direct taxes is quite narrow and difficult to expand. For instance, in India out of 125 crore of population only about 5 crore individuals come within the purview of income tax as incomes of the majority of the people fall below the exemption limit which in 2014-15 budget has been raised to the annual income of ₹ 250,000. Moreover, there is a considerable evasion of income tax. Yield from other direct taxes such as wealth tax, gift tax is quite meagre due to very small coverage, low rates and considerable evasion of them. However, in India due to buoyancy of personal income tax and corporate tax the share of direct taxes in total tax revenue of the central government has greatly gone up to around 60 per cent in 2012-13 from 41 per cent in 2003-04. This reflects sharp improvement in equity of our tax system.

How much tax revenue in developing countries can be raised depends on the two factors (1) *taxable capacity* of the country and (2) tax *effort made by the government.* The tax efforts mean the policy measures are taken by the government to raise revenue so that taxable capacity is fully used. The taxable capacity of an economy depends on the level of its per capita income, the distribution of income among the people. The higher the per capita income and greater the inequalities in income distribution, the larger will be the taxable capacity of the country. Besides, taxable capacity depends on the degree of urbanisation, the size of the industrial sector, and the importance of foreign trade in the economy of the country.

The tax effort depends on the fiscal measures such as income tax, capital gains tax, wealth tax, gift tax, estate duty taken by country to raise tax revenue and how effectively they are implemented. The data regarding tax revenue collected by the government in developing countries on an average is around 20 per cent of GDP as against 31 to 37 per cent of GDP in the developed countries.[6] It is worth mentioning that India lags far behind in regard to tax efforts made as tax revenue as a percentage of GDP is equal to 10 per cent only.[7] In the developing countries, the scope for increasing tax revenues is very limited because a large proportion of the population earns a very low income and falls outside the purview of the tax system. Besides, many exemptions and rebates given by the government in the direct taxes lower the tax base and the collection of tax revenue. In developing countries less than 30 per cent of population is subject to income tax as compared to 70 per cent of population in the developed countries.

Therefore, there is a good deal of scope for raising tax revenue through undertaking reforms. An important objective of tax system in the developing countries is to promote saving so that capital formation is accelerated. The high marginal tax rates, as explained above in the Laffer curve context, often discourage work effort and also to the extent that high marginal tax rates fall on those groups having high marginal propensity to save, the saving rate may fall as marginal tax rate is increased. Besides, several exemptions in personal income tax given by the government are misused by the persons to evade and avoid income tax and wealth tax.

Likewise, corporate income which is a tax on profits of corporate companies is full of several exemptions and rebates given apparently for promoting social objectives are misused by the corporates to illegally reduce their tax liability. For example, in India though corporate income tax rate till 2014-15 was 33 per cent including surcharges, then according to the estimate of the Finance Ministry actually on an average the companies actually pay tax of only 20 per cent of their profits or income. This is because of various exemptions in the corporate tax system. Even then in his budget for 2015-16, the new Finance Minister Mr. Arun Jetly has reduced the corporate tax rate to 25 per cent in a phased manner subject to withdrawal of some exemptions. In our view, this will further reduce the actual income tax rate paid by the companies. This reduction in corporate income tax rate has been done to woo foreign investors to make investment in India. In our view, this is quite inequitable and unjust as individuals have to pay more income tax rate of 33 per cent (including surcharge) on their earned incomes of more than 10 lakh per annum, the corporates will have to pay only 25 per cent. This shows that far from making tax system equitable and buoyant, the government is making it more inequitable. Wages and salary earners are being discriminated against *vis-a-vis* the owners of property and capital. The equity and the need for increasing the saving rate demands that tax system for both individuals and companies should be such as discourages luxury consumption and makes it difficult to evade and avoid taxes.

Besides, the tax reforms are needed for effective taxation of wealth as the ownership of wealth bestows the owners with an inherent taxable capacity regardless of the income it yields. Strangely, instead of making it more effective by plugging its loopholes the Finance Minister in the budget for 2015-16 has abolished the wealth tax and has instead levied 2 per cent surcharge on income of above two crore rupees per annum. Due to large scale evasion of income tax, this move will not serve the end of justice and equity in taxation. A.P. Thirlwall, a renowned development economist has suggested the following four tax reforms in developing countries.[8]

6. See World Bank, *World Development Indicators*, 2011
7. GOI, *Economic Survey*, 2013-14
8. A.P. Thirlwall, *The Economics of Development*, 9th Edition.

1. That overall income (including capital gains) be aggregated and taxed in the same way at a progressive rate but not exceed a maximum marginal rate of say, 50 per cent. Marginal rates above this level will not only discourage incentives but may also be counter productive by encouraging evasion and avoidance.
2. The institution of progressive personal expenditure tax levied on rich individuals who reach the maximum marginal rate of income tax.
3. The imposition of wealth tax and its effective implementation
4. The imposition of a gift tax and its effective imposition.

Role of Indirect Taxes in Resource Mobilisation

As a result of limitations of direct taxes, developing countries have resorted to extensive use of indirect taxes. *In India, almost all commodities have been brought within the net of indirect taxes such as excise duties, service and sales tax. Besides, there are custom duties (i.e., taxes on imports and exports)*. Indirect taxation is an important source of development funds in a developing country such as India. In the last five decades of planned development, revenue from several indirect taxes has been rising . It has been pointed out by some economists that indirect taxes are better suited to the conditions obtaining in developing countries for reducing current consumption and mobilising resources for development. This is because in such countries quite a large proportion of national income tends to be diverted to current consumption instead of being saved and productively invested. The average propensity to consume in such countries is much higher than is the case in advanced countries. Indirect taxes which reduce consumption must thus play a more important part. They will raise the rate of savings which are so essential for economic growth. It may be noted that indirect tax system can also be made progressive by levying higher indirect taxes on income-elastic *luxuries* such as cars, air conditioners, air travel. This will serve the equity objective, apart from making larger contribution to resource mobilisation for economic growth. Similarly, imposing higher indirect tax on harmful commodities such as cigaretless and alcohol will serve a useful social purpose of discouraging their consumption. *"High rates of taxes on commodities with a high income elasticity of demand are quite effective in siphoning a substantial proportion of increase in output into the resources of the public sector needed for development financing and a stiff rate of commodity taxes on luxury articles tends to introduce an element of progressiveness in an otherwise predominantly regressive tax structure in developing countries."*[9]

But in order to make sure that the resources raised through commodity taxes are adequate, it will be necessary to extend their coverage to include some goods of mass consumption. In the poor countries, it is not possible to exempt entirely goods of general and necessary consumption, because they are the only goods that provide a base broad enough to assure an adequate amount of resources. It may be noted that in Indian revenue from indirect taxes has substantially increased during the six decades of development (1951-2010). From a small sum of ₹ 227 crore in 1950-51, the revenue raised from indirect taxes rose to about 4,06,213 crore in 2011-12 (RE). Moreover, the share of indirect takes to total tax revenue at present (2012-2013) is about 40 per cent.

It is thus clear that for mobilisation of resources for growth and capital formation indirect taxes have made an important contribution. But due to reduction in customs duties and union excise duty on the one hand and a large increase in revenue from direct taxes such as personal income tax and corporation tax on the other, share of indirect taxes in total tax revenue of Central government has declined from 78.4 per cent in 1990-91 to 42 per cent in 2011-12. Now, 59 per cent of GDP in India comes through 'services'. Therefore, to increase the tax base

---

9. R.N. Tripathy, *Public Finance in Developing Countries,* 1966, p. 200.

for indirect taxation, all services except only 17 services have been brought in the net of the service tax. In the financial years 2012-13 and 2013-14, revenue from service tax was estimated at ₹ 132601 and ₹ 154630 crore respectively. It is expected that in future service tax will make a substantial conribution to the mobilisation of resources for economic growth. To improve the indirect tax structure, broaden its base and rationalise the rates a single indirect tax called **'Goods and Services Tax (GST)'** is proposed to be introduced which will give a boost to both trade and industry. This new indirect tax GST will replace CENVAT (which is a central excise duty levied by the central government on the basis of value added) and service tax levied by the centre and VAT levied by the State. We will explain GST in detail later in this chapter.

Limitations. But there are some limitations of raising resources through indirect taxes. First, they lead to *cost-push inflation*. The burden of indirect taxes are passed on to the consumers in the form of higher prices charged from them. In India excise duties on sugar, cloth, kerosene oil, petrol etc., has raised the prices and have contributed a good deal to cost-push inflation witnessed in past some years. Secondly, levying of custom duties on imports of capital goods, raw materials used for industrial production have accelerated cost-push inflation in the Indian economy. Thirdly, imposition of custom duties on imports of goods also protect inefficiency in domestic industries. This also contributes to high-cost production and promotes inefficiency. Fourthly, indirect taxes are ***regressive*** in nature; both the rich and poor have to pay the same rate on the taxed commodities. The regressive character of indirect taxes have been attempted to be reduced by imposing higher rates of excise and custom duties on luxury items and smaller rates of duties on goods of mass consumption. However, the need for mobilising greater resources have forced the finance ministers to levy higher indirect taxes even on articles of mass consumption. Lastly, the higher excise duties, customs duties and service tax lead to higher prices of Indian goods and thus adversely affect competitiveness of Indian goods in the foreign markets. Due to these shortcomings of indirect tax the reforms undertaken in India since 1991 seek to bring about a compositional shift from excessive dependence on indirect taxes to direct taxes and provide for increased competitiveness of the Indian Industry.

Perform in the Indirect Tax System: Goods and Service Tax (GST)

An important reform in the indirect tax system is the introduction of Goods and Service Tax (GST). GST will replace all multistage sales or value added taxes such as CENVAT and service tax levied by the centre and the sales tax, or value added tax (VAT), entertainment tax, luxury tax levied by the States. GST is, therefore, a comprehensive tax on goods and services. The introduction of GST will not only simplify the indirect tax system in the country but will also yield more revenue for the government. The significant reason of complexity of the present indirect tax system is related to the existence of various exemptions and multiple rates of CENVAT on various commodities and different rates of sales tax or VAT levied by the States. Since GST is a tax on consumption, it will promote saving. Besides, it will reduce the incidence of evasion. The starting base of central excise duty or CENVAT is narrow and is further eroded by a variety of area specific and conditional and unconditional exemptions. Therefore, the introduction of comprehensive single GST would be appropriate for deepening indirect tax system in India.

It is now widely recognized that GST will be a major milestone for indirect tax reform in India. By replacing all existing indirect taxes the GST will create a national market as it will eliminate the cascading effects of multiple layers of taxation all over the country and facilitate movements of goods and services across state borders. Besides, it will align taxation of imports and exports correctly. This will improve the competitiveness of production and exports from India. The single

GST will also improve tax collection as it will end the long-standing distortion of differential treatment of manufacturing goods and services and ensure uniform removal of exemptions.

A single and transparent GST will reduce the costs of the companies and make our manufacturing export products competitive in the world market.

Exempting real estate, electricity, alchol and petroleum products, a committee headed by Cheif Economic Adviser, Mr Arvind Subramanian has recommended a standard GST rate of 17 to 18 per cent. The actual rate of the tax will be fixed by GST council consisting of representatives of both states and the centre. It has been pointed out if more exemptions are granted, it will not only distort GST tax structure but will push up the GST rate that will fuel inflation. Therefore, there is a real danger of rise in inflation as a result of GST. Besides, rate of service tax is at present 14 per cent, even a single 18 per cent rate of GST on both goods and resources would push up the prices of services and cause services inflation. Services of insurance, telephone, electricity and a host of other services will become much costlier.

51

CHAPTER

Role of Fiscal Policy: Government Borrowing for Financing Development

Government borrowing is another method by which the resources may be mobilised for economic development. When Government's total revenue and capital expenditure exceeds its revenue from taxes and other non-debt receipts, there is deficit in its budget which is called *fiscal deficit*. There are two ways, by which fiscal deficit can be financed. First, to finance this deficit, the Government can borrow from the market through sale of its dated securities or bonds with fixed interest rate. It is generally the banks, insurance companies mutual funds that buy these securities and lend funds to the Government. Second, to meet its deficit the Government can borrow from the Reserve Bank against the treasury bIlls and the Reserve Bank prints new notes against these treasury bills and give it to the Government. In this way money supply in the economy increases. This method involves *monetization* of *deficit* and was previously called *deficit financing* in India. It is now known as money financing of fiscal deficit. In India at present, it is borrowing by the Government or debt financing of fiscal deficit that is used by the Government to finance its fiscal deficit.

Under borrowing, the government issues bonds and sells it. Generally, sale of interest-bearing ›nds to the public is indirect through financial intermediarises such as banks and insurance ›anies. Banks buy the bonds floated by the government with the currency deposits of the Therefore, debt-financing of budget deficit is also known as *bond-financy of budget deficit*. ›orrowed money in this way the government is able to expand its expenditure but at ›e it adds to public debt which has both short-run and long run consequences. It ›ed that budget deficit also comes about when taxes are reduced, keeping govern- constant. This type of budget deficit can also be financed through borrowing ›he banks or public. The government has not only to pay annually interest › has to pay back also the principal sum borrowed for which it may levy

›phasised the expansionary effect of borrowing (*i.e.*, debt-financing) ›e Keynesian model with a fixed price level, the increase in govern- ›rrowed money causes an upward shift in aggregate expenditure is working at less than full-employment level of national ›e economy, the increase in debt-financed government ›n output or income. With the increase in income at › rise which will over time reduce the budget deficit or even ultimately eliminate it so that budget becomes balanced. This can also be illustrated through *IS-LM* model in Fig. 51.1 where *IS* and *LM* curves are drawn, given the money supply in the economy. Y^* is the full-employment level of output. Initially, the equilibrium is at income level Y_0. Now, with debt-financed increase in government expenditure *IS* curve shifts to the right from IS_0 to IS_1 with *LM* curve remaining the same. As a result, as will be seen from Fig. 51.1, national income increases to Y_1. This will bring about increase in tax revenue collected by the government and over time budget deficit will be reduced or even eliminated. It will be seen from Fig. 51.1 that though interest rate also rises but it does not fully offset the expansionary effect of debt-financed increase in government expenditure.

Crowding-out Effect

However, critics have pointed out that government borrowing is largely offset by its *crowding-out effect* on private investment. The crowding-out effect on private investment takes place in a variety of ways. First, it has been pointed out that government's borrowing to finance budget deficit will lead to the increase in demand for lendable funds which will cause the rate of interest to rise. The rise in interest rate will cause private investment to decline. Thus, debt-financed increase in government expenditure, that is, government borrowing crowds out private investment. According to this view, due to crowding-out effect on private investment net expansionary effect of increase in government expenditure is negligible. On the other hand, the society will have to bear the burden of increase in public debt as a result of debt-financed expansion in government expenditure. If budget deficit arises due to reduction in taxes, keeping government expenditure constant, this will also need borrowing by the government to finance the budget dificit and with therefore lead to rise in interest rate causing crowding-out effect on private investment. This also happens because reduction in taxes stimulates consumption expenditure of the people which reduces savings. The decline in savings causes interest rate to rise resulting in fall in private investment.

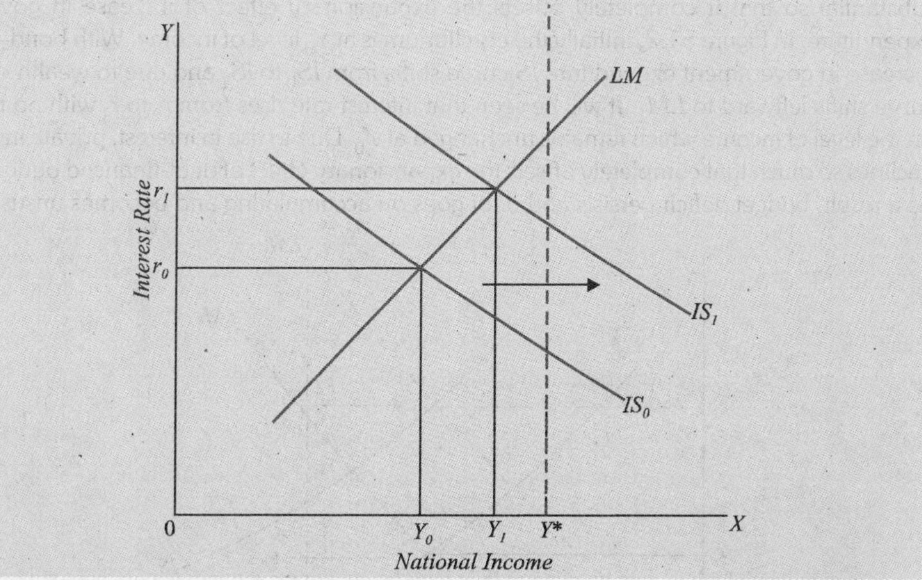

Fig. 51.1. *Expansionary Effect of Increase in Government Expenditure by Borrowing*

Wealth Effect of Government Borrowing (Debt-Financing)

In our above analysis we have not taken into account the *wealth effect* of debt financing. When the government issues bonds to finance its budget deficit, it creates private wealth. This is because bonds are considered as wealth by the people. Patinkin and Friedman in their models include wealth in their money demand function. That is, according to them, demand for money depends on the real value of wealth, apart from other factors. If this wealth effect of bond-financing of budget deficit is recognised, then it exercises an important influence on the dynamic behaviour of the economy. When through debt-financing of budget deficit, more bonds are issued and sold by the government, the wealth of the people increases which will raise the demand for money.[1] The increase in demand for money, money supply remaining the same, causes a leftward shift in the *LM* curve, for instance, from LM_0 to LM_1 in Figure 51.2. This is because borrowing which raises demand for money, given the supply of money, causes interest rate to rise. (Note that in contrast to Government borrowing the financing of Government expenditure through creation of new printed money, causes *LM* curve to the right).

Thus, while with the increase in government expenditure *IS* curve shifts to the right to the new position IS_1 which tends to raise aggregate income, the wealth effect of bonds issued to finance the deficit causes leftward shift in the *LM* curve which tends to raise rate of interest and thereby crowds out private investment. According to Friedman, the wealth effect is quite substantial so that it completely offsets the expansionary effect of increase in government expenditure. In Figure 51.2, initially the equilibrium is at Y_0 level of income. With bond-financed increase in government expenditure *IS* curve shifts from IS_0 to IS_1 and due to wealth effect *LM* curve shifts leftward to LM_1. It will be seen that interest rate rises from r_0 to r_1 with no net effect on the level of income which remains unchanged at Y_0. Due to rise in interest, private investment declines so much that completely offsets the expansionary effect of debt-financed budget deficit. As a result, budget deficit persists and debt goes on accumulating and becomes unsustainable.

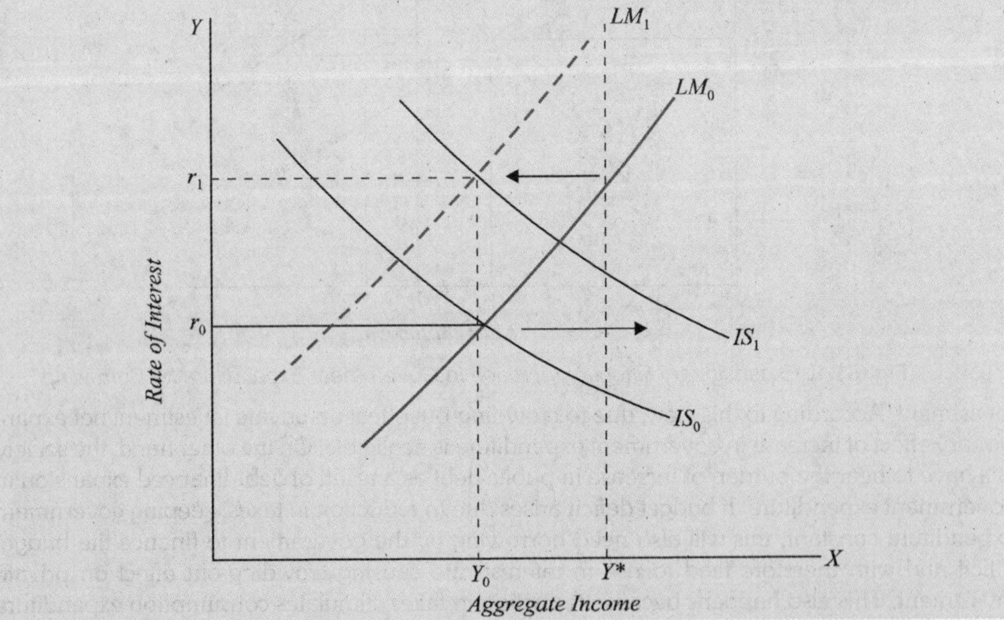

Fig. 51.2. *Borrowing for Government Expenditure with Wealth Effect of Bonds Sold by the Government*

In the above analysis of crowding-out effect of debt-financing it is assumed that price level remains fixed. However, when the aggregate supply function is vertical as is the case when the

1 R. Dombusch, S. Fischer and Startz, *Macroeconomics,* Tata McGraw Hill, 8th edition, p 476.

economy is working at full capacity output (i.e., full-employment level), increase in aggregate demand (*AD*) brought about by increase in government expenditure by borrowing will result in rise in price level, equilibrium income remains unchanged as shown through *AS-AD* model in Fig. 51.3. Since income remains unchanged, tax-revenue will not increase and therefore budget deficit persists and debt will go on accumulating and over time become unsustainable.

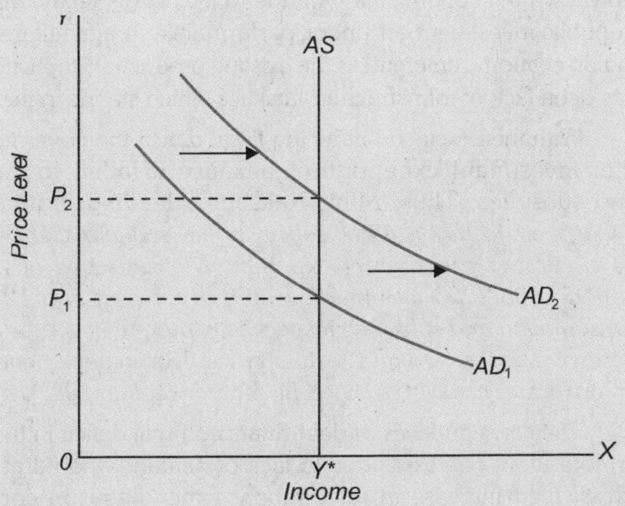

Fig. 51.3. *Rise in Price Level Offsets the Expansionary Effect of Debt Financing of Government Expenditure.*

Conclusion: We have seen above that expansionary effect of debt-financed budget deficit has been challenged on the ground of its crowding-out effect. However, in our view, the crowding-out effect of debt-financing has been below out of all proportions. As a matter of fact, crowding-out effect of debt financing of budget deficit is negligible, especially when the economy is working at less than full-employment level of income. Generally, budget deficit and its financing through floating of bonds is recommend to overcome depression when there is under-employment equilibrium and therefore output gap exists. For planned development in developing countries where there *exists potential for growth*, debt-financing or borrowing by the Government can be used for mobilising resources for projects of economic growth, especially infrastructure without crowding out private investment. *Empirical evidence also shows that wealth effect of sale of bonds is not significant.* As shall be discussed below in detail, even in developing countries where there is gross under-utilisation of resources or when they work at less than their full-production capacity, policy of budget deficits and financing it through debt to a reasonable degree is a useful instrument for stimulating economic growth and raise level of income.

GOVERNMENT BORROWING OR DEBT-FINANCING OF FISCAL DEFICIT: THE CASE OF INDIA

In India there has been a problem of persistent fiscal deficits which has been largely financed by borrowing from the banks and public and thus adding to the public debt. In 1991 as a measure of economic reforms IMF directed that fiscal deficit of the central government should be reduced to achieve economic stability. The economists associated with IMF and World Bank hold the view that large fiscal deficit raises inflation rate of the economy on the one hand and since it is financed largely by borrowing from the market, this raises rate of interest and therefore crowds out private investment and adversely affects economic growth. Besides, it has been pointed out that the persistent budget deficit year after year adds to public debt and as a result ratio of public debt to national income (Debt/GDP ratio) will greatly increase which will land the country in debt trap[2].

2. For this view, see Shankar Acharya, former Chief Economic Advisor who puts forward this view in a forceful manner in 'How Fiscal Deficit Hurts Economic Growth, We will explain in detail this mainstream view later in this chapter.

In view of the above it is appropriate to discuss the above issues relating to debt-financing of Government expenditure in the light of the recent Indian experience. It is worth mentioning that from the years 1997 to 2002-03 and again in 2008 and 2009 the Indian economy experienced slowdown in economic growth due to lack of aggregate demand resulting mainly from the fall in public investment and poor performance in agriculture. In this situation *output gap* in the Indian economy emerged as the existing production capacity was not fully utilised. Besides, there has been lack of infrastructure facilities which stands in the way of raising private investment.

With their focus on reducing fiscal deficit the government reduced its capital expenditure (i.e. investment expenditure) because it failed to curb its consumption expenditure and subsidies. Thus, Mihir Rakshit, a leading Indian macroeconomist, rightly states. "*With their focus on fiscal deficit, policy makers seem to think that what matters primarily is curbing government expenditure irrespective of changes in their composition. The period 1995-2000 was marked by 9.6 per cent and 12.6 per cent growth in government consumption and subsidies respectively, but public sector capital accumulation grew at snail's pace of 1.9 per cent and its two crucial constituents, namely, investment in agriculture and infrastructure actually declined by 5.6 per cent and 0.2 per cent respectively*"[3]

The consequences of debt-financed fiscal deficit in the case of India depends on whether or not output gap exists due to lack of demand and infrastructural facilities. If the output gap exists, then increase in government expenditure on consumption and subsidies will raise aggregate demand and help in utilising more fully the existing production capacity and over time will cause private investment to rise. But this will not raise public saving and public investment and therefore will not result in much higher growth of the economy. This may also raise ratio of public debt to GDP since due to slow growth in GDP, tax collection will not appreciably rise. Mihir Rakshit aptly points out that, "The Indian economy since 1997[3] has also been characterised by output gap, high fiscal deficit and growing debt/GDP ratio. The mainstream view in India is that despite the output gap fiscal deficits crowd out private investment and are unsustainable"[4].

Crowding-in Effect of Public Expenditure. The mainstream view of debt-financing is not correct and has been rightly challenged by some prominent India economists such as Mihir Rakshit, V.N. Pandit and Prabhat Patnaik, among others. Under the circumstances when there exists output-gap and under-utilisation of production capacity, the increase in government expenditure, especially of investment nature, will *crowd in* private investment and speed up rate of economic growth. To quote Mihir Rakshit, "contrary to wide-spread perception among commentators *debt-financing associated with closing the output gap in fact crowds in private investment*.......... crowding in will be much more pronounced in countries like India where government's infrastructural investment favourably affects private investment even while projects are being executed : the fact that highways are being built in some area or that it will soon have abundant supply of power, communication facilities is likely to induce private investors to start setting up new units and expending existing ones even in the shrot run"[5].

When there is output-gap in a developing economy such as India, even increase in government's consumption expenditure will crowd in private investment through the former's demand effect. But, as has been pointed out by Dr. Mihir Rakshit, crowding-in effect of government's investment expenditure will be greater because it expands the infrastructural facilities (i.e., supply-side factors) badly needed for increase in private investment.

3. Mihir Rakshit, "Some Macroeconomics of India's Reforms Experience" in *India's Emerging Economy* (e.d.) Kaushik Basu, Oxford University Press, 2004, p,104.
4. Budget Deficit: Sustainability, Solvancy and Optimality, printed in Amaresh Bagchi, *"Readings in Public Finance"* Oxford University Press, 2005, pp. 342-343.
5. Mihir Rakshit, op. cit., p.345

In our view, the expansionary effect of government's investment expenditure and also its crowding-in effect on private investment in a developing country like India is not confined to the situation when output gap and under-utilisation of capital stock exists due to demand deficiency but also when such an economy functions at its normal capacity. Besides, even in normal times, debt-financed government investment expenditure which brings about rapid economic growth, budget deficits and debt/GDP ratio over time can be reduced. An *important rule of public finance, which is sometimes* described as a ***golden rule*** is that if borrowed money by the government is used for investment or developmental purposes, it leads to growth in GDP or national income. Given the tax rate, this increase in income will ensure collection of more tax revenue possible. As a result, budget deficit or what is also called fiscal deficit will be reduced and debt/GDP ratio will decline. This has actually happened in India.

The viability and sustainability of debt-financed budget deficits in a growing economy must be based on the magnitude of Government investment expenditure (I_g) in the total expenditure ($I_g + G$). Suppose the economy is working at the full capacity output, and government increases its investment expenditure, say, in infrastructure and finances the budget deficit through incurring debt. This increase in government investment expenditure will raise income through both demand effect and capacity effect and will therefore stimulate private investment which depends on change in income (i.e. $Y_1 - Y_{t-1}$). This increase in both government and private investment will over time cause rapid growth in income which in turn will result in more tax revenue. Thus, in this way budget deficit will be reduced with favourable effect on public debt/GDP ratio, if rate of growth in income (GDP) exceeds rate of interest.

It is thus clear that sustainability of budget deficit and public debt (*i.e.* government borrowing) depends on *shifting the composition of government expenditure towards investment.* To quote Mihir Rakshit, "Budgetary viability requires an improvement in revenue balances in the medium term and the long run....... public investment in agriculture aided by crowding-in effect, raises agricultural productivity and acts as a stimulant to a rural economy, brings down poverty and *enables the government to reduce over time expenditure on food or fertilizer subsidies and poverty alleviation measures*. An increase in government investment in rural and urban infrastructural facilities will through increased revenue receipts and decreased subsidies will strengthen budgetary position not only in the medium term and the long run but in the short run as well"[6]. It is interesting to note that when with effect from year 2003 the Government investment expenditure in India had been raised, tax revenue collection significantly increased and also fiscal deficit, revenue deficit and debt/GDP ratio declined. Besides, private investment had also gone up (*i.e.* crowed in) rather than crowding out by increase in debt-financed increase in government expenditure.

Thus, in the 1990s when the focus in our strategy was to reduce fiscal deficit, no matter reducing capital expenditure of the government for this purpose, the Indian economy experienced slowdown in growth and our fiscal situation worsened. On the other hand, when from March 2003 we shifted the focus toward increase in government investment expenditure on power, ports, highways, rural roads in a big way, private investment also croweded in, generated higher economic growth which resulted in lower fiscal deficits and lower debt/GDP ratio.

Now-a-days, the Central Government borrows mostly from the market through sale of its bonds of different maturities carrying different rates of interest by RBI.

Borrowing is the quickest mode of raising funds. Financing through taxation is not so expeditious because passing of tax laws, assessment of taxes based on those laws and their collection involves considerable delay. On the other hand, bonds can be issued any time dur-

6. Mihir Rakshit, op. cit., p.105

ing a year. It is bankes, insurance companies, mutual funds that usually invest their funds in government bonds. **Public borrowing generates additional productive capacity.** The funds raised by public borrowing can be utilised for building up economic infrastructure for the economy through schemes for the development of irrigation, transport, power and communication. They can help also in building up of the agricultural and industrial base of the economy. All such investments facilitate further economic growth. There is no doubt, therefore, that the public borrowing plays a very useful and important role in accelerating economic development of underdeveloped economies. Public debt promotes saving and investment, the two most crucial determinants of economic growth.

But there are three problems concerning government borrowing. First, government borrowing leads to increase is public debt whose burden falls on future generations who have to pay higher taxes to the government for paying back the borrowed funds. Besides, every year the Government has to pay interest on the borrowed funds and these annual interest payments which are very large due to accumulated large public debt generally cause large deficit in revenue account of the Government budget. As a result, a large chunck of new borrowings every year are used to make interest payments. Thirdly, borrowing by the government from the market leads to increase in demand for loanable funds and *causes rise in interet* rate. At a higher interest rate private investment falls. Thus it is often asserted that *Government borrowing crowds out private investment*. However, when there is ample liquidity in the banking system, the banks can make adequate funds available for meeting the demand for funds for the corporate sector.

However, Government borrowing has often been used to finance Governments's current or consumption expenditure as there has been *large revenue deficit* year after year and Government borrowing has been used to meet this revenue deficit with the result that financing of capital expenditure through Government borrowing has been very small. ***Golden rule of Government borrowing*** is that it should be used for financing investment or productive projects so that it yields returns which can be used to pay interest on the borrowed funds as well as pay back the principal amount. In this way Government borrowing would not involve any burden on future generations and instead higher economic growth will occur which will benefit the future generations.

Another problem of Government borrowing to finance large fiscal deficit is that it causes large increase in government expenditure which leads to ***excess demand conditions*** in the immediate future which cause inflation in the economy. Therefore, financial prudence requires that fiscal deficit should be of reasonable degree and the funds borrowed by the Government should be used for investment and productive purposes so that inflationary pressures can be contained.

Obstacles

But there exist a number of obstacles which hinder the success of borrowing policy in developing countries. The resources of the organised financial market may be too inadequate to fulfil the needs both of the private and public sectors. Further, in the financial market the competition for funds between the government and the private sector will raise rate of interest and this will have a highly disincentive effect on the expansion of investment in the private sector. More borrowing by the Government leads to the rise in market rates of interest. The higher interest rates tends to reduce private investment. Therefore, it is often asserted that the *higher borrowing target by the Government crowds out private investment.* In India the rates of interest on loans (on bonds or securities) of Government have been raised quite substantially. Since banks and others prefer to invest in Government securities because they are safe (*i.e.*, riskless). This has reduced funds for private investment. However, in our view, this can be avoided if RBI through its monetary measures ensure adequate availability of funds available with the banks so that rate of interest does not rise when Government borrows from the market.

For the success of government's borrowing policy, it is necessary that financial institutions be developed and extended into the rural areas of the economy in order to inculcate the habit of thrift in the population and to mobilise for productive purposes the amount of savings originating in this sector. Besides, for the mobilisation of savings it will be necessary to check and regulate the diversion of savings into unproductive investment such as real estate, gold and jewellery and inventory accumulation.

Suitable techniques of borrowing must also be devised. For example, bonds issued by the Government should be adjusted to the preferences of the general public; bonds of large denomination and long maturity may be offered to the institutional investors, whereas those of small denomination and short maturity may be reserved for the non-institutional public. If properly devised and conducted small savings campaign can mobilise a sizable amount of resources. Further, the mobilisation of the hoardings of gold and jewellery through government programmes constitutes a highly desirable source of resource mobilisation. Of course, suitable techniques of public borrowing for the mobilisation of these resources have to be evolved. In this connection the announcement by the Finance Minister in his budget speech for 2015-16 to issue gold bonds is a welcome step in this direction.

TYPES OF BUDGET DEFICITS

Government expenditure on goods and services and resources mobilised by it through taxes, etc., are important factors that determine aggregate demand in the economy. When there is a deficit in the budget of the government, it spends more than it collects resources through taxes and non-tax revenue. In recent years there have been huge fiscal deficits in India which have created large excess demand in the economy. This has resulted in inflation or sharp rise in the general level in prices. The deficit may occur either in the revenue budget or capital budget or in both taken together. When there is an overall budget deficit of the Government, it has to be financed by either borrowing from the market or from the Reserve Bank of India which is the nationalised central bank of the country. RBI has the power to create new money, that is, to issue new notes. Thus, to finance its fiscal deficit, the government may borrow from Reserve Bank of India against its own securities. This is only a technical way of creating new money because the government has to pay neither the rate of interest nor the original amount when it borrows from the Reserve Bank of India against its own securities. It is thus clear that fiscal deficit implies that government incurs more expenditure on goods and services than its normal receipts from taxes and non-tax revenue. This excess expenditure by the government is financed by either borrowing from the market or by newly created money which leads to the rise in incomes of the people. This causes the aggregate demand of the community to rise to a greater extent than the actual amount of government borrowing through the operation of what is called Government expenditure multiplier.

There are three types of budget deficit which we explain below:

Revenue Deficit

As mentioned above, the budget has two parts: *Revenue Budget* and *Capital Budget*. Receipts in the revenue account come from such sources as various types of direct and indirect taxes and also from non-tax sources such as interest received on loans given, dividend and profits of public enterprises. The items of expenditure in the revenue account are of the type that represents *collective consumption* of the society and therefore, creates no earning assets. The various types of expenditure on the revenue account are incurred on : (1) Interest payments on public debit, (2) Civil administration, (3) Defence, (4) Subsidies on food, fertilisers, exports and (5) Social services such as education, health, etc.

Revenue deficit refers to the excess of revenue expenditure over revenue receipts. Prudent management of public finance requires that receipts on revenue account should not exceed expenditure on revenue account. In other words, there should be surplus on revenue account so that this surplus should be used for investment in development projects or building assets which yield returns. In fact, surplus on revenue account of the budget represents *public or government savings* which can be used for financing developmental activities. However, in India, for the past several years, there has been deficit on the revenue account. That is, there has been *government dissaving* for the last some years in India. Therefore, borrowed funds from the capital account have been used to meet a part of consumption expenditure of the government. This has bad consequences for the economy. Revenue deficit as percentage of gross domestic product (GDP) has been quite high in recent years. Revenue deficit of the central government of India for the last four years is given in Table 51.1.

Table 51.1: Trends in Budget Deficit of Central Government as % of GDP

	Fiscal deficit	*Revenue deficit*	*Primary deficit*
1996-97	4.1	2.4	–0.2
1997-98	4.8	3.0	0.5
1998-99	5.1	3.8	0.7
1999-2000	5.4	3.5	0.7
2000-01	5.7	4.1	0.9
2001-02	6.2	4.4	1.5
2002-03	5.9	4.4	1.1
Enactment of FRBMA			
2003-04	4.5	3.6	0.0
2004-05	4.0	2.5	–0.1
2005-06	4.0	2.5	0.4
2006-07	3.3	1.9	–0.2
2007-08	2.5	1.1	–0.9
2008-09	6.0	4.5	2.5
2009-10	6.4	5.2	3.1
2010-11	4.8	3.2	1.8
2011-12	5.7	4.4	2.7
2012-13	4.8	3.6	1.8
2013-14	4.5	3.2	1.2
2014-15	4.1	2.9	0.8
2015-16	3.9	2.8	0.7

As per cent of GDP, revenue deficit rose from 2.4 per cent in 1996-97 to 4.4 per cent in 2002-03 but fell to 1.1 per cent in 2007-08 . Fiscal Responsibility Budget Management (FRBM) Act passed in 2003 required to eliminate it by 2008-09. However, due to global financial crisis in 2008, it could not be achieved. As a part of fiscal stimulus package the government increased its expenditure and cut customs and excise duties in 2008 and 2009 to prevent large slowdown of economic growth following the global financial crisis. As a result, revenue deficit rose to 4.5 per cent of GDP in 2008-09 and 5.2% of GDP in 2009-10. Waving of loans of farmers in 2008-09 and rise in salaries of central government employees following the implementation of Sixth Central Payment Commission in 2008 and 2009 also caused the revenue deficit, to go up in 2008-09 and 2009-10.

Since revenue deficit represents *negative savings* of the government it leads to lower investment by the government and slows down economic growth of the country in the long run. Central government has been trying to achieve fiscal consolidation by raising more tax revenue by roll-back of tax concession and withdrawing tax exemptions. As a result, revenue deficit fell to 3.2 per cent of GDP in 2010-11 but again went up to 4.4 per cent of GDP in 2011-12 and 3.6 per cent of GDP in 2012-13. Revenue deficit for 2014-15 was 2.9% of GDP. Government expenditure to meet revenue deficit does not lead to increase in durable assets and therefore does not cause expansion in productive capacity to ensure sustained economic growth in future and for 2015-16 it has been reduced to 2.8% of GDP.

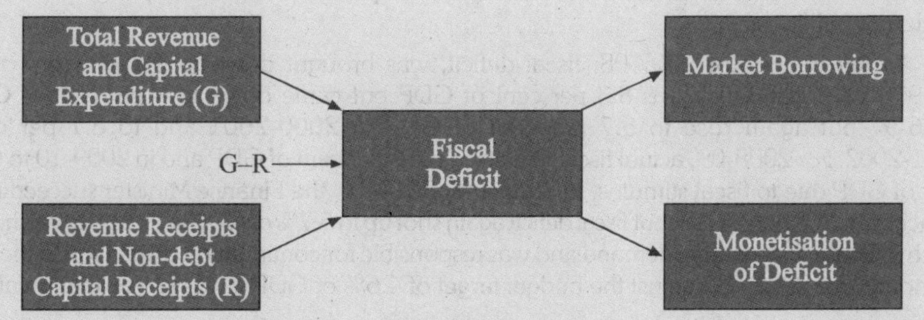

Fig. 51.4. *Financing of Fiscal Deficit*

Fiscal Deficit

Fiscal deficit in the budget is an important measure of deficit. IMF and the World Bank generally prescribe targets for budget deficit in terms of fiscal deficit. *Fiscal deficit is the excess of total expenditure (both on revenue and capital accounts) over revenue receipts and non-debt type of capital receipts such as recoveries of loans.*

Thus,

Fiscal Deficit = *(Total Expenditure both on Revenue Account and Capital Account) – (Revenue Receipts + Non-debt Capital Receipts)*

Fiscal deficit is a more comprehensive measure of budgetary imbalances. Thus, we see that when the government's total expenditure, both revenue and capital expenditure, exceeds its receipts from taxes and other normal non-revenue and non-debt capital resources, *a fiscal deficit* is created. Now, this fiscal deficit can be financed in two ways. First, through borrowing by the government from the market, both inside and outside the country. On this borrowing, the government has to pay rate of interest annually. Apart from that it has to pay back the internal and external debt taken. Secondly, the government can finance the fiscal deficit by borrowing from the Reserve Bank of India which issues new notes against government securities. Thus, government borrowing from the Reserve Bank results in expansion of high powered money in the economy and is in fact *monetisation* of fiscal deficit which, if undertaken to an excessive extent, leads to inflation in the economy. On the other hand, Government borrowing from the market to finance fiscal deficit adds to the public debt and increases burden on future generations on whom heavy taxes have to be imposed for repaying the loans.

In the Table 51.1, fiscal deficit of the Central Government of India has been presented for the last twenty years. Fiscal deficit which was 4.7% of GDP in 1997-98 rose to 5.9% of GDP in 2002-2003 but it fell to 2.5% of GDP in 2007-08. It will be seen from this table that in the Indian economy, prior to 2003-04 fiscal deficit was quite large which led to inflation or rise in prices in the economy on the one hand and increase in public debt on the other. Therefore, it was decided to reduce it to 3 per cent of GDP by the year 2008-09 and Fiscal Responsibility Budget Management (FRBM) Act was passed to discipline Government's fiscal policy and reduce fiscal deficit. Accordingly, the government did not borrow directly from RBI through privately placing bonds with it since 2002 (That is, did not monetise the fiscal deficit since 2002). However, for the years 2008-09 and 2009-10, the Government planned to monetise the deficit to some extent as fiscal deficit greatly went up due to fiscal stimulus packages adopted to overcome recessionary conditions in the Indian economy created by global financial crisis of 2007-09 and it was not considered prudent to finance its fully through borrowing from the market which would cause increase in interest rates and crowd out private investment apart from raising the burden of public debt.

In the budget for 2007-08, fiscal deficit, was brought down to 2.5 per cent of GDP. In 1990-91, fiscal deficit was 8.3 per cent of GDP but came down to 4 per cent of GDP in 1996-97 but again rose to 5.7 per cent of GDP in 2000-2001 and to 6.1 per cent in 2001-2002. For 2008-09, actual fiscal deficit rose to 6 per cent of GDP and in 2009-10 to 6.4 per cent of GDP due to fiscal stimulus. In budget for 2010-11, the Finance Minister succeeded in to reducing it to 4.8 per of GDP but fiscal deficit again shot up to 5.7% of GDP in 2011-12 which caused much increase in aggregate demand and was responsible for continuation of inflation in the Indian economy. For 2012-13 against the budget target of 4.6% of GDP it was feared that fiscal deficit

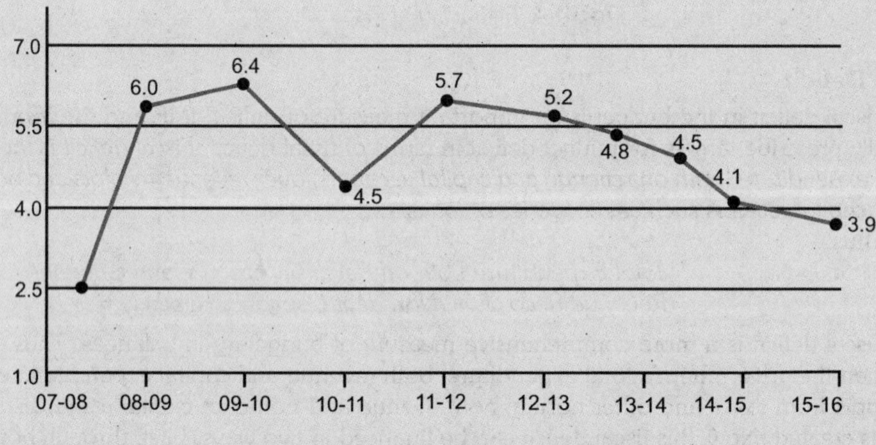

Fig. 51.5. *Gross Fiscal Deficit as % of GDP*

estimated collection of tax revenue as a result of slowdown of the economy and decline in funds from auction of 2G spectrum and disinvestment of certain public sector enterprises. However, Finance Minister succeeded in limiting it to 4.8 per cent of GDP by reducing government expenditure through cutting **plan expenditure** by over ₹ 91000 crore though it was not desirable from growth point of view (see Table 51.1). The fiscal deficit for 2013-14 was 4.5 and for 2014-15 it was 4.1 and for 2015-16 it was 3.9 per cent of GDP. The States in India also have fiscal deficit of around 3 per cent of GDP.

Implications of Large Fiscal Deficit

There are four implications of fiscal deficit. First, a good part of it is financed through borrowing from within and outside the country. This *leads to the increase in public debt and its burden*. Secondly, a part of fiscal deficit is financed through deficit financing, that is, monetisation of fiscal deficit which leads to the creation of new money and *rise in prices or inflation*. To check inflation and achieve price stability, IMF and World Bank have recommended that fiscal deficit of the central government in India should be reduced to 3 per cent of GDP in a phased manner. Thirdly, a very large fiscal deficit especially, large revenue deficit *adversely affects economic growth*. Due to large revenue deficit, a very large part of borrowed funds by the Government is used to finance current consumption expenditure of the Government. As a result, smaller amount of them are left for productive investment in infrastructure and social capital (*i.e.*, education and health) by the Government. This lowers the rate of economic growth. Lastly, more borrowing by the Government leaves less resources for private sector investment.

To reduce fiscal deficit to 3 per cent requires a drastic cut in revenue expenditure which is a difficult task. *In India, attempts have been made to reduce fiscal deficit by curtailing capital expenditure which is incurred on projects of capital formation and other developmental activities.* This is not a desirable way of reducing fiscal deficit because this adversely affects economic growth. For sound management of Government finance there is need to cut revenue expenditure and raise revenue receipts by mobilising resources through taxation. Attempts to reduce fiscal deficit by curtailing capital expenditure, as has been the practice in India adversely affects economic growth and should therefore be avoided.

However, as shall be discussed below, fiscal deficit, even a large one, is not always bad. In times of recessionary situation such as the one that prevailed in 2008-09 and 2009-10, fiscal deficit was needed to fight recession or to prevent slowdown in the economy. All over the world (including the US), the governments resorted to large dozes of fiscal deficit to stimulate the economy and prevent further deepening of recession and more losses of jobs. It was for such a situation when private investment declines that J. M. Keynes recommended that Government should undertake deficit spending on a large scale and finance it either through borrowing or through creation of new printed money to overcome recession and to increase employment. In our view, though undertaking large fiscal deficit in recessionary situation is desirable but in a developing country such as ours borrowed money should be used for *productive purposes* and not frittered away in spending on useless and wasteful projects.

However, from above it should not be understood that any amount of fiscal deficit or government borrowing is good for economic growth and employment generation, Higher fiscal deficit was that is, borrowing by the Government involves payment of interest and *raises the burden of public debt*. The large increase in public debt as a result of Government borrowing involving large interest payments year after year will make the process *unsustainable* and may land the country in debt trap. It may be recalled here the recent experience of European countries such as Greece, Portugal, Spain, Italy which as a result of very high fiscal deficits and Government borrowing in the past have faced *sovereign debt crisis* as they have been unable to pay back not only the principal sum borrowed on its maturity but also interests which are annually due on their debt. As a result, they reached the brink of default on their payments. As much of their accumulated debt came from European banks, no one will give them loans in future in case of defaults. Besides, this posed a damage to unity of European Union which have these highly indebted countries as their members. Therefore, European Central Bank (ECB) and IMF came to their rescue to resolve their debt problem.

However, a fiscal deficit which is *sustainable and of a reasonable amount* is quite desirable. The sustainability of fiscal deficit does not depend only on its amount but also the *quality of expenditure* of the borrowed money. As explained above, fiscal deficit is sustainable if borrowed funds are used for productive investment.

Primary Deficit

Primary deficit is another important concept of budgetary deficit. Primary deficit is a measure of budget deficit which is obtained by deducting interest payments from fiscal deficit. Thus,

Primary Deficit = Fiscal Deficit – Interest Payments

Interest payments on public debt are transfer payments made by the government. The difference between the fiscal deficit and primary deficit shows the importance of interest payments on public debt incurred in the past. Huge interest payments are very largely responsible for causing a large fiscal deficit. In India, in recent years, interest payments on public debt has increased very much. The higher interest payments on the past borrowings by the Government has greatly increased the fiscal deficit. Therefore, primary deficit is much lower than the fiscal deficit. In India, in the year 1993-94 primary deficit was 2.1 per cent of GDP, whereas fiscal deficit was 6.3 per cent of GDP. The primary deficit came down to 0.0 per cent of GDP in 1995-96, went up to 0.7 per cent of GDP in 1999-2000 and to 1.5 per cent in 2001-2002. Primary deficit again fell to around 0.0 per cent of GDP in 2003-04, 2004-05 and 2005-06. It was estimated at –0.9 per cent for 2007-08 and 2.5 per cent of GDP 2008-09. As mentioned above, interest payments is an item of liabilities on the revenue account of the budget. Therefore, if fiscal deficit has to be reduced, interest payments on the revenue account should be reduced which can be done if past public debt is quickly retired by mobilising more resources and curtailing non-developmental public expenditure.

Monetisation of Fiscal Deficit

It may be noted that fiscal deficit can be financed by borrowing from the Reserve Bank of India by the central government against its own securities or treasury bills. The fiscal deficit is financed by borrowing from the Reserve Bank which issues new money or currency against government securities, which leads to the expansion in money supply. In the old terminology, it was known as *deficit financing in India.* Financing the fiscal deficit by issuing new money through borrowing from the Reserve Bank against securities in the new terminology is called *monetisation of fiscal deficit.* It may be noted that in the earlier years separate data regarding the budgetary deficit and therefore, the magnitude of deficit financing undertaken in a year were provided by the government. However, in recent years the data regarding budgetary deficit is not separately provided by the government and it has become a part of fiscal deficit which is shown to be financed by *government borrowing and other new liabilities.* Now, the data regarding these deficits, namely, (1) revenue deficit, (2) fiscal deficit and (3) primary deficit are provided in the budget documents.

HOW FISCAL DEFICIT AFFECTS ECONOMIC GROWTH

How does fiscal deficit affect economic growth is a hotly debated issue. A number of Keynesian economists argue that fiscal deficit promotes growth. In India where in the last some years as between 1997-2003, a good deal of industrial capacity had been lying idle due to lack of aggregate demand, and there had been enough stocks of foodgrains, it was asserted that fiscal deficit would stimulate demand and thereby ensure rapid economic growth. In the economic situation especially from 1997 to 2003 the Indian economy and again in 2008-09 was *demand-constrained economy* and therefore the increase in aggregate demand through larger fiscal deficit would not generate inflationary pressures in such a situation. In such a situation if the increase in public expenditure made possible by large fiscal deficit is used for productive investment, especially for investment in infrastructure and agricultural development, it will boost production and help increase employment opportunities in the economy. In fact, increase in public investment in infrastructure such as irrigation, roads, highways, is doubly beneficial from the viewpoint of accelerating economic growth. It will help in increasing aggregate demand on the one hand and help to reduce supply constraints on economic growth on the other.

So the focus should not be so much on reducing fiscal deficit but on reducing revenue deficit. Recall that revenue deficit is the excess of government revenue expenditure (i.e. current consumption expenditure) over revenue receipts. From the beginning of the nineties since economic reforms have been initiated, there has been large revenue deficits so that a large part of borrowings by the government has been used to bridge the revenue deficit. As a result, capital expenditure on investment in infrastructure and agricultural development as a per cent of GDP declined which adversely affected economic growth.

However, from the above it should not be understood that any amount of fiscal deficit or government borrowing is good for economic growth and employment generation. As explained earlier, higher fiscal deficit, that is, borrowing by the government involves payment of interest and raises the burden of public debt. The large increase in public debt involving large interest payments year after year will not only make the process unsustainable but adversely affect economic growth through reducing investible resources for spending on infrastructure and social sectors. Reviewing the Indian growth scenario World Bank Study concludes "Interest payments consumed less than 20% of total revenues in the pre-crisis period, compared with over 30% during the Ninth Plan period (1997-2002). Revenue deficits doubled from less than 3% in the second half of the 1980s to 6% during the Ninth Plan period and beyond *representing a deterioration in the fiscal stance with spending on social and physical infrastructure crowded out by rising interest and other current payments*"[7].

When revenue and gross fiscal deficits (of the Centre and States Combined) sharply goes up interest payments as per cent of GDP greatly increases. The higher revenue deficits and large interest payments during the nineties caused a drastic decline in capital expenditure and public investment in physical infrastructure (irrigation + power + transport) as compared to the later half of the eighties (1985-86 to 1989-90) while the current expenditure on social services (such as education, health, housing, anti-poverty schemes) remained almost stagnant. This shows fiscal and revenue deficits worked to lower economic growth.

Adverse impact of fiscal deficit on economic growth has been shown through its effect on saving and investment in the Indian economy. For example, Shankar Acharya, a former chief economic adviser to the Government of India, has contended that a large fiscal and revenue deficits after 1996 to 2001-02 as compared to 1995-96 had slowed down economic growth in India[8]. He argues that as a result of fiscal consolidation achieved between 1990-91 and 1995-96, combined fiscal deficit of Centre and States as percentage of GDP declined from 9.4 percent in 1990-91 to 6.5 percent in 1995-96 and revenue deficit fell from 4.2 percent in 1990-91 to 3.2 per cent in 1995-96. This freed resources for private investment and in fact brought about investment boom of 1993-96. Gross domestic investment rose from 22.5 percent of GDP in 1991-92 (to which it had fallen during the crisis) to a peak of 26.8 percent GDP in 1995-96. Gross domestic saving also rose to a record level of 25.1 per cent of GDP in 1995-56. This increase in gross domestic saving and investment, according to Dr. Shankar Acharya, "helped propelled Inida's growth to 7 per cent plus for three successive years in the mid nineties" (1995-96, 1996-97 and 1997-98).

After the mid 1990's, fiscal deficit and revenue deficit increased which caused the decline in gross domestic saving and investment and thereby contributed to slowdown in economic growth. To quote Dr. Shankar Acharya, *"It would be hard to find more telling evidence of the adverse impact of deficits on savings and investment"*[9] Of course, other factors were also dampening investment, including the slowdown in reforms, the higher uncertainties associated with coalition government and a worsening international economic environment. But increased borrowing by government (rising fiscal deficits) and the associated high real interest rates clearly played a role in slowing private investment. The drop in aggregate savings

7. The World Bank, *India : Sustaining Reforms, Reducing Poverty,* Oxford University Press, 2003, pp. 17-18.
8. See his article 'How Fiscal Deficits Hurt Economic Growth, *The Economic Times,* Nov-1, 2001 and 'Why Large Fiscal Deficits are bad for *us CNBC,* January 2003.
9. *Op. cit.*

and investment took its toll of economic growth, which slowed from 7 percent plus of the mid nineties to around 5 percent in recent years"[10]. According to him, high fiscal deficits during the eighties created balance of payments deficits as it was mainly financed by *external commercial borrowing* and therefore did not adversely affect economic growth. But in the later half of nineties rising fiscal deficits were financed by *domestic borrowings* which were largely used to meet current consumption expenditure and resulted in *public dissavings* (see Table 50.3). It may be noted that the implementation during (1997-2000) of Fifth Pay Commission report enhancing the salaries of Government staff both at the Centre and States sharply increased the revenue expenditure of the governments and increased public dissavings. This adversely affected domestic rate of saving and investment and lowered rate of economic growth.

Further, according to Dr. Shankar Acharya, the high and rising fiscal deficits during the period from 1997 to 2002 which resulted in larger government borrowings from the market *preempted the needed resources for investment by the private sector*. This had an adverse effect on private investment and was mainly responsible for slowdown in economic growth.

The high public *debt involves huge interest payments year after year which crowds out essential government expenditure on social sectors such as education, health, housing etc and infrastructure*. This adversely affects economic growth of the country.

Fiscal Deficit and Economic Growth: Our View

However, we do not fully agree with Dr. Shankar Acharya's view which is similar to that of World Bank. They consider only supply-side factors determining economic growth. The fall in growth rate during the period from 1997 to 2002 was largely due to demand recession in the economy caused by (1) reduction in the capital expenditure by Government as a matter of new economic policy initiated since 1991, (2) sluggish performance in agriculture during the period, and (3) world-wide recession during the period. Thus demand recession caused a slowdown in the Ninth Plan period (1999-2002) As a result, gross saving and investment rate and GDP growth slowed down. When capital expenditure of government increased substantially in 2003-04 and 2005-06, with multiplier effect it led to the increase in aggregate demand. This increase in demand also caused increase in private investment and the two together ensured a higher rate of economic growth. In the two years (2005-07) even when Government's capital expenditure as per cent of GDP fell, under pressure of demand it was made up by increase in private investment in the two years 2005-06 and 2006-07 which kept the momentum of higher economic growth.

Thus in our view both supply-side and demand-side factors play a role in determining economic growth. The growth experience of a country cannot be explained by supply-side factors alone. In fact, in 2008 and 2009 as a result of global financial crisis there was economic slowdown in India which caused huge job losses. To prevent the situation from worsening further the Government came out with three fiscal stimulus packages to keep the growth momentum. In these stimulus packages Government raised its expenditure, especially on infrastructure on the one hand and cut taxes on the other to stimulate aggregate demand. To increase its expenditure Government borrowed from the market about ₹ 300,000 crore in 2008-09, ₹ 400,000 crore in 2009-10. As a result, its fiscal deficit went up from 2.7 per cent of GDP in 2007-08 to 6.0 per cent in 2008-09 and 6.4% of GDP in 2009-10. *But this did not produce bad results for the private sector investment,* nor did it result in higher rate of interest. Of course, RBI reduced cash reserve ratio to increase liquidity in the banking system and lowered

10. *Ibid*

its repo rate to enable banks to lower the lending rates of interest. As a matter of fact, increased borrowing and expenditure by the Government in 2008-09 and 2009-10 led to the increase in demand for the products of private sector. Therefore, from May 2009 onward there were signs of revival of the Indian manufacturing sector. Manufacturing sector output grew at 9.6% in Sept. 2009 year-on-year basis and this growth further picked up to 17.6% year-on-year basis in Dec. 2009. Manufacturing sector registered growth of 13.5 per cent in March 2010, 16.5% in April, 2010 and 11.1% in May 2010 year-on-year basis. This shows despite 6.0 per cent fiscal deficit in 2008-09 and 6.4 % in 2009-10 and consequently heavy borrowing by the government in these two years manufacturing output recorded high growth.

Besides, it is because of the fiscal stimulus packages and increase in government expenditure made possible by heavy borrowing and fiscal deficit that India could achieve 6.7 per cent rate of economic growth in 2008-09 and 8.6% in 2009-10 and 8.9% in 2010-11 which is quite high, especially when there were recessionary conditions in the US and Europe. So in our view fiscal deficit of more than 3% in a year is not bad in situation of recession or slowdown in economic growth when there is unutilised potential for expansion of production. All depends on the economic situation in the country and the purposes for which borrowed funds are spent. If there is recession or slowdown in the economy, the fiscal deficit of around 7 per cent of GDP (of both Centre and States combined) is necessary to lift the economy out of recession or to prevent sharp slowdown in the economy. If borrowed funds are spent by the Government for investment or building durable assets, it will lead to the expansion in production capacity and therefore ensure sustained economic growth.

It is evident from above that larger fiscal deficit at the time of recession or economic slowdown far from reducing private saving and investment is helpful for fighting recession or keeping growth momentum of the economy. In fact, the present economic thinking is that even 3 per cent of fiscal deficit of the Central Government of India should be treated as *cyclically adjusted number*; the fiscal deficit should go up at times of recession or economic slowdown and comes down in normal or boom period.

We have explained above the two alternative views regarding the impact of fiscal deficit on our economic growth. One view is of the Keynesian economists who think that in developing economies such as India when they suffer from demand constraint, fiscal deficit provides stimulus to economic growth by bringing about increase in aggregate demand. In the situation prevailing in India from 1997 to 2002, and then in 2008-2009 the Indian economy in fact suffered from lack of aggregate demand for manufactured products. This demand deficiency problem arose due to *bad agricultural performance in some years* (there was a negative agricultural growth in 1995-96, 1997-98 1999-2000 and 2000-01 and 2002-03 and also due to sharp *decline in public sector investment* which started in early nineties following the initiation of economic reforms since 1991.

Thus, during 1997-2002 there was a decline in public investment not only because a good deal of borrowing by the government was used to meet revenue deficit but also because of change in economic policy which aimed at reducing the role of public sector. Besides, public sector investment could not be raised also because of the fiscal policy stance of reducing fiscal deficit as recommended by IMF, World Bank and economists associated with these institutions. In fact the focus of fiscal consolidation was reducing fiscal deficit rather than revenue deficit. In fact, rates of income tax, corporation tax, excise and customs duties were reduced which resulted in fall in tax-GDP ratio till 2001-02 and caused revenue deficit to rise and therefore much of the borrowing by the government was used to bridge the revenue deficit. Thus, the fall in public investment was embedded in the new economic policy of reforms. *Fall in public sector investment resulted in decrease in aggregate demand on the one hand and shortage of infrastructure on the other which caused slowdown in economic growth during the period 1997-2002.* Again in 2008-09 and 2009-10 it was increase in Government expenditure made possible by heavy borrowing and large fiscal deficit that helped India to achieve GDP growth of 6.7% in 2008-09 and 8.6% in 2009-10.

After, 2003-04, the focus of the fiscal strategy of the Government has been to reduce fiscal deficit and revenue deficit by raising more resources through taxes. As a result, the Government succeeded in increasing tax-GDP ratio from 8.1 per cent in 2001-02 to 12.5 per cent in 2007-08, reducing revenue deficit to 1.1% of GDP and fiscal deficit to 2.5 percent in 2007-08. This enabled the Government to raise public setor investment and also private sector investment with the result that investment rate went up to over 36 per cent of GDP in 2007-08. This caused on an average economic growth rate of over 9 per cent in 2005-06, 2006-07 and 2007-08. Thus, *in order to ensure economic growth of 9 percent per annum on a sustained basis, focus should be shifted to reducing revenue deficit.* To reduce revenue deficit, steps should be taken to raise tax-GDP ratio and curtail unproductive consumption expenditure of the government so as to eliminate revenue deficit. The borrowings in the capital account should be used for financing public investment in physical infrastructure and social sectors. This will ensure sustained economic growth at the rate of 9 per cent per annum - the objective fixed under the Twelfth Year Plan (2012-17).

Here it may be recalled the **Golden Rule of Public Finance**, namely, *borrowing by the government should be used only for investment purposes and not to meet excess current consumption expenditure except during times of recession.* In times of recession even government consumption expenditure will promote GDP growth. Thus, the focus on merely reducing fiscal deficit at all times and treat it as fetish is not right. In fact, in a demand-constrained economy, a moderate doze of fiscal stimulus is needed. Fiscal responsibility should not be conceived in ritualistic terms of reducing fiscal deficit alone regardless of its effect on the public investment and the economy. In fact, the increase in public investment in infrastructure will also stimulate private investment. The question of containing Government consumption expenditure, except during periods of recession or economic slowdown, is important but reduction in fiscal deficit should not be elevated to a dogma. A moderate amount of fiscal deficit and associated borrowing is good as long as it is used for increasing public investment in physical infrastructure, education and health of the people. Even foreign investment depends on our success in improving infrastructure.

Government Expenditure Multiplier and Revenue Buoyancy

To control inflation, achievement of fiscal consolidation without compromising growth is essential. But to achieve this requires not only efforts by the government to reduce revenue deficit but also to *properly direct its public expenditure*. In this context the two important economic concepts need to be explained, namely, *government expenditure multiplier*. According to this, an increase in Government expenditure generates the amount of income larger than the original increase in Government expenditure. The ratio of increase in income to the original increase in public expenditure measures the size of government expenditure multiplier. However, different forms of government expenditure have different multiplier effects. For instance, in India public investment expenditure, especially on infrastructure projects, induces increase in private investment thereby increases income directly and also indirectly through multiplier effect. Hence *"the fiscal multiplier of capital expenditure by the government turns out to be much stronger than the fiscal multiplier for current or revenue expenditure"*.[11]

The other relevant economic concept of public finance is of *revenue buoyancy* which represents the percentage increase in revenue that would arise from a given percentage increase in income. In India the tax buoyancy has been on an average is around 1.3 which implies that one per cent increase in GDP leads to an additional 1.3 per cent increase in government revenue".[12]

From above it follows that the government multiplier and revenue buoyancy taken together implies that total revenue is not independent of government spending. The increase in government expenditure not only leads to the higher increase in income but also *higher revenue* for the government and that should be factored into the revenue projections while framing a government budget. Thus, we agree with Prof. Sudipto Mundle that "it is possible to achieve fiscal consolidation (i.e., to reduce fiscal deficit) without compromising growth."[13] For this prupose, the required fiscal strategy is to progressively reduce fiscal deficit to 6 per cent of GDP for the centre and states combined (each to 3% of GDP) on the one hand and at the same time to shift public expenditure in favour of capital expenditure.

But from above it should not be concluded that fiscal deficit and therefore borrowing by the Government can be made with impunity. This is because, as mentioned above, funding fiscal deficit involves interest payments and rising debt burden. It needs to be emphasized that fiscal deficit and government borrowing in normal times should be used for productive investment rather than current revenue (*i.e. consumption) expenditure. The target or limit for fiscal deficit of government cannot be set before hand regardless of the situation in the economy. We think it is improper for Financial Responsibility and Budgetary Management (FRBM) Act to fix the date for achieving 3 percent fiscal deficit by the central government. When a large industrial capacity lies unutilised and the economy is experiencing economic recession or slowdown we can afford to have more than 3 percent central fiscal deficit of the central government to accelerate economic growth. It is worth mentioning that in the USA, there was a record level of fiscal deficits during 2002-03, 2003-04, 2007-08 and 2008-09 caused by cutting back on taxes and raising government expenditure. These fiscal deficits in the USA in fact succeeded in bringing about American recovery and increase in industrial production and employment without much increase in inflation rate.*

11. Sudipto Mundle, "Financing the Deficit" in the *Times of India,* Aug. 26, 2010.
12. *Ibid.*
13. Sudipto Mundle, op. cit.